Criminal Law
Cases and Materials

Criminal Law
Cases and Materials

Third edition

J.C. Smith, CBE, QC, LLD, FBA
Honorary Bencher of Lincoln's Inn;
Honorary Fellow of Downing College, Cambridge;
Professor of Common Law and Head of the
Department of Law, University of Nottingham

Brian Hogan, LLB
of Gray's Inn, Barrister;
Professor of Common Law,
University of Leeds

Butterworths
London
1986

United Kingdom	Butterworth & Co (Publishers) Ltd, 88 Kingsway, LONDON WC2B 6AB and 61A North Castle Street, EDINBURGH EH2 3LJ
Australia	Butterworths Pty Ltd, SYDNEY, MELBOURNE, BRISBANE, ADELAIDE, PERTH, CANBERRA and HOBART
Canada	Butterworths. A division of Reed Inc, TORONTO and VANCOUVER
New Zealand	Butterworths of New Zealand Ltd, WELLINGTON and AUCKLAND
Singapore	Butterworth & Co (Asia) Pte Ltd, SINGAPORE
South Africa	Butterworth Publishers (Pty) Ltd, DURBAN and PRETORIA
USA	Butterworth Legal Publishers, ST PAUL, Minnesota, SEATTLE, Washington, BOSTON, Massachusetts, AUSTIN, Texas and D & S Publishers, CLEARWATER, Florida

British Library Cataloguing in Publication Data

Smith, J.C. (John Cyril)
 Criminal law: cases and materials. — 3rd ed.
 1. Criminal law — England — Cases
 I. Title II. Hogan, Brian
 344.205'0264   KD7868

 ISBN Hardcover 0 406 65824 2
 Softcover 0 406 65825 0

Set by Colset Private Ltd, Singapore
Printed and bound in Great Britain
by Mackays of Chatham Ltd

Preface

Six years have elapsed since the last edition of this book and much has happened to the criminal law in that time. But the event which has had the greatest impact on the present edition was the publication of the draft Criminal Code Bill prepared by a team of academic lawyers (J.C. Smith, I.H. Dennis and E.J. Griew) for the Law Commission and the Report to which the draft Bill is appended. We have re-arranged the materials on general principles of liability in accordance with the structure of the draft Bill. As it purports to be, in the main, a restatement of the general principles of criminal law, we thought the appropriate clauses, together in some cases with the illustrations provided in Schedule 1, to be a valuable introduction of the reader to the principles of the subject which he will then study 'in action' in the cases and materials which follow.

In some instances the codification team (with the approval of the Law Commission) thought it right to incorporate substantial proposals for law reform made by public bodies, usually the Criminal Law Revision Committee or the Law Commission itself. Where this has been done, we thought it more appropriate to place the relevant clauses at the end of the chapter. This enables the reader to compare the present law, as it appears in the cases and materials provided, with that which might one day be enacted.

It is hoped that these arrangements will be helpful in enabling the reader to understand the present law and to criticise it—for some of the illustrations should certainly provoke debate. In particular, it may assist the reader to form a view as to the merits or otherwise of the proposal to codify the criminal law. The debate on this matter is likely to continue for some time and may well still be alive when today's students have become practitioners.

All statutes should be read as a whole and this is particularly so in the case of a Code. It is one of the inevitable limitations—outweighed, we believe, by the advantages—of collections of this kind that they must consist of selections. Reference to the full text of the Code and the Report (Law Com No 143) may sometimes be found desirable. A table of clauses of the draft Bill which are quoted is at p xxi.

There have been significant new cases in every area covered in the book and we have attempted to take full account of these. The impact of the decisions in *Caldwell* [1982] AC 341, *Lawrence* [1982] AC 510 and *Moloney* [1985] 1 All ER 1025 on the fundamental principles of criminal liability is felt at many points. *Ayres* [1984] AC 447 has led to a spate of case-law on conspiracy. *Ghosh* [1982] QB 1053 has solved some problems concerning the meaning of dishonesty but leaves much scope for argument. As we write, the House of Lords appears to be re-considering its attitude to impossibility as it emerged in *Anderton v Ryan* [1985] 1 All ER 138; and it has been invited by the Court of Appeal in *Burke* (see Appendix II) to undertake a fundamental review of the law of duress as a defence to murder. Things are moving rapidly and the book will, no doubt, be out of date in some respects before it is even published; but we have included some of the latest decisions in Appendix II and have attempted to indicate some of the possible future developments.

We thank the holders of the copyright in the various materials who have generously given us permission to reproduce their work in this book. As always, our publishers have earned our gratitude by their patience and help-fulness. Michael Gunn has given us invaluable assistance by reading the proofs and discerning many errors which had escaped us. We are solely responsible for any which may remain. Nor do we forget the students upon whom we have inflicted the second edition for the past six years and whose comments have led us to make changes and, we hope, improvements.

J.C. Smith
Brian Hogan

April 1986

Contents

Chapter 6
Intoxication   85

Chapter 7
The mental element in statutory offences: strict liability   101

Chapter 8
Parties to offences   133

Chapter 9
Vicarious liability and liability of corporations   168

Acknowledgments

The publishers and authors wish to thank the following for permission to reprint material from the sources indicated:

Professor J.A. Andrews: 'The Theft Bill: Robbery' in [1966] Crim LR 524.

Richard Buxton QC: 'Circumstances, Consequences and Attempted Rape' in [1984] Crim LR 25.

Cambridge University Press: Kenny, *Outlines of Criminal Law* (1st edn, 1902; 15th edn, 1946; 19th edn, 1966).

Canada Law Book Inc: Canadian Criminal Cases and Dominion Law Reports.

The Controller of Her Majesty's Stationery Office: Extracts from official reports Cmnd 8932, Cmnd 1728, Cmnd 2977, Cmnd 3909, Cmnd 6244, Cmnd 6733 and Cmnd 7844. Law Commission Working Papers Nos 31 and 50; and Law Commission Reports Nos 29 ('Criminal Damage'), 55 ('Forgery'), 83 ('Defences of General Application') 89 ('The Mental Element in Crime') and 143 ('Codification of the Criminal Law').

Professor Edward Griew: *The Theft Act 1968* (4th edn) and 'Dishonesty and the Jury'.

The Incorporated Council of Law Reporting for England and Wales: *The Law Reports*.

The Incorporated Council of Law Reporting for Northern Ireland: *The Northern Ireland Law Reports*.

Justice of the Peace Ltd: *Justice of the Peace Reports*.

Juta and Company Ltd: *The South African Law Reports*.

Professor Sanford Kadish and the University of California Press. © 1985 by the California Law Review, Vol 73, No 2, p 389. Reprinted by permission.

Kenneth Mason Publications Ltd: *Road Traffic Reports*.

The Law Book Company Ltd: Commonwealth Law Reports.

Legal Studies, The Journal of the Society of Public Teachers of Law, Vol 4, p 88.

The Hon Mr Justice MacKenna: 'The Theft Bill—Blackmail: A Criticism' in [1966] Crim LR 467.

The New Zealand Council of Law Reporting: *New Zealand Law Reports*.

Oxford University Press: *Samples of Lawmaking* (1962) by Lord Devlin, published by Oxford University Press. Reprinted by permission.

J.R. Spencer: 'The Theft Act 1978' in [1979] Crim LR 24 and 'Making off without payment' (a letter) [1983] Crim LR 573.

Stevens and Sons: *Russell on Crime* (12th edn by J.W.C. Turner) and *Crime and the Criminal Law*, by Barbara Wootton.

Sweet & Maxwell Ltd: *The Criminal Appeal Reports* and *The Criminal Law Review*.

Professor Glanville Williams: *The Criminal Law: The General Part* (2nd edn); *The Mental Element in Crime*, 'Assaults and Words' in [1957] Crim LR 219; 'Consent and Public Policy' in [1962] Crim LR 74; and 'Necessity' in [1978] Crim LR 218.

Table of statutes

Page references printed in **bold** type indicate where the section of an Act is set out in part or in full.

Table of clauses of the draft Criminal Code Bill

References are to pages where clauses are set out in part or in full.

Table of cases

Cases are listed under the name of the accused whenever the usual method of citation would cause them to be preceded by the abbreviation "R v" signifying that the prosecution was undertaken by the Crown.

Page references printed in **bold** type indicate that the judgment of a case is set out in part or in full.

PAGE

M

CHAPTER 1

The elements of a crime

1. Actus reus and mens rea

Anyone who thinks about it will readily appreciate that crime ordinarily involves a mental element. Suppose I take your bicycle from the rack in which you have left it, ride it home and put it in my garage. Have I stolen it? The question cannot be answered without considering my state of mind at the time of the taking. Perhaps I mistook your bicycle for my own similar model which I had left in the same shed. Or perhaps I mistakenly supposed that you had said I could borrow the bicycle; or, though I knew it was your bicycle and that I was taking it without your consent, I only intended to borrow it for a day or two. In none of these cases have I stolen it. But, if I knew it was your bicycle and that I did not have your consent and I dishonestly intended to keep it permanently for myself, I am guilty of theft. The act is the same in every case. The difference is in the state of mind with which the act is done. If D, driving his car, runs P down and kills him this will be murder if D did so intending to kill P; manslaughter if, though he wished no harm to anyone, he was taking an obvious and serious risk of causing injury by not looking where he was going; and accidental death if the collision occurred in spite of the fact that he was concentrating on what he was doing and exercising the care that a prudent and reasonably skilful driver should.

Virtually all crimes require proof of a mental element of some sort. It has to be proved with the same degree of strictness as the other elements of the crime as the case of *Woolmington*, p 39, below, demonstrates. Lawyers have long found it convenient to distinguish the mental element for the purposes of exposition of the law and have called it 'mens rea'. This phrase derives from a maxim quoted by Coke in his *Institutes* (ch 1, fo 10) 'Actus non facit reum nisi mens sit rea', an act does not make a man guilty of a crime unless his mind also be guilty. The expression, 'actus reus', is much more recent, having apparently been coined by Kenny in the first edition of his *Outlines of Criminal Law* in 1901 (see Jerome Hall, *General Principles of Criminal Law*, p 222, footnote 24) but it is now used throughout the common law world to designate the elements of an offence other than the mental element. These expressions are only analytical tools. The only thing that exists in law is the crime. Courts and writers use the expressions in different senses and it cannot be asserted that one usage is correct and others wrong. Glanville Williams (*Criminal Law: The General Part* (2nd edn, 1961), p 18) writes:

> '. . . actus reus means the whole definition of the crime with the exception of the mental element—and it even includes a mental element in so far as that is contained in the

1

definition of an act. This meaning of actus reus follows inevitably from the proposition that all the constituents of a crime are either actus reus or mens rea . . .

Actus reus includes, in the terminology here suggested, not merely the whole objective situation that has to be proved by the prosecution, but also the absence of any ground of justification or excuse, whether such justification or excuse be stated in any statute creating the crime or implied by the courts in accordance with general principles (though not including matters of excuse depending on absence of mens rea).' [See also, Williams, *TBCL*, ch 2]

This is a particularly useful description of the concepts but it involves two points of controversy.

(1) The actus reus generally requires proof that the defendant did an act. It is argued that since an act is essentially a voluntary movement and not a spasm or convulsion, 'voluntariness', though a mental element, is part of the actus reus. Moreover, the word that describes the act may imply some further mental element. There are for example many offences where the actus reus consists in possession of proscribed articles. It has long been recognised that 'possess' imports a mental as well as a physical element. (See *Warner*, p 110, below.) Some writers and judges have described these mental elements as part of the mens rea. However, the only thing that really matters is whether they are elements in the crime. If they are, it is immaterial whether they are assigned to the actus reus or to the mens rea.

(2) The second question is whether actus reus should include the absence of justification or excuse. The actus reus of murder may be described as the killing of a human being; but if the killer is the public executioner carrying out his duty to hang a convicted traitor it might seem strange to describe this as an actus reus. Similarly if the killer was acting in lawful self-defence. Where the actor knows of the circumstances of justification it might seem equally strange to describe his state of mind as mens rea. Neither the public executioner nor the person acting in self-defence has a 'guilty mind'. Courts sometimes treat the mental element in the broader sense. In *Gladstone Williams* (1983) 78 Cr App Rep 276, at 280, p 237, below, Lord Lane CJ said:

'The mental element necessary to constitute guilt [of assault] is the intent to apply unlawful force to the victim. We do not believe that the mental element can be substantiated by simply showing an intent to apply force and no more.'

If the defendant believed (though under a mistake) in circumstances which would justify the degree of force he used, he lacked the mens rea for an assault.

There is however something to be said for having terms to describe the particular elements of a crime without thereby invoking all the possible defences. If the Latin expressions are regarded merely as technical terms which do not in themselves necessarily import guilt, the difficulty of so using them disappears. Professor Lanham has said ([1976] Crim LR 276):

'As a matter of analysis we can think of a crime as being made up of three ingredients, actus reus, mens rea and (a negative element) absence of a valid defence.'

According to that view a person may cause an actus reus with mens rea but not be guilty of the crime in question because of the existence of a defence. Gladstone Williams (below) was such a person.

In favour of this approach is the fact that defences also may require mental as well as external elements. For example, the defence of provocation on a murder charge requires evidence of not only provocative facts but also an actual loss of self-control on the part of the defendant (p 321, below). If the object is clarity of exposition, there may, therefore, be something to be said for treating elements of offences and elements of defences separately.

THE DRAFT CRIMINAL CODE BILL

This is the approach of the draft Code (Law Com No 143, 1985). It avoids the Latin terms (their disappearance might be regarded as one of the collateral advantages of codification). It uses—but by way of cross-heading only—the phrase 'external elements of offences' as broadly the equivalent of actus reus in the narrow (Lanham) sense; and the phrase 'fault element' which is defined (cl 5 (1)) to mean

> 'any element of an offence consisting:
> (a) of a state of mind with which a person acts; or
> (b) of a failure to comply with a standard of conduct; or
> (c) partly of such a state of mind and partly of such a failure . . .'

The Report comments:

7.2 *Elements and defences.* Our draft distinguishes between the elements of an offence and defences in a way that may surprise some criminal law theorists.[1] If such a distinction is not to be made, however, the inapplicability of every exception admitted by the definition of an offence must be treated as an element of it. This view of exceptions may be justified on theoretical grounds; but our experience suggests that to adopt it rigorously in the Code would have very unhappy drafting consequences both for the codifier and for the user. This might have to be accepted if distinguishing between elements and defences were to produce serious defects in the law. We do not think that it does. Two matters deserve special mention.

(i) *Mistake.* Until recently a mistaken belief in the existence of a circumstance affording a defence (such as self-defence) would not avail a defendant unless it was a belief held on reasonable grounds. A person who foolishly believed that his victim was attacking him was in a different position from one who foolishly believed that the victim was consenting to what would, but for consent, be an assault.[2] Something therefore turned on whether a matter was a 'definitional element' (such as absence of consent in assault) or a defence. The Code, however, follows recent Court of Appeal authority,[3] as well as recommendations of the Criminal Law Revision Committee[4] and the Law Commission[5], in no longer requiring beliefs as to matters of defence to be reasonably held.[6]

(ii) *Evidential burden and burden of proof.* Clause 17 places upon the prosecution in general the burden of disproving defences as well as of proving the elements of offences. But in relation to a defence that burden does not arise until there is evidence of the defence before the court; the defendant bears the 'evidential burden'. Moreover, the burden of proving a special defence may fall on the defendant.[7] This makes it important for the draftsman of a new offence to decide into which category (element or defence) a particular matter is to fall and to draft accordingly. It is not a ground for dispensing with the distinction between elements and defences at all costs.

1. Glanville Williams, 'Offences and defences' (1982) 2 Legal Studies 233.
2. *Albert v Lavin* [1982] AC 546 (Divisional Court; cf *per* Hodgson J at 562).
3. *R v Gladstone Williams* (1983) 78 Cr App R 276.
4. Fourteenth Report: Offences against the Person (1980), Cmnd 7844, para 283; cf Fifteenth Report: Sexual Offences (1984), Cmnd 9213, paras 5.12–5.16.
5. Report on the Mental Element in Crime (1978), Law Com No 89, paras 90–91.
6. See eg para 13.34, below.
7. Cl 17(4). See para 6.4, above.

2. Constituents of an actus reus

**R v Deller (1952) 36 Cr App Rep 184, Court of Criminal Appeal
(Hilbery, McNair and Streatfeild JJ)**

The appellant was charged with obtaining from C a car No DYW 29 'by falsely pretending that he was the owner of a Standard motor-car No FXF 372, that the said car was free from all encumbrances, that there was no money owing upon the said car, and that he was free to deal with the said car'. The appellant had previously signed documents which purported to effect a sale by him of FXF 372 to Great Western Motors and a hiring back to him by the Central Wagon and Finance Co. If the transaction was in reality a loan to the appellant on the security of the car, it was a bill of sale and void because not registered under the Bills of Sale Act 1878. The appellant was convicted and appealed on the ground that the documents were a bill of sale and that he spoke the truth when he said that the car was free from encumbrances.

[**Hilbery J**, (delivering the judgment of the court) having stated the facts continued:]

It has been argued that, because a document was in existence purporting to represent as between the parties an agreement of hire and purchase, the false pretence was established when the appellant said that it was his car and not encumbered, because he must have believed that and known that there was in existence this agreement. It is to be observed that the false pretence which was alleged was not that he falsely pretended that there was not in existence any hire-purchase agreement in respect of the car; and that in fact he made no such representation was clearly established in the cross-examination of Mr Clarke when before the magistrates, as appears from the depositions.

In those circumstances, if the direction given to the jury was a clear direction that, in the event of their finding that this was in truth a loan transaction on the security of the car and not a genuine sale with a hiring back, the right verdict would be Not Guilty, the verdict of Guilty by the jury would be tantamount to a finding by them that the transaction was not one merely of loan but was in fact a genuine transaction of sale and hiring back to the man who had, prior to that sale, been the owner of the car. Unfortunately, whereas the issue that the jury had to try was correctly put in the summing-up, there was matter later on in the summing-up which, in our opinion, prevents us from taking that view of the verdict and vitiates the summing-up, having regard to the exact terms of the false pretences alleged in the indictment . . . [The judge examined the direction to the jury and continued:] Of course, once the jury came to the conclusion that in fact the transaction was one of loan and not of sale of the car, but loan on the attempted security of the car, the documents as a matter of law were void documents and that the learned Deputy Chairman must have known. But in one and the same breath he was asking the jury to say, if they thought it was a loan, to look upon the documents as being the security for the loan and saying to the jury that, whatever they thought about the strict ownership of the car, when they came to the representation that it was unencumbered, here were these documents which were a charge upon the car. In truth, if they came to the conclusion that the transaction was a loan, as a matter of law the documents were void; they were no more than pieces of paper. The charge to the jury ought to have been: if they came to the conclusion that the documents represented only a transaction of loan on the security of the car, then the documents were all void and of no effect, and the falsity of every one of the alleged representations was not proved because, it may be quite accidentally and, strange as it may sound, dishonestly, the appellant had told the truth. In the circumstances, it seems to us to be quite clear that the jury may well have thought that, although these were documents to cloak a loan transaction and to give a loan transaction the colour of a sale and a hiring back, yet none the less they were a charge on the car, and to say it was unencumbered became a false pretence. Having regard, therefore, to the indictment and the direction in the summing-up, we are of opinion that this conviction must be quashed.

Conviction quashed

Questions

Should Deller have been guilty of an offence? Would it be desirable to have a law stating:

> 'A person who does any act with intent thereby to commit an offence is guilty of an offence and liable to be punished as if he had committed the offence he intended to commit'?

See *Anderton v Ryan*, p 296, below.

3. An act; and automatism

Reduced to its lowest terms, an act is merely a muscular movement—for example, the crooking of a finger. But this is a very narrow view. Reference to an act generally includes some of the circumstances surrounding the movement, and its consequences. For instance, if, when D crooked his finger, it was gripping the trigger of a loaded gun pointing at P's heart, to say that 'D crooked his finger' would be a most incomplete and misleading way of describing what D did. We would naturally say, 'D *shot* P', taking into account the relevant circumstances and consequences. If we say, 'D *murdered* P' we take into account still more circumstances—not only the state of mind with which D pulled the trigger, but also the absence of circumstances of justification or excuse—eg, D was not a soldier in battle shooting at an enemy, P, nor was he acting in self-defence against an aggressor who was attempting to kill him. 'Murder', unlike 'kill', connotes a particular offence and therefore an *actus reus* (including the absence of excuse). The draft Criminal Code Bill recognises that 'act' is a word with a variable meaning and provides as follows:

19 Use of 'act'
A reference in this Act to an 'act' as an element of an offence refers also, where the context permits, to:
(a) any result of the act, and any circumstance in which the act is done or the result occurs, that is an element of the offence;
(b) any omission, state of affairs or occurrence by reason of which a person may be guilty of an offence;
and references to a person's acting or doing an act shall be construed accordingly.

It is sometimes said that the muscular movement is an act only if it is 'willed'—ie, the reflex, spasm or convulsion is not an act at all. This is considered important because it is generally recognised that even offences of strict liability—offences which, it is said, require 'no mens rea'—may not be committed by an involuntary movement. The approach adopted in cl 43 of the draft Code is different:

43 Automatism and physical incapacity:
(1) A person is not guilty of an offence if:
(a) he acts in a state of automatism, that is, his act is a reflex, spasm or convulsion, or occurs while he is in a condition (whether of sleep, unconsciousness, impaired consciousness or otherwise) depriving him of all control of his movements; and
(b) the act or condition is the result neither of anything done or omitted with the fault required for the offence nor of voluntary intoxication.
(2) A person is not guilty of an offence by virtue of an omission to act if:

(a)　he is physically incapable of acting in the way required; and
(b)　his being so incapable is the result neither of anything done or omitted with the fault required for the offence nor of voluntary intoxication.

Clause 43 is explained in the Report as follows:

12.31　*'Automatism'* Is a useful expression for the purposes of the Code as in the common law; and it means essentially the same as it does at common law—an 'involuntary movement of the body or limbs of a person'.[1] For Code purposes such a movement is treated as an 'act' but as one done 'in a state of automatism'. This permits flexible use of the word 'act' as a key term in the Code. Subsection (1)(a) refers to acts of two kinds. There are those over which the person concerned, although conscious, has no control: the 'reflex, spasm or convulsion'. And there are those over which he has no control because of a 'condition' of 'sleep, unconsciousness, impaired consciousness or otherwise'. The reference to 'impaired consciousness' is justified[2] by the facts of several leading cases in which it is far from clear, or even unlikely, that the defendants were entirely unconscious at the time of acts which were treated as automatous.[3] The test must be whether a person lacks power to control his movements and not whether he happens to be completely unconscious.

12.32　*Clause 43(1). Automatism.* The main function of clause 43(1) is to protect a person who acts in a state of automatism from conviction of an offence of strict liability. It is conceded that he does 'the act' specified for the offence; but the clause declares him not guilty. One charged with an offence requiring fault in the form of heedlessness, negligence or carelessness may also have to rely on the clause. On the other hand, a state of automatism will negative a fault requirement of intention or knowledge or (normally) recklessness; a person charged with an offence of violence against another, or of criminal damage, committed when he was in a condition of impaired consciousness, does not rely on this clause for his acquittal but on the absence of the fault element of the offence.

12.33　*Prior fault.* Excepted from the protection of clause 43(1) are cases in which the state of automatism itself is the result of relevant fault on the part of the person affected. Under clause 26(3), for example, a person who is unaware of a risk by reason of voluntary intoxication is credited with the awareness that he would have had if sober; and clause 43(1)(b) ensures that he cannot use clause 43(1) to escape liability for an offence of recklessness. A person charged with an offence that may be committed negligently or carelessly can be convicted if his state of automatism was the result of his own negligent or careless conduct. Paragraph (b) is intended to produce the same results as the common law. In one kind of case, however, it slightly departs from the common law. A driver who falls asleep at the wheel is presently regarded as guilty of careless driving in the period before he falls asleep; he ought to stop at that time.[4] Under the Code he might be convicted even in respect of any period after he falls asleep during which he can be said to be still 'driving'. Clause 43(1), read as a whole, implies that he continues 'driving' until his vehicle comes to rest.

12.34　*Clause 43(2). Physical incapacity.* Subsection (2) provides the necessary corresponding rules for a case in which physical incapacity prevents the doing of that which there is a duty to do. The law does not condemn a person for not doing what cannot possibly be done—unless, once again, it is in a relevant way his fault that he cannot possibly do it.

1. *Watmore v Jenkins* [1962] 2 QB 572 at 586, *per* Winn J.
2. *Pace* Neill J in *Roberts v Ramsbottom* [1980] 1 WLR 823 (a civil case).
3. *R v Charlson* [1955] 1 WLR 317; *R v Kemp* [1957] 1 QB 399; *R v Quick* [1973] QB 910.
4. *Kay v Butterworth* (1945) 173 LT 191.

Ryan v The Queen (1967) 121 CLR 205, High Court of Australia
(Barwick CJ, Taylor, Menzies, Windeyer and Owen JJ)

Ryan entered a service station, pointed a sawn-off rifle at the attendant and demanded money. The rifle was loaded and cocked with the safety catch off. The attendant placed money on the counter. Still pointing the rifle with one hand, Ryan attempted to tie the attendant up. When the attendant moved suddenly Ryan pressed the trigger and shot him dead. At his trial for murder Ryan's defence was that he pressed the trigger involuntarily. He was convicted and his appeal to the High Court of Australia was dismissed.

[**Barwick CJ**, having held that a jury could not dismiss Ryan's account as incredible:]

There were therefore, in my opinion, at least four possible and distinctly different views of the discharge of the gun which, upon all the material before them, could be taken by the jury. First, the applicant's explanation could be disbelieved, and it could be concluded that he had fired the gun intentionally—that is to say, both as a voluntary act and with the intention to do the deceased harm. Second, that he fired the gun voluntarily, not intending to do any harm to the deceased but merely to frighten him as a means of self-protection. Third, that being startled, he voluntarily but in a panic, pressed the trigger but with no specific intent either to do the deceased any harm or to frighten him. Fourth, that being startled so as to move slightly off his balance, the trigger was pressed in a reflex or convulsive, unwilled movement of his hand or of its muscles. I shall later refer to these conclusions of fact as the possible views identifying each by number . . .

An occasion such as the fourth view of the evidence in the instant case (ante) would, in my opinion, be an instance of a deed not the result of a culpable exercise of the will to act. But such an occasion is in sharp contrast to the third view of those facts from which it needs carefully to be distinguished. If voluntariness is not conceded and the material to be submitted to the jury wheresoever derived provides a substantial basis for doubting whether the deed in question was a voluntary or willed act of the accused, the jury's attention must be specifically drawn to the necessity of deciding beyond all reasonable doubt that the deed charged as a crime was the voluntary or willed act of the accused. If it was not then for that reason, there being no defence of insanity, the accused must be acquitted. No doubt care will be taken by the presiding judge that the available material warrants the raising of this specific issue. In doing so, he will of course have in mind that the question for him is whether upon that material a jury would be entitled to entertain a reasonable doubt as to the voluntary quality of the act attributed to the accused. Also, the presiding judge where the circumstances of the case are like those of the instant case will explain the difference between the third and fourth views (ante) so that the jury are given to understand the precise question to which they have relevantly to address themselves. Although a claim of involuntariness is no doubt easily raised, and may involve nice distinctions, the accused, if the material adduced warrants that course, is entitled to have the issue properly put to the jury.

Windeyer J. . . . That an act is only punishable as a crime when it is the voluntary act of the accused is a statement satisfying in its simplicity. But what does it mean? What is a voluntary act? The answer is far from simple, partly because of ambiguities in the word 'voluntary' and its supposed synonyms, partly because of imprecise, but inveterate, distinctions which have long dominated men's ideas concerning the working of the human mind. These distinctions, between will and intellect, between voluntary and involuntary action, may be unscientific and too simple for philosophy and psychology today. However that may be, the difficulty of expressing them in language is obvious and may be illustrated. The word 'involuntary' is sometimes used as meaning an act done seemingly without the conscious exercise of the will, an 'unwilled' act: sometimes as meaning an act done 'unwillingly', that is by the conscious exercise of the will, but reluctantly or under duress so that it was not a 'wilful' act. Words and phrases such as involuntary, unintentional, inadvertent, accidental, unmeditated, unthinking, not deliberate, unwilled and so forth are used by different writers. Their connotations often depend upon their context, and they are used in discussions which seem to drift easily off into psychological questions of consciousness, sanity and insanity and philosophical doctrines of free-will and of events uncontrolled by will. There is a discussion of some aspects of this subject in the American work, *Reflex Action, a Study in the History of Physiological Psychology*. I mention it, not because I profess any knowledge in this field, but because of the readiness with which the phrase 'reflex action' was used in the course of the argument as a presumably exculpatory description of the act of the applicant when he pressed the trigger of the firearm.

The conduct which caused the death was of course a complex of acts all done by the applicant—loading the rifle, cocking it, presenting it, pressing the trigger. But it was the final act, pressing the trigger of the loaded and levelled rifle, which made the conduct lethal. When this was said to be a reflex action, the word 'reflex' was not used strictly in the sense it ordinarily has in neurology as denoting a specific muscular reaction to a particular stimulus of a physical character. The phrase was, as I understood the argument, used to denote rather the probable but unpredictable reaction of a man when startled. He starts. In doing so he may drop something which he is holding, or grasp it more firmly. Doctor Johnson in his Dictionary—and his definition has been in substance repeated by others—said that 'to start' means 'to feel a sudden and involuntary twitch or motion of the animal frame on the apprehension of danger'. The *Oxford Dictionary* speaks of a start as 'a sudden involuntary movement of the body occasioned by surprise, terror, joy or grief . . .'. But assume that the applicant's act was involuntary, in the sense in which the lexicographers use the word, would that, as a matter of law, absolve him from criminal responsibility for its consequences? I do not think so. I do not think that, for present purposes, such an act bears any true analogy to one done under duress, which, although done by an exercise of the will, is said to be involuntary because it was compelled. Neither does it, I think, bear any true analogy to an act done in convulsions or an epileptic seizure, which is said to be involuntary because by no exercise of the will could the actor refrain from doing it. Neither does it, I think, bear any true analogy to an act done by a sleep-walker or a person for some other reason rendered unconscious whose action is said to be involuntary because he knew not what he was doing.

Such phrases as 'reflex action' and 'automatic reaction' can, if used imprecisely and unscientifically, be, like 'blackout', mere excuses. They seem to me to have no real application to the case of a fully conscious man who has put himself in a situation in which he has his finger on the trigger of a loaded rifle levelled at another man. If he then presses the trigger in immediate response to a sudden threat or apprehension of danger, as is said to have occurred in this case, his doing so is, it seems to me, a consequence probable and foreseeable of a conscious apprehension of danger, and in that sense a voluntary act. The latent time is no doubt barely appreciable, and what was done might not have been done had the actor had time to think. But is an act to be called involuntary merely because the mind worked quickly and impulsively?

See also *Bratty v R*, p 196, post.

4. Coincidence of actus reus and mens rea

In order to constitute a crime the actus reus and the mens rea must coincide (a) in point of law and (b) in point of time.

(1) COINCIDENCE IN LAW

All the elements of the crime charged must be proved. It is not therefore sufficient to prove that the defendant caused the actus reus of crime X with the mens rea of crime Y. Cf *Pembliton*, p 81, below. It must be remembered, however, that sometimes the same mens rea is sufficient for two or more crimes; an intention to cause grievous bodily harm is a sufficient mens rea both for the offence of causing such harm with intent contrary to s 18 of the Offences against the Person Act 1861 and for murder. An intention to cause some less than grievous bodily harm is sufficient for the offence maliciously causing grievous bodily harm contrary to s 20 of the Offences against the Person Act 1861 and for manslaughter.

R v Taafe [1984] 1 All ER 747, House of Lords
(Lords Fraser, Scarman, Roskill, Bridge and Brightman)

Lord Scarman. My Lords, the certified question in this appeal by the Crown from the decision of the Court of Appeal quashing the respondent's conviction in the Crown Court at Gravesend neatly summarises the assumed facts on which the recorder ruled that, even if they were proved to the satisfaction of a jury, the respondent would not be entitled to be acquitted. The question is in these terms:

> 'When a defendant is charged with an offence, contrary to section 170(2) of the Customs and Excise Management Act 1979, of being knowingly concerned in the fraudulent evasion of the prohibition on the importation of a controlled drug—Does the defendant commit the offence where he: (a) imports prohibited drugs into the United Kingdom; (b) intends fraudulently to evade a prohibition on importation; but (c) mistakenly believes the goods to be money and not drugs; and (d) mistakenly believes that money is the subject of a prohibition against importation.'

In effect, the recorder answered the question in the affirmative and the Court of Appeal in the negative.

There was no trial, for the respondent changed his plea to guilty after the recorder's ruling. On his appeal against conviction, the judgment of the Court of Appeal was delivered by Lord Lane CJ. The judgment recites the history of the case and the assumptions on which a decision had to be taken (see [1983] 2 All ER 625, [1983] 1 WLR 627). It is unnecessary to burden the House with a repetition of what is there so clearly set forth.

Lord Lane CJ construed the subsection under which the respondent was charged as creating an offence not of absolute liability but as one of which an essential ingredient is a guilty mind. To be 'knowingly concerned' meant, in his judgment, knowledge not only of the existence of a smuggling operation but also that the substance being smuggled into the country was one the importation of which was prohibited by statute. The respondent thought he was concerned in a smuggling operation but believed that the substance was currency. The importation of currency is not subject to any prohibition. Lord Lane CJ concluded ([1983] 2 All ER 625 at 628, [1983] 1 WLR 627 at 631):

> 'He [the respondent] is to be judged against the facts that he believed them to be. Had this indeed been currency and not cannabis, no offence would have been committed.'

Lord Lane CJ went on to ask this question:

> 'Does it make any difference that the [respondent] thought wrongly that by clandestinely importing currency he was committing an offence?'

The Crown submitted that it did. The court rejected the submission: the respondent's mistake of law could not convert the importation of currency into a criminal offence; and importing currency is what it had to be assumed that the respondent believed he was doing.

My Lords, I find the reasoning of Lord Lane CJ compelling. I agree with his construction of s 170(2) of the 1979 Act; and the principle that a man must be judged on the facts as he believes them to be is an accepted principle of the criminal law when the state of a man's mind and his knowledge are ingredients of the offence with which he is charged.

The other Law Lords agreed.

NOTE

Section 170(2) of the Customs and Excise Management Act 1979 provides:

'. . . if any person is, in relation to any goods, in any way knowingly concerned in any fraudulent evasion or attempt at evasion:
(a) of any duty chargeable on the goods;
(b) of any prohibition or restriction for the time being in force with respect to the goods under or by virtue of any enactment; or
(c) of any provision of the Customs and Excise Acts 1979 applicable to the goods,
he shall be guilty of an offence under this section and may be detained.'

If the defendant is mistaken as to the nature of the goods, whether he is guilty will depend on the nature of the mistake. If, on the facts he believed to exist, he would be committing the actus reus of the offence charged and he was in fact committing the actus reus of the same offence, actus reus and mens rea would coincide and he would be guilty. The mistake is immaterial. For example, he believes he is smuggling a crate of Irish whiskey. In fact the crate contains Scotch whisky. He believes he is importing a dutiable item and he is importing a dutiable item. He *knows*, because his belief and the facts coincide in this respect, that he is evading the duty chargeable on the goods in the crate. If the crate contained some item which was not dutiable, there would be no actus reus of the full offence; but it is possible that D might be guilty of an attempt. See p 287, post.

Where D believes that he is smuggling dutiable goods (eg whisky) and the goods are not merely dutiable but prohibited goods (eg cannabis)—or vice versa—it may be different. The answer in principle depends on whether subsection (2) creates a single offence or whether paras (a), (b) and (c) constitute three offences. If there is only one offence D should be guilty. He is committing the actus reus of the offence and he knows that he is committing the actus reus.

In *Taafe* the defendant believed that he was concerned in the importation of something which did not fall within any of the three paragraphs of subsection (2). Consequently, he did not have the mens rea for an offence under the section. He believed that he was committing an offence, but his mistake was one of criminal law. Nor could he have been convicted of an attempt. See p 288, below.

(2) COINCIDENCE IN POINT OF TIME

R v Jakeman (1982) 76 Cr App Rep 223, Court of Appeal, Criminal Division (Eveleigh LJ, Wood and McCullough JJ)

Jakeman (J) booked a flight from Accra to Rome and thence to London. When she checked in at Accra she booked two suitcases through to London. They contained cannabis, the importation of which into the UK is prohibited by s 3(1) of the Misuse of Drugs Act 1971. The flight to Rome was cancelled. The passengers were flown to Paris. J left her luggage there, and flew to Rome and then to London. Customs Officials in Paris assumed the luggage had been misrouted and sent the suitcases to London where the cannabis was discovered. J was convicted under the Customs and Excise Management Act 1979, s 170(2): '. . . if any person is, in relation to any goods, in any way knowingly concerned in any fraudulent evasion . . . (b) of any prohibition . . . for the time being in force with respect to the goods . . . he shall be guilty of an offence.' J's defence was that on leaving Accra she decided to have nothing more to do with the enterprise and so did not collect the suitcases in Paris and tore up the baggage tags. The judge ruled that this was no answer. She appealed.

Wood J. . . . We will deal first with the application for leave to appeal against conviction. Mr Mansfield first submits that the learned judge was wrong in the ruling which he gave. He submits that for the offence under section 170(2) of the 1979 Act, the participation of the applicant and her mens rea must continue throughout the offence—in this case at least until the wheels of the aircraft touched down at Heathrow Airport.

In developing his submission on the first ground of appeal, Mr Mansfield relied upon the applicant's assertion that she had changed her mind immediately on leaving Accra and on the facts that she did not collect her suitcases in Paris, that she tore up the baggage tags on arrival at Heathrow and that she did not seek to claim her suitcases. He submitted that whether one referred to 'withdrawal' or 'abandonment' or 'lack of mens rea' as the necessary ingredient of the defence, assistance was to be obtained from such cases as *Croft* (1944) 29 Cr App R 169, [1944] 1 KB 295 and *Becerra and Cooper* (1975) 62 Cr App R 212. These cases are concerned with accomplices and secondary parties to crime, not to the principal offender, and in the view of this court are not of assistance to test the submission which is made. it is our view that the correct approach is to analyse the offence itself, but before turning to consider the wording of the section as a whole, it is valuable to look at decided cases and to see what assistance can be derived from them.

The following propositions are supported by decisions of this court. First, that the importation takes place when the aircraft bringing the goods lands at an airport in this country. See *Smith (Donald)* (1973) 57 Cr App R 737, 748; [1973] QB 924, 935G. Secondly, acts done abroad in order to further the fraudulent evasion of a restriction on importation into this country are punishable under this section, see *Wall (Geoffrey)* (1974) 59 Cr App R 58, 61; [1974] 1 WLR 930, 934C.

For guilt to be established the importation must, of course, result as a consequence, if only in part, of the activity of the accused. If, for example, in the present case the applicant had taken her two suitcases off the carousel at Charles de Gaulle airport in Paris, removed all the luggage tags, placed the suitcases in a left luggage compartment and thrown the key of that compartment into the Seine, and then subsequently, in a general emergency, all left luggage compartments had been opened, a well-known English travel label had been found on her suitcase and those suitcases had been sent to the Travel Agents' agency, care of Customs and Excise at Heathrow, then that undoubted importation would not be the relevant one for the purposes of a charge against the applicant. . . .

Although the importation takes place at one precise moment—when the aircraft lands—a person who is concerned in the importation may play his part before or after that moment. Commonly, the person responsible for despatching the prohibited drugs to England acts fraudulently and so does the person who removes them from the airport at which they have arrived. Each is guilty. *Wall* (supra) is an example of the former and *Green* (1975) 62 Cr App R 74; [1976] QB 985 of the latter.

There is no doubt, that, putting aside the question of duress, as we have done, the applicant had a guilty mind when at Accra she booked her luggage to London. By that act, she brought about the importation through the instrumentation of innocent agents. In this way, she caused the airline to label it to London, and the labels were responsible for the authorities in Paris sending it on to London.

What is suggested is that she should not be convicted unless her guilty state of mind subsisted at the time of importation. We see no reason to construe the Act in this way. If a guilty mind at the time of importation is an essential, the man recruited to collect the package which has already arrived and which he knows contains prohibited drugs commits no offence. What matters is the state of mind at the time the relevant acts are done, ie at the time the defendant is concerned in bringing about the importation. This accords with the general principles of common law. To stab a victim in a rage with the necessary intent for murder or manslaughter leads to criminal responsibility for the resulting death regardless of any repentance between the act of stabbing and the time of death, which may be hours or days later. This is so even if, within seconds of the stabbing, the criminal comes to his senses and does everything possible to assist his victim. Only the victim's survival will save him from conviction for murder or manslaughter.

The applicant alleged that she repented as soon as she boarded the aircraft; that she deliberately failed to claim her luggage in Paris, that she tore up the baggage tags attached to her ticket and so on, but none of this could have saved her from being held criminally responsible for the importation which she had brought about by deliberate actions committed with guilty intent. Thus, the learned judge was right in the ruling he made. . . .

Appeal dismissed

Questions

1. Do you agree that the defendant would not have been guilty if she had removed the luggage in Paris as envisaged by the judge? D leaves a poisoned apple for his wife, P, intending to kill her. He then repents and conceals the apple. P finds it, eats it and dies. Is D guilty of murder?

2. Was D already guilty of an attempt to commit the offence when, in Accra, she booked the suitcases through to London? Cf Criminal Attempts Act 1981, p 270, below.

3. Is an intention to do a merely preparatory act a sufficient mens rea if, unexpectedly, the preparatory act causes the actus reus of the offence? D prepares a poisoned apple with the intention of giving it to his wife tomorrow. P finds the poisoned apple today, eats it and dies. Or, D is cleaning his gun with the intention of shooting P tomorrow. The gun goes off accidentally and kills P. Is D guilty of murder?

4. See *Wings v Ellis* and question 2, p 120 and p 123, below.

Thabo Meli v R [1954] 1 All ER 373, Privy Council
(Lord Goddard CJ, Lord Reid and Mr L. M. D. de Silva)

The appellants, in accordance with a pre-arranged plan, took a man to a hut, gave him beer so that he was partially intoxicated and then struck him over the head. Believing him to be dead, they took his body and rolled it over a low cliff, dressing the scene to look like an accident. In fact the man was not dead, but died of exposure when unconscious at the foot of the cliff.

Lord Reid. . . . The point of law which was raised in this case can be simply stated. It is said that two acts were done: first, the attack in the hut; and, secondly, the placing of the body outside afterwards—and that they were separate acts. It is said that, while the first act was accompanied by mens rea, it was not the cause of death; but that the second act, while it was the cause of death, was not accompanied by mens rea; and on that ground, it is said that the accused are not guilty of murder, though they may have been guilty of culpable homicide. It is said that the mens rea necessary to establish murder is an intention to kill, and that there could be no intention to kill when the accused thought that the man was already dead, so their original intention to kill had ceased before they did the act which caused the man's death. It appears to their Lordships impossible to divide up what was really one series of acts in this way. There is no doubt that the accused set out to do all these acts in order to achieve their plan, and as parts of their plan; and it is much too refined a ground of judgment to say that, because they were under a misapprehension at one stage and thought that their guilty purpose had been achieved before, in fact, it was achieved, therefore they are to escape the penalties of the law. Their Lordships do not think that this is a matter which is susceptible of elaboration. There appears to be no case, either in South Africa or England, or for that matter elsewhere, which resembles the present. Their Lordships can find no difference relevant to the present case between the law of South Africa and the law of England; and they are of the opinion that by both laws there can be no separation such as that for which the accused contend. Their crime is not reduced from murder to a lesser crime merely because the accused were under some misapprehension for a time during the completion of their criminal plot.

Their Lordships must, therefore, humbly advise Her Majesty that this appeal should be dismissed.

Appeal dismissed

S v Masilela 1968 (2) SA 558, Appellate Division of the Supreme Court of South Africa
(Ogilvie Thompson, Potgieter and Rumpff, JJA)

The appellants assaulted the deceased in his house by striking him over the head and throttling him with a tie. They threw him on his bed and covered him with a blanket. They then ransacked the house until they found some money. After setting fire to, and under, the bed on which the deceased lay and also to other portions of the house, they left with the money and some of the deceased's clothing. Medical evidence showed that the deceased had received potentially serious injuries to his head and neck but that he had died of carbon monoxide poisoning, from the fumes of the fire. At the appellants' trial, it was found that they had acted with 'the subjective intention of killing the deceased by strangling him' but that there was insufficient evidence to prove that they had 'concerted a plan to kill the deceased before they went to his house'. It was assumed in their favour that, when they started the fire, the appellants believed the deceased to be already dead. The question reserved for the Appellate Division was whether, in these circumstances, the appellants were guilty of murder.

[**Ogilvie Thompson JA**, having stated the facts and referred to the arguments and authorities, continued:]

It is, however, important to bear in mind that in *Thabo Meli's* case there would appear to have been a preconceived plan to kill the deceased in the hut and thereafter to simulate an accident by throwing him over a cliff. The decision was, on that ground, distinguished by the Federal Supreme Court in *Chiswibo*, 1961 (2) SA 714 (FC). In that case, the accused had hit the deceased on the head with the blunt side of an axe. The blow rendered the deceased unconscious and the accused, genuinely believing that the deceased was dead, put his body down an ant-bear hole, wherein he died. The trial Court, following the earlier Rhodesian decision in *Shorty*, 1950 SR 280, had convicted Chiswibo of attempted murder and, in an appeal by the Attorney-General as to whether, on the facts, murder had not been committed, the verdict of the trial Court was held to have been correct. In *Shorty's* case, the first accused had violently assaulted the deceased with intent to kill him. Thereafter the first accused, assisted by second and third accused, disposed of the deceased, whom all of the three accused mistakenly believed to be already dead, by putting him down a sewer, where he died of drowning. The first accused was held by Tregold J, to be guilty, not of murder, but of attempted murder, and the second and third accused to be accessories after the fact to attempted murder. In considering *Chiswibo's* case it must be borne in mind that, unlike *Shorty's* case where an express intention to kill was proved, only constructive intention to kill with the axe was established; and, further, that the trial Court had made no finding as to the time which had elapsed between the axe-assault and the placing of the deceased in the ant-bear hole, and no precise finding as to the exact cause of death. As regards this latter, the Court of Appeal proceeded upon the basis that the blow with the axe might not in itself have been fatal, and that 'the death may have been caused by the subsequent interment in the hole' (see p 714G).

In the Court's view, those facts precluded any consideration of the first act being one of the causes of death (see at p 715H).

In *Church* [1965] 2 All ER 72, [p 333, below] the appellant Church, whose van was standing near the bank of a river, had an altercation with a woman in the van and in the course of the ensuing fight knocked her unconscious. He thereafter threw the woman into the river. At his trial for murder, Church deposed that, when he threw the woman into the river, he believed her to be already dead. Medical evidence, however, established that the woman was still alive when she entered the river and that, although she bore marks of grave injuries—inter alia, a battered face and some degree of strangulation—which were likely to have caused unconsciousness and ultimate death, the actual cause of her death was drowning. A jury having convicted him of manslaughter, Church's appeal was dismissed. It is, however, noteworthy that, in the course of delivering the judgment of the Court of Criminal Appeal—which is mainly concerned with the technicalities of the crime 'manslaughter' in English Law, . . . —Edmund Davies J, went out of his way to make express mention of a passage in the trial Judge's summing-up to the jury relating to the charge of murder. After setting out the passage in question and saying that it amounted to a direction to the jury

'in plain terms that they could not convict of murder unless it had been proved that the appellant knew that Mrs Nott was still alive when he threw her into the river or (at least) that he did not then believe she was dead'

the learned Judge, with mention of *Thabo Meli's* case, went on to say:

'We venture to express the view that such a direction was unduly benevolent to the appellant, and that the jury should have been told that it was still open to them to convict of murder, notwithstanding that the appellant may have thought his blows and attempt at strangulation had actually produced death when he threw the body in the river, if they regarded the appellant's behaviour from the moment he first struck her to the moment when he threw her into the river as a series of acts designed to cause death or grievous bodily harm.'

Like *Thabo Meli's* case, *Church*, supra, has also not entirely escaped criticism (see 81 LQR 470 and 82 LQR 193); but, so far as I have been able to ascertain, it is the most recent judicial pronouncement relevant to the enquiry raised by the present appeal.

I revert now to the particular facts of the present case. On the evidence, it is clear that appellants' initial attack upon the deceased consisted of striking him over the head with some undetermined object, immediately followed by the strangling with a neck-tie. Exactly when the deceased's neck was broken, remains undetermined. The only reasonable inference from the evidence is, however, that the head injuries were designed to facilitate the strangling process, and that the broken neck occured at some stage during that process. It was, in my opinion, thus established beyond reasonable doubt that the deceased's head injuries and his broken neck were caused by appellants within the ambit of their proved intention to kill which the learned trial

Judge described as an intention to kill by strangling. From the terms of Nicholas J's judgment as a whole, I entertain no doubt that the finding expressed in the terms that

'the two accused had the subjective intention of killing the deceased by strangling him'

was not intended to confine that intention to strangling alone, to the exclusion of the incidental head and neck injuries, but was intended to comprehend everything done by the appellants up to the stage when they threw the deceased on to his bed.

Unlike some of the examples advanced by the text-book writers when dealing with this subject, no question arises here either of the intervention of any third party or of any subsequent unintentional act. Both the first act (comprising the head and neck assault and the strangling) and the second act (the setting fire to the deceased's bed and house) were intentionally done by the appellants acting in concert. The two acts were closely associated in time and place, and they constituted subsidiary, but integral, parts of the appellants' overall plan to steal money (and other valuables) from the deceased's house and to conceal their crime in the burnt ashes of that dwelling. In that sense, and without as yet seeking to define the ambit of appellants' intention to kill, the facts reveal, in my opinion, a series of acts by the two appellants which constitute a single course of conduct.

Although no direct medical evidence was led upon the point at the trial, the inference is, in my opinion, nevertheless inescapable that the head, neck, and throat injuries suffered by the deceased at the hands of the appellants—hereafter comprehensively called the strangulation injuries—were a material and direct contributory cause of the deceased's dying from carbon-monoxide poisoning. For, on the evidence, the two appellants departed immediately after starting the fire. Had the deceased—who had not been tied up in any way—not been wholly incapacitated in consequence of what the appellants had previously done to him, he would have had no difficulty whatever in escaping from the fire—intentionally started by appellants—long before any question of carbon-monoxide poisoning could have arisen. The vital question, however, remains: was an intentional killing duly proved?

That the first act, as above defined, was committed by appellants with the intention to kill was, as I have already indicated, positively established at the trial. The nature of the second act was such that it would in itself demonstrate an intention to kill were it not for the assumption, made in appellants' favour by the trial court, that, when they started the fire, they believed the deceased to be already dead. In the light of the medical evidence, that belief was erroneous; but the error derived solely from appellants' misconception that they had already achieved their intended killing of the deceased.

Upon the facts as above analysed, the State, in my opinion, duly established its charge of murder against the appellants. That the appellants by their deliberately intended actions caused the death of the deceased is indisputable. To accede, on the facts of the present case, to the contention advanced on behalf of the appellants that, once they erroneously believed that they had achieved their object by strangling the deceased, their proved intention to kill him fell away and can no longer support a charge of murder, would, in my opinion, be wholly unrealistic. (Cf. the extracts, cited above, from the judgments in *Thabo Meli v R*; *Church* and from *Glanville Williams*.) Nor, on the facts of this case, do the principles of our law, in my judgment, compel one to any such unrealistic conclusion. For, as I have pointed out above, the strangulation injuries sustained by the deceased at the hands of the appellants were a directly contributory cause of his death from carbon-monoxide poisoning. Those injuries were—on the express finding of the trial Court—administered by appellants with an intention to kill. In my judgment, it follows that, having regard to the facts as above analysed, the charge of murder was duly made out against both appellants . . .

The conclusion which I have reached may, in a sense, be said to be an extension of the principle of *Thabo Meli's* case, supra, in that in the present case the trial court was unable to find positively that there was a pre-conceived plan to kill the deceased. In my judgment, however, this court should, on the facts of the present case and for the reasons I have given above, not hesitate to make that extension. I am accordingly in full agreement with Nicholas J, that the appellants were guilty of murder even although their intention to kill was concerted, not previously, but as a 'matter of improvisation in the course of the execution of the robbery'. In my judgment, the appellants were rightly convicted of murder. . . .

Potgieter JA, concurred in the above judgment. Rumpff JA, delivered judgment in favour of the State, holding that, in this sort of case, where the accused and nobody else causes the death, the accused's mistake as to the precise manner in which and time when death occurred, is not a factor on which he can rely.

Appeals dismissed

Questions

1. Would the result have been the same if the deceased had been bed-ridden so that he would not have been able to escape from the fire even if he had not been injured?

2. What would the result have been if (i) the appellants had accidentally set the house on fire? (ii) the house had caught fire because of defective wiring as the appellants left? or (iii) the fire had been started by another person, not an accomplice of the appellants?

Attorney General's Reference (No 4 of 1980), [1981] 2 All ER 617
(Ackner LJ, Tudor Evans and Drake JJ)

In the course of an argument on the landing of a maisonette the accused pushed the deceased causing her to fall backwards over a handrail and head first onto the floor below. Almost immediately afterwards the accused tied a rope round the deceased's neck and dragged her upstairs by it. He then placed her in the bath and cut her neck with a knife to let out her blood, with the purpose of cutting up her body and disposing of it, which he then did. The body was never found. The accused was charged with manslaughter. There was evidence that the deceased died either as a result of being pushed down the stairs or by being strangled by the rope or by having her throat cut, but the Crown conceded that it was impossible to prove which of those acts had caused the death. In response to a submission by the defence at the close of the Crown's case that there was no case to go to the jury, the judge decided to withdraw the case from the jury and directed an acquittal on the ground that the Crown had failed to prove the cause of the death. The Attorney General referred to the court for its opinion the question whether, if an accused person killed another by one or other of two or more different acts, each of which was sufficient to establish manslaughter, it was necessary to prove which act caused the death in order to found a conviction.

Ackner LJ. . . . On the above facts this reference raises a single and simple question, viz, if an accused kills another by one or other of two or more different acts each of which, if it caused the death, is a sufficient act to establish manslaughter, is it necessary in order to found a conviction to prove which act caused the death? The answer to that question is No, it is is not necessary to found a conviction to prove which act caused the death. No authority is required to justify this answer, which is clear beyond argument, as was indeed immediately conceded by counsel on behalf of the accused.

What went wrong in this case was that counsel made jury points to the judge and not submissions of law. He was in effect contending that the jury should not convict of manslaughter if the death had resulted from the 'fall', because the push which had projected the deceased over the handrail was a reflex and not a voluntary action, as a result of her digging her nails into him. If, however, the deceased was still alive when he cut her throat, since he then genuinely believed her to be dead, having discovered neither pulse nor sign of breath, but frothy blood coming from her mouth, he could not be guilty of manslaughter because he had not behaved with gross criminal negligence. What counsel and the judge unfortunately overlooked was that there was material available to the jury which would have entitled them to have convicted the accused of manslaughter, whichever of the two sets of acts caused her death. It being common ground that the deceased was killed by an act done to her by the accused and it being conceded that the jury could not be satisfied which was the act which caused the death, they should have been directed in due course in the summing up, to ask themselves the following questions: (i) 'Are we satisfied beyond reasonable doubt that the deceased's "fall" downstairs was the result of an intentional act by the accused which was unlawful and dangerous?' If the answer was No, then they would acquit. If the answer was Yes, then they would need to ask themselves a second question, namely: (ii) 'Are we satisfied beyond reasonable doubt that the act of cutting the girl's throat was an act of gross criminal negligence?' If the answer to that question was No, then they would acquit, but if the answer was Yes, then the verdict would be guilty of manslaughter. The jury would thus have been satisfied that, whichever act had killed the deceased, each was a sufficient act to establish the offence of manslaughter.

The facts of this case did not call for 'a series of acts direction' following the principle in *Thabo Meli v R* [p 12, above]. We have accordingly been deprived of the stimulating questions whether the decision in *R v Church* [p 333, below] correctly extended that principle to manslaughter, in particular to 'constructive manslaughter' and if so whether that view was part of the ratio decidendi.

NOTE

The defendant was certainly guilty of manslaughter if he acted with the fault required on both occasions; but should he not also have been guilty (assuming the *Thabo Meli* principle extends to manslaughter) if he acted with that fault on the first occasion only? If he in fact thereafter killed while disposing of what he believed to be a corpse was not this part of the 'same transaction' (*Thabo Meli*) or 'a series of acts which culminated in death' (*Church*)? But, if the jury were not satisfied with the fault required on the first occasion, acquittal must follow.

CHAPTER 2

Omissions

The draft Criminal Code Bill provides:

20 Liability for omissions

(1) A person does not commit or attempt to commit an offence by omitting to do an act unless:

(a) (i) the enactment creating the offence specifies that it may be committed by such an omission; or

(ii) he is under a duty to do the act and either the offence is murder (section 56), manslaughter (section 57) or intentional serious injury (section 74), or an element of the offence is the detention of another;

and with the fault required for the offence, he omits to do the act; or

(b) either section 27 (supervening fault) or 31(3) (passive encouragement) applies.

(2) For the purposes of subsection (1)(a)(ii), a person is under a duty to do an act where there is a risk that the death of, or serious injury to, or the detention of, another will occur if that act is not done and that person:

(a) (i) is the spouse or a parent or guardian or a child of; or

(ii) is a member of the same household as; or

(iii) has undertaken the care of,

the person endangered and the act is one which, in all the circumstances, including his age and other relevant personal characteristics, he could reasonably be expected to do; or

(b) has a duty to do the act arising from:

(i) his tenure of a public office; or

(ii) any enactment; or

(iii) a contract, whether with the person endangered or not.

As the Report of the Codification Team (Law Com No 143, para 7.6) points out, liability for omissions is exceptional in English criminal law. Stephen in his *Digest of the Criminal Law* (4th edn, 1887), art 212 stated the general rule for offences against the person as follows:

'It is not a crime to cause death or bodily injury, even intentionally, by any omission . . .'

He gave the following famous illustration:

'A sees B drowning and is able to save him by holding out his hand. A abstains from doing so in order that B may be drowned, and B is drowned. A has committed no offence.'

Of course, Stephen went on to state the exceptional cases where the law does impose a duty to act—as, for example, where A is B's parent. When such a person could, by performing his duty, have prevented the proscribed result from happening, he is taken in law to have caused it. Omissions do not cause results in the same obvious sense as acts. Since, ex hypothesi, A does nothing, the evil result would occur in precisely the same way if A did not exist. If A and C, a stranger, walk past the drowning B together, it is impossible to say *as a matter of fact* that A has, and that C has not, caused the death of the child; but, in law, A is taken to have caused it (see the draft Code Bill, cl 21, p 28, below) while C is not responsible.

Two inter-related questions arise: (i) what offences may be committed by omission? and (ii) when an offence may be so committed, who is under a duty to act? When the enactment creating the offence specifies that it may be committed by an omission, it will usually answer the second question as well. For example, s 25 of the Road Traffic Act 1972 provides that the driver of a motor vehicle which has been involved in an accident causing (inter alia) personal injury commits an offence if he fails to stop and, if required, give his name and address to any person having reasonable grounds to require him to do so. Where the enactment makes no provision for omissions, the general principles of criminal law must provide the answers; and cl 20 purports to restate those principles.

The Report explains cl 20(1)(a)(ii) as follows:

7.8   *Paragraph (a) (ii).* This paragraph is based upon the recommendations of the Criminal Law Revision Committee in their Fourteenth Report. Their recommendation 67 is as follows:

'Save where liability for an omission is expressly imposed by statute,
(a)   liability for omissions should be restricted to the offences of murder, manslaughter, causing serious injury with intent, unlawful detention, kidnapping, abduction and aggravated abduction; and
(b)   such liability for omissions should arise only where the omission amounts to a breach of duty to act which is recognised at common law. The common law duties should not be codified (paragraphs 252–255).'

Paragraph (a) (ii) implements that recommendation. It does not specify the detention offences because they are not defined in the Code. It includes all the Committee intended to be included and by implication excludes everything else. They stated:

'It has never been shown to be necessary to include omissions resulting in injury which is not serious even though intentional within the criminal law. A line has to be drawn somewhere and we are of opinion it should be drawn between serious injury and injury.'

The Report justifies this strict limitation on liability for omissions, first, on the ground that this is as far as the common law has gone in imposing duties. It is, however, at present open to the courts to develop the common law by deciding that duties arise in other situations. The enactment of cl 20 might well preclude such development. Second, the Report argues that if, following the recommendations of the CLRC, there is to be no liability for omissions causing less than serious injury to the person, it would be wrong to provide for liability for omissions resulting in damage to property or other interests. These interests cannot be rated more highly than the safety of the person. Where policy does require liability for an omission it should be provided for in the definition of the particular offence.

Three questions may be asked.
(1)   Is it right to preclude the courts from extending liability for omissions?
(2)   Was the CLRC right to draw the line between serious injury and injury?
(3)   Was it right to deduce from the CLRC's recommendation that there should be no liability for criminal damage by omission? Consider the following illustration which the Draft Bill gives of the effect of this proposal and compare *R v Miller*, p 23, post.

20 (v)   D is employed as a night watchman at a factory. His duties are to take all reasonable steps to ensure the safety of the building. D sees that a small fire has broken out. There is an adjacent bucket of sand with which, as he knows, he could easily put out the fire. Having a grievance against his employer, he walks away and lets the fire burn. The factory is destroyed. He is not guilty of arson.

1. The words of the enactment

In deciding whether a statutory offence is capable of being committed by omission the court will obviously have close regard to the words of the enactment. Glanville Williams writes ([1982] Crim LR 773):

> 'In my opinion the courts should not create liability for omissions without statutory authority. Verbs used in defining offences and prima facie implying active conduct should not be stretched by interpretation to include omissions. In general the courts follow this principle. They do not say, for instance, that a person 'wounds' another by failing to save him from being wounded, or 'damages' a building by failing to stop a fire. At least, this has never been decided.'

'Liability for omissions in the criminal law', by J.C. Smith (1984) 4 LS 88, at 97.

Most of the English cases concerning liability for omissions are charges of homicide. Since murder and manslaughter are still common law offences in England, there is no statutory word to construe; but the words 'kill and slay' in an indictment have been held capable of satisfaction by proof of an omission and so has the word 'murder'. [See *Smith* (1869) 11 Cox CC 210 . . .] Lord Campbell CJ, delivering the judgment of the Court for Crown Cases Reserved in *Hughes* (1857) said that '. . . it has never been doubted that if death is the direct consequence of the malicious omission of the performance of a duty (as of a mother to nourish her infant child), this is a case of murder. If the omission was not malicious and arose from negligence only, it is a case of manslaughter only'. [*Hughes* (1857) Dears & Bell 248]

One reason why most of the cases concern manslaughter may well be that manslaughter is a crime which can be committed by negligence. In the case of an omission it will usually be more difficult to prove intention than in the case of an act. Intention was however proved in *Gibbins and Proctor* [(1918) 13 Cr App R 134] where the judge directed the jury that the defendants were guilty of murder if they intentionally withheld food from the child in their care with intent to cause her grievous bodily harm, as a result of which she died. The Court of Criminal Appeal held that this was a correct direction. Suppose that the child had not died but had sustained grievous bodily harm? It is difficult to suppose that the court would not have held the defendants guilty of causing grievous bodily harm with intent to do so contrary to section 18 of the Offences against the Person Act 1861. The commission of this offence, in fact, if not in law, was an essential constituent of the defendants' liability, as the case was left to the jury; and 'cause' is a not inapt word to include liability for omission. There is indeed a serious logical difficulty in not holding the defendant liable for causing grievous bodily harm. The question is whether he was under a duty to act. If he is to be liable for homicide but not for the included non-fatal offence, it seems that we cannot answer the question at the time of the omission but we must wait to see what happens. If the grievous bodily harm results in death, then we will say that he was under a duty to have taken steps to see that this did not happen. But whether or not death occurs may well be a matter of pure chance. Surely the retrospective imposition of a duty is unacceptable. Either the defendant was under a duty at the time he, with the prescribed state of mind, omitted to act, or he was not; and the answer given, in the circumstances of *Gibbins and Proctor*, is that he was under a duty.

What then of other offences against the person? If 'damage', 'destroy', 'kill' and 'slay' may be satisfied by proof of an omission to carry out a duty, why not 'wound' or 'inflict' grievous bodily harm? The answer accepted in English law at least until recently was that (i) the words 'wound' and 'inflict' both imply an assault; and (ii) that 'assault' requires an act and cannot be committed by omission. . . . The assumption that 'assault' requires an act should not go unchallenged. Is there some special magic in the word which distinguishes it from 'kill', 'slay', etc? If D digs a pit with the intention that P should fall into it, and he does, that is said to be an assault. If D is sitting in a corridor and, hearing P running towards him, he puts out his foot with the intention that P shall fall over it, and he does, that is plainly an assault. Should it not equally be an assault if D, having dug the pit with no criminal intention, decides to leave it uncovered so that P will fall into it—which he does? Or if D's legs are already extended and he decides not to draw them back, so that P will fall over them? These seem to be cases where there might properly be held to be a duty to act within the principles of *Miller*—D's act has created the peril and he knows it. If he should happen to cause death, it would seem to be manslaughter, or even murder if he intended to cause grievous bodily harm (it is a very deep pit; or P, as D knows, has very brittle bones). If only grievous bodily harm occurs, he will be liable for causing that. It seems strange that he should escape liability altogether if some lesser degree of harm is caused.

R v Kaitamaki [1980] 1 NZLR 59, New Zealand Court of Appeal

The defendant was charged with rape. His defence was that the victim was consenting, or, at least, that he believed that she was consenting. He stated in evidence that, after he had penetrated the woman, he became aware that she was not consenting. He then continued with the act of intercourse. He was convicted and his appeal was dismissed, Woodhouse J dissenting.

Richmond P and Richardson J. . . . The point raised by Mr MacLean turns upon the true construction of ss 127 and 128 of the Crimes Act 1961. So far as is material those provisions are as follows:

'127. For the purposes of this Part of this Act, sexual intercourse is complete upon penetration'.
'128. (1) Rape is the act of a male person having sexual intercourse with a woman or girl . . . without her consent.'

The first question is whether, in its ordinary and natural meaning, the language of s 128 is apt to refer to a part only of what may be described as one continuous act of intercourse. The trial Judge in the present case obviously thought so, and we agree. The 'act of a male person' referred to in s 128 is not just an act of intercourse. It is the composite act of having intercourse without the woman's consent. Accordingly the conduct of a man who persists in sexual intercourse after he realises that the woman is no longer consenting (or has never consented) may fairly and naturally be described as the 'act of a male person having sexual intercourse with a woman without her consent'. Sexual intercourse is obviously a continuing act and there is no novelty in the concept that a continuing act may become criminal during its progress as a result of a change in the state of mind of the defendant—see *Fagan v Commissioner of Metropolitan Police* [1969] 1 QB 439; [1968] 3 All ER 442. Indeed we did not understand Mr MacLean to argue to the contrary. He relied entirely upon the provisions of s 127, and to those provisions we shall now turn. . . .

In our view the purpose of s 127 is to remove any doubts as to the minimum conduct on the part of an accused person which the prosecution will have to establish in order to prove that he had sexual intercourse with the woman concerned. We are quite unable to accept that its purpose or effect is to remove from the scope of the definition of rape (in s 128) all acts by the accused, subsequent to penetration, which would in ordinary language be described as having sexual intercourse. . . .

We appreciate that the view which we have adopted might, at least in theory, lead to certain results which we would regard as unsatisfactory. We have in mind, for example, a woman suddenly wishing a man to desist at a late stage of intercourse or the failure of a man to fulfil a promise to desist before reaching a climax. At the other end of the scale the view urged upon us by Mr MacLean would lead to equally unsatisfactory results. It must be noted that the slightest degree of penetration is sufficient to bring a case within the s 127 definition of sexual intercourse. If Mr MacLean is correct then a girl who had been seduced into permitting a slight degree of penetration could not cry rape if she were then fully and by violence forced against her obvious wishes and subjected to a complete act of intercourse. Nor could a man be guilty of rape who began to have intercourse in the belief that the woman consented but carried on after he realised that she was not and never had been a consenting party. Some members of the community may take the view that no man should be held guilty of rape unless his initial penetration of the woman's body was without her consent, and unless he knew that such was the case, or was indifferent. Woodhouse J, in the judgment which he is about to deliver, vigorously puts forward that point of view. Others may think it as much a violation of a woman's right to the privacy of her own body if a man continues to have intercourse with her when he knows full well that she desperately wants him to desist. In an area where opinions can differ widely as to what may be just or unjust we are not persuaded that sufficient reason exists for us to depart from what we believe to be the ordinary and natural meaning of the language which Parliament has chosen to define the statutory crime of rape. That language, rather than any popular conception of what is involved in rape, must be decisive of the question which we are called upon to determine.

Woodhouse J. In essence the jury was directed that a man could become guilty of raping a woman during the one act of intercourse to which she had given her prior consent. It means that after he had entered her with consent she could transform his innocent and acceptable conduct into criminal activity of the most serious kind should he fail to meet her sudden indication that he must leave her. It is not explained just how rapidly he would need to act upon that indication to avoid becoming a rapist. But the position certainly must be, if the direction is correct, that in the event of such an indication then the single continuing occasion of intercourse could properly be described as being undertaken both with and without the consent of the woman concerned. If that is correct then with respect I think it is a remarkable extension of what has been the common understanding of this crime for generations.

Early writers spoke of rape in terms of forcible intercourse. Coke, for example, states that 'Rape is when a man hath carnal knowledge of a woman against her will'. It is, of course, a most serious crime of aggression, connoting the subjection of the resistance and will of the woman. In New Zealand the crime is not defined by reference to force or an act done against the will of the complainant. The statutory test of rape is 'the act of a male person having sexual intercourse with a woman or girl . . . *without her consent*'. But the use in that definition of the very practical test of consent as the precondition if the intercourse is to be lawful is simply designed to ensure the inclusion as criminal of those situations where the male has obtained the woman's submission by threats or where there has been no real consent at all. In any event the crime has always been concerned with the criminal invasion of a woman's body by a male; and for my part I cannot understand how any woman could reasonably complain that she had been violated in the gross sense of being raped if she had agreed that her partner could enter her. It may be that after a consensual act of intercourse had commenced physical discomfort or pain could induce a change of mind by the woman concerned or there could be sudden repentance on the part of a young girl that she had yielded to seduction. But surely nothing of this kind could provide the setting for *rape* whatever other offence might then seem to have been committed. And, certainly whatever may be the moral implications, seduction ought never to be confused with rape. It follows, too, that because a man cannot be guilty of the crime unless he is shown to have *intended* intercourse without the woman's consent all these considerations must apply where he has honestly but mistakenly believed that she was willing.

The decision of the New Zealand Court of Appeal was affirmed by the Privy Council, [1985] AC 147, [1984] 2 All ER 435.

Question

The Privy Council held that s 127 of the New Zealand Crimes Act (which corresponds with s 44 of the Sexual Offences Act 1956, p 554, below) merely removes any doubts as to the minimum content of sexual intercourse. It does not define when sexual intercourse ends. Given that it continues until the man withdraws, does it follow that rape is committed when a man who has penetrated with consent declines to withdraw on consent being revoked? Is there a difference between the case where the man penetrates with consent and that where he penetrates wrongly believing that he has consent?

2. Who is under a duty to act?

Though an offence is capable of being committed by omission, it does not follow that everyone is under a duty to act. Clause 20(2) of the Draft Bill purports to restate the law governing the imposition of a duty. Cf Smith & Hogan, p 43, Criminal Law Revision Committee, Fourteenth Report, para 252 and *Stone and Dobinson*, p 343, below and *Dalby*, p 338, post. Should Dalby have been guilty of manslaughter of O'Such by omitting to call an ambulance? Cf *People v Beardsley* (1967) 113 NW 1128 where, on similar facts, a conviction for manslaughter was quashed.

Proposals have often been made for the imposition of a general duty to save others from death or serious injury. A famous early example was the proposal by Edward Livingston for his draft code (never enacted) for Louisiana. It was to the effect that a person shall be guilty of homicide who omits to save life which he could save 'without personal danger or pecuniary loss'. This seems at first sight to be an attractive solution to the 'child in the shallow pool' case. The Commissioners who in 1838 reported on the Indian Penal Code thought the proposal open to serious objection. (Macaulay, *Works*, vol 7, 494). If this were the only test of a duty it would certainly be quite inadequate; the common law duty quite properly requires the person owing it to incur 'pecuniary loss'.

> 'A parent may be unable to procure food for an infant without money. Yet the parent, if he has the means, is bound to furnish the infant with food, and if, by omitting to do so, he voluntarily causes its death, he may with propriety be treated as a murderer'. [Ibid 494–495.]

As a test for an *additional* duty its defects are less obvious; but it would, apparently, have been unacceptable to the Commissioners.

They put the case of a surgeon, the only person in India who could perform a certain operation. If the operation is not performed on a particular patient he will certainly die. The surgeon could perform the operation without personal danger or pecuniary loss—in fact he will be well paid. But, for personal reasons it is extremely inconvenient for him to do so—he wishes to return to Europe or has other plans incompatible with the performance of the operation. The Commissioners thought it self-evident that he should not be guilty of murder. The example is an unusual one, highly unlikely to arise in practice, but not easy to distinguish in principle from the 'shallow pool' case. The difference, if there is one, seems to lie in the immediacy of the impending death in the shallow pool case. If Macaulay's surgeon were to witness an accident and, knowing that he was the only doctor present and that only immediate medical assistance could save an injured man's life, were to pass on because it was inconvenient to stop, it would seem less extravagant to convict him of an offence.

Macaulay excused what he thought might appear to be the excessive leniency of the Commissioners' proposals on the following grounds:

> 'It is indeed, most highly desirable that men should not merely abstain from doing harm to their neighbours, but should render active services to their neighbours. In general, however, the penal law must content itself with keeping men from doing positive harm, and must leave to public opinion, and to the teachers of morality and religion, the office of furnishing men with motives for doing positive good. It is evident that to attempt to punish men by law for not rendering to others all the service which it is their duty to render to others would be preposterous. We must grant impunity to the vast majority of those omissions which a benevolent morality would pronounce reprehensible, and must content ourselves with punishing such omissions only when they are distinguished from the rest by some circumstances which marks them out as peculiarly fit objects of penal legislation.'

Not everyone accepts this point of view. Professor Millner (*Negligence in the Modern Law*, p 33), writing in the context of the civil law of negligence, says:

> 'There is, however, nothing absolute about this immunity from liability, and no reason why changing attitudes should not bring some of the more callous types of indifference within the reach of the law, at least in cases where inaction amounts to calculated indifference to the fate of others, as in the case where an injured pedestrian is left to lie in the path of oncoming traffic by those who know of his plight and could remedy it; or where a

person is allowed, without warning, to cross thin ice or a crumbling bridge by one who is aware that the other, in his innocence is courting disaster; or where a person who, being in a position to take *some* action, yet allows a helpless and solitary invalid to starve to death. It is hard to imagine that anyone would be affronted if the law in such cases were to raise a duty of care in favour of the victim of this kind of callous indifference to the fate of one's fellows.'

Professor Graham Hughes ('Criminal Omissions' (1958) 67 Yale LJ 590 at 634) argues:

'Conventional criticisms of the imposition of a duty to rescue are usually based on objections to compelling one man to serve another, to creating a fear of prosecution which might cause citizens to interfere officiously in the affairs of others, and to the feasibility of imposing liability on a crowd of spectators all of whom had knowledge of the peril but were too selfish to intervene. These objections, however, do not seem to have much merit. To the first, the reply may be made that the evil of interfering with individual liberty by compelling assistance is much outweighed by the good of preserving human life. The second is a speculation which would be difficult to support. The third point appears to pose a real difficulty, but it is no different from a situation which commonly occurs in offences of commission. In a riot, for example, it is difficult if not impossible to bring all the participants to book, but this has never been considered an obstacle to trial and punishment of those who can be reached. If a crowd of spectators stands by and watches a child drown in shallow water, nothing seems objectionable in trying and punishing all who can be tracked down and cannot show a reasonable excuse. To think that such an example of selfish group inertia could exist in our society is distressing, but, if it did, there would be every reason for invoking the criminal law against it.'

3. Supervening fault

Clause 27 of the Draft Code is concerned with a particular type of liability for omission which is not, in terms, limited to particular crimes.

27 Supervening fault
(1) Where it is an offence to be at fault in causing a result, a person who causes the result by an act done without the fault required commits the offence if, after doing the act and with the fault required, he fails to take reasonable steps which might have prevented the result occurring or continuing.
(2) Where it is an offence to be at fault in respect of a state of affairs, a person who was not at fault when the state of affairs arose commits the offence if, with the fault required, he fails to take reasonable steps which might have ended it.

This clause restates and generalises the principle applied by the House of Lords in the following case.

R v Miller [1983] 1 All ER 978, House of Lords
(Lords Diplock, Keith, Bridge, Brandon and Brightman)

The defendant lay on a mattress in a house in which he was a squatter and lit a cigarette. He fell asleep and woke to find the mattress on fire. He went into the next room and went to sleep. The house caught fire and £800 worth of damage was done. He was charged with arson, contrary to s 1(1) and (3) of the Criminal Damage Act 1971, in that he 'damaged by fire a house . . . intending to do damage to such property or recklessly as to whether such property would be damaged'. He was convicted and his appeal to the Court of Appeal was dismissed. He appealed to the House of Lords.

Lord Diplock. The first question is a pure question of causation; it is one of fact to be decided by the jury in a trial on indictment. It should be answered No if, in relation to the fire during the period starting immediately before its ignition and ending with its extinction, the role of the accused was at no time more than that of a passive bystander. In such a case the subsequent questions to which I shall be turning would not arise. The conduct of the parabolical priest and Levite on the road to Jericho may have been indeed deplorable, but English law has not so far developed to the stage of treating it as criminal; and if it ever were to do so there would be difficulties in defining what should be the limits of the offence.

If, on the other hand the question, which I now confine to: 'Did a physical act of the accused start the fire which spread and damaged property belonging to another?', is answered 'Yes', as it was by the jury in the instant case, then for the purpose of the further questions the answers to which are determinative of his guilt of the offence of arson, the conduct of the accused, throughout the period from immediately before the moment of ignition to the completion of the damage to the property by the fire, is relevant; so is his state of mind throughout that period.

Since arson is a result-crime the period may be considerable, and during it the conduct of the accused that is causative of the result may consist not only of his doing physical acts which cause the fire to start or spread but also of his failing to take measures that lie within his power to counteract the danger that he has himself created. And if his conduct, active or passive, varies in the course of the period, so may his state of mind at the time of each piece of conduct. If, at the time of any particular piece of conduct by the accused that is causative of the result, the state of mind that actuates his conduct falls within the description of one or other of the states of mind that are made a necessary ingredient of the offence of arson by s 1(1) of the Criminal Damage Act 1971 (ie intending to damage property belonging to another or being reckless whether such property would be damaged), I know of no principle of English criminal law that would prevent his being guilty of the offence created by that subsection. Likewise I see no rational ground for excluding from conduct capable of giving rise to criminal liability conduct which consists of failing to take measures that lie within one's power to counteract a danger that one has oneself created, if at the time of such conduct one's state of mind is such as constitutes a necessary ingredient of the offence. I venture to think that the habit of lawyers to talk of 'actus reus', suggestive as it is of action rather than inaction, is responsible for any erroneous notion that failure to act cannot give rise to criminal liability in English law.

No one has been bold enough to suggest that if, in the instant case, the accused had been aware at the time that he dropped the cigarette that it would probably set fire to his mattress and yet had taken no steps to extinguish it he would not have been guilty of the offence of arson, since he would have damaged property of another being reckless whether any such property would be damaged.

I cannot see any good reason why, so far as liability under criminal law is concerned, it should matter at what point of time before the resultant damage is complete a person becomes aware that he has done a physical act which, whether or not he appreciated that it would at the time when he did it, does in fact create a risk that property of another will be damaged, provided that, at the moment of awareness, it lies within his power to take steps, either himself or by calling for the assistance of the fire brigade if this be necessary, to prevent or minimise the damage to the property at risk. . . .

My Lords, in the instant case the prosecution did not rely on the state of mind of the accused as being reckless during that part of his conduct that consisted of his lighting and smoking a cigarette while lying on his mattress and falling asleep without extinguishing it. So the jury were not invited to make any finding as to this. What the prosecution did rely on as being reckless was his state of mind during that part of his conduct after he awoke to find that he had set his mattress on fire and that it was smouldering, but did not then take any steps either to try to extinguish it himself or to send for the fire brigade, but simply went into the other room to resume his slumbers, leaving the fire from the already smouldering mattress to spread and to damage that part of the house where the mattress was.

The recorder, in his lucid summing up to the jury (they took 22 minutes only to reach their verdict), told them that the accused, having by his own act started a fire in the mattress which, when he became aware of its existence, presented an obvious risk of damaging the house, became under a duty to take some action to put it out. The Court of Appeal upheld the conviction, but its ratio decidendi appears to be somewhat different from that of the recorder. As I understand the judgment, in effect it treats the whole course of conduct of the accused, from the moment at which he fell asleep and dropped the cigarette onto the mattress until the time the damage to the house by fire was complete, as a continuous act of the accused, and holds that it is sufficient to constitute the statutory offence of arson if at any stage in that course of conduct the state of mind of the accused, when he fails to try to prevent or minimise the damage which will result from his initial act, although it lies within his power to do so, is that of being reckless whether property belonging to another would be damaged. . . .

My Lords, these alternative ways of analysing the legal theory that justifies a decision which has received nothing but commendation for its accord with common sense and justice have, since the publication of the judgment of the Court of Appeal in the instant case, provoked academic controversy. Each theory has distinguished support. Professor J C Smith espouses the 'duty theory' (see [1982] Crim LR 526 at 528); Professor Glanville Williams who, after the decision of the Divisional Court in *Fagan v Metropolitan Police Comr* [below] appears to have been attracted by the duty theory, now prefers that of the continuous act (see [1982] Crim LR 773). When applied to cases where a person has unknowingly done an act which sets in train events that, when he becomes aware of them, present an obvious risk that property belonging to another will be damaged, both theories lead to an identical result; and, since what your Lordships are concerned with is to give guidance to trial judges in their task of summing up to juries, I would for this purpose adopt the duty theory as being the easier to explain to a jury; though I would commend the use of the word 'responsibility', rather than 'duty' which is more appropriate to civil than to criminal law since it suggests an obligation owed to another person, ie the person to whom the endangered property belongs, whereas a criminal statute defines combinations of conduct and state of mind which render a person liable to punishment by the state itself.

While, in the general run of cases of destruction or damage to property belonging to another by fire (or other means) where the prosecution relies on the recklessness of the accused, the direction recommended by this House in *R v Caldwell* is appropriate, in the exceptional case (which is most likely to be one of arson and of which the instant appeal affords a striking example), where the accused is initially unaware that he has done an act that in fact sets in train events which, by the time the accused becomes aware of them, would make it obvious to anyone who troubled to give his mind to them that they present a risk that property belonging to another would be damaged, a suitable direction to the jury would be that the accused is guilty of the offence under s 1(1) of the 1971 Act if, when he does become aware that the events in question have happened as a result of his own act, he does not try to prevent or reduce the risk of damage by his own efforts or if necessary by sending for help from the fire brigade and the reason why he does not is either because he has not given any thought to the possibility of there being any such risk or because having recognised that there was some risk involved he has decided not to try to prevent or reduce it.

Lords Keith, Bridge, Brandon and **Brightman** agreed.

Appeal dismissed

Questions

1. Was the defendant held liable for damaging the house by falling asleep while smoking? Or for damaging the house by failing to take reasonable steps to put out the burning bed?

2. What if the defendant had found that his nine-year-old child had set the bed on fire and had left it to burn? Or the fire had originated in an electrical fault in the wiring of the house when he switched on his electric blanket?

3. What if the defendant's fellow squatter had (a) sustained grievous bodily harm or (b) died in the fire?

Fagan v Metropolitan Police Commissioner [1968] 3 All ER 442, Queen's Bench Division
(Lord Parker CJ, Bridge and James JJ)

The defendant was directed by a constable to park his car close to the kerb. He drove his car on to the constable's foot. The constable said, 'Get off, you are on my foot.' The defendant replied, 'Fuck you, you can wait', and turned off the ignition. He was convicted by the magistrates of assaulting the constable in the execution of his duty and his appeal was dismissed by Quarter Sessions who were in doubt whether the driving on to the foot was intentional or accidental but were satisfied that he 'knowingly, unnecessarily and provocatively' allowed the car to remain on the foot.

James J [with whom **Lord Parker CJ** concurred]. . . . In our judgment, the question arising, which has been argued on general principles, falls to be decided on the facts of the particulars case. An assault is any act which intentionally—or possibly recklessly—causes another person to apprehend immediate and unlawful personal violence. Although 'assault' is an independent crime and is to be treated as such, for practical purposes today 'assault' is generally synonymous with the term 'battery', and is a term used to mean the actual intended use of unlawful force to another person without his consent. On the facts of the present case, the 'assault' alleged involved a 'battery'. Where an assault involved a battery, it matters not, in our judgment, whether the battery is inflicted directly by the body of the offender or through the medium of some weapon or instrument controlled by the action of the offender. An assault may be committed by the laying of a hand on another, and the action does not cease to be an assault if it is a stick held in the hand and not the hand itself which is laid on the person of the victim. So, for our part, we see no difference in principle between the action of stepping on to a person's toe and maintaining that position and the action of driving a car on to a person's foot and sitting in the car while its position on the foot is maintained.

To constitute this offence, some intentional act must have been performed; a *mere* omission to act cannot amount to an assault. Without going into the question whether words alone can constitute an assault, it is clear that the words spoken by the appellant could not alone amount to an assault; they can only shed a light on the appellant's action. For our part, we think that the crucial question is whether, in this case, the act of the appellant can be said to be complete and spent at the moment of time when the car wheel came to rest on the foot, or whether his act is to be regarded as a continuing act operating until the wheel was removed. In our judgment, a distinction is to be drawn between acts which are complete—though results may continue to flow—and those acts which are continuing. Once the act is complete, it cannot thereafter be said to be a threat to inflict unlawful force on the victim. If the act, as distinct from the results thereof, is a continuing act, there is a continuing threat to inflict unlawful force. If the assault involves a battery and that battery continues, there is a continuing act of assault. For an assault to be committed, both the elements of actus reus and mens rea must be present at the same time. The 'actus reus' is the action causing the effect on the victim's mind: see the observations of Parke B, in *R v St George* [(1840) 9 C & P 483 at pp 490, 493]. The 'mens rea' is the intention to cause that effect. It is not necessary that mens rea should be present at the inception of the actus reus; it can be superimposed on an existing act. On the other hand, the subsequent inception of mens rea cannot convert an act which has been completed without mens rea into an assault.

In our judgment, the justices at Willesden and quarter sessions were right in law. On the facts found, the action of the appellant may have been initially unintentional, but the time came when, knowing that the wheel was on the officer's foot, the appellant (i) remained seated in the car so that his body through the medium of the car was in contact with the officer, (ii) switched off the ignition of the car, (iii) maintained the wheel of the car on the foot, and (iv) used words indicating the intention of keeping the wheel in that position. For our part, we cannot regard such conduct as mere omission or inactivity. There was an act constituting a battery which at its inception was not criminal because there was no element of intention, but which became criminal from the moment the intention was formed to produce the apprehension which was flowing from the continuing act. The fallacy of the appellant's argument is that it seeks to equate the facts of this case with such a case as where a motorist has accidentally run over a person and, that action having been completed, fails to assist the victim with the intent that the victim should suffer.

We would dismiss this appeal.

Bridge J. I fully agree with my lords as to the relevant principles to be applied. No mere omission to act can amount to an assault. Both the elements of actus reus and mens rea must be present at the same time, but the one may be superimposed on the other. It is in the application of these principles to the highly unusual facts of this case that I have, with regret, reached a different conclusion from the majority of the court. I have no sympathy at all for the appellant, who behaved disgracefully; but I have been unable to find any way of regarding the facts which satisfied me that they amounted to the crime of assault. This has not been for want of trying; but at every attempt I have encountered the inescapable question: after the wheel of the appellant's car had accidentally come to rest on the constable's foot, what was it that the appellant *did* which constituted the act of assault? However the question is approached, the answer which I feel obliged to give is: precisely nothing. The car rested on the foot by its own weight and remained stationary by its own inertia. The appellant's fault was that he omitted to manipulate the controls to set it in motion again.

Neither the fact that the appellant remained in the driver's seat nor that he switched off the ignition seem to me to be of any relevance. The constable's plight would have been no better, but might well have been worse, if the appellant had alighted from the car leaving the ignition switched on. Similarly, I can get no help from the suggested analogies. If one man accidentally treads on another's toe or touches him with a stick, but deliberately maintains pressure with foot or stick after the victim protests, there is clearly an assault; but there is no true parallel between such cases and the present case. It is not, to my mind, a legitimate use of language to speak of the appellant 'holding' or 'maintaining' the car wheel on the constable's foot. The expression which corresponds to the reality is that used by the justices in the Case Stated. They say, quite rightly, that he 'allowed' the wheel to remain.

With a reluctantly dissenting voice, I would allow this appeal and quash the appellant's conviction.

Appeal dismissed. Leave to appeal to the House of Lords refused.

Questions

1. Was there a 'continuing act' in *Miller* or in *Fagan*? Under the Draft Code (p 23, above) does it matter? Should it matter?

2. D, a motorist without fault on his part, skids on an oil-covered surface and injures P. D stops and sees that P is unconscious and bleeding. He could easily drive P to a nearby hospital. He drives off leaving P by the roadside. P bleeds to death. His life could have been saved had he been driven to the hospital. Is D liable to conviction for (a) manslaughter or (b) causing death by reckless driving according to: (i) *R v Miller* or (ii) the Draft Code, cl 27? Should it be different if D injured P by (i) careless driving or (ii) reckless driving?

NOTE

For a discussion of the duty to act to preserve the life of a handicapped child, see M.J. Gunn and J.C. Smith, '*Arthur's* Case and the Right to Life of a Down's Syndrome Child,' [1985] Crim LR 705.

CHAPTER 3

Causation

The draft Criminal Code Bill provides:

21 Causation
(1) A person causes a result when:
(a) his act makes a more than negligible contribution to its occurrence; or
(b) in breach of duty, he fails to do what he might do to prevent it occurring,
unless in either case some other cause supervenes which is unforeseen, extremely improbable and sufficient in itself to produce the result.
(2) But a person who procures, assists or encourages another to cause a result that is an element of an offence does not himself cause that result so as to be guilty of the offence as a principal except when:
(a) the other is his innocent agent under section 30(2)(*b*) and section 30(3) does not apply; or
(b) the offence consists in the procuring, assisting or encouraging another to cause the result.

Schedule 1 of the Draft Bill provides the following illustrations:

21 (1)(a)   21 (i)   D hits P who falls against Q, knocking Q down. Q suffers injuries from which she later dies. Assuming D intended to cause serious injury to P, but was not aware he might kill, D is guilty of the manslaughter (s 57) of Q. His act has contributed to her death and, by section 28, his intention to cause serious injury to P is to be treated as an intention to cause that result to Q.

                 21 (ii)   It is made a code offence to cause death by 'driving with criminal negligence'. D drives on a main road at an excessive speed to impress his girlfriend P. E drives out of a side road in front of D's car without keeping a proper lookout. P is killed in the ensuing collision. Assuming D and E to have been negligent (see s 22), both are guilty of the offence (irrespective of how civil liability would be apportioned between them) provided that the manner of driving of each was a more than negligible contribution to P's death.

21 (1)(b)   21 (iii)   D, E's mistress, lives with E and P, E's child by his wife. While E is away P falls seriously ill. D, wishing P to die, fails to call a doctor. P dies. P's life might have been prolonged by medical attention. D is guilty of murder (s 56). She is under a duty to act (s 20) and in breach of that duty has failed to do what she might do to prevent death occurring.

21 (1)   21 (iv)   D, the driver of a moving car, produces a knife and tells his passenger P that he intends to have sexual intercourse with her whether she consents or not. Greatly alarmed, P jumps out of the moving car and sustains injury. D may be guilty of intentionally or recklessly causing injury (s 76). His acts have contributed to P's injury notwithstanding that the injury was also caused by P's own act in jumping out of the car. Although this is a supervening cause, it may not be an extremely improbable response to D's behaviour.

                 21 (v)   D stabs P who is taken to hospital. P refuses the blood transfusion which he is told is necessary to save his life. P dies. D has killed P. The refusal of the transfusion may be unforeseen and extremely improbable, but it is not sufficient in itself to cause death. The death would not have occurred without the wound inflicted by D.

                 21 (vi)   D stabs P who is taken to hospital. P is given negligent medical treatment which aggravates his condition and he dies of the ill-treated wound. His life might have been saved by proper treatment. D has killed P. Hospital treat-

ment is unlikely to be negligent but negligent medical treatment is neither extremely improbable nor (save in an exceptional case) sufficient in itself to cause the result of death.

21 (vii) D hits P during a quarrel. P is lying dazed when he is stabbed by E. P dies later. D has not killed P since E's supervening act was unforeseen, extremely improbable and sufficient in itself to cause death.

The Report explains cl 21 as follows:

7.17 *Factual causation*. Under existing law a person's act need not be the sole, or even the major, cause of a harmful result. It is enough that the act is a 'substantial'[1] or 'significant'[2] cause of the result, and in this context this means merely that the accused's contribution must be outside the *de minimis* range.[3] Accordingly it is wrong, for example, to direct a jury that D is not liable if he is less than one-fifth to blame.[4] In subsection (1)(a) we state this requirement in terms that the defendant's act must make a 'more than negligible' contribution to the occurrence of the result. It is of course possible on this test for there to be more than one cause of a result, and illustration 21 (ii) is a case of two persons being independently liable in respect of the same death. As with existing law, this test will take no account of a victim's peculiar susceptibility to harm.[5]

7.18 *Omissions*. It is impossible to apply paragraph (a) of subsection (1) satisfactorily in the case of an omission to act. Ex hypothesi the harmful result has been brought about by a factor such as injury, disease or lack of food the effects of which the defendant has failed (perhaps along with many others) to take steps to prevent. Accordingly, paragraph (b) of subsection (1) provides that a person who has a duty to act (see clause 20) 'causes' a result when in breach of the duty he fails to take the steps he could take to prevent its occurrence.

7.19 *Supervening causes*. The concluding lines of subsection (1) provide that a person does not cause a result by his act or omission if 'some other cause supervenes which is unforeseen, extremely improbable and sufficient in itself to produce the result'. We believe that this restates for criminal law the principles which determine whether intervening acts or events are sufficient to break the chain of causation between the defendant's conduct and the result, or as it is sometimes put, whether in the circumstances the defendant's conduct is a cause in law of the result. According to our provision a person will still be liable if his intended victim suffers injury in trying to escape from the threatened attack unless the victim has done something extremely improbable.[6] Liability will be equally unaffected if the victim refuses medical treatment for a wound caused by the defendant. The refusal may be unforeseeable but it is not sufficient in itself to cause the result of death—in such a case, to use the language of the cases, the original wound is still the 'operating and substantial cause' of death.[7]

7.20 *Improper medical treatment*. A particular instance of an intervening act is improper medical treatment of a person injured by the defendant. There has been some controversy over the extent to which, if ever, such treatment when itself a cause of the harmful result can relieve the original wrongdoer of liability.[8] We believe that no special rule is needed for such cases which can be accommodated under the provision described in the preceding paragraph. In almost all cases improper treatment, although unlikely, will be neither extremely improbable in the circumstances nor sufficient in itself to cause the result. In a very exceptional case, such as *R v Jordan*, it may be both and then the defendant will be held not to have caused the relevant result. Under this provision proper medical treatment can never be a supervening cause sufficient to absolve the defendant.[9]

7.21 *Subsection (2)*. This subsection makes a necessary exception for accessories who participate in a result-crime. But for this provision subsection (1) might have the effect of turning them all into principal offenders with consequential difficulties for clauses 30 and 31. However, this exception must itself be subject to exceptions for cases of innocent agency and offences the elements of which consist of the procuring, assisting or encouraging another to cause a result.

1. *R v Smith* [1959] 2 QB 35; cf *R v Malcherek* [1981] 1 WLR 690.
2. *R v Pagett* (1983) 76 Cr App R 279.
3. *R v Hennigan* [1971] 3 All ER 133; *R v Cato* [1976] 1 WLR 110.
4. *R v Hennigan*, above.
5. See eg *R v Hayward* (1908) 21 Cox CC 692.
6. The rule is occasionally expressed in terms of foreseeability of the victim's attempt to escape (see *R v Roberts* (1971) 56 Cr App R 95), but the effect appears to be the same as the formulation suggested here.
7. *R v Smith*, above; *R v Blaue* [1975] 1 WLR 1411.
8. See *R v Jordan* (1956) 40 Cr App R 152; *R v Smith*, above.
9. As where doctors discontinue the use of a respirator to 'keep alive' a person who has suffered irreversible brain damage at the hands of the defendant, and thereby bring about the victim's death (that is, assuming he is not already dead). See *R v Malcherek*, above.

1. Supervening cause

R v Pagett (1983) 76 Cr App R 279, Court of Appeal, Criminal Division
(Robert Goff LJ, Cantley and Farquharson JJ)

Pagett (P), armed with a shotgun, took a girl, Gail Kinchen (K), who was six months pregnant by him, from the home of her mother and stepfather by force, wounding the stepfather, and violently assaulting her mother. P took K to a block of flats, pursued by the police. The police called on P to come out. Eventually he did so, holding K in front of him as a shield. He approached two police officers and fired the shotgun. The officers fired back instinctively not taking any particular aim. K was struck by three bullets and died. P was convicted of, inter alia, manslaughter. He appealed on the ground that the judge had misdirected the jury that, on these facts, he had caused K's death.

[**Robert Goff LJ** delivered the judgment of the Court:]

We turn to the first ground of appeal, which is that the learned judge erred in directing the jury that it was for him to decide *as a matter of law* whether by his unlawful and deliberate acts the appellant caused or was a cause of Gail Kinchen's death. It is right to observe that this direction of the learned judge followed upon a discussion with counsel, in the absence of the jury; though the appellant, having dismissed his own counsel, was for this purpose without legal representation. In the course of this discussion, counsel for the prosecution referred the learned judge to a passage in Professor Smith and Professor Hogan's *Criminal Law* (4th ed (1978), p 272), which reads as follows:

> 'Causation is a question of both fact and law. D's act cannot be held to be the cause of an event if the event would have occurred without it. The act, that is, must be a *sine qua non* of the event and whether it is so is a question of fact. But there are many acts which are *sine qua non* of a homicide and yet are not either in law, or in ordinary parlance, the cause of it. If I invite P to dinner and he is run over and killed on the way, my invitation may be a *sine qua non* of his death, but no one would say I killed him and I have not caused his death in law. Whether a particular act which is a *sine qua non* of an alleged *actus reus* is also a cause of it is a question of law. Where the facts are admitted the judge may direct the jury that a particular act did, or did not, cause a particular result.'

There follows a reference to *Jordan* [p 31, below].

For the appellant, Lord Gifford criticised the statement of the learned authors that 'Whether a particular act which is a *sine qua non* of an alleged *actus reus* is also a cause of it is a question of law.' He submitted that that question had to be answered by the jury as a question of fact. In our view, with all respect, both the passage in Smith and Hogan's *Criminal Law*, and Lord Gifford's criticism of it, are over-simplifications of a complex matter. . . .

Now the whole subject of causation in the law has been the subject of a well-known and most distinguished treatise by Professors Hart and Honoré, *Causation in the Law*. Passages from this book were cited to the learned judge, and were plainly relied upon by him; we, too, wish to express our indebtedness to it. It would be quite wrong for us to consider in this judgment the wider issues discussed in that work. But, for present purposes, the passage which is of most immediate relevance is to be found in Chapter XII, in which the learned authors consider the circumstances in which the intervention of a third person, not acting in concert with the accused, may have the effect of relieving the accused of criminal responsibility. The criterion which they suggest should be applied in such circumstances is whether the intervention is voluntary, i e whether it is 'free, deliberate and informed.' We resist the temptation of expressing the judicial opinion whether we find ourselves in complete agreement with that definition; though we certainly consider it to be broadly correct and supported by authority. Among the examples which the authors give of non-voluntary conduct, which is not effective to relieve the accused of responsibility, are two which are germane to the present case, viz a reasonable act performed for the purpose of self-preservation, and an act done in performance of a legal duty.

There can, we consider, be no doubt that a reasonable act performed for the purpose of self-preservation, being of course itself an act caused by the accused's own act, does not operate as a *novus actus interveniens*. If authority is needed for this almost self-evident proposition, it is to be found in such cases as *Pitts* (1842) C & M 284, and *Curley* (1909) 2 Cr App R 96. In both these cases, the act performed for the purpose of self-preservation consisted of an act by the victim in attempting to escape from the violence of the accused, which in fact resulted in the victim's death. In each case it was held as a matter of law that, if the victim acted in a reasonable attempt to escape the violence of the accused, the death of the victim was caused by the act of the accused. Now one form of self-preservation is self-defence; for present purposes, we can see no distinction in principle between an attempt to escape the consequences of the accused's act, and a response which takes the form of self-defence. Furthermore, in our judgment, if a reasonable act of self-defence against the act of the accused causes the death of a third party, we can see no reason in principle why the act of self-defence, being an involuntary act caused by the act of the accused, should relieve the accused from criminal responsibility for the death of the third party. Of course, it does not necessarily follow that the accused will be guilty of the murder, or even of the manslaughter, of the third party; though in the majority of cases he is likely to be guilty at least of manslaughter. Whether he is guilty of murder or manslaughter will depend upon the question whether all the ingredients of the relevant offence have been proved; in particular, on a charge of murder, it will be necessary that the accused had the necessary intent, on the principles stated by the House of Lords in *Hyam v DPP* [p 307, below].

No English authority was cited to us, nor we think to the learned judge, in support of the proposition that an act done in the execution of a legal duty, again of course being an act itself caused by the act of the accused, does not operate as a *novus actus interveniens*. . . . Even so, we agree with the learned judge that the proposition is sound in law, because as a matter of principle such an act cannot be regarded as a voluntary act independent of the wrongful act of the accused. A parallel may be drawn with the so-called 'rescue' cases in the law of negligence, where a wrongdoer may be held liable in negligence to a third party who suffers injury in going to the rescue of a person who has been put in danger by the defendant's negligent act. Where, for example, a police officer in the execution of his duty acts to prevent a crime, or to apprehend a person suspected of a crime, the case is surely *a fortiori*. Of course, it is inherent in the requirement that the police officer, or other person, must be acting in the execution of his duty that his act should be reasonable in all the circumstances: see section 3 of the Criminal Law Act 1967. Furthermore, once again we are only considering the issue of causation. If intervention by a third party in the execution of a legal duty, caused by the act of the accused, results in the death of the victim, the question whether the accused is guilty of the murder or manslaughter of the victim must depend on whether the necessary ingredients of the relevant offence have been proved against the accused, including in particular, in the case of murder, whether the accused had the necessary intent.

The principles which we have stated are principles of law. This is plain from, for example, the case of *Pitts* (1842) C & M 284, to which we have already referred. It follows that where, in any particular case, there is an issue concerned with what we have for convenience called *novus actus interveniens*, it will be appropriate for the judge to direct the jury in accordance with these principles. It does not however follow that it is accurate to state broadly that causation is a question of law. On the contrary, generally speaking causation is a question of fact for the jury. Thus in, for example, *Towers* (1874) 12 Cox CC 530, the accused struck a woman; she screamed loudly, and a child whom she was then nursing turned black in the face, and from that day until it died suffered from convulsions. The question whether the death of the child was caused by the act of the accused was left by the judge to the jury to decide as a question of fact. But that does not mean that there are no principles of law relating to causation, so that no directions on law are ever to be given to a jury on the question of causation. On the contrary, we have already pointed out one familiar direction which is given on causation, which is that the accused's act need not be the sole, or even the main, cause of the victim's death for his act to be held to have caused the death.

Appeal dismissed

2. Medical treatment

R v Jordan (1956) 40 Cr App Rep 152, Court of Criminal Appeal
(Hallett, Ormerod and Donovan JJ)

The appellant stabbed a man named Beaumont in a café in Hull on 4 May 1956. Beaumont died in hospital on 12 May. At the trial the pathologist called by the prosecution stated that the cause of death was broncho-pneumonia following penetrating abdominal injury.

In the Court of Criminal Appeal an application was made to call the additional evidence of two doctors to the effect that the wound was not the cause of the death. At the trial it had not occurred to the prosecution, the defence, the judge or the jury that there could be any doubt but that the stab caused death. The Court held, therefore, that the first requisite for the admission of additional evidence, namely that the evidence was not available at the trial, was satisfied.

[Having emphasised that the reception of fresh evidence was to be regarded as 'wholly exceptional' **Hallett J** continued:]

As to the second requisite, namely, that the evidence proposed to be tendered is such that, if the jury had heard that evidence, they might very likely, and indeed probably would, have come to a different verdict, we feel that, if the jury had heard two doctors of the standing of Dr Keith Simpson and Mr Blackburn give evidence that in their judgment death was not due to the stab wound but to something else, the jury might certainly have hesitated very long before saying that they were satisfied that death was due to the stab wound. The jury, of course, would not be bound by medical opinion, but flying in the face of it, particularly in a capital case, is a thing any jury would hesitate to do. When Mr Stanley-Price was trying to assist the court by cross-examining those doctors with a view to showing that they were mistaken in their opinions, and when he told us that he was prepared to tender the evidence of doctors who would, according to his instructions, probably express other opinions, we felt bound to say that the question is not whether we, if we were a jury, would have accepted and acted on the opinions those gentlemen expressed, but whether the jury in all probability would have allowed their verdict to be affected by them.

There is one further aspect that it is important I should emphasise lest this case is cited in some other case. There were two things other than the wound which were stated by these two medical witnesses to have brought about death. The stab wound had penetrated the intestine in two places, but it was mainly healed at the time of death. With a view to preventing infection it was thought right to administer an antibiotic, terramycin.

It was agreed by the two additional witnesses that that was the proper course to take, and a proper dose was administered. Some people, however, are intolerant to terramycin, and Beaumont was one of those people. After the initial doses he developed diarrhoea, which was only properly attributable, in the opinion of those doctors, to the fact that the patient was intolerant to terramycin. Thereupon the administration of terramycin was stopped, but unfortunately the very next day the resumption of such administration was ordered by another doctor and it was recommenced the following day. The two doctors both take the same view about it. Dr Simpson said that to introduce a poisonous substance after the intolerance of the patient was shown was palpably wrong. Mr Blackburn agreed.

Other steps were taken which were also regarded by the doctors as wrong—namely, the intravenous introduction of wholly abnormal quantities of liquid far exceeding the output. As a result the lungs became waterlogged and pulmonary oedema was discovered. Mr Blackburn said that he was not surprised to see that condition after the introduction of so much liquid, and that pulmonary oedema leads to broncho-pneumonia as an inevitable sequel, and it was from broncho-pneumonia that Beaumont died.

We are disposed to accept it as the law that death resulting from any normal treatment employed to deal with a felonious injury may be regarded as caused by the felonious injury, but we do not think it necessary to examine the cases in detail or to formulate for the assistance of those who have to deal with such matters in the future the correct test which ought to be laid down with regard to what is necessary to be proved in order to establish causal connection between the death and the felonious injury. It is sufficient to point out here that this was not normal treatment. Not only one feature, but two separate and independent features, of treatment were, in the opinion of the doctors, palpably wrong and these produced the symptoms discovered at the post-mortem examination which were the direct and immediate cause of death, namely, the pneumonia resulting from the condition of oedema which was found.

The question then is whether it can be said that, if that evidence had been before the jury, it ought not to have, and in all probability would not have, affected their decision. We recognise that the learned judge, if this matter had been before him, would have had to direct the jury correctly on how far such supervening matters could be regarded as interrupting the chain of causation; but we feel that in the end it would have been a question of fact for the jury depending on what evidence they accepted as correct and the view they took on that evidence. We feel no uncertainty at all that, whatever direction had been given to the jury and however correct it had been, the jury would have felt precluded from saying that they were satisfied that death was caused by the stab wound.

For these reasons we come to the conclusion that the appeal must be allowed and the conviction set aside.

Conviction quashed

Questions

1. Was the treatment regarded as the cause of the death because it was 'palpably wrong' or because it was 'not normal'?
2. Should the question whether a wound caused death be decided by (i) the doctors, (ii) the judge, or (iii) the jury? If the question is for the judge or the jury, should medical witnesses be allowed to state whether a death has been caused by an injury or by treatment?
3. Where death has followed after treatment of an injury given bona fide by qualified medical men, should evidence be admissible that it was the medical treatment and not the injury which caused the death?

(See Glanville Williams, 'Causation in Homicide' [1957] Crim LR 429 and 510, and F.E. Camps and J.D.J. Havard, 'Causation in Homicide—A Medical View' [1957] Crim LR 576.)

R v Smith [1959] 2 All ER 193, Courts-Martial Appeal Court
(Lord Parker CJ, Streatfeild and Hinchcliffe JJ)

The appellant was convicted of the murder of Private Creed following a fight in a barracks between men of two regiments. He appealed on the ground (inter alia) that the summing up by the judge-advocate on the question of causation was defective.

[**Lord Parker CJ** delivering the judgment of the court:]

. . . The second ground concerns a question of causation. The deceased man in fact received two bayonet wounds, one in the arm and one in the back. The one in the back, unknown to anybody, had pierced the lung and caused haemorrhage. There followed a series of unfortunate occurrences. A fellow member of his company tried to carry him to the medical reception station. On the way he tripped over a wire and dropped the deceased man. He picked him up again, went a little further, and fell apparently a second time causing the deceased man to be dropped on to the ground. Thereafter he did not try a third time but went for help, and ultimately the deceased man was brought into the reception station. There, the medical officer, Captain Millward, and his orderly were trying to cope with a number of other cases, two serious stabbings and some minor injuries, and it is clear that they did not appreciate the seriousness of the deceased man's condition or exactly what had happened. A transfusion of saline solution was attempted and failed. When his breathing seemed impaired, he was given oxygen and artificial respiration was applied. He died after he had been in the station about an hour, which was about two hours after the original stabbing. It is now known that, having regard to the injuries which the deceased man had in fact suffered, his lung being pierced, the treatment which he was given was thoroughly bad and might well have affected his chances of recovery. There was evidence that there is a tendency for a wound of this sort to heal and for the haemorrhage to stop. No doubt his being dropped on the ground and having artificial respiration applied would halt, or at any rate impede, the chances of healing. Further, there were no facilities whatsoever for blood transfusion, which would have been the best possible treatment. There was evidence that, if he had received immediate and different treatment, he might not have died. Indeed, had facilities for blood transfusion been available and been administered, Dr Camps, who gave evidence for the defence, said that his chances of recovery were as high as seventy-five per cent.

In these circumstances counsel for the appellant urges that, not only was a careful summing-up required, but a correct direction to the court would have been that they must be satisfied that the death of Private Creed was a natural consequence and the sole consequence of the wound sustained by him and flowed directly from it. If there was, says counsel for the appellant, any other cause whether resulting from negligence or not, if, as he contends here, something happened here which impeded the chance of the deceased recovering, then the death did not result from the wound. The court is quite unable to accept that contention. It seems to the court that, if at the time of death the original wound is still an operating cause and a substantial cause, then the death can properly be said to be the result of the wound, albeit that some other cause of death is also operating. Only if it can be said that the original wounding is merely the setting in which another cause operates can it be said that the death does not result from the wound. Putting it in another way, only if the second cause is so overwhelming as to make the original wound merely part of the history can it be said that the death does not flow from the wound. . . .

Counsel for the appellant placed great reliance on *Jordan* (p 31, ante), a decision of the Court of Criminal Appeal, and, in particular, on a passage in the headnote which says:

'. . . that death resulting from any normal treatment employed to deal with a felonious injury may be regarded as caused by the felonious injury, but that the same principle does not apply where the treatment employed is abnormal.'

Reading those words into the present case, counsel for the appellant says that the treatment which Private Creed received from the moment when he was struck until the time of his death was abnormal. The court is satisfied that *Jordan* was a very particular case depending on its exact facts. It incidentally arose in the Court of Criminal Appeal on the grant of an application to call further evidence, and, leave having been obtained, two well-known medical experts gave evidence that in their opinion death had been caused, not by the stabbing, but by the introduction of terramycin after the deceased had shown that he was intolerant to it and by the intravenous introduction of abnormal quantities of liquid. It also appears that, at the time when that was done, the stab wound, which had penetrated the intestine in two places, had mainly healed. In those circumstances the court felt bound to quash the conviction because they could not say that a reasonable jury, properly directed, would not have been able, on that evidence, to say that there had been a break in the chain of causation; the court could uphold the conviction in that case only if they were satisfied that no reasonable jury could have come to that conclusion.

In the present case it is true that the judge-advocate did not, in his summing-up, go into the refinements of causation. Indeed, in the opinion of this court, he was probably wise to refrain from doing so. He left to the court the broad question whether they were satisfied that the wound had caused the death in the sense that the death flowed from the wound, albeit that the treatment which the deceased man received was, in the light of after-knowledge, a bad thing. In the opinion of this court, that was, on the facts of the case, a perfectly adequate summing-up on causation; I say 'on the facts of the case' because, in the opinion of the court, they can only lead to one conclusion: A man is stabbed in the back, his lung is pierced and haemorrhage results; two hours later he dies of haemorrhage from that wound; in the interval there is no time for a careful examination and the treatment given turns out in the light of subsequent knowledge to have been inappropriate and, indeed, harmful. In those circumstances no reasonable jury or court could, properly directed, in our view possibly come to any other conclusion than that the death resulted from the original wound. Accordingly, the court dismisses this appeal.

Appeal dismissed

R v Blaue [1975] 3 All ER 446, Court of Appeal, Criminal Division
(Lawton LJ, Thompson and Shaw JJ)

The appellant was convicted of manslaughter on the ground of diminished responsibility. He had inflicted four serious stab wounds on the deceased, one of which pierced a lung. The deceased, a Jehovah's Witness, refused to have a blood transfusion because it was contrary to her religious beliefs, and acknowledged this refusal in writing, despite the surgeon's advice that without the transfusion she would die. The Crown conceded at the trial that had she had the blood transfusion she would not have died. Blaue appealed on the ground (inter alia) that Mocatta J, following *Holland* (1841) 2 Mood & R 351, in effect directed the jury to find causation proved.

[**Lawton LJ** delivered the judgment of the court:]

. . . In *Holland* [(1841) 2 Mood & R 351] the defendant, in the course of a violent assault, had injured one of his victim's fingers. A surgeon had advised amputation because of danger to life through complications developing. The advice was rejected. A fortnight later the victim died of lockjaw: '. . . the real question is', said Maule J [2 Mood & R at 352], 'whether in the end the wound inflicted by the prisoner was the cause of death?' That distinguished judge left the jury to decide that question as did the judge in this case. They had to decide it as juries always do, by pooling their experience of life and using their common sense. They would not have been handicapped by a lack of training in dialectics or moral theology.

Maule J's direction to the jury reflected the common law's answer to the problem. He who inflicted an injury which resulted in death could not excuse himself by pleading that his victim could have avoided death by taking greater care of himself: see Hale [Pleas of the Crown (1800), pp 427, 428]. The common law in Sir Matthew Hale's time probably was in line with contemporary concepts of ethics. A man who did a wrongful act was deemed *morally* responsible for the natural and probable consequences of that act. Counsel for the appellant asked us to remember that since Sir Matthew Hale's day the rigour of the law relating to homicide has been eased in favour of the accused. It has been—but this has come about through the development of the concept of intent, not by reason of a different view of causation. Well-known practitioner's textbooks, such as *Halsbury's Laws* [3rd edn, vol 10, p 706] and *Russell on Crime* [12th edn (1964), vol 1, p 30], continue to reflect the common law approach. Textbooks intended for students or as studies in jurisprudence have queried the common law rule. See Hart and Honoré, *Causation in the Law* [1959, pp 320, 321], and Smith and Hogan [*Criminal Law* (3rd edn, 1973) p 214].

The physical cause of death in this case was the bleeding into the pleural cavity arising from the penetration of the lung. This had not been brought about by any decision made by the deceased girl but by the stab wound.

Counsel for the appellant tried to overcome this line of reasoning by submitting that the jury should have been directed that if they thought the girl's decision not to have a blood transfusion was an unreasonable one, then the chain of causation would have been broken. At once the question arises—reasonable by whose standards? Those of Jehovah's Witnesses? Humanists? Roman Catholics? Protestants of Anglo-Saxon descent? The man on the Clapham omnibus? But he might well be an admirer of Eleazar who suffered death rather than eat the flesh of swine [See 2 Maccabees, ch 6, vv 18–31] or of Sir Thomas More who, unlike nearly all his contemporaries, was unwilling to accept Henry VIII as Head of the Church in England. Those brought up in the Hebraic and Christian traditions would probably be reluctant to accept that these martyrs caused their own deaths.

As was pointed out to counsel for the appellant in the course of argument, two cases, each raising the same issue of reasonableness because of religious beliefs, could produce different verdicts depending on where the cases were tried. A jury drawn from Preston, sometimes said to be the most Catholic town in England, might have different views about martyrdom to one drawn from the inner suburbs of London. Counsel for the appellant accepted that this might be so; it was, he said, inherent in trial by jury. It is not inherent in the common law as expounded by Sir Matthew Hale and Maule J. It has long been the policy of the law that those who use violence on other people must take their victims as they find them. This in our judgment means the whole man, not just the physical man. It does not lie in the mouth of the assailant to say that his victim's religious beliefs which inhibited him from accepting certain kinds of treatment were unreasonable. The question for decision is what caused her death. The answer is the stab wound. The fact that the victim refused to stop this end coming about did not break the causal connection between the act and death. . . .

Appeal dismissed

R v Malcherek, R v Steel [1981] 2 All ER 422, Court of Appeal, Criminal Division (Lord Lane CJ, Ormrod LJ and Smith J)

In each of these cases the appellant had inflicted severe injuries on a person who, in consequence, was put on a life support machine or ventilator. In each case the doctors in charge, after some time, decided to take the patient off the ventilator. The trial judges withdrew the issue of causation from the jury and both appellants were convicted of murder. They appealed on the ground that the issue should have been left to the jury.

Lord Lane CJ. This is not the occasion for any decision as to what constitutes death. Modern techniques have undoubtedly resulted in the blurring of many of the conventional and traditional concepts of death. A person's heart can now be removed altogether without death supervening; machines can keep the blood circulating through the vessels of the body until a new heart can be implanted in the patient, and even though a person is no longer able to breathe spontaneously a ventilating machine can, so to speak, do his breathing for him, as is demonstrated in the two cases before us. There is, it seems, a body of opinion in the medical profession that there is only one true test of death and that is the irreversible death of the brain stem, which controls the basic functions of the body such as breathing. When that occurs it is said the body has died, even though by mechanical means the lungs are being caused to operate and some circulation of blood is taking place.

We have had placed before us, and have been asked to admit, evidence that in each of these two cases the medical men concerned did not comply with all the suggested criteria for establishing such brain death. Indeed, further evidence has been suggested and placed before us that those criteria or tests are not in themselves stringent enough. However, in each of these two cases there is no doubt that whatever test is applied the victim died; that is to say, applying the traditional test, all body functions, breathing and heartbeat and brain function came to an end, at the latest, soon after the ventilator was disconnected.

The question posed for answer to this court is simply whether the judge in each case was right in withdrawing from the jury the question of causation. Was he right to rule that there was no evidence on which the jury could come to the conclusion that the assailant did not cause the death of the victim?

The way in which the submissions are put by counsel for Malcherek on the one hand and by counsel for Steel on the other is as follows: the doctors, by switching off the ventilator and the life support machine, were the cause of death or, to put it more accurately, there was evidence which the jury should have been allowed to consider that the doctors, and not the assailant, in each case may have been the cause of death.

In each case it is clear that the initial assault was the cause of the grave head injuries in the one case and of the massive abdominal haemorrhage in the other. In each case the initial assault was the reason for the medical treatment being necessary. In each case the medical treatment given was normal and conventional. At some stage the doctors must decide if and when treatment has become otiose. This decision was reached, in each of the two cases here, in circumstances which have already been set out in some detail. It is no part of the task of this court to inquire whether the criteria, the Royal Medical College confirmatory tests, are a satisfactory code of practice. It is no part of the task of this court to decide whether the doctors were, in either of these two cases, justified in omitting one or more of the so called 'confirmatory tests'. The doctors are not on trial: Steel and Malcherek respectively were.

[His Lordship discussed *Jordan* (p 31, above) and *Smith* (p 33, above) and continued:]

In the view of this court, if a choice has to be made between the decision in *R v Jordan* and that in *R v Smith*, which we do not believe it does (*R v Jordan* being a very exceptional case), then the decision in *R v Smith* is to be preferred.

[His Lordship discussed *Blaue* (p 34, above) and continued:]

There is no evidence in the present case here that at the time of conventional death, after the life support machinery was disconnected, the original wound or injury was other than a continuing, operating and indeed substantial cause of the death of the victim, although it need hardly be added that it need not be substantial to render the assailant guilty. There may be occasions, although they will be rare, when the original injury has ceased to operate as a cause at all, but in the ordinary case if the treatment is given bona fide by competent and careful medical practitioners, then evidence will not be admissible to show that the treatment would not have been administered in the same way by other medical practitioners. In other words, the fact that the victim has died, despite or because of medical treatment for the initial injury given by careful and skilled medical practitioners, will not exonerate the original assailant from responsibility for the death. It follows that so far as the ground of appeal in each of these cases relates to the direction given on causation, that ground fails. It also follows that the evidence which it is sought to adduce now, although we are prepared to assume that it is both credible and was not available properly at the trial (and a reasonable explanation for not calling it at the trial has been given), if received could, under no circumstances, afford any ground for allowing the appeal.

The reason is this. Nothing which any of the two or three medical men whose statements are before us could say would alter the fact that in each case the assailant's actions continued to be an operating cause of the death. Nothing the doctors could say would provide any ground for a jury coming to the conclusion that the assailant in either case might not have caused the death. The furthest to which their proposed evidence goes, as already stated, is to suggest, first, that the criteria or the confirmatory tests are not sufficiently stringent and, second, that in the present case they were in certain respects inadequately fulfilled or carried out. It is no part of this court's function in the present circumstances to pronounce on this matter, nor was it a function of either of the juries at these trials. Where a medical practitioner adopting methods which are generally accepted comes bona fide and conscientiously to the conclusion that the patient is for practical purposes dead, and that such vital functions as exist (for example, circulation) are being maintained solely be mechanical means, and therefore discontinues treatment, that does not prevent the person who inflicted the initial injury from being responsible for the victim's death. Putting it in another way, the discontinuance of treatment in those circumstances does not break the chain of causation between the initial injury and the death.

Although it is unnecessary to go further than that for the purpose of deciding the present point, we wish to add this thought. Whatever the strict logic of the matter may be, it is perhaps somewhat bizarre to suggest, as counsel have impliedly done, that where a doctor tries his conscientious best to save the life of a patient brought to hospital in extremis, skilfully using sophisticated methods, drugs and machinery to do so, but fails in his attempt and therefore discontinues treatment, he can be said to have caused the death of the patient.

Appeal and applications dismissed.

On the question, what constitutes death?, see p 303, below.

CHAPTER 4

Proof

The draft Criminal Code Bill provides:

17 Proof
(1) Unless otherwise expressly provided:
(a) the burden of proving every element of an offence and any other fact alleged or relied on by the prosecution shall be on the prosecution;
(b) where evidence is given (whether by the defendant or by the prosecution) of any defence or any other fact relied on by the defendant the burden shall, unless subsection (4) applies, be on the prosecution to prove that an element of the defence or such other fact did not exist.
(2) Evidence is given of a defence or of any other fact alleged or relied on by the defendant when there is such evidence as might lead a court or jury to conclude that there is a reasonable possibility that the elements of the defence or such other fact existed.
(3) Unless otherwise expressly provided:
(a) where the burden of proof is on the prosecution the standard of proof required shall be proof beyond reasonable doubt;
(b) where the burden of proof is on the defendant the standard of proof required shall be proof on the balance of probabilities.
(4) Nothing in this section shall affect the application in relation to any pre-Code offence of section 101 of the Magistrates' Courts Act 1980 or any rule of interpretation whereby the burden of proving a special defence is imposed on the defendant on trial on indictment.

The Report on Codification of the Criminal Law explains this clause as follows:

Clause 17: Burden of Proof
6.1 *Clause 17(1)* states the rule in *Woolmington v DPP*.[1] The burden is on the prosecution to prove all the elements of the offence charged whether by direct or circumstantial evidence and to prove any collateral fact alleged or relied on by the prosecution. Under the present law, where the prosecution allege that the defendant is unfit to plead, they must prove it.[2] Where they tender a confession they must prove that it is voluntary.[3] Where they tender a witness whose competence is challenged they must prove any fact on which they rely to establish his competence.[4] These are instances of the general principle stated in the subsection.
6.2 *Defences and collateral facts.* As under the present law, subsection (1) imposes no burden on the prosecution to disprove a defence until evidence of it is given. Where evidence of a defence emerges in the course of the prosecution's case, the burden is on the prosecution to disprove the defence.[5] Where evidence does not so emerge, the burden is on the defendant to adduce evidence of any defence on which he wishes to rely. Once he has given evidence of a defence, the burden is on the prosecution to disprove it. The same principles apply to collateral facts. If the defendant alleges that he made a confession because a particular inducement was held out to him to confess, he must give evidence of the holding out of that inducement; but when he has done so, it is for the prosecution to prove that it was not held out.
6.3 *Subsection (2). Evidential burden.* This subsection describes what the defendant must do in order to raise the issue of a defence or any other fact. If he tenders such evidence as might lead a court or jury to conclude that there is a reasonable possibility that the elements of a defence existed, the defence must be left to the jury or considered by the magistrates, as the case may be, and upheld if, after taking into account the evidence of the prosecution, they decide that it is reasonably possible that the elements of the defence existed. If the defendant fails to tender such evidence, then the defence will be withdrawn from the jury and magistrates need to consider it no further.

6.4 *Exceptions. Subsections (1) and (4).* Subsection (1) applies only if it is not otherwise expressly provided. It would therefore not affect the numerous enactments relating to pre-Code offences which impose a burden of proof on a balance of probabilities on the defendant. Section 101 of the Magistrates' Courts Act 1980 which imposes a burden of proving defences on the defendant in a summary trial is preserved by subsection (4) but only in relation to pre-Code offences. Section 101 would not apply to Code offences. The burden of disproving special defences in the magistrates' courts would be on the prosecution unless the enactment creating the Code offence and the special defence provided that it should be on the defence.

6.5 Subsection (4) also preserves the rule in *R v Edwards*[6] (that being a 'rule of interpretation whereby the burden of proving a special defence is imposed on the defendant on trial on indictment'), but, again, only in relation to pre-Code offences. The extent of the rule in *R v Edwards* is uncertain. It is sometimes said to be the same as that of section 101; but that is not clear. For example, section 101 seems clearly to apply to section 5(2) of the Criminal Damage Act 1971 so as to impose a burden on the defendant to prove 'a lawful excuse'; but it is by no means clear that the rule for trial on indictments as stated in *R v Edwards* applies. Moreover *R v Edwards* has been much criticised. Subsection (4) recognises the existence of the rule in that case but leaves it open to the courts to determine its limits, or, if thought appropriate, overrule it.

1. [1935] AC 462, HL.
2. *R v Podola* [1960] 1 QB 325, CCA.
3. *R v Thompson* [1893] 2 QB 12, CCR.
4. *R v Yacoob* (1981) 72 Cr App R 313, CA.
5. *Palmer v R* [1971] AC 814, PC.
6. [1975] QB 27, CA at 40. The rule is 'limited to offences arising under enactments which prohibit the doing of an act save in specified circumstances or by persons of specified classes or with special qualifications or with the licence or permission of specified authorities. Whenever the prosecution seeks to rely on this exception, the court must construe the enactment under which the charge is laid. If the true construction is that the enactment prohibits the doing of acts, subject to provisos, exemptions and the like, then the prosecution can rely on the exception.'

1. The presumption of innocence

Woolmington v Director of Public Prosecutions [1935] All ER Rep 1, House of Lords (Lord Sankey LC, Lord Hewart CJ, Lord Atkin, Lord Tomlin and Lord Wright)

After a few months of marriage, the appellant's wife left him and went to live with her mother. The appellant was anxious for her to return but she did not. One morning he called at her mother's house and shot her dead. His story was that he decided to take an old gun which was in the barn at his employer's farm, show it to his wife and tell her that he was going to commit suicide if she did not come back. He sawed off the two barrels and loaded the gun with the two cartridges which were in the barn. He attached a piece of wire flex to the gun so that he could suspend it from his shoulder underneath his coat. When he asked his wife if she would come back, she replied that she was going into service. He then threatened to shoot himself and went on to show her the gun. As he brought it across his waist, it somehow went off. It was, he said, a pure accident.

[**Swift J**, having quoted the passage from Foster's *Crown Law* cited below, directed the jury as follows:]

> 'Once it is shown to a jury that somebody has died through the act of another, that is presumed to be murder, unless the person who has been guilty of the act which causes the death can satisfy a jury that what happened was something less, something which might be alleviated, something which might be reduced to a charge of manslaughter, or was something which was accidental, or was something which could be justified'.

At the end of his summing up he added:

'The Crown has got to satisfy you that this woman, Violet Woolmington, died at the prisoner's hands. They must satisfy you of that beyond any reasonable doubt. If they satisfy you of that, then he has to show that there are circumstances to be found in the evidence which has been given from the witness-box in this case which alleviate the crime so that it is only manslaughter, or which excuse the homicide altogether by showing that it was a pure accident.'

The accused was convicted and his appeal was dismissed by the Court of Criminal Appeal. He appealed to the House of Lords.

[**Lord Sankey, LC**, having stated the facts continued:]

It is true, as stated by the Court of Criminal Appeal, that there is apparent authority for the law as laid down by the learned judge. But your Lordships' House has had the advantage of a prolonged and exhaustive inquiry dealing with the matter in debate from the earliest times, an advantage which was not shared by either of the courts below. Indeed your Lordships were referred to legal propositions dating as far back as the reign of King Canute (994–1035). I do not think it is necessary for the purpose of this opinion to go as far back as that. Rather would I invite your Lordships to begin by considering the proposition of law which is contained in *Foster's Crown Law*, written in 1762, and which appears to be the foundation for the law as laid down by the learned judge in this case. It must be remembered that Sir Michael Foster, although a distinguished judge, is for this purpose to be regarded as a textbook writer, for he did not lay down the doctrine in any case before him, but in an article which is described as 'The Introduction to the Discourse of Homicide'. In the folio edition, published at Oxford at the Clarendon Press in 1762, at p 255, he states:

'In every charge of murder, the fact of killing being first proved, all the circumstances of accident, necessity, or infirmity, are to be satisfactorily proved by the prisoner, unless they arise out of the evidence produced against him; for the law presumeth the fact to have been founded in malice until the contrary appeareth. And very right it is, that the law should so presume. The defendant in this instance standeth upon just the same foot that every other defendant doth: the matters tending to justify, excuse, or alleviate must appear in evidence before he can avail himself of them.'

Now the first part of this passage appears in nearly every textbook or abridgment which has been since written. . . .

The question arises: Is that statement correct law? Is it correct to say, and does Sir Michael Foster mean to lay down, that there may arise in the course of a criminal trial a situation at which it is incumbent upon the accused to prove his innocence? To begin with, if that is what Sir Michael Foster meant, there is no previous authority for his proposition, and I am confirmed in this opinion by the fact that in all the textbooks no earlier authority is cited for it. . . .

If at any period of a trial it was permissible for the judge to rule that the prosecution had established its case and that the onus was shifted on the prisoner to prove that he was not guilty, and that, unless he discharged that onus, the prosecution was entitled to succeed, it would be enabling the judge in such a case to say that the jury must in law find the prisoner guilty and so make the judge decide the case and not the jury, which is not the common law. It would be an entirely different case from those exceptional instances of special verdicts where a judge asks the jury to find certain facts and directs them that on such facts the prosecution is entitled to succeed. Indeed, a consideration of such special verdicts shows that it is not till the end of the evidence that a verdict can properly be found and that at the end of the evidence it is not for the prisoner to establish his innocence, but for the prosecution to establish his guilt. Just as there is evidence on behalf of the prosecution so there may be evidence on behalf of the prisoner which may cause a doubt as to his guilt. In either case, he is entitled to the benefit of the doubt. But while the prosecution must prove the guilt of the prisoner, there is no such burden laid on the prisoner to prove his innocence, and it is sufficient for him to raise a doubt as to his guilt; he is not bound to satisfy the jury of his innocence.

This is the real result of the perplexing case of *Abramovitch* (1912) 7 Cr App Rep 145 which lays down the same proposition, although, perhaps, in somewhat involved language. Juries are always told that, if conviction there is to be, the prosecution must prove the case beyond reasonable doubt. This statement cannot mean that in order to be acquitted the prisoner must 'satisfy' the jury. This is the law as laid down in the Court of Criminal Appeal in *Davies* [1913] 1 KB 573 the head-note of which correctly states that where intent is an ingredient of a crime there is no onus on the defendant to prove that the act alleged was accidental. Throughout the web of the English criminal law one golden thread is always to be seen—that it is the duty of the prosecution to prove the prisoner's guilt subject to what I have already said as to the defence of insanity and subject also to any statutory exception. If, at the end of and on the whole of the case, there is a reasonable doubt, created by the evidence given by either the prosecution or the prisoner, as to whether the prisoner killed the deceased with a malicious intention, the prosecution has not made out the case and the prisoner is entitled to an acquittal. No matter what the charge or where the trial, the principle that the prosecution must prove the guilt of the prisoner is part of the common law of England and no attempt to whittle it down can be entertained. When dealing with a murder case the Crown must prove (*a*) death as the result of a voluntary act of the accused and (*b*) malice of the accused. It may prove malice either expressly or by implication. For malice may be implied where death occurs as the result of a voluntary act of the accused which is (i) intentional and (ii) unprovoked. When evidence of death and malice has been given (this is a question for the jury) the accused is entitled to show by evidence or by examination of the circumstances adduced by the Crown that the act on his part which caused death was either unintentional or provoked. If the jury are either satisfied with his explanation or, upon a review of all the evidence, are left in reasonable doubt whether, even if his explanation be not accepted, the act was unintentional or provoked, the prisoner is entitled to be acquitted. It is not the law of England to say, as was said in the summing up in the present case,

> 'if the Crown satisfy you that this woman died at the prisoner's hands, then he has to show that there are circumstances to be found in the evidence which has been given from the witness-box in this case which alleviate the crime so that it is only manslaughter or which excuse the homicide altogether by showing it was a pure accident.'

Lords Atkin, Hewart, Tomlin and **Wright** concurred.

Appeal allowed

2. Proof or disproof of states of mind

The draft Criminal Code Bill provides:

18 Proof or disproof of states of mind
A court or jury shall not be bound to infer:
(a) that a person intended a result of an act or was aware that it might occur by reason only of its being a probable result of the act; or
(b) that a person was aware or believed that a circumstance existed or might exist by reason only of the fact that a reasonable person would have been aware or would have believed that it existed; or
(c) that a person did not believe that an exempting circumstance existed by reason only of the fact that a reasonable person would not have believed that it existed.
but shall determine by reference to all the evidence whether the person had or (in the case of paragraph (c)) may have had the state of mind in question, drawing such inferences from the evidence as appear proper.

Schedule 1 of the draft Bill provides the following illustrations:

18(a)   18(i)   D sets fire to a house in which, as he knows, P is asleep. P dies in the fire. There was an obvious risk that this would occur. But a finding either that D intended P's death or that he was aware that it might occur depends on a consideration of all the evidence, including the fact that that result was probable and any evidence given by D as to his state of mind.

18(b)   18(ii)   D buys from E, at a very favourable price, goods which E describes to him as 'hot'. D is charged with receiving stolen goods knowing or believing them to be stolen. The court or jury may be satisfied that most people would have realised from the use of the word 'hot' that the goods were stolen. If so, they will take this into account in deciding whether D realised that fact, though they will not be bound to conclude that he did.

18(c)   18(iii)   D is charged with assaulting P. D in evidence says that he misinterpreted a gesture made by P as an act of violence and that he hit P in self-defence. The court or jury are satisfied that there were no reasonable grounds for the mistake D claims to have made. They will take this into account in deciding whether it is possible that D did make that mistake.

The Report on Codification explains the clause as follows:

Clause 18: Proof or disproof of states of mind
6.9 *Paragraphs (a) and (b)* implement the recommendation of the Law Commission that:

> 'the general principle, of which section 8 of the Criminal Justice Act 1967 and section 1(2) of the Sexual Offences (Amendment) Act 1976 are particular applications, should be given statutory formulation.'

The 'general principle' is that if the fault element of an offence includes a state of mind, the defendant himself must be proved to have acted with that state of mind. The fact that a reasonable person would have had that state of mind is merely a factor to be taken into account with any other evidence in deciding whether it should be inferred that the defendant had it.
6.10 *Paragraph (c)* declares the corresponding rule for states of mind that are elements of defences. If a defendant asserts that he believed a circumstance to exist, the fact that a reasonable person would not have believed it to exist is merely a factor for the court or jury to take into account in deciding whether the defendant may have done so.
6.11 The whole provision is strictly speaking otiose. It expresses a truism. But a history of error on the point suggests that it would be wise to include it in the Code.
6.12 *Drafting.* We have drafted this clause in a simpler form than that used in clause 7 of the Law Commission's draft Criminal Liability (Mental Element) Bill. We have also abandoned, as apparently redundant, some phrases inherited by the draft Bill from section 8 of the Criminal Justice Act 1967.

(1) THE CRIMINAL JUSTICE ACT 1967, s 8

Section 8 (p 562, below) was drafted by the Law Commission and included in a Report ('Imputed Criminal Intent: *DPP v Smith*') dealing with the reform of the law of murder, consequent upon the decision in *DPP v Smith* (p 305, below).

The section was not intended by the Law Commission to make any change in the law of murder. In their report, it was followed by a second clause (Smith & Hogan, p 298) which defined the mens rea of murder; but that second clause was never enacted. The change which the Law Commission intended to make in the law of murder was not made. The clause which became s 8 was intended by the Law Commission 'to put on a statutory basis a rule that, *where intent or foresight is required in the criminal law*, such intent or foresight must be subjectively proved . . .' It will be noted that the provision was not intended to require proof of intent or foresight in cases where it was not previously required. It was not intended to alter the definition of the mens rea of crimes. The section, according to any ordinary interpretation, does what it was intended to do. It is concerned with *how* intention or foresight must be proved, not with *when* it must be proved. It changes the law of evidence not the substantive law.

The general principle is that the substantive law to be applied in any case is that which is in force when the act is done. The law of evidence or procedure to be applied is that which is in force at the time of the trial. Section 8 came into force on 1 October 1967. The section was held by the Court of Appeal to be applicable in the case of *Wallett* [1968] 2 QB 367, [1968] 2 All ER 296, where the accused's trial for murder took place on 27 October 1967. The alleged murder took place before 1 October (though the date is not stated in the report). It is thus evident that the Court must have treated the section as making a procedural or evidential reform and not a reform in the substantive law. This seems obviously right. What is less obvious is whether s 8 should have been held to have *any* effect in trials for murder and whether Wallett's conviction for murder was rightly quashed. The alleged misdirection was that the accused was guilty of murder if he acted 'knowing quite well at the time that he was doing something [which] any ordinary person like himself would know was doing [the deceased] really serious bodily harm.' This was held to be wrong because the effect of s 8 was to change the issue from what an ordinary person would know to what the accused knew. The point is that *DPP v Smith* did require an element of intention, which had to be subjectively proved but that was merely the intention to do something unlawful to another, to do an act 'aimed at' another, knowing of the circumstances and natu of the act. Once that was established, according to the House, (p 306, below) 'the sole question is whether the unlawful and voluntary act was of such a kind that grievous bodily harm was the natural and probable result'. The reasonable man was brought in as the test of the nature of the act: 'The only test available for this is what the ordinary responsible man would, in all the circumstances of the case, have contemplated as the natural and probable result.' It is scarcely conceivable that the House had in mind two kinds of intention, one of which (the intention to do something unlawful to another) must be subjectively proved and the other (the intention to cause death or grievous bodily harm) must be objectively proved. In effect, the decision in *Wallett* was that s 8 had amended the law of murder by introducing a new element of intention or foresight into the mens rea. This view, difficult as it is to reconcile with the words of the section which say nothing about the mens rea of murder, appears to have been accepted by the House of Lords in *Hyam v DPP* (p 307, below) and *Moloney* (p 55, below) (though Viscount Dilhorne pointed out that it was not necessary to decide that question) and it seems likely that this interpretation will prevail.

The important point, however, is that this effect is unlikely to be extended outside the law of murder. So in *Lipman*, (p 95, below), the court declined to hold that s 8 had affected the law of manslaughter. The law of murder as laid down in *Smith* and one form of the law of manslaughter both required an unlawful act resulting in the death of a human being, p 332, below. The difference between the two offences was that, for murder the act must be one which reasonable men would realise was likely to cause *grievous* bodily harm, whereas, for manslaughter, it was enough that the reasonable men would foresee *some* bodily harm, not necessarily grievous. Section 8, *Lipman* decided, did not require the substitution of the accused himself for the reasonable man; for the reasonable man was brought in to define 'the type of act from which manslaughter may result, not the intention (real or assumed) of the prisoner.' (See p 95, below.) This view is confirmed by the decision of the House of Lords in *Majewski*, p 87, below.

Section 8 and mistake of fact

Section 8 is concerned only with *results* of actions. If a distinction is taken between foresight of results and knowledge of circumstances, it appears to have no application to the latter. However, as O.W. Holmes J pointed out, knowledge of circumstances and foresight of consequences are inextricably related. Foresight of consequences 'is a picture of a future state of things called up by knowledge of the present state of things, the future being viewed as standing to the present in the relation of effect to cause.' [*The Common Law* (John Harvard Library edn, 1963), p 46.] Because of the circumstance that the gun is loaded, the man at whom it is pointed will be killed when the trigger is pulled. It is impossible to apply s 8 to the results of acts without also applying it to circumstances of this kind. Not all legally relevant circumstances, however, are related to the physical consequences of the act in this way. Some circumstances have no bearing on the *occurrence* of the consequences but are relevant to the *legal effect* of those consequences. The fact that the man at whom the gun is pointed is not 'under the Queen's peace' (he is an enemy soldier in battle) is legally relevant, because it is not murder to kill him. The *consequence* relevant to the law of murder—death of a human being—may occur whether this circumstance exists or not; but if the circumstance does not exist, the consequence is not a crime. Of course, it may perfectly properly be said that 'killing a human being under the Queen's peace' is a different *consequence* from 'killing a human being who is not under the Queen's peace'. If 'results' were interpreted to include *all* legally relevant circumstances then s 8 would have had a far-reaching effect in relation to the defence of mistake; but it has not been so interpreted.

This limitation on the effect of s 8 was important while the courts maintained the opinion that a mistake of fact was no answer to a charge of crime unless it was a reasonable mistake. It is now, however, established by the decision of the House of Lords in *DPP v Morgan*, p 45, below that a mistake *which precludes mens rea* is an answer, even though the mistake is an unreasonable one. The prosecution must establish mens rea and they cannot do so if the defendant was making a mistake, whether reasonably or not, which prevented him from having mens rea. *Morgan* also decided that, at common law, on a charge of rape the prosecution must prove that the defendant knew that the woman was not consenting or was indifferent whether she consented or not. The decision on the law of rape has now been superseded by the Sexual Offences (Amendment) Act 1976 (p 577, below) but *Morgan* remains of great importance on the question of general principle. The decision does for mistake of fact precisely what s 8 does for a failure to foresee results. Like s 8, it does not affect the substantive law of any crime (except rape before the 1976 Act). We must look to the substantive law of the particular offence to find whether knowledge of the existence, or the possibility of the existence, of a particular fact is required and if it is so required, then the defendant is not guilty of that offence if he did not have that knowledge, even though his mistake was entirely unreasonable. When a court holds that a mistake is not a defence because it is an unreasonable mistake, it must be on the ground that the definition of the particular offence does not require knowledge of the existence, or the possibility of the existence of the fact in question. If the bigamy cases, such as *Tolson*, p 105, below, stated the law correctly, it is because the law of bigamy does not require knowledge of the existence, or the possibility of the existence, of the first marriage. It is sufficient that the defendant *ought* to know that his wife is alive, or that the marriage has not been dissolved or annulled, as the case may be; bigamy is an offence of negligence, so far as this element of the crime is concerned.

Cl 18(b) and (c) of the draft Code extends the principle of section 8 to circumstances. Para (b) in effect codifies the principle in *Morgan*. Para (c) applies the same principle to defences. Like section 8 of the Criminal Justice Act 1967, cl 8 is concerned only with proof of states of mind. Whether any state of mind has to be proved can be determined only by reference to the law defining the offence or the defence.

(2) DISPROVING MISTAKE

Director of Public Prosecutions v Morgan [1975] 2 All ER 347, House of Lords (Lord Cross of Chelsea, Lord Hailsham of St. Marylebone, Lord Simon of Glaisdale, Lord Edmund-Davies and Lord Fraser of Tullybelton)

The appellant Morgan was a senior NCO in the Royal Air Force, the other appellants younger and junior members of that service. On the night of the offences Morgan invited the other three to return to his house and suggested to them that they should all have intercourse with his wife, the prosecutrix. The young men, who were complete strangers to Mrs Morgan, were at first incredulous but were persuaded that Morgan's invitation was intended seriously when he told them stories of his wife's sexual aberrations and provided them with contraceptive sheaths to wear. They also said in effect that Morgan told them to expect some show of resistance on his wife's part but that they need not take this seriously since it was a mere pretence whereby she stimulated her own sexual excitement. This part of the conversation was denied by Morgan.

Mrs Morgan's account of what happened, in substance, was that she was awakened from sleep in a single bed in a room which she shared with one of her children. Her husband and the other men in part dragged and in part carried her out on to a landing and thence into another room which contained a double bed. She struggled and screamed and shouted to her son to call the police, but one of the men put a hand over her mouth. Once on the double bed the appellants had intercourse with her in turn, finishing with her husband. During intercourse with the other three she was continuously being held, and this, coupled with her fear of further violence, restricted the scope of her struggles, but she repeatedly called out to her husband to tell the men to stop.

The three men gave evidence of her manifesting her sexual co-operation and enjoyment in a way which could only indicate that she was consenting. Any element of resistance on her part was, according to this account, no more than play acting.

The appellant Morgan's statement to the police was equivocal, but in evidence he asserted that his wife agreed in advance to have intercourse with the three friends he had brought home and, in the event, indicated her pleasure in doing so. According to Morgan, the only protest voiced by his wife related to the fact that one of the men who had intercourse with her was not wearing a contraceptive sheath.

The three younger men were convicted of rape and aiding and abetting rape and Morgan was convicted of aiding and abetting rape. The judge directed the jury that the men were guilty of rape even if they in fact believed that Mrs Morgan consented if such belief was not based on reasonable grounds. They were convicted and their appeal to the Court of Appeal was dismissed.

Lord Cross of Chelsea . . . If the words defining an offence provide either expressly or impliedly that a man is not to be guilty of it if he believes something to be true, then he cannot be found guilty if the jury think that he may have believed it to be true, however inadequate were his reasons for doing so. But, if the definition of the offence is on the face of it 'absolute' and the defendant is seeking to escape his prima facie liability by a defence of mistaken belief, I can see no hardship to him in requiring the mistake—if it is to afford him a defence—to be based on reasonable grounds. As Lord Diplock said in *Sweet v Parsley*, there is nothing unreasonable in the law requiring a citizen to take reasonable care to ascertain the facts relevant to his avoiding doing a prohibited act. To have intercourse with a woman who is not your wife is, even today, not generally considered to be a course of conduct which the law ought positively to encourage and it can be argued with force that it is only fair to the woman and not in the least unfair to the man that he should be under a duty to take reasonable care to ascertain that she is consenting to the intercourse and be at the risk of a prosecution if he fails to take such care. So if the Sexual Offences Act 1956 had made it an offence to have intercourse with a woman who was not consenting to it, so that the defendant could only escape liability by the application of the 'Tolson' principle, I would not have thought the law unjust.

But, as I have said, s 1 of the 1956 Act does not say that a man who has sexual intercourse with a woman who does not consent to it commits an offence; it says that a man who rapes a woman commits an offence. Rape is not a word in the use of which lawyers have a monopoly and the question to be answerèd in this case, as I see it, is whether according to the ordinary use of the English language a man can be said to have committed rape if he believed that the woman was consenting to the intercourse and would not have attempted to have it but for his belief, whatever his grounds for so believing. I do not think that he can. Rape, to my mind, imports at least indifference as to the woman's consent. I think, moreover, that in this connection the ordinary man would distinguish between rape and bigamy. To the question whether a man who goes through a ceremony of marriage with a woman believing his wife to be dead, though she is not, commits bigamy. I think that he would reply 'Yes,—but I suppose that the law contains an escape clause for bigamists who are not really to blame.' On the other hand, to the question whether a man, who has intercourse with a woman believing on inadequate grounds that she is consenting to it, though she is not, commits rape, I think that he would reply 'No . . .' For these reasons, I think that the summing up contained a misdirection.

The question which then arises as to the application of the proviso [to s 2(1) of the Criminal Appeal Act 1968] is far easier of solution . . . The jury obviously considered that the appellants' evidence as to the part played by Mrs Morgan was a pack of lies. So I would apply the proviso and dismiss the appeal.

Lord Hailsham of St Marylebone. . . . The learned judge [at the trial] said: . . .

> 'Further, the Prosecution have to prove that each defendant intended to have sexual intercourse with this woman without her consent. Not merely that he intended to have intercourse with her but that he intended to have intercourse without her consent. Therefore if the defendant believed or may have believed that Mrs Morgan consented to him having sexual intercourse with her, then there would be no such intent in his mind and he would be not guilty of the offence of rape, but such a belief must be honestly held by the defendant in the first place. He must really believe that. And, secondly, his belief must be a reasonable belief; such a belief as a reasonable man would entertain if he applied his mind and thought about the matter. It is not enough for a defendant to rely upon a belief, even though he honestly held it, if it was completely fanciful; contrary to every indication which could be given which would carry some weight with a reasonable man. And, of course the belief must be not a belief that the woman would consent at some time in the future, but a belief that at the time when intercourse was taking place or when it began that she was then consenting to it.'

My first comment upon this direction is that the propositions described 'in the first place' and 'secondly' in the above direction as to the mental ingredient in rape are wholly irreconcilable. In practice this was accepted by both counsel for the appellants and for the respondent, counsel for the appellants embracing that described as 'in the first place' and counsel for the respondent embracing the 'secondly', and each rejecting the other as not being a correct statement of the law. In this, in my view, they had no alternative.

If it be true, as the learned judge says 'in the first place', that the prosecution have to prove that 'each defendant intended to have sexual intercourse without her consent, not merely that he intended to have intercourse with her but that he intended to have intercourse without· her consent,' the defendant must be entitled to an acquittal if the prosecution fail to prove just that. The necessary mental ingredient will be lacking and the only possible verdict is 'not guilty'. If, on the other hand, as is asserted in the passage beginning 'secondly', it is necessary for any belief in the woman's consent to be 'a reasonable belief' before the defendant is entitled to an acquittal, it must either be because the mental ingredient in rape is not 'to have intercourse and to have it without her consent' but simply 'to have intercourse' subject to a special defence of 'honest and reasonable belief', or alternatively to have intercourse without a reasonable belief in her consent. Counsel for the Crown argued for each of these alternatives, but in my view each is open to insuperable objections of principle. No doubt it would be possible, by statute, to devise a law by which intercourse, voluntarily entered into, was an absolute offence, subject to a 'defence' of belief whether honest or honest and reasonable, of which the 'evidential' burden is primarily on the defence and the 'probative' burden on the prosecution. But in my opinion such is not the crime of rape as it has hitherto been understood. The prohibited act in rape is to have intercourse without the victim's consent. The minimum mens rea or guilty mind in most common law offences, including rape, is the intention to do the prohibited act, and that is correctly stated in the proposition stated 'in the first place' of the judge's direction. In murder the situation is different, because the murder is only complete when the victim dies, and an intention to do really serious bodily harm has been held to be enough if such be the case.

The only qualification I would make to the direction of the learned judge's 'in the first place' is the refinement for which, as I shall show, there is both Australian and English authority, that if the intention of the accused is to have intercourse *nolens volens*, that is recklessly and not caring whether the victim be a consenting party or not, that is equivalent on ordinary principles to an intent to do the prohibited act without the consent of the victim.

The alternative version of the learned judge's direction would read that the accused must do the prohibited act with the intention of doing it without an honest and reasonable belief in the victim's consent. This in effect is the version which took up most of the time in argument, and although I find the Court of Appeal's judgment difficult to understand, I think it the version which ultimately commended itself to that Court. At all events I think it the more plausible way in which to state the learned judge's 'secondly'. In principle, however, I find it unacceptable. I believe that 'mens rea' means 'guilty or criminal mind', and if it be the case, as seems to be accepted here that mental element in rape is not knowledge but intent, to insist that a belief must be reasonable to excuse is to insist that either the accused is to be found guilty of intending to do that which in truth he did not intend to do, or that his state of mind, though innocent of evil intent, can convict him if it be honest but not rational . . .

I believe the law on this point to have been correctly stated by Lord Goddard in *Steane* [1947] KB 997 at 1004 (p 60, below), when he said:

> 'if on the totality of the evidence there is room for more than one view as to the intent of the prisoner, the jury should be directed that it is for the prosecution to prove the intent to the jury's satisfaction, and if, on review of the whole evidence, they either think the intent did not exist or they are left in doubt as to the intent, the prisoner is entitled to be acquitted.'

That was indeed, a case which involved a count where a specific, or, as Professor Smith has called it, an ulterior, intent was, and is required to be, charged in the indictment. But, once it be accepted that an intent of whatever description is an ingredient essential to the guilt of the accused I cannot myself see that any other direction can be logically acceptable. Otherwise a jury would in effect be told to find an intent where none existed or where none was proved to have existed. I cannot myself reconcile it with my conscience to sanction as part of the English law what I regard as logical impossibility, and, if there were any authority which, if accepted would compel me to do so, I would feel constrained to declare that it was not to be followed. However for reasons which I will give I do not see any need in the instant case for such desperate remedies. [His Lordship referred to *Tolson* (p 105, below), *Sweet v Parsley* (p 115, below) and *Warner v Metropolitan Police Comr* (p 110, below)].

. . . it is logically impermissible as the Crown sought to do in this case, to draw a necessary inference from decisions in relation to offences where mens rea means one thing, and cases where it means another, and in particular from decisions on the construction of statutes, whether these be related to bigamy, abduction or the possession of drugs, and decisions in relation to common law offences. It is equally impermissible to draw direct or necessary inferences from decisions where the mens rea is, or includes, a state of opinion, and cases where it is limited to intention (a distinction I referred to in *Hyam*, post), or between cases where there is a special 'defence', like self defence or provocation and cases where the issue relates to the primary intention which the prosecution has to prove.

Once one has accepted, what seems to me abundantly clear, that the prohibited act in rape is non-consensual sexual intercourse, and that the guilty state of mind is an intention to commit it, it seems to me to follow as a matter of inexorable logic that there is no room either for a 'defence' of honest belief or mistake, or of a defence of honest and reasonable belief and mistake. Either the prosecution proves that the accused had the requisite intent, or it does not. In the former case it succeeds, and in the latter it fails. Since honest belief clearly negatives intent, the reasonableness or otherwise of that belief can only be evidence for or against the view that the belief and therefore the intent was actually held, and it matters not whether, to quote Bridge J, (see [1975] 2 All ER at 359) 'the definition of a crime includes no specific element beyond the prohibited act'. If the mental element be primarily an intention and not a state of belief it comes within his second proposition and not his third. Any other view, as for insertion of the word 'reasonable' can only have the effect of saying that a man intends something which he does not.

By contrast, the appellants invited us to overrule the bigamy cases from *Tolson* onwards and perhaps also *Prince* (the abduction case) as wrongly decided at least in so far as they purport to insist that a mistaken belief must be reasonable. The arguments for this view are assembled, and enthusiastically argued, by Professor Glanville Williams in his treatise on Criminal Law between pages 176 and 205, and by Messrs Smith and Hogan (see Smith and Hogan, at pp 148, 149 of their textbook (3rd edn)).

Although it is undoubtedly open to this House to reconsider *Tolson* supra and the bigamy cases, and perhaps *Prince* (supra) which may stand or fall with them, I must respectfully decline to do so in the present case. Nor is it necessary that I should. I am not prepared to assume that the statutory offences of bigamy or abduction are necessarily on all fours with rape, and before I was prepared to undermine a whole line of cases which have been accepted as law for so long, I would need argument in the context of a case expressly relating to the relevant offences. I am content to rest my view of the instant case on the crime of rape by saying that it is my opinion that the prohibited act is and always has been intercourse without consent of the victim and the mental element is and always has been the intention to commit that act, or the equivalent intention of having intercourse willy-nilly not caring whether the victim consents or no. A failure to prove this involves an acquittal because the intent, an essential ingredient, is lacking. It matters not why it is lacking if only it is not there, and in particular it matters not that the intention is lacking only because of a belief not based on reasonable grounds. I should add that I myself am inclined to view *Tolson* as a narrow decision based on the construction of a statute, which prima facie seemed to make an absolute offence, with a proviso, related to the seven year period of absence, which created a statutory defence. The judges in *Tolson* decided that this was not reasonable, and, on general jurisprudential principles, imported into the statutory offence words which created a special 'defence' of honest and reasonable belief of which the 'evidential' but not the probative burden lay on the defence. I do not think it is necessary to decide this conclusively in the present case. But if this is the true view there is a complete distinction between *Tolson* and the other cases based in statute and the present.

I may also add that I am not impressed with the analogy based on the decision in *Wilson v Inyang* [1951] 2 KB 799 at 803 which has attracted the attention of some academic authors. That clearly depends on the construction of the words 'wilfully and falsely' where they are used in the relevant statute. Also, though I get some support from what I have been saying from the reasoning of the decision in *Smith* [1974] 1 All ER 632 (p 534, below), I nevertheless regard that case as a decision on the Criminal Damage Act 1971, rather than a decision covering the whole law of criminal liability.

For the above reasons I would answer the question certified in the negative, but would apply the proviso to the Criminal Appeal Act on the ground that no miscarriage of justice has or conceivably could have occurred. In my view, therefore, these appeals should be dismissed.

Lord Fraser of Tullybelton. . . . We were invited to overrule *Tolson* but, as it has stood for over eighty years, and has been followed in many later cases, I would not favour that course. But in my opinion the case is distinguishable from the present. Bigamy was a statutory offence under the Offences against the Person Act 1861, s 57. So far as appears from the words of the section, bigamy was an absolute offence, except for one defence set out in a proviso, and it is clear that the mental element in bigamy is quite different from that in rape. In particular, bigamy does not involve any intention except the intention to go through a marriage ceremony, unlike rape in which I have already considered the mental element. So, if a defendant charged with bigamy believes that his spouse is dead, his belief does not involve the absence of any intent which forms an essential ingredient in the offence, and it is thus not comparable to the belief of a defendant charged with rape that the woman consents. . . . No doubt a rapist, who mistakenly believes that the woman is consenting to intercourse, must be behaving immorally, by committing fornication or adultery. But those forms of immoral conduct are not intended to be struck at by the law against rape; indeed, they are not now considered appropriate to be visited with penalties of the criminal law at all. There seems therefore to be no reason why they should affect the consequences of the mistaken belief. . . .

. . . for the reasons stated by my noble and learned friends, Lord Hailsham and Lord Edmund-Davies, I would apply the proviso to the Criminal Appeal Act 1968, s 2(1), and I would refuse the appeal.

[**Lord Simon of Glaisdale** and **Lord Edmund-Davies** made dissenting speeches.]

Appeal dismissed.

CHAPTER 5

Fault

The draft Criminal Code Bill provides:

22 Fault terms
For the purposes of this Act and of any Code offence:
(a) a person acts in respect of an element of an offence:
    'purposely' when he wants it to exist or occur;
    'intentionally' when he wants it to exist or occur, is aware that it exists or is almost certain that it exists or will exist or occur;
    'knowingly' when he is aware that it exists or is almost certain that it exists or will exist or occur;
    'recklessly' when:
        (i) he is aware of a risk that it exists or will exist or occur; and
        (ii) it is, in the circumstances known to him, unreasonable to take the risk;
    'heedlessly' when:
        (i) he gives no thought to whether there is a risk that it exists or will exist or occur although the risk would be obvious to any reasonable person; and
        (ii) it is in the circumstances unreasonable to take the risk;
(b) a person acts:
    'negligently' when his act is a very serious deviation from the standard of care to be expected of a reasonable person;
    'carelessly' when his act is a deviation from the standard of care to be expected of a reasonable person;
and these and like words shall be construed accordingly unless the context otherwise requires.

Schedule 1 of the draft Bill provides the following illustrations:

22 'Purpose'	22(i)	It is made a Code offence to telephone a false message for the purpose of causing annoyance to another. D telephones P and tells a lie which causes P to cancel a planned holiday. D does this because he believes P will be in danger if he goes on holiday and not because he wants to annoy P (although he knows that P will be annoyed). D does not commit the offence.
'Intention'	22(ii)	D plants a bomb on an aeroplane with the purpose of destroying the aeroplane in flight and recovering the sum for which the cargo is insured. It is not D's purpose to kill the crew; but he is almost certain that they will die. He 'intends' to kill them, within the meaning of section 56 (murder).
	22(iii)	Attempt to commit rape requires an 'intention in respect of all the elements' of rape (s 53(1) and (2)). D attempts to have sexual intercourse with P, who does not consent. He is guilty of attempted rape only if he is aware, or is almost certain, that she does not consent.
'Knowledge'	22(iv)	D is handed a packet by E. The packet contains heroin. D does not open the packet and therefore does not see what it contains. But from all the circumstances he firmly believes that it contains heroin; he has no real doubt about the matter. He is 'knowingly' in possession of heroin.
'Recklessness'	22(v)	D, without justification or excuse, throws a brick at O, who is standing not far from a window belonging to P. D realises that the brick may break the window (or damage some other property belonging to another). He is guilty of recklessly destroying or

damaging the window (s 82(1)) if the brick breaks it. (Compare illustration 22 (vii)).

22(vi)   D, shooting at a bird on his estate, injured P, a poacher who was crouching in the undergrowth. D knew that poachers sometimes operated in this part of the estate and was aware that there was a risk of such injury. Whether D caused the injury recklessly depends on whether it was reasonable for him take the risk. That is the question for the court or jury to decide. They are to have regard to all the circumstances that were known to D (including the size of the risk as, in their opinion, D perceived it).

'Heedlessness'   22(vii)   D, without justification or excuse, throws a brick at O. Any reasonable person would realise that the brick might damage property in the vicinity; but this risk does not occur to D. The brick breaks P's window. D has broken the window heedlessly.

'Negligence'   22(viii)   It is made a Code offence to drive a motor vehicle on a road 'with criminal negligence'. The offence is committed when a person drives in a manner falling far below acceptable driving standards; or when he drives a vehicle that is so defective, or when he himself is so disabled or so incompetent to handle it, that driving it at all is a very serious deviation from acceptable standards of care.

'Recklessness'
'Heedlessness'
'Negligence'
'Carelessness'   22(ix)   D makes a statement which is false.

(a) D is not confident of the truth of the statement; he realises that it may be false. In these circumstances it may be unreasonable to make the statement without first checking its truth; and if so, D, not having checked, acts *recklessly* in respect of the falsity.

(b) D believes the statement to be true. He therefore does not, in making it, act *recklessly* in respect of the falsity. If, however, it would be obvious to any reasonable person that the statement might be false and this possibility does not occur to D, he acts *heedlessly* in respect of the falsity.

(c) D makes the statement *carelessly* if his failure to realise that it is false (whether or not he gave thought to the matter) is judged to render his act in making it a deviation from the standard of care to be expected of a reasonable person. He makes it *negligently* if his failure is judged to render his act a very serious deviation from that standard. Whether his act is negligent or merely careless, or whether he is not at fault within the meaning of terms defined in clause 22, depends on a consideration of all the circumstances.

1. Purpose

The word 'purpose' is rarely used to define the fault element of an offence. One example is to be found in the Official Secrets Act 1911, s 1, which was considered in the following case.

Chandler v Director of Public Prosecutions [1962] 3 All ER 142, House of Lords (Lord Reid, Lord Radcliffe, Lord Hodson, Lord Devlin and Lord Pearce)

The appellants, to demonstrate their opposition to nuclear weapons planned by non-violent action to immobilise the aircraft at an RAF station for a space of six hours. They were convicted of conspiracy to commit a breach of s 1 of the Official Secrets Act 1911, namely to enter a prohibited place for 'a purpose prejudicial to the safety or interests of the state'. The trial judge ruled that they were not entitled to call evidence to show that it would be for the benefit of the country to give up nuclear armament. He directed the jury to convict if they were satisfied that the immediate purpose of the appellants was the obstruction of aircraft. The Court of Criminal Appeal dismissed their appeals against conviction.

Lord Reid. . . . The first word in the section that requires consideration is 'purpose'. One can imagine cases where this word could cause difficulty but I can see no difficulty here. The accused both intended and desired that the base should be immobilised for a time, and I cannot construe purpose in any sense that does not include that state of mind. A person can have two different purposes in doing a particular thing, and even if their reason or motive for doing what they did is called the purpose of influencing public opinion that cannot alter the fact that they had a purpose to immobilise the base. And the statute says 'for any purpose'. There is no question here of the interference with the aircraft being an unintended or undesired consequence of carrying out a legitimate purpose.

Next comes the question of what is meant by the safety or interests of the state. 'State' is not an easy word. It does not mean the government or the executive. 'L'état, c'est moi' was a shrewd remark, but can hardly have been intended as a definition even in the France of the time. And I do not think that it means, as counsel argued, the individuals who inhabit these islands. The statute cannot be referring to the interests of all those individuals because they may differ and the interests of the majority are not necessarily the same as the interests of the state. Again we have seen only too clearly in some other countries what can happen if you personify and almost deify the state. Perhaps the country or the realm are as good synonyms as one can find and I would be prepared to accept the organised community as coming as near to a definition as one can get.

Who then is to determine what is and what is not prejudicial to the safety and interests of the state? The question more frequently arises as to what is or is not in the public interest. I do not subscribe to the view that the government or a minister must always or even as a general rule have the last word about that. But here we are dealing with a very special matter—interfering with a prohibited place which Wethersfield was. The definition in s 3 shows that it must either be closely connected with the armed forces or be a place such that information regarding it or damage to it or interference with it would be useful to an enemy. It is in my opinion clear that the disposition and armament of the armed forces are, and for centuries have been, within the exclusive discretion of the Crown and that no one can seek a legal remedy on the ground that such discretion has been wrongly exercised. . . .

I am prepared to start from the position that, when an Act requires certain things to be established against an accused person to constitute an offence, all of those things must be proved by evidence which the jury accepts, unless Parliament has otherwise provided. But normally such things are facts and where questions of opinion arise they are on limited technical matters on which expert evidence can be called. Here the question whether it is beneficial to use the armed forces in a particular way or prejudicial to interfere with that use would be a political question—a question of opinion on which anyone actively interested in politics, including jurymen, might consider his own opinion as good as that of anyone else. Our criminal system is not devised to deal with issues of that kind. The question therefore is whether this Act can reasonably be read in such a way as to avoid the raising of such issues.

The Act must be read as a whole and paras (c) and (d) of s 3 appear to me to require such a construction. Places to which they refer become prohibited places if a Secretary of State declares that damage, obstruction or interference there 'would be useful to an enemy'. Plainly it is not open to an accused who has interfered with or damaged such a place to a material extent to dispute the declaration of the Secretary of State and it would be absurd if he were entitled to say or lead evidence to show that, although he had deliberately done something which would be useful to an enemy, yet his purpose was not prejudicial to the safety or interests of the state. So here at least the trial judge must be entitled to prevent the leading of evidence and to direct the jury that if they find that his purpose was to interfere to a material extent they must hold that his purpose was prejudicial. If that be so, then, in view of the matters which I have already dealt with, it appears to me that the same must necessarily apply to the present case.

Lord Radcliffe. . . . All controversies about motives or intentions or purposes are apt to become involved through confusion of the meaning of the different terms and it is perhaps not difficult to show by analysis that the ideas conveyed by these respective words merge into each other without a clear line of differentiation. Nevertheless a distinction between motive and purpose, for instance, is familiar enough in ordinary discussion and there are branches of law in which the drawing of such a distinction is unavoidable. The Act of Parliament in this case has introduced the idea of purpose as a determining element in the identification of the offence charged and lawyers therefore, whose function it is to attribute meanings to words and to observe relevant distinctions between different words, cannot escape from this duty merely by saying that 'purpose' is a word which has no sharply defined content. They must do the best they can to find what its content is in the context of this Act. For my part I cannot say that I see any very great difficulty in doing so here. I do not think that the ultimate aims of the appellants in bringing about this demonstration of obstruction constituted a purpose at all within the meaning of the Act. I think that those aims constituted their motive, the reason why they wanted the demonstration, but they did not qualify the purpose for which they approached or sought to enter the airfield. Taking this view, I do not think that the distinction between immediate purposes and long-term purposes is the most satisfactory one that can be made. If the word 'purpose' is retained at all to describe both object and motive, I think that direct and indirect purposes best describe the distinction which should be placed before a jury, since those adjectives are less likely to confuse the issue. In the result, I am of opinion that if a person's direct purpose in approaching or entering is to cause obstruction or interference, and such obstruction or interference is found to be of prejudice to the defence dispositions of the state, an offence is thereby committed, and his indirect purposes or his motives in bringing about the obstruction or interference do not alter the nature or content of his offence.

It is important to note that the case with which we are dealing is one in which the appellants intended to bring about obstruction of the airfield for the sake of having an obstruction. Nothing short of an obstruction would have suited their purpose. That was the kind of demonstration that they desired and it was their intention to use the obstruction as an instrument for furthering their general campaign in favour of nuclear disarmament. I do not regard such a case, in which obstruction is directly intended, as comparable with hypothetical cases put to us in argument in which obstruction, though intended, is only an indirect purpose of entry on a prohibited place. Is a man guilty of an offence, it was asked, if he rushes on to an airfield intending to stop an airplane taking off because he knows that a time bomb has been concealed on board? I should say that he is not, and for the reason that his direct purpose is not to bring about an obstruction but to prevent a disaster, the obstruction that he causes being merely a means of securing that end. . . .

[**Lord Hodson** dismissed the appeal.]

Lord Devlin. . . . . I shall begin by considering the word 'purpose', for both sides have relied on this word in different senses. Broadly, the appellants contend that it is to be given a subjective meaning, and the Crown an objective one.

I have no doubt that it is subjective. A purpose must exist in the mind. It cannot exist anywhere else. The word can be used to designate either the main object which a man wants or hopes to achieve by the contemplated act, or it can be used to designate those objects which he knows will probably be achieved by the act, whether he wants them or not. I am satisfied that in the criminal law in general, and in this statute in particular, its ordinary sense is the latter one. In the former sense it cannot in practice be distinguished from motive which is normally irrelevant in criminal law. Its use in that sense would make this statute quite inept. As my noble and learned friend Lord Reid pointed out during the argument, a spy could secure an acquittal by satisfying the jury that his purpose was to make money for himself, a purpose not in itself prejudicial to the state, and that he was indifferent to all the other consequences of his acts. Accordingly, all the results which a man appreciates will probably flow from his act are classifiable as 'purposes' within the meaning of s 1; and since the statute refers to 'any purpose', the prosecution is entitled to rely on any of them. The next question then is whether the selected purpose is 'prejudicial' or not and that question is in my opinion to be answered objectively.

This construction destroys the appellants' first submission. They argued that the immobilisation of the airfield was only incidental and that their main purpose, and the only one which they desired to achieve, was to further the campaign for nuclear disarmament. So, they said, obstruction was not their 'purpose' within the meaning of the Act. I cannot accept this. Neither can I accept their argument (which was put in the forefront of their case at the trial, though not before this House) that their opinions and beliefs were relevant on the question whether their purpose, whatever it was, was prejudicial or not. That, as I have said, must be determined objectively and none of the appellants was qualified to give expert evidence of fact or opinion.

On the other hand, I cannot accept the argument of the Crown that the word 'purpose', when properly construed, destroys the whole of the appellants' case. The Crown contends in effect that once the immediate purpose has been selected for proof, the only consequences that can be examined in order to see whether it is prejudicial or not are the immediate consequences. A variant of this argument is that the purpose must be confined to acts intended to be done on the prohibited place itself.

My Lords, this in my opinion gives the statute too narrow a meaning and would render criminal acts which could not have been intended to be brought within its scope. The example that the appellants used to demonstrate this was that of a man who in an emergency (and presumably without authority, though I do not know that that matters for the defence of the lawful authority is not made available by this part of the Act) holds up an aeroplane because he believes that a time bomb has been planted in it. It can be said that the removal of the time bomb is a purpose to be fulfilled on the airfield itself. But it is easy to think of other examples (such as police obstructing the air traffic by crossing the runways as a short cut when in pursuit of a criminal), in which that feature is absent. Against this it is said by the Crown that in such cases the purpose is not to interfere with the operation of the airfield but to remove the time bomb or capture the criminal, as the case may be. This, I think, is to employ the argument which when it came from the appellants the Crown rightly condemned as erroneous. It is to assimilate purpose and motive. If it is permissible for a man who has interfered with the running of the airfield to say that all he was doing was trying to capture a criminal, it must also be permissible for him to say that all he was doing was trying to save the state from impending harm.

. . . This statute is concerned with the safety and interests of the state and therefore with the objects of state policy, even though, judged *sub specie aeternatis*, that policy may be wrong. If in this statute these words were given a wider meaning, absurd results would follow. Rebels and high-minded spies could be heard to argue that defeat in battle would serve the best interests of the nation because it would be better off under a different régime. The licence allowed to them would also have to be allowed to traitors. This point was dismissed by counsel for the appellants as theoretical. It was said that no jury would in such circumstances acquit. But even if it be looked at purely on the practical plane, the judge has to decide whether he will allow hours or days to be spent at the trial in giving an accused the opportunity of expounding his political views. The court is not the forum for such a debate and the jury is not the body to determine what the interests of the state should be. . . .

[**Lord Pearce** dismissed the appeal.]

Appeal dismissed.

Questions

1. If a man knows that a particular result will probably be achieved by his act, is that result properly described as 'his purpose' even if he does not want it to occur? What if he knows that the result is a condition precedent to the result he does want to achieve? Or a virtually certain concomitant of what he does want to achieve?

2. Was it open to the jury to consider whether the 'purpose' of obstructing the airfield was prejudicial to the interests of the state, according to (i) Lord Reid, (ii) Lord Radcliffe or (iii) Lord Devlin? Should such a question be open to a jury?

3. Is the hypothetical case of the man obstructing the aircraft containing the bomb distinguishable?

2. Intention

The word, 'intention' and the phrase, 'with intent to' are much more commonly found in the definition of offences than 'purposes'. There has been much controversy as to the proper meaning of intention. Some, including Sir John Salmond and Dr J.W.C. Turner, thought that a result is intended only when it is desired. If that is so, intention is indistinguishable from purpose as that word is defined in the Draft Code, cl 22, and construed by the majority in *Chandler v DPP*. A case in which the words, 'with intent to' were construed in this narrow sense is *Steane*, p 60, below.

At the other extreme, it has sometimes been maintained that a result is intended where it is not desired but is foreseen by a person as a probable result of his act. This opinion appeared to have the approval of a majority of the House of Lords in *Hyam v DPP* [1975] AC 55, p 307, below. The House did not, however decide anything about the nature of intention. They did decide that a person has the mens rea of murder if, when he does the act which kills, he knows that it is highly probable that he will cause death or grievous bodily harm. Ackner J directed the jury to that effect and his direction was held by the majority of the House to be correct. Ackner J described that state of mind as 'the necessary intent'. The House, though agreeing that this was the mens rea of murder, did not decide that it was 'intent'. Lord Hailsham, one of the majority, emphatically said that it was not. Viscount Dilhorne and Lord Cross, though disposed to think it did amount to intention, decided only that it was a sufficient mens rea for murder. The minority differed only as to what it is that must be foreseen. They agreed that it was sufficient that the relevant result (in their opinion, death, not merely grievous bodily harm) should be foreseen as probable. Lord Diplock (one of the minority), however, took a different view of the ratio decidendi because he said in *Whitehouse v Lemon* [1979] AC 617 at 638:

> 'When Stephen (*History of the Criminal Law of England*) was writing in 1883, he did not then regard it as settled law that, where intention to produce a particular result was a necessary element of an offence, no distinction was to be drawn in law between the state of mind of one who did an act because he desired it to produce that particular result and the state of mind of one who, when he did the act, was aware that it was likely to produce that result but was prepared to take the risk that it might do so, in order to achieve some other purpose which provided his motive for doing what he did. It is by now well-settled law that both states of mind constitute 'intention' in the sense in which that expression is used in the definition of a crime whether at common law or in a statute. Any doubts on this matter were finally laid to rest by the decision of this House in *Reg v Hyam* [*Hyam v DPP*] [1975] AC 55.'

In the next case, *Moloney*, the House began with the assumption that the mens rea of murder is an intention to kill or to cause grievous bodily harm. Consequently, the question in issue was the meaning of intention.

Moloney must now be read with *Hancock and Shankland*, Appendix II, below.

R v Moloney [1985] 1 All ER 1025, House of Lords
(Lord Hailsham LC, Lords Fraser, Edmund-Davies, Keith and Bridge)

The appellant (M) and his stepfather (S) drank heavily at the ruby wedding anniversary of the appellant's maternal grandparents. The rest of the family retired at 1.00 am but M and S remained and were heard laughing and talking in an apparently friendly way until nearly 4 am when a shot rang out. M telephoned the police, saying, 'I've just murdered my father.' He stated that they had had a disagreement as to who was quicker at loading and firing a shotgun. At S's request he got two shotguns and cartridges. M was first to load. S said 'I didn't think you'd got the guts, but if you have pull the trigger.' M stated 'I didn't aim the gun. I just pulled the trigger and he was dead.'

Stephen Brown J directed the jury that the prosecution had to prove that M intended to kill S or to cause him some really serious injury. He gave the following direction on intent:

> 'When the law requires that something must be proved to have been done with a particular intent, it means this: a man intends the consequence of his voluntary act (a) when

he desires it to happen, whether or not he foresees that it probably will happen and (b) when he foresees that it will probably happen, whether he desires it or not.'

M was convicted of murder and his appeal was dismissed by the Court of Appeal. He appealed to the House of Lords.

Lord Hailsham LC and Lords Fraser, Edmund-Davies and Keith said that they agreed with the speech of Lord Bridge.

Lord Bridge. . . . The definition of intent on which Stephen Brown J based his initial direction to the jury in this case and which first appeared in the 40th edition but now appears virtually unchanged in the 41st edition of *Archbold Criminal Pleading Evidence & Practice* published in 1982, is, as previously stated, clothed with the spurious authority of quotation marks. I will repeat it here for clarity (para 17–13, p 995):

> 'In law a man intends the consequence of his voluntary act, (a) when he desires it to happen, whether or not he foresees that it probably will happen, or (b) when he foresees that it will probably happen, whether he desires it or not.'

Although in its terms applicable to any offence of specific intent, this so-called definition must be primarily derived from [*Hyam v DPP*] [1975] AC 55. The text embodies a reference to Viscount Dilhorne's opinion, implicit in the passage cited above from p 82 of the report, that in [*Hyam v DPP*] itself, as in the vast majority of cases, an explanation of intent was unnecessary and notes the endorsement of this view to which I have already referred in *Reg v Beer*, 63 Cr App R 222. Apart from copious references to [*Hyam v DPP*], the ensuing citation in support of the claim that the definition 'is in accordance with the great preponderance of authority,' refers to many decided cases in which there are to be found obiter dicta on the subject. But looking on their facts at the decided cases where a crime of specific intent was under consideration, including [*Hyam v DPP*] itself, they suggest to me that the probability of the consequence taken to have been foreseen must be little short of overwhelming before it will suffice to establish the necessary intent. Thus, I regard the *Archbold* definition of intent as unsatisfactory and potentially misleading and one which should no longer be used in directing juries.

The golden rule should be that, when directing a jury on the mental element necessary in a crime of specific intent, the judge should avoid any elaboration or paraphrase of what is meant by intent, and leave it to the jury's good sense to decide whether the accused acted with the necessary intent, unless the judge is convinced that, on the facts and having regard to the way the case has been presented to the jury in evidence and argument, some further explanation or elaboration is strictly necessary to avoid misunderstanding. In trials for murder or wounding with intent, I find it very difficult to visualise a case where any such explanation or elaboration could be required, if the offence consisted of a direct attack on the victim with a weapon, except possibly the case where the accused shot at A and killed B, which any first year law student could explain to a jury in the simplest of terms. Even where the death results indirectly from the act of the accused, I believe the cases that will call for a direction by reference to foresight of consequences will be of extremely rare occurrence. I am in full agreement with the view expressed by Viscount Dilhorne that, in [*Hyam v DPP*] [1975] AC 55, 82 itself, if the issue of intent had been left without elaboration, no reasonable jury could have failed to convict. I find it difficult to understand why the prosecution did not seek to support the conviction, as an alternative to their main submission, on the ground that there had been no actual miscarriage of justice.

I do not, of course, by what I have said in the foregoing paragraph, mean to question the necessity, which frequently arises, to explain to a jury that intention is something quite distinct from motive or desire. But this can normally be quite simply explained by reference to the case before the court or, if necessary, by some homely example. A man who, at London airport, boards a plane which he knows to be bound for Manchester, clearly intends to travel to Manchester, even though Manchester is the last place he wants to be and his motive for boarding the plane is simply to escape pursuit. The possibility that the plane may have engine trouble and be diverted to Luton does not affect the matter. By boarding the Manchester plane, the man conclusively demonstrates his intention to go there, because it is a moral certainty that that is where he will arrive.

I return to the two uncertainties noted by the Criminal Law Revision Committee in [their 14th Report, Cmnd 7844, para 18] as arising from [*Hyam v DPP*] which still remain unresolved. I should preface these observations by expressing my view that the differences of opinion to be found in the five speeches in [*Hyam v DPP*] have, as I believe, caused some confusion in the law in an area where, as I have already indicated, clarity and simplicity are, in my view, of paramount importance. I believe it also follows that it is within the judicial function of your

Lordships' House to lay down new guidelines which will achieve those desiderata, if we can reach broad agreement as to what they should be.

In one sense I should be happy to adopt in its entirety the qualified negative answer proposed by my noble and learned friend on the Woolsack to the certified question in [*Hyam v DPP*] [1975] AC 55, 79, because, if I may [say] so, it seems to me to be supported by the most convincing jurisprudential and philosophical arguments to be found in any of the speeches in [*Hyam v DPP*]. But I have to add at once that there are two reasons why I cannot regard it as providing practical guidance to judges who have to direct juries in the rare cases where foresight of probable consequences must be canvassed with the jury as an element which should affect their conclusion on the issue of intent.

First, I cannot accept that the suggested, criterion that the act of the accused, to amount to murder, must be 'aimed at someone' as explained in *Director of Public Prosecutions v Smith* [1961] AC 290 by Viscount Kilmuir LC, at p 327, is one which would be generally helpful to juries. The accused man in *Director of Public Prosecutions v Smith* was driving a car containing stolen goods. When told to stop by a police constable he accelerated away. The constable clung to the side of his car and the accused, in busy traffic, pursued an erratic course in order to shake the constable off. When finally shaken off, the constable fell in front of another car and was killed. In this context it was, no doubt, entirely apposite to say, as Viscount Kilmuir LC did, at p 327: 'The unlawful and voluntary act must clearly be aimed at someone in order to eliminate cases of negligence or of careless or dangerous driving.' But what of the terrorist who plants a time bomb in a public building and gives timely warning to enable the public to be evacuated? Assume that he knows that, following evacuation, it is virtually certain that a bomb disposal squad will attempt to defuse the bomb. In the event the bomb explodes and kills a bomb disposal expert. In our present troubled times, this is an all too tragically realistic illustration. Can it, however, be said that in this case the bomb was 'aimed' at the bomb disposal expert? With all respect, I believe this criterion would create more doubts than it would resolve.

Secondly, I believe that my noble and learned friend, Lord Hailsham of St Marylebone LC's inclusion in the mental element necessary to a conviction of murder of 'the intention to expose a potential victim,' inter alia, to 'a serious risk that . . . grievous bodily harm will ensue from his acts' ([1975] AC 55, 79) comes dangerously near to causing confusion with at least one possible element in the crime of causing death by reckless driving, and by inference equally of motor manslaughter, as identified by Lord Diplock in the later case of *Reg v Lawrence (Stephen)* [1982] AC 510, 526, 527, where the driving was such 'as to create an obvious and serious risk of causing physical injury to some other person' and the driver 'having recognised that there was some risk involved, had nonetheless gone on to take it.' If the driver, overtaking in a narrow country lane in the face of an oncoming cyclist, recognises and takes not only 'some risk' but a serious risk of hitting the cyclist, is he to be held guilty of murder?

Starting from the proposition established by *Reg v Vickers* [1957] 2 QB 664, as modified by *Director of Public Prosecutions v Smith* [1961] AC 290 that the mental element in murder requires proof of an intention to kill or cause really serious injury, the first fundamental question to be answered is whether there is any rule of substantive law that foresight by the accused of one of those eventualities as a probable consequence of his voluntary act, where the probability can be defined as exceeding a certain degree, is equivalent or alternative to the necessary intention. I would answer this question in the negative. Here I derive powerful support from the speech of my noble and learned friend, Lord Hailsham of St. Marylebone L.C., in [*Hyam v DPP*] [1975] AC 55. He said, at p 75:

> 'I do not, therefore, consider, as was suggested in argument, that the fact that a state of affairs is correctly foreseen as a highly probable consequence of what is done is the same thing as the fact that the state of affairs is intended.'

And again, at p 77:

> 'I do not think that foresight as such of a high degree of probability is at all the same thing as intention, and, in my view, it is not foresight but intention which constitutes the mental element in murder.'

The irrationality of any such rule of substantive law stems from the fact that it is impossible to define degrees of probability, in any of the infinite variety of situations arising in human affairs, in precise or scientific terms. As Lord Reid said in *Southern Portland Cement Ltd v Cooper* [1974] AC 623, 640:

> 'Chance probability or likelihood is always a matter of degree. It is rarely capable of precise assessment. Many different expressions are in common use. It can be said that the occurrence of a future event is very likely, rather likely, more probable than not, not

unlikely, quite likely, not improbable, more than a mere possibility, etc. It is neither practicable nor reasonable to draw a line at extreme probability.'

I am firmly of opinion that foresight of consequences, as an element bearing on the issue of intention in murder, or indeed any other crime of specific intent, belongs, not to the substantive law, but to the law of evidence. Here again I am happy to find myself aligned with my noble and learned friend, Lord Hailsham of St Marylebone LC, in [*Hyam v DPP*] [1975] AC 55, where he said, at p 65: 'Knowledge or foresight is at the best material which entitles or compels a jury to draw the necessary inference as to intention.' A rule of evidence which judges for more than a century found of the utmost utility in directing juries was expressed in the maxim: 'A man is presumed to intend the natural and probable consequences of his acts.' In *Director of Public Prosecutions v Smith* [1961] AC 290 your Lordships' House, by treating this rule of evidence as creating an irrebuttable presumption and thus elevating it, in effect, to the status of a rule of substantive law, predictably provoked the intervention of Parliament by section 8 of the Criminal Justice Act 1967 to put the issue of intention back where it belonged, viz, in the hands of the jury, 'drawing such inferences from the evidence as appear proper in the circumstances.' I do not by any means take the conjunction of the verbs 'intended or foresaw' and 'intend or foresee' in that section as an indication that Parliament treated them as synonymous; on the contrary, two verbs were needed to connote two different states of mind.

I think we should now no longer speak of presumptions in this context but rather of inferences. In the old presumption that a man intends the natural and probable consequences of his acts the important word is 'natural.' This word conveys the idea that in the ordinary course of events a certain act will lead to a certain consequence unless something unexpected supervenes to prevent it. One might almost say that, if a consequence is natural, it is really otiose to speak of it as also being probable.

Section 8 of the Criminal Justice Act 1967 leaves us at liberty to go back to the decisions before that of this House in *Director of Public Prosecutions v Smith* [1961] AC 290 and it is here, I believe, that we can find a sure, clear, intelligible and simple guide to the kind of direction that should be given to a jury in the exceptional case where it is necessary to give guidance as to how, on the evidence, they should approach the issue of intent.

I know of no clearer exposition of the law than that in the judgment of the Court of Criminal Appeal (Lord Goddard CJ Atkinson and Cassels JJ) delivered by Lord Goddard CJ in *Rex v Steane* [1947] KB 997 where he said, at p 1004.

> 'No doubt, if the prosecution prove an act the natural consequence of which would be a certain result and no evidence or explanation is given, then a jury may, on a proper direction, find that the prisoner is guilty of doing the act with the intent alleged, but if on the totality of the evidence there is room for more than one view as to the intent of the prisoner, the jury should be directed that it is for the prosecution to prove the intent to the jury's satisfaction, and if, on a review of the whole evidence, they either think that the intent did not exist or they are left in doubt as to the intent, the prisoner is entitled to be acquitted.'

In the rare cases in which it is necessary to direct a jury by reference to foresight of consequences. I do not believe it is necessary for the judge to do more than invite the jury to consider two questions. First, was death or really serious injury in a murder case (or whatever relevant consequence must be proved to have been intended in any other case) a natural consequence of the defendant's voluntary act? Secondly, did the defendant foresee that consequence as being a natural consequence of his act? The jury should then be told that if they answer yes to both questions it is a proper inference for them to draw that he intended that consequence.

Appeal allowed

NOTE

The passage in *Archbold*, so severely censured by their Lordships, appears to be taken from an article by the late Judge J.H. Buzzard on 'Intent' in [1978] Crim LR 5. As a definition of intention it was criticised (see J.C. Smith, ' "Intent": A Reply' [1978] Crim LR 14) but the state of mind described appeared accurately to represent the opinion of the House in *Hyam* as to the mens rea of murder—and their actual decision if 'highly' is inserted before 'probable'. Lord Hailsham's opinion that the mens rea was an intention to expose another to a serious risk of death or grievous bodily harm from his acts differs in substance only in that it may be wider. A person who knows that his deliberate act will probably kill certainly intends to expose another to a serious risk of death; but would he not also so intend if he knew only that it was *possible* that death might be caused?

Only a few months before *Moloney*, five Law Lords sitting in the Privy Council in *Leung Kam Kwok v R* [1985] Crim LR 227 followed *Hyam*, though they disapproved of the trial judge's use of the word 'likely', saying that the appropriate phrase was 'highly probable' or 'a high degree of probability'. It appears from *Moloney* that it would now be wrong to direct a jury in those terms.

Moloney is expressed to apply to 'specific intents' generally—that is (probably), any requirement of intention as distinct from recklessness or lesser forms of fault—and was soon applied to the 'intent to cause the residential occupier of any premises . . . to give up the occupation of the premises' required by s 1(3)(a) of the Protection from Eviction Act 1977: *AMK (Property Management) Ltd* [1985] Crim LR 600, CA.

Although the Court of Appeal had declined to apply *Hyam* to s 18 of the Offences against the Person Act 1861 in *Belfon* [1976] 3 All ER 46, it appears that some judges, following *Archbold*, may have been directing juries that the defendant had a sufficient intent if he foresaw that serious harm would probably happen. The judge did so in *Bryson* [1985] Crim LR 669 the day before *Moloney* was decided. The direction was held to be wrong. How many defendants must have been convicted on misdirections between *Hyam* and *Moloney*? *Moloney* probably makes no difference so far as attempts at common law (*Mohan* [1976] QB 1) or under the Criminal Attempts Act 1981 (*Pearman* (1984) 80 Cr App Rep 259) are concerned.

The terrorist and the bomb. Lord Bridge's example assumes that the terrorist is guilty of murder. The terrorist intends the bomb squad to attempt to defuse the bomb because he knows that it is a virtually certain result of his act that they will do so. But can it be said that he knows that death or serious injury is virtually certain, highly probable, or even probable? Do officers in charge of bomb squads send their men and themselves to virtually certain death? (If a bomb goes off while being defused, the chances of escaping without serious injury are negligible.) Cf the Fourteenth Report of the Criminal Law Revision Committee where it is proposed that an extention of the law of murder is necessary if the terrorist envisaged is to be guilty of that crime; and see draft Code, cl 56(c), p 348, below.

A possible justification. A result which is desired is intended, even though the actor knows that the chances of achieving it are remote. Because he wants to kill P, he takes great care in aiming a gun at him and pulling the trigger; but P is half a mile away and he knows his chances of hitting him are remote. Surely, he intends to kill P. A result which is known to be an inevitable concomitant of the desired result must also be intended. A much used illustration (see draft Code, illustration 22(ii)) is that of D who plants a bomb in a plane, timed to explode in mid-Atlantic and destroy the cargo in order to enable him to obtain the insurance monies. D wishes the crew no ill—he would be delighted if they should, by some miracle, escape—but he knows that, if his plan succeeds, their deaths are, for all practical purposes, inevitable. It is generally agreed that D intends to kill the crew. Suppose, however, that D knows that this particular type of bomb has a 50% failure rate. There is an even chance that the bomb will not go off. He still intends to destroy the cargo because that is what he wants to do. Does it not follow that he also intends to kill the crew? This is neither a certain result nor a desired result but it is suggested that it is enough that it is the inevitable concomitant of a desired result. Lord Bridge's terrorist of course wants the bomb to go off. If he wants it to go off at a time when he knows the bomb squad will be attempting to defuse it, the case is indistinguishable from that of the bomb in the plane; but if he is merely indifferent whether the squad will be working on the bomb at the time, it is difficult to see that he intends to kill or injure them.

Consider whether cl 22(a) of the draft Code requires amendment to cover the cases discussed in this paragraph.

A narrower construction of intent. Lord Bridge refers to the next case, *Steane*, but does not discuss the nature of 'intent' required by the court in that case.

R v Steane [1947] 1 All ER 813, Court of Criminal Appeal (Lord Goddard CJ, Atkinson and Cassels JJ)

The facts appear in the judgment of the court.

[**Lord Goddard CJ** read the judgment of the court].

The appellant was convicted at the Central Criminal Court before Henn Collins J on an indictment which charged him under the Defence (General) Regulations, reg 2A, with doing acts likely to assist the enemy with intent to assist the enemy . . .

The count on which he was convicted charged him with entering the service of the German Broadcasting System on a date in January 1940, and it was common ground and admitted by the appellant that he did so enter that service and on several occasions broadcast certain matters through that system. . . . [His Lordship described the evidence of threats of internment in a concentration camp and of physical violence which had been made against the appellant and his family] The appellant also asserted again and again and said that he had done so in the written report of 5 July, which, as we have already said, was not produced, that he never had the slightest idea or intention of assisting the enemy and what he did was done to save his wife and children, and that what he did could not have assisted the enemy except in a very technical sense. Unlike the evidence which has been adduced in many other similar cases, there was no record of the actual broadcasts made by the appellant. This again was, no doubt, inevitable, but unfortunate, as the actual tone of the broadcast might have thrown some light on the motives and intentions of the appellant, but, in the opinion of the court, there was undoubtedly evidence from which a jury could infer that the acts done by the appellant were acts likely to assist the enemy.

The far more difficult question that arises, however, is in connection with the direction to the jury with regard to whether these acts were done with the intention of assisting the enemy. The case as opened, and, indeed, as put by the learned judge, appears to this court to be this: A man is taken to intend the natural consequences of his acts. If, therefore he does an act which is likely to assist the enemy, it must be assumed that he did it with the intention of assisting the enemy. Now, the first thing which the court would observe is that where the essence of an offence or a necessary constituent of an offence is a particular intent, that intent must be proved by the Crown just as much as any other fact necessary to constitute the offence. The wording of the regulation itself shows that it is not enough merely to charge a prisoner with doing an act likely to assist the enemy. He must do it with the particular intent specified in the regulation. While, no doubt, the motive of a man's act and his intention in doing the act are in law different things, it is none the less true that in many offences a specific intention is a necessary ingredient and the jury have to be satisfied that a particular act was done with that specific intent, although the natural consequences of the act might, if nothing else was proved, be said to show the intent for which it was done. To take a simple illustration, a man is charged with wounding with intent to do grievous bodily harm. It is proved that he did severely wound the prosecutor. Nevertheless, unless the Crown can prove that the intent was to do the prosecutor grievous bodily harm, he cannot be convicted of that felony. It is always open to the jury to negative by their verdict the intent and to convict only of the misdemeanour of unlawful wounding. Or again, a prisoner may be charged with shooting with intent to murder. Here, again, the prosecution may fail to satisfy the jury of the intent, although the natural consequence of firing, perhaps at close range, would be to kill.

The jury can find in such a case an intent to do grievous bodily harm, or they might find that, if the person shot at was a police constable, the prisoner was not guilty on the count charging intent to murder but was guilty of intent to avoid arrest. The important thing to notice in this respect is that where an intent is charged in the indictment, the burden of proving that intent remains throughout on the prosecution. No doubt, if the prosecution prove an act the natural consequences of which would be a certain result and no evidence or explanation is given, then a jury may, on a proper direction, find that the prisoner is guilty of doing the act with the intent alleged, but if, on the totality of the evidence, there is room for more than one view as to the intent of the prisoner, the jury should be directed that it is for the prosecution to prove the intent to the jury's satisfaction, and if, on a review of the whole evidence, they either think that the intent did not exist or they are left in doubt as to the intent, the prisoner is entitled to be acquitted. . . .

In this case the court cannot but feel that some confusion arose with regard to the question of intent by so much being said in the case with regard to the subject of duress. Duress is a matter of defence where a prisoner is forced by fear of violence or imprisonment to do an act which in itself is criminal. If the act is a criminal act, the prisoner may be able to show that he was forced into doing it by violence, actual or threatened, and to save himself from the consequences of that violence. There is very little learning to be found in any of the books or cases on the subject of duress and it is by no means certain how far the doctrine extends, though we have the authority both of Hale and of Fitzjames Stephen, that, while it does not apply to treason, murder and some other felonies, it does apply to misdemeanours, and offences against these regulations are misdemeanours. But here again, before any question of duress arises, a jury must be satisfied that the prisoner had the intention which is laid in the indictment. Duress is a matter of defence and the onus of proving it is on the accused[1]. As we have already said, where an intent is charged on the indictment, it is for the prosecution to prove it, so the onus is the other way.

Another matter which is of considerable importance in this case, but does not seem to have been brought directly to the attention of the jury, is that very different considerations may apply where the accused at the time he did the acts is in subjection to an enemy power and where he is not. British soldiers who were set to work on the Burma road or, if invasion had unhappily taken place, British subjects who might have been set to work by the enemy digging trenches would, undoubtedly, have been doing acts likely to assist the enemy. It would be unnecessary surely in their cases to consider any of the niceties of the law relating to duress, because no jury would find that merely by doing this work they were intending to assist the enemy. In our opinion, it is impossible to say that where acts were done by a person in subjection to the power of another, especially if that other be a brutal enemy, an inference that he intended the natural consequences of his acts must be drawn merely from the fact that he did them. The guilty intent cannot be presumed and must be proved. The proper direction to the jury in this case would have been that it was for the prosecution to prove the criminal intent, and that, while the jury would be entitled to presume that intent if they thought that the act was done as the result of the free, uncontrolled action of the accused, they would not be entitled to presume it if the circumstances showed that the act was done in subjection to the power of the enemy or was as equally consistent with an innocent intent as with a criminal intent, eg a desire to save his wife and children from a concentration camp. They should only convict if satisfied by the evidence that the act complained of was, in fact, done to assist the enemy and if there was doubt about the matter, the prisoner was entitled to be acquitted. . . .

Appeal allowed

1. This dictum goes too far. The accused who wishes to set up duress may bear an evidential burden; but once he has introduced evidence of duress, the burden of disproving it lies on the Crown: *Gill* [1963] 2 All ER 688, [1963] 1 WLR 841.

Glanville Williams, *The Mental Element in Crime*, commenting on *Steane*, p 21

The chief English authority against the view that intention may be held to include foresight of certainty is *Steane*[1]. Although this is frequently cited as an important authority in discussions of intention, its importance derives chiefly from its rejection of the proposition that a person is to be deemed to intend the natural consequence of his acts. The actual decision in *Steane* seems highly disputable; it could have been reached more readily and more acceptably by recognising duress as a defence. Undoubtedly the element of duress caused the Court of Criminal Appeal to be sympathetic towards the defendant; and in cases where such sympathy is absent, foresight of certainty (or knowledge of existing circumstances) is regularly taken to be equivalent to intention. Thus in *Arrowsmith v Jenkins*[2], the defendant's knowledge that a meeting she was addressing was obstructing the highway made her guilty of 'wilfully' obstructing the highway, even though she had no particular desire to create an obstruction as such.

Lord Denning's treatment of *Steane* in his Lionel Cohen lecture[3] seems hard to reconcile with his principal thesis, which is that the word 'intent' in law includes recklessness unless there is some statutory indication of a narrower meaning. I should have thought that this view would have led him to disapprove the decision in *Steane*, but Lord Denning agrees with it; and the reason he gives is that the statutory offence of doing an act likely to assist the enemy with intent to assist the enemy obviously required desire or purpose. 'This man Steane had no desire or purpose to assist the enemy. The Gestapo had said to him: ''If you don't obey, your wife and children will be put in a concentration camp.'' So he obeyed their commands. It would be very hard to convict him of an 'intent to assist the enemy' if it was the last thing he desired to do.'

I cannot myself see that the statutory language rebutted Lord Denning's wide meaning of 'intention' if there is such a wide meaning. As a matter of policy, the draftsman would surely have wished to catch the man who did an act knowing that it was likely to assist the enemy, but not caring whether it did so or not; and he has not used any language to negative this meaning except the overriding phrase 'with intent to assist the enemy', which Lord Denning does not regard as sufficient to negative recklessness. However, let me assume, with Lord Denning, that the formula is restricted to acts done with intent (in the sense of desire or purpose) to assist the enemy. Steane's predominant intent was to save his family, and in order to do that he broadcast for the enemy. On any intelligible use of language, he intentionally (purposely) broadcast. He did not broadcast by mistake or accident or in a state of automatism. If it is thought too strong to say that he desired to broadcast, at least he knew he was broadcasting, which is enough to establish wilfulness or intent. No doubt he did so reluctantly, as the lesser of two evils; but many people go to work in the morning for precisely the same reason.

But, it may be said, it is not enough to assert that Steane intentionally broadcast; what has to be established is that he intended to assist the enemy. On this, there may be an initial doubt whether he assisted the enemy. The enemy presumably hoped and thought that the broadcasts would assist them, but it would be hard to determine whether or not the broadcasts did so. The answer to this doubt is that the notion of assisting the enemy as used in the statute is obviously not limited to acts that can be shown to have assisted the enemy to win a military victory or otherwise to have promoted their cause. It would be no defence to a traitor to show that a campaign in which he assisted the enemy turned out to be disastrous to the enemy and caused them to lose the war. 'Assisting the enemy' means assisting the enemy in the war effort, whether the outcome is successful or not, Steane's intentional participation in the enemy broadcasts was an intentional assistance to the enemy, whether or not the broadcasts in fact helped them. It could perhaps be said that Steane desired to help the enemy in this way in order to save his family; but even if this formula is objected to, he certainly knew that he was assisting the enemy's war project, and therefore intentionally assisted the enemy. The case can either be regarded as one of voluntary action in known circumstances, or as taking part in the causation of a result (the transmission of radio waves) which is foreseen as certain; on either view it is one of intention.

The concept of intention cannot distinguish between the man who assists the enemy in order to save his family and the man who assists the enemy in order to earn a packet of cigarettes. It is only the law of duress that can make a distinction. That is why Steane should have been acquitted by reason of the defence of duress, and not because he lacked intent to assist the enemy.

1. See p 60, above.
2. [1963] 2 QB 561; [1963] 2 All ER 210. For a criticism of some of the language used in the judgment see 79 LQR 331.
3. *Responsibility before the Law* (Jerusalem, Israel, 1961) 27.

NOTE

Steane does not stand alone in construing 'intent' as, in effect, synonymous with purpose. In *Ahlers* [1915] 1 KB 616 a German consul who assisted German nationals to return home after the declaration of war in 1914 was held to intend to do his duty as consul and not to intend to aid the king's enemies. In *Thorne v Motor Trade Association* [1937] AC 797, [1937] 3 All ER 157, HL Lord Atkin thought that to put a trader's name on a 'stop list' so that his business would certainly be ruined might be 'an act done in lawful furtherance of business interests, and . . . without any express intent to injure the person whose name is published'. In *Sinnasamy Selvanayagam v R* [1951] AC 83 the Privy Council thought that if D remained in occupation of his home in defiance of a lawful order to quit, knowing that the owner of the property would be annoyed, his 'dominant intention' was simply to retain his home and he was not guilty of an offence under the Ceylon Penal Code of remaining in occupation with intent to annoy the owner. (This was obiter since the court declined to find that the defendant contemplated that he would induce in the mind of the 'owner' (a government superintendent) 'an emotion so inappropriate to a government officer and so unprofitable, as annoyance').

Are the expressions 'express intent' and 'dominant intention' simply a way of describing purpose? But if a person's purpose is to achieve consequence (a) and he knows that he can do so only by achieving consequence (b), does he not intend to achieve consequence (b)? Cf Smith & Hogan, *Criminal Law* (3rd edn), pp 42–44 (a passage omitted in later editions because of the decision in *Hyam*).

3. Recklessness and negligence

The word 'reckless' seems to have been used in the statutory definition of offences only comparatively recently but the concept is an old one. Unfortunately, the word is used in the present law in two quite distinct senses. These are distinguished in the draft Code, cl 22 (p 50, above) as 'recklessness' and 'heedlessness', but the latter term is not currently used in the law. The leading cases on the two types of recklessness are *Cunningham* [1957] 2 QB 396, [1957] 2 All ER 412, below, and *Caldwell* [1982] AC 341, [1981] 1 All ER 961, p 68, below. 'Cunningham recklessness' corresponds to recklessness in the draft Code, and 'Caldwell recklessness' to heedlessness.

R v Cunningham [1957] 2 All ER 412, Court of Criminal Appeal
(Byrne, Slade and Barry JJ)

In his summing-up, the learned judge directed the jury as follows:

You will observe that there is nothing there about 'with intention that that person should take it'. He has not got to intend that it should be taken; it is sufficient that by his unlawful and malicious act he causes it to be taken. What you have to decide here, then, is whether, when he loosed that frightful cloud of coal gas into the house which he shared with this old lady, he caused her to take it by his unlawful and malicious action.

'Unlawful' does not need any definition. It is something forbidden by law. What about 'malicious'? 'Malicious' for this purpose means wicked—something which he has no business to do and perfectly well knows it. 'Wicked' is as good a definition as any other which you would get.

The facts which face you (and they are uncontradicted and undisputed; the prisoner has not gone into the box to seek to give any particular explanation) are these. Living in the house, which was now two houses but which had once been one and had been rather roughly divided, the prisoner quite deliberately, intending to steal the money that was in the meter—there it is (indicating Exhibit 1)—broke the gas meter away from the supply pipes and thus released the mains supply of gas at large into that house. When he did that he knew that this old lady and her husband were living next door to him. The gas meter was in a cellar. The wall which divided his cellar from the cellar next door was a kind of honeycomb wall through which gas could very well go, so that when he loosed that cloud of gas into that place he must have known perfectly well that gas would percolate all over the house. If it were part of this offence—which it is not—that he intended to poison the old lady, I should have left it to you to decide, and I should have told you that there was evidence on which you could find that he intended that, since he did an action which he must have known would result in that. As I have already told you, it is not necessary to prove that he intended to do it; it is quite enough that what he did was done unlawfully and maliciously.

Byrne J, having stated the facts and referred to *Pembliton* (p 81, post), *Latimer* (p 82, post), *Faulkner* (1877) 13 Cox CC 550 and *Martin* (p 366, post), continued:

We have considered those cases, and we have also considered, in the light of those cases, the following principle which was propounded by the late Professor C.S. Kenny in the first edition of his *Outlines of Criminal Law* published in 1902, and repeated in the sixteenth edition, edited by Mr J.W. Cecil Turner, and published in 1952 (ibid, at p 186):

'. . . in any statutory definition of a crime "malice" must be taken not in the old vague sense of 'wickedness' in general, but as requiring either (i) an actual intention to do the particular *kind* of harm that in fact was done, or (ii) recklessness as to whether such harm should occur or not (i e the accused has foreseen that the particular kind of harm might be done, and yet has gone on to take the risk of it). It is neither limited to, nor does it indeed require, any ill-will towards the person injured.'

The same principle is repeated by Mr Turner in his tenth edition of *Russell on Crime*. We think that this is an accurate statement of the law. It derives some support from the judgments of Lord Coleridge CJ, and Blackburn J, in *Pembliton*. In our opinion, the word 'maliciously' in a statutory crime postulates foresight of consequence. [His Lordship quoted the direction (above) of the trial judge.]

With the utmost respect to the learned judge, we think it is incorrect to say that the word 'malicious' in a statutory offence merely means wicked. We think the learned judge was, in effect, telling the jury that if they were satisfied that the appellant acted wickedly—and he had clearly acted wickedly in stealing the gas meter and its contents—they ought to find that he had acted maliciously in causing the gas to be taken by Mrs Wade so as thereby to endanger her life. In our view, it should have been left to the jury to decide whether, even if the appellant did not intend the injury to Mrs Wade, he foresaw that the removal of the gas meter might cause injury to someone but nevertheless removed it. We are unable to say that a reasonable jury, properly directed as to the meaning of the word 'maliciously' in the context of s 23 [See s 23 of the Offences against the Person Act 1861, p 542, below], would, without doubt, have convicted.

In these circumstances, this court has no alternative but to allow the appeal and quash the conviction.

Appeal allowed

Question

Is it sufficient on a charge under s 23 that the accused foresaw 'injury' to someone or is it necessary to prove that he foresaw danger to life or grievous bodily harm? Cf *Mowatt*, below.

R v Mowatt [1967] 3 All ER 47, Court of Appeal, Criminal Division (Diplock LJ, Brabin and Waller JJ)

The facts are stated in the final paragraph of the judgment.

[**Diplock LJ**, having cited the passage from *Kenny* (above) which was approved in *Cunningham*, continued:]

This generalisation is not, in our view, appropriate to the specific alternative statutory offences described in s 18 and s 20 of the Offences against the Person Act 1861, and s 5 of the Prevention of Offences Act 1851, and if used in that form in the summing-up is liable to bemuse the jury. In s 18 the word 'maliciously' adds nothing. The intent expressly required by that section is more specific than such element of foresight of consequences as is implicit in the word 'maliciously' and in directing a jury about an offence under this section the word 'maliciously' is best ignored. In the offence under s 20, and in the alternative verdict which may be given on a charge under s 18—for neither of which is any specific intent required—the word 'maliciously' does import on the part of the person who unlawfully inflicts the wound or other grievous bodily harm an awareness that his act may have the consequence of causing some physical harm to some other person. That is what is meant by 'the particular kind of harm' in the citation from Professor Kenny's *Outlines of Criminal Law*. It is quite unnecessary that the accused should have foreseen that his unlawful act might cause physical harm of the gravity described in the section, ie a wound or serious physical injury. It is enough that he should have foreseen that some physical harm to some person, albeit of a minor character might result.

In many cases in instructing a jury on a charge under s 20 of the Act of 1861, or on the alternative verdict which may be given under that section when the accused is charged under s 18, it may be unnecessary to refer specifically to the word 'maliciously'. The function of a summing-up is not to give the jury a general dissertation on some aspect of the criminal law, but to tell them what are the issues of fact on which they must make up their minds in order to determine whether the accused is guilty of a particular offence. There may, of course, be cases where the accused's awareness of the possible consequences of this act is genuinely in issue. *Cunningham* [see p 63, above] is a good example. But where the evidence for the prosecution, if accepted, shows that the physical act of the accused which caused the injury to another person was a direct assault which any ordinary person would be bound to realise was likely to cause some physical harm to the other person (as, for instance, an assault with a weapon or the boot or violence with the hands) and the defence put forward on behalf of the accused is not that the assault was accidental or that he did not realise that it might cause some physical harm to the victim, but is some other defence such as that he did not do the alleged act or that he did it in self-defence, it is unnecessary to deal specifically in the summing-up with what is meant by the word 'maliciously' in the section. It can only confuse the jury to invite them in the summing-up to consider an improbability not previously put forward and to which no evidence has been directed, to wit—that the accused did not realise what any ordinary person would have realised was a likely consequence of his act, and to tell the jury that the onus lies, not on the accused to establish, but on the prosecution to negative, that improbability, and to go on to talk about presumptions. To a jury who are not jurisprudents that sounds like jargon. In the absence of any evidence that the accused did not realise that it was a possible consequence of his act that some physical harm might be caused to the victim, the prosecution satisfy the relevant onus by proving the commission by the accused of an act which any ordinary person would realise was likely to have that consequence. There is no issue here to which the jury need direct their minds and there is no need to give to them any specific directions about it. . . . As regards the blows seen by the police to be struck, viz., the appellant's sitting astride the complainant and raining a series of blows on his face, lifting him up and casting him down again, the only issues before the jury was whether that happened at all and, if so, whether they were inflicted with intent to do grievous bodily harm. If the jury accepted that it did happen, then clearly any ordinary man would realise that some physical harm would be sustained by the victim, even though he might not have any specific intent to break the skin or cause serious physical injury. In the view of this court, this was clearly a case where in relation to the lesser offence of which the appellant was convicted it was quite unnecesssary for the learned judge to give the jury any instructions on the meaning of the word 'maliciously'. . . . This appeal is accordingly dismissed.

Appeal dismissed

Questions

1. An accused person (and the prosecutor) may now make formal admissions of any fact of which oral evidence may be given in any criminal proceedings and the admission is conclusive evidence of the fact admitted: Criminal Justice Act 1967, s 10. Where there is no such admission, is it proper for the judge to omit to direct the jury that they must be satisfied that a particular ingredient of the offence charged is proved, because the accused has not specifically denied that that element was present?

2. In the light of s 8 of the Criminal Justice Act 1967, (p 562, below) is it now correct to say that 'the prosecution satisfy the relevant onus by proving the commission by the accused of an act which any ordinary person would realise was likely to have that consequence'?

3. Is it correct to say that in s 18 (p 541, below) the word 'maliciously' adds nothing? Consider, for example, a charge of wounding with intent to resist lawful apprehension.

4. Is it right that foresight of physical harm of a minor character should be a sufficient mens rea on charge of maliciously causing grievous bodily harm? (Cf Buxton, 'Negligence and Constructive Crime' [1969] Crim LR 112 and Brett J in *Prince* (p 102, below).

NOTE

In *Grimshaw* [1984] Crim LR 108, CA, D heard P make an insulting remark to her boyfriend. She struck P and the glass he was holding went into the bridge of his nose and caused extensive eye injuries. She was convicted of inflicting grievous bodily harm contrary to s 20 of the Offences against the Person Act 1861. In answer to a question by the jury, the judge said that it was enough if D ought to have foreseen that some physical harm, although of a minor character might result from her act. The Court of Appeal allowed her appeal. In *Mowatt* (above, first paragraph) Diplock LJ twice used the phrase, 'should have foreseen', but the Court said that, when read in its context, this meant 'did foresee'. It was a jury's view of what a defendant foresaw, not their view of what as a reasonable man, he ought to have foreseen, that was material. [In the passage in question Diplock LJ was concerned only with the question of what it is that the defendant must have foreseen.]

W (A Minor) v Dolbey [1983] Crim LR 681, Queen's Bench Division (Robert Goff LJ and Forbes J)

Robert Goff LJ. The appellant was convicted of an offence under section 20 of the Offences Against the Person Act 1861 in that he, on 11 June 1982, at Sound in Cheshire, unlawfully and maliciously wounded Philip John Rimmer contrary to that section.

. . . The appellant was a young man born on 12 June 1966, which makes him just under 16 at the time of the incident. It appears that on 11 June 1982, he took from home an air rifle which belonged to his elder brother. He had not been given proper instruction in the use of the gun, but he had seen his brother use it. It seems he had a number of pellets with him. With the gun he shot at a number of bottles.

Later on he walked towards a farm. When he got there, Philip Rimmer was standing at the barn door. The appellant lay down on the ground and pointed the gun at Rimmer. Rimmer told the appellant to put the gun down. The appellant then stood up and walked towards Rimmer and when he was about 25 feet away from him he stood there, put the rifle to his shoulder and aimed at Rimmer. Rimmer forcefully told the Appellant to desist and the Appellant then said: 'There is nothing in the gun, I have got no pellets'. He then pulled the trigger. There was a pellet in the gun. He fired at Rimmer and struck him on the forehead between the eyes. By striking Rimmer on the forehead, the pellet caused a wound which required hospital treatment.

The magistrates found that the appellant did indeed believe the gun to be unloaded at the time when he aimed at Rimmer, because he believed that he had used his last pellet shooting at the bottles. The magistrates found as a fact that the appellant honestly had this belief at the time of the offence. The magistrates also found that the appellant did not open the gun to ascertain it was unloaded before aiming it at the victim, but believed at that time that the weapon was not loaded. It appears from a later passage in the case that they formed the view that the appellant ignored the risk that the gun might be loaded before pulling the trigger . . .

[His Lordship stated that the magistrates found that the fact that the appellant ignored the risk that the gun might be loaded was sufficient to constitute the malicious intent required, following *Caldwell*, p 68, below and *Lawrence* p 72, below. He discussed those cases and *Cunningham*, p 63, above, and continued:]

. . . in my judgment Lord Diplock was concerned to distinguish the meaning of the word 'maliciously' as used in the Offences against the Person Act 1861 from the meaning of the word 'reckless' as used in section 1 of the Criminal Damage Act 1971. No guidance can be derived from the definition of the latter word in Lord Diplock's speech in the consideration of the problem in the present case. It also follows that it was the view of Lord Diplock that *R v Cunningham* was still good law so far as the subject matter of that case was concerned, and that what he was saying in *Caldwell* was not considered by him to have any impact on either the decision or the reasoning in that case. So we can put on one side the definition of 'reckless' in *Caldwell* and it follows from what Lord Diplock said that we are simply concerned with the meaning of the word 'maliciously' used as a term of art, as he put it, in the criminal law.

That being so, referring again to the case of *Cunningham*, it appears from the passage which I have quoted from the judgment of Mr Justice Byrne that the word 'maliciously' postulates foresight of consequence. That means, in the ordinary sense of the words, that the accused person must have actually foreseen, as it was put by Professor Kenny, that a particular kind of harm might be done.

Here, Mr Clegg submitted, on the facts as known to the accused, the gun was not loaded, because he honestly believed that the gun was not loaded. Therefore, says Mr Clegg, this young man, Woodward, did not foresee the risk of any harm happening at all to Rimmer if he pointed the gun at him and pulled the trigger, however foolhardy the ordinary man might think that act to have been.

For the respondent, Mr Collins made the following submission. He said:

'Let us stand back and look at what Woodward did. Here he picked up a gun, pointed it at Rimmer and pulled the trigger in the belief, honestly held, that the gun was not loaded. But if we look further into the matter and ask ourselves the question: "Why did he form the view that the gun was not loaded", the answer must be: "Because he did not bother to check the gun and see if there was a pellet in the gun." He simply assumed, on the basis of his recollection, that the gun was not loaded without checking it.'

Mr Collins submitted that, if the facts are looked at in that way, it can be seen that this young man recklessly disregarded the risk of the gun being loaded and therefore was reckless as to the possible consequence that if the gun was loaded, Rimmer might be injured. In my judgment, however, this submission is contrary to authority; because, as I read the decision of the Court of Criminal Appeal in *Cunningham*, what is required is actual foresight, on the facts known to the accused person; that the particular kind of harm might be done. If there was not such foresight, then it is not permissible to ask the question: 'Why did the accused not appreciate that there was such a risk?' and then on an investigation of the circumstances form an opinion as to whether his action could be described as reckless. It is not to be forgotten that the relevant authority is one which has been described by Lord Diplock as authority on the meaning of 'malice' as a term of art, not on the meaning of the word 'reckless'.

In my judgment, on the findings of fact in this case Woodward did not foresee that any physical harm might come to Rimmer at all, however foolhardy he was in pointing the gun at Rimmer and pulling the trigger without checking to see if the gun was loaded.

Forbes J agreed.

Conviction quashed

(1) 'CALDWELL RECKLESSNESS' — 'HEEDLESSNESS'

R v Caldwell [1981] 1 All ER 961, House of Lords
(Lord Wilberforce, Lord Diplock, Lord Edmund-Davies, Lord Keith of Kinkel and Lord Roskill)

Lord Wilberforce. My Lords, I would dismiss the appeal and answer the certified questions as suggested by my noble and learned friend Lord Edmund-Davies.

Lord Diplock. My Lords, the facts that gave rise to this appeal are simple. The respondent had been doing work for the proprietor of a residential hotel. He considered that he had a grievance against the proprietor. One night he got very drunk and in the early hours of the morning he decided to revenge himself on the proprietor by setting fire to the hotel, in which some ten guests were living at the time. He broke a window and succeeded in starting a fire in a ground room floor; but fortunately it was discovered and the flames were extinguished before any serious damage was caused. At his trial he said that he was so drunk at the time that the thought that there might be people in the hotel whose lives might be endangered if it were set on fire had never crossed his mind.

He was indicted at the Central Criminal Court on two counts of arson under s 1(1) and (2) respectively of the Criminal Damage Act 1971. [His Lordship cited s 1 p 575, below].

Count 1 contained the charge of the more serious offence under s 1(2) which requires intent to endanger the life of another or recklessness whether the life of another would be endangered. To this count the respondent pleaded not guilty. He relied on his self-induced drunkenness as a defence on the ground that the offence under sub-s (2) was one of 'specific intent' in the sense in which that expression was used in speeches in this House in *Director of Public Prosecutions v Majewski* [p 87, below]. Count 2 contained the lesser offence under s 1(1) to which the respondent pleaded guilty.

The recorder directed the jury that self-induced drunkenness was not a defence to count 1, and the jury convicted him on this count. The recorder sentenced him to three years' imprisonment on count 1 but passed no sentence on count 2, the lesser offence, to which he had pleaded guilty. On appeal the Court of Appeal held that her direction to the jury as to the effect of self-induced drunkenness on the charge in count 1 was wrong. They set aside the conviction on that count: but left the sentence of three years' imprisonment unchanged as they considered it to be an appropriate sentence on count 2. So it was only a Pyrrhic victory for the respondent; but it left the law on criminal damage and drunkenness in a state of some confusion.

The question of law certified for the opinion of this House was:

> 'Whether evidence of self-induced intoxication can be relevant to the following questions—(a) Whether the defendant intended to endanger the life of another; and (b) Whether the defendant was reckless as to whether the life of another would be endangered, within the meaning of Section 1(2)(b) of the Criminal Damage Act 1971.'

The question recognises that under s 1(2)(b) there are two alternatives states of mind as respects endangering the life of another, and that the existence of either of them on the part of the accused is sufficient to constitute the mens rea needed to convert the lesser offence under s 1(1) into the graver offence under s 1(2). One is intention that a particular thing should happen in consequence of the actus reus, viz that the life of another person should be endangered (this was not relied on by the Crown in the instant case). The other is recklessness whether the particular thing should happen or not. The same dichotomy of mentes reae, intention and recklessness, is to be found throughout the section: in sub-s (1) and para (a) of sub-s (2) as well as in para (b); and 'reckless' as descriptive of a state of mind must be given the same meaning in each of them.

My Lords, the Criminal Damage Act 1971 replaced almost in their entirety the many and detailed provisions of the Malicious Damage Act 1861. Its purpose, as stated in its long-title was to *revise* the law of England and Wales as to offences of damage to property. As the brevity of the Act suggests, it must have been hoped that it would also simplify the law.

In the 1861 Act, the word consistently used to describe the mens rea that was a necessary element in the multifarious offences that the Act created was 'maliciously', a technical expression, not readily intelligible to juries, which became the subject of considerable judicial exegesis. This culminated in a judgment of the Court of Criminal Appeal in *R v Cunningham* [His Lordship cited the passage from *Kenny* approved by the Court of Criminal Appeal (p 64, above)].

My Lords, in this passage Professor Kenny was engaged in defining for the benefit of students the meaning of 'malice' as a term of art in criminal law. To do so he used ordinary English words in their popular meaning. Among the words he used was 'recklessness', the noun derived from the adjective 'reckless', of which the popular or dictionary meaning is 'careless, regardless, or heedless of the possible harmful consequences of one's acts'. It presupposes that, if thought were given to the matter by the doer before the act was done, it would have been apparent to him that there was a real risk of its having the relevant harmful consequences; but, granted this, reckless-ness covers a whole range of states of mind from failing to give any thought at all to whether or not there is any risk of those harmful consequences, to recognising the existence of the risk and nevertheless deciding to ignore it. Conscious of this imprecision in the popular meaning of recklessness as descriptive of a state of mind, Professor Kenny, in the passage quoted, was as it seems to me, at pains to indicate by the words in brackets the particular species within the genus, reckless states of mind, that constituted 'malice' in criminal law. This parenthetical restriction on the natural meaning of recklessness was necessary to an explanation of the meaning of the adverb 'maliciously' when used as a term of art in the description of an offence under the Malicious Damage Act 1861 (which was the matter in point in *R v Cunningham*) but it was not directed to and consequently has no bearing on the meaning of the adjective 'reckless' in s 1 of the Criminal Damage Act 1971. To use it for that purpose can, in my view, only be misleading.

My Lords, the restricted meaning that the Court of Appeal in *R v Cunningham* had placed on the adverb 'maliciously' in the Malicious Damage Act 1861 in cases where the prosecution did not rely on an actual intention of the accused to cause the damage that was in fact done called for a meticulous analysis by the jury of the thoughts that passed through the mind of the accused at or before the time he did the act that caused the damage, in order to see on which side of a narrow dividing line they fell. If it had crossed his mind that there was a risk that someone's property might be damaged but, because his mind was affected by rage or excitement or confused by drink, he did not appreciate the seriousness of the risk or trusted that good luck would prevent its happening, this state of mind would amount to malice in the restricted meaning placed on that term by the Court of Appeal; whereas if, for any of these reasons, he did not even trouble to give his mind to the question whether there was any risk of damaging the property, this state of mind would not suffice to make him guilty of an offence under the Malicious Damage Act 1861.

Neither state of mind seems to me to be less blameworthy than the other; but, if the difference between the two constituted the distinction between what does and what does not in legal theory amount to a guilty state of mind for the purpose of a statutory offence of damage to property, it would not be a practicable distinction for use in a trial by jury. The only person who knows what the accused's mental processes were is the accused himself, and probably not even he can recall them accurately when the rage or excitement under which he acted has passed, or he has sobered up if he were under the influence of drink at the relevant time. If the accused gives evidence that because of his rage, excitement or drunkenness the risk of particular harmful consequences of his acts simply did not occur to him, a jury would find it hard to be satisfied beyond reasonable doubt that his true mental process was not that, but was the slightly different mental process required if one applies the restricted meaning of 'being reckless as to whether' something would happen, adopted by the Court of Appeal in *R v Cunningham*.

My Lords, I can see no reason why Parliament when it decided to revise the law as to offences of damage to property should go out of its way to perpetuate fine and impracticable distinctions such as these, between one mental state and another. One would think that the sooner they were got rid of the better.

When cases under s 1(1) of the new Act, in which the Crown's case was based on the accused having been 'reckless as to whether . . . property would be destroyed or damaged', first came before the Court of Appeal, the question as to the meaning of the expression 'reckless' in the context of that subsection appears to have been treated as soluble simply by posing and answering what had by then, unfortunately, become an obsessive question among English lawyers: is the test of recklessness subjective or objective? The first two reported cases, in both of which judgments were given off the cuff, are *R v Briggs* [1977] 1 All ER 475, [1977] 1 WLR 605n and *R v Parker* [1977] 2 All ER 37, [1977] 1 WLR 600. Both classified the test of reckless-ness as subjective. This led the court in *R v Briggs* [1977] 1 All ER 475 at 477–478, [1977] 1 WLR 605n at 608 to say: 'A man is reckless in the sense required when he carries out a deliberate act knowing that there is some risk of damage resulting from the act but neverthe-less continues in the performance of that act.' This leaves over the question whether the risk of damage may not be so slight that even the most prudent of men would feel justified in taking it, but it excludes that kind of recklessness that consists of acting without giving any thought at all to whether or not there is any risk of harmful consequences of one's act, even though the risk is great and would be obvious if any thought were given to the matter by the doer of the act. *R v Parker*, however, opened the door a chink by adding as an alternative to the actual knowledge of the accused that there is some risk of damage resulting from his act and his going on to take it, a mental state described as 'closing his mind to the obvious fact' that there is such a risk (see [1977] 2 All ER 37 at 40, [1977] 1 WLR 600 at 604).

R v Stephenson [1979] 2 All ER 1198, [1979] QB 695, the first case in which there was full argument, though only on one side, and a reserved judgment, slammed the door again on any less restricted interpretation of 'reckless' whether particular consequences will occur than that originally approved in *Briggs*. The appellant, a tramp, intending to pass the night in a hollow in the side of a haystack, had lit a fire to keep himself warm; as a result of this the stack itself caught fire. At his trial, he was not himself called as a witness but a psychiatrist gave evidence on his behalf that he was schizophrenic and might not have had the same ability to foresee or appreciate risk as a mentally normal person. The judge had given to the jury the direction on the meaning of reckless that had been approved in *R v Parker*. The argument for the appellant on the appeal was that this let in an objective test whereas the test should be entirely subjective. It was buttressed by copious citation from previous judgments in civil and criminal cases where the expressions 'reckless' or 'recklessness' had been used by judges in various contexts. Counsel for the Crown expressed his agreement with the submissions for the appellant. The judgment of the court contains an analysis of a number of the cited cases, mainly in the field of civil law. These cases do not disclose a uniform judicial use of the terms; and as respects judicial statements made before the current vogue for classifying all tests of legal liability as either objective or subjective they are not easily assignable to one of those categories rather than the other. The court, however, reached its final conclusion by a different route. It made the assumption that although Parliament in replacing the 1861 Act by the 1971 Act had discarded the word 'maliciously' as descriptive of the mens rea of the offences of which the actus reus is damaging property, in favour of the more explicit phrase 'intending to destroy or damage any such property or being reckless as to whether any such property would be destroyed', it nevertheless intended the words to be interpreted in precisely the same sense as that in which the single adverb 'maliciously' had been construed by Professor Kenny in the passage that received the subsequent approval of the Court of Appeal in *R v Cunningham*.

My Lords, I see no warrant for making any such assumption in an Act whose declared purpose is to revise the then existing law as to offences of damage to property, not to perpetuate it. 'Reckless' as used in the new statutory definition of the mens rea of these offences is an ordinary English word. It had not by 1971 become a term of legal art with some more limited esoteric meaning than that which it bore in ordinary speech, a meaning which surely includes not only deciding to ignore a risk of harmful consequences resulting from one's acts that one has recognised as existing, but also failing to give any thought to whether or not there is any such risk in circumstances where, if any thought were given to the matter, it would be obvious that there was.

If one is attaching labels, the latter state of mind is neither more nor less 'subjective' than the first. But the label solves nothing. It is a statement of the obvious; mens rea is, by definition, a state of mind of the accused himself at the time he did the physical act that constitutes the actus reus of the offence; it cannot be the mental state of some non-existent, hypothetical person.

Nevertheless, to decide whether someone has been 'reckless' whether harmful consequences of a particular kind will result from his act, as distinguished from his actually intending such harmful consequences to follow, does call for some consideration of how the mind of the ordinary prudent individual would have reacted to a similar situation. If there were nothing in the circumstances that ought to have drawn the attention of an ordinary prudent individual to the possibility of that kind of harmful consequence, the accused would not be described as 'reckless' in the natural meaning of that word for failing to address his mind to the possibility; nor, if the risk of the harmful consequences was so slight that the ordinary prudent individual on due consideration of the risk would not be deterred from treating it as negligible, could the accused be described as 'reckless' in its ordinary sense if, having considered the risk, he decided to ignore it. (In this connection the gravity of the possible harmful consequences would be an important factor. To endanger life must be one of the most grave.) So to its extent, even if one ascribes to 'reckless' only the restricted meaning, adopted by the Court of Appeal in *Stephenson* and *Briggs*, of foreseeing that a particular kind of harm might happen and yet going on to take the risk of it, it involves a test that would be described in part as 'objective' in current legal jargon. Questions of criminal liability are seldom solved by simply asking whether the test is subjective or objective.

In my opinion, a person charged with an offence under s 1(1) of the 1971 Act is 'reckless as to whether or not any property would be destroyed or damaged' if (1) he does an act which in fact creates an obvious risk that property will be destroyed or damaged and (2) when he does the act he either has not given any thought to the possibility of there being any such risk or has recognised that there was some risk involved and has none the less gone on to do it. That would be a proper direction to the jury; cases in the Court of Appeal which held otherwise should be regarded as overruled.

Where the charge is under s 1(2) the question of the state of mind of the accused must be approached in stages, corresponding to paras (a) and (b). The jury must be satisfied that what the accused did amounted to an offence under s 1(1), either because he actually intended to destroy or damage the property or because he was reckless (in the sense that I have described) whether it might be destroyed or damaged. Only if they are so satisfied must the jury go on to consider whether the accused also either actually intended that the destruction or damage of the property should endanger someone's life or was reckless (in a similar sense) whether a human life might be endangered.

Turning now to the instant case, the first stage was eliminated by the respondent's plea of guilty to the charge under s 1(1). Furthermore he himself gave evidence that his actual intention was to damage the hotel in order to revenge himself on the proprietor. As respects the charge under s 1(2) the prosecution did not rely on an actual intent of the respondent to endanger the lives of the residents but relied on his having been reckless whether the lives of any of them would be endangered. His act of setting fire to it was one which the jury were entitled to think created an obvious risk that the lives of the residents would be endangered; and the only defence with which your Lordships are concerned is that the respondent had made himself so drunk as to render him oblivious of that risk. If the only mental state capable of constituting the necessary mens rea for an offence under s 1(2) were that expressed in the words 'intending by the destruction or damage to endanger the life of another', it would have been necessary to consider whether the offence was to be classified as one of 'specific' intent for the purposes of the rule of law which this House affirmed and applied in *Director of Public Prosecutions v Majewski* [1976] 2 All ER 142, [1977] AC 443; and this it plainly is. But this is not, in my view, a relevant inquiry where 'being reckless as to whether the life of another would be thereby endangered' is an alternative mental state that is capable of constituting the necessary mens rea of the offence with which he is charged.

The speech of Lord Elwyn-Jones LC in *Majewski*, with which Lord Simon, Lord Kilbrandon and I agreed, is authority that self-induced intoxication is no defence to a crime in which recklessness is enough to constitute the necessary mens rea (see [1976] 2 All ER 142 at 150–151, [1977] AC 443 at 474–475). The charge in *Majewski* was of assault occasioning actual bodily harm and it was held by the majority of the House, approving *R v Venna* [1975] 3 All ER 788 at 794, [1976] 1 QB 421 at 428, that recklessness in the use of force was sufficient to satisfy the mental element in the offence of assault. Reducing oneself by drink or drugs to a condition in which the restraints of reason and conscience are cast off was held to be a reckless course of conduct and an integral part of the crime. Lord Elwyn-Jones LC accepted as correctly stating English law the provision in §2.08 (2) of the American Model Penal Code:

> 'When recklessness establishes an element of the offence, if the actor, due to self-induced intoxication, is unaware of a risk of which he would have been aware had he been sober, such unawareness is immaterial.'

So, in the instant case, the fact that the respondent was unaware of the risk of endangering the lives of residents in the hotel owing to his self-induced intoxication would be no defence if that risk would have been obvious to him had he been sober.

My Lords, the Court of Appeal in the instant case regarded the case as turning on whether the offence under s 1(2) was one of 'specific' intent or 'basic' intent. Following a recent decision of the Court of Appeal by which it was bound, *R v Orpin* [1980] 2 All ER 321 [1980] 1 WLR 1050, it held that the offence under s 1(2) was one of specific intent in contrast to the offence under s 1(1) which was of basic intent. This would be right if the only mens rea capable of constituting the offence were an actual intention to endanger the life of another. For the reasons I have given, however, classification into offences of specific and basic intent is irrelevant where being reckless whether a particular harmful consequence will result from one's act is a sufficient alternative mens rea. . . .

I would give the following answers to the certified questions: (a) if the charge of an offence under s 1(2) of the Criminal Damage Act 1971 is framed so as to charge the defendant only with *intending* by the destruction or damage [of the property] to endanger the life of another', evidence of self-induced intoxication can be relevant to his defence; (b) if the charge is, or includes, a reference to his 'being reckless as to whether the life of another would thereby be endangered', evidence of self-induced intoxication is not relevant.

[**Lord Edmund-Davies** concurred in the result but held that recklessness had been correctly defined in the 'much respected decision of *Cunningham*' and in *Stephenson*.]

[**Lord Keith of Kinkel** and **Lord Roskill** agreed with **Lord Diplock.**]

Appeal dismissed

For criticism of the decision see commentary, [1981] Crim LR 393. Griew [1981] Crim LR 743; Syrota [1982] Crim LR 97: Glanville Williams, 'Recklessness Redefined' [1981] CLJ 252.

R v Lawrence [1981] 1 All ER 974, House of Lords
(Lord Hailsham of St Marylebone LC, Lord Diplock, Lord Fraser of Tullybelton, Lord Roskill and Lord Bridge of Harwich)

Lawrence was convicted of causing death by reckless driving. The Court of Appeal quashed his conviction for misdirection, but certified three points of law of general public importance for the decision of the House of Lords: (1) was mens rea involved in the offence of driving recklessly? (2) if yes, what was the mental element required: and (3) was the following a proper direction?:

> 'A driver is guilty of driving recklessly if he deliberately disregards the obligation to drive with due care and attention or is indifferent whether he does so and thereby creates a risk of an accident which a driver driving with due care and attention would not create'?

[**Lord Hailsham** made a speech dismissing the appeal.]

Lord Diplock. . . . The context in which the word 'reckless' appears in s 1 of the Criminal Damage Act 1971 differs in two respects from the context in which the word 'recklessly' appears in ss 1 and 2 of the Road Traffic Act 1972, as now amended. In the Criminal Damage Act 1971 the actus reus, the physical act of destroying or damaging property belonging to another, is in itself a tort. It is not something that one does regularly as part of the ordinary routine of daily life, such as driving a car or a motor cycle. So there is something out of the ordinary to call the doer's attention to what he is doing and its possible consequences, which is absent in road traffic offences. The other difference in context is that in s 1 of the Criminal Damage Act 1971 the mens rea of the offences is defined as being reckless whether particular harmful consequences would occur, whereas in ss 1 and 2 of the Road Traffic Act 1972, as now amended, the possible harmful consequences of which the driver must be shown to have been heedless are left to be implied from the use of the word 'recklessly' itself. In ordinary usage 'recklessly' as descriptive of a physical act such as driving a motor vehicle which can be performed in a variety of different ways some of them entailing danger and some of them not, refers not only to the state of mind of the doer of the act when he decides to do it but also qualifies the manner in which the act itself is performed. One does not speak of a person acting 'recklessly', even though he has given no thought at all to the consequences of his act unless the act is one that presents a real risk of harmful consequences which anyone acting with reasonable prudence would recognise and give heed to. So the actus reus of the offence under ss 1 and 2 is not simply driving a motor vehicle on a road, but driving it in a manner which in fact creates a real risk of harmful consequences resulting from it. Since driving in such a manner as to do no worse than create a risk of causing inconvenience or annoyance to other road users constitutes the lesser offence under s 3, the manner of driving that constitutes the actus reus of an offence under ss 1 and 2 must be worse than that; it must be such as to create a real risk of causing physical injury to someone else who happens to be using the road or damage to property more substantial than the kind of minor damage that may be caused by an error of judgment in the course of parking one's car. . . .

I turn now to the mens rea. My task is greatly simplified by what has already been said about the concept of recklessness in criminal law in *R v Caldwell*. Warning was there given against adopting the simplistic approach of treating all problems of criminal liability as soluble by classifying the test of liability as being either 'subjective' or 'objective'. Recklessness on the part of the doer of an act does presuppose that there is something in the circumstances that would have drawn the attention of an ordinary prudent individual to the possibility that his act was capable of causing the kind of serious harmful consequences that the section which creates the offence was intended to prevent and that the risk of those harmful consequences occurring was not so slight that an ordinary prudent individual would feel justified in treating them as negligible. It is only when this is so that the doer of the act is acting 'recklessly' if, before doing the act, he either fails to give any thought to the possibility of there being any such risk or, having recognised that there was such risk, he nevertheless goes on to do it.

In my view, an appropriate instruction to the jury on what is meant by driving recklessly would be that they must be satisfied of two things: first, that the defendant was in fact driving the vehicle in such a manner as to create an obvious and serious risk of causing physical injury to some other person who might happen to be using the road or of doing substantial damage to property; and, second, that in driving in that manner the defendant did so without having given any thought to the possibility of there being any such risk or, having recognised that there was some risk involved, had none the less gone on to take it.

It is for the jury to decide whether the risk created by the manner in which the vehicle was being driven was both obvious and serious and, in deciding this, they may apply the standard of the ordinary prudent motorist as represented by themselves.

If satisfied that an obvious and serious risk was created by the manner of the defendant's driving, the jury was entitled to infer that he was in one or other of the states of mind required to constitute the offence and will probably do so; but regard must be given to any explanation he gives as to his state of mind which may displace the inference.

My Lords, in *Allan v Patterson*, 1980 SLT 77, Lord Emslie in the High Court of Justiciary did apply the label 'objective' to the test of whether a driver was driving recklessly within the meaning of s 3 of the Act. While for reasons set out in greater detail in my speech in *R v Caldwell* I think it is desirable in all cases of criminal liability to avoid the use of the label. I do not think that, having regard to the likelihood that the jury will draw the inference to which I have referred, the practical result of approaching the question of what constitutes driving recklessly in the way that was adopted by the Lord Justice-General in *Allan v Patterson* is likely to be any different from the result of instructing a jury in some such terms as I have suggested above. The same Act applies to both countries; it would be unfortunate if the interpretation put on it by the Scottish courts differed from that put on it by the courts in England and Wales.

I would give the following answers to the questions certified by the Court of Appeal: 1. mens rea is involved in the offence of driving recklessly; 2. the mental element required is that, before adopting a manner of driving that in fact involves an obvious and serious risk of causing physical injury to some other person who may happen to be using the road or of doing substantial damage to property, the driver has failed to give any thought to the possibility of there being any such risk, or, having recognised that there was some risk involved, has none the less gone on to take it; 3. the *Murphy* direction is wrong in the respects referred to earlier.

Since the deputy circuit judge gave to the jury, what was substantially the *Murphy* direction itself and also a somewhat confused version of it and both of these stated the law too unfavourably to the driver, this appeal must in my view be dismissed.

[**Lords Fraser, Roskill** and **Bridge** agreed with **Lords Hailsham** and **Diplock**.]

Appeal dismissed

(2) AN 'OBVIOUS RISK' — OBVIOUS TO WHOM?

Elliott v C (a minor) [1983] 2 All ER 1005, Queen's Bench Division (Robert Goff LJ and Glidewell J)

Glidewell J. . . . . The respondent was a schoolgirl who had reached the age of 14 years in May 1982. She lived with her foster mother and was in a remedial class at school. On the evening of 15 June 1982 the respondent went out with an older girl friend. She hoped to stay the night at the friend's home, but was not able to do so. The respondent did not return to her own home but stayed out all night, not sleeping for the whole night.

At about 5 am on 16 June 1982 the respondent entered Mr Davies's garden shed. She found the white spirit in its plastic container. She poured white spirit onto the carpet on the floor of the shed and threw two lighted matches onto the spirit, the second of which ignited it. The fire immediately flared up out of control and the respondent left the shed.

[**Glidewell J** quoted **Lord Diplock's** 'model direction' in *Caldwell* (p 70), and continued:]

As I have said, the magistrates accepted that they were bound to follow the model direction of Lord Diplock which I have read. It was, however, argued before them, and again before us by counsel for the respondent (to whom, and to counsel for the appellant, the court is much indebted for their arguments) that when, in the first part of his test, Lord Diplock referred to 'an act which in fact creates an obvious risk that property will be destroyed or damaged', he meant a risk which was obvious to the particular defendant. This argument was accepted by the magistrates and is set out by them in the following passages in para 7 of the case stated:

'H.   That while the respondent had realised that the contents of the bottle which contained white spirit were possibly inflammable, she had not handled it before and had not appreciated how explosively it would burn and immediately become out of her control, thereby destroying the shed and contents and also placing her own life at risk.

I.   That the respondent had given no thought at the time that she started the fire to the possibility of there being a risk that the shed and contents would be destroyed by her actions. That in the circumstances this risk would not have been obvious to her or been appreciated by her if she had given thought to the matter.

J.   We were unable to form any conclusion on the question why she had started the fire.

K.   That in reaching our findings set out herein we had due regard to the age and understanding of the respondent, her lack of experience of dealing with inflammable spirit and the fact that she must have been tired and exhausted at the time.

L.   That we accepted the interpretation of the effect of the decision in the case of *R v Caldwell* put forward on behalf of the respondent.

M.   That in particular we found it implicit in the decision in that case that a defendant should only be held to have acted recklessly by virtue of his failure to give any thought to an obvious risk that property would be destroyed or damaged, where such risk would have been obvious to him if he had given any thought to the matter.

N.   Accordingly having regard to our findings set out above, we found the respondent not guilty of the charge and dismissed the information.'

Before us, counsel for the appellant has argued forcefully that the magistrates were wrong to adopt that interpretation of the decision in *Caldwell*. He submits that the phrase 'creates an obvious risk' means that the risk is one which must have been obvious to a reasonably prudent man, not necessarily to the particular defendant if he or she had given thought of it. It follows, says counsel, that if the risk is one which would have been obvious to a reasonably prudent person, once it has also been proved that the particular defendant gave no thought to the possibility of there being such a risk, it is not a defence that because of limited intelligence or exhaustion she would not have appreciated the risk even if she had thought about it.

It is right to say, as counsel for the appellant pointed out to us, that there are passages in the speech of Lord Diplock in *Caldwell* which suggest that his Lordship was indeed using the phrase 'creates an obvious risk' as meaning, 'creates a risk which was obvious to the particular defendant.' Thus, his Lordship said ([1981] 1 All ER 961 at 964 [1982] AC 341 at 351):

'Among the words [Professor Kenny] used was "recklessness", the noun derived from the adjective "reckless," of which the popular or dictionary meaning is "careless, regardless, or heedless of the possible harmful consequences of one's acts". It presupposes that, if thought were given to the matter by the doer before the act was done, it would have been apparent to him that there was a real risk of its having the relevant harmful consequences . . .'

Speaking of another earlier decision of the Court of Appeal, in *R v Briggs* [1977] 1 All ER 475, [1977] 1 WLR 605n, he said ([1981] 1 All ER 961 at 965, [1982] AC 341 at 353): '. . . even though the risk is great and would be obvious if any thought were given to the matter by the doer of the act.'

He said ([1981] 1 All ER 961 at 967, [1982] AC 341 at 355):

'So, in the instant case, the fact that the respondent was unaware of the risk of endangering the lives of residents in the hotel owing to his self-induced intoxication would be no defence if that risk would have been obvious to him had he been sober.'

The last passage was based on the earlier decision of the House of Lords in *R v Majewski* [1976] 2 All ER 142, [1977] AC 443, a decision relating to the effect of self-induced intoxication on intent. But, quite apart from the Majewski test, the decision of the majority in *Caldwell* that intoxication, even if it resulted in the defendant not thinking at all whether there was a risk that property or life would be endangered, nevertheless did not take him out of the state of mind properly described as 'reckless' is only consistent in my view with their Lordships meaning by the phrase 'creates an obvious risk' creates a risk obvious to the reasonably prudent person.

That the submission of counsel for the appellant is correct is to my mind, however, put beyond a peradventure by two later decisions of the House of Lords. [His Lordship cited Lord Diplock's discussion of 'reckless' in *Lawrence*, p 72, above, and *Miller*, p 25, above].

In the light of these last two authorities, we are in my judgment bound to hold that the word reckless in s 1 of the Criminal Damage Act 1971 has the meaning ascribed to it by counsel for the appellant. It is only fair to the magistrates in the present case to say that it seems that they were not referred to the decision in *R v Lawrence*, and *R v Miller* had not, when they reached their decision, been heard by the House of Lords. . . .

Robert Goff LJ. I agree with the conclusion reached by Glidewell J, but I do so simply because I believe myself constrained to do so by authority. I feel moreover that I would be lacking in candour if I were to conceal my unhappiness about the conclusion which I feel compelled to reach. In my opinion, although of course the courts of this country are bound by the doctrine of precedent, sensibly interpreted, nevertheless it would be irresponsible for judges to act as automatons, rigidly applying authorities without regard to consequences. Where therefore it appears at first sight that authority compels a judge to reach a conclusion which he senses to be unjust or inappropriate, he is, I consider, under a positive duty to examine the relevant authorities with scrupulous care to ascertain whether he can, within the limits imposed by the doctrine of precedent (always sensibly interpreted), legitimately interpret or qualify the principle expressed in the authorities to achieve the result which he perceives to be just or appropriate in the particular case. I do not disguise the fact that I have sought to perform this function in the present case.

[**Goff LJ** quoted Lord Diplock's model direction and continued:]

Now, if that test is applied literally in the present case, the conclusion appears inevitable that, on the facts found by the magistrates, the respondent was reckless whether the shed and contents would be destroyed; because first she did an act which created an obvious risk that the property would be destroyed, and second she had not given any thought to the possibility of there being any such risk.

Yet, if I next pause (as I have done, in accordance with what I conceive to be my proper function) and ask myself the question: would I, having regard only to the ordinary meaning of the word, consider this girl to have been, on the facts found, *reckless* whether the shed and contents would be destroyed, my answer would, I confess, be in the negative. This is not a case where there was a deliberate disregard of a known risk of damage or injury of a certain type or degree; nor is it a case where there was mindless indifference to a risk of such damage or injury, as is expressed in common speech in the context of motoring offences (though not, I think, of arson) as 'blazing on regardless'; nor is it even a case where failure to give thought to the possibility of the risk was due to some blameworthy cause, such as intoxication. This is a case where it appears that the only basis on which the accused might be held to have been reckless would be if the appropriate test to be applied was purely objective: a test which might in some circumstances be thought justifiable in relation to certain conduct (eg reckless driving), particularly where the word 'reckless' is used simply to characterise the relevant conduct. But such a test does not appear at first sight to be appropriate to a crime such as that under consideration in the present case, especially as recklessness in that crime has to be related to a particular consequence. I therefore next ask myself the question whether I can, consistently with the doctrine of precedent, sensibly interpreted, legitimately construe or qualify the principle stated by Lord Diplock in *Caldwell* so as to accommodate what I conceive to be appropriate result on the facts of the present case, bearing in mind that those facts are very different from the facts under consideration by the House of Lords in *Caldwell*, where the defendant had set fire to a hotel when in a state of intoxication.

Here again, it would be unrealistic if I were to disguise the fact that I am well aware that the statement of principle by Lord Diplock in *Caldwell* has been the subject of comment, much of it critical, in articles written by jurists; and that I have studied certain of these articles with interest. I find it striking that the justices, in reaching their conclusion in the present case, have done so (no doubt in response to an argument advanced on the respondent's behalf) by imposing on Lord Diplock's statement of principle a qualification similar to one considered by Professor Glanville Williams in his article 'Recklessness Redefined' (1981) 40 CLJ 252 at 270-271. This is that a defendant should only be regarded as having acted recklessly by virtue of his failure to give any thought to an obvious risk that property would be destroyed or damaged, where such risk would have been obvious to *him* if he had given any thought to the matter. However, having studied Lord Diplock's speech, I do not think it would be consistent with his reasoning to impose any such qualification. I say that not only because this qualification does not appear in terms in his conclusion which I have already quoted, but also because, when considering earlier in his speech Professor Kenny's definition of recklessness (which he rejected as being too narrow), Lord Diplock expressly adverted to the fact that that definition presupposed that 'if thought were given to the matter by the doer before the act was done, it would have been apparent to *him* that there was a real risk of its having the relevant harmful consequences . . .' (see [1981] 1 All ER 961 at 964, [1982] AC 341 at 351; my emphasis). It seems to me that, having expressly considered that element in Professor Kenny's test, and having (as I think) plainly decided to omit it from his own formulation of the concept of recklessness, it would not now be legitimate for an inferior court, in a case under this particular subsection, to impose a qualification which had so been rejected by Lord Diplock himself. It follows that for that reason alone I do not feel able to uphold the reasoning of the magistrates in the present case. But I wish to add that, for my part, I doubt whether this qualification can be justified in any event. Where there is no thought of the consequences, any further inquiry necessary for the purposes of establishing guilt should prima facie be directed to the question why such thought was not given, rather than to the purely hypothetical question of what the particular person would have appreciated had he directed his mind to the matter. . . .

Appeal allowed. Leave to appeal refused

The House of Lords refused a petition for leave to appeal: [1983] 1 WLR 951.

R v Stephen Malcom R (1984) 79 Cr App Rep 334, Court of Appeal, Criminal Division
(Ackner LJ, Bristow and Popplewell JJ)

The appellant when aged 15 committed a series of burglaries. He and his accomplices believed that a woman and her daughter had 'grassed' on them. They made three petrol bombs from milk bottles and threw them at the woman's house near the daughter's bedroom, causing loud bangs and sheets of flame. The appellant said that they did not intend to injure but only to frighten. He did not realise that if the bomb had gone through the daughter's window it might have killed her. He was convicted of arson contrary to s 1 (2) (b) of the Criminal Damage Act 1971, p 575, below having pleaded guilty when the judge rejected a submission that he should tell the jury that the appellant was reckless only if he did an act which created a risk obvious to someone of his age and with such of his characteristics as would affect his appreciation of the risk.

Ackner LJ, having discussed *Elliott v C*:

In the face of that difficult situation, Mr Timms sought to induce us to adopt a *via media*. He said he accepted it would be wrong to ask the question whether the defendant himself was aware of the risk, but it would be right to inquire whether a person of the age of the defendant and with his characteristics which might be relevant to his ability to foresee the risk, would have appreciated it. He drew our attention in particular to the submission made by the prosecution before the justices in *Elliott's* case (1983) 77 Cr App R 103; [1983] 1 WLR 939 (see p 110 and p 940 respectively) 'that in relation to the defendant aged 14 years, the proper approach was whether such risk would have been obvious to a normal 14 year old child.' Therefore he said he was not seeking to relate the test to the particular defendant, but merely, so to speak, to a class of which he is a member. This, he says, provides him with the same logical basis of approach to the reasonable man or the reasonably prudent person as *DPP v Camplin* [p 321, below] had suggested. We do not think that that *via media* was for one moment in the mind of Lord Diplock. The opportunity so to ingraft this important modification on the principle which he had enunciated had arisen in the subsequent cases and would have been just the sort of point (if it was a valid one) which we would have expected the House of Lords to have desired to have dealt with, thus clearing up the position, when they had the opportunity to do so when considering whether or not to give leave in *Elliott's* case (supra). If they had desired to say, for instance, that the age of the defendant was a factor to which particular regard must be had in applying the test, then *Elliott* was just the sort of case to do that, excising, if appropriate, any reference to any other ephemeral characteristics such as exhaustion from which the girl was said to be suffering. But they did not take that opportunity. We do not think that we should seek by this subtlety to avoid applying principles which we also have difficulty in accepting. We respectfully share the regrets voiced by Robert Goff LJ that in essence 'recklessness' has now been construed synonymously with 'carelessness.' Like the Editor of the current edition of *Archbold* (41st ed) at para 17–25(5), we find difficulty in reconciling the following excerpts from the speech of Lord Hailsham LC with Lord Diplock's conclusion in *R v Lawrence* with which he agreed. Lord Hailsham said at 73 Cr App R 1, 6; [1982] AC 510, 520:

'It only surprises me that there should have been any question regarding the existence of *mens rea* in relation to the words "reckless" "recklessly" or "recklessness." Unlike most English words it has been in the English language as a word in general use at least since the eighth century AD almost always with the same meaning, applied to a person or conduct evincing a state of mind stopping short of deliberate intention, and going beyond mere inadvertence, or in its modern, though not its etymological and original sense, mere carelessness.'

The excerpt from the speech of Lord Diplock is at p 10 and p 525 respectively, where he refers to *Caldwell's* case (supra) and says:

'The conclusion reached by the majority was that the adjective "reckless" when used in a criminal statute, i e the Criminal Damage Act 1971, had not acquired a special meaning as a term of legal art, but bore its popular or dictionary meaning of careless, regardless, or heedless of the possible harmful consequences of one's acts. The same must be true of the adverbial derivative "recklessly".'

We therefore dismiss the appeal against conviction.

Appeal dismissed

(3) RECKLESSNESS IN RAPE

R v Satnam S, R v Kewal S, p 400, below

Questions

1. In this case authority for the view that *Caldwell* applies only to recklessness as to results, not to recklessness as to circumstances?
2. Does the phrase, 'couldn't care less', adequately encapsulate the concept of recklessness? Consider a man who is aware that the woman with whom he is about to have intercourse may not be consenting. Fervently hoping that she is consenting, he proceeds to have intercourse. He does care (though not enough); but is he reckless?
3. Is there a distinction between 'indifferent' and 'couldn't care less'? Can 'indifferent' be grafted on to the *Caldwell* test, as was proposed in *Pigg*?

A person's act is 'reckless' only if it creates an obvious risk—or, as it mysteriously becomes in *Lawrence*, an obvious *and serious* risk—of causing the relevant result. But obvious to whom? *Caldwell* appears to be ambiguous on the point. Is it sufficient that it would have been obvious to a reasonable and prudent man who gave thought to the matter? Or is it necessary that it would have been obvious to the particular defendant had he directed his mind to the matter? As Glidewell J pointed out in *Elliott v C* there are certainly passages in *Caldwell* which suggest that we have to consider the particular defendant. The passages which he cites from that case for the contrary view are not really decisive. Every one agrees that there is an objective element in recklessness, whether of the *Cunningham* or the *Caldwell* variety. As the draft Code has it, in all cases it must be 'unreasonable to take the risk'. Arguably, in the passages in question Lord Diplock was referring to this element. If the risk would not have been obvious to the reasonable man giving thought to the matter, this is not a case of recklessness—there is no need to look any further.

But this is not incompatible with a further requirement—would the risk have been obvious to the particular defendant had he thought about it? The passages in *Caldwell* might thus be reconciled; but the same is not true of *Lawrence*, as Glidewell J makes clear; the standard to be applied by the jury is that of the 'ordinary prudent motorist as represented by themselves'.

Would it have made better law if the ambiguity in *Caldwell* had been resolved the other way? Ought the proposed Code to provide for such a form of fault, either instead of or in addition to, 'heedlessness'? For example:

'A person acts in respect of an element of an offence— -------ly when—

(i) he gives no thought to whether there is a risk that it exists or will exist or occur when, if he had given thought to the matter, the risk would have been obvious to him.'

In applying such a test the court would obviously take into account the fact that the defendant was a schizophrenic (as in *Stephenson* (discussed p 70 above)) or a backward fourteen-year-old girl (as in *Elliott v C*, p 73, above). Clearly also the court would not take into account the fact that the defendant was intoxicated (cf cl 26 of the draft Code which would be amended to provide for this); but what about other temporary conditions such as the fact that the defendant had been out all night without any food or sleep?

Problems involved in introducing an additional variety of fault are (i) that there is shortage of suitable words to describe fault elements. 'Heedless' is perhaps not a very happy expression to describe *Caldwell* recklessness but it was the best the Codification team could find and it would be necessary to find yet another word; and (ii) the law may become over-refined. On what criterion would the legislator choose between three forms of risk-taking? And think of the problems of judge and jury confronted with an indictment covering three offences involving the three different concepts, and perhaps criminal negligence as well. Would a better solution be to *replace* 'heedlessness' as currently defined in the draft Code with the alternative concept? There is only one case in which the courts appear to have applied such a concept. *Hudson* [1966] 1 QB 448, [1965] 1 All ER 721 p 403, below; but see also Professor Hart's persuasive article, 'Mens Rea and Criminal Responsibility' in *Oxford Essays in Jurisprudence*, p 29.

(4) RECKLESSNESS AND CULPABILITY

In *Caldwell* (p 68, above), Lord Diplock suggested that there is no difference in culpability between a defendant who has given no thought to the possibility that there might be a risk and one who knows there is a risk and decides to take it. Do you agree? Consider the case of the South Wales busdriver who in 1982 attempted to drive his 13 ft 9 in. double decker under a railway bridge 10 ft 6 in height, killing six people and injuring several others. (See *The Times*, 7/10/82, 2/11/82 and 13/1/83) It appears that he had driven the route regularly for ten years but had never taken a double-decker on the route before. When he hit the bridge he thought, 'My God, a double-decker.' He knew he was driving a double-decker because, only two stops before the crash, he had told passengers boarding the bus that there was plenty of room upstairs. But, as he approached the bridge, he had apparently forgotten that he was driving a double-decker. It was stated at the inquest that the Director of Public Prosecutions did not consider there was evidence for a charge of manslaughter or causing death by dangerous (meaning, presumably 'reckless', dangerous driving having been abolished) driving. The driver subsequently pleaded guilty to driving without due care and attention.

The risk would have been obvious to a reasonable man who stopped to think and the driver did not think. Was not this plainly *Caldwell* recklessness? But how would you rate the culpability of the driver with that of another who, approaching a low bridge, muses, 'Am I driving a double-decker today? I really can't remember,' and then proceeds to drive the double-decker into the bridge?

See also the similar case of Fl-Lt Lawrence who, while flying his Phantom aircraft over Germany, fired a side-winder missile and shot down an RAF Jaguar aircraft. ((1983) Times, 13 January). At the time Lawrence had completely forgotten that he was flying with live weapons. According to the expert evidence, 'He didn't forget, in the sense that his long-term memory did retain the information. He was not aware at the time he had released the side-winder that he had weapons on the aircraft.' Again, compare the pilot's culpability with that of one who, realising that the plane may be armed with live missiles, decides to take a chance and press the button.

4. Knowledge in the criminal law

These cases raise a more general problem about knowledge in the criminal law. Does a person 'know' a fact which is not present to his mind at the relevant moment, though he is quite capable of recalling it—as the bus-driver recalled that he was driving a double-decker at the moment of impact? Professor Glanville Williams at one time thought he does. The following passage in the first edition of his *Textbook* (p 79) does not appear in the second edition but it is not clear whether he has changed his mind. He is discussing *Parker* (see p 69, above). D, in a telephone kiosk, being frustrated by his inability to get through, twice slammed the telephone down on to its cradle. On the second occasion he smashed it. Charged with criminal damage, he said that he did not realise at the time he acted that he was likely to break the telephone. The Court of Appeal held he was rightly convicted because 'a man is reckless when he carried out the deliberate act knowing or closing his mind to the obvious fact that there is some risk of damage resulting from that act, but nevertheless continued the performance of that act.'

> 'The facts were so eloquent of recklessness that the appeal might well have been dismissed on the ground that no miscarriage of justice had actually occurred, even if the direction was regarded as misleading. Parker must have slammed the receiver down extremely hard to break the plastic, and it is impossible to believe that he did not know the risk of damaging it. It is a misunderstanding of the legal requirement to suppose that this knowledge of risk must be a matter of conscious awareness at the moment of the act. We grow up in a world in which we come to know, from the earliest age, that things are broken by rough treatment. Some things are more resistant than others: one could, in a temper, kick a farm tractor or the wheel of a lorry without doing damage. But is there anyone who does not know that a telephone receiver can be damaged by being violently slammed down? The fact that it is slammed down because of a feeling of frustration is nothing to the purpose.'

If this is right, what was all the fuss over *DPP v Smith* (p 42 above) about? If, when Smith was sitting quietly at home, relaxed in his armchair, someone had said to him, 'Jim, if you were to drive off in your car at top speed in a busy street with a copper clinging to the bonnet, do you think it is likely that he would suffer serious injury?' would not his reply have been an unprintable affirmative? The Court of Appeal in that case, however, thought that the relevant question was what *Smith* thought in a moment of panic and the ten seconds which the whole episode occupied. Was not this right?

5. Transferred fault and defences

The draft Criminal Code Bill provides:

28 Transferred fault and defences
(1) In determining whether a person is guilty of an offence, his intention to cause, or his recklessness whether he causes, a result in relation to a person or thing capable of being the victim or subject-matter of the offence is to be treated as an intention to cause or, as the case may be, recklessness whether he causes that result in relation to any other person or thing affected by his conduct.
(2) Any defence on which a person might have relied on a charge of an offence in relation to a person or thing within his contemplation is open to him on a charge of the same offence in relation to a person or thing not within his contemplation.

Schedule 1 of the draft Bill provides the following illustrations:

28(1)   28(i)   D does an act by which he intends to injure O. He misses O but injures P, whom he does not intend to injure or have in mind as likely to be injured. He is guilty of intentionally causing injury to another under section 76. He may be convicted of this offence on an indictment or information alleging an intention to injure P.

28(ii) D, intending to frighten O, plants a bomb to explode where he expects O to be. He realises that O may be seriously injured. D's child, P, comes to the place at the time of the explosion and is killed. D is guilty of manslaughter (under s 57 (1)(c)).

28(iii) D wishes to injure O. He aims a blow at P, believing him to be O. He is guilty of attempting to injure P (under s 53 (1)). If he hits and injures P, he is guilty of intentionally injuring him (under s 76).

28(2)   28(vi) D, under provocation, aims a shot at O with intent to kill him. The shot misses O and kills P. D may raise the plea of provocation under section 60.

The Report on Codification explains the clause as follows:

Clause 28: Transferred fault and defences
9.27 This clause restates the doctrine known as 'transferred intent' and provides a corresponding rule as to 'transferred' defences.
9.28 *Subsection (1). Transferred fault.* A general statement on transferred fault has the following practical justifications.

(i)   Where a person intends to affect one person or thing (X) and actually affects another (Y), he may be charged with an offence of attempt in relation to X; or it may be possible to satisfy a court or jury, without resort to the doctrine, that he was reckless with respect to Y. But an attempt charge may be impossible (where it is not known until trial that the defendant claims to have had X and not Y in contemplation); or inappropriate (as not describing the harm done adequately for labelling or sentencing purposes). Moreover, recklessness with respect to Y may be insufficient to establish the offence or incapable of being proved. The rule stated by this subsection overcomes these difficulties.

(ii) The drafting of particular offences is simplified. This is illustrated by our redrafting (in clause 82) of section 1 of the Criminal Damage Act 1971. [Discussed in this respect in para 16.3, below].

9.29 *Transfer 'only within the same crime'.* [Cf Williams, *Criminal Law, The General Part* 2nd ed (1961), 128.] If an offence can be committed only in respect of a particular class of person or thing, the actor's intention or recklessness, to be 'transferred', must relate to such a person or thing—that is, in the words of the subsection, to 'a person or thing capable of being the victim or subject-matter of the offence'. [Cf *R v Pembliton* (1874) LR 2 CCR 119]. If, on the other hand, the person or thing actually affected is not so capable, the external elements of the offence are not made out and the question of transferring the actor's fault does not arise.

9.30 *Wording of offences and charges.* The subsection treats an intention to affect X as an intention to affect Y (who is actually affected). So where an offence requires an affecting of a person with intention to affect him (as opposed to 'any person'), there can still be a conviction; and a charge of an offence committed against Y with intent to affect Y can be proved by evidence of an intent to affect X. Existing authority is not consistent on these points [See the comment on *R v Monger* [1973] Crim LR 301 at 302]; but the proposed solution is in keeping with the best authority.

9.31 *Mistake as to victim.* Clause 28(1) is so worded as to deal also with the case of an irrelevant mistake about the identity of the victim or subject-matter of an offence. The argument, 'I thought Y was X; I intended to hit X; therefore I did not intend to hit Y', hardly needs a statutory answer; but this provision incidentally provides one.

9.32 *Subsection (2). Transferred defences.* This provision for the transfer of defences will be useful for the avoidance of doubt. It enables a person who affects an uncontemplated victim to rely on a defence that would have been available to him if he had affected the person or thing he had in contemplation. It is wide enough to apply consistently with a provision such as a clause 47(8) (force against innocent persons), which restricts a defence of lawful force against a person's body to a case where the force is directed against a person to be arrested or one whose unlawful conduct provokes the defensive force. If permissible force is directed against such a person (X), the actor would have a defence if that force found its target; so clause 28(2) gives the actor the same defence if he misses X and hits Y (who was outside his contemplation).

R v Pembliton [1874–80] All ER Rep 1163, Court for Crown Cases Reserved (Lord Coleridge CJ, Blackburn and Lush JJ and Pigott and Cleasby BB)

Case Stated by the recorder of Wolverhampton.

At the quarter sessions of the peace held at Wolverhampton on 8 January 1874, Henry Pembliton was indicted for that he

> 'unlawfully and maliciously did commit damage, injury, and spoil upon a window in the house of Henry Kirkham,'

contrary to s 51 of the Malicious Damage Act 1861.

On the night of 6 December 1873, the prisoner was drinking with others at a public-house called 'The Grand Turk' kept by the prosecutor. At about 11 o'clock pm the whole party were turned out of the house for being disorderly, and they then began to fight in the street and near the prosecutor's window, where a crowd of from 40 to 50 persons collected. The prisoner, after fighting some time with persons in the crowd, separated himself from them, and removed to the other side of the street, where he picked up a large stone, and threw it at the persons he had been fighting with. The stone passed over the heads of those persons, and struck a large plate glass window in the prosecutor's house, and broke it, thereby doing damage to the extent of £7 12s 9d. The jury, after hearing evidence on both sides, found that the prisoner threw the stone which broke the window, but that he threw it at the people he had been fighting with, intending to strike one or more of them with it, but not intending to break the window. They returned a verdict of 'guilty'. The recorder respited the sentence, and admitted the prisoner to bail, and prayed the judgment of the Court for Crown Cases Reserved, whether, on the facts stated, and the finding of the jury, the prisoner was rightly convicted or not.

Lord Coleridge C. I am of opinion that this conviction must be quashed. [His Lordship stated the facts, referred to ss 51 and 58 of the Malicious Damage Act 1861 and continued:] It seems to me that, in both these sections, what was intended to be provided against by the Act is the wilfully doing an unlawful act, and that that act must be wilfully and intentionally done on the part of the person doing it to render him liable to be convicted. Without saying that, on these facts, if the jury had found that the prisoner had been guilty of throwing the stone recklessly, knowing that there was a window near which it might probably hit, I should have been disposed to interfere with the conviction, yet, as they have found that he threw the stone at the people he had been fighting with intending to strike them and not intending to break the window, I think that the conviction must be quashed. I do not intend to throw any doubt on the cases which have been cited and which show what is sufficient to constitute malice in the case of murder. They rest on the principles of the common law, and have no application to a statutory offence.

Blackburn J. I am of the same opinion. . . . A person may be said to act maliciously when he wilfully does an unlawful act without lawful excuse. The question here is can the prisoner be said, when he not only threw the stone unlawfully but broke the window unintentionally, to have unlawfully and maliciously broken the window? I think that there was evidence on which the jury might have found that he unlawfully and maliciously broke the window, if they had found that he was aware that the natural and probable consequence of his throwing the stone was that it might break the glass window, on the principle that a man must be taken to intend what is the natural and probable consequence of his acts. But the jury have not found that the prisoner threw the stone, knowing that, on the other side of the men he was throwing at, there was a glass window, and that he was reckless whether he did or did not break the window. On the contrary, they have found that he did not intend to break the window. I think, therefore, that the conviction must be quashed.

Pigott B. I am of the same opinion.

Lush J. I also think that, on this finding of the jury, we have no alternative but to hold that the conviction must be quashed. The word 'maliciously' means an act done either actually or constructively with a malicious intention. The jury might have found that the prisoner did intend actually to break the window or constructively to do so, that he knew that the stone might probably break it when he threw it. But they have not so found.

Cleasby B, concurred.

Conviction quashed

Questions

1. Would the judges have upheld the conviction for breaking the window of the pub if there had been a finding:
(a) that the appellant *ought* to have known that it was probable that the stone would break the window?
(b) that he *actually knew* that it was probable that the stone would break the window?
(c) that he threw the stone at the closed window of a *carriage* in which one of his enemies was seated intending to injure that person? See *Latimer,* below.
2. According to Blackburn J, 'A person may be said to act maliciously when he wilfully does an unlawful act without lawful excuse'. Why was not the appellant, then, acting maliciously? What qualification must be made to the proposition of Blackburn J?
3. What would be the result today? (See Criminal Damage Act 1971, p 575, below.) Is Blackburn J's statement of 'the principle that a man must be taken to intend what is the natural and probable consequence of his acts' materially different from s 8 of the Criminal Justice Act 1967? (p 562, below, p 42, above).

**R v Latimer [1886–90] All ER Rep 386, Court for Crown Cases Reserved
(Lord Coleridge CJ, Lord Esher MR, Bowen LJ, Field and Manisty JJ)**

Case Stated by the recorder for the borough of Devonport.
    At the quarter sessions for the borough of Devonport held on 10 April 1886, the prisoner was indicted for unlawfully and maliciously wounding Ellen Rolston. The evidence showed that the prosecutrix kept a public-house in Devonport; that on Sunday, 14 February 1886, the prisoner, who was a soldier, and a man named Horace Chapple were in the public-house, and a quarrel

took place, and that eventually the prisoner was knocked down by the man Chapple. The prisoner subsequently went out into a yard at the back of the house. In about five minutes the prisoner came back hastily through the room in which Chapple was still sitting having in his hand his belt which he had taken off. As the prisoner passed he aimed a blow with his belt at Chapple and struck him slightly, but the belt bounded off and struck the prosecutrix, who was talking to Chapple, cutting her face open and wounding her severely. At the close of the case the recorder left these questions to the jury: (i) Was the blow struck at Chapple in self-defence to get through the room, or unlawfully and maliciously? (ii) Did the blow so struck, in fact wound Ellen Rolston? (iii) Was the striking Ellen Rolston purely accidental, or was it such a consequence as the prisoner should have expected to follow from the blow he aimed at Chapple? The jury found: (i) That the blow was unlawful and malicious. (ii) That the blow did in fact wound Ellen Rolston. (iii) That the striking of Ellen Rolston was purely accidental, and not such a consequence of the blow as the prisoner ought to have expected. Upon these findings the recorder directed a verdict of Guilty to be entered to the first count, but respited judgment and admitted the prisoner to bail to come up for judgment at the next sessions. The question for the consideration of the court was, whether upon the facts and the findings of the jury the prisoner was rightly convicted of the offence for which he was indicted.

Lord Coleridge CJ. . . . The Master of the Rolls has pointed out that these very sections are in substitution for and correction of the earlier statute of 9 Geo 4, c 31. where it was necessary that the act should have been done with intent to maim, disfigure, or disable 'such person', showing that the intent must have been to injure the person actually injured. Those words are left out in the later statute, the Offences against the Person Act 1861, and the words are 'wound any other person'. I cannot see that there could be any question, but for *R v Pembliton*. I think that that case was properly decided; but upon a ground which renders it clearly distinguishable from the present case. That is to say, the Malicious Damage Act 1861, which was under discussion in *Pembliton* makes an unlawful injury to property punishable in a certain way. In that case the jury and the facts expressly negatived that there was any intent to injure any property at all; and the court held that, in a statute which created it an offence to injure property, there must be an intention to injure property in order to support an indictment under that statute. But for that case counsel for the appellant is out of order, and I, therefore, think that this conviction should be sustained.

Bowen LJ. I am also of opinion that this conviction should be affirmed. It is quite clear that this offence was committed without any malice in the mind of the prisoner, and that he had no intention of wounding Ellen Rolston. The only difficulty that arises from *Pembliton*, which was a case under the Malicious Damage Act 1861, which does not deal with all malice in general, but with malice towards property; and all that case holds is, that though the prisoner would have been guilty of acting maliciously within the common law meaning of the term, still he was not guilty of acting maliciously within the meaning of a statute which requires a malicious intent to injure property. Had the prisoner meant to strike a pane of glass, and without any reasonable expectation of doing so injured a person, it might be said that the malicious intent to injure property was not enough to sustain a prosecution under this statute. But, as the jury found that the prisoner intended to wound Chapple, I am of opinion that he acted maliciously within the meaning of the Offences against the Person Act 1861.

Lord Esher MR, Field and Manisty JJ, agreed that the conviction should be affirmed.

Conviction affirmed

R v Mitchell [1983] 2 All ER 427, Court of Criminal Division (Purchas LJ, Talbot and Staughton JJ)

Staughton J. The facts alleged by the prosecution at the trial were briefly as follows. On 26 March 1981 Mitchell, who was aged 22 at the time, was in a busy post office at Tottenham. An altercation arose when he tried to force himself into a queue or in some other way to be served before those who had been waiting longer than he had. A Mr Edward Smith, who was aged 72, spoke to him about his behaviour. There was some argument, and Mitchell hit Mr Smith in the mouth, causing him to stagger back and hit the back of his head against a glass panel above the post office counter. The glass panel shattered. Mr Smith recovered and moved forward. Mitchell then either hit Mr Smith again or else threw him, so that he fell into other people who were waiting in the post office. Mr Smith fell against Mrs Anne Crafts, a lady aged 89. Both Mr Smith and Mrs Crafts fell to the ground. Mr Smith suffered a bruise in the back of his head, and his lower lip was cut and swollen, Mrs Crafts suffered a broken femur. She was taken to hospital, and on 31 March 1981 an operation was performed to replace her hip joint. She appeared to make a satisfactory recovery, but on 2 April 1981 she died suddenly. The cause of death was pulmonary embolism caused by thrombosis of the left leg veins, which in turn was caused by fracture of the femur. [Mitchell appealed against conviction for manslaughter. His Lordship stated that the main question argued was whether the person at whom the act is aimed must also be the person whose death is caused. He referred to various leading cases on manslaughter and continued:] The only authority (if such it be) which we have found to be directly in point is *Russell on Crime* (12th edn, 1964) vol 1, p 588 citing the 1839 Commissioners on Criminal Law:

> 'Involuntary homicide, which is not by misadventure, includes all cases where, without intention to kill or do great bodily harm, or wilfully to endanger life, death occurs in any of the following instances: Where death results from any unlawful act or omission done or omitted with intent to hurt the person of another, whether the mischief light on the person intended, or on any other person; where death results from any wrong wilfully occasioned to the person of another; where death results from any unlawful act or unlawful omission, attended with risk of hurt to the person of another; where death results from want of due caution either in doing an act, or neglecting to prevent mischief, which the offender is bound by law to prevent.'

We can see no reason of policy for holding that an act calculated to harm A cannot be manslaughter if it in fact kills B. The criminality of the doer of the act is precisely the same whether it is A or B who dies. A person who throws a stone at A is just as guilty if, instead of hitting and killing A, it hits and kills B. Parliament evidently held the same view in relation to the allied offence of unlawful and malicious wounding contrary to s 20 of the Offences against the Person Act 1861: see *R v Latimer* (1886) 17 QBD 359. We accordingly reject the argument of counsel for Mitchell that, because Mitchell's acts were aimed at Mr Smith, it cannot have been manslaughter when they caused the death of Mrs Crafts.

CHAPTER 6

Intoxication

The draft Criminal Code Bill provides:

26 Intoxication

(1) Evidence of involuntary intoxication shall be taken into account in determining whether a person acted with the fault required for the offence with which he is charged.

(2) Evidence of voluntary intoxication shall be taken into account in determining whether a person acted with a fault element (however described) consisting in a state of mind other than recklessness or heedlessness.

(3) Where an offence requires a fault element (however described) of recklessness or heedlessness a person who was voluntarily intoxicated shall be treated as having been aware of any risk of which he would have been aware had he been sober.

(4) Where the definition of a fault element or of a defence refers, or requires reference, to the state of mind or conduct to be expected of a reasonable person, such person shall be understood to be one who is not intoxicated.

(5) Where a person becomes intoxicated with a view to doing an act specified in the definition of an offence and, while intoxicated, does that act, he shall be treated as having done it intentionally.

(6) In determining whether a person believed that an exempting circumstance existed, there shall be taken into account:

(a) any evidence of involuntary intoxication;

(b) any evidence of voluntary intoxication, except that where:

    (i) the offence charged involves a fault element of recklessness, heedlessness, criminal negligence or carelessness, or requires no fault; or

    (ii) the person became intoxicated with a view to committing the offence charged,

    he shall be treated as if he knew that the exempting circumstance did not exist if he would have known this had he been sober.

(7) Subsections (3) and (6)(b)(i) do not apply:

(a) to murder (to which section 57(1)(b) applies); or

(b) to the case (to which section 38(1)(b) applies) where the person's unawareness or belief arises from a combination of mental disorder and voluntary intoxication.

(8) (a) 'Intoxicant' means alcohol or any other thing which, when taken into the body, may impair awareness or control.

(b) 'Voluntary intoxication' means the intoxication of a person by an intoxicant which he takes, otherwise than properly for a medicinal purpose, knowing that it is an intoxicant; and 'involuntary intoxication' means any other intoxication.

(c) For the purposes of this section, a person 'takes' an intoxicant if he permits it to be administered to him.

(9) An intoxicant, although taken for a medicinal purpose, is not properly so taken if:

(a) (i) it is not taken on medical advice; or

    (ii) it is taken on medical advice but the taker fails then or thereafter to comply with any condition forming part of the advice; and

(b) the taker is aware that the taking, or the failure, as the case may be, may result in his doing an act capable of constituting the offence in question;

and accordingly intoxication resulting from such taking or failure is voluntary intoxication.

(10) [Where a defendant adduces or relies on evidence that he was involuntarily intoxicated it shall be for him to prove that the alleged intoxication was involuntary.]

1. Intoxication and proof of the mental element

This clause is based primarily upon the recommendations of the Criminal Law Revision Committee in their Fourteenth Report, Part VI (1980). The principal recommendation was that in offences of which recklessness is an element the defendant's failure to appreciate a risk because of voluntary intoxication should be immaterial. The decision in *Caldwell* (1981), p 68, above, appears to have brought the existing law into line with this recommendation. Lord Edmund-Davies, dissenting, said [1981] 1 All ER at 972:

> 'My Lords, it was recently predicted that "There can hardly be any doubt that *all* crimes of recklessness except murder will now be held to be crimes of basic intent within *Majewski*" (see Glanville Williams, *Textbook of Criminal Law* (1978, p 431)). That prophecy has been promptly fulfilled by the majority of your Lordships. . . .'

Clause 26 is therefore offered as a statement of the present law with the modifications indicated in the following passages from the Report:

9.9 *Subsections (2) to (6)* deal with the effect of voluntary intoxication. Generally, the relevance of evidence of intoxication is to show that the defendant lacked some mental element which is required for the offence charged. The recommendations of the Criminal Law Revision Committee require a distinction to be drawn between recklessness and other prescribed mental states. The Committee, reporting before the decision in *R v Caldwell* [[1981] AC 341] were not able to make any recommendation about the fault element designated "heedlessness" in the Code. Whether this is properly described as a state of mind has been much debated. [See particularly Glanville Williams, 'Recklessness Redefined' [1981] CLJ 252 at 256–258.] It is unnecessary to consider the rights and wrongs of the debate. It is clear that, for the purposes of this section, if, and insofar as, it involves a mental element, heedlessness must be classed with recklessness. Subsections (2) and (3) are drafted accordingly. For the effect, see illustration 26 (iii) in Schedule 1.

'26 (3).   26 (iii) A statute makes it an offence heedlessly to cause injury to a person by driving a motor vehicle. D drove his car in such a manner that the risk of causing injury would be obvious to any reasonable person. D says that he gave thought to the question whether there was a risk of causing injury and decided there was none. If this is true, he was not heedless; but, if he was voluntarily intoxicated and would have been aware of the risk had he been sober, he will be treated as having been aware of it. If he had been aware of it, he would have been reckless. A requirement of heedlessness is satisfied by recklessness (s 23(2)) and be may therefore he convicted of heedlessly causing injury.'

9.10 *Subsection (2). Mental elements other than recklessness and heedlessness.* When the offence requires proof of other mental elements such as purpose, intention or knowledge, evidence of voluntary intoxication is to be treated like any other evidence tending to show that the defendant lacked the mental element in question. The same mental element may be described by different terminology in pre-Code offences and perhaps in post-Code legislation. The subsection will apply to any mental element, however described, other than recklessness or heedlessness. For example, where the term "wilfully" is used to mean "intentionally", subsection (2) will apply. If, however, "wilfully" is construed to include recklessness [Cf *R v Sheppard* [1981] AC 394.], then subsection (3) will apply. If any offences requiring "malice" survive the enactment of the Code, they too will be governed by subsection (3) since "maliciously" is satisfied by proof of recklessness, as defined in section 22. [*W v Dolbey* [1983] Crim LR 681, DC; *R v Grimshaw* [1984] Crim LR 109, CA]

9.11 *Subsection (3). Recklessness and heedlessness.* This subsection applies to any offence requiring a fault element of recklessness or heedlessness even where the offence also requires, expressly or by implication, an element of purpose, intention or knowledge. A charge of rape, being reckless whether the woman consented', implies an intention to have sexual intercourse. If the defendant claims that, because he was intoxicated, he was not aware that the woman might not be consenting he is to be treated as if he were so aware and may be convicted of rape.

A defendant who was intoxicated may, however, deny that he intended to do any act at all, having no control over, or awareness of, his movements. Charged with recklessly causing serious injury by beating a woman, he says that because of his drugged condition he was unconscious.

[Cf *R v Lipman* [1970] 1 QB 152] Clause 43 (1) (b) makes it clear that he cannot rely on his condition if it arises from voluntary intoxication. Had he been sober, he would have been aware that there was a risk that acts of the kind he did might cause serious injury. He is to be treated as having beaten the woman, being aware of any risk of causing serious injury of which he would have been aware had he been sober.

(1) INTOXICATION AND MURDER

When *Hyam*, p 55, above represented the law, murder was regarded by Professor Williams (see the passage quoted by Lord Edmund-Davies above) and the CLRC as a crime of recklessness requiring special provision to exclude the intoxicated killer, lacking mens rea, from liability. Such a provision would also be required under the Code which, following the CLRC, provides for a variety of reckless murder. Under the present law, as stated in *Moloney*, p 55, above no special provision is required. Murder may not be committed by recklessness; it requires a 'specific intent'.

The Report continues:

9.15 *Subsection (6). Belief in exempting circumstances.* Just as a person may, because of intoxication, lack the mental element required for an offence, so he may have the mental element required for a defence—as when, being drunk, he mistakenly believes that P is making a murderous attack on him and retaliates, as he supposes, in self-defence. Again it is necessary to distinguish between involuntary and voluntary intoxication. Evidence of involuntary intoxication is to be treated like any other evidence tending to show that the defendant held any belief or other state of mind which is an element of a defence.

9.16 Where intoxication is voluntary, its effect depends on the fault element of the offence charged. This follows the recommendation of the Criminal Law Revision Committee: [Fourteenth Report, paras 276–278.]

'. . . in offences in which recklessness constitutes an element of the offence, if the defendant because of a mistake due to voluntary intoxication holds a belief which, if held by a sober man, would be a defence to the charge, but which the defendant would not have held had he been sober, the mistaken belief should be immaterial.'

If this is to be the rule for offences which may be committed recklessly, it must apply *a fortiori* to offences requiring a lower degree of fault. Subsection (6) (b) (i) therefore provides that, where the offence charged involves a fault element of recklessness, heedlessness, criminal negligence or carelessness, or requires no fault, the defendant is to be treated as if he knew the exempting circumstance did not exist if he would have known this had he been sober. The effect is to reverse *Jaggard v Dickinson* [[1981] QB 527]. This is justified, not only on the ground that it follows from the Committee's recommendations, but also because that decision creates an indefensible anomaly [Smith and Hogan, *Criminal Law* 5th ed (1983), 195–196.] which it would be wrong to perpetuate in the Code

(2) 'SPECIFIC' AND 'BASIC' INTENT

Director of Public Prosecutions v Majewski [1976] 2 All ER 142 House of Lords (Lord Elwyn-Jones LC, Lord Diplock, Lord Simon of Glaisdale, Lord Kilbrandon, Lord Salmon, Lord Edmund-Davies and Lord Russell of Killowen)

The appellant was convicted on three counts of assault occasioning actual bodily harm and on three counts of assault on a police constable in the execution of his duty. The evidence which was largely undisputed showed that the offences were committed in the Bull public house in Basildon and that during a fierce struggle Majewski shouted at the police: 'You pigs, I'll kill you all, you f. . . . pigs, you bastards.' He had consumed large quantities of drugs and alcohol shortly before the offences. He was a drug-addict, and admitted that he had previously 'gone paranoid' but said that this was the first time he had 'completely blanked out.' He claimed not to have known what he was doing. The medical evidence suggested that such a state, called 'pathological intoxication' was possible but unlikely: it was quite possible for an intoxicated person to know what he was doing at the time and to suffer an 'amnesic patch' later. Judge Petre directed the jury to 'ignore the subject of drink and drugs as being in any way a defence' to the assaults. An appeal to the House of Lords was unanimously dismissed.

Lord Elwyn-Jones LC. . . . If a man consciously and deliberately takes alcohol and drugs not on medical prescription, but in order to escape from reality, to go 'on a trip', to become hallucinated, whatever the description may be, and thereby disables himself from taking the care he might otherwise take and as a result by his subsequent actions causes injury to another—does our criminal law enable him to say that because he did not know what he was doing he lacked both intention and recklessness and accordingly is entitled to an acquittal?

Originally the common law would not and did not recognise self-induced intoxication as an excuse. Lawton LJ [[1975] 3 All ER 296 at 305, 306.] spoke of the 'merciful relaxation' to that rule which was introduced by the judges during the 19th century, and he added:

> 'Although there was much reforming zeal and activity in the 19th century Parliament never once considered whether self-induced intoxication should be a defence generally to a criminal charge. It would have been a strange result if the merciful relaxation of a strict rule of law had ended, without any Parliamentary intervention, by whittling it away to such an extent that the more drunk a man became, provided he stopped short of making himself insane, the better chance he had of an acquittal . . . The common law rule still applied but there were exceptions to it which Lord Birkenhead LC [*Director of Public Prosecutions v Beard*] tried to define by reference to specific intent.'

There are, however, decisions of eminent judges in a number of Commonwealth cases in Australia and New Zealand (but generally not in Canada nor in the United States), as well as impressive academic comment in this country, to which we have been referred, supporting the view that it is illogical and inconsistent with legal principle to treat a person who of his own choice and volition has taken drugs and drink, even though he thereby creates a state in which he is not conscious of what he is doing, any differently from a person suffering from the various medical conditions like epilepsy or diabetic coma and who is regarded by the law as free from fault. However, our courts have for a very long time regarded in quite another light the state of self-induced intoxication. The authority which for the last half century has been relied on in this context has been the speech of Lord Birkenhead LC in *Director of Public Prosecutions v Beard* [[1920] AC at 494, [1920] All ER Rep at 25]:

> 'Under the law of England as it prevailed until early in the nineteenth century voluntary drunkenness was never an excuse for criminal misconduct; and indeed the classic authorities broadly assert that voluntary drunkenness must be considered rather an aggravation than a defence. This view was in terms based upon the principle that a man who by his own voluntary act debauches and destroys his will power shall be no better situated in regard to criminal acts than a sober man.'

Lord Birkenhead LC made an historical survey of the way the common law from the 16th century on dealt with the effect of self-induced intoxication on criminal responsibility. This indicates how, from 1819 on, the judges began to mitigate the severity of the attitude of the common law in such cases as murder and serious violent crime when the penalties of death or transportation applied or where there was likely to be sympathy for the accused, as in attempted suicide. Lord Birkenhead LC [[1920] AC at 499, 500, [1920] All ER Rep at 27, 28] concluded that (except in cases where insanity was pleaded) the decisions he cited:

> 'establish that where a specific intent is an essential element in the offence, evidence of a state of drunkenness rendering the accused incapable of forming such an intent should be taken into consideration in order to determine whether he had in fact formed the intent necessary to constitute the particular crime. If he was so drunk that he was incapable of forming the intent required he could not be convicted of a crime which was committed only if the intent was proved. . . . In a charge of murder based upon intention to kill or to

do grievous bodily harm, if the jury are satisfied that the accused was, by reason of his drunken condition, incapable of forming the intent to kill or to do grievous bodily harm . . . he cannot be convicted of murder. But nevertheless unlawful homicide has been committed by the accused, and consequently he is guilty of unlawful homicide without malice aforethought, and that is manslaughter: per Stephen J in *Doherty's* case [(1887) 16 Cox CC 306 at 307]. [He concluded the passage:] the law is plain beyond all question that in cases falling short of insanity a condition of drunkenness at the time of committing an offence causing death can only, when it is available at all, have the effect of reducing the crime from murder to manslaughter.'

From this it seemed clear—and this is the interpretation which the judges have placed on the decision during the ensuing half-century—that it is only in the limited class of cases requiring proof of specific intent that drunkenness can exculpate. Otherwise in no case can it exempt completely from criminal liability.

Unhappily what Lord Birkenhead LC [[1920] AC at 500, [1920] All ER Rep at 28] described as 'plain beyond question' becomes less plain in the later passage in his speech [[1920] AC at 504, [1920] All ER Rep at 30] on which counsel for the appellant not unnaturally placed great emphasis. It reads:

'I do not think that the proposition of law deduced from these earlier cases is an exceptional rule applicable only to cases in which it is necessary to prove a specific intent in order to constitute the graver crime—e g, wounding with intent to do grievous bodily harm or with intent to kill. It is true that in such cases the specific intent must be proved to constitute the particular crime, but this is, on ultimate analysis, only in accordance with the ordinary law applicable to crime, for, speaking generally (and apart from certain special offences), a person cannot be convicted of a crime unless the mens was rea. Drunkenness, rendering a person incapable of the intent, would be an answer, as it is for example in a charge of attempted suicide.'

Why then would it not be an answer in a charge of manslaughter, contrary to the earlier pronouncement [[1920] AC at 499, [1920] All ER Rep at 27]? In my view these passages are not easy to reconcile, but I do not dissent from the reconciliation suggested by my noble and learned friend Lord Russell of Killowen. Commenting on the passage in 1920 shortly after it was delivered, however, Stroud [(1920) 36 LQR at 270] wrote:

'The whole of these observations . . . suggest an extension of the defence of drunkenness far beyond the limits which have hitherto been assigned to it. The suggestion, put shortly, is that drunkenness may be available as a defence, upon any criminal charge, whenever it can be shown to have affected mens rea. Not only is there no authority for the suggestion; there is abundant authority, both ancient and modern, to the contrary.'

It has to be said that it is on the latter footing that the judges have applied the law before and since *Beard's* case [[1920] AC 479, [1920] All ER Rep 21] and have taken the view that self-induced intoxication, however gross and even if it has produced a condition akin to automatism, cannot excuse crimes of basic intent such as the charges of assault which have given rise to the present appeal.

[His Lordship discussed *A-G for Northern Ireland v Gallagher* (p 93, below) and *Bratty v A-G for Northern Ireland* (p 196, below)]

The seal of approval is clearly set on the passage of the *Beard* decision. In no case has the general principle of English law as described by Lord Denning in *Gallagher's* case and exposed again in *Bratty's* case [[1963] AC 386, [1961] 3 All ER 523] been overruled in this House and the question now to be determined is whether it should be.

I do not for my part regard that general principle as either unethical or contrary to the principles of natural justice. If a man of his own volition takes a substance which causes him to cast off the restraints of reason and conscience, no wrong is done to him by holding him answerable criminally for any injury he may do while in that condition. His course of conduct in reducing himself by drugs and drink to that condition in my view supplies the evidence of mens rea, of guilty mind certainly sufficient for crimes of basic intent. It is a reckless course of conduct and recklessness is enough to constitute the necessary mens rea in assault cases: see *Venna* [[1975] 3 All ER 788 at 793] per James LJ. The drunkenness is itself an intrinsic, an integral part of the crime, the other part being the evidence of the unlawful use of force against the victim. Together they add up to criminal recklessness. On this I adopt the conclusion of Stroud [[1920] 36 LQR at 273] that:

'It would be contrary to all principle and authority to suppose that drunkenness [and what is true of drunkenness is equally true of intoxication by drugs] can be a defence for crime in general on the ground that "a person cannot be convicted of a crime unless the *mens* was *rea*". By allowing himself to get drunk and thereby putting himself in such a condition as to be no longer amenable to the law's commands, a man shows such regard-lessness as amounts to mens rea for the purpose of all ordinary crimes.'

This approach is in line with the American Model Code [section 2.08(2)]:

> 'When recklessness establishes an element of the offence, if the actor, due to self-induced intoxication, is unaware of a risk of which he would have been aware had he been sober, such unawareness is immaterial.'

Acceptance generally of intoxication as a defence (as distinct from the exceptional cases where some additional mental element above that of ordinary mens rea has to be proved) would in my view undermine the criminal law and I do not think that it is enough to say, as did counsel for the appellant, that we can rely on the good sense of the jury or of magistrates to ensure that the guilty are convicted. It may well be that Parliament will at some future time consider, as I think it should, the recommendation in the Butler Committee Report on Mentally Abnormal Offenders [(1975) Cmnd 6244] that a new offence of 'dangerous intoxication' should be created. But in the meantime it would be irresponsible to abandon the common law rule, as 'mercifully relaxed', which the courts have followed for a century and a half . . .

The final question that arises is whether s 8 of the Criminal Justice Act 1967 has had the result of abrogating or qualifying the common law rule. That section emanated from the consideration the Law Commission gave to the decision of the House in *Director of Public Prosecutions v Smith* [[1961] AC 290, [1960] 3 All ER 161]. Its purpose and effect was to alter the law of evidence about the presumption of intention to produce the reasonable and probable consequences of one's acts. It was not intended to change the common law rule. In referring to 'all the evidence' it meant all the *relevant* evidence. But if there is a substantive rule of law that in crimes of basic intent, the factor of intoxication is irrelevant (and such I hold to be the substantive law), evidence with regard to it is quite irrelevant. Section 8 does not abrogate the substantive rule and it cannot properly be said that the continued application of that rule contravenes the section. For these reasons, my conclusion is that the certified question should be answered Yes, that there was no misdirection in this case and that the appeal should be dismissed.

My noble and learned friends and I think it may be helpful if we give the following indication of the general lines on which in our view the jury should be directed as to the effect on the criminal responsibility of the accused of drink or drugs or both, whenever death or physical injury to another person results from something done by the accused for which there is no legal justification and the offence with which the accused is charged is manslaughter or assault at common law or the statutory offence of unlawful wounding under s 20, or of assault occasioning actual bodily harm under s 47 of the Offences against the Person Act 1861.

In the case of these offences it is no excuse in law that, because of drink or drugs which the accused himself had taken knowingly and willingly, he had deprived himself of the ability to exercise self-control, to realise the possible consequences of what he was doing or even to be conscious that he was doing it. As in the instant case, the jury may be properly instructed that they 'can ignore the subject of drink or drugs as being in any way a defence to' charges of this character.

Lord Diplock said that he agreed with the speech of Lord Elwyn-Jones LC and with the analysis by Lord Russell (p 92, below) of the speech of Lord Birkenhead in *Director of Public Prosecutions v Beard*.

Lord Simon. . . . I still have the temerity to think that the concept of 'crime of basic intent' is a useful tool of analysis; and I explained what I meant by it in the passage in *Morgan* [[1975] 2 All ER at 363, 364] generously cited by my noble and learned friend, Lord Elwyn-Jones LC. It stands significantly in contrast with 'crime of specific intent' as that term was used by Stephen's Digest and by Lord Birkenhead LC in *Beard* [[1920] AC 479, [1920] All ER Rep 21]. The best description of 'specific intent' in this sense that I know is contained in the judgment of Fauteux J in *George* [(1960) 128 CCC 289 at 301]:

> 'In considering the question of mens rea, a distinction is to be made between (i) intention as applied to acts considered in relation to their purposes and (ii) intention as applied to acts apart from their purposes. A general intent attending the commission of an act is, in some cases, the only intent required to constitute the crime while, in others, there must be, in addition to that general intent, a specific intent attending the purpose for the commission of the act.'

In short, where the crime is one of 'specific intent' the prosecution must in general prove that the purpose for the commission of the act extends to the intent expressed or implied in the definition of the crime . . .

As I have ventured to suggest, there is nothing unreasonable or illogical in the law holding that a mind rendered self-inducedly insensible (short of *M'Naghten* [*M'Naghten's case* (1843) 10 Cl & Fin 200, [1843-60] All ER Rep 229 [p 188, below]] insanity), through drink or drugs, to the nature of a prohibited act or to its probable consequences is as wrongful a mind as one which consciously contemplates the prohibited act and foresees its probable consequences (or is reckless whether they ensue). The latter is all that is required by way of mens rea in a crime of basic intent. But a crime of specific intent requires something more than contemplation of the prohibited act and foresight of its probable consequences. The mens rea in a crime of specific intent requires proof of a purposive element. This purposive element either exists or not; it cannot be supplied by saying that the impairment of mental powers by self-induced intoxication is its equivalent, for it is not. So that the 19th century development of the law as to the effect of self-induced intoxication on criminal responsibility is juristically entirely acceptable; and it need be a matter of no surprise that Stephen stated it without demur or question.

Lord Kilbrandon said that he agreed with the speech of Lord Elwyn-Jones.

Lord Salmon. . . . an assault committed accidentally is not a criminal offence. A man may, e g, thoughtlessly throw out his hand to stop a taxi, or open the door of his car and accidentally hit a passer-by and perhaps unhappily cause him quite serious bodily harm. In such circumstances, the man who caused the injury would be liable civilly for damages but clearly he would have committed no crime. It is, I agree, possible to commit assault and other crimes of violence recklessly, not caring whether or not what you do causes injury. There are no doubt some contexts, e g, commercial contracts in which the words 'very carelessly' and 'recklessly' are synonymous, but I do not think that this is usually true in the context of the criminal law, except perhaps in the case of manslaughter. I do not, however, wish to take up your Lordships' time in discussing this topic further for it is hardly relevant to the question before this House.

There are many cases in which injuries are caused by pure accident. I have already given examples of such cases: to these could be added injuries inflicted during an epileptic fit, or whilst sleep-walking, and in many other ways. No one, I think, would suggest that any such case could give rise to criminal liability.

It is argued on behalf of the appellant that a man who makes a vicious assault may at the material time have been so intoxicated by drink or drugs that he no more knew what he was doing than did any of the persons in the examples I have given and that therefore he too cannot be found guilty of a criminal offence.

To my mind there is a very real distinction between such a case and the examples I have given. A man who by voluntarily taking drink and drugs gets himself into an aggressive state in which he does not know what he is doing and then makes a vicious assault can hardly say with any plausibility that what he did was a pure accident which should render him immune from any criminal liability. Yet this in effect is precisely what counsel for the appellant contends that the learned judge should have told the jury.

A number of distinguished academic writers support this contention on the ground of logic. As I understand it, the argument runs like this. Intention, whether special or basic (or whatever fancy name you choose to give it), is still intention. If voluntary intoxication by drink or drugs can, as it admittedly can, negative the special or specific intention necessary for the commission of crimes such as murder and theft, how can you justify in strict logic the view that it cannot negative a basic intention, e g, the intention to commit offences such as assault and unlawful wounding? The answer is that in strict logic this view cannot be justified. But this is the view that has been adopted by the common law of England, which is founded on common sense and experience rather than strict logic. There is no case in the 19th century when the courts were relaxing the harshness of the law in relation to the effect of drunkenness on criminal liability in which the courts ever went so far as to suggest that drunkenness, short of drunkenness producing insanity, could ever exculpate a man from any offence other than one which required some special or specific intent to be proved . . .

[His Lordship cited the passage from the speech of Lord Birkenhead in *Beard* which was also quoted by Lord Elwyn-Jones LC, pp 88–89, above] and continued: But then he illustrates his proposition by referring to the crime of attempted suicide which, in my view, does require a specific intent. A man may cut his throat but he could not be convicted of attempted suicide unless it were proved that he did so with the specific intention of killing himself. I am inclined to think that Lord Birkenhead LC was meaning to point out that drunkenness was relevant to all cases in which it was necessary to prove a specific intent and was not confined to those cases in which, if the prosecution failed to prove such an intent, the accused could still be convicted of a lesser offence. I confess that I find the passage somewhat obscure but I prefer the construction which makes it consistent with rather than contradictory of the first part of the speech. There can be no doubt that that is how it was understood by the judges, who continued to direct juries in the same way as they always had done and as the learned judge did in the present case. Many distinguished academic writers however, from Stroud (with disapproval) to Professor Glanville Williams (with approval), put the same construction on this passage of Lord Birkenhead LC's speech as that for which counsel for the appellant contends.

If, however, Lord Birkenhead LC and the distinguished Law Lords sitting with him had intended to make the suggested drastic change in the law, I feel confident that they would have made it crystal clear that they were doing so. This would have been to ensure that the judges would not make the mistake of continuing to sum up this topic along the lines they had summed up for about a century before *Beard's* case [[1920] AC 479, [1920] All ER Rep 21] and have continued so to sum up ever since . . .

Lord Edmund-Davies made a speech dismissing the appeal.

[**Lord Russell of Killowen**, having cited the passage from *Beard* quoted by Lords Elwyn-Jones and Salmon:]

. . . In my opinion this passage is not to be taken as stating in effect the opposite of the whole previous tenor of the speech in the course of denying the applicability of the statement in *Meade* [[1909] 1 KB 895]. The clue to the cited passage appears to me to be in the words 'in order to constitute the graver crime'. In my opinion the passage cited does no more than to say that special intent cases are not restricted to those crimes in which the absence of a special intent leaves available a lesser crime embodying no special intent, but embrace all cases of special intent even though no alternative lesser criminal charge is available. And the example given of attempted suicide is just such a case.

The second aspect of *Beard* [[1920] AC 479, [1920] All ER Rep 21] to which I have referred relates to two passages. The first [[1920] AC at 504, 505, [1920] All ER Rep at 30] is:

> 'My Lords, drunkenness in this case could be no defence unless it could be established that Beard at the time of committing the rape was so drunk that he was incapable of forming the intent to commit it, which was not in fact, and manifestly, having regard to the evidence, could not be contended. For in the present case the death resulted from two acts or from a succession of acts, the rape and the act of violence causing suffocation. These acts cannot be regarded separately and independently of each other. The capacity of the mind of the prisoner to form the felonious intent which murder involves is in other words to be explored in relation to the ravishment; and not in relation merely to the violent act which gave effect to the ravishment.'

The second [[1920] AC at 507, [1920] All ER Rep at 31] is: 'There was certainly no evidence that he was too drunk to form the intent of committing rape.'

In my opinion these passages do not indicate an opinion that rape is a crime of special intent. All that is meant is that conscious rape is required to supply 'the felonious intent which murder involves'. For the crime of murder special or particular intent is always required for the necessary malice aforethought. This may be intent to kill or intent to cause grievous bodily harm: or in a case such as *Beard* of constructive malice, this required the special intent *consciously to commit* the violent felony of rape in the course and furtherance of which the act of violence causing death took place. *Beard* therefore, in my opinion does not suggest that rape is a crime of special or particular intent.

I too would dismiss this appeal.

Appeal dismissed

Questions

1. Is the decision confined to the case where 'a man consciously and deliberately takes alcohol and drugs . . . in order to escape from reality, to go "on a trip", to become hallucinated . . .'? Or does it apply to cases of ordinary social drinking?

2. If 'specific intent' requires proof of a 'purposive element' is (a) murder, (b) rape or (c) taking a conveyance without the consent of the owner (see *MacPherson* [1973] RTR 157) a crime of specific intent?

3. Was it justifiable to uphold the conviction on the ground that the appellant was reckless? Was there any finding that he was reckless in the sense in which that term is used in *Venna* (p. 355, below) at the time he took the drink?

4. If 'the drunkenness is itself an intrinsic, an integral part of the crime', can the prosecution make out their case by adducing evidence that the defendant was drunk?

5. Are you convinced by Lord Russell's explanation of the controversial passage in Lord Birkenhead's speech in *Beard*?

(3) CALDWELL AND INTOXICATION

In *Caldwell* [1981] 1 All ER 961 at 968, p 68, above, Lord Diplock said:

> '. . . classification into offences of specific and basic intent is irrelevant where being reckless whether a particular harmful consequence will result from one's act is a sufficient alternative mens rea.'

This is right where, as in *Caldwell*, there is an obvious risk and the defendant has not give any thought to the possibility of it. However intoxicated he is, he has the fault required for the crime and is liable. But, if he gave thought to the question whether there was a risk and decided there was none, he was not 'reckless' under either limb of the definition in that case. If he was sober, he must be acquitted. What if he was drunk and came to the conclusion that there was no risk because he was drunk? Is he likely to be acquitted of an offence of recklessness? He can be convicted only by invoking the classification and holding that the offence is one 'of basic intent'.

D, who is drunk, points an airgun at a window. E says, 'Careful! You might break that window.' 'Not a chance,' says D. 'I have checked the gun and it is not loaded.' He pulls the trigger and breaks the window. Because he was drunk he failed to notice the pellet. Is he guilty of causing criminal damage?

2. Drinking 'with intent'

Attorney-General for Northern Ireland v Gallagher [1961] 3 All ER 299, House of Lords
(Lord Reid, Lord Goddard, Lord Tucker, Lord Denning and Lord Morris of Borth-y-Gest)

The facts appear sufficiently in the speech of Lord Denning. The Court of Criminal Appeal in Northern Ireland quashed the conviction for murder because the Lord Chief Justice, in their view, had directed the jury to apply the M'Naghten test [p 188, below] not to the time when the accused killed his wife but to the morning of that day, before he opened the bottle of whisky.

[**Lord Tucker**, with whom **Lords Goddard** and **Reid** agreed, held that the jury had not been misdirected.]

Lord Denning. My Lords, every direction which a judge gives to a jury in point of law must be considered against the background of facts which have been proved or admitted in the case. In this case the respondent did not give evidence himself. And the facts proved against him were: He had a grievance against his wife. She had obtained a maintenance order against him and had been instrumental in getting him detained in a mental hospital. He had made up his mind to kill his wife. He bought a knife for the purpose and a bottle of whisky—either to give himself Dutch courage to do the deed or to drown his conscience after it. He did in fact carry out his intention. He killed his wife with the knife and drank much of the whisky before or after he killed her. There were only two defences raised on his behalf: (i) Insanity; (ii) Drunkenness. . . .

My Lords, this case differs from all others in the books in that the respondent, whilst sane and sober, before he took to the drink, had already made up his mind to kill his wife. This seems to me to be far worse—and far more deserving of condemnation—than the case of a man who, before getting drunk, has no intention to kill, but afterwards in his cups, whilst drunk, kills another by an act which he would not dream of doing when sober. Yet, by the law of England, in this latter case his drunkenness is no defence even though it has distorted his reason and his will-power. So why should it be a defence in the present case? And is it made any better by saying that the man is a psychopath? The answer to the question is, I think, that the case falls to be decided by the general principle of English law that, subject to very limited exceptions, drunkenness is no defence to a criminal charge nor is a defect of reason produced by drunkenness. This principle was stated by Sir Matthew Hale in his *Pleas of the Crown*, Vol 1, p 32, in words which I would repeat here:

'This vice [drunkenness] doth deprive men of the use of reason, and puts many men into a perfect, but temporary phrenzy . . . by the laws of England such a person shall have no privilege by this voluntary contracted madness, but shall have the same judgment as if he were in his right senses.'

This general principle can be illustrated by looking at the various ways in which drunkenness may produce a defect of reason: (a) It may impair a man's powers of perception so that he may not be able to foresee or measure the consequences of his actions as he would if he were sober. Nevertheless, he is not allowed to set up his self-induced want of perception as a defence. Even if he did not himself appreciate that what he was doing was dangerous, nevertheless, if a reasonable man in his place, who was not befuddled with drink, would have appreciated it, he is guilty; see *Meade* [[1909] 1 KB 895], as explained in *Director of Public Prosecutions v Beard* [see p 88, above]. (b) It may impair a man's power to judge between right or wrong, so that he may do a thing when drunk which he would not dream of doing while sober. He does not realise he is doing wrong. Nevertheless, he is not allowed to set up his self-induced want of moral sense as a defence. In *Beard's* case Lord Birkenhead LC distinctly ruled that it was not a defence for a drunken man to say he did not know he was doing wrong. (c) It may impair a man's power of self-control so that he may more readily give way to provocation than if he were sober. Nevertheless, he is not allowed to set up his self-induced want of control as a defence. The acts of provocation are to be assessed, not according to their effect on him personally, but according to the effect they would have on a reasonable man in his place. The law on this point was previously in doubt (see the cases considered in *Beard's* case), but it has since been resolved by *McCarthy* [[1954] 2 All ER 262], *Bedder v Director of Public Prosecutions* [see p 322, below] and s 3 of the Homicide Act, 1957.

The general principle which I have enunciated is subject to two exceptions: (i) If a man is charged with an offence in which a specific intention is essential (as in murder, though not in manslaughter), then evidence of drunkenness, which renders him incapable of forming that intent, is an answer; see *Beard's* case. This degree of drunkenness is reached when the man is rendered so stupid by drink that he does not know what he is doing (see *Moore* [(1852) 3 Car & Kir 319]) as where, at a christening, a drunken nurse put the baby behind a large fire, taking it for a log of wood (18 Gentleman's Magazine, 1748, p 570); and where a drunken man thought his friend (lying in his bed) was a theatrical dummy placed there and stabbed him to death ((1951) Times, 13 January). In each of those cases it would not be murder. But it would be manslaughter. (ii) If a man by drinking brings on a distinct disease of the mind such as delirium tremens, so that he is temporarily insane within the M'Naghten rules, that is to say, he does not at the time know what he is doing or that it is wrong, then he has a defence on the ground of insanity; see *Davis* [(1881) 14 Cox CC 563], and *Beard's* case.

Does the present case come within the general principle or the exceptions to it? It certainly does not come within the first exception. The respondent was not incapable of forming an intent to kill. Quite the contrary. He knew full well what he was doing. He formed an intent to kill, he carried out his intention and he remembered afterwards what he had done. And the jury, properly directed on the point, have found as much, for they found him guilty of murder. Then does the case come within the second exception? It does not to my mind; for the simple reason that he was not suffering from a disease of the mind brought on by drink. He was suffering from a different disease altogether. As the Lord Chief Justice observed in his summing-up: 'If this man was suffering from a disease of the mind, it wasn't of a kind that is produced by drink'. So we have here a case of the first impression. That man is a psychopath. That is, he has a disease of the mind which is not produced by drink. But it is quiescent. And, whilst it is quiescent, he forms an intention to kill his wife. He knows it is wrong, but still he means to kill her. Then he gets himself so drunk that he has an explosive outburst and kills his wife. At that moment he knows what he is doing but he does not know it is wrong. So in that respect—in not knowing it is wrong—he has a defect of reason at the moment of killing. If that defect of reason is due to the drink, it is no defence in law. But, if it is due to the disease of the mind, it gives rise to a defence of insanity. No one can say, however, whether it is due to the drink or to the disease. It may well be due to both in combination. What guidance does the law give in this difficulty? That is, as I see it, the question of general public importance which is involved in this case.

My Lords, I think the law on this point should take a clear stand. If a man, whilst sane and sober, forms an intention to kill and makes preparation for it, knowing it is a wrong thing to do, and then gets himself drunk so as to give himself Dutch courage to do the killing, and whilst drunk carries out his intention, he cannot rely on this self-induced drunkenness as a defence to a charge of murder, nor even as reducing it to manslaughter. He cannot say that he got himself into such a stupid state that he was incapable of an intent to kill. So, also, when he is a psychopath, he cannot by drinking rely on his self-induced defect of reason as a defence of insanity. The wickedness of his mind before he got drunk is enough to condemn him, coupled with the act which he intended to do and did do. A psychopath who goes out intending to kill, knowing it is wrong, and does kill, cannot escape the consequences by making himself drunk before doing it. That is, I believe, the direction which the Lord Chief Justice gave to the jury and which the Court of Criminal Appeal found to be wrong. I think that it was right, and for this reason I would allow the appeal. I would agree, of course, that if, before the killing, he had discarded his intention to kill or reversed it—and then got drunk—it would be a different matter. But when he forms the intention to kill and without interruption proceeds to get drunk and carry out his intention, then his drunkenness is no defence, and none the less so because it is dressed up as a defence of insanity. There was no evidence in this case of any interruption, and there was no need for the Lord Chief Justice to mention it to the jury.

I need hardly say, of course, that I have here only considered the law of Northern Ireland. In England, a psychopath such as this man might now be in a position to raise a defence of diminished responsibility under s 2 of the Homicide Act 1957. . . .

I would allow this appeal and restore the conviction of murder.

Appeal allowed

NOTE

1. Archbold (41st edn) para 17–52, commenting on *Gallagher's* case:

'If A with the intention of killing B enrages a gorilla with the result that the gorilla in fact kills B, A is clearly guilty of murder and, under the old law, as a principal in the first degree. What difference does it make if for the gorilla he substitutes himself?'

3. Intoxication causing automatism

R v Lipman [1969] 3 All ER 410, Court of Appeal, Criminal Division
(Widgery and Fenton Atkinson LJJ and James J)

The facts appear in the judgment. Milmo J directed the jury:

'He would be guilty of manslaughter if the jury were to find either—(1) that he must have realised before he got himself into the condition he did by taking the drugs, that acts such as those he subsequently performed and which resulted in the death, were dangerous; or (2) that the taking of the drugs which the defendant took that night was dangerous and that the [defendant] must have realised that by taking them he was incurring a risk of some harm, not necessarily serious harm, to some other person or persons; or (3) that in taking these drugs in the circumstances in which he took them, the [defendant] was grossly negligent and reckless and this involves the jury considering whether or not he thought that what he was doing was safe so far as other people were concerned'. [See [1970] 1 QB 152.]

The jury found the defendant not guilty of murder but guilty of manslaughter by reason of grounds (1) and (3) above. The defendant appealed.

[**Widgery LJ** delivered the judgment of the court:]

Both the applicant and the victim were addicted to drugs and on the evening of 16 September 1967 both took a quantity of a drug known as LSD. Early on the morning of 18 September the applicant (who is a United States citizen) hurriedly booked out of his hotel and left the country. On the following day (19 September) Delbarre's landlord found her dead in her room. She had suffered two blows on the head causing haemorrhage of the brain, but she died of asphyxia as a result of some eight inches of sheet having been crammed into her mouth.

The applicant was returned to this country by extradition proceedings, and at the trial he gave evidence of having gone with Delbarre to her room and there experienced what he described as an LSD 'trip'. He explained how he had the illusion of descending to the centre of the earth and being attacked by snakes, with which he had fought. It was not seriously disputed that he had killed the victim in the course of this experience, but he said he had no knowledge of what he was doing and no intention to harm her. He was charged with murder, but the jury evidently accepted that he lacked the necessary intention to kill or to do grievous bodily harm, As to manslaughter, the jury was directed that it would suffice for the Crown to prove that:

> '. . . he must have realised, before he got himself into the condition he did by taking the drug, that acts such as those he subsequently performed and which resulted in the death were dangerous'.

In this court counsel for the applicant contends that this was a misdirection, and that the jury should have been directed further that it was necessary for the Crown to prove that the applicant had intended to do acts likely to result in harm, or foresaw that harm would result from what he was doing.

For the purposes of criminal responsibility we see no reason to distinguish between the effect of drugs voluntarily taken and drunkenness voluntarily induced. As to the latter there is a great deal of authority. [His Lordship quoted from the speeches of Lord Birkenhead in *Beard's* case and Lord Denning, in *Bratty's* case [see p 196, below] and *Gallagher's* case [see p 93, above]]

These authorities show quite clearly, in our opinion, that it was well established that no specific intent was necessary to support a conviction for manslaughter based on killing in the course of an unlawful act and that, accordingly, self-induced drunkenness was no defence to such a charge.

In a case of manslaughter by neglect, however, it has been recognised that some mental element must be established, and for this I turn to *Andrews v Director of Public Prosecutions* [see p 341, below]. In that case Lord Atkin dealt in some detail with the mental element involved in manslaughter by neglect. [His Lordship cited a passage from Lord Atkin's speech, p 342, below.]

It is to be observed that in that case there are two references to mens rea; and the next case in which a similar reference is made is *Church* [see p 333, below]. This seems to be the first case in which a reference to mens rea occurs when the killing was the result of an allegedly unlawful act, and the crucial passage appears in the judgment of Edmund Davies J. Before I turn to that passage, I should say that in *Church* the appellant, who threw the unconscious body of the victim into a river where she drowned, pleaded that he thought she was already dead. The jury were directed that if they thought that that was the state of the prisoner's mind the proper verdict was manslaughter, and this direction was criticised by the Court of Criminal Appeal on the ground that on the facts of that case it was equivalent to saying the commission of any unlawful act from which death resulted would be manslaughter. [His Lordship cited a passage from the judgment of Edmund Davies J, p 334, below]

This passage forms the basis of the applicant's submission before us, namely, that by 1965 (the date of *Church*) it had become recognised that guilt of manslaughter derived from the accused's having intended or foreseen that some harm should befall the victim as a result of his action. It is accepted in this argument that at that time the so-called objective test was applied to the state of the accused's mind, so that the issue was concluded against him if ordinary sober and reasonable people would recognise that harm was likely to be caused. But it is nevertheless maintained that the theoretical basis of guilt was the accused's supposed intent or foresight.

The final step in the argument is that s 8 of the Criminal Justice Act 1967 has replaced the objective test by a subjective one, so that the jury are now required to consider the actual state of the accused's own mind at the relevant time. [His Lordship quoted s 8, p 562, below].

If the applicant's argument be sound, it follows that we have come a long way since *Director of Public Prosecutions v Beard* [see p 88, above] and that events have moved very fast. In our judgment, there is a flaw in the applicant's argument; and the flaw lies in the assumption that *Church* introduced a new element of intent or foreseeability into this type of manslaughter. All that the judgment in *Church* says in terms is that whereas, formerly, a killing by any unlawful act amounted to manslaughter, this consequence does not now inexorably follow unless the unlawful act is one in which ordinary sober and responsible people would recognise the existence of risk. The development recognised by *Church* relates to the type of act from which a charge of manslaughter may result, not in the intention (real or assumed) of the prisoner. It is perhaps unfortunate that a reference to mens rea, which had been found unhelpful by Lord Atkin, was repeated in *Church*, and to give it the effect now contended for would be contrary to *Director of Public Prosecutions v Beard* and the other authorities which we have cited. The decision in *Church* was referred to in this court later in *Lamb* [see p 334, below] where the accused had pointed a revolver at the victim in the belief, as he said, that there was no round in the chamber, but the revolver had fired and the victim was killed. It was pointed out in this court that no unlawful act on the part of the prisoner had been proved in the absence of the necessary intent to constitute an assault. But this is intention of a different kind. Even if intent has to be proved to constitute the unlawful act, no specific further intent is required to turn that act into manslaughter. Manslaughter remains a most difficult offence to define because it arises in so many different ways and, as the mental element (if any) required to establish it varies so widely, any general reference to mens rea is apt to mislead.

We can dispose of the present application by reiterating that when the killing results from an unlawful act of the accused no specific intent has to be proved to convict of manslaughter, and self-induced intoxication is accordingly no defence. Since in the present case the acts complained of were obviously likely to cause harm to the victim (and did, in fact, kill her) no acquittal was possible and the verdict of manslaughter, at the least, was inevitable.

Appeal dismissed

Questions

1. Why is it relevant whether a man knows it is dangerous to cram eight inches of bedsheet into a woman's mouth if he has no idea that he is going to do such an act?

2. The cases appear to distinguish between (i) manslaughter by an unlawful act and (ii) manslaughter by 'gross negligence' or 'recklessness' p 332, below. Which of these doctrines was invoked by (a) Milmo J, in his direction and (b) the Court of Appeal in upholding the conviction?

3. According to (i) Milmo J's summing up and (ii) the Court of Appeal, was the act for which Lipman was responsible (a) the taking of the drugs or (b) the acts done to Delbarre? If they differ, which is right?

4. The court concedes, 'even if intent has to be proved to constitute the unlawful act . . .' Was any intent proved with respect to the unlawful acts done to Delbarre?

4. Reckless intoxication

R v Hardie [1984] 3 All ER 848, Court of Appeal, Criminal Division
(Parker LJ, Stuart-Smith and McCowan JJ)

The defendant's relationship with the woman with whom he was living broke down and she left him. He became upset and took several tablets of valium, a sedative drug, belonging to the woman. Later he started a fire in the bedroom of the flat while the woman and her daughter were in the sitting room. Charged with an offence under s 1(2) of the Criminal Damage Act 1971, he argued that the effect of the drug was to prevent him having the mens rea. The judge directed the jury that this could be no defence because the drug was self-administered. He appealed on grounds of misdirection.

Parker LJ. . . . In *R v Bailey* [1983] 2 All ER 503, [1983] 1 WLR 760 this court had to consider a case where a diabetic had failed to take sufficient food after taking a normal dose of insulin and struck the victim over the head with an iron bar. The judge directed the jury that the defence of automatism, i e that the mind did not go with the act, was not available because the incapacity was self-induced. It was held that this was wrong on two grounds: (a) because on the basis of *DPP v Majewski* it was clearly available to the offence embodying specific intent and (b) because although self-induced by the omission to take food it was also available to negative the other offence which was of basic intent only.

Having referred to *DPP v Majewski* and *R v Lipman* Griffiths LJ, giving the considered judgment of the court, said ([1983] 2 All ER 503 at 507, [1983] 1 WLR 760 at 764–765):

> 'It was submitted on behalf of the Crown that a similar rule should be applied as a matter of public policy to all cases of self-induced automatism. But it seems to us that there may be material distinctions between a man who consumes alcohol or takes dangerous drugs and one who fails to take sufficient food after insulin to avert hypoglycaemia. It is common knowledge that those who take alcohol to excess or certain sorts of drugs may become aggressive or do dangerous or unpredictable things; they may be able to foresee the risks of causing harm to others, but nevertheless persist in their conduct. But the same cannot be said, without more, of a man who fails to take food after an insulin injection. If he does appreciate the risk that such a failure may lead to aggressive, unpredictable and uncontrollable conduct and he nevertheless deliberately runs the risk or otherwise disregards it, this will amount to recklessness. But we certainly do not think that it is common knowledge, even among diabetics, that such is a consequence of a failure to take food; and there is no evidence that it was known to this appellant. Doubtless he knew that if he failed to take his insulin or proper food after it he might lose consciousness, but as such he would only be a danger to himself unless he put himself in charge of some machine such as a motor car, which required his continuous conscious control. In our judgment, self-induced automatism, other than that due to intoxication from alcohol or drugs, may provide a defence to crimes of basic intent. The question in each case will be whether the prosecution has proved the necessary element of recklessness. In cases of assault, if the accused knows that his actions or inaction are likely to make him aggressive, unpredictable or uncontrolled with the result that he may cause some injury to others and he persists in the action or takes no remedial action when he knows it is required, it will be open to the jury to find that he was reckless.'

In the present instance the defence was that the valium was taken for the purpose of calming the nerves only, that it was old stock and that the appellant was told it would do him no harm. There was no evidence that it was known to the appellant or even generally known that the taking of valium in the quantity taken would be liable to render a person aggressive or incapable of appreciating risks to others or have other side effects such that its self-administration would itself have an element of recklessness. It is true that valium is a drug and it is true that it was taken deliberately and not taken on medical prescription, but the drug is, in our view, wholly different in kind from drugs which are liable to cause unpredictability or aggressiveness. It may well be that the taking of a sedative or soporific drug will, in certain circumstances, be no answer, for example in a case of reckless driving, but if the effect of a drug is merely soporific or sedative the taking of it, even in some excessive quantity, cannot in the ordinary way raise a *conclusive* presumption against the admission of proof of intoxication for the purpose of disproving mens rea in ordinary crimes, such as would be the case with alcoholic intoxication or incapacity or automatism resulting from the self-administration of dangerous drugs.

In the present case the jury should not, in our judgment, have been directed to disregard any incapacity which resulted or might have resulted from the taking of valium. They should have been directed that if they came to the conclusion that, as a result of the valium, the appellant was, at the time, unable to appreciate the risks to property and persons from his actions they should then consider whether the taking of the valium was itself reckless. We are unable to say what would have been the appropriate direction with regard to the elements of recklessness in this case for we have not seen all the relevant evidence, nor are we able to suggest a model direction, for circumstances will vary infinitely and model directions can sometimes lead to more rather than less confusion. It is sufficient to say that the direction that the effects of valium were necessarily irrelevant was wrong.

Appeal allowed

Questions

1. Are drugs to be divided into two categories—alcohol and 'dangerous' drugs which attract the operation of *Majewski* and other drugs which do not?
2. Is it permissible for the court to apply a 'conclusive presumption' of recklessness in the light of s 8 of the Criminal Justice Act 1967?
3. Cf *Elliott v C (A Minor)*, p 73, above. If it is not an answer to a charge under s 1(2) of the Criminal Damage Act 1971 to say, 'I was not aware of the risk and would not have been aware of it even if I had given thought to the matter because I am a backward fourteen-year-old and at the time I as cold, tired and hungry,' why should it be an answer to say 'I was not aware of the risk because I had been taking valium'?

5. Intoxication and defences

Jaggard v Dickinson [1980] 3 All ER 716, Queen's Bench Division
Donaldson LJ and Mustill J.

The defendant lived in a house belonging to one, Heyfron. Making her way home drunk, she went by mistake to the wrong house, found it locked and did damage by breaking in. She was charged with an offence under s 1(1) of the Criminal Damage Act 1971. She relied on s 5(2) of the Act, p 575, below, saying that she believed that Heyfron would have consented to her doing the damage in the circumstances. The magistrates held that this drunken belief could not be a defence.

Mustill J. . . . It is convenient to refer to the exculpatory provisions of s 5(2) as if they created a defence whilst recognising that the burden of disproving the facts referred to by the subsection remains on the prosecution. The magistrates held that the appellant was not entitled to rely on s 5(2) since the belief relied on was brought about by a state of self-induced intoxication.

In support of the conviction counsel for the respondent advanced an argument which may be summarised as follows. (i) Where an offence is one of 'basic intent', in contrast to one of 'specific intent,' the fact that the accused was in a state of self-induced intoxication at the time when he did the acts constituting the actus reus does not prevent him from possessing the mens rea necessary to constitute the offence: see *Director of Public Prosecutions v Morgan* [p 45, above] *Director of Public Prosecutions v Majewski* [p 87, above] (ii) Section 1(1) of the 1971 Act creates an offence of basic intent: see *R v Stephenson* [1979] 2 All ER 1198, [1979] QB 695. (iii) Section 5(3) has no bearing on the present issue. It does not create a separate defence, but is no more than a partial definition of the expression 'without lawful excuse' in s 1(1). The absence of lawful excuse forms an element in the mens rea: see *R v Smith* [1974] 1 All ER 632 at 636, [1974] QB 354 at 360 [p 534, below]. Accordingly, since drunkenness does not negative mens rea in crimes of basic intent, it cannot be relied on as part of a defence based on s 5(2).

Whilst this is an attractive submission, we consider it to be unsound, for the following reasons. In the first place, the argument transfers the distinction between offences of specific and of basic intent to a context in which it has no place. The distinction is material where the defendant relies on his own drunkenness as a ground for denying that he had the degree of intention or recklessness required in order to constitute the offence. Here, by contrast, the appellant does not rely on her drunkenness to displace an inference of intent or recklessness; indeed she does not rely on it at all. Her defence is founded on the state of belief called for by s 5(2). True, the fact of the appellant's intoxication was relevant to the defence under s 5(2) for it helped to explain what would otherwise have been inexplicable, and hence lent colour to her evidence about the state of her belief. This is not the same as using drunkenness to rebut an inference of intention or recklessness. Belief, like intention or recklessness, is a state of mind; but they are not the same states of mind.

It was, however, urged that we could not properly read s 5(2) in isolation from s 1(1), which forms the context of the words 'without lawful excuse' partially defined by s 5(2). Once the words are put in context, so it is maintained, it can be seen that the law must treat drunkenness in the same way in relation to lawful excuse (and hence belief) as it does to intention and recklessness, for they are all part of the mens rea of the offence. To fragment the mens rea, so as to treat one part of it as affected by drunkenness in one way and the remainder as affected in a different way, would make the law impossibly complicated to enforce.

If it had been necessary to decide whether, for all purposes, the mens rea of an offence under s 1(1) extends as far as an intent (or recklessness) as to the existence of a lawful excuse, I should have wished to consider the observations of James LJ, delivering the judgment of the Court of Appeal in *R v Smith* [1974] 1 All ER 632 at 636, [1974] QB 354 at 360. I do not however find it necessary to reach a conclusion on this matter and will only say that I am not at present convinced that, when these observations are read in the context of the judgment as a whole, they have the meaning which the respondent has sought to put on them. In my view, however, the answer to the argument lies in the fact that any distinctions which have to be drawn as to the relevance of drunkenness to the two subsections arises from the scheme of the 1971 Act itself. No doubt the mens rea is in general indivisible, with no distinction being possible as regards the effect of drunkenness. But Parliament has specifically isolated one subjective element, in the shape of honest belief, and has given it separate treatment and its own special gloss in s 5(3). This being so, there is nothing objectionable in giving it special treatment as regards drunkenness, in accordance with the natural meaning of its words.

Appeal allowed

Questions

1. Why did not s 101 of the Magistrates' Courts Act 1980, p 582, below, apply so as put the onus of proving the defence on the defendant?

2. Would the defendant have been liable if she had believed (through intoxication or otherwise) that the house was her own? Cf *Smith*, p 534, below. Would it be sensible for the law to distinguish between the two cases? Cf Codification Report, p 87, above.

3. Is there a distinction between using intoxication to rebut an inference of recklessness and to rebut evidence of belief? What if the belief is that there is no risk?

4. Did *Smith*, p 534, below, decide that the absence of lawful excuse forms an element in the mens rea?

The mental element in statutory offences: strict liability

1. Meaning of strict liability

Most offences are now defined by statute. It is a question of construction whether the offence requires a mental element and, if so, what that mental element is. Often the definition uses a word or a phrase—'knowingly', 'with intent to', 'recklessly', 'wilfully', 'dishonestly', and so on—which gives guidance to the court. See Smith & Hogan chapter 7. Often the definition uses a verb or noun which imports a mental element of some kind—'permits', 'appropriates', 'possesses', are examples—so that there cannot be an actus reus without that mental element. See Smith & Hogan pp 30–31.

It does not follow that, where no word or phrase importing a mental element is used, the court will find that mens rea is not required. On the contrary the courts have frequently asserted that there is a presumption in favour of mens rea which must be rebutted by the prosecution; but the application of this presumption has been far from consistent.

There are many offences known as offences of strict liability or absolute prohibition where it is commonly said that 'no mens rea' need be proved. As the cases in this chapter will show, this usually means that mens rea need not be proved with respect to one or more elements of the offence. It does not mean that no mental element whatever need be proved. Lord Edmund-Davies in *Whitehouse v Lemon* [1979] 1 All ER 898 at 920 cited the statement in Smith & Hogan (5th edn), p 920 that 'an offence is regarded—and properly regarded—as one of strict liability if no mens rea need be proved as to a single element in the actus reus.' The single element is, however, usually one of crucial importance so the effect is that a person with no moral culpability may be convicted. The latest (at the time of writing) of a long line of cases imposing liability without fault is *Pharmaceutical Society of Great Britain v Storkwain Ltd* [1985] 3 All ER 4, DC. The Medicines Act 1968, s 58(2) provides that no person shall sell by retail specified medicinal products except in accordance with a prescription given by an appropriate medical practitioner. The defendant supplied specified drugs on prescriptions purporting to be signed by Dr Irani. The prescriptions were forged. There was no finding that the defendants acted dishonestly, improperly or even negligently. So far as appeared, the forgery was sufficient to deceive the sellers without any short-coming on their part. Yet the Divisional Court directed the magistrate to convict. The Court cited the following summary of principles stated by Lord Scarman, giving the advice of Privy Council in *Gammon (Hong Kong) Ltd v A-G of Hong Kong* [1984] 2 All ER 503:

> '(1) there is a presumption of law that mens rea is required before a person can be held guilty of a criminal offence; (2) the presumption is particularly strong where the offence is

"truly criminal" in character; (3) the presumption applies to statutory offences, and can be displaced only if this is clearly or by necessary implication the effect of the statute; (4) the only situation in which the presumption can be displaced is where the statute is concerned with an issue of social concern; public safety is such an issue; (5) even where a statute is concerned with such an issue, the presumption of mens rea stands unless it can be shown that the creation of strict liability will be effective to promote the objects of the statute by encouraging greater vigilance to prevent the commission of the prohibited act.'

The court said that the statute applied to an issue of social concern (what statute imposing criminal liability does not?) and public safety; and strict liability would be effective to promote its objects. The Appeal Committee of the House of Lords has granted leave to appeal.

The courts will much more readily impose strict liability where the statute (as in this case) regulates a particular activity involving potential danger to public health, safety or morals than where it applies to citizens generally. Such offences are sometimes known as 'regulatory' or 'public welfare' offences.

Prince (below) is usually considered to be the seminal case on strict liability (though, as appears, some of the judges at least thought their judgments gave 'full scope to the doctrine of mens rea'). *Prince* must be read with *Tolson*, p 105, below and *Tolson* in the light of *Gould*, p 107, below. The latter cases are concerned with bigamy, a crime of perhaps not great practical importance at the present day but one which lent itself to the elucidation of principles of criminal liability. It was not until *Warner*, p 110, below, in 1968 that strict liability was first considered by the House of Lords; and that and the subsequent decisions of the House must now be regarded as the most authoritative source of such principles as it is possible to discern in this branch of the law.

R v Prince [1874–80] All ER Rep 881, Court for Crown Cases Reserved
(Cockburn CJ, Kelly CB, Bramwell B, Blackburn, Mellor and Lush JJ, Cleasby B, Brett, Grove, Denman, Quain and Archibald JJ, Pollock and Amphlett BB, Field and Lindley JJ)

The accused was charged under s 55 of the Offences against the Person Act 1861 which provided:

> 'Whosoever shall unlawfully take or cause to be taken any unmarried girl, being under the age of sixteen years, out of the possession and against the will of her father or mother or of any other person having the lawful care or charge of her, shall be guilty of a misdemeanour . . .'.

See now Sexual Offences Act 1956, s 20 p 551, below.

The girl, Annie Phillips, though proved by her father to be not yet 14, looked very much older than 16, and the jury found upon reasonable evidence that before the defendant took her away she had told him that she was 18, and that the defendant bona fide believed that statement, and that such belief was reasonable.

Denman J stated a case whether, under these circumstances, a conviction was right; and the Court reserved the case for the consideration of all the judges.

[**Bramwell B**, read a judgment to which **Kelly CB, Cleasby B, Grove J, Pollock B**, and **Amphlett B**, assénted.]

. . . It is impossible to suppose that a person taking a girl out of her father's possession against his will is guilty of no offence within the statute unless he, the taker, knows she is under 16—that he would not be guilty if the jury were of opinion he knew neither one way nor the other. Let it be then that the question is whether he is guilty where he knows, as he thinks, that she is over 16. This introduces the necessity for reading the statute with some strange words introduced; as thus: 'Whosoever shall take any unmarried girl being under the age of sixteen, and not believing her to be over the age of sixteen, out of the possession', etc. Those words are not there, and the question is whether we are bound to construe the statute as though they were, on account of the rule that mens rea is necessary to make an act a crime.

I am of opinion that we are not, nor as though the word 'knowingly' was there, and for the following reasons. The act forbidden is wrong in itself, if without lawful cause. I do not say illegal, but wrong. I have not lost sight of this, that though the statute probably principally aims at seduction for carnal purposes, the taking may be by a female, with a good motive. Nevertheless, though there may be cases which are not immoral in one sense, I say that the act forbidden is wrong. Let us remember what is the case supposed by the statute. It supposes that there is a girl—it does not say a woman, but a girl something between a child and a woman—it supposes she is in the possession of her father or mother, or other person having lawful care and charge of her, and it supposes there is a taking, and that that taking is against the will of the person in whose possession she is. It is, then, a taking of a girl in the possession of someone, against his will. I say that done without lawful cause is wrong, and that the legislature meant it should be at the risk of the taker, whether or not the girl was under 16. I do not say that taking a woman of 50 from her brother's or even father's house is wrong. She is at an age when she has a right to choose for herself; she is not a girl, nor of such tender age that she can be said to be in possession of or under the care or in the charge of anyone. If I am asked where I draw the line, I answer at when the female is no longer a girl in anyone's possession. But what the statute contemplates, and what I say is wrong, is the taking of a female of such tender years that she is properly called a girl, and can be said to be in another's possession, and in that other's care or charge. No argument is necessary to prove this; it is enough to state the case. The legislature has enacted that if anyone does this wrong act he does it at the risk of the girl turning out to be under 16. This opinion gives full scope to the doctrine of mens rea. If the taker believed he had the father's consent, though wrongly, he would have no mens rea. So if he did not know she was in anyone's possession, nor in the care or charge of anyone. In those cases he would not know he was doing the act forbidden by the statute, an act which, if he knew she was in the possession and care or charge of anyone, he would know was a crime or not according as she was under 16 or not. He would know he was doing an act wrong itself, whatever was his intention, if done without lawful cause. In addition to these considerations one may add that the statute does use the word 'unlawfully', and does not use the words 'knowingly or not believing to the contrary'. If the question was whether his act was unlawful there would be no difficulty as it clearly was not lawful.

This view of the section, to my mind, is much strengthened by a reference to other sections of the same statute.

The learned judge then considered ss 50, 51 and 56 of the Act (see the judgment of Blackburn J, below) and continued: The same principle applies in these cases. In *Forbes and Webb* [(1865) 10 Cox CC 362] a man was held liable for assaulting a police officer in the execution of his duty, though he did not know he was a police officer. Why? because the act was wrong in itself. So also in the case of burglary; could a person charged claim an acquittal on the ground that he believed it was past 6 a m when he entered, or in housebreaking that he did not know the place broken into was a house? As to the case of marine stores it was held properly that there was no mens rea where the person charged with the possession of naval stores with the Admiralty mark did not know the stores he had bore the mark: *Sleep* [(1861) Le & Ca 44 (CCR)]; because there is nothing prima facie wrong or immoral in having naval stores unless they are so marked. But suppose someone told him there was a mark, and he had said he would chance whether or not it was the Admiralty mark. So in the case of the carrier with the game in his possession, unless he knew he had it, there would be nothing done or permitted by him, no intentional act or omission. So of the vitriol senders there was nothing wrong in sending such packages as were sent unless they contained vitriol: *Hearne v Garton* [(1859) 2 E & E 66] . . . I think the conviction should be affirmed.

[**Blackburn J** read the following judgment to which **Cockburn CJ, Mellor, Quain, Lush, Archibald, Field** and **Lindley JJ,** assented:]

. . . The question, therefore, is reduced to whether the words in s 55 of the Offences against the Person Act 1861, that whosoever shall unlawfully take 'any unmarried girl being under the age of sixteen, out of the possession of her father' are to be read as if they were 'being under the age of sixteen, and he knowing she was under that age'. No such words are contained in the statute, nor is there the word 'maliciously', 'knowingly', or any other word used that can be said to involve a similar meaning. The argument in favour of the prisoner must, therefore, entirely proceed on the ground that in general a guilty mind is an essential ingredient in a crime, and that where a statute creates a crime the intention of the legislature should be presumed to be to include 'knowingly' in the definition of the crime, and the statute should be read as if that word were inserted. unless the contrary intention appears. We need not inquire at present whether the canon of construction goes quite so far as above stated, for we are of opinion that the intention of the legislature sufficiently appears to have been to punish the abductor unless the girl, in fact, was of such an age as to make her consent an excuse irrespective of whether he knew her to be too young to give an effectual consent, and to fix that age at 16.

The section in question is one of a series of enactments beginning with s 50 forming a code for the protection of women 'and the guardians of young women. These enactments are taken with scarcely any alteration from the repealed statute, the Offences against the Person Act 1828, which had collected them into a code from a variety of old statutes all repealed by it. Section 50 enacts that:

> 'Whosoever shall unlawfully and carnally know and abuse any girl under the age of ten years, shall be guilty of felony.'

By s 51:

> 'Whosoever shall unlawfully and carnally know and abuse any girl being above the age of ten years and under the age of twelve years, shall be guilty of a misdemeanour.'

It seems impossible to suppose that the intention of the legislature in those two sections could have been to make the crime depend upon the knowledge of the prisoner of the girl's actual age. It would produce the monstrous result that a man who had carnal connection with a girl in reality not quite ten years old, but whom he, on reasonable grounds, believed to be a little more than ten, was to escape altogether. He could not, in that view of the statute, be convicted of the felony, for he did not know her to be under ten. He could not be convicted of the misdemeanour because she was, in fact, not above the age of ten. It seems to us that the intention of the legislature was to punish those who had connection with young girls, though with their consent, unless the girl was, in fact, old enough to give a valid consent. The man who has connection with a child relying on her consent does it at his peril if she is below the statutable age.

Section 55, on which the present case arises, uses precisely the same words as those in ss 50 and 51, and must be construed in the same way, . . .

Conviction affirmed

Questions

1. *Prince* has been generally treated as the leading case on strict liability: but did the judges intend to dispense with *mens rea* as they understood it?
2. Bramwell B and Blackburn J pointed to the consequences for ss 50 and 51 of the Act which they thought to be involved in acceptance of the defendant's argument. Did these consequences necessarily follow? (See now Sexual Offences Act 1956, ss 5 and 6, p 549, below.)
3. How would the judges have decided the case if the defendant had believed on reasonable grounds:
(i)   that he had the parents' consent; or
(ii) that the girl was in no one's custody; or
(iii) that the girl was a boy; or
(iv) that the girl was married?
4. What if the defendant had been the girl's maiden aunt and had removed her from the custody of her parents because she believed on reasonable grounds that they were bringing her up in an immoral atmosphere?

2. Strict liability and negligence in bigamy

**R v Tolson [1886–90] All ER Rep 26, Court for Crown Cases Reserved
(Lord Coleridge CJ, Denman J, Pollock B, Field J, Huddleston B, Manisty,
Hawkins, Stephen, Cave, Day, A L Smith, Wills, Grantham and Charles JJ)**

The accused's husband deserted her on 13 December 1881. She and her father made inquiries about him and learned from his elder brother and from general report that he had been lost on a vessel bound for America, which went down with all hands. On 10 January 1887 the accused, supposing herself to be a widow, went through a ceremony of marriage with another man. In December 1887, Tolson returned from America.

[**Wills J** (with whom **Charles J** concurred) and **Cave J** (with whom **Day** and **A L Smith JJ** concurred) delivered judgments holding that the conviction should be quashed.]

Stephen J [with whom **Grantham J** concurred]: For the purpose of settling a question which had been debated for a considerable time, and on which I thought the decisions were conflicting, and not as the expression of my own opinion, I directed the jury at the trial of the accused woman that a belief in good faith and on reasonable grounds in the death of one party to a marriage was not a defence to the charge of bigamy against the other who married again within seven years. I passed a nominal sentence on the accused, and I stated, for the decision of this court, a case which reserved the question whether my decision was right or wrong. I am of opinion that the conviction should be quashed, as the direction I gave was wrong, and that I ought to have told the jury that the defence raised for the prisoner was valid.

My view of the subject is based upon a particular application of the doctrine usually, though I think not happily, described by the phrase *non est reus, nisi mens sit rea*. Though this phrase is in common use, I think it most unfortunate, and not only likely to mislead, but actually misleading, on the following grounds. It naturally suggests that, apart from all particular definitions of crimes, such as thing exists as a mens rea, or 'guilty mind', which is always expressly or by implication involved in every definition. This is obviously not the case, for the mental elements of different crimes differ widely. Mens rea means in the case of murder, malice aforethought; in the case of theft, an intention to steal; in the case of rape, an intention to have forcible connection with a woman, without her consent; and in the case of receiving stolen goods, knowledge that the goods were stolen. In some cases it denotes mere inattention. For instance, in the case of manslaughter by negligence it may mean forgetting to notice a signal. It appears confusing to call so many dissimilar states of mind by one name. It seems contradictory indeed to describe a mere absence of mind as a mens rea or guilty mind. The expression again is likely to and often does mislead. To an unlegal mind it suggests that by the law of England no act is a crime which is done from laudable motives, in other words, that immorality is essential to crime. It will, I think, be found that much of the discussion of the law of libel in *Shipley* [(1784) 4 Doug KB 73] proceeds upon a more or less distinct belief to this effect. It is a topic frequently insisted upon in reference to political offences, and it was urged in a recent notorious case of abduction, in which it was contended that motives said to be laudable were an excuse for the abduction of a child from its parents. . . . The principle involved appears to me, when fully considered, to amount to no more than this. The full definition of every crime contains expressly or by implication a proposition as to a state of mind. Therefore, if the mental element of any conduct alleged to be a crime is proved to have been absent in any given case, the crime so defined is not committed; or, again, if a crime is fully defined, nothing amounts to that crime which does not satisfy that definition. Crimes are in the present day much more accurately defined by statute or otherwise than they formerly were. The mental element of most crimes is marked by one of the words 'maliciously', 'fraudulently', 'negligently', or 'knowingly', but it is the general—I might, I think, say the invariable—practice of the legislature to leave unexpressed some of the mental elements of crime. In all cases whatever, competent age, sanity, and some degree of freedom from some kinds of coercion are assumed to be essential to criminality, but I do not believe they are ever introduced into any statute by which any particular crime is defined. The meaning of the words 'malice', 'negligence', and 'fraud' in relation to particular crimes has been ascertained by numerous cases. Malice means one thing in relation to murder; another in relation to the Malicious Mischief Act [?Malicious Damage Act 1861], and a third in relation to libel, and so of fraud and negligence.

With regard to knowledge of fact, the law, perhaps, is not quite so clear, but it may, I think, be maintained that in every case knowledge of facts is to some extent an element of criminality as much as competent age and sanity. To make an extreme illustration, can anyone doubt that a man who, though he might be perfectly sane, committed what would otherwise be a crime in a state of somnambulism, would be entitled to be acquitted? And why is this? Simply because he would not know what he was doing. A multitude of illustrations of the same sort might be given. I will mention one or two glaring ones. *Levett's* case [(1638) cited Cro Car at p 538, 1 Hale PC 474] decides that a man who making a thrust with a sword at a place where, upon reasonable grounds, he supposes a burglar to be, killed a person who was not a burglar was held not to be a felon though he might be (it was not decided that he was) guilty of killing *per infortunium*, or possibly, *se defendendo*, which then involved certain forfeitures. In other words, he was in the same situation as far as regarded the homicide as if he had killed a burglar. In the decision of the judges in *M'Naghten's Case* [see p 188, below], it is stated that if under an insane delusion one man kills another and if the delusion was such that it would, if true, justify or excuse the killing, the homicide would be justified or excused. This could hardly be if the same were not law as to a sane mistake. A bona fide claim of right excuses larceny, and many of the offences against the Malicious Mischief Act [?Malicious Damage Act 1861]. Apart, indeed from the present case, I think it may be laid down as a general rule that an alleged offender is deemed to have acted under that state of facts which he in good faith and on reasonable grounds believed to exist when he did the act alleged to be an offence. I am unable to suggest any real exception to this rule, nor has one ever been suggested to me . . .

I will now proceed to deal with the arguments which are supposed to lead to the opposite result. It is said, first, that the words of the Offences against the Person Act 1861, s 57, are absolute, and that the exceptions which that section contains are the only ones which are intended to be admitted, and this it is said is confirmed by the express proviso in the section—an indication which is thought to negative any tacit exception. It is also supposed that *Prince* decided on s 55, confirms this view. I will begin by saying how far I agree with these views. First, I agree that the case turns exclusively upon the construction of s 57 of the Act of 1861. Much was said to us in argument on the old statute, the Bigamy Act 1603. I cannot see what this has to do with the matter. Of course, it would be competent to the legislature to define a crime in such a way as to make the existence of any state of mind immaterial. The question is solely whether it has actually done so in this case. In the first place I will observe upon the absolute character of the section. It appears to me to resemble most of the enactments contained in the Consolidation Acts of 1861, in passing over the general mental elements of crime which are pre-supposed in every case. Age, sanity, and more or less freedom from compulsion, are always presumed, and I think it would be impossible to quote any statute which in any case specifies these elements of criminality in the definition of any crime. It will be found that either by using the words wilfully and maliciously, or by specifying some special intent as an element of particular crimes, knowledge of fact is implicitly made part of the statutory definition of most modern definitions of crimes, but there are some cases in which this cannot be said. Such are s 55, on which *Prince* was decided, s 56, which punishes the stealing of 'any child under the age of fourteen years', s 49, as to procuring the defilement of any 'woman or girl under the age of twenty-one', in each of which the same question might arise as in *Prince*. To this I may add some of the provisions of the Criminal Law Amendment Act 1885 [repealed by Sexual Offences Act 1956]. Reasonable belief that a girl is 16 or upwards is a defence to the charge of an offence under ss 5, 6, and 7, but this is not provided for as to an offence against s 4, which is meant to protect girls under 13.

It seems to me that as to the construction of all these sections *Prince* is a direct authority. It was the case of a man who abducted a girl under 16, believing, on good grounds, that she was above that age. Brett J was against the conviction. His judgment establishes at much length, and, as it appears to me, unanswerably, the principle above explained, which he states as follows (LR 2 CCR at p 170)

> 'That a mistake of facts on reasonable grounds, to the extent that, if the facts were as believed, the acts of the prisoner would make him guilty of no offence at all, is an excuse, and that such an excuse is implied in every criminal charge and every criminal enactment in England'.

Lord Blackburn, with whom nine other judges agreed, and Lord Bramwell, with whom seven others agreed, do not appear to me to have dissented from this principle, speaking generally; but they held that it not apply fully to each part of every section to which I have referred. Some of the prohibited acts they thought the legislature intended to be done at the peril of the person who did them, but not all. . . . All the judges, therefore, in *Prince* agreed on the general principle, though they all, except Brett J, considered that, the object of the legislature being to prevent a scandalous and wicked invasion of parental rights (whether it was to be regarded as illegal apart from the statute or not), it was to be supposed that they intended that the wrongdoer should act at his peril. . . .

. . . The application of this to the present case appears to me to be as follows. The general principle is clearly in favour of the prisoner, but how does the intention of the legislature appear to have been against her? It could not be the object of Parliament to treat the marriage of widows as an act to be, if possible, prevented as presumably immoral. The conduct of the woman convicted was not in the smallest degree immoral, it was perfectly natural and legitimate. Assuming the fact to be as she supposed, the infliction of more than a nominal punishment on her would have been a scandal. Why, then, should the legislature be held to have wished to subject her to punishment at all? If such a punishment is legal, the following among many other cases might occur: A number of men in a mine are killed, and their bodies are disfigured and mutilated, by an explosion; one of the survivors secretly absconds, and it is supposed that one of the disfigured bodies is his. His wife sees his supposed remains buried; she marries again. I cannot believe that it can have been the intention of the legislature to make such a woman a criminal; the contracting of an invalid marriage is quite misfortune enough. It appears to me that every argument which showed, in the opinion of the judges in *Prince*, that the legislature meant seducers and abductors to act at their peril, shows that the legislature did not mean to hamper what is not only intended, but naturally and reasonably supposed by the parties, to be a valid and honourable marriage, with a liability to seven years' penal servitude. . . .

[**Hawkins J** and **Lord Coleridge CJ** held that the conviction should be quashed. **Manisty, Denman** and **Field JJ**, and **Pollock** and **Huddleston BB**, that it should be affirmed.]

Conviction quashed

Questions

1. Did Mrs Tolson *intend* to do an act which was criminal, or unlawful in the civil law, or immoral? Should she have been found guilty under any of the principles stated by the judges in *Prince*?

2. Are *Tolson* and *Prince* properly distinguishable? (Manisty J with whom four judges concurred said that he was 'absolutely unable' to distinguish the cases.)

R v Gould [1968] 1 All ER 849 Court of Appeal, Criminal Division (Diplock, LJ, Widgery and Blain JJ)

The appellant, at the time of his second marriage honestly believed that his first marriage had been dissolved and had reasonable grounds for that belief. He wrongly believed that a decree absolute dissolving his first marriage had been granted. His first wife was still alive. He appealed against his conviction for bigamy contrary to s 57 of the Offences against the Person Act 1861, p 546, post.

[**Diplock LJ**, having stated the terms of s 57, continued:]

The enacting words which are absolute in their terms, set out the three elements in the offence: (a) a married person; (b) going through the form or ceremony of marriage with another person; (c) during the life of his or her spouse. The circumstances referred to in the first two parts of the proviso relate to element (b) and element (c) respectively and are true exceptions, that is to say, but for the proviso they would fall within the enacting words which precede it, but the second two parts which refer to cases where the former marriage has been dissolved or declared void at the time of the second marriage are not exceptions. They subtract nothing from and add nothing to the enacting words, for a person whose former marriage has been dissolved or avoided is no longer a married person and element (a) in the offence is absent. . . .

In *Wheat, Stocks* [[1921] 2 KB 119, [1921] All ER Rep 602] the accused's mistaken belief related to element (a). He claimed to have had at the time of his second marriage ceremony an honest and reasonable belief that his former marriage had been dissolved. The Court of Criminal Appeal, consisting of five judges, held that this belief, had it been proved, would have been no defence. They sought to distinguish *Tolson* on the ground that that decision turned on the presence of the exception relating to seven years' absence as indicating that an honest belief in the death of the former spouse before the seven years had elapsed was a defence, which, but for the exception, it would not have been. This, however, is almost exactly the converse of the reasoning of the judges in *Tolson*. The court in *Wheat, Stocks* also accepted the argument of the Attorney-General that

> '. . . this exception creates or involves a presumption of death, which, unless rebutted by the prosecution, entitles the accused to an acquittal—in other words, the accused is presumed to believe in such circumstances that the former wife or husband is dead at the time of the second marriage, and therefore has no intention of doing the act forbidden by the statute'.

This reasoning, however, with great respect, does not bear analysis. The accused has no need to rely on any presumption of death; it is for the prosecution to prove in every case of bigamy that the former spouse was alive at the time of the second marriage. Nor does the proviso depend on the accused's belief in the death of the former spouse but on his lack of knowledge that the former spouse was alive. In the case of a young and healthy spouse who goes abroad there may be no reason whatever for believing that he or she is dead. An honest accused may freely admit that he believed his former spouse to be alive at the time of the second marriage, as long as he did not *know* her to be so at any time within the previous seven years. This was pointed out in terms by Cave J, in *Tolson* and was the very reasoning which persuaded Lord Coleridge CJ that the first exception did not qualify the application to the enacting words of the general presumption that mens rea is a necessary ingredient in the offence. On this reasoning which, with great respect, not only misinterprets the judgments in *Tolson* but also is in itself fallacious, the court in *Wheat, Stocks* expressed their opinion that

> '. . . this decision is not in conflict with the decision of the majority of the judges in *Tolson*, but is in accord with the principle of the judgment in *Prince* [see p 102, above]'.

We, however, agree with Latham CJ in [*Thomas v R* (1937) 59 CLR 279, High Court of Australia] that these two English decisions of courts of co-ordinate jurisdiction are in conflict. *Tolson* decides that mens rea is a necessary ingredient of the felony described in the enacting words despite their absolute terms. *Wheat, Stocks* decides the contrary. *Prince*, which was discussed at length in *Tolson* was decided on another statute which the court held was intended to punish abduction of a girl without her father's consent—an act which the court regarded as *mala in se*; whereas the legislature in 1861 cannot be thought to have regarded the act of marrying for a second time as *mala in se* after a previous marriage had ceased to subsist. . . .

Once it is accepted, as it has been in *King*[1], that the offence is not an absolute one and that honest and reasonable belief in fact affecting the matrimonial status of the defendant which, if true, would make his second marriage lawful and innocent can constitute a defence, there can in our view be no possible ground in justice or in reason for drawing a distinction between facts the result of which would be that he was innocent because he did not come withing the enacting words at all, and facts the result of which would be that he was excluded from the enacting words by the proviso. Given that the belief is formed honestly and on reasonable grounds, there can be no difference on grounds of moral blameworthiness or of public policy between a mistaken belief that a decree absolute has been granted, as in *Wheat, Stocks* and one that it has not, as in *King*. Indeed, it needs little ingenuity to postulate circumstances in which the existence of a decree absolute would make the defendant's first purported marriage void ab initio as the absence of a decree absolute would have done in *King*, and *Thomas v R*[2]. To draw such fine distinctions would we think, in the words of Dixon J:

> '. . . lead to consequences which would not only be contrary to principle but which would be discreditable to our system of criminal law'.

We think that *Wheat, Stocks* was wrongly decided. We agree with the High Court of Australia that it conflicts with *Tolson*. In this respect we respectfully differ from the opinion expressed by the Court of Criminal Appeal in *King*, but our decision is in conformity with the result arrived at in *King* and those parts of the reasoning which led to that result. The prosecution accept that the appellant at the time of the second marriage did honestly believe that his former marriage had been dissolved and that he had reasonable grounds for that belief. This appeal is, accordingly, allowed and the conviction quashed. I should like to say how much we are indebted to both counsel for argument in this case, it was of great assistance to us.

Appeal allowed. Conviction quashed

1. [1964] 1 QB 285, [1965] 3 All ER 561, CCA. D was charged with marrying C in the lifetime of B. His defence was that at the time of the marriage with B he believed that his previous marriage to A had not been dissolved. The defence was rejected on the ground only that he had no reasonable grounds for that belief.
2. (1937) 59 CLR 279 (High Court of Australia).

Question

Would the result have been the same in *Gould* if the appellant had believed honestly but without reasonable grounds that his first marriage had been dissolved? Suppose he had been informed that he had been granted a decree nisi of divorce and understood this to mean that he was divorced, and the decree was never made absolute?

NOTES

Wheat is overruled, but the kind of reasoning on which it was based is to be found in other cases which stand in the law. This is to the effect that there was sufficient mens rea because there was an intention to do 'the act forbidden by statute'. See *Kat v Diment* [1951] 1 KB 34, [1950] 2 All ER 657. In *Wheat* Avory J said:

> 'In *Tolson* the person accused believed on reasonable grounds that her husband was dead; therefore she did not intend at the time of the second marriage to do the act forbidden by the statute—namely, *to marry during his life* . . . In our opinion the maxim [*sc. actus non facit reum nisi mens sit rea*] in its application to this statute is satisfied if the evidence establishes an intention on the part of the person accused to do the act forbidden by the statute—namely, *"being married, to marry during the life of the former wife or husband"*. . .'

It will be observed that the two italicised passages give different definitions of the 'act forbidden by statute'. Which is correct? What is the effect of applying the reasoning in respect of each definition to the facts of *Wheat*?

The process of reasoning which was employed (though somewhat inconsistently) by Avory J in *Wheat* was discussed (though not in relation to that case) by Devlin J in a lecture in 1958. ('Statutory Offences', reprinted in *Samples of Law-making* (1962) 67 at 78).

'Statutory Offences' by Devlin J, 4 JSPTL (NS) 206 at 212

. . . it is said that there must be mens rea but that it is supplied by the intent to do the forbidden act. This phrase, as Dr Glanville Williams has shown, does not stand up to analysis. Take, for example, the offence of selling adulterated milk. The forbidden act is selling *adulterated* milk: it is not selling milk. So the reasoning has to go something like this:

    (1) I intend to sell this can of milk;
    (2) This can of milk is adulterated;
    (3) Therefore I intend to sell adulterated milk.

So it is said, there is an intent to do the forbidden act.

One ought not to brush aside the conception simply because it is expressed in that inelegant way. The conception is a workable one. Mens rea consists of two elements. It consists first of all of the intent to do an act, and secondly of a knowledge of the circumstances that makes that act a criminal offence. Take, for example, firing a gun within forty yards of the highway. There must be an intention to do it—there must be an intention to pull the trigger. If the trigger is pulled accidentally, then without going any further, there is no mens rea. But there must also be a knowledge of the circumstances that make the act forbidden—a knowledge that you are standing within forty yards of the highway. What this formula does is to call the act, as distinct from knowledge of its circumstances and effects, the forbidden act. In every case of crime you have to identify one act that makes the crime; the man's state of mind has to be determined at the time of that act. What was his knowledge of the circumstances and his intention at that time? It is difficult to find a convenient word for the act; let me call it the cardinal act, because the crime hinges on its commission. It is the deed that is at the heart of the crime. That is what those who have stated the law in this form intend it to mean. The effect of stating the law in this way is that if you do the cardinal act, eg the act of selling, you do it at your peril. The prosecution need not prove that you knew of any of the factors that make the selling criminal.

This is one way of stating what is meant by absolute liability in statutory offences. But it is a way which involves a state of mind. It means that you have got deliberately to do the cardinal act and then the intentional doing of that act supplies the mens rea. You cannot sell milk in your sleep, but there are some things that you can do in semi-conscious state and it is those things which have begun to raise the problem of what is the proper way of stating the law. Is it that the doing of the act supplies the mens rea? Or is it simply that state of mind is quite immaterial and that there is no need for the prosecution to prove any intent at all? Stephen J stated it in the second way as long ago as 1889 in *Tolson* (1889) 23 QBD 168. More recently Goddard CJ has put it both ways; in the first way in 1951 in *Kat v Diment* [1951] 1 KB 34,[1950] 2 All ER 657 and in the second way in the following year in *Gardner v Akeroyd* [1952] 2 QB 743,[1952] All ER 306. This difference is not merely of theoretical interest to students of law; it may be of prime importance, though only in a minority of cases. Last year in *Hill v Baxter* [1958] 1 QB 277, [1958] 1 All ER 193, the justices acquitted a man of dangerous driving and of failing to conform to traffic signals because they held he was in a state of automatism and did not know what he was doing. This brought up the point quite acutely though, as it turned out, it was not specifically dealt with. The facts raised the question of whether you were to say that the state of mind was immaterial or whether you were to say that there must be an intent at least to drive. Two of the judges in the Divisional Court arrived at their conclusion without dealing with the point specifically but, I think, by assuming that state of mind was immaterial; and the third judge, whom I must confess to be myself, evaded the issue. Thus these two schools of thought have never been formally arrayed in opposition one to another. . . .

3. Strict liability and drug offences

Warner v Metropolitan Police Commissioner [1968] 2 All ER 356, House of Lords (Lord Reid, Lord Morris of Borth-y-Gest, Lord Guest, Lord Pearce and Lord Wilberforce)

The appellant, a floor-layer, sold scent as a side-line. He went to a cafe and inquired whether anything had been left for him. The proprietor told him there was something under the counter. The appellant found two boxes there and took them away. He was stopped by the police. One box contained scent, the other 20,000 tablets containing amphetamine sulphate, a prohibited drug under the Drugs (Prevention of Misuse) Act 1964. He was charged with being in possession of a prohibited drug, contrary to s 1 of the Act. The appellant said that he assumed that both boxes contained scent. The jury were directed that lack of knowledge of what the box contained went only to mitigation. The jury returned a verdict of guilty after three minutes. The chairman asked the jury whether they thought the appellant knew he had possession of drugs. The foreman answered that he did not know, he had not asked the jury. At the chairman's invitation, the jury retired again and shortly returned to say that they found that the appellant did know. The chairman made it clear that this was his own view and sentenced Warner to two years imprisonment. The Court of Appeal dismissed his appeal against conviction and sentence. On appeal to the House of Lords, it was held that the jury had been misdirected but that no reasonable jury would have accepted the appellant's story and the conviction was upheld under the proviso to s 4(1) of the Criminal Appeal Act 1907.

Lord Reid. . .I understand that this is the first case in which this House has had to consider whether a statutory offence is an absolute offence in the sense that the belief, intention, or state of mind of the accused is immaterial and irrelevant. It appears from the authorities that the law on this matter is in some confusion, there being at least two schools of thought. So I think it necessary to begin by making some observations of a general character.

There is no doubt that for centuries mens rea has been an essential element in every common law crime or offence. Equally there is no doubt that Parliament, being sovereign, can create absolute offences if so minded; but we were referred to no instance where Parliament in giving statutory form to an old common law crime has or has been held to have excluded the necessity to prove mens rea. There is a number of statutes going back for over a century where Parliament in creating a new offence has transferred the onus of proof so that, once the facts necessary to constitute the crime have been proved, the accused will be held to be guilty unless he can prove that he had no mens rea. We were not referred, however, to any except quite recent cases in which it was held that it was no defence to a charge of a serious and truly criminal statutory offence to prove absence of mens rea.

On the other hand there is a long line of cases in which it has been held with regard to less serious offences that absence of mens rea was no defence. Typical examples are offences under public health, licensing and industrial legislation. If a person sets up as say a butcher, a publican, or manufacturer and exposes unsound meat for sale, or sells drink to a drunk man or certain parts of his factory are unsafe, it is no defence that he could not by the exercise of reasonable care have known or discovered that the meat was unsound, or that the man was drunk or that his premises were unsafe. He must take the risk and when it is found that the statutory prohibition or requirement has been infringed he must pay the penalty. This may well seem unjust, but it is a comparatively minor injustice and there is good reason for it as affording some protection to his customers or servants or to the public at large. Although this man might be able to show that he did his best, a more skilful or diligent man in his position might have done better, and when we are dealing with minor penalties which do not involve the disgrace of criminality it may be in the public interest to have a hard and fast rule. Strictly speaking there ought perhaps to be a defence that the defect was truly latent so that no one could have discovered it; but the law has not developed in that way, and one can see the difficulty if such a defence were allowed in a summary prosecution. These are only quasi-criminal offences and it does not really offend the ordinary man's sense of justice that moral guilt is not of the essence of the offence.

[His Lordship reviewed the authorities and continued:]

The only thing that makes me hesitate about this case is the severity of the penalty and the fact that this would be regarded as a truly criminal and disgraceful offence, so that a stigma would attach to a person convicted of it. Applicants for employment, permits or other advantages are often asked whether they have been convicted of any offence. Admission of a conviction of an ordinary offence of this class ought not to be too seriously regarded—and the conviction might be of the man's company and not of the man himself. A man who had, however, to admit a conviction with regard to dangerous drugs might be at a grave disadvantage, and this might not be removed by an explanation that he had only suffered a small penalty. He might even be dismissed by his employer. This makes me hesitate to impute to Parliament an intention to deprive persons accused of these offences of the defence that they had no mens rea. I would think it difficult to convince Parliament that there was any real need to convict a man who could prove that he had neither knowledge of what was being done nor any grounds for suspecting that there was anything wrong.

I dissent emphatically from the view that Parliament can be supposed to have been of the opinion that it could be left to the discretion of the police not to prosecute, or that if there was a prosecution justice would be served by only a nominal penalty being imposed . . . The object of this legislation is to penalise possession of certain drugs. So if mens rea has not been excluded what would be required would be the knowledge of the accused that he had prohibited drugs in his possession. It would be no defence, though it would be a mitigation, that he did not intend that they should be used improperly. And it is a commonplace that, if the accused had a suspicion but deliberately shut his eyes, the court or jury is well entitled to hold him guilty. Further, it would be pedantic to hold that it must be shown that the accused knew precisely which drug he had in his possession. Ignorance of the law is no defence and in fact virtually everyone knows that there are prohibited drugs. So it would be quite sufficient to prove facts from which it could properly be inferred that the accused knew that he had a prohibited drug in his possession. That would not lead to an unreasonable result. In a case like this Parliament, if consulted, might think it right to transfer the onus of proof so that an accused would have to prove that he neither knew nor had any reason to suspect that he had a prohibited drug in his possession; I am unable to find sufficient grounds for imputing to Parliament an intention to deprive the accused of all rights to show that he had no knowledge or reason to suspect that any prohibited drug was on his premises or in a container which was in his possession.

It was suggested in argument that it may always be a defence, even to an absolute offence, to prove absence of mens rea. There are some dicta to that effect, but I do not think that your lordships would introduce such a far reaching doctrine without statutory authority. When we are dealing with the original type of absolute offence—a person engaging in a business where he does certain things at the peril of a pecuniary penalty—it is clearly established that absence of mens rea is no defence. And a right to prove absence of mens rea would sometimes go too far. Mens rea or its absence is a subjective test, and any attempt to substitute an objective test for serious crime has been successfully resisted. If, however, there is to be a halfway house between the common law doctrine and absolute liability, there could be an objective test: not whether the accused knew, but whether a reasonable man in his shoes would have known or have had reason to suspect that there was something wrong. I would not support an objective test where the ordinary member of the public is concerned, but it is not unreasonable to say that if a person engages in some particular business he must behave as, and have the capacity of, the ordinary reasonable man. . . .

In considering what is the proper construction of a provision in any Act of Parliament which is ambiguous one ought to reject that construction which leads to an unreasonable result. As a legal term 'possession' is ambiguous at least to this extent: there is no clear rule as to the nature of the mental element required. All are agreed that there must be some mental element in possession, but there is no agreement as to what precisely it must be. Indeed the view which prevailed in *R v Ashwell* [[1885] 16 QBD 190] and was approved in *Hudson* [[1943] KB 458, [1943] 1 All ER 642] went so far that a person who received a sovereign thinking it to be a shilling was held not to possess the sovereign until he discovered the mistake. There it was argued that 'possession' in this context should be given a popular and not a legal meaning; but even if that were a legitimate way to construe a well-known legal term, I think that it would lead to the same ambiguity. If the ordinary reasonable man were asked what he thought 'possession' meant in this context he would probably say that is a puzzle for the lawyers, and if he ventured his own opinion he might say it meant control; but if asked whether the innkeeper controls the contents of a box handed to him for safekeeping, I think that he would most probably say 'No'.

Lockyer v Gibb was relied on by the Court of Appeal as the case most nearly in point. There the accused had been in a café with some people when the police came in. A man, whom apparently she did not know, gave her a bottle containing tablets 'to look after for him'. She put them at the bottom of her shopping bag and when she went out she was stopped by the police. She was prosecuted under a regulation made under the Dangerous Drugs Act 1965 for being in possession of a scheduled drug. The magistrate held that there was a possibility that she did not know that the tablets contained any of the scheduled drugs. She may have been a very stupid woman, for I would think that any normal person being given a bottle of tablets in such circumstances would know perfectly well that the tablets must contain prohibited drugs which the man did not want the police to find in his possession. With regard to possession Lord Parker CJ, said:

> 'In my judgment, it is quite clear that a person cannot be said to be in possession of some article which he or she does not realise is, or may be, in her handbag, in her room, or in some other place over which she had control. That, I should have thought, is elementary, if something were slipped into one's basket and one had not the vaguest notion it was there at all, one could not possibly be said to be in possession of it.'

I entirely agree; but that destroys any contention that mere physical control or custody without any mental element is sufficient to constitute possession under that enactment. If something is slipped into my bag I have as much physical control over it as I have over anything else in my bag. I can carry it where I will and I can transfer the whole contents of my bag to some other person without ever realising that this particular thing is included. Then, however, Lord Parker went on to say:

> '. . .in my judgment, under this provision, while it is necessary to show that the appellant knew she had the articles which turned out to be a drug, it is not necessary that she should know that in fact it was a drug of a particular character.'

With that I cannot agree for reasons which I have already given. I do not think that this distinction will bear critical examination and I do not know what the result would be on this view if, in the present case, both the scent and the drugs had been in the same parcel. The appellant, if his story were accepted, would have rightly believed that the parcel contained scent, but would have been ignorant of the fact that drugs had been slipped in with the scent. Could it be right that if the appellant had taken possession of the parcel of scent and thereafter the drugs had been slipped in without his knowledge he would be innocent (which is Lord Parker's view), but that if the drugs had been slipped in without his knowledge before he took possession then he would be guilty? That seems to me to be quite unreasonable and it seems to me to be equally unreasonable that the fact that there were two parcels and not one should make all the difference between guilt and innocence.

If this case is to be decided on this narrower ground I accept the view of my noble and learned friends, Lord Pearce and Lord Wilberforce. It enables justice to be done in all cases which resemble this case. But it still leaves subject to injustice persons who in innocent circumstances take into their possession what they genuinely and reasonably believe to be an ordinary medicine, if in fact the substance turns out to be a prohibited drug. Nevertheless this ground is sufficient to show that the learned trial judge must be held to have misdirected the jury in the present case.

[**Lord Morris** held that the accused could be convicted of possession of a prohibited drug only if it were proved that he was knowingly in control of the substance or container in circumstances which enabled him to know or discover (or could have enabled him, had he so wished, to know or discover) what it was that he had, before assuming control of it or continuing to be in control of it.]

[**Lord Guest** held that possession of the parcel amounted to possession of the contents and no proof need be given of the knowledge of the nature of the contents.]

[**Lord Pearce**, having considered certain authorities and held that Lord Parker CJ in *Lockyer v Gibb* was right to hold that a person did not have possession of something which had been 'slipped into his bag' without his knowledge continued:].

One may, therefore, exclude from the 'possession' intended by the Act of 1964 the physical control of articles which have been 'planted' on him without his knowledge; but how much further is one to go? If one goes to the extreme length of requiring the prosecution to prove that 'possession' implies a full knowledge of the name and nature of the drug concerned, the efficacy of the Act is seriously impaired, since many drug pedlars may in truth be unaware of this. I think that the term 'possession' is satisfied by a knowledge only of the existence of the thing itself and not its qualities, and that ignorance or mistake as to its qualities is not an excuse. This would comply with the general understanding of the word 'possess'. Though I reasonably believe the tablets which I possess to be aspirin, yet if they turn out to be heroin I am in possession of heroin tablets. This would be so I think even if I believed them to be sweets. It would be otherwise if I believed them to be something of a wholly different nature. At this point a question of degree arises as to when a difference in qualities amounts to a difference in kind. That is a matter for a jury who would probably decide it sensibly in favour of the genuinely innocent but against the guilty.

The situation with regard to containers presents further problems. If a man is in possession of the contents of a package, prima facie his possession of the package leads to the strong inference that he is in possession of its contents; but can this be rebutted by evidence that he was mistaken as to its contents? As in the case of goods that have been 'planted' in his pocket without his knowledge, so I do not think that he is in possession of contents which are quite different in kind from what he believed. Thus the prima facie assumption is discharged if he proves (or raises a real doubt in the matter) either (a) that he was a servant or bailee who had no right to open it *and* no reason to suspect that its contents were illicit or were drugs or (b) that although he was the owner he had no knowledge of (including a genuine mistake as to) its actual contents or of their illicit nature and that he received them innocently and also that he had had no reasonable opportunity since receiving the package of acquainting himself with its actual contents. For a man takes over a package or suit-case at risk as to its contents being unlawful if he does not immediately examine it (if he is entitled to do so). As soon as may be he should examine it and if he finds the contents suspicious reject possession by either throwing them away or by taking immediate sensible steps for their disposal. . . .

The direction to which the appellant was entitled would, in my opinion, be approximately as follows. The Drugs (Prevention of Misuse) Act 1964 forbids possession of these drugs. Whether he possessed them with an innocent or guilty mind or for a laudable or improper purpose is immaterial, since he is not allowed to possess them. If he possessed them, he is guilty. If a man has physical control or possession of a thing that is sufficient possession under the Act of 1964 provided that he knows that he has the thing; but a man does not (within the meaning of the Act of 1964) possess things of whose existence he is unaware. The prosecution have here proved that he possessed the parcel, but have they proved that he possessed its contents also? There is a very strong inference of fact in any normal case that a man who possesses a parcel also possesses its contents, an inference on which a jury would in a normal case be justified in finding possession. A man who accepts possession of a parcel normally accepts possession of the contents. That inference, however, can be disproved or shaken by evidence that, although a man was in possession of a parcel, he was completely mistaken as to its contents and would not have accepted possession had he known what kind of thing the contents were. A mistake as to the qualities of the contents, however, does not negative possession. Many people possess things of whose exact qualities they are unaware. If the accused knew that the contents were drugs or were tablets, he was in possession of them, though he was mistaken as to their qualities. Again if, though unaware of the contents, he did not open them at the first opportunity to ascertain (as he was entitled to do in this case) what they were, the proper inference is that he was accepting possession of them. (It would be otherwise if he had no right to open the parcel.) Again, if he suspected that there was anything wrong about the contents when he received the parcel, the proper inference is that he was accepting possession of the contents by not immediately verifying them. (This would, in my opinion, apply also to a bailee.)

In the present case you may think that the difference between scent and tablets is a sufficient difference in kind to entitle the accused to an acquittal if on the whole of the evidence it appears that he may have genuinely believed that the parcel contained scent, and that he may not have had any suspicions that there was anything illicit in the parcel, and that he had no opportunity of verifying its contents. For in that case it is not proved that he was in possession of the contents of the parcel.

The appellant has, therefore, been deprived of the chance of putting before the jury a defence which was in theory open to him on the facts of this case; but the evidence against him was so strong that no jury properly directed would have acquitted him. In my opinion, therefore, the proviso should be applied and I would dismiss the appeal.

Lord Wilberforce held that there was one single question to be answered—'what kind of control with what mental element does the Act intend to prohibit?' On the question of making clear to the jury what is required in order to establish possession, he associated himself with the observations of Lord Pearce.

Appeal dismissed

Questions

1. Can we properly distinguish 'quasi-criminal offences' from crimes involving the 'disgrace of criminality' as Lord Reid suggests? On what principle should the line be drawn? On which side of the line would the following offences fall:
    careless driving;
    driving while uninsured against third party liability;
    the sale by a butcher of meat unfit for human consumption;
    the sale by a licensee of alcohol to (i) a drunken man; (ii) a constable on duty?
2. The judges got into great difficulties over the concept of possession. Would any of these difficulties have arisen if the offence had been interpreted to require mens rea?
3. D is found carrying a sealed package which contains heroin. How would the judges have dealt with him if he believed:
    (i) the box was empty;
    (ii) the box contained aspirin or, sweets or, jewellery or, stolen jewellery or, explosives or, something, but he had no idea what?
4. When *Warner* was tried, the offence was understood to be one of strict liability, requiring no mental element as to the nature of the thing (in fact, a drug) which was in the defendant's control. Was there any reason why the

jury should have given any thought to the question whether he knew that the boxes contained drugs? Was the chairman right to ask the jury their opinion? Was the opinion of the jury (given after they had returned their verdict) of any value? Should evidence have been admitted as to the defendant's knowledge, or lack of it, at the trial?

Sweet v Parsley, [1969] 1 All ER 347, House of Lords
(Lord Reid, Lord Morris of Borth-y-Gest, Lord Pearce, Lord Wilberforce and Lord Diplock)

Miss Sweet, a schoolteacher, was the sub-tenant of a farm in Oxfordshire. Finding it impracticable to travel into Oxford, she let the rooms in the farmhouse to tenants at low rentals allowing them the common use of the kitchen. She retained one room for her own use and visited the farm occasionally to collect rent and see that all was well. The police found evidence that cannabis was smoked in the farmhouse. She was convicted by the magistrates of being concerned in the management of premises which were used for the purpose of smoking cannabis, contrary to s 5(b) of the Dangerous Drugs Act 1965. The magistrates found that 'she had no knowledge whatever that the house was being used for the purpose of smoking cannabis' and that 'once or twice when staying overnight at the farmhouse the appellant shouted if there was excessive noise late at night but otherwise she did not exercise any control over the tenants except that she collected rent from them? Miss Sweet's appeal to the Divisional Court was dismissed. She appealed to the House of Lords.

Lord Reid. . . . How has it come about that the Divisional Court has felt bound to reach such an obviously unjust result? It has, in effect, held that it was carrying out the will of Parliament because Parliament has chosen to make this an absolute offence. And, of course, if Parliament has so chosen, the courts must carry out its will, and they cannot be blamed for any unjust consequences. But has Parliament so chosen? I dealt with this matter at some length in *Warner v Metropolitan Police Comr* [p 110, above]. On reconsideration I see no reason to alter anything which I there said. But I think that some amplification is necessary. Our first duty is to consider the words of the Act; if they show a clear intention to create an absolute offence, that is an end of the matter. But such cases are very rare. Sometimes the words of the section which creates a particular offence make it clear that mens rea is required in one form or another. Such cases are quite frequent. But in a very large number of cases there is no clear indication either way. In such cases there has for centuries been a presumption that Parliament did not intend to make criminals of persons who were in no way blameworthy in what they did. That means that, whenever a section is silent as to mens rea, there is a presumption that, in order to give effect to the will of Parliament, we must read in words appropriate to require mens rea.

Where it is contended that an absolute offence has been created, the words of Alderson B in *A-G v Lockwood* [(1842) 9 M & W 378 at 398] have often been quoted:

'The rule of law, I take it, upon the construction of all statutes, and therefore applicable to the construction of this, is, whether they be penal or remedial, to construe them according to the plain literal and grammatical meaning of the words in which they are expressed unless that construction leads to a plain and clear contradiction of the apparent purpose of the act or to some palpable and evident absurdity.'

That is perfectly right as a general rule and where there is no legal presumption. But what about the multitude of criminal enactments where the words of the Act simply make it an offence to do certain things but where everyone agrees that there cannot be a conviction without proof of mens rea in some form? This passage, if applied to the present problem, would mean that there is no need to prove mens rea unless it would be 'a plain and clear contradiction of the apparent purpose of the Act' to convict without proof of mens rea. But that would be putting the presumption the wrong way round; for it is firmly established by a host of authorities that mens rea is an essential ingredient of every offence unless some reason can be found for holding that that is not necessary. It is also firmly established that the fact that other sections of the Act expressly require mens rea, for example because they contain the word 'knowingly', is not in itself sufficient to justify a decision that a section which is silent as to mens rea creates an absolute offence. In the absence of a clear indication in the Act that an offence is intended to be an absolute offence, it is necessary to go outside the Act and examine all relevant circumstances in order to establish that this must have been the intention of Parliament. I say 'must have been', because it is a universal principle that if a penal provision is reasonably capable of two interpretations, that interpretation which is most favourable to the accused must be adopted.

What, then, are the circumstances which it is proper to take into account? In the well known case of *Sherras v De Rutzen* [[1895] 1 QB 918 at 924; [1895–99] All ER Rep 1167 at 1169], Wright J only mentioned the subject-matter with which the Act deals. But he was there dealing with something which was one of a class of acts which 'are not criminal in any real sense, but are acts which in the public interest are prohibited under a penalty'. It does not in the least follow that, when one is dealing with a truly criminal act, it is sufficient merely to have regard to the subject-matter of the enactment. One must put oneself in the position of a legislator. It has long been the practice to recognise absolute offences in this class of quasi-criminal acts, and one can safely assume that, when Parliament is passing new legislation dealing with this class of offences, its silence as to mens rea means that the old practice is to apply. But when one comes to acts of a truly criminal character, it appears to me that there are at least two other factors which any reasonable legislator would have in mind. In the first place, a stigma still attaches to any person convicted of a truly criminal offence, and the more serious or more disgraceful the offence the greater the stigma. So he would have to consider whether, in a case of this gravity, the public interest really requires that an innocent person should be prevented from proving his innocence in order that fewer guilty men may escape. And equally important is the fact that, fortunately, the press in this country are vigilant to expose injustice, and every manifestly unjust conviction made known to the public tends to injure the body politic by undermining public confidence in the justice of the law and of its administration. But I regret to observe that, in some recent cases where serious offences have been held to be absolute offences, the court has taken into account no more than the wording of the Act and the character and seriousness of the mischief which constitutes the offence.

The choice would be more difficult if there were no other way open than either mens rea in the full sense or an absolute offence; for there are many kinds of case where putting on the prosecutor the full burden of proving mens rea creates great difficulties and may lead to many unjust acquittals. But there are at least two other possibilities. Parliament has not infrequently transferred the onus as regards mens rea to the accused, so that, once the necessary facts are proved, he must convince the jury that, on balance of probabilities, he is innocent of any criminal intention. I find it a little surprising that more use has not been made of this method; but one of the bad effects of the decision of this House in *Woolmington v Director of Public Prosecutions* [p 39, above] may have been to discourage its use. The other method would be in effect to substitute in appropriate classes of cases gross negligence for mens rea in the full sense as the mental element necessary to constitute the crime. It would often be much easier to infer that Parliament must have meant that gross negligence should be the necessary mental element than to infer that Parliament intended to create an absolute offence. A variant of this would be to accept the view of Cave J in *Tolson* [p 105, above]. This appears to have been done in Australia where authority appears to support what Dixon J said in *Proudman v Dayman* [(1941) 67 CLR 536]

> 'As a general rule an honest and reasonable belief in a state of facts which, if they existed, would make the defendant's act innocent affords an excuse for doing what would otherwise be an offence.'

It may be that none of these methods is wholly satisfactory, but at least the public scandal of convicting on a serious charge persons who are in no way blameworthy would be avoided.

If this section means what the Divisional Court have held that it means, then hundreds of thousands of people who sublet part of their premises or take in lodgers or are concerned in the management of residential premises or institutions are daily incurring a risk of being convicted of a serious offence in circumstances where they are in no way to blame. For the greatest vigilance cannot prevent tenants, lodgers or inmates or guests whom they bring in from smoking cannabis cigarettes in their own rooms. It was suggested in argument that the appellant brought this conviction on herself because it is found as a fact that, when the police searched the premises, there were people there of the 'beatnik fraternity'. But surely it would be going a very long way to say that persons managing premises of any kind ought to safeguard themselves by refusing accommodation to all who are of slovenly or exotic appearance, or who bring in guests of that kind. And, unfortunately, drug taking is by no means confined to those of unusual appearance. Speaking from a rather long experience of membership of both Houses, I assert with confidence that no Parliament within my recollection would have agreed to make an offence of this kind an absolute offence if the matter had been fully explained to it. So, if the court ought only to hold an offence to be an absolute offence where it appears that that must have been the intention of Parliament, offences of this kind are very far removed from those which it is proper to hold to be absolute offences.

I must now turn to the question what is the true meaning of s 5 of the Act of 1965. [His Lordship held that the 'purpose' referred to in s 5 of the 1965 Act was the purpose of the management and, as the appellant had no such purpose, the conviction must be quashed.]

[**Lords Morris** and **Pearce** held that it was necessary to prove that the accused had knowledge of the particular purpose to which the premises were being put in order to secure a conviction, and that the appeal should be allowed.]

Lord Wilberforce held that the 'purpose' which must be proved under the section must be that of the manager; and that the appeal should be allowed.

[**Lord Diplock**, having held, following *Tolson*, p 105 ante, that criminal statutes are to be read subject to the implication that a necessary element in the offence is the absence of a belief held honestly and on reasonable grounds, went on:]

This implication stems from the principle that it is contrary to a rational and civilised criminal code, such as Parliament must be presumed to have intended, to penalise one who has performed his duty as a citizen to ascertain what acts are prohibited by law (*ignorantia juris non excusat*) and has taken all proper care to inform himself of any facts which would make his conduct lawful. Where penal provisions are of general application to the conduct of ordinary citizens in the course of their everyday life, the presumption is that the standard of care required of them in informing themselves of facts which would make their conduct unlawful, is that of the familiar common law duty of care. But where the subject-matter of a statute is the regulation of particular activity involving potential danger to public health, safety or morals, in which citizens have a choice whether they participate or not, the court may feel driven to infer an intention of Parliament to impose, by penal sanctions, a higher duty of care on those who choose to participate and to place on them an obligation to take whatever measures may be necessary to prevent the prohibited act, without regard to those considerations of cost or business practicability which play a part in the determination of what would be required of them in order to fulfil the ordinary common law duty of care. But such an inference is not lightly to be drawn, nor is there any room for it unless there is something that the person on whom the obligation is imposed can do directly or indirectly, by supervision or inspection, by improvement of his business methods or by exhorting those whom he may be expected to influence or control, which will promote the observance of the obligation (see *Lim Chin Aik v R* [1963] AC 160 at 174, [1963] 1 All ER 223 at 228).

The numerous decisions in the English courts since *Tolson* [see p 105, above] in which this later inference has been drawn rightly or, as I think, often wrongly, are not easy to reconcile with others where the court has failed to draw the inference, nor are they always limited to penal provisions designed to regulate the conduct of persons who choose to participate in a particular activity as distinct from those of general application to the conduct of ordinary citizens in the course of their everyday life. It may well be that, had the significance of *Tolson* been appreciated here, as it was in the High Court of Australia, our courts, too would have been less ready to infer an intention of Parliament to create offences for which honest and reasonable mistake was no excuse. Its importance as a guide to the construction of penal provisions in statutes of general application was recognised by Dixon J in *Maher v Musson* [(1934) 52 CLR 100 at 104], and by the majority of the High Court of Australia in *Thomas v R* [(1937) 59 CLR 279]. It is now regularly adopted in Australia as a general principle of construction of statutory provisions of this kind.

By contrast, in England the principle laid down in *Tolson* has been overlooked until recently (see *Gould* [p 107, above]) partly because the ratio decidendi was misunderstood by the Court of Criminal Appeal in *Wheat, Stocks* [[1921] 2 KB 119; [1921] All ER Rep 602], and partly, I suspect, because the reference in *Tolson* to the mistaken belief as being a 'defence' to the charge of bigamy was thought to run counter to the decision of your Lordships' House in *Woolmington v Director of Public Prosecutions* [p 39, above]. That expression might have to be expanded in the light of what was said in *Woolmington's* case, though I doubt whether a jury would find the expansion much more informative than describing the existence of the mistaken belief as a defence to which they should give effect unless they felt sure either that the accused did not honestly hold it or, if he did, that he had no reasonable grounds for doing so.

Woolmington's case affirmed the principle that the onus lies on the prosecution in a criminal trial to prove all the elements of the offence with which the accused is charged. It does not purport to lay down how that onus can be discharged as respects any particular elements of the offence. This, under our system of criminal procedure, is left to the common sense of the jury. *Woolmington's* case did not decide anything so irrational as that the prosecution must call evidence to prove the absence of any mistaken belief by the accused in the existence of facts which, if true, would make the act innocent, any more than it decided that the prosecution must call evidence to prove the absence of any claim of right in a charge of larceny. The jury is entitled to presume that the accused acted with knowledge of the facts, unless there is some evidence to the contrary originating from the accused who alone can know on what belief he acted and on what ground the belief if mistaken was held. What *Woolmington's* case did decide is that, where there is any such evidence, the jury, after considering it and also any relevant evidence called by the prosecution on the issue of the existence of the alleged mistaken belief, should acquit the accused unless they feel sure that he did not hold the belief or that there were no reasonable grounds on which he could have done so. This, as I understand it, is the approach of Dixon J, to the onus of proof of honest and reasonable mistaken belief as he expressed it in *Proudman v Dayman* [(1941) 67 CLR 536]. Unlike the position where a statute expressly places the onus of proving lack of guilty knowledge on the accused, the accused does not have to prove the existence of mistaken belief on the balance of probabilities; he has to raise a reasonable doubt as to its non-existence.

It has been objected that the requirement laid down in *Tolson* and the *Bank of New South Wales v Piper* [[1897] AC 383] that the mistaken belief should be based on reasonable grounds introduces an objective mental element into mens rea. This may be so, but there is nothing novel in this. The test of the mental element of provocation which distinguishes manslaughter from murder has always been at common law and now is by statute the objective one of the way in which a reasonable man would react to provocation. There is nothing unreasonable in requiring a citizen to take reasonable care to ascertain the facts relevant to his avoiding doing a prohibited act.

[His Lordship then held that the 'purpose' to be proved was that of the person concerned in the management and, since the appellant had no knowlege of the use of the premises for smoking cannabis, the appeal should be allowed.]

Appeal allowed

Questions

1. Is it a 'bad effect' of *Woolmington v Director of Public Prosecutions* (p 39, above) that it has discouraged the courts from putting an onus of proof on the accused? Cf *R v City of Sault Ste Marie*, p 127, below.
2. Did *Woolmington* decide anything about mistaken beliefs? Particularly, did it decide that an unreasonably mistaken belief is no defence?
3. Why should an unreasonable failure to foresee results amount to a defence (Criminal Justice Act 1967, s 8, p 42, above) and an unreasonable failure to know facts not do so?

NOTES

In *Fernandez* [1970] Crim LR 277, CA, a merchant seaman was convicted of possessing cannabis when he was given a package to bring into England and he took it, having an idea that it might contain marijuana cigarettes and appreciating that he might get into trouble with the customs authorities if it were discovered. He claimed that he did not know the package contained drugs. The Court of Appeal held that the law laid down in *Warner v Metropolitan Police Comr* was not affected by the decision in *Sweet v Parsley*. 'In "package cases" the position could be summarised as follows: prima facie the prosecution satisfy the onus on them by proving that the accused was in physical control of articles which were dangerous drugs. But if the suggestion is made that he was mistaken as to the nature of the goods then it may be necessary to consider what his mental state was. For example, if it is clear that he did not know precisely what the contents of the package were but nevertheless his conduct indicated that he was prepared to take it into his possession whatever it was then no difficulty arose in regard to proving that he was in possession of the contents for all purposes. Similarly if the accused took the package into his possession in a situation in which he should certainly have been put on inquiry as to the nature of what he was carrying and yet he deliberately failed to pursue an inquiry and accepted the goods in circumstances which must have pointed the finger of suspicion at their nature and at the propriety of carrying them, then it was a proper inference that he accepted them whatever they were and it was not open to him to say that he was not in possession of the goods because he did not know what they were.' However in *Patel* [1970] Crim LR 274, CA, where the charge was one of *aiding and abetting* the possession of cannabis, it was held that an intention to aid in the possession of the thing, whatever it might be, was not enough; it must be proved that the accused knew he was aiding possession of a dangerous drug (cf. p 153, post). In *Irving* [1970] Crim LR 642, CA, the accused was found in possession of a bottle which contained stomach pills and an amphetamine tablet. He said that the tablet had been prescribed for his wife and she must have put it in the bottle by accident when she was refilling it with stomach pills for his use and that he had no idea it was there. It was held the jury had been wrongly directed that, if he was knowingly in possession of the bottle, he was in possession of the contents; it was akin to the case where a drug is slipped into a person's pocket without his knowledge.

These were 'container' cases. In *Marriott* [1970] 1 All ER 595, CA, the accused was convicted of being in possession of cannabis when he had a penknife with 0.03 grains of cannabis resin, representing at most one thirtieth of a single cannabis cigarette, adhering to a broken blade. A direction that the accused was guilty if he knew he was in possession of the penknife, even if he did not know that there was foreign matter adhering to the knife was held to be wrong. It was necessary at least to prove that he knew that there was some foreign matter adhering to the knife. The court thought it may be that no further mens rea was necessary—so that the accused would be guilty if he believed on reasonable grounds that the matter was tobacco or toffee—though, 'Perhaps the law does not go as far as that'.

Misuse of Drugs Act 1971, ss 4, 5, 6, 8, 9 and 28, p 573, below

NOTES ON THE MISUSE OF DRUGS ACT 1971

1. Since nothing in s 28 is to prejudice any defence which it is open to a person to raise apart from the section, it seems still open to the accused to submit that the prosecution have not proved that he was in possession of the drug in question. The onus of proving possession is on the Crown: *Ashton-Rickardt* [1978] 1 All ER 173. Does s 28 affect a case like that discussed in *Lockyer v Gibb* where the defence is that the drug was slipped into the accused's basket without his knowledge? It is for the prosecution to prove possession and if the jury think D's story may reasonably be true, can they then be satisfied beyond reasonable doubt that he was in possession or must they acquit? Suppose then the accused says that he knew he had the thing in question but (to adopt Lord Pearce's formulation) was 'completely mistaken' as to its character and not merely making a mistake as to quality. If he is believed, he was not in possession. Must he, then, be acquitted if the jury think his story may reasonably be true?—ie does the onus of proof remain with the Crown?

See *Colyer* [1974] Crim LR 243 (Judge Stinson).

2. The Act, by s 2, divides controlled drugs into three classes, A, B, and C; and Sch 2 to the Act specifies into which class each drug falls. The maximum punishment which may be inflicted for the various offences under the Act is prescribed in Sch 4 and varies according to the class of drug involved. For example, on a charge of possessing a controlled drug, contrary to s 5 (2), the maxima are: Class A drug: 7 years; Class B drug: 5 years; Class C drug: 2 years.

Questions

1. How would *Warner's* case (p 110, above) and *Sweet v Parsley* (p 115, above) be decided under the Misuse of Drugs Act 1971?

2. If the facts of *Irving* and *Marriott* (p 119, above) were to recur after the Act came into force:

(a)   Would it be for Irving to prove that he did not know that the tablet was in the bottle or for the Crown to prove that he did know it was there?

(b)   Would it be for Marriott to prove that he did not know there was anything on the knife or for the Crown to prove that he did? If he had said that he knew there was something on the knife but thought it was toffee, where would the onus of proof lie?

3. F and G call on H to collect some drugs. H, by mistake, hands them the wrong boxes. Consequently F has a box containing pethidine (a Class A drug) which he believes to contain pemoline (a class C drug) and G has a box containing pemoline which he believes to contain pethidine. F and G have no authority to possess any controlled drugs. Of what offences, or attempts to commit offences, may F and G be convicted and to what punishments are they liable? See note 2, above.

4.   Trade description and pollution offences

Wings Ltd v Ellis [1984] 3 All ER 577, House of Lords
(Lord Hailsham LC, Lords Keith, Scarman, Brandon and Templeman)

Wings Ltd published a brochure which was inaccurate in two respects. It stated that the Sea Shells Hotel in Sri Lanka was air conditioned; and it included a photograph of a room which was a room of superior quality in another hotel. At the time of publication Wings Ltd were unaware of these errors. Shortly afterwards, they discovered the errors and took steps to correct them. Subsequently a Mr Wade read the uncorrected brochure and, after his holiday, complained that he had been misled. Section 14 (1) of the Trade Descriptions Act 1968 provides:

> 'It shall be an offence for any person in the course of any trade or business—(a) to make a statement which he knows to be false; or (b) recklessly to make a statement which is false; as to any of the following matters, that is to say,— (i) the provision in the course of

any trade or business of any services, accommodation or facilities; (ii) the nature of any services, accommodation or facilities provided in the course of any trade or business; (iii) the time at which, manner in which or persons by whom any services, accommodation or facilities are so provided; (iv) the examination, approval or evaluation by any person of any services, accommodation or facilities so provided; or (v) the location or amenities of any accommodation so provided.'

Wings Ltd were convicted (i) under s 14 (1) (a) of making a statement which they knew to be false that the hotel was air-conditioned and (ii) under s 14 (1) (b) of recklessly making a statement (by the photograph) which was false as to the nature of the accommodation.

The Divisional Court (Robert Goff LJ and Mann J) quashed both convictions, conviction (i) because, although the required knowledge could exist when the statement was read, the offence was not committed when the defendant had done all that could reasonably be expected to neutralise the error, applying *Miller*, p 23, above; and conviction (ii) because there was no evidence that any person whose mind could be said to be the directing mind and will of the company (see the *Tesco* case, p 181, below) had been reckless by failing to have regard to the truth or falsity of the statement. The prosecutor appealed against the quashing of the conviction of offence (i) only.

[**Lord Scarman**, having held that the statutory defence provisions in ss 23 and 24 of the Act (on which the defendant did not rely) were applicable to the offences under s 14 and having referred to (inter alia) *Sweet v Parsley*, p 115, above, and *Gammon (Hong Kong) Ltd v A-G of Hong Kong* [1984] 2 All ER 503 at 507 p 101, above]:

In the light of the foregoing it is now necessary to determine the proper construction to be put on the words of s 14(1)(a). The necessary ingredients of the offence as formulated in the subsection are that (1) a person in the course of a trade or business (2) makes a statement (3) which he knows to be false (4) as to the provision in the course of trade or business of any services, accommodation or facilities. The respondent submits that the essence of the offence is knowingly making a false statement. The appellant submits that it suffices to prove that the statement was made on a person's behalf in the course of his business and that its content was false to the knowledge of the person carrying on the business.

My Lords, I accept the appellant's construction as correct. First, it advances the legislative purpose embodied in the Act, in that it strikes directly against the false statement irrespective of the reason for, or explanation of, its falsity. It involves, of course, construing the offence as one of strict liability to the extent that the offence can be committed unknowingly, i e without knowledge of the act of statement; but this is consistent with the social purpose of a statute in the class to which this Act belongs. And the strictness of the offence does no injustice: the accused, if he has acted innocently, can invoke and prove one of the statutory defences. Second, the appellant's submission has the advantage of following the literal and natural meaning of the words used. The subsection says not that it is an offence knowingly to make the statement but that it is an offence to make the statement.

The respondent's counsel, however, in support of his submission made a number of telling points. None of them is, in my judgment, strong enough to overcome the difficulties in his way. First, he relied on the general principles governing the interpretation of the provisions of a criminal statute. They are, however, for the reasons already developed, not applicable to this statute, Second, he submitted that he who makes a statement must as a matter of common sense know that he is making it. This is not so, however, when one is dealing, as in this statute, with statements made in the course of a trade or business. It would stultify the statute if this submission were to be upheld. Third, he contrasted the wording of para (a) with para (b). Paragraph (b) provides that it is an offence 'recklessly' to make the false statement. The inference arises, therefore, that the offence under para (a) requires proof of a deliberate false statement. This, with respect, I believe to be his best point, but it cannot prevail against all the indications to which I have referred in favour of the interpretation put on para (a) by the appellant.

But this is not the end of the respondent's case. There remains the question: did the respondent make any statement at all as to the air-conditioning of the hotel bedroom on 13 January when Mr Wade read it? The respondent's submission was that such a statement was made only once, on publication of the brochure in May 1981. The importance of the question is not only that the prosecution pinned its case to 13 January 1982 but that in May 1981 the company did not know the statement was false whereas in January 1982 it did know it was false.

This submission was not open to the respondent company before the magistrates or in the Divisional Court. The Court of Appeal had decided in *R v Thomson Holidays Ltd* [1974] 1 All ER 823, [1974] QB 592 that a new statement is made on every occasion that an interested member of the public reads it in a brochure published by a company engaged in attracting his custom. The court considered that communication is the essence of statement. My Lords, I think *R v Thomson Holidays Ltd* was correctly decided, even though I do not accept the totality of the court's reasoning. A statement can consist of a communication to another; and in the context of this Act and the circumstances of this class of business I have no hesitation in accepting the court's view that communication by an uncorrected brochure of false information to someone who is being invited to do business in reliance on the brochure is to make a statement within s 14(1)(a). But there can be statements which are not communicated to others. It was unnecessary for the Court of Appeal to hold that communication was of the essence, and to that extent only I think the court erred.

The respondent's case that it only made one statement, i e on publication of the brochure, is as fallacious in its way as is the view of the Court of Appeal that without communication there is no statement. I have no doubt that a statement as to the air-conditioning in the hotel was made when the brochure was published. But further statements to the same effect were made whenever persons did business with the respondent on the strength of the uncorrected brochure, which so far from being withdrawn continued to be the basis on which the respondent was inviting business. There is no injustice in this being the effect of the statute. If the respondent believed that there was no default on its part when the false description was communicated to Mr Wade, it should have admitted that the offence was committed and called evidence to establish a s 23 or s 24 defence. Instead, the respondent chose to argue that no offence had been committed at all, an argument which for reasons I have given, I believe to be unsustainable.

Accordingly I hold that the respondent company did make a statement as to the air-conditioning to Mr Wade on 13 January 1982. This conclusion renders it unnecessary to deal with the ingenious, if far-fetched, analogy which the respondent sought to draw between this case and your Lordships' analysis of a 'result crime' in the arson case of *R v Miller* [p 23, above], and which found favour with the Divisional Court. I will say only that to construe the words 'to make a statement which he knows to be false' in the context of this Act as being capable of covering a physical act of statement completed or perfected at a later date by a damaging result when it is read appears to me to be an unhelpful and over-elaborate approach to the interpretation of an Act intended to protect the public by provisions which the public can understand without a lawyer at their elbow. Making a statement consists of the act of statement. If it has consequences, so be it; the consequences are not the statement.

For these reasons I would make answer to the certified point of law as follows. A statement which was false was made by the respondent company in the course of its business when it was read by Mr Wade, an interested member of the public doing business with the respondent company on the basis of the statement. The offence was committed on that occasion because the respondent company then knew that it was false to state that the hotel accommodation was air-conditioned. The fact that the respondent was unaware of the falsity of the statement when it was published as part of the brochure in May 1981 is irrelevant. If the respondent believed it was innocent of fault, it was open to it to prove lack of fault. It did not do so.

Like my noble and learned friend Lord Brandon (whose speech in draft I have had the opportunity of reading), I cannot think, though I understand the genuine difficulties which faced the respondent, that it was improper to prosecute in this case

I would allow the appeal.

[In allowing the appeal **Lord Hailsham** said that he had great sympathy with the defendant in that it was guilty of an offence which any ordinary reader would think was fraudulent when it was not; and with the Divisional Court in striving to avoid what it called ('not without reason') an absurdity. **Lord Brandon**, allowing the appeal, said that the statement in the brochure was one that continued to be made so long as it continued in circulation without effective correction.]

Appeal allowed

Questions

1. Was it reasonable to construe the section so that s 14 (1) (a) imposes strict liability (subject to the statutory defence) whereas s 14 (1) (b) requires recklessness? See G. Stephenson and R. Taylor, 48 MLR 340.

2. Cf *Jakeman*, p 10, above. Suppose the defendant had despatched the suitcases from Accra, not knowing that they contained cannabis but had learned this fact while the plane was in flight. Would she have been 'knowingly concerned' in the fraudulent importation of the drug?

Alphacell Ltd v Woodward [1972] AC 824, House of Lords
(Lord Wilberforce, Viscount Dilhorne, Lord Pearson, Lord Cross of Chelsea and Lord Salmon)

The appellant's business involved the washing of manilla fibres in water which was thereby polluted. The polluted water was piped to two settling tanks on the river bank. In the tanks were two pumps, designed to prevent overflow into the river, which sucked the water into a reservoir so that it could be re-used. If the tanks did overflow, the polluted water went into the river via a channel provided for that purpose. The pumps were inspected each weekend. The pumps became obstructed by brambles, ferns and leaves. Consequently the tanks overflowed into the river. The appellants were convicted of causing polluted matter to enter the river contrary to s 2(1) of the Rivers (Prevention of Pollution) Act 1951. The justices made no finding that the appellants knew of the overflow or that they had been negligent. The conviction was upheld by the Divisional Court (Bridge J dissenting).

Lord Wilberforce. . . . .In my opinion, 'causing' here must be given a common sense meaning and I deprecate the introduction of refinements, such as causa causans, effective cause or novus actus. There may be difficulties where acts of third persons or natural forces are concerned but I find the present case comparatively simple. The appellants abstract water, pass it through their works where it becomes polluted, conduct it to a settling tank communicating directly with the stream, into which the polluted water will inevitably overflow if the level rises over the overflow point. They plan, however, to recycle the water by pumping it back from the settling tank into their works; if the pumps work properly this will happen and the level in the tank will remain below the overflow point. It did not happen on the relevant occasion due to some failure in the pumps.

In my opinion, this is a clear case of causing the polluted water to enter the stream. The whole complex operation which might lead to this result was an operation deliberately conducted by the appellants and I fail to see how a defect in one stage of it, even if we must assume that this happened without their negligence, can enable them to say they did not cause the pollution. In my opinion, complication of this case by infusion of the concept of mens rea, and its exceptions, is unnecessary and undesirable. The section is clear, its application plain. I agree with the majority of the Divisional Court [[1972] 1 QB 127; [1971] 2 All ER 910] who upheld the conviction, except that rather than say that the actions of the appellants were *a cause* of the pollution I think it more accurate to say that the appellants caused the polluting matter to enter the stream. . .

The actual question submitted to this House under the Administration of Justice Act 1960, s 1 (2) is:

> 'Whether the offence of causing polluting matter to enter a stream contrary to section 2 of the Rivers (Prevention of Pollution) Act 1951 can be committed by a person who has no knowledge of the fact that polluting matter is entering the stream and has not been negligent in any relevant respect.'

The answer to this, I suggest, should be 'Yes', it being understood that the test is whether the person concerned caused or knowingly permitted the poisonous, noxious or polluting matter to enter the stream. As, in my opinion, the appellant did so cause, I would dismiss the appeal.

[Viscount Dilhorne and **Lords Pearson** and **Cross of Chelsea** made speeches dismissing the appeal.]

Lord Salmon. . . . . The appellants clearly did not cause the pollution intentionally and we must assume that they did not do so negligently. Nevertheless, the facts, so fully and clearly stated by my noble and learned friend, Viscount Dilhorne, to my mind make it obvious that the appellants in fact caused the pollution. If they did not cause it, what did? There was no intervening act of a third party nor was there any act of God to which it could be attributed. The appellants had been responsible for the design of the plant; everything within their works was under their control; they had chosen all the equipment. The process which they operated required contaminated effluent being pumped round their works until it came to rest in an open tank which they sited on the river bank. If the pumps which they had installed in this tank failed to operate efficiently the effluent would necessarily overflow into the river. And that is what occured. It seems plain to me that the appellants caused the pollution by the active operation of their plant. They certainly did not intend to cause pollution but they intended to do acts which caused it. What they did was something different in kind from the passive storing of effluent which could not discharge into the river save by an act of God or, as in *Impress (Worcester) Ltd v Rees*, by the active intervention of a stranger, the risk of which could not reasonably have been foreseen. . . .

The appellants contend that even if they caused the pollution still they should succeed since they did not cause it intentionally or knowingly or negligently. Section 2 (1) (a) of the Rivers (Prevention of Pollution) Act 1951 is undoubtedly a penal section. It follows that if it is capable of two or more meanings then the meaning most favourable to the subject should be adopted. Accordingly, so the argument runs, the words 'intentionally or 'knowingly' or 'negligently' should be read into the section immediately before the word 'causes'. I do not agree. It is of the utmost public importance that our rivers should not be polluted. The risk of pollution, particularly from the vast and increasing number of riparian industries, is very great. The offences created by the 1951 Act seem to me to be prototypes of offences which 'are not criminal in any real sense, but acts which in the public interest are prohibited under a penalty': *Sherras v De Rutzen* [[1895] 1 QB 918 at 922; [1895–99] All ER Rep 1167 at 1169] per Wright J referred to with approval by my noble and learned friends, Lord Reid and Lord Diplock, in *Sweet v Parsley* [p 115, above]. I can see no valid reason for reading the word 'intentionally', 'knowingly' or 'negligently' into s 2 (1) (a) and a number of cogent reasons for not doing so. In the case of a minor pollution such as the present, when the justices find that there is no wrongful intention or negligence on the part of the defendant, a comparatively nominal fine will no doubt be imposed. This may be regarded as a not unfair hazard of carrying on a business which may cause pollution on the banks of a river. The present appellants were fined £20 and ordered to pay in all £24 costs. I should be surprised if the costs of pursuing this appeal to this House were incurred to the purpose of saving these appellants £43.

If this appeal succeeded and it were held to be the law that no conviction could be obtained under the 1951 Act unless the prosecution could discharge the often impossible onus of proving that the pollution was caused intentionally or negligently, a great deal of pollution would go unpunished and undeterred to the relief of many riparian factory owners. As a result, many rivers which are now filthy would become filthier still and many rivers which are now clean would lose their cleanliness. The legislature no doubt recognised that as a matter of public policy this would be most unfortunate. Hence s 2 (1) (a) which encourages riparian factory owners not only to take reasonable steps to prevent pollution but to do everything possible to ensure that they do not cause it.

Appeal dismissed

Questions

1. Viscount Dilhorne, like Lord Salmon, thought the Act dealt with acts 'not criminal in any real sense'. Is it possible to distinguish between 'real crimes' and 'quasi-crimes'? Does Parliament make any such distinction? Cf *Warner v Metropolitan Police Comr*, p 110, above.
2. A repetition or continuation of an offence under s 2 (1) is punishable with six months imprisonment. If D, who has a previous conviction, is charged with another offence under the Act, is it still 'not criminal in any real sense'?
3. Should the criminal law require a person to do more than is reasonable to prevent a particular harm occurring?
4. Lord Pearson pointed out: 'There was no intervening act of a trespasser and no act of God. There was not even any unusual weather or freak of nature.' Lord Cross also appears to have thought the decision might have been different if there had been such evidence. Why?

5. R.W.L. Howells (35 MLR p 663) writes:

> 'The appellants' contention was, in essence that having set up a system which would, in ordinary circumstances, prevent pollution, they were entitled to provide a "second line" system for the disposal of their effluent into the river, in the event of an unforeseen failure of their "first line" system. Disposal into the river would be, at the same time, the simplest and cheapest for them, as well as the very activity the Act was designed to prevent. An alternative, but obviously less convenient, "second line" system would have been one that provided for the automatic stopping of their operation whenever their effluent recovery system failed. But it was obviously far more economic for the company, in the event of a pump failure, to continue their operations, and to take their chance with a plea that they had not "caused" pollution within section 2 (a) when their effluent had emptied itself into the river.'

Looked at this way, might it be said that the appellants had *intentionally* caused the pollution?—The provision of the channel into the river showed that, in a certain event, which they thought to be unlikely and hoped to prevent, they intended the effluent to flow into the river. A conditional intention is still intention. Was the case then, one of strict liability?

5. Liability without an act

The cases so far considered in this chapter all involved the commission of an act by the defendant. But Parliament can do anything and has occasionally enacted that a person may be liable because something happens to him in certain circumstances—ie, he 'is found' in a particular situation.

R v Larsonneur (1933) 97 JP 206, Court of Criminal Appeal
(Lord Hewart CJ, Avory and Humphreys JJ)

On 14 March 1933, the appellant, who was a French citizen, landed at Folkestone with a French passport, which was endorsed 'Leave to land granted at Folkestone this day on condition that the holder does not enter any employment, paid or unpaid, while in the United Kingdom.' On 22 March 1933, the condition was varied by the following endorsement signed by an Under-Secretary of State: 'The condition attached to the grant of leave to land is hereby varied so as to require departure from the United Kingdom not later than the 22nd March 1933.'

The appellant went on that day to the Irish Free State. An order for her deportation therefrom was made by the executive authorities of that country, and on 20 April she was brought to Holyhead in the custody of the Irish Free State police. There she was handed over to the Holyhead police and detained by them until the arrival of a police officer from London. On the following day she was taken to London in custody, and on 22 April she was charged before a police magistrate there.

At the trial, on a charge under art 18 (1) (b) of the Aliens Order 1920 (below) the jury returned a verdict of 'Guilty through circumstances beyond her own control', and the Chairman passed a sentence of three days' imprisonment and made an order recommending the appellant for deportation.

By the Aliens Order 1920, art 1 (3): 'Leave shall not be given to an alien to land in the United Kingdom unless he complies with the following conditions, that is to say . . . (g) he has not been prohibited from landing by the Secretary of State.'

By art 1 (4), as amended by SR & O No 326 of 1923, and No 715 of 1931: '. . . an alien who is found in the United Kingdom at any time after the expiration of the period limited by any such condition shall for the purposes of this Order be deemed to be an alien to whom leave to land has been refused. . . .'

By art 18 (1) (b), as amended by SR & O No 326 of 1923: 'If any alien, having landed in the United Kingdom in contravention of art 1 of this Order, is at at any time found within the United Kingdom, he shall be guilty of an offence against this Order.'

The judgment of the Court was delivered by

Lord Hewart CJ. In fact, the appellant went to the Irish Free State and afterwards, in circumstances which are perfectly immaterial, so far as this appeal is concerned, came back, to Holyhead. She was at Holyhead on 21 April 1933, practically a month after the day limited by the condition on her passport.

In these circumstances, it seems to be quite clear that art 1(4) of the Aliens Order 1920 (as varied by the Orders of 1923 and 1931), applies. The appellant was, therefore, on 21 April 1933, in the position in which she would have been if she had been prohibited from landing by the Secretary of State and, that being so, there is no reason to interfere with the finding of the jury. She was found here and was, therefore, deemed to be in the class of persons whose landing had been prohibited by the Secretary of State, by reason of the fact that she had violated the condition on her passport. The appeal, therefore, is dismissed and the recommendation for deportation remains.

Appeal dismissed

Questions

Did the offence consist in 'being found' or in 'landing and being found'? If the latter, was the court justified in saying that the circumstances in which Larsonneur came back to Holyhead were 'perfectly immaterial'? 'Being found' may not require a voluntary act on the part of the accused, but is that also true of 'landing'?

Larsonneur no longer stands alone. In *Winzar v Chief Constable of Kent* (1983) Times, 28 March, D was taken to hospital on a stretcher but was found to be drunk and told to leave. When he was seen slumped on a seat in the corridor the police were called and they took him to a police car parked in the hospital forecourt on W Road and drove him to the police station. He was convicted of being found drunk in a highway, W Road, and his conviction was upheld by the Divisional Court. 'Found drunk' meant perceived to be drunk. It was enough that he was present in a highway and there perceived to be drunk. 'Perceive' means to become aware of. Did the police become aware of D's state in the highway? Or in the hospital or its forecourt?

Larsonneur has been generally condemned by the writers but it is defended by D.J. Lanham [1976] Crim LR 276. He considers why the accused should have been denied the 'most readily acceptable' of all defences, physical compulsion.

Clear though compulsion may be as a defence it is, unlike infancy, not an absolute defence. It may, at least with regard to certain types of crime, be defeated if the defendant has been at fault in bringing about the situation which has exposed him to compulsion. An authority for this proposition is the Australian case *O'Sullivan v Fisher*.[1] D was in effect charged with being found drunk in a public place. He had been forced from private premises into a public place by police officers. Reed J accepted that the offence charged was strict in the sense that it was not necessary to prove that D intended to get drunk or to be in the public place. The learned judge ruled however that compulsion [2] was capable of being a defence. His Honour considered three types of case:

(a) where the defendant was forced into the public place by unlawful force;
(b) where the defendant was arrested and taken into the public place;
(c) where the defendant was ejected from the private place by lawful force.

In the first two cases the judge thought that compulsion would be a defence. In the third case compulsion would provide no excuse.

The first and third cases are clear. If a man gets drunk in his own house and is kidnapped by terrorists and taken into the street there can be no possible justification for denying him the defence of compulsion. If a man trespasses in his neighbour's house and drinks himself silly he cannot plead compulsion if his neighbour lawfully decants him into the street. Case (b) however may need qualification. If the defendant is drunk in his own house and is unexpectedly arrested there by the police and is taken into the street he should have the defence whether he is guilty of the crime for which the arrest is made or not. But if the defendant is on the run from the police and gets himself drunk on private premises when his arrest is imminent, he should not be able to rely on the defence.

Though Reed J did not express himself in these terms it is suggested that the principle which emerges from the case of *O'Sullivan v Fisher* is that in cases of strict liability a person can rely on the defence of compulsion unless he has culpably brought about the situation in which the compulsion was used. He will, for example, lose the defence if the compulsion was reasonably foreseeable.

1. [1954] SASR 33.
2. The term 'duress' was used in the case. The line between duress and physical compulsion is a thin one and the distinction between the defences is irrelevant for present purposes.

Having examined the evidence in the case. Professor Lanham concludes that Larsonneur brought upon herself the act of compulsion which led to her being charged.

No one could claim that *Larsonneur* stood as a shining example of English jurisprudence. But it can hardly be regarded as the last word in judicial depravity. If Miss Larsonneur had been dragged kicking and screaming from France into the United Kingdom by kidnappers and the same judgment had been given by the Court of Criminal Appeal, the defence of unforeseeable compulsion would truly have been excluded and the case would be the worst blot on the pages of the modern criminal law. But she wasn't and it wasn't and it isn't.

6. A Canadian approach

R v City of Sault Ste Marie (1978) 85 DLR (3d) 161, 40 CCC (2d) 353, Supreme Court of Canada
(Laskin CJC, Maitland, Ritchie, Spence, Pigeon, Dickson, Beetz, Estey and Pratte JJ)

The defendant was convicted of an offence contrary to s 32(1) of the Ontario Water Resources Act, RSO 1970, c 332, of discharging, causing to be discharged, or permitting to be discharged or deposited materials into a body of water or on the shore or bank thereof, or in such place that might impair the quality of the water. The defendant had entered into an agreement with a private company for the disposal of the city's garbage and as a result of the manner of disposal of the garbage nearby bodies of water were polluted. The Divisional Court quashed the conviction on the ground (inter alia) that the offence of causing or permitting a discharge requires proof of mens rea. On further appeal the Ontario Court of Appeal agreed with the Divisional Court on the issue of mens rea, the majority holding that there was insufficient evidence of mens rea to uphold the conviction. On further appeal by the Crown and the accused to the Supreme Court of Canada, held, the appeals should be dismissed and a new trial ordered.

[The judgment of the Court was delivered by **Dickson J:**]

The mens rea point

The distinction between the true criminal offence and the public welfare offence is one of prime importance. Where the offence is criminal, the Crown must establish a mental element, namely, that the accused who committed the prohibited act did so intentionally or recklessly, with knowledge of the facts constituting the offence, or with wilful blindness toward them. Mere negligence is excluded from the concept of the mental element required for conviction. Within the context of a criminal prosecution a person who fails to make such inquiries as a reasonable and prudent person would make, or who fails to know facts he should have known, is innocent in the eyes of the law.

In sharp contrast, 'absolute liability' entails conviction on proof merely that the defendant committed the prohibited act constituting the actus reus of the offence. There is no relevant mental element. It is no defence that the accused was entirely without fault. He may be morally innocent in every sense, yet be branded as a malefactor and punished as such.

Public welfare offences obviously lie in a field of conflicting values. It is essential for society to maintain, through effective enforcement, high standards of public health and safety. Potential victims of those who carry on latently pernicious activities have a strong claim to consideration. On the other hand, there is a generally held revulsion against punishment of the morally innocent.

Public welfare offences evolved in mid-19th century Britain (*Woodrow* (1846) 15 M & W 404, and *Stephens* (1866) LR 1 QB 702) as a means of doing away with the requirement of mens rea for petty police offences. The concept was a judicial creation, founded on expediency. That concept is now firmly embedded in the concrete of Anglo-American and Canadian jurisprudence, its importance heightened by the ever-increasing complexities of modern society.

Various arguments are advanced in justification of absolute liability in public welfare offences. Two predominate. Firstly, it is argued that the protection of social interests requires a high standard of care and attention on the part of those who follow certain pursuits and such persons are more likely to be stimulated to maintain those standards if they know that ignorance or mistake will not excuse them. The removal of any possible loophole acts, it is said, as an incentive to take precautionary measures beyond what would otherwise be taken, in order that mistakes and mishaps be avoided. The second main argument is one based on administrative efficiency. Having regard to both the difficulty of proving mental culpability and the number of petty cases which daily come before the Courts, proof of fault is just too great a burden in time and money to place upon the prosecution. To require proof of each person's individual intent would allow almost every violator to escape. This, together with the glut of work entailed in proving mens rea in every case would clutter the docket, and impede adequate enforcement as virtually to nullify the regulatory statutes. In short, absolute liability, it is contended, is the most efficient and effective way of ensuring compliance with minor regulatory legislation and the social ends to be achieved are of such importance as to override the unfortunate by-product of punishing those who may be free of moral turpitude. In further justification, it is urged that slight penalties are usually imposed and that conviction for breach of a public welfare offence does not carry the stigma associated with conviction for a criminal offence.

Arguments of greater force are advanced against absolute liability. The most telling is that it violates fundamental principles of penal liability. It also rests upon assumptions which have not been, and cannot be, empirically established. There is no evidence that a higher standard of care results from absolute liability. If a person is already taking every reasonable precautionary measure, is he likely to take additional measures, knowing that however much care he takes, it will not serve as a defence in the event of breach? If he has exercised care and skill, will conviction have a deterrent effect upon him or others? Will the injustice of conviction lead to cynicism and disrespect for the law, on his part and on the part of others? These are among the questions asked. The argument that no stigma attaches does not withstand analysis, for the accused will have suffered loss of time, legal costs, exposure to the processes of the criminal law at trial and, however one may downplay it, the opprobrium of conviction. It is not sufficient to say that the public interest is engaged and, therefore, liability may be imposed without fault. In serious crimes, the public interest is involved and mens rea must be proven. The administrative argument has little force. In sentencing, evidence of due diligence is admissible and therefore the evidence might just as well be heard when considering guilt . . .

Public welfare offences involve a shift of emphasis from the protection of individual interests to the protection of public and social interests . . . The unfortunate tendency in many past cases has been to see the choice as between two stark alternatives: (i) full mens rea or (ii) absolute liability. In respect of public welfare offences (within which category pollution offences fall) where full mens rea is not required, absolute liability has often been imposed. English jurisprudence has consistently maintained this dichotomy: see 'Criminal Law, Evidence and Procedure', 11 Hals, 4th edn, pp 20-2, para 18. There has, however, been an attempt in Australia, in many Canadian Courts, and indeed in England to seek a middle position, fulfilling the goals of public welfare offences while still not punishing the entirely blameless. There is an increasing and impressive stream of authority which holds that where an offence does not require full mens rea it is nevertheless a good defence for the defendant to prove that he was not negligent. . . .

There is nothing in *Woolmington's* case, as I comprehend it, which stands in the way of adoption, in respect of regulatory offences, of a defence of due care, with burden of proof resting on the accused to establish the defence on the balance of probabilities.

It may be suggested that the introduction of a defence based on due diligence and the shifting of the burden of proof might better be implemented by legislative act. In answer, it should be recalled that the concept of absolute liability and the creation of a jural category of public welfare offences are both the product of the judiciary and not of the Legislature. The development to date of this defence, in the numerous decisions I have referred to, of Courts in this country as well as in Australia and New Zealand, has also been the work of Judges. The present case offers the opportunity of consolidating and clarifying the doctrine.

The correct approach, in my opinion, is to relieve the Crown of the burden of proving mens rea, having regard to *Pierce Fisheries* and to the virtual impossibility in most regulatory cases of proving wrongful intention. In a normal case, the accused alone will have knowledge of what he has done to avoid the breach and it is not improper to expect him to come forward with the evidence of due diligence. This is particularly so when it is alleged, for example, that pollution was caused by the activities of a large and complex corporation. Equally, there is nothing wrong with rejecting absolute liability and admitting the defence of reasonable care.

In this doctrine it is not up to the prosecution to prove negligence. Instead, it is open to the defendant to prove that all due care has been taken. This burden falls upon the defendant as he is the only one who will generally have the means of proof. This would not seem unfair as the alternative is absolute liability which denies an accused any defence whatsoever. While the prosecution must prove beyond a reasonable doubt that the defendant committed the prohibited act, the defendant must only establish on the balance of probabilities that he has a defence of reasonable care.

I conclude, for the reasons which I have sought to express, that there are compelling grounds for the recognition of three categories of offences rather than the traditional two:

1. Offences in which mens rea, consisting of some positive state of mind such as intent, knowledge, or recklessness, must be proved by the prosecution either as an inference from the nature of the act committed, or by additional evidence.

2. Offences in which there is no necessity for the prosecution to prove the existence of mens rea; the doing of the prohibited act prima facie imports the offence, leaving it open to the accused to avoid liability by proving that he took all reasonable care. This involves consideration of what a reasonable man would have done in the circumstances. The defence will be available if the accused reasonably believed in a mistaken set of facts which, if true, would render the act or omission innocent, or if he took all reasonable steps to avoid the particular event. These offences may properly be called offences of strict liability. Mr. Justice Estey so referred to them in *Hickey's* case.

3. Offences of absolute liability where it is not open to the accused to exculpate himself by showing that he was free of fault.

Offences which are criminal in the true sense fall in the first category. Public welfare offences would, prima facie, be in the second category. They are not subject to the presumption of full mens rea. An offence of this type would fall in the first category only if such words as 'wilfully', 'with intent', 'knowingly', or 'intentionally' are contained in the statutory provision creating the offence. On the other hand, the principle that punishment should in general not be inflicted on those without fault applies. Offences of absolute liability would be those in respect of which the Legislature had made it clear that guilt would follow proof merely of the proscribed act. The over-all regulatory pattern adopted by the Legislature, the subject-matter of the legislation, the importance of the penalty, and the precision of the language used will be primary considerations in determining whether the offence falls into the third category.

7. Which way ahead?

The draft Criminal Code Bill provides:

24 General requirement of fault

(1) Unless a contrary intention appears, a person does not commit a Code offence unless he acts intentionally, knowingly or recklessly in respect of each of its elements other than fault elements.

(2) A contrary intention appears in relation to an element only if the terms of the enactment creating the offence indicate:

  (a) that some other fault is required in respect of that element; or

  (b) that no fault is required in respect of that element; or

  (c) that a person does not commit the offence if in relation to that element he has or does not have a specified state of mind or complies with a specified standard of conduct.

The Report on Codification explains the clause as follows:

Clause 24: General requirement of fault

8.29 *The need for the clause.*   A provision creating an offence should ordinarily specify the fault required for the offence or expressly provide that the offence is one of strict liability in respect of one or more identified elements. Cf Law Com No 89, para 75. It is necessary, however, to have a general rule for the interpretation of any offence the definition of which does not state, in respect of one or more elements, whether fault is required or what degree of fault is required. The absence of a consistent rule of interpretation has been a regrettable source of uncertainty in English law. This clause provides such a rule.

8.30 *Application of the clause.*   The clause (like clause 22) applies only to Code offences, so as not to disturb the settled interpretation or understanding of existing legislation.

8.31 *Clause 24(1).*   This subsection produces the same result as clause 5 (2) and (3) of the draft Bill [The draft Bill appended to Law Com No 89] (though it does so in simpler style). It imposes a presumption, in respect of every element of an offence, that liability depends upon fault of the degree of recklessness at least. That presumption is no doubt more controversial now than it was in 1978, when Law Com No 89 was published. For since that time some offences requiring at least 'recklessness' for their commission have been so interpreted that heedlessness (as it is defined in clause 22) will suffice. [See para 8.19]. If Parliament, when the Code is enacted, considers that that interpretation achieved an appropriate scope for the serious offences to which it applied, it may, consistently, wish in this clause to specify heedlessness as the presumed fault requirement for the future. That is a point for others to consider. There is no need for purposes of the present draft to depart from the Law Commission's recommendation.

8.32 *Drafting.*   The subsection refers to three degrees of fault (intention, knowledge, recklessness) in the alternative. Since a requirement of recklessness will be satisfied by intention or knowledge (clause 23 (2)), the subsection could refer to recklessness alone. The method adopted, however, is justified on the score of clarity. Moreover, the definition of any offence to which the subsection applies will thus refer to the alternative modes of fault; and this will permit any of the alternatives to be alleged in a particular case.

8.33 *Clause 24 (2).*   This subsection follows clause 5 (4) of the draft Bill in specifying how the application of subsection (1) may be excluded. Hitherto the courts have relied upon a wide and varying range of considerations as a basis for inferring Parliament's intention. Those considerations have included, for example, the nature of the offence itself and the size of the available penalty. The resulting uncertainty has been a notorious feature of the criminal law [Cf Law Com No 89, paras 29–39]; and the intention which is said to be divined by the judicial process has often been one that could only rhetorically be attributed to Parliament. Under subsections (1) and (2), by contrast, it will be possible to refer more accurately to 'the intention of Parliament' and to identify that intention without difficulty. The provision creating an offence will normally state expressly, for every element of an offence, what fault is required for liability, or that no fault is required (strict liability), or that liability is excluded in certain circumstances relevant to fault. Failing such express provision, or some other indication of like effect, the presumption stated by subsection (1) will apply. Our draft (perhaps more clearly than the draft Bill) permits 'the terms of the enactment creating the offence' to 'indicate' the exclusion of subsection (1). This admits reference to the statutory context of the particular provision concerned; a contrast between adjacent sections of an Act, for example, or between different parts of the same section, might exceptionally 'indicate' quite plainly the intended meaning of one of them. But only the 'terms' of the enactment are admissible aids for this purpose.

Crime and The Criminal Law by Barbara Wootton

Nothing has dealt so devastating a blow at the punitive conception of the criminal process as the proliferation of offences of strict liability; and the alarm has forthwith been raised. Thus Dr J.Ll. J. Edwards has expressed the fear that there is a real danger that the 'widespread practice of imposing criminal liability independent of any moral fault' will result in the criminal law being regarded with contempt. 'The process of basing criminal liability upon a theory of absolute prohibition', he writes, 'may well have the opposite effect to that intended and lead to a weakening of respect for the law' [Edwards, J.Ll.J., *Mens Rea in Statutory Offences* (Macmillan) 1955, p 247]. Nor, in his view, is it an adequate answer to say that absolute liability can be tolerated because of the comparative unimportance of the offences to which it is applied and because, as a rule, only a monetary penalty is involved; for, in the first place, there are a number of important exceptions to this rule (drunken driving for example); and, secondly, as Dr Edwards himself points out, in certain cases the penalty imposed by the court may be the least part of the punishment. A merchant's conviction for a minor trading offence may have a disastrous effect upon his business.

Such dislike of strict liability is not by any means confined to academic lawyers. In the courts, too, various devices have been used to smuggle mens rea back into offences from which, on the face of it, it would appear to be excluded. To the lawyer's ingenious mind the invention of such devices naturally presents no difficulty. Criminal liability, for instance, can attach only to voluntary acts. If a driver is struck unconscious with an epileptic seizure, it can be argued that he is not responsible for any consequences because his driving thereafter is involuntary: indeed he has been said not to be driving at all. If on the other hand he falls asleep, this defence will not serve since sleep is a condition that comes on gradually, and a driver has an opportunity and a duty to stop before it overpowers him. Alternatively, recourse can be had to the circular argument that anyone who commits a forbidden act must have intended to commit it and must, therefore, have formed a guilty intention. As Lord Devlin puts it, the word 'knowingly' or 'wilfully' can be read into acts in which it is not present; although as his Lordship points out this subterfuge is open to the criticism that it fails to distinguish between the physical act itself and the circumstances in which this becomes a crime [Devlin, Lord, *Samples of Law Making* (OUP, 1962) pp 71–80, p 109, above]. All that the accused may have intended was to perform an action (such as firing a gun or driving a car) which is not in itself criminal. Again, in yet other cases such as those in which it is forbidden to permit or to allow something to be done the concept of negligence can do duty as a watered down version of mens rea for how can anyone be blamed for permitting something about which he could not have known?

All these devices, it cannot be too strongly emphasised, are necessitated by the need to preserve the essentially punitive function of the criminal law. For it is not, as Dr Edwards fears, the criminal law which will be brought into contempt by the multiplication of offences of strict liability, so much as this particular conception of the law's function. If that function is conceived less in terms of punishment than as a mechanism of prevention these fears become irrelevant. Such a conception, however, apparently sticks in the throat of even the most progressive lawyers. Even Professor Hart, in his Hobhouse lecture on *Punishment and the Elimination of Responsibility* [Hart, H.L.A., *Punishment and the Elimination of Responsibility* (Athlone Press 1962) pp 27, 28.] seems to be incurably obsessed with the notion of punishment, which haunts his text as well as figuring in his title. Although rejecting many traditional theories, such as that punishment should be 'retributive' or 'denunciatory', he nevertheless seems wholly unable to envisage a system in which sentence is not automatically equated with 'punishment'. Thus he writes of 'values quite distinct from those of retributive punishment which the system of responsibility does maintain, and which remain of great importance even if our aims in *punishing* are the forward-looking aims of social protection'; and again 'even if we *punish* men not as wicked but as nuisances . . .' while he makes many references to the principle that liability to punishment must depend on a voluntary act. Perhaps it requires the naivete of an amateur to suggest that the forward-looking aims of social protection might, on occasion, have absolutely no connection with punishment.

If, however, the primary function of the courts is conceived as the prevention of forbidden acts, there is little cause to be disturbed by the multiplication of offences of strict liability. If the law says that certain things are not to be done, it is illogical to confine this prohibition to occasions on which they are done from malice aforethought; for at least the material consequences of an action, and the reasons for prohibiting it, are the same whether it is the result of sinister malicious plotting, of negligence or of sheer accident. A man is equally dead and his relatives equally bereaved whether he was stabbed or run over by a drunken motorist or by an incompetent one; and the inconvenience caused by the loss of your bicycle is unaffected by the question whether or no the youth who removed it had the intention of putting it back, if in fact he had not done so at the time of his arrest. It is true, of course, as Professor Hart has argued [op cit, pp 29,30], that the material consequences of an action by no means exhaust its effects. 'If one person hits another, the person struck does not think of the other as *just* a cause of pain to him . . . If the blow was light but deliberate, it has a significance for the person struck quite different from an accidental much heavier blow.' To ignore this difference, he argues, is to outrage 'distinctions which not only underlie morality, but pervade the whole of our social life'. That these distinctions are widely appreciated and keenly felt no one would deny. Often perhaps they derive their force from a purely punitive or retributive attitude; but alternatively they may be held to be relevant to an assessment of the social damage that results from a criminal act. Just as a heavy blow does more damage than a light one, so also perhaps does a blow which involves psychological injury do more damage than one in which the hurt is purely physical.

The conclusion to which this argument leads is, I think, not that the presence or absence of the guilty mind is unimportant, but that mens rea has, so to speak—and this is the crux of the matter—*got into the wrong place*. Traditionally, the requirement of the guilty mind is written into the actual definition of a crime. No guilty intention, no crime, is the rule. Obviously this makes sense if the law's concern is with wickedness: where there is no guilty intention, there can be no wickedness. But it is equally obvious, on the other hand, that an action does not become innocuous merely because whoever performed it meant no harm. If the object of the criminal law is to prevent the occurrence of socially damaging actions, it would be absurd to turn a blind eye to those which were due to carelessness, negligence or even accident. The question of motivation is *in the first instance* irrelevant.

But only in the first instance. At a later stage, that is to say, after what is now known as a conviction, the presence or absence of guilty intention is all-important for its effect on the appropriate measures to be taken to prevent a recurrence of the forbidden act. The prevention of accidental deaths presents different problems from those involved in the prevention of wilful murders. The results of the actions of the careless, the mistaken, the wicked and the merely unfortunate may be indistinguishable from one another, but each case calls for a different treatment. Tradition, however, is very strong, and the notion that these differences are relevant only after the fact has been established that the accused committed the forbidden act seems still to be deeply abhorrent to the legal mind. Thus Lord Devlin, discussing the possibility that judges might have taken the line that all 'unintentional' criminals might be dealt with simply by the imposition of a nominal penalty, regards this as the 'negation of law'. 'It would', [Devlin, Lord, *Samples of Law Making* (OUP, 1962) p 73] he says, 'confuse the function of mercy which the judge is dispensing when imposing the penalty with the function of justice. It would have been to deny to the citizen due process of law because it would have been to say to him, in effect: "Although we cannot think that Parliament intended you to be punished in this case because you have really done nothing wrong, come to us, ask for mercy, and we shall grant mercy" . . . . In all criminal matters the citizen is entitled to the protection of the law . . . and the mitigation of penalty should not be adopted as the prime method of dealing with accidental offenders.'

Within its own implied terms of reference the logic is unexceptionable. If the purpose of the law is to dispense punishment tempered with mercy, then to use mercy as a consolation for unjust punishment is certainly to give a stone for bread. But these are not the implied terms of reference of strict liability. In the case of offences of strict liability the presumption is not that those who have committed forbidden actions must be punished, but that appropriate steps must be taken to prevent the occurrence of such actions.

Question

Do you prefer Lady Wootton's way forward or that embodied in the draft Criminal Code? For a criticism of Lady Wootton's views, see J.C. Smith, 'Responsibility in Criminal Law', in Barbara Wootton, *Essays in Her Honour* (ed Bean and Whynes, 1986), p 141.

CHAPTER 8

Parties to offences

1. Principals

The draft Criminal Code Bill provides:

29 Parties to offences
A person may be guilty of an offence as a principal or as an accessory.

30 Principals
(1) A person is guilty of an offence as a principal if, with the fault required for the offence, he:
(a) does the act or acts specified for the offence; or
(b) does at least one such act, any other such acts being done by another.
(2) For the purposes of subsection (1), a person does an act not only when he does it himself but also when:
(a) an act of another is attributed to him under section 33; or
(b) he does the act by an innocent agent, that is, by one whom he procures, assists or encourages to do it and who is not guilty of the offence because:
  (i) he is under ten years of age; or
  (ii) he is suffering from mental disorder; or
  (iii) he does the act without the fault required for the offence; or
  (iv) he has a defence.
(3) A person is not guilty of an offence as a principal by reason of an act that he does by an innocent agent if:
(a) the offence can be committed only by a person complying with a particular description which does not apply to him; or
(b) the offence is defined in terms implying that that act must be done by the offender personally;
and a person who is not guilty of an offence as a principal by virtue only of this subsection is guilty of that offence as an accessory.

Schedule 1 of the draft Bill provides the following illustrations:

30 (1)(a)	30 (i)	It is an offence (robbery) for a person to steal, using force or the threat of force in order to do so. D orders P, a wages clerk, to drop the money he is carrying and threatens to use violence if P does not obey. P drops the money and D takes it. D is guilty of robbery as a principal.
30 (1)(b)	30 (ii)	As in illustration 30 (i) except that the money is taken by E acting in concert with D. D and E are guilty of robbery as principals.
30 (2)(a) and **33 (b)**	30 (iii)	It is made a Code offence for a person to sell to the prejudice of the purchaser any food which is not of the nature or quality demanded by the purchaser. No fault is required for this offence. E, an assistant in D's shop, sells a mouldy pie to P. D and E are guilty of the offence as principals.
30 (2)(b)	30 (iv)	It is offence (burglary) for a person to enter a building as a trespasser with intent to steal therein. D instructs his son E, aged nine, to climb through a window of a house and take some jewellery. E does so while D keeps watch outside. E is not guilty of burglary because he is under ten years of age (s 36). D is guilty of burglary as a principal.
	30 (v)	D encourages E to trip up P. D knows, but E does not, that P suffers from a bone condition which makes him peculiarly vulnerable to

fractures. D intends that P shall break his leg. E foresees only that P may be cut or bruised by the fall. E trips P who breaks his leg in the fall. E is guilty of recklessly causing injury (s 76), but is not guilty of the more serious offences under sections 74 and 75 since he lacks both intention and recklessness in respect of the causing of serious injury. D is guilty as a principal of intentionally causing serious injury.

30 (3)(a)   30 (vi)   It is an offence for a licensee knowingly to supply alcohol to a police officer on duty. D induces E, a licensee, to supply alcohol to P, a police officer on duty. If E does not know that P is on duty he is not guilty of the offence. D cannot be guilty of the offence as a principal acting by an innocent agent because he is not a licensee, and thus he does not comply with the description of the class of persons who can commit this offence. He is guilty of the offence as an accessory.

30 (3)(b)   30 (vii) A man commits rape when he has sexual intercourse with a woman without her consent, either knowing that she does not consent to it, or being reckless whether she consents to it. D induces E to have intercourse with P by telling E that P will consent to it despite her apparent reluctance. E then has intercourse with P believing, despite her protests, that she is consenting. E is not guilty of rape because his mistake negatives the fault element of knowledge of or recklessness as to non-consent. D cannot be guilty of rape as a principal acting by an innocent agent because the definition of the offence implies personal conduct on the part of the principal offender. He is guilty of rape as an accessory.

The Report explains clauses 29 and 30 as follows:

Clause 29: Parties to offences

10.2 *Principal and accessory*. This clause restates the present law by providing that a person may be guilty of an offence either as a principal offender or as an accessory. Since each type of participant is guilty of the offence each is liable to the same penalties.

10.3 *Terminology*. The use of the terms principal and accessory to indicate different modes of participation in an offence was proposed in Working Paper No 43 [Proposition 1]. This usage is familiar and convenient. There are a number of reasons for maintaining a distinction between these modes of participation. An accessory is not normally indicated directly as an offender by the law creating the offence, so a special provision is needed to make him guilty of it. Secondly, the fault elements are different for a principal and an accessory. Indeed a principal may be convicted of some offences in the absence of any fault on his part, but an accessory can never be guilty in the absence of fault. Thirdly, an accessory may not be liable for an offence, despite an apparent act of participation, where he is a 'victim', or where he has effectively withdrawn from participation, or where the principal has gone beyond the scope of the common purpose.

Clause 30: Principals

10.4 *Persons who are principals*. This clause provides that a person is a principal offender in three types of case. In summary, these are when he commits an offence by his own act (subsection (1)), when he commits it by virtue of being vicariously liable for the act of another (subsection (2) (a)) and when he commits it by an innocent agent (subsection (2) (b)). These cases represent existing law and their continuation was proposed in Working Paper No 43 [Proposition 2]. There are two situations, however, in which the doctrine of innocent agency cannot operate satisfactorily, and a special rule is provided for these in subsection (3). . . .

10.6 *Subsection (2)(a): liability for the act of another*. There are two cases where a person may be guilty of an offence as a principal despite the fact that he did not perform any of the relevant acts himself. As indicated above, the first arises when a person is liable for the act of another which is attributed to him. Provision for the continued application of the doctrine of vicarious liability (as this form of liability is generally labelled) is made in clause 33. Both that clause and the subsection permit the attribution to another of acts only (including of course any mental element implicit in the relevant verb, such as 'sell'). They will not permit the attribution to a person of another's fault, so a person may not have attributed to him the knowledge of his employee who 'knowingly sells'. This is in accordance with the requirement in subsection (1) that for a person to be guilty as a principal he must act with the fault specified for the offence. The consequences for the doctrine of vicarious liability are discussed in paragraph 10.29 below.

10.7 *Subsection (2)(b): innocent agency*. The second case in which a principal does not himself perform the acts specified for the offence arises when they are done by his innocent agent. An innocent agent is one who is procured, assisted or encouraged to do the relevant acts but who is not guilty of the offence because he is a child, or suffers from mental disorder, or lacks the fault required for the offence or has a defence (for example, of duress). The doctrine of innocent agency thus enables culpability as a principal to attach to the person who was the real perpetrator of the offence in question. It is particularly appropriate for a person who procures a child or a person suffering from mental disorder to do criminal acts. Retention of the doctrine was proposed in Working Paper No 43.

10.8 *The semi-innocent agent*. The provision here will extend to what may be termed the 'semi-innocent agent'. He is a person who does an act specified for an offence with some degree of fault, but who lacks the fault required for the offence with which the person who procured, assisted or encouraged him to act is charged. Such an agent is being manipulated in the same way as one who is entirely blameless, and the fact that he may be guilty of some lesser offence should not be an argument for reducing the seriousness of the offence contemplated by the principal. An effect of our provision, therefore, will be to reverse *R v Richards* [below]. Under the subsection Richards would be guilty of wounding with intent as a principal acting by an innocent agent. (See also illustration 30 (v)) [p 133, above].

10.9 *Subsection (3)*. Working Paper No 43 identified two cases for which the doctrine of innocent agency is inappropriate [see Proposition 3]. A person who cannot comply with a particular description specified for a person committing the offence (for example 'licensee') should not be guilty of the offence as a principal, even where he has procured an innocent person of that description to do the relevant act. Nor should a person be guilty as a principal of an offence requiring personal conduct on the part of the offender (for example rape, or driving without due care and attention) where he has procured an innocent person to do the physical act involved. One method of dealing with such exceptional cases is to create specific offences of procuring, assisting or encouraging a person to act in a certain way. This method is cumbersome, time-consuming and potentially inefficient, since it is always possible that certain cases may be overlooked in drawing up the new offences. A more satisfactory solution is a special rule creating liability as an accessory. The subsection provides accordingly. A person who would be guilty as a principal acting by an innocent agent but for the fact that the case falls within one of these two categories is nevertheless guilty as an accessory. Such a solution was suggested by the Criminal Law Revision Committee [Working Paper on Sexual Offences (1980), para 26] and by the Court of Appeal in *R v Cogan and Leak* [[1976] QB 217]. In this case the court held also that Leak, a married man, could be guilty of raping his own wife through the innocent agency of Cogan's body. The reasoning on this point has attracted much criticism and it is submitted that liability as an accessory is preferable. *R v Bourne* [(1952) 36 Cr App R 125] affords another example of the utility of the provision. A husband who forced his wife to have connection with a dog could be convicted as an accessory to bestiality.

2. Innocent and semi-innocent agents

R v Richards (Isabelle), [1973] 3 All ER 1088, Court of Appeal, Criminal Division (James LJ, Kilner Brown and Boreham JJ)

The appellant told two men, 'I wanted them to beat up [her husband] bad enough to put him in hospital for a month.' She offered them £5 to do so. She proposed to give a signal by putting on the kitchen light when her husband went to work. There was a power cut at the time, so, instead, she held up a candle at the kitchen window. The two men attacked the husband and caused a laceration on his scalp which required two stitches but no serious injury.

The appellant and the two men were arraigned on an indictment containing two counts: (1) wounding with intent contrary to s 18 of the Offences against the Person Act 1861 and (2) unlawful wounding contrary to s 20 of the same Act (p 541, below). The appellant was convicted on the first count. The two co-accused were acquitted on the first count and convicted on the second. The appellant appealed against conviction and sentence.

[**James LJ**, having referred to authorities cited by counsel for the Crown:]

Then (without attempting to cite in any detail all the authorities to which we have been referred, for it is not necessary to do so in the light of the view we have formed as to the facts of this particular case), counsel for the Crown invites our attention to the book on criminal law by Professors Smith and Hogan[1], in particular a section which deals with accomplices. After reference to Russell[2] and again citing from Hawkins[3], one finds this[4]:

'. . . if there were malice in the abettor, and none in the person who struck the party it will be murder as to the abettor, and manslaughter only as to the other'.

There the person who is an abettor, using the old word again, not actually doing the physical act himself, is said to be guilty of the more serious crime than the crime of which the person acting is guilty. But it is right to observe that Hawkins, the authority for that proposition there cited, confines that to a case in which the person who is said to be capable of being guilty of the more serious offence is an abettor, a different situation from one who is in the position of an accessory, though as to accessories Hawkins thought, it is said[5]:

'that the abettor might be guilty of a greater crime than the principal in the first degree, he was emphatic that the rule was otherwise with respect to accessories before the fact'.

Hawkins said[6]:

'I take it to be an uncontroverted rule [that the offence of the accessory can never rise higher than that of the principal]; it seeming incongruous and absurd that he who is punished only as a partaker of the guilt of another, should be adjudged guilty of a higher crime than the other'.

Again citing from Hawkins in a passage which puts in a very short compass an essential part of counsel for the Crown's argument[7]:

'The true principle, it is suggested [counsel says this is right] is that where the principal has caused an actus reus, the liability of each of the secondary parties should be assessed according to his own mens rea. If there is no actus reus, then certainly no one can be convicted'.

We have been helpfully invited again to look at the cases of *Anthony*[8], *Humphreys and Turner*[9], and the passage in Archbold[10] is drawn to our attention where it is said, citing as authority for the proposition *Burton*[11]:

'If an aider and abettor and a principal in an offence are indicted together as principals, the aider and abettor may be convicted, although the principal is acquitted'.

Counsel for the Crown says that here one can properly look at the actus reus, that is the physical blows struck on Mr Richards, and separately at the intention with which the blows were struck. The appellant, he says, is responsible for the blows being struck, the actus reus, because they were struck at her request by the co-accused. If, as counsel says is the case, the specific intention of the appellant was different from the specific intention, if any, proved to be entertained on the part of the co-accused, then it is proper that the appellant should be convicted of the s 18 offence if that specific intention goes so far as to amount to intent to cause grievous bodily harm, although that intention was never in the minds of the persons who committed the acts at her request.

We do not take that view. Looking at the facts of this case the acts were perpetrated at some distance from where the appellant was. She was not truly in a position which would earlier have been described as an abettor of those who did the acts. There is proved on the evidence in this case one offence and one offence only, namely, the offence of unlawful wounding without the element of specific intent. We do not think it right that one could say that that which was done can be said to be done with the intention of the appellant who was not present at the time and whose intention did not go to the offence which was in fact committed. That is the short point in the case as we see it. If there is only one offence committed, and that is the offence of unlawful wounding, then the person who has requested that offence to be committed, or advised that that offence be committed, cannot be guilty of a graver offence than that in fact which was committed. . . .

Conviction quashed; verdict of guilty of unlawful wounding substituted. Sentence of six months imprisonment quashed and a sentence of six months imprisonment suspended for two years operative from the date of judgment substituted therefor

1. *Criminal Law* (3rd edn, 1973) pp 105, 106.
2. *Russell on Crime* (12th edn, 1964) p 128.
3. *Pleas of the Crown* (8th edn, 1824) vol 2, p 439.
4. *Criminal Law* (3rd edn, 1973) p 106.

5. Smith and Hogan, *Criminal Law* (3rd edn, 1973) p 107.
6. *Pleas of the Crown* (8th edn, 1824), vol 2, p 442.
7. Smith and Hogan, *Criminal Law* (3rd edn, 1973), p 107.
8. [1965] 2 QB 189; [1965] 1 All ER 440.
9. [1965] 3 All ER 689.
10. Archbold's *Criminal Pleading, Evidence and Practice* (38th edn, 1973) p 1562, para 4136.
11. (1875), 13 Cox CC 71.

Note: See *Burke*, Appendix II, below.

Questions

1. What did Hawkins mean by 'a higher crime'? Cf Smith, 'Aid, Abet, Counsel or Procure' in *Reshaping the Criminal Law* (ed Glazebrook, 1978) 120 at 128.

2. What would have been the position if the appellant had shouted encouragement to the two co-accused as they attacked her husband? *Should it make any difference to the result whether assistance or encouragement is given shortly before, or at the time of the commission of the offence?*

'Complicity Cause and Blame: A Study in the Interpretation of Doctrine' by S.H. Kadish (1985) 73 Cal Law Rev 323 at 388:

. . . the greater liability of the secondary party can be supported only where some feature of the primary party's action is not volitional in the full sense, so that the former can be said to have caused it by using the latter as his instrument. This limitation is illustrated in *Regina v Richards*. The case has been criticized,[1] and insofar as the decision rested on the distinction between whether the secondary party was present or not, the criticism is well taken.[2] But the decision is supportable, it would seem, on the ground that Mrs Richards did not *cause* the actions of the men.

Critics of the *Richards* decision have taken a different view. Smith and Hogan, for example, argue by analogy to a person, D, who gives poison to another E, to administer to the deceased, telling E it is an emetic that will cause only discomfort. They argue that if D had told E that the poison was medicine the deceased needed, D would unquestionably be guilty of murder. It should make no difference that D told E the poison was an emetic, which, since E's action would then have been an intentional assault, would have made E guilty of manslaughter. They conclude: 'The true principle . . . is that where the principal has caused an *actus reus*, the liability of each of the secondary parties should be assessed according to his own *mens rea*.'[3]

Their conclusion that D is liable for murder is sound, but the generalization they adduce to support it is questionable. It is not a 'true principle' that the secondary party's liability is assessed according to his own mens rea when the primary party 'has caused an actus reus.' This is true only when the secondary party can be said to have caused the actions of the primary party, thereby bringing into play the doctrine of causation which, unlike the doctrine of complicity, does not rest on a derivative theory of liability. In Smith and Hogan's hypothetical this is the case, since D used E as his unwitting instrument. But it is not the case with Mrs Richards. She made no misrepresentation to the men she hired. They were not her unwitting instruments, but freely chose to act as they did. Hence their actions, as such, could not be attributed to Mrs Richards. The innocent-agency doctrine is inapplicable because she did not cause their action.[4]

[*NB* notes have been renumbered here. Cross references are to original note numbers in article.]
1. See J. Smith & B. Hogan, supra note 130, at 140; G. Williams, supra note 10, at 373–74.
2. See supra text accompanying note 191.
3. J. Smith & B. Hogan, supra note 130, at 140; see also Note, *Proof of Principal Offences and Liability of Secondary Party*, 90 Law Q Rev 314, 318 (1974).
4. The same argument applies to Professor Williams' criticism of the *Richards* case. See G. Williams, supra note 10, at 373–74.

Question

Is it true to say that Mrs Richards did not cause D's and E's action?

R v Bourne (1952) 36 Cr App Rep 125, Court of Criminal Appeal
(Lord Goddard CJ, Hilbery and Slade JJ)

Bourne was convicted of aiding and abetting his wife to commit buggery with a dog. The wife stated in her evidence that she had been terrorised into submission and that the acts were entirely against her will. On appeal it was argued (i) that there was no finding that Bourne was present when the act was done and therefore no aiding and abetting; (ii) that the wife could not have been convicted as she was acting under the coercion of her husband; she was not a principal but a victim, so that there was no crime to aid and abet, citing *Tyler* (1838) 8 C & P 616 (where Lord Denman CJ, directed that the accused could not be convicted of murder as principals in the second degree since Thom, who had killed the deceased and shot himself, would probably have been entitled to be acquitted of murder on the ground of insanity. The accused were however convicted as principals in the first degree.)

Lord Goddard CJ. The case against the appellant was that he was a principal in the second degree to the crime of buggery which was committed by his wife, because if a woman has connection with a dog, or allows a dog to have connection with her, that is the full offence of buggery. She may be able to show that she was forced to commit the offence. I will assume that the plea of duress could have been set up by her on the evidence, and in fact we have allowed Mr Green to argue this case on the footing that the wife would have been entitled to be acquitted on the ground of duress. The learned judge left no question to the jury on duress, but the jury have found that she did not consent. Assuming that she could have set up duress, what does that mean? It means that she admits that she has committed the crime but prays to be excused from punishment for the consequences of the crime by reason of the duress, and no doubt in those circumstances the law would allow a verdict of Not Guilty to be entered. I have only to read a passage from *Blackstone's Commentaries* (Vol 4, p 27) to show that that is the true position:

> 'The same principle which excuses those who have no mental will in the perpetration of an offence protects from the punishment of the law those who commit crimes in subjection to the power of others, and not as the result of an uncontrolled free action proceeding from themselves. Thus, if A by force takes the hand of B in which is a weapon, and therewith kills C, A is guilty of murder, but B is excused; but if a merely moral force is used, as threats, duress of imprisonment, or even an assault to the peril of his life, in order to compel him to kill C, it is no legal excuse.'

See also 1 Hale's Pleas of the Crown, pp 44, 51. That means that duress is not a legal excuse for murder. There may be certain doctrines with regard to murder which do not apply to other cases, but I am willing to assume for the purpose of this case, and I think my brethren are too, that if this woman had been charged herself with committing the offence, she could have set up the plea of duress, not as showing that no offence had been committed, but as showing that she had no mens rea because her will was overborne by threats of imprisonment or violence so that she would be excused from punishment. But the offence of buggery whether with man or beast does not depend upon consent; it depends on the act, and if an act of buggery is committed, the felony is committed.

A point is raised here that the appellant was charged with being not merely an accessory before the fact but with being an aider and abettor. So he was, because the charge is: 'you being present aided and abetted, counselled and procured.' The only questions that were left to the jury by the learned judge, and he was not asked to leave any more, were these: (1) 'Did the prisoner on a day in or about the month of September 1949, in the County of Stafford cause his wife Adelaide Bourne to have carnal knowledge of a dog?' and the jury have found that he did. (2) 'Are you satisfied that she did not consent to having such carnal knowledge?' The answer of the jury was. 'Yes, we are satisfied she did not consent.' Then the same two questions were asked with regard to the other day on which an offence was alleged to have been committed.

In the opinion of the court, there is no doubt that the appellant was properly indicted for being a principal in the second degree to the commission of the crime of buggery. That is all that it is necessary to show. The evidence was, and the jury by their verdict have shown they accepted it, that he caused his wife to have connection with a dog, and if he caused his wife to have connection with a dog he is guilty, whether you call him an aider and abettor or an accessory, as a principal in the second degree. For that reason, this appeal fails and is dismissed.

Appeal dismissed

Questions

1. *Does* a person who sets up the defence of duress (p 205, below, and cf *Steane*, p 60, above) admit that he has committed the crime? If, in particular circumstances, the law allows a verdict of Not Guilty to be entered, has a crime been committed?

2. It has been suggested that Bourne could well have been convicted of the substantive crime as principal in the first degree, acting through the innocent agency of his wife. Do you agree?

3. Sir Rupert Cross argues (69 LQR 354) that Bourne's conviction for aiding and abetting was consonant with the old learning on the subject.

> 'The wife committed the "actus reus" with the "mens rea" required by the definition of the crime in question, and the husband participated in that "mens rea". Lord Goddard CJ might have stated the distinction between the case before him and *Tyler and Price* in some such words as the following: "the wife could have set up the plea of duress, not as showing that she did not intend to do the prohibited act with knowledge that it was wrong, but as showing that her will was overborne".'

Is this a better way of rationalising the case?

4. How would the theories discussed in questions 2 and 3 deal with the following case referred to by Cross at 69 LQR 358: A, a bachelor, induces a married woman to believe, on reasonable grounds, but contrary to the facts known to him, that her husband is dead, whereupon she goes through a ceremony of marriage with A. Can A be convicted of bigamy? Cf Smith & Hogan, ch 8, heads 1, 11.

R v Cogan and Leak [1975] 2 All ER 1059, Court of Appeal, Criminal Division (Lawton, James LJJ and Bristow J)

The appellants were convicted of rape, Cogan as a principal, and Leak as 'being aider and abettor to the same offence'. Leak had terrorised his wife into submitting to sexual intercourse with Cogan. The jury found that Cogan believed that Mrs Leak was consenting but that he had no reasonable grounds for this belief. Under the decision of the Court of Appeal in *Morgan* (p 45, above), which stood at the time of the trial, such an unreasonable belief was no defence. Following the decision of the House of Lords in *DPP v Morgan* (p 45, above) Cogan's conviction was quashed. The judge had directed the jury that, even if Cogan was not guilty (ie if he had reasonable grounds for his belief), they were still entitled to convict Leak.

Lawton LJ. Leak's appeal against conviction was based on the proposition that he could not be found guilty of aiding and abetting Cogan to rape his wife if Cogan was acquitted of that offence as he was deemed in law to have been when his conviction was quashed: see s 2 (3) of the Criminal Appeal Act 1968. Counsel for Leak conceded, however, that this proposition had some limitations. The law on this topic lacks clarity as a perusal of some of the textbooks shows: see Smith and Hogan, *Criminal Law* [3rd edn (1973), pp 106–109]; Glanville Williams, *Criminal Law* [2nd edn (1961), pp 386–390, 406–408]; and *Russell on Crime* [12th edn (1964), vol 1, p 128]. We do not consider it appropriate to review the law generally because, as was said by this court in *Quick, Paddison* [[1973] QB 910 at 923, [1973] 3 All ER 347 at 356], when considering this kind of problem:

> 'The facts of each case . . . have to be considered and in particular what is alleged to have been done by way of aiding and abetting.'

The only case which counsel for Leak submitted had a direct bearing on the problem of Leak's guilt was *Walters v Lunt* [[1951] 2 All ER 645]. In that case the respondents had been charged under the Larceny Act 1916, s 33 (1), with receiving from a child aged seven years, certain articles knowing them to have been stolen. In 1951 a child under eight years was deemed in law to be incapable of committing a crime; it followed that at the time of receipt by the respondents the articles had not been stolen and that the charge had not been proved. That case is very different from this because here one fact is clear—the wife had been raped. Cogan had had sexual intercourse with her without her consent. The fact that Cogan was innocent of rape because he believed that she was consenting does not affect the position that she was raped.

Her ravishment had come about because Leak had wanted it to happen and had taken action to see that it did by persuading Cogan to use his body as the instrument for the necessary physical act. In the language of the law the act of sexual intercourse without the wife's consent was the actus reus; it had been procured by Leak who had the appropriate mens rea, namely his intention that Cogan should have sexual intercourse with her without her consent. In our judgment it is irrelevant that the man whom Leak had procured to do the physical act himself did not intend to have sexual intercourse with the wife without her consent. Leak was using him as a means to procure a criminal purpose.

Before 1861 a case such as this, pleaded as it was in the indictment, might have presented a court with problems arising from the old distinctions between principals and accessories in felony. Most of the old law was swept away by s 8 of the Accessories and Abettors Act 1861 and what remained, by s 1 of the Criminal Law Act 1967. The modern law allowed Leak to be tried and punished as a principal offender. In our judgment he could have been indicted as a principal offender. It would have been no defence for him to submit that if Cogan was an 'innocent' agent, he was necessarily in the old terminology of the law a principal in the first degree, which was a legal impossibility as a man cannot rape his own wife during cohabitation. The law no longer concerns itself with niceties of degrees in participation in crime; but even if it did, Leak would still be guilty. The reason a man cannot by his own physical act rape his wife during cohabitation is because the law presumes consent from the marriage ceremony: see Hale [Pleas of the Crown, vol 1, p 629]. There is no such presumption when a man procures a drunken friend to do the physical act for him. Hale CJ put this case in one sentence:

> 'tho in marriage she hath given up her body to her husband, she is not to be by him prostituted to another'.

Had Leak been indicted as a principal offender, the case against him would have been clear beyond argument. Should he be allowed to go free because he was charged with 'being aider and abettor to the same offence'? If we are right in our opinion that the wife had been raped (and no one outside a court of law would say that she had not been), then the particulars of offence accurately stated what Leak had done, namely he had procured Cogan to commit the offence.

Appeal dismissed

3. Accessories

The draft Criminal Code Bill provides:

31 Accessories

(1) A person is guilty of an offence as an accessory—

(a) where the offence is committed by a principal, if he procures, assists or encourages the commission of the offence and does so with the fault specified in subsection (4); or

(b) if section 30 (3) or section 35 (1) (liability of officer of corporation) applies.

(2) In determining whether a person is guilty of an offence as an accessory it is immaterial that the principal is unaware of that person's act of procurement or assistance.

(3) For the purposes of this section, encouragement includes encouragement arising from a failure by a person to take reasonable steps to exercise any authority he has to control the relevant acts of the principal in order to prevent the commission of the offence.

(4) A person has the fault referred to in subsection (1) (a) if he—

(a) intends that what he does shall, or is aware that it will or may, cause, assist or encourage the principal to do an act of the kind he does and in the circumstances specified for the offence; and

(b) where a result is an element of the offence, is, in respect of that element, at fault in the way required for liability as a principal.

(5) For the purposes of subsection (4), and subject to subsection (6), it is immaterial that the accessory does not know the particulars of the offence committed by the principal.

(6) Notwithstanding section 28 (1) (transferred fault), a person who assists or encourages a principal in pursuance of an agreement between them that an offence shall be committed in relation to a particular person or thing is not guilty as an accessory to an offence intentionally committed by the principal in relation to some other person or thing.

(7) A person is not guilty of an offence as an accessory by reason of anything he does—

(a) with the purpose of preventing the commission of the offence or of nullifying its effects; or

(b) only because he believes that he is under a legal obligation to do it.

(8) Where the purpose of an enactment creating an offence is the protection of a class of persons no member of that class who is a victim of such an offence can be guilty of that offence as an accessory.

(9) A person who has procured, assisted or encouraged the commission of an offence is not guilty as an accessory if after his act and before the commission of the offence he took all reasonable steps to prevent it.

Schedule 1 of the draft Bill provides the following illustrations:

31 (1) and (4)	31 (i)	It is an offence to use an overloaded lorry on the highway. D, a weighbridge operator at a colliery, hands over a ticket to E, the driver of a lorry which has just been loaded with coal. The ticket records the weight of the load which is in excess of that permitted for the lorry. D knows that possession of the ticket will enable E to leave the colliery and drive the lorry on the highway. E does so. E is guilty of the offence as a principal. D is guilty as an accessory.
	31 (ii)	D hears screams and the sounds of a struggle from E's room. He enters and watches silently while E rapes P. D is guilty of rape as an accessory if his presence is an encouragement to E to commit the rape and if he knows that his presence will or may encourage E to do so.
31 (2)	31 (iii)	It is an offence for a person to drive a motor vehicle on a road with a level of alcohol in his blood in excess of that permitted. D, knowing that E will shortly be driving home, surreptitiously laces E's drinks. E drives home with an excessive level of alcohol in his blood. If the definition of the offence indicates that no fault is required on the part of the driver E is guilty of the offence as a principal. D is guilty as an accessory. (If fault of the driver is required and E is acquitted D is guilty of the offence as an accessory by virtue of s 30 (3)).
31 (3)	31 (iv)	It is an offence to consume alcohol on licensed premises outside permitted hours. D, a licensee, fails to take steps to collect the drinks of customers who are drinking in his public house outside the permitted hours. D may be guilty as an accessory to the offence committed by the customers.
31 (4)(a)	31 (v)	D is ordered to drive E to a remote public house. He knows that E is a member of an illegal organisation and that E is 'on a job'. He knows further that E has with him in the car the means for mounting an attack upon the public house inevitably involving danger to life or damage to property. E has a bomb with him in the car and throws it into the public house. D is guilty as an accessory of possession of explosives with intent and doing an act with intent to cause an explosion. He intends that his act of driving E to the scene shall assist E to do whatever acts, among those which D knows E may do, E has in mind.
	31 (vi)	It is made an offence to sell a house at a price in excess of a permitted maximum. D and E are partners in a firm of solicitors acting for the builder of a house. E advises the builder that he may lawfully sell the house at a price which is in fact above the maximum permitted. D has no knowledge of the transaction. E is guilty as an accessory to the offence committed by the builder. His mistaken interpretation of the law is no defence (s 25). D is not guilty. Even if D knows that the firm is acting for the builder, he does not know that the firm is assisting the builder to act in the circumstances specified for the offence.
	31 (vii)	It is an offence dishonestly to obtain property belonging to another by a deliberate or reckless deception. At D's suggestion E tells P that a picture which E is selling is painted by Constable. Neither D nor E

knows whether this statement is true. It is false. P buys the picture in reliance on the statement. E is guilty of dishonestly obtaining the price by deception. D is guilty as an accessory because he encourages E and is reckless whether E obtains the price by deception.

31 (viii) D and E agree to assault P using their fists. During the assault E stabs P with a knife which D does not know E is carrying. P dies from the wound. E is guilty of murder under section 56 if he intended the stabbing to kill or if he intended it to cause serious injury and was aware that it might kill. D is not guilty as an accessory to murder because he did not intend to assist or encourage E to do the kind of act (stabbing) E did. He is not guilty of manslaughter as an accessory for the same reason. He is guilty of assault (s 77) and an attempt to commit an offence under section 74 or 76 if he intended the assault to cause serious injury or injury respectively.

31 (4)(b)   31 (ix) A person commits manslaughter under section 57 (1)(c) when he kills being reckless whether death or serious injury be caused. D and E agree that E shall put a certain substance in P's drink. D believes that it will cause P diarrhoea and vomiting but he does not foresee that P may suffer death or serious injury. E realises that the substance may cause serious injury to P. E puts the substance into P's drink and P dies. E is guilty of manslaughter. D is not guilty as an accessory to manslaughter. Although he encouraged E to act as he did, in respect of the result of death D did not have the fault required for a principal. D is guilty as an accessory to recklessly causing injury (s 76) and administering a substance without consent (s 80).

31 (5)   31 (x) D lends E oxy-acetylene equipment, knowing that E intends to use it to break into premises. E uses it a week later to break into a bank in London. D is guilty as an accessory to burglary. He intended to assist E to do the acts specified for the offence and it is immaterial that he did not know which premises were to be entered and when.

31 (6)   31 (xi) D advises E, who wants to kill his wife, to give her a poisoned apple. E does so, but his wife passes the apple to their child in E's presence. D is not present. E remains silent, not wishing to reveal his criminal intention, while the child eats the apple. The child dies. E is guilty of murder (s 56). D is not guilty as an accessory to murder of the child but is guilty of conspiracy to murder E's wife (s 52).

31 (7)(a)   31 (xii) E and F agree to carry out a robbery at a warehouse. They approach D for assistance. Unknown to them D is an informer. D supplies advice in order to learn details of the plan. He subsequently passes the details to the police in the expectation that they will prevent the robbery. The police fail to arrive in time and the robbery takes place. D is not guilty as an accessory.

31 (xiii) As in illustration 31 (xii) except that D supplies a van for removal of the stolen goods. D has fitted the van with a signalling device to enable the police to track it to the premises of the intended handler of the goods. If the robbery takes place D is not guilty as an accessory. His assistance was given with the purpose of nullifying the effects of the offence (that is, of enabling the goods to be recovered).

31 (7)(b)   31 (xiv) D hands over a jemmy to E on request, knowing that E intends to commit a burglary with it. In fact the jemmy belongs to E and D believes that he is legally obliged to return it. If this is his sole reason for giving it up he will not be guilty as an accessory to any subsequent burglary committed by E.

31 (8)   31 (xv) It is an offence to have sexual intercourse with a girl under sixteen, and her consent is no defence. E has intercourse with D, a girl under sixteen, who consents to the intercourse. D is not guilty as an accessory to E's offence.

31 (9)   31 (xvi) D and E agree to burn down an empty building. D procures petrol which he gives to E. D later repents of the plan and informs E of his decision to take no further part in it. E sets fire to the building using the petrol. E is guilty of arson (s 82 (1) and (3)). D is guilty as an accessory. Despite his repentance and withdrawal from the plan he has not taken reasonable steps to prevent the arson. The result would be different if beforehand he informed the police of E's intentions.

The Report explains cl 31 as follows:

Clause 31: Accessories

10.10 *Persons liable as accessories.* This clause states the law on accessory liability. In summary, subsection (1)(a) specifies the acts sufficient for the purpose in the usual case and subsection (1)(b) give necessary cross-references to the special accessory provisions set out in clause 30(3), mentioned above and 35(1) (liability of officer of corporation). Subsections (2) and (3) restate existing law on the scope of the acts sufficient for accessoryship. Subsection (4) sets out the fault element, and subsections (5) and (6) restate existing law on the scope of the rules relating to the fault of accessories. The remaining subsections (7), (8) and (9) deal with a number of limitations on the liability of an accessory which are not directly related to the elements of act and fault. . . .

10.13 *Passive encouragement.* A person does not become an accessory to an offence merely because he omits to take steps to prevent it. However, a person who has a special authority over the acts of others, arising, for example, by virtue of his management of premises or his ownership of a chattel, may incur accessory liability through a failure to exercise that authority to prevent an offence taking place on those premises or through use of the chattel. This failure to act may then be regarded as encouragement of the offence. Subsection (3) restates existing law by allowing for these cases. We think it is unnecessary and unwise to attempt to provide a comprehensive list of cases in which this special authority may exist.

The Working Party suggested a rule which was effectively the converse of the one provided here, on the ground that it was necessary to prevent erosion of the general principle of no criminal liability for a mere omission. [See Working Paper No 43, Proposition 6 (4)]. Such a rule would have the effect of reversing the decisions in a number of cases [For example, *Du Cros v Lambourne* [1907] 1 KB 40; *Tuck v Robson* [1970] 1 WLR 741], and the Working Party suggested that special provision might be needed for cases of persons in positions of special responsibility who permitted others to commit offences. It appears that this proposal was not well received on consultation on the Working Paper. Most commentators found nothing objectionable in the present law and did not share the Working Party's fear of erosion of the general principle.

10.14 *Fault element for accessories.* Subsection (4) restates the fault element necessary for liability as an accessory. A number of points require comment.

   (i)   The word 'cause' is used in paragraph (a) to convey the same notion as 'procure' in subsection (1), because the latter word does not read harmoniously in this context.

  (ii)   The proposition in paragraph (a) that the accessory has sufficient fault if he knows that what he does '*may* cause, assist or encourage . . .' is designed to cover cases of recklessness. Recklessness may be as to the circumstances specified for the offence (*Carter v Richardson* [[1974] RTR 314] and see illustration 31 (vii)), or as to the offences which the principal is proposing to commit (see *DPP for Northern Ireland v Maxwell* [[1978] 1 WLR 1350], illustration 31 (v)).

 (iii)   Illustration 31 (viii) shows that where the principal goes outside the 'common purpose', in the sense of doing acts of a different kind from those agreed to or contemplated by the accessory, the latter will not be liable in respect of the offence so committed. Under the present law, for example, an assault with knives is regarded as a different kind of act from an assault with fists [*Davies v DPP* [1954] AC 378; *R v Anderson and Morris* [1966] 2 QB 110] and the subsection enables this distinction to be maintained. We think it is impossible to be precise as to the application of this principle. Occasionally, in the Code a concept has to be used which has an irreducible minimum of uncertainty in its application, and the concept used here to restate existing law may require further development by the courts. A related type of case, where the principle does do the kind of act agreed but does it deliberately in relation to an uncontemplated victim, is dealt with by a separate provision in subsection (6).

 (iv)   An offence sometimes requires that a certain result be caused. Under the present law for a person to be liable as an accessory he must have in respect of that result the fault required for a principal. Hence he cannot be guilty of murder at common law in the absence of an intention that the victim shall be killed or suffer grievous bodily harm or foresight that the principal's act is likely to cause death or grievous bodily harm [*R v Betts and Ridley* (1930) 22 Cr App R 148]. However, he may be liable for manslaughter even though he did not intend or even foresee the causing of death as the result of the principal's unlawful act [*R v Baldessare* (1930) 22 Cr App R 70]. Paragraph (b) of the subsection restates the general principle for the Code. An application of it is given in illustration 31 (ix).

  (v)   The proposals relating to the fault element for accessories which were put forward by the Working Party were extensive and elaborate and are now somewhat out of date. (See Working Paper No 43, Proposition 7.) We hope that this subsection, when read together with subsections (5) and (6), offers a simpler and clearer method of dealing with this complex topic. . . .

10.16 *Principal's change of plan.* The 'common purpose' doctrine applies to relieve an accessory from liability where the principal does an act of the kind agreed but does it deliberately against a different victim. An early example is *R v Saunders and Archer* [(1576) 2 Plowden 473; 75 ER 706], which forms the basis of illustration 31 (xi). Under subsection (5) an accessory need not generally know the identity of the victim, hence he would still be guilty, for example, if the plan accidentally miscarried and took effect against a different victim. This would have been the position in *Saunders and Archer* if Saunders had been absent when his wife passed on the apple, ie, the case would have been one of 'transferred intention' (see clause 28) and Archer would have been liable as an accessory to the murder of the child. However, the common law has consistently taken the view that it is different when the principal takes a deliberate decision to let the plan miscarry. The subsection gives effect to this and so qualifies subsection (5). . . .

10.17 *Subsection (7).* The subsection largely restates existing law. Paragraph (a) provides for the case of the police informer or undercover agent who gives assistance, or does some other act of participation, towards the commission of an offence, but whose purpose is to frustrate the offence. If his plan fails and the offence is committed before the police can intervene he is not an accessory. Likewise, where his act is designed to enable the police to intervene after a theft or similar offence to nullify the effects of the offence (by recovering the stolen property and arresting the participants), he should not be guilty of the offence himself. The paragraph follows the proposal made in Working Paper No 43.

There has been some controversy over cases where a person in possession of an article hands it over to another knowing that the other intends to commit an offence using the article. The question is whether there should be accessory liability even where the recipient has or may have a legal claim to the article. The point is covered in paragraph (b) which makes the answer depend on the state of mind of the transferor. If he believes that he is under a legal obligation to hand over the article, and this is his only reason for so acting, he should not be liable for a subsequent offence involving the article. The case is analogous to a claim of right. It would be going too far to impose a positive duty to resist the transfer, particularly where the transferor could not be certain that an offence would be committed.

10.18 *Protected persons.* Subsection (8) restates a well-established principle, of which *R v Tyrrell* [[1894] 1 QB 710] is the leading illustration. Continuation of this principle was proposed in Working Paper No 43 [Proposition 8] and it has subsequently received the support of the Criminal Law Revision Committee in their Report on Sexual Offences [Fifteenth Report (1984), Cmnd 9213, 101–103].

10.19 *Incidental participation.* Working Paper No 43 (Proposition 8) suggested a generalisation of the principle referred to in the previous paragraph. The Working Party proposed that a person should not become an accessory to an offence 'if the offence is so defined that his conduct in it is inevitably incidental to its commission and such conduct is not expressly penalised'. It was noted that English law at present only applies such a rule where the party whose conduct is 'incidental' is a victim of an offence created for his or her protection. The spectator who pays to watch an obscene performance and the knowing buyer of goods from an unlicensed seller are (probably) not exempt from accessory liability. It appears that the balance of opinion on consultation on the Working Paper was against extending immunity in these cases, and it seems right that the spectator or buyer who incites the commission of the offence should not be protected from prosecution. The passive spectator may not be liable in any event if he does nothing to encourage the offence, and other cases of 'incidental' participation can be dealt with by prosecutorial discretion. Accordingly, the Code makes no express provision for such cases.

10.20 *Withdrawal from participation.* Subsection (9) attempts to resolve a matter of some uncertainty in existing law. At present it is unclear to what extent a person who has done acts sufficient to make him an accessory to an offence can escape liability by withdrawing or repenting of his participation before the offence is committed. Working Paper No 43 suggested a rule in wider terms than the subsection (see Proposition 9), but this was not generally well-received on consultation. Critics argued that to allow an alternative of withdrawal in the form of simple communication of that fact to the principal was too generous. It was unrelated to any notion of the accessory undoing his act of participation and was too weak to be justified on the ground that the public interest in the prevention of crime supports a defence of withdrawal. We think the rule stated in the subsection offers the best and simplest solution. It is consistent with the provision for police informers and undercover agents in subsection (7) (a) and allows for flexibility in its application.

(1) AIDING, ABETTING, COUNSELLING OR PROCURING

The Accessories and Abettors Act 1861, s 8, p 540, below

The Magistrates Courts' Act 1980, s 44, p 582, below

Attorney-General's Reference (No 1 of 1975) [1975] 2 All ER 684, Court of Appeal, Criminal Division
(Lord Widgery CJ, Bristow and May JJ)

The facts appear in the question for the court.

[**Lord Widgery CJ** delivered the following judgment of the court:]

This case comes before the court on a reference from the Attorney-General under s 36 of the Criminal Justice Act 1972, and by his reference he asks the following question:

> 'Whether an accused who surreptitiously laced a friend's drinks with double measures of spirits when he knew that his friend would shortly be driving his car home, and in consequence his friend drove with an excess quantity of alcohol in his body and was convicted of the offence under the Road Traffic Act 1972 s 6 (1) is entitled to a ruling of no case to answer on being later charged as an aider and abettor, counsellor and procurer, on the ground that there was no shared intention between the two, that the accused did not by accompanying him or otherwise positively encourage the friend to drive, or on any other ground.'

The language in the section which determines whether a 'secondary party', as he is sometimes called, is guilty of a criminal offence committed by another embraces the four words 'aid, abet, counsel or procure'. The origin of those words is to be found in s 8 of the Accessories and Abettors Act 1861 which provides:

> 'Whosoever shall aid, abet, counsel, or procure the commission of any misdemeanor, whether the same be a misdemeanor at common law or by virtue of any Act passed or to be passed, shall be liable to be tried, indicted, and punished as a principal offender.'

Thus, in the past, when the distinction was still drawn between felony and misdemeanor, it was sufficient to make a person guilty of a misdemeanor if he aided, abetted, counselled or procured the offence of another. When the difference between felonies and misdemeanors was abolished in 1967, s 1 of the Criminal Law Act 1967 in effect provided that the same test should apply to make a secondary party guilty either of treason or felony.

Of course it is the fact that in the great majority of instances where a secondary party is sought to be convicted of an offence there has been a contact between the principal offender and the secondary party. Aiding and abetting almost inevitably involves a situation in which the secondary party and the main offender are together at some stage discussing the plans which they may be making in respect of the alleged offence, and are in contact so that each knows what is passing through the mind of the other.

In the same way it seems to us that a person who counsels the commission of a crime by another, almost inevitably comes to a moment when he is in contact with that other, when he is discussing the offence with that other and when, to use the words of the statute, he counsels the other to commit the offence.

The fact that so often the relationship between the secondary party and the principal will be such that there is a meeting of minds between them caused the trial judge in the case from which this reference is derived to think that this was really an essential feature of proving or establishing the guilt of the secondary party and, as we understand his judgment, he took the view that in the absence of some sort of meeting of minds, some sort of mental link between the secondary party and the principal, there could be no aiding, abetting or counselling of the offence within the meaning of the section.

So far as aiding, abetting and counselling is concerned we would go a long way with that conclusion. It may very well be, as I said a moment ago, difficult to think of a case of aiding, abetting or counselling when the parties have not met and have not discussed in some respects the terms of the offence which they have in mind. But we do not see why a similar principle should apply to procuring. We approach s 8 of the 1861 Act on the basis that the words should be given their ordinary meaning, if possible. We approach the section on the basis also that if four words are employed here, 'aid, abet, counsel or procure', the probability is that there is a difference between each of those four words and the other three, because, if there were no such difference, then Parliament would be wasting time in using four words where two or three would do. Thus, in deciding whether that which is assumed to be done under our reference was a criminal offence we approach the section on the footing that each word must be given its ordinary meaning.

To procure means to produce by endeavour. You procure a thing by setting out to see that it happens and taking the appropriate steps to produce that happening. We think that there are plenty of instances in which a person may be said to procure the commission of a crime by another even though there is no sort of conspiracy between the two, even though there is no attempt at agreement or discussion as to the form which the offence should take. In our judgment the offence described in this reference is such a case.

If one looks back at the facts of the reference: the accused surreptitiously laced his friend's drink. This is an important element and, although we are not going to decide today anything other than the problem posed to us, it may well be that in similar cases where the lacing of the drink or the introduction of the extra alcohol is known to the driver quite different considerations may apply. We say that because where the driver has no knowledge of what is happening, in most instances he would have no means of preventing the offence from being committed. If the driver is unaware of what has happened, he will not be taking precautions. He will get into his car seat, switch on the ignition and drive home and, consequently, the conception of another procuring the commission of the offence by the driver is very much stronger where the driver is innocent of all knowledge of what is happening, as in the present case where the lacing of the drink was surreptitious.

The second thing which is important in the facts set out in our reference is that following and in consequence of the introduction of the extra alcohol, the friend drove with an excess quantity of alcohol in his blood. Causation here is important. You cannot procure an offence unless there is a causal link between what you do and the commission of the offence, and here we are told that in consequence of the addition of this alcohol the driver, when he drove home, drove with an excess quantity of alcohol in his body.

Giving the words their ordinary meaning in English, and asking oneself whether in those circumstances the offence has been procured, we are in no doubt that the answer is that it has. It has been procured because, unknown to the driver and without his collaboration, he has been put in a position in which in fact he has committed an offence which he never would have committed otherwise. We think that there was a case to answer and that the trial judge should have directed the jury that an offence is committed if it is shown beyond reasonable doubt that the accused knew that his friend was going to drive, and also knew that the ordinary and natural result of the additional alcohol added to the friend's drink would be to bring him above the recognised limit of 80 milligrammes per 100 millilitres of blood.

It was suggested to us that, if we held that there may be a procuring on the facts of the present case, it would be but a short step to a similar finding for the generous host, with somewhat bibulous friends, when at the end of the day his friends leave him to go to their own homes in circumstances in which they are not fit to drive and in circumstances in which an offence under the Road Traffic Act 1972 is committed. The suggestion has been made that the host may in those circumstances be guilty with his guests on the basis that he has either aided, abetted, counselled or procured the offence.

The first point to notice in regard to the generous host is that that is not a case in which the alcohol is being put surreptitiously into the glass of the driver. That is a case in which the driver knows perfectly well how much he has to drink and where to a large extent it is perfectly right and proper to leave him to make his own decision.

Furthermore, we would say that if such a case arises, the basis on which the case will be put against the host is, we think, bound to be on the footing that he has supplied the tool with which the offence is committed. This of course is a reference back to such cases as those where oxyacetylene equipment was bought by a man knowing it was to be used by another for a criminal offence [*Bainbridge*, p 147, below]. There is ample and clear authority as to the extent to which supplying the tools for the commission of an offence may amount to aiding and abetting for present purposes.

Accordingly, so far as the generous host type of case is concerned we are not concerned at the possibility that difficulties will be created, as long as it is borne in mind that in those circumstances the matter must be approached in accordance with well-known authority governing the provision of the tools for the commission of an offence, and never forgetting that the introduction of the alcohol is not there surreptitious, and that consequently the case for saying that the offence was procured by the supplier of the alcohol is very much more difficult.

Our decision on the reference is that the question posed by the Attorney-General should be answered in the negative.

Determination accordingly

Questions

1. Can there be a case of aiding, abetting or counselling where the parties have not met and have not discussed the offence? Cf *Mohan* [1976] QB 1, p 271, below.

2. Is it fair to assume that Parliament intended the four words to have different meanings? Cf Smith, 'Aid, Abet, Counsel or Procure' in *Reshaping the Criminal Law* (ed Glazebrook, 1978) 120.

3. Is causation an essential constituent of all types of secondary participation?

4. Is the case of the generous host properly distinguishable?

R v Calhaem [1985] 2 All ER 266, Court of Appeal
(Parker LJ, Tudor Evans J and Sir John Thompson)

The prosecution alleged that Calhaem (C) hired Zajac (Z) to murder Mrs Rendell (R), C's rival for the affections of her solicitor. Z, the principal witness for the prosecution, testified to the hiring and said that he went to R's house, armed but with no intention of killing her; that he intended only to act out a charade so that C and R would think an attempt had been made; but that, when R screamed, he went berserk and killed her. On C's application for leave to appeal, it was argued, inter alia, that the judge had misdirected the jury by not telling them that, as in the case of procuring, the counselling by C must have been a 'substantial cause' of the killing.

[**Parker LJ**, having cited *A-G's Reference (No 1 of 1975)*, above, continued:]

We must therefore approach the question raised on the basis that we should give to the word 'counsel' its ordinary meaning, which is, as the judge said, 'advise', 'solicit', or something of that sort. There is no implication in the word itself that there should be any causal connection between the counselling and the offence. It is true that, unlike the offence of incitement at common law, the actual offence must have been committed, and committed by the person counselled. To this extent there must clearly be, first, contact between the parties, and, second, a connection between the counselling and the murder. Equally, the act done must, we think, be done within the scope of the authority or advice, and not, for example, accidentally when the mind of the final murderer did not go with his actions. For example, if the principal offender happened to be involved in a football riot in the course of which he laid about him with a weapon of some sort and killed someone who, unknown to him, was the person whom he had been counselled to kill, he would not, in our view, have been acting within the scope of his authority; he would have been acting entirely outside it, albeit what he had done was what he had been counselled to do.

Question

What is the difference between 'connection' and cause?

(2) SECONDARY PARTICIPATION IN A 'TYPE' OF CRIME

R v Bainbridge [1959] 3 All ER 200, Court of Criminal Appeal
(Lord Parker CJ, Byrne and Winn JJ)

[**Lord Parker CJ**, delivered the following judgment of the court:]

The appellant in this case was convicted at the Central Criminal Court of being accessory before the fact to office-breaking and was sentenced to four years' imprisonment. He now appeals against his conviction only on a point of law.

The facts were these. On the night of 30 October 1958, the Stoke Newington branch of the Midland Bank was broken into by cutting the bars of a window, the doors of the strong room and of a safe inside the strong room. They were opened by means of oxygen cutting equipment and nearly £18,000 was stolen. The cutting equipment was all left behind, and it was later found that that cutting equipment so left behind by the thieves had been purchased by the appellant some six weeks earlier. The case against him was that he had bought this cutting equipment on behalf of one or more of the thieves with the full knowledge that it was going to be used, if not against the Stoke Newington branch of the Midland Bank, at any rate for the purposes of breaking and entering premises. The appellant's case, as given in his evidence, was this: 'True, I had bought this equipment from two different firms. I had gone there with a man called Shakeshaft to buy it for him. As a result of conversation which I had with him, I was suspicious that he wanted it for something illegal. I thought it was for breaking up stolen goods which Shakeshaft had received, and, as the result, in making those purchases I gave false names and addresses; but I had no knowledge that the equipment was going to be used for any such purpose as that for which it was used.'

The complaint here is that Judge Aarvold, who tried the case, gave the jury a wrong direction in regard to what it was necessary for them to be satisfied of in order to hold the appellant guilty of being an accessory before the fact. The passages in question are these:

> 'To prove that, the prosecution have to prove these matters; first of all, they have to prove that the felony itself was committed. Of that there is no doubt. That is not contested. Secondly, they have to prove that the [appellant] knew that a felony of that kind was intended and was going to be committed, and with that knowledge he did something to help the felons commit the crime. The knowledge that is required to be proved in the mind of [the appellant] is not the knowledge of the precise crime. In other words, it need not be proved that he knew that the Midland Bank, Stoke Newington branch, was going to be broken and entered, and money stolen from that particular bank, but he must know the type of crime that was in fact committed. In this case it is a breaking and entering of premises and the stealing of property from those premises. It must be proved that he knew that that sort of crime was intended and was going to be committed. It is not enough to show that he either suspected or knew that some crime was going to be committed, some crime which might have been a breaking and entering or might have been disposing of stolen property or anything of that kind. That is not enough. It must be proved that he knew that the type of crime which was in fact committed was intended.'

There are other passages to the same effect; in particular, when the jury returned for further directions before they came to their verdict, the learned judge said this:

> 'If in fact, before it has happened, [the appellant], knowing what is going to happen, with full knowledge that a felony of that kind is going to take place, deliberately and wilfully helps it on its way, he is an accessory . . . If he was not present he would not be guilty as a principal, but then you would have to decide whether he helped in purchasing this equipment for Shakeshaft knowing full well the type of offence for which it was going to be used, and, with that knowledge, buying it and helping in that way.'

Counsel for the appellant, who argued this case very well, contended that that direction was wrong. As he put it, in order that a person should be convicted of being accessory before the fact, it must be shown that, at the time when he bought the equipment in a case such as this, he knew that a particular crime was going to be committed; and by 'a particular crime' counsel meant that the premises in this case which were going to be broken into were known to the appellant and contemplated by him, and not only the premises in question but the date when the crime was going to occur; in other words, that he must have known that on a particular date the Stoke Newington branch of the Midland Bank was intended to be broken into.

The court fully appreciates that it is not enough that it should be shown that a person knew that some illegal venture was intended. To take this case, it would not be enough if the appellant knew—he says that he only suspected—that the equipment was going to be used to dispose of stolen property. That would not be enough. Equally, this court is quite satisfied that it is unnecessary that knowledge of the intention to commit the particular crime which was in fact committed should be shown, and by 'particular crime' I am using the words in the same way as that in which counsel for the appellant used them, namely, on a particular date and particular premises.

It is not altogether easy to lay down a precise form of words which will cover every case that can be contemplated. But, having considered the cases and the law, this court is quite clear that the direction of Judge Aarvold in this case cannot be criticised. Indeed, it might well have been made with the passage in Foster's *Crown Cases* (3rd edn) (1792) at p 369, in mind, because there the learned author says:

> 'If the principal totally and substantially varieth, if being solicited to commit a felony of one kind he *wilfully and knowingly* committeth a felony of another, *he* will stand single in that offence, and the person soliciting will not be involved in his guilt. For on *his* part it was no more than a fruitless ineffectual temptation.'

The converse of course is that, if the principal does not totally and substantially vary the advice or the help and does not wilfully and knowingly commit a different form of felony altogether, the man who has advised or helped, aided or abetted, will be guilty as an accessory before the fact.

Judge Aarvold in this case, in the passages to which I have referred, makes it clear that there must be not merely suspicion but knowledge that a crime of the type in question was intended, and that the equipment was bought with that in view. In his reference to the felony of the type intended it was, as he states, the felony of breaking and entering premises and the stealing of property from those premises. The court can see nothing wrong in that direction.

Appeal dismissed

Questions

1. Is this case authority for the proposition that the supplier of equipment for use in committing a particular type of crime is liable for all crimes of that type which are committed by the person supplied, using that equipment? Does the fact that the equipment was left behind suggest that it was for use on one occasion only?

2. A South African judge, Schreiner JA, suggests that the supplier of an implement to a burglar may be liable only for those offences which he knew, or perhaps ought to have known, were specifically in the contemplation of the burglar when he gave it to him: *Toni* 1941 (1) SA 109 at 116 (AD). Is this a workable test? What if no specific offences are contemplated by the burglar or no specific offences are known by the supplier to be contemplated by the burglar at the time of supply of the implement?

3. D knows that E makes his living by armed robberies. He supplies E with a revolver and ammunition. Is D liable for murder if E with the revolver deliberately shoots (i) a policeman who is impeding his escape after a robbery; (ii) his wife, with whom he has had a sudden quarrel?

4. D knows that E is a burglar. He supplies him with a jemmy. E, using the jemmy, breaks into D's mother's house and steals. D is furious. Is he liable for burglary? What if E had committed the burglary in D's house?

NOTE

See Law Commission Working Paper No 43, Proposition 10:

> 'Where a principal is helped in the commission of more than one offence by a single act of help, the accessory who afforded that help shall not, after having been convicted of one or more of such offences, be convicted of another of such offences of equal or lesser gravity.'

(A proposition not adopted in the draft Code, p 140, above.)

Director of Public Prosecutions for Northern Ireland v Maxwell [1978] 3 All ER 1140, House of Lords
(Viscount Dilhorne, Lord Hailsham of St Marylebone, Lord Edmund-Davies, Lord Fraser of Tullybelton and Lord Scarman)
Court of Criminal Appeal in Northern Ireland [1978] 3 All ER 1151 Note
(Lowry LCJ, Jones and McGonigal LJJ)

The appellant, a member of the Ulster Volunteer Force, proscribed in Northern Ireland, had guided terrorists to the Crosskeys Inn by leading them in his car. The trial judge found that the appellant knew there was to be 'an attack on the Crosskeys bar, not a casual or social visit or mere reconnaissance' and that 'the attack would be one of violence in which people would be endangered or premises seriously damaged.' However the appellant did not know precisely what offence was to be committed. Although the appellant was charged as a principal in the offence, of planting a pipe bomb in the Crosskeys Inn, contrary to s 3 (a) of the Explosive Substances Act 1883, the true nature of his rôle was that of an aider and abettor. He appealed against conviction on the ground that he must be shown to have known the type of crime intended to be committed and the kind of means of offence being carried to the scene.

Lowry LCJ [delivering the judgment of the Court of Criminal Appeal in Northern Ireland]. . . . Suppose the intending principal offender (whom I shall call 'the principal') tells the intended accomplice (whom I shall call 'the accomplice') that he means to shoot A or else leave a bomb at A's house and the accomplice agrees to drive the principal to A's house and keep watch while there, it seems clear that the accomplice would be guilty of aiding and abetting whichever crime the principal committed, because he would know that one of two crimes was to be committed, he would have assisted the principal and he would have intended to assist him. Again, let us suppose that the principal tells the accomplice that the intention is to murder A at one house but, if he cannot be found or the house is guarded, the alternative plan is to go to B's house and leave a bomb there or thirdly to rob a particular bank (or indeed murder somebody, or bomb somebody's house or rob any bank, as to which see *Bainbridge* ([1960] 1 QB 129, [1959] 3 All ER 200) and requests the accomplice to make a reconnaissance of a number of places and report on the best way of gaining access to the target. The accomplice agrees and makes all the reconnaissances and reports, and the principal then, without further communication, selects a target and commits the crime. It seems clear that, whichever crime the principal commits, all the ingredients of the accomplice's guilt are present. In each of these examples the accomplice knows exactly what is contemplated and the only thing he does not know is to which particular crime he will become an accessory when it is committed. His guilt springs from the fact that he contemplates the commission of one (or more) of a number of crimes by the principal and he intentionally lends his assistance in order that such a crime will be committed. In other words, he knows that the principal is committing or about to commit one of a number of specified illegal acts and with that knowledge he helps him to do so.

The situation has something in common with that of two persons who agree to rob a bank on the understanding, either express or implied from conduct (such as the carrying of a loaded gun by one person with the knowledge of the other), that violence *may* be resorted to. The accomplice knows, not that the principal *will* shoot the cashier, but that he may do so; and if the principal does shoot him, the accomplice will be guilty of murder. A different case is where the accomplice has only offence A in contemplation and the principal commits offence B. Here the accomplice, although morally culpable (and perhaps guilty of conspiring to commit offence A), is not guilty of aiding and abetting offence B. The principle with which we are dealing does not seem to us to provide a warrant, on the basis of combating lawlessness generally, for convicting an alleged accomplice of *any* offence which, helped by his preliminary acts, a principal may commit. The relevant crime must be within the contemplation of the accomplice and only exceptionally would evidence be found to support the allegation that the accomplice had given the principal a completely blank cheque. . . .

The facts found here show that the appellant, as a member of an organisation which habitually perpetrates sectarian acts of violence with firearms and explosives, must, as soon as he was briefed for his role, have contemplated the bombing of the Crosskeys Inn as not the only possibility but one of the most obvious possibilities among the jobs which the principals were likely to be undertaking and in the commission of which he was intentionally assisting. He was therefore in just the same situation, so far as guilty knowledge is concerned, as a man who had been given a list of jobs and told that one of them would be carried out. And so he is guilty of the offence alleged against him in count 1 . . .

[The Court certified the following point of law of general importance:

> 'If the crime committed by the principal, and actually assisted by the accused, was one of a number of offences, one of which the accused knew the principal would probably commit, is the guilty mind which must be proved against an accomplice thereby proved against the accused?'

The House of Lords dismissed the appeal. All of their Lordships approved the judgment of Lowry LCJ. Lord Edmund-Davies said that to do more than approve it would be a sleeveless errand; but he agreed with the view (below) of Viscount Dilhorne.]

Viscount Dilhorne. . . . No objection could be taken to the form of these counts as by statute [Accessories and Abettors Act 1861, s 8; Criminal Law Act 1967, s 1 (2)] aiders and abettors can be charged as principals, but the particulars to each count give no indication of the case the prosecution intended to present and which the appellant had to meet. In the particulars to the first count, he is charged with placing the bomb in the Crosskeys Inn; in the particulars to the second with having had it in his possession or under his control. The prosecution did not attempt to prove that he had placed the bomb or that he had been present when the bomb was put in the inn, nor was any attempt made to establish that at any time he had the bomb in his possession or under his control. It is desirable that the particulars of the offence should bear some relation to the realities and where, as here, it is clear that the appellant was alleged to have aided and abetted the placing of the bomb and its possession or control, it would in my opinion have been better if the particulars of offence had made that clear.

[**Lord Scarman** (having quoted from the judgment of Lowry CJ)] **Lowry LCJ** continues:

> 'The relevant crime must be within the contemplation of the accomplice and only exceptionally would evidence be found to support the allegation that the accomplice had given the principal a completely blank cheque.'

The principle thus formulated has great merit. It directs attention to the state of mind of the accused: not what he ought to have in contemplation, but what he did have. It avoids definition and classification, while ensuring that a man will not be convicted of aiding and abetting any offence his principal may commit, but only one which is within his contemplation. He may have in contemplation only one offence, or several; and the several which he contemplates he may see as alternatives. An accessory who leaves it to his principal to choose is liable, provided always the choice is made from the range of offences from which the accessory contemplates the choice will be made. Although the court's formulation of the principle goes further than the earlier cases, it is a sound development of the law and in no way inconsistent with them. I accept it as good judge-made law in a field where there is no statute to offer guidance.

Appeal dismissed

(3) PRINCIPAL EXCEEDING AUTHORITY

S v Robinson 1968 (1) SA 666, Supreme Court of South Africa, Appellate Division (Steyn CJ, Potgieter and Holmes JJA)

Because of dire financial distress and for the purpose of insurance gain to his widow and to avoid imprisonment for fraud, the deceased conspired with Robinson (the first appellant), his wife (the second appellant) and Esterhuizen (the third appellant) that he be shot. Robinson was to do the shooting and the deceased agreed to go on with the plan 'no matter what happens'. Robinson drove the deceased to the agreed place. At the last minute, the deceased withdrew his consent to die. Robinson then shot him. The three appellants were convicted of murder.

Steyn CJ. . . . The remark by the deceased 'No matter what happens, we must go through with it', is explained by the fact that, on at least one previous occasion, an attempt to execute the murder as planned and desired by the deceased had been frustrated, because the deceased's courage failed him and he declined to go through with it. Although the use of the word 'we' renders it less clear, this remark was in all probability intended to convey to the first appellant that he must not be deterred from the deed if the deceased should once again revoke his consent to be killed. What is perfectly clear from this evidence, is that the deceased did in fact, by saying that he could not go through with it at all, resile from the pact of murder by consent. When, in spite of that, the first appellant shot him, he was no longer a consenting or willing party. He had countermanded the arrangement, at least as between himself and the second and third appellants. He had been the author and originator of that arrangement and his willingness and desire to be killed, was an essential feature of it. There can be no doubt that, had it not been for his own wish and readiness to die, no such arrangement would have come into existence, and there can, I think, equally be no doubt that death without his consent was no part of it. He was, as all concerned must have been aware, in control of the situation he had created for himself and at liberty at any time to withdraw from it. It was precisely as a result of this that the earlier attempt had failed. Because he could not go through with it, the first appellant desisted. It is true that on the day of his death the second appellant, his wife, after he had suggested suicide by both of them, told him that, because such suicide would not achieve the purposes of his death, he 'must go through with it'. That amounted to no more than an implied exhortation not to flinch again from being killed. I cannot find in it a variation of the then existing arrangement, having the effect that he was to be killed whether or not he withdrew his consent at the crucial moment, and there is no ground for holding that it was so intended by the second appellant or so understood by the third appellant, or that anything to that effect was conveyed to the first appellant, who was not present on this occasion. The witness Kleynhans does not say that the third appellant displayed any dissatisfaction when the above-mentioned report was made to him, but that takes the matter no further. Assuming that his assent may be inferred from the absence of evidence of dissatisfaction, acquiescence, without protest ex post facto in what the first appellant had done, would not show that it was part of the common purpose. Had the deceased not told the first appellant that they must go through with it, no matter what happens, it may well be that the latter would again have refrained from the fatal deed. The common purpose was murder with the consent of the victim. In shooting the deceased after he had retracted his consent, the first appellant acted outside the common purpose. There is no evidence to show or from which it could be inferred with any certainty that the second and third appellants foresaw the possibility that the first appellant might kill the deceased even if he withdrew his consent, and that they were reckless whether or not he did so kill him. It follows that an intention on their part that the deceased was to be murdered also in such an event, has not been proved. The suggestion that the deceased was so drunk that his withdrawal of consent is to be ignored is without substance. From his remarks and reactions, as described by the first appellant, it is quite clear that he knew full well what the two of them were about. In the result, the second and third appellants have, in my opinion, not been shown to be guilty of murder.

But that is not the end of the matter. When the deceased told the appellants that they were to go through with it, no matter what happened, that did not have the effect of cancelling the arrangement of murder by consent. It merely added, as between the deceased and the first appellant, an instruction to proceed even if consent should be revoked. Had the deceased not retracted and had he been killed with his consent, it could hardly have been contended that this added instruction removed the killing from the ambit of the common purpose. Up to the point where the deceased recoiled from execution of the common purpose and said that he could not go through with it at all, the first appellant was applying himself to the achievement of that purpose. As the deceased, in relief, fell forward with his head on to the steering wheel, the first appellant pulled the trigger. The inference is justified that at that stage he had the revolver in his hand, ready to shoot. That he then had the firm intention to kill is obvious from the fact that a moment later he fired the fatal shot. In relation to the common purpose, there was, shortly before the shot was fired, a completed attempt to murder in the execution of that purpose. The fact that the first appellant proceeded beyond his attempt to a murder without consent, does not mean that at this stage he had not committed the crime of attempted murder with consent. In my view the second and third appellants cannot be absolved from complicity in this crime of attempted murder. . . .

[**Potgieter JA** concurred in the judgment of Steyn CJ.]

Holmes JA. . . . What is needed here is a robust conspectus of the circumstances as a whole. . . . looking squarely at the whole train of events, the conspiracy was fulfilled in death, and there is no room for exquisite niceties of logic about the exact limits of the mandate in the conspiratorial common purpose. The three members of the trial Court held that the appellants were all equally a party to this planned and urgently sought death. On the facts, I consider as a matter of justice that the trial Court was entitled to come to that conclusion, and there is no basis for disturbing it.

To hold that, in the known desperate circumstances of the deceased, his final instruction (ie to go through with it 'whatever happens') took the matter outside the conspiracy of death, would in my view be at odds with the realities; and it would produce an air of artificiality . . .

Questions

1. Is the opinion of the majority preferable to that of Holmes JA?

2. A employs B to follow his wife C and, if he finds she is committing adultery, to kill her. B finds that C is not committing adultery. He nevertheless kills her. What is the liability of A?

3. The draft Code (see para 10.16 of the Report) leaves a case like *Robinson* to be decided on the interpretation of cl 31 (4) and (5), as a suitable matter for 'judicial development'. Should the codifiers have offered a solution and, if so, what should it be?

(4) ACCESSORY'S KNOWLEDGE OF FACTS

Johnson v Youden [1950] 1 All ER 300, King's Bench Division
(Lord Goddard CJ, Humphreys and Lynskey JJ)

It was an offence under s 7 (1) of the Building Materials and Housing Act 1945 for a builder to sell a house at a price in excess of that fixed by the local authority in the licence to build the house. The three respondents, partners in a firm of solicitors, were charged with aiding and abetting a builder in an offence under this section and acquitted. The prosecutor appealed by way of case stated.

Lord Goddard CJ. . . . In this case the builder had a licence which entitled him to sell the house for £1,025. He induced a railway porter to agree to buy the house for £1,275, ie £250 more than the controlled price, and he instructed a firm of solicitors, in which the three respondents are partners, to act as his solicitors for the sale. The builder was charged with an offence against s 7 (1) of the Act of 1945 and was convicted, but the three respondents were acquitted on charges of aiding and abetting him.

In regard to the respondents, the justices found that, until 6 April 1949, none of them knew anything about the extra £250 which the builder was receiving, and that the first two respondents, Mr Henry Wallace Youden and Mr George Henry Youden, did not know about it at any time, as the builder deliberately concealed the fact and even refused to give the purchaser a receipt for that £250. The justices, therefore, were right, in our opinion, in dismissing the information against the first two respondents on the ground that they could not be guilty of aiding and abetting the commission of the offence as they did not know of the matter which constituted the offence. If they had known that the builder was receiving the extra £250 and had continued to ask the purchaser to complete, they would have committed an offence by continuing to assist the builder to offer the property for sale, contrary to the provisions of s 7 (1) of the Act of 1945, and, as ignorance of the law is no defence, they would have been guilty of the offence even if they had not realised that they were committing an offence, but a person cannot be convicted of aiding and abetting the commission of an offence if he does not know of the essential matters which would constitute the offence.

In regard to their partner, Mr Brydone, the third respondent, the facts are different. Until 6 or 7 April 1949, he was as ignorant as were his partners that the builder had insisted on receiving £250 beyond what he was entitled to charge, but on 6 April he received a letter from the purchaser's solicitor saying:

> 'I duly received your letter of 26 March informing me that you are ready to settle at any time and that the amount payable on completion is £925.'

The sum was £925, because the controlled price was £1,025, and £100 had been paid as deposit. The letter continued:

> 'I think I ought to let you know the reason why I have not as yet proceeded to completion. It is that I have felt compelled to report to the town clerk what I consider to be a breach by your client of the provisions of s 7 of the Building Materials and Housing Act 1945.'

This letter naturally put the third respondent, who was dealing with the matter, on inquiry, and he thereupon read the relevant provisions of the Act of 1945 and also spoke to the builder who told him a story which, even if it were true, was on the face of it obviously a colourable evasion of the Act. The builder's story was that he had placed the extra £250 in a separate deposit account and that it was to be spent on payment for work as and when he (the builder) would be lawfully able to execute it in the future on the house on behalf of the purchaser.

It seems impossible to imagine that anyone could believe such a story. Who has ever heard of a purchaser, when buying a house from a builder, putting money into the builder's hands because he may want some work done thereafter? I think that the third respondent could not have read s 7 (5) of the Act as carefully as he should have done, because I cannot believe that any solicitor, or even a layman, would not understand that the bargain which the builder described was just the kind of transaction which the Act prohibits. Section 7 (5) provides:

> 'In determining for the purposes of this section the consideration for which a house has been sold or let, the court shall have regard to any transaction with which the sale or letting is associated . . .'

If the third respondent had read and appreciated those words he would have seen at once that the extra £250 which the builder was getting was in regard to a transaction with which the sale was associated, and was, therefore, an unlawful payment. Unfortunately, however, he did not realise it, but either misread the Act or did not read it carefully, and on the following day he called on the purchaser to complete. He was, therefore, clearly aiding and abetting the builder in the offence which the builder was committing. The result is that, so far as the first two respondents are concerned, the appeal fails and must be dismissed, but, so far as the third respondent is concerned, the case must go back to the justices with an intimation that an offence has been committed, and there must be a conviction.

Humphreys J. I agree.

Lynskey J. I also agree.

Appeal dismissed in respect of the first two respondents and allowed in respect of the third respondent. Case remitted to the justices with a direction to convict the third respondent. No order as to costs.

Questions

1. Brydone's fault seems to have been that, on this occasion, he was not as good at, or perhaps as careful in, statutory interpretation, as he ought to have been. Is that a good ground for convicting him as an aider and abettor?
2. If Brydone had consulted his partners and they had all concluded that the proposed transaction would be lawful and should proceed, would they have been guilty of conspiracy? Cf Criminal Law Act 1977, s 1, p 528, below.

**Ferguson v Weaving [1951] 1 All ER 412, King's Bench Division
(Lord Goddard CJ, Hilbery and Devlin JJ)**

The respondent was the licensee of a hotel with several rooms in which intoxicating liquor was served. She was charged with aiding, abetting, counselling and procuring customers to consume liquor after hours, and acquitted. She had given signals to indicate the approach, and arrival, of closing time. (The law did not then allow 'drinking-up time'). Waiters, in breach of the instructions given by the respondent, failed to collect glasses from the offending customers in the concert room. She was performing her duties in another part of the hotel; and the magistrate found that she had done everything she could to see that the requirements of the law were complied with. The prosecutor appealed.

[**Lord Goddard CJ**, reading the judgment of the Court:]

The argument for the appellant may be summarised as follows. If the respondent herself had been present or had knowledge that the customers were consuming liquor after hours and took no steps to prevent it, she would be aiding and abetting the offence. Although she herself was not present and had no knowledge, yet, as she had placed waiters in charge of the concert room and had, as it was said, delegated the management of the room to them, their knowledge was her knowledge, and she was accordingly, guilty of aiding and abetting.

The first thing to observe is that, while s 4 of the Licensing Act 1921 prohibits a licensee from selling or supplying either by himself or his servants intoxicating liquor outside permitted hours, and also prohibits the consumption in licensed premises of any intoxicating liquor after those hours, it does not make it an offence in the licensee to suffer or permit the consumption of liquor after hours. While it may seem curious that Parliament did not make this an offence in a licensee, nothing would be gained by discussing whether the omission appears to be deliberate or accidental. The fact remains that consuming liquor after hours is only a substantive offence in the consumer. At the same time, there can be no doubt that, if a licensee consciously permits consumption after hours, it would amount to aiding and abetting the offence, but we have now to consider whether, as the section does not create a substantive offence in the licensee, she can be convicted of aiding and abetting by imputing to her the knowledge of her servants.

There can be no doubt that this court has more than once laid it down in clear terms that before a person can be convicted of aiding and abetting the commission of an offence he must at least know the essential matters which constitute the offence; see, for instance, *Johnson v Youden* [see p 153, above]. The magistrate in this case has acquitted the respondent of any knowledge of the matters which constituted the principal offence, but it is said that the cases establish that the knowledge of her servants must be imputed to her, and that there are many cases in which a licensee has been convicted although he himself did not know the facts constituting the offence is, of course, beyond question. There are certain offences under the Licensing Acts which arise because the statute imposes an absolute prohibition, for instance, the offence of selling liquor to a drunken person. In *Cundy v Le Cocq* [(1884) 13 QBD 207] it was held that the prohibition against selling to such a person imposed by s 13 of the Licensing Act 1872, now replaced by s 75 of the Licensing (Consolidation) Act 1910, is absolute and that knowledge of the condition of the person served is not necessary to constitute the offence. On the other hand, there are many offences in which it is necessary to show either that the licensee suffered or permitted the offence to take place, or that he knowingly permitted matters which constitute an offence. There is no material difference between permitting or suffering something and knowingly allowing it to take place, for, as was said in *Somerset v Hart* ((1884) 12 QBD 360):

'How can a man suffer a thing to be done when he does not know of it?'

The difference between an absolute prohibition and a prohibition against permitting or suffering was pointed out by Collins J in *Somerset v Wade* [[1894] 1 QB 574], where, under other words in the same section as was under consideration in *Cundy v Le Cocq*, the licensee was prosecuted not for selling to a drunken person but for permitting drunkenness on licensed premises. As it was there proved that the licensee did not know that the person in question was drunk the court held he could not be convicted of permitting drunkenness, though they approved the decision in *Cundy v Le Cocq* because the prohibition against selling to a drunken person was absolute.

We now turn to the cases in which knowledge has been imputed to a licensee because of the knowledge of his manager or servant. It is unnecessary to go through them all because the principle which applies was laid down, not for the first time, in *Linnett v Metropolitan Police Comrs* [[1946] KB 290; [1946] 1 All ER 380]. All the cases on the subject were quoted and, in giving judgment, I said ([1946] 1 All ER 382):

'The principle does not, in my opinion, depend merely upon the legal relationship between the two persons, the person who actually permitted with knowledge and the person who is convicted although he had no actual knowledge. The point does not, as I say, depend merely on the fact that the relationship of master and servant exists; it depends on the fact that the person who is responsible in law as the keeper of the house, or the licensee of the house if the offence is under the Licensing Act [1872], has chosen to delegate his duties, powers and authority to somebody else.'

We will assume for the purpose of this case that the respondent had delegated to the waiters the conduct and management of the concert room, and if the Act of 1921 had made it an offence for a liccnsee knowingly to permit liquor to be consumed after hours then the fact that she had delegated the management and control of the concert room to the waiters would have made their .knowledge her knowledge. In this case there is no substantive offence in the licensee at all. The substantive offence is committed only by the customers. She can aid and abet the customers if she knows that the customers are committing the offence, but we are not prepared to hold that knowledge can be imputed to her so as to make her, not a principal offender, but an aider and abettor. So to hold would be to establish a new principle in criminal law and one for which there is no authority. If Parliament had desired to make a licensee guilty of an offence by allowing persons to consume liquor after hours it would have been perfectly easy so to provide in the section. A doctrine of criminal law that a licensee who has knowledge of the facts is liable as a principal in the second degree is no reason for holding that, if she herself had no knowledge of the facts but someone in her employ and to whom she may have entrusted the management of the room did know them, this makes her an aider and abettor. As no duty is imposed on her by the section to prevent the consumption of liquor after hours there was no duty in this respect that she could delegate to her employees. While it may be that the waiters could have been prosecuted for aiding and abetting the consumers, as to which we need express no opinion, we are clearly of opinion that the respondent could not be. To hold the contrary would, in our opinion, be an unwarranted extension of the doctrine of vicarious responsibility in criminal law. The appeal will be dismissed with costs.

Appeal dismissed

NOTE

In connection with Lord Goddard's remarks on delegation and vicarious responsibility, compare *Vane v Yiannopoullos* p 171, below.

Questions

1. Why should the knowledge of the waiters be imputed to the licensee where the licensee is charged as a principal and not where he is charged as an abettor? If the licensee should be treated as if he knew that which he does not know for the one purpose, why not for the other?
2. If the Licensing Act had made it an offence for a licensee to permit liquor to be consumed after hours, would Weaving have been guilty of that offence?

**National Coal Board v Gamble [1958] 3 All ER 203, Queen's Bench Division
(Lord Goddard CJ, Slade and Devlin JJ)**

The Board was convicted of having aided, abetted, counselled and procured the commission of the offence of using a motor lorry on a road with a load weighing more than that permitted, in contravention of the Motor Vehicles (Construction and Use) Regulations, 68 and 104, 1955. The lorry was driven by one Mallender whose employers were convicted of the offence as principals. The Board appealed by way of case stated. The facts appear sufficiently in the judgment of Devlin J.

[**Lord Goddard** delivered judgment dismissing the appeal.]

Devlin J. A person who supplies the instrument for a crime or anything essential to its commission aids in the commission of it; and if he does so knowingly and with intent to aid, he abets it as well and is therefore guilty of aiding and abetting. I use the word 'supplies' to comprehend giving, lending, selling or any other transfer of the right of property. In a sense a man who gives up to a criminal a weapon which the latter has a right to demand from him aids in the commission of the crime as much as if he sold or lent the article, but this has never been held to be aiding in law (see *Lomas* (1913) 110 LT 239, and *Bullock* [1955] 1 All ER 15). The reason, I think, is that in the former [Sic. Presumably 'latter' is intended.] case there is in law a positive act and in the latter [Sic. Presumably 'former' is intended.] only a negative one. In the transfer of property there must be either a physical delivery or a positive act of assent to a taking; but a man who hands over to another his own property on demand, although he may physically be performing a positive act, in law is only refraining from detinue. Thus in law the former act is one of assistance voluntarily given and the latter is only a failure to prevent the commission of the crime by means of a forcible detention, which would not even be justified except in the case of felony. Another way of putting the point is to say that aiding and abetting is a crime that requires proof of mens rea, that is to say, of intention to aid as well as of knowledge of the circumstances, and that proof of the intent involves proof of a positive act of assistance voluntarily done. These considerations make it necessary to determine at what point the property in the coal passed from the Coal Board and what the Coal Board's state of knowledge was at that time. If the property had passed before the Coal Board knew of the proposed crime, there was nothing they could legally do to prevent the driver of the lorry from taking the overloaded lorry out on to the road. If it had not, then they sold the coal with knowledge that an offence was going to be committed.

The Coal Board called no evidence, so that a good deal was left to inference; but the conclusions of fact reached by the magistrates have not been seriously disputed. The Coal Board had an instalment contract with the Central Electricity Authority for a supply of coal to be delivered at the colliery into lorries sent by a carrier on behalf of the authority. The quantity of each instalment was not prescribed and the inference is that the Coal Board were to deliver and the carrier to receive as much as each lorry could carry (which means of course as much as it could legally and safely carry) until the contract quantity was exhausted. The method of delivery was for the lorry to be loaded by hopper and then to proceed to a weighbridge; there were off-loading facilities if the load was found to be overweight. At the weighbridge a ticket was issued in accordance with the Weights and Measures Act 1889, s 21 (1), which provides that where any quantity of coal exceeding two hundredweight is delivered by means of any vehicle to any purchaser, the seller of the coal shall deliver or send by post to the purchaser or his servant, before any part of the coal is unloaded, a ticket or note in the prescribed form. On this occasion the carrier's lorry was driven by one Mallender and its maximum legal load (after allowing for the tare weight) was 11 tons 12 hundredweights. It was loaded at the hopper, Mallender telling the operator when to stop. Mallender then took the lorry to the weighbridge. The weighbridge operator, one Haslam, weighed the lorry and its load and informed Mallender that his load was nearly four tons overweight. Haslam asked Mallender whether he intended taking the load and Mallender said he would risk it; he then took the weight ticket from Haslam and left the colliery.

In these circumstances prima facie the property in the coal passed on delivery to the carrier in accordance with r 5 of s 18 of the Sale of Goods Act 1893. If the delivery was complete after loading and before weighing, the Coal Board had not until after delivery any knowledge that an offence had been committed; but where weighing is necessary for the purpose of the contract, as for example in order to ascertain the price of an instalment, the property does not pass until the weight has been agreed. . . .

It was contended on behalf of the Coal Board that Haslam had no option after weighing but to issue the ticket for the amount then in the lorry. I think that this contention is unsound. In the circumstances of this case the loading must be taken as subject to adjustment; otherwise, if the contract were for a limited amount, the seller might make an over-delivery or an under-delivery which could not thereafter be rectified and the carrier might be contractually compelled to carry away a load in excess of that legally permitted. I think that the delivery of the coal was not completed until after the ascertained weight had been assented to and some act was done signifying assent and passing the property. The property passed when Haslam asked Mallender whether he intended to take the load and Mallender said he would risk it and when the mutual assent was, as it were, sealed by the delivery and acceptance of the weight ticket. Haslam could, therefore, after he knew of the overload have refused to transfer the property in the coal.

This is the conclusion to which the justices came. Counsel for the Coal Board submits that it does not justify a verdict of guilty of aiding and abetting. He submits, first, that even if knowledge of the illegal purpose had been acquired before delivery began, it would not be sufficient for the verdict; and secondly, that if he is wrong about that, the knowledge was acquired too late, and the Coal Board was not guilty of aiding and abetting simply because Haslam failed to stop the process of delivery after it had been initiated.

On his first point counsel submits that the furnishing of an article essential to the crime with knowledge of the use to which it is to be put does not of itself constitute aiding and abetting; there must be proved in addition a purpose or motive of the defendant to further the crime or encourage the criminal. Otherwise, he submits, there is no mens rea.

I have already said that in my judgment there must be proof of intent to aid. I would agree that proof that the article was knowingly supplied is not conclusive evidence of intent to aid. *Fretwell* ((1862) Le & Ca 161) is authority for that. *Steane* p 60, above, in which the defendant was charged with having acted during the war with intent to assist the enemy contrary to the defence regulations then in force, makes the same point. But prima facie—and *Steane* makes this clear also—a man is presumed to intend the natural and probable consequences of his acts and the consequence of supplying essential material is that assistance is given to the criminal. It is always open to the defendant, as in *Steane* to give evidence of his real intention; but in this case the defence called no evidence. The prima facie presumption is therefore enough to justify the verdict, unless it is the law that some other mental element besides intent is necessary to the offence.

This is what counsel for the Coal Board argues, and he describes the additional element as the purpose or motive of encouraging the crime. No doubt evidence of an interest in the crime or of an express purpose to assist it will greatly strengthen the case for the prosecution, but an indifference to the result of the crime does not of itself negative abetting. If one man deliberately sells to another a gun to be used for murdering a third, he may be indifferent whether the third man lives or dies and interested only in the cash profit to be made out of the sale, but he can still be an aider and abettor. To hold otherwise would be to negative the rule that mens rea is a matter of intent only and does not depend on desire or motive.

The authorities, I think, support this conclusion, though none has been cited to us in which the point has been specifically argued and decided. The Lord Chief Justice has quoted the statement of the law in *Ackroyds Air Travel Ltd v Director of Public Prosecutions* ([1950] 1 All ER 933), which is consistent with the results reached in the earlier cases of *Cook v Stockwell* ((1915) 84 LJKB 2187) and *Cafferata v Wilson, Reeve v Wilson* ([1936] 3 All ER 149) and with the later case of *Bullock* ([1955] 1 All ER 15). The same principle has been applied in civil cases where the seller has sued on a contract for the supply of goods which he knew were to be used for an illegal purpose. In some of the authorities there is a suggestion that he could recover on the contract unless it appeared that in addition to knowledge of the purpose he had an interest in the venture and looked for payment to the proceeds of the crime. In *Pearce v Brooks* ((1866) LR 1 Exch 213) Pollock, CB (ibid, at p 217) stated the law as follows:

> '. . . I have always considered it as settled law, that any person who contributes to the performance of an illegal act by supplying a thing with the knowledge that it is going to be used for that purpose, cannot recover the price of the thing so supplied. If, to create that incapacity, it was ever considered necessary that the price should be bargained for or expected to be paid out of the fruits of the illegal act (which I do not stop to examine), that proposition has been overruled by the cases I have referred to [viz, *Cannan v Bryce* (1819) 3 B & Ald 179 and *M'Kinnell v Robinson* (1838) 3 M & W 434], and has now ceased to be law.'

The case chiefly relied on by counsel for the Coal Board was *Coney* ((1882) 8 QBD 534). In this case the defendants were charged with aiding and abetting an illegal prize fight at which they had been present. The judgments all refer to 'encouragement', but it would be wrong to conclude from that that encouragement is necessary to every form of aiding and abetting. Presence on the scene of the crime without encouragement or assistance is no aid to the criminal; the supply of essential material is. Moreover, the decision makes it clear that encouragement can be inferred from mere presence. Cave J, who gave the leading judgment, said of the summing-up (ibid, at p 543):

> 'It may mean either that mere presence unexplained is evidence of encouragement, and so of guilt, or that mere presence unexplained is conclusive proof of encouragement, and so of guilt. If the former is the correct meaning, I concur in the law so laid down, if the latter, I am unable to do so.'

This dictum seems to me to support the view which I have expressed. If voluntary presence is prima facie evidence of encouragement and therefore of aiding and abetting, it appears to me to be a fortiori that the intentional supply of an essential article must be prima facie evidence of aiding and abetting.

As to counsel for the Coal Board's alternative point, I have already expressed the view that the facts show an act of assent made by Haslam after knowledge of the proposed illegality and without which the property would not have passed. If some positive act to complete delivery is committed after knowledge of the illegality, the position in law must, I think, be just the same as if the knowledge had been obtained before the delivery had been begun. Of course, it is quite likely that Haslam was confused about the legal position and thought that he was not entitled to withhold the weight ticket. There is no mens rea if the defendant is shown to have a genuine belief in the existence of circumstances which, if true, would negative an intention to aid; see *Wilson v Inyang* ([1951] 2 KB 799, [1951] 2 All ER 237). This argument, however, which might have been the most cogent available to the defence, cannot now be relied on, because Haslam was not called to give evidence about what he thought or believed. . . .

[**Slade J** dissented, holding that an aider and abettor must be shown to have assisted or encouraged and that 'assist' and 'encourage' necessarily import motive. There was no evidence that Haslam was inspired by a desire to encourage Mallender to commit the offence.]

Appeal dismissed

NOTES

1. The court accepted the Board's invitation to identify the Board with their servant and to treat the Board as answerable for the servant's offence. Slade J felt doubtful of the court's jurisdiction to do so on a criminal charge. But for this invitation, the Board could not have been convicted. It could not be held vicariously liable for aiding and abetting, as distinct from committing the offence in question (see *Ferguson v Weaving*, p 154, above) and Haslam was much too inferior a servant for his acts to be regarded as the acts of the Board. See *John Henshall (Quarries) Ltd v Harvey* [1965] 2 QB 233 and *Tesco Supermarkets Ltd v Nattrass* (p 181, below).

2. Professor Williams argues, relying principally on *Hodgson v Temple* (1813) 5 Taunt 181, that a seller can enforce a sale of goods made in the ordinary course of business although he knew of the buyer's illegal purpose, at least if the illegality is a minor one and does not involve great immorality; and that this inevitably implies that he is not a party to a crime (CLGP, p 372). Other civil cases hold that the seller may not sue on the contract but Professor Williams thinks it is settled that *Hodgson v Temple* is the case which would be followed today. A different view however is taken (without discussion) by Treitel, *Law of Contract* (5th edn) p 320, note 35; Williston, *Contracts*, Revised ed., sections 1754-6. Professor Williams distinguishes sale from letting on the ground that the letter is involved more continuously in the known illegality than the seller. *Pearce v Brooks* was a case of hire purchase though no distinction was drawn between letting and sale and Devlin J treats it as an authority on 'supply' which would cover both. Is the distinction between sale and hire a valid one?

3. Should we distinguish between major illegalities known to be contemplated by buyers which would both disable the seller from suing on the contract and make him liable for the buyer's crime—and minor illegalities which would not disable the seller from suing and would leave him free from criminal liability? On what principle should the distinction be based? See Smith [1972B] CLJ 197, 208-211. Devlin J distinguishes sharply between the sale or loan of an article on the one hand and the surrender of an article to its owner on the other. It follows that there is a distinction between one who enters into an agreement to sell or to let, knowing from the start of the illegal purpose of the buyer or hirer, and one who only discovers that illegal purpose after the transaction has passed the point at which the other party acquires proprietary rights. Is this a valid distinction?

Questions

1. D agrees (*a*) to sell (*b*) to let on hire his car to E. D knows that E intends to drive the car himself and—(i) has no licence to drive; or (ii) has no insurance against third party risks; or (iii) is disqualified; or (iv) is subject to epileptic fits. Is D liable for offences that E commits by driving the car? (Cf Smith & Hogan, ch. 8, heads 1, 7)

2. D agrees (*a*) to sell (*b*) to let, his house to E. D knows that E intends to use the house (i) as a brothel (cf. Sexual Offences Act, 1956, s 34, Smith & Hogan, p 431); (ii) as a residence for his mistress (cf *Upfill v Wright* [1911] 1 KB 506, where it was held that the landlord could not recover the rent because he knew that the tenant had such an immoral purpose); (iii) as a centre for espionage. Is D liable for offences that E commits in the house?

3. In *Lomas*, the accused was held to be not guilty of aiding and abetting a burglary by returning to the burglar, one King, a jemmy which the accused had borrowed from him. How do you think Devlin J would have dealt with an action by King in detinue to recover his jemmy from Lomas? See the Report on Codification, 10.17, p 144, above.

NOTE

In *Lynch* (1974), p 211, below, the Court of Criminal Appeal in Northern Ireland dismissed an appeal against conviction for murder as an aider and abettor. The appellant had set up the defence of duress, contending that he drove the killers to the scene of the crime only because he believed that, otherwise, he would have been shot. On appeal, it was argued that the trial judge misdirected the jury in the following passage:

> 'If, of course, a man knows that a certain crime is intended to be committed, and it is committed and he has physically participated, then there is no question but that he is guilty. He has aided and abetted.'

Lowry CJ, giving the opinion of the majority said:

> 'To abet means "to encourage" or "to instigate" and in modern English is used only in a bad sense. Therefore it may be contended that someone who aids and abets an offence must be seen both to assist and to encourage its commission, in other words both to give intentional physical assistance and intentional encouragement and that the latter activity involves a specific intent, namely that the primary actor should be encouraged to commit the offence. In order to consider this point, one must first analyse the ingredients of aiding and abetting separately from the context of duress . . .
> The learned authors of Smith and Hogan suggest (3rd edn, p 93 note 5) that "aid" and "abet" are synonymous, as are also "counsel" and "procure". In support of this view, we have not found any case where a person has been acquitted on the ground that he was not shown to have *both* aided *and* abetted, and we have also observed the disjunctive word "or" in section 8 of the Accessories and Abettors Act, 1861. Smith and Hogan say (p 94):
>> "An 'abettor' (meaning an aider or abettor—see p 93, note 5) is one who is present assisting *or* encouraging the principal at the time of the commission of the offence."
>> (our italics).
> In *Clarkson* [1971] 3 All ER 344, Megaw LJ, delivering the judgment of the Court-Martials Appeal Court, cited with approval an extract from the judgment of Hawkins J in *Coney* (1882) 8 QBD 534 at 558, where the judge set out the circumstances in which a jury would be justified in finding that a person "wilfully encouraged *and so* aided and abetted." If such a finding leads to guilt, then it would be strange if a person who knowingly and voluntarily *aids* is not equally guilty.
> We conclude that, when presence and physical participation are proved, the only element remaining to be established is knowledge that the acts which are to be done will probably result in the death or serious personal injury of a third person. If intention has to be proved, then it is enough to prove intent to assist and this is done, as Ackner J told the

jury in *Hyam's* case, by proving participation together with the knowledge already mentioned. On either basis we consider that the learned judge's direction at p 218 was adequate.'

Lowry CJ's judgment on this point was approved by the House of Lords, [1975] 1 All ER 913.

Callow v Tillstone (1900) 83 LT 411, Queen's Bench Division
(Lawrence and Kennedy JJ)

A heifer belonging to a farmer, Lintott, became very ill in consequence of eating yew leaves. Lintott killed the heifer which would probably have died in a few minutes. Callow, a veterinary surgeon, accompanied by Lintott and Grey, a butcher, examined the carcase and certified that it was sound and healthy. The examination was negligently conducted. If Callow had exercised due care, he must have discovered that the meat was unsound. Grey exposed the meat for sale and was convicted by the justices of exposing for sale meat which was unsound and unfit for human consumption. Subsequently Callow was convicted by the justices of aiding and abetting Grey's offence. The justices found that Callow had been guilty of negligence and that such negligence had caused the exposure of the unsound meat for sale. The justices stated a case, asking 'Was the negligence of which the justices found Callow had been guilty sufficient to support the conviction for aiding and abetting . . .?'

Lawrence J. In this case we have no doubt that the justices came to a wrong conclusion in finding that the appellant Callow was guilty of the offence charged against him. What they had found him guilty of was only negligence, and the question now arises upon that finding whether Callow, who was the veterinary surgeon called in in the case, can be found guilty of aiding and abetting the exposing for sale of this unsound meat, when all that the justices find against him is negligence. The justices found that Callow had been guilty of negligence and thereby abetted Grey, and upon that they convicted him. We think that is not sufficient, and the case of *Benford v Simms* [1898] 2 QB 641 is very strong to show that it is not sufficient. In that case, where there was a conviction, the defendant, a veterinary surgeon, had—according to the finding of the justices—knowingly counselled the owner of a horse to cause the act of cruelty in question and Channell J says at the end of his judgment, that the decision of the court in that case 'afforded no ground whatever for supposing that a veterinary surgeon who gives a wrong opinion and commits an error in judgment is liable to be convicted of cruelty if the effect of his opinion being followed is that the act of cruelty does in fact result'. I think, therefore, the appeal must be allowed.

Kennedy J: I am entirely of the same opinion. It seems to me that all that is found by the justices against the appellant is negligence, and to my mind a person cannot be convicted of aiding and abetting the commission of this offence upon such a finding. In this case the appellant gave his certificate, one is bound to assume, quite honestly, and therefore it seems to me he ought not to be convicted under s 5 of aiding and abetting the exposing of the meat for sale.

Appeal allowed. Conviction quashed

Questions

1. It is clear that it would have been no defence for the butcher to show that he was exercising all proper care reasonably relying on the skill and judgment of the vet, and had no means of knowing that the meat was unsound: *Hobbs v Winchester Corpn* [1910] 2 KB 471, CA (a decision to which Kennedy LJ was a party). In such a case, what is the justification for convicting the butcher who is blameless while acquitting the veterinary surgeon who is the cause of the commission of the offence?

2. If the policy of strict liability requires the conviction of a blameless principal, why does it not equally require the conviction of a blameless secondary party?—let alone a negligent secondary party?

(5) ABETTING BY INACTIVITY

R v Allan [1963] 2 All ER 897, Court of Criminal Appeal
(Edmund Davies, Marshall and Lawton JJ)

The appellants were convicted of making an affray and appealed on the ground of misdirection.

[**Edmund Davies J** read the judgment of the Court:]

. . . The legal point that calls for determination is as to the learned judge's direction regarding the proof necessary before an accused person may properly be convicted of making an affray, but the criticism made of it involves consideration of matters which have an importance which reaches beyond the confines of the law as to affrays. The learned judge had caused to be typed out copies of his direction which were handed to the jury and, one may take it, this was carefully studied by them and operated to guide their deliberations, as it was intended to do. The direction was in the following terms:

'1. An affray is a fight between two or more people in a public street that is likely to terrify passers-by or residents. 2. Every person who is a party to an affray is guilty of an offence. 3. Mere presence at the fight does not make a person a party to it, even if he does nothing to stop it; nor is he a party to it if he tries to stop the fight and restore the Queen's Peace, or if he tries to defend someone from being hurt, because it is lawful to intervene for this purpose. 4. Every person is, however, a party and guilty who: (i) agrees that such a fight should take place and, in pursuance of that agreement, is later present at it; *or* (ii) without such agreement unlawfully joins in such a fight, or, being present, chose to remain present, either (*a*) knowing that his continued presence encouraged the fight, *or* (*b*) intending to join in the fight if his help was needed by his side'.

No criticism has been, or properly could be, levelled against para 1, para 2, para 3 and para 4(i) of that direction, nor as to the direction in para 4(ii) that a person unlawfully joining in an affray is guilty, notwithstanding the absence of prior agreement. Paragraph 4(ii)(*a*) is, however, attacked as containing what learned counsel described as 'a concealed dichotomy'. This highly alarming concept fortunately does not call for comment, and, we can turn forthwith to consider the more telling attack made on para 4(ii)(*b*). In effect, it amounts to this: that the learned judge thereby directed the jury that they were in duty bound to convict an accused who was proved to have been present and witnessing an affray if it was also proved that he nursed an intention to join in if help was needed by the side which he favoured, and this notwithstanding that he did nothing by words or deeds to evince his intention and outwardly played the role of a purely passive spectator. It was said that, if that direction is right, where A and B behave themselves to all outward appearances in an exactly similar manner, but it be proved that A had the intention to participate if needs be, whereas B had no such intention, then A must be convicted of being a principal in the second degree to the affray, whereas B should be acquitted. To do that, it is objected, would be to convict A on his thoughts, even though they found no reflection in his actions. For the Crown, on the other hand, it is contended that the direction was unimpeachable, and that, in the given circumstances, a jury doing its duty would be bound to convict A of aiding and abetting in an affray, even though he uttered no word of encouragement and acted throughout in exactly the same manner as all the other spectators of what was happening. . . .

Applying these passages to the direction in the present case, we have come to the conclusion that, in effect, the trial judge here dealt with facts which, at most, might provide some evidence of encouragement as amounting to conclusive proof of guilt. The jury were in terms told that a man who chooses to remain at a fight, nursing the secret intention to help if the need arose, but doing nothing to evince that intention, *must* in law be held to be a principal in the second degree and that, on these facts being proved, the jury would have no alternative but to convict him. In our judgment, that was a misdirection. As Cave J said in *Coney* [(1882) 8 QBD at 540], 'Where presence is prima facie not accidental it is evidence, but no more than evidence, for the jury', and it remains no more than evidence for the jury even when one adds to presence at an affray a secret intention to help. No authority in support of the direction given in the present case has been cited to us. The passage in *Young* [(1838) 8 C & P 644 at 652] cited in *Coney* [(1882) 8 QBD at 541], is incomplete, and reference to the report itself makes clear that Vaughan J was there dealing with presence at a fight as the result of a previous arrangement. The only other case cited by the Crown, *Wilcox v Jeffery* [below] turned on special facts very different from the present, and is one from which we think no general principle can be deduced. In the present case, the trial judge dealt with matters of evidence from which encouragement (and, therefore, guilty participation) might be inferred if—but only if—the jury thought fit to do so as necessarily amounting in law to proof that guilt was established. In our judgment, this amounted to a misdirection, and one, unfortunately, of a basic kind.

Appeals allowed

R v Clarkson and Carroll [1971] 3 All ER 344, Courts-Martial Appeal Court (Megaw LJ, Geoffrey Lane and Kilner Brown JJ)

The appellants, soldiers, entered a room in their barracks in which a girl was being raped by other soldiers. They were charged with aiding and abetting the rape. There was no evidence that either had done any act or uttered any word which involved direct physical participation or verbal encouragement. They appealed on the ground of misdirection by the judge-advocate.

[**Megaw LJ** delivered the judgment of the Court:]

Coney [(1882) 8 QBD 534] decided that non-accidental presence at the scene of the crime is not conclusive of aiding and abetting. The jury has to be told by the judge, or as in this case the court-martial has to be told by the judge-advocate, in clear terms what it is that has to be proved before they can convict of aiding and abetting; what it is of which the jury or the court-martial, as the case may be, must be sure as matters of inference before they can convict of aiding and abetting in such a case where the evidence adduced by the prosecution is limited to non-accidental presence (His Lordship quoted from *Coney* [(1882) 8 QBD 534 at 557, 558]). It is not enough, then, that the presence of the accused has, in fact, given encouragement. It must be proved that he *wilfully* encouraged. In such a case as the present, more than in many other cases where aiding and abetting is alleged, it was essential that that element should be stressed; for there was here at least the possibility that a drunken man with his self-discipline loosened by drink, being aware that a woman was being raped, might be attracted to the scene and might stay on the scene in the capacity of what is known as a voyeur; and, while his presence and the presence of others might in fact encourage the rapers or discourage the victim, he himself, enjoying the scene or at least standing by assenting, might not intend that his presence should offer encouragement to rapers and would-be rapers and discouragement to the victim; he might not realise that he was giving encouragement; so that, while encouragement there might be, it would not be a case in which, to use the words of Hawkins J [(1882) 8 QBD 534 at 558] the accused person wilfully encouraged. [His Lordship quoted *Allan*, p 162, above.]

From that it follows that mere intention is not in itself enough. There must be an intention to encourage; and there must also be encouragement in fact, in cases such as the present case.

Appeals allowed

Wilcox v Jeffery [1951] 1 All ER 464, King's Bench Division (Lord Goddard CJ, Humphreys and Devlin JJ)

Lord Goddard CJ. This is a case stated by the metropolitan magistrate at Bow Street Magistrate's Court before whom the appellant, Herbert William Wilcox, the proprietor of a periodical called *Jazz Illustrated*, was charged on an information that 'on 11 December 1949, he did unlawfully aid and abet one Coleman Hawkins in contravening art 1 (4) of the Aliens Order 1920, by failing to comply with a condition attached to a grant of leave to land, to wit, that the said Coleman Hawkins should take no employment paid or unpaid while in the United Kingdom, contrary to art 18 (2) of the Aliens Order 1920'. Under the Aliens Order, art 1 (1), it is provided that

'. . . an alien coming . . . by sea to a place in the United Kingdom—(a) shall not land in the United Kingdom without the leave of an immigration officer . . .'

It is provided by art 1 (4) that:

'An immigration officer, in accordance with general or special directions of the Secretary of State, may, by general order or notice or otherwise, attach such conditions as he may think fit to the grant of leave to land, and the Secretary of State may at any time vary such conditions in such manner as he thinks fit, and the alien shall comply with the conditions so attached or varied . . .'

If the alien fails to comply, he is to be in the same position as if he has landed without permission, ie he commits an offence.

The case is concerned with the visit of a celebrated professor of the saxophone, a gentleman by the name of Hawkins who was a citizen of the United States. He came here at the invitation of two gentlemen of the name of Curtis and Hughes, connected with a jazz club which enlivens the neighbourhood of Willesden. They, apparently, had applied for permission for Mr Hawkins to land and it was refused, but, nevertheless, this professor of the saxophone arrived with four French musicians. When they came to the airport, among the people who were there to greet them was the appellant. He had not arranged their visit, but he knew they were coming and he was there to report the arrival of these important musicians for his magazine. So, evidently, he was regarding the visit of Mr Hawkins as a matter which would be of interest to himself and the magazine which he was editing and selling for profit. Messrs Curtis and Hughes arranged a concert at the Princes Theatre, London. The appellant attended that concert as a spectator. He paid for his ticket. Mr Hawkins went on the stage and delighted the audience by playing the saxophone. The appellant did not get up and protest in the name of the musicians of England that Mr Hawkins ought not to be here competing with them and taking the bread out of their mouths or the wind out of their instruments. It is not found that he actually applauded, but he was there having paid to go in, and, no doubt, enjoying the performance, and then, lo and behold, out comes his magazine with a most laudatory description, fully illustrated, of this concert. On those facts the magistrate has found that he aided and abetted.

Reliance is placed by the prosecution on *Coney* [see pp 158, 160, above].

There was not accidental presence in this case. The appellant paid to go to the concert and he went there because he wanted to report it. He must, therefore, be held to have been present, taking part, concurring, or encouraging, whichever word you like to use for expressing this conception. It was an illegal act on the part of Hawkins to play the saxophone or any other instrument at this concert. The appellant clearly knew that it was an unlawful act for him to play. He had gone there to hear him, and his presence and his payment to go there was an encouragement. He went there to make use of the performance, because he went there, as the magistrate finds and was justified in finding, to get 'copy' for his newspaper. It might have been entirely different, as I say, if he had gone there and protested, saying: 'The musicians' union do not like you foreigners coming here and playing and you ought to get off the stage'. If he had booed, it might have been some evidence that he was not aiding and abetting. If he had gone as a member of a *claque* to try to drown the noise of the saxophone, he might very likely be found not guilty of aiding and abetting. In this case it seems clear that he was there, not only to approve and encourage what was done, but to take advantage of it by getting 'copy' for his paper. In those circumstances there was evidence on which the magistrate could find that the appellant aided and abetted, and for these reasons I am of opinion that the appeal fails.

Humphreys J. I agree that there was evidence sufficient to justify the finding of the magistrate.

Devlin J. I agree, and I wish to add only a word on the application of *Coney*. Counsel for the appellant sought to distinguish that case on the facts inasmuch as in *Coney* the performance, which was a prize fight, was illegal from beginning to end, whereas in the case we are considering the bulk of the concert was quite legal, the only part of the performance which was illegal being that which involved Mr Hawkins. That, however, is not, in my judgment, a distinction which affects the application to this case of the principle in *Coney*. It may well be that if a spectator goes to a concert he may explain his presence during an illegal item by saying that he hardly felt it necessary to get up and go out and then return when the performance resumed its legality, if I may so call it. It is conceivable that in such circumstances (and I should wish to consider it further if it ever arose) the presence of a person during one item might fall within the accidental or casual class which was envisaged by Cave J. Here there was abundant evidence, apart from the mere fact of the appellant's presence, that he was making use of this item in the performance and that his attendance at that item was, therefore, deliberate. In those circumstances I think the principle in *R v Coney* applies, and that the magistrate was justified in drawing the inference which he did draw.

Appeal dismissed with costs

Questions

1. Fred and George go to a public house on Saturday night. They know that during the evening an obscene performance lasting half-an-hour will be given. Fred, who only drinks lemonade, goes because he relishes an obscene show. George, who is not interested in the show, is only there for the beer. The licensee is convicted of keeping a disorderly house. Are Fred and George guilty of abetting him?

2. Cf Law Commission Working Paper No 43, Proposition 8.

> 'A person does not become an accessory to an offence if the offence is so defined that his conduct in it is inevitably incidental to its commission and such conduct is not expressly penalised.' If this were law, would *Wilcox v Jeffery* be overruled?

(6) ACCESSORY'S FORESIGHT OF CONSEQUENCES

Chan Wing-siu v The Queen [1984] 3 All ER 877, Privy Council (Lords Keith, Bridge, Brandon and Templeman and Sir Robin Cooke)

The three appellants were convicted in Hong Kong of murder and wounding with intent. They went to the deceased's flat to commit a robbery, armed with knives. The deceased was stabbed to death and his wife was wounded. The judge directed the jury that they could convict each of the accused on both counts if he was proved to have had in contemplation that a knife might be used by one of his co-adventurers with the intention of inflicting serious bodily injury.

Sir Robin Cooke. . . . . A line of relevant English authorities from 1830 onwards was considered by the Court of Criminal Appeal in *R v Anderson and Morris* [1966] 2 All ER 644, [1966] 2 QB 110. Delivering the judgment of a court of five, Lord Parker CJ accepted a submission by Geoffrey Lane QC, and stated the law as follows, in terms very close to those reported ([1966] 2 QB 110 at 114) to have been formulated by counsel:

> '. . . where two persons embark on a joint enterprise, each is liable for the acts done in pursuance of that joint enterprise, and that includes liability for unusual consequences if they arise from the execution of the agreed joint enterprise but (and this is the crux of the matter) . . . if one of the adventurers goes beyond what has been tacitly agreed as part of the common enterprise, his co-adventurer is not liable for the consequences of that unauthorised act. Finally . . . it is for the jury in every case to decide whether what was done was part of the joint enterprise, or went beyond it and was in fact an act unauthorised by that joint enterprise.'

(See [1966] 2 All ER 644 at 647, [1966] 2 QB 110 at 118–119.)

In England it appears not to have been found necessary hitherto to analyse more elaborately the test which the jury have to apply. But, in association with the modern emphasis on subjective tests of criminal guilt, the matter has been examined by appellate courts in Australia and New Zealand. In *Johns v R* (1980) 143 CLR 108 the High Court of Australia rejected an argument that at common law an accessory before the fact is not liable for the crime, although contemplated by him as an act which might be done in the course of the venture, unless it was more probable than not that the criminal act charged would take place. Stephen J in his judgment (at 122) and Mason, Murphy and Wilson JJ in a joint judgment (at 130–131) approved the following statement by Street CJ in the Supreme Court of New South Wales:

> '. . . an accessory before the fact bears, as does a principal in the second degree, a 'criminal liability for an act which was within the contemplation of both himself and the principal in the first degree as an act which might be done in the course of carrying out the primary criminal intention—an act contemplated as a possible incident of the originally planned particular venture.'

The joint judgment added that such an act is one which falls within the parties' own purpose and design precisely because it is within their contemplation and is foreseen as a possible incident of the execution of their planned enterprise. Stephen J, taking a phrase from *Howard on Criminal Law* (3rd edn, 1967), spoke of contemplation by the parties of a 'substantial risk' that the killing would occur. The same phrase was used by the High Court in a case of extraordinary facts, *Miller v R* (1980) 55 ALJR 23. There approval was given to a direction to the effect that the accused was guilty of murder if the common plan included the possible murder of girls, so that the parties to the plan contemplated as a substantial risk the murder of any girl who was picked up, even though it was not contemplated that murder would occur in the course of every drive.

Those two Australian authorities were cited to, and strongly influenced, the Hong Kong Court of Appeal in the present case. In *R v Gush* [1980] 2 NZLR 92, delivering a judgment of the New Zealand Court of Appeal, Richmond P applied the approach in *Johns v R* when interpreting a provision in a statutory code (s 66 (2) of the Crimes Act 1961) making a person liable as a party 'if the commission of that offence was known to be a probable consequence of the prosecution of the common purpose'. After discussing the range of meanings which 'probable' may bear, he said (at 95) that the statutory objects would be largely frustrated if in this provision the word was treated as meaning more probable than not. Instead the court in *R v Gush* preferred the interpretation that, in the particular context, 'probable' denoted an event that could well happen.

In agreement with the courts in Hong Kong, Australia and New Zealand, their Lordships regard as wholly unacceptable any argument that would propose, as any part of the criteria of the guilt of an accomplice, whether on considering in advance the possibility of a crime of the kind in the event actually committed by his co-adventurers he thought that it was more than an even risk. The concession that the contingency in which the crime is committed need not itself be foreseen as more probable than not, while virtually inevitable in the light of the reasoning in *Johns v R* and the other cases, complicates the argument without improving it. What public policy requires was rightly identified in the submissions of the Crown. Where a man lends himself to a criminal enterprise knowing that potentially murderous weapons are to be carried, and in the event they are in fact used by his partner with an intent sufficient for murder, he should not escape the consequences by reliance on a nuance of prior assessment, only too likely to have been optimistic.

On the other hand, if it was not even contemplated by the particular accused that serious bodily harm would be intentionally inflicted, he is not a party to murder. This is reflected in a passage in the speech of Viscount Simonds LC in *Davies v DPP* [1954] 1 All ER 507 at 514, [1954] AC 378 at 401:

> '. . . I can see no reason why, if half a dozen boys fight another crowd, and one of them produces a knife and stabs one of the opponents to death, all the rest of his group should be treated as accomplices in the use of a knife and the infliction of mortal injury by that means, unless there is evidence that the rest intended or concerted or at least contemplated an attack with a knife by one of their number, as opposed to a common assault. If all that was designed or envisaged was in fact a common assault, and there was no evidence that Lawson, a party to that common assault, knew that any of his companions had a knife, then Lawson was not an accomplice in the crime consisting in its felonious use.'

The test of mens rea here is subjective. It is what the individual accused in fact contemplated that matters. As in other cases where the state of a person's mind has to be ascertained, this may be inferred from his conduct and any other evidence throwing light on what he foresaw at the material time, including of course any explanation that he gives in evidence or in a statement put in evidence by the prosecution. It is no less elementary that all questions of weight are for the jury. The prosecution must prove the necessary contemplation beyond reasonable doubt, although that may be done by inference as just mentioned. If, at the end of the day and whether as a result of hearing evidence from the accused or for some other reason, the jury conclude that there is a reasonable possibility that the accused did not even contemplate the risk, he is in this type of case not guilty of murder or wounding with intent to cause serious bodily harm.

In some cases in this field it is enough to direct the jury by adapting to the circumstances the simple formula common in a number of jurisdictions. For instance, did the particular accused contemplate that in carrying out a common unlawful purpose one of his partners in the enterprise might use a knife or a loaded gun with the intention of causing really serious bodily harm? . . .

In cases where an issue of remoteness does arise it is for the jury (or other tribunal of fact) to decide whether the risk *as recognised by the accused* was sufficient to make him a party to the crime committed by the principal. Various formulae have been suggested, including a substantial risk, a real risk, a risk that something might well happen. No one formula is exclusively preferable; indeed it may be advantageous in a summing up to use more than one. For the question is not one of semantics. What has to be brought home to the jury is that occasionally a risk may have occurred to an accused's mind, fleetingly or even causing him some deliberation, but may genuinely have been dismissed by him as altogether negligible. If they think there is a reasonable possibility that the case is in that class, taking the risk should not make that accused a party to such a crime of intention as murder or wounding with intent to cause grievous bodily harm. The judge is entitled to warn the jury to be cautious before reaching that conclusion; but the law can do no more by way of definition; it can only be for the jury to determine any issue of that kind on the facts of the particular case.

The present case not being in that class, their Lordships agree with the Court of Appeal that the attack on the summing up fails and will humbly advise Her Majesty that the appeals should be dismissed.

Appeals dismissed

NOTE

In *Jubb and Rigby* [1984] Crim LR 616, a similar case where the defendants were charged with murder, the judge used the phrase, 'may or [might] well involve killing'. The Court of Appeal, dismissing the appeal, said that this meant 'probably involve killing' and that this had to be made clear to the jury. In future it would be preferable for the judges to use a constant phrase and 'probably' would be the right word. Is this different in effect from *Chan Wing-siu*?

In the light of these cases, does cl 31 (4) (b) of the draft Code, p 140, above, correctly state the law? The fault required for murder is intention to kill or cause serious injury (*Moloney*, p 55, above). Is it necessary to prove that the accessory had such an intention? Or is it enough that to prove that he knew that there was a risk that (or it was probable that) the principal would act with such an intention?

CHAPTER 9

Vicarious liability and liability of corporations

1. Vicarious liability

The draft Criminal Code Bill provides:

33 Vicarious liability
An element of a Code offence may be attributed to a person by reason of an act done by another only if that other is:
(a) specified in the definition of the offence as a person whose act may be so attributed; or
(b) acting within the scope of his employment or authority and the definition of the offence specifies the element in terms which apply to both persons; or
(c) his innocent agent under section 30(2)(b).

Schedule 1 of the draft Bill provides the following illustrations:

33 (a)   **33** (i)   It is made a Code offence for the holder of a justices' licence whether by himself, his servant or agent to supply intoxicating liquor on licensed premises outside permitted hours. No fault is required for this offence. D is the licensee of a public house. E, his barman, serves a drink to a friend outside the permitted hours. In the absence of any special defence D is guilty of the offence as a principal. Assuming fault on E's part, E is guilty as an accessory.

33 (b)   **33** (ii)   It is made a Code offence for a person to sell goods to which a false trade description is applied. No fault is required for this offence. E, an assistant employed in D's shop, sells a ham as a "Scotch" ham. D has previously given instructions that such hams are not to be sold under any specific name of place of origin. The ham is in fact an American ham. Both D and E are guilty of the offence as principals.

The Report explains cl 33 as follows:

Clause 33: Vicarious liability
10.25 *Cases in which one person may be liable for the act of another*. A person may sometimes be held to have committed an offence not by reason of anything he himself has done, but by reason of an act done by another, either (paragraph (a)) because the statute creating the offence expressly so provides, or (paragraph (b)) as a result of the extended interpretation given by the courts to certain words in the definition of the offence. Such words are usually verbs like 'sell', 'use', 'possess' and so on, and their extended interpretation means that both the actual seller, user and possessor and the principal on whose behalf he is acting are held to commit the offence. The offences covered by these paragraphs are often said, though inexactly, to impose 'vicarious liability'. There is no principle underlying these cases. Their existence is simply the product of statutory interpretation. However, there are certain limits to the interpretative process involved and these are set out in paragraph (b). Paragraph (c) of the subsection cross-refers to a type of case of liability for the act of another which is dealt with in clause 30 (2) (innocent agency).
10.26 *Limits of vicarious liability*. Paragraph (b) provides for two conditions to be satisfied before a provision may be interpreted as applying to a person who did not himself do the prohibited act. The relevant element of the offence must be expressed in terms which are apt for the defendant as well as the person who in fact acted, and some well-known examples are given in the previous paragraph. Secondly, the person who in fact acted must have done so within the scope of his employment or authority (that is, as the defendant's agent). These conditions are in

accordance with the results reached in the great majority of cases, and we take the view that in their absence and in the absence of express provision there can be no justification for imposing vicarious liability. Under existing law an employee may disobey an express instruction from his employer and yet still be held to be acting within the scope of his employment.[1] Illustration 33(ii) anticipates that the same result will be reached under the Code.

10.27 Two particular types of case require further comment. The Law Commission's Working Party proposed that in principle vicarious liability should be restricted to cases where there is a relationship of employer and employee between the defendant and the person who acts.[2] However, the word 'employee' was to be defined to include a person acting with the consent of the defendant 'as if he were . . . employed by him'. In this way the Working Party proposed to extend vicarious liability to cases where a member of the defendant's family or friend performed the relevant act for the defendant at his request. We think it is right to provide for such cases, but it should not be done by characterising them as types of 'employment'. They are cases where one person is acting for another as his agent. To avoid artificiality the reference to a person 'acting within the scope of authority' is apt for the purpose.

10.28 Such a reference extends of course to cases in which the person acting is doing so not merely at the defendant's request but for valuable consideration as an independent contractor. The Working Party proposed to exclude independent contractors from the scope of vicarious liability, and drafted a restrictive definition of the word 'agent' accordingly. We have not adopted the proposal. It would change the present law[3] and we are not convinced that the case for change has been made out. We can see no real difference in principle between a person who, for example, 'uses' the defendant's vehicle as his employee, and a person who 'uses' the defendant's vehicle on a single occasion because the defendant has asked him or paid him to do so.

Our draft clause allows for cases such as *Quality Dairies (York) Ltd v Pedley* and *F E Charman Ltd v Clow*[4] to be decided as they were. It does not follow that liability for the acts of independent contractors will be extended or made general. The second part of paragraph (b) enables the court to exclude liability in appropriate cases. It is one thing to hold that a person carrying on a business of supplying milk[5] or heavy building materials[6] 'uses' a vehicle if he employs an independent contractor to supply those things in the contractor's vehicle. It would be quite another thing to hold that a householder 'uses' the removal van owned by the firm of removers whom he employs to carry his furniture to a new residence. The draft also leaves open the possibility that, where an independent contractor does an act incidental to the act he was engaged to do, he will be held not to have acted within the scope of his authority.

1. See e g *Coppen v Moore (No 2)* [1898] 2 QB 306.
2. Working Paper No 43, Proposition 4.
3. A principal has been held liable for the act of his independent contractor in such cases as *Quality Dairies (York) Ltd v Pedley* [1952] 1 KB 275 and *F E Charman Ltd v Clow* [1974] 1 WLR 1384.
4. See n 3.
5. As in *Quality Dairies (York) Ltd v Pedley*, above, n 3.
6. As in *F E Charman Ltd v Clow*, above, n 3.

(1) DOING AN ACT THROUGH ANOTHER

Coppen v Moore (No 2) [1898] 2 QB 306, Divisional Court
(Lord Russell CJ, Sir FH Jeune P, Chitty LJ, Wright, Darling and Channell JJ.)

Under s 2 (2) of the Merchandise Marks Act 1887 it was an offence to sell goods to which a false trade description had been applied. The appellant who owned six shops sent the following instruction to each shop:

'Most important.
Please instruct your assistants most explicitly that the hams described in list as breakfast hams must not be sold under any specific name of place or origin. That is to say, they must not be described as 'Bristol,' 'Bath,' 'Wiltshire,' or any such title, but simply as breakfast hams. Please sign and return.'

An assistant in one of the shops sold one of the hams (an American ham) as 'a Scotch ham'. The appellant appealed from his conviction of the offence.

Lord Russell CJ, having acepted that the general principle is 'Nemo reus est nisi mens sit rea', said that it was subject to exceptions:

But by far the greater number of exceptions engrafted upon the general rule are cases in which it has been decided that by various statutes criminal responsibility has been put upon masters for the acts of their servants. Amongst such cases is *Mullins v Collins* [LR 9 QB 292], where a licensed victualler was convicted of an offence under s 16 of the Licensing Act, 1872, for supplying liquor to a constable on duty, although this was done by his servant without the knowledge of the master. Again, in *Bond v Evans* [21 QBD 249], a licensed victualler was convicted of an offence against s 17 of the same Act, where gaming had been allowed in the licensed premises by the servant in charge of the premises although without the knowledge of his master. The decisions in these and in other like cases were based upon the construction of the statute in question. The Court in fact came to the conclusion that, having regard to the language, scope, and object of those Acts, the Legislature intended to fix criminal responsibilty upon the master for acts done by his servant in the course of his employment, although such acts were not authorized by the master, and might even have been expressly prohibited by him.

The question, then, in this case, comes to be narrowed to the simple point, whether upon the true construction of the statute here in question the master was intended to be made criminally responsible for acts done by his servants in contravention of the Act, where such acts were done, as in this case, within the scope or in the course of their employment. In our judgment it was clearly the intention of the Legislature to make the master criminally liable for such acts, unless he was able to rebut the primâ facie presumption of guilt by one or other of the methods pointed out in the Act. Take the facts here, and apply the Act to them. To begin with, it cannot be doubted that the appellant sold the ham in question, although the transaction was carried out by his servants. In other words, he was the seller, although not the actual salesman. . . .

In answer, then, to the question which alone is put to us, namely, whether upon the facts stated the decision of the magistrates convicting the appellant was in point of law correct, our answer is that in our judgment it was. When the scope and object of the Act are borne in mind, any other conclusion would to a large extent render the Act ineffective for its avowed purposes. The circumstances of the present case afford a convenient illustration of this. The appellant, under the style of the 'London Supply Stores,' carries on an extensive business as grocer and provision dealer, having, it appears, six shops or branch establishments, and having also a wholesale warehouse. It is obvious that, if sales with false trade descriptions could be carried out in these establishments with impunity so far as the principal is concerned, the Act would to a large extent be nugatory. We conceive the effect of the Act to be to make the master or principal liable criminally (as he is already, by law, civilly) for the acts of his agents and servants in all cases within the sections with which we are dealing where the conduct constituting the offence was pursued by such servants and agents within the scope or in the course of their employment, subject to this: that the master or principal may be relieved from criminal responsibility where he can prove that he had acted in good faith and had done all that it was reasonably possible to do to prevent the commission by his agents and servants of offences against the Act.

Appeal dismissed

NOTE

Cf *Wings Ltd v Ellis* p 120, above.

(2) THE DELEGATION PRINCIPLE

Coppen v Moore was concerned with an offence of strict liablity. The defendant, in fact and law, had sold a ham to which a false trade description had been applied; and that was the offence. The courts have gone even further in their zeal to prevent a statutory offence from being 'rendered nugatory'. Where the defendant has delegated the performance of a statutory duty to another, they have sometimes held that not only the acts but also the mens rea of the delegate are to be imputed to him. A good example is *Allen v*

Whitehead which is discussed below, p 174. The principle was considered by the House of Lords in the next case.

Vane v Yiannopoullos [1964] 3 All ER 820, House of Lords
(Lord Reid, Lord Evershed, Lord Morris of Borth-y-Gest, Lord Hodson and Lord Donovan)

Respondent was the holder of a restaurant licence. A condition of the licence was that liquor should not be sold except to persons taking meals. The restaurant was on two floors. While the respondent was on one floor, conducting the business of the restaurant, a waitress on the other floor sold liquor to customers who had not ordered a meal. The waitress had been instructed to serve liquor only to customers ordering a meal. The respondent did not know of these sales.

A charge of knowingly selling intoxicating liquor to persons to whom he was not entitled to sell, contrary to s 22 of the Licensing Act 1961, was dismissed by the justices. The prosecutor's appeal was dismissed by the Divisional Court on the ground that the respondent had not delegated to the waitress the management of the business. The prosecutor appealed.

Lord Reid. . . . . The appellant maintains that under this section there is vicarious responsibility, so that the licence holder must he held guilty if a servant employed to sell liquor sells knowingly to a person to whom the licence holder is not permitted to sell, and that it is no defence that the accused had forbidden the servant so to sell and did not know of or connive at the sale. The appellant does not dispute that it is the general rule in criminal cases that an accused person cannot be convicted unless he has mens rea; but he maintains that the authorities have established a principle of interpretation of the provisions of the Licensing Acts that, where a licence holder is prohibited from doing or suffering certain things, vicarious responsibility must be inferred, so that the knowledge of the servant must be imputed to the licence holder whatever be the terms of the section under which he is prosecuted. His counsel frankly agreed that, but for this principle, a man charged with knowingly selling could not be convicted unless it was shown that he knew what his servant was doing or at least connived or shut his eyes to facts indicating that the servant was doing wrong or disobeying his orders.

The offence charged in this case is a new offence created for the first time by s 22 of the Act of 1961 and it must be observed that in the immediately preceding section, s 21 (1), it is enacted that 'the holder of the licence or his servant shall not knowingly sell intoxicating liquor to a person under eighteen. . .'. The appellant denies that the contrast between this provision and that in s 22, 'If the holder of a justices' on-licence knowingly sells or supplies intoxicating liquor to persons. . .', has any relevance. Section 21 (1) enables the servant himself to be prosecuted if he is the guilty person, but, to be consistent, the appellant must and does argue that if a servant does this without the knowledge of the licence holder then the prosecutor can prosecute under s 21 both the servant and the innocent licence holder—the servant because he has directly infringed the section, and the licence holder because he is vicariously responsible for the servant's acts. I doubt whether any authority however strong would justify your lordships reaching a result so contrary to the ordinary principles of construction and to the fundamental principle that an accused person cannot be convicted without proof of mens rea, unless from a consideration of the terms of the statute and other relevant circumstances it clearly appears that that must have been the intention of Parliament.

I shall not deal in detail with the cases on which the appellant has to rely. They are all more than 60 years old and with one exception they dealt with provisions in which the word 'knowingly' did not occur. The courts relied on the fact that it must have been known to Parliament that the things prohibited would frequently be done by servants of the licence holder and that in many cases the licence holder would have no knowledge of what his servant had done or at least that it would be very difficult to prove his knowledge or connivance. As there was no provision making the servant himself liable to prosecution, it would be impossible to enforce the law adequately if it was necessary in every case to prove mens rea in the licence holder. Those were strong arguments, and, as there was nothing in the wording of the relevant sections to exclude vicarious responsibility, I think that the courts were well justified in construing the sections as they did. The only case in which the word 'knowingly' occurred in the relevant section was *Avards v Dance*[1], where the offence was knowingly suffering gaming to take place, and it was suggested—it was no more than a suggestion—that, if the licence holder left someone else in charge, he might be answerable.

There are four cases[2] since 1903 where the word 'knowingly' did occur in the relevant section, but they do not support the contention of the appellant in this case. There the courts adopted a construction which on any view I find it hard to justify. They drew a distinction between acts done by a servant without the knowledge of the licence holder while the licence holder was on the premises and giving general supervision to his business, and acts done without the knowledge of the licence holder but with the knowledge of a person whom the licence holder had left in charge of the premises. In the latter case they held that the knowledge of the person left in charge must be imputed to the licence holder. If that distinction is valid then I agree with the Divisional Court[3] that, on the facts of this case, there was not that 'delegation' by the accused necessary to make him answerable for the servant having acted against the orders of the accused.

Counsel for the appellant strenuously argued that this distinction is illogical and not warranted by any statutory provision. He maintained that if a licence holder entrusts to his wine waiter the duty of selling intoxicating liquor that is sufficient delegation and that, if the wine waiter disobeys his orders and sells to persons to whom he ought not to sell, there is nothing to justify the licence holder being acquitted, if he happens to have gone out leaving the wine waiter in charge. If this were a new distinction recently introduced by the courts I would think it necessary to consider whether a provision that the licence holder shall not knowingly sell can ever make him vicariously liable by reason of the knowledge of some other person; but this distinction has now been recognised and acted on by the courts for over half a century. It may have been unwarranted in the first instance, but I would think it now too late to upset so long-standing a practice.

It is, however, quite another matter to extend a long-standing anomaly particularly because there may in this matter be good practical reasons for requiring a licence holder to be specially careful about the person whom he chooses to leave in charge in his absence. One might have expected to find in the Licensing Acts some provisions regulating the position in the common case of a licence holder being absent from the licensed premises during the permitted hours, but there appears to be none. So, if the courts have in effect legislated to fill the gap, I think that we should leave matters as they are. . . .

I can find nothing to require your lordships to give to the recent enactment with which we are concerned in the present case such an unusual meaning as would be necessary to support the appellant's case. This appeal must, therefore, be dismissed. In accordance with the terms imposed when giving to appeal the appellant must pay the respondent's costs.

[**Lord Evershed** having stated the facts and the issues, continued:]

It is, of course, a well-established proposition of the English criminal law that as a general rule the existence of mens rea is an essential requisite to a finding of guilt on the part of one accused of a criminal offence. None-the-less it appears to have now been established in the course of the numerous cases decided during the past century, to which counsel for the appellant alluded in his careful and elaborate argument, that where offences are charged under legislation such as that involved in the present case—e g licensing legislation—an exception to the general rule has been accepted, so that persons holding licences or exercising powers or duties under legislation of the character to which I have alluded have been held guilty of the statutory offences formulated in the legislation in the absence of any mens rea on their part. I have used the word 'accepted': and though it may be difficult to assert complete coherence in all the cases—particularly having regard to the considerable variation in the terminology of the numerous statutes which have been involved—yet it seems to me now impossible to reject the general conclusion which I have formulated, namely, that in statutes of the kind with which your lordships are here concerned an exception to the general common law rule will (for better or worse) be accepted if, on the general terms of the statute, liability on the part of the licensee is required to give practical effect to the legislative intention. [Lord Evershed went on to hold that no 'knowledge was proved against the licensee and that there was no sufficient evidence of such delegation as would render him liable on that ground'.]

[**Lord Morris of Borth-y-Gest** found it unnecessary to express any opinion on the delegation cases and held that, as a matter of construction, in the context of s 22 (1), the presence of the word 'knowingly' requires knowledge in the licensee. The interpretation urged by the appellant involved reading words into the subsection which were not there.]

[**Lord Hodson**, having stated the arguments continued:]

In this case the Divisional Court held[4] that there had been no delegation of authority in the sense in which the word has been used in *Emary v Nolloth*[5] and in succeeding cases which have followed, because here the licensee was himself controlling the premises and had given direct instructions to the persons in his employment (including the waitress who served the liquor in contravention of the terms of licence) that these terms had to be strictly observed. The distinction is a narrow one and the extent of the delegation may raise difficult questions, but it has never so far been extended so as to cover the case where the whole of the authority of the licensee has not been transferred to another: contrast this case where no more than a partial delegation has occurred. I agree with your lordships that, even if the 'delegation cases' are to remain undisturbed, so as to give the word 'knowingly' as applied to the licensee a meaning which embraces the licensee or his substitute, there is no justification for enlarging the ambit of the section so as to embrace the activities of any servant who is in breach of the provisions of a licence or of a statutory requirement. . . .

The charge . . . was laid under s 22 (1)(a) of the Act of 1961 which creates the following offence.

> 'If (a) the holder of a justices' on-licence knowingly sells or supplies intoxicating liquor to persons to whom he is not permitted by the conditions of the licence to sell or supply it . . . he shall be guilty of an offence under this section.'

One must compare and contrast the language of the preceding section, s 21, which provides that 'the holder of the licence *or his servant* shall not knowingly sell intoxicating liquor to a person under eighteen . . .'. It would be strange if the words 'or his servant' which appear in s 21 but do not appear in s 22 were to be implied in the latter section from which they would seem to have been deliberately excluded.

Your lordships are not I think driven to such a conclusion, and I would dismiss the appeal.

Lord Donovan. . . . The rule that there may be liability in certain cases on an otherwise innocent licensee, if he has delegated sufficient control of the premises to the person who actually commits the offence, but no liability if he has delegated insufficient control, is a rule which so far I have failed to spell out of any Act of Parliament cited to us. In the present case it is, fortunately, not necessary to pronounce on its validity. Like my noble and learned friends, I think that the case can and should be decided on the language of s 22 (1)(a) alone: since it is sufficiently clear by itself not to need elucidation by reference to the outside aids to which the appellant has been obliged to resort. If a decision that 'knowingly' means 'knowingly' will make the provision difficult to enforce, the remedy lies with the legislature.

Appeal dismissed

1. (1862) 26 JP 437.
2. *Emary v Nolloth* [1903] 2 KB 264, [1900–03] All ER Rep 606; *McKenna v Harding* (1905) 69 JP 354; *Allen v Whitehead* [1930] 2 KB 211, [1929] All ER Rep 13; and *Linnett v Metropolitan Police Comr* [1946] KB 290, [1946] 1 All ER 380.
3. [1964] 2 All ER at 823.
4. [1964] 2 All ER at 823.
5. [1903] 2 KB at 269; [1900–03] All ER Rep at 608.

R v Winson [1968] 1 All ER 197, Court of Appeal, Criminal Division (Lord Parker CJ, Salmon LJ and Widgery J)

The appellant was a director of a company which owned a club and the holder of a justices' on-licence in respect of the club. It was a term of the licence that liquor should not be sold to anyone who had been a member for less than 48 hours. Liquor was sold in breach of this term. At the material times the club was run by a manager appointed by the managing director. The appellant, who also held licences in respect of three other premises, visited the club only occasionally. He was charged under s 161(1) of the Licensing Act 1964, which reproduced s 22 of the Licensing Act 1961 (above).

[**Lord Parker CJ,** having stated the facts, referred to *Vane v Yiannopoullos* (p 171, above) and the fact that the Lords Morris and Donovan thought that, if the doctrine of delegation was part of the law, it could not apply to s 22 of the 1961 Act: but that Lords Reid and Evershed thought that, if there had been delegation, it would have applied to s 22. His Lordship continued:]

Accordingly, it seems to the court that their lordships in *Vane v Yiannopoullos* were equally divided on this point. It is, therefore, necessary to look a little further back into the inception of this doctrine. It is to be observed in the first instance that this doctrine is something quite independent of the principles which come into play when Parliament has created an absolute offence. When an absolute offence has been created by Parliament, then the person on whom a duty is thrown is responsible, whether he has delegated or whether he has acted through a servant; he is absolutely liable regardless of any intent or knowledge or mens rea. The principle of delegation comes into play, and only comes into play, in cases where, though the statute uses words which import knowledge, or intent such as in this case 'knowingly' or in some other cases 'permitting' or 'suffering' and the like, cases to which knowledge is inherent, nevertheless it has been held that a man cannot get out of the responsibilities which have been put on him by delegating those responsibilities to another.

Though not the first case by any means on the subject, the first case to which attention is drawn is that of *Allen v Whitehead* [[1930] 1 KB 211, [1929] All ER Rep 13]. The offence in question there was knowingly permitting or suffering prostitutes to meet together on premises, contrary to s 44 of the Metropolitan Police Act 1839. In that case, the occupier and licensee of a refreshment house did not manage the refreshment house himself but employed a manager for that purpose. A number of women known to the manager to be prostitutes resorted to the refreshment house. In that case, as here, the occupier and licensee said 'It was not knowingly on my part, I was not there, I had appointed a manager.' Lord Hewart CJ, said this [[1930] 1 KB at 220, [1929] All ER Rep at 16]:

> '. . . I think that this provision in this statute would be rendered nugatory, if the contention raised on behalf of this respondent were held to prevail. That contention was that, as the respondent did not himself manage the refreshment house, had no personal knowledge that prostitutes met together and remained therein, had not been negligent in failing to notice these facts, and had not wilfully closed his eyes to the facts, he could not, in law, be held responsible.'

He went on to say [[1930] 1 KB at 221, [1929] All ER Rep at 16]:

> '. . . he had transferred to the manager the exercise of discretion in the conduct of the business, and it seems to me that the only reasonable conclusion is, regard being had to the purposes of this Act, that knowledge in the manager was knowledge in the keeper of the house.'

Branson J, put the matter very succinctly. He said [[1930] 1 KB at 221, 222, [1929] All ER Rep at 17]:

> 'I agree. The essence of the respondent's case was that he had no personal knowledge of the fact that prostitutes were meeting and remaining upon these premises. It is found that his manager knew, and it is said in *Somerset v Hart* [(1884) 12 QBD 360 at 362], that a man may put another in his position, so as to represent him for the purpose of knowledge. I think that is what the respondent has done here, and that consequently his contention fails.'

It is just worth referring to *Somerset v Hart* itself, if only because that was decided on the basis that there had been no valid delegation. The offence there concerned gaming, that the licensee of premises had suffered gaming to take place on the premises. In fact he had not delegated the management to anybody else, but a servant of his employed on the premises, without any connivance or wilful blindness on the part of the licensee, had suffered gaming to take place. In the course of the argument, Lord Coleridge CJ said [(1884) 12 QBD at 362]:

> 'How can a man suffer a thing done when he does not know of it? It is true that a man may put another in his position so as to represent him for the purpose of knowledge, but there is no evidence of such delegation here.'

In his judgment, Lord Coleridge CJ, said [(1884) 12 QBD at 364]:

> 'I quite agree that the provisions of an Act which is passed in the interests of public morality and order should receive a reasonably liberal construction. I do not say that proof of actual knowledge on the part of the landlord is necessary. Slight evidence might be sufficient to satisfy the magistrates that the landlord might have known what was

taking place if he had pleased, but where no actual knowledge is shown there must, as it seems to me, be something to show either that the gaming took place with the knowledge of some person clothed with the landlord's authority, or that there was something like connivance on his part, that he might have known but purposely abstained from knowing.'

Finally, of the more important authorities on this point, there is *Linnett v Metropolitan Police Comr* [[1946] KB 290; [1946] 1 All ER 380]. The offence there was 'knowingly permitting disorderly conduct, contrary to s 44 of the Metropolitan Police Act 1839'. In fact the licensee of the premises had absented himself from the premises and left the control to another man. It was held that, although he, the licensee, had no knowledge, the man he had appointed manager or controller did have knowledge and that, on the principle of delegation, he the licensee, was liable. Lord Goddard CJ said [[1946] KB at 294, 295; [1946] 1 All ER at 382]:

> 'The point does not, as I say, depend merely on the fact that the relationship of master and servant exists; it depends on the fact that the person who is responsible in law as the keeper of the house, or the licensee of the house if the offence is under the Licensing Act, has chosen to delegate his duties, powers and authority to somebody else.'

He went on to refer to *Somerset v Hart* and pointed out that in that case there had been no delegation of control, but that it was merely a case, as indeed was *Vane v Yiannopoullos*, of a servant acting behind the back of the licensee. He ended up by saying [[1946] KB at 295, 296; [1946] 1 All ER at 382, 383]:

> 'Where there is such delegation [that is true delegation] then the knowledge of the servant or agent becomes that of the master or principal. In this case there was no relationship of master and servant between the appellant and Baker. They were joint licensees. If one licensee chooses to say to his co-licensee, although not his servant: 'We are both licensees and both keepers of this house, but I am not going to take any part in the management of this house, I leave the management to you', he is putting his co-licensee into his own place to exercise his own powers and duties and he must, therefore, accept responsibility for what is done or known by his co-licensee in that exercise. That is the principle which underlies all the cases to which I have referred. I am far from saying, and I do not wish it to be thought that I am saying, that where a statute provides that in any business a certain act permitted by the manager shall be an offence on the part of the manager if it is done with his knowledge, that if that act takes place whilst the manager himself is carrying on that business and is in charge of that business but without his knowledge, so that he was powerless to prevent it, that person necessarily commits the offence. But if the manager chooses to delegate the carrying on of the business to another, whether or not that other is his servant, then what that other does or what he knows must be imputed to the person who put the other into that position.'

That is the doctrine of delegation which does form part our law, and no one in the House of Lords has said that it does not. I should add that reference was made to a Scottish case since the decision of the House of Lords in *Vane's* case, that of *Noble v Heatley* [1967 SLT 26]. The court can get no assistance from that case, if only because it was a decision that this doctrine of delegation, though as I said part of the law of England, formed no part of the law of Scotland.

Accordingly, one comes back to the question whether this well established doctrine applies to s 161 of the Licensing Act 1964—a matter on which their lordships in *Vane's* case were divided. This court can see no valid distinction between the earlier cases, whether they concern prostitutes, drunkenness or gaming, and the provisions in this section. Parliament must be taken, when this section was originally introduced in 1961 [in s 22 of the Licensing Act 1961] and continued in 1964, to know that the doctrine of delegation had been applied in number of licensing cases, and that the principle of those case was that a man cannot get out of the responsibilities and duties attached to a licence by absenting himself. The position of course is quite different if he remains in control. It would be only right that he should not be liable if a servant behind his back did something which contravened the terms of the licence. If, however, he wholly absents himself leaving somebody else in control, he cannot claim that what has happened has happened without his knowledge if the delegate has knowingly carried on in contravention of the licence. Indeed, with all respect to Lord Morris and Lord Donovan, it is difficult to see how s 22 of the Act of 1961 differs in essential respects from the sections in other Acts dealt with in the earlier cases. The general principle in the opinion of this court must be applicable to a licensing case under this section as it is applicable in the other cases.

Finally, in a recent case since *Vane's* case, namely, *Ross v Moss* [[1965] 2 QB 396, [1965] 3 All ER 145], while intimating that the matter remained open for argument and decision in the future, I did venture to suggest [[1965] QB at 407, 408, [1965] 3 All ER at 149] that in the present state of authority the principle of delegation would seem to apply to an offence against this section.

Accordingly, for the reasons that I have endeavoured to state, this court has come to the conclusion that this appeal fails and must be dismissed.

Appeal dismissed

Problem

While Dan, the licensee of The Bell, is answering the telephone, Bess, the barmaid, sells liquor (a) to Plod, a constable on duty; and (b) to Scott, a drunken person. Bess knows that Plod is on duty, but is quite reasonably unaware that Scott is drunk. See Licensing Act 1964, ss 172 (3) ('The holder of a justices' license shall not sell intoxicating liquor to a drunken person'.) and 178 (The holder of a justices' licence commits an offence if he 'supplies any liquor . . . to any constable on duty'.); and *Sherras v de Rutzen* and *Cundy v Le Cocq* discussed pp 116, 124, 155, above. Consider the liability of Bess and Dan.

Report on Codification of the Criminal Law

10.29   *The delegation principle.* The courts have interpreted some offences requiring knowledge (notably licensees' offences) so as to permit a person's conviction on the basis of the act and knowledge of one to whom he had delegated management of premises or of any activity. This 'delegation principle' was regarded as anomalous by members of the House of Lords in *Vane v Yiannopoullos* [[1965] AC 486] and the Law Commission's Working Party proposed its abolition. [Working Paper No 43, pp 29–31] The Code gives effect to this proposal by subsection (1) of clause 30 which states that to be guilty as a principal a person must act with the fault specified for the offence. Accordingly, a person charged with 'knowingly selling' must be proved to have had the requisite knowledge. The knowledge of another cannot be attributed to him under clause 33 because this clause, read with clause 30 (2), shows that only the *acts* of another may be attributed to the defendant. Thus the 'delegation principle' will not apply to Code offences unless the particular offence expressly provides that a person can commit the offence although personally lacking the fault specified by the definition of the offence.

2. Liability of a corporation

The draft Criminal Code Bill provides:

34 Corporations
(1) A corporation may be guilty of an offence not involving a fault element by reason of:
(a) an act done by its employee or agent as provided by section 33 [p 168, above]; or
(b) an omission, state of affairs or occurrence that is an element of the offence.
(2) A corporation may be guilty:
(a) as a principal, of an offence involving a fault element; or
(b) as an accessory, of any offence,
   only if one of its controlling officers, acting within the scope of his office and with the fault required, is concerned in the offence.
(3) (a) 'Controlling officer' of a corporation means a person participating in the control of the corporation in the capacity of a director, manager, secretary or other similar officer (whether or not he was validly appointed to his office).
(b) In this subsection 'director', in relation to a corporation established by or under any enactment for the purpose of carrying on under national ownership any industry or part of an industry or undertaking, being a corporation whose affairs are managed by the members thereof, means a member of the corporation.
(c) Whether a person acting in a particular capacity is a controlling officer is a question of law.

(4) A controlling officer is concerned in an offence if he does, procures, assists, encourages or fails to prevent the acts specified for the offence.

(5) For the purposes of subsection (4), a controlling officer fails to prevent an act when he fails to take steps that he ought to take:

(a) to ensure that the act is not done; or

(b) where the offence may be constituted by an omission to do an act or by a state of affairs or occurrence, to ensure that the omission is not made or to prevent or end the state of affairs or occurrence.

(6) A controlling officer does not act 'within the scope of his office' if he acts with the intention of doing harm or of concealing harm done by him or another to the corporation.

(7) A corporation cannot be guilty of murder or of any other offence not punishable with a fine.

(8) A corporation has a defence consisting of or including:

(a) a state of mind only if:

(i) all controlling officers who are concerned in the offence; or

(ii) where no controlling officer is so concerned, all other employees or agents who are so concerned, have that state of mind;

(b) the absence of a state of mind only if no controlling officer with responsibility for the subject-matter of the offence has that state of mind;

(c) compliance with a standard of conduct required of the corporation itself only if it is complied with by the controlling officers with responsibility for the subject-matter of the offence.

Schedule 1 of the draft Bill provides the following illustrations:

34 (1)   34 (i) It is an offence to use a motor vehicle on a road in breach of construction and use regulations. No fault is required. C, an employee of D Ltd, drives one of its lorries on a road. The lorry's condition does not comply with the regulations. D Ltd commits the offence.

    34 (ii) If dark smoke is emitted from a chimney, the occupier of the building is guilty of an offence although he is not at fault. D Ltd. occupies a factory from the chimney of which dark smoke is emitted. It commits the offence.

34 (2)–(5)   34 (iii) C, a director of D Ltd, conspires with others to obtain by deception for D Ltd payments of a subsidy to which it is not entitled. D Ltd is a party to the conspiracy and to any subsequent offence of obtaining the subsidy by deception.

    34 (iv) The carriage of a coach party without a special licence is an offence if, as the carrier knows or ought to know, the trip has been publicly advertised. A theatre club books a coach trip with D Ltd. The club then advertises spare seats in the local newspaper. C, a director of D Ltd, sees the advertisement and realises that it may relate to a company trip. He takes no action. The trip goes ahead without a special licence. If C ought to have discovered the facts, D Ltd. is guilty of the offence.

34 (8)(a)(i)   34 (v) D Ltd. owns a sheep farm. C, a director, acting as such, orders the killing of a neighbouring farmer's dog. D Ltd is not guilty of an offence under section 82 (1) (destroying or damaging property) if C believes the circumstances to be such that the killing would be justifiable for the

		protection of the company's sheep (see s 89).
34 (8)(a)(ii)	34 (vi)	The manager of a store belonging to D Ltd finds a controlled drug among groceries which have just been delivered to the store. He takes possession of it, intending to deliver it to the police. D Ltd may rely upon this intention on a charge under the Misuse of Drugs Act 1971, s 5 (1), of possessing the drug (see s 5 (4)(b) of that Act).
34 (8)(b) and (c)	34 (vii)	D Ltd. has a parcel of heroin in its warehouse. It is guilty of having a controlled drug in its possession, unless it neither knows nor suspects nor has reason to suspect that the parcel contains such a drug (see Misuse of Drugs Act 1971, s 28 (2)). No director of D Ltd with responsibility for warehousing operations knows or suspects or has reason to suspect that fact. D Ltd is not guilty.
34 (8)(c)	34 (viii)	Goods are supplied in a store belonging to D Ltd although safety regulations prohibit their supply. This is an offence under the Consumer Safety Act 1978, s 2, unless D Ltd can prove that it took all reasonable precautions and exercised all due diligence to avoid committing the offence. This requires the company to show that no fault on the part of controlling officers was involved in failing to maintain effective systems designed to avoid such an offence.

The Report explains cl 34 as follows:

11.4 *Clause 34 (1). Offences of strict liability.* Vicarious liability for offences of strict liability may attach to corporations as to other persons. Or a corporation may, for example, be the occupier of a building from a chimney of which dark smoke is emitted; or its activities may cause polluting matter to enter a stream. Then, like any other person, it can be liable for the emission or for causing the pollution, without fault on its part.[1] These propositions are confirmed by subsection (1).

11.5 *Clause 34 (2). Offences involving fault.* The attribution to a corporation of criminal liability for an offence involving fault is achieved by indentifying the corporation with its 'directing mind and will'—that is, with those of its human agents whose acts and states of mind are (in law) its acts and states of mind.[2] This metaphysical notion of the common law has to be translated into legislative terms without resort to puzzling or misleading metaphor and with as much definition as the subject—matter will allow. The translation is made by subsections (2)-(5). The primary statement is in subsection (2): what is required to make a corporation liable, in any case in which fault is an element, is that 'one of its controlling officers, acting within the scope of his office and with the fault required, is concerned in the offence'. There are several phrases here which require elaboration.

11.6 *Clause 34 (3). 'Controlling officer'* is defined in subsection (3) as:

'a person participating in the control of the corporation in the capacity of a director, manager, secretary or other similar officer (whether or not he was validly appointed to his office)'.

We believe that this (ignoring the parenthesis) comes as close as possible to the meaning of 'directing mind and will' as explained in the opinions in the *Tesco* case. The phrase 'director, manager, secretary or other similar officer' is taken from the common-form provision for the imposition of liability on company officers, which was recognised by members of the House of Lords as providing a useful indication of the persons concerned.[3] Viscount Dilhorne referred to the person or persons 'in actual control of the operations of the company'.[4] Any of them 'participates' in such control. He may do so as a member of the board of directors, as managing director, or perhaps as some other superior officer (to adapt the language of Lord Reid); or by virtue of a delegation of directors' powers.[5]

11.7 *Invalid appointment*. We follow a hint in Working Paper No 44 in not requiring the controlling officer to be validly appointed.[6] An over-constitutional test for the identification of 'controlling officers' would put a premium on disregard of the formalities of appointment and delegation. This aspect of our definition rebels against some dicta in *Tesco*.[7]

11.8 *Question of law*. It is the judge's duty to direct the jury as to the facts necessary to identify a particular person with a defendant company.[8] For it is 'a question of law whether . . . a person in doing particular things is to be regarded as the company . . .'[9] Subsection (3) (c) declares accordingly.

11.9 *'One of its controlling officers, acting . . . with the fault required.'* This formula in subsection (2) gives effect to the provisional view of the Working Party, which we believe to be right, that 'a corporation should not be taken as having any required mental element unless at least one of its controlling officers has the whole mental element required for the offence'.[10]

11.10 *Clause 34 (4) and (5)*. *'Is concerned in the offence'*. This shorthand expression in subsection (2) is explained in subsections (4) and (5). There are several ways in which a controlling officer may by his activity or inactivity render a corporation guilty of an offence.

(i)   He may *do the acts* specified for the offence. It would be simpler to refer to the officer's committing the offence; but this is not possible, because the offence may be one that only the corporation can commit as principal.

(ii) He may *be a party to* the acts of others—by procuring, assisting or encouraging those acts.

(iii) He may *fail to prevent* relevant acts (of other controlling officers or of subordinates) or relevant events. It seems clear on principle that a company must be guilty of a fraud offence if its managing director knows that company personnel (not being controlling officers) are defrauding customers and turns a blind eye to what is going on. The perpetrators cannot be said to be 'encouraged' by his inactivity unless they know of his knowledge. So an additional expression is needed. 'Fails to prevent'[11] will cover this kind of case and also some cases involving offences of omission or 'situational offences'. Some positive duty of a company may be entrusted to a subordinate; but he omits (and therefore the company omits) to do what is required; or a subordinate's actions give rise to a state of affairs capable of constituting an offence on the company's part. If in either case the offence requires fault, the company's liability depends upon some culpable failure on the part of a controlling officer. Subsection (5) makes the point as clear as possible with an explanation of 'fails to prevent'. the subsection must of course be read together with the reference to 'the fault required' in subsection (2).

11.11 *'Acting within the scope of his office.'* This phrase in subsection (2) embraces a number of limitations on corporate liability.

(i)   *The officer must be acting as such*. A corporation is not liable for what is done by any of its officers in a personal capacity.[12]

(ii) *The officer must be acting within his sphere*. If only some of the functions of management are delegated to a controlling officer, the criminal liability of the corporation on the basis of identification with him should be limited to his activities in connection with those functions.[13]

(iii) *Clause 34 (6). The officer must not be acting against the corporation*. Subsection (6) declares that an act done by an officer with the intention of harming the corporation is not done 'within the scope of his office'. This will lay to rest the 'inequitable'[14] decision of *Moore v I Bresler Ltd*.[15]

11.12 *Offences that a corporation cannot commit*. Three groups of offences require consideration.

(i)   *Clause 34 (7). Offences not punishable with a fine*. The conventional view is that there can be no question of liability if there can be no punishment. Subsection (7), reflecting this view, declares that a corporation cannot be guilty of murder or of any other offence not punishable with a fine.

(ii) *Offences requiring natural persons as principals*. Sexual offences, bigamy, driving offences (as opposed to offences of 'using' vehicles): these, no doubt, cannot be committed by corporations as principal. Accessory liability, on the other hand, is perfectly possible in theory, however unlikely in practice with some of these offences; and in the case of driving offences it has been known.[16] No statutory statement seems called for on either point.

(iii) *Perjury*. It is very doubtful whether a corporation can commit perjury as a principal, since only a human being can take an oath (or, because he has no religious belief or his religion prohibits oath-taking, affirm).[17] A corporation can, of course, be guilty of perjury as an accessory. We do not consider that express provision on the matter is necessary; but the point may bear further consideration in the context of a modernisation of offences against the administration of justice.[18]

(iv) *Conspiracy.* If a company director, acting as such, decides to perpetrate a fraud, he does not thereby conspire with the company. This is because no 'agreement' (the essential feature of conspiracy) is involved, not because of any limitation on corporate liability. See illustration 52 (iii). The point does not call for statement in the present clause.[19]

11.13 *Clause 34 (8). Defences.* The leading case of *Tesco Supermarkets Ltd v Nattrass*[20] was concerned with a statutory defence of a particular type—namely, a defence under the Trade Descriptions Act 1968 that the offence charged was due to the act or default of another person and that the defendant took all reasonable precautions and exercised all due diligence to avoid the commission of such an offence by himself or any person under his control.[21] The manager of the Tesco store where the infringement of the Act occurred was held to be 'another person' within the first limb of this defence. The company brought itself within the second limb by showing that there had been no failure in the matter of precautions or diligence on the part of those in control of its operations; the company had established an effective system of command and control. Defences are of many kinds, however, and the *Tesco* case seems not to be capable of direct application to all of them. We believe that it is necessary to distinguish, as subsection (8) does, between three classes of defence.

11.14 *Defence involving a state of mind (subsection (8) (a)).* A rule is required as to who must entertain a belief, or have any other state of mind, that affords a defence to an offence charged against a corporation. The possible cases fall into two groups.

(i) *Controlling officers concerned.* There are those in which controlling officers are 'concerned in the offence', in the sense established by subsections (4) and (5). In such cases the corporation must be able to rely on the states of mind of those officers, and it cannot matter that other persons concerned in the transaction do not have the belief or intention required for the defence. Such a rule derives readily enough from the *Tesco* case by analogy.

(ii) *No controlling officer involved.* But that case is not, we believe, adequate authority for denying a corporation a defence when everyone concerned in the transaction has the required state of mind. It should not matter that no controlling officer is so concerned and that therefore none has the state of mind. See illustration 34 (vi) in Schedule 1.

11.5 *Defence involving the absence of a state of mind (subsection (8) (b)).* The Misuse of Drugs Act 1971, section 28 (2), usefully illustrates this class of defence as well as the third class. On a charge of possessing a controlled drug, it is a defence that the possessor neither knew nor suspected nor had reason to suspect that the thing possessed was a controlled drug. The burden of proving this defence is on the defendant. It would be oppressive to require every director of a company to be called as a witness to deny knowledge or suspicion. It should be enough that no controlling officer with relevant responsibilities knew or suspected that the company was in possession of a controlled drug.

11.16 *Defence involving compliance with a standard of conduct (subsection (8) (c)).* The fact that no relevant controlling officer has reason to suspect that the company is in possession of a controlled drug will complete the defence under section 28 of the 1971 Act. This is an example of 'compliance with a standard of conduct'. Some such expression is needed if the Code is not at this point to become impossibly particularistic. The *Tesco* decision has to be codified by way of a succinct answer to the very general question: what, in the case of a corporation, constitutes compliance with a standard of conduct? Not that a defendant employer (corporate or otherwise) must always show that his own conduct fell within the terms of a statutory exception to liability; a corporation (like any other defendant) may be able to rely on the conduct of the very person for whose act it would otherwise be liable. All depends upon the terms of the defence in question. But if a specified standard must, on the true interpretation of the statute, be complied with by the defendant personally, what does this require of a defendant corporation? The *Tesco* case is authority for the proposition that such a defence is made out if the standard is complied with by the corporation's controlling officers. This means in practice that relevant controlling officers (which may in some contexts mean the board of directors as a whole) did not fall below the stipulated standard in connection with the matter in question. Subsection (8) (c) states the rule accordingly. It is illustrated in Schedule 1 by reference to a 'due diligence' defence simpler than that in issue in the *Tesco* case: see illustration 34 (viii). It will be seen that such an example has to be given in very general terms.

1. See, respectively, Clean Air Act 1956, s 1; Control of Pollution Act 1974, s 31 (1) (a).

2. *Tesco Supermarkets Ltd v Nattrass* [1972] AC 153.
3. Ibid. at 180, 187–188, 190–191, 201.
4. Ibid. at 187.
5. Ibid. at 171.
6. Working Paper No 44, para 40.
7. [1972] AC 153 at 199–200, per Lord Diplock.
8. *R v Andrews Weatherfoil Ltd* [1972] 1 WLR 118; applying dictum of Lord Reid in *Tesco Supermarkets Ltd v Nattrass* [1972] AC 153 at 173.
9. [1972] AC 153 at 170, per Lord Reid.
10. Working Paper No 44, para 39d.
11. The word 'connives' (used in a similar context in cl 35) will not do here. It implies at least recklessness; whereas a corporation's liability for an offence of negligence or carelessness may be based on a controlling officer's merely negligent or careless failure to know what is going on or to act as he should act with such knowledge.
12. Cf Working Paper No 44, para 39b.
13. Ibid.
14. Ibid. para 39c.
15. [1944] 2 All ER 515. The decision may not have survived *Attorney General's Reference (No 2 of 1982)* [1984] QB 624; shareholders and directors charged with theft from a company they control cannot, on the ground of identification with the company, claim the company's consent to their acts.
16. See eg *R v Robert Millar (Contractors) Ltd* [1970] 2 QB 54.
17. Cf *Penn-Texas Corporation v Murat Anstalt* [1964] 1 QB 40 at 53–56, per Willmer LJ.
18. See (1979), Law Com No 96, Offences Relating to Interference with the Course of Justice. The offence of perjury proposed by cl 3 of the draft Administration of Justice (Offences) Bill appended to that Report might in some of its forms be committed by a corporation as principal.
19. Cf *R v McDonnell* [1966] 1 QB 233 (no conspiracy between a company and its sole controller).
20. [1972] AC 153.
21. Trade Descriptions Act 1968, s 24 (1).

**Tesco Supermarkets Ltd v Nattrass [1971] 2 All ER 127, House of Lords
(Lord Reid, Lord Morris of Borth-y-Gest, Viscount Dilhorne, Lord Pearson
and Lord Diplock)**

The facts appear in the speech of Lord Reid.

Lord Reid. My Lords, the appellants own a large number of supermarkets in which they sell a wide variety of goods. The goods are put out for sale on shelves or stands, each article being marked with the price at which it is offered for sale. The customer selects the articles he wants, take them to the cashier, and pays the price. From time to time the appellants, apparently by way of advertisement, sell 'flash packs' at prices lower than the normal price. In September 1969 they were selling Radiant washing powder in this way. The normal price was 11d but these packs were marked and sold at 2s 11d. Posters were displayed in the shops drawing attention to this reduction in price. These prices were displayed in the appellants' shop at Northwich on 26 September. Mr Coane, an old age pensioner, saw this and went to buy a pack. He could only find packs marked 3s 11d. He took one to the cashier who told him that there were none in stock for sale at 2s 11d. He paid 3s 11d and complained to an inspector of weights and measures. This resulted in a prosecution under the Trade Descriptions Act 1968 and the appellants were fined £25 and costs. Section 11 (2) provides:

> 'If any person offering to supply any goods gives, by whatever means, any indication likely to be taken as an indication that the goods are being offered at a price less than that at which they are in fact offered he shall, subject to the provisions of this Act, be guilty of an offence.'

It is not disputed that that section applies to this case. The appellants relied on s 24 (1) which provides:

> 'In any proceedings for an offence under this Act it shall, subject to subsection (2) of this section, be a defence for the person charged to prove—(a) that the commission of the offence was due to a mistake or to reliance on information supplied to him or to the act or default of another person, an accident or some other cause beyond his control; and (b)

that he took all reasonable precautions and exercised all due diligence to avoid the commission of such an offence by himself or any person under his control.'

The relevant facts as found by the justices were that on the previous evening a shop assistant, Miss Rogers, whose duty it was to put out fresh stock found that there were no more of the specially marked packs in the stock. There were a number of packs marked with the ordinary price so she put them out. She ought to have told the shop manager Mr Clement, about this but she failed to do so. Mr Clement was responsible for seeing that the proper packs were on sale, but he failed to see to this although he marked his daily return 'All special offers OK'. The justices found that if he had known about this he would either have removed the poster advertising the reduced price or given instructions that only 2s 11d was to be charged for the packs marked 3s 11d. Section 24 (2) requires notice to be given to the prosecutor if the accused is blaming another person and such notice was duly given naming Mr Clement.

In order to avoid conviction the appellants had to prove facts sufficient to satisfy both parts of s 24 (1) of the 1968 Act. The justices held that they:

> 'had exercised all due diligence in devising a proper system for the operation of the said store and by securing so far as was reasonably practicable that it was fully implemented and thus had fulfilled the requirements of s 24 (1) (b).'

But they convicted the appellants because in their view the requirements of s 24 (1) (a) had not been fulfilled; they held that Mr Clement was not 'another person' within the meaning of that provision. The Divisional Court [[1971] 1 QB 133; [1970] 3 All ER 357] held that the justices were wrong in holding that Mr Clement was not 'another person'. The respondent did not challenge this finding of the Divisional Court so I need say no more about it than that I think that on this matter the Divisional Court was plainly right. But that court sustained the conviction on the ground that the justices had applied the wrong test in deciding the requirements of s 24 (1) (b) had been fulfilled. In effect that court held that the words 'he took all reasonable precautions . . .' do not mean what they say; 'he' does not mean the accused, it means the accused and all his servants who were acting in a managerial or supervisory capacity. . . . In my judgment the main object of these provisions must have been to distinguish between those who are in some degree blameworthy and those who are not, and to enable the latter to escape from conviction if they can show that they were in no way to blame. I find it almost impossible to suppose that Parliament or any reasonable body of men would as a matter of policy think it right to make employers criminally liable for the acts of some of their servants but not for those of others and I find it incredible that a draftsman, aware of that intention, would fail to insert any words to express it. But in several cases the courts, for reasons which it is not easy to discover, have given a restricted meaning to such provisions. It has been held that such provisions afford a defence if the master proves that the servant at fault was the person who himself did the prohibited act, but that they afford no defence if the servant at fault was one who failed in his duty of supervision to see that his subordinates did not commit the prohibited act. Why Parliament should be thought to have intended this distinction or how as a matter of construction these provisions can reasonably be held to have that meaning is not apparent.

In some of these cases the employer charged with the offence was a limited company. But in others the employer was an individual and still it was held that he, though personally blameless, could not rely on these provisions if the fault which led to the commission of the offence was the fault of a servant in failing to carry out his duty to instruct or supervise his subordinates. Where a limited company is the employer difficult questions do arise in a wide variety of circumstances in deciding which of its officers or servants is to be identified with the company so that his guilt is the guilt of the company.

I must start by considering the nature of the personality which by a fiction the law attributes to a corporation. A living person has a mind which can have knowledge or intention or be negligent and he has hands to carry out his intentions. A corporation has none of these; it must act through living persons, though not always one or the same person. Then the person who acts is not speaking or acting for the company. He is acting as the company and his mind which directs his acts is the mind of the company. There is no question of the company being vicariously liable. He is not acting as a servant, representative, agent or delegate. He is an embodiment of the company or, one could say, he hears and speaks through the persona of the company, within his appropriate sphere, and his mind is the mind of the company. If it is a guilty mind then that guilt is the guilt of the company. It must be a question of law whether, once the facts have been ascertained, a person in doing particular things is to be regarded as the company or merely the company's servant or agent. In that case any liability of the company can only be a statutory or vicarious liability.

In *Lennard's Carrying Co Ltd v Asiatic Petroleum Co Ltd* [[1915] AC 705, [1914–15] All ER Rep 280] the question was whether damage had occurred without the 'actual fault or privity' of the owner of a ship. The owners were a company. The fault was that of the registered managing owner who managed the ship on behalf of the owners and it was held that the company could not dissociate itself from him so as to say that there was no actual fault or privity on the part of the company. Viscount Haldane LC said [[1915] AC at 713, 714, [1914–15] All ER Rep at 283]:

'For if Mr Lennard was the directing mind of the company, then his action must, unless a corporation is not to be liable at all, have been an action which was the action of the company itself within the meaning of s 502 . . . It must be upon the true construction of that section in such a case as the present one that the fault or privity is the fault or privity of somebody who is not merely a servant or agent for whom the company is liable upon the footing respondent superior, but somebody for whom the company is liable because his action is the very action of the company itself.'

Reference is frequently made to the judgment of Denning LJ in *H L Bolton (Engineering) Co Ltd v TJ Graham & Sons Ltd* [[1957] 1 QB 159 at 172, [1956] 3 All ER 624 at 630]. He said:

'A company may in many ways be likened to a human body. It has a brain and nerve centre which controls what it does. It also has hands which hold the tools and act in accordance with directions from the centre. Some of the people in the company are mere servants and agents who are nothing more than hands to do the work and cannot be said to represent the mind or will. Others are directors and managers who represent the directing mind and will of the company, and control what it does. The state of mind of these managers is the state of mind of the company and is treated by the law as such.'

In that case the directors of the company only met once a year; they left the management of the business to others, and it was the intention of those managers which was imputed to the company. I think that was right. There have been attempts to apply Denning LJ's words to all servants of a company whose work is brain work, or who exercise some managerial discretion under the direction of superior officers of the company. I do not think that Denning LJ intended to refer to them. He only referred to those who 'represent the directing mind and will of the company, and control what it does'.

I think that is right for this reason. Normally the board of directors, the managing director and perhaps other superior officers of a company carry out the functions of management and speak and act as the company. Their subordinates do not. They carry out orders from above and it can make no difference that they are given some measure of discretion. But the board of directors may delegate some part of their functions of management giving to their delegate full discretion to act independently of instructions from them. I see no difficulty in holding that they have thereby put such a delegate in their place so that within the scope of the delegation he can act as the company. It may not always be easy to draw the line but there are cases in which the line must be drawn. *Lennard's* case was one of them.

In some cases the phrase alter ego has been used. I think it is misleading. When dealing with a company the word alter is I think misleading. The person who speaks and acts as the company is not alter. He is identified with the company. And when dealing with an individual no other individual can be his alter ego. . . . In the next two cases a company was accused and it was held liable for the fault of a superior officer. In *Director of Public Prosecutions v Kent and Sussex Contractors Ltd* [[1944] KB 146, [1944] 1 All ER 119] he was the transport manager. In *ICR Haulage Ltd* [[1944] KB 551, [1944] 1 All ER 691] it was held that a company can be guilty of common law conspiracy. The act of the managing director was held to be the act of the company. I think that a passage in the judgment is too widely stated [[1944] KB at 559, [1944] 1 All ER at 695].

'Whether in any particular case there is evidence to go to a jury that the criminal act of an agent, including his state of mind, intention, knowledge or belief is the act of the company, and in cases where the presiding judge so rules whether the jury are satisfied that it has been so proved, must depend on the nature of the charge, the relative position of the officer or agent and the other relevant facts and circumstances of the case.'

This may have been influenced by the erroneous views expressed in the two *Hammett* cases [(1931) 145 LT 638, [1931] All ER Rep 70]. I think that the true view is that the judge must direct the jury that if they find certain facts proved then as a matter of law they must find that the criminal act of the officer, servant or agent including his state of mind, intention, knowledge or belief is the act of the company. I have already dealt with the considerations to be applied in deciding when such a person can and when he cannot be identified with the company. I do not see how the nature of the charge can make any difference. If the guilty man was in law identifiable with the company then whether his offence was serious or venial his act was the act of the company but if he was not so identifiable then no act of his, serious or otherwise, was the act of the company itself. . . .

What good purpose could be served by making an employer criminally responsible for the misdeeds of some of his servants but not for those of others? It is sometimes argued—it was argued in the present case—that making an employer criminally responsible, even when he has done all that he could to prevent an offence, affords some additional protection to the public because this will induce him to do more. But if he has done all he can how can he do more? I think that what lies behind this argument is a suspicion that justices too readily accept evidence that an employer has done all he can to prevent offences. But if justices were to accept as sufficient a paper scheme and perfunctory efforts to enforce it they would not be doing their duty—that would not be 'due diligence' on the part of the employer. Then it is said that this would involve discrimination in favour of a large employer like the appellants against a small shopkeeper. But that is not so. Mr Clement was the 'opposite number' of the small shopkeeper and he was liable to prosecution in this case. The purpose of this Act must have been to penalise those at fault, not those who were in no way to blame.

The Divisional Court [[1971] 1 QB 133, [1970] 3 All ER 357] decided this case on a theory of delegation. In that they were following some earlier authorities. But they gave far too wide a meaning to delegation. I have said that a board of directors can delegate part of their functions of management so as to make their delegate an embodiment of the company within the sphere of the delegation. But here the board never delegated any part of their functions. They set up a chain of command through regional and district supervisors, but they remained in control. The shop managers had to obey their general directions and also to take orders from their superiors. The acts or omissions of shop managers were not acts of the company itself.

In my judgment the appellant established the statutory defence, I would therefore allow this appeal.

[**Lord Morris of Borth-y-Gest, Viscount Dilhorne Lord Pearson** and **Lord Diplock** made speeches allowing the appeal.]

Appeal allowed

Questions

1. See note, 'A Blow against Enterprise Liability', by R. W. L. Howells in (1971) 34 MLR 676 and consider the answers to the following questions raised by the note:

    (a) '. . . the longstanding proposition that an employer remained criminally liable for the conduct of a servant to whom he had delegated the performance of a statutory duty on his behalf has been confined to situations in which artificial persons have to delegate performance of their legal duties to human agents. Possibly this may be extended to situations in which natural persons delegate the full and unfettered management of their business to responsible agents.'

Does the decision go as far as stated in the first sentence?

    (b) 'It is suggested that a first principle for the enforcement of legislation such as the Trade Descriptions Act is that those who profit from contraventions of the law are those who should feel the weight of the legal penalties.'

Is this a sound first principle? Is it infringed by the decision?

2. Was there anything to be said for the rejected distinction between liability for the servant who is at fault in committing the actual offence and liability for the servant who fails in his duty of supervision?

3. Are all statutory duties delegable? Abel, the owner of a business, delegates the entire management of it to Baker. Baker intentionally applies a false trade description to goods and services supplied by the business. Abel is charged with (i) an offence under s 1 (1) of the Trade Descriptions Act 1968; (ii) an offence under s 14 (1) (a) of that Act; (iii) attempting to obtain the price of goods by deception, contrary to s 15 of the Theft Act 1968 (p 569, below).

[Section 1 (1) of the Trade Descriptions Act provides: 'Any person who in the course of a trade or business—(a) applies a false trade description to any goods . . . shall . . . be guilty of an offence; and s 14 (1): 'It shall be an offence for any person in the course of any trade or business—(a) to make a statement which he knows to be false.']

For which of these offences, if any, is Abel liable? (Suppose that he omits to plead the defence under s 24 or is unable to prove that he exercised the diligence required by that section.)

4. If only some statutory duties are delegable, how do we distinguish between delegable and non-delegable duties? Should delegable duties be confined to those which are imposed upon designated individuals (eg 'the holder of a justices' licence')? Or to those imposed by statutes relating to 'public welfare'? Or to so-called quasi-criminal offences?

5. What justificiation is there for imposing corporate criminal liability? Consider particularly a corporation administering a nationalised industry.

CHAPTER 10

Mental abnormality

1. Fitness to plead

R v Podola [1959] 3 All ER 418, Court of Criminal Appeal
(Lord Parker CJ, Hilbery, Donovan, Ashworth and Paull JJ)

Podola, being indicted for capital murder, raised a preliminary issue that he was unfit to plead owing to loss of memory of events prior to and including the time of the alleged homicide. Edmund Davies J ruled that there was an onus of proof on a balance of probabilities on the defendant to establish his unfitness. The jury found that the defendant was not suffering from a genuine loss of memory. The trial proceeded and Podola was found guilty of capital murder. The Home Secretary, being of the opinion that the question of onus of proof on the preliminary issue ought to be considered by the Court of Criminal Appeal, referred the whole case to the Court under s 19 (a) of the Criminal Appeal Act 1907.

[**Lord Parker CJ**, having ruled that the question specifically referred to the Court involved by necessary implication the question whether the alleged amnesia could in law bring the accused within the scope of s 2 of the Criminal Lunatics Act 1800, continued:]

We deal first with the matter specifically referred to us, namely the question as to onus of proof. The relevant words in s 2 of the Criminal Lunatics Act 1800, are as follows:

> '. . . if any person indicted for any offence shall be insane, and shall upon arraignment be found so to be by a jury lawfully empanelled for that purpose, so that such person cannot be tried upon such indictment . . .'

Those words do not indicate how or by whom the question of the accused person's sanity is to be raised. But it is now well established that the question may be raised either by the prosecution or by the defence or by the court itself. Indeed, if a court becomes aware, either before or during a trial, that the accused person's sanity is doubtful, it is the duty of the court to have the the doubt resolved before beginning or continuing the trial. For the purpose of deciding whether a person is 'insane . . . so that he cannot be tried upon the indictment' a jury is empanelled and as counsel for the appellant emphasised, the procedure before that jury is an inquiry and not a trial. In most cases in which this course is taken, there is no contest between the prosecution and the defence as to the accused person's insanity, and the evidence to that effect is unchallenged. In such cases, although the jury must be satisfied of the accused person's insanity before so finding, the question of onus of proof is not a live issue. But cases have arisen of which the present one is an example, where either the prosecution or the defence has challenged the alleged insanity, and in a case in Scotland (*Russell v H M Advocate* [1946 JC 37]), to which more detailed reference will be made later, the court itself refused to give effect to a plea in bar of trial put forward on behalf of the defence and not contested by the prosecution.

It was contended by counsel for the appellant that, inasmuch as the proceedings on the issue of insanity are an inquiry and not a trial, it is wrong to introduce any principle as to onus of proof, derived from proceedings properly regarded as trials. We do not agree with this contention. In our judgment the right principles may be stated as follows:

1. In all cases in which a preliminary issue as to the accused person's sanity is raised, whether that issue is contested or not, the jury should be directed to consider the whole of the evidence and to answer the question 'Are you satisfied on that evidence that the accused person is insane so that he cannot be tried on the indictment?' If authority were needed for the principle, it is to be found in the very words of the section itself, quoted above.

2. If the contention that the accused is insane is put forward by the defence and contested by the prosecution, there is in our judgment a burden on the defence of satisfying the jury of the accused's insanity. In such a case, as in other criminal cases in which the onus of proof rests on the defence, the onus is discharged if the jury are satisfied on the balance of probabilities that the accused's insanity has been made out.

3. Conversely, if the prosecution alleges and the defence disputes insanity, there is a burden on the prosecution of establishing it. . . .

It is not suggested in this case that the appellant could not plead to the indictment, or that he did not know that he had the right of challenge, or that he could not follow the evidence given, but counsel for the appellant submitted strongly that, where there was the partial obliteration of memory alleged in this case, a prisoner could not make a proper defence and could not 'comprehend' the details of the evidence within the meaning of the words used in *Pritchard* [(1836) 7 C&P 303 at 304]. So far as 'making a proper defence' is concerned, it is important to note that the words do not stand alone, but form part of a sentence the whole of which is 'whether he is of sufficient intellect to comprehend the course of proceedings on the trial, so as to make a proper defence'. In other words this passage itself defines what Alderson B meant by 'making a proper defence'. As to the word 'comprehend' we do not think that this word goes further in meaning than the word 'understand'. In our judgment the direction given by Alderson B is not intended to cover and does not cover a case where the prisoner can plead to the indictment and has the physical and mental capacity to know that he has the right of challenge and to understand the case as it proceeds.

[His Lordship then referred to two Scottish cases and concluded:]

It is true that in the case of a deaf mute the word 'insane' does not strictly apply, but . . . the practice of including as coming within the word the case of persons who, from mental or physical infirmity cannot follow what is happening in a case is in accordance with reason and common sense. We cannot see that it is in accordance either with reason or common sense to extend the meaning of the word to include persons who are mentally normal at the time of the hearing of the proceedings against them and are perfectly capable of instructing their solicitors as to what submission their counsel is to put forward with regard to the commission of the crime . . .

Appeal dismissed

Questions

1. Is it right that a person should be liable to indefinite detention when it has been established only that he is unfit to plead and not that he has done anything wrong? Is s 4 of the Criminal Procedure (Insanity) Act 1964 (p 557, below) a sufficient safeguard?

2. Would it be preferable to try the accused person notwithstanding his unfitness? (See 'A Proposal for the Abolition of the Incompetency Plea,' By Burt and Morris, 40 Univ of Chic LR 66.)

Criminal Procedure (Insanity) Act 1964, s 4

4   Unfitness to plead [see p 557, below]

Criminal Appeal Act 1968, s 15

UNFITNESS TO STAND TRIAL

15   Right to appeal against finding of disability [see p 564, below]

2. The M'Naghten rules

M'Naghten's Case (1843) 10 Clark and Finnelly 200

M'Naghten was charged with the murder by shooting of Edward Drummond. He pleaded not guilty. Medical evidence was called on behalf of the prisoner to prove that he was not, at the time of committing the act, in a sound state of mind. The evidence was to the effect that persons of otherwise sound mind might be affected by morbid delusions and that the prisoner was in that condition; that a person labouring under a morbid delusion might have a moral perception of right and wrong, but that in the case of the prisoner it was a delusion which carried him away beyond the power of his own control, and left him with no such perception; and that he was not capable of exercising any control over acts which had connection with his delusion: that it was the nature of the disease with which the prisoner was affected, to go on gradually until it had reached a climax, when it burst forth with irresistible intensity: that a man might go on for years quietly, though at the same time under its influence, but would all at once break out into the most extravagant and violent paroxysms.

Some of the witnesses who gave this evidence had previously examined the prisoner, others had never seen him till he appeared in court, and they formed their opinions on hearing the evidence given by other witnesses.

[**Tindal CJ** directed the jury:]

The question to be determined is whether at the time the act in question was committed, the prisoner had or had not the use of his understanding, so as to know that he was doing a wrong or wicked act. If the jurors should be of opinion that the prisoner was not sensible, at the time he committed it, that he was violating the laws of both God and man, then he would be entitled to a verdict in his favour: but if, on the contrary, they were of opinion that when he committed the act he was in a sound state of mind, then their verdict must be against him.

Verdict, Not guilty, on the ground of insanity.

This verdict was made the subject of debate in the House of Lords and it was determined to take the opinion of all the judges on the law governing such cases. The judges attended on two occasions and, on the second occasion, five questions were put to them.

[**Maule CJ** having referred to the difficulty which he felt about answering hypothetical questions on which he had heard no argument and his fear that the answers might embarrass the administration of criminal justice, stated that he would have been glad if his learned brethren would have joined him in praying their Lordships to excuse them from answering the questions. Maule J then offered his own answers.]

Tindal CJ. The first question proposed by your Lordships is this: 'What is the law respecting alleged crimes committed by persons afflicted with insane delusion in respect of one or more particular subjects or persons: as, for instance, where at the time of the commission of the alleged crime the accused knew he was acting contrary to law, but did the act complained of with a view, under the influence of insane delusion, of redressing or revenging some supposed grievance or injury, or of producing some supposed public benefit?'

In answer to which question, assuming that your Lordships' inquiries are confined to those persons who labour under such partial delusions only, and are not in other respects insane, we are of opinion that, notwithstanding the party accused did the act complained of with a view, under the influence of insane delusion, of redressing or revenging some supposed grievance or injury, or of producing some public benefit, he is nevertheless punishable according to the nature of the crime committed, if he knew at the time of committing such crime that he was acting contrary to law; by which expression we understand your Lordships to mean the law of the land.

Your Lordships are pleased to inquire of us, secondly, 'What are the proper questions to be submitted to the jury, where a person alleged to be afflicted with insane delusion respecting one or more particular subjects or persons, is charged with the commission of a crime (murder, for example), and insanity is set up as a defence?' And, thirdly, 'In what terms ought the question to be left to the jury as to the prisoner's state of mind at the time when the act was committed?' And as these two questions appear to us to be more conveniently answered together, we have to submit our opinion to be, that the jurors ought to be told in all cases that every man is to be presumed to be sane, and to possess a sufficient degree of reason to be responsible for his crimes, until the contrary to be proved to their satisfaction; and that to establish a defence on the ground of insanity, it must be clearly proved that, at the time of the committing of the act, the party accused was labouring under such a defect of reason, from disease of the mind, as not to know the nature and quality of the act he was doing; or, if he did know it, that he did not know he was doing what was wrong. The mode of putting the latter part of the question to the jury on these occasions has generally been, whether the accused at the time of doing the act knew the difference between right and wrong: which mode, though rarely, if ever, leading to any mistake with the jury, is not, as we conceive, so accurate when put generally and in the abstract, as when put with reference to the party's knowledge of right and wrong in respect to the very act with which he is charged. If the question were to be put as to the knowledge of the accused solely and exclusively with reference to the law of the land, it might tend to confound the jury, by inducing them to believe that an actual knowledge of the law of the land was essential in order to lead a conviction; whereas the law is administered upon the principle that every one must be taken conclusively to know it, without proof that he does know it. If the accused was conscious that the act was one which he ought not to do, and if that act was at the same time contrary to the law of the land, he is punishable; and the usual course therefore has been to leave the question to the jury, whether the party accused had a sufficient degree of reason to know that he was doing an act that was wrong: and this course we think is correct, accompanied with such observations and explanations as the circumstances of each particular case may require.

The fourth question which your Lordships have proposed to us is this: 'If a person under an insane delusion as to existing facts, commits an offence in consequence thereof, is he thereby excused?' To which question the answer must of course depend on the nature of the delusion: but, making the same assumption as we did before, namely, that he labours under such partial delusion only, and is not in other respects insane, we think he must be considered in the same situation as to responsibility as if the facts with respect to which the delusion exists were real. For example, if under the influence of his delusion he supposes another man to be in the act of attempting to take away his life, and he kills that man, as he supposes, in self-defence, he would be exempt from punishment. If his delusion was that the deceased had inflicted a serious injury to his character and fortune, and he killed him in revenge for such supposed injury, he would be liable to punishment.

The question lastly proposed by your Lordships is: 'Can a medical man conversant with the disease of insanity, who never saw the prisoner previously to the trial, but who was present during the whole trial and the examination of all the witnesses, be asked his opinion as to the state of the prisoner's mind at the time of the commission of the alleged crime, or his opinion whether the prisoner was conscious at the time of doing the act that he was acting contrary to law, or whether he was labouring under any and what delusion at the time?' In answer thereto, we state to your Lordships, that we think the medical man, under the circumstances supposed, cannot in strictness be asked his opinion in the terms above stated, because each of those questions involves the determination of the truth of the facts deposed to, which it is for the jury to decide, and the questions are not mere questions upon a matter of science, in which such evidence is admissible. But where the facts are admitted or not disputed, and the question becomes substantially one of science only, it may be convenient to allow the question to be put in that general form, though the same cannot be insisted on as a matter of right.

Trial of Lunatics Act 1883 (as amended by the Criminal Procedure (Insanity) Act 1964

2   Special verdict where accused found guilty, but insane at date of act or omission charged, and orders thereupon [see p 547, below]

Criminal Appeal Act 1968

APPEAL IN CASES OF INSANITY

12.   Appeal against verdict of not guilty by reason of insanity [see p 564, below]

R v Clarke [1972] 1 All ER 219, Court of Appeal, Criminal Division
(Lord Widgery CJ, Sachs LJ, and Ackner J)

The applicant selected various items in a supermarket and put them into the wire basket provided. Before she went to the checkout, she transferred three items into her own bag so that, when she presented the basket, these items were not in it and were not paid for. She was charged with stealing them. Her defence was that she had no intent to steal. She suffered from diabetes and had various domestic problems. There was evidence that, prior to the alleged theft, she had behaved absent-mindedly in the home. She said that she must have put the articles in her bag in a moment of absent-mindedness. Her doctor and a consultant psychiatrist were called and testified that she was suffering from depression which one of them accepted to be a minor mental illness which could produce absent-mindedness consistent with her story.

Ackner J. Unfortunately the medical witnesses were pressed to, what it seems to us, an unreasonable degree to explain the workings of this particular illness. The psychiatrist stated that what happens in these cases is 'that there is a patchy state of affairs, and the consciousness, if you like, goes off at times and comes on again, changing every few minutes and not in proper control of the patient'.

The effect of this evidence on the assistant recorder was to convince him that the defence was in truth a defence of 'not guilty by reason of insanity' under the *M'Naghten* rules [p 188, above]. He was undoubtedly influenced to this decision by the evidence that the depression was an illness which he translated as meaning also a disease and by the fact that on the medical evidence, as he understood it, a possible explanation was that there had been a total lack of consciousness at the moment when the offence was committed. In order to sustain a defence under the *M'Naghten* rules it is necessary to show that the party accused was labouring under *such a defect of reason from the disease of the mind as not to know the nature and quality of the act he was doing* or if he did know, that he did not know that what he was doing was wrong.

It may be that on the evidence in this case the assistant recorder was entitled to the view that the appellant suffered from a disease of the mind but we express no concluded view on that. However, in our judgment the evidence fell very far short either of showing that she suffered from a defect of a reason or that the consequences of that defect in reason, if any, were that she was unable to know the nature and quality of the act she was doing. The *M'Naghten* rules relate to accused persons who by reason of a disease of the mind are deprived of the power of reasoning. They do not apply and never have applied to those who retain the power of reasoning but who in moments of confusion or absent-mindedness fail to use their powers to the full. The picture painted by the evidence was wholly inconsistent [sic] with this being a woman who retained her ordinary powers of reason but who was momentarily absent-minded or confused and acted as she did by failing to concentrate properly on what she was doing and by failing adequately to use her mental powers.

Because the assistant recorder ruled that the defence put forward had to be put forward as a defence of insanity, although the medical evidence was to the effect that it was absurd to call anyone in the appellant's condition insane, defending counsel felt constrained to advise the appellant to alter her plea from not guilty to guilty so as to avoid the disastrous consequences of her defence, as wrongly defined by the assistant recorder, succeeding. Thus the appellant in this case ultimately pleaded guilty solely by reason of the assistant recorder's ruling. . . . The conviction is accordingly quashed.

Appeal allowed

R v Windle [1952] 2 All ER 1, Court of Criminal Appeal
(Lord Goddard CJ, Jones and Parker JJ)

[**Lord Goddard CJ** delivered the following judgment of the court:]

The appellant was convicted before Devlin J at Birmingham Assizes of the murder of his wife. He is a man of little resolution and weak character who was married to a woman 18 years older than himself. His married life was very unhappy. His wife, in the opinion of the doctors, though they never saw her, must have been certifiable, and was always talking about committing suicide.

The appellant became obsessed with this and discussed it with his workmates until they were tired of hearing him, and on one occasion, just before this crime was committed, one of them said 'Give her a dozen aspirins'. On the day of the crime the appellant seems to have given the woman 100 aspirin tablets, which was a fatal dose. Later, he told the police that he supposed he would be hanged for it.

The defence at the trial was that he was insane and that the jury should return a special verdict to that effect, but Devlin J ruled that there was no issue of insanity to be left to the jury. There was some evidence that the prisoner suffered from some defect of reason or disease of the mind. The doctor called for the defence said it was a form of communicated insanity known as *folie à deux* which arises when a person is in constant attendance on a person of unsound mind. [His lordship quoted the M'Naghten Rules.]

The argument in this appeal really has been concerned with what is meant by the word 'wrong'. The evidence that was given on the issue of insanity was that of the doctor called by the appellant and that of the prison doctor who was called by the prosecution. Both doctors expressed without hesitation the view that when the appellant was administering this poison to his wife he knew he was doing an act which the law forbade. I need not put it higher than that. It may well be that in the misery in which he had been living with this nagging and tiresome wife who constantly expressed the desire to commit suicide, he thought she was better out of the world than in it. He may have thought it was a kindly act to put her out of her sufferings or imagined sufferings, but the law does not permit such an act as that. There was some exceedingly vague evidence that the appellant was suffering from a defect of his reason owing to his communicated insanity, and, if the only question in the case had been whether the appellant was suffering from a disease of the mind, that question must have been left to the jury because there was some evidence of it, but that was not the question. The question, as I endeavoured to point out in giving judgment in *Rivett* [(1950) 34 Cr App Rep 87], in all these cases is one of responsibility. A man may be suffering from a defect of reason, but, if he knows that what he is doing is wrong—and by 'wrong' is meant contrary to law—he is responsible. Counsel for the appellant suggested that the word 'wrong' as it is used in the M'Naghten rules did not mean contrary to law, but had some qualified meaning—morally wrong—and that, if a person was in a state of mind through a defect of reason that he thought that what he was doing, although he knew it was wrong in law, was really beneficial, or kind, or praiseworthy, that would excuse him.

Courts of law, however, can only distinguish between that which is in accordance with the law and that which is contrary to law. There are many acts which, we all know, to use an expression to be found in some of the old cases, are contrary to the law of God and man. In the Decalogue are the commandments: 'Thou shall not kill' and 'Thou shall not steal'. Such acts are contrary to the law of man and they are contrary to the law of God. In regard to the Seventh Commandment: 'Thou shall not commit adultery', it will be found that, so far as the criminal law is concerned, though that act is contrary to the law of God, it is not contrary to the law of man.

The test must be whether an act is contrary to law. In *Rivett* I referred to the Trial of Lunatics Act 1883, s 2 (1) of which provides:

> 'Where in any indictment or information any act or omission is charged against any person as an offence, and it is given in evidence on the trial of such person for that offence that he was insane, so as not to be responsible, according to law, for his actions at the time when the act was done or omission made, then if it appears to the jury before whom such person is tried that he did the act or made the omission charged, but was insane as aforesaid at the time when he did or made the same, the jury shall return a special verdict . . .'

I emphasise again that the test is responsibility 'according to law'. . . . Devlin J was right to withdraw the case from jury. This appeal fails.

Appeal dismissed

(1) INSANITY AND AUTOMATISM

R v Kemp [1956] 3 All ER 249, Bristol Assizes
(Devlin J)

The accused was charged with causing grievous bodily harm to his wife by striking her with a hammer. It was accepted that at the time of the act the accused was suffering from arteriosclerosis and that he did not know what he was doing—that he did not know the nature and quality of his act. One doctor, called by the prosecution, gave as his opinion that this was due to melancholia, a disease of the mind, which was induced by the disease of arteriosclerosis. Two other doctors, one called by the prosecution and the other by the defence, gave as their opinions that whereas arteriosclerosis can cause degeneration of the brain cells which would in time amount to disease of the mind, in the present case that stage had not been reached, and that at the time when he committed the act the accused suffered from a congestion of blood in the brain (due to the arteriosclerosis) which caused a temporary loss of consciousness as a result of which he acted irrationally and irresponsibly. It was therefore submitted by the defence that although the accused did not know the nature and quality of his act, he was not suffering from a disease of the mind and was not, therefore, insane within the test laid down in *M'Naghten's Case* ((1843) 10 C1 & Fin 200), p 188, above.

Devlin J. [His Lordship referred to *Charlson* [1955] 1 All ER 859, discussed by Lord Denning p 197, below and continued:] In that case the doctors were apparently agreed that the accused was not suffering from any disease of the mind which would render him insane at the time of the commission of the acts. The present case is in my judgment entirely different, because here the doctors are not so agreed and the whole question that I have to determine, which was not considered in that case, is what is meant by 'disease of the mind' within the meaning of the M'Naghten rules? . . .
The broad submission that was made to me on behalf of the defence was that this is a physical disease and not a mental disease, that arteriosclerosis is primarily a physical not a mental condition; but that argument does not go so far as to suggest that for this purpose those diseases that affect the mind can be strictly divided into those that are physical in origin and those that are mental in origin. That there is such a distinction is clear from the evidence. I should think that it would probably be recognised by medical men that there are mental diseases which have an organic cause; that there are disturbances of the brain which can be traced to some hardening of the arteries, to some degeneration of the brain cells or to some physical condition which accounts for mental derangement. It would probably be recognised that there are diseases functional in origin about which it is not possible to point to any physical cause but simply to say that there has been a mental derangement of the functioning of the mind, such as melancholia, schizophrenia and many other of those diseases which are primarily handled by psychiatrists, but that distinction is rightly not pressed as part of the argument for the defence in the present case. The distinction between the two categories is irrelevant for the purposes of the law, which is not concerned with the origin of the disease or the cause of it but simply with the mental condition which has brought about the act. It does not matter, for the purposes of the law, whether the defect of reasoning is due to a degeneration of the brain or to some other form of mental derangement. That may be a matter of importance medically, but it is of no importance to the law which merely has to consider the state of mind in which the accused is, not how he got there.
The distinction that emerges from the evidence of the doctor called by the defence, and which has been argued by counsel for the defence, is different. It is that arteriosclerosis is something which is capable, as I understand it, of becoming a mental disease but in the present case has not yet become one. It has not yet created any degeneration of the brain and the argument is that it is merely interfering temporarily with the working of the brain by cutting off the supply of blood in the same way as concussion might. The test, therefore, that I am invited to apply is to say that this disease at this stage is purely physical; when it interferes with the brain cells so that they degenerate it then becomes a disease of the mind. There again I should think that is a very difficult and complicated principle to apply for the purposes of the law. I should think that it would be a matter of some difficulty medically to determine precisely at what point degeneration of the brain sets in and it would mean that the verdict depended on the medical evidence. It is the effect which is produced on the mind and not the precise cause of producing it which is relevant. Moreover, the Trial of Lunatics Act 1883, is not in any way concerned with the brain but with the mind, in the sense that the term is ordinarily used when speaking of the mental faculties of reasoning, memory and understanding, particularly in the present case the faculties of reasoning and understanding. If one read for 'disease of the mind' 'disease of the brain' it would follow that in many cases pleas of insanity would not be established because it would not be established that the brain had been affected either by degeneration of the cells or in any other way. In my judgment the condition of the brain is irrelevant and so is the question whether the disease is

curable or incurable, or whether it is temporary or permanent. There is no warranty for introducing those considerations into the definition of the M'Naghten rules. Either temporary or permanent insanity is sufficient to satisfy them.

I therefore accept the argument of counsel for the prosecution. He stresses the order of the words [ie in the rule stated in *M'Naghten's Case*] that I have to apply, namely:

> ' . . . the party accused was labouring under such a defect of reason, from disease of the mind, as not to know the nature and quality of the act he was doing.'

It is not labouring under a disease of the mind which produces the defect of reasoning, but the paramount thing that has to be looked for is the defect of reasoning. The prime thing is to determine what is admitted in the present case, namely, whether or not there is a defect of reasoning, and in my judgment the words 'from disease of the mind' are not to be construed as if they were put in for the purposes of distinguishing between diseases of the mind and diseases of the body, diseases which had mental or physical origin, but they were put in primarily for the purpose of limiting the effect of the words 'defect of reason'. A defect of reason is by itself normally enough to make the act irrational and therefore to deny responsibility in law, but it was not intended by that rule that it should apply to defects of reason which were caused simply by brutish stupidity without rational power. It was not intended that the law should say of a person: 'Although with a healthy mind he nevertheless had been brought up in such a way that he had never learned to exercise his reason, and therefore he is suffering from a defect of reason.' The main object, in my judgment, was that it should be decided whether there was a defect of reason which had been caused by a disease affecting the mind; if it were so decided, then there would be insanity within the meaning of the rule in *M'Naghten's Case*. The hardening of the arteries is a disease which is shown on the evidence to be capable of affecting the mind in such a way as to cause a defect, temporarily or permanently, of its reasoning and understanding, and is thus a disease of the mind within the meaning of the rule. I shall therefore direct the jury that it matters not whether they accept the medical evidence of the prosecution or the defence, but that on the whole of the medical evidence they ought to find that there is a disease of the mind within the meaning of the rule.

[After the jury had heard speeches of counsel and the summing-up they returned a verdict of guilty but insane. Devlin J then ordered the accused to be kept in strict custody until Her Majesty's pleasure should be known.]

Order accordingly

R v Quick and Paddison [1973] 3 All ER 347, Court of Appeal, Criminal Division
(Lawton LJ, Mocatta and Milmo JJ)

The appellants were nurses employed at a mental hospital. They were convicted of assault occasioning actual bodily harm to a paraplegic spastic patient at the hospital. Quick called medical evidence to show that he was diabetic and that at the time of the alleged assault he was suffering from hypoglycaemia and was unaware of what he was doing. He submitted that the evidence established a defence of automatism. Bridge J ruled that the defence raised was one of insanity, whereupon Quick changed his plea to guilty. Paddison was convicted by the jury on the basis that he had abetted Quick. Quick appealed on the ground that the judge's ruling was wrong and that a diabetic in a temporary and reversible condition of hypoglycaemia was not, while in that condition, suffering from any defect of reason from disease of the mind.

[**Lawton LJ**, delivering the judgment of the court, reviewed the evidence, referred to the dictum of Lord Denning in *Bratty* (pp 197, 198, below) that:

> ' . . . any mental disorder which has manifested itself in violence and is prone to recur is a disease of the mind. At any rate it is the sort of disease for which a person should be detained in hospital rather than be given an unqualified acquittal';

and continued:

If this opinion is right and there are no restricting qualifications which ought to be applied to it, Quick was setting up a defence of insanity. He may have been at the material time in a condition of mental disorder manifesting itself in violence. Such manifestations had occurred before and might recur. The difficulty arises as soon as the question is asked whether he should be detained in a mental hospital? No mental hospital would admit a diabetic merely because he had a low sugar reaction; and common sense is affronted by the prospect of a diabetic being sent to such a hospital when in most cases the disordered mental condition can be rectified quickly by pushing a lump of sugar or a teaspoonful of glucose into the patient's mouth.

The 'affront to common sense' argument, however, has its own inherent weakness, as counsel for the Crown pointed out. If an accused is shown to have done a criminal act whilst suffering from a 'defect of reason from disease of the mind,' it matters not 'whether the disease is curable or incurable . . . temporary or permanent' (see *Kemp* [see p 191, above], per Devlin J). If the condition is temporary, the Secretary of State may have a difficult problem of disposal; but what happens to those found not guilty by reason of insanity is not a matter for the courts.

In *Kemp*, where the violent act was alleged to have been done during a period of unconsciousness arising from arteriosclerosis, counsel for the accused submitted that his client had done what he had during a period of mental confusion arising from a physical, not a mental disease. Devlin J rejected this argument saying:

'It does not matter, for the purposes of the law, whether the defect of reasoning is due to a degeneration of the brain or to some other form of mental derangement. That may be a matter of importance medically, but it is of no importance to the law, which merely has to consider the state of mind in which the accused is, not how he got there.'

Applied without qualification of any kind, Devlin J's statement of the law would have some surprising consequences. Take the not uncommon case of the rugby player who gets a kick on the head early in the game and plays on to the end in a state of automatism. If, whilst he was in that state, he assaulted the referee it is difficult to envisage any court adjudging that he was not guilty by reason of insanity. Another type of case which could occur is that of the dental patient who kicks out whilst coming round from an anaesthetic. The law would be in a defective state if a patient accused of assaulting a dental nurse by kicking her whilst regaining consciousness could only excuse himself by raising the defence of insanity.

In *Hill v Baxter* [[1958] 1 QB 277, [1958] 1 All ER 193] the problem before the Divisional Court was whether the accused had put forward sufficient evidence on a charge of dangerous driving to justify the justices adjudging that he should be acquitted, there having been no dispute that at the time when his car collided with another one he was at the driving wheel. At the trial the accused had contended that he became unconscious at a result of being overcome by an unidentified illness. The court (Lord Goddard CJ, Devlin and Pearson JJ) allowed an appeal by the prosecution against the verdict of acquittal. In the course of examining the evidence which had been put forward by the accused the judges made some comments of a general nature. Lord Goddard CJ [[1958] 1 QB at 282, [1958] 1 All ER at 195], referred to some observations of Humphreys J in *Kay v Butterworth* [(1945) 173 LT 191] which seemed to indicate that a man who became unconscious whilst driving due to the onset of a sudden illness should not be made liable at criminal law and went as follows [[1958] 1 QB at 282, [1958] 1 All ER at 195]:

'I agree that there may be cases when circumstances are such that the accused could not really be said to be driving at all. Suppose he had a stroke or an epileptic fit, both instances of what may properly be called Act of God; he might well be in the driver's seat even with his hands on the wheel but in such a state of unconsciousness that he could not be said to be driving . . . . In this case, however, I am content to say that the evidence falls far short of what would justify a court holding that this man was in some automatous state'.

Lord Goddard CJ did not equate unconsciousness due to a sudden illness, which must entail the malfunctioning of the mental processes of the sufferer, with disease of the mind, and in our judgment no one outside a court of law would. Devlin J in his judgment [[1958] 1 QB at 285, [1958] 1 All ER at 197] accepted that some temporary loss of consciousness arising *accidentally* (the italics are ours) did not call for a verdict based on insanity. It is not clear what he meant by 'accidentally'. The context suggests that he may have meant 'unexpectedly' as can happen with some kinds of virus infections. He went on as follows[1]:

'If, however, disease is present the same thing may happen again and therefore since 1800 the law has provided that persons acquitted on this ground should be subject to restraint.'

If this be right anyone suffering from a tooth abscess who knows from past experience that he reacts violently to anaesthetics because of some constitutional bodily disorder which can be attributed to disease might have to go on suffering or take the risk of being found insane unless he could find a dentist who would be prepared to take the risk of being kicked by a recovering patient. It seems to us that the law should not give the words 'defect of reason from disease of the mind' a meaning which would be regarded with incredulity outside a court. . . .

In this quagmire of law seldom entered nowadays save by those in desperate need of some kind of defence, *Bratty v A-G for Northern Ireland* provides the only firm ground. Is there any discernible path? We think there is—judges should follow in a common sense way their sense of fairness. This seems to have been the approach of the New Zealand Court of Appeal in *Cottle* [[1958] NZLR 999] and of Sholl J in *Carter* [[1959] VR 105]. In our judgment no help can be obtained by speculating (because that is what we would have to do) as to what the judges who answered the House of Lord's questions in 1843 [see p 188, above] meant by disease of the mind, still less what Sir Matthew Hale meant in the second half of the 17th century [(1682) Vol I, Ch IV]. A quick backward look at the state of medicine in 1843 will suffice to show how unreal it would be to apply the concepts of that age to the present time. Dr Simpson had not yet started his experiments with chloroform, the future Lord Lister was only 16 and laudanum was used and prescribed like aspirins are today. Our task has been to decide what the law means now by the words 'disease of the mind'. In our judgment the fundamental concept is of a malfunctioning of the mind caused by disease. A malfunctioning of the mind of transitory effect caused by the application to the body of some external factor such as violence, drugs, including anaesthetics, alcohol and hypnotic influences cannot fairly be said to be due to disease. Such malfunctioning, unlike that caused by a defect of reason from disease of the mind, will not always relieve an accused from criminal responsibility. A self-induced incapacity will not excuse (see *Lipman* [see p 95, above]) nor will one which could have been reasonably foreseen as a result of either doing, or omitting to do something, as for example, taking alcohol against medical advice after using certain prescribed drugs, or failing to have regular meals whilst taking insulin. From time to time difficult borderline cases are likely to arise. When they do, the test suggested by the New Zealand Court of Appeal in *Cottle* is likely to give the correct result, viz can this mental condition be fairly regarded as amounting to or producing a defect of reason from disease of the mind?

In this case Quick's alleged mental condition, if it ever existed, was not caused by his diabetes but by his use of the insulin prescribed by his doctor. Such malfunctioning of his mind as there was, was caused by an external factor and not by a bodily disorder in the nature of a disease which disturbed the working of his mind. It follows in our judgment that Quick was entitled to have his defence of automatism left to the jury and that Bridge J's ruling as to the effect of the medical evidence called by him was wrong. Had the defence of automatism been left to the jury, a number of questions of fact would have had to be answered. If he was in a confused mental condition, was it due to a hypoglycaemic episode or to too much alcohol? If the former, to what extent had he brought about his condition by not following his doctor's instructions about taking regular meals? Did he know that he was getting into a hypoglycaemic episode? If Yes, why did he not use the antidote of eating a lump of sugar as he had been advised to do? On the evidence which was before the jury Quick might have had difficulty in answering these questions in a manner which would have relieved him of responsibility for his acts. We cannot say, however, with the requisite degree of confidence, that the jury would have convicted him. It follows that his conviction must be quashed on the ground that the verdict was unsatisfactory.

If Quick's conviction is quashed, what happens to Paddison's having regard to the fact that he was said to have aided and abetted Quick? The quashing of Quick's conviction amounts in law to an acquittal. Can Paddison be deemed to have aided and abetted someone who has been adjudged not guilty? As a general proposition of law, the answer to this question is a qualified, Yes. The facts of each case, however, have to be considered and in particular what is alleged to have been done by way of aiding and abetting. In this case the allegation against Paddison was encouragement by conduct. The case against him was that he knew what Quick was going to do and encouraged him to do it by getting the other patients out of the way. If Quick acted without conscious volition, it is most unlikely that Paddison would have known what he intended to do. The quashing of Quick's conviction in our judgment introduces an element of unreality into the verdict against Paddison. It follows that the verdict too must be quashed as being unsatisfactory.

Appeals allowed

Questions

1. What would have been the result if the court had found that it was the diabetes and not the insulin which caused the automatism?

2. Is it accurate to say that 'a self-induced incapacity will not excuse'? Did not a self-induced incapacity excuse to some extent even in Lipman (p 95, above)? He was not convicted of murder.
3. Was the incapacity not 'self-induced' in the present case? Quick administered the insulin to himself. What difference would it have made if his condition had been brought about by failure to follow the doctor's instructions about regular meals?

Bratty v Attorney-General for Northern Ireland [1963] AC 386; [1961] 3 All ER 523, House of Lords
(Viscount Kilmuir LC, Lord Tucker, Lord Denning, Lord Morris of Borth-y-Gest and Lord Hodson)

The accused killed a girl whom he was driving in his car by taking off her stocking and strangling her with it. He gave evidence that a 'blackness' came over him and that 'I didn't know what I was doing. I didn't realise anything.' There was evidence that he might have been suffering from psychomotor epilepsy which could cause ignorance of the nature and quality of acts done. At the trial the defences of automatism and insanity were raised. The trial judge refused to leave the defence of automatism to the jury. The jury rejected the defence of insanity. The Court of Criminal Appeal in Northern Ireland dismissed an appeal against conviction for murder. The appellant appealed to the House of Lords.

[**Viscount Kilmuir LC** made a speech dismissing the appeal.]

[**Lord Tucker** agreed.]

Lord Denning. My Lords, in *Woolmington v Director of Public Prosecutions* Viscount Sankey LC said:

> 'When dealing with a murder case the Crown must prove (a) death as the result of a voluntary act of the accused and (b) malice of the accused.'

The requirement that it should be a voluntary act is essential, not only in a murder case, but also in every criminal case. No act is punishable if it is done involuntarily: and an involuntary act in this context—some people nowadays prefer to speak of it as 'automatism'—means an act which is done by the muscles without any control by the mind such as a spasm, a reflex action or a convulsion; or an act done by a person who is not conscious of what he is doing such as an act done whilst suffering from concussion or whilst sleep-walking. The point was well put by Stephen J in 1889:

> '. . . can anyone doubt that a man who, though he might be perfectly sane, committed what would otherwise be a crime in a state of somnambulism, would be entitled to be acquitted? And why is this? Simply because he would not know what he was doing';

see *Tolson* [see p 105, above]. The term 'involuntary act' is, however, capable of wider connotations: and to prevent confusion it is to be observed that in the criminal law an act is not to be regarded as an involuntary act simply because the doer does not remember it. When a man is charged with dangerous driving, it is no defence for him to say 'I don't know what happened. I cannot remember a thing': see *Hill v Baxter* [[1958] 1 QB 277, [1958] 1 All ER 193]. Loss of memory afterwards is never a defence in itself, so long as he was conscious at the time; see *Russell v HM Advocate* [1946 JC 37]; *Podola* [see p 186, above]. Nor is an act to be regarded as an involuntary act simply because the doer could not control his impulse to do it. When a man is charged with murder, and it appears that he knew what he was doing, but that he could not resist it, then his assertion 'I couldn't help myself' is no defence in itself: see *A-G for South Australia v Brown* [[1960] AC 432, [1960] 1 All ER 734]: though it may go towards a defence of diminished responsibility, in places where that defence is available, see *Byrne* [see p 316, below]: but it does not render his act involuntary so as to entitle him to an unqualified acquittal. Nor is an act to be regarded as an involuntary act simply because it is unintentional or its consequences are unforeseen. When a man is charged with dangerous driving, it is no defence for him to say, however truly, 'I did not mean to drive dangerously'. There is said to be an absolute prohibition against that offence, whether he had a guilty mind or not (see *Hill v Baxter* per Lord Goddard CJ), but even though it is absolutely prohibited, nevertheless he has a defence if he can show that it was an involuntary act in the sense that he was unconscious at the time and did not know what he was doing (see *HM Advocate v Ritchie* [1926 JC 45], *Minor* [(1955) 15 WWR (NS) 433] and *Cooper v McKenna, ex p Cooper* [[1960] Qd R 406]).

Another thing to be observed is that it is not every involuntary act which leads to a complete acquittal. Take first an involuntary act which proceeds from a state of drunkenness. If the drunken man is so drunk that he does not know what he is doing, he has a defence to any charge, such as murder or wounding with intent, in which a specific intent is essential, but he is still liable to be convicted of manslaughter or unlawful wounding for which no specific intent is necessary; see *Beard's* case [see p 88, below]. Again, if the involuntary act proceeds from a disease of the mind, it gives rise to a defence of insanity, but not to a defence of automatism. Suppose a crime is committed by a man in a state of automatism or clouded consciousness due to a recurrent disease of the mind. Such an act is no doubt involuntary, but it does not give rise to an unqualified acquittal, for that would mean that he would be let at large to do it again. The only proper verdict is one which ensures that the person who suffers from the disease is kept secure in a hospital so as not to be a danger to himself or others. That is, a verdict of guilty but insane.

Once you exclude all the cases I have mentioned, it is apparent that the category of involuntary acts is very limited. So limited indeed that until recently there was hardly any reference in the English books to this so-called defence of automatism. There was a passing reference to it in 1951 in *Harrison-Owen* [[1951] 2 All ER 726] where a burglar, who broke into houses, said he did not know what he was doing. I should have thought that, in order to rebut this defence, he could have been cross-examined about his previous burglaries: but the Court of Criminal Appeal ruled otherwise. I venture to doubt that decision. The next is the singular case of *Charlson* [[1955] 1 All ER 859]. Stanley Charlson, a devoted husband and father, hit his ten-year-old son on the head with a hammer and threw him into the river and so injured him. There was not the slightest cause for the attack. He was charged with causing grievous bodily harm with intent, and with unlawful wounding. The evidence pointed to the possibility that Charlson was suffering from a cerebral tumour in which case he would be liable to a motiveless outburst of impulsive violence over which he would have no control at all. Now comes the important point—no plea of insanity was raised, but only the defence of automatism. Barry J directed the jury in these words [[1955] 1 All ER at 864]:

> 'If he did not know what he was doing, if his actions were purely automatic and his mind had no control over the movement of his limbs, if he was in the same position as a person in an epileptic fit and no responsibility rests on him at all, then the proper verdict is "not guilty" . . .'

On that direction the jury found him not guilty. In striking contrast to *Charlson* is *Kemp* [see p 191, above] . . .

My Lords, I think that Devlin J was quite right in *Kemp* in putting the question of insanity to the jury, even though it had not been raised by the defence. When it is asserted that the accused did an involuntary act in a state of automatism, the defence necessarily puts in issue the state of mind of the accused man: and thereupon it is open to the prosecution to show what his true state of mind was. The old notion that only the defence can raise a defence of insanity is now gone. The prosecution are entitled to raise it and it is their duty to do so rather than allow a dangerous person to be at large. The Trial of Lunatics Act 1883, s 2, says that where 'it is given in evidence' that the person was insane, the jury shall return a verdict of guilty but insane. It does not say that the defence alone can give such evidence. The prosecution can give it. And in either case inasmuch as the verdict is one of acquittal, see *Felstead v R* [[1914] AC 534], it should be decided on the balance of probabilities. So it has been held in England that where a man sets up a defence of diminished responsibility, the prosecution are entitled to show that he was insane; see *Bastian* [[1958] 1 All ER 568n]: and conversely when a man sets up insanity, the prosecution are entitled to give evidence of diminished responsibility; see *Nott* [(1958) 43 Cr App Rep 8].

On the other point discussed by Devlin J namely, what is a 'disease of the mind' within the M'Naghten rules, I would agree with him that this is a question for the judge. The major mental diseases, which the doctors call psychoses, such as schizophrenia, are clearly diseases of the mind. But in *Charlson*, Barry J seems to have assumed that other diseases such as epilepsy or cerebral tumour are not diseases of the mind, even when they are such as to manifest themselves in violence. I do not agree with this. It seems to me that any mental disorder which has manifested itself in violence and is prone to recur is a disease of the mind. At any rate it is the sort of disease for which a person should be detained in hospital rather than be given an unqualified acquittal.

It is to be noticed that in *Charlson* and *Kemp* the defence raised only automatism, not insanity. In the present case the defence raised both automatism and insanity. And herein lies the difficulty because of the burden of proof. If the accused says he did not know what he was doing, then, so far as the defence of automatism is concerned, the Crown must prove that the act was a voluntary act; see *Woolmington's* case. But so far as the defence of insanity is concerned, the defence must prove that the act was an involuntary act due to disease of the mind; see *M'Naghten's Case*. This apparent incongruity was noticed by Sir Owen Dixon, Chief Justice of the High Court of Australia, in an address which is to be found in 31 Australian Law Journal 255 and it needs to be resolved. The defence here say: Even though we have not proved that the act was involuntary, yet the Crown have not proved that it was a voluntary act: and that point at least should have been put to the jury.

My Lords, I think that the difficulty is to be resolved by remembering that, whilst the *ultimate* burden rests on the Crown of proving every element essential in the crime, nevertheless in order to prove that the act was a voluntary act, the Crown is entitled to rely on the *presumption* that every man has sufficient mental capacity to be responsible for his crimes: and that if the defence wish to displace that presumption they must give some evidence from which the contrary may reasonably be inferred. Thus a drunken man is presumed to have the capacity to form the specific intent necessary to constitute the crime, unless evidence is given from which it can reasonably be inferred that he was incapable of forming it; see the valuable judgment of the Court of Justiciary in *Kennedy v HM Advocate* [1944 JC at 177] which was delivered by the Lord Justice-General (Lord Normand). So also it seems to me that a man's act is presumed to be a voluntary act unless there is evidence from which it can reasonably be inferred that it was involuntary. To use the words of Devlin J the defence of automatism 'ought not to be considered at all until the defence has produced at least prima facie evidence', see *Hill v Baxter* [[1958] 1 QB at 285; [1958] 1 All ER at 196]; and the words of North J in New Zealand 'unless a proper foundation is laid', see *Cottle* [[1958] NZLR at 1025]. The necessity of laying this proper foundation is on the defence: and if it is not so laid, the defence of automatism need not be left to the jury, any more than the defence of drunkenness (*Kennedy v HM Advocate* [1944 JC 171]), provocation (*Gauthier* [(1943) 29 Cr App Rep 113]) or self-defence (*Lobell* [[1957] 1 QB 547; [1957] 1 All ER 734]) need be.

What, then, is a proper foundation? The presumption of mental capacity of which I have spoken is a provisional presumption only. It does not put the legal burden on the defence in the same way as the presumption of sanity does. It leaves the legal burden on the prosecution, but nevertheless, until it is displaced, it enables the prosecution to discharge the ultimate burden of proving that the act was voluntary. Not because the presumption is evidence itself, but because it takes the place of evidence. In order to displace the presumption of mental capacity, the defence must give sufficient evidence from which it may reasonably be inferred that the act was involuntary. The evidence of the man himself will rarely be sufficient unless it is supported by medical evidence which points to the cause of the mental incapacity. It is not sufficient for a man to say 'I had a black-out': for 'black-out' as Stable J said in *Cooper v McKenna* [[1960] Qd R at 419] 'is one of the first refuges of a guilty conscience, and a popular excuse'. The words of Devlin J in *Hill v Baxter* [[1958] 1 QB at 285, [1958] 1 All ER at 197] should be remembered:

> 'I do not doubt that there are genuine cases of automatism and the like, but I do not see how the layman can safely attempt without the help of some medical or scientific evidence to distinguish the genuine from the fraudulent'.

When the only cause that is assigned for an involuntary act is drunkenness, then it is only necessary to leave drunkenness to the jury, with the consequential directions, and not to leave automatism at all. When the only cause that is assigned for it is a disease of the mind, then it is only necessary to leave insanity to the jury, and not automatism. When the cause assigned is concussion or sleepwalking, there should be some evidence from which it can reasonably be inferred before it should be left to the jury. If it is said to be due to concussion, there should be evidence of a severe blow shortly beforehand. If it is said to be sleepwalking, there should be some credible support for it. His mere assertion that he was asleep will not suffice. Once a proper foundation is thus laid for automatism, the matter becomes at large and must be left to the jury. As the case proceeds, the evidence may weigh first to one side and then to the other: and so the burden may appear to shift to and fro. But at the end of the day the legal burden comes into play and requires that the jury should be satisfied beyond reasonable doubt that the act was a voluntary one. . . . There was [in the present case] no evidence of automatism apart from insanity. There was therefore no need for the judge to put it to the jury. . . . I would therefore dismiss the appeal.

[**Lord Morris of Borth-y-Gest** made a speech dismissing the appeal with which **Lord Hodson** agreed.]

Appeal dismissed

Problem

Dan and Ed are jointly charged with murder. Each says that he was unaware of what he was doing at the material time. Dan because he was suffering from psychomotor epilepsy, Ed because he was sleepwalking. Each defence is supported by medical evidence. How should the judge direct the jury? If the jury, having considered the evidence, return to inform the judge that they consider that both defences are, as likely as not, true, and ask for further directions, what should the judge tell them? Is the result satisfactory?

R v Sullivan [1983] 2 All ER 673, House of Lords
(Lords Diplock, Scarman, Lowry, Bridge and Brandon)

Lord Diplock. My Lords, the appellant, a man of blameless reputation, has the misfortune to have been a lifelong sufferer from epilepsy. There was a period when he was subject to major seizures known as grand mal; but as a result of treatment which he was receiving as an out-patient of the Maudsley Hospital from 1976 onwards, these seizures had, by the use of drugs, been reduced by 1979 to seizures of less severity known as petit mal, or psychomotor epilepsy, though they continued to occur at a frequency of one or two per week.

One such seizure occurred on 8 May 1981, when the appellant, then aged 51, was visiting a neighbour, Mrs Killick, an old lady aged 86 for whom he was accustomed to perform regular acts of kindness. He was chatting there to a fellow visitor and friend of his, a Mr Payne aged 80, when the epileptic fit came on. It appears likely from the expert medical evidence about the way in which epileptics behave at the various stages of a petit mal seizure that Mr Payne got up from the chair to help the appellant. The only evidence of an eye-witness was that of Mrs Killick, who did not see what had happened before she saw Mr Payne lying on the floor and the appellant kicking him about the head and body, in consequence of which Mr Payne suffered injuries severe enough to require hospital treatment.

As a result of this occurrence the appellant was indicted on two counts: the first was of causing grievous bodily harm with intent, contrary to s 18 of the Offences against the Person Act 1861; the second was of causing grievous bodily harm, contrary to s 20 of the Act. At his trial, which took place at the Central Criminal Court before his Honour Judge Lymbery QC and a jury, the appellant pleaded not guilty to both counts. Mrs Killick's evidence that he had kicked Mr Payne violently about the head and body was undisputed and the appellant himself gave evidence of his history of epilepsy and his absence of all recollection of what had occurred at Mrs Killick's flat between the time that he was chatting peacefully to Mr Payne there and his returning to the flat from somewhere else to find that Mr Payne was injured and that an ambulance had been sent for. The prosecution accepted his evidence as true. There was no cross-examination.

Counsel for the appellant wanted to rely on the defence of automatism or, as Viscount Kilmuir LC had put in *Bratty v A-G for Northern Ireland* [1961] 3 All ER 523 at 530, [1963] AC 386 at 405, 'non-insane' automatism, that is to say that he had acted unconsciously and involuntarily in kicking Mr Payne, but that when doing so he was not 'insane' in the sense in which that expression is used as a term of art in English law, and in particular in s 2 of the Trial of Lunatics Act 1883, as amended by s 5 of the Criminal Procedure (Insanity) Act 1964. As was decided unanimously by this House in *Bratty's* case, before a defence of non-insane automatism may properly be left to the jury some evidential foundation for it must first be laid. The evidential foundation that counsel laid before the jury in the instant case consisted of the testimony of two distinguished specialists from the neuropsychiatry epilepsy unit at the Maudsley Hospital, Dr Fenwick and Dr Taylor, as to the pathology of the various stages of a seizure due to psychomotor epilepsy. Their expert evidence, which was not disputed by the prosecution, was that the appellant's acts in kicking Mr Payne had all the characteristics of epileptic automatism at the third or post-ictal stage of petit mal, and that, in view of his history of psychomotor epilepsy and the hospital records of his behaviour during previous seizures, the strong probability was that the appellant's acts of violence towards Mr Payne took place while he was going through that stage.

The evidence as to the pathology of a seizure due to psychomotor epilepsy can be sufficiently stated for the purposes of this appeal by saying that after the first stage, the prodram, which precedes the fit itself, there is a second stage, the ictus, lasting a few seconds, during which there are electrical discharges into the temporal lobes of the brain of the sufferer. The effect of these discharges cause him in the post-ictal stage to make movements which he is not conscious that he is making, including, and this was a characteristic of previous seizures which the appellant had suffered, automatic movements of resistance to anyone trying to come to his aid. These movements of resistance might, though in practice they very rarely would, involve violence. . . .

[His Lordship stated that the judge had ruled that, he would direct the jury that, if they accepted this evidence, they would be bound to return a verdict of not guilty by reason of insanity, whereupon the appellant changed his plea to guilty of assault occasioning actual bodily harm and was sentenced to three years probation. He reviewed the M'Naghten rules and *Bratty*, p 196, above and continued:]

In the instant case, as in *Bratty's* case, the only evidential foundation that was laid for any finding by the jury that the appellant was acting unconsciously and involuntarily when he was kicking Mr Payne was that when he did so he was in the post-ictal stage of a seizure of psychomotor epilepsy. The evidential foundation in the case of Bratty, that he was suffering from psychomotor epilepsy at the time he did the act with which he was charged, was very weak and was rejected by the jury; the evidence in the appellant's case, that he was so suffering when he was kicking Mr Payne, was very strong and would almost inevitably be accepted by a properly directed jury. It would be the duty of the judge to direct the jury that if they did accept that evidence the law required them to bring in a special verdict and none other. The governing statutory provision is to be found in s 2 of the Trial of Lunatics Act 1883. This says 'the jury *shall* return a special verdict'.

My Lords, I can deal briefly with the various grounds on which it has been submitted that the instant case can be distinguished from what constituted the ratio decidendi in *Bratty's* case, and that it falls outside the ambit of the M'Naghten Rules.

First, it is submitted the medical evidence in the instant case shows that psychomotor epilepsy is not a disease of the mind, whereas in *Bratty's* case it was accepted by all the doctors that it was. The only evidential basis for this submission is that Dr Fenwick said that in medical terms to constitute a 'disease of the mind' or 'mental illness', which he appeared to regard as interchangeable descriptions, a disorder of brain functions (which undoubtedly occurs during a seizure in psychomotor epilepsy) must be prolonged for a period of time usually more than a day, while Dr Taylor would have it that the disorder must continue for a minimum of a month to qualify for the description 'a disease of the mind'.

The nomenclature adopted by the medical profession may change from time to time; Bratty was tried in 1961. But the meaning of the expression 'disease of the mind' as the cause of 'a defect of reason' remains unchanged for the purposes of the application of the M'Naghten Rules. I agree with what was said by Devlin J in *R v Kemp* [1956] 3 All ER 249 at 253, [1957] 1 QB 399 at 407 that 'mind' in the M'Naghten Rules is used in the ordinary sense of the mental faculties of reason, memory and understanding. If the effect of a disease is to impair these faculties so severely as to have either of the consequences referred to in the latter part of the rules, it matters not whether the aetiology of the impairment is organic, as in epilepsy, or functional, or whether the impairment itself is permanent or is transient and intermittent, provided that it subsisted at the time of commission of the act. The purpose of the legislation relating to the defence of insanity, ever since its origin in 1880, has been to protect society against recurrence of the dangerous conduct. The duration of a temporary suspension of the mental faculties of reason, memory and understanding, particularly if, as in the appellant's case, it is recurrent, cannot on any rational ground be relevant to the application by the courts of the M'Naghten Rules, though it may be relevant to the course adopted by the Secretary of State, to whom the responsibility for how the defendant is to be dealt with passes after the return of the special verdict of not guilty by reason of insanity.

To avoid misunderstanding I ought perhaps to add that in expressing my agreement with what was said by Devlin J in *R v Kemp*, where the disease that caused the temporary and intermittent impairment of the mental faculties was arteriosclerosis, I do not regard that judge as excluding the possibility of non-insane automatism, for which the proper verdict would be a verdict of not guilty, in cases where temporary impairment not being self-induced by consuming drink or drugs, results from some external physical factor such as a blow on the head causing concussion or the administration of an anaesthetic for therapeutic purposes. I mention this because in *R v Quick* [1973] 3 All ER 347, [1973] QB 910 Lawton LJ appears to have regarded the ruling in *R v*

Kemp as going as far as this. If it had done, it would have been inconsistent with the speeches in this House in *Bratty's* case, where *R v Kemp* was alluded to without disapproval by Viscount Kilmuir LC and received the express approval of Lord Denning. The instant case, however, does not in my view afford an appropriate occasion for exploring possible causes of non-insane automatism.

The only other submission in support of the appellant's appeal which I think it necessary to mention is that, because the expert evidence was to the effect that the appellant's acts in kicking Mr Payne were unconscious and thus 'involuntary' in the legal sense of that term, his state of mind was not one dealt with by the M'Naghten Rules at all, since it was not covered by the phrase 'as not to know the nature and quality of the act he was doing'. Quite apart from being contrary to all three speeches in this House in *Bratty's* case, the submission appears to me, with all respect to counsel, to be quite unarguable. Dr Fenwick himself accepted it as an accurate description of the appellant's mental state in the post-ictal stage of a seizure. The audience to whom the phrase in the M'Naghten Rules was addressed consisted of peers of the realm in the 1840s when a certain orotundity of diction had not yet fallen out of fashion. Addressed to an audience of jurors in the 1980s it might more aptly be expressed as: he did not know what he was doing.

My Lords, it is natural to feel reluctant to attach the label of insanity to a sufferer from psychomotor epilepsy of the kind to which the appellant was subject, even though the expression in the context of a special verdict of not guilty by reason of insanity is a technical one which includes a purely temporary and intermittent suspension of the mental faculties of reason, memory and understanding resulting from the occurrence of an epileptic fit. But the label is contained in the current statute, it has appeared in this statute's predecessors ever since 1800. It does not lie within the power of the courts to alter it. Only Parliament can do that. It has done so twice; it could do so once again.

Sympathise though I do with the appellant, I see no other course open to your Lordships than to dismiss this appeal.

[The other Law Lords agreed.]

Appeal dismissed

(2) REFORM OF THE LAW

See EJ Griew, 'Let's implement Butler on Mental Disorder and Crime', [1984] CLP 47 and the Butler Report on *Mentally Abnormal Offenders* (Cmnd 6244, 1975).

The draft Criminal Code Bill provides:

38 Mental disorder verdict

(1) A mental disorder verdict shall be returned where:

(a) the defendant is proved to have committed an offence but it is proved on the balance of probabilities (whether by the prosecution or by the defendant) that he was at the time suffering from severe mental illness or severe subnormality; or

(b) (i) the defendant is found not to have committed an offence on the ground only that, by reason of mental disorder or a combination of mental disorder and intoxication, he acted or may have acted in a state of automatism, or without the fault required for the offence, or believing that an exempting circumstance existed; and

(ii) it is proved on the balance of probablities (whether by the prosecution or by the defendant) that he was suffering from mental disorder at the time of the act.

(2) (a) 'Mental disorder' means mental illness, arrested or incomplete development of mind, psychopathic disorder, and (subject to paragraph (b)) any other disorder or disability of mind.

(b) 'Mental disorder' does not include:

(i) intoxication, whether voluntary or involuntary; or

(ii) any disorder caused by illnesss, injury, shock or hypnosis, or occurring during sleep, unless it is a feature of a condition (whether continuing or recurring) that may cause a similar disorder on another occasion.

(c) 'Psychopathic disorder' means a persistent disorder or disability of mind (whether or not including significant impairment of intelligence) which results in abnormally aggressive or seriously irresponsible conduct.

(d) 'Return a mental disorder verdict' means:
    (i) in relation to trial on indictment, return a verdict that the defendant is not guilty on evidence of mental disorder; and
    (ii) in relation to summary trial, dismiss the information on evidence of mental disorder.

Schedule 1 of the draft Bill provides the following illustrations:

38 (1) (a).	38 (i)	D intentionally sets fire to P's house when suffering from mental illness with one or more of the severe features listed in section 38 (2) (e). On a charge of arson he is entitled to a mental disorder verdict.
38 (1)(b) and (2).	38 (ii)	D is charged with intentionally causing injury to P. He was unaware of his violent act. It occurred when he was in a state of impaired consciousness during an epileptic episode of a kind to which he is prone. The impairment of consciousness was a 'disorder of mind' caused by illness but liable to recur. A mental disorder verdict must be returned. The court has power to make any of a number of orders or to discharge D.
38 (1)(b).	38 (iii)	The same charge as in illustration 38 (ii). A similar explanation of the attack is given. The medical evidence leads the court or jury to think that the explanation may be true; D must therefore be acquitted. But they are not satisfied (on the whole of the medical evidence, including any adduced by the prosecution) that it is in fact true; so there will not be a mental disorder verdict, mental disorder not having been proved.
38 (2)(b)(i).	38 (iv)	The same charge as in illustration 38 (ii). There is evidence that D, who suffers from diabetes, had taken insulin on medical advice. This had caused a fall in his blood-sugar level which deprived him of control or awareness of his movements. If D is acquitted, a mental disorder verdict is not appropriate. His 'disorder of mind' was caused by the insulin, an 'intoxicant' (see s 26 (8) (a)). It was therefore a case of 'intoxication' and not of 'mental disorder'.
38 (2)(b)(ii).	38 (v)	The same charge as in illustration 38 (ii). There is evidence that D's violent act occurred while he was asleep. If this may be true he will be acquitted. If it is proved that the 'sleep-walking' episode was a feature of an underlying condition and might recur, the acquittal will be in the form of a mental disorder verdict; if not, it will be an ordinary acquittal.

3. Disposal

The proposals by the codification team assume that the recommendations of the Butler Committee as to the disposal of mentally disordered persons will have been implemented. These are that, for both persons found 'unfit to plead' or (as *Butler* would have it, 'under disability in relation to the trial') and those found not guilty on evidence of mental disorder, the court should have the following powers:

(a) an order for in-patient treatment in hospital with or without a restriction order;
(b) an order for hospital out-patient treatment;
(c) an order for forfeiture of any firearm, motor vehicle, etc, used in crime;
(d) a guardianship order;
(e) any disqualification (e g from driving) normally open to the court to make on conviction;
(f) discharge without any order.
The usual criteria for the making of orders under (a), (b) and (d) should be observed.

The Report explains cl 38 as follows:

12.5   Clause 38 gives effect to the main substantive proposal in Chapter 18 of the Butler Report: namely, to substitute for the existing 'special verdict' based on insanity within the meaning of the

M'Naghten Rules a verdict of 'not guilty on evidence of mental disorder', to be returned in either of two kinds of situation. One situation is that in which the defendant committed the offence charged but was at the time suffering from severe mental disorder (clause 38(1)(a)). The other is that in which evidence of the defendant's mental disorder at the time of his act is the reason why he is not proved to have committed the offence charged (clause 38(1)(b)). On the return of a mental disorder verdict the court would have flexible disposal powers (see paragraph 12.29 below), the availability of which would undoubtedly give clause 38 greater practical importance than the insanity defence now has.

12.6 *Clause 38(1)(a)*. The defendant has done the act specified for the offence with the fault required. He has no defence other than that he was suffering from severe mental illness or severe subnormality. The proposal that he should be acquitted on proof of such severe disorder is controversial. The Butler Committee acknowledged that:

> 'it is theoretically possible for a person to be suffering from a severe mental disorder which has in a causal sense nothing to do with the act or omission for which he is being tried';

but they found it 'very difficult to imagine a case in which one could be sure of the absence of any such connection'. [Ibid, para 18.29] The Committee proposed, in effect, an irrebuttable presumption that there was a sufficient connection between the severe disorder and the offence. This certainly simplifies the tasks of psychiatric witnesses and the court. Some people, however, take the view that it would be wrong in principle that a person should escape conviction if, although severely mentally ill, he has committed a rational crime which was uninfluenced by his illness and for which he ought to be liable to be punished. They believe that the prosecution should be allowed to persuade the jury (if it can) that the offence and the disorder were unconnected. If such a person were to remain ill at the time of his conviction, he could of course be made the subject of a hospital order. There is undoubtedly force in this point of view. We have been bound to draft in accordance with the Butler Committee's proposal; but clause 38 could readily be amended to reflect the view of the Committee's critics if that view should prevail.

12.7 *'Severe mental illness'*, for the purpose of this exemption from criminal liability, ought, in the Butler Committee's view, to be closely defined and restricted to serious cases of psychosis (as that term is currently understood). The Committee recommended, as the preferable mode of definition, the identification of 'the abnormal mental phenomena which occur in the various mental illnesses and which when present would be regarded by common consent as being evidence of severity'. [Ibid para 18.30-18.36] The definition offered by the Committee is reproduced in subsection (2) (e). It is placed in square brackets because it is certain to receive close professional scrutiny and may well call for amendment before it is enacted.

12.8 *'Severe subnormality'*. The Butler Committee adopted this category of disorder from the Mental Health Act 1959, section 4. Its definition in that Act was apt for the Committee's purpose. But the expression 'severe mental impairment' has since replaced 'severe subnormality' in mental health legislation (the latter term having fallen out of favour). 'Severe mental impairment' has the following meaning:

> 'a state of arrested or incomplete development of mind which includes severe impairment of intelligence and social functioning and is associated with abnormally aggressive or seriously irresponsible conduct on the part of the person concerned'. [Mental Health Act 1983, s 1 (1)]

The new definition is not a happy one for present purposes; exemption from criminal liability on the ground of severe mental handicap ought not to be limited to a case where the handicap is associated with aggressive or irresponsible conduct. It is clear that further consideration will have to be given both to terminology and to definition at this point. Meanwhile we have simply followed the Butler Committee and the definition in the Mental Health Act 1959.

12.9 *Evidence of severe mental disorder*. Clause 38 (3), providing that such evidence must be given by appropriately qualified doctors, is as recommended by the Butler Committee. [Butler Report, para 18.37.]

12.10 *Clause 38 (1) (b)*. Evidence of mental disorder may be the reason why the court or jury is at least doubtful whether the defendant acted with the fault required for the offence. The Butler Committee recommended that, although in such a case there must be an acquittal, this acquittal should be in the qualified form "not guilty on evidence of mental disorder" where it is proved that the defendant was in fact suffering from mental disorder at the time of his act. [Ibid para 47 of Summary of Recommendations.] Subsection (1) (b) gives effect to this recommendation.

CHAPTER 11

General defences

1. Report on codification of the criminal law

General defences

13.8 Clauses 45 to 49 are concerned with defences to crimes generally. There are many rules, both common law and statutory, which, in particular circumstances, require, justify or excuse the doing of acts which, in the absence of those circumstances, would be criminal offences. Some of these rules, like the defence of duress, have been developed particularly in relation to criminal law but many of them are part of the civil as well as of the criminal law. Whether the issue arises in a civil or a criminal court, the conduct in question is equally required, justified or excused, as the case may be. Examples are the law relating to the chastisement of children or that which would justify a surgeon in operating on an unconcious patient without his consent. If particular conduct is required, justified or excused by the civil law, it would clearly be wrong for it to amount to an offence. The converse, however, does not follow. The criminal law might properly afford a defence when the civil law does not, as in cases where the defendant's unreasonable mistake negatives the fault which must be proved to convict him of crime although he is left liable in the civil law for his negligence. The Code must assume the continued existence of rules of this kind. It would be impossible to list them all and therefore some general provision is required. It is provided by clauses 48 and 49.

48   Act authorised by law
(1) A person does not commit an offence by doing an act which, in the circumstances which exist or which he believes to exist, he is authorised to do by:
(a) the judgment or order of a competent court or tribunal; or
(b) the law governing the execution of legal process; or
(c) the law governing the armed forces or the lawful conduct of war; or
(d) the law defining the duties or functions of a public officer or the assistance to be rendered to such an officer in the performance of his duties; or
(e) any other rule of law imposing a public duty.
(2) In this section 'armed forces' means any of the naval, military or air forces of the Crown.

49   Act justified or excused by law
(1) A person does not commit an offence by doing an act which is justified or excused by:
(a) any enactment; or
(b) any rule of the common law, except insofar as the rule is inconsistent with this or any other enactment.
(2) Nothing in this Act shall limit any power of the courts to determine the existence, extent or application of any rule of the common law referred to in subsection (1) and continuing to apply after the commencement of this Act.

13.9 *Particularity and generality of the clauses.* Clause 49 alone would be sufficient to incorporate by reference all general defences. To rely solely on this clause, however, would be quite incompatible with codification. It would leave a mass of detailed rules to the common law and various statutes and would fail to resolve inconsistencies and uncertainties. The general provision in clause 49 is necessary for the reason given below; but it is far from sufficient. Where rules concerning particular defences are established, the Code must state them. Clause 48 requires special mention at this point because it is also expressed in general terms, though less general than those of clause 49. It relates to a category of defence which has long been recognised in the books [See below, para 13.58] and is not different in principle from the defences spelt out in more detail in clauses 45 to 47. It is more particular than clause 48 and therefore merits inclusion on the principle that the Code should be as informative as possible. It directs the reader to particular areas of the civil law which are relevant.

13.10 *Development of common law defences.* Common law principles of justification and excuse are not static. They are developed by the judges as occasion arises and attitudes change. The development of the law relating to duress in recent years is a striking example of this. Clause 49 preserves the power of the courts to determine the existence, extent and application of any justification or excuse provided by the common law. Similar provisions are to be found in section 7 (3) of the Canadian Criminal Code and Section 20 of the New Zealand Crimes Act 1961. The case (in our opinion, overwhelming) for the inclusion of a provision of this kind was made by Stephen J. in 1880, defending the corresponding provision of the Draft Code of 1879. The relevant passage is conveniently quoted in the Criminal Law Review for 1978 [Glanville Williams, 'Necessity' [1978] Crim LR 128 at 129] and need not be repeated here.

13.11 *Definitive and open-ended defences.* In the case of some defences, the law appears to have attained such a degree of maturity and completeness that a definitive statement of it is possible. Duress, in our opinion, has now reached that stage and clause 45 (following a recommendation of the Law Commission [(1977) Law Com No 83,Part II]) provides such a statement. Any further development of the defence of duress would have to be made by Parliament. It is otherwise with necessity. Though we have taken the exceptional course of departing from a recommendation of the Law Commission [(1977) Law Com No 83, Part IV] in proposing a limited defence of necessity, this defence is left open-ended, to be developed or not as the courts may decide. It may be noted that the examples given by Stephen of cases where the courts should have this power all fall under the broad head of necessity.

13.12 *The potential of clause 49* is not limited to necessity. The courts have occasionally recognised impossibility of compliance with the law as a good defence. [Smith and Hogan, *Criminal Law* 5th ed (1983), 220.] Again, the limits of any such defence are extremely uncertain. The authorities do not justify the statement of any general principle which could be incorporated into the Code. The cases represent the law for the particular offences in issue and no more. What would be wrong, for the reasons so cogently developed by Stephen, would be for the Code arbitrarily to put an end to this and other possible developments, such as a defence of superior orders [Ibid at 219] or '*de minimis*'. If the stage were reached at which it was possible to enunciate a general principle, then that principle should be incorporated into the Code at its next revision.

13.13 *The use of 'unlawfully' and 'without lawful excuse'.* General defences are sometimes thought to be admitted into the present law by the use of the words 'unlawfully' or 'without lawful excuse' in the definition of offences. There is no consistency in this usage and it may well be that the same principles would apply even if no such words were used. [Williams, *The Criminal Law, The General Part* 2nd ed (1961), 28–29.] We noted that the Criminal Law Revision Committee proposed to rely on the word 'unlawful' in the statutory definition of murder to cover the phrase, 'under the Queen's Peace', in the traditional common law definition. [Fourteenth Report, Cmnd 7844, para 38.] Although that phrase is never mentioned in connection with any crime other than homicide, the principle is equally applicable to a large number of crimes. It is not only killing but also wounding and other injuries to the person, imprisonment, and appropriation of and damage to property which are justified when they are committed against the Queen's enemies in the lawful conduct of war. If 'unlawful' is necessary to achieve this result in homicide, it is equally necessary in many crimes.

13.14 *'Unlawfully' and 'without lawful excuse' unnecessary in the Code.* The use of the word 'unlawfully' in the definition of crimes has been justly criticised [Williams, *The Criminal Law, The General Part* 2nd ed (1961), 27]. We found that consistent use of it would cause considerable drafting difficulties, sometimes requiring its repetition within the same sentence. The use of 'without lawful excuse' would present even greater problems. Moreover, the Code can and should be more specific. Defences such as duress and necessity which are defined in the Code will, by their terms, apply to offences generally. Other matters of justification or excuse are made generally applicable by clauses 48 and 49. These clauses ensure that it is unnecessary to use the word 'unlawfully' or any similar word or phrase in the definition of any Code offence.

2. Duress

The draft Criminal Code Bill provides:

45   Defence of duress
(1) A person is not guilty of an offence when he does an act under duress.
(2) A person does an act under duress if:

(a) he does it because he believes:
    (i) that a threat has been made to kill or cause serious injury to himself or another if the act is not done; and
    (ii) that the threat will be carried out immediately if he does not do the act or, if not immediately, before he can obtain official protection; and
    (iii) that there is no other way of preventing the threat being carried out; and
(b) the threat is one which in all the circumstances (including any of his personal characteristics that affect its gravity) he could not reasonably be expected to resist.
(3) The fact that any official protection available in the circumstances might be ineffective to prevent the threat being carried out is immaterial.
(4) Subsection (1) does not apply to a person who has knowingly and without reasonable excuse exposed himself to the risk of such a threat.
(5) A wife has no defence (except under this section) by virtue of having done an act under the coercion of her husband.

The Report explains the clause as follows:

13.15 The Law Commission's Report on Defences of General Application (Law Com No 83) proposes for the Code a defence of duress, applicable to all offences, similar to that available at common law. A draft Criminal Liability (Duress) Bill appended to the Report gives effect to the proposal. Our clause follows the Law Commission's recommendations and the method of the draft Bill, save in a few respects.
13.16 The function of *subsection (1)* is simply to make available the phrase 'acting under duress' for use elsewhere (as in clause 47 (3)).
13.17 *Subsection (2)* states the elements of the defence. It adapts clause 1 (3) of the draft Bill to the style of the Code. The following departures from the Bill should be mentioned.
(i) According to the Law Commission draft, there must be an *actual* threat of harm, which the actor may wrongly *believe* to be one of death or serious injury. We do not understand this distinction. Consistently with what is provided for other defences (compare clause 44 as to special defences and, for example, clause 47), a person should be able to rely for the defence on all the facts as he believes them to be. It would be strange if a person seeking to rely on the defence of duress were in a worse position in this respect than one relying (by way of defence to a murder charge) on a supposed provocation.
(ii) We refer to 'serious injury' where the draft Bill has 'serious personal injury (physical or mental)'. The intended meaning is the same, as is made clear in paragraph 15.43 below.
(iii) The draft Bill refers to the actor's having to act before he can 'have any real opportunity of seeking official protection'. We substitute 'before he can obtain official protection.' It is clear from subection (3) that this does not mean effective protection; but we believe that the question must be whether the actor believes that he can make actual contact with the police or other relevant authorities and ask for protection, not whether he had a chance to look for a policeman (as 'seeking' might be taken to suggest). (We do not think that a definition of 'official protection' is necessary; contrast clause 1 (6) of the draft Bill.)
(iv) The passage in clause 1 (3) of the draft Bill corresponding to our subsection (2) (b) refers to 'any of his personal circumstances which are relevant'. We think that our reference to 'personal characteristics' that effect the 'gravity' of the threat is more precise and informative.
13.18 *Subection (3)* corresponds to clause 1 (4) of the draft Bill. We should not be justified in rejecting the recommendation of the Law Commission that the possible ineffectiveness of any protection that might be available to the person under duress is immaterial. But we beg leave to doubt whether this recommendation is sound. A person's belief that the authorities will be unable to give him effective protection against the duressor is surely relevant to the effect of the threat on his freedom of action. We do not think that it can properly be ignored as one of the circumstances in the light of which the question whether he could reasonably be expected to resist the threat is to be answered.
13.19 *Subsection (4)* (voluntary exposure to risk of duress) corresponds to clause 1 (5) of the draft Bill. It is very much shorter than clause 1 (5) but we believe it has the same effect.
13.20 *Subsection (5)* (no separate defence of marital coercion) corresponds to clause 3 (1) of the draft Bill.

R v Hudson and Taylor [1971] 2 All ER 244, Court of Appeal, Criminal Division (Lord Parker CJ, Widgery LJ and Cooke J)

The accused, girls aged 17 and 19 respectively, were the principal prosecution witnesses at the trial of one, Wright, on a charge of wounding. They both failed to identify Wright and testified that they did not know him. Wright was acquitted. At their trial for perjury the accused admitted that their evidence was false and set up the defence of duress. Hudson said that she had been approached before the trial of Wright by men, including one, Farrell, who had a reputation for violence and warned that they would 'cut her up' if she 'told on' Wright. Hudson passed this on to Taylor, who had also been warned by other girls. The accused were frightened and decided to tell lies to avoid the consequences. Their decision was confirmed when, on arriving in court, they saw Farrell in the gallery.

The recorder directed that the defence of duress was not open because there was no present immediate threat capable of being carried out there and then, since the accused were in court in the presence of the judge and the police. On appeal the Crown argued that the ruling could be upheld on the additional ground that the accused should have neutralised the threat by seeking police protection when they came to court or beforehand.

[**Lord Widgery CJ**, having stated the facts, continued:]

. . . We have been referred to large number of authorities and to the views of writers of text books. Despite the concern expressed in 2 Stephen's *History of the Criminal Law in England* [Vol 2, p 107], that it would be:

> '. . . a much greater misfortune for society at large if criminals could confer impunity upon their agents by threatening them with death or violence if they refused to execute their commands . . .'

it is clearly established that duress provides a defence in all offences including perjury (except possibly treason or murder as a principal) if the will of the accused has been overborne by threats of death or serious personal injury so that the commission of the alleged offence was no longer the voluntary act of the accused. This appeal raises two main questions; first, as to the nature of the necessary threat and, in particular, whether it must be 'present and immediate'; secondly, as to the extent to which a right to plead duress may be lost if the accused has failed to take steps to remove the threat as, for example, by seeking police protection.

It is essential to the defence of duress that the threat shall be effective at the moment when the crime is committed. The threat must be a 'present' threat in the sense that it is effective to neutralise the will of the accused at that time. Hence an accused who joins a rebellion under the compulsion of threats cannot plead duress if he remains with the rebels after the threats have lost their effect and his own will has had a chance to re-assert itself (*McGrowther's case* [(1746) Fost 13] and *A-G v Whelan* [[1934] IR 518]). Similarly a threat of future violence may be so remote as to be insufficient to overpower the will at the moment when the offence was committed, or the accused may have elected to commit the offence in order to rid himself of a threat hanging over him and not because he was driven to act by immediate and unavoidable pressure. In none of these cases is the defence of duress available because a person cannot justify the commission of a crime merely to secure his own peace of mind.

When, however, there is no opportunity for delaying tactics, and the person threatened must make up his mind whether he is to commit the criminal act or not, the existence at that moment of threats sufficient to destroy his will ought to provide him with a defence even though the threatened injury may not follow instantly, but after an interval. This principle is illustrated by *Subramaniam v Public Prosecutor* [[1956] 1 WLR 965], when the appellant was charged in Malaya with unlawful possession of ammunition and was held by the Privy Council to have a defence of duress, fit to go to the jury, on his plea that he had been compelled by terrorists to accept the ammunition and feared for his safety if the terrorists returned.

In the present case the threats of Farrell were likely to be no less compelling, because their execution could not be effected in the court room, if they could be carried out in the streets of Salford the same night. Insofar, therefore, as the recorder ruled as a matter of law that the threats were not sufficiently present and immediate to support the defence of duress we think that he was in error. He should have left the jury to decide whether the threats had overborne the will of the appellants at the time when they gave the false evidence.

Counsel for the Crown, however, contends that the recorder's ruling can be supported on another ground, namely, that the appellants should have taken steps to neutralise the threats by seeking police protection either when they came to court to give evidence, or beforehand. He submits on grounds of public policy that an accused should not be able to plead duress if he had the opportunity to ask for protection from the police before committing the offence and failed to do so. The argument does not distinguish cases in which the police would be able to provide effective protection, from those when they would not, and it would, in effect, restrict the defence of duress to cases where the person threatened had been kept in custody by the maker of the threats, or where the time interval between the making of the threats and the commisssion of the offence had made recourse to the police impossible. We recognise the need to keep the defence of duress within reasonable bounds but cannot accept so severe a restriction on it. The duty, of the person threatened, to take steps to remove the threat does not seem to have arisen in an English case but in a full review of the defence of duress in the Supreme Court of Victoria (*Hurley* and *Murray* [[1967] VR 526]), a condition of raising the defence was said to be that the accused 'had no means, with safety to himself, of preventing the execution of the threat'.

In the opinion of this court it is always open to the Crown to prove that the accused failed to avail himself of some opportunity which was reasonably open to him to render the threat ineffective, and that on this being established the threat in question can no longer be relied on by the defence. In deciding whether such an opportunity was reasonably open to the accused the jury should have regard to his age and circumstances, and to any risks to him which may be involved in the course of action relied on.

In our judgment the defence of duress should have been left to the jury in the present case, as should any issue raised by the Crown and arising out of the appellants' failure to seek police protection. The appeals will, therefore, be allowed and the convictions quashed.

Appeals allowed

Question

Is a sufficiently grave threat capable of amounting to duress in all cases where the accused knows that police will not be able to offer effective and indefinite protection if he goes to them?

NOTE

The defence of duress applies if the defendant would not have committed the crime *but for* threats of death or grievous bodily harm. It is wrong to direct a jury that such threats must be the sole reason for the defendant's acts: *Valderrama–Vega* [1985] Crim LR 220 CA. The defendant, charged with importation of prohibited drugs, may have been subjected to 'Mafia–type threats' and motivated by his need to obtain money and fear of disclosure of his homosexuality as well as the threats of death or grievous bodily harm.

R v Graham [1982] 1 All ER 801, Court of Appeal, Criminal Division
(Lord Lane CJ, Taylor and McCullough JJ)

The appellant (G) was a practising homosexual living in 'a bizarre ménage a trois' with his wife (W) and another homosexual, King (K). G suffered from an anxiety state. He was taking valium which, according to medical evidence, would make him more susceptible to bullying. K was a violent man and had in 1978 tipped G and W off a settee because they were embracing and he was jealous. G knew K had been guilty of other acts of violence. On 27 June 1980 K attacked W with a knife. W then went to G's mother's home. G and K stayed drinking heavily while G also took valium. K suggested getting rid of the wife once and for all. G induced her to return by pretending that he had cut his wrists. She knelt beside him, as he lay face down on the floor pretending to be seriously hurt. K put a percolator flex round her neck, saying, 'What's it like to know you are going to die?'. She put up her hands to the flex. K told G to pull on one end of the flex. He did so, he said, only because he was afraid of K. The plug which he was pulling came off the flex, leaving it in doubt whether his act made any contribution to W's death. G was convicted of murder.

Lord Lane CJ. . . . . The Crown at the trial conceded that, on those facts, it was open to the defence to raise the issue of duress. In other words, they were not prepared to take the point that the defence of duress is not available to a principal in the first degree to murder. Consequently, the interesting question raised by the decisions in *Lynch v DPP for Northern Ireland* [1975] 1 All ER 913, [1975] AC 653, and *Abbott v R* [1976] 3 All ER 140, [1977] AC 755 was not argued before us. We do not have to decide it. We pause only to observe that the jury would no doubt have been puzzled to learn that whether the appellant was to be convicted of murder or acquitted altogether might depend on whether the plug came off the end of the percolator flex when he began to pull it.

There are other possible aspects of the defence of duress which do not arise for decision in this case, namely: (1) whether in murder, duress, if available, excuses a defendant from criminal liability altogether or only reduces his offence to manslaughter; (2) whether in murder a fear of physical injury (rather than one of death) can ever amount to duress; (3) to what extent fear of death or injury to persons other than the defendant may be relied on; and (4) whether a fear of false imprisonment may be relied on.

The direction which the judge gave to the jury required them to ask themselves two questions. First, a subjective question which the judge formulated thus: 'Was this man at the time of the killing taking part because he feared for his own life or personal safety as a result of the words or the conduct on the part of King, either personally experienced by him, or genuinely believed in by him?' Neither side in the present appeal has taken issue with the judge on this question. We feel, however, that for purposes of completeness, we should say that the direction appropriate in this particular case should have been in these words: 'Was this man at the time of the killing taking part because he held a well-grounded fear of death (or serious physical injury) as a result of the words or conduct on the part of King?' The bracketed words may be too favourable to the defendant. The point was not argued before us.

The judge then went on to direct the jury that if the answer to that first question was 'Yes', or 'He may have been', the jury should then go on to consider a second question importing an objective test of reasonableness. This is the issue which arises in this appeal. Counsel for the appellant contends that no second question arises at all; the test is purely subjective. He argues that if the appellant's will was in fact overborne by threats of the requisite cogency, he is entitled to be acquitted and no question arises to whether a reasonable man, with or without his characteristics, would have reacted similarly.

Counsel for the Crown, on the other hand, submits that such dicta as can be found on the point are in favour of a second test; this time an objective test. He argues that public policy requires this and draws an analogy with provocation. He submits that while the judge was right to pose a second question, he formulated it too favourably to the appellant. The question was put to the jury in the following terms:

> 'Taking into account all the circumstances of the case, including the age, sex, sexual propensities and other characteristics personal to the defendant, including his state of mind and the amount of drink or drugs he had taken, was it reasonable for the defendant to behave in the way he did, that is to take part in the murder of his wife as a result of the fear present at the time in his mind? The test of reasonableness in this context is: would the defendant's behaviour in all the particular circumstances to which I have just referred reflect the degree of self-control and firmness of purpose which everyone is entitled to expect that his fellow citizens would exercise in society as it is today?'

If the references to drink and drugs had been omitted, the judge's phraseology would have been in line with the direction given in cases of provocation (see *DPP v Camplin* [1978] 2 All ER 168, [1978] AC 705 and *R v Newell* (1980) 71 Cr App R 331). By using those words the judge introduced, says counsel for the Crown, transitory factors and self-induced factors peculiar to the appellant and having no place in an objective test.

There is no direct binding authority on the questions whether the test is solely subjective or, if objective, how it is to be formulated. The point did not arise for decision in *Lynch's* case but Lord Wilberforce cited, with apparent approval, 'as a statement of principle' a passage from the judgment of Rumpff J in *State v Goliath* 1972 (3) SALR 465 at 480 which included the following words:

'. . . it seems to me to be irrational . . . to exclude compulsion as a complete defence to murder if the threatened party was under such a strong duress that a reasonable person would not have acted otherwise under the same duress.'

(See [1975] 1 All ER 913 at 929, [1975] AC 653 at 683.)

A little later Lord Wilberforce went on ([1975] 1 All ER 913 at 930, [1975] AC 653 at 684–685):

'The judges have always assumed responsibility for deciding questions of principle relating to criminal liability and guilt and particularly for setting the standards by which the law expects normal men to act. In all such matters as capacity, sanity, drunkenness, coercion, necessity, provocation, self-defence, the common law, through the judges, accepts and sets the standards of right-thinking men of normal firmness and humanity at a level at which people can accept and respect.'

Lord Morris referred to 'the standards of honest and reasonable men' of which the law should take account (see [1975] 1 All ER 913 at 917, [1975] AC 653 at 670).

Lord Edmund-Davies referred, with apparent approval, to a passage from the judgment of Murnaghan J in *A-G v Whelan* [1934] IR 518 at 526 as follows:

'Threats of immediate death or serious personal violence so great as to overbear the ordinary power of human resistance should be accepted as a justification for acts which would otherwise be criminal.'

(See [1975] 1 All ER 913 at 952, [1975] AC 653 at 711.)

Lord Simon mentioned 'subjectivity', but only in relation to belief in the existence of the threat not in regard to the defendant's conduct in reaction to the threat.

In *Archbold's Criminal Pleading, Evidence and Practice* (40th edn, 1979) para 1449e it is stated tentatively that the threats must be 'of such gravity that they might well have caused a reasonable man placed in the same situation to act as he did'.

Smith and Hogan's *Criminal Law* (4th edn, 1978) p 205 states the law in this way:

'*Subjective or Objective?* Since duress is a concession to human frailty and some are more frail than others so, it is arguable, the standard should vary. Probably, however, the standard of resolution and fortitude required is fixed by the law. It is for the law to lay down standards of conduct. Under provocation, D must display a reasonable degree of self-restraint. When actually attacked, D may used only a reasonable degree of force in self-defence. In blackmail, P is expected to display a measure of fortitude and not to be affected by trivial threats. Probably, then, a person under duress must display reasonable fortitude and has no defence unless the threat is one which might have affected a reasonably resolute man.'

The Law Commission in their report on *Defences of General Application* (1977, Law Com No 83) para 2.28 make the following observations:

'It may be said that the whole test as to whether the requirements of duress exist should be subjective, but we feel that this would create too wide a defence. Serious personal injury can cover a wide range of threatened harm, and if the defence is to be available even in respect of the most serious offences, it would be unsatisfactory in the final event to dispense with some objective assessment of whether the defendant could reasonably have been expected to resist the threat. The solution which is adopted by section 2.09 (1) of the American Law Institute's Model Penal Code is to provide that the threat of unlawful force (which is left undefined) must be that "which a person of reasonable firmness in his situation would have been unable to resist." Whether the words "in his situation" comprehend more than the surrounding circumstances, and extend to the characteristics of the defendant himself, it is difficult to say, and for that reason we would not recommend without qualification the adoption of that solution. We think that there should be an objective element in the requirements of the defence so that in the final event it will be for the jury to determine whether the threat was one which the defendant in question could not reasonably have been expected to resist. This will allow the jury to take into account the nature of the offence committed, its relationship to the threats which the defendant believed to exist, the threats themselves and the circumstances in which they were made, and the personal characteristics of the defendant. The last consideration is, we feel, a most important one. Threats directed against a weak, immature or disabled person may well be much more compelling than the same threats directed against a normal healthy person.'

As a matter of public policy, it seems to us essential to limit the defence of duress by means of an objective criterion formulated in terms of reasonableness. Consistency of approach in defences to criminal liability is obviously desirable. Provocation and duress are analogous. In provocation the words or actions of one person break the self-control of another. In duress the words or actions of one person break the will of another. The law requires a defendant to have the self-control reasonably to be expected of the ordinary citizen in his situation. It should likewise require him to have the steadfastness reasonably to be expected of the ordinary citizen in his situation. So too with self-defence, in which the law permits the use of no more force than is reasonable in the circumstances. And, in general, if a mistake is to excuse what would otherwise be criminal, the mistake must be a reasonable one.

It follows that we accept counsel for the Crown's submission that the direction in this case was too favourable to the appellant. The Crown having conceded that the issue of duress was open to the appellant and was raised on the evidence, the correct approach on the facts of this case would have been as follows: (1) was the defendant, or may he have been, impelled to act as he did because, as a result of what he reasonably believed King had said or done, he had good cause to fear that if he did not so act King would kill him or (if this is to be added) cause him serious physical injury? (2) if so, have the prosecution made the jury sure that a sober person of reasonable firmness, sharing the characteristics of the defendant, would not have responded to whatever he reasonably believed King said or did by taking part in the killing? The fact that a defendant's will to resist has been eroded by the voluntary consumption of drink or drugs or both is not relevant to this test.

We doubt whether the Crown were right to concede that the question of duress ever arose on the facts of this case. The words and deeds of King relied on by the defence were far short of those needed to raise a threat of the requisite gravity. However, the Crown having made the concession, the judge was right to pose the second objective question to the jury. His only error lay in putting it too favourably to the appellant.

The appeal is dismissed.

Appeal dismissed.

See *Burke*, Appendix II, below.

Question

1. Should the defendant who sets up duress be judged on the facts as he reasonably believed or (where there is a difference) on the facts as he actually believed them to be? Cf *Gladstone Williams*, p 236, below. Is there a proper distinction between duress and self–defence in this respect? What if the mistake of fact is caused by intoxication?

2. In what respects would Lord Lane's 'correct approach' be modified by the enactment of cl 45 of the draft Criminal Code?

Lynch v Director of Public Prosecutions for Northern Ireland [1975] 1 All ER 913, House of Lords
(Lord Morris of Borth-y-Gest, Lord Wilberforce, Lord Simon of Glaisdale, Lord Kilbrandon, Lord Edmund-Davies)

The appellant was summoned by Meehan, a well-known and ruthless gunman, and ordered to drive Meehan and his accomplices to a place where they intended to kill, and did kill a policeman. The appellant remained in the car while the shooting took place and drove the gunmen away afterwards. There was evidence that it would be perilous to disobey Meehan and, on the occasion in question, he gave his instructions in a manner which indicated that he would tolerate no disobedience. The appellant testified that he believed that, if he had disobeyed the instructions, he would have been shot. He was convicted of murder and appealed. His appeal was dismissed by the Court of Criminal Appeal for Northern Ireland.

Lord Morris of Borth-y-Gest made a speech allowing the appeal.

Lord Wilberforce. . . . Does then the law forbid admission of a defence of duress on a charge of murder whether as a principal in the first degree or as a principal in the second degree or as an accessory? Consistently with the method normal in the development of the common law, an answer to this question must be sought in authority, and in the principles on which established authority is based. I look first at the principle. The principle on which duress is admitted as a defence is not easy to state. Professor Glanville Williams [*Criminal Law* (2nd edn, 1961) p 751] indeed doubts whether duress fits in to any accepted theory; it may, in his view, stand by itself altogether outside the definition of will and act. The reason for this is historical. Duress emerged very early in our law as a fact of which account has to be taken, particularly in times of civil strife where charges of treason were the normal consequence of defeat, long before the criminal law had worked out a consistent or any theory of mens rea or intention. At the present time, whatever the ultimate analysis in jurisprudence may be, the best opinion, as reflected in decisions of judges and in writers, seems to be that duress per minas is something which is superimposed on the other ingredients which by themselves would make up an offence, i e on the act and intention. *Coactus volui* sums up the combination: the victim completes the act and knows that he is doing so; but the addition of the element of duress prevents the law from treating what he has done as a crime. . . .

I referred above to judicial decisions; it is certainly the case that, in recent years, and subsequently to Stephen's *History of the Criminal Law of England* (and in spite of that eminent author's views) the defence of duress has been judicially admitted in relation to a variety of crimes: inter alia, treason, receiving, stealing, malicious damage, arson, perjury. In all of these crimes there would have to be proved, in addition to an actus reus, an element of intention. Yet this defence has been admitted. This makes it clear beyond doubt, to my mind, that if the defence is to be denied in relation to murder, that cannot be because the crime of murder—as distinct from other crimes—involves the presence of intention; it must be for some other reason. If the proposition is correct at all that duress prevents what would otherwise constitute a crime for attracting criminal responsibility, then that should be correct whatever the crime.

What reason then can there be for excepting murder? One may say—as some authorities do (cf *A-G v Whelan* per Murnaghan J, [[1934] IR 518 at 526] *Hurley and Murray* per Smith J [[1967] VR 526 at 543]) that murder is the most heinous of crimes: so it may be, and in some circumstances, a defence of duress in relation to it should be correspondingly hard to establish. Indeed, to justify the deliberate killing by one's own hand of another human being may be something that no pressure or threat even to one's own life which can be imagined can justify—no such case ever seems to have reached the courts. But if one accepts the test of heinousness, this does not, in my opinion, involve that all cases of what is murder in law must be treated in the same way. Heinousness is a word of degree, and that there are lesser degrees of heinousness, even of involvement in homicide, seems beyond doubt. An accessory before the fact, or an aider or abettor, may (not necessarily must) bear a less degree than the actual killer: and even if the rule of exclusion is absolute, or nearly so in relation to the latter, it need not be so in lesser cases. Nobody would dispute that the greater the degree of heinousness of the crime, the greater and less resistable must be the degree of pressure, if pressure is to excuse. Questions of this kind where it is necessary to weigh the pressures acting on a man against the gravity of the act he commits are common enough in the criminal law, for example with regard to provocation and self-defence: their difficulty is not a reason for a total rejection of the defence. To say that the defence may be admitted in relation to some degrees of murder, but that its admission in cases of direct killing by a first degree principal is likely to be attended by such great difficulty as almost to justify a ruling that the defence is not available, is not illogical. It simply involves the recognition that by sufficiently adding to the degrees, one may approach an absolute position.

So I find no convincing reason, on principle, why, if a defence of duress in the criminal law exists at all, it should be absolutely excluded in murder charges whatever the nature of the charge; hard to establish, yes, in case of direct killing so hard that perhaps it will never be proved; but in other cases to be judged, strictly indeed, on the totality of facts. Exclusion, if not arbitrary, must be based either on authority or policy. I shall deal with each.

[His Lordship examined the authorities and continued:]

The conclusion which I deduce is that although, in a case of actual killing by a first degree principal the balance of judicial authority at the present time is against the admission of the defence of duress, in the case of lesser degrees of participation, the balance is, if anything, the other way. At the very least, to admit the defence in such cases involves no departure from established decisions. . . .

The broad question remains how this House, clearly not bound by any precedent, should now state the law with regard to this defence in relation to the facts of the present case. I have no doubt that it is open to us, on normal judicial principles, to hold the defence admissible. We are here in the domain of the common law; our task is to fit what we can see as principle and authority to the facts before us, and it is no obstacle that these facts are new. The judges have always assumed responsibility for deciding questions of principle relating to criminal liability and guilt and particularly for setting the standards by which the law expects normal men to act. In all such matters as capacity, sanity, drunkenness, coercion, necessity, provocation, self-defence, the common law, through the judges, accepts and sets the standards of right-thinking men of normal firmness and humanity at a level which people can accept and respect. The House is not inventing a new defence; on the contrary, it would not discharge its judicial duty if it failed to define the law's attitude to this particular defence in particular circumstances. I would decide that the defence is in law admissible in a case of aiding and abetting murder, and so in the present case. I would leave cases of direct killing by a principal in the first degree to be dealt with as they arise.

It is said that such persons as the appellant can always be safeguarded by action of the executive which can order an imprisoned person to be released. I firmly reject any such argument. A law, which requires innocent victims of terrorist threats to be tried for murder and convicted as murderers, is an unjust law even if the executive, resisting political pressures, may decide, after it all, and within the permissible limits of the prerogative to release them. Moreover, if the defence is excluded in law, much of the evidence which would prove the duress would be inadmissible at the trial, not brought out in court, and not tested by cross-examination. The validity of the defence is far better judged by a jury, after proper direction and a fair trial, than by executive officials; and if it is said that to allow the defence will be to encourage fictitious claims of pressure I have enough confidence in our legal system to believe that the process of law is a better safeguard against this than enquiry by a Government department.

I would allow the appeal . . .

Lord Simon of Glaisdale. . . . In my opinion no distinction can be based on the degree of participation. I have already rehearsed the arguments in support of the concept of duress as a defence (absence of moral blameworthiness and the inappropriateness of punishment in such circumstances); there are no different arguments relating to 'necessity' as a defence: and none affords any ground for distinguishing between principals in the first or second degrees respectively. It is, with all respect, irrational to say, 'The man who actually pulls the trigger is in a class by himself: he is outside the pale of any such defence as I am prepared to countenance'. He cannot on any sensible ground be put in a class by himself: the man who pulls the trigger because his child will be killed otherwise is deserving of exactly the same consideration as the man who merely carries the gun because he is frightened. Moreover, in general, as Smith and Hogan state in this very connection [*Criminal Law* (3rd edn, 1973) p 166]:

> 'The difficulty about adopting a distinction between the principal and secondary parties as a rule of law is that the contribution of the secondary party to the death may be no less significant than that of the principal.'

So the question must be faced whether there is a sustainable distinction in principle between 'necessity' and duress as defences to a charge of murder as a principal. In the circumstances where either 'necessity' or duress is relevant, there is both actus reus and mens rea. In both sets of circumstances, there is power of choice between two alternatives; but one of those alternatives is so disagreeable that even serious infraction of the criminal law seems preferable. In both the consequences of the act is intended, within any permissible definition of intention. The only difference is that in duress the force constraining the choice is a human threat, whereas in 'necessity' it can be any circumstances constituting a threat to life (or, perhaps, limb). Duress is, thus considered, merely a particular application of the doctrine of 'necessity': see Glanville Williams's *Criminal Law* [(2nd edn, 1961) p 760]. In my view, therefore, if your Lordships were to allow the instant appeal, it would be necessary to hold that *Dudley and Stephens* [(1884) 14 QBD 273, [1881-5] All ER Rep 61; p 219, below] either was wrongly decided or was not a decision negativing 'necessity' as a defence to murder; and, if the latter, it would be further incumbent, I think, to define 'necessity' as a criminal defence, and lay down whether it is a defence to all crimes, and if not why not. It would, in particular, be necessary to consider Hale's dissent from Bacon as to the starving man stealing a loaf of bread. It would be a travesty of justice and an invitation to anarchy to declare that an innocent life may be taken with impunity if the threat to one's own life is from a terrorist but not when from a natural disaster like ship- or plane-wreck. . . .

If the first question for your Lordships' consideration is to be answered Yes, it is overturning the consensus of centuries. I am all for recognising frankly that judges do make law. And I am all for judges exercising this responsibility boldly at the proper time and place—that is, where they can feel confident of having in mind, and correctly weighed, all the implications of their decision, and where matters of social policy are not involved which the collective wisdom of Parliament is better suited to resolve (see *Morgans v Launchbury* [1973] AC 127 at 136, 137, [1972] 2 All ER 606 at 610. I can hardly conceive of circumstances less suitable than the instant for five members of an appellate committee of your Lordships' House to arrogate to ourselves so momentous a law-making initiative . . . .

[**Lord Kilbrandon** held that to allow a defence of duress to a charge of murder would be to change the law; that no distinction could be made between principals in the first and principals in the second degree; and that the appeal should be dismissed.]

Lord Edmund-Davies, [having found the basis of duress to be correctly stated by Professor Glanville Williams (see p 212, above) and asked why duress should not be available in murder, concluded:]

Having considered the available material to the best of my ability, I find myself unable to accept that any ground in law, logic, morals or public policy has been established to justify withholding the plea of duress in the present case. To say, as Murnaghan J did, in *A-G v Whelan* [[1934] IR at 526] that: 'Murder is a crime so heinous that . . . in such a case the strongest duress would not be any justification,' is, with respect, to beg the whole question. That murder has a unique gravity most would regard as not open to doubt, but the degree of legal criminality or blameworthiness involved in participation therein depends on all the circumstances of the particular case, just as it does whenever the actus reus and the mens rea necessary to constitute any other offence is established. In homicide, the law already recognises degrees of criminality, notwithstanding that unlawful killing with malice aforethought has unquestionably taken place. In non-homicidal cases, the degree of criminality or blameworthiness can and should be reflected in the punishment meted out, a course which the mandatory life sentence for murder prohibits. And in relation to *all* offences ('except possibly treason and murder as a principal', as Lord Parker CJ said in *Hudson* [[1971] 2 QB at 206, [1971] 2 All ER at 246]), a person committing them is entitled to be completely acquitted if at the material time he was acting under the threat of death or serious bodily harm. Professor J.C. Smith has rightly observed that [[1974] Crim LR 352]:

> 'To allow a defence to crime is not to express approval of the action of the accused person but only to declare that it does not merit condemnation and punishment.'

For the reasons I have sought to advance, I can find no valid ground for preventing the appellant Lynch from presenting the plea of duress, and I would therefore be for allowing his appeal. By doing so, I consider that this House would be paying due regard to those 'contemporary views of what is just, what is moral, what is humane', which my noble and learned friend, Lord Diplock, described in *Hyam v Director of Public Prosecutions* [[1974] 2 All ER at 65, [1974] 2 WLR at 631] as constituting 'the underlying principle which is the justification for retaining the common law as a living source of rules binding on all members of contemporary society in England'.

Appeal allowed: new trial ordered

Abbott v R [1976] 3 All ER 140, Privy Council
(Lord Wilberforce, Lord Hailsham of St Marylebone, Lord Kilbrandon, Lord Salmon and Lord Edmund-Davies)

The appellant was induced to take part in the murder of Gale Benson as a result of threats against his own and his mother's life made by one Malik, who was subsequently hanged for murder. In his view Malik's 'respectability' made complaint to the police futile. He dug a hole for the body, and held the victim as she was stabbed by another man. She was left dying in the hole, which was then filled in by the appellant and three other men while the deceased was still alive. Death was caused by (1) the stab wound and (2) the inhalation of dirt. Lord Salmon said it was 'clearly hopeless' to argue that the appellant was only a principal in the second degree. The appellant argued unsuccessfully that duress was available as a defence to a principle in the first degree.

Lord Salmon. . . . Whilst their Lordships feel bound to accept the decision of the House of Lords in *Lynch v Director of Public Prosecutions for Northern Ireland* (p 211 above) they find themselves constrained to say that had they considered (which they do not) that that decision was an authority which required the extension of the doctrine to cover cases like the present, they would not have accepted it.

Their Lordships will now consider the question whether *Lynch v Director of Public Prosecutions for Northern Ireland* can properly be regarded as any authority for the proposition advanced on behalf of the appellant that duress affords him a complete defence although he was a principal in the first degree, having clearly taken an active, prominent and indispensable part in the actual killing of Gale Benson.

The majority of the noble and learned Lords who decided *Lynch v Director of Public Prosecutions for Northern Ireland* certainly said nothing to support the contention now being made on behalf of the appellant. At best, from the appellant's point of view, they left the point open. Indeed, there are passages in some of their speeches which suggest that duress can be of no avail to a charge of murder as principal in the first degree . . . [His Lordship quoted from the speeches in *Lynch*.]

It seems to their Lordships that if one adds these passages from the speeches of Lord Morris of Borth-y-Gest and Lord Wilberforce to those of Lord Simon of Glaisdale and Lord Kilbrandon, who dissented in *Lynch v Director of Public Prosecutions for Northern Ireland*, the majority of the House was of the opinion that duress is not a defence to a charge of murder against anyone proved to have done the actual killing. However this may be, their Lordships are clearly of the opinion that in such a case, duress, as the law now stands, affords no defence. For reasons which will presently be explained their Lordships, whilst loyally accepting the decision in *Lynch's* case, are certainly not prepared to extend it.

When Lord Simon of Glaisdale and Lord Kilbrandon stated in their dissenting speeches in *Lynch v Director of Public Prosecutions for Northern Ireland* that the drawing of an arbitrary line between murder as a principal in the first degree and murder as a principal in the second degree cannot be justified either morally or juridically, they clearly meant that since, rightly, it had always been accepted that duress was not a defence to a charge of murder as a principal in the first degree, the cases and dicta (eg Bray CJ in *Brown and Morley* and *Kray* [[1970] 1 QB 125, [1969] 3 All ER 941]) which suggested that duress could amount to a defence to a charge of murder in the second degree should not be followed. The noble and learned Lords were clearly not conceding that if, contrary to their view, duress were capable of being a defence to a charge of murder as a principal in the second degree it should therefore be capable of being a defence to a charge of murder as a principal in the first degree . . .

Prior to the present case it has never even been argued in England or any other part of the Commonwealth that duress is a defence to a charge of murder by a principal in the first degree. The only case in which such a view was canvassed is *S v Goliath* [1972 (3) SA 1]; this was a case decided under a mixture of Roman-Dutch and English law after South Africa had left the Commonwealth. From time immemorial it has been accepted by the common law of England that duress is no defence to murder, certainly not to murder by a principal in the first degree. . . .

Counsel for the appellant has argued that the law presupposes a degree of heroism of which the ordinary man is incapable and which therefore should not be expected of him and that modern conditions and concepts of humanity have rendered obsolete the rule that the actual killer cannot rely on duress as a defence. Their Lordships do not agree. In the trials of those responsible for wartime atrocities such as mass killings of men, women or children, inhuman experiments on human beings, often resulting in death, and like crimes, it was invariably argued for the defence that these atrocities should be excused on the ground that they resulted from superior orders and duress: if the accused had refused to do these dreadful things, they would have been shot and therefore they should be acquitted and allowed to go go free. This argument has always been universally rejected. Their Lordships would be sorry indeed to see it accepted by the common law of England.

It seems incredible to their Lordships that in any civilised society, acts such as the appellant's, whatever threats may have been made to him, could be regarded as excusable or within the law. We are not living in a dream world in which the mounting wave of violence and terrorism can be contained by strict logic and intellectual niceties alone. Common sense surely reveals the added dangers to which in this modern world the public would be exposed, if the change in the law proposed on behalf of the appellant were effected. It might well, as Lord Simon of Glaisdale said in *Lynch v Director of Public Prosecutions for Northern Ireland*, prove to be a charter for terrorists, gang leaders and kidnappers. A terrorist of notorious violence might, eg threaten death to A and his family unless A obeys his instructions to put a bomb with a time fuse set by A in a certain passenger aircraft and/or in a thronged market, railway station or the like. A, under duress, does obey his instructions and as a result, hundreds of men, women and children are killed or mangled. Should the contentions made on behalf of the appellant be correct, A would have a complete defence and, if charged, would be bound to be acquitted and set at liberty. Having now gained some real experience and expertise, he might again be approached by the terrorist who would make the same threats and exercise the same duress under which A would then give a repeat performance, killing even more men, women and children. Is there any limit to the number of people you may kill to save your own life and that of your family?

We have been reminded that it is an important part of the judge's role to adapt and develop the principles of the common law to meet the changing needs of time. Their Lordships, however, are firmly of the opinion that the invitation extended to them on behalf of the appellant goes far beyond adapting and developing the principles of the common law. What has been suggested is the destruction of a fundamental doctrine of our law which might well have far-reaching and disastrous consequences for public safety, to say nothing of its important social, ethical and maybe political implications. Such a decision would be far beyond their Lordships' powers even if they approved—as they certainly do not—of this revolutionary change in the law proposed on behalf of the appellant. Judges have no power to create new criminal offences nor, in their Lordships' opinion, for the reasons already stated, have they the power to invent a new defence to murder which is entirely contrary to fundamental legal doctrine, accepted for hundreds of years without question. If a policy change of such fundamental nature were to be made it could, in their Lordships' view, be made only by Parliament . . .

[Lord Wilberforce and Lord Edmund-Davies dissenting:] . . .

. . . The dreadful circumstances leading up to and culminating in the death of Gale Benson at the hands of the appellant and others have been related in the majority judgment. They are such as to establish clearly that the appellant was a principal in the first degree to her murder. The sole question of law is whether it is open to such an accused to plead that he acted under duress. For the purposes of this appeal, it is unnecessary to consider what *sort* of duress or how *much* duress. If the Crown is right, there is no let-out for any principal in the first degree, even if the duress be so dreadful as would be likely to wreck the morale of most men of reasonable courage, and even were the duress directed not against the person threatened but against other innocent people (in the present case, the appellant's mother) so that considerations of mere self-preservation are not operative. That is indeed 'a blueprint for heroism' (*S v Goliath* [1971 (3) SA 1]). The question is whether it is also the common law, which, being indivisible, has to be applied in Trinidad and Tobago as in Great Britain. In our opinion it is not. . . .

Something must be said about the significance attached by the majority of their Lordships to the absence of any direct decision that it is open to principals in the first degree to murder to advance a plea of duress. As to this, two observations need to be made: (i) There is little use in looking back earlier than 1838 [*R v Tyler and Price* (1838) 8 C & P 616], for until then an accused could not give evidence on his own behalf; and to advance such a plea without any opportunity of explaining to the jury why he acted as he did would be to attempt something foredoomed to failure. It is significant, too, that the increasingly humane attitude of the courts in relation to duress has developed since the gag on accused persons was removed. (ii) As was pointed out in *Lynch v Director of Public Prosecutions*, the balance of such judicial authority as exists was against the admission of the defence of duress in cases of first degree murder. But this balance was a weak one and one which both of us thought might have to yield in an actual case. While there are in the law reports a number of obiter dicta (that is in cases where murder was not charged) to the effect that duress is not available in murder, apparently in only one case has it been directly so held. The one exception is nearly 140 years old, *Tyler and Price* [(1838) 8 C & P at 620], where Lord Denman CJ, using unqualified terms which certainly cannot be regarded as accurately stating the law of today, said: 'It cannot be too often repeated that the apprehension of personal danger does not furnish any excuse for assisting in doing any act which is illegal.' Apart from the unqualified and therefore unacceptable generality of those words, the decision is for additional reasons an unsatisfactory guide to the proper outcome of the present appeal: see *Lynch's* case [[1975] AC 713 at 714, [1975] 1 All ER 954 at 955]. It has further to be borne in mind that the present case involved a feature (viz threats of death to an innocent third person) which has not been considered in the United Kingdom or, so far as we are aware, elsewhere in the Commonwealth except in the Victoria case of *Hurley and Murray* [[1967] VR 526].

Lynch v Director of Public Prosecutions for Northern Ireland having been decided as it was, the most striking feature of the present appeal is the lack of any indication, in the judgment of the majority, *why* a flat declaration that in no circumstances whatsoever may the actual killer be absolved by a plea of duress makes for sounder law and better ethics. In truth, the contrary is the case. For example, D attempts to kill P but, though injuring him, fails. When charged with attempted murder he may plead duress (*Fegan* [(1974) 20 September (unreported)] and several times referred to in *Lynch's* case). Later P dies and D is charged with his murder: if the majority of their Lordships are right, he now has no such plea available. Again, no one can doubt that our law would today allow duress to be pleaded in answer to a charge, under s 18 of the Offences against the Person Act 1861, of wounding with intent. Yet, here again, should the victim die after the conclusion of the first trial, the accused when faced with a murder charge would be bereft of any such defence. It is not the mere lack of logic that troubles one. It is when one stops to consider why duress is *ever* permitted as a defence even to charges of great gravity that the lack of any moral reason justifying its *automatic* exclusion in such cases as the present becomes so baffling—and so important . . .

To hold that a principal in the first degree in murder is never in any circumstances to be entitled to plead duress, whereas a principal in the second degree may, is to import the possibility of grave injustice into the common law. Such a conclusion should not be arrived at unless supported by compelling authority or by the demands of public policy shown to operate differently in the two cases. There are no authorities compelling this Board so to hold, nor are these reasons of public policy present in this case which are lacking in the case of principals in the second degree. It has to be said with all respect that the majority opinion of their Lordships amounts, in effect, to side-stepping the decision in *Lynch v Director of Public Prosecutions for Northern Ireland* and, even were that constitutionally appropriate, to do it without advancing cogent grounds . . .

Appeal dismissed

Questions

1. Were Lords Simon and Kilbrandon right when, in *Lynch*, they held that no rational or sensible distinction could be drawn between principals in the first and principals in the second degree? Cf *Burke*, Appendix II, below.

2. Is one who holds a victim while he is stabbed a principal in the first or second degree? Cf the case where the victim of rape is held down. Was the defendant a principal in the first degree because he held the victim or because he heaped earth on her?

3. Malik directed the operation but did not take an active part in the killing. If he had been acting under duress, would he have had a defence? Would it be right that he should have a defence and the actual killers not?

4. If duress is not a defence to murder as a principal in the first degree, it would appear that it is not regarded as an excuse for forming an intent to kill or to cause grievous bodily harm or to do an unlawful act to another, knowing that it is likely to cause death or grievous bodily harm. Should duress then be a defence (a) to attempted murder? (b) to causing grievous bodily harm with intent, contrary to s 18 of the Offences against the Person Act 1861? (c) to malicious wounding, contrary to s 20 of that Act?

5. Acting under duress, D strikes P with an iron bar. He is charged with causing P grievous bodily harm with intent, but is acquitted on the ground of duress. P then dies. D is indicted for his murder. Is the act which was previously held to be excusable now inexcusable?

6. Is *Dudley and Stephens* (p 219, below) overruled with respect to (i) the actual killer? (ii) an abettor?

R v Fitzpatrick [1977] NI 20, Court of Criminal Appeal in Northern Ireland (Lowry LCJ and Jones LJ)

The appellant voluntarily joined the IRA, which he knew to be an illegal organisation, in 1975. He attempted to leave later in the year, but was induced by threats against himself and his mother not only to remain with the organisation but also to take part in an armed robbery. In the course of this he shot the deceased. The appellant was convicted of murder, robbery and of belonging to a proscribed organisation contrary to s 19 (i)(a) of the Northern Ireland (Emergency Provisions) Act 1973. The only defence raised was duress. The trial judge held that the prosecution had failed to prove beyond reasonable doubt that such threats were not made, or that, if they were, they had not influenced him. Nevertheless, he rejected the availability of the defence of duress, citing Stephen's History of the Criminal Law of England:

> 'If a man chooses to expose and still more if he chooses to submit himself to illegal compulsion, it may not operate even in mitigation of punishment. It would surely be monstrous to mitigate the punishment of a murderer on the ground that he was a member of a secret society by which he would have been assassinated if he had not committed murder.' (Vol 2, p 108)

The grounds of appeal were that the judge had wrongly directed himself, 1(a) that duress was not available as a defence to a person who voluntarily joined a terrorist organisation which engaged in violence and 1(b) if the first ground of appeal failed, that the defendant's attempts to dissociate himself from the organisation were of no avail. (The second and third grounds of appeal are omitted.)

Lowry LCJ. . . . Counsel on both sides have informed us that the point is devoid of judicial authority and we have not found anything to suggest the contrary. Therefore we have to decide, in the absence of judicial decisions, what is the common law. Assistance may be sought from the opinions of textwriters, judicial dicta and the reports of Commissions and legal committees, and from analogies with legal systems which share our common law heritage, with a view to considering matters of general principle and arriving at the answer . . .

[His Lordship considered the Canadian Criminal Code s 17, the New Zealand Crimes Act 1961 s 24, the Queensland Criminal Code (1899) s 31 (4) and the similar Western Australian Code, the Tasmanian Criminal Code s 20, the New York Penal Code (1967) s 35, the Royal Commission Draft Code (1879) s 23, Perkins on Criminal Law (1957) p 843 and the Law Commission's Working Paper No 55 paragraph 26, and continued:]

We consider that the widespread adoption of such limiting provisions with regard to duress shows that the framers of the codes and drafts which we have mentioned considered that this exclusory doctrine was already part of the common law and the Law Commission's recommendation indicates the view of a distinguished body of jurists, (whose recommendations are in general favourable to duress as a defence), that participation in unlawful associations or conspiracies should disqualify the accused from relying on it . . .

The drawing up by the framers of penal codes of lists of offences reflects a widely shared opinion that the common law refuses to recognise a defence of duress in regard to the most heinous crimes and the exclusion of duress as a defence to a person who has in the predicated circumstances joined an unlawful association is in our opinion equally attributable to the view that such exclusion also reflected the common law . . .

[His Lordship quoted extensively from the speeches of the House of Lords in *Director of Public Prosecutions v Lynch*, and continued:]

If a person behaves immorally by, for example, committing himself to an unlawful conspiracy, he ought not to be able to take advantage of the pressure exercised on him by his fellow criminals in order to put on when it suits him the breastplate of righteousness. An even more rigorous view which, as we have seen, prevails in the United States, but does not arise for consideration in this case, is that, if a person is culpably negligent or reckless in exposing himself to the risk of being subjected to coercive pressure, he too loses the right to call himself innocent by reason of his succumbing to that pressure.

A practical consideration is that, if some such limit on the defendant's duress does not exist, it would be only too easy for every member of an unlawful conspiracy and for every member of a gang except the leader to obtain an immunity denied to ordinary citizens. Indeed, the better organised the conspiracy and the more brutal its internal discipline, the surer would be the defence of duress for its members. It can hardly be supposed that the common law tolerates such an absurdity.

In making this last observation we are not saying that the ease with which a defence can be put up is a reason for not allowing that defence and impartially considering it when made. Still less do we subscribe to any doctrine that, when society is threatened, the ordinary protection of the common law can, except by statute, be withheld even from those who are alleged to have conspired against it: 'Amid the clash of arms the laws are not silent.' On the other hand what we are contemplating here is the possibility that any band of criminals could so organise their affairs in advance as to confer mutual immunity in respect of any crime to which duress provides a defence . . .

The learned trial judge summarised at page 6 of his judgment the facts to which he applied the principle of non-availability of duress. While adopting his reasoning, we guard ourselves against the use of any expression which might tend to confine the application of that principle to illegal, in the narrow sense of proscribed, organisations. A person may become associated with a sinister group of men with criminal objectives and coercive methods of ensuring that their lawless enterprises are carried out and thereby voluntarily expose himself to illegal compulsion, whether or not the group is or becomes a proscribed organisation.

Nor indeed, so far as the facts are concerned, do we consider that the evidence of the nature and activities of the relevant organisation has necessarily to be the same formal and precise character as it apparently was in this case.

As to ground 1 (b), which we have set out above but which did not seem to be pressed in this court, here again we agree with the trial judge. To say that the appellant could revive for his own benefit the defence of duress by trying to leave the organisation is no more cogent an argument than saying that he tried unavailingly to resist the order to carry out a robbery. In each case the answer is the same: if a person voluntarily exposes and submits himself, as the appellant did, to illegal compulsion, he cannot rely on the duress to which he has voluntarily exposed himself as an excuse either in respect of the crimes he commits against his will or in respect of his continued but unwilling association with those capable of exercising upon him the duress which he calls in aid . . .

Appeal dismissed

3. Necessity

R v Dudley and Stephens [1881–5] All ER Rep 61, Queen's Bench Division (Lord Coleridge CJ, Grove and Denman JJ, Pollock and Huddleston BB)

The two accused, with a third man and the deceased, a 17 year old boy, were cast away in an open boat, 1,600 miles from land. When they had been eight days without food and six days without water, the accused killed the boy, who was weak and unable to resist but did not assent to being killed. The men fed upon his body and blood for four days when they were picked up by a passing vessel. At the trial for murder, the jury found by a special verdict that if the men had not fed upon the boy they would probably not have survived the four days; that the boy was likely to have died first; that at the time of the act there was no reasonable prospect of relief; that it appeared to the accused that there was every probability that they would die of starvation unless one of the castaways was killed; that there was no appreciable chance of saving life except by killing; but that there was no greater necessity for killing the boy than any of the three men. The finding of the jury was referred to the Queen's Bench Division for its decision.

[Lord Coleridge CJ, having referred to the special verdict continued:]

. . . this is clear, that the prisoners put to death a weak and unoffending boy upon the chance of preserving their own lives by feeding upon his flesh and blood after he was killed, and with a certainty of depriving him of any possible chance of survival. The verdict finds in terms that: 'if the men had not fed upon the body of the boy, they would probably not have survived . . .' and that 'the boy, being in a much weaker condition, was likely to have died before them.' They might possibly have been picked up next day by a passing ship; they might possibly not have been picked up at all; in either case it is obvious that the killing of the boy would have been an unnecessary and profitless act. It is found by the verdict that the boy was incapable of resistance, and, in fact, made none; and it is not even suggested that his death was due to any violence on his part attempted against, or even so much as feared by, them who killed him . . . .

[His Lordship dealt with objections taken by counsel for the prisoners which do not call for report, and continued.]

First, it is said that it follows, from various definitions of murder in books of authority—which definitions imply, if they do not state, the doctrine—that, in order to save your own life you may lawfully take away the life of another, when the other is neither attempting nor threatening yours, nor is guilty of any illegal act whatever towards you or anyone else. But, if these definitions be looked at, they will not be found to sustain the contention. The earliest in point of date is the passage cited to us from Bracton, who wrote in the reign of Henry III . . . . But in the very passage as to necessity, on which reliance has been placed, it is clear that Bracton is speaking of necessity in the ordinary sense, the repelling by violence—violence justified so far as it was necessary for the object—any illegal violence used towards oneself. If, says Bracton (Lib iii, Art De Corona, cap 4, fol 120), the necessity be *'evitabilis et evadere posset absque occisione, tunc erit reus homicidii'*—words which show clearly that he is thinking of physical danger, from which escape may be possible, and that *'inevitabilis necessitas,'* of which he speaks as justifying homicide, is a necessity of the same nature.

It is, if possible, yet clearer that the doctrine contended for receives no support from the great authority of Lord Hale. It is plain that in his view the necessity which justifies homicide is that only which has always been, and is now, considered a justification. He says (1 Hale, PC 491):

'In all these cases of homicide by necessity, as in pursuit of a felon, in killing him that assaults to rob, or comes to burn or break a house, or the like, which are in themselves no felony.'

Again, he says that the necessity which justifies homicide is of two kinds:

'(1) That necessity which is of private nature; (2) That necessity which relates to the public justice and safety. The former is that necessity which obligeth a man to his own defence and safeguard; and this takes in these inquiries: 1.   What may be done for the safeguard of a man's own life;'

and then follow three other heads not necessary to pursue. Lord Hale proceeds (1 Hale PC 478):

'1. As touching the first of these, viz, homicide in defence of a man's own life, which is usually styled se defendendo.'

It is not possible to use words more clear to show that Lord Hale regarded the private necessity which justified, and alone justified, the taking the life of another for the safeguard of one's own to be what is commonly called self-defence. But if this could be even doubtful upon Lord Hale's words, Lord Hale himself has made it clear, for, in the chapter in which he deals with the exemption created by compulsion or necessity, he thus expresses himself (1 Hale PC 51):

'If a man be desperately asaulted, and in peril of death, and cannot otherwise escape, unless to satisfy his assailant's fury he will kill an innocent person then present, the fear and actual force will not acquit him of the crime and punishment of murder if he commit the fact, for he ought rather to die himself than to kill an innocent; but if he cannot otherwise save his own life, the law permits him in his own defence to kill the assailant, for, by the violence of the assault and the offence committed upon him by the assailant himself, the law of nature and necessity hath made him his own protector *cum debito moderamine inculpatae tutelae.'*

But, further still, Lord Hale, in the following chapter (1 Hale PC 54), deals with the position asserted by the casuists, and sanctioned, as he says by Grotius and Puffendorf, that in a case of extreme necessity, either of hunger or clothing,

'theft is no theft, or at least not punishable as theft, and some even of our own lawyers have asserted the same; but I take it that here in England that rule, at least by the laws of England, is false, and, therefore, if a person, being under necessity for want of victuals or clothes, shall upon the account clandestinely and *animo furandi* steal another man's goods, it is a felony and a crime by the laws of England punishable with death.'

If, therefore, Lord Hale is clear, as he is, that extreme necessity of hunger does not justify larceny, what would he have said to the doctrine that it justified murder?

It is satisfactory to find that another great authority, second probably only to Lord Hale, speaks with the same unhesitating clearness on this matter. [His Lordship referred to *Foster's Discourse on Homicide*, chapter 3, and other authorities.]

There remains the authority of Stephen J who both in his *Digest* (art 32) and in his *History of the Criminal Law* (vol 2, p 108) uses language perhaps wide enough to cover this case. The language is somewhat vague in both places, but it does not in either place cover this case of necessity, and we have the best authority for saying that it was not meant to cover it. If it had been necessary we must with true deference have differed from him; but it is satisfactory to know that we have, probably at least, arrived at no conclusion in which, if he had been a member of the court, he would have been unable to agree. Neither are we in conflict with any opinion expressed upon this subject by the learned persons who formed the commission for preparing the Criminal Code. They say on this subject:

'We are not prepared to suggest that necessity should in every case be a justification; we are equally unprepared to suggest that necessity should in no case be a defence. We judge it better to leave such questions to be dealt with when, if ever, they arise in practice by applying the principles of law to the circumstances of the particular case.'

It would have been satisfactory to us if these eminent persons could have told us whether the received definitions of legal necessity were, in their judgment, correct and exhaustive, and, if not, in what way they should be amended; but as it is we have, as they say, 'to apply the principles of law to the circumstances of this particular case.'

It is admitted that the deliberate killing of this unoffending and unresisting boy was clearly murder, unless the killing can be justified by some well-recognised excuse admitted by the law. It is further admitted that there was in this case no such excuse, unless the killing was justified by what has been called necessity. But the temptation to the act which existed here was not what the law has ever called necessity. Nor is this to be regretted. Though law and morality are not the same, and though many things may be immoral which are not necessarily illegal, yet the absolute divorce of law from morality would be of fatal consequence, and such divorce would follow if the temptation to murder in this case were to be held by law an absolute defence of it. It is not so.

To preserve one's life is generally speaking, a duty, but it may be the plainest and the highest duty to sacrifice it. War is full of instances in which it is a man's duty not to live, but to die . . . . It is not correct, therefore, to say that there is any absolute and unqualified necessity to preserve one's life . . . . It it enough in a Christian country to remind ourselves of the Great Example which we profess to follow.

It is not needful to point out the awful danger of admitting the principle which has been contended for. Who is to be the judge of this sort of necessity? By what measure is the comparative value of lives to be measured? Is it to be strength, or intellect, or what? It is plain that the principle leaves to him who is to profit by it to determine the necessity which will justify him in deliberately taking another's life to save his own. In this case the weakest, the youngest, the most unresisting was chosen. Was it more necessary to kill *him* than one of the grown men? The answer be, No. . . .

There is no path safe for judges to tread but to ascertain the law to the best of their ability, and to declare it according to their judgment, and if in any case the law appears to be too severe on individuals, to leave it to the Sovereign to exercise that prerogative of mercy which the Constitution has entrusted to the hands fittest to dispense it. It must not be supposed that, in refusing to admit temptation to be an excuse for crime, it is forgotten how terrible the temptation was, how awful the suffering, how hard in such trials to keep the judgment straight and the conduct pure. We are often compelled to set up standards we cannot reach ourselves, and to lay down rules which we could not ourselves satisfy. But a man has no right to declare temptation to be an excuse, though he might himself have yielded to it, nor allow compassion for the criminal to change or weaken in any manner the legal definition of the crime. . . .

The Lord Chief Justice thereupon passed sentence of death in the usual form.[The prisoners were afterwards respited and their sentence commuted to one of six months' imprisonment without hard labour.]

Judgment for the Crown

Questions

1. Should it have been a defence if the boy had consented to die? Andanaes (GPCL of Norway, 171): 'Even though consent generally has no impunitive effect in murder ([Norwegian] Penal Code, s 236, para 2), the situation is different when there is both a necessity situation *and* consent.'

2. Should it be a defence that many lives would be saved by the sacrifice of one? Andanaes (GPCL of Norway, 169) thinks not: 'It would conflict with the general attitude towards the inviolability of human life to interfere in this way with the course of events.'

3. A is injured and needs an immediate blood transfusion to save his life. B is the only person who can be found with the same rare blood group. He refuses to give any blood. May B be overpowered and the blood taken without his consent?

4. Should the criminal law 'set up standards we [?reasonable men] cannot reach ourselves'? Cf *Lynch v Director of Public Prosecutions for Northern Ireland*, p 211, above.

See, on *Dudley and Stephens*, A.W.B. Simpson, *Cannibalism and the Common Law* (1984).

London Borough of Southwark v Williams [1971] 2 All ER 175, Court of Appeal, Civil Division
(Lord Denning MR, Edmund-Davies and Megaw LJJ)

The defendants, two homeless families, were unable to obtain housing. With the help of a squatters' association, they made an orderly entry into houses owned by the borough council. The council obtained an order for possession. The defendants appealed and relied, inter alia, on the defence of necessity.

Lord Denning MR. . . . I will next consider the defence of 'necessity'. There is authority for saying that in case of great and imminent danger, in order to preserve life, the law will permit of an encroachment on private property. That is shown by *Mouse's* case [(1608) 12 Co Rep 63], where the ferryman at Gravesend took 47 passengers into his barge to carry them to London. A great tempest arose and all were in danger. Mr Mouse was one of the passengers. He threw a casket belonging to the plaintiff overboard so as to lighten the ship. Other passengers threw other things. It was proved that, if they had not done so, the passengers would have been drowned. It was held by the whole court that 'in any case of necessity, for the safety of the lives of the passengers' it was lawful for Mr Mouse to cast the casket out of the barge. The court said it was like the pulling down of a house, in time of fire, to stop it spreading; which has always been held justified *pro bono publico*.

The doctrine so enunciated must, however, be carefully circumscribed. Else necessity would open the door to many an excuse. It was for this reason that it was not admitted in *Dudley and Stephens* [see p 219, above], where the three shipwrecked sailors, in extreme despair, killed the cabin-boy and ate him to save their own lives. They were held guilty of murder. The killing was not justified by necessity. Similarly, when a man who is starving enters a house and takes food in order to keep himself alive. Our English law does not admit the defence of necessity. It holds him guilty of larceny. Lord Hale said [Hale's *Pleas of the Crown*, i 54] that 'if a person, being under necessity for want of victuals or clothes, shall upon that account clandestinely, and *animus furandi*, steal another man's food, it is felony'. The reason is because, if hunger were once allowed to be an excuse for stealing, it would open a way through which all kinds of disorder and lawlessness would pass. So here. If homelessness were once admitted as a defence to trespass, no one's house could be safe. Necessity would open a door which no man could shut. It would not only be those in extreme need who would enter. There would be others who would imagine that they were in need, or would invent a need, so as to gain entry. Each man would say his need was greater than the next man's. The plea would be an excuse for all sorts of wrongdoing. So the courts must, for the sake of law and order, take a firm stand. They must refuse to admit the plea of necessity to the hungry and the homeless; and trust that their distress will be relieved by the charitable and the good. Applying these principles, it seems to me in the circumstances of these squatters are not such as to afford any justification or excuse in law for their entry into these houses. We can sympathise with the plight in which they find themselves. We can recognise the orderly way in which they made their entry. But we can go no further. They must make their appeal for help to others, not to us. . . .

[**Edmund-Davies LJ** delivered judgment dismissing the appeal and **Megaw LJ** agreed.]

Appeal dismissed

**Buckoke v Greater London Council [1971] 2 All ER 254, Court of Appeal,
Civil Division
(Lord Denning MR, Sachs and Buckley LJJ)**

The Chief Officer of the London Fire Brigade issued brigade order 144/8 which pointed out that drivers were obliged to obey traffic lights but stated that a driver responding to an emergency call must observe certain conditions if he decided to proceed against a red light when responding to an emergency call; that the onus of avoiding an accident was on the driver; and that no call was so urgent as to justify the risk of a collision preventing the vehicle from reaching its destination and perhaps blocking the road for other essential services. The Fire Brigades Union objected to the order on the ground that it encouraged drivers to break the law. Twenty firemen (the plaintiffs) refused to travel with drivers who would not give an assurance that they would never cross a red light. Disciplinary proceedings were taken against the plaintiffs who sought an injunction restraining the disciplinary proceedings and requiring the order to be countermanded. Plowman J refused the injunction.

[**Lord Denning MR**, having held that on a strict reading of the statute a fireman is bound to obey traffic lights like anyone else; and pointing out that, while there is a statutory exemption from the speed limit, there is no exemption from traffic lights, continued:]

The defence of necessity
During the argument I raised the question: might not the driver of a fire engine be able to raise the defence of necessity? I put this illustration. A driver of a fire engine with ladders approaches the traffic lights. He sees 200 yards down the road a blazing house with a man at an upstairs window in extreme peril. The road is clear in all directions. At that moment the lights turn red. Is the driver to wait for 60 seconds, or more, for the lights to turn green? If the driver waits for that time, the man's life will be lost. I suggested to both counsel that the driver might be excused in crossing the lights to save the man. He might have the defence of necessity. Both counsel denied it. They would not allow him any defence in law. The circumstances went to mitigation, they said and did not take away his guilt. If counsel are correct—and I accept that they are—nevertheless such a man should not be prosecuted. He should be congratulated.

Mitigating the rigour of the law
Accepting that the law, according to the strict letter of it, does compel every driver to stop at the red light, no matter how great the emergency, even when there is no danger, then the question arises: can the chief officer of the fire brigade issue an order authorising his men to depart from the letter of the law?

This raises an important question. It is a fundamental principle of our constitution, enshrined in the Bill of Rights (1688), that no one, not even the Crown itself, has the 'power of dispensing with laws or the execution of laws'. But this is subject to some qualification. When a law has become a dead letter, the police need not prosecute. Nor need the justices punish. They can give an absolute discharge. So also when there is a technical breach of the law in which it would be unjust to inflict any punishment whatever. The commissioner of police may properly in such a case make a policy decision directing his men not to proceed: see *R v Metropolitan Police, ex parte Blackburn* [1968] 2 QB 118 at 136; [1968] 1 All ER 763 at 769 where it was said that a chief officer of police can 'make policy decisions and give effect to them, as, for instance, was often done when prosecutions were not brought for attempted suicide'. So in this case, I have no doubt that the commissioner of police could give directions to his men—he may indeed have done so, for aught I know—that they need not prosecute when the driver of a fire engine crosses the lights, so long as he uses all care and there is no danger to others. This would be a justifiable policy decision so as to mitigate the strict rigour of the law. If any police officer, notwithstanding this direction, should prosecute for this technical offence, I would expect the justices to give the driver an absolute discharge under s 7 of the Criminal Justice Act 1948. Thus by administrative action, backed by judicial decision, an exemption is grafted on to the law. . . .

Sachs and Buckley LJJ delivered judgments dismissing the appeal.

Appeal dismissed

Questions

1. Lord Denning said 'we have grafted an exception on to the strictness of the law so as to mitigate the rigour of it'. Is this case an authority in favour of, or against a defence of necessity in the criminal law?

2. Even if a general defence of necessity exists, it is capable of exclusion by statute. Since legislation then exempted fire engines from speed limits but not from traffic lights, was not such a defence impliedly excluded? (The Traffic Signs Regulations and General Directions 1975 (SI 1975 No 1536), reg 34 (1)(b) now provides a qualified exemption from compliance with traffic lights for fire brigade, ambulance or police vehicles.)

R v Bourne [1939] 1 KB 687, [1938] 3 All ER 615, Central Criminal Court (Macnaghten J)

A young girl, not quite fifteen years of age, was pregnant as the result of rape. A surgeon of the highest skill, openly, in one of the London hospitals, without fee, performed the operation of abortion. He was charged under the Offences against the Person Act 1861, s 58, with unlawfully procuring the abortion of the girl.

[**Macnaghten J** directed the jury as follows:] . . .

The question that you have got to determine is whether the Crown has proved to your satisfaction beyond reasonable doubt that the act which Mr Bourne admittedly did was not done in good faith for the purpose only of preserving the life of the girl. If the Crown has failed to satisfy you of that, Mr Bourne is entitled, by the law of this land, to a verdict of acquittal. On the other hand, if you are satisfied beyond all real doubt that Mr Bourne did not do it in good faith for the purpose only of preserving the life of the girl, your verdict should be a verdict of guilty.

There has been much discussion before you as to the meaning of the words 'preserving the life of the mother'. I will deal with that in a moment, but, before doing so, I fully agree with the criticism of Mr Oliver that the Infant Life (Preservation) Act 1929, is dealing with the case—indeed, I think I explained it to you yesterday—where the child is killed while it is being delivered from the body of the mother. It provides that no one is to be found guilty of the offence created by the Act—namely, 'child destruction'—unless it is proved that:

> '. . . the act which caused the death of the child was not done in good faith for the purpose only of preserving the life of the mother'.

Those words express what, in my view, has always been the law with regard to the procuring of an abortion, and, although not expressed in s 58 of the Act of 1861, they are implied by the word 'unlawful' in that section. No person ought to be convicted under s 58 of the Act of 1861 unless the jury are satisfied the act was not done in good faith for the purpose only of preserving the life of the mother. My view is that it has always been the law that, on a charge of procuring abortion, the Crown have got to prove that the act was not done in good faith for the purpose of preserving the life of the mother. It is said—and, I think, rightly—that this is a case of great importance to the public, and more especially to the medical profession, but you will observe that it has nothing to do with the ordinary cases of procuring abortion to which I have already referred. In those cases, the operation is performed by a person of no skill, with no medical qualifications, and there is no pretence that it is done for the preservation of the mother's life. Cases of that sort are in no way affected by the consideration of the question that is put before you. In the ordinary cases, no question of that sort can arise. It is obvious that that defence could not be available to the professional abortionist. As I say, you have heard a great deal of discussion as to the difference between danger to life and danger to health. It may be that you are more fortunate than I am, but I confess that I have felt great difficulty in understanding what the discussion really meant. Life depends upon health, and it may be that health is so gravely impaired that death results. There was one question that was asked by the Attorney-General in the course of his cross-examination of Mr Bourne, where the matter was put thus:

'I suggest to you, Mr Bourne, that there is a perfectly clear line—there may be border-line cases—there is a clear line of distinction between danger to health and danger to life?'

That is the question that the Attorney-General put, and he assumes that it is so. Is it? Of course there are maladies that are a danger to health without being a danger to life. Rheumatism, I suppose, is not a danger to life, but a danger to health. Cancer is plainly a danger to life. But is there a perfectly clear line of distinction between danger to life and danger to health? I should have thought not. I should have thought that impairment of health might reach a stage where it was a danger to life. The answer of Mr Bourne was:

'I cannot agree without qualifying it. I cannot say just yes or no. I can say there is a large group whose health may be damaged, but whose life almost certainly will not be sacrificed. There is another group at the other end whose life will be definitely in very great danger'.

Then he added:

'There is a large body of material between those two extremes in which it is not really possible to say how far life will be in danger, but we find, of course, that the health is depressed to such an extent that their life is shortened, such as in cardiac cases, so that you may say that their life is in danger, because death might occur within measurable distance of the time of their labour.'

He is speaking of a case such as this. If that is a view which commends itself to you, so that you cannot say that there is this division into two separate classes with a dividing line between them, then it may be that you will accept the view that Mr Oliver put forward when he invited you to give to the words 'for the purpose of preserving the life of the mother' a wide and liberal view of their meaning. I would prefer the word 'reasonable' to the words 'wide and liberal'. Take a reasonable view of the words 'for the preservation of the life of the mother'. I do not think that it is contended that those words mean merely for the preservation of the life of the mother from instant death. There are cases, we were told—and indeed I expect you know cases from your own experience—where it is reasonably certain that a woman will not be able to deliver the child with which she is pregnant. In such a case, where the doctor expects, baseing his opinion upon the experience and knowledge of the profession, that the child cannot be delivered without the death of the mother, in those circumstances the doctor is entitled—and, indeed, it is his duty—to perform this operation with a view to saving the life of the mother, and in such a case it is obvious that the sooner the operation is performed the better. The law is not that the doctor has got to wait until the unfortunate woman is in peril of immediate death and then at the last moment snatch her from the jaws of death. He is not only entitled, but it is his duty, to perform the operation with a view to saving her life.

Here let me diverge for one moment to touch upon a matter that has been mentioned to you—namely, the various views which are held by different people with regard to this operation. Apparently there is a great divergence of view even in the medical profession itself. Some there may be, for all I know, who hold the view that the fact that the woman desires the operation to be performed is a sufficient justification for it. That is not the law. The desire of a woman to be relieved of her pregnancy is not justification for performing the operation. On the other hand, no doubt there are people who, from what are said to be religious reasons, object to the operation being performed at all, in any circumstances. That is not the law either. On the contrary, a person who holds such an opinion ought not to be a doctor practising in that branch of medicine, for, if a case arose where the life of the woman could be saved by performing the operation and the doctor refused to perform it because of some religious opinion, and the woman died, he would be in grave peril of being brought before this court on a charge of manslaughter by negligence. He would have no better defence than would a person who, again for some religious reason, refused to call in a doctor to attend his child, where a doctor could have been called in and the life of the child saved. If the father, for a so-called religious reason, refused to call in a doctor, he also would be answerable to the criminal law for the death of his child. I mention those two extreme cases merely to show that the law—whether or not you think it a reasonable law is immaterial—lies at any rate between those two. It does not permit of the termination of pregnancy except for the purpose of preserving the life of the mother. As I have said, I think that those words ought to be construed in a reasonable sense, and, if the doctor is of opinion, on reasonable grounds and with adequate knowledge, that the probable consequence of the continuance of the pregnancy will be to make the woman a physical or mental wreck, the jury are quite entitled to take the view that the doctor, who, in those circumstances, and in that honest belief, operates, is operating for the purpose of preserving the life of the woman. . . . (The jury found the accused not guilty.)

Questions

1. Was Macnaghten J applying a defence of necessity?
2. Why was Macnaghten J so concerned about interpreting the words, 'for the purpose only of preserving the life of the mother,' since they did not appear in the statute under consideration?
3. Consider the Abortion Act 1967, p 563, below. D, a doctor, procures an abortion because E is holding a pistol at his head. There is no other justification for the abortion. Is D guilty of an offence under s 58? (See particularly s 5 (2) of the Abortion Act 1967.)
4. D is a former medical practitioner who was disqualified for immoral conduct. While on holiday in a remote place he was called to a cottage to see a pregnant woman. He formed the opinion—and the opinion was well-founded—that an immediate abortion was necessary in order to preserve the life of the mother. There was no time to summon other aid. He performed the operation with skill and the woman's life was saved. Is D guilty of an offence under s 58?
5. If necessity would justify the doing of a particular act, does it follow that there is a *duty* to do that act? Would Bourne have been guilty of an offence if he had declined to perform the operation and the girl had died or suffered serious bodily harm? Cf. Abortion Act 1967, s 4, p 564, below.

Perka et al v The Queen (1984) 13 DLR (4th) 1, Supreme Court of Canada

The accused were charged with possession of narcotics. They raised the defence of necessity, alleging that their cargo of of marijuana was destined for Alaska and that problems with the vessel and deteriorating weather caused them to make for the Canadian shore where the ship ran aground. Fearing that the vessel was about to capsize, the captain ordered the men to off-load the cargo. The defence was left to the jury and the accused were acquitted but an appeal was allowed by the British Columbia Court of Appeals. On appeal to the Supreme Court the Crown contended that the trial judge erred in leaving the defence of necessity to the jury. The Supreme Court dismissed the appeal.

Dickson J. . . . . I retain the scepticism I expressed in *Morgentaler*, supra, at p 497 CCC, p 209 DLR, p 678 SCR. It is still my opinion that, '[n]o system of positive law can recognize any principle which would entitle a person to violate the law because on his view the law conflicted with some higher social value'. The *Criminal Code* has specified a number of identifiable situations in which an actor is justified in committing what would otherwise be a criminal offence. To go beyond that and hold that ostensibly illegal acts can be validated on the basis of their expediency, would import an undue subjectivity into the criminal law. It would invite the courts to second-guess the Legislature and to assess the relative merits of social policies underlying criminal prohibitions. Neither is a role which fits well with the judicial function. Such a doctrine could well become the last resort of scoundrels and, in the words of Edmund Davies LJ in *Southwark London Borough Council v Williams et al*, [1971] Ch 734 [at p 746], it could 'very easily become simply a mask for anarchy'.

Conceptualized as an 'excuse', however, the residual defence of necessity is, in my view, much less open to criticism. It rests on a realistic assessment of human weakness, recognizing that a liberal and humane criminal law cannot hold people to the strict obedience of laws in emergency situations where normal human instincts, whether of self-preservation or of altruism, overwhelmingly impel disobedience. The objectivity of the criminal law is preserved; such acts are still wrongful, but in the circumstances they are excusable. Praise is indeed not bestowed, but pardon is, when one does a wrongful act under pressure which, in the words of Aristotle in *The Nicomachean Ethics* (translator Rees, p 49), 'overstrains human nature and which no one could withstand'.

George Fletcher, *Rethinking Criminal Law*, describes this view of necessity as 'compulsion of circumstances' which description points to the conceptual link between necessity as an excuse and the familiar criminal law requirement that in order to engage criminal liability, the actions constituting the *actus reus* of an offence must be voluntary. Literally, this voluntariness requirement simply refers to the need that the prohibited physical acts must have been under the conscious control of the actor. Without such control, there is, for purposes of the criminal law, no act. The excuse of necessity does not go to voluntariness in this sense. The lost Alpinist who, on the point of freezing to death, breaks open an isolated mountain cabin is not literally behaving in an involuntary fashion. He has control over his actions to the extent of being physically capable of abstaining from the act. . . .

Realistically, however, his act is not a 'voluntary' one. His 'choice' to break the law is no true choice at all; it is remorselessly compelled by normal human instincts. This sort of involuntariness is often described as 'moral or normative involuntariness'. Its place in criminal theory is described by Fletcher at pp 804–5 as follows:

'The notion of voluntariness adds a valuable dimension to the theory of excuses. That conduct is involuntary—even in the normative sense—explains why it cannot fairly be punished. Indeed, HLA Hart builds his theory of excuses on the principle that the distribution of punishment should be reserved for those who voluntarily break the law. Of the arguments he advances for this principle of justice, the most explicit is that it is preferable to live in a society where we have the maximum opportunity to choose whether we shall become the subject of criminal liability. In addition Hart intimates that it is ideologically desirable for the government to treat its citizens as self-actuating, choosing agents. This principle of respect for individual autonomy is implicitly confirmed whenever those who lack an adequate choice are excused for their offenses.'

I agree with this formulation of the *rationale* for excuses in the criminal law. In my view, this *rationale* extends beyond specific codified excuses and embraces the residual excuse known as the defence of necessity. At the heart of this defence is the perceived injustice of punishing violations of the law in circumstances in which the person had no other viable or reasonable choice available; the act was wrong but it is excused because it was realistically unavoidable.

Punishment of such acts, as Fletcher notes at p 813, can be seen as purposeless as well as unjust:

'. . . involuntary conduct cannot be deterred and therefore it is pointless and wasteful to punish involuntary actors. This theory . . . of pointless punishment, carries considerable weight in current Anglo-American legal thought.'

Relating necessity to the principle that the law ought not to punish involuntary acts leads to a conceptualization of the defence that integrates it into the normal rules for criminal liability rather than constituting it as a *sui generis* exception and threatening to engulf large portions of the criminal law. Such a conceptualization accords with our traditional legal, moral and philosophic views as to what sorts of acts and what sorts of actors ought to be punished. In this formulation it is a defence which I do not hesitate to acknowledge and would not hesitate to apply to relevant facts capable of satisfying its necessary prerequisites.

[His Honour considered the limitations on the defence and continued:]

(f) *Preliminary conclusions as to the defence of necessity*

It is now possible to summarize a number of conclusions as to the defence of necessity in terms of its nature, basis and limitations:

(1) the defence of necessity could be conceptualized as either a justification or an excuse;
(2) it should be recognized in Canada as an excuse, operating by virtue of s 7(3) of the *Criminal Code*;
(3) necessity as an excuse implies no vindication of the deeds of the actor;
(4) the criterion is the moral involuntariness of the wrongful action;
(5) this involuntariness is measured on the basis of society's expectation of appropriate and normal resistance to pressure;
(6) negligence or involvement in criminal or immoral activity does not disentitle the actor to the excuse of necessity:
(7) actions or circumstances which indicate that the wrongful deed was not truly involuntary do disentitle;
(8) the existence of a reasonable legal alternative similarly disentitles; to be involuntary the act must be inevitable, unavoidable and afford no reasonable opportunity for an alternative course of action that does not involve a breach of the law;
(9) the defence only applies in circumstances of imminent risk where the action was taken to avoid a direct and immediate peril;

(10)   where the accused places before the court sufficient evidence to raise the issue, the onus is on the Crown to meet it beyond a reasonable doubt.

4. Reform of the law

'Necessity' by Glanville Williams [1978] Crim LR 128

The Law Commission, pursuing the goal of a criminal code on a piecemeal basis, makes two proposals on the defence of necessity [Law Com No 83, Part IV]. First, that no attempt should be made to establish the defence by legislation. Secondly, that the proposed Act should expressly abolish any such defence as may exist at common law. The second proposal is much the more surprising, and it is conveniently considered first.

The second proposal seems to exhibit a misunderstanding of the rationale of codification. This is to enable the citizen to know (at least if he takes legal advice) what conduct is penalised, so that he may not have to guess whether what he does is punishable. There will always be a degree of uncertainty in the application of the law, but the object is to take from the courts their powers of extending the area of legal prohibition except to the extent that these powers are inherent in the judicial process. Of late years the courts have themselves surrendered their power to add to offences under the head of public mischief, but they retain the power of extensive interpretation of common law crimes of vague ambit, like public mischief and the corruption of public morals. Reducing these offences to statutory form will clarify them one way or the other.

It by no means follows that it should be any part of the purpose of a code to get rid of open-ended defences, or to fetter the power of the courts to create new defences in the name of the common law. That the courts have power to enlarge defences is sometimes denied by the judges, just as they deny in terms their power to enlarge offences; but history records some examples of the former activity as well as innumerable examples of the latter.

The Draft Code of 1879 recognised this distinction of policy. It contained two sections (5 and 19), one removing the power of the judges to create new crimes and the other preserving judicial creativity in respect of justifications and excuses. The proposal was immediately criticised by Cockburn LCJ on the ground that the arguments for exhaustive codification of offences applied equally to defences. Stephen, the architect of the code, replied to this criticism in a notable article. [See the Nineteenth Century for January 1880, pp 152–157. I am indebted to Sir Rupert Cross for calling my attention to this article.] He first distinguished two meanings of the term 'common law': a body of relatively fixed principles resulting from judicial decisions, and the qualified power of the judges to make new law under the fiction of declaring existing law, or in other words 'not a part of the law actually existing, but law which has only a potential existence—that which, if the case should ever occur, the judges would declare to be the law.' Stephen thought it justifiable to save the common law in the second sense in respect of defences, though not in respect of offences. The central passage of his argument is worth quoting rather fully.

'It appears to me that the two proposed enactments stand on entirely different principles. After the experience of centuries, and with a Parliament sitting every year, and keenly alive to all matters likely to endanger the public interest, we are surely in a position to say the power of declaring new offences shall henceforth be vested in Parliament only. The power which has at times been claimed for the judges of declaring new offences cannot be useful now, whatever may have been its value in earlier times.

On the other hand it is hardly possible to foresee all the circumstances which might possibly justify or excuse acts which might otherwise be crimes. A long series of authorities have settled certain rules which can be put into a distinct and convenient form, and it is of course desirable to take the opportunity of deciding by the way minor points which an examination of the authorities shows to be still open. In this manner rules can be laid down as to the effect of infancy, insanity, compulsion, and ignorance of law, and also as to the cases in which force may lawfully be employed against the person of another; but is it therefore wise or safe to go so far as to say that no other circumstances than those expressly enumerated shall operate by way of excuse or justification for what would otherwise be a crime? To do so would be to run a risk, the extent of which it is difficult to estimate, of producing a conflict between the Code and the moral feelings of the public. Such a conflict is upon all possible grounds to be avoided. It would, if it occurred, do more to discredit codification than anything which could possibly happen, and it might cause serious evils of another kind. Cases sometimes occur in which public opinion is at once violently excited and greatly divided, so that conduct is regarded as criminal or praiseworthy according to the sympathies of excited partisans. If the Code provided that nothing should amount to an excuse or justification which was not within the express words of the Code, it would, in such a case, be vain to allege that the conduct of the accused person was justifiable; that, but for the Code, it would have been legally justifiable; that every legal analogy was in its favour; and that the omission of an express provision about it was probably an oversight. I think such a result would be eminently unsatisfactory. I think the public would feel that the allegations referred to ought to have been carefully examined and duly decided upon.

To put the whole matter very shortly, the reason why the common law definitions of offences should be taken away, whilst the common law principles as to justification and excuse are kept alive, is like the reason why the benefit of a doubt should be given to a prisoner. The worst result that could arise from the abolition of the common law offences would be the occasional escape of a person morally guilty. The only result which can follow from preserving the common law as to justification and excuse is, that a man morally innocent, not otherwise protected, may avoid punishment. In the one case you remove rusty spring-guns and man-traps from unfrequented plantations, in the other you decline to issue an order for the destruction of every old-fashioned drag or life-buoy which may be found on the banks of a dangerous river, but is not in the inventory of the Royal Humane Society. This indeed does not put the matter strongly enough. The continued existence of the undefined common law offences is not only dangerous to individuals, but may be dangerous to the administration of justice itself. By allowing them to remain, we run the risk of tempting the judges to express their disapproval of conduct which, upon political, moral, or social grounds, they consider deserving of punishment, by declaring upon slender authority that it constitutes an offence at common law; nothing, I think, could place the bench in a more invidious position, or go further to shake its authority. . . .

Besides the well-known matters dealt with by the Code, there are a variety of speculative questions which have been discussed by ingenious persons for centuries, but which could be raised only by such rare occurrences that it may be thought pedantic to legislate for them expressly beforehand, and rash to do so without materials which the course of events has not provided. Such cases are the case of necessity (two shipwrecked men on one plank), the case of a choice of evils (my horses are running away, and I can avoid running over A only by running over B), and some others which might be suggested. . . .

Any ingenious person may divert himself, as Hecato did, by playing with such questions. The Commission acted on the view that in practice the wisest answer to all of them is to say, 'When the case actually happens it shall be decided;' and this is effected by the preservation of such parts of the common law as to justification and excuse as are not embodied in the Code. Fiction apart, there is at present no law at all upon the subject, but the judges will make one under the fiction of declaring it, if the occasion for doing so should ever arise.'

The effect of abolishing the defence of necessity
The defence of necessity at present exists in the law under a number of disguises. The necessity to administer drugs with lethal effect in order to overcome extreme pain in terminal cases is disguised under the theory that when death occurs it is not a consequence of the administration of the drug. The theory will not stand examination, but the legal result must be secured somehow. Necessity can also come in under cover of doctrines of negligence and dishonesty, and in statutes containing saving phrases like 'without reasonable cause' and 'unlawfully.' An express abolition of the defence of necessity would not prevent it being recognised in these covert ways. But what about situations when these expedients fail?

Take as an example the one case in which necessity, or something indistinguishable from it, has been judicially recognised in modern times: *Johnson v Phillips* [1975] 3 All ER 682. (It perhaps says something about the attitude of the bench to legal defences that this solitary decision represents an acceptance of necessity as a reason not for acquitting but for convicting.) The defendant stopped his car behind an ambulance in a narrow one-way street, and refused to comply with the request of a police officer to reverse to the next street in order to allow for the passage of further ambulances to remove injured people. He was convicted of obstructing the officer in the execution of his duty; and the Divisional Court pointed out that it was the officer's duty to protect life and property, which justified the order even though it involved a breach of the letter of the law. On a narrow interpretation, the decision justifies the driver in reversing in such circumstances only when required to do so by the police. But is it seriously suggested that a driver would be guilty of an offence if he reversed on his own initiative in order to allow the passage of ambulances? And what defence could he possibly have under the present law except that of necessity? Is it really proposed that that defence should be taken away from him?

Take next the facts of a case in which the defence of necessity was not even raised. A passenger in a car who had gone to sleep in it in a state of intoxication woke to find the driver gone and the car coasting downhill. He steered it to the grass verge to avoid a possible collision, and for this was convicted of driving under the influence of drink. Do we expect such a person to remain passive while a fatal accident takes place? The Law Commission say that in respect of minor offences 'it would be preferable for no defence to be available,' but such a conclusion needs to be supported by far more convincing arguments than they have produced.

The draft Criminal Code Bill provides:

46   Defence of necessity
(1) Without prejudice to the generality of section 49, a person is not guilty of an offence when he does an act out of necessity, as defined in subsection (2).
(2) A person does an act out of necessity if:
(a) he does it believing that it is immediately necessary to avoid death or serious injury to himself or another; and
(b) the danger which he believes to exist is such that in all the circumstances (including any of his personal characteristics that affect its gravity) he could not reasonably be expected to act otherwise.
(3) This section does not apply:
(a) to a person who uses force for any of the purposes referred to in section 47(1) or 89; or
(b) to a person who acts in the belief that a threat of a kind described in section 45(2)(a)(i) (duress) has been made; or
(c) to a person who has knowingly and without reasonable excuse exposed himself to the danger.

The Report explains the clause as follows:

13.25 *Law Commission's Report.* The recommendations of the Law Commission in Law Com No 83, on the subject of necessity as a defence were, quite simply:

> 'There should be no general defence of necessity and, if any such general defence exists at common law, it should be abolished.' [(1974), Law Com No 83, para 6.4]

This was in striking contrast to the provisional proposals of the Law Commission's Working Party, who had made a case for a general defence available to a person who believes that his conduct is necessary to avoid some greater harm that he faces, that harm being 'out of all proportion' to the harm actually caused by his conduct. [Working Paper No 55; for summary of this provisional proposal, see para 57.] In view of the difficulties which the Law Commission found with this suggestion [Law Com No 83, 25–31], it would not be appropriate for us now to revive it; nor, in fact, do we wish to do so. On the other hand, the Commission's own negative proposals have attracted severe criticism. [See Williams [1978] Crim LR 128; Huxley, ibid. 141.] Two criticisms in particular will point the way towards our own suggested solution to the very difficult problem that necessity presents to a codifier.
(i) *The analogy with duress.* The impact of some situations of imminent peril upon persons affected by them is hardly different in kind from that of threats such as give rise to the defence of duress. The late Professor Cross was moved to describe the proposal to 'provide for a defence of duress while excluding any general defence of necessity' as 'the apotheosis of absurdity'. [28 Univ. of Toronto LJ 377 (cited by Williams, *Textbook of Criminal Law* 2nd ed (1983), 602)].
(ii) *Saving the common law.* The critics are agreed that, if there is to be no general defence of necessity, the power of the judges at common law to recognise a situation of necessity as affording a defence must be preserved. It will not do either to suppose that all offences can or will be so drafted as to incorporate all appropriate exceptions for cases of necessity, or to leave any residue of cases not taken care of in this way to the discretion of the prosecutor or the sentencing court. We have already referred [See above, para 13.10] to the case made by Stephen J a century ago, with particular reference to cases of necessity, for a Code provision allowing for the development of defences.
13.26 *The solution proposed.* Necessity is not a topic to which we can apply our normal procedure of restatement, for which the present law does not provide suitable material. [In particular, 'such reference to the defence as there has been in recent cases is either contradictory

or uncertain in effect' [Law Com No 83, para 4.1.] We cannot ourselves conduct a law reform exercise and propose a general defence of necessity of our own devising. And, as indicated above, we cannot support the Law Commission's totally negative proposals. In these circumstances our main proposal is that necessity should remain a matter of common law. That is, to the extent that the defence is now recognised, it should be unaffected by the Criminal Code Act; and (probably more important, because the present status of the defence is so limited and uncertain) the courts should retain the power that they now have to develop or clarify the defence. Necessity, that is to say, would fall within the general saving for common law defences declared by clause 49. Our only specific necessity provision is clause 46, which admits a defence in circumstances so closely analogous to those of the duress defence that it might indeed be 'the apotheosis of absurdity' to admit the one and to deny the other. The kind of situation catered for by clause 46 has, indeed, sometimes been called 'duress of circumstances'.

13.27 *Clause 46(1)* provides the phrase 'acting out of necessity' for use elsewhere. The opening words ('Without prejudice to the generality of section 49 . . . ') make clear that application or development of the necessity defence under clause 49 will not be 'inconsistent with this . . . Act' (see clause 49 (1) (b)). In this respect clause 46 deliberately differs from clause 45, which states the whole of the duress defence.

13.28 *Clause 46(2)* states the elements of the defence. Like duress, it is limited to cases where death or serious injury is threatened. The danger must be imminent. Like duress, the defence is limited 'by means of an objective criterion formulated in terms of reasonableness' [Per Lord Lane CJ in *R v Graham* [1982] 1 WLR 294 at 300]; though once again the standard of conduct required is that applicable to one having the actor's personal characteristics so far as they affect the gravity of the danger.

13.29 *Clause 46(3)*. Paragraphs (a) and (b) avoid the overlap between this and other defences that would otherwise occur. Paragraph (c) sustains the analogy with duress by excluding the case where the actor has knowingly and without reasonable excuse exposed himself to the danger.

5. The use of force in public or private defence

The draft Criminal Code Bill provides:

47 Use of force in public or private defence
(1) A person does not commit an offence by using such force as, in the circumstances which exist or which he believes to exist, is immediately necessary and reasonable:
(a) to prevent or terminate crime, or effect or assist in the lawful arrest of an offender or suspected offender or of a person unlawfully at large;
(b) to prevent or terminate a breach of the peace;
(c) to protect himself or any other person from unlawful force or unlawful injury;
(d) to prevent or terminate the unlawful imprisonment of himself or any other person;
(e) to protect property (whether belonging to himself or another) from unlawful appropriation, destruction or damage; or
(f) to prevent or terminate a trespass to his person or his property.
(2) In this section, except where the context otherwise requires, 'force' includes, in addition to force against a person:
(a) force against property;
(b) a threat of force against person or property; and
(c) the detention of a person without the use of force.
(3) For the purposes of this section, an act is ''unlawful'' notwithstanding that a person charged with an offence in respect of it would be acquitted on the ground only that he:
(a) was under ten years of age;
(b) lacked the fault required for the offence or believed that an exempting circumstance existed;
(c) was acting under duress or out of necessity; or
(d) was in a state of automatism or suffering from mental disorder.
(4) A breach of the peace occurs when, by unlawful violence, harm is done to a person, or in his presence to his property, or a person fears on reasonable grounds that unlawful violence likely to cause such harm is imminent.
(5) A person does not commit an offence by doing an act immediately preparatory to the use of such force as is referred to in subsection (1).
(6) Subsection (1)(c) applies also to the use of force to resist or prevent an act which is not unlawful where:

(a) the person using force believes it to be immediately necessary to prevent injury to himself or another; and

(b) the act to be resisted or prevented is not unlawful only because it is done in pursuance of a reasonable but mistaken suspicion or belief.

(7) A person who believes circumstances to exist which would otherwise justify or excuse the use of force under subsection (1) has no defence if:

(a) he knows that the force is used against a constable or a person assisting a constable; and

(b) the constable is acting in the execution of his duty,

unless he believes the force to be immediately necessary to prevent injury to himself or another.

(8) Where force is directed against a person's body, subsection (1) applies only if that person is or is believed to be the person to be arrested or a party to the act or state of affairs to be prevented or terminated.

(9) Subsection (1) does not apply where a person causes unlawful conduct or an unlawful state of affairs with a view to using force to resist or terminate it; but subsection (1) may apply although the occasion for the use of force arises only because he does anything he may lawfully do, knowing that such an occasion may arise.

(10) In determining whether the use of force by a person in defence of person or property was immediately necessary and reasonable, regard shall be had to any opportunity he had to retreat before using force.

(11) A threat of force may be reasonable although the use of the force would not be.

(12) This section is without prejudice to the generality of section 89 (criminal damage: protection of person or property) or any other special defence.

Schedule 1 of the Draft Bill provides the following illustrations:

47 (1)(a) and (c)	47 (i)	D shoots P who is about to attack him with a knife. If this action is necessary and reasonable to prevent P from killing or causing serious injury to D, D commits no offence, even though he is unaware that P is armed with a knife, or is about to attack.
	47 (ii)	D shoots P whom he believes to be about to attack him with a knife. If this action would have been necessary and reasonable to prevent P killing or causing serious injury to D, had D's belief been true, D commits no offence, even if P was unarmed, or was not in fact about to attack.
47 (1)(b) and (4)	47 (iii)	During a strike, D, a police constable, uses force to prevent P, one of a large number of strikers, from approaching a works entrance. If D's action is necessary and reasonable to prevent workers entering the premises from being put in fear of unlawful violence to themselves or their property, D commits no offence.
47 (3)(a)	47 (iv)	D, a shopkeeper, sees P, whom he knows to be under the age of 10, take a watch from the counter and run off with it. D seizes P and takes the watch from him by force. If it is necessary to use force to prevent P from appropriating the watch and the force used is reasonable, D commits no offence.
47 (3)(b)	47 (v)	D's tenant, P, is about to destroy certain fixtures in the leased premises. P wrongly believes that the fixtures belong to him. Although P lacks the fault for the offence of causing criminal damage to property belonging to another, D may use reasonable and necessary force to protect his property.
	47 (vi)	Wrongly believing that D is about to attack him, P makes what he believes to be a counter-attack on D. If P is using no more force than would be necessary and reasonable if the circumstances were as he believed them to be, he is not committing any offence; but D may use necessary and reasonable force to repel P's attack.
47 (3)(c)	47 (vii)	Believing that he will be killed if he does not obey orders to "knee-cap" D, P attempts to do so. Even if P would have a defence of duress to a charge of causing serious injury, D may use reasonable and necessary force in self-defence.
47 (5)	47 (viii)	P, an armed criminal, shoots a policeman who drops his revolver. D, a bystander, fearing that P is about to shoot him, picks up the revolver to use it in self-defence. D is not guilty of being in possession of a firearm without a firearm certificate; or of having with him an offensive weapon, contrary to the Prevention of Crime Act 1953.

47 (6)	47 (ix)	P, a police officer, reasonably but wrongly believing D to be an armed, dangerous criminal, X, points a revolver at him. D, believing that he is about to be shot, strikes P and severely injures him. If, in the light of D's belief, this action is necessary and reasonable to prevent injury to D, he commits no offence, even though P is acting lawfully and D knows that.
47 (7)	47 (x)	P, a constable, is arresting Q. D, who believes that P has no grounds for making the arrest, uses force against P to free Q. In fact P has reasonable grounds for suspecting that Q has committed an arrestable offence. D has no defence under this section to a charge of assault or causing injury.
	47 (xi)	As in (x), but D also believes that P is about to injure Q. If the force used by D would have been necessary and reasonable to prevent the apprehended injury to a person wrongfully arrested, D commits no offence.
47 (8)	47 (xii)	D, a police officer driving a patrol car in pursuit of a notorious rapist, crosses a pedestrian crossing against a red light and kills or injures a pedestrian. The facts that it is necessary to cross the light (ie, otherwise the rapist would escape) and that a jury might regard it as a reasonable thing to do, do not amount to a defence under this section to a charge involving proof of an intention to cause injury or serious injury to the person.
	47 (xiii)	A notorious rapist is making an escape in a car. D, a police constable, seeing no other way of preventing the rapist's escape, commandeers P's car, threatens P with his truncheon when P demurs, and rams the rapist's car causing damage to P's car. If this is necessary to prevent the rapist's escape and a reasonable thing to do. D commits no offence.
47 (9)	47 (xiv)	A gang of white youths, looking for a fight, shout taunts at a group of black youths until the black youths attack them. D, a white youth, is attacked by P, a black youth, with a knife. D, who also has a knife, stabs P and kills or injures him. D has no defence under subsection (1) to a charge of murder, manslaughter or causing injury.
	47 (xv)	Members of a political group, X, hold a lawful meeting. They know from experience that they are almost certain to be attacked by members of the rival group, Y. They are so attacked, and D, a member of the X group, kills or injures P, a member of the Y group. D may rely on subsection (1).

The Report explains the clause as follows:

13.30 This clause defines circumstances in which a person has a defence to a charge of committing a crime involving the use of force. It applies to the use of force against property as well as against the person, to threats of force and to the detention of a person without the use of force. The clause could be involved, for example, on a charge of murder or any violent offence against the person, or any offence of criminal damage to property.

13.31 The clause states principles of the criminal law. It does not (as section 3 of the Criminal Law Act 1967 does) affect civil liability in any way. A person may have a defence under the section yet remain liable in damages for assault or negligence.

13.32 The present law on the subject-matter of the clause is to be found in a variety of sources. Self-defence and the defence of others are governed by the common law as is the use of force to prevent a breach of the peace or a trespass. Defence of property is governed by the provisions of the Criminal Damage Act 1971; and the use of force in the prevention of crime by section 3 of the Criminal Law Act 1967.

13.33 The substance of the present law varies according to the circumstances in respects which are impossible to defend. If a person is charged with damaging property belonging to another and his defence is that he was defending his own property the Criminal Damage Act 1971 applies and the test is whether he *believed* that what he did was reasonable; but if his defence is that he was defending his person, or that of another, the test at common law is whether what he did *was* reasonable. If he is charged with criminal damage by killing or injuring an aggressive dog, the test will vary according to whether he was defending his trousers or his leg—and he is likely to have a better chance of acquittal if it was his trousers. Clause 47 (together with clause 89) would eliminate such absurd distinctions by the application of a common principle to all cases of this kind.

13.34 *The principle.* Section 3 (1) of the Criminal Law Act 1967 provides that:

'A person may use such force as is reasonable in the circumstances in the prevention of crime, or in effecting or assisting in the lawful arrest of offenders or suspected offenders or of persons unlawfully at large.'

Where the use of force is reasonable in the circumstances the user commits no criminal offence or civil wrong. Where it is unreasonable, he is probably liable in tort but it does not follow that he commits a criminal offence because questions of *mens rea* arise in the criminal trial which are irrelevant in the civil proceedings. The case of *R v Gladstone Williams* [(1983) 78 Cr App R 276 CA] has established that a person charged with a crime has a defence of self-defence at common law if he uses such force as is reasonable *in the circumstance as he believes them to be* in the defence of himself or any other person. The court made it clear that the defence applies even though the use of that force was unreasonable in the actual circumstances; and even if the defendant's belief was not based on reasonable grounds. In so deciding the court held that a recommendation made by the Criminal Law Revision Committee for reform in fact represents the existing law. [Fourteenth Report (1980), Cmnd 7844, 119–122.] Clause 47 follows *Gladstone Williams* and the Committee by using the words, 'in the circumstances . . . which he believes to exist.'

13.35 *The 'Dadson principle'.* The test in *R v Gladstone Williams*, like that proposed in the Criminal Law Revision Committee's report, is stated exclusively in terms of the defendant's belief. As expressed, it would not apply where the defendant was unaware of existing circumstances which, if he knew of them, would justify his use of force. In this respect the test accords with that applied in *R v Dadson* [(1850) 2 Den 35; 169 ER 407]. The defendant was charged with shooting at P, an escaping felon, with intent to cause him grievous bodily harm. He was unaware of the facts constituting the felony. He argued unsuccessfully that the force was justifiable because it was used to arrest an escaping felon. The court held that the alleged felony, 'being unknown to the prisoner', constituted no justification.

13.36 *The Criminal Law Act 1967 and the Police and Criminal Evidence Bill.* On the other hand, section 2 (2) of the Criminal Law Act 1967 provides that:

'Where an arrestable offence has been committed, any person may arrest without warrant anyone who is, or whom he, with reasonable cause, suspects to be in the act of committing an arrestable offence.'

It seems clear that the arrest is lawful if the arrested person is in fact committing an arrestable offence, even though the arrester does not, with reasonable cause, suspect that he is doing so. The subsection provides alternative justifications. Subsection (3) (arrest where an arrestable offence has been committed) and (5) (arrest of person about to commit an arrestable offence) of the 1967 Act are in similar terms; and the dual nature of the justification for arrest is emphasised by the form of the Police and Criminal Evidence Bill, clause 21 (arrest without warrant for arrestable and other offences). These provisions, when read with section 3 of the 1967 Act [above, para 13.34], seem to exclude (and, we understand, were intended to exclude) the *Dadson* principle so far as force used to make an arrest in concerned. We think that there is much to be said in favour of the *Dadson* principle but that sections 2 and 3 of the Criminal Law Act 1967, reinforced by the Police and Criminal Evidence Bill, preclude us from adopting it so far as force used in making an arrest is concerned. We considered whether force used in making an arrest should be distinguished from the other cases but concluded that this is impracticable. A person making an arrest is frequently also acting in the prevention of crime; and a person acting in the prevention of crime is frequently also acting in self-defence or in the defence of others. To have different rules according to the purpose of the user of force when the purposes may be indistinguishable would defeat one of the primary objects of codification, namely the enactment of a consistent and coherent body of law. We therefore concluded that the *Dadson* principle must be excluded, throughout. This is achieved by subsection (1) which provides a defence if the force is immediately necessary and reasonable either in the circumstances which exist or in those which the defendant believes to exist.

13.37 *Necessity and reasonableness objectively determined,* The force used must be 'immediately necessary and reasonable' in the circumstances which exist or which the defendant believes to exist. The test of necessity and reasonableness is objective. This is in accordance with the Criminal Law Revision Committee's proposal [Fourteenth Report (1980), Cmnd 7844, 119–122] and *R v Gladstone Williams* [(1983) 78 Cr App R 276, CA]. It changes the law as stated in the Criminal Damage Act 1971, section 5. Under that section, the defendant has a lawful excuse if, when he destroys or damages property belonging to another, he believes that other property is in immediate need of protection and he believes that the means of protection adopted are reasonable having regard to all the circumstances; and it is immaterial whether his belief is justified or not if it is honestly held (section 5 (3)). Under that provision it is the defendant's judgment whether the force used was reasonable which governs. Under clause 47 it is the judgment of the court or jury. It is wrong in principle, in our view, for the law to afford greater protection to a person's trousers than his leg, or his spectacles than his eye. The special defence provided by clause 89 (defence of protection or property) [see below, para 16.15] is in some respects wider than provided by clause 47 but the test of 'necessary and reasonable' in that clause is also objective. . . .

13.45 *Clause 47(6).* This subsection provides for the case where force is lawfully but mistakenly used against an innocent person, and the defendant—the innocent person or someone coming to his defence—uses force which he believes to be immediately necessary to prevent injury to himself or the innocent third party, as the case may be. For example, P, a police officer, reasonably but wrongly believing D to be an armed, dangerous criminal, X, points a revolver at him. D seizes P's wrist and twists it until he drops the revolver. P's act is lawful in every sense. It is not a case within subsection (3) where P merely has a defence to a criminal charge. The effect of subsection (6) is that D is not guilty of an offence if he believes the use of force to be immediately necessary and if the force used is, in the circumstances which exist or which he believes to exist, immediately necessary and reasonable. This is so although D is aware of all the circumstances giving rise to P's reasonable suspicion. (If he were not aware of those circumstances, he could simply rely on subsection (1)—the force would, in the circumstances which he *believed* to exist, be used to prevent *unlawful* injury.)

13.46 We have found no authority for this proposition. There is, indeed, a dictum to the contrary [per *Lowry LCJ* in *R v Browne* [1973] NI 96 at 107]; but it seems right in principle that an innocent person should not commit an offence by using reasonable and necessary force to prevent injury to himself. The subsection would leave entirely open the question of civil liability. . . .

13.49 *Clause 47(7).* This subsection limits the defence where the force is used against a person known to be a constable or a person assisting a constable. If the defendant, because of a mistake of fact, believes the constable is acting outside the execution of his duty, he would, but for this subsection, be entitled to use reasonable force to resist. The subsection is therefore necessary to incorporate the effect of *R v Fennell* [[1971] 1 QB 428, p 383, below].

If the constable is in fact acting in the execution of his duty the defendant may not use force to resist unless he believes circumstances to exist which (but for this subsection) would justify the use of force *and* he believes the force to be immediately necessary to prevent injury to himself or another. The principle underlying *Fennell* appears to be that the citizen should submit to arrest and other acts which are unlikely to cause injury and which are done by a policeman in the execution of his duty, even if the citizen believes them to be unlawful. If he uses force to resist arrest, he does so at his peril if it turns out that the constable is acting in the execution of his duty.

13.50 *Clause 47(8).* This subsection offers a solution to a point on which there appears to be little authority. To what extent should a person acting in the prevention of crime, etc, be immune from conviction where he causes injury to an innocent person or his property? Section 3 of the Criminal Law Act 1967 is not, in terms, confined to the use of force against a person acting unlawfully. Is a constable, pursuing an offender, entitled to knock down an innocent person who inadvertently gets in his way? Or to seize an innocent person's car to make a road block to stop escaping bank robbers?

13.51 Section 2(6) of the Criminal Law Act 1967 provides that:

> 'For the purposes of arresting a person under any power conferred by this section a constable may enter (if need be, by force) and search any place where that person is or where the constable, with reasonable cause, suspects him to be.'

If force used in accordance with this subsection damages the property of an innocent third party, it appears that the constable will commit no civil or criminal offence. If an innocent person's house is not immune from reasonable and necessary damage done by an arresting officer it would be surprising if his personal property were immune.

13.52 In principle it seems obviously right that the police, or anyone else, should not be guilty of an offence of damage to property if it is necessary to cause that damage to save an innocent person from death or serious injury at the hands of a criminal. This would in any event be covered by clause 46 (defence of necessity) but damage done to prevent lesser harms would not. Subsection (8), by implication, leaves it open to the courts to hold that damage to property or a threat of force against the person is excused as being necessary and reasonable for the purposes mentioned in subsection (1). This would leave entirely open the question of civil liability. The subsection would, however, exclude the defence where force was directed against an innocent person. We recognise that this is a controversial proposal and will require further discussion, particularly as it would inevitably imply that the person using force would also be civilly liable. It would mean that a police officer would be guilty of battery if he pushed aside a pedestrian who happened to be in his way while he was pursuing a dangerous criminal.

13.53 *Clause 47(9)*. In *R v Browne* [[1973] NI 96 at 107] Lowry LCJ said, with regard to self-defence:

> 'The need to act must not have been created by the conduct of the accused in the immediate context of the incident which was likely or intended to give rise to that need,'

It is clearly right that a person should not be able to invoke the defence if he has deliberately provoked the attack with a view to using force to resist or terminate it; and subsection (9) so provides. It seems to be going too far, however, to say that the defendant may not act in self-defence because his conduct was likely (or even foreseen to be likely) to give rise to that need. This part of the dictum would infringe the important principle of *Beatty v Gillbanks* [(1882) 9 QBD 308], and is not followed. Instead, that principle is preserved by the second part of the subsection. When the Salvation Army embarked on their famous march they must have known well enough that they were likely to be attacked by the Skeleton Army. They were nevertheless entitled to march and presumably to defend themselves if unlawfully attacked. In *R v Field* [[1972] Crim LR 435] it was held that a person is not deprived of his right to self-defence because he goes to a place where he may lawfully go, knowing that he is likely to be attacked. The underlying principle appears to be a general one—there is no reason why the right should be confined to taking part in processions or going to particular places; so the subsection applies to anything that the person relying on the defence may lawfully do.

13.54 The effect of the subsection as a whole then is that the defendant may not rely on the defence if it was his purpose to provoke an attack; but he may do so if this was not his purpose even if he knew that he would almost certainly be attacked.

13.55 *Clause 47(10)*. This subsection states the law as laid down in *R v McInnes* [[1971] 1 WLR 1600 CA]. It does not require as a condition of the defence that the defendant 'must demonstrate that he is prepared to temporise and disengage and perhaps to make some physical withdrawal', as stated in *R v Julien* [[1969] 1 WLR 839. The dictum in *Julien* has since been disapproved in *Bird* [1985] 2 All ER 513, CA]. The circumstances in which force is used in self-defence may vary greatly and sometimes there will be no question of 'temporising'. The only way to deal with this matter seems to be to leave it to the court or jury to determine whether it was reasonable, in the light of all the circumstances of the case, to stand and fight.

13.56 *Clause 47(11)*. This subsection states the effect of *R v Cousins* [[1982] QB 526].

13.57 *Clause 47(12)*. The special defence to charges of offences of criminal damage provided by clause 89 (protection of person or property) overlaps the general defence provided by clause 47 and this subsection makes it clear that clause 89 is to be given its full effect.

**R v Gladstone Williams (1983) 78 Cr App Rep 276, Court of Appeal,
Criminal Division
(Lord Lane CJ, Skinner and McCowan JJ)**

One, M, saw a youth rob a woman in a street. He caught the youth who escaped and then caught him again and knocked him to the ground. The youth was calling for help. The appellant who saw only the later stages of the incident, intervened. M said, falsely, that he was a police officer but was unable to produce a warrant card when the appellant requested it. The appellant punched M, as he said, to save the youth from further beating. He was charged with assault occasioning actual bodily harm. The recorder directed the jury that the appellant might have an excuse if he had a belief based on reasonable grounds that M was acting unlawfully.

[**Lord Lane CJ**, having held that the recorder had failed to make it clear that the onus of proof was on the prosecution to eliminate the possibility that the appellant was acting under a mistake of fact:]

. . . we turn to consider the second point.

One starts off with the meaning of the word 'assault.' 'Assault' in the context of this case, that is to say using the word as a convenient abbreviation for assault and battery, is an act by which the defendant, intentionally or recklessly, applies unlawful force to the complainant. There are circumstances in which force may be applied to another lawfully. Taking a few examples: first, where the victim consents, as in lawful sports, the application of force to another will, generally speaking, not be unlawful. Secondly, where the defendant is acting in self-defence: the exercise of any necessary and reasonable force to protect himself from unlawful violence is not unlawful. Thirdly, by virtue of section 3 of the Criminal Law Act 1967, a person may use such force as is reasonable in the circumstances in the prevention of crime or in effecting or assisting in the lawful arrest of an offender or suspected offender or persons unlawfully at large. In each of those cases the defendant will be guilty if the jury are sure that first of all he applied force to the person of another, and secondly that he had the necessary mental element to constitute guilt.

The mental element necessary to constitute guilt is the intent to apply unlawful force to the victim. We do not believe that the mental element can be substantiated by simply showing an intent to apply force and no more.

What then is the situation if the defendant is labouring under a mistake of fact as to the circumstances? What if he believes, but believes mistakenly, that the victim is consenting, or that it is necessary to defend himself, or that a crime is being committed which he intends to prevent? He must then be judged against the mistaken facts as he believes them to be. If judged against those facts or circumstances the prosecution fail to establish his guilt, then he is entitled to be acquitted.

The next question is, does it make any difference if the mistake of the defendant was one which, viewed objectively by a reasonable onlooker, was an unreasonable mistake? In other words should the jury be directed as follows: 'Even if the defendant may have genuinely believed that what he was doing to the victim was either with the victim's consent or in reasonable self-defence or to prevent the commission of crime, as the case may be, nevertheless if you, the jury, come to the conclusion that the mistaken belief was unreasonable, that is to say that the defendant as a reasonable man should have realised his mistake, then you should convict him.'

It is upon this point that the large volume of historical precedent with which Mr Howard threatened us at an earlier stage is concerned. But in our judgment the answer is provided by the judgment of this Court in *Kimber* (1983) 77 Cr App R 225; [1983] 1 WLR 1118, by which, as already stated, we are bound. There is no need for me to rehearse the facts, save to say that that was a case of an alleged indecent assault upon a woman. Lawton LJ deals first of all with the case of *Albert v Lavin* (1981) 72 Cr App R 178; [1982] AC 546; then at p 229 and p 1122 of the respective reports:

> 'The application of the *Morgan* principle ((1975) 61 Cr App R 136; [1976] AC 182) to offences other than indecent assault on a woman will have to be considered when such offences come before the courts. We do, however, think it necessary to consider two of them because of what was said in the judgment. The first is a decision of the Divisional Court in *Albert v Lavin* (1981) 72 Cr App R 178; [1982] AC 546. The offence charged was assaulting a police officer in the execution of his duty, contrary to section 51 of the Police Act 1964. The defendant in his defence contended, inter alia, that he had not believed the police officer to be such and in consequence had resisted arrest. His counsel analysed the offence in the same way as we have done and referred to the reasoning in *Director of Public Prosecutions v Morgan*. Hodgson J delivering the leading judgment, rejected this argument and in doing so said, at p 190 and p 561 of the respective reports: "In my judgment Mr Walker's ingenious argument fails at an earlier stage. It does not seem to me that the element of unlawfulness can properly be regarded as part of the definitional elements of the offence. In defining a criminal offence the word 'unlawful' is surely tautologous and can add nothing to its essential ingredients. . . And no matter how strange it may seem that a defendant charged with assault can escape conviction if he shows that he mistakenly but unreasonably thought his victim was consenting but not if he was in the same state of mind as to whether his victim had a right to detain him, that in my judgment is the law." We have found difficulty in agreeing with this reasoning'—and I interpolate, so have we—'even though the judge seems to be accepting that belief in consent does entitle a defendant to an acquittal on a charge of assault. We cannot accept that the word 'unlawful' when used in a definition of an offence is to be regarded as 'tautologous.' In our judgment the word 'unlawful' does import an essential element into the offence. If it were not there social life would be unbearable, because every touching would amount to a battery unless there was an evidential basis for a defence. This case was considered by the House of Lords. The appeal was dismissed, but their Lordships declined to deal with the issue of belief.'

That is the end of the citation from *Kimber* supra in so far as it is necessary for the second point. I read a further passage from p 230 and p 1123 respectively which sets out the proper direction to the jury, and is relevant to the first leg of the appellant's argument in this case. It reads as follows: 'In our judgment the learned recorder should have directed the jury that the prosecution had to make them sure that the appellant never had believed that Betty was consenting. As he did not do so, the jury never considered an important aspect of his defence.'

We respectfully agree with what Lawton LJ said there with regard both to the way in which the defence should have been put and also with regard to his remarks as to the nature of the defence. The reasonableness or unreasonableness of the defendant's belief is material to the question of whether the belief was held by the defendant at all. If the belief was in fact held, its unreasonableness, so far as guilt or innocence is concerned, is neither here nor there. It is irrelevant. Were it otherwise, the defendant would be convicted because he was negligent in failing to recognise that the victim was not consenting or that a crime was not being committed and so on. In other words the jury should be directed first of all that the prosecution have the burden or duty of proving the unlawfulness of the defendant's actions; secondly, if the defendant may have been labouring under a mistake as to the facts, he must be judged according to his mistaken view of the facts; thirdly, that is so whether the mistake was, on an objective view, a reasonable mistake or not.

In a case of self-defence, where self-defence or the prevention of crime is concerned, if the jury came to the conclusion that the defendant believed, or may have believed, that he was being attacked or that a crime was being committed, and that force was necessary to protect himself or to prevent the crime, then the prosecution have not proved their case. If however the defendant's alleged belief was mistaken and if the mistake was an unreasonable one, that may be a powerful reason for coming to the conclusion that the belief was not honestly held and should be rejected.

Even if the jury come to the conclusion that the mistake was an unreasonable one, if the defendant may genuinely have been labouring under it, he is entitled to rely upon it.

We have read the recommendations of the Criminal Law Revision Committee, Part IX, paragraph 72(a), in which the following passage appears: 'The common law defence of self-defence should be replaced by a statutory defence providing that a person may use such force as is reasonable in the circumstances as he believes them to be in the defence of himself or any other person.' In the view of this Court that represents the law as expressed in *DPP v Morgan* (supra) and in *Kimber* (supra) and we do not think that the decision of the Divisional Court in *Albert v Lavin* (supra) from which we have cited can be supported.

For those reasons this appeal must be allowed and the conviction quashed.

Appeal allowed

NOTE

Since the conviction had to be quashed for misdirection on the onus of proof, it is arguable that the above passage is obiter; but it was applied by the Court of Appeal in *Jackson* [1985] RTR 257 at 262–263 and referred to with approval in *Asbury* [1986] Crim LR 258, CA.

Palmer v R [1971] 1 All ER 1077, Privy Council
(Lord Morris of Borth-y-Gest, Lord Donovan and Lord Avonside)

The appellant was indicted for murder in Jamaica. He never suggested that he had killed in self-defence but as there was evidence that made possible the view that whoever fired might have done so in self-defence, the judge properly left the issue of self-defence to the jury. He directed them that to found this defence 'the force used must not be by way of revenge and he must have believed on reasonable grounds that the force used by him was necessary to prevent or resist the attack and in deciding whether it was reasonably necessary to have used as much force as was used regard must be had to all the circumstances of the case'. The judge told the jury that only two verdicts were open to them—guilty of murder or not guilty. On appeal to the Privy Council, Lord Morris stated that the only question raised for determination was whether in cases where on a charge of murder an issue of self-defence is left to the jury it will in all cases be obligatory to direct the jury that if they found the accused, while intending to defend himself, had used more force than was necessary in the circumstances they should return a verdict of manslaughter. Having reviewed the authorities, in particular *Howe* (1958) 100 CLR 448, he continued, speaking of that case:

It will thus be seen that the Full Court of South Australia had posed two questions as being the relevant questions where a plea of self-defence would succeed in toto but for the use of excessive force by the person attacked: (1) was more force used than a reasonable man would consider necessary? (2) if so, did the accused nevertheless honestly believe that such excessive force was necessary? and both questions would have to be answered in the affirmative to justify a verdict of manslaughter. Three members of the High Court of Australia (Sir Owen Dixon CJ, McTiernan and Fullager JJ) agreed in substance with the Full Court.

On the assumption that an attack of a violent and felonious nature, or at least of an unlawful nature, was made or threatened so that a person under attack or threat of attack reasonably feared for his life or the safety of his person from injury, violation or indecent or insulting usage so that occasion had arisen entitling a person to resort to force to repel force or apprehended force, then Sir Owen Dixon CJ, stated that the law was as follows [(1958) 100 CLR at 460, 461]:

> 'Had he used no more force than was proportionate to the danger in which he stood, or reasonably supposed he stood, although he thereby caused the death of his assailant he would not have been guilty either of murder or manslaughter. But assuming that he was not entitled to a complete defence to a charge of murder, for the reason only that the force or violence which he used against his assailant or apprehended assailant went beyond what was needed for his protection or what the circumstances could cause him reasonably to believe to be necessary for his protection, of what crime does he stand guilty? Is the consequence of the failure of his plea of self-defence on that ground that he is guilty of murder or does it operate to reduce the homicide to manslaughter? There is no clear and definite judicial decision providing an answer to this question but it seems reasonable in principle to regard such a homicide as reduced to manslaughter, and that view has the support of not a few judicial statements to be found in the reports.'

. . . In the year before *Howe* [(1958) 100 CLR 448] was decided occurred *McKay* [[1957] VR 560]. This was a trial for murder in the State of Victoria though no issue as to self-defence arose in the case. McKay was caretaker of a poultry farm outside Melbourne belonging to his father. For a considerable time there had been nightly thefts of fowls from the farm, and a system of alarm bells was installed which would ring in the farmhouse if an intruder entered the pens. The bells did so ring on the morning of 9 September 1956 as daylight was breaking. McKay rose, took a loaded rifle with him, and saw a man named Wicks some 50 yards away carrying some fowls. He fired one shot at him, intending he said, to hit Wicks in the leg. Wicks ran away, and when he had run some five yards McKay fired another shot at him. Wicks thereupon dropped the fowls, but continued running. McKay fired another three shots, and later discovered Wicks behind a hedge either dead or in a dying condition. It seemed probable that one of the last three shots had killed him by penetrating the heart. To a neighbour who by this time had joined him, McKay said: 'Serve him right. He was pinching fowls.' He added that when he fired he did not care whether he killed the man or not. To the police however he said that he only meant to wound the man and not kill him, and he fired because he did not want the man to get away. He again made this assertion in a statement from the dock at his trial. The trial judge directed the jury that if they thought that McKay fired with the intention of killing Wicks and that when he fired he did so out of feelings of revenge or a desire to punish, he was guilty of murder. But if McKay was honestly exercising his legal right to prevent the escape of a man who had committed a felony, and that the killing was unintentional, but the means used were far in excess of what was proper in the circumstances, then McKay was guilty of manslaughter. He was convicted of manslaughter. McKay appealed to the Supreme Court of Victoria alleging a misdirection on the law which had deprived him of the chance of acquittal. The appeal was, by a majority of two to one dismissed. An application by McKay to the High Court of Australia for special leave to appeal was also dismissed. In giving the leading judgment in the Supreme Court of Victoria Lowe J formulated six propositions dealing with the law relating to justifiable homicide. The sixth was in these terms [[1957] VR at 563]:

> 'If the occasion warrants action in self-defence or for the prevention of felony or the apprehension of the felon, but the person taking action acts beyond the necessity of the occasion and kills the offender, the crime is manslaughter—not murder.'

This proposition was quoted with approval by the High Court in *Howe*. Taylor J, however pointed out that the proposition so formulated was not in any way limited to cases where it appears that the accused entertained an honest belief that the force used, though excessive on any reasonable view, was necessary. He added [(1958) 100 CLR at 467]:

'This distinction is of significance and reflection upon it provides grounds for thinking that the test proposed by the Full Court is erroneous.'

. . . In their Lordships' view the defence of self-defence is one which can be and will be readily understood by any jury. It is a straightforward conception. It involves no abstruse legal thought. It requires no set words by way of explanation. No formula need be employed in reference to it. Only common sense is needed for its understanding. It is both good law and good sense that a man who is attacked may defend himself. It is both good law and good sense that he may do, but may only do, what is reasonably necessary. But everythin', will depend on the particular facts and circumstances. Of these a jury can decide. It may in some cases be only sensible and clearly possible to take some simple avoiding action. Some at*acks may be serious and dangerous. Others may not be. If there is some relatively minor attack it would not be common sense to permit some action of retaliation which was wholly out of proportion to the necessities of the situation. If an attack is serious so that it puts someone in immediate peril then immediate defensive action may be necessary. If the moment is one of crisis for someone in imminent danger he may have to avert the danger by some instant reaction. If the attack is all over and no sort of peril remains then the employment of force may be by way of revenge or punishment or by way of paying off an old score or may be pure aggression. There may no longer be any link with a necessity of defence. Of all these matters the good sense of a jury will be the arbiter. There are no prescribed words which must be employed in or adopted in a summing-up. All that is needed is a clear exposition, in relation to the particular facts of the case, of the conception of necessary self-defence. If there has been no attack then clearly there will have been no need for defence. If there has been an attack so that defence is reasonably necessary it will be recognised that a person defending himself cannot weigh to a nicety the exact measure of his necessary defensive action. If a jury thought that in a moment of unexpected anguish a person attacked had only done what he honestly and instinctively thought was necessary that would be most potent evidence that only reasonable defensive action had been taken. A jury will be told that the defence of self-defence, where the evidence makes its raising possible, will only fail if the prosecution show beyond doubt that what the accused did was not by way of self-defence. But their Lordships consider . . . that if the prosecution have shown that what was done was not done in self-defence then that issue is eliminated from the case. If the jury consider that an accused acted in self-defence or if the jury are in doubt as to this then they will acquit. The defence of self-defence either succeeds so as to result in an acquittal or it is disproved in which case as a defence it is rejected. In a homicide case the circumstances may be such that it will become an issue whether there was provocation so that the verdict might be one of manslaughter. Any other possible issues will remain. If in any case the view is possible that the intent necessary to constitute the crime of murder was lacking then that matter would be left to the jury.

For the reasons which they have set out their Lordships have humbly advised Her Majesty that the appeal should be dismissed.

Appeal dismissed

Criminal Law Act 1967, s 3, p 558, below.

2   **Arrest without warrant, Police and Criminal Evidence Act 1984, s 24, p 590, below**

R v McInnes [1971] 3 All ER 295, Court of Appeal, Criminal Division (Edmund-Davies LJ, Lawton and Forbes JJ)

In a fight between 'greasers' and 'skinheads' the appellant, a greaser, stabbed and killed a skinhead. In a statement, he said, 'I let him have it.' At the trial, his defence was that the killing was an accident. He said that he had held the knife at his hip, warning the deceased not to come any closer, and that the deceased ran straight on to the knife. He appealed on the ground that the summing up did not deal adequately with, inter alia, excessive force used in self-defence.

[Edmund-Davies LJ reading the judgment of the court:]

The final criticism levelled against the summing-up is that the learned judge wrongly failed to direct the jury that, if death resulted from the use of excessive force by the appellant in defending himself against the aggressiveness of the deceased, the proper verdict was one of not guilty of murder but guilty of manslaughter. Certainly no such direction was given, and the question that arises is whether its omission constitutes a defect in the summing-up.

The Privy Council decision in *Palmer v R* [[1971] 1 All ER 1077, [1971] 2 WLR 831] provides high persuasive authority which we, for our part, unhesitatingly accept, that there is certainly *no* rule that, in every case where self-defence is left to the jury, such a direction is called for. But where self-defence fails on the ground that the force used went clearly beyond that which was reasonable in the light of the circumstances as they reasonably appeared to the accused, is it the law that the inevitable result must be that he can be convicted of manslaughter only, and not of murder? It seems that in Australia that question is answered in the affirmative (see Professor Colin Howard's article, 'Two Problems in ℥xcessive Defence' [(1968) 84 LQR 343]), but not, we think, in this country. On the contrary, if self-defence fails for the reason stated, it affords the accused no protection at all. But it is important to stress that the facts on which the plea of self-defence is unsuccessfully sought to be based may nevertheless serve the accused in good stead. They may, for example, go to show that he may have acted under provocation or that, although acting unlawfully, he may have lacked the intent to kill or cause serious bodily harm, and in that way render the proper verdict one of manslaughter. . . .

Section 3 (1) of the Criminal Law Act 1967 provides: 'A person may use such force as is reasonable in the circumstances in the prevention of crime . . .', and in our judgment the degree of force permissible in self-defence is similarly limited. Deliberate stabbing was so totally unreasonable in the circumstances of this case, even on the appellant's version, that self-defence justifying a complete acquittal was not relied on before us, and rightly so. Despite the high esteem in which we hold our Australian brethren, we respectfully reject as far as this country is concerned the refinement sought to be introduced that, if the accused, in defending himself during a fisticuffs encounter, drew out against his opponent (who he had no reason to think was armed) the deadly weapon which he had earlier unsheathed and then 'let him have it', the jury should have been directed that, even on those facts, it was open to them to convict of manslaughter. They are, in our view, the facts of this case. It follows that in our judgment no such direction was called for.

In the result, we hold that, on abundant evidence and following a summing-up which is not open to substantial criticism, the jury arrived at a verdict which ought not to be disturbed. We accordingly dismiss this appeal.

Appeal dismissed

NOTE

See *The People v Dwyer* [1972] IR 416, discussed [1975] CLJ 14.

Questions

1. Where the assailant is committing an offence, should there be room for the application of different rules governing the force used in reply, according to whether the person attacked was acting (i) in self-defence or (ii) in the prevention of crime? What should the difference in the rules be? (Cf C Harlow, 'Self-Defence: Public Right or Private Privilege', [1974] Crim LR 528.)

2. Dan, seeing Paul make a violent attack on Dan's wife, goes to her aid and in the course of a struggle, kills Paul. Was Dan acting in private defence or in the prevention of crime? Or both? Does it matter?

3. Albert, a madman who believes that other men are wild animals, escapes from an asylum. While he is making a violent attack on Gert, Robert, a policeman kills him, being unable to overpower him in any other way. Is the position regulated by s 3 of the Criminal Law Act? If not, what is the relevant law?

4. Peter's car breaks down late at night on a lonely road. He attempts unsuccessfully to repair it. Still carrying a spanner in his hand, he knocks at the door of a cottage to seek help. Dan, who lives alone in the cottage and is terrified of burglars opens the door. He takes Peter for a burglar and the spanner for a weapon. In a panic he hits Peter with the golf club with which he has armed himself and kills him.

Assume that it would have been reasonable at that time and place to strike that blow at an armed burglar, but that a reasonable man would have been able to discern that Peter was not an armed burglar. Has Dan a defence (a) to a charge of homicide? (b) to a civil action for negligence?

R v Hussey (1924) 18 Cr App Rep 160, Court of Criminal Appeal (Lord Hewart CJ, Avory and Salter JJ)

Appeal against conviction and sentence.

Appellant was convicted on 13 November 1924, before Acton J at the Central Criminal Court of unlawful wounding, and was sentenced to twelve months' imprisonment with hard labour.

Marston Garsia for the appellant (under s 10 of the Criminal Appeal Act 1907), who was present. In June, 1924, appellant rented a room at Brixton from a Mrs West. In July Mrs West purported to give him an oral notice to quit, which he contended was not a valid notice. Because he refused to vacate the room Mrs West, a woman named Mrs Gould, and a man named Crook, armed with a hammer, a spanner, a poker and a chisel, tried to force their way into the room, the door of which the appellant had barricaded. A panel of the door was broken, and appellant thereupon fired through the opening and Mrs Gould and Crook were wounded. At no place in the summing-up was the attention of the jury drawn to the distinction in law between what is permissible in self-defence and what is permissible in defence of one's house: Archbold's *Criminal Pleading, Evidence and Practice*, 26th edn p 887. On the contrary, the matter was treated throughout as if only the law of self-defence was applicable.

Eustace Fulton for the Crown. The question now raised was never urged at the trial, where the defence was that the violence used by appellant was necessary to protect his life and that of his wife and children. The rule of law referred to in Archbold (above) is a very ancient one, and belonged to the days when persons went out with armed retainers to seize other persons' lands. It is no longer to be observed. Appellant made no attempt to use lesser methods. With a proper direction the jury would have come to the same conclusion.

The Lord Chief Justice. No sufficient notice had been given to appellant to quit his room, and therefore he was in the position of a man defending his house. In Archbold's *Criminal Pleading, Evidence and Practice*, 26th edn p 887, it appears that:

> 'In defence of a man's house, the owner or his family may kill a trespasser who would forcibly dispossess him or it, in the same manner as he might, by law, kill in self-defence a man who attacks him personally; with this distinction, however, that in defending his home he need not retreat, as in other cases of self-defence, for that would be giving up his house to his adversary.'

That is still the law, but not one word was said about that distinction in the summing-up, which proceeded on the foundation that the defence was the ordinary one of self-defence. The jury, by their verdict, negatived felonious intent, and with a proper direction they might have come to a different conclusion. This appeal must therefore be allowed.

Conviction quashed

Questions

1. Hussey was acting in the defence of his home. Was he also acting in the prevention of crime? (Cf Criminal Law Act 1977, s 6.) Should it make any difference to the amount of force he might lawfully use?

2. Would it have been different if the assailants had intended, not to dispossess Hussey, but to gatecrash a party he was giving?

3. Would it be reasonable to stand and fight in defence of the home when it would be unreasonable not to retreat if the attack was directed at the defendant's person?

4. Al and Ben try to burst open the door of Dan's ground floor room, intending to tar-and-feather him. Dan could easily escape through the window. He fires a shotgun through the door and wounds Al. Is he guilty of unlawful wounding?

CHAPTER 12

Incitement

The draft Criminal Code Bill provides:

51 Incitement to commit an offence

(1) A person is guilty of incitement to commit an offence or offences if:

(a) he encourages any other person to do an act or acts which, if done with the fault required for the offence or offences, will involve the commission of the offence or offences by the other person; and

(b) he intends that the other person shall commit the offence or offences.

(2) Subject to section 55(1), 'offence' in this section means any offence triable in England and Wales other than:

(a) conspiracy (under section 52 or any other enactment);

(b) attempt (under section 53 or any other enactment).

(3) Where the purpose of an enactment creating an offence is the protection of a class of persons no member of that class who is the intended victim of such an offence can be guilty of incitement to commit that offence.

(4) A person cannot be guilty of incitement to commit an offence if the only person whom he incites to commit the offence is his spouse.

(5) A person may be convicted of incitement to commit an offence notwithstanding that the identity of the person incited is unknown.

(6) A person may be guilty as an accessory to the incitement by another of a third person to commit an offence; but it is not an offence under this section or under any enactment referred to in subsection (7) to incite another to assist, encourage or procure the commission of an offence by a third person.

(7) This section shall apply in determining whether a person is guilty of an offence of incitement to commit a specified offence created by any enactment other than this section; but conduct which is an offence under any other such enactment shall not also be an offence under this section.

Schedule 1 of the draft Bill provides the following illustrations

51 (1)	51 (i)	D offers E money to shoot P in the leg. E refuses. D is guilty of inciting E intentionally to cause injury (s 76) and, if the injury he intends is 'serious', of inciting E intentionally to cause serious injury (s 74).
	51 (ii)	It is an offence dishonestly to handle stolen goods knowing or believing them to be stolen. D suggests to E that E should purchase a gold watch for £5 from F who is offering it for sale in a public house. D knows that the watch is stolen and believes that E knows this also. D is guilty of inciting E to handle stolen goods.
	51 (iii)	D tells E, aged nine, to put a certain powder in P's drink 'to make him feel ill'. D is not guilty of inciting E to administer a substance without consent (s 80); even if E does this act with the fault required (knowledge that the substance is capable of interfering substantially with the other's bodily functions) he will not commit the offence because he is under ten (s 36). D may be guilty of attempting to commit the offence by an innocent agent depending on whether he has done an act which is more than merely preparatory to the commission of the offence.
51 (3)	51 (iv)	It is an offence to have sexual intercourse with a girl under the age of sixteen. D, a girl aged fifteen, proposes to E that he should have intercourse with her. D is not guilty of inciting the commission of an offence by E. If

intercourse does take place she is not guilty as an accessory to E's offence (s 31 (8)).

51 (5) 51 (v) It is an offence (burglary) to enter a building as a trespasser with intent to steal therein. D, the secretary of an animal welfare organisation, writes an article in the organisation's newsletter describing methods of breaking into laboratories in order to release into the wild animals used for research. D is guilty of incitement to burglary if his article is an encouragement to its readers to commit that offence and if he intends that one or more of them shall do so.

51 (6) 51 (vi) E writes a note to F ordering him to kill P. The note is delivered to F by D who knows its contents. D is guilty as an accessory to E's offence of incitement to murder.

51 (vii) D, who knows that F intends to commit a burglary, suggests to E that E should leave a ladder at a convenient place so as to facilitate F's entry to the building. D is not guilty of inciting E to commit an offence as he does not encourage E to commit burglary as a principal. If E does place the ladder as suggested and F uses it to effect an entry D and E will be guilty of burglary as accessories (s 31 (1) and (2)).

The Report on Codification explains the clause as follows:

14.6 *The fault requirement for incitement.* Paragraph (b) of subsection (1) provides that the incitor is guilty if 'he intends that the other person shall commit the offence or offences'. In relation to conspiracy and attempt Parliament has now determined that intention is the requisite fault element. [But see *Anderson*, p 256, below] We take the view that the interests of consistency and simplicity indicate the same rule for incitement. Under this paragraph therefore it would have to be proved that the incitor intended any consequences specified by the definition of the offence incited and knew of any specified circumstances. These requirements are implicit in the use of the word 'intend' in this context (see clause 22) and we do not think that any further definition is necessary. Also implicit is a third requirement peculiar to incitement. In order for a person to intend another to commit what will be an offence by the other, he (the incitor) must know or believe that the person incited will act with whatever fault is required for the offence. In *R v Curr*[1] the Court of Appeal quashed convictions for inciting women to commit offences under the Family Allowances Act 1945 because the prosecution failed to prove that the women (who had done the acts incited) had the mental element required for such offences. We share the view of the Law Commission's Working Party that the decision states the wrong test.[2] It is not necessary that any offence should be committed or even intended by the person incited, therefore it is irrelevant and confusing to ask whether that person had the mental element for the offence. The correct test is whether the incitor knows or believes that, if the incited person is induced to act, he will do so with the fault specified for the offence. In this respect we propose to depart from the decision in *Curr*.[3]

If the incitor does not know or believe that the person incited will act with the required fault, but nonetheless intends that the external elements of the offence shall occur, then he may be guilty of attempting to commit the offence through an innocent agent. The act of encouragement will in most cases amount to a more than preparatory act as required by clause 53, and the requisite intent for an attempt is present. The Working Party envisaged that a person who incites a child under ten to shoplift would be guilty in this way of an attempt to steal through an innocent agent.[4] We agree. . . .

14.8 *Protected persons.* Subsection (3) restates for incitement the principle deriving from *R v Tyrrell* which has been referred to already in connection with clause 31 (8). The principle was applied to conspiracy by section 2 (1) of the Criminal Law Act 1977, now restated in clause 52 (4). It has recently received the support of the Criminal Law Revision Committee.

14.9 *Spouses.* Section 2 (2) (a) of the Criminal Law Act 1977 provides in effect that a person cannot be guilty of conspiracy if the only other person with whom he agrees to commit an offence is his spouse. The rule is restated in clause 52 (5). We think that for consistency a similar rule should be provided for incitement. It would be anomalous if a person could be liable for inciting his wife to commit an offence, while enjoying an exemption from conspiracy if she agreed to his plan. Subsection (4) provides accordingly. . . .

14.11 *Accessories and incitement.* Under existing law it is probable that a person may aid, abet, counsel or procure another to incite a third person to commit an offence, but that incitement to aid, abet, etc is not an offence known to the law. Subsection (6) restates this position for the Code. The subsection is consistent with clause 53 (6) which makes a similar provision in the case of an attempt to commit an offence. The latter provision restates the decision of the Court of Appeal in *R v Dunnington*, construing section 1 (1) and (4) of the Criminal Attempts Act 1981.

1. [1968] 2 QB 944.
2. Working Paper No 50, Para 93.
3. The Working Party proposed that recklessness as to the mental element of the person incited should be sufficient. This proposal has been overtaken by the Parliamentary decisions to make the other preliminary offences crimes of intention only. As indicated above, we regard these decisions as settling the policy for incitement also.
4. Working Paper No 50, para 102.

R v Curr [1967] 1 All ER 478, Court of Appeal, Criminal Division
(Lord Parker CJ, Salmon LJ and Fenton Atkinson J)

The appellant was a trafficker in family allowance books. He advanced money to married women with large families on the security of their books and got them to sign some of the vouchers. He employed a team of women agents to cash the vouchers, pocketed the proceeds in repayment of the loan and returned the books. He handled about 40 to 80 books a week and made about 800% per annum on the transactions. He admitted that he knew that he was not entitled to receive the family allowance payments. He appealed from his convictions for inciting to commit offences contrary to s 9 (b) of the Family Allowances Act 1945 (incitement to commit a summary offence is now triable only summarily: Magistrates' Courts Act 1980, s 45) and of conspiring to commit offences contrary to that section. Section 9 (b) provides:

> 'If any person— . . . (b) obtains or receives any sum as on account of an allowance, either as in that person's own right or as on behalf of another, knowing that it was not properly payable, or not properly receivable by him or her; that person shall be liable on summary conviction to imprisonment for a term not exceeding three months or to a fine not exceeding £50 or both such imprisonment and such fine.'

Fenton Atkinson J. Counsel for the appellant's argument was that, if the woman agent in fact has no guilty knowledge, knowing perhaps nothing of the assignment, or supposing that the appellant was merely collecting for the use and benefit of the woman concerned, then she would be an innocent agent, and, by using her services in that way, the appellant would be committing the summary offence himself, but would not be inciting her to receive money knowing that it was not receivable by her. He contends that it was essential to prove, to support this charge, that the woman agent in question in this transaction affecting a Mrs Currie, knew that the allowances were not properly receivable by her. Counsel for the Crown's answer to that submission was that the woman agent must be presumed to know the law, and, if she knew the law, she must have known, he contends, that the allowance was not receivable by her. [His Lordship referred to regulations providing that the allowance was receivable only by the wife or husband except during a short period of illness.]

In our view, the argument for the Crown here gives no effect to the word 'knowing' in the section, and in our view the appellant could be guilty on count 3 only if the woman agent sent to collect the allowance knew that the action which she was asked to carry out amounted to an offence. As has already been said, the appellant himself clearly knew that his conduct in the matter was illegal and contrary to s 9 (b), but it was essential in our view for the jury to consider the knowledge, if any, of the woman agent. When the assistant recorder dealt with this count, he referred to soliciting in this way:

> 'Solicited means encouraged or incited another person to go and draw that money which should have been paid, you may think, to Mrs Currie.'

He then dealt with ignorance of the law being no excuse. He went on to deal with statutory offences, and read s 4 of the Family Allowances Act 1945, telling the jury in effect that, apart from the case of sickness, nobody else could legally receive these allowances, and then he went on to consider the position of the appellant, asking the rhetorical question whether he could be heard to say with his knowledge of this matter and his trafficking in these books that it was not known to be wrong to employ an agent to go and collect the family allowances. He never followed that, however, with the question of the knowledge of the women agents, and in the whole of the summing-up dealing with this matter he proceeded on the assumption that either guilty knowledge in the woman was irrelevant, or alternatively, that any woman agent must be taken to have known that she was committing an offence under s 9 (b). If the matter had been left on a proper direction for the jury's consideration, they might well have thought that the women agents, other than Mrs Nicholson, whom they acquitted, must have known very well that they were doing something wrong; some of them were apparently collecting as many as ten of these weekly payments. The matter, however, was never left to them for their consideration, and here again, so it seems to this court, there was a vital matter where the defence was not left to the jury at all and there was no sufficient direction; it would be quite impossible to say that, on a proper direction, the jury must have convicted on this count.

[His Lordship held that the convictions for conspiracy must also be quashed as the jury had not been told that both parties to the alleged conspiracy must have known that the money was not properly payable.]

Appeal allowed. Convictions quashed

Questions

1. On the incitement charge, was the proper question whether the collectors knew that they were not entitled to collect the allowance or whether Curr believed that they knew that they were not entitled? Or must both questions be answered? See p 245, above. Consider the following case. D urges E to take possession of certain goods. The goods, as D knows, are stolen goods. D believes that E also knows the goods to be stolen but in fact E does not know this. Is D guilty of inciting E to handle stolen goods?

2. Was mistake of law (as to who is entitled to receive a family allowance) regarded as a defence in this case? If so, is it necessary in such a case for the prosecution to prove that the accused knew it was an *offence* improperly to receive a family allowance?

R v Whitehouse [1977] 3 All ER 737, Court of Appeal, Criminal Division
(Scarman and Geoffrey Lane LJJ and Donaldson J)

The defendant pleaded guilty to a charge of incitement of his 15-year-old daughter to commit incest with him. Under s 11 of the Sexual Offences Act 1956 (p 550, below) it is an offence for a woman of 16 or over to permit (inter alios) her father to have intercourse with her but a girl aged 15 cannot commit incest. The court held that it had jurisdiction to entertain an appeal against conviction and continued:

Scarman LJ. It is of course accepted by the Crown that at common law the crime of incitement consists of inciting another person to commit a crime. When one looks at this indictment in the light of the particulars of the offence pleaded, one sees that it is charging the accused man with inciting a girl to commit a crime which in fact by statute she is incapable of committing. If therefore the girl was incapable of committing the crime alleged, how can the accused be guilty of the common law crime of incitement? The Crown accepts the logic of that position and does not seek in this court to rely on s 11 of the 1956 Act or to suggest that this man could be guilty of inciting his daughter to commit incest, to use the old phrase, as a principal in the first degree. But the Crown says that it is open to them on this indictment to submit that it covers the offence of inciting the girl to aid and abet the man to commit the crime of incest on her. Section 10 of the 1956 Act makes it an offence for a man to have sexual intercourse with a woman whom he knows to be his daughter, and the Crown says that on this indictment it is possible to say that the accused has committed an offence known to the law, the offence being that of inciting his daughter under the age of 16 to aid and abet him to have sexual intercourse with her . . .

There is no doubt of the general principle, namely that a person, provided always he or she is of the age of criminal responsibility, can be guilty of aiding or abetting a crime even though it be a crime which he or she cannot commit as a principal in the first degree. There are two famous illustrations in the books of this principle. A woman can aid and abet a rape so as herself to be guilty of rape, and a boy at an age where he is presumed impotent can nevertheless aid and abet a rape. The cases, which are very well known, are first in time *R v Eldershaw* [(1828) 3 C & P 396]. In that case Vaughan B, in the course of a six line judgment, the brevity of which I wish I could emulate, says: 'This boy being under fourteen, he cannot, by law, be found guilty of a rape, except as a principal in the second degree.' So much for the boy. The position in regard to a woman is stated by Bowen LJ [*R v Ram and Ram* (1893) 17 Cox CC 609] in one line and a half, where two prisoners, a Mr and Mrs Ram, were indicted jointly for rape on Annie Edkins of the age of 13. It was submitted that the woman could not be indicted for rape. Bowen LJ declined to quash the indictment for rape as against the female prisoner. Those cases clearly establish, and have been regarded for a very long time as establishing, the general principle to which I have referred.

But what if the person alleged to be aiding and abetting the crime is herself the victim of the crime?. . .

The question in our judgment is determined by authority. It is, strictly speaking, persuasive authority only because it deals with a different Act of Parliament, but it is a decision by a strong court which has declared a principle which is as applicable to the statutory provision with which we are concerned as to that with which that case was concerned. The case is *R v Tyrrell* [[1894] 1 QB 710, [1891–4] All ER Rep 1215]. It was a decision of the Court for Crown Cases Reserved and it was a five judge court, consisting of Lord Coleridge CJ, Mathew, Grantham, Lawrence and Collins JJ. The headnote reads as follows [[1894] 1 QB 710]:

> 'It is not a criminal offence for a girl between the ages of thirteen and sixteen to aid and abet a male person in committing, or to incite him to commit, the misdemeanour of having unlawful carnal knowledge of her contrary to s 5 of the Criminal Law Amendment Act 1885.'

It is necessary to look at the facts. I take them from the report. The defendant was tried and convicted on an indictment charging her with having unlawfully aided and abetted, counselled and procured the commission by one Thomas Ford of the misdemeanour of having unlawful carnal knowledge of her while she was between the ages of 13 and 16, and it was proved at the trial that the girl did aid and abet, solicit or incite the man to commit the misdemeanour made punishable by s 5 of the 1885 Act. Lord Coleridge CJ in giving judgment said [[1894] 1 QB 710 at 712, cf [1891–4] All ER Rep 1215 at 1215, 1216]:

> '[The Act] was passed for the purpose of protecting women and girls against themselves. At the time it was passed there was a discussion as to what point should be fixed as the age of consent. That discussion ended in a compromise, and the age of consent was fixed at sixteen. With the object of protecting women and girls against themselves the Act of Parliament has made illicit connection with a girl under that age unlawful; if a man wishes to have such illicit connection he must wait until the girl is sixteen otherwise he breaks the law; but it is impossible to say that the Act, which is absolutely silent about aiding or abetting, or soliciting or inciting, can have intended that the girls for whose protection it was passed should be punishable under it of the offences committed upon themselves.'

The other four judges agreed with Lord Coleridge CJ.

In our judgment it is impossible, as a matter of principle, to distinguish *R v Tyrrell* from the present case. Clearly the relevant provisions of the Sexual Offences Act 1956 are intended to protect women and girls. Most certainly s 11 is intended to protect girls under the age of 16 from criminal liability, and the Act as a whole exists, insofar as it deals with women and girls exposed to sexual threat, to protect them. The very fact that girls under the age of 16 are protected from criminal liability for what would otherwise be incest demonstrates that this girl who is said to have been the subject of incitement was being incited to do something which, if she did it, could not be a crime by her.

I refer to s 1 of the Indecency with Children Act 1960. By that section any person, and I leave out the immaterial words, who incites a child under the age of 14 to an act of gross indecency shall be liable on conviction on indictment to imprisonment for a term not exceeding two years. Had his daughter been under the age of 14, the accused would have been guilty of this statutory incitement, and on a plea of guilty that would have been the end of the matter. It is noted that in the earlier 1975 indictment there was included a count under s 1 of the 1960 Act to which he did in fact plead guilty. But the gap remains between the age of 14 and the age of 16. It may be that the legislature will consider it desirable to stop that the gap . . . .

Appeals against conviction allowed. Appeal against sentence allowed; sentence varied.

NOTES

Should the case have been disposed of on the short ground that incitement to aid and abet is not an offence known to the law? See draft Code, cl 51 (6), p 244, above, and Report, para 14.11, p 245, above. Parliament responded quickly to the suggestion for legislation. The Criminal Law Act 1977, s 54 provided that 'It is an offence for a man to incite to have sexual intercourse with him a girl under the age of sixteen whom he knows to be his grand-daughter, daughter or sister.' Whitehouse's plea of guilty could now be sustained; but consider the following cases:

(i) Dan incites his 15-year-old daughter, Poppy, to have sexual intercourse with (a) her 18-year-old brother, (b) an unrelated 18-year-old man.

(ii) Dan incites Peggy, who is a defective within the meaning of the Sexual Offences Act 1956, ss 7 and 9 (p 549, below) to have sexual intercourse with him.

In *Sirat* [1986] Crim LR 245 the Court of Appeal held that an indictment will lie for incitement to incite unless it amounts to an incitement to conspire in which case it is no longer an offence by virtue of the Criminal Law Act 1977, s 5 (7), p 580, below.

CHAPTER 13

Conspiracy

1. Statutory and common law conspiracy

Conspiracy at common law was defined as an agreement to do an unlawful act or a lawful act by unlawful means. The word 'unlawful' included not only all crimes triable in England and Wales, even summary offences, but also some torts, fraud, the corruption of public morals and the outraging of public decency, whether or not the acts in question amounted to crimes when done by an individual. The Law Commission has declared its ultimate aim that the crime of conspiracy should be limited to agreements to commit crimes. The Criminal Law Act 1977, p 578, below, goes a long way towards achieving that aim. It does not go the whole way because it was thought that, to do so in the present state of the criminal law, would leave unacceptably wide gaps. Two types of conspiracy at common law were therefore preserved:
(i) conspiracy to defraud (s 5 (2))
(ii) conspiracy to corrupt public morals or outrage public decency (s 5 (3)).

So far as the second exception is concerned, the relationship between common law and statutory conspiracy is clearly defined by the Act, s 5 (3) (b). The agreement is a conspiracy at common law only if it 'would not amount to or involve the commission of an offence if carried out by a single person otherwise than in pursuance of an agreement.' If it would amount to or involve the commission of an offence then it is a conspiracy to commit that offence, contrary to s 1 of the 1977 Act.

There is no corresponding provision for conspiracy to defraud. On the contrary, s 5 (2) provides that

> 'Subsection (1) [which abolishes conspiracy at common law] shall not affect the offence of conspiracy at common law so far as relates to conspiracy to defraud, and section 1 above shall not apply in any case where the agreement in question amounts to a conspiracy to defraud at common law.'

This seems, very plainly, to preserve the whole of the common law of conspiracy to defraud and to make it clear that any such conspiracy is not a statutory conspiracy contrary to s 1. This was surprising because conspiracies to steal and commit other offences of dishonesty were conspiracies to defraud at common law (see *Scott*, discussed p 254, below). Thus a very large and important area of the law of conspiracy would be outside the terms of the 1977 Act.

The result was that in *Duncalf* [1979] 2 All ER 1116, CA it was held that s 5 (2) and (3) should not be 'literally construed'.

> '. . . a sensible construction can, as we think, be given to both s 5 (2) and s 5 (3) as preserving the old law to, but only to, such extent as is necessary to ensure that a lacuna was not left in the law by s 1 (1).'

If the agreement was to commit a crime, there was no lacuna, so the common law was not preserved and the agreement was a statutory and not a common law conspiracy. The same limitation was imposed *by the court* on conspiracy to defraud as is imposed *by the Act* on common law conspiracy to corrupt public morals or outrage public decency. The reader may judge whether this is a permissible way to construe a statute.

Duncalf was not acceptable to all courts. Earlier, Drake J in *Quinn* [1978] Crim LR 750 had held that the words of the Act should be given their natural meaning and this was also the opinion of the Court of Appeal in *Walters* (1979) 69 Cr App R 115. In *Ayres* (1983) 148 JP 458, [1984] Crim LR 165, the Court of Appeal followed *Walters* and held that the appellant was properly convicted of conspiracy to defraud although the agreement was to obtain property by deception which was an offence under s 15 of the Theft Act 1968. He appealed to the House of Lords.

R v Ayres [1984] 1 All ER 619, House of Lords
(Lord Fraser of Tullybelton, Lord Scarman, Lord Bridge of Harwich, Lord Brandon of Oakbrook and Lord Templeman)

Lord Bridge. . . . . Before turning to the authorities and arguments bearing on this conflict of opinion, it is well to remove one source of misunderstanding. Some judicial dicta on the subject might be understood as suggesting that the choice whether to prosecute for a statutory conspiracy under s 1 of the 1977 Act or for a common law conspiracy to defraud is one dictated by convenience and that in many cases both options may be open. It was indeed argued for the Crown before your Lordships that the two offences are not mutually exclusive. I have no hesitation at the outset in rejecting this argument. Section 5(2) of the 1977 Act, which preserves conspiracy to defraud at common law as an exception to the general abolition of the offence of common law conspiracy by s 5(1) concludes with the words: '. . . and section 1 above shall not apply in any case where the agreement in question amounts to a conspiracy to defraud at common law.' I can see no escape from the stark choice of alternatives which this plain language imposes. According to the true construction of the 1977 Act, an offence which amounts to a common law conspiracy to defraud must be charged as such and not as a statutory conspiracy under s 1. Conversely a s 1 conspiracy cannot be charged as a common law conspiracy to defraud. It is, in my opinion, of considerable importance to bear in mind the implications of the fact that the offences are thus mutually exclusive in approaching the problem of construction. [Having considered the authorities, his Lordship continued:]

My Lords, the passing of the 1977 Act followed the publication in March 1976 of the Law Commission's Report on Conspiracy and Criminal Law Reform (Law Com No 76). It is legitimate to look at that report to ascertain the mischief which the statute was intended to remedy. To attempt briefly to paraphrase and summarise, without quoting, I read the report as identifying the defect in the previous law of criminal conspiracy as arising from the uncertainty as to what might constitute the subject matter of an agreement amounting to a criminal conspiracy, which, in general terms, could only be eliminated by restriction of criminal conspiracies to agreements to commit substantive criminal offences. But as a gloss on this main theme, the report recognised that an unqualified restriction of criminal conspiracies to such agreements might leave gaps in the law in certain areas, including fraud, which only the retention of the common law conspiracy offence could cover. This reading of the Law Commission's report seems to me to lend powerful support to the construction adopted in *R v Duncalf* of ss 1(1) and 5(2) of the 1977 Act.

Further considerations point to the same conclusion. Adopting a purposive approach to construction, it is difficult indeed to suppose that Parliament, whilst limiting the punishment of conspirators generally to the maximum appropriate to the substantive offences they had conspired to commit and giving them the added protection of requiring approval from the Director of Public Prosecutions to their prosecution if the substantive offences in question were summary offences, should have intended to deny both these advantages to any person agreeing to commit a substantive offence involving an element of fraud, however trivial that offence might be.

It remains to consider whether any light is thrown on the point at issue by comparing the language of s 5(2) with that of s 5(3). The latter provides:

'Subsection (1) above shall not affect the offence of conspiracy at common law if and in so far as it may be committed by entering into an agreement to engage in conduct which—(a) tends to corrupt public morals or outrages public decency; but (b) would not amount to or involve the commission of an offence if carried out by a single person otherwise than in pursuance of an agreement.'

No comparable limitation to that imposed by sub-s (3)(b) applies to the provision that sub-s (1) (abolishing the offence of conspiracy at common law) 'shall not affect the offence of conspiracy at common law so far as relates to conspiracy to defraud'.

So far as one can judge from the short report of *R v Quinn*, Drake J seems to have based his ruling primarily on this distinction in the statutory language applied to the two common law conspiracy offences preserved by the 1977 Act. I do not, with respect, find this convincing. By itself sub-s (3)(b) seems fully to support the view that the underlying policy of Pt 1 of the 1977 Act was to preserve the offence of conspiracy at common law only to the extent necessary to avoid leaving a lacuna in the law. The question then arises why a similar limitation was not imposed expressly on the scope of the preserved common law offence of conspiracy to defraud. I believe the answer to be this. Agreements entered into for a fraudulent purpose may take an almost infinite variety of forms. In some cases it may be impossible to say of such an agreement whether or not carrying the agreement into effect would have involved the commission of any substantive offence. To constitute an offence of conspiracy under s 1 of the 1977 Act, the agreement must be:

'that a course of conduct shall be pursued which will necessarily amount to or involve the commission of any offence or offences by one or more of the parties to the agreement if the agreement is carried out in accordance with their intentions. . .'

If s 5(2) had imposed on the preserved common law offence of conspiracy to defraud a restriction in comparable terms to those used in s 5(3)(b) this would have left in limbo those conspiracies to defraud where the evidence left in doubt the question whether the execution of the agreement would or would not necessarily have involved the commission of some substantive offence by one or more of the conspirators.

For these reasons, and for those expressed in the extract quoted above from the judgment of the court in *R v Duncalf*, with which I respectfully agree, I conclude that the phrase 'conspiracy to defraud' in s 5(2) of the 1977 Act must be construed as limited to an agreement which, if carried into effect, would not necessarily involve the commission of any substantive criminal offence by any of the conspirators. I would accordingly answer the certified question in the affirmative.

The effect of this ruling should not, I believe, create undue difficulty for prosecutors or judges. In the overwhelming majority of conspiracy cases it will be obvious that performance of the agreement which constitutes the conspiracy would necessarily involve, and frequently will in fact have already involved, the commission of one or more substantive offences by one or more of the conspirators. In such cases one or more counts of conspiracy, as appropriate, should be charged under s 1 of the 1977 Act. Only the exceptional fraudulent agreements will need to be charged as common law conspiracies to defraud, when either it is clear that performance of the agreement constituting the conspiracy would not have involved the commission by any conspirator of any substantive offence or it is uncertain whether or not it would do so. In case of doubt, it may be appropriate to include two counts in the indictment in the alternative.

[The House upheld the conviction under the proviso to s 2(1) of the Criminal Appeal Act 1968 on the ground that no actual miscarriage of justice had occurred.]

Appeal dismissed

When considering whether to indict for conspiracy to defraud the prosecutor must now always ask himself whether the carrying out of the alleged agreement would necessarily amount to or involve the commission of any offence. If it would, then he must indict for conspiracy to commit that offence and not for conspiracy to defraud. If it would not, then it may be a conspiracy to defraud. Similarly, in deciding whether a person was properly indicted for conspiracy to defraud, the court must first ask itself that question: *Hollinshead* [1985] 2 All ER 769 at p 777, per Lord Brandon. Where the acts agreed to be done are a combination of offences and frauds not amounting to offences, the conspiracy is a conspiracy to commit those offences: *Tonner* [1985] 1 All ER 807, CA.

If the defendants have agreed to defraud A by an act which would not constitute an offence against A if done by an individual, an indictment for conspiring to defraud A will, nevertheless, not lie if the act would necessarily amount to or involve an offence against B. The agreement must be charged as a conspiracy to commit that offence. In *Cooke and Sutcliffe* [1985] Crim LR 215 British Rail stewards plotted to sell their own food on trains and to retain the proceeds, thus defrauding British Rail of the profit they should have made. This was probably not a substantive offence against British Rail. Though the stewards would be bound to account for their ill-gotten gains, British Rail had no proprietary interest in them: Smith, *Law of Theft* (5th edn) para 75. But the defendants' conduct, according to the court, would necessarily amount to or involve an offence of going equipped to cheat the passengers, contrary to s 25 of the Theft Act 1968: see *Doukas*, p 456, below. Yet the court declined to apply the proviso to s 2 (1) of the Criminal Appeal Act 1968:

> 'Unlike *Ayres*, where the proviso was applied, because the particulars of the common law conspiracy inevitably required a finding by a jury of the commission of the statutory offence, no such construction could be applied to the present indictment as charging an offence to deceive the customers—a necessary ingredient of the s 25 offence.'

Does this contradict the reason for holding that the indictment for conspiracy to defraud would not lie?

2. Crime or fraud to be committed by third party

An agreement will amount to a statutory conspiracy only if carrying it out will necessarily amount to or involve the commission of an offence *by one or more of the parties to the conspiracy*. In *Hollinshead*, below, the Court of Appeal held that, in this respect, the Act did no more than restate the common law; so that there could be no conspiracy to defraud where the fraud contemplated was to be carried out, not by any party to the agreement, but by a third party: [1985] 1 All ER 850 at 857. The defendants had agreed to supply 'black boxes' to a man (in fact an undercover policeman) who was expected to resell them to persons unknown who would use them to defraud electricity boards. (The black box reverses the flow of current so as to make it appear that less electricity has been used. It has no other use.) The Court of Appeal also refused leave to proceed on another count (count 1) alleging a statutory conspiracy to aid, abet, counsel or procure an offence under s 1 of the Theft Act 1968, p 565, below, following Smith & Hogan *Criminal Law* (5th edn), pp 234–235 and holding that an agreement to aid, etc, is not a conspiracy under the 1977 Act. (Cf draft Code, cl 52(7), p 268, post.) The prosecution obtained leave to appeal to the House of Lords.

R v Hollinshead [1985] 2 All ER 769, House of Lords
(Lords Fraser, Diplock, Roskill, Bridge and Brandon)

Lord Roskill. The real question, as already stated, is whether in order to secure conviction on count 2 it was necessary to aver and prove a dishonest agreement by the respondents actually to use the black boxes, the submission being that it was not enough to show only an intention that such a dishonest use should follow their dishonest manufacture and sale.

My Lords, in my view, with all respect to those who have taken a different view, this submission is contrary to authority. I start with the decision of this House in *Scott v Comr of Police for the Metropolis* [1974] 3 All ER 1032, [1975] AC 819. It is to be observed that that case was decided before the passing of the 1977 Act. Scott was charged with two offences. First, he was charged with conspiracy to defraud and, second, with conspiracy to infringe s 21(1)(a) of the Copyright Act 1956. He ultimately pleaded guilty to both and was sentenced on both counts (see [1974] 3 All ER 1032 at 1033, [1975] AC 819 at 822). In this connection I have the permission of my noble and learned friend Lord Bridge to say that he was in error in saying in his speech in *R v Ayres* that the conspiracy under consideration in *Scott v Comr of Police for the Metropolis* did not involve the commission of any identifiable offence (see [1984] 1 All ER 619 at 622, [1984] AC 447 at 454). But the House was not there concerned with what would now be called a statutory conspiracy. Indeed, since *R v Ayres* the two counts would be mutually exclusive and Scott could not have been convicted on both. That is, however, of no importance in the present case. The importance of the decision in *Scott v Comr of Police for the Metropolis* lies in the conclusion summarised in the headnote ([1975] AC 819 at 820):

> '(3) That the common law offence of conspiracy to defraud was not limited to an agree-ment between two or more persons to deceive the intended victim and by such deceit to defraud him; and accordingly, as deceit was not an essential ingredient of the offence, the count was not bad in law and the appellant had been rightly convicted.'

Viscount Dilhorne said ([1974] 3 All ER 1032 at 1038, [1975] AC 819 at 839): 'One must not confuse the object of a conspiracy with the means by which it is intended to be carried out.' Lord Diplock said ([1974] 3 All ER 1032 at 1040, [1975] AC 819 at 841):

> '(2) Where the intended victim of a 'conspiracy to defraud' is a private individual the purpose of the conspirators must be to cause the victim economic loss by depriving him of some property or right, corporeal or incorporeal, to which he is or would or might become entitled. The intended means by which the purpose is to be achieved must be dis-honest. They need not involve fraudulent misrepresentation such as is needed to constitute the civil tort of deceit. Dishonesty of any kind is enough.'

In *A-G's Reference (No 1 of 1982)* [1983] 2 All ER 721, [1983] QB 751 (the whisky label case) the Court of Appeal (Lord Lane CJ, Taylor and McCowan JJ) was primarily concerned with the question of jurisdiction to try persons for conspiracy which had been entered into in England but which was to be carried out abroad though that conspiracy would cause economic damage to persons in England. The court held that there was no such jurisdiction. But it is apparent from a passage in the judgment of that court delivered by Lord Lane CJ that but for the question of jurisdiction the former defendants would have been guilty of conspiracy to defraud. Lord Lane CJ said ([1983] 2 All ER 721 at 724, [1983] QB 751 at 757):

> 'In each case, to determine the object of the conspiracy, the court must see what the defendants actually agreed to do. Had it not been for the jurisdictional problem we have no doubt that the charge against these conspirators would have been conspiracy to defraud potential purchasers of the whisky, for that was the true object of the agreement.'

The dishonest agreement there under considerations was to produce, label and distribute bottles of whisky so as to represent them as containing whisky of a well-known brand which in fact they did not contain. The object, as Lord Lane CJ said, was to defraud potential purchasers of the whisky outside this country.

In my view the respondents were liable to be convicted of conspiracy to defraud because they agreed to manufacture and sell and thus put into circulation dishonest devices, the sole purpose of which was to cause loss, just as the former defendants in the case just referred to would, apart from the jurisdictional problem, have been liable to be convicted of conspiracy to defraud because they agreed dishonestly to produce, label and distribute bottles of whisky, the sole pur-pose of the sale of which was to defraud potential purchasers of those bottles. . . .

I can deal with the question raised in connection with count 1 more briefly. As was pointed out in *R v Ayres* [1984] 1 All ER 619 at 622, [1984] AC 447 at 455 in the passage, to which I have already referred, offences of statutory conspiracy and of common law conspiracy to defraud are mutually exclusive. It follows that, if your Lordships agree with me that the respondents were properly convicted on count 2 of conspiracy to defraud, this conclusion presupposes that the respondents could not properly have been convicted on count 1 of the statutory conspiracy there charged. The Court of Appeal was of the opinion that they could not have been so convicted for the reason that s 1(1) of the 1977 Act did not, on its true construction, make a charge of conspiracy to aid, abet, counsel or procure possible in law. The foundation for this view is a passage in Smith and Hogan *Criminal Law* (5th edn, 1983) pp 234–235, which is quoted in full in the judgment by Hodgson J and with which the Court of Appeal expressed complete agreement (see [1985] 1 All ER 850 at 857–858, [1985] 2 WLR 761 at 770–771).

My Lords, I do not find it necessary to consider whether or not this view is correct for this reason. Even if such a charge of conspiracy to aid, abet, counsel or procure were possible in law, I can see no evidence whatever that the respondents ever agreed so to aid, abet, counsel or procure or indeed did aid, abet, counsel or procure those who as the ultimate purchasers or possessors of the black boxes were destined to be the actual perpetrators of the intended frauds on electricity boards. It follows that on no view could the respondents have been convicted on count 1 even if that count were sustainable in law. This last question is obviously one of some difficulty and a case in which that question arose for direct decision is likely to be a rarity. I suggest that in any future case in which that question does arise it should be treated as open for consideration de novo, as much may depend on the particular facts of the case in question.

(**Lords Fraser, Diplock, Bridge** and **Brandon** agreed.)

Appeal allowed

Questions

1. Was it true to say that it was the *purpose* of the alleged conspirators to cause economic loss to the electricity boards? Suppose that the buyer (not being a policeman or other entrapper) having bought and paid for the boxes, were to see the error of his ways and destroy them, would the defendants have considered the enterprise a failure? Would it be more realistic to say that it was their *intention* that the boards should be defrauded because this was a natural consequence of what they did? Cf *Moloney*, p 55, above. In conspiracy cases the courts frequently refer to a requirement of 'purpose' but their actions seem to belie their words. See commentaries on *A-G's Reference No 1 of 1982*, [1983] Crim LR 534 and *MacPherson and Watts* [1985] Crim LR 508; p 267, below.
2. Lord Roskill said that he could see no evidence whatever of an agreement to aid, abet, etc. Yet he also held that 'the manufacture and sale was for the dishonest purposes of enabling those black boxes to be used by persons other than the respondents to the detriment of the intended victim.' If that is not aiding, etc, what is?
3. If an agreement to aid and abet is a statutory conspiracy it cannot be a common law conspiracy: *Ayres*, p 251, above. Does the decision (as distinct from the dicta) suggest that an agreement to aid and abet is not a statutory conspiracy? See draft Code Bill, cl 52(7), p 268, below.

3. Intention and conspiracy

The Law Commission Report on Conspiracy and Criminal Law Reform (Law Com No 76, 1976), on which the Part 1 of the Criminal Law Act 1977 was based, includes a full discussion of the mental element to be required for conspiracy (paras 1.25–1.41). The Law Commission's conclusion on the common law was that:

'. . . it is reasonably clear from such authority as there is that what the law requires before a charge of conspiracy can be proved against a defendant is that *he should intend to bring about any consequences prohibited by the offence* and should have full knowledge of all the circumstances or facts which need to be known to enable him to know that the agreed course of conduct will result in a crime.' (Authors' italics.)

The Commission thought that this was what the law ought to be: 'We think that the law should require full intention and knowledge before a conspiracy can be established.' Their recommendation (5), para 7.2 reads:

> 'A person should be guilty of conspiracy if he agrees with another person that an offence shall be committed. *Both must intend that any consequence in the definition of the offence will result* and both must know of the existence of any state of affairs which it is necessary for them to know in order to be aware that the course of conduct agreed upon will amount to the offence.' (Authors' italics)

The Report included a draft Bill, implementing the Commission's intentions. Clause 1, which became section 1 of the 1977 Act, included the phrase, 'in accordance with their intentions', which was discussed by the House of Lords in the next case.

R v Anderson [1985] 2 All ER 961, House of Lords
(Lords Scarman, Diplock, Keith, Bridge and Brightman)

The appellant was remanded in custody with Ahmed Andaloussi. He confidently expected to be released on bail but Andaloussi was awaiting trial for very serious drug offences. The appellant agreed with Andaloussi's brother Mohamed and Mohamed Assou to participate in a scheme to effect Andaloussi's escape from prison. The appellant was to supply diamond wire capable of cutting through metal bars to be smuggled into prison. He received £2,000 on account and admitted that he intended to supply the wire on payment of a further £10,000 but said that he would then have left for Spain and taken no further part in the scheme, which he believed could not possibly succeed. His submission that he lacked the mental element for conspiracy to commit the crime of escape was rejected by the trial judge and the Court of Appeal. That court held (1) that a person who agrees with two or more others, who do intend to carry out the agreement, but who has a secret intention himself to participate only in part, is guilty of an offence under s 1 (1) of the Criminal Law Act 1977; and (2), if he is not guilty as a principal offender, then he may be convicted of aiding and abetting the conspiracy..He appealed to the House of Lords and both points of law were certified for decision.

Lord Bridge. The 1977 Act, subject to exceptions not presently material, abolished the offence of conspiracy at common law. It follows that the elements of the new statutory offence of conspiracy must be ascertained purely by interpretation of the language of s 1(1) of the 1977 Act. For purposes of analysis it is perhaps convenient to isolate the three clauses each of which must be taken as indicating an essential ingredient of the offence as follows: (1) 'if a person agrees with any other person or persons that a course of conduct shall be pursued' (2) 'which will necessarily amount to or involve the commission of any offence or offences by one or more of the parties to the agreement' (3) 'if the agreement is carried out in accordance with their intentions'.

Clause (1) presents, as it seems to me, no difficulty. It means exactly what is says and what it says is crystal clear. To be convicted, the party charged must have agreed with one or more others that 'a course of conduct shall be pursued'. What is important is to resist the temptation to introduce into this simple concept ideas derived from the civil law of contract. Any number of persons may agree that a course of conduct shall be pursued without undertaking any contractual liability. The agreed course of conduct may be a simple or an elaborate one and may may involve the participation of two or any larger number of persons who may have agreed to play a variety of roles in the course of conduct agreed.

Again, clause (2) could hardly use simpler language. Here what is important to note is that it is not necessary that more than one of the participants in the agreed course of conduct shall commit a substantive offence. It is, of course, necessary that any party to the agreement shall have assented to play his part in the agreed course of conduct, however innocent in itself, knowing that the part to be played by one or more of the others will amount to or involve the commission of an offence.

It is only clause (3) which presents any possible ambiguity. The heart of the submission for the appellant is that in order to be convicted of conspiracy to commit a given offence the language of clause (3) requires that the party charged should not only have agreed that a course of conduct shall be pursued which will necessarily amount to or involve the commission of that offence by himself or one or more other parties to the agreement, but must also be proved himself to have intended that the offence should be committed. Thus, it is submitted here that the appellant's case that he never intended that Andaloussi should be enabled to escape from prison raised an issue to be left to the jury, who should have been directed to convict him only if satisfied that he did so intend. I do not find it altogether easy to understand why the draftsman of this provision chose to use the phrase 'in accordance with their intentions'. But I suspect the answer may be that this seemed a desirable alternative to the phrase 'in accordance with its terms' or any similar expression, because it is a matter of common experience in the criminal courts that the 'terms' of a criminal conspiracy are hardly ever susceptible of proof. The evidence from which a jury may infer a criminal conspiracy is almost invariably to be found in the conduct of the parties. This was so at common law and remains so under the statute. If the evidence in a given case justifies the inference of an agreement that a course of conduct should be pursued, it is a not inappropriate formulation of the test of the criminality of the inferred agreement to ask whether the further inference can be drawn that a crime would necessarily have been committed if the agreed course of conduct had been pursued in accordance with the *several* intentions of the parties. Whether that is an accurate analysis or not, I am clearly driven by consideration of the diversity of roles which parties may agree to play in criminal conspiracies to reject any construction of the statutory language which would require the prosecution to prove an intention on the part of each conspirator that the criminal offence or offences which will necessarily be committed by one or more of the conspirators if the agreed course of conduct is fully carried out should in fact be committed. A simple example will illustrate the absurdity to which this construction would lead. The proprietor of a car hire firm agrees for a substantial payment to make available a hire car to a gang for use in a robbery and to make false entries in his books relating to the hiring to which he can point if the number of the car is traced back to him in connection with the robbery. Being fully aware of the circumstances of the robbery in which the car is proposed to be used he is plainly a party to the conspiracy to rob. Making his car available for use in the robbery is as much a part of the relevant agreed course of conduct as the robbery itself. Yet, once he has been paid, it will be a matter of complete indifference to him whether the robbery is in fact committed or not. In these days of highly organised crime the most serious statutory conspiracies will frequently involve an elaborate and complex agreed course of conduct in which many will consent to play necessary but subordinate roles, not involving them in any direct participation in the commission of the offence or offences at the centre of the conspiracy. Parliament cannot have intended that such parties should escape conviction of conspiracy on the basis that it cannot be proved against them that they intended that the relevant offence or offences should be committed.

There remains the important question whether a person who has agreed that a course of conduct will be pursued which, if pursued as agreed, will necessarily amount to or involve the commission of an offence is guilty of statutory conspiracy irrespective of his intention, and, if not, what is the mens rea of the offence. I have no hesitation in answering the first part of the question in the negative. There may be many situations in which perfectly respectable citizens, more particularly those concerned with law enforcement, may enter into agreements that a course of conduct shall be pursued which will involve commission of a crime without the least intention of playing any part in furtherance of the ostensibly agreed criminal objective, but rather with the purpose of exposing and frustrating the criminal purpose of the other parties to the agreement. To say this is in no way to encourage schemes by which police act, directly or through the agency of informers, as agents provocateurs for the purpose of entrapment. That is conduct of which the courts have always strongly disapproved. But it may sometimes happen, as most of us with experience in criminal trials well know, that a criminal enterprise is well advanced in the course of preparation when it comes to the notice either of the police or of some honest citizen in such circumstances that the only prospect of exposing and frustrating the criminals is that some innocent person should play the part of an intending collaborator in the course of criminal conduct proposed to be pursued. The mens rea implicit in the offence of statutory conspiracy must clearly be such as to recognise the innocence of such a person, notwithstanding that he will, in literal terms, be obliged to agree that a course of conduct be pursued involving the commission of an offence.

I have said already, but I repeat to emphasise its importance, that an essential ingredient in the crime of conspiring to commit a specific offence or offences under s 1(1) of the 1977 Act is that the accused should agree that a course of conduct be pursued which he knows must involve the commission by one or more of the parties to the agreement of that offence or those offences. But, beyond the mere fact of agreement, the necessary mens rea of the crime is, in my opinion, established if, and only if, it is shown that the accused, when he entered into the agreement, intended to play some part in the agreed course of conduct in furtherance of the criminal purpose which the agreed course of conduct was intended to achieve. Nothing less will suffice; nothing more is required.

Applying this test to the facts which, for the purposes of the appeal, we must assume, the appellant, in agreeing that a course of conduct be pursued that would, if successful, necessarily involve the offence of effecting Andaloussi's escape from lawful custody, clearly intended, by providing diamond wire to be smuggled into the prison, to play a part in the agreed course of conduct in furtherance of that criminal objective. Neither the fact that he intended to play no further part in attempting to effect the escape, nor that he believed the escape to be impossible, would, if the jury had supposed they might be true, have afforded him any defence.

(Lords Scarman, Diplock, Keith and **Brightman** agreed.)

Appeal dismissed

Questions

1. Unlike the Court of Appeal, the House did not insist that there must be two parties who do intend to carry out the agreement. What if only one intends to do so? Or none?

2. Was there a valid reason for not giving the words 'in accordance with their intentions' their natural meaning? Does the decision carry out the intention of Parliament (who must be taken to have read the Report presented to them by the Law Commission)?

3. Is there any warrant in the words of the Act for the opinion that a person is guilty of conspiracy only if he intended to play some part in the furtherance of the criminal purpose? A incites B to murder C and B agrees to do so. A intends to do nothing more. Is this not a conspiracy to murder?

4. Cf the draft Code Bill, cl 52 (1) (b) and (7). Would these provisions (a) implement the proposals of the Law Commission regarding intention and (b) make adequate provision for cases such as *Anderson* and Lord Bridge's example of the car-hire firm?

4. Corruption of public morals and outraging public decency

Shaw v Director of Public Prosecutions [1961] 2 All ER 446, House of Lords (Viscount Simonds, Lord Reid, Lord Tucker, Lord Morris of Borth-y-Gest and Lord Hodson)

The appellant published a booklet entitled 'The Ladies' Directory' with the object of enabling prostitutes to ply their trade. The booklet contained names and addresses and sometimes photographs of prostitutes and in some cases abbreviations indicating the type of conduct in which the woman would indulge. The women paid for the advertisements to be inserted. He was convicted on three counts: (i) conspiracy to corrupt public morals; (ii) living wholly or in part on the earnings of prostitution, contrary to s 30 (1) of the Sexual Offences Act 1956 and (iii) publishing an obscene article contrary to s 2 (1) of the Obscene Publications Act 1959. His appeal to the Court of

Criminal Appeal was dismissed. That Court held that conduct calculated and intended to corrupt public morals was an indictable misdemeanour at common law and that it followed that an agreement to do so was a conspiracy; s 2 (4) of the Obscene Publications Act 1959 (Smith & Hogan, ch 18, 3) did not prohibit the prosecution of the appellant for conspiracy because that offence consisted in an agreement to corrupt, and did not 'consist of the publication' of the booklets. The appellant appealed against his conviction on the first and second counts.

The following extracts from the speeches of their Lordships relate only to the conspiracy charge.

[**Viscount Simonds**, having asserted that, contrary to the appellant's submission conspiracy to corrupt public morals is an offence known to the common law, continued:]

Need I say, my Lords, that I am no advocate of the right of the judges to create new criminal offences? . . .

But I am at a loss to understand how it can be said either that the law does not recognise a conspiracy to corrupt public morals or that, though there may not be an exact precedent for such a conspiracy as this case reveals, it does not fall fairly within the general words by which it is described. I do not propose to examine all the relevant authorities. That will be done by my noble and learned friend. The fallacy in the argument that was addressed to us lay in the attempt to exclude from the scope of general words acts well calculated to corrupt public morals just because they had not been committed or had not been brought to the notice of the court before. It is not thus that the common law has developed. We are, perhaps, more accustomed to hear this matter discussed on the question whether such and such a transaction is contrary to public policy. At once the controversy arises. On the one hand it is said that it is not possible in the twentieth century for the court to create a new head of public policy, on the other it is said that this is but a new example of a well-established head. In the sphere of criminal law, I entertain no doubt that there remains in the courts of law a residual power to enforce the supreme and fundamental purpose of the law, to conserve not only the safety and order but also the moral welfare of the state, and that it is their duty to guard it against attacks which may be the more insidious because they are novel and unprepared for. That is the broad head (call it public policy if you wish) within which the present indictment falls. It matters little what label is given to the offending act. To one of your Lordships it may appear an affront to public decency, to another, considering that it may succeed in its obvious intention of provoking libidinous desires, it will seem a corruption of public morals. Yet others may deem it aptly described as the creation of a public mischief or the undermining of moral conduct. The same act will not in all ages be regarded in the same way. The law must be related to the changing standards of life, not yielding to every shifting impulse of the popular will but having regard to fundamental assessments of human values and the purposes of society. Today a denial of the fundamental Christian doctrine, which in past centuries would have been regarded by the ecclesiastical courts as heresy and by the common law as blasphemy, will no longer be an offence if the decencies of controversy are observed. When Lord Mansfield, speaking long after the Star Chamber had been abolished, said [In *Delaval* (1763) 3 Burr 1434 at 1438] that the Court of King's Bench was the *custos morum* of the people and had the superintendency of offences *contra bonos mores*, he was asserting, as I now assert, that there is in that court a residual power, where no statute has yet intervened to supersede the common law, to superintend those offences which are prejudicial to the public welfare. Such occasions will be rare, for Parliament has not been slow to legislate when attention has been sufficiently aroused. But gaps remain and will always remain since no one can foresee every way in which the wickedness of man may disrupt the order of society. Let me take a single instance to which my noble and learned friend, Lord Tucker, refers. Let it be supposed that, at some future, perhaps, early, date homosexual practices between adult consenting males are no longer a crime. Would it not be an offence if, even without obscenity, such practices were publicly advocated and encouraged by pamphlet and advertisement? Or must we wait until Parliament finds time to deal with such conduct? I say, my Lords, that, if the common law is powerless in such an event, then we should no longer do her reverence. But I say that her hand is still powerful and that it is for Her Majesty's judges to play the part which Lord Mansfield pointed out to them.

I have so far paid little regard to the fact that the charge here is of conspiracy. But, if I have correctly described the conduct of the appellant, it is an irresistible inference that a conspiracy between him and others to do such acts is indictable. It is irrelevant to this charge that s 2 (4) of the Obscene Publications Act 1959, might bar proceedings against him if no conspiracy were alleged. It may be thought superfluous, where that Act can be invoked, to bring a charge also of conspiracy to corrupt public morals, but I can well understand the desirability of doing so where a doubt exists whether obscenity within the meaning of the Act can be proved. . . .

The appeal on both counts should, in my opinion, be dismissed.

Lord Reid [dissenting]. . . . There are two competing views. One is that conspiring to corrupt public morals is only one facet of a still more general offence, conspiracy to effect public mischief; and that, like the categories of negligence, the categories of public mischief are never closed. The other is that, whatever may have been done two or three centuries ago, we ought not now to extend the doctrine further than it has already been carried by the common law courts. Of course I do not mean that it should only be applied in circumstances precisely similar to those in some decided case. Decisions are always authority for other cases which are reasonably analogous and are not properly distinguishable. But we ought not to extend the doctrine to new fields. I agree with R.S. Wright, when he says (*Law of Criminal Conspiracies and Agreements*, p 86):

> 'there appear to be great theoretical objections to any general rule that agreement may make punishable that which ought not to be punished in the absence of agreement.'

And I think, or at least I hope, that it is now established that the courts cannot create new offences by individuals. So far at least I have the authority of Lord Goddard CJ, in delivering the opinion of the court in *Newland* [[1954] 1 QB 158 at 167; [1953] 2 All ER 1067 at 1072] . . .

Every argument against creating new offences by an individual appears to me to be equally valid against creating new offences by a combination of individuals. But there is this historical difference. The judges appear to have continued to extend the law of conspiracy after they had ceased to extend offences by individuals. Again I quote from R.S. Wright (*Law of Criminal Conspiracies and Agreements*, p 88):

> 'In an imperfect system of criminal law the doctrine of criminal agreements for acts not criminal may be of great practical value for the punishment of persons for acts which are not, but which ought to be made punishable irrespectively of agreement.'

Even if there is still a vestigial power of this kind, it ought not, in my view, to be used unless there appears to be general agreement that the offence to which it is applied ought to be criminal if committed by an individual. Notoriously there are wide differences of opinion today how far the law ought to punish immoral acts which are not done in the face of the public. Some think that the law already goes too far, some that it does not go far enough. Parliament is the proper place, and I am firmly of opinion the only proper place, to settle that. When there is sufficient support from public opinion, Parliament does not hesitate to intervene. Where Parliament fears to tread it is not for the courts to rush in. . . .

In my judgment, the House is in no way bound and ought not to sanction the extension of 'public mischief' to any new field, and certainly not if such extension would be in any way controversial. Public mischief is the criminal counterpart of public policy, and the criminal law ought to be even more hesitant than the civil law in founding on it in some new aspect . . . as I understood counsel for the Crown, he did not argue that these advertisements were obscene libels, and that must mean that merely reading them does not tend to deprave or corrupt—if it did, they would be obscene libels by virtue of the definition in the Act, conspiracy to publish them would obviously be a crime, and the point now in controversy would never have arisen. So, any depraving and corrupting must be the result of resorting to the prostitutes. Prostitution is not an offence; it is not said that the woman or any man resorting to her is guilty of any offence. The argument is that, if two or more persons (who may include the prostitute herself) combine to issue such an invitation to members of the public, they are guilty of an offence. It could not matter whether the invitation was made by words or in some other way. So both Pearce and Brooks in *Pearce v Brooks* [(1866) LR 1 Exch 213] would today be guilty of an indictable offence by reason of having acted in concert to enable Brooks to attract men for the purpose of prostitution. That seems to me to be novel doctrine. It hardly seems to accord with views expressed in the *Mogul* series of cases [[1892] AC 25] to which I referred earlier, and I cannot believe that it is right.

But the advertisements also contain much more objectionable matter. The particulars refer to inducing readers to take part in 'other disgusting and immoral acts' and with this I think there must be coupled the reference in the intent charged to 'inordinate' desires. The evidence shows that the invitations were to resort to certain of the prostitutes for the purpose of certain forms of perversion. That I would think to be an offence for a different reason. I shall not examine the authorities, because I think that they establish that it is an indictable offence to say or do or exhibit anything in public which outrages public decency, whether or not it also tends to corrupt and deprave those who see or hear it. In my view, it is open to a jury to hold that a public invitation to indulge in sexual perversion does so outrage public decency as to be a punishable offence. If the jury in this case had been properly directed, they might well have found the appellant guilty for this reason. And the offence would be the same whether the invitation was made by an individual or by several people acting in concert. But it appears to me to be impossible to say the same with regard to ordinary prostitution. The common law has never treated the appearance of a prostitute in public as an indictable offence, however obvious her purpose might be, and an Act of Parliament has been found necessary to stop the nuisance of prostitutes parading in the public street. . . .

[**Lord Tucker, Lord Morris** and **Lord Hodson** made speeches dismissing the appeal.]

Appeal dismissed

Knuller Ltd v Director of Public Prosecutions [1972] 2 All ER 898, House of Lords
(Lord Reid, Lord Morris of Borth-y-Gest, Lord Diplock, Lord Simon of Glaisdale and Lord Kilbrandon)

The appellants published a magazine, the International Times, which contained on inner pages columns of advertisements headed 'Males'. Most of the advertisements were inserted by homosexuals for the purpose of attracting persons who would indulge in homosexual activities. The magazine had a circulation of over 30,000 copies. It was not disputed that a great many copies found their way into the hands of young students and schoolboys, but the prosecution did not make any point of the fact that it was likely that males under 21 would reply to the advertisements.

The appellants were charged in two counts. The first count alleged a conspiracy to corrupt public morals. The particulars were that the appellants conspired by means of the advertisements:

> 'to induce readers thereof to meet those persons inserting such advertisements for the purpose of sexual practices taking place between such male persons and to encourage readers thereof to indulge in such practices, with intent thereby to debauch and corrupt the morals as well of youth as divers other liege subjects of Our Lady the Queen.'

The second count alleged a conspiracy to outrage public decency by the publication of the 'lewd, disgusting and offensive' advertisements.

The appellants were convicted on both counts and their appeals to the Court of Appeal were dismissed.

Lord Reid. [having said that it was technically correct that s 2 (4) of the Obscene Publications Act does not exclude prosecution for the offence of corrupting morals but that the distinction seemed to him to offend against the policy of the Act; and that, if the draftsman had foreseen *Shaw's* case, he might well have drafted the subsection differently] . . . The matter was raised in the House of Commons on 3 June 1964 when the Solicitor-General gave an assurance, repeating an earlier assurance, that a conspiracy to corrupt public morals would not be charged so as to circumvent the statutory defence in s 4. That does at least show that Parliament has not been entirely satisfied with *Shaw's* case [[1962] AC 220, [1961] 2 All ER 446, p 258, above]. It is not for me to comment on the undesirability of seeking to alter the law by undertakings or otherwise than by legislation. But I am bound to say that I was surprised to learn that nothing effective had been done to bring this undertaking to the notice of the legal profession. Very experienced senior counsel in this case had never heard of it. It was not said that the course of the present case would have been different if counsel had known of the undertaking. But I cannot avoid an uneasy suspicion that ignorance of it may have effected the conduct of some other prosecution for this crime.

Although I would not support reconsidering *Shaw's* case I think that we ought to clarify one or two matters. In the first place conspiracy to corrupt public morals is something of a misnomer. It really means to corrupt the morals of such members of the public as may be influenced by the matter published by the accused.

Next I think that the meaning of the word 'corrupt' requires some clarification. One of my objections to the *Shaw* decision is that it leaves too much to the jury. I recognise that in the end it must be for the jury to say whether the matter published is likely to lead to corruption. But juries, unlike judges, are not expected to be experts in the use of the English language and I think that they ought to be given some assistance. In *Shaw's* case a direction was upheld in which the trial judge said [[1962] AC at 290; [1961] 2 All ER at 466]

> 'And, really, the meaning of debauched and corrupt is again, just as the meaning of the word induce is, essentially a matter for you. After all the arguments, I wonder really whether it means in this case and in this context much more than lead astray morally.'

I cannot agree that that is right. 'Corrupt' is a strong word and the jury ought to be reminded of that, as they were in the present case. The Obscene Publications Act 1959 appears to use the words 'deprave' and 'corrupt' as synonymous, as I think they are. We may regret that we live in a permissive society but I doubt whether even the most staunch defender of a better age would maintain that all or even most of those who have at one time or in one way or another been led astray morally have thereby become depraved or corrupt. I think that the jury should be told in one way or another that although in the end the question whether matter is corrupting is for them, they should keep in mind the current standards of ordinary decent people.

I can now turn to the appellants' second argument. They say that homosexual acts between adult males in private are now lawful so it is unreasonable and cannot be the law that other persons are guilty of an offence if they merely put in touch with one another two males who wish to indulge in such acts. But there is a material difference between merely exempting certain conduct from criminal penalties and making it lawful in the full sense. Prostitution and gaming afford examples of this difference. So we must examine the provisions of the Sexual Offences Act 1967 to see just how far it altered the old law. It enacts subject to limitation that a homosexual act in private shall not be an offence but it goes no further than that. Section 4 shows that procuring is still a serious offence and it would seem that some of the facts in this case might have supported a charge under that section.

I find nothing in the Act to indicate that Parliament thought or intended to lay down that indulgence in these practices is not corrupting. I read the Act as saying that, even though it may be corrupting, if people choose to corrupt themselves in this way that is their affair and the law will not interfere. But no licence is given to others to encourage the practice. So if one accepts *Shaw's* case as rightly decided it must be left to each jury to decide in the circumstances of each case whether people were likely to be corrupted. In this case the jury were properly directed and it is impossible to say that they reached a wrong conclusion. It is not for us to say whether or not we agree with it. So I would dismiss the appeal as regards the first count.

The second count is conspiracy to outrage public decency, the particulars, based on the same facts being that the appellants conspired with persons inserting lewd, disgusting and offensive advertisements in the magazine 'by means of the publication of the said magazine containing the said advertisements to outrage public decency'.

The crucial question here is whether in this generalised form this is an offence known to the law. There are a number of particular offences well known to the law which involve indecency in various ways but none of them covers the facts of this case. We were informed that a charge of this character has never been brought with regard to printed matter on sale to the public. The recognised offences with regard to such matter are based on its being obscene, i e likely to corrupt or deprave. The basis of the new offence, if it is one, is quite different. It is that ordinary decent-minded people who are not likely to become corrupted or depraved will be outraged or utterly disgusted by what they read. To my mind questions of public policy of the utmost importance are at stake here.

I think that the objections to the creation of this generalised offence are similar in character to but even greater than the objections to the generalised offence of conspiracy to corrupt public morals. In upholding the decision in *Shaw's* case [[1962] AC 220; [1961] 2 All ER 446] we are, in my view, in no way affirming or lending any support to the doctrine that the courts still have some general or residual power either to create new offences or so to widen existing offences as to make punishable conduct of a type hitherto not subject to punishment. Apart from some statutory offences of limited application, there appears to be neither precedent nor authority of any kind for punishing the publication of written or printed matter on the ground that it is indecent as distinct from being obscene. To say that published matter offends against public decency adds nothing to saying that it is indecent. To say, as is said in this charge, that it outrages public decency adds no new factor; it seems to me to mean no more than that the degree of indecency is such that decent members of the public who read the material will not merely feel shocked or disgusted but will feel outraged. If this charge is an attempt to introduce something new into the criminal law it cannot be saved because it is limited to what a jury might think to be a high degree of indecency.

There are at present three well-known offences of general application which involve indecency: indecent exposure of the person, keeping a disorderly house, and exposure or exhibition in public of indecent things or acts. The first two are far removed from sale of indecent literature and I can see no real analogy with the third.

Indecent exhibitions in public have been widely interpreted. Indecency is not confined to sexual indecency; indeed it is difficult to find any limit short of saying that it includes anything which an ordinary decent man or woman would find to be shocking, disgusting and revolting. And 'in public' also has a wide meaning. It appears to cover exhibitions in all places to which the public have access either as of right or gratis or on payment. There is authority to the effect that two or more members of the public must be able to see the exhibition at the same time, but I doubt whether that applies in all cases. We were not referred to any case where the exhibition consisted of written or printed matter but it may well be that public exhibition of an indecent notice or advertisement would be punishable.

But to say that an inside page of a book or magazine exposed for sale is exhibited in public seems to me to be going far beyond both the general purpose and intendment of this offence and any decision or even dictum in any case. I need not go farther because this offence is not charged and it was not argued that it could have been charged in this case.

I must now consider what the effect would be if this new generalised crime were held to exist. If there were in any book, new or old, a few pages or even a few sentences which any jury could find to be outrageously indecent, those who took part in its publication and sale would risk conviction. I can see no way of denying to juries the free hand which *Shaw's* case gives them in cases of conspiracy to corrupt public morals. There would be no defence based on literary, artistic or scientific merit. The undertaking given in Parliament with regard to obscene publications would not apply to this quite different crime. Notoriously many old works, commonly regarded as classics of the highest merit, contain passages which many a juryman might regard as outrageously indecent. It has been generally supposed that the days for Bowdlerising the classics were long past, but the introduction of this new crime might make publishers of such works think twice. It may be said that no prosecution would ever be brought except in a very bad case. But I have expressed on previous occasions my opinion that a bad law is not defensible on the ground that it will be judiciously administered. To recognise this new crime would go contrary to the whole trend of public policy followed by Parliament in recent times. I have no hesitation in saying that in my opinion the conviction of the appellants on the second count must be quashed.

Lords Morris, Simon and Kilbrandon agreed that the conviction on count 1 should be upheld. Lord Diplock, dissenting, thought it should be quashed.

Lords Diplock, Simon and Kilbrandon agreed that the conviction on count 2 should be quashed. Lord Diplock agreed with Lord Reid that there was no such offence as a conspiracy to outrage public decency. Lords Simon, Kilbrandon and Morris held that the authorities established an offence of outraging public decency and it followed that that it was a conspiracy to agree to commit it; but Lords Simon and Kilbrandon held that 'outrage' was a very strong word, going considerably beyond offending the susceptibilities of, or even shocking, reasonable people; and the jury had not been adequately directed to that effect, so the conviction must be quashed. Lord Morris thought the jury had been fairly and sufficiently directed and would have dismissed the appeal.

Appeal dismissed on count 1. Appeal allowed on count 2.

5. Conspiracy with a foreign element

Director of Public Prosecutions v Doot [1973] 1 All ER 940 House, of Lords (Lord Wilberforce, Viscount Dilhorne, Lord Pearson, Lord Kilbrandon and Lord Salmon)

The five respondents, all American citizens, were parties to an agreement made either in Belgium or Morocco to import cannabis resin into England with the object of re-exporting it from there to the United States. No part of the agreement was made in England. By s 2 of the Dangerous Drugs Act 1965 it was unlawful to import cannabis resin into the United Kingdom without a licence. The respondents had no licence. They concealed the cannabis resin in three separate vans which were then shipped to England. The cannabis was discovered by customs officers in one of the vans when it arrived at Southampton; the other vans were subsequently traced and the cannabis found in them. The respondents were convicted, inter alia, of conspiracy to import dangerous drugs, the particulars of the offence alleging that between certain dates 'in Hampshire and elsewhere' they had conspired together 'fraudulently to evade the prohibition imposed by the Dangerous Drugs Act 1965, on the importation of a dangerous drug, namely cannabis resin, into the United Kingdom'. On appeal against conviction on the conspiracy count the Court of Appeal quashed the conviction holding that the English courts had no jurisdiction to try the offence charged since the essence of the offence was the agreement between the respondents to do the unlawful act, the offence was complete when the agreement had been made, and the agreement had been made abroad. The Crown appealed.

[**Lord Wilberforce** made a speech, allowing the appeal.]

Viscount Dilhorne. . . .The conclusion to which I have come after consideration of these authorities and of many others to which the House was referred but to which I do not think it is necessary to refer is that though the offence of conspiracy is complete when the agreement to do the unlawful act is made and it is not necessary for the prosecution to do more than prove the making of such an agreement, a conspiracy does not end with the making of the agreement. It continues so long as the parties to the agreement intend to carry it out. It may be joined by others, some may leave it. Proof of acts done by the accused in this country may suffice to prove there was at the time of those acts a conspiracy in existence in this country to which they were parties and if that is proved, then the charge of conspiracy is within the jurisdiction of the English courts, even though the initial agreement was made outside the jurisdiction.

For the reasons I have stated, in my opinion this appeal should be allowed and the convictions of the respondents on count 1 restored.

[**Lord Pearson** made a speech, allowing the appeal. **Lord Kilbrandon** agreed that the appeal should be allowed.]

Lord Salmon. . . . It is obvious that a conspiracy to carry out a bank robbery in London is equally a threat to the Queen's peace whether it is hatched, say, in Birmingham or in Brussels. Accordingly, having regard to the special nature of the offence a conspiracy to commit a crime in England is, in my opinion, an offence against the common law even when entered into abroad, certainly if acts in furtherance of the conspiracy are done in this country. There can in such circumstances be no doubt that the conspiracy is in fact as well as in theory a real threat to the Queen's peace.

I recognise that the proposition that a conspiracy entered into abroad to commit a crime in England may be an offence under our law appears perhaps to be an exception to the well established general rule that 'all crime is local' and that our criminal law does not, as a rule, extend to acts done abroad: *Macleod v A-G for New South Wales* [[1891] AC 455]. Such acts may or may not be criminal under the law of the state in which they are committed. If they are not criminal under that law and do no harm here nor amount to a conspiracy to commit a crime here, it would be contrary to the rules of international comity to punish a foreigner and pointless to punish a British subject who had committed such an act abroad and then come to this country. The criminal law of England exists to protect this realm and all those within it, e g an agreement made in England to commit an unlawful act constitutes the crime of conspiracy only if the act is unlawful by the laws of England. It is not enough that it is unlawful only by the law of the country in which it is to be committed: *Board of Trade v Owen* [[1957] AC 602; [1957] 1 All ER 411].

If a conspiracy is entered into abroad to commit a crime in England, exactly the same public mischief is produced by it as if it had been entered into here. It is unnecessary for me to consider what the position might be if the conspirators came to England for an entirely innocent purpose unconnected with the conspiracy. If, however, the conspirators come here and do acts in furtherance of the conspiracy, e g by preparing to commit the planned crime, it cannot, in my view, be considered contrary to the rules of international comity for the forces of law and order in England to protect the Queen's peace by arresting them and putting them on trial for conspiracy whether they are British subjects or foreigners and whether or not conspiracy is a crime under the law of the country in which the conspiracy was born. It was unusual until recently to have any direct evidence of conspiracy. Conspiracy was usually proved by what are called overt acts, being acts from which an antecedent conspiracy is to be inferred. Where and when the conspiracy occurs is often unknown and seldom relevant. Today, however, it is possible to have direct evidence such as tape recordings of oral agreements. Suppose a case in which evidence existed of a conspiracy hatched abroad by bank robbers to raid a bank in London, or by terrorists to carry out some violent crime at an English airport, or by drug pedlars to smuggle large quantities of dangerous drugs on some stretch of the English coast. Suppose the conspirators came to England for the purpose of carrying out the crime and were detected by the police reconnoitring the place where they proposed to commit it, but doing nothing which by itself would be illegal, it would surely be absurd if the police could not arrest them then and there but had to take the risk of waiting and hoping to be able to catch them as they were actually committing or attempting to commit the crime. Yet that is precisely what the police would have to do if a conspiracy entered into abroad to commit a crime here were not in the circumstances postulated recognised by our law as a criminal offence which our courts had any jurisdiction to try.

I do not believe that any civilised country, even assuming that its own laws do not recognise conspiracy as a criminal offence, could today have any reasonable objection to its nationals being arrested, tried and convicted by English courts in the circumstances to which I have referred. Today, crime is an international problem—perhaps not least, crimes connected with the illicit drug traffic—and there is a great deal of co-operation between the nations to bring criminals to justice. Great care also is taken by most countries to do nothing which might help their own nationals to commit what would be crimes in other countries, see, e g s 3 (2) of the Dangerous Drugs Act 1965. . . .

Appeal allowed

Fraud with a foreign element presents an increasing problem. It may raise difficult issues as to the relation between statutory and common law conspiracy. In *A-G's Reference (No 1 of 1982)* [1983] 2 All ER 721, [1983] Crim LR 534 the defendants were charged with conspiracy to defraud X Co by causing loss by unlawful labelling, sale and supply of whisky, falsely purporting to be 'X label' products. The agreement was made in England but the whisky was to be sold in Lebanon. The trial judge held that he had no jurisdiction to try the indictment because the contemplated crime in Lebanon (obtaining by deception from the purchasers of the whisky) would not have been indictable in England. On the Attorney General's reference, the Court of Appeal held that the judge was right. Lord Lane CJ said (at [1983] 2 All ER 724):

The real question must in each case be what [was] the true object of the agreement entered into by the conspirators? In our judgment, the object here was to obtain money from prospective purchasers of whisky in the Lebanon by falsely representing that it was X Co's whisky. It may well be that, if the plan had been carried out, some damage could have resulted to X Co, but that would have been a side effect or incidental consequence of the conspiracy, and not its object. There may be many conspiracies aimed at particular victims which in their execution result in loss or damage to third parties. It would be contrary to principle, as well as being impracticable for the courts, to attribute to defendants constructive intentions to defraud third parties based on what the defendants should have foreseen as probable or possible consequences. In each case, to determine the object of the conspiracy, the court must see what the defendants actually agreed to do. Had it not been for the jurisdictional problem, we have no doubt that charge against these conspirators would have been conspiracy to defraud potential purchasers of the whisky, for that was the true object of the agreement. Accordingly we reject the first argument.

Counsel for the Attorney General's alternative approach is more bold. She asks us to lay down a different test from that propounded in *Board of Trade v Owen*, which she suggests is inappropriate to the facts of this case. The new test proposed is this. If a conspiracy to defraud, although to be wholly carried out abroad, would cause injury to an individual or company within the jurisdiction, it is indictable here. Counsel for the Attorney General contends that the protection of economic interest in this country against injury by fraud here or abroad is a legitimate and proper function of the criminal law.

The only semblance of support for her proposal is a dictum at the end of Lord Tucker's speech in *Board of Trade v Owen* [1957] 1 All ER 411 at 422, [1957] AC 602 at 634. After stating the general test already cited, he went on:

> 'In so deciding I would, however, reserve for future consideration the question whether a conspiracy in this country which is wholly to be carried out abroad may not be indictable here on proof that its performance would produce a public mischief in this country or injure a person here by causing him damage abroad.'

[His Lordship referred to Lord Wilberforce in *Doot* [1973] 1 All ER 940 at 943.]

If. . . .Lord Tucker's limitation to conspiracies entered into in England were removed, the new test would be immensely wide. Whenever a fraudulent conspiracy made abroad and to be carried out abroad sent ripples back to England washing over and damaging some economic interest here, an indictment would lie.

We can find no grounds in authority or principle for so holding. If it is necessary to enlarge the present jurisdiction, which we think it is not, then that is a matter for Parliament. Accordingly, we reject counsel for the Attorney General's second argument.

In *Tomsett* [1985] Crim LR 369 the London branch of a Swiss bank had transferred $7,000,000 to New York to earn overnight interest. The money should have been returned to London the next day. D, a telex operator employed by the Swiss Bank, sent a telex from its office in London diverting the money plus interest to another bank in New York for an account at its Geneva branch, which D2 had opened a month earlier. To cover this up, a second telex appeared to have been sent to New York shortly afterwards, giving the correct destination for the money, but was 'killed' before it was transmitted. The defendants' conviction for conspiring to steal the money was quashed. Although it is convenient to speak of the 'money', the property involved was a thing in action, the debt owed by the New York bank to the London branch of the Swiss bank. A thing in action is a legal concept (p 418, below) and is held to be situated in the country where the debtor or other person against whom a claim exists resides: Dicey, *Conflict of Laws* (10th edn), pp 528–530. Thus the alleged conspiracy was an agreement to steal property in New York.

Both the whisky label case and *Tomsett* might have been decided differently if the courts had been prepared to adopt a broader view of the nature of fraud. The case for it has been put as follows (by JCS in 'Theft, Conspiracy and Jurisdiction: *Tarling's* case' [1979] Crim LR 221 at 223):

> Whereas theft and obtaining by deception are defined in terms or the effect of the defendant's act on property, 'defraud' prima facie relates to the effect on the victim. It is something that happens to him. He is in some way wrongfully injured, usually by being impoverished.
>
> 'Now, I think that there are one or two things that can be said with confidence about the meaning of this word 'defraud' It requires a person as its object: that is, defrauding involves doing something to someone. Although in the nature of things it is almost invariably associated with the obtaining of an advantage for the person who commits the fraud, it is the effect upon the person who is the object of the fraud that ultimately determines its meaning.' (*Welham v DPP* [1961] AC 103 at p 123, per Lord Radcliffe.)
>
> Just as a man can be killed or wounded only in the place where he is, so arguably, he can be impoverished, or defrauded only in the place where he is. It might be objected that, if this is right, it provides too easy a way round jurisdictional limitations in the case of agreements to commit offences of dishonesty. If A and B agree in Germany to obtain by deception in Germany property owned by C who is in England, it is clear that an English court would hold that it had no jurisdiction to try a charge of conspiracy to obtain property by deception. Can this limitation be evaded

simply by framing the charge as one of conspiracy to defraud C? It seems rather unlikely that the courts would hold that their jurisdiction was so much greater than it has long been assumed to be. More probably, where the fraud consists in causing economic loss, it will be held to have been committed in the place where the victim's proprietary interest is situated.

It will be seen that in the whisky label case Lord Lane CJ drew a distinction between the 'true object' of the conspiracy and a 'side effect or incidental consequence' of it. However, in these cases the *object* of the conspirators is obviously to make a profit. The fact that someone will inevitably suffer a corresponding loss might be described as an incidental or side effect but it is nevertheless commonly regarded as a sufficient fraud. In *Scott v Metropolitan Police Comr* [1975] AC 819, [1974] 3 All ER 1032 discussed above, p 254, the defendants were convicted of conspiracy to defraud 'such companies and persons as might be caused loss by the unlawful copying and distribution of films the copyright in which and the distribution rights of which belonged to the companies and persons . . .'. In *Scott's case* the defendants temporarily deprived the companies of their films but it will be noted that this temporary deprivation was not the fraud alleged. The whole plan in that case was carried out in England, so no problem of jurisdiction arose; but the loss alleged as the fraud would seem to have been exactly the same if the films had been taken abroad and copied there. It is fraud, according to *Scott*, to deprive a person of property 'to which . . . he might become entitled'. There are two ways in which the copyright owners might be held to be so deprived: (i) because of the circulation of the pirated copies, they would sell fewer legitimate copies; and (ii) the defendants would be bound to account to the owners for the profits they made by selling the pirated copies (*Reading v A-G* [1951] AC 507, [1951] 1 All ER 617) and they clearly intended to deprive the owners of that money. *If* there was fraud in *Cooke and Sutcliffe* (p 253, above) it was of a similar nature. British Rail failed to sell so much food as they should; and they were to be deprived of the profits made by the defendants. And, similarly, in the whisky label case.

These losses may be 'side effect or incidental consequences' but are they not inevitable consequences of the success of the conspiracy and undoubtedly known to be such, by the conspirators? If so, are they not 'intended' by them (p 54–62, above)? Is it really necessary to prove that it was the 'object' or 'purpose' of the defendants to cause loss? If it were, how many conspiracies to defraud would there be? Does not the practice of the courts show that intention is enough? In *Anderson*, p 256, above, the House of Lords has now held that even intention need not be proved.

In *McPherson and Watts* [1985] Crim LR 508, CA, the appellants, using stolen cheque books and guarantee cards, obtained payment on a number of cheques in Germany. The cheques were drawn on the Nat West Bank which, through the cards, had guaranteed payment. The trial judge rejected a submission that the counts were not triable because the conspiracy had been carried out abroad. The convictions were quashed because he failed to leave to the jury the question whether it had been the appellants' object to defraud banks in England. Lawton LJ, however, seemed to recognise that intention would have been enough:

> 'The probability is that a jury [if the question had been left to them] would have concluded that both these appellants appreciated that what they did and what they were planning to do would inevitably and directly, defraud the English banks.'

Notice that the case for holding that there would be fraud in England is here stronger than in the whisky label case or in *Tomsett*, because the effect was to cause the English bank to act to its detriment—ie to pay out on the forged cheques. If, however, this constituted an offence under the Theft Act 1968, s 16 (2) (b) see *Charles*, p 455, below, then it was a conspiracy to commit that offence and not a conspiracy to defraud.

6. The draft Criminal Code Bill and conspiracy

The authors of the draft Code assumed that common law conspiracies will have been abolished and the gap filled by the creation of suitable substantive offences by the time a codification Bill is presented to Parliament. The draft Bill therefore avoids many of the troubles which plague the present law. It provides:

52 Conspiracy to commit an offence.
(1) A person is guilty of conspiracy to commit an offence or offences if:
(a) he agrees with any other person or persons that an act or acts shall be done which, if done, will involve the commission of the offence or offences by one or more of the parties to the agreement; and
(b) he and at least one other party to the agreement intend that the offence or offences shall be committed.
(2) For the purposes of subsection (1), an intention that an offence shall be committed is an intention in respect of all the elements of the offence.
(3) Subject to section 55(1), 'offence' in this section means any offence triable in England and Wales, provided that:
(a) it extends to an offence of murder which would not be so triable;
(b) it does not include a summary offence, not punishable with imprisonment, constituted by an act or acts agreed to be done in contemplation or furtherance of a trade dispute (within the meaning of the Trade Union and Labour Relations Act 1974).
(4) Where the purpose of an enactment creating an offence is the protection of a class of persons no member of that class who is the intended victim of such an offence can be guilty of conspiracy to commit that offence.
(5) A person cannot be guilty of conspiracy to commit an offence if the only other person or persons with whom he agrees is or are throughout the currency of the agreement:
(a) his spouse;
(b) a child under ten years of age;
(c) an intended victim of that offence who is a member of such a class of persons as is referred to in subsection (4).
(6)(a) An offence of conspiracy subsists until the agreed act or acts is or are done or until all or all save one of the parties to the agreement have abandoned the intention that such act or acts shall be done.
(b) A person may become a party to a subsisting offence of conspiracy by joining the agreement constituting the offence.
(7) A person may be guilty as an accessory to a conspiracy by others; but it is not an offence under this section or under any enactment referred to in subsection (9) to agree to assist, encourage or procure the commission of an offence by a person who is not a party to the agreement.
(8) A person may be convicted of conspiracy to commit an offence notwithstanding that:
(a) no other person has been or is charged with such conspiracy;
(b) the identity of any other party to the agreement is unknown;
(c) any other person appearing from the indictment to have been a party to the agreement has been or is acquitted of such conspiracy, unless in all the circumstances his conviction is inconsistent with the acquittal of the other.
(9) This section shall apply in determining whether a person is guilty of an offence of conspiracy to commit a specified offence created by any enactment other than this Act; but conduct which is an offence under any other such enactment shall not also be an offence under subsection (1).

Schedule 1 of the draft Bill provides, inter alia, the following illustrations:

52 (1) and (2a)	52 (iv)	It is an offence (abduction) for a person acting without lawful authority or excuse to take an unmarried girl under the age of sixteen out of the possession of her parent or guardian against his will. D agrees to help E to elope with P. D knows that P's father has forbidden contact between E and P but believes P to be eighteen. P is in fact fifteen. D and E are not guilty of conspiracy to abduct P. D does not act intentionally in respect of P's age (s 22), and therefore does not intend that the offence shall be committed.
52 (4) and (5)(c)	52 (v)	As in illustration 51 (iv) [p 244, above]. D and E are not guilty of conspiracy to commit the offence
52 (6)	52 (vi)	D and E agree that an armed robbery shall be carried out by a person to be recruited by E. E subsequently hires F to carry out the robbery. D, E and F are guilty of conspiracy to rob.
52 (7)	52 (vii)	It is an offence to escape from prison. E and F agree to effect the escape of G, a prisoner. D agrees to supply a car to be used in the escape and is paid £500. He does not intend to supply the car or that the agreement to effect the escape should be carried out. D is guilty as an accessory to the conspiracy of E and F.
	52 (viii)	D and E know that F intends to burgle the house where they are employed. Without F's knowledge they agree to leave a ladder positioned so as to facilitate F's entry to the house. They are not guilty of conspiracy to be accessories to the commission of burglary by F.
52 (8)(a) and (b)	52 (ix)	As in illustration 52 (vi). F is charged with conspiracy with persons unknown to rob. It is immaterial that D and E are not charged or that their identity is unknown.
52 (8)(c)	52 (x)	The facts are as in illustration 52 (vi). D, E and F are charged with conspiracy to rob. There is some circumstantial evidence against all three and a confession admissible only against F. D and E are acquitted and F is convicted. F's conviction is not inconsistent in the circumstances with the acquittal of D and E. If the evidence against D and E were substantially the same, and D were convicted and E acquitted, D's conviction would be inconsistent in the circumstances with E's acquittal.

CHAPTER 14

Attempt

The law of attempts to commit crime is now to be found in the Criminal Attempts Act 1981, p 586, below which repealed the common law. It will be noted that the Act begins with the words, 'If, with intent to commit an offence to which this section applies . . .'. The next case, *Whybrow*, states that, in attempt, the intent is 'the principal ingredient of the crime.' It is convenient then to begin with a consideration of the mens rea of attempt. The Act offers no definition of 'intent' (cf the draft Code, cl 22, p 50 above and cl 53(2), p 285, below) but in *Pearman* [1984] Crim LR 675 the Court of Appeal could see no reason why the Act should have altered the common law in this respect and applied *Mohan*, p 271, below and it is clear that *Whybrow* also represents the present law.

R v Whybrow (1951) 35 Cr App Rep 141, Court of Criminal Appeal (Lord Goddard CJ, Hilbery, Finnemore, Slade and Devlin JJ)

The appellant was convicted of attempted murder of his wife. The case for the prosecution was that he had administered an electric shock to her while she was in a bath, by means of an apparatus connecting a soap dish with the mains power supply. The appellant's explanation of the apparatus was that it was to provide an earth for a wireless set in his bedroom and that, if she did get an electric shock, it was an accident. He appealed against his conviction on the ground of misdirection.

Goddard LCJ. . . . The case lasted two days and the learned Judge's summing-up, so far as the facts were concerned, was meticulously careful and meticulously accurate, but unfortunately he did, in charging the jury, confuse in his mind for a moment the direction given to a jury in a case of murder with the direction given to a jury in a case of attempted murder. In murder the jury is told—and it has always been the law—that if a person wounds another or attacks another either intending to kill or intending to do grievous bodily harm, and the person attacked dies, that is murder, the reason being that the requisite malice aforethought, which is a term of art, is satisfied if the attacker intends to do grievous bodily harm. Therefore, if one person attacks another, inflicting a wound in such a way that an ordinary, reasonable person must know that at least grievous bodily harm will result, and death results, there is the malice aforethought sufficient to support the charge of murder. But, if the charge is one of attempted murder, the intent becomes the principal ingredient of the crime. It may be said that the law, which is not always logical, is somewhat illogical in saying that, if one attacks a person intending to do grievous bodily harm and death results, that is murder, but that if one attacks a person and only intends to do grievous bodily harm, and death does not result, it is not attempted murder, but wounding with intent to do grievous bodily harm. It is not really illogical because, in that particular case, the intent is the essence of the crime while, where the death of another is caused, the necessity is to prove malice aforethought, which is supplied in law by proving intent to do grievous bodily harm . . . .

The learned Judge, as I say, had in his mind the charge which is given to a jury in a case of

270

murder. . . . There is no question that that was a misdirection, and the jury should have been told that the essence of the offence was the intent to murder . . .

[The court concluded that there had been no substantial miscarriage of justice and dismissed the appeal under the proviso to s 4 of the Criminal Appeal Act 1907.]

R v Mohan [1975] 2 All ER 193, Court of Appeal, Criminal Division (James LJ, Talbot and Michael Davies JJ)

The appellant was convicted on count 2 of an indictment of attempting by wanton driving to cause bodily harm to be done to a police constable. The judge directed the jury that it must be proved that the appellant 'must have realised at the time that he was driving that such driving . . . was likely to cause bodily harm if he went on, or he was reckless as to whether bodily harm was caused. It is not necessary to prove an intention actually to cause bodily harm.'

[**James LJ**, giving the judgment of the Court, said:]

The first question we have to answer is: what is the meaning of 'intention' when that word is used to describe the mens rea in attempt? It is to be distinguished from 'motive' in the sense of an emotion leading to action: it has never been suggested that such a meaning is appropriate to 'intention' in this context. It is equally clear that the word means what is often referred to as 'specific intent' and can be defined as 'a decision to bring about a certain consequence' or as the 'aim'. In *Hyam* [p 307, below] Lord Hailsham (at p 332) cited with approval the judicial interpretation of 'intention' or 'intent' applied by Asquith LJ, in *Cunliffe v Goodman* [1950] 2 KB 237 at 253. 'An "intention" to my mind connotes a state of affairs which the party intending—I will call him X—does more than merely contemplate: it connotes a state of affairs which, on the contrary, he decides so far as in him lies to bring about and which, in point of possibility, he has a reasonable prospect of being able to bring about by his own act of volition.'

If that interpretation of 'intent' is adopted as the meaning of mens rea in the offence of attempt it is not wide enough to justify the direction in the present case. The direction, taken as a whole, can be supported as accurate only if the necessary mens rea includes not only specific intent but also the state of mind of one who realises that, if his conduct continues, the likely consequence is the commission of the complete offence and who continues his conduct in that realisation, or the state of mind of one who, knowing that continuation of his conduct is likely to result in the commission of the complete offence, is reckless as to whether or not that is the result. [His Lordship considered *Hyam* (p 307, below) and continued:]

We do not find in the speeches of their Lordships in the case of *Hyam* anything which binds us to hold that mens rea in the offence of attempt is proved by establishing beyond reasonable doubt that the accused knew or correctly foresaw that the consequences of his act unless interrupted would 'as a high degree of probability', or would be 'likely' to, be the commission of the complete offence. Nor do we find authority in that case for the proposition that a reckless state of mind is sufficient to constitute the mens rea in the offence of attempt.

Prior to the enactment of the Criminal Justice Act 1967, s 8, the standard test in English Law of a man's state of mind in the commission of an act was the foreseeable or natural consequence of the act. Therefore it could be said that when a person applied his mind to the consequences that did happen and foresaw that they would probably happen he intended them to happen, whether he wanted them to happen or not. So knowledge of the foreseeable consequence could be said to be a form of 'intent'. [His Lordship read s 8, (p 562, below).]

Thus, upon the question whether or not the accused had the necessary intent in relation to a charge of attempt, evidence tending to establish directly, or by inference, that the accused knew or foresaw that the likely consequence, and, even more so, the highly probable consequence, of his act—unless interrupted—would be the commission of the completed offence, is relevant material for the consideration of the jury. In our judgment, evidence of knowledge of likely consequences, or from what knowledge of likely consequences can be inferred, is evidence by which intent may be established but it is not, in relation to the offence of attempt, to be equated with intent. If the jury find such knowledge established they may and, using common sense, they probably will find intent proved, but it is not the case that they must do so.

An attempt to commit crime is itself an offence. Often it is a grave offence. Often it is as morally culpable as the completed offence which is attempted but not in fact committed.

Nevertheless it falls within the class of conduct which is preparatory to the commission of a crime and is one step removed from the offence which is attempted. The Court must not strain to bring within the offence of attempt conduct which does not fall within the well established bounds of the offence. On the contrary, the Court must safeguard against extension of those bounds save by the authority of Parliament. The bounds are presently set requiring proof of specific intent, a decision to bring about, in so far as it lies within the accused's power, the commission of the offence which it is alleged the accused attempted to commit, no matter whether the accused desired that consequence of his act or not.

In the present case the final direction was bad in law. Not only did the judge maintain the exclusion of 'intent' as an ingredient of the offence in Count 2 but he introduced an alternative basis for a conviction which did not and could not constitute the necessary mens rea . . .

Appeal on count 2 allowed

Questions

1. ' . . . P and D are walking at the edge of a cliff; they both see a watch lying on the path in front of them, and both plunge forward to get it. P is the more powerful and swifter man and will infallibly reach the watch first unless D takes extreme measures. D therefore gives P a sudden and treacherous push which he intends to result in P's falling over the cliff. He knows full well that if he is successful in his plan, P will certainly be killed . . . . There is no reason why D should not be guilty of attempted murder': Glanville Williams, *The Mental Element in Crime*, p 24. Do you agree?

2. D sets fire to P's house in order to frighten P away from the neighbourhood. D does not want to kill P but he knows that it is probable that P will be killed in the blaze. P survives. Is D guilty of attempted murder? Cf. *Hyam*, p 307, below.

1. Intention and circumstances

It is clear that intention is required as to any result in the actus reus—in *Whybrow*, death, in *Mohan* bodily harm. What is less clear is whether intention is also required as to circumstance. It is arguable that a person has 'an intent to commit an offence' if he intends to produce the relevant result and is reckless whether the circumstances necessary to constitute the crime exist, where such recklessness is sufficient for the complete offence. A man intends to have sexual intercourse with a woman, being aware that she may not be consenting to his doing so. If he succeeds he will be guilty of rape. If he fails, should he be guilty of an attempt? In *Pigg* [1982] 2 All ER 591, CA it was held, though perhaps *obiter*, that this amounted to attempted rape at common law but it has not been decided whether this continues to be an offence under the Sexual Offences (Amendment) Act 1976, p 577, below. The Law Commission, rejecting the earlier view of their Working Party, considered that a distinction between circumstances and results was unworkable and proposed that intention should be required as to all the elements of the offence. The draft Code, cl 53 (2), p 285, below, would make this entirely clear: but some think it is not so under the Act. In *DPP v Morgan* [1975] 2 All ER 347 at 357 Lord Hailsham said

' . . . if the intention of the accused is to have intercourse nolens volens, that is recklessly and not caring whether the victim be a consenting party or not, that is equivalent on ordinary principles to *an intent to do the prohibited act without the consent of the victim.'* (Authors' italics)

It is by no means impossible then that the state of mind described by Lord Hailsham might be held to be an intent to commit rape within the meaning of the Act. Professor Williams has argued that this is right: [1983] Crim LR 365. Richard Buxton QC takes the opposite view [1984] Crim LR 25. He argues at p 33:

The law under the Criminal Attempts Act

Pigg is, of course, an authority on the law as it stood before the 1981 Act. The case did not, *pace* Dr Williams,[1] *decide* that recklessness can be sufficient mens rea in a case of attempt, because it was assumed on both sides and never argued that recklessness as to the woman's consent sufficed for conviction; but admittedly the acceptance of that assumption points strongly to recklessness as to consent having been the pre-Act law. One could well wish that, the government having decided that that law should be altered and intention be required as to *all* elements in the actus reus, some more expansive form of words had been adopted in the 1981 Act than 'intent to commit an offence.' But, in interpreting those words, there are, it is submitted, absolutely no grounds for following the analysis advocated by Dr Williams.

We should first mention two arguments on which we do not rely, although both of them would have to be taken very seriously by a court hearing a charge of attempt where the prosecution followed Dr Williams in arguing that reckless as to a 'circumstance' (for instance, as to the woman's consent in attempted rape) was enough to achieve a conviction. It would be difficult, in view of the terms of the 1981 Act, to say that Dr Williams' arguments are so clearly correct that the tribunal was not left in real doubt as to what that Act means. Any such doubt must be resolved in favour of the accused, by interpreting the Act as incorporating the more lenient rule as to *mens rea* favoured by the Law Commission.[2] Second, that ambiguity well justifies reference to the long title of the Act, as 'the plainest of all the guides to the general objectives of a statute.'[3] Dr Williams suggests that the Act gives no indication of a Parliamentary intention to change the law[4], but the description of the Act in its long title as 'an Act to amend the law of England and Wales as to attempts to commit offences' at least justifies the observation that no one should be surprised if the Act indeed turns out to have amended the law as it was believed to be in *Pigg*.

The foregoing are, however, arguments that need only be deployed if the court is in doubt as to what the 1981 Act requires the prosecution to prove as the *mens rea* applicable to a charge of attempt. But on the plain wording of the Act there is no scope for any such doubt. While, as we have said, the phrase 'intent to commit an offence' could be more happily put, it is impossible to interpret it other than as requiring 'intent' as to every element constituting the crime. Dr Williams argues[5] that 'intention in law generally implies a requirement of knowledge of circumstances [but] it may bear a different meaning in connection with a particular crime; *Pigg* shows that this was so for attempts at common law.' But that, with respect, is simply not correct. *Pigg* showed, to quote Dr Williams' description of the case higher up the same page, that attempted rape could be committed by a person who was *reckless* as to the woman's consent. Particularly after *Caldwell* it is surely clear that recklessness is in law a different state of mind from intent. At the least, *Pigg* certainly does not suggest that a requirement of *intent* is satisfied by a finding of recklessness, nor can a court construing a statute that speaks of intent substitute for intent a requirement only of recklessness.

A court construing the 1981 Act would, therefore, have no ground for requiring of the accused anything other than 'intent' as to every element in the completed crime. Since intent includes knowledge, the accused's state of mind in regard to the woman's consent in attempted rape must be knowledge that she did not consent, as the Law Commission recommended. The true position is indeed summarised in a cogent exchange in the *Textbook*:

' "May an offence be so worded as to require intention as to consequences but to be satisfied with recklessness as to circumstances?" "Yes, of course, if the law expressly says so. A problem arises only if the law requires intention to the offence and does not provide for recklessness as to circumstances. There is a strong argument in point of principle for saying that in such a case knowledge of (or belief in) circumstances is required, not merely recklessness." '

Dr Williams admittedly expresses some fears as to whether the courts will always see the force of the principle referred to; but in our view a court would and indeed must follow the stated principle when interpreting the requirement of 'intent' in the Criminal Attempts Act.

1. [1983] Crim LR 373.
2. See *Liew Sai Wah v Public Prosecutor* [1969] 1 AC 295 at 301, per Viscount Dilhorne; *DPP v Ottewell* [1970] AC 642 at 649, per Lord Reid; *Bloxham* [1983] 1 AC 109 at 114E, HL.
3. *Black-Clawson Ltd v Papierwerke AG* [1975] AC 591 at 647F, per Lord Simon of Glaisdale.
4. [1983] Crim LR 373.
5. Ibid.

Though the discussion has centred largely on attempted rape, it should be noted that it relates to all offences which may be committed by recklessness as to circumstances. The offence of obtaining by deception contrary to s 15 of the Theft Act 1968 may be committed by a reckless deception. If, in order to induce P to buy his car, D states that it has had only one previous owner, having no idea whether this statement is true or false, and P is thereby persuaded to buy the car, D has obtained the price by deception if the statement is untrue. If P is not persuaded, is D guilty of an attempt to obtain?

2. The actus reus of attempt

The actus reus of attempt cannot be defined with the same precision as the actus reus of a substantive offence. It can take as many forms as there are substantive offences. It may, moreover, be an objectively innocent act. D puts sugar in P's tea. There is nothing wrong with that—P likes sweet tea. But D believes, mistakenly, that the sugar is arsenic and intends to kill P. He is guilty of attempted murder, the actus reus of the attempt being that objectively innocent act. It will be recalled that Lord Goddard in *Whybrow*, p 270, above, described the intent as the principal ingredient of the offence of attempt. It is not however the only ingredient. Something must be done to put the intent into execution. The question is, how much? The law has always distinguished mere acts of preparation from attempts. It was said at common law that the act had to be sufficiently proximate to the complete offence. The doctrine of proximity excluded from liability acts which some thought should entail guilt. A conspicuous example is *Robinson*, below. The 1981 Act, p 586, below, following the recommendations of the Law Commission, makes no attempt to state a test of proximity. It merely requires that the act done by the defendant should be 'more than merely preparatory to the commission of the offence'.

The only well-settled rule of common law was that if D had done the last act which, as he knew, was necessary to achieve the consequence alleged to be attempted, he was guilty. Every act preceding the last one might quite properly be described as 'preparatory'. The assassin crooks his finger round the trigger *preparatory* to pulling it. If every preparatory act were to be regarded as outside the scope of the offence the effect of the Act would be to narrow the offence. It was well recognised at common law that some prior acts were sufficiently proximate: see *White*, p 278 below but cf *Ilyas*, p 276, below. Though it has been argued that the word 'merely' does no more than add emphasis (Griew, annotations to *Current Law Statutes*), it seems that it has a key role. Not all preparatory acts are excluded; only those that are *merely* preparatory; and it is thought that the assassin's crooking of the finger, though preparatory, would not be regarded as *merely* preparatory.

The reason, it appears, is that he is now engaged in the commission of the offence—as Rowlatt J put it in *Osborn* (1919) 84 JP 63, he is 'on the job'.

Whether the act is more than merely preparatory is a question of fact: s 4(4). In a jury trial it is for the judge to decide whether there is sufficient evidence to support such a finding.

R v Robinson [1915] 2 KB 342, Court of Criminal Appeal
(Lord Reading CJ, Bray and Lush JJ)

The appellant was a jeweller. A policeman passing his shop heard someone inside shout, 'I am bound and gagged. Open the door.' The policeman whistled for assistance and then broke in. The appellant was found with his legs and one hand tied with cords. He said that after locking the door of the shop the previous evening he had been knocked on the head. The safe was open and empty. He said, 'They have cleared me out.' The police not being satisfied, took him to the station and searched his premises. They found the jewellery concealed in a recess at the back of the safe. The appellant admitted that he had insured his stock for £1200 and that he had staged the burglary with a view to making a claim. He was convicted of attempting to obtain the money by false pretences and appealed.

Lord Reading CJ. On those facts it was not disputed that the appellant had arranged a fraudulent scheme with the object of its being used to obtain money on the policy from the underwriters, and the only question was whether, the police having intervened and prevented its execution, the offence of attempting to obtain the money had been committed. If he had made a claim of the money from the underwriters, or had communicated to them the facts of the pretended burglary upon which a claim was to be subsequently based, he clearly could have been convicted of an attempt to obtain the money. It seems to the Court upon consideration of the authorities that there is no real difficulty in formulating the principle of law which is applicable to cases of this kind. A safe guide is to be found in the statement of the law which is laid down by Parke B in *Reg v Eagleton* [(1855) Dears CC 515 at p 538]:

> 'The mere intention to commit a misdemeanour is not criminal. Some act is required, and we do not think that all acts towards committing a misdemeanour are indictable. Acts remotely leading towards the commission of the offence are not to be considered as attempts to commit it, but acts immediately connected with it are.'

The difficulty lies in the application of that principle to the facts of the particular case. In some cases it is a difficult matter to determine whether an act is immediately or remotely connected with the offence of which it is alleged to be an attempt. In other cases the question is easier of solution, as for instance in *Reg v Button* [[1900] 2 QB 597]. There upon the evidence there was a false pretence made directly to the race authorities with the intent to make them part with the prize, and one which, but for the fact of the fraud being discovered, would necessarily have had that effect. In the present case the real difficulty lies in the fact that there is no evidence of any act done by the appellant in the nature of a false pretence which ever reached the minds of the under-writers, though they were the persons who were to be induced to part with the money. The evidence falls short of any communication of such a pretence to the underwriters or to any agent of theirs. The police were not acting on behalf of the underwriters. In truth what the appellant did was preparation for the commission of a crime, not a step in the commission of it. It consisted in the preparation of evidence which might indirectly induce the underwriters to pay; for if the police had made a report that a burglary had taken place,—and that was presumably what the appellant intended,—it may very well be that the underwriters would have paid without further inquiry. But there must be some act beyond mere preparation if a person is to be charged with an attempt. Applying the rule laid down by Parke B, we think that the appellant's act was only remotely connected with the commission of the full offence, and not immediately connected with it. If we were to hold otherwise we should be going further than any case has ever yet gone, and should be opening the door to convictions for acts which are not at present criminal offences. We think the conviction must be quashed, not on the technical ground that no information or evidence as to the property lost was given to the underwriters as required by the policy, but upon the broad ground that no communication of any kind of the false pretence was made to them.

Appeal allowed

Had Robinson done an act which was 'more than merely preparatory' to the commission of obtaining money by false pretences (or deception)? If he had not, what of the defendant in *Comer v Bloomfield* (1970) 55 Cr App Rep 305? He owned a van worth about £35 and insured only in respect of third party risks. He crashed the van and pushed the wrecked vehicle into some woods so as to conceal it. The following day, he reported to the police that the van had been stolen the night before. A week after the crash, the respondent gave a circumstantial story to the police of how the van had been stolen. The same day he wrote to his insurers: 'I have had my van stolen . . . I would be pleased to know if I could make a claim for stolen van . . . ' Later the respondent admitted the truth and on being asked why he had falsely reported the van to be stolen, said: 'Well, it was a write-off. I thought I would have a few bob off the insurance.' He was charged with attempting to obtain money by deception but the justices were of opinion that the letter amounted only to an inquiry and was therefore not sufficiently proximate to the offence to amount to an attempt. The prosecutor appealed by way of case stated. The Divisional Court held that the justices were entitled to conclude that the respondent's acts were not sufficiently proximate and dismissed the appeal. The letter was 'no more than a preliminary inquiry to sound the position and see if a claim could effectively be put forward at all.' Was this more than 'merely preparatory'? Would it have been if the letter had said (i) 'I wish to make a claim for my stolen van. Please send me a claim form'? or (ii) 'My van has been stolen. I claim its value (£35) under my insurance'? Cf the next case.

R v Ilyas (1983) 78 Cr App Rep 17, Court of Appeal
(Purchas LJ, Tudor Evans and Peter Pain JJ)

In 1980 the appellant reported to the police that his car had been stolen and telephoned his insurers informing them of the theft. He went to the insurers' office and obtained a claim form but he never completed it. It appears that he knew the car had not been stolen. He was convicted of attempting to obtain property from the insurers by deception (NB, at common law, not under the 1981 Act) and appealed, inter alia, on the ground that the judge should have withdrawn the case from the jury for lack of evidence.

[**Tudor Evans J**, giving the judgment of the court:]

There is high authority to support Miss Thomas's submission. In *Eagleton* (1854–1855) Dears CC 515, 6 Cox CC 559, Parke B, delivering the judgment of a court of nine judges, said, at p 538 and p 571 respectively:

> 'The mere intention to commit a misdemeanour is not criminal, some act is required; and we do not think that all acts towards committing a misdemeanour are indictable. Acts remotely leading towards the commission of the offence are not to be considered as attempts to commit it; but acts immediately connected with it are; and if in this case after the credit with the relieving officer for the fraudulent overcharge, any further step on the part of the defendant had been necessary to obtain payment, as the making out a further account, or producing the vouchers to the board, we should have thought that the obtaining credit in account with the relieving officer would not have been sufficiently proximate to the obtaining of the money. But on the statement in this case, no other act on the part of the defendant would have been required. It was the last act depending on himself towards the payment of the money and therefore it ought to be considered as an attempt.'

The concluding parts of this passage seem to us to be a clear statement of law that before an act or acts can be considered to be sufficiently proximate, a defendant must have carried out every act which depended on himself.

This test was adopted by Lord Diplock in *Director of Public Prosecutions v Stonehouse*, p 278, below.

[Having referred to the test stated in *Davey v Lee*, below, the judge continued:]

We do not find it necessary to decide which of the two tests we consider to be correct in law because we are of the opinion that whichever is applied, the learned judge should have withdrawn the case from the jury. The acts which the appellant carried out pursuant to his dishonest intention were that he reported his vehicle to the police as having been stolen and he reported the false loss to his insurers and obtained a claim form. Nothing further was done by him or on his behalf. Judged by the test in *Eagleton* (supra) as approved by Lord Diplock in *DPP v Stonehouse*, the appellant had plainly not done every act which it was necessary for him to do to achieve the result he intended.

Equally, tested by the language of the judgments in *Davey v Lee* (below), we are of the opinion that the appellant's acts were remote from the commission of the offence. The offence charged was a dishonest attempt to obtain money from an insurance company. All that the appellant had done was to obtain a claim form. That act and all other acts which preceded it in point of time, seem to us to be merely preparatory and remote from the contemplated offence. This is a sufficient ground for quashing the conviction.

Appeal allowed

Davey v Lee [1967] 2 All ER 423, Queen's Bench Division
(Lord Parker CJ, Diplock LJ and Ashworth J)

The appellants were convicted of attempting to steal a quantity of metal. They were found by the police outside the perimeter of a compound. At the eastern end of the compound was a copper store containing the metal in question. The compound contained, in addition to the copper store, other stores, an office building and dwelling-houses. At its eastern end the compound was surrounded by an outer wire fence, a fence of six strands of heavy barbed wire, a fence of four strands of insulated wire and finally a chain link fence. All the fences had been cut. Wire cutters were found in the appellants' van and bolt croppers were found at a point near where something had been thrown from the van. All four types of wire could have been cut by the bolt croppers, only the insulated wire by the wire cutters.

The appellants did not give evidence. The justices were satisfied by the evidence that the appellants intended to break and enter the compound and to steal therein in the vicinity of the place where the fences had been attacked such copper as was removable, with or without the use of bolt croppers, but that they were interrupted by Motor Patrol Constable Jane when they had very nearly completed the last of the steps necessary to break into the compound for the purpose of carrying out their intention. Quarter Sessions dismissed an appeal.

Lord Parker CJ. . . . A helpful definition is given in para 4104 in Archbold's *Pleading, Evidence and Practice* (36th edn), where it is stated in this form:

'It is submitted that the actus reus necessary to constitute an attempt is complete if the prisoner does an act which is a step towards the commission of the specific crime, which is immediately and not merely remotely connected with the commission of it, and the doing of which cannot reasonably be regarded as having any other purpose than the commission of the specific crime.'

It seems to me that the facts of this case fully come within the test, and that the magistrates were undoubtedly right in the view they formed. I would dismiss this appeal.

[**Diplock LJ** and **Ashworth J** agreed.]

Appeal dismissed

Questions

1. Has the test stated in *Archbold* any relevance to the question whether the act was more than merely preparatory? (It is omitted from the current (41st) edition, para 28-54, which does not even mention *Davey v Lee*.

2. Was the act more than merely preparatory to theft? Were the appellants in the course of committing the offence—or 'on the job'? But suppose that they had confessed to an intention to rape the compound manager's wife. Was the act more than merely preparatory to that?

R v White [1908–10] All ER Rep 340, Court of Criminal Appeal
(Lord Alverstone CJ, Bray and Pickford JJ)

The appellant's mother was found dead sitting on a sofa. Beside her was a glass three parts filled with a drink called nectar. The glass also contained two grains of cyanide of potassium. Her death was due to heart failure due to fright or some external cause. There was no evidence to show that she had taken any of the liquid and the quantity of poison in the glass was, even if she had taken the whole, insufficient to cause her death.

The appellant was indicted for murder and convicted of attempted murder. He appealed.

[**Bray J** (delivering the judgment of the court), having held that there was evidence on which the jury could find that the appellant had put the poison in the glass and reviewed the evidence of his intent, continued:]

He, therefore, perfectly well knew the deadly character of this poison, and supposed that a very small quantity would produce an instant effect. Upon consideration of all the evidence, including the denial of the prisoner that he had put anything into the wine glass at all, we are of opinion that there was sufficient evidence to warrant the jury also in coming to the conclusion that the appellant put the cyanide in the glass with intent to murder his mother.

The next point made was that, if he put it there with that intent, there was no attempt at murder; that the jury must have acted upon a suggestion of the learned judge in his summing up that this was one, the first or some later, of a series of doses which he intended to administer and so cause her death by slow poisoning, and if they did act on that suggestion there was no attempt at murder, because the act of which he was guilty—viz, the putting of poison in the wine glass—was a completed act and could not be and was not intended by the appellant to have the effect of killing her at once. It could not kill unless it were followed by other acts which he might never have done. There seems no doubt that the learned judge in effect did tell the jury that, if this was a case of slow poisoning, the appellant would be guilty of the attempt to murder. We are of opinion that this direction was right, and that the completion or attempted completion of one of a series of acts intended by a man to result in killing is an attempt to murder even although this completed act would not, unless followed by the other acts, result in killing. It might be the beginning of the attempt, but would none the less be an attempt. While saying this, we must say also that we do not think it likely the jury acted on this suggestion, because there was nothing to show that the administration of small doses of cyanide of potassium would have a cumulative effect; we think it much more likely, having regard to the statement made by the prisoner to the witness Carden, that the appellant supposed he had put sufficient poison in the glass to kill her. This, of course would be an attempt to murder. . . .

Appeal dismissed

Director of Public Prosecutions v Stonehouse [1977] 2 All ER 909, House of Lords
(Lord Diplock, Viscount Dilhorne, Lord Salmon, Lord Edmund-Davies and Lord Keith of Kinkel)

The appellant, a well-known public figure, was convicted of thirteen offences of dishonesty and on five charges of attempting by deception to enable another to obtain property contrary to s 15 of the Theft Act 1968. The appellant had insured his life for £125,000 with five different life insurance companies. On 20 November 1974 he faked his death by drowning in Miami so that his wife, who was not a party to the plan, could claim the policy moneys. The news of his 'death' was, as he intended, quickly transmitted to England by the media, but his wife made no claim on any of the policies. Five weeks later the appellant was discovered in Australia and extradited. His appeal was dismissed by the Court of Appeal which certified that the following point of law of public importance was involved in the decision:

'Whether the offence of attempting on 20 November 1974 to obtain property in England by deception, the final act alleged to constitute the offence of attempt having occurred outside the jurisdiction of the English courts is triable in an English court, all the remaining acts necessary to constitute the complete offence being intended to take place in England.'

Lord Diplock. . . . . So I start by considering the territorial element in [the jurisdiction of the English courts] to try the complete crime; for on this and on the corresponding offence under s 32 of the Larceny Act 1916, which has been replaced by s 15 of the Theft Act 1968, there is long-standing authority to the effect that in a 'result-crime' the English courts have jurisdiction to try the offence if the described consequence of the conduct of the accused which is part of the definition of the crime took place in England. . . .

In those reported cases where the false representations have been made abroad but the property has been obtained in England, the property has been obtained by the offender himself and this has in fact involved some physical act in England by the the offender or by someone else, not necessarily an accomplice but possibly an innocent agent or bailee accepting possession or control of the property on the offender's behalf. In the instant case if the crime which the accused was charged with attempting to commit had been completed, he would have enabled another person, Mrs Stonehouse, to obtain the property, viz the policy moneys, for herself and no further act would have needed to be done in England by the accused himself or anyone acting on his behalf. Should this make any difference? In my opinion it does not. The basis of the jurisdiction under the terminatory theory is not that the accused has done some physical act in England, but that his physical acts, wherever they were done, have caused the obtaining of the property in England from the person to whom it belonged. Whether he has caused it to be obtained for himself through the instrumentality of an innocent agent, such as the Post Office, acting on his behalf, or has caused it to be obtained by an innocent third party cannot in my view make any difference to the jurisdiction of the English court to try the offence.

My Lords, if this be the principle on which the English courts would have had jurisdiction to try the complete offence which the accused was charged with attempting to commit, that principle is broad enough to cover also their jurisdiction to try the inchoate offence of attempting to commit it. The accused had done all the physical acts lying within his power that were needed to comply with the definition of a complete crime justiciable by an English court; and his state of mind at the time he did them also satisfied the definition of that crime. All that was left was for him not to be found out before the intended consequence could occur. Once it is appreciated that territorial jurisdiction over a 'result-crime' does not depend on acts done by the offender in England but on consequences which he causes to occur in England, I see no ground for holding that an attempt to commit a crime which, if the attempt succeeded, would be justiciable in England does not fall within the jurisdiction of the English courts, notwithstanding that the physical acts intended to produce the proscribed consequences in England were all of them done abroad. . . .

If in order to found jurisdiction it were necessary to prove that something had been actually caused to happen in England by the acts done by the offender abroad a qualified answer to the certified question would be called for. I do not think that it is necessay. So I would answer with an unqualified Yes.

I can deal much more briefly with the two other points of law relied on on behalf of the accused. The constituent elements of the inchoate crime of an attempt are a physical act by the offender sufficiently proximate to the complete offence and an intention on the part of the offender to commit the complete offence. Acts that are merely preparatory to the commission of the offence, such as, in the instant case, the taking out of the insurance policies, are not sufficiently proximate to constitute an attempt. They do not indicate a fixed irrevocable intention to go on to commit the complete offence unless involuntarily prevented from doing so. As it was put in the locus classicus *Eagleton*[1]:

'The mere intention to commit a misdemeanour is not criminal, some act is required; and we do not think that all acts towards committing a misdemeanour are indictable. Acts remotely leading towards the commission of the offence are not to be considered as attempts to commit it; but acts immediately connected with it are . . .'

In other words the offender must have crossed the Rubicon and burnt his boats.

In the instant case, as I have pointed out, the accused by 20 November 1974 had done all the physical acts lying within his power that were needed to enable Mrs Stonehouse to obtain the policy moneys if all had gone as he had intended. There was nothing left for him to do thereafter except to avoid detection of his real identity. That was the day on which he crossed his Rubicon and burnt his boats.

In my opinion it is quite unarguable that, given the necessary intention, those acts were not sufficiently proximate to the complete offence of obtaining property by deception to be capable in law of constituting an attempt to commit the offence. On the contrary they clearly do constitute such an attempt in law. At the trial indeed the judge so regarded the matter. He directed the jury in the following terms: . . . (His Lordship quoted from the direction and continued:) So he did not leave it to the jury to decide whether the acts of the accused in Florida on 20 November 1974 were sufficiently 'proximate' to constitute an attempt.

The Court of Appeal took the view, which I understand is shared by all your Lordships, that what the accused did on 20 November 1974 was so obviously sufficiently proximate to constitute an attempt that no reasonable jury could have any doubt about it; a contrary finding could only be perverse. The Court of Appeal held that in those circumstances it was proper for the judge to tell the jury that if the facts alleged were proved they should find the accused guilty of the attempt charged. With this I agree . . .

In directing the jury that the only acts of the accused of which there is evidence are outside the range of proximity which any reasonable person could regard as conforming to that concept as a constituent element in the common law offence of attempt, the judge is exercising his responsibility as controller of the trial to prevent its resulting in a perverse verdict which would call for correction by the Court of Appeal under s 2 (1) (a) of the Criminal Appeal Act 1968. If the acts of the accused lay beyond the other extreme of the range of proximity within which any reasonable person could doubt that they conformed to that concept as a constituent element in the offence of attempt, a verdict of acquittal on the ground that the acts of the accused were not sufficiently proximate would also be perverse.

When in either case any opinion to the contrary would be equally perverse, why, if the judge is bound to tell the jury that particular acts of the accused are so remotely connected with the intended offence that they do not amount in law to an attempt to commit it, should the judge be forbidden to tell the jury that particular acts of the accused, if established, are so closely connected with the offence that they do amount in law to an attempt to commit it?

It has been suggested by counsel for the prosecution that the difference lies in the accused being entitled to be protected against being *convicted* on a verdict that is perverse but is entitled to his chance of a perverse verdict of *acquittal*. This cynical view of justice and the jury system is inconsistent with the test applied by the Court of Appeal under the proviso to s 2 (1) of the Criminal Appeal Act 1968 in deciding to uphold a conviction, notwithstanding that the trial judge has made an error in summing-up, on the ground that no substantial miscarriage of justice has actually occurred as a result of his error.

[**Viscount Dilhorne** agreed with Lord Diplock that the judge had not misdirected the jury by instructing them that the facts proved constituted an attempt.]

[**Lord Salmon** held that the judge had misdirected the jury by not leaving it to them to decide whether the facts proved amounted to an attempt, but since no reasonable jury could have failed so to find, the proviso to s 2 (1) of the Criminal Appeal Act 1968 should be applied.]

[**Lord Edmund-Davies** referred to *Robinson*, p 275, above, and continued:]

The court there founded its judgment on the well-known statement of Parke B in *Eagleton*[2] that 'Acts remotely leading towards the commission of the offence are not to be considered as attempts to commit it, but acts immediately connected with it are'. But it is open to doubt whether that dictum was properly applied in *Robinson*, a decision which has been said to be 'as favourable to the accused as any that can be found in English law; it seems to be too favourable' (Glanville Williams, *Criminal Law: The General Part*[3]). In my respectful judgment, the ruling that there cannot be a conviction for an attempt to obtain by false pretences (or, now, of obtaining by deception) unless the pretence or the deception has come to the knowledge of the intended victim should not be followed, and the court was wrong in treating all preceding acts as mere preparation and therefore as not amounting to perpetration of an attempt to commit the full offence.

The much-cited *Eagleton*[4] has itself been criticised as going further than is called for, in stressing the necessity for the act charged to be 'immediately connected' with the full offence: see, for example, Archbold's *Pleading, Evidence and Practice in Criminal Cases*[5]. In his *Digest of the Criminal Law*[6] Stephen laid it down that: 'An attempt to commit a crime is an act done with intent to commit that crime, and forming part of a series of acts which would constitute its actual commission if it were not interrupted.' That definition has been repeatedly cited with judicial approval, as by Byrne J in *Hope v Brown*[7] and by the Divisional Court in *Davey v Lee*[8]. But, as Lord Parker CJ observed in the latter case[9], Stephen's definition 'does not help to define the point of time at which the series of acts begins'. Professor Glanville Williams has added[10] . and rightly in my judgment, that:

> 'This definition, notwithstanding its judical commendation, is too narrow, because it is now settled that one may attempt a crime by impossible means, in which case the attempt is doomed to failure quite apart from interruption. It is, also, too wide, because many acts that have been held to be mere preparation were part of a series of acts that would have constituted the actual commission of the crime if it were not interrupted.'

In the present case, while conceding that the mere act of taking out the insurance policies was, at most, only an act of preparation, counsel for the prosecution submitted:

> 'Where a crime is not completed, the principal may be indicted for an attempt to commit the crime, provided that (a) it is capable of being committed and (b) he has himself or by his agent performed an act or acts which show that he is trying to commit the crime, as distinct from merely getting ready to commit it.'

This was a commendable endeavour to embrace the elements (1) of intention, (2) of the necessity for the overt acts charged to be part of a series of acts which would constitute the full offence if uninterrupted, and (3) of proximity, which Lord Hailsham of St Marylebone LC said in *Haughton v Smith*[11] were the true ingredients of a criminal attempt and which I respectfully adopt in the present case.

But what, for my part, I am not prepared to adopt is the view sometimes advanced (e g Glanville Williams, *Criminal Law (The General Part)*[12] and Smith and Hogan, *Criminal Law*[13]) that a man *must* be guilty of an attempt if he has done the last act which he expects to do and which it is necessary for him to do to achieve the consequence aimed at. That is probably based on the observation of Parke B in *Eagleton*[14], regarding a charge of attempting to obtain money from guardians of the poor by false pretences, that:

> 'no other act on the part of the defendant would have been required. It was the last act *depending on himself*, towards the payment of the money, and *therefore* it ought to be considered as an attempt'. (Italics supplied.)

But even so, the wrongdoer may not have progressed a sufficient distance along the intended path, and his actions may still amount (as in *Hope v Brown*) to no more than mere 'preparation'. As Lord Widgery CJ pointed out in the instant case, he may have been given merely 'jobs of a kind which were obviously preparatory and not proximate'. What has always to be borne in mind, as I think, is the nature of the *full* offence alleged to have been attempted. In the instant case, it would not have been that by deception the appellant dishonestly obtained a cheque from an insurance company by falsely pretending that he had died, for such a charge would be manifestly ridiculous; and, even if it were not, one can well imagine it being argued, on the lines of *Robinson*, that what the appellant did in Miami did not go beyond mere preparation. But the charge actually laid was based on one of the extended meanings of 'obtain' contained in s 15 (2) of the Theft Act 1968, viz 'enabling another to obtain'. So, had it been carried through to completion and not being interrupted by his being recognised and arrested in Australia, the full offence charged would have been that the appellant dishonestly and by deception enabled his wife to obtain insurance money by the false pretence that he had drowned. Towards the commission of *that* offence, the faking of his death (a) was intended to produce that result; (b) was the final act that he could perform, and (c) went a substantial distance towards the attainment of his goal. In short, in my judgment it was sufficiently proximate thereto to constitute the attempts charged in count 17 to 21. . . .

[His Lordship held that the judge ought to have left it to the jury to say whether the facts constituted an attempt but, since no reasonable jury could have decided otherwise, the proviso should be applied.]

My Lords, the erroneous direction in the instant case is but one example of a prevalent (though fortunately not universal) tendency in our courts in these days to withdraw from the jury issues which are solely theirs to determine. The tendency has been deplored, notably by Lord Devlin in commenting on *Larkin*[15]: see his *Trial by Jury*[16]. It has been markedly evinced in cases arising under the Road Traffic Acts, and this despite the earlier warning of Lord Parker CJ in *Waters*[17]: see, for example, *Kelly*[18]('driving or attempting to drive') and *Morris*[19] ('accident'). Whether this tendency springs from distrust of the jury's capacity or from excessive zeal in seeking to simplify their task, it needs careful watching, and there are welcome signs that judges are awakening to that fact: see, for example, *Guttridge*[20], *Clemo*[21] and *Martin*[22]. And it has to be said that, while the possibility of a perverse verdict cannot be wholly eliminated, the risk that directions to convict may lead to quashings can be obviated by clarity in identifying the contested issue, by commenting on the evidence (maybe even in strong terms, provided that they fall short of a direction, as Lord Devlin stressed in *Chandler v Director of Public Prosecutions*[23]), and by then trusting the jury to play their constitutional part in the criminal process . . .

[**Lord Keith of Kinkel**, having quoted from the judgment of the Court of Appeal in *Baxter* [1971] 2 All ER at 362, continued:]

. . . I would myself prefer to rest the matter not so much on the proposition that the offence is a continuing one, or on the alternative proposition, also favoured by Sachs LJ, that part of the offence is committed within the jurisdiction, as on the principle that an offence is committed if the effects of the act intentionally operate or exist within the jurisdiction. This would be the situation if a bomb or a letter sent from abroad were found anywhere within the jurisdiction. Its presence at that spot would be an intended effect of the act of despatching it. In my opinion it is not the present law of England that an offence is committed if no effect of an act done abroad is felt here, even though it was the intention that it should be. Thus if a person on the Scottish bank of the Tweed, where it forms the border between Scotland and England, were to fire a rifle at someone on the English bank, with intent to kill him, and actually did so, he would be guilty of murder under English law. If he fired with similar intent but missed his intended victim, he would be guilty of attempted murder under English law, because the presence of the bullet in England would be an intended effect of his act. But if he pressed the trigger and his weapon misfired, he would be guilty of no offence under the law of England, provided at least that the intended victim was unaware of the attempt, since no effect would have been felt there. If, however, the intended victim were aware of the rifle being pointed at him, and was thus put into a state of alarm, an effect would have been felt in England and a crime would have been committed there. The result may seem illogical, and there would appear to be nothing contrary to international comity in holding that an act done abroad intended to result in damage in England, but which for some reason independent of the actor's volition had no effect there, was justiciable in England. But if that were to be the law, I consider that it would require to be enacted by Parliament . . .

[His Lordship held that the jury had been misdirected but that the proviso should be applied.]

Appeal dismissed

1. (1855) Dears CC 515 at 538.
2. (1855) Dears CC 515 at 538.
3. 2nd edn (1961), p 627.
4. (1855) Dears CC 515.
5. 39th edn (1976), para 4105.
6. 9th edn (1950), p 24, art 29.
7. [1954] 1 All ER 330 at 332.
8. [1968] 1 QB 366, [1967] 2 All ER 423.
9. [1968] 1 QB 366 at 370, [1967] 2 All ER 423 at 425.
10. 'Police Control of Intending Criminals,' [1955] Crim LR 66 at 68.
11. [1975] AC 476 at 492, [1973] 3 All ER 1109 at 1114.
12. 2nd edn (1961), p 622.
13. 3rd edn (1973), p 198.
14. (1855) Dears CC 515 at 538.
15. [1943] 1 KB 174, [1943] 1 All ER 217.
16. Revised edition (1966), p 186, appendix II.
17. (1963) 47 Cr App Rep 149.
18. [1970] 2 All ER 198.
19. [1972] 1 All ER 384.
20. [1973] RTR 135.
21. [1973] RTR 176n.
22. (1972) 57 Cr App Rep 279.
23. [1964] AC 763 at 804, [1962] 3 All ER 142 at 154.

Questions

1. D, in Miami, posts a letter addressed to P in England. The letter contains a false pretence designed to persuade P to send D money. The letter is destroyed in a fire in Miami. Is D guilty of an offence justiciable in England, according to Lord Diplock or Lord Keith? Should he be guilty of such an offence?

2. If Mrs Stonehouse had been (she was not) a party to the fraud, would the answer to the question whether Stonehouse's acts were sufficiently proximate have been the same? (Cf commentary, below.)

3. D overhears E and F plotting to steal from the office where he works. In order to facilitate their plan he leaves open the window through which he believes they intend to enter and leaves the keys to the strong room in an unlocked drawer. E and F change their minds and do not carry out the plan. Is D guilty of an attempt to commit any crime? What if G finds the window open, enters, takes the keys and steals from the strong room? Cf *Davis* [1977] Crim LR 542.

4. Is the criticism by Lord Edmund-Davies of the 'last act' doctrine valid?

5. Should the judge be able to direct the jury that particular facts, if proved, amount to an attempt to commit a crime?

Commentary by JCS on *DPP v Stonehouse* [1977] Crim LR 544 at 547.

In the present case, the scheme had advanced no farther than in *Comer v Bloomfield*. It does not necessarily follow that that case is wrongly decided. There is an important difference between the facts of the two cases. Stonehouse's plan involved the use of an innocent agent, his wife. Bloomfield's plan did not. All that Stonehouse had to do, having staged his death, was to remain concealed; the claim would be made by his wife. Bloomfield had to fill in and despatch a claim form. Stonehouse was much nearer to the end of his part in the enterprise than Bloomfield and nearer still than Robinson. It is argued below that, where the alleged principal offender has done, or attempted to do, the last act which it is intended that he should do and which it is necessary for him to do in order to achieve the consequence alleged to be attempted, this must be sufficiently proximate. Having disappeared, Stonehouse had to stay out of the way long enough for it to be inferred that he was dead and for his wife to make a claim. If she had in fact made a claim, the case would have been clear, but she did not. This, however, was, in the nature of the scheme, a matter over which he could exercise no control—he was supposed to be dead. He had done all he could do up to the moment of his discovery—and was continuing to do so. That must surely be sufficiently proximate.

It is interesting to note that it would have been quite different if his wife had been a party to the fraudulent scheme. On this hypothesis, she would have been the principal in the first degree in the proposed fraud and she had done nothing to further it. As an aider and abettor the defendant could have been guilty of an offence only if the principal had committed the *actus reus*, at least of attempt. It is possible to be guilty of aiding and abetting an attempt, but there is no such offence as an attempt to aid and abet, except where aiding and abetting is the principal offence, as in the Suicide Act 1961—Cf *McShane* [1977] Crim LR 737. Therefore, even though the defendant had completely performed his part of the scheme, he would have been guilty of no offence. . . . if the defendant's wife had been an accomplice, his part would have consisted only in doing preparatory acts. The attempt, on this hypothesis, was to be committed by the wife. Since however, the wife was in fact innocent, the defendant himself was the principal in the first degree in the proposed crime. It appears that an act which is insufficiently proximate when done as an abettor may be an attempt when done as the intending principal acting through an innocent agent.

(iii) *The 'last act' doctrine.* No satisfactory general test for determining whether an act is sufficiently proximate to amount to an attempt has ever been formulated but it has been said that there is at least one rule that can be asserted with confidence—that if the defendant has done the last act which he intends to do and which it is necessary for him to do in order to achieve the consequence alleged to be attempted, he has gone far enough. See Glanville Williams, *The Criminal Law*, *The General Part*, (2nd ed) p 622; Smith and Hogan, *Criminal Law* (3rd ed), p 198. Lord Edmund-Davies casts doubt on even this rule (p 167). He refers to *Eagleton* (1855) Dears CC 515, where the Court, in holding the accused to be rightly convicted of an attempt, said that he had done the last act, *depending on himself*, towards the completion of the crime. Lord Edmund-Davies says that even though the accused may have done the last act depending on himself, he may not have gone far enough. That last act may be no more than preparation. He quotes Lord Widgery in the Court of Appeal as pointing out that a defendant may have been given merely 'jobs of a kind which were obviously preparatory and proximate.' These remarks evidently relate to secondary parties, and it is respectfully agreed that the last act done by a secondary party does not necessarily amount to an attempt. As pointed out above, the acts done by the defendant in the present case, though his last acts, would not have been sufficiently proximate under *Comer v Bloomfield* if he had been a secondary party; but he was a principal acting through an innocent agent, so the majority had no difficulty in holding him to be guilty without casting any doubt on *Comer v Bloomfield*, still less on *Robinson*.

Where the defendant is to be the principal offender, it must surely be true to say that his last act is sufficiently proximate. It is now or never. If there is no attempt at this point, then it seems that the crime is one which cannot be attempted. There may be a few such crimes but they are rare. See Smith and Hogan, *Criminal Law* (3rd ed), p 206 [see 5th edn, p 267]. It is submitted that there could be no serious doubt that the accused's last act was sufficiently proximate where, if his intention had been effectuated, he would have been the direct cause of the actus reus. It might be argued that it is different where the accused is acting through an innocent agent: that the accused is guilty of an attempt only when *the agent* has done a sufficiently proximate act. If that is right, either the present case or *Comer v Boomfield* is wrongly decided; but it is submitted that it is not right. If D hands poison to his *accomplice*, telling him to administer it tomorrow night to P, that might well be thought too remote to be an attempt to murder; but if D hands poison to an *innocent agent*, telling him that it is a medicine which he must administer to P tomorrow, it is submitted that D is guilty of an attempt to murder.

Eagleton was a case of innocent agency. The defendant made false statements as to the weight of loaves he had supplied to poor persons, thereby causing the relieving officer to enter a credit in his favour which would have led, without further action on the defendant's part, to his being paid money to which he was not entitled. If the relieving officer had been an accomplice whose entries would have deceived the paying officer, the defendant's statement would probably not have been an attempt.

Lord Edmund-Davies also referred to *Hope v Brown* [1954] 1 All ER 330. This case, which is criticised by Professor Glanville Williams at [1956] Crim LR 66 and 68, is a questionable decision, particularly in the light of the present case. In a shop managed by the defendant were found packages of meat bearing tickets marked with the correct price. In a drawer was found another set of tickets, marked with higher prices, prices above the maximum then permitted by law. The defendant had prepared this second set of tickets and instructed a girl to change them before delivering the meat. The Divisional Court held that this was not an attempt to sell meat at an excessive price. It would have been different, they thought, if the offending tickets had been affixed to the meat. The girl was apparently not charged and presumably she was an innocent agent. Even if she was a party to the illegality, the defendant was probably the principal offender because the girl was not a 'seller.' It appears that the defendant had done the last act intended to be done, and necessary to be done, by him. If the girl had been uninterrupted and had done as he told her, the offence would have been completed, at the latest, when she delivered the meat. At least as much, probably more, had to happen in the present case before the crime was complete. The defendant had to stay out of the way, his wife had to make a claim, the claim had to be scrutinised by the insurance company's officials, the company had to satisfy itself that the defendant was dead, payment had to be authorised and made. A possible distinction is that the girl in *Hope v Brown* was under the immediate supervision of the defendant who could have intervened at any moment. But Mr Stonehouse could also have intervened at any moment, simply by announcing that he was alive. It is thought that *Hope v Brown* is difficult to reconcile with the present case and is probably wrongly decided.

3. The Code Bill on attempts

Clause 53 of the Code Bill is substantially a restatement of the Criminal Attempts Act 1981 in the style and language of the Code. It provides:

53 Attempt to commit an offence.

(1) A person who, with the intention of committing an indictable offence, does an act that is more than merely preparatory to the commission of the offence is guilty of attempt to commit the offence.

(2) An 'intention of committing an offence' means an intention in respect of all the elements of the offence.

(3) 'Act' in this section includes an omission only where the offence intended is one to which section 20 (1) (a) applies.

(4) Where there is evidence to support a finding that an act was more than merely preparatory to the commission of the offence intended, the question whether that act was more than merely preparatory is a question of fact.

(5) Subject to section 55 (1), this section applies to any offence which, if it were completed, would be triable in England and Wales as an indictable offence, other than:

    (a) conspiracy (under section 52 or any other enactment);

    (b) offences under section 4 (1) (assisting offenders) or 5 (1) (accepting or agreeing to accept consideration for not disclosing information about an arrestable offence) of the Criminal Law Act 1967.

(6) A person may be guilty as an accessory to an attempt by another to commit an offence; but it is not an offence under this section or under any enactment referred to in subsection (7) (a) to attempt to assist, encourage or procure the commission of an offence by another.

(7) (a) In determining whether a person has committed an offence created by an enactment other than this section of attempt to commit a specified offence, this section shall apply with the substitution in subsection (1) of a reference to the specified offence for the words 'an indictable offence'.

    (b) Conduct which is an offence under any other such enactment shall not also be an offence under this section.

The draft does, however, seek to clarify the law in a number of respects as explained in the Report:

14.30 *The fault requirement for attempt*. Subsection (1) restates the Act by stipulating that for an attempt a person must have the 'intention' of committing an offence. This accords with the recommendation of the Law Commission who thought that 'the concept of the mental element in attempt should be expressed as an intent to bring about each of the constituent elements of the offence attempted. Put more simply, this may be stated as an intent to commit the offence attempted' [Law Com No 102, para 2.14]. However, some doubt has arisen about the interpretation of section 1 (1) of the Act as a result of the decision of the Court of Appeal in *R v Pigg* [[1982] 1 WLR 762]. In that case a conviction for attempted rape was upheld on the basis that the accused was reckless whether the woman consented to intercourse. The case was decided on the common law, but it has been argued [see Glanville Williams, op cit 409] that the principle involved—that where recklessness as to a circumstance suffices for the substantive offence it should suffice for the attempt—should apply under the Act also. We take the view that this would be contrary to the considered proposal of the Law Commission and inconsistent with the fault requirements proposed for the other preliminary offences. Accordingly subsection (2) seeks to resolve the matter by providing that the intention required for an attempt is an intention in respect of all the elements of the offence. In the case of attempted rape, for example, this means that it would have to be proved that the accused was aware or was almost certain that the woman was not consenting.

14.31 *Attempt by omission*. The extended meaning given to the word 'act' in the Code allows for the possibility of an attempt being committed by an omission. The general view is that the interpretation of 'act' in the Criminal Attempts Act 1981 is not so extensive, although it was the intention of the Government that in certain cases an attempt by omission could be charged under the Act. [See Dennis in [1982] Crim. L.R. 7–8.] We take the view that in the two types of case set out in clause 20 (1) (a) it would be appropriate to allow for the possibility of an attempt by omission. Subsection (3) provides accordingly. Such cases are likely to be rare, but where there is clear evidence, for example, of an attempt to cause the death of a child or elderly member of the household by starvation or neglect, it seems right that a charge of attempted murder should be available.

14.34 *Accessories and attempts*. The principle underlying section 1 (4) (b) of the Criminal Attempts Act 1981 is that it is not an offence to attempt to aid, abet etc. an offence which is actually committed. The provision is not aptly worded, however, since aiding, abetting etc. is not as such an offence in the same sense as the other offences referred to In *R v Dunnington* [[1984] QB 472] the Court of Appeal was faced with the argument that the provision had in fact achieved the quite different effect of abolishing liability for aiding and abetting an attempt. After referring to the Law Commission's Report on Attempt, the court concluded that as a matter of construction section 1 (4) did not have the effect contended for, and that it continued to be possible for a person to be liable as an accomplice to an attempt. Subsection (6) restates this principle together with a clarification of the intended effect of section 1 (4) (b).

Schedule 1 of the draft Bill provides the following illustrations:

53 (1) and (4)	53 (i)	D puts poison in P's tea with the intention of killing P. J throws the tea away before P drinks it. D will be guilty of attempted murder (s 56) if his act is capable in law of being more than merely preparatory to the murder of P and the jury then find that it was in fact more than merely preparatory to the commission of that offence.
53 (1) and (2)	53 (ii)	It is an offence (rape) for a man to have sexual intercourse with a woman without her consent, either knowing that she does not consent to it, or being reckless whether she consents to it. D, who is voluntarily intoxicated, tries to have sexual intercourse with P but fails. P does not consent to intercourse with D. D claims that because he was intoxicated he gave no thought to whether P was consenting to intercourse. D is not guilty of attempted rape; he was neither aware nor almost certain that P was not consenting to intercourse (s 22 (a): intention).
53 (3)	53 (iii)	D has custody of P, her mentally handicapped child by her divorced husband. E moves in to live with D and P. The police visit the house some weeks later and find P emaciated and very ill. D and E confess that, hoping P would die, they had agreed not to feed P or to call medical attention when P fell ill. D (P's parent) and E (a member of the same household as P) are guilty of the attempted murder of P.
53 (6)	53 (iv)	As in illustration 53 (i). The poison is supplied to D by E, who knows of D's intention. Assuming that D is guilty of attempted murder, E is guilty as accessory to D's attempt.
	53 (v)	D, knowing that E intends to burgle the house where D is employed, leaves a ladder positioned so as to facilitate E's entry to the house. The ladder is subsequently blown over by the wind and E does not see it. E enters the house using a duplicate key. D is not guilty of an attempt to be an accessory to the burglary committed by E.

Attempt and impossibility: a very recent development

At p 595 below, the facts of *Shivpuri* are summarised and it is indicated that, at the time of writing, an appeal had been heard by the House of Lords and their decision was awaited. It was given on 15 May 1986.

Lord Bridge, having quoted section 1 of the Criminal Attempts Act 1981, p 586, below, continued:

"Applying this language to the facts of the case, the first question to be asked is whether the appellant intended to commit the offences of being knowingly concerned in dealing with and harbouring drugs of Class A or Class B with intent to evade the prohibition on their importation. Translated into more homely language the question may be rephrased, without in any way altering its legal significance, in the following terms: did the appellant intend to receive and store (harbour) and in due course pass on to third parties (deal with) packages of heroin or cannabis which he knew had been smuggled into England from India? The answer is plainly yes, he did. Next, did he in relation to each offence, do an act which was more than merely preparatory to the commission of the offence? The act relied on in relation to harbouring was the receipt and retention of the packages found in the lining of the suitcase. The act relied on in relation to dealing was the meeting at Southall station with the intended recipient of one of the packages. In each case the act was clearly more than preparatory to the commission of the *intended* offence; it was not and could not be more than merely preparatory to the commission of the *actual* offence, because the facts were such that the commission of the actual offence was impossible. Here then is the nub of the matter. Does the 'act which is more than merely preparatory to the commission of the offence' in section 1(1) of the Act of 1981 (the actus reus of the statutory offence of attempt) require any more than an act which is more than merely preparatory to the commission of the offence which the defendant intended to commit? Section 1(2) must surely indicate a negative answer; if it were otherwise, whenever the facts were such that the commission of the actual offence was impossible, it would be impossible to prove an act more than merely preparatory to the commission of that offence and subsections (1) and (2) would contradict each other.

This very simple, perhaps over simple, analysis leads me to the provisional conclusion that the appellant was rightly convicted of the two offences of attempt with which he was charged. But can this conclusion stand with *Anderton v Ryan* (p 296, below)? The appellant in that case was charged with an attempt to handle stolen goods. She bought a video recorder believing it to be stolen. On the facts as they were to be assumed it was not stolen. By a majority the House decided that she was entitled to be acquitted. I have re-examined the case with care. If I could extract from the speech of Lord Roskill or from my own speech a clear and coherent principle distinguishing those cases of attempting the impossible which amount to offences under the statute from those which do not, I should have to consider carefully on which side of the line the instant case fell. But I have to confess that I can find no such principle.

Running through Lord Roskill's speech and my own in *Anderton v Ryan* is the concept of 'objectively innocent' acts which, in my speech certainly, are contrasted with 'guilty acts.' A few citations will make this clear. ... [His Lordship quoted from the speeches of Lord Roskill and himself and continued]

If we fell into error, it is clear that our concern was to avoid convictions in situations which most people, as a matter of common sense, would not regard as involving criminality. In this connection it is to be regretted that we did not take due note of para 2.97 of the Law Commission's report (Criminal Law: Attempt, and Impossibility in Relation to Attempt, Conspiracy and Incitement (1980) (Law Commission No 102)) which preceded the enactment of the Act of 1981, which reads:

'If it is right in principle that an attempt should be chargeable even though the crime which it is sought to commit could not possibly be committed, we do not think that we should be deterred by the consideration that such a change in our law would also cover some extreme and exceptional cases in which a prosecution would be theoretically possible. An example would be where a person is offered goods at such a low price that he believes that they are stolen, when in fact they are not; if he actually purchases them, upon the principles which we have discussed he would be liable for an attempt to handle stolen goods. Another case which has been much debated is that raised in argument by Bramwell B. in *R v Collins* (1864) 9 Cox CC 497. If A takes his own umbrella, mistaking it for one belonging to B and intending to steal B's umbrella, is he guilty of attempted theft? Again, on the principles which we have discussed he would in theory be guilty, but in neither case would it be realistic to suppose that a complaint would be made or that a prosecution would ensue.'

The prosecution in *Anderton v Ryan* itself falsified the Commission's prognosis in one of the 'extreme and exceptional cases.' It nevertheless probably holds good for other such cases, particularly that of the young man having sexual intercourse with a girl over 16, mistakenly believing her to be under that age, by which both Lord Roskill and I were much troubled.

However that may be, the distinction between acts which are 'objectively innocent' and those which are not is an essential element in the reasoning in *Anderton v Ryan* and the decision, unless it can be supported on some other ground, must stand or fall by the validity of this distinction. I am satisfied on further consideration that the concept of 'objective innocence' is incapable of sensible application in relation to the law of criminal attempts. The reason for this is that any attempt to commit an offence which involves 'an act which is more than merely preparatory to the commission of the offence' but for any reason fails, so that in the event no offence is committed, must *ex hypothesi*, from the point view of the criminal law, be 'objectively innocent.' What turns what would otherwise, from the point of view of the criminal law, be an innocent act into a crime is the intent of the actor to commit an offence. I say 'from the point of view of the criminal law' because the law of tort must surely here be quite irrelevant. A. puts his hand into B.'s pocket. Whether or not there is anything in the pocket capable of being stolen, if A. intends to steal, his act is a criminal attempt; if he does not so intend, his act is innocent. A. plunges a knife into a bolster in a bed. To avoid the complication of an offence of criminal damage, assume it to be A.'s bolster. If A. believes the bolster to be his enemy B. and intends to kill him, his act is an attempt to murder B.; if he knows the bolster is only a bolster, his act is innocent. These considerations lead me to the conclusion that the distinction sought to be drawn in *Anderton v Ryan* between innocent and guilty acts considered 'objectively' and independently of the state of mind of the actor cannot be sensibly maintained.

Another conceivable ground of distinction which was to some extent canvassed in argument, both in *Anderton v Ryan* and in the instant case, though no trace of it appears in the speeches in *Anderton v Ryan*, is a distinction which would make guilt or innocence of the crime of attempt in a case of mistaken belief dependent on what, for want of a better phrase, I will call the defendant's dominant intention. According to the theory necessary to sustain this distinction, the appellant's dominant intention in *Anderton v Ryan* was to buy a cheap video recorder; her belief that it was stolen was merely incidental. Likewise in the hypothetical case of attempted unlawful sexual intercourse, the young man's dominant intention was to have intercourse with the particular girl; his mistaken belief that she was under 16 was merely incidental. By contrast, in the instant case the appellant's dominant intention was to receive and distribute illegally imported heroin or cannabis.

Whilst I see the superficial attraction of this suggested ground of distinction, I also see formidable practical difficulties in its application. By what test is a jury to be told that a defendant's dominant intention is to be recognised and distinguished from his incidental but mistaken belief? But there is perhaps a more formidable theoretical difficulty. If this ground of distinction is relied on to support the acquittal of the appellant in *Anderton v Ryan*, it can only do so on the basis that her mistaken belief that the video recorder was stolen played no significant part in her decision to buy it and therefore she may be acquitted of the intent to handle stolen goods. But this line of reasoning runs into head-on collision with section 1(3) of the Act of 1981. The theory produces a situation where, apart from the subsection, her intention would not be regarded as having amounted to any intent to commit an offence. Section 1(3)(*b*) then requires one to ask whether, if the video recorder had in fact been stolen, her intention would have been regarded as an intent to handle stolen goods. The answer must clearly be yes, it would. If she had bought the video recorder knowing it to be stolen, when in fact it was, it would have availed her nothing to say that her dominant intention was to buy a video recorder because it was cheap and that her knowledge that it was stolen was merely incidental. This seems to me fatal to the dominant intention theory.

I am thus led to the conclusion that there is no valid ground on which *Anderton v Ryan* can be distinguished. I have made clear my own conviction, which as a party to the decision (and craving the indulgence of my noble and learned friends who agreed in it) I am the readier to express, that the decision was wrong. What then is to be done? If the case is indistinguishable, the application of the strict doctrine of precedent would require that the present appeal be allowed. Is it permissible to depart from precedent under the *Practice Statement* (*Judicial Precedent*) [1966] 1 WLR 1234 notwithstanding the especial need for certainty in the criminal law? The following considerations lead me to answer that question affirmatively. First, I am undeterred by the consideration that the decision in *Anderton v Ryan* was so recent. The Practice Statement is an effective abandonment of our pretention to infallibility. If a serious error embodied in a decision of this House has distorted the law, the sooner it is corrected the better. Secondly, I cannot see how, in the very nature of the case, anyone could have acted in reliance on the law as propounded in *Anderton v Ryan* in the belief that he was acting innocently and now find that, after all, he is to be held to have committed a criminal offence. Thirdly, to hold the House bound to follow *Anderton v Ryan* because it cannot be distinguished and to allow the appeal in this case would, it seems to me, be tantamount to a declaration that the Act of 1981 left the law of criminal attempts unchanged following the decision in *R v Smith (Roger)* [1975] AC 476. Finally, if, contrary to my present view, there is a valid ground on which it would be proper to distinguish cases similar to that considered in *Anderton v Ryan*, my present opinion on that point would not foreclose the option of making such a distinction in some future case.

I cannot conclude this opinion without disclosing that I have had the advantage, since the conclusion of the argument in this appeal, of reading an article by Professor Glanville Williams entitled 'The Lords and Impossible Attempts, or *Quis Custodiet Ipsos Custodes?*' [1986] CLJ 33. The language in which he criticises the decision in *Anderton v Ryan* is not conspicuous for its moderation, but it would be foolish, on that account, not to recognise the force of the criticism and churlish not to acknowledge the assistance I have derived from it.

I would answer the certified question in the affirmative and dismiss the appeal."

Lord Hailsham LC agreed with Lord Bridge but added that he would have been prepared to distinguish *Anderton v Ryan*: the *sole* intent of the instant appellant was to defeat the customs prohibition. In *Anderton v Ryan* the only intention of Mrs Ryan was to buy a particular video cassette recorder at a knock-down price and the fact that she believed it to be stolen formed no part of that intention. It was a belief, assumed to be false and not an intention at all.

Lord Elwyn Jones and Lord Mackay agreed with the Lord Chancellor and with Lord Bridge.

Lord Scarman agreed with Lord Bridge.

NOTE

Much of Chapter 15, below, is irrelevant to liability for attempt, as a result of *Shivpuri. Haughton v Smith* and *Anderton v Ryan* no longer apply to attempts; and it is highly probable that those cases and *DPP v Nock*, below, p 294, no longer apply to conspiracy. All of these cases however continue to be relevant to the question of incitement to do something impossible, which is still governed by common law: *Fitzmaurice* [1983] 1 All ER 189.

CHAPTER 15

Impossibility and preliminary offences

If it is impossible to commit a crime, no one can be convicted of committing it, but it does not follow that no one can be convicted of inciting another, or conspiring, or attempting to commit it. As a matter of fact, people do from time to time incite, conspire and attempt to do what is impossible. The problem arises most often in connection with attempt. It might naturally be expected that the same general principles would apply to solve the problem in all three of these closely related offences. As will appear, it is improbable that this is so in the existing law.

The draft Code Bill, however, offers a solution common to each of the offences:

54 Impossibility and preliminary offences
(1) A person may be guilty of incitement, conspiracy or attempt to commit an offence although the commission of the offence is impossible, if it would be possible in the circumstances which he believes or hopes exist or will exist at the relevant time.
(2) Subsection (1) applies to:
(a) Offences under sections 51, 52 and 53;
(b) any offence created by any other enactment of incitement, conspiracy or attempt to commit a specified offence.

The clause was believed by its authors to represent the existing law for attempts and statutory conspiracy as stated in the Criminal Attempts Act 1981, ss 1 (2) and (3) and 5 (1), though not for incitement or common law conspiracy. The authors thought it would be absurd for the Code to perpetuate such distinctions and the Bill therefore applies the principle, which the authors believed had been so recently approved by Parliament, to all cases. It has since been decided by the House of Lords in *Anderton v Ryan*, p 296, below, that the law in relation to attempts is not as stated in the clause. Whether the clause represents the law for statutory conspiracy is uncertain. It certainly does not do so in relation to common law conspiracy and incitement. It is necessary to analyse the nature of the problem and, as it occurs most often in connection with attempts, it is best done in relation to those offences. (The analysis which follows is derived from an article by JCS, 'Attempts, Impossibility and the Test of Rational Motivation' in *Auckland Law School Centenary Lectures* (1983) 25)

The principal characteristic of an attempt is that the attempter is trying, striving, to achieve some result. He has an objective which he wishes to attain. We cannot conceive of an attempt where the actor does not have some objective in view. Secondly, the concept of attempt involves failure or, if not failure, incompleteness of some kind. Naturally enough, charges of attempt to commit a crime are usually brought only when the accused has failed, or is believed to have failed, to achieve his objective. If he has succeeded, he will naturally be charged with the full offence. It is often said that attempt involves failure;[1] but this is not necessarily so. It is well established that it is no defence to a charge of attempt for the defendant to show that he went on to complete the crime.[2] This is perfectly logical, for the greater includes the less. In the great majority of successful crimes there was a point at which the defendant had committed an attempt and the complete crime includes this, even though it was completed only a matter of seconds later. An attempt may, then, be a failure to commit, or a proximate step towards the successful commission of, an offence.

Since sane men do not attempt what they know to be impossible, it follows that, in all cases of attempts to do the impossible, the defendant was labouring under a mistake of some kind. The cases may conveniently be divided into three categories according to the kind of mistake that the defendant was making.

(1) Where the defendant is making a mistake about the criminal law.

He is making no mistake about any material fact, but he believes his objective to be criminal when it is not. The objective is not impossible of attainment and, when it is attained, no crime will have been committed. His conduct is in no sense a failure nor is it a proximate step towards the commission of an offence. For example:

D is living in a jurisdiction where it was formerly illegal for a man of any age to have homosexual relations. It is now permissible for adult males to have homosexual relations in private. D (aged 21), being unaware that the law has been changed, engages in homosexual relations in private. He believes he is committing a criminal offence. He accomplishes his objective. The enterprise is in no sense a failure. It was not his purpose to commit crime.
D has sexual intercourse with a 17 year-old-girl, believing that the criminal law forbids sexual intercourse with girls under the age of 18. He is wrong. The age is 16. The accomplished objective is not criminal. D, believing that it is unlawful to shoot rabbits in May, shoots a rabbit on May 1. The law allows rabbits to be shot in May. There is nothing unlawful in what he has done.

It is generally agreed that these examples do not amount to attempts to commit crimes in law. This is surely right. There is no actus reus for the act done is lawful. If mens rea means (or includes) an intention to cause, or to take the risk of causing, a result which the law forbids, there is no mens rea, for the result intended by the defendant is not one which the law forbids. A belief that an act is a criminal offence is not mens rea or part of it.[3] Only one writer, so far as is known, has argued that these cases should amount to attempts. Professor Brett[4] argued that, because the defendant has shown that he is prepared to defy the law, he should be liable to conviction, provided that there is some crime to which his conduct can be related

(2) Where the defendant, because he is making a mistake of fact[5], believes his objective to be criminal when it is not.

The prototype of this case is that posed by Bramwell B, in *Collins* in 1864.[6] D takes an umbrella, intending to steal it. It turns out to be his own. D, we will suppose, has lost his umbrella. He believes it has been stolen. On leaving his Club one rainy day he decides to help himself to an umbrella left in the stand at the Club entrance. He intends to steal the umbrella from the owner, whoever he may be. When he gets home he finds that there is a mark inside the umbrella which proves conclusively that it is his own umbrella, the one he had thought to be stolen. It had, all along, been in the Club where he absent-mindedly left it six months ago. He has the intention to steal, but he does nothing wrong. Many similar cases may be put.

'D has sexual intercourse with a girl believing her to be 13—a criminal intention. In fact she is 18. He commits no offence against the criminal law.
Or, he believes the girl of 18 to be a mental defective. If that were true, the intercourse would be criminal. But it is not true. She is quite normal. D goes through a ceremony of marriage, having no doubt that his wife is alive. He intends to commit bigamy. But, five minutes before the ceremony, she was run down and killed. The marriage ceremony is perfectly lawful.
D buys a valuable painting in a junk shop for an absurdly low price. He has no doubt that it is stolen goods, but he is wrong. The shopkeeper acquired it lawfully and had no idea of its value. D intended to receive stolen goods but he has done nothing wrong.'

There is a much stronger case for conviction in these cases than in the first group.
  (a) These persons do have the mens rea of the various offences—dishonestly to appropriate an umbrella belonging to another; to have sexual intercourse with a girl under the age of 16; to have sexual intercourse with a mental defective; to marry during the life of a spouse; to receive stolen goods. It follows from this that:
  (b) Morally, the actor is just as bad as the person who actually commits the offence and;

(c) he is as dangerous as the person who actually commits the offence to whatever interest it is that the particular law is designed to protect.

On the other hand, in these cases the actor succeeds in doing the precise thing that he sets out to do. He accomplishes his objective. The transaction is complete—and it is not a crime. These are cases neither of failure nor of a proximate step towards the successful commission of a crime. The umbrellaless defendant decided to acquire that umbrella and did so. It was no part of his purpose that the umbrella should belong to another—he had no umbrella and he wanted to, and did, acquire one. He wanted to have sexual intercourse with that girl and did so. It would be very surprising if Head,[7] the man who actually had sexual intercourse with the woman whom he mistakenly believed to be a defective said, when he learned that, after all, she was not a defective, 'Dammit, I've failed.' The intending bigamist would hardly be disappointed to discover that he had lawfully married the object of his desire instead, as he thought, of committing an offence. Certainly the receiver of the painting will not be disappointed to learn that his bargain is a lawful one.

Because the defendant achieves (or would, if not interrupted, achieve) his objective without committing a crime, it is argued that he should not be guilty of an indictable attempt. Since the deed is done and is not a crime, the defendant should not be liable to conviction merely for his criminal intention. Fletcher[8] argues in favour of his test of rational motivation,

> 'first, that the test appears to be in tune with judicial intuitions that still reign in Anglo-American case-law; and secondly, that this analysis of attempting, based upon the ordinary usage of the words 'trying' and 'attempting', carries out the objectivist programme of grounding liability in an act of attempting that is conceptually separable from the actor's intent.'

(3) Where the defendant's objective, if it could be attained, would be a crime and, because he is making a mistake of fact, he believes it to be possible when it is not.

These are cases of failure, where, if the defendant had succeeded, he would have committed a crime. Because of the decision of the House of Lords in *Haughton v Smith*,[9] this third group must be divided into two sub-categories, though it may be thought that no rational distinction can be made between them.

Sub-category (a) is that where the defendant has used inadequate means to achieve his objective.

With intent to kill, he administers a dose of poison (or what he believes to be poison) which could not possibly kill anyone. With intent to steal, he uses a jemmy to break into a safe which could never be opened with such an implement. With intent to obtain money by deception, he writes a letter containing a false pretence to a person who knows the truth in the matter and could not possibly be deceived by it. The defendant in these cases intends to murder, to steal, to obtain by deception. His objective is the result constituting the commission of the crime. He will, inevitably, fail to attain his objective.

Sub-category (b) includes all other cases where it is in fact impossible to attain the defendant's criminal objective.

They are principally cases where the alleged subject-matter does not exist or lacks some essential characteristic. Defendant, intending to steal money, puts his hand into a pocket, or searches a wallet, which contains no money. His objective is the commission of theft but, inevitably, he will fail to do so. With intent to kill P, he fires a hail of bullets into P's bed. The bed is empty. It should make no difference whether P is lying under the bed, having taken evasive action in nick of time, or is downstairs making himself a cup of cocoa, or is enjoying a good night's sleep 50 miles away. Indistinguishable is the case where D shoots at a tree stump, believing it to be his deadly enemy. The only difference is that, in the latter case, it is more difficult to prove the intention to kill. There is no such difficulty, however, if it is proved that he is hunting his enemy through swirling mist on a moor. Into the same category falls the case of the man who, with intent to kill, shoots at a person who is already dead. His purpose is to kill and he fails. Similarly with the American case of *Guffey*.[10] Defendant shot at what he believed to be a deer. In fact it was not a living animal, but a stuffed one. His conviction for attempting to kill a protected animal out of season was quashed. But if, as seems certain, he was seeking venison for dinner or for sale, he certainly failed in his objective—and it would have been a crime had he succeeded. On the other hand, the theory fits perfectly with *People v Siu*[11] where D initiated negotiations to get possession of heroin. A sheriff's deputy handed him a package containing talcum powder. Undeniably this was a failure to achieve a criminal objective. Siu did not get what he wanted. Similarly with the New Zealand case of *Jay*[12] where the would-be purchaser of cannabis was handed a bag containing hedge-clippings. A variation of the 'umbrella case' would fall within the third category. Defendant sees a celebrity, P, leave his umbrella in the umbrella stand of a club. He has an overwhelming desire to possess something belonging to P and resolves to steal his umbrella. When an opportunity occurs, he surreptitiously takes from the stand the umbrella which he believes to be that left by P, but P's umbrella has already been removed. It is a second, different, umbrella and, when he gets it home, D finds that it is his own, lost, umbrella. Here he has painly failed to achieve his objective. If he had succeeded, he would have been guilty of theft.

1. Hall, *General Principles of Criminal Law* at p 557:'. . . attempt implies failure . . .'; Fletcher *Rethinking Criminal Law*. at p 131:'Attempts are cases of failure'.
2. Smith and Hogan, *Criminal Law*, p 265.
3. This is the logical consequence of the rule that ignorance of the criminal law is no defence.
4. *An Inquiry into Criminal Guilt* (1963), at pp 128–129.
5. Or a mistake of civil law where the offence includes a legal concept like 'being married' in bigamy.
6. 9 Cox CC 497 at p 498.
7. *Director of Public Prosecutions v Head* [1959] AC 83.
8. Op cit, at p 163.
9. [1975] AC 476.
10. 1262 SW 2d 152 (Mo App) (1953).
11. (1945) 126 Cal App 2d 41.
12. [1974] 2 NZLR 204.

According to *Haughton v Smith*, only cases in category 3 (a) constituted indictable attempts. Cases in categories 1, 2 and 3 (b) were not offences. The House of Lords held that the same principles applied to common law conspiracy in *DPP v Nock* [1978] 2 All ER 654; and the Court of Appeal held that they were also applicable to incitement in *Fitzmaurice* [1983] 1 All ER 189; so it appears that *Haughton v Smith* continues to apply to these offences at the present day. Attempts are, however, now governed by the Criminal Attempts Act 1981 and though it has been held that the Act did not achieve the result intended by its authors (which is encapsulated in cl 54 of the draft Bill, p 287, above), it so modified the law that cases in category 3 (b) will also constitute offences. The range of liability is summarised in the following diagram.

Impossibility In Preliminary Offences

1. Where, because D is making a mistake about the criminal law, he believes his objective to be criminal when it is not.			
2. Where, because D is making a mistake of fact, he believes his objective to be criminal when it is not.			Possibly statutory conspiracy.
3. Where D's objective is criminal but impossible of attainment because: (a) he uses inadequate means; or	Incitement and common law conspiracy.	Attempts and, possibly, statutory conspiracy.	And incitement, conspiracy and attempt under the
(b) An element in the definition of the crime is missing, e g the subject-matter lacks some essential characteristic or does not exist.			Criminal Code Bill cl 54

D may be convicted of an attempt ▨

D may not be convicted of an attempt ☐

Haughton v Smith [1973] 3 All ER 1109, House of Lords.
(Lord Hailsham of St Marylebone LC, Lord Reid, Lord Morris of Borth-y-Gest, Viscount Dilhorne and Lord Salmon)

A quantity of corned beef was stolen in Liverpool. Some days later an overloaded van was noticed by the police travelling south. They stopped the van and found the stolen corned beef. With the object of catching the intended receivers, the van (partly unloaded) was allowed to go on its way with two policemen concealed inside and a disguised policeman beside the driver. The van was met at a rendezvous by the respondent and another, evidently by arrangement, and driven on to London under the respondent's direction, but with the police still on board. The respondent played a prominent part in assisting in the disposal of the van and its contents. The members of the gang, including the respondent were then arrested. The respondent was convicted of attempting to handle stolen goods by dishonestly attempting to assist in the disposal of the goods for the benefit of others knowing or believing the goods to be stolen, contrary to s 22 of the Theft Act 1968. His conviction was quashed by the Court of Appeal. The prosecutor obtained leave to appeal to the House of Lords.

Lord Hailsham of St Marylebone LC. . . . I was at first inclined to think that s 22 of the Theft Act 1968 was drafted in such a way as to permit the construction that to be stolen for the purpose of s 22 (1) it was sufficient that the goods had been stolen without continuing to be stolen at the time of the handling, provided, of course, that the accused believed them at the time of the handling to be stolen. I thought that the expression 'believed' in the subsection aided the view that it could cover a state of facts where the defendant believed the goods to be stolen when they were not in fact still stolen at that moment of time. But, on consideration, I am sure that this would be a false construction, and that the expression 'believed' was inserted to guard against acquittals which had taken place under the former Larceny Act when it was necessary to prove knowledge that the goods were stolen and belief was not enough. If I were not already certain that this was the true meaning of s 22 (1), the provisions of s 24, and, in particular, s 24 (3), would, I think, clinch the matter. In my view, it is plain that, in order to constitute the offence of handling, the goods specified in the particulars of offence must not only be believed to be stolen, but actually continue to be stolen goods at the moment of handling. Once this is accepted as the true construction of the section, I do not think that it is possible to convert a completed act of handling, which is not itself criminal because it was not the handling of stolen goods, into a criminal act by the simple device of alleging that it was an attempt to handle stolen goods on the ground that at the time of handling the accused falsely believed them still to be stolen. In my opinion, this would be for the courts to manufacture a new criminal offence not authorised by the legislature.

This would be enough to decide the result of this appeal, but both counsel invited us to take a wider view of our obligations, and, once the question was discussed by the Court of Appeal [[1973] 2 All ER 896, [1973] 2 WLR 942] in general terms and since I believe that the result of our decision is to overrule a number of decided cases, at least to some extent, I feel bound to accede to this invitation. The question certified by the Court of Appeal was:

'If stolen goods are returned to lawful custody and thus cease to be stolen by virtue of s 24 (3) of the Theft Act 1968, can a person who subsequently dishonestly handles goods believing them to be stolen be guilty of the offence of attempting to handle stolen goods?'

I have already given a negative answer to this question, but the range of the discussion before us demands a wider consideration of the principles involved. . . .

I note that in the New Zealand case of *Donnelly* [[1970] NZLR 980], which, except insofar as it relates to the construction of the relevant New Zealand statutes, is very much on all fours with this, Turner J adopts a six-fold classification. He says [[1970] NZLR at 990, 991]:

'He who sets out to commit a crime may in the event fall short of the complete commission of that crime for any one of a number of reasons. *First*, he may, of course, simply change his mind before committing any act sufficiently overt to amount to an attempt. *Second*, he may change his mind, but too late to deny that he had got so far as an attempt. *Third*, he may be prevented by some outside agency from doing some act necessary to complete commission of the crime—as when a police officer interrupts him while he is endeavouring to force the window open, but before he has broken into the premises. *Fourth*, he may suffer no such outside interference, but may fail to complete the commission of the crime through ineptitude, inefficiency or insufficient means. The jemmy which he has brought with him may not be strong enough to force the window open. *Fifth*, he may find that what he is proposing to do is after all impossible—not because of insufficiency of means, but because it is for some reason physically not possible, whatever means be adopted. He who walks into a room intending to steal, say a specific diamond ring, and finds that the ring is no longer there but has been removed by the owner to the bank, is thus prevented from committing the crime which he intended, and which, but for the supervening physical impossibility imposed by events he would have committed. *Sixth*, he may without interruption efficiently do every act which he set out to do, but may be saved from criminal liability by the fact that what he has done, contrary to his own belief at the time, does not after all amount in law to a crime.'

On the whole, though I hope it will never be subjected to too much analysis, as it is merely a convenient exposition and illustration of classes of case which can arise, I find this classification more satisfactory than Lord Widgery CJ's dual classification. Applying the three principles derived from my primary definitions, I would seek to obtain the following results. (1) In the first case no criminal attempt is committed. At the relevant time there was no mens rea since there had been a change of intention, and the overt acts relied on would be preparatory and not immediately connected with the completed offence. (2) In the second case there is both mens rea and an act connected immediately with the offence. An example would be an attempted rape where the intended victim was criminally assaulted, but the attacker desisted at the stage immediately before he had achieved penetration. It follows that there is a criminal attempt. (3) The third case is more difficult because, as a matter of fact and degree, it will depend to some extent on the stage at which the interruption takes place, and the precise offence the attempt to commit which is the subject of the charge. In general, however, a criminal attempt is committed, assuming that the proximity test is passed. (4) In the fourth case there is ample authority for the proposition that, assuming the proximity test is passed, a criminal attempt is committed. But here casuistry is possible. Examples were given in argument of shots at an intended victim which fail because he is just out of range or because, as in the case of the well-known popular novel, *The Day of the Jackal*, the intended victim moves at the critical moment, or when a dose of poison insufficient to kill is administered with intent to murder. In all these cases the attempt is clearly criminal. (5) The fifth case is more complicated. It is clear that an attempt to obtain money by a false pretence which is not in fact believed, is criminal notwithstanding that the consequences intended were not achieved see *Hensler* [(1870) 22 LT 691]. The same would be true of an attempted murder when the victim did not actually die for whatever reason. But I do not regard these as true, or at least not as typical, examples of the fifth class. They belong rather to the fourth, since the criminal had done all that he intended to do, and all that was necessary to complete the crime was an act or event wholly outside his control. The case of *M'Pherson* [(1857) Dears & B 197], where the conviction was quashed, may be regarded as simply a case where a man was charged with one thing and convicted of another. But both the facts and the reasoning of the judges are much closer to the example postulated by Turner J in *Donnelly* [[1970] NZLR 980] as typical of the fifth class, though Turner J's own opinion to the effect that the attempt is criminal depends on the terms of the New Zealand statute and has no application to English law. In *M'Pherson* the reasoning of the English judges on English law was to the contrary. Cockburn CJ said [(1857) Dears & B at 201]:

> 'Here the prisoner had the intention to steal before he went into the house; but when he got there the goods specified in the indictment were not there; how then could he attempt to steal those goods? There can be no attempt *asportare* unless there is something *asportare*.'

Bramwell B, anticipating the decision in *Collins*, [(1864) 9 Cox CC 497], said [(1857) Dears & B at 201]:

> 'The argument that a man putting his hand into an empty pocket might be convicted of attempting to steal, appeared to me at first plausible; but suppose a man, believing a block of wood to be a man who was his deadly enemy, struck it a blow intending to murder, could he be convicted of attempting to murder the man he took it to be?'

. . . I regard the reasoning in *M'Pherson* [(1857) Dears & B 197] and *Collins* as sound and in general I would consider that 'attempts' in Turner J's fifth class of case are not indictable in English law, and I consider that the purported overruling of *Collins* needs further consideration.

In addition to the reported cases, we postulated in argument a number of real and imaginary instances of this class. In *The Empty Room*, Sherlock Holmes's enemy, Colonel Maron, was induced to fire at a wax image of the detective silhouetted in the window, though Holmes prudently rejected Inspector Lestrade's advice to prefer a charge of attempted murder and so the matter was never tested; in *White* [[1910] 2 KB 124, [1908–10] All ER Rep 340; p 278, above], a man who put a small quantity of cyanide in a wine glass, too small to kill, was held guilty of attempted murder. This was an example of the fourth of Turner J's cases and therefore criminal. But *quaere*, what would have been the position if the glass administered had contained pure water, even though the accused believed falsely that it contained cyanide? We discussed the situation when a would-be murderer attempts to assassinate a corpse, or a bolster in a bed, believing it to be the living body of his enemy, or when he fires into an empty room believing that it contained an intended victim; and we had our attention drawn to an American case where the accused fired at a peephole in a roof believed to be in use by a watching policeman who was in fact a few yards away. In most of these cases, a statutory offence of some kind (e g discharging a firearm with intent to endanger life) would be committed in English law, but in general I would think that a charge of an attempt to commit the common law offence of murder would not lie since, if the contemplated sequence of actions had been completed (as in some of the supposed instances they were) no substantive offence could have been committed of the type corresponding to the charge of attempt supposed to be laid. I get some support for this view from the summing-up of Rowlatt J in *Osborn* [(1919) 84 JP 63]. But I prefer to rest on the principle above stated, since *Osborn* was couched in more popular language than is appropriate to what has become a somewhat theoretical discussion. At the end of the day there must be a question of fact for the jury. The judge may direct them what facts, if established, could constitute an attempt, or would be evidence of an attempt. The jury alone can decide whether there was an attempt.

Turner J's [[1970] NZLR 980 at 991] sixth class of case was where a man efficiently does:

'without interruption . . . every act which he set out to do, but may be saved from criminal liability by the fact that what he has done, contrary to his own belief at the time, does not after all amount in law to a crime.'

. . . I have already explained that I consider that the present appeal fails on the proper construction of s 22 of the Theft Act 1968. But I think that this is a special example of a wider principle, and I agree with Turner J's conclusion about it.

In *Collins* [(1864) 9 Cox CC at 498] Bramwell B put the rhetorical question:

'Suppose a man takes away an umbrella from a stand with intent to steal it, believing it not to be his own, but it turns out to be his own, could he be convicted of attempting to steal?'

In *Villensky* [(1892) 2 QB 597 at 498] Lord Coleridge CJ, in circumstances not unlike the present, following *Dolan* [(1855) Dears CC 436], held that prisoners could not be indicted under the old law for receiving stolen goods, and made no reference to the possibility of a conviction for attempt.

In *Williams* [[1893] 1 QB 320 at 321] the same Lord Chief Justice said that a boy below the age at which he could be properly indicted for rape could not be convicted on the same facts for an attempt. I do not agree with the contrary opinion of Hawkins J, in the same case, even though it was possibly supported by the rest of the court. The same reasoning would apply to a case of unlawful carnal knowledge (cf *Waite* [[1892] 2 QB 600]), whether, as there, it was the male who was by reason of age incapable in law of committing the offence, or the female who was in law incapable by reason of her age of having it committed against her, and it would not, in my view, matter in the latter case that the male falsely believed her to be under age. Support for his view is to be found in *Director of Public Prosecutions v Head* [[1959] AC 83; [1958] 1 All ER 679], which was a charge of a completed offence in relation to a mental defective, but counsel for the respondent made considerable play with the argument *a silentio* to be derived from the fact that no one suggested the possibility of a conviction for an attempt. In my view, it is a general principle that Turner J's sixth class of attempts are not criminal, not because the acts are not proximate or because the intention is absent, but because the second of the three propositons I derive from the two judicial definitions I cited above is not satisfied. The acts are not part of a series 'which would constitute the actual commission of the offence if it were not interrupted'. In this event the often discussed question whether the legal impossibility derives from a mistake of fact or law on the part of the accused is hardly relevant.

The discussion enables me to deal with the cases cited in the judgment of the Court of Appeal [[1973] 2 All ER 896]. Like Lord Widgery CJ, I disagree with the decision in *People of the State of California v Rojas* [(1961) 10 Cal, Rptr 465] and prefer the decisions in *Donnelly* [[1970]

NZLR 980] and *People of the State of New York v Jaffe* [(1906) 185 NY 497] overruling the decisions in the lower courts [cf (1906) 98 NY Supp 486]. I agree with the decision in *Percy Dalton (London) Ltd* [[1949] LJR 1626], and particularly with the quotation from Birkett J [[1949] LJR at 1630] cited by Lord Widgery CJ [[1973] 2 All ER at 900], in the present case, where he said:

> 'Steps on the way to the commission of what would be a crime, if the acts were completed, may amount to attempts to commit that crime, to which, unless interrupted, they would have led; but steps on the way to the doing of something which is thereafter done, and which is no crime, cannot be regarded as attempts to commit a crime.'

I would add to the last sentence a rider to the effect that equally steps on the way to do something which is thereafter *not* completed, but which if done would not constitute a crime cannot be indicted as attempts to commit that crime. It is, of course, true that, at least in theory, some villains will escape by this route. But in most cases they can properly be charged with something else—statutory offences like breaking and entering with intent, etc., or loitering with intent, etc., using an instrument with intent, etc., discharging or possessing a firearm with intent, etc., or as here, common law offences like conspiring to commit the same offence as that the attempt to commit which is charged, or even committing a substantive offence of a different kind, as here, stealing or attempting to steal.

[**Lord Reid, Lord Morris of Borth-y-Gest** and **Viscount Dilhorne** made speeches dismissing the appeal and **Lord Salmon** dismissed the appeal for the reasons given by **Lord Hailsham**.]

Appeal dismissed

Director of Public Prosecutions v Nock and Alsford [1978] 2 All ER 654 House of Lords.
(Lord Diplock, Lord Edmund-Davies, Lord Russell of Killowen, Lord Keith of Kinkel and Lord Scarman)

The appellants were convicted of conspiracy to commit an offence, contrary to s 4 (2) of the Misuse of Drugs Act 1971, of producing a controlled drug. They had agreed to extract cocaine from a powder in their possession which they believed to be a mixture of cocaine and lignocaine. Had this been so the agreement could have succeeded, but the powder was, in fact, lignocaine hydrochloride which contained no cocaine. The alleged conspiracy was therefore impossible of commission.

Lord Scarman. . . . On these facts the appellants submit that the evidence reveals no 'conspiracy at large', by which they mean an agreement in general terms to produce cocaine if and when they could find a suitable raw material, but only the limited agreement, to which I have referred. Counsel for the appellants concedes that, if two or more persons decide to go into business as cocaine producers, or, to take another example, as assassins for hire (eg 'Murder Incorporated'), the mere fact that in the course of performing their agreement they attempt to produce cocaine from a raw material which could not possibly yield it or, in the second example, stab a corpse, believing it to be the body of a living man, would not avail them as a defence: for the performance of their general agreement would not be rendered impossible by such transient frustrations. But performance of the limited agreement proved in this case could not in any circumstances have involved the commission of the offence created by the statute.

The answer sought to be made by the Crown (and accepted by the Court of Appeal) is that the offence of conspiracy is committed when an agreement to commit, or to try to commit, a crime is reached, whether or not anything is, or can be, done to perform it. It is wrong, on their view, to treat conspiracy as a 'preliminary' or 'inchoate' crime, for its criminality depends in no way on its being a step towards the commission of the substantive offence (or, at common law, the unlawful act). On this view of the law the scope of agreement is irrelevant: all that is needed to constitute the crime is the intention to commit the substantive offence and the agreement to try to do so.

If the Court of Appeal is right, *Haughton v Smith* [[1975] AC 476, [1973] 3 All ER 1109] can have no application in cases of conspiracy . . .

It was, somewhat half-heartedly, suggested by the Crown that the House might reconsider the decision, which we were told is causing difficulties in some respects. It is, however, a very recent decision; and a unanimous one reached after full argument which brought to the attention of this House the relevant case law and exposed the difficulties. More importantly, the decision is, in my respectful opinion, correct in principle. I would not question the decision, though its proper limits may have to be considered. The House decided the case on two grounds, either of which would have sufficed, standing alone to support the decision, but both of which commended themselves to the House. They may be described as the statutory (and narrower) ground and the common law principle.

The statutory ground was provided by ss 22 and 24 (3) of the Theft Act 1968. The offence being considered by the House was one of attempting to handle stolen goods. At the time of the attempted handling, the goods had been (this was conceded) restored to lawful custody. The House ruled that, in the case of a statutory offence [[1975] AC 476 at 498, [1973] 3 All ER 1109 at 1119, per Lord Reid]:

> 'The only possible attempt would be to do what Parliament has forbidden. But Parliament has not forbidden that which the accused did, i e handling goods which have ceased to be stolen goods . . . Here the mens rea was proved but there was no actus reus so the case is not within the scope of the section.'

With all respect to the Court of Appeal, there is no difficulty in applying this line of reasoning to a case in which the allegation is not an attempt but a conspiracy to commit a statutory offence. First, there is no logical difficulty in applying a rule that an agreement is a conspiracy to commit a statutory offence only if it is an agreement to do that which Parliament has forbidden. It is no more than the application of the principle that an actus reus as well as mens rea must be established. And in the present case there was no actus reus, because there was no agreement on a course of conduct forbidden by the statute. Secondly, the application of such a rule is consistent with principle. Unless the law requires the actus reus as well as mens rea to be proved, men, whether they be accused of conspiracy or attempt, will be punished for their guilty intentions alone. I conclude the consideration of this ground of decision with a further quotation from Lord Reid's speech [[1975] AC 476 at 500, [1973] 3 All ER 1109 at 1121]: 'But such a radical change in the principles of our law should not be introduced in this way even if it were desirable.'

The second ground of decision, the common law principle, can be summarised in words which commended themselves to all the noble and learned Lords concerned with the case. In *Percy Dalton (London) Ltd* [[1949] LJR 1626 at 1630] Birkett J giving the judgment of the Court of Criminal Appeal said:

> 'Steps on the way to the commission of what would be a crime, if the acts were completed, may amount to attempts to commit that crime, to which, unless interrupted, they would have led; but steps on the way to the doing of something, which is thereafter done, and which is no crime, cannot be regarded as attempts to commit a crime.'

In his speech Lord Hailsham LC [[1975] AC 476 at 497, [1973] 3 All ER 1109 at 1118] added the rider (a logical one) to the effect 'that equally steps on the way to do something which is thereafter *not* completed, but which if done would not constitute a crime cannot be indicted as attempts to commit that crime'. As in the case of the statutory ground, there is no logical difficulty in the way of applying this principle to the law relating to conspiracy provided it is recognised that conspiracy is a 'preliminary' or 'auxiliary' crime. And again, as with the statutory ground, common sense and justice combine to require of the law that no man should be punished criminally for the intention with which he enters an agreement unless it can also be shown that what he has agreed to do is unlawful.

The Crown's argument, as developed before your Lordships, rests, in my judgment, on a misconception of the nature of the agreement proved. This is a case not of an agreement to commit a crime capable of being committed in the way agreed on, but frustrated by a supervening event making its completion impossible, which was the Crown's submission, but of an agreement on a course of conduct which could not in any circumstances result in the statutory offence alleged, i e the offence of producing the controlled drug, cocaine.

I conclude therefore that the two parallel lines of reasoning on which this House decided *Haughton v Smith* apply equally to criminal conspiracy as they do to attempted crime.

Our attention was also drawn to two cases, on which it may be helpful to comment very briefly. In *McDonough* [(1962) 47 Cr App Rep 37] the Court of Criminal Appeal held that an incitement to receive stolen goods was complete on the making of the incitement even though there were no stolen goods, perhaps, even no goods at all. In *Haggard v Mason* [[1976] 1 All ER 337, [1976] 1 WLR 187] the Divisional Court held that the offence of offering to supply a controlled drug was committed, even though the drug in fact supplied was not a controlled drug. Neither of these cases infringes the principle of *Haughton v Smith*; for in each, as was pointed out in *Haggard v Mason* the offence was complete. In *McDonough* the actus reus was the making of the incitement and in *Haggard's* case [[1976] 1 All ER 337 at 339] it was the making of the offer.

[**Lords Diplock, Edmund-Davies, Russell of Killowen** and **Keith of Kinkel** agreed with the speech of **Lord Scarman.**]

Anderton v Ryan [1985] 2 All ER 355, House of Lords.
(Lords Fraser, Edmund-Davies, Keith, Roskill and Bridge)

The defendant bought a video recorder for £110. Later she said to the police, 'I may as well be honest, it was a stolen one I bought. . .' She was charged with handling the recorder knowing it to be stolen and, secondly, with attempting to handle it contrary to s 1(1) of the Criminal Attempts Act 1981, p 586, below. The prosecution offered no evidence on the first charge. On the second charge the magistrates were not satisfied that the recorder had in fact been stolen though the defendant believed it had. They dismissed the charge. The Divisional Court allowed the prosecution's appeal. The defendant appealed to the House of Lords.

Lord Edmund-Davies (dissenting). . . . My Lords, in my judgment the Divisional Court came to the correct conclusion. If, on the contrary, the submission advanced on behalf of the appellant is right, the legislature has substantially missed its mark, for it was and is common knowledge that (to take as an example merely the facts of the present case) Parliament intended by the 1981 Act that a person who dishonestly handles goods, mistakenly believing that they are stolen goods, should for the future be liable to conviction for attempted handling.

Section 1 (4) provides: 'This section applies to any offence which, if it were completed, would be triable in England and Wales as an indictable offence . . .' I shall later indicate why, in my judgment, the appellant clearly intended to handle stolen goods. She also took steps which were 'more than merely preparatory' to the offence of handling, for in her belief that the goods were stolen she bought the recorder and received it into her custody. So she had the mens rea and, as far as she could and thought (though mistakenly), she committed the actus reus of the full offence of handling, though in reality a piece of the actus reus of handling '*stolen goods*' was missing.

But, since the recorder was not in reality stolen, are the facts nevertheless sufficient for the charge of *attempted* handling? In developing the view that the proper answer is No, Professor Hogan has observed ([1984] Crim LR 584 at 589–590):

> '. . . [Mrs Ryan] attempted to handle non-stolen goods believing that they were stolen. That is not an offence known to the law and cannot be an offence to which section 1 of the Act applies. To convict Mrs Ryan would be to contravene the principle of legality; a person, however evil his or her intentions may be, cannot be convicted unless he or she does, or fails to do, something which constitutes the *actus reus* of a defined crime. . . Mrs Ryan got what she wanted for what she wanted was the video recorder at a very low price, and in so doing did not handle stolen goods; if she is to be properly convicted of an attempt the requirement for proof that the goods were stolen still stands and cannot be satisfied by proof that Mrs Ryan thought they were stolen.'

I have set out this extensive quotation because Professor Hogan's article was cited and adopted by the appellant's counsel. I desire to make the following brief comments on it. (1) In my judgment the quoted passage reveals an unsound approach to the new law of attempts introduced by the 1981 Act, which by s 6(1) abolished for all purposes the common law relating to the offence of attempt. It is not right to say that the appellant 'attempted to handle non-stolen goods'. Her own words disclosed that what she attempted was to handle stolen goods, and to the best of her belief she accomplished that very act, an act which undoubtedly constitutes 'an offence to which [s 1 of the Act] applies' (s 1(1)). (2) I naturally accept that what is intended must be something which, if accomplished, would have brought about the actus reus of a defined crime, but at the same time I bear in mind that, in ascertaining what was intended, s 1(3) requires that the facts are to be taken as if they had been as the actor *believed* them to be. (3) Professor Hogan earlier said: '. . . it can be accepted that Mrs Ryan had mens rea.' Then what mens rea did she have? In my judgment clearly the mens rea of one intending to handle stolen goods, for from its attractively low price she 'supposed' that the recorder was stolen and acting on the supposition she bought and received it. As Professor Glanville Williams neatly puts it ((1985) 135 NLJ 337):

'If the defendant received a *stolen* article believing it to be *clean*, you would not say that he intended to receive a stolen article. So when he receives a *clean* article believing it to be *stolen*, you should not say that he intended to receive a clean article.'

My Lords, I hold that the appellant's case fails to have full and proper regard for the impact of s 1(2) and (3) of the 1981 Act. The section wins no prize for lucidity, but its effect when considered in its entirety is that a person may now be guilty of attempting an offence even though the facts are such that commission of the full offence is impossible, *provided* that, 'if the facts of the case had been as he believed them to be' (see s 1(3)(b)), he would be regarded as having made an attempt to commit that offence. In dealing with any attempt charge other than those expressly excluded by the Act, the court has now to take the facts as the defendant believed them to be. If, on those supposed *facts* (as contrasted with supposed *law*), he would be guilty of an attempt, the Act makes him guilty of it. Taking the facts of the present case before the Act a piece of the actus reus would have been missing for both handling and attempted handling, viz the goods were not stolen; that is to say the decision in *Haughton v Smith* [1973]3 All ER 1109, [1975] AC 476 would have applied. Today that piece is still missing and accordingly there can again be no conviction for handling. Nevertheless, the appellant is not in the position of one who, in the words of my noble and learned friend Lord Bridge, 'embarks on and completes a course of conduct which is objectively innocent', nor is she to be convicted 'solely on the ground that the person mistakenly believes facts which, if true, would make that course of conduct a complete crime'. The legality of her conduct now falls to be judged by applying the Act, her belief being vitally relevant not only to her intent but also to the quality of law in her 'objective' actions. Thus considered, her 'more than merely preparatory' conduct was, in my respectful judgment, certainly not 'innocent'. On the contrary, contaminated by and performed in furtherance of her criminal objective, her conduct now constitutes the actus reus of the new statutory offence of attempted handling.

My Lords, I believe that acceptance of the appellant's case would reduce the sonority of s 6(1) of the Act to a mere tinkle. In my judgment the legislature has succeeded in doing what in the main it set out to do, namely to effect a radical change in the law of attempts as it had been declared in *Haughton v Smith*. Professor Hogan, while agreeing that such was the main purpose of the Act, concludes that there has been 'a spectacular failure of legislative intent' (see [1984] Crim LR 584 at 591). Although the drafting of s 1 has been criticised, for the reasons already stated I hold that there has been no such failure and I would therefore dismiss the appeal.

[Lord Roskill, having referred to the citation in *Haughton v Smith* of the analysis made by Turner J in *Donnelly* (p 291, above):]

The reasoning of Lord Hailsham LC in relation to the fifth class and his analysis of the decided cases happily absolves me from the necessity of traversing the same ground once more. He reached the conclusion ([1973] 3 All ER 1109 at 1117, [1975] AC 476 at 495):

'. . . in general I regard the reasoning in *R v M'Pherson* (1857) Dears & B 197, 169 ER 975 and *R v Collins* (1864) 9 Cox CC 497 as sound and in general I would consider that "attempts" in Turner J's fifth class of case are not indictable in English law . . .'

Lord Reid emphatically rejected the argument that cases within the fifth class constituted attempts. He said ([1973] 3 All ER 1109, [1975] AC 476 at 498):

'It is said that if the accused does not know the true facts but erroneously believes the facts to be such that his conduct would be an offence if the facts had been as he believes them to be, then he is guilty of an attempt to commit the offence. In the case of a statutory offence that appears to me to be clearly wrong. The only possible attempt would be to do what Parliament has forbidden. But Parliament has not forbidden that which the accused did, i e handling goods which have ceased to be stolen goods. The section [i e s 22 of the Theft Act 1968] defines both the actus reus and the mens rea required to constitute the offence. Both must be proved. Here the mens rea was proved but there was no actus reus so the case is not within the scope of the section.'

I need not quote similar passages from the speech of Viscount Dilhorne.

So far as the sixth class is concerned, the House unanimously held that in this class of case also no offence was committed. The House adopted as correct the statement of law in *R v Percy Dalton (London) Ltd* (1949) 33 Cr App R 102 at 110:

'Steps on the way to the commission of what would be a crime, if the acts were completed, may amount to attempts to commit that crime, to which, unless interrupted, they would have led; but steps on the way to the doing of something, which is thereafter done, and which is no crime cannot be regarded as attempts to commit a crime.'

Lord Reid, in a well-known passage in *Haughton v Smith* [1973] 3 All ER 1109 at 1121, [1975] AC 476 at 500, dealt with the matter thus:

> 'I would not, however, decide the matter entirely on logical argument. The life blood of the law is not logic but common sense. So I would see where this theory takes us. A man lies dead. His enemy comes along and thinks he is asleep, so he stabs the corpse. The theory inevitably requires us to hold that the enemy has attempted to murder the dead man. The law may sometimes be an ass but it cannot be so asinine as that.'

This then was the state of the law regarding cases falling within the fifth and sixth classes before the enactment of the 1981 Act. Plainly, before that Act was passed, the appellant could not have been convicted of attempting dishonestly to handle stolen goods because, had she attained her objective, she could not in law have been guilty of dishonestly handling stolen goods, the goods by concession not being stolen goods. Can she now be convicted of that offence?

The answer depends on to what extent the 1981 Act has altered the law. [His Lordship cited the long title and sections 1 and 6.]

The principle which I have stated at the outset of this speech, that where more than one construction of a statute is possible that preferred should be the construction which eliminates the 'mischief' at which the statute was directed, must not be carried to extremes. The facts of *Haughton v Smith* were most unusual. The problems to which the decision of this House gave rise were many. It by no means follows that Parliament in its efforts to solve some at least of those problems intended by this legislation to solve them all, or to ensure that if those unusual facts were to be repeated in the future a defendant in the same position as Smith should be convicted when before this legislation he would have been entitled to acquittal. Loyalty to the principle should not require the adoption of a construction which leads to manifestly absurd results unless, of course, the draftsman's language compels that conclusion. I have already quoted Lord Reid's observations about the possible asininity of the law of the field. For my part I decline to construe a statute designed to amend 'the law . . . as to attempts' and thus to reform it so as to make it sensible and simple in its future application as having that result. It must, however, be said that the language used in the statute is such as to make the attainment of common sense and the avoidance of asininity at one and the same time almost impossible of achievement. [His Lordship referred to s 1 (2) and (3).] Subsection (2) is seemingly aimed at cases such as that of the pickpocket who puts his hand into an empty pocket. *In fact* (I emphasise those words) he never could have achieved his ambition because the pocket was empty. The commission of the full offence was never possible not because of any lack of intent (mens rea) or indeed lack of relevant physical action (actus reus) on the part of the pickpocket. But because he was attempting to do that which was factually impossible it was said that he must be acquitted. That happily is now a matter of past controversy. Subsection (2) has at least removed the viability of what became known as the pickpocket's defence. It is against that background that I turn to consider sub-s (3). . .

I take the case of a defendant intending to kill another by stabbing him or by shooting him in bed only to find after the knife has been plunged or the revolver fired that the assumed and intended victim was a pillow. Such a defendant I am glad to think could now be successfully charged with and convicted of attempted murder. . . . After long consideration of the difficulties to which the drafting gives rise, I have come to the conclusion, in agreement with my noble and learned friend Lord Bridge, that, if the action is innocent and the defendant does everything he intends to do, sub-s (3) does not compel the conclusion that erroneous belief in the existence of facts which, if true, would have made his completed act a crime makes him guilty of an attempt to commit that crime. I also think that likewise a defendant who is possessed of a like erroneous belief and who after doing innocent acts which are more than merely preparatory to fulfilling his intention for some reason subsequently fails to achieve that which he intends is not liable to be convicted of an attempt to commit a crime.

If the contrary proposition be correct, some remarkable results follow. Let me take only one example. A young gentleman is determined on sexual intercourse with a young lady whom he erroneously believes to be under 16. She is in fact 18. He succeeds in his ambition. Before sub-s (3) was enacted he was clearly not guilty of any offence. Since the enactment of sub-s (3), his completed act is still itself not a completed offence. I find it impossible to believe that it was intended by sub-s (3) that he should be liable to be found guilty of attempting to have unlawful sexual intercourse with a girl under 16 merely because of his erroneous belief. I find it equally impossible to believe that in those circumstances Parliament intended that he should be liable to conviction for an attempt to commit that offence in a case where, for some reason, he failed at the last moment to achieve his ambition.

I do not stop to speculate what Lord Reid might have thought or, indeed, have said about legislation which led to such a result.

In my view, much clearer and one might say much more drastic language would be required to achieve that last result. Without presuming to redraft the subsection, I would at least have expected to have found some such provision as:

'If a person does an act which, if the facts were as that person believed them to be, would amount to an offence to which this section applies, he shall be guilty of attempting to commit that offence.'

Lord Bridge. . . . The question may be stated in abstract terms as follows. Does s 1 of the 1981 Act create a new offence of attempt where a person embarks on and completes a course of conduct, which is objectively innocent, solely on the ground that the person mistakenly believes facts which, if true, would make that course of conduct a complete crime? If the question must be answered affirmatively it requires convictions in a number of surprising cases: the classic case, put by Bramwell B in *R v Collins* (1864) 9 Cox CC 497 at 498, of the man who takes away his own umbrella from a stand, believing it not to be his own with intent to steal it; the case of the man who has consensual intercourse with a girl over 16 believing her to be under that age; the case of the art dealer who sells a picture which he represents to be and which is in fact a genuine Picasso, but which the dealer mistakenly believes to be a fake.

The common feature of all these cases, including that under appeal, is that the mind alone is guilty, the act is innocent. I should find it surprising that Parliament, if intending to make this purely subjective guilt criminally punishable, should have done so by anything less than the clearest express language, and, in particular, should have done so in a section aimed specifically at inchoate offences.

I agree with my noble and learned friend Lord Roskill that sub-ss (1) and (4) of s 1 of the 1981 Act provide a statutory substitute for the common law offence of attempt abolished by s 6. It seems to me possible to find ample substance and content in sub-ss (2) and (3), reversing aspects of the law of attempt which emerge from *Smith*'s case, without straining them to make the present appellant guilty of any offence. It is sufficient to say of sub-s (2) that it is plainly intended to reverse the law, originally declared in *R v Collins*, mistakenly thought to have been overruled by *R v Brown* (1889) 24 QBD 357, but reaffirmed in *Smith*'s case, that the pickpocket who puts his hand in an empty pocket commits no offence. Putting the hand in the pocket is the guilty act, the intent to steal is the guilty mind, the offence is appropriately dealt with as an attempt, and the impossibility of committing the full offence for want of anything in the pocket to steal is declared by the subsection to be no obstacle to conviction. The precise scope of sub-s (3) is more difficult to delineate and I will not be so rash as to attempt to identify to which of the numerous hypothetical cases discussed in *Smith*'s case it would apply; but I have no difficulty in giving an example of my own to which it certainly would. A wages clerk collects £10,000 in cash from the bank every Friday in a suitcase. An informer tells the police that a thief plans on a particular Friday to snatch the case and steal the money. The police set a trap, but, in case the thief should escape, arrange that the bank will fill the suitcase with torn strips of newspaper. The thief snatches the suitcase intending to throw it away and take the money which he believes it contains. At common law his only offence is stealing the torn pieces of newspaper. The effect of s 1(1) and (3) of the 1981 Act is that he is guilty of attempting to steal £10,000. Here again there is a guilty act 'more than merely preparatory to the commission of the offence' under sub-s (1). Apart from sub-s (3) his intention would not be regarded as an intention to steal £10,000. By sub-s (3) his erroneous belief requires that his intention should be so regarded. It follows that the section enables him to be convicted of attempting to steal £10,000.

It seems to be that sub-ss (2) and (3) are in a sense complementary to each other. Subsection (2) covers the case of a person acting in a criminal way with a general intent to commit a crime in circumstances where no crime is possible. Subsection (3) covers the case of a person acting in a criminal way with a specific intent to commit a particular crime which he erroneously believes to be, but which is not in fact, possible. Given the criminal action, the appropriate subsection allows the actor's guilty intention to be supplied by his subjective but mistaken state of mind, notwithstanding that on the true facts that intention is incapable of fulfilment. But, if the action is throughout innocent and the actor has done everything he intended to do, I can find nothing in either subsection which requires me to hold that his erroneous belief in facts which, if true, would have made the action a crime makes him a guilty of an attempt to commit that crime.

[**Lords Fraser** and **Keith** agreed with the speeches of **Lord Roskill** and **Lord Bridge.**]

Appeal allowed

Note: see *Shivpuri* and *Tulloch*, Appendix II, below.

1. The principle of legality

Lord Edmund-Davies quoted Professor Hogan's opinion that the conviction of Ryan would contravene the principle of legality (no one shall be convicted of doing something which has not been declared by the law to be an offence). For another point of view see commentary (by JCS) on the decision, [1985] Crim LR 504, 505:

But in the present case, there was no suggestion that [Ryan] was making any mistake other than one of fact. She believed certain events to have taken place which, in the absence of proof, we must assume did not take place. No one suggested that she was under any misapprehension as to the terms of section 22 of the Theft Act or any other rule of law. It is desirable to be clear about this because of the misleading label 'legal impossibility' which is sometimes applied to cases of this kind. Similarly, argument about the 'principle of legality' . . . is wholly beside the point. It is a matter of the construction of the statute. If Parliament has said that it is to be an offence to do *any* more than merely preparatory act with intent to commit an offence, the law may be criticised for being too wide-ranging; but the conviction of the person who does any such act with that intent cannot be criticised for breaching the principle of legality. That person is convicted in accordance with the previously declared law, not contrary to it. . . .

2. The argument from absurdity

Referring to two examples given by Lord Roskill (p 298 above) the commentary concludes:

So, the man who, with intent to murder, plunges the knife into the lump in the bed is guilty of attempted murder if it is a pillow but not guilty (only an ass could think otherwise) if it is a corpse. Is this 'the attainment of common sense and the avoidance of asininity' which was his Lordship's aim? The uninitiated might have thought that corpse-stabber was, if anything, rather closer to murder than the pillow-stabber.

3. Would Haughton v Smith now be decided in the same way?

All the judges in *Anderton v Ryan* thought this was the effect of the decision; but the commentary suggests this deserves further consideration:

Like [Ryan], Roger Smith mistakenly believed that the goods he was receiving were stolen goods; but Smith's mistake was of a more complex character than that. It was of a kind quite different from that of a buyer of an article in a junk shop who simply assumes, because of the low price and the shady atmosphere of the place, that the article has been stolen. The goods had been stolen in Smith's case and he knew it. His mistake was that he did not know that the police had taken possession of the goods. In the present case, the appellant succeeded in doing precisely what she set out to do and it is for this reason, it is submitted, that she is acquitted. Smith's enterprise was a success in the limited sense that he received the very goods he intended to receive; but in another, more substantial, sense it was a failure. He would have given a very dusty answer if, as the police took him away, someone had congratulated him on the success of the enterprise. In effect, Smith received goods *from the police*. The police had assumed control of them and his erstwhile accomplices were now acting as agents of the police. His objective was to receive the goods from his accomplices and it had in fact been foiled. The enterprise was a failure; and if it had succeeded it would have been a crime. According to the proposed test then, it is distinguishable from the present case. Lord Roskill says that the facts were unusual; but there are many similar cases in the law reports of England, the Commonwealth and the United States. It appears indeed to be the commonest instance of this type of problem, much more important in practice than the stabbing of pillows or corpses.

4. The effect on statutory conspiracy and incitement

The commentary observes:

The House gave no consideration to the possible implications for conspiracy. Section 1(1) of the Criminal Law Act 1977 as amended by section 5(1)(b) of the Criminal Attempts Act provides that a person is guilty of conspiracy if he agrees with another that a course of conduct shall be pursued which, if the agreement were carried out in accordance with their intentions, would necessarily amount to or involve the commission of an offence, 'but for the existence of facts which render the commission of the offence . . . impossible.' Clearly one would expect 'impossible' to bear the same meaning when used in relation to two such closely-related offences as conspiracy and attempt in the same statute. It is, however, argued in Smith and Hogan, *Criminal Law* (5th ed), pp 230–233, that, in order to avoid absurdity, the ambiguous phrase, 'course of conduct,' must be construed to include the intended consequences and the material circumstances which the parties believe will exist as well as the physical acts designed to cause the consequences. If this is right, the Law Commission solution to impossibility was already implicit in the definition of conspiracy as originally enacted in the Criminal Law Act 1977 and section 5(1)(b) was strictly unnecessary but should be regarded as an 'avoidance of doubt' provision. If this is right, we now have different tests for impossibility in cases of attempt and statutory conspiracy and yet a third test for common law conspiracy and incitement (cf *Fitzmaurice* [1983] 1 All ER 189) where *Smith (Roger)* in its full horror still prevails. Clause 54(1) of the Draft Criminal Code (Law Com No 143, 1985) would restore the Law Commission test for attempts and apply it to the whole range of inchoate offences, thus introducing much needed consistency into the law; 'A person may be guilty of incitement, conspiracy or attempt to commit an offence although the commission of the offence is impossible, if it would be possible in the circumstances which he believes or hopes exist or will exist at the relevant time.'

NOTE

Fitzmaurice was followed in *Sirat* [1986] Crim LR 245, CA, p 249, above.

CHAPTER 16

Murder

1. Homicide

The actus reus of murder and manslaughter is generally the same. It is the unlawful killing of any person 'under the Queen's Peace', the death following within a year and a day of the infliction of the fatal injury.

2. Causing death

It must be proved that the defendant caused the death of the deceased person. The most common source of problems of causation in the criminal law is homicide. The leading cases have been considered, above, p 30–37, and reference may be made to these. The 'year-and-a-day' rule is peculiar to homicide. Its origin lies in the difficulty of proving that the defendant's act was the cause of death when there was a long interval between injury and death. The Criminal Law Revision Committee wrote (14th Report) on this:

39. A killing cannot amount to murder unless death occurs within a year and a day of the infliction of injury. The longer the gap between the injury and death the more difficult it is to decide whether the injury is a cause of death. We reaffirm the view expressed in our Working Paper (paragraph 44) that, although with the advance of medical science it is arguably no longer necessary to retain the year-and-a-day rule, it would be wrong for a person to remain almost indefinitely at risk of prosecution for murder. A line has to be drawn somewhere and in our opinion the present law operates satisfactorily. When death follows over a year after the infliction of injury the killer does not necessarily escape justice. He may be charged with attempted murder or causing grievous bodily harm with intent, both of which are punishable, and, if our recommendations are accepted, will continue to be punishable, with life imprisonment. Accordingly, we recommend that a killing should not amount to murder unless death follows before the expiration of a year after the day on which the injury was inflicted.

40. In the majority of cases of murder the act which causes death (for example, the firing of a gun) and the infliction of injury (for example, the entry of a bullet into the victim's body) occur almost at the same time. In some cases, however, this is not so: the act which later causes injury may occur a substantial period of time before the actual infliction of injury. A decision therefore has to be made whether time should run from the act or the infliction of injury. A case that directly raises the issue is where a person places in a deserted building a booby-trap bomb which explodes more than a year later, killing a person instantly. If time were to run from the placing of the bomb, the killing could not be murder; it could be murder if time ran from the explosion. In such a case it would be wrong if a verdict of murder could not be returned. We have already explained that the year-and-a-day rule exists only to avoid uncertainties which may arise in cases where a person survives the infliction of injury upon him for a substantial time. In view of this, we recommend that time should run from the infliction of injury as opposed to the act which causes death. Where pre-natal injury is inflicted, time should run from birth.

3. A person 'in being'

The victim of homicide must have been born and not have died before the defendant's act took effect. Although this principle is discussed exclusively in connection with homicide, it is probably applicable to offences against the person generally. As to birth, the Committee (14th Report) wrote:

35. The common law definition of birth (for the purposes of offences against the person) has not been the subject of judicial review or comment for a long time. The last reported case on the subject that we can trace occurred in 1874. We have examined not only the common law test of birth but also the statutory formulation in the Infant Life (Preservation) Act 1929 which provides that the offence of child destruction may apply only to the killing of a child 'before it has an existence independent of its mother'. In our opinion the test of independent existence should be adopted. It also seems to us right that there should be an ascertainable point up to which the killing of a child would be child destruction under the Infant Life (Preservation) Act 1929 after which the law of homicide would apply. We therefore recommend that for a killing to constitute murder (or manslaughter or infanticide) the victim should have been born and have an existence independent of its mother.

As to death:

37. We have considered whether there should be a statutory definition of death. A memorandum issued by the honorary secretary of the Conference of Medical Royal Colleges and Faculties in the United Kingdom on 15 January 1979 refers to an earlier report of the Conference which expressed their unanimous opinion that "brain death" could be diagnosed with certainty. The memorandum states that the report published by the Conference has been widely accepted and says that the identification of brain death means that a patient is truly dead, whether or not the function of some organs, such as a heart beat, is still maintained by artificial means. Brain death is said to be when all the functions of the brain have permanently and irreversibly ceased. We are however extremely hesitant about embodying in a statute (which is not always susceptible of speedy amendment) an expression of present medical opinion and knowledge derived from a field of science which is continually progressing and inevitably altering its opinions in the light of new information. If a statutory definition of death were to be enacted there would, in our opinion, be a risk that further knowledge would cause it to lose the assent of the majority of the medical profession. In that event, far from assisting the medical profession, for example in cases of organ transplants, the definition might be a hindrance to them. Moreover, while there might be agreement that the statutory definition was defective, there might be differences of view about the proper content of any new definition. An additional reason for not recommending a definition of death is that such definition would have wide repercussions outside offences against the person and the criminal law. A legal definition of death would also have to be applicable in the civil law. It would be undesirable to have a statutory definition confined only to offences against the person, which is the extent of our present remit. For these reasons therefore we are not recommending the enactment of a definition of death.

See also *Malcherek*, p 35, above.

The draft Code Bill implements the Committee's opinion in the following clause:

69 Causing death

For the purposes of sections 56 to 62, 65 and 67, a person does not cause the death of another unless:

(a) that other has been born and has an existence independent of his mother when his death occurs (whether or not he was born or had an independent existence at the time of the infliction of any injury causing death); and

(b) the death occurs within a year and a day after the day on which any act causing death was done by that person or on which any fatal injury resulting from such an act was sustained by that other (and, where the fatal injury was done to an unborn child, within a year and a day after the day on which he was born and had an independent existence).

4. Murder: the mental element

The leading case on the mental element in murder is now *Moloney*, p 55, above. This proceeds on the assumption that the mental element required is an intention to kill or to cause grievous (i e 'really serious') bodily harm and is concerned exclusively with deciding the meaning of intention. As noted above, p 55, in an earlier case, *Hyam*, p 307, below, the House approached the matter differently. *Hyam* still requires consideration. The starting point must however be section 1 of the Homicide Act 1957, p 555, below, and the interpretation of it in the next case.

R v Vickers [1957] 2 All ER 741, Court of Criminal Appeal
(Lord Goddard CJ, Hilbery, Byrne, Slade and Devlin JJ)

The appellant broke into the cellar of a shop which was occupied by an old woman of seventy-three, a Miss Duckett, intending to steal money. At the shop Miss Duckett carried on a prosperous business of grocer and tobacconist, and she lived alone on the same premises in two rooms above the shop; she was a small woman and the appellant, who lived in lodgings a short distance away, knew that she was deaf. While the appellant was in the cellar Miss Duckett came down the stairs leading to it and saw the appellant. She asked him what he was doing and came towards him, whereupon the appellant attacked her with his fists and struck her several blows; she fell down. The medical evidence was that Miss Duckett was struck by ten to fifteen blows and was kicked in the face by the appellant, and that death was caused by shock due to general injuries; the medical evidence was also that the degree of force necessary to inflict the injuries sustained by Miss Duckett would be moderately severe to quite slight force.

The appellant now appealed against his conviction inter alia on the ground that the judge misdirected the jury when he told them that malice aforethought could be implied if the victim was killed by a voluntary act done with the intention of causing grievous bodily harm.

[**Lord Goddard CJ** delivering the judgment of the court:]

. . . The point that is raised is this: s 1(1) of the Act of 1957 says: [His Lordship quoted the subsection.]. The marginal note of s 1, which of course is not part of the section, but may be looked at as some indication of the purpose, is: 'Abolition of "constructive malice" '.

'Constructive malice' is an expression that has crept into the law—I do not think that it will be found in any particular decision but it is to be found in the text-books—and is something different from implied malice. The expression 'constructive malice' is generally used and the best illustration of constructive malice which is generally given is that if a person caused death during the course of his carrying out a felony which involved violence, that always amounted to murder. There were cases in which a man was not intending to cause death, as for instance where a mere push was given which would never have been considered in the ordinary way as one which would cause death, but the person pushed fell down and most unfortunately struck his head or fell down the stairs and broke his neck, yet if the act were done, for example, in the course of burglary, it amounted to murder. Take the case of rape. If a man raped a woman and in order to overcome her resistance proceeded to strangle her, the fact that he might only have used a moderate degree of violence in the strangling, in holding her throat, would have been no defence. If he did cause death it would have been murder because he caused death during the commission of the offence of rape. Another instance of constructive malice which was always held sufficient to amount to murder was the killing of a police officer in the execution of his duty. If a prisoner was resisting arrest, although he might use only a moderate degree of violence on a police officer, yet if he caused the death of the officer from some unusual or perhaps extraordinary reason, he was, before the Act of 1957, guilty of murder. Murder is, of course, killing with malice aforethought and 'malice aforethought' is a term of art. Malice aforethought has always been defined in English law as either an express intention to kill such as could be inferred when a person, having uttered threats against another, produced a lethal weapon and used it on him, or an implied intention to kill, as where the prisoner inflicted grievous bodily harm, that is to say, harmed the victim by a voluntary act intended to harm him and the victim died as the result of that grievous bodily harm. If a person does an act on another which amounts to the infliction of grievous bodily harm he cannot say that he did not intend to go so far. It is put as *malum in se* in the old cases and he must take the consequences. If he intends to inflict grievous bodily harm and that person dies, that has always been held in English law, and was at the time when the Act of 1957 was passed, sufficient to imply the malice aforethought which is a necessary constituent of murder.

It will be observed that s 1 preserves the implied malice as well as express malice and the words 'where a person kills another in the course or furtherance of some other offence' cannot in our opinion refer to the infliction of the grievous bodily harm, if the case which is made against the prisoner is that he killed a person by having assaulted the person with intent to do grievous bodily harm and from the bodily harm which he inflicted that person dies. The furtherance of some other offence must refer to the offence that he was committing or endeavouring to commit other than the killing, otherwise there would be no sense in it. It was always the English law that if death were caused by a person in the course of committing a felony involving violence, that was murder. Therefore, in this particular case it is perfectly clear that the words 'where a person kills another in the course or furtherance of some other offence' must be attributed to the burglary which the appellant was committing. The killing was in the course or furtherance of that burglary. He killed that person in the course of the burglary because he realised that the victim recognised him and he therefore inflicted grievous bodily harm on her, perhaps only intending to render her unconscious, but he did intend to inflict grievous bodily harm by the blows he inflicted on her and by kicking her in the face, of which there was evidence.

Section 1 (1) of the Act of 1957 then goes on:

> 'the killing shall not amount to murder unless done with the same malice aforethought (express or implied) as is required for a killing to amount to murder when not done in the course or furtherance of another offence.'

It would seem clear, therefore, that what the legislature is providing is that where there is a killing, though it may be done in the course or furtherance of another offence, that other offence must be ignored. The other offence is not taken into consideration. What has to be considered are the circumstances of the killing; and if the killing would amount to murder by reason of the express or implied malice then that person is guilty of capital murder. It is not enough that he killed in the course of the felony unless the killing is done in a manner which would amount to murder ignoring the felony which is committed. It seems to the court, therefore, that here you have a case of a burglar attacking a householder to prevent recognition. The householder died as the result of blows inflicted on her—blows or kicks or both—and if s 1 of the Act of 1957 had not been passed there could be no doubt that the man would have been guilty of murder. He is guilty of murder because he has killed a person with the necessary malice aforethought being implied from the fact that he intended to do grievous bodily harm.

I will now briefly refer to the summing-up of Hinchcliffe J, which the court thinks is quite impeccable. . . .

The court desires to say quite firmly that in considering the construction of s 1(1), it is impossible to say that the doing of grievous bodily harm is the other offence which is referred to in the first line and a half of the sub-section. It must be shown that independently of the fact that the accused is committing another offence, that the act which caused the death was done with malice aforethought as implied by law. The existence of express or implied malice is expressly preserved by the Act of 1957 and, in our opinion, a perfectly proper direction was given by Hinchcliffe J, to the jury, and accordingly this appeal fails and is dismissed.

Appeal dismissed

Director of Prosecutions v Smith [1960] 3 All ER 161, House of Lords (Viscount Kilmuir LC, Lord Goddard, Lord Tucker, Lord Denning and Lord Parker of Waddington)

The respondent was driving a car in which there was stolen property. While he was stopped by a police officer on point duty, another officer came to the driver's window and spoke to the respondent. As a result of what he saw in the back of the car, this constable told the respondent to draw into the near side. The respondent began to do so and the constable walked beside the car. Then the respondent suddenly accelerated and made off down an adjoining road. The constable succeeded in hanging on to the car which pursued an erratic course until the constable was thrown off in the path of a vehicle which ran over him, causing him fatal injuries.

At his trial for capital murder, the respondent maintained that he had no intention of killing or causing serious injury to the constable. Donovan J directed the jury, '. . . if you are satisfied that . . . he must, as a reasonable man, have contemplated that grievous bodily harm was likely to result to that officer . . . and that such harm did happen and the officer died in consequence, then the accused is guilty of capital murder'.

The jury returned a verdict of guilty. The Court of Criminal Appeal quashed his conviction on the ground of misdirection. The Crown appealed to the House of Lords.

[**Viscount Kilmuir LC**, having quoted from the summing-up, continued:]

The main complaint is that the learned judge was there applying what is referred to as an objective test, namely, the test of what a reasonable man would contemplate as the probable result of his acts, and, therefore, would intend, whereas the question for the jury, it is said, was what the respondent himself intended. This, indeed, was the view of the Court of Criminal Appeal . . .

Putting aside for a moment the distincion which the Court of Criminal Appeal were seeking to draw between results which were 'certain' and those which were 'likely', they were saying that it was for the jury to decide, whether, having regard to the panic in which he said he was, the respondent in fact at the time contemplated that grievous bodily harm would result from his actions or, indeed, whether he contemplated anything at all. Unless the jury were satisfied that he in fact had such contemplation, the necessary intent to constitute malice would not, in their view, have been proved. This purely subjective approach involves this, that, if an accused said that he did not in fact think of the consequences and the jury considered that might well be true, he would be entitled to be acquitted of murder.

My Lords, the proposition has only to be stated thus to make one realise what a departure it is from that on which the courts have always acted. The jury must of course in such a case as the present make up their minds on the evidence whether the accused was unlawfully and voluntarily doing something to someone. The unlawful and voluntary act must clearly be aimed at someone in order to eliminate cases of negligence or of careless or dangerous driving. Once, however, the jury are satisfied as to that, it matters not what the accused in fact contemplated as the probable result, or whether he ever contemplated at all, provided he was in law responsible and accountable for his actions, i e was a man capable of forming an intent, not insane within the M'Naghten Rules and not suffering from diminished responsibility. On the assumption that he is so accountable for his actions, the sole question is whether the unlawful and voluntary act was of such a kind that grievous bodily harm was the natural and probable result. The only test available for this is what the ordinary, responsible man would, in all the circumstances of the case, have contemplated as the natural and probable result. That, indeed, has always been the law and I would only make a few citations. . . .

[His Lordship referred to various authorities and continued.]

My Lords, the law being as I have endeavoured to define it, there seems to be no ground on which the approach by the trial judge in the present case can be criticised. Having excluded the suggestion of accident, he asked the jury to consider what were the exact circumstances at the time as known to the respondent and what were the unlawful and voluntary acts which he did towards the police officer. The learned judge then prefaced the passages of which complaint is made by saying, in effect, that if, in doing what he did, he must as a reasonable man have contemplated that serious harm was likely to occur then he was guilty of murder. My only doubt concerns the use of the expression 'a reasonable man', since this to lawyers connotes the man on the Clapham omnibus by reference to whom a standard of care in civil cases is ascertained. In judging of intent, however, it really denotes an ordinary man capable of reasoning who is responsible and accountable for his actions, and this would be the sense in which it would be understood by a jury.

Another criticism of the summing-up and one which found favour in the Court of Criminal Appeal concerned the manner in which the trial judge dealt with the presumption that a man intends the natural and probable consequences of his acts. I will cite the passage again:

> 'The intention with which a man did something can usually be determined by a jury only by inference from the surrounding circumstances including the presumption of law that a man intends the natural and probable consequences of his acts.'

It is said that the reference to this being a presumption of law without explaining that it was rebuttable amounted to a misdirection. Whether the presumption is one of law or of fact or, as has been said, of common sense, matters not for this purpose. The real question is whether the jury should have been told that it was rebuttable. In truth, however, as I see it, this is merely another way of applying the test of the reasonable man. Provided that the presumption is applied, once the accused's knowledge of the circumstances and the nature of his acts have been ascertained, the only thing that could rebut the presumption would be proof of incapacity to form an intent, insanity or diminished responsibility. In the present case, therefore, there was no need to explain to the jury that the presumption was rebuttable. . . .

Before leaving this part of the case, I should mention that the Court of Criminal Appeal in their judgment drew a distinction between serious harm which was 'certain' to result and serious harm which was 'likely' to result. . . . My Lords, there is, in my opinion, no warrant for such a distinction and no authority can be adduced in support thereof. Indeed, counsel for the respondent did not, in your Lordships' House, seek to support the disjunction. . . .

[His Lordship held that, in both the law of murder and statutory offences, 'grievous bodily harm' means no more and no less than 'really serious bodily harm', disapproving *Ashman* (1858) 1 F & F 88.]

In the result, the appeal should, in my opinion, be allowed and the conviction of capital murder restored.

[**Lord Goddard, Lord Tucker, Lord Denning** and **Lord Parker of Waddington** agreed.]

Appeal allowed

Questions

1. Did the House of Lords apply a subjective or an objective test to (i) the accused's knowledge of the circumstances and the nature of his act and (ii) the consequences of his act?

2. Is the distinction made, between knowledge and foresight a sound distinction? Why should we apply a subjective test to the one and an objective test to the other? If unreasonable ignorance of a fact and inability to foresee a consequence have the same effect on blameworthiness (do they?) why should one lead to an acquittal and the other to conviction and (presumably) punishment?

Hyam v Director of Public Prosecutions [1974] 2 All ER 41, House of Lords (Lord Hailsham of St Marylebone LC, Viscount Dilhorne, Lord Diplock, Lord Cross of Chelsea and Lord Kilbrandon)

The facts appear in the speech of Lord Hailsham.

Lord Hailsham LC: . . . The facts are simple, and not in dispute. In the early hours of Saturday, 15 July 1972, the appellant set fire to a dwelling-house in Coventry by deliberately pouring about a half gallon of petrol through the letterbox and igniting it by means of a newspaper and a match. The house contained four persons, presumably asleep. They were a Mrs Booth and her three children, a boy and the two young girls who were the subjects of the charges. Mrs Booth and the boy escaped alive through a window. The two girls died as the result of asphyxia by the fumes generated by the fire. The appellant's motive (in the sense in which I shall use the word 'motive') was jealousy of Mrs Booth whom the appellant believed was likely to marry a Mr Jones of whom the appellant herself was the discarded, or partly discarded, mistress. Her account of her actions, and her defence, was that she had started the fire only with the intention of frightening Mrs Booth into leaving the neighbourhood, and that she did not intend to cause death or grievous bodily harm. The judge directed the jury:

> 'The prosecution must prove, beyond all reasonable doubt, that the accused intended to (kill or) do serious bodily harm to Mrs Booth, the mother of the deceased girls. If you are satisfied that when the accused set fire to the house she knew that it was highly probable that this would cause (death or) serious bodily harm then the prosecution will have established . . . the necessary intent. It matters not if her motive was, as she says, to frighten Mrs Booth.'

The judge explained that he had put brackets round the words 'kill or' and 'death or' because he advised the jury to concentrate on the intent to do serious bodily harm rather than the intent to kill.

There were other passages in the summing-up to the same effect, but this was the vital passage, and the judge reduced it to writing and caused the jury to retire with it into the jury room. As the case proceeded, it is the only passage in the judge's summing-up to which I need draw attention, and gives rise to the only point which was argued before your Lordships' House. The Court of Appeal [(1973) 3 All ER 842] dismissed the appeal 'not without some reluctance', and, in giving leave to appeal to the House of Lords, certified that it involved the following point of law of general public importance, namely, the question:

> 'Is malice aforethought in the crime of murder established by proof beyond reasonable doubt that when doing the act which led to the death of another the accused knew that it was highly probable that that act would result in death or serious bodily harm?

This is the only question which, in my view, it is necessary to consider and the whole appeal is, therefore, within a fairly narrow compass. . . .

[Having considered *DPP v Smith* and s 8 of the Criminal Justice Act 1967, his Lordship continued:]

At the end of the day there are, I think, two reasons against formally overruling *Director of Public Prosecutions v Smith* in virtue of our Practice Direction as suggested by the authors of Smith and Hogan. The first is that in view of the diversity of interpretation it is difficult to know exactly what one is overruling. Indeed, if the extreme minimalising interpretations be adopted, there is little or nothing to overrule or indeed little enough to require the intervention of Parliament in 1967. The second is that there are at least two passages in *Director of Public Prosecutions v Smith* of permanent value which on any view ought not to be overruled. The first is the passage at the end of Viscount Kilmuir LC's opinion [[1961] AC at 335, [1960] 3 All ER at 172] which disposes at least in this context of the doctrine of *Ashman* [(1858) 1 F & F 88] regarding the nature of grievous bodily harm, and thus excludes the possibility of 'murder by pinprick'. The second is the earlier passage [[1961] AC at 327, [1960] 3 All ER at 176] where Viscount Kilmuir LC says:

> 'The unlawful and voluntary act must clearly be aimed at someone in order to eliminate cases of negligence or of careless or dangerous driving.'

There is also a more important third element latent in the decision to which I will return later, and which seems to justify the result, if not all the reasoning.

The view taken above of *Director of Public Prosecutions v Smith* and of the 1967 Act is not enough to dispose of the present appeal. For, whatever may be said by way of criticism of the crucial passage in the judge's direction, it was impeccable at least in this, that it applied the jury's mind to a subjective test of what was the state of the mind of the accused. The question raised by Ackner J's charge to the jury is not whether he revived the passages in *Director of Public Prosecutions v Smith* which seems to suggest an objective test, but (i) whether, on the assumption that the test is subjective, foresight of the probable consequences is an alternative species of malice aforethought to intention, or, as Pearson LJ clearly suggests in *Hardy v Motor Insurers' Bureau* [[1964] 2 QB at 764, [1964] 2 All ER at 749], whether foresight of the probable consequence is only another way of describing intention and (ii) on the assumption that foresight can be used as an alternative or equivalent of intention whether a high degree of probability in that which is foreseen is enough. . . .

I know of no better judicial interpretation of 'intention' or 'intent' than that given in a civil case by Asquith LJ (*Cunliffe v Goodman* [[1950] 2 KB 237 at 253, [1950] 1 All ER 720 at 724]) when he said:

'An "intention," to my mind, connotes a state of affairs which the party "intending"—I will call him X—does more than merely contemplate. It connotes a state of affairs which, on the contrary, he decides, so far as in him lies, to bring about, and which, in point of possibility, he has a reasonable prospect of being able to bring about, by his own act of volition.'

If this be a good definition of 'intention' for the purposes of the criminal law of murder, and so long as it is held to include the means as well as the end and the inseparable consequences of the end as well as the means, I think it is clear that 'intention' is clearly to be distinguished alike from 'desire' and from foresight of the probable consequences. As the Law Commission pointed out in their disquisition ['Imputed Criminal Intent (*Director of Public Prosecutions v Smith*)', pp 14, 15, para 18 (12 December 1966)] on *Director of Public Prosecutions v Smith*, a man may desire to blow up an aircraft in flight in order to obtain insurance moneys. But if any passengers are killed he is guilty of murder, as their death will be a moral certainty if he carries out his intention. There is no difference between blowing up the aircraft and intending the death of some or all of the passengers. On the other hand, the surgeon in a heart transplant operation may intend to save his patient's life, but he may recognise that there is at least a high degree of probability that his action will kill the patient. In that case he intends to save his patient's life, but he foresees as a high degree of probability that he will cause his death, which he neither intends nor desires, since he regards the operation not as a means to killing his patient, but as the best, and possibly the only, means of ensuring his survival. . . .

I do not, therefore consider, as was suggested in argument, that the fact that a state of affairs is correctly foreseen as a highly probable consequence of what is done is the same thing as the fact that the state of affairs is intended. The highest that it can be put in the context of the present set of facts is that what was intended was to expose the inhabitants of the house to the serious risk of death or grievous bodily harm and not actually to cause death or grievous bodily harm. I do not think that these propositions are identical.

But this, again, does not dispose of the matter. Another way of putting the case for the Crown was that, even if it be conceded that foresight of the probable consequences is not the same thing as intention, it can, nevertheless, be an alternative type of malice aforethought, equally effective as intention to convert an unlawful killing into murder. This view, which is inconsistent with the view that foresight of a high degree of probability is only another way of describing intention, derives some support from the way in which the proposition is put in Stephen's Digest where it is said that malice aforethought for the purpose of the law of murder includes a state of mind in which there is:

'knowledge that the act which causes death will probably cause the death of, or grievous bodily harm to, some person, whether such person is the person actually killed or not, although such knowledge is accompanied by indifference whether death or grievous bodily harm is caused or not, or by a wish that it may not be caused'.

If this is right, Ackner J's direction can be justified on the grounds that such knowledge is itself a separate species of malice aforethought, and not simply another way of describing intention. . . .

I must, however, qualify the negative answer I have proposed to the question certified as of general public importance. For the reason I have given, I do not think that foresight as such of a high degree of probability is at all the same thing as intention, and, in my view, it is not foresight but intention which constitutes the mental element in murder. It is the absence of intention to kill or cause grievous bodily harm which absolves the heart surgeon in the case of the transplant, notwithstanding that he foresees as a matter of high probability that his action will probably actually kill the patient. It is the presence of an actual intention to kill or cause grievous bodily harm which convicts the murderer who takes a very long shot at his victim and kills him notwithstanding that he thinks correctly as he takes his aim that the odds are very much against his hitting him at all.

But what are we to say of the state of mind of a defendant who knows that a proposed course of conduct exposes a third party to a serious risk of death or grievous bodily harm, without actually intending those consequences, but nevertheless and without lawful excuse deliberately pursues that course of conduct regardless whether the consequences to his potential victim take place or not? In that case, if my analysis be correct, there is not merely actual foresight of the probable consequences, but actual intention to expose his victim to the risk of those consequences whether they in fact occur or not. Is that intention sufficient to reduce the crime to manslaughter notwithstanding a jury's finding that they are sure that it was the intention with which the act was done? In my opinion, it is not, and in this my opinion corresponds with the opinion of the Commissioners on the Criminal Law [See Fourth Report of Her Majesty's

Commissioners on Criminal Law (8 March 1839), p xx] when they said, 'Again, it appears to us that it ought to make no difference in point of legal distinction whether death results from a direct intention to kill, or from wilfully doing an act of which death is the probable consequence'. And again in a later passage [Ibid, p xxiv], 'It is the *wilful exposure* of life to peril that constitutes the crime'. The heart surgeon exposes his patient to the risk, but does everything he can to save his life, regarding his actions as the best or only means of securing the patient's survival. He is, therefore, not exposing his patient to the risk without lawful excuse or regardless of the consequences. The reckless motorist who is guilty of manslaughter, but not murder, is not at least ordinarily aiming his actions at anyone in the sense explained in *Director of Public Prosecutions v Smith*. If he were, it is quite possible that, as in *Director of Public Prosecutions v Smith*, he might be convicted of murder. In the field of guilty knowledge it has long been accepted both for the purposes of criminal and civil law that 'a man who deliberately shuts his eyes to the truth will not be heard to say that he did not know it'. (See per Lord Reid in *Southern Portland Cement v Cooper* [[1974] 1 All ER at 93; [1974] 2 WLR at 158].) Cannot the same be said of the state of intention of a man who, with actual appreciation of the risks and without lawful excuse, wilfully decides to expose potential victims to the risk of death or really serious injury regardless of whether the consequences take place or not? This seems to me to be the truth underlying the statement of the law in Stephen's *Digest*, the summing-up of Cockburn CJ in *Desmond* [(1868) Times, 28 April], and of Avory J in *Lumley* [(1911) 76 JP 208] and of those phrases in *Director of Public Prosecutions v Smith* in which it seems to be said that a rational man must be taken to intend the consequences of his acts. It is not a revival of the doctrine of constructive malice or the substitution of an objective for a subjective test of knowledge or intention. It is the man's actual state of knowledge and intent which, as in all other cases, determines his criminal responsibility. Nor, for the like reason, does this set up an irrebuttable presumption. It simply proclaims the moral truth that if a man, in full knowledge of the danger involved, and without lawful excuse, deliberately does that which exposes a victim to the risk of the probable grievous bodily harm (in the sense explained) or death, and the victim dies, the perpetrator of the crime is guilty of murder and not manslaughter to the same extent as if he had actually intended the consequence to follow, and irrespective of whether he wishes it. That is because the two types of intention are morally indistinguishable, although factually and logically distinct, and because it is therefore just that they should bear the same consequences to the perpetrator as they have the same consequences for the victim if death ensues. . . .

I therefore propose the following propositions in answer to the question of general public importance.

(1) Before an act can be murder it must be 'aimed at someone' as explained in *Director of Public Prosecutions v Smith*, and must in addition be an act committed with one of the following intentions, the test of which is always subjective to the actual defendant: (i) The intention to cause death; (ii) The intention to cause grievous bodily harm in the sense of that term explained in *Director of Public Prosecutions v Smith*, i e really serious injury; (iii) Where the defendant knows that there is a serious risk that death or grievous bodily harm will ensue from his acts, and commits those acts deliberately and without lawful excuse, the intention to expose a potential victim to that risk as the result of those acts. It does not matter in such circumstances whether the defendant desires those consequences to ensue or not and in none of these cases does it matter that the act and the intention were aimed at a potential victim other than the one who succumbed.

(2) Without an intention of one of these three types the mere fact that the defendant's conduct is done in the knowledge that grievous bodily harm is likely or highly likely to ensue from his conduct is not by itself enough to convert a homicide into the crime of murder. Nevertheless, for the reasons I have given in my opinion the appeal fails and should be dismissed.

Viscount Dilhorne. . . . Whether or not it be that the doing of the act with the knowledge that certain consequences are highly probable is to be treated as establishing the intent to bring about those consequences, I think it is clear that for at least 100 years such knowledge has been recognised as amounting to malice aforethought. In my opinion, it follows the second contention advanced on behalf of the appellant is rejected, that the question certified should be answered in the affirmative.

While I do not think that it is strictly necessary in this case to decide whether such knowledge established the necessary intent, for, if Ackner J was wrong about that, it is not such a mis-direction as would warrant the quashing of the conviction as, even if it did not establish intent, it was correct in that such knowledge amounted to malice aforethought, I am inclined to the view that Ackner J was correct. A man may do an act with a number of intentions. If he does it deliberately and intentionally, knowing when he does it that it is highly probable that grievous bodily harm will result, I think most people would say and be justified in saying that whatever other intentions he may have had as well, he at least intended grievous bodily harm.

I think, too, that if Ackner J had left the question of intent in the way in which it is left in the vast majority of cases, namely, was it proved that the accused had intended to kill or to do grievous bodily harm, no reasonable jury could on the facts of this case have come to any other conclusion than that she had intended to do grievous bodily harm, bearing in mind her knowledge and the fact that, before she set fire to the house, she took steps to make sure that Mr Jones was not in it as she did not want to harm him. If the normal direction had been given, much litigation would have been avoided.

[His Lordship went on to hold that the words 'grievous bodily harm' must be given their ordinary meaning. To substitute 'bodily injury known to the offender to be likely to cause death' would be a task for Parliament; but he shared the view that it would not lead to any great difference in the day-to-day administration of the law.]

For these reasons in my opinion this appeal should be dismissed.

Lord Diplock. . . . . This appeal raises two separate questions. The first is common to all crimes of this class. It is: what is the attitude of mind of the accused towards the particular evil consequence of his physical act that must be proved in order to constitute the offence? The second is special to the crime of murder. It is: what is the relevant evil consequence of his physical act which causes death, towards which the attitude of mind of the accused must be determined on a charge of murder?

On the first question I do not desire to say more than I agree with those of your Lordships who take the uncomplicated view that in crimes of this class no distinction is to be drawn in English law between the state of mind of one who does an act because he desires it to produce a particular evil consequence and the state of mind of one who does an act knowing full well that it is likely to produce the consequence although it may not be the object he was seeking to achieve by doing the act. What is common to both these states of mind is willingness to produce the particular evil consequence: and this, in my view, is the mens rea needed to satisfy a requirement, whether imposed by statute or existing at common law, that in order to constitute the offence with which the accused is charged he must have acted with 'intent' to produce a particular evil consequence or, in the ancient phrase which still survives in crimes of homicide, with 'malice aforethought'.

[His Lordship held that an intention to cause serious bodily harm was not enough. There must be an intention to do an act likely to endanger life. An intention to cause serious bodily harm was enough from 1803, when Lord Ellenborough's Act created the statutory felony of causing grievous bodily harm with intent to cause such harm, until the Homicide Act 1957 came into force. Under the doctrine of constructive malice, the intention to commit that felony was a sufficient mens rea for murder; but the doctrine was now abolished. It was necessary to determine the state of the law in 1803 and decide how the common law would have developed if that Act had not been passed. In his opinion, *Vickers* p 304, above, was wrongly decided.]

Lord Cross of Chelsea. . . . . Stephen's definition covers four states of mind. A(1) an intent to kill, (2) knowledge that the act in question will probably cause death. B(1) an intent to cause grievous bodily harm, (2) knowledge that the act in question will probably cause grievous bodily harm. Counsel for the appellant argued strenuously that there was a great gulf fixed between A(1) and B(1) on the one hand, and A(2) and B(2) on the other, and that unless the accused believed that the consequences in question were certain to ensue one ought not to equate mere foresight of consequences with an intention to produce them. Even if one views the matter simply from the point of view of linguistics I am not sure that the ordinary man would agree. If, for example, someone parks a car in a city street with a time bomb in it which explodes and injures a number of people I think that the ordinary man might well argue as follows: 'The man responsible for this outrage did not injure these people unintentionally; he injured them intentionally. So he can fairly be said to have intentionally injured them—that is to say, to have intended to injure them. The fact that he was not certain that anyone would be injured is quite irrelevant;—(after all, how could he possibly be certain that anyone would be injured?)—and the fact that, although he foresaw that it was likely that some people would be injured, it was a matter of indifference to him whether they were injured or not (his object being simply to call attention to Irish grievances and to demonstrate the power of the IRA) is equally irrelevant.' But I can see that a logician might object that the ordinary man was using the word 'intentionally' with two different shades of meaning, and I am prepared to assume that as a matter of the correct use of language the man in question did not intend to injure those who were in fact injured by his act. But we are not debating a problem of linguistics; we are asking ourselves whether Stephen was right in saying that the states of mind labelled A(2) and B(2) constitute 'malice aforethought'. The first question to be answered is whether if an intention to kill—using intention in the strict sense of the word—is murder—as it plainly is—doing an unlawful act with knowledge that it may well cause death ought also to be murder. I have no doubt whatever that it ought to be. On this point I agree entirely with the view expressed by Cockburn CJ in the passage in his summing-up in *Desmond* [(1868) Times 28 April, 11 Cox CC 146] which is quoted by my noble and learned friend, Lord Hailsham of St Marylebone. Turning now to the states of mind labelled B(1) and (2)—*if* it is the law that an intention to cause grievous bodily harm—using intention in the strict sense of the word—is 'malice aforethought', whether or not one realises that one's act may endanger life, then I think that it is right that the doing of an act which one realises may well cause grievous bodily harm should also constitute malice aforethought whether or not one realises that one's act may endanger life. No doubt many people think that Stephen's four categories ought to be reduced to two (namely, an intention to kill and a willingness to endanger life), and my noble and learned friend, Lord Diplock, whose speech I have had the advantage of reading, thinks that since the passing of the Homicide Act 1957 it has been open to the courts to declare that this is in fact the law. But to achieve that result it would be necessary for us to over-rule *Vickers* and that part of the decision in *Director of Public Prosecutions v Smith* which approved *Vickers*. . . . In the result, therefore, I think that the only criticism which can be directed against Ackner J's summing-up is that by the insertion of the word 'highly' before 'probable' it was unduly favourable to the appellant.

[His Lordship said that he had not appreciated until a late stage that it was being argued that *Vickers* was wrongly decided. Lord Diplock might well be right in so thinking; but Viscount Dilhorne might be right in thinking *Vickers* correct. Without the fullest possible argument he was not prepared to decide; but *on the footing that* Vickers *was rightly decided*, the appeal should be dismissed]

[**Lord Kilbrandon** made a speech agreeing with **Lord Diplock.**]

Appeal dismissed

Questions

1. Is there a distinction between (i) doing an act actually foreseeing that it will probably cause death or grievous bodily harm to P and (ii) doing an act intending to expose P to the risk of probable death or grievous bodily harm? (Lord Hailsham, p 310, ante.)
2. Does Lord Hailsham adequately explain why the heart surgeon is not guilty of murder? He does not intend to kill or cause grievous bodily harm, but does he not intend to expose his victim to a serious risk of those consequences?

R v Cunningham [1981] 2 All ER 863, House of Lords
(Lord Hailsham LC, and Lords Wilberforce, Simon, Edmund-Davies and Bridge)

The appellant attacked the deceased in a pub and hit him repeatedly with a chair. The deceased died from his injuries. The judge directed the jury that the appellant was guilty of murder if he intended to cause really serious harm. The Court of Appeal dismissed his appeal and he appealed to the House of Lords, relying on the speeches of Lords Diplock and Kilbrandon in *Hyam*, p 307, above.

Lord Hailsham LC. . . . The real nerve of Lord Diplock's argument, however, does, as it seems to me, depend on the importance to be attached to the passing in 1803 of Lord Ellenborough's Act (43 Geo 3 c 58) by which, for the first time, wounding with the intent to inflict grievous bodily harm became a felony. This, Lord Diplock believes, rendered it possible to apply the doctrine of 'felony murder' as defined in Stephen's category (c), abolished in 1957, to all cases of felonious wounding, where death actually ensued from the wound. The abolition of 'felony murder' in 1957 was thus seen to enable the judiciary to pursue the mental element in murder behind the curtain imposed on it by the combined effect of the statutory crime of felonious wounding and the doctrine of constructive malice, and so to arrive at a position in which the mental element could be redefined in terms either of an intention to kill, or an intention actually to endanger human life, to correspond with the recommendations of the Fourth Report of Her Majesty's Commissioners on Criminal Law (8th March 1839).

It seems to me, however, that this highly ingenious argument meets with two insuperable difficulties. I accept that it appears to be established that the actual phrase 'grievous bodily harm', if not an actual coinage by Lord Ellenborough's Act, can never be found to have appeared in print before it, though it has subsequently become current coin, and has passed into the general legal jargon of statute law, and the cases decided thereon. But counsel, having diligently carried us through the institutional writers on homicide, starting with Coke, and ending with East, with several citations from the meagre reports available, only succeeded in persuading me at least that, even prior to Lord Ellenborough's Act of 1803, and without the precise label 'grievous bodily harm', the authors and the courts had consistently treated as murder, and therefore unclergiable, any killing with intent to do serious harm, however described, to which the label 'grievous bodily harm', as defined by Viscount Kilmuir LC in *Director of Public Prosecutions v Smith* [1960] 3 All ER 161 at 171, [1961] AC 290 at 334, reversing the 'murder by pinprick' doctrine arising from *R v Ashman* (1858) 1 F & F 88, 175 ER 638, could properly have been applied. It would be tedious to pursue the citations all in detail. We were referred successively to 3 Co Inst 47–52, 1 Hale PC 424–477, 1 Hawk PC 85–88, 4 Bl Com 191–201, Foster's Discourse on Homicide (Crown Law) 255–267 and 1 East PC 103, 214–233. But the further we went into these passages the more hopeless appeared to be the view that, irrespective of constructive malice, malice aforethought had ever been limited to the intention to kill or endanger life. On the contrary, these authorities reinforced the conclusion arrived at by Stephen's original Note XIV (in the Sturge edition Note VIII). This is the more striking in that the last few lines of the note demonstrate clearly that the possible combined effect of the felony-murder rule and the existence of a statutory crime of felonious wounding was consciously present to the author's mind.

There is a second difficulty in the way of treating Lord Ellenborough's Act as providing the kind of historical watershed demanded by Lord Diplock's speech and contended for in the instant appeal by the appellant's counsel. This consists in the fact that, though the nineteenth century judges might in theory have employed the felony-murder rule to apply to cases where death ensued in the course of a felonious wounding, they do not appear to have done so in fact. No case was cited where they did so. On the contrary, there appears to be no historical discontinuity between criminal jurisprudence before and after 1803. Stephen never so treated the matter (either in his text, or, except in the last few lines, in his Note XIV). It was not so treated in the Australian case of *La Fontaine v R* (1976) 136 CLR 62 (after *Hyam*, but in a jurisdiction in which the constructive malice rule still applied). It was pointed out by counsel for the Crown that the relevant felony created by Lord Ellenborough's Act was limited to cutting or stabbing and did not extend, for example, to beating, which would effectively have excluded the felony-murder doctrine from many cases where death ensued from an act intended to inflict grievous bodily harm. For myself, I think that there is a logical difficulty not based on this narrow point of construction, which prevented the judges from adopting the principle. Felonious wounding intrinsically involves proof by the prosecution of the requisite intention and therefore gives no added force to the earlier law, if I have correctly interpreted the learning before 1803. The way is thus clear on any view to accept as decisive what I myself had always understood to be the law prior to 1957. This is contained in the statement of Lord Goddard CJ representing the court of five judges in *Vickers* [1957] 2 QB 664 at 670; cf [1957] 2 All ER 741 at 743 [p 304, above].

R v Moloney, p 55, above, Hancock and Shankland, Appendix II, below

Moloney and *Hancock* must now be regarded as the leading cases on the mens rea of murder. In the light of those cases, consider whether the following directions would now be correct:

1. 'If D knew that there was a serious risk that death or grievous bodily harm would ensue from his acts and he committed those acts deliberately and without lawful excuse, his intention to expose P to that risk as a result of those acts is an intention to murder.' (Cf Lord Hailsham, p 310, above).

2. 'If when D did the act which killed P he knew that it was *likely* (cf Lord Diplock, p 311, above) [or *probable* (cf Lord Cross, p 311, above); or *highly probable* (cf Viscount Dilhorne, p 310, above)] that it would cause grievous bodily harm, he is guilty of murder.'

Is *Hyam* impliedly overruled? If Ackner J's direction to the jury were given on the same facts today, could the conviction be upheld?

The Criminal Law Revision Committee was of the opinion that, if a definition of intention similar to that propounded in *Hyam* were adopted, it would be necessary to make special provision if the terrorist bomber were to be guilty of murder. Their recommendation is incorporated in the draft Criminal Code Bill, cl 56 (c), p 348, below.

CHAPTER 17

Manslaughter

Manslaughter is a complex crime of no less than five varieties. It covers three cases where the defendant kills with the fault required for murder but, because of the presence of a particular extenuating circumstance recognised by law, the offence is reduced to manslaughter. These cases are traditionally known as 'voluntary manslaughter'. The other cases—'involuntary manslaughter'—consist of homicides committed with a fault element less than that required for murder but recognised by the common law as sufficient to found liability for homicide. It should be emphasised that there is only one offence. Whether the defendant is guilty of the voluntary or the involuntary variety, he is convicted simply of manslaughter. It makes no difference that some of the jury think the defendant guilty of one variety and others think him guilty of another variety or other varieties. The right verdict is guilty of manslaughter. The only qualification to this is that, where diminished responsibility has been left to the jury, it is the practice for the judge to invite the jury to inform him when giving their verdict of guilty of manslaughter whether it is on that ground. A life sentence is mandatory for murder but for manslaughter the maximum is life and there is no minimum. It is an offence which may be committed with a wide variety of culpability and sometimes may be properly dealt with by a fine or a conditional or absolute discharge.

The law might be summarised as follows:

A person is guilty of manslaughter where:

(a) he kills or is a party to the killing of another with the fault required for murder (*Moloney*, p 55, above) but he acted:
   (i) under diminished responsibility (Homicide Act 1957, s 2) or
   (ii) under provocation (s 3 of the Homicide Act 1957 and *Camplin* p 321, below); or
   (iii) in pursuance of a suicide pact (Homicide Act 1957, s 4) or

(b) he is not guilty of murder by reason only of the fact that, because of voluntary intoxication, he lacked the fault required, (*Majewski*, p 87, above) or

(c) he kills another:
   (i) by an unlawful and dangerous act as defined in *Newbury and Jones*, p 336, below); or
   (ii) being reckless (as defined in *Caldwell* p 68, above) whether personal injury be caused to another.

1. Diminished responsibility

Homicide Act 1957, s 2, p 555, below

2   Persons suffering from diminished responsibility

R v Byrne [1960] 3 All ER 1, Court of Criminal Appeal
(Lord Parker CJ, Hilbery and Diplock JJ)

[**Lord Parker CJ** read the following judgment of the court:]

The appellant was convicted of murder before Stable J at Birmingham Assizes and sentenced to imprisonment for life. The victim was a young woman whom he strangled in the YWCA hostel, and after her death he committed horrifying mutilations on her dead body. The facts as to the killing were not disputed, and were admitted in a long statement made by the appellant. The only defence was that in killing his victim the appellant was suffering from diminished responsibility as defined by s 2 of the Homicide Act 1957, and was accordingly guilty, not of murder, but of manslaughter.

Three medical witnesses were called by the defence, the senior medical officer at Birmingham prison and two specialists in psychological medicine. Their uncontradicted evidence was that the appellant was a sexual psychopath, that he suffered from abnormality of mind, as, indeed, was abundantly clear from the other evidence in the case, and that such abnormality of mind arose from a condition of arrested or retarded development of mind or inherent causes. The nature of the abnormality of mind of a sexual psychopath, according to the medical evidence, is that he suffers from violent perverted sexual desires which he finds it difficult or impossible to control. Save when under the influence of his perverted sexual desires, he may be normal. All three doctors were of opinion that the killing was done under the influence of his perverted sexual desires, and, although all three were of opinion that he was not insane in the technical sense of insanity laid down in the rules in *M'Naghten's Case* [see p 188, above], it was their view that his sexual psychopathy could properly be described as partial insanity.

In his summing-up the learned judge, after summarising the medical evidence, gave to the jury a direction of law, on the correctness of which this appeal turns. He told the jury that, if on the evidence they came to the conclusion that the facts could be fairly summarised as follows:

> '(i) from an early age [the appellant] has been subject to these perverted, violent desires and in some cases has indulged his desires; (ii) the impulse or urge of these desires is stronger than normal impulse or urge of sex to such an extent that the subject finds it very difficult or perhaps impossible in some cases to resist putting the desire into practice; (iii) the act of killing this girl was done under such impulse or urge; and (iv) setting aside these sexual addictions and practices, [the appellant] was normal in every other respect'

—those facts, with nothing more, would not bring a case within the section and 'do not constitute such abnormality of mind as substantially to impair a man's mental responsibility for his acts'. He went on to say:

> 'In other words, mental affliction is one thing. The section is there to protect them. The section is not there to give protection where there is nothing else than what is vicious and depraved.'

Taken by themselves those last words are unobjectionable, but it is contended on behalf of the appellant that the direction, taken as a whole, involves a misconstruction of the section, and had the effect of withdrawing from the jury an issue of fact which it was peculiarly their province to decide.

Section 2 of the Homicide Act 1957, is dealing with the crime of murder in which there are, at common law, two essential elements: (i) the physical act of killing another person, and (ii) the state of mind of the person who kills or is a party to the killing, namely, his intention to kill or to cause grievous bodily harm. Section 2 (1) does not deal with the first element. It modified the existing law as respects the second element, that is, the state of mind of the person who kills or is a party to a killing. Before the passing of the Homicide Act 1957, a person who killed or was party to a killing could escape liability for murder—as for any other crime requiring mens rea—if he showed that at the time of the killing he was insane within the meaning of the M'Naghten Rules [see p 188, above], that is,

'. . . that . . . [he] was labouring under such a defect of reason, from disease of the mind, as not to know the nature and quality of the act he was doing; or, if he did know it, that he did not know he was doing what was wrong.'

If established, this defence negatives mens rea and the accused was, and still is, entitled to a special verdict of 'guilty of the act but insane' at the time of doing the act, which is an acquittal of any crime. The test is a rigid one: it relates solely to a person's intellectual ability to appreciate (a) the physical act that he is doing, and (b) whether it is wrong. If he has such intellectual ability, his power to control his physical acts by exercise of his will is irrelevant.

The ability of the accused to control his physical acts by exercise of his will was relevant before the passing of the Homicide Act 1957, in one case only: that of provocation. Loss of self-control on the part of the accused so as to make him for the moment not master of his mind had the effect of reducing murder to manslaughter if (i) it was induced by an act or series of acts done by the deceased to the accused, and (ii) such act or series of acts would have induced a reasonable man to lose his self-control and act in the same manner as the accused acted (see *Duffy* [see [1949] 1 All ER 932]). Whether loss of self-control induced by provocation negatived the ordinary presumption that a man intended the natural ordinary consequences of his physical acts so that in such a case the prosecution had failed to prove the essential mental element in murder (namely, that the accused intended to kill or to inflict grievous bodily harm) is academic for the purposes of our consideration. What is relevant is that loss of self-control has always been recognised as capable of reducing murder to manslaughter, but that the criterion has always been the degree of self-control which would be exercised by a reasonable man, that is to say, a man with a normal mind.

It is against that background of the existing law that s 2 (1) of the Homicide Act 1957, falls to be construed. To satisfy the requirements of the subsection the accused must show (a) that he was suffering from an abnormality of mind; and (b) that such abnormality of mind (i) arose from a condition of arrested or retarded development of mind or any inherent causes or was induced by disease or injury, and (ii) was such as substantially impaired his mental responsibility for his acts in doing or being a party to the killing. 'Abnormality of mind', which has to be contrasted with the time-honoured expression in the M'Naghten Rules 'defect of reason', means a state of mind so different from that of ordinary human beings that the reasonable man would term it abnormal. It appears to us to be wide enough to cover the mind's activities in all its aspects, not only the perception of physical acts and matters and the ability to form a rational judgment whether an act is right or wrong, but also the ability to exercise will-power to control physical acts in accordance with that rational judgment. The expression 'mental responsibility for his acts' points to a consideration of the extent to which the accused's mind is answerable for his physical acts which must include a consideration of the extent of his ability to exercise will-power to control his physical acts.

Whether the accused was at the time of the killing suffering from any 'abnormality of mind' in the broad sense which we have indicated above is a question for the jury. On this question medical evidence is, no doubt, of importance, but the jury are entitled to take into consideration all the evidence including the acts or statements of the accused and his demeanour. They are not bound to accept the medical evidence if there is other material before them which, in their good judgment, conflicts with it and outweighs it. The aetiology of the abnormality of mind (namely, whether it arose from a condition of arrested or retarded development of mind or any inherent causes or was induced by disease or injury) does, however, seem to be a matter to be determined on expert evidence. Assuming that the jury are satisfied on the balance of probabilities that the accused was suffering from 'abnormality of mind' from one of the causes specified in the parenthesis of the subsection, the crucial question nevertheless arises: Was the abnormality such as substantially impaired his mental responsibility for his acts in doing or being a party to the killing? This is a question of degree and essentially one for the jury. Medical evidence is, of course, relevant but the question involves a decision, not merely whether there was some impairment of the mental responsibility of the accused for his acts, but whether such impairment can properly be called 'substantial', a matter on which juries may quite legitimately differ from doctors.

Furthermore, in a case where the abnormality of mind is one which affects the accused's self-control, the step between 'he did not resist his impulse' and 'he could not resist his impulse' is, as the evidence in this case shows, one which is incapable of scientific proof. A fortiori, there is no scientific measurement of the degree of difficulty which an abnormal person finds in controlling his impulses. These problems, which in the present state of medical knowledge are scientifically insoluble, the jury can only approach in a broad, common-sense way. This court has repeatedly approved directions to the jury which have followed directions given in Scots cases where the doctrine of diminished responsibility forms part of the common law. We need not repeat them.

They are quoted in *Spriggs* [[1958] 1 QB 270; [1958] 1 All ER 300]. They indicate that such abnormality as 'substantially impairs his mental responsibility' involves a mental state which in popular language (not that of M'Naghten Rules) a jury would regard as amounting to partial insanity or being on the border-line of insanity.

It appears to us that the learned judge's direction to the jury that the defence under s 2 of the Act was not available, even though they found the facts set out in No (ii) and No (iii) of the learned judge's summary [see p 316, above], amounted to a direction that difficulty or even inability of an accused person to exercise will-power to control his physical acts could not amount to such abnormality of mind as substantially impaired his mental responsibility. For the reasons which we have already expressed, we think that this construction of the Act is wrong. Inability to exercise will-power to control physical acts, provided that it is due to abnormality of mind from one of the causes specified in the parenthesis in the subsection, is, in our view, sufficient to entitle the accused to the benefit of the section; difficulty in controlling his physical acts, depending on the degree of difficulty, may be. It is for the jury to decide on the whole of the evidence whether such inability or difficulty has, not as a matter of scientific certainty but on the balance of probabilities, been established and, in the case of difficulty, whether the difficulty is so great as to amount in their view to a substantial impairment of the accused's mental responsibility for his acts. The direction in the present case thus withdrew from the jury the essential determination of fact which it was their province to decide.

As already indicated, the medical evidence as to the appellant's ability to control his physical acts at the time of the killing was all one way. The evidence of the revolting circumstances of the killing and the subsequent mutilations, as of the previous sexual history of the appellant, pointed, we think plainly, to the conclusion that the appellant was what would be described in ordinary language as on the border-line of insanity or partially insane. Properly directed, we do not think that the jury could have come to any other conclusion than that the defence under s 2 of the Homicide Act 1957, was made out. The appeal will be allowed and a verdict of manslaughter substituted for the verdict of murder. The only possible sentence, having regard to the tendencies of the appellant, is imprisonment for life. The sentence will, accordingly, not be disturbed.

Appeal allowed.
Sentence confirmed

Barbara Wootton, Commenting on Byrne (Crime and the Criminal Law), p 74

Apart from admiration of the optimism which expects common sense to make good the deficiencies of science, it is only necessary to add that the problem would seem to be insoluble, not merely in the present, but indeed in any, state of medical knowledge. Improved medical knowledge may certainly be expected to give better insight into the origins of mental abnormalities, and better predictions as to the probability that particular types of individuals will in fact 'control their physical acts' or make 'rational judgments'; but neither medical nor any other science can ever hope to prove whether a man who does not resist his impulses does not do so because he cannot or because he will not. The propositions of science are by definition subject to empirical validation; but since it is not possible to get inside another man's skin, no objective criterion which can distinguish between 'he did not' and 'he could not' is conceivable.

Logic, experience and the Lord Chief Justice thus all appear to lead to the same conclusion—that is to say, to the impossibility of establishing any reliable measure of responsibility in the sense of a man's ability to have acted otherwise than as he did. After all, every one of us can say with St. Paul (who, as far as I am aware, is not generally suspected of diminished responsibility) 'the good that I would I do not: but the evil which I would not, that I do'.

Questions

1. Is it true that we can never be satisfied beyond reasonable doubt that a man could have resisted an impulse to commit crime? Is it a good reason for not acting on such a belief that it cannot be scientifically validated?

2. In dealing with a person who is not alleged to be mentally abnormal, a jury can draw on its own experience in deciding what he must have known or foreseen, and whether he could have chosen to act differently. Is this so in the case of a person alleged to be mentally abnormal? Is it justifiable to draw conclusions as to the validity of theories of criminal responsibility generally, from an analysis of cases concerned with diminished responsibility?

3. If an accused person proves that he did not merely find it difficult, but that he was *unable* to control his acts, is his responsibility merely 'diminished'? Should such a person be convicted of manslaughter?

R v Atkinson (John) [1985] Crim LR 314, Court of Appeal
(Lord Lane CJ, Boreham and Macpherson JJ)

The appellant, aged 18, together with other youths stole spirits which they drank and later burgled a house occupied by a 77 year old woman, who disturbed them and shouted for help. The appellant threatened to kill her if she did not stop shouting, punched her in the back of the head and then beat her including stamping on her face and she died of a fractured skull. In February 1984 he was tried on a charge of murder. He did not give evidence and a defence of diminished responsibility was advanced. Medical evidence was that he had grossly arrested or retarded development of mind and that alcohol had played a part in the events. The jury were directed to pose themselves the questions, first, whether they thought it more probable than not that at the time of the killing his responsibility was substantially impaired by the fact that he was suffering from arrested or retarded development; and, if they thought that drink had something to do with it, secondly, whether that was the substantial cause, the root cause, of his inability to control himself at the time of the killing. He was convicted of murder. He appealed on the ground of misdirection on diminished responsibility.

Held, dismissing the appeal, that at the trial in February the trial judge had, so to speak, to anticipate what the Court of Appeal would say in *R v Gittens* [1984] QB 698. *Gittens* was reported and commented on by Professor J.C. Smith at [1984] Crim LR 553-554, where he stated that the two questions for the jury, in logical sequence, would seem to be: 'Have the defence satisfied you on the balance of probabilities—that if the defendant had not taken drink—(i) he would have killed as he in fact did? And (ii) he would have been under diminished responsibility when he did so?' The Court would like respectfully and gratefully to agree with Professor Smith's analysis, which put the matter clearly and in a way which could be understood by all. In the direction to the jury the judge was, in effect, posing the questions posed by Professor Smith in his commentary, although the other way round. The question for the jury was: if the appellant had not taken drink would he have killed as in fact he did? The jury were entitled to answer the question as they had. The direction of the authorities was to be drawn to the medical reports, which were ordered to be appended to the transcript.

(1) REFORM OF THE LAW

Criminal Law Revision Committee, Fourteenth Report (Cmnd 7844, 1980), para 91

The wording of section 2 has created problems for doctors, judges and juries. Psychiatrists are sometimes expected by lawyers to testify in terms that go outside their professional competence. They are required to testify whether the defendant's abnormality of mind substantially impaired his mental responsibility. The section refers to mental responsibility, which is a legal concept not a medical one; and the jury have to consider as a question of fact whether the abnormality of mind, which is a medical concept, has substantially impaired the defendant's mental responsibility. Some jurors probably have difficulty in understanding these concepts. It is the duty of judges to explain the meaning of section 2 to juries: it is not enough for them to read out the section (*Terry* [1961] 2 QB 314).

92. The Butler Committee considered and reported upon the defence of diminished responsibility and how it has worked in practice [Report of the Committee on Mentally Abnormal Offenders; Cmnd 6244, chapter 19]. They recommended that, if the mandatory life sentence of murder is retained, the definition of diminished responsibility in section 2 of the Homicide Act 1957 should be reworded in order to remove some of the difficulties of interpretation. They suggested the following.

> 'Where a person kills or is party to the killing of another, he shall not be convicted of murder if there is medical or other evidence that he was suffering from a form of mental disorder as defined in section 4 of the Mental Health Act 1959 and if, in the opinion of the jury, the mental disorder was such as to be an extenuating circumstance which ought to reduce the offence to manslaughter.'

There can be no doubt that the wording of section 2 of the Homicide Act 1957 is unsatisfactory. We agree that the suggested rewording referred to above provides a more easily recognisable diagnostic framework for doctors giving evidence, and the task of judges would be made easier. However, when we considered the rewording we had two reservations. First, we were concerned about the requirement that the defendant, when he killed, must be suffering 'from a form of mental disorder as defined in section 4 of the Mental Health Act 1959 . . .'. The Butler Committee were of opinion that this rewording would not materially alter the practical effect of the section. Initially, however, we felt some doubt about whether the rewording might be to some extent restrictive and leave outside the revised definition some offenders who are now regarded by the courts as falling within section 2. The kind of case we had in mind was the depressed father who kills a severely handicapped subnormal child or a morbidly jealous person who kills his or her spouse. In our experience such defendants are not necessarily suffering from a mental disorder of such a kind as to justify the making of a hospital order and are commonly dealt with by the courts, following the section 2 verdict, under the ordinary sentencing provisions applicable to manslaughter, for example, by a relatively short custodial sentence or a conditional discharge or probation order. Because of our doubts, this matter was further considered by the medical advisers to the Department of Health and Social Security, who have advised that the proposed rewording would not exclude the kind of cases we had in mind. Having looked at the matter again, we are satisifed that this view is right having regard to the wide terms in which the definition of mental disorder in section 4 of the Mental Health Act 1959 [Section 4(1) provides 'In this Act "mental disorder" means mental illness, arrested or incomplete development of mind, psychopathic disorder, and any other disorder or disability of mind; and "mentally disordered" shall be construed accordingly.'] is drafted. We now accept that the types of mental disturbance we had in mind would be within the definition of mental disorder in section 4 of the Act of 1959, and therefore within the rewording proposed by the Butler Committee for section 2 of the Homicide Act 1957, notwithstanding that they fall outside the criteria in section 60 of the Act of 1959 and are not such as to justify the making of a hospital order.

93. Our other reservation with regard to the Butler Committee's rewording of the section is that we think that in one respect it may be too lax. . . . The judge would have to give some guidance to the jury as to what extenuating circumstances ought to reduce the offence, and in practice that means that the mental disorder has to be substantial enough to reduce the offence to manslaughter. We consider that the definition should be tightened up so as to include that ingredient upon which the jury will have to be directed, which will give to the jury the necessary guidance. A form of wording which in our opinion tightens up the latter part of such a to be a substantial enough reason to reduce the offence to manslaughter'.

(2) CODIFICATION OF THE LAW

The Codification report follows the recommendations of the Criminal Law Revision Committee (paras 15.9–15.15) except that the term 'mental abnormality' is used instead of 'mental disorder' because the latter phrase is defined more narrowly in cl 38 for the purpose of mental disorder verdicts. Clause 58 provides:

58   Diminished responsibility

(1) This section applies where the person who kills or is a party to the killing of another is

suffering from a form of mental abnormality which is a substantial enough reason to reduce his offence to manslaughter.

(2) In this section 'mental abnormality' means mental illness, arrested or incomplete development of mind, psychopathic disorder, and any other disorder or disability of mind, except intoxication.

(3) Where the person suffering from mental abnormality is also intoxicated this section applies only where it would apply if he were not intoxicated.

2. Provocation

Director of Public Prosecutions v Camplin [1978] 2 All ER 168, House of Lords (Lord Diplock, Lord Morris of Borth-y-Gest, Lord Simon of Glaisdale, Lord Fraser of Tullybelton and Lord Scarman)

The facts appear in the speech of Lord Diplock with whom Lords Fraser and Scarman agreed. Lords Simon and Morris made speeches dismissing the appeal.

Lord Diplock. My Lords, for the purpose of answering the question of law on which this appeal will turn only a brief account is needed of the facts that have given rise to it. The respondent, Camplin, who was 15 years of age, killed a middle-aged Pakistani, Mohammed Lal Khan, by splitting his skull with a chapati pan, a heavy kitchen utensil like a rimless frying pan. At the time the two of them were alone together in Khan's flat. At Camplin's trial for murder before Boreham J his only defence was that of provocation so as to reduce the offence to manslaughter. According to the story that he told in the witness box but which differed materially from that which he had told to the police, Khan had buggered him in spite of his resistance and had then laughed at him, whereupon Camplin had lost his self-control and attacked Khan fatally with the chapati pan.

In his address to the jury on the defence of provocation, counsel for Camplin had suggested to them that when they addressed their minds to the question whether the provocation relied on was enough to make a reasonable man do as Camplin had done, what they ought to consider was not the reaction of a reasonable adult but the reaction of a reasonable boy of Camplin's age. The judge thought that this was wrong in law. So in this summing-up he took pains to instruct the jury that they must consider whether:

> 'the provocation was sufficient to make a reasonable man in like circumstances act as the defendant did. Not a reasonable boy, as [counsel for Camplin] would have it, or a reasonable lad; it is an objective test—a reasonable man.'

The jury found Camplin guilty of murder. On appeal the Court of Appeal, Criminal Division [[1978] QB 254, [1978] 1 All ER 1236], allowed the appeal and substituted a conviction for manslaughter on the ground that the passage I have cited from the summing-up was a misdirection. The court held that [[1978]1 All ER 1236]:

> 'the proper direction to the jury is to invite the jury to consider whether the provocation was enough to have made a reasonable person of the same age as the appellant in the same circumstances do as he did.'

The point of law of general public importance involved in the case has been certified as being:

> 'Whether, on the prosecution for murder of a boy of 15, where the issue of provocation arises, the jury should be directed to consider the question, under s 3 of the Homicide Act 1957, whether the provocation was enough to make a reasonable man do as he did by reference to a "reasonable adult" or by reference to a "reasonable boy of 15".'

My Lords, the doctrine of provocation in crimes of homicide has always represented an anomaly in English law. In crimes of violence which result in injury short of death, the fact that the act of violence was committed under provocation, which has caused the accused to lose his self-control, does not affect the nature of the offence of which he is guilty: it is merely a matter to be taken into consideration in determining the penalty which it is appropriate to impose: whereas in homicide provocation effects a change in the offence itself from murder, for which the penalty is fixed by law (formerly death and now imprisonment for life), to the lesser offence of manslaughter, for which the penalty is in the discretion of the judge.

The doctrine of provocation has a long history of evolution at common law. Such changes as there had been were entirely the consequence of judicial decision until Parliament first intervened by passing the Homicide Act 1957. Section 3 deals specifically with provocation and alters the law as it had been expounded in the cases, including three that had been decided comparatively recently in this House, namely *Mancini v Director of Prosecutions* [[1942] AC 1, [1941] 3 All ER 272], *Holmes v Director of Public Prosecutions* [[1946] AC 588, [1946] 2 All ER 124] and *Bedder v Director of Public Prosecutions* [[1954] 2 All ER 801]. One of the questions in this appeal is to what extent propositions as to the law of provocation that are laid down in those cases, and in particular in *Bedder*, ought to be treated as being of undiminished authority despite the passing of the Homicide Act 1957.

For my part I find it instructive to approach this question by a brief survey of the historical development of the doctrine of provocation at common law. Its origin at a period when the penalty for murder was death is to be found, as Tindal CJ, echoing Sir Michael Foster [See *Broadfoot's Case* (1743) Fost 154], put it in *Hayward* [(1833) 6 C & P 157 at 159], in 'the law's compassion to human infirmity'. The human infirmity on which the law first took compassion in a violent age when men bore weapons for their own protection when going about their business appears to have been chance medley or a sudden falling out at which both parties had recourse to their weapons and fought on equal terms. Chance medley as a ground of provocation was extended to assault and battery committed by the deceased on the accused in circumstances other than sudden falling out. But with two exceptions actual violence offered by the deceased to the accused remained the badge of provocation right up to the passing of the 1957 Act. The two exceptions were the discovery by a husband of a wife in the act of committing adultery and the discovery by a father of someone committing sodomy on his son; but these apart, insulting words or gestures unaccompanied by physical attack did not in law amount to provocation.

The 'reasonable man' was a comparatively late arrival in the law of provocation. As the law of negligence emerged in the first half of the 19th century he became the anthropomorphic embodiment of the standard of care required by the law. It would appear that Keating J in *Welsh* [(1869) 11 Cox CC 336] was the first to make use of the reasonable man as the embodiment of the standard of self-control required by the criminal law of persons exposed to provocation, and not merely as a criterion by which to check the credibility of a claim to have been provoked to lose his self-control made by an accused who at that time was not permitted to give evidence himself. This had not been so previously and did not at once become the orthodox view. In his Digest of the Criminal Law [(1877).] and his History of the Criminal Law [(1883).] Sir James Fitzjames Stephen makes no reference to the reasonable man as providing a standard of self-control by which the question whether the facts relied on as provocation are sufficient to reduce the subsequent killing to manslaughter is to be decided. He classifies and defines the kinds of conduct of the deceased that alone are capable in law of amounting to provocation and appears to treat the questions for the jury as being limited to (1) whether the evidence establishes conduct by the deceased that falls within one of the defined classes and, if so, (2) whether the accused was thereby actually deprived of his self-control.

The reasonable man referred to by Keating J [(1869) 11 Cox CC 336 at 338.] was not then a term of legal art nor has it since become one in criminal law. He (or she) has established his (or her) role in the law of provocation under a variety of different sobriquets in which the noun 'man' is frequently replaced by 'person' and the adjective 'reasonable' by 'ordinary', 'average' or 'normal'. At least from as early as 1914 (see *R v Lesbini* [[1914] 3 KB 1116]), the test of whether the defence of provocation is entitled to succeed has been a dual one: the conduct of the deceased to the accused must be such as (1) might cause in any reasonable or ordinary person and (2) actually causes in the accused a sudden and temporary loss of self-control as the result of which he commits the unlawful act that kills the deceased. But until the 1957 Act was passed there was a condition precedent which had to be satisfied before any question of applying this dual test could arise. The conduct of the deceased had to be of such a kind as was capable in law of constituting provocation; and whether it was or was not a question for the judge, not for the jury. This House so held in *Mancini* where it also laid down a rule of law that the mode of resentment, as for instance the weapon used in the act that caused the death, must bear a reasonable relation to the kind of violence that constituted the provocation.

It is unnecessary for the purposes of the present appeal to spend time on a detailed account of what conduct was or was not capable in law of giving rise to a defence of provocation immediately before the passing of the 1957 Act. It had remained much the same as when Stephen was writing in the last quarter of the 19th century. What, however, is important to note is that this House in *Holmes* had recently confirmed that words alone, save perhaps in circumstances of a most extreme and exceptional nature, were incapable in law of constituting provocation.

My Lords, this was the state of law when *Bedder* fell to be considered by this House. The accused had killed a prostitute. He was sexually impotent. According to his evidence he had tried to have sexual intercourse with her and failed. She taunted him with his failure and tried to get away from his grasp. In the course of her attempts to do so she slapped him in the face, punched him in the stomach and kicked him in the groin, whereupon he took a knife out of his pocket and stabbed her twice and caused her death. The struggle that led to her death thus started because the deceased taunted the accused with his physical infirmity; but in the state of the law as it then was, taunts unaccompanied by any physical violence did not constitute provocation. The taunts were followed by violence on the part of the deceased in the course of her attempt to get away from the accused, and it may be that this subsequent violence would have a greater effect on the self-control of an impotent man already enraged by the taunts than it would have had on a person conscious of possessing normal physical attributes. So there might be some justification for the judge to instruct the jury to ignore the fact that the accused was impotent when they were considering whether the deceased's conduct amounted to such provocation as would cause a reasonable or ordinary person to lose his self-control. This indeed appears to have been the ground on which the Court of Criminal Appeal [[1954] 2 All ER 801 at 803.] had approved the summing-up when they said:

'. . . no distinction is to be made in the case of a person who, though it may not be a matter of temperament is physically impotent, is conscious of that impotence, *and therefore mentally liable to be more excited unduly* if he is "twitted" or attacked on the subject of that particular infirmity.'

This statement, for which I have myself supplied the emphasis, was approved by Lord Simonds LC speaking on behalf of all the members of this House who sat on the appeal; but he also went on to lay down the broader proposition that [[1954] 2 All ER 801 at 803, 804]:

'It would be plainly illogical not to recognise an unusually excitable or pugnacious temperament in the accused as a matter to be taken into account but yet to recognise for that purpose some unusual physical characteristic, be it impotence or another.'

Section 3 of the 1957 Act is in the following terms:

'Where on a charge of murder there is evidence on which the jury can find that the person charged was provoked (whether by things done or by things said or by both together) to lose his self-control, the question whether the provocation was enough to make a reasonable man do as he did shall be left to be determined by the jury; and in determining that question the jury shall take into account everything both done and said according to the effect which, in their opinion, it would have on a reasonable man.'

My Lords, this section was intended to mitigate in some degree the harshness of the common law of provocation as it had been developed by recent decisions in this House. It recognises and retains the dual test: the provocation must not only have caused the accused to lose his self-control but also be such as might cause a reasonable man to react to it as the accused did. Nevertheless it brings about two important changes in the law. The first is it abolishes all previous rules of law as to what can or cannot amount to provocation and in particular the rule of law that, save in the two exceptional cases I have mentioned, words unaccompanied by violence could not do so. Secondly it makes it clear that if there was any evidence that the accused himself at the time of the act which caused the death in fact lost his self-control in consequence of some provocation however slight it might appear to the judge, he was bound to leave to the jury the question, which is one of opinion not of law, whether a reasonable man might have reacted to that provocation as the accused did.

I agree with my noble and learned friend, Lord Simon of Glaisdale, that since this question is one for the opinion of the jury the evidence of witnesses as to how they think a reasonable man would react to the provocation is not admissible.

The public policy that underlay the adoption of the 'reasonable man' test in the common law doctrine of provocation was to reduce the incidence of fatal violence by preventing a person relying on his own exceptional pugnacity or excitability as an excuse for loss of self-control. The rationale of the test may not be easy to reconcile in logic with more universal propositions as to the mental element in crime. Nevertheless it has been preserved by the 1957 Act but falls to be applied now in the context of a law of provocation that is significantly different from what it was before the Act was passed.

Although it is now for the jury to apply the 'reasonable man' test, it still remains for the judge to direct them what, in the new context of the section, is the meaning of this apparently inapt expression, since powers of ratiocination bear no obvious relationship to powers of self-control. Apart from this the judge is entitled, if he thinks it helpful, to suggest considerations which may influence the jury in forming their own opinions as to whether the test is satisfied; but he should make it clear that these are not instructions which they are required to follow: it is for them and no one else to decide what weight, if any, ought to be given to them.

As I have already pointed out, for the purposes of the law of provocation the 'reasonable man' has never been confined to the adult male. It means an ordinary person of either sex, not exceptionally excitable or pugnacious, but possessed of such powers of self-control as everyone is entitled to expect that his fellow citizens will exercise in society as it is today. A crucial factor in the defence of provocation from earliest times has been the relationship between the gravity of provocation and the way in which the accused retaliated, both being judged by the social standards of the day. When Hale was writing in the 17th century pulling a man's nose was thought to justify retaliation with a sword; when *Mancini* was decided by this House, a blow with a fist would not justify retaliation with a deadly weapon. But so long as words unaccompanied by violence could not in common law amount to provocation the relevant proportionality between provocation and retaliation was primarily one of degrees of violence. Words spoken to the accused before the violence started were not normally to be included in the proportion sum. But now that the law has been changed so as to permit of words being treated as provocation, even though unaccompanied by any other acts, the gravity of verbal provocation may well depend on the particular characteristics or circumstances of the person to whom a taunt or insult is addressed. To taunt a person because of his race, his physical infirmities or some shameful incident in his past may well be considered by the jury to be more offensive to the person addressed, however equable his temperament, if the facts on which the taunt is founded are true than it would be if they were not. It would stultify much of the mitigation of the previous harshness of the common law in ruling out verbal provocation as capable of reducing murder to manslaughter if the jury could not take into consideration all those factors which in their opinion would affect the gravity of taunts and insults when applied to the person to whom they are addressed. So to this extent at any rate the unqualified proposition accepted by this House in *Bedder* that for the purposes of the 'reasonable man' test any unusual physical characteristics of the accused must be ignored requires revision as a result of the passing of the 1957 Act.

That he was only 15 years of age at the time of the killing is the relevant characteristic of the accused in the instant case. It is a characteristic which may have its effects on temperament as well as physique. If the jury think that the same power of self-control is not to be expected in an ordinary, average or normal boy of 15 as in an older person, are they to treat the lesser powers of self-control possessed by an ordinary, average or normal boy of 15 as the standard of self-control with which the conduct of the accused is to be compared?

It may be conceded that in strict logic there is a transition between treating age as a characteristic that may be taken into account in assessing the gravity of the provocation addressed to the accused and treating it as a characteristic to be taken into account in determining what is the degree of self-control to be expected of the ordinary person with whom the accused's conduct is to be compared. But to require old heads on young shoulders is inconsistent with the law's compassion of human infirmity to which Sir Michael Foster ascribed the doctrine of provocation more than two centuries ago. The distinction as to the purpose for which it is legitimate to take the age of the accused into account involves considerations of too great nicety to warrant a place in deciding a matter of opinion, which is no longer one to be decided by a judge trained in logical reasoning but by a jury drawing on their experience of how ordinary human beings behave in real life.

There is no direct authority prior to the Act that states expressly that the age of the accused could not be taken into account in determining the standard of self-control for the purposes of the reasonable man test, unless this is implicit in the reasoning of Lord Simonds LC in *Bedder*. The Court of Appeal distinguished the instant case from that of *Bedder* on the ground that what it was there said must be ignored was an unusual characteristic that distinguished the accused from ordinary normal persons, whereas nothing could be more ordinary or normal than to be aged 15. The reasoning in *Bedder* would, I think, permit of this distinction between normal and abnormal characteristics, which may affect the powers of self-control of the accused; but for reasons that I have already mentioned the proposition stated in *Bedder* requires qualification as a consequence of changes in the law effected by the 1957 Act. To try to salve what can remain of it without conflict with the Act could in my view only lead to unnecessary and unsatisfactory complexity in a question which has now become a question for the jury alone. In my view *Bedder*, like *Mancini* and *Holmes*, ought no longer to be treated as an authority on the law of provocation.

In my opinion a proper direction to a jury on the question left to their exclusive determination by s 3 of the 1957 Act would be on the following lines. The judge should state what the question is, using the very terms of the section. He should then explain to them that the reasonable man referred to in the question is a person having the power of self-control to be expected of an ordinary person of the sex and age of the accused, but in other respects sharing such of the accused's characteristics as they think would affect the gravity of the provocation to him, and that the question is not merely whether such a person would in like circumstances be provoked to lose his self-control but also would react to the provocation as the accused did.

I accordingly agree with the Court of Appeal that the judge ought not to have instructed the jury to pay no account to the age of the accused even though they themselves might be of opinion that the degree of self-control to be expected in a boy of that age was less than in an adult. So to direct them was to impose a fetter on the right and duty of the jury which the 1957 Act accords to them to act on their own opinion on the matter.

I would dismiss this appeal.

Appeal dismissed

R v Newell (1980) 71 Cr App Rep 331, Court of Appeal
(Lord Lane LCJ, Park and Lincoln JJ)

The appellant, a chronic alcoholic, was very depressed by the defection of a young woman with whom he had been living for some time and to whom he was strongly attached. When he and his friend, Mike, were both very drunk, Mike made derogatory remarks about the woman which, it was alleged, caused him to lose his self-control and kill Mike. The judge asked the jury, 'Would a sober man in relation to that drunken observation, batter his friend over the head with a nearly two pound weight ashtray?' Mike received 22 heavy blows. On appeal it was submitted that the judge should have directed as follows:

'Do you consider that the accused, being emotionally depressed and upset, as he was, and in the physical condition of a chronic alcoholic, was reasonably provoked by the words used and reacted in a way in which he might reasonably be expected to have acted, on the basis that he had had a very large amount to drink and had had a suicidal overdose of drugs four days previously, and that he was in a state of toxic confusion?'

[**Lord Lane CJ** referred to the New Zealand decision in *McGregor* [1962] NZLR 1069 and s 169 of the New Zealand Crimes Act 1961 which reads:]

'(1) Culpable homicide that would otherwise be murder may be reduced to manslaughter if the person who caused the death did so under provocation. (2) Anything done or said may be provocation if—(a) In the circumstances of the case it was sufficient to deprive a person having the power of self-control of an ordinary person, but otherwise having the characteristics of the offender, of the power of self-control; and (b) It did in fact deprive the offender of the power of self-control and thereby induced him to commit the act of homicide. (3) Whether there is any evidence of provocation is a question of law. (4) Whether, if there is evidence of provocation, the provocation was sufficient as aforesaid, and whether it did in fact deprive the offender of the power of self-control and thereby induced him to commit the act of homicide, are questions of fact.'

[His Lordship continued:]

In *McGregor* supra the judgment of the court was delivered by North J, and contains the following passage which appears to us to be entirely apt to the situation in the instant case:

'The Legislature has given us no guide as to what limitations might be imposed, but perforce there must be adopted a construction which will ensure regard being had to the characteristics of the offender without wholly extinguishing the ordinary man. The offender must be presumed to possess in general the power of self-control of the ordinary man, save in so far as his power of self-control is weakened because of some particular characteristic possessed by him. It is not every trait or disposition of the offender that can be invoked to modify the concept of the ordinary man. The characteristic must be something definite and of sufficient significance to make the offender a different person from the ordinary run of mankind, and have also a sufficient degree of permanence to warrant its being regarded as something constituting part of the individual's character or personality. A disposition to be unduly suspicious or to lose one's temper readily will not suffice, nor will a temporary or transitory state of mind such as a mood of depression, excitability or irascibility. These matters are either not of sufficient significance or not of sufficient permanency to be regarded as "characteristics" which would enable the offender to be distinguished from the ordinary man. The "unusually excitable or pugnacious individual" spoken of in *Lesbini* (1914) 11 Cr App R 7, [1914] 3 KB 1116 is no more entitled to special consideration under the new section than he was when that case was decided. Still less can a self-induced transitory state be relied upon, as where it arises from the consumption of liquor. The word "characteristics" in the context of this section is wide enough to apply not only to physical qualities but also to mental qualities and such more indeterminate attributes as colour, race and creed. It is to be emphasised that of whatever nature the characteristic may be, it must be such that it can fairly be said that the offender is thereby marked off or distinguished from the ordinary man of the community. Moreover, it is to be equally emphasised that there must be some real connection between the nature of the provocation and the particular characteristic of the offender by which it is sought to modify the ordinary man test. The words or conduct must have been exclusively or particularly provocative to the individual because, and only because, of the characteristic. In short, there must be some direct connection between the provocative words or conduct and the characteristic sought to be invoked as warranting some departure from the ordinary man test. Such a connection may be seen readily enough where the offender possesses some unusual physical peculiarity though he might in all other respects be an ordinary man, provocative words alluding for example to some infirmity or deformity from which he was suffering might well bring about a loss of self-control. So too, if the colour, race or creed of the offender be relied on as constituting a characteristic, it is to be repeated that the provocative words or conduct must be related to the particular characteristic relied upon. Thus, it would not be sufficient, for instance, for the offender to claim merely that he belongs to an excitable race, or that members of his nationality are accustomed to resort readily to the use of some lethal weapon. Here again, the provocative act or words require to be directed at the particular characteristic before it can be relied upon. Special difficulties, however, arise when it becomes necessary to consider what purely mental peculiarities may be allowed as characteristics.

In our opinion it is not enough to constitute a characteristic that the offender should merely in some general way be mentally deficient or weak-minded. To allow this to be said would, as we have earlier indicated, deny any real operation to the reference made in the section to the ordinary man, and it would, moreover, go far towards the admission of a defence of diminished responsibility without any statutory authority in this country to sanction it. There must be something more, such as provocative words or acts directed to a particular phobia from which the offender suffers. Beyond that, we do not think it is advisable that we should attempt to go.'

That passage, and the reasoning therein contained, seem to us to be impeccable. It is not only expressed in plain, easily comprehended language; it represents also, we think, the law of this country as well as that of New Zealand. In the present case the only matter which could remotely be described as a characteristic was the appellant's condition of chronic alcoholism. Assuming that that was truly a characteristic (and we expressly make no determination as to that), nevertheless it had nothing to do with the words by which it is said that he was provoked. There was no connection between the derogatory reference to the appellant's girl friend and the suggestion of a possible homosexual act and his chronic alcoholism. It had nothing at all to do with the words by which it is said that he was provoked.

If the test set out in *McGregor* (supra) is applied, the learned judge in the instant case was right in not inviting the jury to take chronic alcoholism into account on the question of provocation.

The other matters advanced by Mr Ashe Lincoln as being characteristics which the jury should have been invited to consider, in examining what a reasonable man might or would have done, are not characteristics at all. The appellant's drunkenness, or lack of sobriety, his having taken an overdose of drugs and written a suicide note a few days previously, his grief at the defection of his girl friend, and so on, are none of them matters which can properly be described as characteristics. They were truly transitory in nature, in the light of the words and reasoning of North J, in *McGregor's* case (supra).

Appeal dismissed

R v Ibrams and Gregory (1981) 74 Cr App Rep 154, Court of Appeal

The appellants and a young woman, A, had been bullied and terrorised by Monk over a period up to and including Sunday, 7 October. They had been unable to obtain effective police protection. Anticipating that there would be a repetition of Monk's behaviour on Sunday, 14 October, on Wednesday, 10 October the three made a plan. On Sunday Monk was to be got drunk and to be encouraged to take A to his bed. She would slip the catch on the door and leave a signal for the appellants who would attack him and break his arms and legs. The plan was carried out meticulously and Monk was killed. The appellants were convicted of murder. They appealed on the ground that the judge had wrongly withdrawn the defence of provocation from the jury.

Lawton LJ. . . . At an early stage in his submissions Mr Carter was asked by the Court whether he knew of any case where there had been a substantial interval of time between the last act of provocation and the killing, and he was unable to call our attention to any such case. The nearest he was able to get to such a case was *Davies (Peter)* (1975) 60 Cr App R 253, [1975] QB 691. In that case the provocation had consisted of an adulterous relationship between the defendant's wife and her lover. The wife had been shot on a day when she was meeting her lover to the knowledge of the defendant. The trial judge let the provocation go to the jury, but complaint was made of the trial that he had misdirected them about the effects of the provocation. In the course of the judgment of this Court in *Davies's* case at p 259 and p 702 respectively it was pointed out that letting the provocation go to the jury was perhaps over-lenient towards the defendant. That is the view which we take of that case. There is nothing in the reports comparable to the time-interval which occurred in this case. On the other hand, none of the cases to which we have been referred provides provocation as grave as in this case. Mr Carter submitted that it followed that in those circumstances the nature of the provocation—the quality of it, so to speak—may lead to a loss of self-control extending over a longish period of time.

There are, it seems to us, three answers to that proposition. The first is to be found in the history of the law relating to provocation which was set out in the speech of Lord Diplock in *Director of Public Prosecutions v Camplin* (1978) 67 Cr App R 14; [1978] AC 705. That history shows that, in the past at any rate, provocation and loss of self-control tended to be regarded by the courts as taking place with a very short interval of time between the provocation and the loss of self-control. But Lord Diplock in the course of his speech went a little further with regard to this matter. At p 19 and p 716 respectively, having reviewed section 3 of the Homicide Act 1957, he said, referring to the section:

> 'Secondly it makes it clear that if there was any evidence that the accused himself at the time of the act which caused the death in fact lost his self-control in consequence of some provocation however slight it might appear to the judge, he was bound to leave to the jury the question, which is one of opinion not of law: Whether a reasonable man might have reacted to that provocation as the accused did'.

In our judgment, Lord Diplock clearly thought that the loss of self-control must occur at or about the time of the act of provocation.

Here the last act of provocation was on Sunday, October 7. It was not in any way suggested that the dead man had provoked anybody on the night of his death. In fact, when Gregory and Ibrams went into the bedroom he was asleep. The first blow he received was inflicted on him by Gregory, and it dazed him but did not knock him unconscious. He was able to sit up in bed, and he was then attacked by Ibrams. Nothing happened on the night of the killing which caused Ibrams to lose his self-control. There having been a plan to kill Monk, his evidence that when he saw him all the past came to his mind does not, in our judgment, provide any evidence of loss of self-control.

In our judgment, the matter is really concluded by the summing-up to the jury of Devlin J (as he then was) in *Duffy* [1949] 1 All ER 932n, which was approved by the Court of Criminal Appeal. There is a passage in the summing-up so approved which is referred to time and time again in cases and in the textbooks; but, whether we look at the whole of the summing-up or at those parts of it which were approved by the Court of Criminal Appeal, it appears that there was another passage which is directly relevant to the facts of this case. The part which has been referred to many times with approval, and in particular with the approval of this Court in *Whitfield* (1976) 63 Cr App R 39, 42, is as follows:

'Provocation is some act or series of acts done by the dead man to the accused which would cause in any reasonable person and actually causes in the accused, a sudden and temporary loss of self-control, rendering the accused so subject to passion as to make him for the moment not master of his mind.'

That passage refers to 'a sudden and temporary loss of self-control,' which has to be of such a kind as to make the accused for the moment not master of his mind.

Later in the same summing-up, in another passage which was also approved by the Court of Criminal Appeal in *Duffy* (supra), are these words: ([1949] 1 All ER at p 932H)

'Indeed, circumstances which induce a desire for revenge are inconsistent with provocation, since the conscious formulation of a desire for revenge means that a person has had time to think, to reflect, and that would negative a sudden temporary loss of self-control, which is of the essence of provocation.'

Appeal dismissed

Philips v R (1968) 53 Cr App Rep 132, Privy Council
(Lord Hodson, Lord Guest and Lord Diplock)

The appellant, who had been convicted of the murder of his mistress, appealed to the Court of Appeal for Jamaica on the ground that the direction of the trial judge on provocation was erroneous. The direction was in the following terms:

'If you are satisfied, if you find that the accused did commit the act as a result of provocation, you will have to consider the retaliation as against the type of provocation that he received. You have to determine whether the provocation under which the accused was labouring was enough to make a reasonable person do as the accused did. In deciding this question you must consider the provocation received and the manner of the retaliation, and ask whether a reasonable person provoked in the way that the accused was provoked would retaliate in the way that the accused retaliated. If a reasonable person would not retaliate in the way that the accused retaliated, the defence of provocation cannot avail the accused because the standard fixed by law is that of the reasonable man, and you, the jury, must be satisfied not only that the accused was so provoked that he lost his self-control and retaliated, but that a reasonable person would have lost his self-control in the same circumstances and do as the accused did. . . .'

The Court upheld the appellant's contention that the direction of the trial judge was wrong in law, but dismissed the appeal on the ground that no substantial miscarriage of justice had actually occurred. The appellant obtained special leave to appeal to the Privy Council.

Lord Diplock. . . . . The test of provocation in the law of homicide is two-fold. The first, which has always been a question of fact for the jury, assuming that there is any evidence upon which they can so find, is: 'Was the defendant provoked into losing his self-control?' The second, which is one not of fact but of opinion, 'Would a reasonable man have reacted to the same provocation in the same way as the defendant did?' . . .

Before their Lordships, counsel for the appellant contended, not as a matter of construction but as one of logic, that once a reasonable man had lost his self-control his actions ceased to be those of a reasonable man and that accordingly he was no longer fully responsible in law for them whatever he did. This argument is based on the premise that loss of self-control is not a matter of degree but is absolute: there is no intermediate stage between icy detachment and going berserk. This premise, unless the argument is purely semantic, must be based upon human experience and is, in their Lordships' view, false. The average man reacts to provocation according to its degree with angry words, with a blow of the hand, possibly, if the provocation is gross and there is a dangerous weapon to hand, with that weapon. It is not insignificant that the appellant himself described his own instantaneous reaction to the victim's provocation in spitting on his mother as: 'I spin around quickly was to punch her with my hand.'

In that part of his direction which the Court of Appeal held to be objectionable, the learned judge followed closely the actual words of the section and made it clear to the jury that it was their responsibility, not his, to decide whether a reasonable man would have reacted to the provocation in the way that the appellant did. In their Lordships' view this was an impeccable direction.

Since the passing of the legislation, it may be prudent to avoid the use of the precise words of Viscount Simon's in *Mancini v Director of Public Prosecutions* 'the mode of resentment must bear a reasonable relationship to the provocation' unless they are used in a context which makes it clear to the jury that this is not a rule of law which they are bound to follow, but merely a consideration which may or may not commend itself to them. But their Lordships would repeat that it is the effect of the summing-up as a whole that matters and not any stated verbal formula used in the course of it.

As already pointed out, the learned judge in the instant case did not use the *Mancini* (supra) formula at all. He made it abundantly clear to the jury that it was their function and theirs alone to decide whether or not a reasonable man would have reacted to the provocation in the way the appellant did. In their Lordships' view the Court of Appeal of Jamaica should have dismissed the appeal on the ground that there was no error in the summing-up on provocation. The question of the application of the proviso to s 16 (1) of the Jamaica Judicature (Court of Appeal) Law, does not therefore arise.

For these reasons their Lordships humbly advised Her Majesty that this appeal should be dismissed.

Appeal dismissed

Question

How is the view that the 'reasonable relationship' principle is not a rule of law but merely a consideration which may or may not commend itself to the jury to be reconciled with the words of the section, 'enough to make a reasonable man do as he did'?

Edwards v R [1973] 1 All ER 152, Privy Council
(Lord Wilberforce, Lord Pearson, Lord Salmon, Sir Edward McTiernan and Sir Richard Wild)

The appellant followed Dr Coombe from Australia to Hong Kong with the intention of blackmailing him. He went to see Coombe in his hotel bedroom for that purpose. He claimed that Coombe swore at him, attacked him with a knife and inflicted several wounds; that the appellant then wrested the knife from Coombe and stabbed him in a fit of 'white hot' passion. At his trial for murder. Rigby CJ directed that the defence of provocation was not available. The Full Court of the Supreme Court of Hong Kong held that this was a misdirection but upheld the conviction on the ground that no miscarriage of justice had occurred. The appellant appealed to the Privy Council.

Lord Pearson. . . .Rigby CJ said to the jury:

> '. . . in my view the defence of provocation cannot be of any avail to the accused in this case. Provocation . . . is undoubtedly a valid legal defence in certain circumstances, but you might well think that it ill befits the accused in this case, having gone there with the deliberate purpose of blackmailing this man—you may well think that it ill befits him to say out of his own mouth that he was provoked by any attack. In my view the defence of provocation is not one which you need consider in this case.'

That direction was held by the Full Court to be erroneous in relation to the facts of this case, and their Lordships agree with the Full Court. No authority has been cited with regard to what may be called 'self-induced provocation'. On principle it seems reasonable to say that (1) a blackmailer cannot rely on the predictable results of his own blackmailing conduct as constituting provocation sufficient to reduce his killing of the victim from murder to manslaughter, and the predictable results may include a considerable degree of hostile reaction by the person sought to be blackmailed, for instance vituperative words and even some hostile action such as blows with a fist; (2) but if the hostile reaction by the person sought to be blackmailed goes to extreme lengths it might constitute sufficient provocation even for the blackmailer; (3) there would in many cases be a question of degree to be decided by the jury.

In the present case, if the appellant's version of the facts be assumed to be correct, Dr Coombe, the person sought to be blackmailed, did go to extreme lengths, in that he made a violent attack on the appellant with a knife, inflicting painful wounds and putting the appellant's life in danger. There was evidence of provocation and it was fit for consideration by the jury: see *Parker v R* [[1964] AC 1369 at 1392; [1964] 2 All ER 641 at 652]. The burden of proof would be on the prosecution to satisfy the jury that the killing was unprovoked. If the evidence raised in their minds a reasonable doubt whether it was provoked or not, the proper verdict would be a conviction for manslaughter: see *Bullard v R* [[1957] AC 635; [1961] 3 All ER 470n]. . . .

Appeal allowed. Conviction of murder reduced to manslaughter

NOTE

The Hong Kong Homicide Ordinance (cap 339) adopts the provisions of s 3 of the Homicide Act 1957 (p 555, below) verbatim. The Ordinance has been in force since 1963.

In *Leung Ping-Fat v R* (1973) 3 HKLJ 342 the applicant and three others entered a coffin shop and demanded money. In the fight which followed, K, a member of the staff of the shop was killed. The applicant's defence was that K had attacked him with a wooden pole and that he had stabbed in self-defence. The judge directed that if the jury were satisfied that K had been killed in the course of resisting a robber, the defences of provocation and self-defence were not open to the applicant. It was held (Huggins, McMullin and Pickering JJ) that the application for leave to appeal must be dismissed, following *Edwards v R* (p 329, above). The deceased's behaviour had never exceeded the limits of the obviously predictable results of the applicant's initial conduct and the trial judge was therefore justified in withholding the issue of provocation from the jury.

Questions

1. As a fact, an accused might lose his self-control as the result of an attack predictably caused by his own wrongful act. Is it right for the judge, in view of s 3 of the Homicide Act, to withdraw such a case from the jury?

2. If—contrary to *Edwards and Leung Ping-Fat*—s 3 precludes the judge from withdrawing such a case from the jury, may he tell them that, in deciding whether the provocation was enough to make a reasonable man do as he did, they should ignore evidence of conduct predictably provoked by the accused's own wrongdoing? Or would this be contrary to the provision in the section that the jury shall take into account '*everything both done and said* according to the effect which *in their opinion* it would have on a reasonable man'?

3. By whom should the provocation be predictable?—the accused or a reasonable man?

4. If, in *Leung Ping-Fat*, K was acting in self-defence and therefore lawfully, could his acts amount in law to provocation? Cf Howard, *Australian Criminal Law* (2nd edn), p 93: 'The law would be self-contradictory if a

lawful act could amount to provocation.' Is this so? Why should not the law recognise (if it be the fact) that P's lawful act was likely to make an ordinary person lose his self-control?

See, generally, A.J Ashworth, 'Self-induced Provocation and the Homicide Act' [1973] Crim LR 483.

3. Suicide pacts and complicity in suicide

Homicide Act 1957, s 4, p 556, below

Suicide Act 1961, p 556, below

Questions

1. Don decides to commit suicide. He closes his eyes and throws himself from a fifth floor window into the street below. He lands on Paul. Paul's neck is broken and he dies. Don breaks both his legs but, after six months in hospital, is now fully recovered. Is Don guilty of any offence?

2. Dick and Dora agree that they will die together. They are found in a gas-filled room. Dora is dead, but Dick recovers. Dick cannot remember who turned on the gas-tap and there is no evidence on the point. Can Dick be convicted of an offence under the Suicide Act or under s 4 of the Homicide Act? Might it be different if Dora had been shot and it was impossible to prove whether she shot herself or was shot by Dick?

3. Eric and Ernie, who belong to a strange religious sect, agree that they will inflict mutilations on each other, amounting to grievous bodily harm. They believe that this will put them in a state of grace. They carry out their agreement. Are they guilty of an offence? (See pp 357–362, post) If Ernie dies of the injuries inflicted by Eric, is Eric guilty of homicide?

4. Kevin, a prisoner, announces that he will neither eat nor drink until he is released or he dies. Leo, the prison governor, tells the prison staff that Kevin's wishes are to be respected that he is to be offered neither food nor drink unless he asks for it. Kevin asks for nothing and dies. Is Leo guilty of an offence? Cf. p 362, post.

R v McShane (1977) 66 Cr App Rep 97, Court of Appeal, Criminal Division (Orr, Browne LJJ and Willis J)

The appellant was in some financial difficulty. Her grandmother had left a large part of her estate in trust for the appellant, but provided that the appellant's mother should receive the income from that estate for her life. The appellant's mother was elderly and ill, and had often talked of committing suicide. On at least three occasions the appellant had left fatal doses of pills with her mother, and on the last was heard to advise her that 'Whisky with barbiturates is fatal.' The appellant was convicted of an attempt to counsel or procure her mother's suicide. She argued that this was not an offence known to the law.

[Orr LJ read the judgment of the court:]

. . . The answer to that ground is, in our judgment, that every attempt to commit an offence is an offence at common law, whether the crime attempted is one by statute or at common law (See *Archbold*, (39th edn) paragraph 4100 and the authorities there cited). It follows in our judgment that the appellant was properly charged under count 1 with an offence of attempting to aid or abet, counsel or procure the suicide of Mrs Mott and none the less so because the crime defined in section 2(1) of the Act 1961 is itself of the nature of an attempt . . .

Appeal dismissed

Questions

1. Why was the defendant charged with an attempt and not with the full offence of counselling suicide?
2. *Is* the crime defined in s 2 (1) in the nature of an attempt? Can there be an attempt to attempt?
3. Does the case establish a general principle that there can be an attempt to aid and abet? Cf *Stonehouse*, p 278 above and [1977] Crim LR 542, 544 and 738.

NOTE

For proposed amendments to the law, see the draft Code Bill, cll 64,65 and 66, p 348, below.

4. Involuntary manslaughter

The difficulties of defining involuntary manslaughter were described by Lord Atkin in the leading case of *Andrews v DPP* [1937] AC 576, [1937] 2 All ER 552, p 341, below.

> 'My Lords, of all crimes manslaughter appears to afford most difficulties of definition, for it concerns homicide in so many and so varying conditions. From the early days, when any homicide involved penalty, the law has gradually evolved "through successive differentiations and integrations" until it recognises murder on the one hand, based mainly, though not exclusively, on an intention to kill, and manslaughter on the other hand, based mainly, though not exclusively, on the absence of intention to kill, but the presence of an element of "unlawfulness" which is the elusive factor.'

Andrews' case did little to diminish the uncertainty as to the boundaries of the offence in its various forms. The matter has been the subject of extensive recent debate (see articles in [1983] Crim LR 764 and 767 and [1984] Crim LR 467 and 476) especially as to the impact of *Caldwell*, p 68, above, and the new test of recklessness there propounded. It may be that this has in fact resulted in a simplification of the law—p 340, below. However, involuntary manslaughter certainly continues to take at least two distinct forms. The first is known as 'constructive manslaughter'. Parallel to the doctrine of constructive murder (death caused in the course of committing a felony was murder), abolished by s 1 (1) of Homicide Act 1957, there existed a doctrine that death caused in the course of an unlawful act, not amounting to a felony, was manslaughter. The act was at one time sufficiently 'unlawful' for this purpose if it was a tort. In the case of *Fenton* (1830) 1 Lew CC 179 Tindal CJ directed the jury that throwing stones down a mine shaft was a trespass and therefore it followed that the defendant was guilty of manslaughter when the stone broke some scaffodding with the result that a corf overturned and miners were killed. Even in the nineteenth century, some judges found this doctrine unacceptable. Consider the next case.

(1) CONSTRUCTIVE MANSLAUGHTER

R v Franklin (1883) 15 Cox CC 163, Sussex Assizes

The defendant on the West Pier at Brighton, took up 'a good sized box' from a refreshment-stall and wantonly threw it into the sea. It struck T who was swimming underneath and caused his death. The prosecution, citing *Fenton*, above, urged that throwing the refreshment stall-keeper's box into the sea was an unlawful act and it followed that, if it caused death, that was manslaughter.

[Field, J, having consulted **Mathew J]**

I am of opinion that the case must go to the jury upon the broad ground of negligence and not upon the narrow ground proposed by the learned counsel, because it seems to me—and I may say that in this view my brother Mathew agrees—that the mere fact of a civil wrong committed by one person against another ought not to be used as an incident which is a necessary step in a criminal case. I have a great abhorrence of constructive crime. We do not think the case cited by the counsel for the prosecution is binding upon us in the facts of this case, and, therefore, the civil wrong against the refreshment-stall keeper is immaterial to this charge of manslaughter. I do not think that the facts of this case bring it clearly within the principle laid down by Tindal CJ in *Reg v Fenton*. If I thought this case was in principle like that case I would, if requested, state a case for the opinion of the Court of Criminal Appeal. But I do not think so.

It was not disputed that the prisoner threw the box over the pier, that the box fell upon the boy, and the death of the boy was caused by the box falling upon him.

Gill, for the prisoner, relied upon the point that there was not proved such negligence as was criminal negligence on the part of the prisoner.

Field J, in summing up the case to the jury, went carefully through the evidence, pointing out how the facts as admitted and proved affected the prisoner upon the legal question as he had explained it to them.

The jury returned a verdict of guilty of manslaughter.

Guilty

The prisoner was sentenced to two months' imprisonment.

The 'broad ground of negligence' is considered below. *Franklin* is a greatly respected decision but it has the authority of only a first instance ruling and it was concerned only to reject the argument that a civil wrong is sufficiently 'unlawful'. It left open the question of whether any crime, however trivial, is enough. The matter was considered in the next case.

R v Church [1965] 2 All ER 72, Court of Criminal Appeal
(Edmund-Davies, Marshall and Widgery JJ)

The appellant, according to his account, took a woman, Mrs Nott, to his van for sexual purposes. He was unable to satisfy her. She reproached him and slapped his face. They had a fight and he knocked her out. He tried unsuccessfully for about half an hour to wake her, panicked, dragged her out of the van and put her in the river. Mrs Nott was drowned.

At the trial, for the first time, the appellant said that he thought she was dead when he put her in the water. The judge directed the jury that if Nott in fact was alive when thrown into the river, whether the appellant knew it or not, that was manslaughter. The jury convicted him of manslaughter.

[**Edmund Davies J**. having cited the judge's direction on this issue:]

Such a direction is not lacking in authority; see, for example, *Shoukatallie v R* [[1962] AC 81; [1961] 3 All ER 996], in Lord Denning's opinion [[1962] AC at 86,92; [1961] 3 All ER 998, 1001], and Dr Glanville Williams' *Criminal Law* (2nd ed) at p 173. Nevertheless, in the judgment of this court it was misdirection. It amounted to telling the jury that, whenever any unlawful act is committed in relation to a human being which resulted in death there must be, at least, a conviction for manslaughter. This might at one time have been regarded as good law: see, for example, *Fenton* [(1830) 1 Lew CC 179]. It appears to this court, however, that the passage of years has achieved a transformation in this branch of the law and, even in relation to manslaughter, a degree of mens rea has become recognised as essential. To define it is a difficult task, and in *Andrews v Director of Public Prosecutions* [[1937] AC 576 at 582; [1937] 2 All ER 552 at 555; p 332 above] Lord Atkin spoke of the element of "unlawfulness" which is the elusive factor'. Stressing that we are here leaving entirely out of account those ingredients of homicide which might justify a verdict of manslaughter on the grounds of (a) criminal negligence, or (b) provocation or (c) diminished responsibility, the conclusion of this court is that an unlawful act causing the death of another cannot, simply because it is an unlawful act, render a manslaughter verdict inevitable. For such a verdict inexorably to follow, the unlawful act must be such as all sober and reasonable people would inevitably recognise must subject the other person to, at least, the risk of some harm resulting therefrom, albeit not serious harm. . . .

If such be the test, as we adjudge it to be, then it follows that, in our view, it was a misdirection to tell the jury simpliciter that it mattered nothing for manslaughter whether or not the appellant believed Mrs Nott to be dead when he threw her in the river. . . .

[The court dismissed the appeal on the ground that judge's direction on criminal negligence was an adequate one and, quite apart from that, the principle of *Thabo Meli*, p 12, above applied to manslaughter (following Glanville Williams, *The Criminal Law* (2nd edn), p 174) and the jury were entitled to regard the appellant's conduct as a series of acts which culminated in her death.]

Appeal dismissed

R v Lamb [1967] 2 All ER 1282, Court of Appeal, Criminal Division (Sachs LJ, Lyell and Geoffrey Lane JJ)

The appellant, in jest, pointed at his best friend a revolver with five chambers. It had bullets in two of the chambers but neither of these was opposite the barrel. He thought it was safe to pull the trigger. His friend was also treating the matter as a joke. Lamb pulled the trigger and shot his friend dead. The revolver functioned in such a way that, when the trigger was pulled, the chambers rotated, bringing the loaded chamber opposite the barrel, before the firing pin struck. The appellant was charged with manslaughter and set up the defence of accident. The judge directed that the pointing of the revolver and pulling of the trigger was an unlawful act even if there was no intent to injure or alarm and that the jury did not need to consider whether the pointing of the gun was an assault.

[**Sachs LJ**, reading the judgment of the court:]

Counsel for the Crown, however, had at all times put forward the correct view that for the act to be unlawful it must constitute at least what he then termed 'a technical assault'. In this court, moreover, he rightly conceded that there was no evidence to go to the jury of any assault of any kind. Nor did he feel able to submit that the acts of the appellant were on any other ground unlawful in the criminal sense of that word. Indeed no such submission could in law be made: if, for instance, the pulling of the trigger had had no effect because the striking mechanism or the ammunition had been defective no offence would have been committed by the appellant.

Another way of putting it is that mens rea being now an essential ingredient in manslaughter (compare *Andrews v Director of Public Prosecutions* [[1937] AC 576 at 582; [1937] 2 All ER 552 at 555, 556; p 332, above ante] and *Church* [[1966] 1 QB at 70; [1965] 2 All ER at 76; p 333, ante) this could not in the present case be established in relation to the first ground except by proving that element of intent without which there can be no assault. It is perhaps as well to mention that when using the phrase 'unlawful in the criminal sense of that word' the court has in mind that it is long settled that it is not in point to consider whether an act is unlawful merely from the angle of civil liabilities. That was first made clear in *Franklin* [(1883) 15 Cox CC 163]. The relevant extracts from this and from later judgments are collected in *Russell on Crime* (11th edn, 1958), pp 651–658. The whole of that part of the summing-up which concerned the first ground was thus vitiated by misdirections based on an erroneous concept of the law; and the strength with which that ground was put to the jury no doubt stemmed from the firm view of the trial judge, expressed more than once in the course of the discussion on law in relation to the undisputed facts: 'How can there be a defence to the charge of manslaughter? Manslaughter requires no intent.' . . . [His Lordship discussed the judge's direction on criminal negligence.] The general effect of the summing-up was thus to withdraw from the jury the defence put forward on behalf of the appellant. When the gravamen of a charge is criminal negligence—often referred to as recklessness—of an accused, the jury have to consider amongst other matters the state of his mind, and that includes the question of whether or not he thought that that which he was doing was safe. In the present case it would, of course, have been fully open to a jury, if properly directed, to find the accused guilty because they considered his view as to there being no danger was formed in a criminally negligent way. But he was entitled to a direction that the jury should take into account the fact that he had indisputably formed this view and that there was expert evidence as to this being an understandable view. Strong though the evidence of criminal negligence was, the appellant was entitled as of right to have his defence considered but he was not accorded this right and the jury was left without a direction on an essential matter. Those defects of themselves are such that the verdict cannot stand. . . .

Appeal allowed

Questions

1. What would have been the position if:

(i) the accused had intended to alarm his friend by pointing the gun but the friend was not alarmed?

(ii) The accused did not intend to alarm his friend but the friend was in fact alarmed?

2. Did the court consider that proof of criminal negligence requires proof of a state of mind? Could the defendant, in the view of the court, be guilty though he believed his conduct was perfectly safe?

3. Why was it necessary for the jury to consider, on the negligence ground, what the accused himself thought?

R v Larkin [1943] 1 All ER 217, Court of Criminal Appeal
(Viscount Caldecote CJ, Humphreys and Asquith JJ)

The woman with whom the appellant was living died from a throat wound inflicted by the appellant. He found her at a drinking party with a man, Nielsen, with whom she had been committing what would have been adultery if she had in fact been married to the appellant. He went away, brooded on the matter and returned with a razor. He stated in evidence that his only intention was to terrify Nielsen with the razor but the woman, groggy with drink, swayed against him and her throat was cut by accident.

[At the trial for murder, **Oliver J** directed the jury:]

'A man who rushes into a house flourishing a naked razor and wounds someone, even accidentally, is still guilty of manslaughter if that person dies . . . I have told you the law is for me, and I will tell you on my responsibility that in threatening a man with a naked razor because you wanted to scare him, however good reason you may have for disliking him, you are doing an unlawful act.'

Humphreys J. Perhaps it is as well that once more the proposition of law should be stated which has been stated for generations by judges and, so far as we are aware, never disputed or doubted. If a person is engaged in doing a lawful act, and in the course of doing that lawful act behaves so negligently as to cause the death of some other person, then it is for the jury to say, upon a consideration of the whole of the facts of case, whether the negligence proved against the accused person amounts to manslaughter, and it is the duty of the presiding judge to tell them that it will not amount to manslaughter unless the negligence is of a very high degree; the expression most commonly used is unless it shows the accused to have been reckless as to the consequences of the act. That is where the act is lawful. Where the act which a person is engaged in performing is unlawful, then, if at the same time it is a dangerous act, that is, an act which is likely to injure another person, and quite inadvertently he causes the death of that other person by that act, then he is guilty of manslaughter. If, in doing that dangerous and unlawful act, he is doing an act which amounts to a felony he is guilty of murder, and he is equally guilty of murder if he does the act with the intention of causing grievous bodily harm to the person whom, in fact, he kills . . .

Appeal dismissed

Director of Public Prosecutions v Newbury and Jones [1976] 2 All ER 365, House of Lords
(Lord Diplock, Lord Simon of Glaisdale, Lord Kilbrandon, Lord Salmon and Lord Edmund-Davies)

The facts appear in the speech of Lord Salmon, with which all their Lordships agreed.

Lord Salmon. My Lords, on 11 October 1974 the train travelling from Pontypridd to Cardiff was approaching a bridge which crossed the railway line. The guard was sitting next to the driver of the train in the front cab. The driver noticed the heads of three boys above the parapet of the bridge. He saw one of the boys push something off the parapet towards the oncoming train. This proved to be part of a paving stone which some workmen had left on the parapet. It came through the glass window of the cab in which the driver and the guard were sitting, struck the guard and killed him. There was ample evidence that just as the train was about to reach the bridge the two appellants, who were each about 15 years of age, were jointly concerned in pushing over the parapet the piece of paving stone which killed the guard. They were jointly charged with manslaughter and after a very fair and lucid summing-up, each was found guilty. Both of them appealed against conviction and sentence and their appeals against conviction were dismissed. The appellants now appeal to this House. The point of law certified to be of general public importance is:

'Can a defendant be properly convicted of manslaughter, when his mind is not affected by drink or drugs, if he did not foresee that his act might cause harm to another?'

The learned trial judge did not direct the jury that they should acquit the appellants unless they were satisfied beyond a reasonable doubt that the appellants had foreseen that they might cause harm to someone by pushing the piece of paving stone off the parapet into the path of the approaching train. In my view the learned trial judge was quite right not to give such a direction to the jury. The direction which he gave is completely in accordance with established law, which, possibly with one exception to which I shall presently refer, has never been challenged. In *Larkin* [[1943] 1 All ER 217 at 219] Humphreys J said:

'Where the act which a person is engaged in performing is unlawful, then if at the same time it is a dangerous act, that is, an act which is likely to injure another person, and quite inadvertently he causes the death of that other person by that act, then he is guilty of manslaughter.'

I agree entirely with Lawton LJ that that is an admirably clear statement of the law which has been applied many times. It makes it plain (a) that an accused is guilty of manslaughter if it is proved that he intentionally did an act which was unlawful and dangerous and that that act inadvertently caused death and (b) that it is unnecessary to prove that the accused knew that the act was unlawful or dangerous. This is one of the reasons why cases of manslaughter vary so infinitely in their gravity. They may amount to little more than pure inadvertence and sometimes to little less than murder.

I am sure that in *Church* Edmund Davies J, in giving the judgment of the court, did not intend to differ from or qualify anything which had been said in *Larkin*. Indeed he was restating the principle laid down in that case by illustrating the sense in which the word 'dangerous' should be understood. Edmund Davies J said [[1966] 1 QB at 70, [1965] 2 All ER at 76]:

> 'For such a verdict [guilty of manslaughter] inexorably to follow, the unlawful act must be such as all sober and reasonable people would inevitably recognise must subject the other person to, at least, the risk of some harm resulting therefrom, albeit not serious harm.'

The test is still the objective test. In judging whether the act was dangerous, the test is not did the accused recognise that it was dangerous but would all sober and reasonable people recognise its danger. . . .

Appeal dismissed

Questions

1. Since the judge did not direct the jury that it must be proved that the defendant foresaw harm to anyone the question for the House was whether a person doing what the defendants did but not foreseeing harm to anyone could properly be convicted. What is the 'unlawful act' which such a person commits?

2. Is *Lamb* reconcilable with the present decision? Why is foresight of injury to alarm of P necessary if D points a revolver at P but not necessary if he throws a paving stone from a parapet?

R v Cato [1976] 1 All ER 260, Court of Appeal, Criminal Division
(Lord Widgery CJ, O'Connor and Jupp JJ)

The appellant was convicted of manslaughter and of administering a noxious thing contrary to s 23 of the Offences against the Person Act 1861. The appellant had injected the deceased with a mixture of heroin and water from a syringe several times throughout the night. The intoxication eventually caused his respiratory system to cease to function. The deceased himself prepared the strength of the mixture of each 'fix', just as the appellant prepared those fixes which the deceased was to give him. An appeal to the Court of Appeal was dismissed.

Lord Widgery CJ. . . . The trial judge left the manslaughter charge to the jury on the two alternative bases which the Crown had suggested, and it will be appreciated at once what they were. The first alternative was that the death was caused by the injection and the consequent intrusion of morphine into the body, and that was an unlawful act so that the killing was the result of an unlawful act and manslaughter on that footing.

The next matter, I think, is the unlawful act. Of course on the approach to manslaughter in this case it was necessary for the prosecution to prove that Farmer had been killed in the course of an unlawful act. Strangely enough, or it may seem strange to most of us, although the possession or supply of heroin is an offence, it is not an offence to take it, and although supplying it is an offence, it is not an offence to administer it. At least it is not made to be an offence, and so counsel for Cato says there was no unlawful act here. That which Cato did—taking Farmer's syringe already charged and injecting the mixture into Farmer as directed—is not an unlawful act, says counsel for Cato because there is nothing there which is an offence against the Misuse of Drugs

Act 1971, and when he shows us the terms of the section it seems that that is absolutely right.

Of course if the conviction on count 2 remains (that is the charge under s 23 of the Offences against the Person Act 1861, of administering a noxious thing), then that in itself would be an unlawful act. The prohibition in that Act would be enough in itself, and it is probably right to say that as we are going to uphold the conviction on count 2, as will appear presently, that really answers the problem and destroys the basis of counsel for Cato's argument.

But since he went to such trouble with the argument, and in respect for it, we think we ought to say that had it not been possible to rely on the charge under s 23 of the 1861 Act, we think there would have been an unlawful act here, and we think the unlawful act would be described as injecting the deceased Farmer with a mixture of heroin and water which at the time of the injection Cato had unlawfully taken into his possession. As I say, it is not really necessary to rely on that because of our views on the other count, but we would not wish it to be thought that we had felt counsel for Cato's argument on this point would have succeeded had it been effectively open to him. So much then for the unlawful act.

[His Lordship considered the judge's direction on recklessness and held that it was satisfactory.]

Appeal dismissed

R v Dalby [1982] 1 All ER 916, Court of Appeal
(Waller LJ, Jupp and Waterhouse JJ)

[**Waller LJ** read the judgment of the court:]

The appellant, aged 25, and Stefan O'Such were both drug addicts and had been friends for some years. On Friday, 2 May 1980, after he had been staying with O'Such and his wife in their flat in Bournemouth for about a week, the appellant lawfully obtained, on prescription, 32 tablets of diconal. They were to be taken two every four hours, i e 8 per day. During his journey back to the flat, the appellant swallowed a number of tablets. At 8 pm shortly after his return, he supplied O'Such with some tablets: the evidence was unclear as to how many but probably four at that time and four or eight more later. The appellant and O'Such each injected himself intravenously and they then went out shortly after 9.30 pm to a discotheque where they parted company. The evidence was that O'Such met another friend at the discotheque who helped him administer an intravenous injection, of an unspecified substance, shortly before midnight and later a second intravenous injection.

When the appellant returned to the flat at about 2 am O'Such was already asleep on a settee in the living room and the appellant went to sleep himself. He was woken by Mrs O'Such at 8 am and both of them attempted to wake O'Such but without success. Mrs O'Such asked the appellant whether an ambulance should be called but he said No. When the appellant went out at 1.30 pm, O'Such was still asleep. At 3 pm Mrs O'Such called an ambulance and when the ambulance attendants arrived some five minutes later they found O'Such was dead.

The Crown case was that the appellant was guilty of manslaughter because he had supplied diconal unlawfully, that it was a dangerous act and caused O'Such's death, or alternatively that the appellant owed a duty of care to O'Such and was grossly negligent in not calling an ambulance at an earlier stage.

Before this court, the argument proceeded on the former of those two alternatives because it was agreed that if the direction concerning an unlawful act that was dangerous, causing the death of O'Such was in error, then the appeal must succeed.

The judge directed the jury that there were five questions which they had to consider: first, did the appellant supply the diconal; second, did he intend to supply the diconal; third, was the supply of diconal to O'Such an unlawful act? No question arises about those three questions because the answer was clearly Yes in each case. The fourth and fifth questions were dealt with by the judge as follows: 'Was the supply of the diconal a dangerous act, because manslaughter is by a dangerous and unlawful act. By a dangerous act, we mean any act which subjects the victim to the risk of some harm, not necessarily serious harm. The test for whether the act was dangerous or not is an objective one.' Then the fifth question was posed: 'The fifth and last question you will ask yourself is whether the supply of the diconal was a substantial cause of the victim's death. It does not have to be the only cause of death, but it has to be a substantial cause of death, by which we mean a cause which is not merely trivial.' The judge then went on to discuss with the jury the question of whether or not it could be a substantial cause of death when it was O'Such who administered the diconal to himself.

The argument before this court has not centred on the precise words of the judge. It was submitted on behalf of the appellant: (1) that the unlawful act must be one directed at the victim; the supply of drugs in this case was not such a direct act; (2) that the supply of drugs can be harmless or extremely harmful according to the manner in which the victim deals with them; (3) that the drugs in this case were taken voluntarily by the victim in a form, i e intravenously, and in a quantity which together made them extremely dangerous and resulted in death; the line of causation was therefore broken between the unlawful act of supplying drugs and the death resulting from intravenous injection of too great a quantity of them.

Clearly there may be circumstances which would justify a finding of criminal negligence resulting in death which would found a case of manslaughter but this part of the argument is not concerned with negligence.

The earlier authorities show than any unlawful act resulting in death would justify a verdict of manslaughter but modern authorities have restricted this form of manslaughter to unlawful acts which are dangerous.

[His Lordship referred to *Larkin*, p 335, above, *Church*, p 333, above and *Newbury*, p 336, above.]

There are several reported cases of manslaughter where the conduct which led to the death of the victim was not a direct act but these have been cases of manslaughter by negligence. In *R v Markuss* (1864) 4 F & F 356, 176 ER 598 a herbalist prescribed a cure for a cold which killed the patient and in *R v Benge* (1865) 4 F & F 504, 176 ER 665 a foreman platelayer placed his flagman at too short a distance from the approaching train with the result that somebody was killed. In such cases, it is necessary to prove gross negligence. In the well-known words of Lord Hewart CJ in *R v Bateman* (1925) 94 LJKB 791 at 793-794, [1925] All ER Rep 45 at 48, he said:

> ': . . in order to establish criminal liability the facts must be such that, in the opinion of the jury, the negligence of the accused went beyond a mere matter of compensation between subjects and showed such disregard for the life and safety of others as to amount to a crime against the State and conduct deserving punishment.'

But in all the reported cases of manslaughter by an unlawful and dangerous act, the researches of counsel have failed to find any case where the act was not a direct act.

The difficulty in the present case is that the act of supplying a controlled drug was not an act which caused direct harm. It was an act which made it possible, or even likely, that harm would occur subsequently, particularly if the drug was supplied to somebody who was on drugs. In all the reported cases, the physical act has been one which inevitably would subject the other person to the risk of some harm from the act itself. In this case, the supply of drugs would itself have caused no harm unless the deceased had subsequently used the drugs in a form and quantity which was dangerous.

It is interesting to note that in Smith and Hogan *Criminal Law* (4th edn, 1978) p 274, when discussing intervening causes, a number of examples are cited, but the whole discussion is based on an original injury followed by some other intervening act.

In the judgment of this court, the unlawful act of supplying drugs was not an act directed against the person of O'Such and the supply did not cause any direct injury to him. The kind of harm envisaged in all the reported cases of involuntary manslaughter was physical injury of some kind as an immediate and inevitable result of the unlawful act, e g a blow on the chin which knocks the victim against a wall causing a fractured skull and death, or threatening with a loaded gun which accidentally fires, or dropping a large stone on a train (see *DPP v Newbury*) or threatening another with an open razor and stumbling with death resulting (see *R v Larkin*).

In the judgment of this court, where the charge of manslaughter is based on an unlawful and dangerous act, it must be an act directed at the victim and likely to cause immediate injury, however slight.

In his certificate giving leave to appeal, the judge posed this question:

> 'In the circumstances in which the intravenous consumption of a dangerous drug is a substantial cause of the death of the deceased, does the unlawful act of supply of the dangerous drug by the defendant to the deceased per se constitute the actus reus of the offence of manslaughter?'

For the reasons given, the answer to that question is No. . . .

Appeal allowed. Conviction of manslaughter quashed.

Note: see *Goodfellow*, Appendix II, below.

Questions

1. Did Dalby cause O'Such's death? Does the case decide he did not?
2. *If* Dalby caused the death for the purposes of 'reckless' or 'gross negligence manslaughter', must he not also have done so for the purposes of 'unlawful act' manslaughter?
3. Can the 'directed at' requirement be reconciled with *Newbury* where it was held that the defendant need not know that his act was dangerous? Is the requirement affected by *Moloney* (p 55, above)?
4. Is *Markuss* distinguishable? Presumably the patient did not know the dangerous nature of 'the cure' he took.
5. Cf *Pagett*, p 30, above. Was it not just as likely that O'Such would take the drug and suffer harm as that the police would shoot Gail when Pagett used her as a shield? If the latter result was caused by D, why not the former?

(2) RECKLESS MANSLAUGHTER

Over a period of many years in manslaughter cases the courts have used the expressions, 'negligence'—usually qualified by an epithet, such as 'gross'—and 'recklessness' in an undefined and imprecise way. There has beeı. a great deal of debate whether the test was subjective or objective, or partly subjective and partly objective; and whether there were two or more tests of this variety of manslaughter. The fifth edition of Smith and Hogan, for example, makes a distinction between *manslaughter by gross negligence* where the negligence must be whether death or serious injury be caused, and *reckless manslaughter* where *it would suffice to* prove recklessness whether any personal injury or, possibly, any injury to 'health or welfare' be caused. This analysis was founded on the case-law. Since that edition was written, however, the *Caldwell* test has been held to be applicable to manslaughter by the House of Lords in two cases, *Goverment of the United States of America v Jennings* [1983] AC 624, [1982] 3 All ER 104 and *Seymour* [1983] 2 All ER 1058, and by the Privy Council in *Kong Cheuk Kwan v R* [1985] NLJ Rep 753. 'Gross negligence' is part of the *Caldwell* test; the risk must be one which would have been *obvious* to a reasonable and prudent person who gave thought to the matter. The defendant who fails to give thought is grossly negligent but this fault is now comprehended within the *Caldwell* test.

There are, however, two elements of doubt. (i) What of the person who *does* give thought to the matter and decides that there is no risk when the reasonably prudent person would have been aware that there was a serious risk? He is not reckless within either limb of the *Caldwell* test. But he might well be thought to be grossly negligent. Take the boy in *W v Dolbey*, p 66, above. He had decided that there was no risk and so as not *Caldwell*-reckless; but it might well be thought that this was a grossly negligent decision—that a reasonably prudent person would have been aware that there was a risk of causing at least some personal injury. If the pellet had entered the victim's eye and killed him, this might well have been held to be manslaughter before *Caldwell*. Consider, for example, the application of the '*Bateman* test', pp 342 and 345, below. But it is now at least doubtful whether that test represents the law. (ii) It remains to be seen whether the courts are prepared to apply the *Caldwell* test in its full rigour to manslaughter where they are concerned with a person lacking the capacity of the normal adult—the schizophrenic tramp in *Stephenson*, the backward, tired, cold and hungry fourteen-year-old girl in *Elliott v C* and the ordinary fifteen-year-old boy in *Stephen M.R.*, pp 70, 73 and 76, above. If they had caused death, would they be guilty of manslaughter?

As to the first of these points, *Caldwell* would effect some relaxation of the severity of the law; but, as regards the second, it might well have the opposite effect. In the law of tort, according to *Clerk and Lindsell* (15th edn, 1982) para 2.33, 'it will be a question of fact whether [the defendant] is of such an age that he ought to have foreseen'; and the test of gross negligence in the criminal law has generally been stated to require a higher degree of culpability than the civil law. *Caldwell*, as interpreted in *Elliott v C* and *W v Dolbey*, appears to impose a stricter test.

It is too early to discard the pre-*Caldwell* case law but it must now be read carefully in the light of *Seymour* and *Kong Cheuk Kwan*.

Andrews v Director of Public Prosecutions [1937] AC 576; [1937] 2 All ER 552, House of Lords
(Lord Atkin, Lord Thankerton, Lord Wright and Lord Roche)

The appellant, an employee of Leeds corporation, was sent to assist a corporation bus which had broken down about three or four miles away at 10.30 pm on a Saturday night. Driving fast, over 30 mph, in a van, he overtook a car and, driving well over on the off-side of the road, struck a man, Craven, who was crossing the road. Craven was carried forward on the bonnet, thrown off and run over. The appellant did not stop. He was convicted of manslaughter and appealed on the ground of misdirection in that the judge had told the jury that they must convict if the appellant caused death by driving recklessly or in a dangerous manner, contrary to the Road Traffic Act 1930, s 11 (see now Road Traffic Act 1972, ss 1 and 2.)

[**Lord Atkin**, having stated the facts, continued:]

In the present case it is necessary to consider manslaughter only from the point of view of an unintentional killing caused by negligence, ie the omission of a duty to take care. I do not propose to discuss the development of this branch of the subject as treated in the successive treatises of Coke, Hale, Foster and East, and in the judgments of the courts to be found either in directions to juries by individual judges, or in the more considered pronouncements of the body of judges which preceded the formal Court of Crown Cases Reserved. Expressions will be found which indicate that to cause death by lack of due care will amount to manslaughter; but, as manners softened and the law became more humane, a narrower criterion appeared. After all, manslaughter is a felony, and was capital, and men shrank from attaching the serious consequences of a conviction for felony to results produced by mere inadvertence. The stricter view became apparent in prosecutions of medical men, or men who professed medical or surgical skill, for manslaughter by reason of negligence. As an instance I will cite *Williamson* [(1807) 3 C & P 635], where a man who practised as an accoucheur, owing to a mistake in his observation of the actual symptoms, inflicted on a patient terrible injuries from which she died. Lord Ellenborough said:

> 'To substantiate that charge [of manslaughter] the prisoner must have been guilty of criminal misconduct, arising either from the grossest ignorance or the most criminal inattention'.

The word 'criminal' in any attempt to define a crime is perhaps not the most helpful, but it is plain that Lord Ellenborough meant to indicate to the jury a high degree of negligence. So at a much later date in *Bateman* [(1925) 94 LKJB 791], a charge of manslaughter was made against a qualified medical practitioner in circumstances similar to those of Williamson's case. In a considered judgment of the court, Lord Hewart LCJ, after pointing out that, in a civil case, once negligence is proved the degree of negligence is irrelevant, said, at p 793:

> 'In a criminal court, on the contrary, the amount and degree of negligence are the determining question. There must be mens rea'.

After citing *Cashill v Wright*, a civil case, Lord Hewart LCJ proceeds:

> 'In explaining to juries the test which they should apply to determine whether the negligence, in the particular case, amounted or did not amount to a crime, judges have used many epithets, such as 'culpable', 'gross', 'wicked', 'clear', 'complete'. But, whatever epithet be used and whether an epithet be used or not, in order to establish criminal liability the facts must be such that, in the opinion of the jury, the negligence of the accused went beyond a mere matter of compensation between subjects and showed such disregard for the life and safety of others, as to amount to a crime against the State and conduct deserving punishment.'

Here, again, I think, with respect, that the expressions used are not, indeed they probably were not intended to be, a precise definition of the crime. I do not myself find the connotations of mens rea helpful in distinguishing between degrees of negligence, nor do the ideas of crime and punishment in themselves carry a jury much further in deciding whether, in a particular case, the degree of negligence shown is a crime, and deserves punishment. But the substance of the judgment is most valuable, and, in my opinion, is correct. In practice, it has generally been adopted by judges in charging juries all cases of manslaughter by negligence, whether in driving vehicles or otherwise. The principle to be observed is that cases of manslaughter in driving motor cars are but instances of a general rule applicable to all charges of homicide by negligence. Simple lack of care such as will constitute civil liability is not enough. For the purpose of the criminal law there are degrees of negligence, and a very high degree of negligence is required to be proved before the felony is established. Probably of all the epithets that can be applied 'reckless' most nearly covers the case. It is difficult to visualise a case of death caused by 'reckless' driving, in the connotation of that term in ordinary speech, which would not justify a conviction for manslaughter, but it is probably not all-embracing, for 'reckless' suggests an indifference to risk, whereas the accused may have appreciated the risk, and intended to avoid it, and yet shown in the means adopted to avoid the risk such a degree of negligence as would justify a conviction. If the principle of *Bateman's* case is observed, it will appear that the law of manslaughter has not changed by the introduction of motor vehicles on the road. Death caused by their negligent driving, though unhappily much more frequent, is to be treated in law as death caused by any other form of negligence, and juries should be directed accordingly.

If this view be adopted, it will be easier for judges to disentangle themselves from the meshes of the Road Traffic Acts. Those Acts have provisions which regulate the degree of care to be taken in driving motor vehicles. They have no direct reference to causing death by negligence. Their prohibitions, while directed, no doubt, to cases of negligent driving, which, if death be caused, would justify convictions for manslaughter, extend to degrees of negligence of less gravity. Section 12 of the Road Traffic Act imposes a penalty for driving without due care or attention. This would apparently cover all degrees of negligence. Section 11 imposes a penalty for driving recklessly, or at a speed or in a manner which is dangerous to the public. There can be no doubt that this section covers driving with such a high degree of negligence as that, if death were caused, the offender would have committed manslaughter. But the converse is not true, and it is perfectly possible that a man may drive at a speed or in a manner dangerous to the public, and cause death, and yet not be guilty of manslaughter. The legislature appears to recognise this by the provision in the Road Traffic Act 1934, s 34, that, on an indictment for manslaughter, a man may be convicted of dangerous driving. But, apart altogether from any inference to be drawn from s 34, I entertain no doubt that the statutory offence of dangerous driving may be committed, though the negligence is not of such a degree as would amount to manslaughter if death ensued. As an instance, in the course of argument it was suggested that a man might execute the dangerous manoeuvre of drawing out to pass a vehicle in front with another vehicle meeting him, and be able to show that he would have succeeded in his calculated intention but for some increase of speed in the vehicles in front: a case very doubtfully of manslaughter, but very probably of dangerous driving. I cannot think of anything worse for users of the road than the conception that no one could be convicted of dangerous driving unless his negligence was so great that, if he had caused death, he must have been convicted of manslaughter. It therefore would appear that, in directing the jury in a case of manslaughter, the judge should in the first instance charge them substantially in accordance with the general law, i e requiring the high degree of negligence indicated in *Bateman's* case, and then explain that such degree of negligence is not necessarily the same as that which is required for the offence of dangerous driving, and then indicate to them the conditions under which they might acquit of manslaughter and convict of dangerous driving. A direction that all they had to consider was whether death was caused by dangerous driving within the Road Traffic Act 1930, s 11, and no more, would, in my opinion, be a misdirection.

In dealing with the summing-up in the present case, I feel bound to say, with every respect to the learned and very careful judge, that there are passages which are open to criticism. In particular, at the beginning of his charge to the jury, he began with the statement that, if a man kills another in the course of doing an unlawful act, he is guilty to manslaughter, and then proceeded to ascertain what the unlawful act was by considering the Road Traffic Act 1930, s 11. If the summing-up rested there, there would have been misdirection. There is an obvious difference in the law of manslaughter between doing an unlawful act and doing a lawful act with a degree of carelessness which the legislature makes criminal. If it were otherwise, a man who, while driving without due care and attention, killed another, would *ex necessitate* commit manslaughter. But as the summing-up proceeded the learned judge reverted to, and I think rested the case on, the principles which have been just stated. On many occasions he directed the attention of the jury to the recklessness and high degree of negligence which the prosection alleged to have been proved, and which would justify them in convicting the accused. On consideration of the summing-up as a whole, I am satisfied that the true question was ultimately left to the jury.

[**Lords Thankerton, Wright, Finlay** and **Roche** concurred.]

Appeal dismissed

Questions

1. Is the test laid down by Lord Atkin objective or subjective? Does it require the prosecution to prove anything about the actual state of mind of the accused at the time of the killing?

2. Is there 'an obvious difference in the law of manslaughter between doing an unlawful act and doing a lawful act with a degree of carelessness which the legislature makes criminal'? What is it?

3. If Craven had been severely injured but had lived (at least for a year and a day) Andrews, while of course guilty of dangerous driving, would have been guilty of no criminal offence against the person. Why does the fact of death make such a difference? Should it do so? Should it be a crime to cause non-fatal personal injuries by gross negligence? What about negligent damage to property?

4. Is the 'Bateman test', quoted by Lord Atkin, a useful test of negligence? Is it circular? Does it leave the jury to determine a question of law?

R v Stone and Dobinson [1977] 2 All ER 341, Court of Appeal, Criminal Division (Geoffrey Lane LJ, Nield and Croom-Johnson JJ)

The appellants were convicted of manslaughter. The first appellant's sister, who was described as 'eccentric in many ways' and 'morbidly and unnecessarily anxious about putting on weight', became infirm while lodging with the appellants. She remained immobile in bed for several weeks, and eventually died of toxaemia from infected bed sores and prolonged immobilisation. The appellants made no more than a half-hearted attempt to secure her medical attention. The first appellant was 'partially deaf, almost totally blind and had no appreciable sense of smell' and of 'low average intelligence'. The second appellant, his mistress, was 'ineffectual and somewhat inadequate', and the first appellant's son [Cyril], who lived at home, was 'mentally subnormal'.

[**Geoffrey Lane LJ** read the judgment of the court:

. . . There is no dispute, broadly speaking, as to the matters on which the jury must be satisfied before they can convict of manslaughter in circumstances such as the present. They are: (1) that the defendant undertook the care of a person who by reason of age or infirmity was unable to care for himself; (2) that the defendant was grossly negligent in regard to his duty of care; (3) that by reason of such negligence the person died. It is submitted on behalf of the appellants that the judge's direction to the jury with regard to the first two items was incorrect.

At the close of the Crown's case submissions were made to the judge that there was no, or no sufficient, evidence that the appellants, or either of them, had chosen to undertake the care of Fanny.

That contention was advanced by counsel for the appellant before this court as his first ground of appeal. He amplified the ground somewhat by submitting that the evidence which the judge had suggested to the jury might support the assumption of a duty by the appellants did not, when examined, succeed in doing so. He suggested that the situation here was unlike any reported case. Fanny came to this house as a lodger. Largely, if not entirely due to her own eccentricity and failure to look after herself or feed herself properly, she became increasingly infirm and immobile and eventually unable to look after herself. Is it to be said, asks counsel for the appellants rhetorically, that by the mere fact of becoming infirm and helpless in these circumstances, she casts a duty on her brother and Mrs Dobinson to take steps to have her looked after or taken to hospital? The suggestion is that, heartless though it may seem, this is one of those situations where the appellants were entitled to do nothing; where no duty was cast on them to help, any more than it is cast on a man to rescue a stranger from drowning, however easy such a rescue might be.

This court rejects that proposition. Whether Fanny was a lodger or not she was a blood relation of the appellant Stone; she was occupying a room in his house; Mrs Dobinson had undertaken the duty of trying to wash her, of taking such food to her as she required. There was ample evidence that each appellant was aware of the poor condition she was in by mid-July. It was not disputed that no effort was made to summon an ambulance or the social services or the police despite the entreaties of Mrs Wilson and Mrs West. A social worker used to visit Cyril. No word was spoken to him. All these were matters which the jury were entitled to take into account when considering whether the necessary assumption of a duty to care for Fanny had been proved.

This was *not* a situation analagous to the drowning stranger. They *did* make efforts to care. They tried to get a doctor; they tried to discover the previous doctor. Mrs Dobinson helped with the washing and the provision of food. All these matters were put before the jury in terms which we find it impossible to fault. The jury were entitled to find that the duty had been assumed. They were entitled to conclude that once Fanny became helplessly infirm, as she had by 19 July, the appellants were, in the circumstances, obliged either to summon help or else to care for Fanny themselves.

Counsel for the appellants' second submission presents greater difficulty. It is that the judge's direction on the nature of the negligence or recklessness required was wrongly stated. This is how the matter was left to the jury. [His Lordship quoted from the direction.]

The appellant's contention is that the Crown in order to succeed must show recklessness on the part of the defendant; that recklessness in this context means foresight of the likelihood or possibility of death or serious injury and a determination nevertheless to persist in the omission to provide care. We were referred to a number of 19th century decisions which are historically interesting but of small practical assistance. Counsel for the appellants relied principally on the decision of this court in *Lowe* [[1973] QB 702, [1973] 1 All ER 805]. In that case there were two counts, one alleging manslaughter of a child on the grounds that the defendants' cruelty alleged under the second count caused its death, and the second count charging cruelty to a child by wilfully neglecting it so as to cause unnecessary suffering or injury to health under the Children and Young Persons Act 1933, s 1 (1). The judge had directed the jury that if they found the appellant guilty on the second count they must find him guilty under the first count of manslaughter, even though they acquitted him of recklessness.

That was held to be a misdirection. Phillimore LJ, [[1973] QB 702 at 709, [1973] 1 All ER 805 at 809], delivering the judgment of the court, went on say this:

> 'Now in the present case the jury negatived recklessness. How then can mere neglect albeit wilful amount of manslaughter? This court feels that there is something inherently unattractive in a theory of constructive manslaughter. It seems strange that an omission which is wilful solely in the sense that it is not inadvertent, the consequences of which are not in fact foreseen by the person who is neglectful, should if death results, automatically give rise to an indeterminate sentence. . .'

Counsel for the appellants submits that that passage is support for his argument that there must be an appreciation by the defendant of the risk of death or serious injury before a conviction for manslaughter in these circumstances can result. We disagree. The court is saying simply that there must be proved the necessary high degree of negligence, and a direction which fails to emphasise that requirement will be defective. It is to *Andrews v Director of Public Prosecutions* [[1937] AC 576, [1937] 2 All ER 552] that one must turn to discover the definition of the requisite degree of negligence. Lord Atkin [[1937] AC 576 at 582, [1937] 2 All ER 552 at 555] cites, with approval, the words of Hewart CJ in *R v Bateman* [(1925) 94 LJKB 791] and goes on to say this [see p 342, above]:

'Simple lack of care such as will constitute civil liability is not enough. . .'

It is clear from that passage that indifference to an obvious risk and appreciation of such risk, coupled with a determination nevertheless to run it, are both examples of recklessness.

The duty which a defendant has undertaken is a duty of caring for the health and welfare of the infirm person. What the Crown has to prove is a breach of that duty in such circumstances that the jury feel convinced that the defendant's conduct can properly be described as reckless. That is to say a reckless disregard of danger to the health and welfare of the infirm person. Mere inadvertence is not enough. The defendant must be proved to have been indifferent to an obvious risk of injury to health, or actually to have foreseen the risk but to have determined nevertheless to run it.

The direction given by the judge was wholly in accord with these principles. If any criticism is to be made it would be that the direction was unduly favourable to the defence. The appeals against conviction therefore fail. . . .

Appeal dismissed

Questions

1. What is the difference between (i) indifference to an obvious risk and (ii) appreciation of such a risk, coupled with a determination nevertheless to run it? (Cf Farrier, (1978) 41 MLR 211, Williams, *TBCL 229-233*, Smith, [1977] Crim LR 167 and *Smith* [1979] Crim LR 251 (Griffiths J)).

2. Was Phillimore LJ wrong in *Lowe* when he implied that 'mere neglect albeit wilful' could not amount to manslaughter?

3. The court rejects the view that recklessness, in the law of manslaughter, requires foresight of death or serious injury. Does the court require foresight of any injury?

4. What is meant by 'welfare'?

5. Dobinson was sentenced to 18 months' imprisonment suspended for two years. The Court of Appeal reduced Stone's sentence from three years to twelve months, saying that a sentence of immediate imprisonment was 'unavoidable if for nothing else at least to mark the public disapproval of such behaviour'. Was this right?

R v Seymour [1983] 2 All ER 1058, House of Lords
(Lords Diplock, Fraser, Roskill, Bridge and Templeman)

Following a quarrel with Mrs B with whom he had been living, S met her driving a car in the opposite direction from which he was driving a lorry. There was a slight collision. B got out of the car and approached the lorry. S, allegedly intending only to push her car out of the way, drove up against the car so violently that it was moved ten to twenty feet and one of its tyres was forced off. B was crushed between the two vehicles, sustained severe injuries and died a week later. S was convicted of manslaughter and sentenced to 5 years' imprisonment. His appeal against conviction (there was no appeal against sentence) was dismissed by the Court of Appeal. He appealed to the House of Lords.

[**Lord Roskill**, having referred to the creation of the offence of causing death by reckless or dangerous driving by the Road Traffic Act 1956 (because of the reluctance of juries to convict motorists of manslaughter), its re-enactment in the Road Traffic Act 1972, s 1 (1) and replacement by the Criminal Law Act 1977 (p 577, below) under which it is now an offence to cause death by reckless, but not by dangerous, driving:]

This enactment in due course gave rise to two questions. First, what was the meaning of the word 'reckless' in this new section? Or, to put the same point in other words, what was the proper direction for the trial judge to give to a jury as to the test to be applied in determining whether or not a person charged under this section was guilty of the offence charged? Second, and in particular having regard to the speech of Lord Atkin in *Andrews v DPP* [1937] 2 All ER 552 at 557, [1937] AC 576 at 584, did the common law offence of manslaughter by reckless driving of a motor vehicle survive the enactment of s 50 of the 1977 Act, for if it did so survive there would be two offences, one at common law and the other by statute which, since the ingredients of each were indistinguishable, would be co-extensive, though one carried the maximum penalty of imprisonment for life, and the other of five years' imprisonment only.

[His Lordship referred to *Caldwell*, p 68, above and *Lawrence*, p 72, above, quoted from the latter and continued:]

As to the second question, there had been, as Watkins LJ said in giving the judgment of the Court of Appeal, Criminal Division in the present case, a body of opinion which thought that the common law offence of manslaughter by the reckless driving of a motor vehicle must be taken to have been impliedly repealed by s 50 of the 1977 Act, or possibly earlier. That view was taken by the Divisional Court in *Jennings* [1982] 3 All ER 104, [1982] 1 WLR 949. But your Lordships' House in that case unanimously held otherwise. The argument founded on implied repeal was rejected for the reasons given in my speech (see [1982] 3 All ER 104 at 113–117, [1983] AC 624 at 639–644) which I will not repeat. But I added:

'No doubt the prosecuting authorities today would only prosecute for manslaughter in the case of death caused by the reckless driving of a motor vehicle on a road in a very grave case.'

My Lords, *Jennings* was decided on 29 July 1982, over a year after Mrs Burrows's death and some six months after the appellant's trial at Northampton Crown Court. This trial also preceded the hearing of *Jennings* in the Divisional Court. As already stated, the appellant was charged only with manslaughter, no doubt because of the view which the prosecuting authorities took of the gravity of the case. Your Lordships were told that a plea of guilty to the statutory offence, which had that also been charged, was proffered but was rejected by counsel for the Crown. I agree with the view of the Court of Appeal that this was an entirely proper course for counsel for the Crown to have adopted. The jury was, of course, unaware of this fact.

After the close of the evidence, counsel for the appellant invited the judge not to give the jury what I will call for brevity the '*Lawrence* direction' simpliciter, arguing that that direction was applicable only where the statutory offence was charged. He submitted that where the common law offence of manslaughter was charged, the jury should be directed that the Crown must further prove that the appellant recognised that some risk was involved and had none the less proceeded to take that risk.

The judge rejected the submission and gave the *Lawrence* direction subject only to the omission of any reference to the 'obvious and serious risk . . . of doing substantial damage to property': see *R v Lawrence* [1981] 1 All ER 974 at 982, [1982] AC 510 at 526. In my view, he was entirely right not to refer to damage to property, a reference to which was irrelevant in this case and might well have confused the jury. His admirably clear direction not only properly reflected the decision of this House in *R v Lawrence* but also Lord Atkin's speech in *Andrews v DPP*. I quote the relevant passage. . .

As already stated, the appellant was convicted. He appealed and his appeal to the Court of Appeal was dismissed. By the date of the appeal *Jennings* had been decided in your Lordships' House. The reasons given for the dismissal of his appeal were in substance, that since your

Lordships' House had held that the ingredients of the common law and statutory offences were identical, the *Lawrence* direction, which was appropriate when the statutory offence was charged, must be equally appropriate when the common law offence of manslaughter was charged. The Court of Appeal, Criminal Division granted the appellant a certificate in the following terms:

> 'Where manslaughter is charged and the circumstances of the offence are that the victim was killed as the result of the reckless driving of the defendant on a public highway; should the trial Judge give the jury the direction suggested in *R v Lawrence* in its entirety; or should the direction be that only a recognition by the defendant that some risk was involved and he had none-the-less gone on to take it would be sufficient to establish the commission of the offence?' . . .

My Lords, I would accept the submission of counsel for the Crown that once it is shown that the two offences co-exist it would be quite wrong to give the adjective 'reckless' or the adverb 'recklessly' a different meaning according to whether the statutory or the common law offence is charged. 'Reckless' should today be given the same meaning in relation to all offences which involve 'recklessness' as one of the elements unless Parliament has otherwise ordained. That this has been so in the past is shown by the respective decisions of the Court of Criminal Appeal and the Court of Appeal, Criminal Division in *R v Church* [1965] 2 All ER 72 at 75, [1966] 1 QB 59 at 68 and *R v Lowe* [1973] 1 All ER 805 at 808, [1973] QB 702 at 708, to neither of which was attention of this House drawn in either *R v Caldwell* or *R v Lawrence*. This was also clearly the view taken by the Court of Appeal, Criminal Division in *R v Pigg* [1982] 2 All ER 591 esp at 597–599, [1982] 1 WLR 762 esp at 770–772 per Lord Lane CJ, with all of whose reasoning I respectfully agree.

In truth, the argument of counsel for the appellant is an attempt to overcome an anomaly resulting from the amendment of the law in 1977, an amendment made not for the purpose of effecting a reform of substantive law but, as my noble and learned friend Lord Diplock pointed out in his speech in *R v Lawrence* [1981] 1 All ER 947 at 980–981, [1982] AC 510 at 524, in connection with the redistribution of criminal business between the Crown Court and magistrates' courts. The very difficulty which counsel for the appellant encountered in trying to distinguish between a defendant who gave no thought to a risk to which he was indifferent and who even if he had thought of that risk would have acted in precisely the same way and a defendant who gave no thought to a risk because it never crossed his mind that the risk existed is eloquent of the need to prescribe a simple and single meaning of the adjective 'reckless' and the adverb 'recklessly' throughout the criminal law unless Parliament has otherwise ordained in a particular case. That simple and single meaning should be the ordinary meaning of those words as stated in this House in *R v Caldwell* and in *R v Lawrence*.

Parliament must however be taken to have intended that 'motor manslaughter' should be a more grave offence than the statutory offence. While the former still carries a maximum penalty of imprisonment for life, Parliament has thought fit to limit the maximum penalty for the statutory offence to five years' imprisonment, the sentence in fact passed by the trial judge on the appellant on his conviction for manslaughter. This difference recognises that there are degrees of turpitude which will vary according to the gravity of the risk created by the manner of a defendant's driving. In these circumstances your Lordships may think that in future it will only be very rarely that it will be appropriate to charge 'motor manslaughter': that is where, as in the instant case, the risk of death from a defendant's driving was very high. . . .

In England and Wales it is for the prosecution and not for the court to decide what charge or charges should be made against a particular defendant. The prosecution is entitled to consider all the circumstances of the case before so deciding. In the instant case the prosecution properly charged manslaughter and manslaughter alone. In doing so the prosecution took the risk that a jury might have refused to convict the appellant of that crime though on the evidence it is difficult to see how any reasonable jury could have acquitted him of that offence. But had he been acquitted he would have gone unpunished even though the jury might have convicted him of the statutory offence had that been charged.

In my opinion that consideration cannot justify the joinder of both charges in a single indictment. In future if in any case in England and Wales any such joinder should occur I think it must behove the trial judge to require the prosecution to elect on which of the two counts in the indictment they wish to proceed and not to allow the trial to proceed on both counts. This may result in a different practice prevailing in England and Wales from that which has prevailed in Scotland, a part of the United Kingdom over which no criminal jurisdiction is exercised by this House. But since it is clear that the substantive law is the same in both countries, differences in practice may be thought to be not of great importance.

I would therefore answer the certified question as follows: 'Where manslaughter is charged and the circumstances are that the victim was killed as a result of the reckless driving of the defendant on a public highway, the trial judge should give the jury the direction suggested in *R v Lawrence* but it is appropriate also to point out that in order to constitute the offence of manslaughter the risk of death being caused by the manner of the defendant's driving must be very high.'

I would dismiss this appeal.

Appeal dismissed

Questions

1. The Lawrence direction requires proof of 'an obvious and serious risk of causing physical injury'—not, be it noted, death or even *serious* physical injury. If it is right to give the *Lawrence* direction on a charge of manslaughter, can it also be right to tell the jury 'that in order to constitute the offence of manslaughter the risk of death being caused must be very high'?

2. If manslaughter did require a high risk of death would there not be every justification for having a second count for causing death by reckless driving? A jury which was satisfied that there was an obvious risk of causing injury might not be satisfied that here was a high risk of causing death.

3. Lord Fraser said, 'Although the ingredients of the two offences are the same, the degree of recklessness required for the conviction of the statutory offence is less than that required for conviction of the common law crime.' Is not this self-contradictory?

Kong Cheuk Kwan v R [1985] NLJ Rep 753, Privy Council
(Lords Fraser, Roskill, Bridge and Brandon and Sir Owen Woodhouse)

The appellant was in command of one of two hydrofoils which collided at full speed in fine sunny weather. Two passengers were killed. The appellant, with other officers, was convicted of manslaughter and his conviction was upheld by the Hong Kong Court of Appeal. In accordance with *Archbold* (41st edn), second supp, para 20–49, the judge directed the jury as follows:

the defendant . . ., is guilty of manslaughter if the Crown have proved beyond reasonable doubt, firstly, that at the time he caused the deceased's death and, of course, you must be satisfied that each of the accused did cause the deceased's death, there was something in the circumstances which would have drawn the attention of an ordinary prudent individual and in this case you would consider the ordinary prudent deck officer or helmsman in the position of the defendant, to the possibility that his conduct was capable of causing some injury albeit not necessarily serious to the deceased including injury to health, which does not apply here, and that the risk was not so slight that an ordinary prudent individual would feel justified in treating it as negligible and that, secondly, before the act or omission which caused the deceased's death, the defendant either failed to give any thought to the possibility of there being any such risk or having recognised that there was such a risk he, nevertheless, went on to take the risk, or was guilty of such a high degree of negligence in the means that he adopted to avoid the risk as to go beyond a mere matter of compensation between subjects and showed in your opinion, such disregard for the life and safety of others as to amount to a crime against the State and conduct deserving punishment.

Lord Roskill (giving the judgment of the Board):

With profound respect this direction cannot be supported. There is (as in the paragraph in the Supplement to *Archbold*) confusion between (1) causing death by an illegal act of violence, (2) what was said in *R v Caldwell*, (3) what was said in *R v Lawrence* and (4) what had half a century previously been said by the Court of Criminal Appeal in *R v Bateman* [1925] 19 Cr App R 8 . . . It is to be observed that from beginning to end of the summing up neither the word 'reckless' nor the word 'recklessness' ever appears.

Their Lordships have been gravely concerned that the source of this erroneous direction should have appeared in the Second Supplement of the 41st edition of *Archbold*, especially as the paragraph numbered (7) purported to reflect the decisions of the House of Lords in *R v Caldwell* and *R v Lawrence* . . .

Though *R v Caldwell* and *R v Lawrence* are referred to in the preface to the 41st edition as 'extraordinary decisions' (a view which the editor is of course at liberty to express in his preface if he so wishes) they are understandably not referred to in the original text of para 20-49 though there is a passing reference to them in the final sentence of para 20-49. No doubt it was this ommission which necessitated the addition of para (7) in the Second Supplement. But the view, whether correct or not, that the two decisions are 'extraordinary' cannot justify complete misrepresentation as to their effect in a text book of great authority widely used in England and Wales and elsewhere as in Hong Kong where the relevant criminal law is the same.

It thus becomes necessary for their Lordships to restate the current position though in so doing they are largely repeating what was said in those two decisions which have themselves since been applied in two further decisions in the House of Lords, *Jennings v US Government* [1982] 3 All ER 104 and *R v Seymour* [1983] 2 All ER 1058. In *R v Caldwell* the House was concerned with and only with the meaning of the word 'reckless' in the statutory context of s 1 of the Criminal Damage Act 1971. Any relationship between 'recklessness' in arson cases and 'recklessness' in cases of causing death by reckless driving or of motor manslaughter was not there under consideration. The crucial passage is in the speech of Lord Diplock ([1981] 1 All ER 961 at 966-967) with which the other members of the majority of the House agreed . . . Lord Diplock was in that passage thus stating (in part) a negative proposition. He was dealing with the factual situation where there was nothing to alert the ordinary prudent individual to the possibility of harmful consequences or where that possibility was so slight that the individual could properly treat the risk as negligible. Such conduct was not 'reckless' within the ordinary meaning of that ordinary English word.

Their Lordships now move to *R v Lawrence*. There the House was dealing with death caused by reckless driving. The House unanimously accepted that view of the majority in *R v Caldwell* as to the meaning of 'reckless' and of 'recklessness'. It applied that ruling to the statutory offence causing death by reckless driving and suggested a model direction in such cases.

Lord Diplock ([1981] 1 All ER 974 at 982) on this occasion [spoke] for all the Lords then present [in stating the appropriate instruction to the jury on what is meant by driving recklessly].

Their Lordships emphasise that in this passage Lord Diplock was speaking of an obvious and serious risk of causing physical injury created by the defendant. He was not there concerned to deal with cases where the conduct complained of was of a defendant's reaction or lack of reaction to such a risk created by another person . . .

Their Lordships are of the view that the present state of the relevant law in England and Wales and thus in Hong Kong is clear. The model direction suggested in *R v Lawrence*, and held in *R v Seymour* to be equally applicable to cases of motor manslaughter, requires first, proof that the vehicle was in fact being driven in such a manner as to create an obvious and serious risk of causing physical injury to another and second, that the defendant so drove either without having given any thought to the possibility of there being such a risk or having recognised that there was such a risk nevertheless took it. Once that direction is given, it is for the jury to decide whether or not on their view of the evidence the relevant charge has been proved.

In principle their Lordships see no reason why a comparable direction should not have been given in the present case . . . Unfortunately this direction was not given. The direction given and its source in the Second Supplement, in the passage which reads "his conduct was capable of causing some injury albeit not necessarily serious to the deceased . . . and that the risk was not so slight that an ordinary prudent individual would feel justified in treating it as negligible" has been taken from Lord Diplock's negative proposition. This has then been turned round and the proposition treated as an affirmative statement of the relevant risk. With all respect, that cannot be justified and in their Lordships, view vitiates the direction. The first part of the second limb purports to repeat in part the model direction in *R v Lawrence* but unhappily that direction is vitiated by the reference back to the statement of the nature of this risk to which their Lordships have already referred. The second part of the second limb appears to be a throwback to

R v Bateman. Though Lord Atkin in his speech in *R v Andrews* [1937] AC 576 at 583 did not disapprove of what was there said, he clearly thought that it was better to use the word 'reckless' rather than to add to the word 'negligence' various possible vituperative epithets. Their Lordships respectfully agree. Indeed they further respectfully agree with the comment made by Watkins LJ in delivering the judgment of the Court of Appeal (Criminal Division) *R v Seymour* (1983) 76 Cr App R 211 at 216 . . .

Appeal allowed

In the passage referred to in *Seymour*, Watkins LJ expressed the court's view that 'it is no longer necessary or helpful to make references to compensation or negligence.' Thus, the much-used 'Bateman test', p 342, above appears to be no longer law; and it is likely that there is no separate category of 'gross negligence manslaughter'.

5. Homicide under the draft Code

The draft Code incorporates the reforms proposed by the Criminal Law Revision Committee in their Fourteenth Report (Cmnd 7844). The clauses relating to homicide are as follows:

56 Murder
A person who kills another:
(a) intending to kill; or
(b) intending to cause serious injury and being aware that he may kill; [or
(c) intending to cause fear of death or serious injury and being aware that he may kill,]
is guilty of murder, unless section 58, 60, 61, 65 or 67 applies.

57 Manslaughter
(1) A person is guilty of manslaughter where:
(a) he kills or is a party to the killing of another with the fault specified in section 56 but section 58 (diminished responsibility), 60 (provocation) or 61 (use of excessive force) applies; or
(b) he is not guilty of murder by reason only of the fact that, because of voluntary intoxication, he is not aware that death may be caused or believes that an exempting circumstance exists; or
(c) he kills another:
    (i) intending to cause serious injury; or
    (ii) being reckless whether death or serious injury will be caused.
(2) Where section 58 applies the jury shall return a verdict of 'guilty of manslaughter by reason of diminished responsibility' and in any other case they shall return a verdict of 'guilty of manslaughter'.

[For cl 58 see p 320, above.]

60 Provocation
This section applies where:
(a) the person who kills or is a party to the killing of another is provoked (whether by things done or by things said or by both and whether by the deceased person or by another) to lose his self-control; and
(b) the provocation is, in all the circumstances (including any of his personal characteristics that effect its gravity), sufficient ground for the loss of self-control.

61 Use of excessive force
This section applies where the person kills or is a party to the killing of another by the use of force which he believes to be necessary and reasonable to effect a purpose referred to in section 47 (use of force in public or private defence) but which exceeds the force which is necessary and reasonable in the circumstances which exist and (where there is a difference) in those which he believes to exist.

62 Jurisdiction over murder and manslaughter
A person is guilty of murder or manslaughter (if section 56 or 57 applies) where:
(a) he causes a fatal injury to another person to occur within the ordinary limits of criminal

jurisdiction, whether his act is done within or outside and whether the death occurs within or outside those limits:
(b) he kills another person anywhere in the world by an act done within the ordinary limits of criminal jurisdiction; or
(c) being a British citizen, he kills another person anywhere in the world by an act done anywhere in the world.

63 Attempted manslaughter
A person who attempts or is a party to an attempt to kill another, where section 58, 60 or 61 would apply if death were caused, is not guilty of attempted murder but is guilty of attempted manslaughter.

64 Liability of party not having defence
The fact that one person is, by virtue of section 58, 60, 61, 63 or 67, not guilty of murder or attempted murder shall not affect the question whether any other person is so guilty.

65 Killing in pursuance of suicide pact
(1) A person who, with the fault specified in section 56, kills another or is a party to the other being killed by a third person is not guilty of murder but is guilty of an offence under this section if he is acting in pursuance of a suicide pact between him and the other.
(2) 'Suicide pact' means a common agreement between two or more persons having for its object the death of all of them, whether or not each is to take his own life, but nothing done by a person who enters into a suicide pact shall be treated as done by him in pursuance of the pact unless it is done while he has the settled intention of dying in pursuance of the pact.
(3) A person who in pursuance of a suicide pact attempts or is a party to an attempt to kill another is not guilty of attempted murder but is guilty of an attempt to commit an offence under this section.

66 Complicity in suicide
A person who procures, assists or encourages suicide committed or attempted by another is guilty of an offence.

67 Infanticide
(1) A woman who, with the fault specified in section 56 or section 57 (1)(c), kills or is a party to the killing of her child by an act done when the child is under the age of twelve months and when the balance of her mind is disturbed by reason of the effect of giving birth or of circumstances consequent upon that birth, is not guilty of murder or manslaughter but is guilty of infanticide.
(2) A woman who, in the circumstances specified in subsection (1), attempts or is a party to an attempt to kill her child is not guilty of attempted murder but is guilty of attempted infanticide.
(3) A woman may be convicted of infanticide (or attempted infanticide) although the jury is uncertain whether the child had been born and had an existence independent of her when his death occured (or, in the case of an attempt, when the act was done).

68 Threat to kill or cause serious injury
A person who makes to another a threat, intending that other to fear that it will be carried out, to kill or cause serious injury to that other or a third person is guilty of an offence.

[For cl 69, see p 303, above]

70 Abortion
A person who terminates the pregnancy of a woman otherwise than in accordance with the provisions of section 1 of the Abortion Act 1967 is guilty of an offence.

71 Self-abortion
(1) A pregnant woman who terminates her pregnancy otherwise than in accordance with the provisions of section 1 of the Abortion Act 1967 is guilty of an offence.
(2) Notwithstanding section 54 (impossibility), a woman who is not pregnant cannot be guilty of an attempt to commit an offence under this section.

72 Supplying article for abortion
A person who supplies or procures any article knowing that it is to be used with intent to terminate the pregnancy of a woman, whether she is pregnant or not, commits an offence.

CHAPTER 18

Non-fatal offences against the person

The development of the law relating to non-fatal offences against the person has not been a model of logical consistency. In the past the Legislature has tended to respond to particular problems by the creation of particular offences. The outcome is that there is a plethora of offences which include such oddities as preventing a clergyman from celebrating divine service (Offences against the Person Act 1861, s 36) and impeding persons endeavouring to escape from wrecks (ibid, s 17). This chapter deals with the principal offences including assault and battery and certain aggravated assaults.

Proposals for the reform of the law have been made by the CLRC (Fourteenth Report, *Offences against the Person*, Cmnd 7844, 1980) and the draft Criminal Code contains provisions relating to most of the offences in this section.

1. Assault and battery

Offences against the Person Act 1861, ss 42, 43, 47, p 545–546, below

(1) THE ELEMENTS OF ASSAULT AND BATTERY

East, 1 PC 406 (following Hawkins, 1 PC (1716) 133):

'An assault is any attempt or offer with force and violence to do a corporal hurt to another, whether from malice or wantonness; as by striking at him, or even by holding up one's fist at him in a threatening or insulting manner, or with such other circumstances as denote at the time an intention, coupled with a present ability of using actual violence against his person; as by pointing a weapon at him within the reach of it. Where the injury is actually inflicted, it amounts to a battery, (which includes an assault); and this, however small it may be; as by spitting in a man's face, or any way touching him in anger without any lawful occasion. But if the occasion were merely accidental and undesigned, or if it were lawful, and the party used no more force than was reasonably necessary to accomplish the purpose, as to defend himself against a prior assault, or to arrest the other, or make him desist from some wrongful act or endeavour, or the like; it is no assault or battery in the law, and the party may justify the force; and any matter in justification or excuse, such as *son assault demesne*, may upon an indictment be given in evidence under the general issue: and the defendant who is charged with an assault and battery, may be found guilty of the one and acquitted of the other. But *son assault demesne* is no excuse, if the retaliation by the defendant were excessive, and bore no proportion to the necessity, or the provocation received.'

Tuberville v Savage (1669) 1 Mod Rep 3, King's Bench

Action of *assault, battery* and *wounding*. The evidence to prove a provocation was, that the plaintiff put his hand upon his sword and said, *'If it were not assize-time, I would not take such language from you.'*—The question was, If that were an assault?—The Court agreed that it was not; for the declaration of the plaintiff was, that he would not assault him, the Judges being in town; and *the intention* as well as *the act* makes an assault. Therefore if one strike another upon the hand, or arm, or breast in discourse, it is no assault, there being no *intention* to assault; but if one, intending to assault, strike *at* another and miss him, this is an assault: so if he hold up his hand against another in a threatening manner and say nothing, it is an assault.—In the principal case the plaintiff had judgment.

'Assault and Words' by Glanville Williams, [1957] Crim LR 219 at 220

The rule in *Tuberville v Savage*, that words may negative or end an assault, was misapplied in *Blake v Barnard* (1840) 9 C & P 626, where the facts given in evidence were that D presented a pistol at P and said: 'If you are not quiet I will blow your brains out.' According to the report (which may not be accurate), Lord Abinger, in summing up, directed the jury that 'if the defendant, at the time he presented [the pistol] added words showing that it was not his intention to shoot the plaintiff, that would be no assault.' Although literally unimpeachable, this direction was totally inadequate having regard to the evidence that the jury had to consider. There was a great difference between the words used in *Tuberville v Savage* and those used in the case at bar. In the former case, the declaration of the desire to kill was made subject to an extraneous condition ('If it were not assize-time'), which was known to the other party not to be fulfilled. The unfulfilled condition therefore nullified the threat. But in the present case, the threat was conditional upon the way the plaintiff thereafter behaved; in order to avoid being killed he had to keep quiet, and his conduct was therefore constrained by the threat. The plaintiff, in other words, was subject to the fear that if he spoke he would be shot. It is submitted that in these circumstances the presentation of the pistol was an assault. Otherwise, indeed, the highwayman who says 'Your money or your life', at the same time presenting a weapon, would not be guilty of assault at common law—a proposition which it is impossible to believe. . . .

But, according to some authorities, a menace will equally be an assault even if the defendant merely demanded an act to which he had a legal right—if the menace was an improper way of enforcing his legal right. For example, a trespasser may be ejected by force, but only by moderate force, not amounting to death or serious bodily harm. A threat to cause serious harm to a trespasser if he does not leave is held to be an assault. In *Read v Coker* (1853) 13 CB 850, D, the occupier of premises, told P to leave, and on his failure to do so collected together some men, who mustered round P, tucking up their sleeves, and threatened to break his neck if he did not leave. P, fearing that they would carry out their threat, departed. It was held that D was liable for assault. P became a trespasser on his failure to leave, but it would not have been lawful to break his neck, or to inflict any other serious harm upon him, or to use any force against him except what was necessary for his ejection. The threats went beyond that, and therefore constituted an assault.

The correctness of this decision on the particular facts is perhaps not entirely beyond question. Although it is true that only moderate force may be used to eject trespassers, it does not follow that a threat to use immoderate (extreme) force should be held to be unlawful. For a mere threat to use immoderate force, not carried out, might be held to be moderate force. If one looks at the situation realistically, there is less affront to the dignity in being merely threatened with having one's neck broken if one does not leave, than in being hustled out by main force. It is strange if the latter is lawful and the former unlawful. Even if the occupier has gone so far as to threaten the trespasser with a gun, there would seem to be no pressing necessity to regard such an act as anything more than the use of moderate force within the meaning of the rule relating to the ejection of trespassers. It seems, however, that the courts are committed to the opposite view. In *Osborn v Veitch* (1858) 1 F & F 317, Willes J ruled that it was unlawful to point a gun at a man in order to restrain him from making an unlawful arrest.

Another query on *Read v Coker* is whether the court was not too naive in taking literally the threat to break P's neck. Whatever this expression meant in 1853, one may doubt whether it should today be understood to mean what it says . . .

Can assault be by words?

It is stated in nearly all the books on criminal law and the law of tort that words cannot make an assault. The judicial authority for this supposed rule is of the slightest: little more than a direction to the jury in *Meade and Belt* (1823) 1 Lew CC 184 at 185. Its main support derives from uncritical repetition by legal writers. A moment's reflection will reveal severe objections. For one thing, the opinion would deny the possibility of an assault (as opposed to a battery) in pitch darkness, when a gesture cannot be seen but menacing words can be heard. There seems to be no reason for denying to plain words the legal effect that will be given to a gesture, whether the words are spoken in the dark or otherwise. Mention has already been made of *Genner v Sparkes* [(1704) 1 Salk 79], where a merely symbolical gesture—a gesture that was intended to be read as a conditional threat—was held to be an assault. Why should not express words be treated in the same way, without the gesture? The other English case which has just been discussed, *Read v Coker*, may be used to reinforce the argument. There, the defendant through his servants used express language to the effect that they would break the plaintiff's neck if he did not leave, and this threat was held to be an assault. It is true that there was a gesture in addition to the words used, namely the act of the men in gathering round and tucking up their sleeves. But although this gesture doubtless added effect to the words, and showed beyond a doubt the immediacy of the threat, it is hard to see why it should be legally required where the other essentials of assault are present. If a highwayman, visibly armed, says: 'Your money or your life', should he escape the consequences of the law of assault merely because he does not trouble to point his pistol at his victim? If the pistol obviously lies loaded to his hand, he surely need not reach for it to constitute an assault. Nor need there be a pistol at all. If D says to P: 'Be quiet, or I will knock your block off,' or if, behind P's back, he says: 'Don't turn round or I shoot', such a threat ought to be accounted an assault (even though, in the second case, D is not in fact armed).

How can this opinion be reconciled with the traditional statement that words do not make an assault? It is submitted that the statement is true only as a restatement of the rule that an assault involves the apprehension of immediate force. A verbal threat of force in the future is not assault, not because it is verbal but because it is not immediate. A verbal threat of immediate force has all the essential elements of an assault, particularly where it is uttered with the intention of imposing a present restraint upon the conduct of the victim. There is nothing in the English decisions contrary to this view. . . .

NOTES AND QUESTIONS

1. In *Byrne* [1968] 3 CCC 179, Br Col CA, it was held there was no assault where the appellant entered a bank with a coat over his arm and said to Miss Eacrett, the cashier, 'I've got a gun, give me all your money or I'll shoot.' Robertson JA, said, at p 188,

> 'The report does not state in what position the appellant was holding his arm. When sentencing him the Magistrate said, "You simulated that you were carrying a gun under a jacket that was draped over your arm by *telling* [my italics] the cashier 'I've got a gun, give me all your money or I'll shoot.' " In the absence of evidence to the contrary, I must give the appellant the benefit of the doubt and assume that he was not holding or moving his arm in such a way as to simulate that he was pointing a gun at Miss Eacrett . . . If a man standing within arm's length of another says to him "I'm going to punch you in the nose" and does nothing, he does not thereby commit an assault; but, if he accompanies his words with the clenching of his fist and the drawing back of his arm, he does thereby commit an assault.'

Cf *Wilson* [1955] 1 All ER 744 at 745, CCA, where Lord Goddard CJ said, 'He [the appellant] called out "Get out knives", which itself would be an assault . . .'

Traditional definitions of assault (cf the definition approved in *Fagan*, p 356, below) have imported the requirement that the threat be of 'immediate' violence. Immediacy is of course a matter of degree; a threat of violence at some remote future time would not be an assault but a threat to take effect 'within a second or two of time' would clearly be sufficiently immediate: *Stephens v Myers* (1830) 4 C & P 349. In *Logdon v DPP* [1976] Crim LR 121, DC, a Customs official, P, who called on D concerning VAT payments, was told by D that she would be held prisoner until money which he claimed was owing to him by Customs was returned. D also showed P a revolver he had in a drawer and said it was loaded but then handed it to her pointing out that it was a replica. On a charge of assault D contended that he neither had the intention nor ability to carry out his threat and that it was all a joke. Affirming his conviction the court said, '. . . the offence of assault was a threat by a person to inflict unlawful force on another and that the offence was committed when by some physical act the threatener intentionally or recklessly caused the other to believe such force was about to be inflicted . . . .' See also *Halliday* (1889) 61 LT 701, [1886–90] All ER Rep 1028, and following Note, below p 366.

2. Ought not the question in *Byrne* to have been whether Miss Eacrett believed that the appellant had a gun on his person and was intended so to believe by the appellant?

3. Where during the course of an argument, as in *Tuberville v Savage*, one man places his hand on his sword, is it realistic to require the other party to undertake a precise linguistic analysis of the accompanying words before making up his mind to draw his own sword and strike first? Cf. *Light* (1857) Dears & B 332, where it was held that D was guilty of an assault in raising a shovel over his wife's head while saying, 'Were it not for the bloody police-man outside, I would split your head open.'

4. Was there in *Logdon* a threat of immediate violence? P was apparently frightened. Is it enough to be frightened? What if P had not been frightened? Suppose D telephones P to tell her that it won't be long before he gets her and that she will not look so pretty when he is through with her. Is this an assault? Ought it to be an assault?

R v Venna [1975] 3 All ER 788, Court of Appeal, Criminal Division (James and Ormrod LJJ and Cusack J)

The appellant and others were creating a disturbance in a public street. The police were sent for and during a scuffle which ensued as the police sought to arrest him, the appellant kicked out with his feet. In so doing he struck the hand of an officer and caused a fracture which resulted in his being convicted of an assault occasioning actual bodily harm.

[James LJ read the following judgment of the court:. . .]

The second substantial ground of appeal relates to the conviction of assault occasioning actual bodily harm. Having summed up to the jury the issue of self-defence in relation to the alleged assault, the judge directed them in these terms, and I read from the transcript:

'However, you would still have to consider, on this question of assault by Venna, whether it was an accident. If he is lashing out . . . Let me put it this way. [Counsel] on behalf of Venna says "Well, he is not guilty of an assault because it was neither inten-tional nor reckless. It was a pure accident that he happened to hit the officer", and that is quite right. If you hit somebody accidentally, it cannot be a criminal offence so you have got to ask yourselves, "Was this deliberate, or was it reckless?" If it was, then he is guilty. To do an act deliberately hardly needs explanation. If you see somebody in front of you and you deliberately kick him on the knee, that is a deliberate act and, no two ways about it, that is an assault but it can equally well be an assault if you are lashing out, knowing that there are people in the neighbourhood or that there are likely to be people in the neighbourhood and, in this case, it is suggested that he had two people by his arms and he knew that he was being restrained so as to lead to arrest. If he lashes out with his feet, knowing that there are officers about him and knowing that by lashing out he will probably or is likely to kick somebody or hurt his hand by banging his heel down on it, then he is equally guilty of the offence. Venna can therefore be guilty of the offence in count three in the indictment if he deliberately brought his foot down on Police Constable Spencer's hand or if he lashed out simply reckless as to who was there, not caring an iota as to whether he kicked somebody or brought his heel down on his hands.'

Counsel for the appellant argued that the direction is wrong in law because it states that the mental element of recklessness is enough, when coupled with the actus reus of physical contact, to constitute the battery involved in assault occasioning actual bodily harm. Recklessness, it is argued, is not enough; there must be intention to do the physical act the subject matter of the charge. Counsel relied on *R v Lamb* [[1967] 2 QB 981, [1967] 2 All ER 1282] and argued that an assault is not established by proof of a deliberate act which gives rise to consequences which are not intended.

In *Fagan v Metropolitan Police Comr*, it was said [[1969] 1 QB 439 at 440; p 25, above, [1968] 3 All ER 442 at 442]: 'An assault is any act which intentionally or possibly recklessly causes another person to apprehend immediate and unlawful personal violence'. In *Fagan* [[1969] 1 QB 439, [1968] 3 All ER 422] it was not necessary to decide the question whether proof of recklessness is sufficient to establish the mens rea ingredient of assault. That question falls for decision in the present case. Why it was considered necessary for the Crown to put the case forward on the alternative bases of 'intention' and 'recklessness' is not clear to us. This resulted in the direction given in the summing-up.

On the evidence of the appellant himself, one. would have thought that the inescapable inference was that the appellant intended to make physical contact with whoever might try to restrain him. Be that as it may, in the light of the direction given, the verdict may have been arrived at on the basis of 'recklessness'. Counsel for the appellant cited *Ackroyd v Barett* [(1894) 11 TLR 115] in support of his argument that recklessness, which falls short of intention, is not enough to support a charge of battery, and argued that, there being no authority to the contrary, it is now too late to extend the law by a decision of the courts and that any extension must be by the decision of Parliament.

Counsel for the appellant sought support from the distinction between the offences which are assaults and offences which by statute include the element contained in the word 'maliciously', e g unlawful and malicious wounding contrary to s. 20 of the Offences against the Person Act 1861, in which recklessness will suffice to support the charge: see *Cunningham* [[1957] 2 QB 396, [1957] 2 All ER 412]. Insofar as the editors of textbooks commit themselves to an opinion on this branch of the law, they are favourable to the view that recklessness is or should logically be sufficient to support the charge of assault or battery: see Glanville Williams [*Criminal Law* (2nd edn, 1961), p 65, para 27]; Kenny [*Outlines of Criminal Law* (19th edn, 1966), p 218, para 164]; Russell [*Russell on Crime* (12th edn 1964), vol 1, p 656] and Smith and Hogan [*Criminal Law* (3rd edn, 1973), pp 283, 286].

We think that the decision in *Ackroyd v Barett* is explicable on the basis that the facts of the case did not support a finding of recklessness. The case was not argued for both sides. *Bradshaw* [(1878) 14 Cox CC 83] can be read as supporting the view that unlawful physical force applied recklessly constitutes a criminal assault. In our view the element of mens rea in the offence of battery is satisfied by proof that the defendant intentionally or recklessly applied force to the person of another. If it were otherwise, the strange consequence would be that an offence of unlawful wounding contrary to s. 20 of the Offences against the Person Act 1861 could be established by proof that the defendant wounded the victim either intentionally or recklessly, but if the victim's skin was not broken and the offence was therefore laid as an assault occasioning actual bodily harm contrary to s. 47 of 1861 Act, it would be necessary to prove that the physical force was intentionally applied.

We see no reason in logic or in law why a person who recklessly applies physical force to the person of another should be outside the criminal law of assault. In many cases the dividing line between intention and recklessness is barely distinguishable. This is such a case. In our judgment the direction was right in law; this ground of appeal fails. . . .

For these reasons we dismiss the appeal.

Appeal dismissed

NOTE

In *Cole v Turner* (1705) 6 Mod Rep 149, it was said that the least touching of another in anger constituted a battery; hence it would be a battery to knock rudely against someone while passing in the street, but not to touch another gently when passing in a narrow passage. It was accordingly held in *Coward v Baddeley* (1859) 28 LJ Ex 260, that there was no assault when a spectator at a fire touched a fireman on the shoulder to attract his attention in order to tell him that the efforts of his men were spreading the fire rather than containing it. The trial judge, Bramwell B, had directed the jury that in order to constitute an assault or battery there must be a hostile intention. As to that counsel argued, 'The intention is immaterial; if there be a touch, and that against the will of the person touched, there is a battery.' But Bramwell B's direction was apparently approved. Cf *State v Hemphill* 78 SE 167 (1913), SC of North Carolina, where it was held that the defendant was not guilty of an assault where, at the request of the prosecutrix's grandmother, he laid his hand gently on the prosecutrix for the purpose of inducing her to return home and to quit the company of designing men. Walker J said,

> 'If we are restricted to the defendant's testimony, it would appear that he did not intend to injure the prosecutrix, or to do any violence to her person . . . The jury may conclude that his object was one of persuasion rather than coercion. He saw her plight . . . and wished to relieve her of its evil consequences. If so, it was an act of kindness and mercy to her, rather than one of hostility.'

Cf *Donnelly v Jackman* [1970] 1 All ER 987, DC p 373, below; *Faulkner v Talbot*, p 402, below.

Question

May the touching of another amount to an assault though it is not done in anger? If one touches another in anger is that necessarily an assault?

(2) CONSENT AS A DEFENCE TO OFFENCES INVOLVING AN ASSAULT

Outlines of Criminal Law by Kenny, (15th edn) at p 181
(Footnotes omitted)

There is, further, a justification for acts that are done by consent of the person assaulted; unless the force be a breach of the peace, or be causelessly dangerous. *Volenti non fit injuria*. Hence seduction is no assault, either in the law of crime or even in that of tort.

But the consent must be given freely (i e without force, fear or fraud), and by a sane and sober person, so situated as to be able to form a reasonable opinion upon the matter to which consent is given. 'Fraud vitiates consent'; if the fraud relate to a fundamental *fact*, like the identity of the deceiver, or the nature of the assault. Accordingly an imposter, who, by pretending to be a surgeon, induces an invalid to submit to be operated upon by him, will be guilty of assault, notwithstanding the consent which was nominally given. As regards the mental capacity to consent, it may be mentioned that, in the case of indecent assaults, the legislature has established a definite rule as to age, by enacting that consent given by a child of either sex under sixteen years of age shall not constitute a defence . . . And, again, even the most complete consent, by the most competent person, will not suffice to legalise an assault which there are public grounds for prohibiting. Thus consent is no defence, criminally, for any assault that involves some extreme and causeless injury to life, limb, or health; or even one that constitutes a mere breach of the peace; nor for any assault likely to cause bodily harm (whether extreme or not) and not justified by any good reason, e g sport, lawful chastisement, etc. If, therefore, one of the parties to a duel is injured, his consent is no excuse. Yet it is uncertain at what degree of danger the law thus takes away a man's right to consent to be placed in situations of peril (as, for instance, by allowing himself to be wheeled in a barrow along a tight-rope). But in the case of a surgical operation carried out by a competent surgeon, however great be the risk, there will usually be adequate cause for running it; and so the patient's consent will be full justification for what would otherwise be an aggravated assault. And even injuries which are occasioned in the course of a mere game, if it be a lawful one and be played with due care, are not regarded as causeless.

In *Clarence* (1888) 22 QBD 23, [1886–90] All ER Rep 133 D, knowing that he was suffering from gonorrhea, had intercourse with his wife and infected her. His wife would not have consented had she known that he was so suffering. D's conviction for an assault occasioning actual bodily harm was quashed. In his judgment, Wills J said (at p 27):

First, was he guilty of an assault? In support of a conviction it is urged that even a married woman is under no obligation to consent to intercourse with a diseased husband; that had the wife known that her husband was diseased she would not have consented; that the husband was guilty of a fraud in concealing the fact of his illness; that her consent was, therefore, obtained by fraud and so was no consent at all, and, as the act of coition would imply an assault if done without consent, he can be convicted. This reasoning seems to me eminently unsatisfactory. That consent obtained by fraud is no consent at all is not true as a general proposition either in fact or in law. If a man meets a woman in the street and knowingly gives her bad money in order to procure her consent to intercourse with him, he obtains her consent by fraud, but it would be childish to say that she did not consent. In respect of a contract fraud does not destroy the consent; it only makes it revocable. Money or goods obtained by false pretences still become the property of the fraudulent obtainer unless and until the contract is revoked by the person defrauded, and it has never been held that, as far as regards the application of criminal law, the repudiation of the contract had a retrospective effect or there would have been no distinction between obtaining money under false pretences and theft . . .

We are thus introduced, as it seems to me, to a set of very subtle metaphysical questions: If we are invited to apply the analogy of the cases in which a man has procured intercourse by personating a husband, or by representing that he was performing a surgical operation, we have to ask ourselves whether the procurement of intercourse by suppressing the fact that the man is diseased is more nearly allied to the procurement of intercourse by misrepresentation as to who the man is, or as to what is being done, or to misrepresentations of a thousand kinds in respect of which it has never yet occurred to anyone to suggest that intercourse so procured was an assault or a rape. There are plenty of such instances in which the knowledge of the truth would have made the victim as ready to accept the embraces of a man stricken with smallpox or leprosy. Take, for example, the case of a man without a single good quality, a gaol bird, heartless, mean, and cruel, without the smallest intention of doing anything but possessing himself of the person of his victim, but successfully representing himself as a man of good family and connections prevented by some temporary obstacle from contracting an immediate marriage, and with conscious hypocrisy acting the part of a devoted lover, and in this fashion, or perhaps under the guise of affected religious fervour, effecting the ruin of his victim. In all that induces consent there is not less difference between the man to whom the woman supposes she is yielding herself and the man by whom she is really betrayed, than there is between the man bodily sound and the man afflicted with a contagious disease.

Is there to be a distinction in this respect between an act of intercourse with a wife who on this special occasion would have had a right to refuse her consent, and certainly would have refused it had she known the truth, and the intercourse taking place under the general consent inferred from a bigamous marriage obtained by the false representation that the man was capable of contracting a legal marriage? In such a case the man can give no title of wife to the woman whose person he obtains by the false representation that he is unmarried, and by a ceremony which, under the circumstances, is absolutely void. Where is the difference between consent obtained by the suppression of the fact that the act of intercourse may produce a foul disease, and consent obtained by the suppression of the fact that it will certainly make the woman a concubine, and while destroying her status as a virgin withhold from her the title and rights of a wife? Where is the distinction between the mistake of fact which induces the woman to consent to intercourse with a man supposed to be sound in body, but not really so, and the mistake of fact which induces her to consent to intercourse with a man whom she believes to be her lawful husband but who is not? Many women would think that, of two cruel wrongs, the bigamist had committed the worse . . .

NOTES AND QUESTIONS

1. In *Bolduc and Bird* [1967] 3 CCC 294, SC of Can, D, a doctor who was about to conduct a vaginal examination, asked the patient if she minded the presence of E, who was represented by D to be a medical intern seeking experience. She agreed and E, who was in fact a lay friend of D and was there merely to satisfy his prurient interest, remained present throughout the examination. Quashing the convictions of D and E for indecent assault the court said, 'There was no fraud on [D's] part as to what he was supposed to do and in what he actually did. The complainant knew that [E] was present and consented to his presence. The fraud that was practised on her was not as to the nature and quality of what was done but was as to [E's] identity as a medical intern. His presence as distinct from some overt act by him was not an assault.' Spence J, dissenting, said, at 299, 'Let us examine for a moment what was the consent obtained from the complainant. Surely . . . it was consent to the examination by [D] . . . in the presence of a doctor, not a mere medical student or a layman . . . She only gave this consent to such a serious invasion of her privacy on the basis that [E] was a doctor intending to commence practice and who desired practical experience . . . That was the consent which the complainant granted.'

2. Would it have made any difference if (i) in *Clarence* the wife had asked for, and received, a specific assurance from the husband that he was not suffering from any venereal disease; and (ii) in *Bolduc and Bird* E had, with the patient's permission, sounded her chest with a stethoscope?

3. Were the wife in *Clarence* and the patient in *Bolduc and Bird* so situated, to use Kenny's words, 'as to be able to form a reasonable opinion upon the matter to which consent is given'?

4. Viewed as a matter of principle, ought consent to be vitiated (a) only where the victim has made a fundamental mistake, or (b) wherever the victim would not have consented had he known the true facts? Cf burglary (p 492, below) where an entry to premises secured by fraud may be regarded as trespassory.

5. Should it be a crime intentionally or recklessly to communicate venereal disease? Or any other disease? See Adrian Lynch, 'Criminal Liability for Transmitting Disease' [1978] Crim LR 612.

Attorney General's Reference (No 6 of 1980) [1980] 2 All ER 1057, Court of Appeal (Lord Lane CJ, Phillips and Drake JJ)

[**Lord Lane CJ** read the following opinion of the court:]

This is a reference to the court by the Attorney General under s 36 of the Criminal Justice Act 1972. The point of law on which the court is asked to give its opinion is as follows:

> 'Where two persons fight (otherwise than in the course of sport) in a public place can it be a defence for one of those persons to a charge of assault arising out of the fight that the other consented to fight?'

The facts out of which the reference arises are these. The respondent, aged 18, and a youth aged 17 met in a public street and argued together. The respondent and the youth decided to settle the argument there and then by a fight. Before the fight the respondent removed his watch and handed it to a bystander for safe keeping and the youth removed his jacket. The respondent and the youth exchanged blows with their fists and the youth sustained a bleeding nose and bruises to his face caused by blows from the respondent.

Two issues arose at the trial: (1) self-defence and (2) consent. The judge directed the jury in part as follows:

> 'Secondly, if both parties consent to a fight then that fight may be lawful. In that respect I disagree with [counsel for the prosecution's] description of the law. It may well be that a fight on the pavement is a breach of the peace or fighting in public or some other offence but it does not necessarily mean that both parties are guilty of an assault. So that if two people decide to fight it out with their fists then that is not necessarily an assault. If they use weapons or something of that nature, other considerations apply. So you have to consider those two matters in this case. Was [the youth] acting in self-defence? Was this a case of both parties agreeing to fight and using only reasonable force?'

Thus the jury were directed that the respondent would, or might, not be guilty of assault if the victim agreed to fight, and the respondent only used reasonable force. The respondent was acquitted.

Leading counsel who appeared for the Attorney General at the hearing of the reference submitted that this direction was incorrect, that the answer to the point of law was No, and that if an act (ordinarily constituting an assault) is unlawful per se no amount of consent can render it lawful. Thus an act committed in public might, he submitted, be an assault, even though it would not be if committed in private, since if committed in public it would be a breach of the peace and for that reason unlawful.

Counsel as amicus curiae drew the attention of the court to the relevant authorities and textbooks. He pointed out that though the conclusions in the cases are reasonably consistent the reasons for them are not.

For convenience we use the word 'assault' as including 'battery', and adopt the definition of James J in *Fagan v Metropolitan Police Comr* [1968] 3 All ER 442 at 445, [1969] 1 QB 439 at 444, namely 'the actual intended use of unlawful force to another person without his consent', to which we would respectfully add 'or any other lawful excuse'.

We think that it can be taken as a starting point that it is an essential element of an assault that the act is done contrary to the will and without the consent of the victim; and it is doubtless for this reason that the burden lies on the prosecution to negative consent. Ordinarily, then, if the victim consents, the assailant is not guilty.

But the cases show that the courts will make an exception to this principle where the public interest requires: see *R v Coney* (1882) 8 QBD 534 (the prize-fight case). The eleven judges were of the opinion that a prize-fight is illegal, that all persons aiding and abetting were guilty of assault, and that the consent of the actual fighters was irrelevant. Their reasons varied as follows: Cave J, that the blow was struck in anger and likely to do corporal hurt, as opposed to one struck in sport, not intended to cause bodily harm; Mathew J, the dangerous nature of the proceedings; Stephen J, what was done was injurious to the public, depending on the degree of force and the place used; Hawkins J, the likelihood of a breach of the peace, and the degree of force and injury; Lord Coleridge CJ, breach of the peace and protection of the public.

The judgment in *R v Donovan* [1934] 2 KB 498, [1934] All ER Rep 207 (beating for the purposes of sexual gratification), the reasoning in which seems to be tautologous, proceeds on a different basis, starting with the proposition that consent is irrelevant if the act complained of is 'unlawful . . . in itself', which it will be if it involves the infliction of bodily harm.

Bearing in mind the various cases and the views of the textbook writers cited to us, and starting with the proposition that ordinarily an act consented to will not constitute an assault, the question is: at what point does the public interest require the court to hold otherwise?

In answering this question the diversity of view expressed in the previous decisions, such as the two cases cited, make some selection and a partly new approach necessary. Accordingly we have not followed the dicta which would make an act (even if consensual) an assault if it occurred in public, on the ground that it constituted a breach of the peace, and was therefore itself unlawful. These dicta reflect the conditions of the times when they were uttered, when there was little by way of an established police force and prize-fights were a source of civil disturbance. Today, with regular policing, conditions are different. Statutory offences, and indeed byelaws, provide a sufficient sanction against true cases of public disorder, as do the common law offences of affray etc. Nor have we followed the Scottish case of *Smart v HM Advocate* 1975 SLT 65, holding the consent of the victim to be irrelevant on a charge of assault, guilt depending on the 'evil intent' of the accused, irrespective of the harm done.

The answer to this question, in our judgment, is that it is not in the public interest that people should try to cause or should cause each other actual bodily harm for no good reason. Minor struggles are another matter. So, in our judgment, it is immaterial whether the act occurs in private or in public; it is an assault if actual bodily harm is intended and/or caused. This means that most fights will be unlawful regardless of consent.

Nothing which we have said is intended to cast doubt on the accepted legality of properly conducted games and sports, lawful chastisement or correction, reasonable surgical interference, dangerous exhibitions etc. These apparent exceptions can be justified as involving the exercise of a legal right, in the case of chastisement or correction, or as needed in the public interest, in the other cases.

Our answer to the point of law is No, but not (as the reference implies) because the fight occurred in a public place, but because, wherever it occurred, the participants would have been guilty of assault (subject to self-defence) if (as we understand was the case) they intended to and/or did cause actual bodily harm.

The point of law referred to us by the Attorney General has revealed itself as having been the subject of much interesting legal and philosophical debate, but it does not seem that the particular uncertainty enshrined in the reference has caused practical inconvenience in the administration of justice during the law few hundred years. We would not wish our judgment on the point to be the signal for unnecessary prosecutions.

Determination accordingly

NOTES AND QUESTIONS

1. In *Donovan* ([1934] All ER Rep 207 at 210) the court said,

'If an act is unlawful in the sense of being in itself a criminal act, it is plain that it cannot be rendered lawful because the person to whose detriment it is done consents to it. No person can licence another to commit a crime. So far as the criminal law is concerned, therefore, where the act charged is itself unlawful, it can never be necessary to prove absence of consent on the part of the person wronged in order to obtain the conviction of the wrongdoer.'

It was this reasoning which Lord Lane considered to be tautologous. But is it any more satisfactory to say that people should not inflict actual bodily harm 'for no good reason'? No doubt purely cosmetic surgery would be accepted as a good reason. But in *Adesanya* (noted in [1983] Crim LR 720) D was convicted of an assault occasioning actual bodily harm where she incised the cheeks of her two sons aged 14 and 9, as she claimed with their consent, in accordance with Nigerian tribal custom. If, however, someone fully and freely consents to such incisions for tribal, cosmetic or religious reasons, why cannot these be good reasons?

2. Commenting on *Clarence* and *Donovan*, Lynch says ([1978] Crim LR 612 at 613):

'1. A has intercourse with B. A knows that he (A) suffers from VD. He does not inform B of this, and B becomes infected. There can be no liability under sections 20 and 47 [of the Offences against the Person Act], as A has not assaulted B (*Clarence*). 2. A has intercourse with B. Prior to intercourse, A informs B that he has VD. B decides to have intercourse and risk becoming infected, arguing that if she does contract it she can easily have it cured. Paradoxically, it may be that A is liable here under section 20 or 47, depending upon whether the variety of VD is classified as [actual bodily harm] or [grievous bodily harm]. This follows from the law's attitude to the 'victim's' fully aware consent to the injury in circumstances which do not meet with social (or judicial) approval (or, at least, meet with positive disapproval).'

Do you agree?

3. *Other defences to offences involving an assault*
Under certain circumstances the use of force on the person of another is justified even though that other does not consent to it. Obvious instances include the use of force incidental to a lawful arrest, p 231, above, and in self-defence and defence of property, p 242, above. It is also lawful for parents to punish

their children, and for a teacher to chastise children in his care; the circumstances in which such punishment may be inflicted and its degree must be governed by standards currently prevailing in the community.

In *Leigh v Gladstone* (1909) 26 TLR 139, a civil action for assault arising from the forcible feeding of a suffragette whilst in prison, Lord Alverstone, CJ, in directing the jury said,

> 'It was the duty, both under the [prison] rules and apart from the rules, of the officials to preserve the health and lives of the prisoners, who were in custody of the Crown . . . If Dr Helby had allowed the plaintiff to fast for a few days longer and she had died in consequence, what answer could he have made? It was said that the treatment had failed. That had nothing to do with the case, for there was evidence that it had been successfully continued in some cases for two and half years, and they [the jury] had heard that two other ladies who were also guilty of this wicked folly—for it was a wicked folly to attempt to starve themselves to death—had completed their full sentences although fed by force'.

The jury, after considering the matter for two minutes, returned a verdict for the defendants.

Rule 17(1) of the Prison Rules, SI 1964/388 provides that 'The medical officer of a prison shall have the care of the health, mental and physical, of the prisoners in that prison'. Suicide is no longer a crime, p 556, below and as to abetting suicide see p 331, above.

Questions

Suppose that a Home Secretary were to amend the Prison Rules and direct that any prisoner who goes on hunger strike was no longer to be forcibly fed. Bloggs, a prisoner, goes on hunger strike and suffers seriously in health. Has any offence been committed by the officials taking no action to prevent this consequence? Would it make any difference to your answer if Bloggs starved himself to death?

2. Assault occasioning actual bodily harm

Offences against the Person Act, s 47, p 546, below

**R v Miller [1954] 2 All ER 529, Winchester Assizes
(Lynskey J)**

The defendant was charged with raping his wife and also with an assault occasioning actual bodily harm.

[Having dealt with the rape charge (see p 392, below) **Lynskey J** continued:]

With regard to the second count, which is a charge of assault occasioning actual bodily harm, the proposition is put forward by counsel for the defence that the defendant, having the right to marital intercourse, is entitled, for the purpose of exercising that right, to use as much force as is reasonably necessary to enable him to do so. I have heard no case cited to support that proposition, but *Jackson* ([1891] 1 QB 671) which was mentioned, is, in my view, rather against it. In that case a husband had obtained an order for the restitution of conjugal rights against his wife, and she was ordered to return to him. She did not return, whereupon the husband, with the assistance of an articled clerk, took possession of the person of the wife and took her off to his house, and thereafter he detained her there. She was allowed the run of the house, but was not allowed to leave the premises. The husband said that he had a right to her society, and that his general rights included the right to marital intercourse, and he claimed that he had a right to do what he did. The wife, or someone on her behalf, took out process for habeas corpus, and the Court of Appeal held that, although the husband had a right to his wife's society, and although he had a decree of the court for the restitution of conjugal rights, he was not entitled to use force for the purpose of enforcing his rights.

It seems to me, on the reasoning of that case, that, although the husband has a right to marital intercourse and the wife cannot refuse her consent, and although, if he does have intercourse against her actual will, it is not rape, nevertheless he is not entitled to use force or violence for the purpose of exercising that right. If he does so, he may make himself liable to the criminal law, not for the offence of rape, but for whatever other offence the facts of the particular case warrant. If he should wound her, he might be charged with wounding or causing actual bodily harm, or he may be liable to be convicted of common assault. The result is that in the present case I am satisfied that the second count is a valid one and must be left to the jury for their decision. The point was taken that there is no evidence of bodily harm. The bodily harm alleged is said to be the result of the defendant's actions, and they were, if the jury accept the evidence, that he threw the wife down three times. There is evidence that afterwards she was in a hysterical and nervous condition, but it is submitted by counsel for the defendant that that is not 'actual bodily harm'. According to Archbold's *Criminal Pleading, Evidence and Practice*, 32nd edn, p 959:

> 'Actual bodily harm includes any hurt or injury calculated to interfere with the health or comfort of the prosecutor . . .'

There was a time when shock was not regarded as bodily hurt, but the day has gone by when that could be said. It seems to me now that, if a person is caused hurt or injury resulting, not in any physical injury, but in an injury to the state of his mind for the time being, that is within the definition of 'actual bodily harm'. On that point I would leave the case to the jury.

Verdict: 'Guilty' on the second count

R v Roberts [1971] 56 Cr App Rep 95, Court of Appeal, Criminal Division (Stephenson LJ, Thompson and Bridge JJ)

The complainant, a woman of twenty-one, agreed to travel with the appellant in his car to a party. She claimed that during the journey he grabbed at her, ordered her to take off her clothes and then started to pull at her coat. She opened the car door and jumped out, and was subsequently treated in hospital for the concussion and grazing which she suffered.

The judgment of the court was delivered by:

Stephenson LJ. . . . . In those circumstances, the jury had to make up their minds, first of all, whether the appellant had indecently assaulted this girl; and after a direction to the jury of which no complaint is made, or could be made, the jury acquitted him, as has been said, on that charge.

Next, they had to consider: was the appellant guilty of an assault occasioning her actual bodily harm? Of course, for that to be established, it had to be established that he was responsible in law and in fact for her injuries caused by leaving in a hurry the moving car, and it is the Chairman's direction with regard to the law on the second count which leads to this appeal . . .

The only question is: was there a misdirection by the Chairman which led them to that conclusion, or compelled that conclusion on their part?—and the way in which that is put in the grounds of appeal which Mr Carus has pursued before us is that the Chairman was wrong in law when he told the jury 'if you are satisfied that he tried to pull off her coat and as a result she jumped out of the moving car, then your verdict is Guilty'. He failed to tell the jury that they must be satisfied that the cause of her injuries was the action of the appellant, and not the fact that she was under the influence of alcohol, or any other reason. Then he goes on to submit that the learned Chairman was wrong in failing to tell the jury that they must be satisfied that the appellant foresaw that she might jump out as a result of his touching her, before they convicted. And there is a complaint, not really pursued in this Court, that the judge failed to direct the jury that they might find the appellant guilty of common assault.

We have been helpfully referred to a number of reported cases, some well over a century old, of women jumping out of windows, or jumping or throwing themselves into a river, as a consequence of threats of violence or actual violence. The most recent case is the case of *Lewis* [1970] Crim LR 647. An earlier case is that of *Beech* (1912) 107 LT 461, which was a case of a woman jumping out of a window and injuring herself and of a man who had friendly relations with her, whom she knew and might have had reason to be afraid of, being prosecuted for inflicting grievous bodily harm upon her, contrary to s 20 of the Offences against the Person Act. In that case the Court of Criminal Appeal (at p 200) approved the direction given by the trial judge in these terms: 'Will you say whether the conduct of the prisoner amounted to a threat of causing injury to this young woman, was the act of jumping the natural consequence of the conduct of the prisoner, and was the grievous bodily harm the result of the conduct of the prisoner?' That, said the Court, was a proper direction as far as the law went, and they were satisfied that there was evidence before the jury of the prisoner causing actual bodily harm to the woman. 'No-one could say,' said Darling J when giving the judgment of the Court, 'that if she jumped from the window it was not a natural consequence of the prisoner's conduct. It was a very likely thing for a woman to do as the result of the threats of a man who was conducting himself as this man indisputably was.'

This Court thinks that that correctly states the law, and that Mr Carus was wrong in submitting to this Court that the jury must be sure that a defendant, who is charged either with inflicting grievous bodily harm or assault occasioning actual bodily harm, must foresee the actions of the victim which result in the grievous bodily harm, or the actual bodily harm. That, in the view of this Court, is not the test. The test is: Was it the natural result of what the alleged assailant said and did, in the sense that it was something that could reasonably have been foreseen as the consequence of what he was saying or doing? As it was put in one of the old cases it had got to be shown to be his act, and if of course the victim does something so 'daft', in the words of the appellant in this case, or so unexpected, not that this particular assailant did not actually foresee it but that no reasonable man could be expected to foresee it, then it is only in a very remote and unreal sense a consequence of his assault, it is really occasioned by a voluntary act on the part of the victim which could not reasonably be foreseen and which breaks the chain of causation between the assault and the harm or injury. . .

The Court has come to the conclusion, after the assistance of the arguments of counsel on both sides, that the judge was right to tell the jury that it was their duty to convict if they accepted the evidence of the girl, and there was no misdirection involved in his telling them just that. For those reasons, the Court finds no misdirection in the summing-up, and nothing in the grounds of complaint made on behalf of the appellant, and this appeal against conviction must be dismissed.

Appeal dismissed

3. Malicious wounding and causing grievous bodily harm

Offences against the Person Act 1861, ss 18 and 20, p 541, below

For the purposes of s 20 a 'wound' requires a breach in the continuity of the whole skin so that a mere abrasion of the skin does not suffice. It extends to a breaking of the continuity of the skin of an inner cavity of the body such as the mouth but it does not extend to an injury which causes the rupture of an internal blood vessel or internal bleeding of some kind: *C (a minor) v Eisenhower* [1984] QB 331, [1983] 3 All ER 230, QB. No doubt 'wound' bears the same meaning within s 18 even though the harm might be relatively trivial whereas other bodily harm must be 'grievous' to fall within the section. Grievous bodily harm means no more and no less than really serious bodily harm: *DPP v Smith* [1961] AC 290, [1960] 3 All ER 161, p 305, above; *Metharam* [1961] 3 All ER 200, CCA. Where s 18 uses the word 'cause' s 20 uses 'inflict'. 'Inflict' might be thought to be narrower than 'cause' (certainly it could not be wider) and there have been two schools of thought about the meaning of 'inflict'. One school held that infliction required an assault. The majority in *Clarence* (p 358, above) thought that D could not be convicted of inflicting grievous bodily harm on his wife because he had not assaulted her. He might have been convicted under s 18 of causing grievous bodily harm since harm may be caused without an assault. The other school of thought was that infliction did not require an assault. In *Wilson and Jenkins* [1984] AC 242, [1983] 3 All ER 448, the House of Lords settled the difference in favour of the latter view. The issue, a procedural one, was whether by virtue of s 6(3) of the Criminal Law Act 1967 (which provides, essentially, that on a charge of offence A, there may be a conviction for offence B if the allegations in A amount to or include the allegations for offence B) a person charged with inflicting grievous bodily harm contrary to s 20 could be convicted of an assault occasioning actual bodily harm. Lord Roskill, with whom all their Lordships agreed, said this (at p 454):

> . . . What, then, are the allegations expressly or impliedly included in a charge of 'inflicting grievous bodily harm'. Plainly that allegation must, so far as physical injuries are concerned, at least impliedly if not indeed expressly, include the infliction of 'actual bodily harm' because infliction of the more serious injuries must include the infliction of the less serious injuries. But does the allegation of 'inflicting' include an allegation of 'assault'? The problem arises by reason of the fact that the relevant English case law has proceeded along two different paths. In one group it has, as has already been pointed out, been held that a verdict of assault was a possible alternative verdict on a charge of inflicting grievous bodily harm contrary to s 20. In the other group grievous bodily harm was said to have been inflicted without any assault having taken place, unless of course the offence of assault were to be given a much wider significance than is usually attached to it. This problem has been the subject of recent detailed analysis in the Supreme Court of Victoria in *R v Salisbury* [1976] VR 452. In a most valuable judgment (I most gratefully acknowledge the assistance I have derived from that judgment in preparing this speech) the full court drew attention, in relation to comparable legislation in Victoria, to the problems which arose from this divergence in the mainstream of English authority. The problem with which your Lordships' House is now faced arose in *R v Salisbury* in a different way from the present appeals. There, the appellant was convicted of an offence against the Victorian equivalent of s 20. He appealed on the ground that the trial judge had refused to leave to the jury the possibility of convicting him on that single charge of assault occasioning actual bodily harm or of common assault. The full court dismissed the appeal on the ground that at common law these latter offences were not 'necessarily included' in the offence of 'inflicting grievous bodily harm'. The reasoning leading to this conclusion is plain ([1976] VR 452 at 461):
>
> > 'It may be that the somewhat different wording of s 20 of the English Act has played a part in bringing about the existence of the two lines of authority in England, but, be that as it may, we have come to the conclusion that, although the word "inflicts" . . . does not have as wide a meaning as the word "causes" . . . the word "inflicts" does have a wider meaning than it would have if it were construed so that inflicting grievous bodily harm always involved assaulting the victim. In our opinion, grievous bodily harm may be inflicted . . . either where the accused has directly and violently "inflicted" it by assaulting the victim, or where the accused has "inflicted" it by doing something, intentionally, which, though it is not itself a direct application of force to the body of the victim, does directly result in force being applied violently to the body of the victim, so that he suffers grievous bodily harm. Hence, the lesser misdemeanours of assault occasioning actual bodily harm and common assault . . . are not necessarily included in the misdemeanour of inflicting grievous bodily harm . . .'
>
> This conclusion was reached after careful consideration of English authorities such as *R v Taylor* (1869) LR 1 CCR 194, *R v Martin* (1881) 8 QBD 54, [1881–5] All ER Rep 699, *R v Clarence* (1888) 22 QBD 23, [1886–90] All ER Rep 133, *R v Halliday* (1889) 61 LT 701, [1886–90] All ER Rep 1028. My Lords, it would be idle to pretend that these cases are wholly consistent with each other, or even that, as in *R v Clarence*, though there was a majority in favour of quashing the conviction then in question, the judgments of those judges among the thirteen present who formed the majority are consistent with each other. Some of these cases were not argued on both sides. Others are very inadequately reported and different reports vary. Thus Stephen J, who was in the majority in *R v Clarence* 22 QBD 23 at 41, [1886–90] All ER Rep 133 at 143, described the infliction of grievous bodily harm in these words:
>
> > 'The words appear to me to mean the direct causing of some grievous injury to the body itself with a weapon, as by a cut with a knife, or without a weapon, as by a blow with the fist, or by pushing a person down. Indeed, though the word "assault" is not used in the

section, I think the words imply an assault and battery of which a wound or grievous bodily harm is the manifest immediate and obvious result. This is supported by *Reg v Taylor* . . .'

But Wills J, also in the majority, was clearly of the view that grievous bodily harm could be inflicted without an assault, as for example, by creating panic. On the other hand, in *R v Taylor*, where the accused was charged on two counts, one under each limb of s 20, the jury convicted him of common assault. Kelly CB said that each count was for an offence which necessarily included an assault, and a verdict of guilty of common assault was upheld. *R v Taylor* is not easy to reconcile with the later cases unless it is to be supported on the basis of the wounding count in the indictment. In *R v Martin*, on the other hand, there was no reference to the issue whether the accused's conduct in creating panic among a theatre audience constituted assault. He did an unlawful act calculated to cause injury and injury was thereby caused. He was thus guilty of an offence against s 20.

My Lords, I doubt whether any useful purpose would be served by further detailed analysis of these and other cases, since to do so would only be to report less felicitously what has already been done by the full court of Victoria in *R v Salisbury*. I am content to accept, as did the full court, that there can be an infliction of grievous bodily harm contrary to s 20 without an assault being committed. . . .

The House of Lords appears to have accepted that grievous bodily harm was 'inflicted' in *Martin* (1881) 8 QBD 54, CCR, where D, shortly before the end of a performance in a theatre, switched out the staircase lights and placed an iron bar across the doorway thus causing injury to patrons in the ensuing panic; and in *Halliday* (1896) 61 LT 701, where D so frightened his wife that in order to escape imminent harm she jumped from a bedroom window and injured herself in the fall. Convictions under s 20 have been upheld where a wife who had locked herself in the matrimonial home broke her legs when she jumped from an upstairs window following D's, her husband's, threats and the sound of breaking glass in another room (*Lewis* [1970] Crim LR 647, CA); and where P, having been threatened by D and others, ran off pursued by the others but not by D, injured his hand when he thrust it through a public house door in seeking refuge (*Cartledge v Allen* [1973] Crim LR 530, DC). While the House of Lords in *Wilson* did not attempt an exhaustive definition of 'inflict' it may be that it is now co-extensive with 'cause'. The *Oxford English Dictionary* gives 'cause' as a meaning of 'inflict'. So can it be said that in *Clarence* D 'inflicted' grievous bodily harm on his wife?

Consider *Mowatt* [1968] 1 QB 421, [1967] 3 All ER 47, which is set out above p 64 (together with the observations thereon in *Grimshaw* [1984] Crim LR 609, p 66, above); and *W (a minor) v Dolbey* [1983] Crim LR 681, which is set out above, p 66.

The intent required for the s 18 offence was considered by the Court of Appeal in *Bryson* [1985] Crim LR 669. Following an altercation outside a pub between the defendant and members of a coach party, the defendant drove off in his car and knocked down four members of the coach party. Three of them were seriously injured and wounded. The defendant claimed that his reclining seat suddenly went back and that his foot slipped from the clutch but there was other evidence tending to show that he had deliberately driven at the men and he was convicted of wounding with intent. The court, though upholding the defendant's conviction by applying the proviso, said this:

. . . Their verdict inevitably implies that the jury rejected the defendant's account completely. Verdicts of at least unlawful wounding had necessarily to follow. The only remaining question was whether the wounding was done with intent to cause grievous bodily harm.

The learned recorder told the jury early in the summing-up that self-defence would be a lawful excuse for wounding, but that it was not suggested on behalf of the appellant; next, that the

Crown had to prove that the driving was deliberate and not accidental. She then instructed the jury, if they came to the conclusion that the wounding was by a deliberate act of the appellant to go on and ask themselves: 'Is it proved that that deliberate act was done with the intention of causing . . . grievous bodily harm, or to translate into more modern language, to do some really serious harm'. An almost exactly similar direction was given at the end of the summing-up. But in both instances the learned recorder added a reference to foreseeability.

It is sufficient to quote the second instance—almost the last words before the jury retired. . . .

> 'If you come to the conclusion that it was a deliberate piece of driving, then you have to ask yourselves the next question, what was the intention of the man who deliberately drove in that way. If you come to the conclusion that it was an intention, either a deliberate intention or an intention in the terms I have told you yesterday of foreseeing that the consequences of his actions would probably result in injury, whether he wished that injury or not, that in law is an intention to cause the harm which happened'.

Forty minutes after their retirement the jury sent a note asking for a written definition of each category. We take that to mean of each type of offence.

With the assistance of counsel the learned recorder drafted three questions. The final result was agreed by counsel. For the second question, which dealt with intent, they used the definition given in paragraph 17–13 of *Archbold*. The first question was to establish whether the appellant was in control of the car and driving it. The second question then reads:

> 'If the answer to (1) is that it is surely proved that he *was* driving, then if he foresaw that the consequence of his driving was that serious harm would probably happen, whether he desired it or not, he intended to cause grievous bodily harm and is guilty of counts 1, 2 and 3'.

The third question deals with the alternative verdict of unlawful wounding and reads:

> 'If the answer to (2) is that you cannot be sure that he foresaw that serious harm would probably result from his driving e g through panic, but nevertheless he foresaw that some physical harm might result, then he is not guilty of wounding with intent to cause grievous bodily harm but guilty of the alternative offences of unlawful wounding.'

[The court referred to *Moloney* [1985] 1 All ER 1025, p 55, above and continued:]

In the present case, the appellant's *motive* may have been panic, whilst his *desire* was to get away from an ugly crowd scene, and his *objective* was to pass the bus and (for all we know) to telephone the police. The appellant did in fact dial '999' as soon as he got home. But what was his *intention?* Did it include doing serious injury to whoever might be in his way on the road?

If that was how the jury might have looked at it, this is a case covered by Lord Bridge . . . when he said:

> 'I do not, of course, by what I have said in the foregoing paragraph, mean to question the necessity, which frequently arises, to explain to a jury that intention is something quite distinct from motive or desire. But this can normally be quite simply explained by reference to the case before the court or, if necessary, by some homely example.'

The vice of the written direction on which the jury reached their verdict in this case is that it equates foresight 'that serious harm would *probably* happen' with intention to cause grievous bodily harm. As a matter of law, following the decision in *R v Moloney*, the step from 'foresight' to 'intention' is one of inference to be taken by the jury. Here the judge took the step herself.

NOTES AND QUESTIONS

1. What is the mens rea of (i) an assault occasioning actual bodily harm contrary to s 47; (ii) malicious wounding contrary to s 20; and (iii) causing grievous bodily harm contrary to s 18?

2. Elliott, 'Frightening a Person into Injuring Himself' [1974] Crim LR 15, 23, concludes that 'where the charge is under section 20, foresight of some harm, albeit of a minor character, is certainly enough; foresight of fear in the victim is probably enough, and foresight of grievous bodily harm is certainly not essential.' Do you agree? See *Flack v Hunt* [1980] Crim LR 44.

3. In the light of recommendations made by the CLRC, the draft Criminal Code restates the law as follows:

74   Intentional serious injury
(1) A person who intentionally causes serious injury to another is guilty of an offence.
(2) A person may be guilty of an offence under subsection (1) if either:
(a) the act causing serious injury is done; or
(b) the serious injury occurs,
within the ordinary limits of criminal jurisdiction.

75   Reckless serious injury
A person who recklessly causes serious injury to another is guilty of an offence.

76   Intentional or reckless injury
A person who intentionally or recklessly causes injury to another is guilty of an offence.

77   Assault
(1) A person who intentionally or recklessly:
(a) applies force to or causes any impact on the body of another, or
(b) causes another to fear that any such force or impact is imminent, without that other's consent or, where the act is likely or intended to cause injury to another, with or without that other's consent, is guilty of an assault.
(2) A person does not commit an offence under subsection (1) by an act done to another with his consent if it is a reasonable act to do in the course of a lawful game, sport, entertainment or medical treatment or is otherwise justified or excused by any provision or rule referred to in section 49.

Would Clarence be guilty of an assault under cl 77, or of an offence under cll 74, 75 or 76?

4. Administering poison etc

Offences against the Person Act 1861, ss 23 and 24, p 542, below

R v Cunningham [1957] 2 All ER 412, Court of Criminal Appeal

The case is set out at p 63, above.

R v Cato [1976] 1 All ER 260, Court of Appeal, Criminal Division
(Lord Widgery CJ, O'Connor and Jupp JJ)

The appellant, with P's consent, administered heroin to him with a syringe causing his death. He was convicted of manslaughter and of an offence under s 23.

Lord Widgery CJ [delivering the judgment of the court, dealt with the conviction for manslaughter, p 337, above, and continued:]

Thus, a number of things have to be proved in order to establish the offence [under s 23] and the two which are relevant to the argument of counsel for Cato are 'maliciously' and 'noxious'. The thing must be a 'noxious thing' and it must be administered 'maliciously'.
    What is a noxious thing, and in particular is heroin a noxious thing? The authorities show that an article is not to be described as noxious for present purposes merely because it has a potentiality for harm if taken in an overdose. There are many articles of value in common use which may be harmful in overdose, and it is clear on the authorities when looking at them that one cannot describe an article as noxious merely because it has that aptitude. On the other hand, if an article is liable to injure in common use, not when an overdose in the sense of an accidental excess is used but is liable to cause injury in common use, should it then not be regarded as a noxious thing for present purposes?

When one has regard to the potentiality of heroin in the circumstances which we read about and hear about in our courts today we have no hesitation in saying that heroin is a noxious thing and we do not think that arguments are open to an accused person in a case such as the present, whereby he may say: 'Well the deceased was experienced in taking heroin: his tolerance was high', and generally to indicate that the heroin was unlikely to do any particular harm in a particular circumstance. We think there can be no doubt, and it should be said clearly, that heroin is a noxious thing for the purposes of s 23.

[The court considered *Cunningham* [1957] 2 All ER 412 at 413 in a passage which is set out above, p 64, and continued:]

No doubt this is correct in the *Cunningham* type of case where the injury to the victim was done indirectly; done, as it was in that case, by the escape of gas making itself felt in the wholly different part of the house. No doubt if the injury to the victim is indirect, then the element of foresight arises and the element of foresight will be taken from the words of Byrne J in *Cunningham*. But these problems do not arise when the act complained of is done directly to the person of the victim, as it was in this case. We think in this case where the act was entirely a direct one that the requirement of malice is satisfied if the syringe was deliberately inserted into the body of Farmer, as it undoubtedly was, and if Cato at a time when he so inserted the syringe knew that the syringe contained a noxious substance. That is enough, we think, in this type of direct injury case to satisfy the requirement of maliciousness.

Appeal dismissed

R v Hill, [1985] Crim LR 384; Court of Appeal Criminal Division transcript from 'Lexis'
(Robert Goff LJ, Mars-Jones and Drake JJ)

The appellant, who admitted he was a homosexual who was attracted to young boys, gave Tenuate Dospan tablets to boys of 13 and 11. These tablets were available only on prescription as slimming tablets and a side effect of them, of which the appellant was aware, was that taken at the wrong time or in excess of the appropriate dose they could cause sleeplessness. The prosecution's case was that the appellant's intention in giving the tablets was to disinhibit the boys so as to cause them to lose their natural reserve and more inclined to do things that otherwise they would not do. One of the boys who stayed with the appellant spent a sleepless night but the appellant made no sexual advances. The appellant was convicted on two counts under s 24 of administering a noxious thing with intent to injure, aggrieve or annoy.

[**Robert Goff LJ** read the judgment of the court:]

. . . Mr Baillie on behalf of the appellant accepted that these Tenuate Dospan tablets were 'a noxious thing' and that the appellant had 'administered or caused that noxious thing to be taken' within the meaning of section 24 of the Offences against the Person Act 1861. The sole remaining issue for the jury to consider was whether the prosecution had proved that the appellant administered the tablets with intent to injure, aggrieve or annoy these two boys.

Although those alternatives appear in the indictment, the argument in the court below was directed solely to an 'intent to injure' and the only ground of appeal relied upon by Mr Baillie before this court was that:

'The learned Judge erred in directing the jury that an intention on the part of the Appellant to keep awake the alleged victims was capable of amounting to an intention to injure.'

There is no doubt that the learned judge did direct the jury in those terms in the course of his summing up. The learned judge referred to the element of intent in these words:

'It is the final element which is very much in point, because what the prosecution have to do is to make you sure that at the time of these tablets were given to the boys the accused man had the intention of causing injury to them.

Now, what does 'causing injury' mean in this sense? It does not mean causing a possible injury as you might cause an injury if you take a knife and you stab somebody and blood spurts all over the place. It does not mean that at all. The injury can be caused to a body externally. It can be caused by making the body malfunction. Injury can be caused by affecting those parts of the body or the metabolism in the body which may make the body function in a way different from that which it normally does.

Of course you might cause injury in the sense of causing harm to somebody if you give them something which keeps them awake. We know from the medical evidence that one of the effects of taking this drug—which is intended as an aid to slimming—is to keep awake the person who takes it. This may be a very important point in this case, because the prosecution say this is the one of the areas of harm which was done to these boys. Obviously the body needs sleep. We all need our sleep every day in order to keep our bodies functioning normally. Nature tells us when the body is in need of rest. Nature tells us that by making us fall asleep quite naturally when the relevant time has come. More particularly, children need more sleep than does an adult because they are expending so much more energy during the day, running about as they do. If the body is persuaded not to fall asleep at the relevant time and it goes on beyond that, expending itself and using up energy to keep awake when normally the body should be asleep, it may well be that you would think that this is causing harm to the body, causing injury to the body in the sense of harm, and that is one of the points suggested by the prosecution.

The other way in which the prosecution suggest that harm was caused to these young boys is that they were disinhibited; in other words, they were made to lose the natural reserve which they have, disinhibited in the sense that they were made to feel lively and on top of the world and more inclined to do things they otherwise would not have done. The prosecution say if somebody administers a substance to a young boy which has that effect, then it is causing harm to him because it is leaving him open to a situation which otherwise would not exist. So the prosecution say there are two forms of harm which were befalling these two young boys. One of them was the fact that they were being kept awake. Secondly they were being disinhibited and, thirdly, say the prosecution, this drug was being administered in a considerable overdose on this occasion.'

Having regard to the earlier part of that passage from his summing up, the judge appears to have directed the jury that an intention to keep these boys awake was by itself sufficient to constitute an intent to injure. There are other passages later in his summing up which are to the same effect. It was the submission of Mr Baillie that this direction was erroneous in point of law.

Mr Baillie's submission raises a point of some little difficulty on the construction of the relevant section, which is section 24 of the Offences Against the Person Act 1861. That section provides as follows: [his Lordship read s 24]. . . .

It is plain that there are a number of elements in the offence created under the section. These are:
(1) The accused must have acted unlawfully and maliciously.
(2) The actus reus of the offence is that the accused must have
—administered to, or caused to be administered to or taken by
—any other person
—any poison or other destructive or noxious thing.
(3) The mens rea is that the accused must have had an intent to injure, aggrieve or annoy such person.

For the purposes of the present case, it is not necessary for us to consider the actus reus; for it is conceded that the tablets in question did constitute noxious things within the section, and that the accused had administered them to the boys or caused them to be taken by the boys. Furthermore, this court has already given guidance on the meaning of the words 'noxious thing' in *R v Marcus* [1981] 1 WLR 774. It is enough for present purposes to record that, in that case, a wide meaning was given to those words. In particular, it was held that it is not necessary that the substance in question should be injurious to bodily health; the word 'noxious' is, in its context, wide enough to embrace things which, though not injurious to health, are objectionable or unwholesome. Furthermore, in considering whether the thing in question is noxious, 'the jury has to consider the very thing which on the facts is administered or sought to be administered both as to quality and to quantity.'

Nor do we have to consider, on this appeal, the requirement that the accused must have acted unlawfully. However, since the two boys appear to have willingly swallowed the tablets in question, we think it right to observe that, in our opinion, the expression 'unlawfully' here bears its ordinary meaning of without lawful justification or excuse; and that, in ordinary circumstances, the consent of the person to whom the thing is administered will render the act lawful. However, this will not be so if, for example, the act itself is such that consent will not render it lawful (see *R v Cato* [1976] 1 WLR 110) or where the person is too young to give his or her consent.

With these preliminary observations, we turn to the meaning of the words 'with intent to injure, aggrieve or annoy', and in particular the words 'with intent to injure', upon which the judge concentrated when directing the jury in the present case.

We have no doubt that, in considering whether in any particular case the accused acted 'with intent to injure', it is necessary to have regard not merely to his intent upon the person to whom it is administered, but to his whole object in acting as he has done. The accused may, in one case, administer the noxious thing with the intent that it would itself injure the person in question; but in another case he may have an ulterior motive, as for example when he administers a sleeping pill to a woman with an intent to rape her when she is comatose. In either case he will, in our judgment, have an intent to injure the person in question, within the words in the section. By way of contrast, if a husband puts a sleeping draught in his wife's nightcap, without her knowledge, because he is worried that she has been sleeping badly and wishes to give her a decent night's sleep, he will commit no offence. So, in each case it is necessary to ask the question: Did the accused have the intention, in administering the noxious thing, to injure the person in question? And in each case it is necessary to look, not just at his intention as regards the immediate effect of the noxious thing upon that person, but at the whole object of the accused. If his intention, so understood, is that the noxious thing should itself injure the person in question, then that is enough; but it will also be enough if he has an ulterior motive that the person should, as a result of taking the noxious thing, suffer injury. Within this latter category there will, in our judgment, fall those cases where the accused intends, in administering the noxious thing, thereby to achieve or facilitate an act of unlawful sexual interference with the person in question—unlawful, either because it is not consented to (as, for example, in the case of rape), or because the law forbids it (as, for example, in the case of sexual intercourse with girls under the age of 16, or of unlawful homosexual activity). In such cases the accused does, we consider, have an intent to injure the person in question within the meaning of those words in the section.

While holding that such intent falls within the words 'intent to injure' in the section, we do not think it necessary or right to attempt to attach a definitive meaning to those words in this judgment. It may very well be that if, for example, the accused administers a sleeping pill to a person with a view to stealing his property while he is asleep, he will have an intent to injure that person, for the purposes of the section, in the sense of an intent to deprive him of his property. Such an attempt appears to us, at first sight, to fall more naturally within the words 'intent to injure' than the words 'intent to aggrieve' appear to be directed to cases where the intention is to cause distress, and to deprive another person of his property is, we incline to think not merely distressing, but also injurious to the victim. But we need to express no final opinion on the point, which does not arise in the present case, and on which we have heard no argument. We mention it only to show that our decision is intended to indicate that certain categories of case fall within the words 'intent to injure', rather than to provide a complete definition of those words.

Turning to the judge's direction to the jury in the present case, we feel driven to hold that it was not correct in law to direct the jury that an intent to keep a person awake constitutes of itself an intent to injure within the section, any more than it would be correct in law to direct a jury that intent to cause a person to fall asleep constitutes of itself an intent to injure. If that were right, a husband who, with every good intention, slips a sleeping pill into his wife's cup of tea at night to give her a good night's sleep, will commit a criminal offence. We cannot think that that is the law. It is necessary, as we have already indicated, to direct the jury to have regard to the whole object of the accused in order to consider whether, on the facts of the particular case, the accused did intend to injure the person in question; but the mere fact that the accused intended that that person should be kept awake, or should fall asleep, is not of itself necessarily enough. It follows that we accept Mr Baillie's submission that, in the present case, there was a material misdirection to the jury on this point.

We recognise that, on the evidence in the present case, it was open to the jury to convict the appellant on the basis that he administered the tablets to the boys with the intention of injuring them, in that he intended to disinhibit them and thereby facilitate indulgence in unlawful homosexual activity with them. This was, as we understand it, one of the two alternative ways in which the case was left to the jury by the judge. Had this been the only way in which he did so, his summing up would not have been left open to criticism; but as he left the case to the jury on two alternative bases, one of which was correct in law and the other was not, we cannot tell on which basis the jury decided to convict the appellant, and it follows that his conviction cannot stand.

For these reasons, the appeal will be allowed and the conviction will be quashed.

Appeal allowed, conviction quashed

NOTES AND QUESTIONS

1. In *Weatherall* [1968] Crim LR 115 (Judge Brodrick), D administered Tuinal to his wife to make her sleep more soundly so that he could search her handbag for letters which he thought might prove her guilty of adultery. The judge ruled that there was no evidence of an intent to annoy or aggrieve. Can the ruling stand with *Hill*?

2. Suppose that when Cunningham (p 63, above) pulled the gas meter from the wall he had realised that the gas would escape into the adjoining house but had thought that the occupants would be no more than mildly discomfited. Could he be convicted of the offences under s 23 and s 24?

3. Does it make sense for the purposes of s 23 to draw, as was done in *Cato*, a distinction between injuries directly and indirectly done? Where the injury is directly done, in what precise respect does Lord Widgery see the mens rea as differing from a case where the injury is caused indirectly?

5. Assaults etc on constables

Police Act 1964, s 51, p 558, below

(1) ACTING IN THE EXECUTION OF DUTY

English law contains no comprehensive statement of a constable's duties. In the form of attestation required of all constables (Police Act 1964, Sch 2) the constable declares that he will 'cause the peace to be kept and prevent all offences against the persons and properties of Her Majesty's subjects'. But this is only a statement of his primary duties and in order to effect these (cf *Final Report of the Royal Commission on the Police*, Cmnd 1728, 1962, para 57) he has ancillary duties to investigate crime, to question witnesses and suspects, to preserve evidence, to execute warrants of search and arrest and so on. The Royal Commission concluded that the police 'have by long tradition a duty to befriend anyone who needs their help' but the relevant duty must relate to something which the constable is by law required, authorised or empowered to do; it can hardly be supposed that a constable is legally obliged to tell the time to a passer-by. But a constable on beat duty does not cease to be acting in the execution of his duty because he pauses to tell someone the time.

Coffin v Smith (1980) 71 Cr App Rep 221, Queen's Bench Division
(Donaldson LJ and Bristow J)

Two police constables were summoned to a boys' club by the youth leader. A disco, to which entry was restricted, was about to start and the youth leader was anxious that people not invited, including the defendants, should leave the premises. Outside the club the defendants were told by the police to move on. Their response was to become abusive and then to assault the constables. It was accepted that up to this stage no criminal offence had been committed inside or outside the club. The justices upheld a submission of no case to answer on the grounds that the constables were not acting in the execution of their duty.

Donaldson LJ. . . . .I am bound to say, speaking for myself, that when I read this case through overnight, I regarded this decision as prima facie perverse and incomprehensible. We have had the advantage today of very full argument from Mr Staddon, for the defendants, who plainly considers, and quite firmly considers, that this case raises an issue of considerable constitutional importance. I can well understand the justices, having been told that there was such an issue involved here and having been exposed to the skill with which his arguments were no doubt deployed there as they were deployed before us, reaching the decision that they did reach. I remain however of opinion that it was wholly and completely wrong. Let me justify that.

The whole basis of Mr Staddon's argument is that a police officer is not in the execution of his duty if he is doing something that he is not compelled by law to do. He relies upon two old cases. The first is *Prebble and Others* (1858) 1 F & F 325, a *nisi prius* decision briefly reported. There the prisoners were indicted for assaulting a constable in the execution of his duty, and also for common assault. It appears that some persons were drinking at a late hour of the night in a barn attached to a public house and the landlord desired the constable to clear them out. While he was doing so the prisoners assaulted him.

In the words of Bramwell B at pp 325, 326

> 'The people were doing nothing illegal, nor contrary to any Act of Parliament, and there-fore the constable was not acting in the execution of his duty as such, although what he did may have been very laudable and proper. It would have been otherwise had there been a nuisance or disturbance of the public peace, or any danger of a breach of the peace.'

The second is *Roxburgh* (1871) 12 Cox CC 8, a decision of Cockburn J. It appears from the report that

> 'The prisoner had been drinking at a public house and was so much the worse for liquor that the publican desired to get him out and called in a constable. The man had wanted to go to bed, and the publican had assented to this, but the man desired a light, with which, on account of his condition, the publican refused to entrust him. Thereupon the prisoner said he would leave, and then said he would not, and upon this the publican desired the prosecutor to assist in ejecting him which he attempted to do. In resisting him the prisoner inflicted a serious injury, for which he was indicted. The defence was, that the violence used by the prosecutor was unlawful, as he had no right to use force to eject the prisoner, and was acting beyond his duty in doing so. . . .'

Cockburn J. said at p 9 that

> 'although, no doubt, the prosecutor might not have been acting—strictly speaking—in the execution of his duty as a police officer, since he was not actually obliged to assist in ejecting the prisoner, yet he was acting quite lawfully in doing so; for the landlord had a right to eject the prisoner under the circumstances, and the prosecutor might lawfully assist him in so doing.'

It must of course be appreciated that those decisions were under a different statute, slightly differently worded. They are authorities supporting the proposition for which Mr Staddon contended, but I do not for my part think that they can be regarded as good law today. The modern law on the subject is, I think, to be found in two different cases. The first is a decision of the Court of Criminal Appeal, *Waterfield and Lynn* (1963) 48 Cr App R 42; [1964] 1 QB 164, where Ashworth J delivering the judgment of the Court, at p 47 and 170 respectively said:

> 'In the judgment of this court it would be difficult, and in the present case it is unnecessary, to reduce within specific limits the general terms in which the duties of police constables have been expressed. In most cases it is probably more convenient to consider what the police constable was actually doing and in particular whether such conduct was prima facie an unlawful interference with a person's liberty or property. If so, it is then relevant to consider whether (a) such conduct falls within the general scope of any duty imposed by statute or recognised at common law and (b) whether such conduct, albeit within the general scope of such a duty, involved an unjustifiable use of powers associated with the duty.'

Applying that basis, it is quite clear that these constables were on duty, they were in uniform, and they were not doing anything which was prima facie any unlawful interference with a person's liberty or property.

Further guidance on the scope of the police officer's duty in this context is I think to be derived from the judgment of Lord Parker CJ in *Rice v Connolly* [1966] 2 QB 414, and the passage to which I would like to refer is at p 419:

'It is also in my judgment clear that it is part of the obligations and duties of a police constable to take all steps which appear to him necessary for keeping the peace, for preventing crime or for protecting property from criminal injury. There is no exhaustive definition of the powers and obligations of the police, but they are at least those, and they would further include the duty to detect crime and to bring an offender to justice.'

In a word a police officer's duty is to be a keeper of the peace and to take all necessary steps with that in view. These officers, just like the ordinary officer on the beat, were attending a place where they thought that their presence would assist in the keeping of the peace. I know that Mr Staddon says 'Oh no, this is all part and parcel of the assistance which they gave to the youth leader in ejecting these people.' Even if that was so, they would have been doing no more than a police officer's duty in all the circumstances. In fact it is clear that there was a break. Both the respondents went away and came back. The officers were in effect simply standing there on their beat in the execution of their duty when they were assaulted. This is a very clear case indeed. . . .

[**Bristow J** agreed.]

Appeal allowed. Case not remitted.

In *Waterfield* [1964] 1 QB 164, [1963] 3 All ER 659, CCA, P, a constable, had been informed that a car had been involved in a serious offence. Acting on the instructions of a superior officer, he attempted to prevent D, the owner of the car, from removing it from the place on the road where it was parked. D drove the car at P, thus assaulting him, in order to remove it. The court held that P was not 'entitled' to prevent removal of the car and therefore was not acting in the execution of his duty. The difficulty with the case is that the judgment nowhere specifies in what respect P's act was unlawful. Cf P.J. Fitzgerald [1965] Crim LR 23 at 34:

'In this case the court held that preventing the removal of [D's] car was not an act in the execution of [P's] duty, on the ground that it was an act which he was not entitled to do . . . [T]his latter proposition is only true if [P's] act was either criminal or tortious and it is not clear that it was either.'

Perhaps another way to look at *Waterfield* is to ask what did D do that was unlawful? A citizen has no general legal duty to assist the police, and D may have done no more than use reasonable force to do what he was entitled to do, namely, drive away in his car.

The actual decision in *Waterfield* may be affected by the coming into force of the Police and Criminal Evidence Act 1984. Under this Act police are given powers to seize anything that is evidence in relation to an offence and it is necessary to seize it to prevent it being concealed, lost, altered or destroyed. Thus if the car bore evidence of a collision implicating D in reckless driving, the police might lawfully seize the car to prevent the evidence being removed.

In *Betts v Stevens* [1910] 1 KB 1, DC, it was held that constables who were operating a speed trap were acting in the execution of their duty so that the appellant, who had been warning approaching motorists of the existence of the trap, was properly convicted of obstructing the police. It was argued by the appellant that the police had no statutory or common law duty to collect evidence relating to offences which they thought to have been committed. Lord Alverstone CJ, said that

'where you have got the evidence of a superior officer, and the superior officer telling the policeman to do certain things . . . it seems to me impossible to say that, because the statute does not expressly say that the policeman may use the particular means for obtaining the required evidence that he does use, it is not his duty to obtain it by those means, and that the person who frustrates him . . . is not guilty of obstructing him in the execution of his duty.'

These five police officers,' said Bucknill J, 'were on duty in the ordinary sense of that term, and their duty was to act together and assist each other in obtaining proof of the speed of certain cars which were travelling on the road.'

Clearly a constable cannot be acting in the execution of his duty where his act is unlawful since it cannot be his duty to do an unlawful act. Hence a constable is not acting in the execution of his duty where he challenges someone to a fight: *Whiteside v Gamble* [1968] Crim LR 560.

Donnelly v Jackman [1970] 1 All ER 987, Queen's Bench Division (Lord Parker CJ, Ashworth and Talbot JJ)

[**Talbot J** delivered the first judgment at the invitation of **Lord Parker CJ**:]

. . . The facts found by the justices were these; at about 11.15 am on Saturday, 5 April, the appellant was lawfully walking along a pavement when PC Roy Grimmett in uniform came up to him for the purposes of making enquiries about an offence which the officer had cause to believe the appellant had committed or might have committed. The officer spoke to the appellant asking him if he could have a word with him. The appellant ignored that request, and continued to walk along the pavement away from the officer. The officer followed close behind him, and apparently repeatedly asked him to stop and speak to him. At one stage the officer tapped the appellant on the shoulder, and apparently shortly after that the appellant turned round and in turn tapped the officer on the chest saying 'Now we are even, copper?'

It became apparent to the officer, so the finding proceeds, that the appellant had no intention of stopping to speak to him. The officer then again touched the appellant on the shoulder with the intention of stopping him, whereupon the appellant then turned round and struck the officer with some force. The finding is that the officer did not touch the appellant for the purpose of making any formal arrest or charge, but solely for the purpose of speaking to him. Following the striking of the officer, the appellant was arrested for assaulting the officer in the execution of his duty and taken to the police station. The justices convicted the appellant, finding the summons proved.

The principal question it seems to me is whether the officer was acting in the execution of his duty, and a secondary question, whether anything he did caused him to cease to be acting in the execution of his duty. When considering what the duties of the officer were, I do not think that I can do better than cite the words of Lord Parker CJ, in *Rice v Connolly* [[1966] 2 QB 414 at 419; [1966] 2 All ER 649 at 651], when he said:

> 'It is also in my judgment clear that it is part of the obligations and duties of a police constable to take all steps which appear to him necessary for keeping the peace, for preventing crime or for protecting property from criminal injury.'

Furthermore, in considering the problem whether the officer went outside the ambit of his duties so as to be ceasing to be acting therein, I would refer to the words of Ashworth J taken from *Waterfield, Lynn* [[1964] 1 QB 164 at 170; [1963] 3 All ER 659 at 661; p 374, above], and this is the way it was put:

> 'In the judgment of this court it would be difficult, and in the present case it is unnecessary, to reduce within specific limits the general terms in which the duties of police constables have been expressed. In most cases it is probably more convenient to consider what the police constable was actually doing and in particular whether such conduct was prima facie an unlawful interference with a person's liberty or property. If so, it is then relevant to consider whether (a) such conduct falls within the general scope of any duty imposed by statute or recognised at common law and (b) whether such conduct, albeit within the general scope of such a duty, involved an unjustifiable use of powers associated with the duty.'

The main point taken by counsel for the appellant is that the result of what the officer did was such that he was not acting in the execution of his duty. He had, argued counsel, no right to stop the appellant or any other person other than by arrest. In support of his argument he cited several authorities in which officers, whilst it is alleged acting in the execution of their duties, had been assaulted, in which the court had found that in fact that was not so, they were not acting in the execution of their duties. The first one was *Davis v Lisle* [[1936] 2 KB 434; [1936] 2 All ER 213].

That was a case where a police officer, taking these facts from the headnote, believing that an offence had been committed by the servant of the appellant of causing an obstruction on the highway with a motor lorry, was making enquiries, and he went to the appellant's garage and he went into the garage. The appellant asked him to leave and as a result of not leaving he was assaulted. It was held that even if the respondent police officer had a right to go into the garage and make enquiries he became a trespasser after he had been told to leave, and henceforward was not acting in the execution of his duty.

That seems to me a very different case from the present one which we are considering. There the police officer had gone so far as to make himself a trespasser. The other authority quoted by counsel for the appellant was *Kenlin v Gardiner* [[1967] 2 QB 510; [1966] 3 All ER 931]. There two schoolboys apparently were visiting a number of premises and caused certain police officers to be suspicious; the police officers therefore went up to make enquiries, they said that they were police officers and asked the boys what they were calling on these houses for. Apparently the boys were acting perfectly innocently and had a perfectly lawful reason for what they were doing. However, the upshot of it was that they became alarmed and the police officers seized them by arms, with the result that these boys retaliated and assaulted the police officers. There again in my judgment the facts of that case are vastly different from those that we are considering because there each officer had taken hold of one of the boys and had in fact detained him.

Turning to the facts of this matter, it is not very clear what precisely the justices meant or found when they said that the officer touched the appellant on the shoulder, but whatever it was that they really did mean, it seems clear to me that they must have felt that it was a minimal matter by the way in which they treated this matter and the result of the case. When one considers the problem: was this officer acting in the course of his duty, in my view one ought to bear in mind that it is not every trivial interference with a citizen's liberty that amounts to a course of conduct sufficient to take the officer out of the course of his duties. In my judgment the facts that the justices found in this case do not justify the view that the officer was not acting in the execution of his duty when he went up to the appellant and wanted to speak to him. Therefore the assault was rightly found to be an assault on the officer whilst acting in the execution of his duties, and I would dismiss this appeal.

Ashworth J. I agree.

Lord Parker CJ. I agree.

Appeal dismissed

NOTES AND QUESTIONS

1. Do you agree with the court in *Donnelly v Jackman* that the facts of *Kenlin v Gardiner* were 'vastly different'? Cf David Lanham [1974] Crim LR 288 at 292,

> 'If the defendant in *Donnelly v Jackman* had gently brushed the police officer aside, would he have been guilty of any offence? If not could the police officer have continued to pursue him tapping him, at technical intervals, trivially on the shoulder until he had his undivided attention? Could the policeman . . . follow him to his home and remain there, taking care that his trespasses were trivial, until his questions were answered? Can the defendant in such cases continue to resist each trivial trespass with the minimum force necessary? Is there a stage at which a number of trivial trespasses amount to a substantial trespass?'

Consider *Bentley v Brudzinski* [1982] Crim LR 825, DC, which is factually very similar to *Donnelly v Jackman*. P, a constable, who was looking for a stolen vehicle, stopped two barefoot runners, D and E. They stayed, reluctantly but voluntarily, with P for some ten minutes while he made some abortive inquiries. They then decided to go home but as they made to go P signalled to another officer, Q, who had just appeared on the scene and who knew nothing of what had transpired, that he wished to talk to D. When Q placed his hand on D's shoulder to attract his attention, D hit him. The court agreed with the justices finding that D had no case to answer. The justices were entitled to find as a matter of fact (is it a matter of fact?) that the interference with D's liberty was sufficient to take the constable's act outside the scope of his duties. The act of Q here was really P's act since Q was ignorant of what had happened and had acted as P's agent. So how trivial is trivial? Is it clear that Q was not acting in the execution of his duty? He arrived on the scene in the course of his duties, received what to all appearances was a reasonable request from a fellow officer that he wanted a word with D and tapped D on the shoulder to attract his attention. What's wrong with that?

2. Suppose that in *Coffin v Smith* D and E were still in the club when the police arrived but were refusing to leave, thereby constituting themselves trespassers. The police, using no more force than necessary, then help the club's youth leader to evict them? Is it clear that the police are acting in the execution of their duty if no breach of the peace is anticipated?

3. Is a constable acting in the execution of his duty whenever he is (i) on duty; or (ii) acting under the orders of a superior officer; or (iii) both?

(2) THE MEANING OF OBSTRUCTION

Green v Moore [1982] 1 All ER 428, Queen's Bench Division (Donaldson LJ and Skinner J)

[**Donaldson LJ** read the following judgment of the court:]

This appeal is concerned with a conflict between two principles. The first is that the prevention of crime is to be encouraged and is certainly not an activity which is contrary to law. The second is that it is illegal to obstruct the police acting in the execution of their duty.

The facts were highly unusual. The respondent was a probationer constable of the Gwent Constabulary. He was also a 'regular' at the Castle Hotel, Chepstow. In the latter capacity he was aware that the landlord did not give a high priority to the strict observance of licensing hours, although the respondent denied that he himself ever drank after hours. The landlord had also assisted him from time to time in the line of police duty by providing him with information.

On 27 June 1980, a police support group with the appellant, Sgt Moore, in charge visited Chepstow with a view to investigating the manner in which the licensee of the Castle Hotel conducted his premises and his observance or otherwise of licensing hours. In furtherance of this investigation, Pc Davies of the support group went into the bar of the Castle Hotel during licensing hours. He was in plain clothes and was to remain there until after hours if drinking continued so long. In this event he was to leave the premises at 11.45 pm, thus enabling uniformed officers to enter through the door by which he left.

At about 10 pm the appellant asked a local police officer, Pc Pidgeon, to be near the Castle Hotel at 11.45 pm. Shortly afterwards Pc Pidgeon met the respondent and, according to the respondent, told him that the support group was in the area and suggested by a nod and a wink that the respondent should acquaint the landlord of the Castle Hotel of the support group's activities. Whether this account of the part played by Pc Pidgeon is true is immaterial. Suffice it to say that at about 10.30 pm, and well before closing time, the respondent went to the Castle Hotel, sent for the landlord to come outside and told him that the support group was in Chepstow.

What happened next was predictable. There was a marked change in the attitude of staff and customers inside the hotel towards Pc Davies, who was a stranger. Previously it had been very amiable. Thereafter it was not. Furthermore the landlord adhered strictly to the licensing laws permitting drinking only until 11 pm with ten minutes for drinking up and the bar was clear by 11.15 pm.

The respondent was charged and convicted by the Cwmbran magistrates of wilfully obstructing the appellant and other officers of the Gwent Constabulary support group acting in the execution of their duty, contrary to s 51(3) of the Police Act 1964.

He appealed to the Crown Court at Newport and his appeal was heard by his Honour Judge Hopkin Morgan QC and justices. He was successful and the police now appeal to this court by case stated.

Let me at once pay tribute to the wholly admirable reserved judgment of the judge which has been of the greatest assistance. He analysed all the cases and came to the conclusion that for this offence to be made out it was essential for the prosecution to prove that at the time when the alleged obstruction took place the person helped by that obstruction was in the course of committing or had already committed an offence. This conclusion was based on the decisions of this court in *Bastable v Little* [1907] 1 KB 59 and *Betts v Stevens* [1910] 1 KB 1. On the facts of the instant case, no offence had been committed at the time of the alleged obstruction. The judge also concluded that at that time the members of the support group were not acting in the execution of their duty. They were not going to be so acting until, and unless, at 11.45 pm they had reason to enter the hotel to investigate a suspected breach of the licensing laws.

Bastable v Little is the earliest in the relevant line of the cases. It has elements which seem idiosyncratic today. Thus Lord Alverstone CJ said (at 62):

> 'Suppose a party of men are engaged in the offence of night poaching, and a person passing near warns them that the police are coming, I think it is clear that that could not be held to be an offence within this section. We must not allow ourselves to be warped by any prejudice against motor cars, and so strain the law against them.'

The offence charged was obstructing constables in the execution of their duty as such constables, contrary to s 2 of the Prevention of Crimes Amendment Act 1885. The police had set up a series of speed traps in London Road, Croydon. Mr Little occupied himself giving warning signals to drivers approaching the traps, thus ensuring that they did not exceed the speed limit. The ratio of the decision is without doubt that there was no evidence that the drivers were exceeding the speed limit at the time when they received Mr Little's signals, although all slowed down. Darling J made this point and added (at p 63):

> 'In my opinion it is quite easy to distinguish the cases where a warning is given with the object of preventing the commission of a crime from the cases in which the crime is being committed and the warning is given in order that the commission of the crime should be suspended while there is danger of detection, with the intention that the commission of the crime should be re-commenced as soon as the danger of detection is past.'

In *Betts v Stevens* the facts were indistinguishable from those in *Bastable v Little*, save that (a) the cars were exceeding the speed limit of 20 mph when they received the warning which was given by an Automobile Association patrolman, and (b) police officers were observing the cars at the place where the warning was given and the speed trap was intended to provide confirmatory evidence of their opinion that the speed limit had been exceeded. The patrolman was convicted. The court distinguished *Bastable v Little* on the ground that, contrary to the position in *Bastable's* case, the motorists were exceeding the speed limit before they entered the measured distance and that the action of the patrolman prevented the police from obtaining confirmatory evidence by timings over that distance. Both Darling and Bucknill JJ, the former expressly and the latter impliedly, stated that the gist of the offence lay in the intention with which the acts complained of were done. If the intention was simply to prevent the commission of crime, no offence was committed. It was otherwise if the intention was to prevent the commission of crime only at a time when there was a danger of detection.

The judge was also referred to and considered three other authorities. One was *R v Britton* [1973] RTR 502. A motorist was exceeding the speed limit and a police constable signalled him to stop. He did not do so and a high speed chase ensued. Eventually the motorist reached his home and dashed inside, but not before the police officer had called out a requirement that he provide a specimen of breath. On entering the house the motorist asked his mother to impede the entry of the police until such time as he had consumed a bottle of beer. This ploy was successful in the sense that it then became impossible to carry through the breathalyser procedure. However, the motorist was charged with the offence of attempting to defeat the course of justice. He was convicted on indictment and appealed to the Court of Appeal, Criminal Division. In giving the judgment of the court, Lord Widgery CJ said (at 507):

> '[Counsel for the defendant] in reply has said that if [counsel for the Crown's] formulation of the principle is right, it will take the scope of this offence to unacceptable limits. He cites the case of the motorist leaving a public house, seeing a police officer standing outside, the going back to warn all those in the public house that they had better either walk home or defer their departure until the police officer has gone. I do not for a moment accept that that conduct is criminal *within the terms of the offence with which we are presently dealing*, and we draw a distinction between that case and the present by pointing out that the statutory course upon which justice had embarked in the present

case had not been embarked upon in [counsel for the defendant's] example.' (Our emphasis.)

We do not think that *R v Britton* assists. Lord Widgery CJ advisedly limited his remarks to the offence of attempting to defeat the course of justice and, in that context, it is understandable that no offence can be committed until circumstances have arisen in which it can be said that justice has embarked on a course.

The second authority was *Hinchliffe v Sheldon* [1955] 3 All ER 406, [1955] 1 WLR 1207. The son of the licensee of a public house returned after closing time and warned his parents that the police were outside. He told them: 'Make sure you are clear before you open the door.' The son was convicted of wilfully obstructing a constable in the execution of his duty, notwithstanding that it was not proved that any offence had been committed by the licensee although there were obviously ample grounds for suspicion. The judge distinguished that authority on the basis that in the instant case no offence could have been committed, because the tip-off was given before the expiration of licensing hours. With respect, that is not entirely accurate since it is quite possible to commit offences during licensing hours, for example, by serving drink to those who are drunk or by giving short measure.

Finally, the judge was referred to and considered *Rice v Connolly* [1966] 2 All ER 649 at 651, [1966] 2 QB 414 at 419 where Lord Parker CJ said:

> 'What the prosecution have to prove is that there was an obstructing of a constable, that the constable was at the time acting in the execution of his duty, and that the person obstructing did so wilfully. To carry the matter a little further, it is in my view clear that "obstruct" in s 51(3) [of the Police Act 1964] is to do any act which makes it more difficult for the police to carry out their duty. That description of obstructing I take from the case of *Hinchliffe v Sheldon*. It is also in my judgment clear that it is part of the obligations and duties of a police constable to take all steps which appear to him to be necessary for keeping the peace, for preventing crime or for protecting property from criminal injury. There is no exhaustive definition of the powers and obligations of the police, but they are at least those, and they would further include the duty to detect crime and to bring an offender to justice.'

Judge Hopkin Morgan concluded his judgment by saying:

> 'Our basic concern is *Bastable v Little*. We can see no reason why, or even how, we could distinguish it, as Mr Eccles urged. We can see no reason why the principle expressed in that case should not apply to the present appeal. It is a fact, as far as counsel have been able to establish (and I know that they worked hard on this) that no later case has criticised the decision given in *Bastable v Little*. Accordingly, we are of the view that the law is that the person helped by the alleged obstruction must, at the time of the alleged obstruction, be in the course of committing, or must have already committed, an offence. That was not the situation here. At 10.30 that night, the landlord of the Castle Hotel did not commit an offence, and could not have committed an offence, against licensing laws.'

If *Bastable v Little* has never yet been criticised, this is a situation which is capable of being remedied. It seems to us to be a very curious decision based on a highly eccentric view of the facts. The decision seems to have proceeded on the basis that prior to the warning the motorists concerned had not exceeded the speed limit and that the warning was intended to discourage them from ever so doing. If that were indeed the position, we would agree that no offence was committed. Far from obstructing the police in the execution of their duty, Mr Little would have been assisting them in one of their most important duties, namely, crime prevention. But a more realistic view of the facts is that the warning was based on a lively anticipation that even if the motorists were not then exceeding the speed limit, they were likely to do so over the measured distance and the warning was intended to discourage them from doing so until after they had passed out of the area of the police trap. However, the court never considered that hypothesis. We cannot see any distinction between a warning given in order that the commission of a crime may be suspended whilst there is danger of detection, which is an offence (see *Betts v Stevens*) and one which is given in order that the commission of a crime may be postponed until after the danger of detection has passed. We are, of course, bound by *Bastable v Little* and it must be left to others to consider overruling it. However, it is an authority which, in our judgment, should be strictly confined to the facts as the court found them.

In our view the law requires a court which is considering a charge of wilfully obstructing a police officer in the execution of his duty to ask itself the three questions propounded by Lord Parker CJ in *Rice v Connolly* [1966] 2 All ER 649 at 651, [1966] 2 QB 414 at 419:

1. *Was there any obstruction of a constable?*

Pc Davies who was in the bar of the hotel to observe how the landlord normally conducted his business was quite plainly obstructed in the execution of that duty because, as was clear from the changed attitude of staff and customers, the tip-off created a changed situation. Similarly, the rest of the support group were obstructed because they were deprived of the opportunity of seeing whether, in normal circumstances, the landlord would observe the statutory closing hours. The obstruction was none the less an obstruction because it was so successful that the group had to abandon their intended activity before closing time.

2. *Was the constable acting lawfully in the execution of his duty?*

Pc Davies was clearly acting lawfully in the execution of his duty. The fallacy in the judge's reasoning, induced by *Bastable v Little*, was to think that the only lawful duty of a constable is to detect offences which are being or have been committed. Police constables maintain the Queen's peace in many different ways besides by criminal investigation. They patrol beats. They direct traffic. Is it really to be said that a police constable on point duty is not acting in the execution of his duty and that someone who wilfully obstructs his field of vision is not obstructing him in the execution of that duty? Of course not.

The other members of the support group were also acting lawfully in the execution of their duty whilst cruising round Chepstow and would have been so acting in keeping close observation on the hotel at and after closing time.

3. *Was the obstruction intended to obstruct the constables in the execution of their duty?*

The distinction between action which is and action which is not intended to obstruct a constable in the execution of his duty is well illustrated by the facts in *Willmott v Atack* [1976] 3 All ER 794, [1977] 1 QB 498. Mr Willmott got in the way of police officers trying to force an arrested man to get into a police car and thereby quite clearly obstructed them. His purpose was, however, to assist the police by persuading the man to go quietly. He was acquitted. However, on the facts of the present case, it is quite clear that the respondent's intention was to assist the landlord and not the police.

This view of the law is similar to that adopted by the Court of Appeal of British Columbia in *R v Westlie* (1971) 2 CCC (2d) 315. There plain clothes officers were patrolling the streets of one of the less salubrious parts of Vancouver in order to see whether any of the citizens were begging or committing other offences. Mr Westlie frustrated all their efforts by walking with them and explaining to all who were interested that they were 'undercover pigs' and 'undercover fuzz'. There was no evidence that at the time any crimes were being committed in that part of Vancouver, which is not perhaps surprising. *Bastable v Little* was cited to the court, but Mr Westlie was convicted.

The appeal will be allowed and the matter remitted to the Crown Court to continue the hearing.

Appeal allowed; case remitted to Crown Court for further hearing.

NOTES AND QUESTIONS

1. In *Rice v Connolly* it was held that D did not obstruct the police, who were investigating breaking offences, by refusing to answer, or answering incompletely, their questions and by refusing to accompany the police to a police box for the purposes of identification. In *Ricketts v Cox* (1981) 74 Cr App Rep 298, DC, the police approached D with a view to seeking his assistance with regard to a serious offence which had been committed in the area. D was extremely hostile, abusive and unco-operative. The police were acting lawfully in seeking to put questions to D and the court held that there was 'no possible shadow of a doubt' that D had obstructed the police for which he had no lawful excuse. But can it make a sensible difference that D couches his refusal to co-operate in the most intemperate language?

2. Suppose that in *Green v Moore* the landlord had been a meticulous observer of the licensing laws. But since the support group had decided to include his pub in their investigations the respondent had warned him about their intended visit. Obstruction?

3. Don, a law student, overhears police officers questioning Ed, a sociology student, about the burning down of the university library. Don says to Ed, 'You ought to know that you are not obliged to answer their questions, and if you take my advice you'll keep your mouth shut.' Ed thereupon refuses to answer any more questions. Has Don obstructed the police?

(3) MENS REA

R v Reynhoudt [1962] ALR 483, High Court of Australia (Dixon CJ, Kitto, Taylor, Menzies and Owen JJ)

[**Dixon CJ** and **Kitto J** delivered a judgments in favour of dismissing the appeal.]

Taylor J. Section 40 of the Crimes Act 1958 (Vic) provides, inter alia, that whosoever assaults any member of the police force in the due execution of his duty shall be guilty of a misdemeanour. The respondent was convicted of this offence, it having been proved upon his trial that he assaulted a constable of police whilst the latter was attempting to arrest him according to law. But upon appeal to the Court of Criminal Appeal it was contended that the trial had miscarried because the chairman of general sessions had instructed the jury that it was not incumbent upon the prosecution to prove that the accused knew, at the time, that the person whom he was alleged to have assaulted was an officer of the police force. Once the assault was proved it was sufficient, the learned chairman said, 'for the Crown to prove he was, in fact, a policeman and that he was acting in pursuance of his duty.' Having regard to the circumstances relating to the several offences of which the accused was found guilty it is unlikely in the extreme that the jury would have had any doubt that he knew that the person whom he assaulted was an officer of police acting in the due course of his duty. But the issue of knowledge on the part of the respondent was not left to the jury and the Court of Criminal Appeal quashed the conviction on the charge referred to. . . .

Their Honours' view, it seems to me, rests primarily upon the proposition as they stated it, at p 748, that it is proper to assume that 'the common law requirements that the assault must be intentional is to be carried forward into these aggravating elements of the new offence'. Any other conclusion they thought might well place the citizen in a position of grave embarrassment. Further, they did not perceive any legislative intention to displace what they called the common law rule but, on the contrary, they found in the expression 'wilfully', as applied to 'obstructs', an express indication that the onus is upon the Crown to establish, not only that any alleged obstruction itself is intentional, but that it is accompanied by an intent to obstruct a member of the police force in the due execution of his duty. 'It was', they thought, at p 749, 'probably thought unnecessary to introduce any like word before "assaults" or "resists" because the crime of assault and the very word "resists" already import the notion of intention'. But, to my mind, the use of the word 'wilfully' before 'obstructs' was intended to serve a very particular purpose and its presence in the section is of no assistance in solving the problem with which we are concerned. 'Obstruction' is a much wider word than either 'assault' or 'resist', which expressions are themselves sufficient to define the quality of the prohibited acts and, no doubt, it was thought to be not unimportant to make it clear that, in relation to obstruction, the section was concerned, not with all acts which might in fact constitute an obstruction, but only those which constitute intentional obstructions. That being so the presence in the composite phrase of the word 'wilfully' throws no reflected light on 'assaults' or 'resists' and provides no foundation for the construction for which the respondent contends.

There is, however, much to be said for the primary and fundamental ground upon which their Honours proceeded. Indeed, as Jordan CJ pointed out in *Turnbull* (1943) 44 SR (NSW) 108—after referring to the observations of Cave J in *Tolson* (1889) 23 QBD 168 at 181—there is much to be said for the proposition that if the courts had adhered to the principle that the proof of statutory offences involved as an element of proof that the accused knew that he was in fact doing the criminal act with which he was charged, that branch of the criminal law dealing with statutory offences might be free from some of the difficulties which, on the present state of the authorities, are inevitably encountered. 'If,' his Honour said, p 109, 'it [that principle] had been steadily insisted upon, persons sponsoring a bill by which it was sought to penalize a man for doing something, notwithstanding that he did not and could not know that he was doing it, would very soon have learned that it was necessary to disclose this on the face of the bill either in express terms or by words conveying so necessary an implication of intention in that behalf as to leave no room for doubt about their purpose. If the Legislature were prepared to allow such a provision, it would pass it; if it disapproved of it, it would strike it out. In either case, the result would be perfectly clear; the Legislature would know exactly what it was doing, and people would know exactly how they stood'. But, as his Honour said, that course had not been followed and he made reference to the 'multitudes of reported cases . . . many of them irreconcilable, in which the common law rule has been treated as excluded or not excluded upon judge-made *indicia* derived from cases in which there has often been a difference of opinion as to so-called necessary implications'. However, in my view, it is difficult, for reasons which will appear, to say that the legislature failed to make its meaning clear when it enacted s 40. . . .

The history of the provision with which we are concerned is traced in the judgment of my brother Owen and he has referred to like English legislation which the Victorian legislature adopted. What emerges is that legislation in what is for all material purposes identical with the provision with which we are concerned has been in operation in Victoria for nearly one hundred years. The relevant provisions were the subject of consolidating re-enactments in 1890, 1915, 1928 and finally in 1958. For a like period in England, decisions have stood which have accorded a fixed interpretation to provisions similar to those with which we are concerned. The first of these—*Forbes and Webb* (1865) 10 Cox CC 362—was a case where the accused were indicted for assaulting two constables in the execution of their duty and the submission was made that, since there was no evidence in the Crown case tending to show that the accused knew that the victims were police officers, the case should be withdrawn from the jury. The submission was rejected the recorder observing that 'The offence was, not assaulting them knowing them to be in execution of their duty, but assaulting them being in the execution of their duty'. Standing by itself the decision may not be of the greatest authority but apart from *Galvin's Case* (No 2) and two other cases—one in South Africa and one in Canada which I shall presently mention—it has never been questioned by the decision of any court. On the contrary, some 10 years later it was quite plainly approved in a judgment prepared by Bramwell B, and to which Kelly LCB, Cleasby B, Grove J, Pollock B, and Amphlett B, assented. Then, in 1909, its authority was expressly reserved in *Maxwell and Clanchy* (1900) 2 Cr App Rep 26, and, finally, it was followed by Maxwell Turner J, in *Mark* [1961] Crim LR 173. In the last-mentioned case it was expressly said, in relation to the facts of that case, that the accused was entitled to be acquitted if he showed that he had acted with the genuine belief, honestly and reasonably held, that the person assaulted was in the act of committing a felony or breach of the peace. This ruling was in accord with what Professor Paton calls the 'liberal approach' (Paton, *Jurisprudence*, p 371), that is to say that mens rea is not entirely 'eclipsed' (cf *Chajutin v Whitehead* [1938] 1 KB 506, [1938] 1 All ER 159) and what Dixon J in *Thomas v R* (1937) 59 CLR 279 at p 304, called the Mikado rule does not apply, but that the accused will be entitled to an acquittal if he makes out of the defence of mistake on reasonable grounds. The same principle was applied by this Court in cases such as *Maher v Musson* (1934) 52 CLR 100, and in England in *Sherras v De Rutzen* [1895] 1 QB 918.

On many occasions the failure of the legislature to make its meaning plain has been justifiably deplored but, to my mind, such a complaint is without validity when the legislature has adopted language to which a specific and precise meaning has been assigned without serious question for a great many years. This, of course, is precisely the position in this case and I find it impossible now to say that on the various occasions when the substance of s 40 has been enacted and re-enacted the legislature intended something other than its settled meaning. The South African and Canadian cases to which I referred previously—*Wallendorf* [1920] SALR 383, and *McLeod* (1954) 111 Can CC 106—have, however, adopted a different interpretation. But there is some divergence between the views expressed in those two cases and also between those decisions and the views expressed in the decision of the Court of Criminal Appeal in Victoria in the second *Galvin Case*. I have had the opportunity of reading what my brother Owen has said about these cases and I agree with his observations. They do not, in my view, afford any ground for departing from the fixed meaning which the English authorities have given to legislation in the form of s 40. In the circumstances, I am of the opinion that special leave should be granted and the appeal upheld.

[**Menzies** and **Owen JJ**, delivered judgments upholding the appeal.]

Special leave to appeal granted. Appeal allowed.

R v Fennell [1970] 3 All ER 215, Court of Appeal, Criminal Division
(Widgery and Fenton Atkinson LJJ, and Eveleigh J)

[**Widgery LJ** read the judgment of the court:]

The appellant was convicted at Portsmouth Quarter Sessions of assault on a police constable and sentenced to six months' imprisonment. He appeals against conviction and sentence by leave of the single judge.

On a Saturday night in September 1969, at about 11.15 pm, fighting broke out amongst 30 to 40 youths outside a public house in Portsmouth. Two policemen attempted to break up the fight and they were later reinforced by others. The police attempted to make arrests but were hampered by interference from other participants in the fighting. The appellant and his son, Clive, were present at the scene and in due course Clive became involved in the fighting. A police officer tried to arrest Clive, but said that he was very violent, kicking out in all directions, and even at one stage kicking his own mother when she tried to calm him. The appellant had lost sight of Clive for a few moments and came upon him when he was being restrained by two or more officers. The appellant spoke to a police sergeant, telling him to release Clive as the latter had done no wrong, and there was a conflict of evidence as to the sergeant's reply. According to the sergeant, he said that Clive had been arrested and must go to the station, whereas the appellant said the sergeant had told him to take Clive home. The appellant also said that the officers were using excessive force on Clive, and the upshot of it was that the appellant approached one of the officers and told him that the appellant would hit him unless Clive was released. As the officer did not respond, the appellant hit him a deliberate blow on the jaw.

The appellant seems to have run a number of defences at the trial contending that he was justified in using reasonable force, either to secure the release of his son because the initial arrest was unlawful, or in defence of his son at a time when the latter was in imminent danger of being injured by use of excessive force. The jury rejected these two defences and no further question arises on them. A further defence which the appellant wished to raise was that, even if the officers had not, in fact, exceeded their powers, he genuinely believed on reasonable grounds that the restraint of his son was unlawful and was thus justified in using reasonable force to free him. The deputy recorder ruled that this could not amount in law to a defence to the charge, and the question for this court is whether this ruling was correct.

It was accepted in the court below that, if the arrest had been, in fact, unlawful, the appellant would have been justified in using reasonable force to secure the release of his son. This proposition has not been argued before us and we will assume without deciding it, that it is correct. Counsel for the appellant referred us to a number of authorities concerned with the use of force in self-defence, and pointed out that a sufficient justification was there established if the accused genuinely believed on reasonable grounds that a relative or friend was in imminent danger of injury, even though that belief was based on an honest mistake of fact: *Chisam* [(1963) 47 Cr App Rep 130]. Counsel then contended that, by a parity of reasoning, a father who used force to effect the release of his son from custody was justified in so doing if he honestly believed on reasonable grounds that (contrary to the fact) the arrest was unlawful. We do not accept that submission. The law jealously scrutinises all claims to justify the use of force and will not readily recognise new ones. Where a person honestly and reasonably believes that he or his child is in imminent danger of injury, it would be unjust if he were deprived of the right to use reasonable force by way of defence merely because he had made some genuine mistake of fact. On the other hand, if the child is in police custody and not in imminent danger of injury, there is no urgency of the kind which requires an immediate decision, and a father who forcibly releases the child does so at his peril. If in fact the arrest proves to be lawful, the father's use of force cannot be justified. In our view, therefore, the deputy recorder gave a correct ruling and we dismiss the appeal against conviction.

Appeal against conviction dismissed

Hills v Ellis [1983] 1 All ER 667, Queen's Bench Division
(Griffiths LJ and McCullough J)

Griffiths LJ. This is an appeal by way of case stated from a decision of the justices sitting for the petty sessional division of Edmonton, who convicted this appellant of the offence of wilfully obstructing a police officer in the execution of his duty contrary to s 51(3) of the Police Act 1964.

The facts found by the justices were as follows. On Saturday, 2 January 1982 the appellant and a friend of his were in Park Lane, Tottenham, having just left a football match which had taken place at the Tottenham Hotspur football ground. The appellant saw a fight between two men and he formed the view that one of the men was the innocent party in the fight. He then saw Pc Robert Grey go up and arrest the man whom this appellant thought to be the innocent party. The appellant approached with the intention of intervening on the part of the arrested man. In order to attract the attention of the arresting officer, and in an effort to overcome the noise of the crowd leaving the match, the appellant addressed the officer in a raised voice, but due to the noise, the officer failed to hear what the appellant said. The appellant then grabbed the officer by the elbow in order to draw the officer's attention to the fact that, in the appellant's opinion, he was arresting the wrong man, and that he was in a position to provide cogent evidence, if they wished to have it, which might make the officer revise his decision to arrest the person he was trying to apprehend. The respondent, who is also a police officer, saw the appellant addressing Pc Grey in a raised voice and also saw the appellant grab Pc Grey by the elbow. The respondent warned the appellant that he should stop and that failure to do so might lead to his arrest for obstructing Pc Grey. However, the appellant persisted in his behaviour, and thereupon he was arrested by the respondent and charged.

Those are the salient facts found by the justices, and on those facts they expressed the following opinion:

> 'We were of opinion that the appellant in intervening in the processes of arrest had conducted himself in an excited and agitated fashion. That the manner in which the appellant interfered in the process of arrest failed to take into account the problems of the police officer in making an arrest against the background of many people leaving the football ground when violence amongst football supporters is a prevalent phenomenon. Seen in this light the appellant's actions were intrusive and a considerable impediment of the police officer in making his arrest.'

I interject here to say that it has never been suggested, either before the justices or in this court, that the officer was not making a lawful arrest. It was never suggested, despite the opinion of this appellant, that the officer did not have reasonable grounds for arresting the man he was trying to apprehend. . . .

In presenting his submissions on behalf of this appellant, counsel has referred the court first to the decision of the Divisional Court in *Rice v Connolly* [1966] 2 All ER 649 at 651–652, [1966] 2 QB 414 at 419 in which Lord Parker CJ considered the ingredient of this offence. He said:

> 'What the prosecution have to prove is that there was an obstructing of a constable, that the constable was at the time acting in the execution of his duty, and that the person obstructing did so wilfully. To carry the matter a little further, it is in my view clear that to "obstruct" in s. 51(3) [of the Police Act 1964] is to do any act which makes it more difficult for the police to carry out their duty.'

I pause there. There can be no doubt in this case that there was an obstruction within the meaning of that definition. The appellant was actually grabbing hold of the officer when in very difficult conditions, at the end of a football match, he was trying to arrest a man. Lord Parker LJ then continued to consider the element of wilfulness in the offence, and he said:

> The only remaining element of the alleged offence, and the one on which in my judgment this case depends, is whether the obstructing of which the appellant was guilty was a wilful obstruction. "Wilful" in this context in my judgment means not only "intentional" but also connotes something which is done without lawful excuse, and that indeed is conceded by counsel. . .'

What is submitted in this case on behalf of the appellant is that his action was not wilful in the sense of being done without lawful excuse, because he had a moral duty to draw to the attention of the officer that he was arresting the wrong man. I cannot accept that submission. Here was an officer, acting in the course of his duty, arresting a man. It would be quite intolerable if citizens, who may genuinely believe the wrong man was arrested, were entitled to lay hands on the police and obstruct them in that arrest because they thought that some other person should be arrested. One has only got to state the proposition to see the enormous abuse to which any such power on the part of the citizen might be put. A private citizen has no lawful excuse to interfere with a lawful arrest by a police officer. Accordingly, he was acting without lawful excuse within the definition as stated by Lord Parker CJ in *Rice v Connolly*.

The only other authority cited in support of the appellant's submission is *Willmott v Atack* [1976] 3 All ER 794, [1977] QB 498. The facts in that case were very different. A police officer was attempting to restrain a man under arrest and to get him into a police car. The defendant intervened, not with the intention of making it more difficult for the police officer to get the man into the police car, but with the intention of helping the officer. But due to the clumsiness of his intervention, the man in fact escaped. There is no doubt that in those circumstances the first part of the definition of 'wilfully obstructing' has been fulfilled. The officer had, in fact, been obstructed, but the court held that it had not been a wilful obstruction. Croom-Johnson J expressed the view of the court in the following way ([1976] 3 All ER 794 at 800, [1977] QB 498 at 504–505):

> 'When one looks at the whole context of s 51, dealing as it does with assaults on constables in sub-s (1) and concluding in sub-s (3) with resistance and wilful obstruction in the execution of the duty, I am of the view that the interpretation of this subsection for which the appellant contends is the right one. It fits the words "wilfully obstructs" in the context of the subsection, and in my view there must be something in the nature of a criminal intent of the kind which means that it is done with the idea of some form of hostility to the police with the intention of seeing that what is done is to obstruct, and that it is not enough merely to show that he intended to do what he did and that it did, in fact, have the result of the police being obstructed.'

The appellant's counsel argues from that passage that, as the motive here was merely to correct a policeman's error, it cannot be said that he, the appellant, was acting with any hostility towards the police. But in my view, the phrase 'hostility towards the police' in that passage means no more than that the actions of the defendant are aimed at the police. There can be no doubt here that his action in grabbing the policeman's arm was aimed at that policeman. It was an attempt to get that policeman to desist from the arrest that he was making. In my view, this is as clear a case as we can have of obstructing a police officer in the course of his duty, and the justices came to the right decision. But as always, one finds the justices took a very sensible view of the overall circumstances, and being satisfied of the appellant's overall motive, they gave him an absolute discharge.

For the reasons I have given, I would dismiss this appeal.

McCullough J. I agree. The submissions on behalf of the appellant, both here and below, are based on what it was submitted were his motives and lack of hostility towards the policeman. Those references to motives and hostility were clearly based on *Willmott v Atack* [1976] 3 All ER 794, [1977] QB 498, which I regard as a difficult case. . . .

I am uncertain what Croom-Johnson J had in mind when he used the word 'hostility' in the passage cited by Griffiths LJ. Hostility suggests emotion and motive, but motive and emotion are alike irrelevant in criminal law. What matters is intention, that is what state of affairs the defendant intended to bring about. What motive he had while so intending is irrelevant.

What is meant by an 'intention to obstruct'? I would construe 'wilfully obstructs' as doing deliberate actions with the intention of bringing about a state of affairs which, objectively regarded, amount to an obstruction as that phrase was explained by Lord Parker CJ in *Rice v Connolly* [1966] 2 All ER 649 at 651, [1966] 2 QB 414 at 419, ie making it more difficult for the police to carry out their duty. The fact that the defendant might not himself have called that state of affairs an obstruction is, to my mind, immaterial. This is not to say that it is enough to do deliberate actions which, in fact, obtruct; there must be an intention that those actions should result in the further state of affairs to which I have been referring.

If I may give an example. D interferes while a police officer, P, is arresting X, and delays the arrest. It is not enough that his deliberate actions in fact delay the arrest. If D intends to prevent P from arresting X, then D is guilty because it is his intention to do that which, objectively regarded, amounts to an obstruction, that is to say, to prevent the arrest. D's motives for wanting to prevent the arrest are immaterial. He is guilty even though he feels no hostility to the officer. He is guilty even though he believes the officer is arresting the wrong man. He is guilty even though he does not appreciate that interfering with the arrest amounts to what would be regarded objectively as an obstruction.

It may very well be that what I have been endeavouring to express would accord with Croom-Johnson J's opinion. I am not certain that May J in his three paragraph judgment was adopting what Croom-Johnson J had said about hostility. But even if he was, I think that what I have said can stand with his judgment. Lord Widgery CJ's judgment is in two sentences. He did not adopt the reasoning of the other two judges. He merely said that the question posed should be answered in the negative. The question is in the form:

> '. . . whether . . . it is sufficient for the Prosecution to prove that the Defendant wilfully did an act which obstructed the police officer in the execution of his duty, or must the prosecution further prove that. . .'

(See [1976] 3 All ER 794 at 798, [1977] QB 498 at 502.)

It is quite plain that, in saying that the question must be answered in the negative, Lord Widgery CJ was referring only to the first part of the question.

The facts found by the Crown Court in *Willmott v Atack* are not easy to reconcile with one another. Although it is said (see [1976] 3 All ER 794 at 796, [1977] QB 498 at 499) that Willmott attempted to interfere and in doing so pushed the officer in the throat while he was holding and restraining the other man, Howe, who was under arrest, the court did not see that as an assault (see [1976] 3 All ER 794 at 796, [1977] QB 498 at 500); and although Willmott's actions were to be found to be deliberate, the court did not anywhere say in terms that he was trying to prevent the arrest or secure the man's release. For these reasons it is, in my judgment, impossible to derive much assistance from the facts of that case.

It is to be noted that in *Green v Moore* [1982] 1 All ER 428 at 433, [1982] QB 1044 at 1052 Donaldson LJ in speaking of *Willmott v Atack*, and when comparing the facts of the case he was considering with *Willmott v Atack*, did not speak in terms of hostility.

When one comes to the facts of this case, all the essentials are present. The appellant deliberately grabbed the officer. In so doing he intended to intervene on behalf of the person whom the officer was arresting. He intended to cause the officer to revise his decision to arrest that man. It is therefore clear that he intended to do that which in fact amounted to an obstruction of the officer, namely to interfere with his actions in arresting and detaining the man. His motive for intending to interfere in this way is irrelevant. The fact that he may have harboured no feeling of hostility towards the officer is likewise irrelevant. So too, it is irrelevant whether or not he realised that interfering with an arrest was an obstruction as that word is generally understood.

In my judgment this appeal fails.

Appeal dismissed.

NOTES AND QUESTIONS

1. What is the mens rea of the offence of assaulting a constable in the execution of his duty? Is it enough that D has the mens rea of common assault only? cf *Gladstone Williams* (1983) 78 Cr App Rep 276, CA, p 236, above. There it was said by Lord Lane CJ (at p 280),

> 'The mental element [*sc* in assault] necessary to constitute guilt is the intent to apply unlawful force to the victim. We do not believe that the mental element can be substantiated by simply showing an intent to apply force and no more. What then is the situation if the defendant is labouring under a mistake of fact as to the circumstances? What if he believes, but believes mistakenly, that the victim is consenting, or that it is necessary to defend himself, or that a crime is being committed which he intends to prevent? He must then be judged against the mistaken facts as he believes them to be. If judged against those facts or circumstances the prosecution fail to establish his guilt, then he is entitled to be acquitted. . . . If the belief was in fact held, its unreasonableness, so far as guilt or innocence is concerned, is neither here nor there. It is irrelevant.'

Is there, then, a different definition of assault when the victim is a constable acting in the execution of his duty? Did Fennell intend to apply *unlawful* force?

2. In *Willmott v Atack* the charge of assaulting the constable was dismissed by the Crown Court though no reasons for this appear. On the facts as given, what possible defences might the appellant have had to such a charge?

3. Can *Willmott v Atack* stand with *Hills v Ellis*? Is there a distinction between D 'helping' the police to make what D believes to be a lawful arrest, and E 'helping' the police to desist from making an arrest which E believes to be unlawful?

4. The Draft Criminal Code Bill s 78 provides for assaults on constables as follows:

> A person who assaults a constable acting in the execution of his duty, or anyone assisting a constable so acting, knowing that or being reckless whether the person assaulted or the

person being assisted is a constable, is guilty of an offence, whether or not he is or ought to be aware that the constable is so acting.

This section must be read in conjunction with s 47 (which is set out above, p 231), and particular attention is drawn to s 47(6) and illustrations 47(viii)–(xiii).

6. Affray

Affray, a common law misdemeanour for which punishment by imprisonment or fine is at the discretion of the court, might be said properly to belong to offences commonly described as offences against public order, a category which includes such offences at common law as unlawful assembly, rout and riot, and such statutory offences as those arising under the Public Order Act 1936 and the Race Relations Act 1965. But there is no legal category of offences against public order, and affray may just as readily be regarded as a half-brother to assault. The offence of affray, after spending many years in the legal lumber room, has been pressed back into regular service.

Attorney General's Reference (No 3 of 1983) [1985] 1 All ER 501, Court of Appeal (Lord Lane CJ, Boreham and Tudor Price JJ)

Lord Lane CJ. The Court of Appeal is asked to give its opinion on the following related points of law:

'(i) On a charge of affray, where the unlawful fighting or violence occurred in a public place, do the prosecution have to prove not only (a) that it would have (or might reasonably be expected to have) terrified a bystander or person within earshot of reasonable firm character, but also either (b) the presence of a bystander or person within earshot, or (c) a reasonable likelihood of a member of the public coming within sight or earshot?

(ii) In what circumstances, if any, may an innocent victim or intended victim of fighting or violence or an innocent participant in it constitute a "bystander" for the purposes of (i)(b) above?'

In September 1981 five defendants appeared before the Crown Court at Leeds charged with affray, and certain other offences which are immaterial to the present argument. Submissions (with which we deal in detail hereafter), were made by defending counsel that there was no case for the defendants to answer so far as the affray was concerned; the judge upheld those submissions and the defendants were accordingly acquitted of affray.

On 29 June 1983 the present reference was filed with the Registrar of Criminal Appeals by the Attorney General.

The facts, in so far as they are material, were as follows. The incident took place in a public place, namely the car park at the rear of a public house at night shortly after the end of 'drinking-up time'. The defendants attacked a group of innocent youths. The ensuing mêlée was undoubtedly such as would have terrified a bystander of reasonably firm character.

There was no evidence that there was anybody in the car park or within earshot of it apart from the two groups of youths, and it is said that there was no reasonable likelihood of any other person coming within sight or earshot of the fighting. G was a member of the group of innocent youths. He himself was not attacked. However he did pull one of the defendants off a companion of his; he also collided with another defendant who was kicking a further companion of his; this was as he, G, ran off to telephone to the police.

The submission made by counsel for the defence was based on the following grounds: (i) The prosecution had to prove *not only* (a) that the fighting would have (or might reasonably be expected to have) terrified a bystander or person within earshot of reasonably firm character, *but also* either (b) the actual presence of a bystander or person within earshot or (c) the reasonable likelihood of a member of the public coming within sight or earshot. (ii) Since G and the other members of the 'innocent group' were victims and/or participants in the fighting, none of them could constitute a 'bystander' for the purpose of completing proof of the offence. Therefore, since the prosecution had failed to adduce any evidence of the actual presence of a bystander and no sufficient evidence of the likelihood of one appearing, their case must fail.

Prosecuting counsel submitted that (i) since the fighting took place in a public place, the prosecution only had to prove that it would have (or might reasonably be expected to have) terrified a bystander or person within earshot of reasonably firm character and did not have to prove the actual presence of a bystander or the reasonable likelihood of one materialising. (ii) Alternatively, if the prosecution did have to prove actual or likely presence, (1) G could constitute a bystander and (2) there was enough evidence of the likelihood of a member of the public coming within sight or earshot to constitute a prima facie case.

Counsel for the Attorney General has taken us through the recent history of the offence of affray to demonstrate how the courts have gradually defined and refined it. We think it may be useful to set out in summary form the various cases.

R v Sharp [1957] 1 All ER 577, [1957] 1 QB 552 decided firstly that on a charge of making an affray in a public place there is no necessity to call direct evidence of any person having been put in fear; it is sufficient to prove such circumstances that reasonable people might have been intimidated or frightened by the fighting and/or violence. (But see Lord Hailsham LC in *Taylor v DPP* [1973] 2 All ER 1108 at 1112, [1973] AC 964 at 987:

> '. . . it is essential to stress that the degree of violence required to constitute the offence of affray must be such as to be calculated to terrify a person of reasonably firm character. This should not be watered down. Thus it is arguable that the phrase "*might* be frightened or intimidated" may be too weak. The violence must be such as to be *calculated* to terrify (that is, might reasonably be expected to terrify) not simply such as *might* terrify a person of the requisite degree of firmness.'

Secondly, a person who merely defends himself against the attack of another and does not himself attack is not guilty of affray.

Button v DPP, Swain v DPP [1965] 3 All ER 587, [1966] AC 591, apart from containing a very useful and detailed history by McKenna J of the offence of affray from earliest times, decided that there was no requirement that the affray should be committed in a public place, despite decisions to the contrary over the previous century. These had crept into the law by error.

In *R v Scarrow* (1968) 52 Cr App R 591 it was decided that there is no requirement for the prosecution to prove that one defendant has fought with another. The offence may be committed though the persons attacked did not resist or retaliate. Lord Parker CJ said (at 596):

> 'It may well be that if two people fight and one is acting in self-defence, that man cannot be said to be guilty of an affray, but it would appear to this court that there is no reason why his attacker, whether acting alone or jointly with another attacker, should not be held guilty of the affray.'

R v Summers (1972) 56 Cr App R 604 covered much of the same ground as *R v Scarrow*, but in addition is authority for the proposition that one of the innocent parties attacked by the defendant is capable of being regarded as a member of the public, a potential subject of the necessary terror.

The questions raised by this reference however have been the subject of direct consideration in only one case, namely a charge to the jury by Paull J in *R v Mapstone* [1963] 3 All ER 930n, [1964] 1 WLR 439n. This was a case where a fight had taken place in a public house during opening hours. The judge directed the jury that they had to be satisfied that the particular defendant took part in a fight in a public place or road in such a way as might well frighten any members of the public who might be present. He went on ([1963] 3 All ER 930 at 931)

> ' "Affray" is an old English word, not one we use very often today, but what it means is this that a number of people, two will do, start fighting in a public road or place in such a way that people who may be present may well get frightened. The old English word used to be "terrified". So what the prosecution has to prove . . . is, first of all, that that accused person took part in a fight in a public place . . . Secondly, that the fighting that went on was such as might well frighten any ordinary person passing by. The prosecution has not got to prove that anyone *was* frightened; the prosecution has not got to prove that someone was passing by; but the prosecution must prove that the character of the fighting which was going on was such that it might well frighten.' (Our emphasis.)

This direction has now of course to be read in the light of *Button v DPP, Swain v DPP* in that the fighting may be in a private place, and also of Lord Hailsham LC's observations in *Taylor v DPP*, to both of which we have referred.

Counsel appearing as amicus curiae submits primarily that affray is a well-defined common law offence which should be kept within its historical bounds and should not be allowed, so to speak, to overflow into areas more properly covered by the offence of riot. His suggestion is that if there is no requirement for the prosecution to prove the actual or likely presence of a bystander available to be terrified, then the whole basis of the offence, namely fighting to the terror of the public, is lost. He does however concede that presence or likely presence does not have to be proved by direct evidence. It may be by inference. He gives the example of a fight in a public street in a town, where it would, he suggests, be proper to draw the inference that some member of the public was there or likely to be there to witness the fight.

We deal first with that proposition, namely that the actual or likely presence of a bystander is one of the essential elements which the prosecution must prove.

We have had our attention drawn to the following obiter dicta. *Taylor v DPP* was a case which was primarily concerned with the question whether one person fighting unlawfully could properly be convicted of an affray. It was held that he could, and that if one person was acting unlawfully it was not necessary to inquire whether others participating were acting lawfully or not. However in the course of his speech Lord Reid had this to say about the problem with which we are here concerned ([1973] 2 All ER 1108 at 1114–1115, [1973] AC 964 at 989–990):

> 'The question of terror does not arise in this case but as it was much referred to in argument and is an essential element in the offence, I think that I must say a word about it. Undoubtedly if people are present it is not necessary to prove by their evidence that they were terrified. It is enough if the circumstances are such that ordinary people like them would have been terrified. I say "would" not "might" have been. But I am much more doubtful about suggestions in some cases that no one but the combatants need be present at all or even within earshot: that it is enough that if someone had been present he would have been terrified. As terror is an essential ingredient of the offence I think that there can be no difference in principle between violence in a public or a private place. But that is a matter which can be decided when it arises.'

Lord Hailsham LC on the other hand said ([1973] 2 All ER 1108 at 1112–1113, [1973] AC 964 at 987–988):

> 'We were invited to express an opinion as to the extent to which persons must be proved to have been present in order to satisfy the ingredient of terror. I do not think that, on the facts of the present case, where many persons were in fact present and some were in fact terrified, it is desirable to explore this in depth. It is possible that where the fight takes place in a public street it is not necessary to prove the actual presence of bystanders, of persons within earshot or that they were actually terrified. It may be enough to show that the violence used was of such a kind to render the street unusable by persons of reasonable firmness by reason of the terror it was liable to cause. I am not, for example, prepared to say that a fight between rival gangs on the front of a seaside resort, or a duel with lethal weapons on Putney Heath, would not be an affray if the prosecution failed to establish the presence of bystanders or their actual terror. But in a private place it would be surprising if affray could be complete without the actual presence of onlookers or audience to be frightened by the sight or sound of what was occurring. This must clearly be considered of importance since the decision in *Button* [1965] 3 All ER 587, [1966] AC 591. These are matters which must be canvassed in the light of cases where the facts are such as to raise the issues.'

Kamara v DPP [1973] 2 All ER 1242, [1974] AC 104 was concerned with unlawful assembly rather than affray, but Lord Hailsham LC had this to say ([1973] 2 All ER 1242 at 1248, [1974] AC 104 at 116):

> 'No doubt unlawful assembly differs from an affray, because, unlike affray, it implies a common purpose, and because, unlike affray, actual violence is unnecessary provided the public peace is endangered, but in my view it is analogous to affray in that (1) it need not be in a public place and (2) that the essential requisite in both is the presence or likely presence of innocent third parties, members of the public not participating in the illegal activities in question. It is their presence, or the likelihood of it, and the danger to their security in each case which constitutes the threat to public peace and the public element necessary to the commission of each offence.'

We respectfully agree with the dictum of Lord Hailsham LC in *Taylor v DPP* [1973] 2 All ER 1108 at 1112–1113, [1973] AC 964 at 987–988, and, in so far as they are relevant, the terms of the directions to the jury by Paull J in *R v Mapstone*. Certainly, so far as fighting in a public place is concerned, it would be wrong to allow guilt or innocence to depend on the chance presence or absence of an uninvolved member of the public. The essence of affray is participation in unlawful violence in fighting of such a kind as is calculated to cause any person of reasonable firmness who might witness it to be terrified, for example by reason of fear for his or her own safety. There will in most cases be evidence available from actual uninvolved bystanders as to the nature and degree of the violence being exhibited, but the absence of such evidence does not mean that the prosecution must fail. It would be strange were it otherwise, because uninvolved members of the public are likely, if they are wise, to make themselves scarce at the first signs of trouble. It would scarcely be just if this fact allowed defendants to escape conviction.

Nor do we consider it necessary for the prosecution to prove the reasonable likelihood that members of the public might come on the scene. Quite apart from the practical difficulties of proving a 'likelihood' of that nature, it involves the jury in what is little more than a guessing game. As the Law Commission say in Working Paper No 82 (Offences against Public Order) para 4.27:

> '. . . Furthermore, it may be argued that a "public place" is by definition a place where a member of the public may be, and that the extra requirement of reasonable likelihood of the presence of others therefore involves an arbitrary qualification of the scope of that term. . .'

If counsel appearing as amicus curiae is right in his concession that in some cases the jury may properly infer the presence of a bystander from the nature of the place, and in some cases they may not, that would involve the court or jury in the task of deciding whether the public place was or was not sufficiently public for the inference to be drawn. This would, to say the least, be a difficult exercise.

In the light of those conclusions it is not strictly necessary for us to tackle the question of whether, assuming the bystander to be necessary for proof of the offence, G in the present case can be regarded as a bystander. However a simple example serves to demonstrate the absurdity of the situation if he could not be so regarded. G stands terrified, the sole spectator of the fighting and having nothing to do with either batch of contestants. At that point he is undoubtedly a bystander and the offence of affray is complete. The fighting then becomes more widespread and G is himself attacked. If the arguments put forward by defending counsel in the present case are correct, the affray then ceases because there is no uninvolved spectator/bystander. The attack on G then ceases and the situation becomes less serious but fighting continues, does the offence of affray then start again?

It seems to us clear that in any event the innocent victims of an affray may themselves fill the role of the so-called bystander. The opposite conclusion would lead to absurdity.

We have employed the word 'bystander' throughout this judgment as a convenient abbreviation and in deference to what seems to have become common usage. The word has however connotations which make it not altogether apt. We use it in the sense of 'innocent member of the public within sight or earshot of the fighting'.

We reject as impracticable the distinction which counsel appearing as amicus curiae seeks to draw between persons who are the intended victims of those unlawfully fighting on the one hand and those on the other hand who are, as he describes it, 'merely sucked into the mêlée'.

We summarise our views as follows. In order to establish the offence of affray in a public place, the Crown must establish that: (i) there was unlawful fighting or unlawful violence used by one or more than one person against another or others, or there was an unlawful display of force by one or more than one person without actual violence, and (ii) the unlawful fighting, violence or display of force was such that a bystander of reasonable firmness and courage (whether or not present or likely to be present) might reasonably be expected to be terrified.

We do not consider it either necessary or desirable in this opinion to embark on any discussion about fighting in places which are not public.

The answers to the questions posed are therefore as follows: (i) No. (ii) In all circumstances, so far as we are able to see.

Opinion accordingly.

NOTES AND QUESTIONS

1. In the above case the court refrained from expressing any opinion about fighting in places not open to the public. Suppose that in the privacy of his own house D makes a violent attack on his wife which terrifies her. If, as the court thought, the innocent victim of the fighting can constitute a bystander where the fight takes place in public, is there any logical ground on which a fight in a private place can be treated differently? If it is treated differently would it follow that if D's daughter was present when the attack was made on his wife what is an affray would cease to be so if D attacked the daughter?

2. The display of violence most usually takes the form of fighting but it would be unwise to conclude that it is confined to fighting. In *Taylor v DPP* [1978] 2 All ER 1108 at 1111 Lord Hailsham thought that nothing less than 'an unlawful participation in a violent breach of the peace' would suffice. This is allied to the requirement that the violence must be such as to *terrify*; it is not enough that bystanders would be upset, alarmed or frightened. What then of a party of football supporters who charge through a shopping precinct shouting obscenities, causing those who are fleet of foot to get out of their way and knocking aside those who are not? 'To my mind,' said Lord Hailsham in *Taylor* (at p 1112) 'it is essential to stress that the degree of violence . . . must be such as to be calculated to terrify a person of reasonably firm character. This should not be watered down.' Does this mean that in the shopping precinct there would be no affray if only old age pensioners and women with small children were terrified? Is 'terror' a meaningful concept?

3. What is the mens rea of an affray?

4. Ought affray to have been left in the legal lumber room? The Law Commission (Working Paper No 82, *Offences against Public Order*, paras 2.4–2.14) while pointing out that the range of offences other than affray for dealing with fighting in public was considerable, nevertheless thought that its abolition would leave a significant gap in the law. The essence of affray was seen by the Commission as fighting which caused alarm to the public; it was essentially an offence against public order. The Commission accordingly proposes to retain the offence though it would receive a more precise statutory definition.

CHAPTER 19

Sexual offences

1. Rape

Sexual Offences Act 1956, ss 1–4, 44, and Sexual Offences (Amendment) Act 1976, pp 548 and 577, below.

The actus reus of rape requires proof of (i) sexual intercourse which is (ii) unlawful and (iii) without the consent of the woman.

(1) SEXUAL INTERCOURSE

See s 44 of the Sexual Offences Act 1956 and s 7(2) of the Sexual Offences (Amendment) Act 1976. Rape is confined to penetration per vaginam. The Criminal Law Revision Committee (*Fifteenth Report*, Sexual Offences, Cmnd 9213, 1984, para 2.45) provisionally concluded that the offence should not be extended to the insertion of the penis in other body orifices or to the insertion of objects in the vagina since it was undesirable that the definition of a serious offence should become out of step with popular understanding.

While intercourse is complete on penetration, the current view appears to be that it continues so long as penetration is maintained (*Kaitamaki* [1985] AC 147, [1984] 2 All ER 435, PC, p 20, above).

(2) UNLAWFUL SEXUAL INTERCOURSE

R v Steele (1976) 65 Cr App Rep 22, Court of Appeal, Criminal Division (Geoffrey Lane LJ, Nield and Croom-Johnson JJ)

Shortly after the appellant married the complainant their marriage began to flounder and the wife left him to live in the nurses' home of the hospital where she worked. In proceedings commenced by the wife, the appellant undertook not to molest her and not to approach or enter the nurses' home. The appellant subsequently entered the home where he had intercourse with his wife without, as it was alleged, her consent. He was convicted of rape.

The judgment of the court was delivered by:

Geoffrey Lane LJ . . . Mr McCowan, on behalf of the appellant in this Court. . . . says that in the circumstances of this case, the fact that the appellant is married to the complainant is a bar to any conviction to rape. He concedes that there are occasions when a husband may be found guilty of raping his wife. This, he submits, is not one of them. . . .

As a general principle, there is no doubt that a husband cannot be guilty of rape upon his wife. the reason is Sir Matthew Hale's *Pleas of the Crown*, Vol 1 at p 629 is stated in this way: '. . . by

392

their mutual matrimonial consent and contract the wife hath given up herself in this kind unto her husband, which she cannot retract.' No doubt in times gone by there were no circumstances in which the wife could be held to have retracted the overall consent which, by the marriage ceremony, she gave to sexual intercourse with her husband. Researches have failed to reveal any exception to the general rule until 1949: that was the case of *Clarke* (1949) 33 Cr App R 216 decided by Byrne J. In *Clarke*, there was in existence at the time of the alleged rape, a separation order on the grounds of the prisoner's persistent cruelty towards his wife. That separation order was in force and it contained a clause that the wife was no longer bound to cohabit with the prisoner. Cohabitation had not been resumed. The learned judge ruled that in those circumstances the wife's consent had been revoked. He said at p. 218:

'The position, therefore, was that the wife, by process of law, namely, by marriage, had given consent to the husband to exercise the marital right during such time as the ordinary relations created by the marriage contract subsisted between them, but by a further process of law, namely, the justices' order, her consent to marital intercourse was revoked.'

The next case in point of time was the decision by Lynskey J in *Miller* [1954] 2 QB 282, 38 Cr App R 1. In that case, the only relevant action which the wife had taken was to file a petition for divorce on the grounds of adultery. There had been, it seems, some sort of hearing of that petition in which the wife had given evidence but the hearing was adjourned for the attendance of the husband. Subsequently, the husband met her and had sexual intercourse with her without her consent. He was indicted for rape and also for assault occasioning actual bodily harm. Lynskey J at p 290 and p 8, 9 of the respective reports, held that the mere filing of a petition for a divorce, even though there had been a partial hearing of that petition, without any order from the Court at all, was not sufficient to revoke the wife's consent and consequently the husband was entitled to have intercourse, albeit by force, with his wife without being guilty of rape although, in certain circumstances, he might be guilty of inflicting harm and violence upon her.

The third decision is that of *O'Brien (Edward)*, a decision of Park J reported in [1974] 3 All ER 663. In that case, the wife was granted a decree nisi and it was after that decree that the husband had intercourse with her by force. It was held by the learned judge that the decree nisi effectively terminated the wife's consent to marital intercourse. Therefore, the husband was liable to be convicted of rape.

In this case, the circumstances are of course different from any of those in the three cases to which I have referred. Here there has been no decree of the Court, here there has been no direct order of the Court compelling the husband to stay away from his wife. There has been an undertaking by the husband not to molest his wife. The question which the Court has to decide is this. Have the parties made it clear, by agreement between themselves, or has the Court made it clear by an order or something equivalent to an order, that the wife's consent to sexual intercourse with her husband implicit in the act of marriage, no longer exists? A separation agreement with a non-cohabitatic.1 clause, a decree of divorce, a decree of judicial separation, a separation order in the justices' court containing a non-cohabitation clause and an injunction restraining the husband from molesting the wife or having sexual intercourse with her are all obvious cases in which the wife's consent would be successfully revoked. On the other hand, the mere filing of a petition for divorce would clearly not be enough, the mere issue of proceedings leading up to a magistrates' separation order or the mere issue of proceedings as a preliminary to apply for an ex parte injunction to restrain the husband would be enough because the Court is making an order wholly inconsistent with the wife's consent and an order, breach of which would or might result in the husband being punished by imprisonment.

What then of the undertaking in lieu of an injunction? It is, in the judgment of this Court, the equivalent of an injunction. It is given to avoid, amongst other things, the stigma of an injunction. Breach of it is enforceable by the Court and may result in imprisonment. It is, in effect equivalent to the granting of an injunction. Indeed, whether one considers this as equivalent to the order of the Court or the equivalent of an agreement between the parties, it does not matter. It may indeed have aspects of both. The effect is to eliminate the wife's matrimonial consent to intercourse. That is the judgment of the Court on that first point. Therefore, there is no bar to this man being found guilty of rape if the other ingredients of the offence are successfully proved by the prosecution.

[The Court found on point 2 of the appeal that the trial judge had failed to direct the jury on the lines directed in *Director of Public Prosecutions v Morgan*, p 45, above, and quashed the conviction of rape, finding it was not a case for the application of the proviso to section 2(1) of the Criminal Appeal Act 1968. . . .]

Appeal allowed. Conviction quashed.

The requirement that the intercourse be unlawful merely preserves the common law rule that a husband cannot rape his wife during the subsistence of cohabitation. Cohabitation for this purpose is ended only by an order made or acknowledged by a court, or by a formal separation agreement even if it does not contain a non-molestation clause: *Roberts* [1986] Crim LR 188. Even when the parties are cohabiting there are circumstances (eg where the husband is suffering from a venereal disease) where intercourse without consent may constitute cruelty for the purposes of matrimonial law (*Foster v Foster* [1921] P 438) and in *Clarence* (1888) 22 QBD 23 at 41 Stephen J characterised such conduct as unlawful. Presumably even Hale could not maintain in such a case that the wife 'hath given up herself in this kind to her husband' but would it be rape?

The CLRC (Cmnd 9213, para 2.55) favoured extending the law to all cases where the husband and wife had ceased cohabitation. But there are real difficulties in defining cohabitation for this purpose and the Committee decided, by a narrow majority, that in the absence of a satisfactory definition of cohabitation the law should be left as it is.

(3) THE ABSENCE OF CONSENT

Papadimitropoulos v R (1957) 98 CLR 249, High Court of Australia (Dixon CJ, McTiernan, Webb, Kitto and Taylor JJ)

The Court delivered the following written judgment:

The applicant for special leave to appeal in this case was convicted before Gavan Duffy J, on 17 April 1957 of rape with mitigating circumstances and sentenced to four years' imprisonment. The case made against him was that he had obtained the actual consent of the woman to his having carnal knowledge of her by a fraudulent pretence which made it no consent at all. . . .

It appears that since the events upon which the charge depends Dina Karnezi has married, and at the trial she was Dena Arvaniti. She is described as a Greek girl who has not learned to speak English. For some three months she had been employed at a factory in Fitzroy. On the morning of 14 June 1956, accompanied by the applicant, who is also a Greek but who speaks English intelligibly, she saw the manager. They requested that she should have a week off saying that they had been married that morning. Mrs Arvaniti's story was that she met the applicant in Australia and that four or five days later he asked her to marry him. He bought her a ring and got her to wear it in the street. On the morning of 14 June 1956 he asked her to go to the registry office and get married . . . Mrs Arvaniti said that on the morning of 14 June 1956, which was in fact a Thursday, in compliance with the applicant's request she went with him accompanied by her two cousins and an aunt, none of whom spoke English, to the registry office in Queen Street, Melbourne. There she and the applicant signed a card and a form which had been filled in by the officer on information supplied in English by the applicant. The two documents were produced at the trial and identified by her and were respectively a notice of intention that the marriage would be celebrated and an information paper giving the particulars for registration and for the filling in of the marriage certificate. Mrs Arvaniti said that then the applicant, speaking to her of course in Greek, told her that they were married. Next they went to her employer, as already stated, to obtain leave, and after that to his employer for the like purpose. Having done that they went to obtain a room at what is presumably a lodging house. It was in Brunswick Street, Fitzroy and was conducted by a Mrs Fatouris. According to Mrs Fatouris, the applicant had already bespoken the room for himself and his intended wife, and on this occasion the applicant introduced the girl as his wife and said that they had been married that morning at the registry. That night they went into occupation of the room. They lived there together for the next four days, during which, according to the evidence of Mrs Arvaniti, they had sexual intercourse two or three times. On the Sunday morning he told her that they had to go to the registry again at 3 pm on the following day to collect a paper, a document. Early on Monday morning he left and did not return. She then discovered that there had not been a marriage ceremony . . . Gavan Duffy J directed the jury that rape consisted in having carnal knowledge of a woman without her consent; but, in law, if the girl did believe that the accused had become her husband by marriage and acquiesced in sexual intercourse with him on that basis and would not have so acquiesced otherwise, and that belief of hers had been brought about by the accused representing to her that they were married, he knowing they were not, and with the intention of persuading her to consent to sexual intercourse with him as her husband, then there would be no consent at all . . .

On application to the Full Court of the Supreme Court sitting as a Court of Criminal Appeal for leave to appeal that court was divided in opinion. Lowe and O'Bryan JJ were of opinion that the direction to the jury was correct and that it was open to the jury to find that the woman's consent was vitiated by fraud and amounted to no consent. Monahan J adopted a contrary conclusion. In the elaborate reasons which were given in the joint judgment of Lowe and O'Bryan JJ on the one hand and by Monahan J on the other hand the distinction was accepted between a consent given under a deception or mistake as to the thing itself, that is to say as to the act of intercourse, and a consent to that act itself induced by a deception or mistake as to a matter antecedent or collateral thereto. Under the first heading come the cases in which the woman is deluded into supposing that she is undergoing medical treatment, and the cases where in the dark she is induced to assume that her husband is the man with whom she is having intercourse. Under the second heading comes consent induced by fraudulent representations made by the man as to his wealth, position or freedom to marry the woman. Consent obtained by frauds of the latter character is nevertheless a consent. But Lowe and O'Bryan JJ were of opinion that a misrepresentation as to the performance of the marriage ceremony fell under the former head. Their Honours said: 'A mistake of such a kind in our opinion makes the act which took place essentially different from that to which she supposed she was consenting. What she was consenting to was a marital act, an act to which in her mistaken belief she was in duty bound to submit. What she got was an act of fornication—an act wholly different in moral character. On principle it seems to us that the consent relied on is no real consent at all and should afford no help to the applicant.' On the other hand Monahan J, speaking of the two classes of cases given above as examples of the first heading, said: 'I have no more difficulty in understanding the essential difference between the act consented to and the act done in the personation cases than I have in understanding the same essential differences in the acts which have been considered in the medical cases. My difficulty arises when I am asked to say that there is the same essential difference between the act consented to and the act done in this case; the sexual act was the act to which the prosecutrix intended to consent and the prisoner was the person with whom she consented to perform the act.'

The modern history of the crime of rape shows a tendency to extend the application of the constituent elements of the offence. The '*violenter et felonice rapuit*' of the old Latin indictment is now satisfied although there be no use of force: *Bourke* [[1915] VLR 289]. The '*contra voluntatem suam*' requires only a negative absence of consent (as to the need of the man's being aware of the absence of consent, see *Lambert* [[1919] VLR 205 at 213]). The '*violenter et felonice carnaliter cognovit*' is established if there has been some degree of penetration although slight, and no more force has been used than is required to effect it: *Bourke* [[1915] VLR 289]; *Burles* [[1947] VLR 392].

There has been some judicial resistance to the idea that an actual consent to an act of sexual intercourse can be no consent because it is vitiated by fraud or mistake. The key to the difficulty may perhaps be found in a brief sentence of Cussen J in *Lambert* [[1919] VLR at 212]: 'Now, carnal knowledge is merely the physical fact of penetration though, of course, there canno̠t be consent even to that without some perception of what is about to take place.'

In 1822 Bayley J reserved for the consideration of the twelve judges the case of one Jackson who had been convicted before him of burglary with intent to commit rape. Jackson had entered a dwelling house by night in the absence of the householder with the intention of personating him and deceiving his wife into submitting to sexual intercourse with him. As he was proceeding to his purpose she discovered the deception and he made off, 'four judges thought, that having carnal knowledge of a woman whilst she was under the belief of its being her husband would be a rape, but the other eight judges thought it would not: and Dallas CJ pointed out forcibly the difference between compelling a woman against her will, when the abhorrence which would naturally arise in her mind was called into action, and beguiling her into consent and co-operation; but several of the eight judges intimated that if the case should occur again they would advise the jury to find a special verdict': *Jackson* [(1822) Russ & Ry 487]. The case did occur again. In *Saunders* [(1838) 8 C & P 265] it appeared that the person had got into a married woman's bed and by personating her husband had connection with her. Bayley J directed the jury that he was bound to tell them that the charge of rape was not made out 'as the crime was not committed against the will of the prosecutrix, as she consented believing it to be her husband'. Alderson B, applied the same law in a similar case in the same year: *Williams* [(1838) 8 C & P 286]. Twelve years later a case arose for the consideration of the judges in which a prisoner who was a medical man had been convicted of assault on evidence that he had induced a girl of fourteen years of age to submit to his having connection with her by leading her to believe that it was but 'medical treatment for the ailment under which she laboured': the conviction was affirmed: *Case* [(1850) 1 Den 580]. In 1854 another case was reserved for the judges in which a prisoner had been convicted of rape on evidence that he impersonated the woman's husband and so obtained her assent to sexual intercourse. The judges declined to permit the question to be re-opened and followed *Jackson's* case: *Clarke* [(1854) Dears CC 397].

In 1868 the Court of Crown Cases Reserved quashed a conviction of rape based on a similar impersonation. 'It falls,' said Bovill CJ, for the judges, 'within the class of cases which decide that, when consent is obtained by fraud, the act does not amount to rape': *Barrow* [(1868) LR 1 CCR 156]. In *Young* [(1878) 38 LT 540] the court upheld a conviction of a man who had connection with a sleeping woman who, when she first woke, thought the man was her husband, and then discovering it was not threw him off. In the course of the reasons doubts were raised about the decisions beginning with *Jackson's* case. In Ireland the court refused to follow the reasoning: *Dee* [(1884) 15 Cox CC 579]. In the meantime the Court of Crown Cases Reserved in *Flattery* [(1887) 2 QBD 410] had questioned the decision in *Barrow's Case*. The facts resembled those in *Case* [(1850) 1 Den 580] except that the prisoner was not a medical man but a quack, and the representations about his giving some form of treatment were put to the mother as well as the girl, and in a form which might well have excited the mother's suspicions. Field J said: 'The question is one of consent, or not consent; but the consent must be to sexual connexion. There was no such consent.' This decision was strongly criticised by Sir James Fitzjames Stephen in his *Digest of the Criminal Law*, 3rd edn (1883), at p 185, on the ground that it almost overruled the principle 'that where consent is obtained by fraud the act does not amount to rape'. At this point a declaration of the law was made by statute. Section 4 of the Criminal Law Amendment Act 1885 after reciting that doubts had been entertained whether a man who induces a married woman to permit him to have connection with her by personating her husband is or is not guilty of rape, enacted and declared that every such offender should be deemed to be guilty of rape (cf now Sexual Offences Act 1956, s 1(2)).

The next judicial step was taken in the case of *Clarence* [(1888) 22 QBD 23, p 358, above]. The decision was simply that a husband who infects his wife with venereal disease is not thereby guilty of inflicting grievous bodily harm. But this led to the judges giving much consideration to what was involved in the wife's consent, ignorant as she was of her husband's condition. The judgments contain many observations which are pertinent to the distinction upon which this case turns. For example, in the judgment of Wills J, there is to be found, to say the least of it, a dyslogistic description of a fraud that will afford no basis for treating the woman's consent as a nullity and the act of intercourse as rape. 'Take, for example', said his Lordship 'the case of a man without a single good quality, a gaol-bird, heartless, mean and cruel, without the smallest intention of doing anything but possessing himself of the person of his victim, but successfully representing himself as a man of good family and connections prevented by some temporary obstacle from contracting an immediate marriage, and with conscious hypocrisy acting the part of a devoted lover, and in this fashion, or perhaps under the guise of affected religious fervour, effecting the ruin of his victim' [(1888) 22 QBD at 29, 30]. The conception which Wills J had of what sufficed to vitiate consent is expressed as follows: 'The essence of rape is, to my mind, the penetration of the woman's person without her consent. In other words it is, roughly speaking, where the woman does not intend that the sexual act shall be done upon her either at all, or, what is pretty much the same thing, by the particular individual doing it, and an assault which includes penetration does not seem to me under such circumstances to be anything but rape' [(1888) 22 QBD at 34]. Stephen J [(1888) 22 QBD at 43] refers to the conflict between the decision in *Barrow* and the Irish decision in *Dee* and remarks that the decisions were examined minutely in the latter case. Stephen J proceeded: 'I think they justify the observation that the only sorts of fraud which so far destroy the effect of a woman's consent as to convert a connection consented to in fact into a rape are frauds as to the nature of the act itself, or as to the identity of the person who does the act' [(1888) 22 QBD at 44]. Field J speaks of the woman's consenting to the act of intercourse yet not consenting to it in its actual nature and conditions, and he again says that a consent obtained to one is not a consent to an act of a different nature [(1888) 22 QBD at 60, 61].

In *Williams* [[1923] 1 KB 340] a new version of the 'medical treatment' cases was dealt with by the Court of Criminal Appeal. This time it was a singing master and the pretence was that the treatment was for breathing. Possibly the case went a little further than *Case* and *Flattery* but, if so, that is only with reference to the complexion the facts were given. The materiality of the case lies only in a broad statement which Lord Hewart CJ, quoted from a text book. ' "A consent or submission obtained by fraud is, it would seem, not a defence to rape or cognate offences" ' [[1923] 1 KB at 347]. It is interesting to notice that this statement is the contradictory of that of Sir James Fitzjames Stephen in the note in his *Digest* quoted above, in which he describes the principle to be 'that where consent is obtained by fraud the act does not amount to rape'. It is the contradictory too of that made by Bovill CJ in *Barrow* also quoted above. From what has been said already, however, it should be clear enough that the truth lies between the two opposing generalisations.

In the language of a note to the Canadian decision of *Harms* [[1944] 2 DLR 61], fraud in the inducement does not destroy the reality of the apparent consent; fraud in the factum does. The note distinguishes 'between the type of fraud which induces a consent that would not otherwise have been obtained but which is none the less a valid consent and the type of fraud which prevents any real consent from existing'. The same distinction exists in relation to fraud inducing marriage itself. In *Moss v Moss* [(1897) P 263], Lord St Helier as he afterwards became, said:

'It has been repeatedly stated that a marriage may be declared null on the ground of fraud or duress. But, on examination, it will be found that this is only a way of amplifying the proposition long ago laid down (*Fulwood's* case [(1638) Cro Car 482 at 488, 493]) that the voluntary consent of the parties is required. In the case of duress with regard to the marriage contract as with regard to any other, it is obvious that there is an absence of a consenting will. But when in English law fraud is spoken of as a ground for avoiding a marriage, this does not include such fraud as induces a consent, but is limited to such fraud as procures the appearance without the reality of consent' [(1897) P 263 at 268, 269] . . .

It must be noted that in considering whether an apparent consent is unreal it is the mistake or misapprehension that makes it so. It is not the fraud producing the mistake which is material so much as the mistake itself. But if the mistake or misapprehension is not produced by the fraud of the man, there is logically room for the possibility that he was unaware of the woman's mistake so that a question of his mens rea may arise. So in *Lambert*, Cussen J, 'It is plain that, though in these cases the question of consent or non-consent is primarily referable to the mind of the woman, if she has really a mind, yet the mind of the man is also affected by the facts which indicate want of consent or possible want of capacity to consent' [(1919) VLR at 213]. For that reason it is easy to understand why the stress has been on the fraud. But that stress tends to distract the attention from the essential inquiry, namely, whether the consent is no consent because it is not directed to the nature and character of the act. The identity of the man and the character of the physical act that is done or proposed seem now clearly to be regarded as forming part of the nature and character of the act to which the woman's consent is directed. That accords with the principles governing mistake vitiating apparent manifestations of will in other chapters of the law.

In the present case the decision of the majority of the Full Court extends this conception beyond the identity of the physical act and the immediate conditions affecting its nature to an antecedent cause—the existence of a valid marriage. In the history of bigamy that has never been done. The most heartless bigamist has not been considered guilty of rape. Mock marriages are no new thing. Before the Hardwicke Marriage Act it was a fraud easily devised and readily carried out. But there is no reported instance of an indictment for rape based on the fraudulent character of the ceremony. No indictment of rape was founded on such a fraud. Rape, as a capital felony, was defined with exactness, and although there has been some extension over the centuries in the ambit of the crime, it is quite wrong to bring within its operation forms of evil conduct because they wear some analogy to aspects of the crime and deserve punishment. The judgment of the majority of the Full Court of the Supreme Court goes upon the moral differences between marital intercourse and sexual relations without marriage. The difference is indeed so radical that it is apt to draw the mind away from the real question which is carnal knowledge without consent. It may well be true that the woman in the present case never intended to consent to the latter relationship. But, as was said before, the key to such a case as the present lies in remembering that it is the penetration of the woman's body without her consent to such penetration that makes the felony. The capital felony was not directed to fraudulent conduct inducing her consent. Frauds of that kind must be punished under other heads of the criminal law or not at all; they are not rape. To say that in the present case the facts which the jury must be taken to have found amount to wicked and heartless conduct on the part of the applicant is not enough to establish that he committed rape. To say that in having intercourse with him she supposed that she was concerned in a perfectly moral act is not to say that the intercourse was without her consent. To return to the central point; rape is carnal knowledge of a woman without her consent: carnal knowledge is the physical fact of penetration; it is the consent to that which is in question; such a consent demands a perception as to what is about to take place, as to the identity of the man and the character of what he is doing. But once the consent is comprehending and actual the inducing causes cannot destroy its reality and leave the man guilty of rape . . .

The appeal should be allowed and the conviction quashed.

Appeal allowed. Conviction quashed

Obviously there is no consent where the victim is physically overborne and it cannot be sensibly argued that the victim consents because she offers no physical resistance when she is threatened with violence if she does not. In *Olugboja* [1982] QB 320, [1981] 3 All ER 443, CA, counsel for D's argument that rape was confined to cases where consent was vitiated by threats of violence either to her or a near relative was rejected by the court. '[T]he question now is simply:' said the court (at p 448), 'at the time of the sexual intercourse did the woman consent to it? It is not necessary for the prosecution to prove that what might otherwise appear to have been consent was in reality merely submission induced by force, fear or fraud, although one or more of these factors will no doubt be present in the majority of cases of rape.' The court recognised that while 'consent' is an ordinary English word it covered a wide range of states of mind ranging from actual desire on the one hand to reluctant acquiescence on the other. Accordingly a jury might need to be directed on the difference between consent and submission for while every consent involves a submission it did not follow that submission involved consent (see *Day* (1841) 9 C & P 722 at 724 per Coleridge J).

It seems to be established that it is rape to have intercourse with a woman who is asleep (*Fletcher* (1859) Bell CC 63) or who has been rendered insensate by drink or drugs (*Camplin* (1845) 1 Den 89). In such cases the intercourse is without the victim's consent but has it been accomplished by 'force, fear or fraud'? Does it have to be? What of a police officer who secures the woman's submission by threatening to report her for an offence if she does not? Winn J once ruled (see *Olugboja* at p 446) that the police officer had no case to answer on a charge of rape but in *Wellard* (1978) 67 Cr App Rep 364 at 368, the court noted, without comment, that D had previously been convicted of rape where he had pretended to be a security officer and had secured the victim's submission to sexual intercourse by saying that otherwise he would inform the police and her parents that she had been having intercourse in a public place. Does the victim in such cases as these any more consent than the victim who submits to avoid personal violence? If not, what of the actress who submits to sexual intercourse by a film producer who tells her that otherwise she will not get a part in the film? Is it a possible distinction that the actress gets what she wants (the part in the film) whereas in the *Wellard* situation she merely avoids what she does not want (disclosure to police and parents)? Is it helpful to talk of a distinction between consent and submission? Do the actress and the girl in *Wellard* consent or merely submit?

There are similar problems with fraud. At present the only fraud recognised as vitiating consent is deception as to the nature of the act and impersonation of a husband. As to the former the cases (see *Case* (1850) 1 Den 580, *Flattery* [1877] 2 QBD 410, and *Williams* [1923] 1 KB 340 which are discussed in *Papadimitropoulos*) have consistently held this to be rape. On the other hand Willes J once said that a consent produced by mere animal instinct would be sufficient to prevent the act from being rape (*Fletcher* (1859) Bell CC 63 at 70) but it is not clear what he meant by this and in fact he joined in affirming D's conviction for rape where D had had intercourse with a 13-year-old girl of weak intellect, incapable of distinguishing right from wrong who was not shown to have offered any resistance.

As to personation it is now settled by statute (now Sexual Offences Act 1956, s 1(2)) that a man who effects intercourse by personating the husband is guilty of rape. As appears from the discussion in *Papadimitropoulos* the decisions are conflicting on this issue and the issue assumes importance if D effects intercourse by personating the victim's boyfriend. Ought this to be rape? If yes, how is it to be distinguished from *Papadimitropoulos*? The victim in *Papadimitropoulos* because of D's fraud thought she was engaging in lawful sexual intercourse capable of producing legitimate offspring; the victim who submits to intercourse by one personating her boyfriend knows that she is engaging in unlawful sexual intercourse. Is there any convincing reason why it should not be rape in the one case but rape in the other?

The CLRC (Cmnd 9213, para 2.20) concluded that it should be rape to effect sexual intercourse by personation (whether of a husband or another man) or by fraud as to the nature of the act but not otherwise. At the Working Paper stage some members had favoured dispensing altogether with fraud in rape and this view was supported both by a majority of members of the Policy Advisory Committee and by the majority of commentators on the Working Paper. As to submission through force or fear the CLRC thought this should be restricted to threats of force against the victim or any other person and it should not be rape if there was no such threat or where the threat could only be carried out at some time in the future. Note that under s 2 of the Sexual Offences Act 1956 it is an offence to procure a woman by threats or intimidation to have sexual intercourse, and under s 3 it is an offence so to procure a woman by false pretences or false representations. The CLRC favours the retention of both offences, presently punishable with two years' imprisonment but proposed that the punishment on the s 2 offence be increased to five years.

The offences under ss 2 and 3, though not often used in practice, provide necessary supplements to the offence of rape in those cases which do not fall within the definition of rape ought nevertheless to be proscribed. The case instanced (p 398, above) of the police officer who secures the victim's submission to sexual intercourse by threatening otherwise to report the victim for an offence, if it is not already rape, ought to be proscribed and clearly falls within s 2. Threats may vary in seriousness from a threat to dismiss the victim from employment to a threat not to take the victim to a dance. The analogy of blackmail suggests itself (p 484, below) so the threat must be of such a nature as to overbear the mind of a woman of normal stability and courage.

Similarly s 3 extends to cases of sexual intercourse obtained by fraud not falling within the definition of rape. *Papadimitropoulos* would seem to fall within the section since there the victim would not have consented but for being deceived into thinking she was married. The test would seem to be whether, but for the false pretence or representation, the victim would not have consented to the intercourse. Suppose then that D obtains the victim's consent by telling her that it will improve her voice. The analogy with obtaining property by deception (p 451, below) suggests that the undue gullibility of the victim is no defence but an analogy with s 2 might suggest that the pretence should be one which would influence a reasonable woman. Which is to be preferred?

(4) MENS REA

Director of Public Prosecutions v Morgan [1975] 2 All ER 347, House of Lords

The case is set out at p 45, above.

After *Morgan* and following the Heilbron Report (Cmnd 6352, 1975) rape was defined in s 1(1) of the Sexual Offences (Amendment) Act 1976 (p 577, below) to include the case where D is reckless as to whether the victim consents. There is no doubt that the Heilbron Group had in mind *Cunningham* recklessness (p 63, above) but the decision in *Caldwell* (p 68, above) ran counter to that intention. For a while the Court of Appeal sought to accommodate *Caldwell* though it involved the preposterous contemplation of a man having sexual intercourse giving no thought to whether the victim was consenting.

R v Satnam, R v Kewal (1983) 78 Cr App Rep 149, Court of Appeal, Criminal Division
(Dunn LJ, Bristow J and Sir John Thompson)

[The following facts are taken from the judgment.]

The victim was a 13-year-old white girl, although she looked older, who worked part-time in a shop where Satnam, aged 31, also worked. Some minor familiarities had taken place between them. She had met Kewal, aged 30, once. She had been a virgin prior to the offences.

At about 7.00 pm, on January 25 1981, Satnam offered her a lift in Kewal's car to the shop to do some cleaning. As there were no lights on there she agreed that they should drive round for a time, although she said she had to be home by 9.00 pm. There followed two incidents when both appellants had sexual intercourse with her or attempted to do so. In each case one got into the back of the car with the girl and had intercourse while the other drove. In between the incidents they stopped, once at a public house and once at an off-licence to buy some Bacardi. On neither occasion did the girl try to run away or make any complaint. During the second incident Satnam failed to have sexual intercourse because he was drunk, but Kewal had sexual intercourse with her for a long time. During both incidents the girl kicked and struggled and told them to leave her alone, but they removed her underclothes and persisted. . . .

When questioned she said quite calmly: 'They had intercourse with me,' and went on to say she had tried to stop them but they were too strong. . . .

Both gave evidence. Satnam said that he had had sexual intercourse once with her agreement. On the second occasion she seemed to want it, but he could not manage it. Kewal said that on both occasions he thought she wanted it. . . .

[**Bristow J** read the judgment of the Court:]

On February 1, 1982, at Stafford Crown Court before his Honour Judge Taylor the appellants were both convicted of rape, being reckless as to consent, and of aiding and abetting the other to commit such rape. They were both acquitted of rape, knowing there to be no consent, and of aiding and abetting the other to commit such rape. They were both sentenced to five years' imprisonment on each count, concurrent. . . .

The question of law is whether, in directing the jury as to the state of mind of the appellants in 'reckless' rape, the judge should have left to the jury the question whether they genuinely though mistakenly believed that the victim was consenting to sexual intercourse; and whether the judge was right to direct them that it was sufficient, in order to prove recklessness, if it was obvious to an ordinary observer that she was not consenting. On November 4, 1983, we allowed the appeals and quashed the convictions. We now give our reasons.

[His Lordship stated the facts and continued:] The judge plainly took a great deal of trouble in his direction as to the law, and in fairness to him it must be said that when he summed up, on February 1, 1982, the law was in an uncertain state. *R v Caldwell* (1981) 73 Cr App R 13, [1982] AC 341 and *R v Lawrence* (1981) 73 Cr App R 1, [1982] AC 510 had recently been decided, and *Pigg* (1982) 74 Cr App R 352 was not decided until February 5, 1982.

The judge rightly pointed out that there was no dispute that sexual intercourse had in fact taken place. He went on to deal impeccably with the elements of consent by the girl and the knowledge of the appellants which was relevant to the counts on which they were acquitted. He then turned to the element of recklessness and said this:

'Members of the jury, a person is reckless in this context: if there was an obvious reason, in the circumstances as the jury find them to be, if there was an obvious reason that the girl was not in fact willing to have sexual intercourse, that is to say, obvious to every ordinary observer, and the defendant either did not apply his mind to that reason at all, for whatever reason, or, applied his mind to the reason, but carried on having sexual intercourse with her, or trying to, that is recklessness.'

He then repeated that direction and gave no further direction as to the necessary elements to be proved in the crime of reckless rape.

Two grounds of appeal were relied on in this Court. (1) That the judge should have directed the jury that a genuine though mistaken belief that the girl was consenting offered a defence to a charge of reckless rape; (2) that the judge erred in referring to an 'ordinary observer' in his direction as to recklessness, and that he should have directed the jury that it was necessary to prove that each appellant was actually aware of the possibility that the girl was not consenting before they could find him reckless.

So far as the first ground was concerned, it was accepted by Mr Smith for the Crown that he could not support the summing-up in the absence of a direction as to belief. In *Thomas* (1982) 77 Cr App R 63 Lord Lane CJ said, at p 65:

'In this particular case, the judge should have spelt out in terms that a mistaken belief that the woman was consenting, however unreasonable it may appear to have been, is an answer to the charge, and that it is for the prosecution to eliminate the possibility of such a mistake if they are to succeed. He should then have gone on to deal with the matters set out in section 1(2) of the 1976 Act. As it was the jury were left without any guidance on the matter.'

The same situation arose here. The jury were left without any guidance on the matter of belief and on that ground alone we would allow the appeal.

We turn now to consider the second ground, i e the direction as to recklessness. Strictly it may be said that this point has already been decided in *Bashir* (1982) 77 Cr App R 59, 62 where Watkins LJ said:

'As recently as the fifth of this month, Lord Lane CJ in *Thomas* (supra) restated the definition of "reckless" as applied to the offence of rape. He said (1982) 77 Cr App R 63, 66: "A man is reckless if either he was indifferent and gave no thought to the possibility that the woman might not be consenting, in circumstances where, if any thought had been given to the matter, it would have been obvious that there was a risk she was not, or, he was aware of the possibility that she might not be consenting but nevertheless persisted, regardless of whether she consented or not." He was in almost exact form repeating the definition of "reckless" in relation to rape which he had provided in the case of *Pigg* (1982) 74 Cr App R 352. It will be noted that that definition allows of none other than a subjective approach to the state of mind of a person of whom it is said he acted recklessly in committing a crime. It was incumbent therefore on the trial judge in the present case to ensure that he provided the jury with this kind of definition of the word "reckless." '

Mr Tayler on behalf of the appellants submitted, in his able argument, that the use of the word 'obvious' in its context in both *Pigg* (supra) and *Thomas* (supra) gives rise to a possible ambiguity. 'Obvious' to whom? If it meant obvious to any reasonable person that would introduce an objective test, and Mr Tayler submitted that the authorities properly understood do not warrant such a conclusion. He invited us in effect to clarify the situation which has developed since *Caldwell* (supra) and *Lawrence* (supra), as he said that judges up and down the country are now in a state of some confusion as to the state of the law. He submitted that the direction of recklessness in *Pigg* (supra) was in any event obiter.

As Robert Goff LJ said in *Elliott v C (a minor)* (1983) 77 Cr App R 103, 119, [1983] 1 WLR 939, 950, with reference to the suggested direction in *Pigg* (supra):

'Now it cannot be disguised that the addition of the words "was indifferent and" constituted a gloss upon the definition of recklessness proposed by Lord Diplock in *R v Caldwell* (supra). Furthermore, if it were legitimate to interpret Lord Diplock's speech in relation to a case arising not under section 1 of the Sexual Offences (Amendment) Act 1976, but under section 1(1) of the Criminal Damage Act 1971, the effect would be that the second question posed by the magistrates in the case now before this court would be answered in the affirmative, and the appeal would be dismissed; because there is no finding of fact that this defendant in the case before us was indifferent to the risk of destruction by fire of the shed and its contents. This is an approach which I would gladly adopt, if I felt that I was free to do so. However, I do not consider that it is open to this Court, in a case arising under the very subsection to which Lord Diplock's speech was expressly directed, to impose this qualification, which I feel would in this context constitute too substantial a departure from the test proposed by him.'

The instant case, unlike *Elliott* (supra), is not concerned with the Criminal Damage Act 1971 but with the Sexual Offences (Amendment) Act 1976, and the Court is considering recklessness in the context of rape and not in the context of criminal damage. We feel we are therefore free to review the situation so far as it is governed by relevant authority, and accepting as we do that there is an ambiguity in the suggested direction in *Pigg*, which was in any event obiter.

Mr Tayler took as his starting point *Director of Public Prosecutions v Morgan* (1975) 61 Cr App R 136; [1976] AC 182, a decision of the House of Lords on the very question of rape, which was not overruled by either *Caldwell* or *Lawrence* and is binding on this Court. Lord Hailsham said at p 151 and p 215 of the respective reports:

'I am content to rest my view of the instant case on the crime of rape by saying that it is my opinion that the prohibited act is and always has been intercourse without consent of the victim and the mental element is and always has been the intention to commit that act, or the equivalent intention of having intercourse willy-nilly not caring whether the victim consents or no. A failure to prove this involves an acquittal because the intent, an essential ingredient, is lacking. It matters not why it is lacking if only it is not there, and in particular it matters not that the intention is lacking only because of a belief not based on reasonable grounds.'

In the Report of the Advisory Group on the Law of Rape (The Heilbron Committee) Command Paper 6352 1975, the following 'Recommendations for declaratory legislation' were made:

'81. Notwithstanding our conclusions that *Morgan's* case (supra) is right in principle, we nevertheless feel that legislation is required to clarify the law governing intention in rape cases, as it is now settled. We think this for two principal reasons. The first is that it would be possible in future cases to argue that the question of recklessness did not directly arise for decision in *Morgan's* case, in view of the form of the question certified: to avoid possible doubts the ruling on recklessness needs to be put in statutory form. 82. Secondly, it would be unfortunate if a tendency were to arise to say to the jury "that a belief, however unreasonable, that the woman consented, entitled the accused to acquittal." Such a phrase might tend to give an undue or misleading emphasis to one aspect only and the law, therefore, should be statutorily restated in a fuller form which would obviate the use of those words. 83. We think that there would be advantage if this matter could also be dealt with by a statutory provision which would—(i) declare that (in cases where the question of belief is raised) the issue which the jury have to consider is whether the accused at the time when sexual intercourse took place believed that she was consenting, and (ii) make it clear that, while there is no requirement of law that such a belief must be based on reasonable grounds, the presence or absence of such grounds is a relevant consideration to which the jury should have regard, in conjunction with all other evidence, in considering whether the accused genuinely had such a belief.'

There followed the Sexual Offences (Amendment) Act 1976 [his Lordship read s 1].

We think that in enacting those provisions Parliament must have accepted the recommendations of the Heilbron Committee, so that the provisions are declaratory of the existing law as stated in *DPP v Morgan* (supra).

Any direction as to the definition of rape should therefore be based upon section 1 of the 1976 Act and upon *DPP v Morgan* (supra), without regard to *R v Caldwell* (supra) or *R v Lawrence* (supra), which were concerned with recklessness in a different context and under a different statute.

The word 'reckless' in relation to rape involves a different concept to its use in relation to malicious damage or, indeed, in relation to offences against the person. In the latter cases the foreseeability, or possible foreseeability, is as to the consequences of the criminal act. In the case of rape the foreseeability is as to the state of mind of the victim. . . .

In summing-up a case of rape which involves the issue of consent, the judge should, in dealing with the state of mind of the defendant, first of all direct the jury that before they could convict of rape the Crown had to prove either that the defendant knew the woman did not want to have sexual intercourse, or was reckless as to whether she wanted to or not. If they were sure he knew she did not want to they should find him guilty of rape knowing there to be no consent. If they were not sure about that, then they would find him not guilty of such rape and should go on to consider reckless rape. If they thought he might genuinely have believed that she did want to, even though he was mistaken in his belief, they would find him not guilty. In considering whether his belief was genuine, they should take into account all the relevant circumstances (which could at that point be summarised) and ask themselves whether, in the light of those circumstances, he had reasonable grounds for such a belief. If, after considering those circumstances, they were sure he had no genuine belief that she wanted to, they would find him guilty. If they came to the conclusion that he could not care less whether she wanted to or not, but pressed on regardless, then he would have been reckless and could not have believed that she wanted to, and they would find him guilty of reckless rape. . . .

Appeals allowed. Convictions of rape quashed.

Questions

1. In *Seymour* [1983] 2 All ER 1058 at 1064, p 345, above Lord Roskill said that ' "Reckless" should today be given the same meaning [*sc* the *Caldwell* meaning] in relation to all offences which involve "recklessness" as one of the elements unless Parliament has otherwise ordained.' Can it be sensibly argued that Parliament has 'otherwise ordained' in the context of s 1 of the Sexual Offences (Amendment) Act? If not, is there any other reason why *Caldwell* recklessness should not apply to rape?
2. What of the defendant who says, 'Well I thought she was consenting but really I could not have cared less because I would have gone ahead anyway'?
3. Viewed as a matter of principle what would be wrong with a rule in rape that required that the defendant's belief should be honestly entertained on reasonable grounds? If a man going through a ceremony of marriage has to take reasonable care to ascertain the facts relevant to his avoiding the commission of a prohibited act, why shouldn't a man indulging in sexual intercourse take reasonable care to ascertain whether the woman is consenting?

(5) BOYS UNDER 14

There is a long established and irrebuttable presumption that a boy under 14 cannot commit rape nor any offence involving sexual intercourse. Hale (1 PC 630) said that 'as to this fact the law presumes him impotent as well as wanting discretion.' The rule is indefensible. The CLRC found that boys under 14 did commit acts which would be rape were they over 14 and that it was a matter of public concern that they could not be convicted of rape. The CLRC accordingly recommended the abolition of the presumption (Cmnd 9213, para 2.48). A boy over ten and under 14 may, if he has mischievous discretion, be convicted of indecent assault and of aiding and abetting rape.

2. Indecent assault and indecency with children

Sexual Offences Act 1956, ss 14 and 15, pp 550–551, below; and Indecency with Children Act 1960, s 1, p 556, below

Generally consent is a defence to these offences except that it is provided that a person under sixteen or who is a defective cannot give any consent which would prevent an act being an assault for the purposes of these sections.

If D does not know and has no reason to suspect that P is a defective, P's consent is a defence though P is in fact a defective. In *Hudson* [1966] 1 QB 448, [1965] 1 All ER 721, CA, where D had, or attempted to have, intercourse with an 18-year-old defective girl it was held the trial judge was wrong to direct the jury that they might convict if they were satisfied that there existed facts or circumstances which would have given the ordinary man possessed of his reason, grounds to suspect that the girl was a defective. The proper test was subjective, that is to say that if D establishes on a balance of probabilities that he himself had no reason to suspect then he was entitled to an acquittal.

There is no similar provision with respect to persons under sixteen so that it is clear that *Prince* (1875) LR 2 CCR 154, (p 102, above) is applicable and even a reasonable belief that P is over that age is no defence.

Where a man under 24 is charged under s 6 with intercourse with a girl under 16 and establishes a defence on the ground that he reasonably believed her to be over 16, he may be convicted on a second count for an indecent assault under s 14. In *Laws* (1928) 21 Cr App Rep 45 at 46 the Court of Criminal Appeal stigmatised as 'grotesque' a situation which offered the man a defence on the major but not the minor charge but the anomaly was re-enacted in the 1956 consolidation.

Faulkner v Talbot [1981] 3 All ER 468, Queen's Bench Division.
(Lord Lane CJ, Boreham and Drake JJ)

Lord Lane CJ. . . . . The way in which the case arises is this. The appellant was convicted by the justices on 5th February 1980 of indecent assault on a boy, who was then aged 14 years, contrary to s 15(1) of the Sexual Offences Act 1956. The events happened at the appellant's home, and there is no dispute as to the material facts. The 14-year-old boy was living in the appellant's home, having left his parents. The appellant and the boy watched a horror film on the television; the boy was scared, or said he was scared, by the film. As a result of that the appellant told the boy that he could sleep with her if he wished. That he chose to do.

Once they were in bed together, the appellant invited the boy to have sexual intercourse with her. The boy's account, in so far as it was material, was this: the appellant tried to put her hand on his penis, but he would not let her. She then pulled the boy on top of her; she took hold of his penis and put it inside her vagina. On those facts the charge was laid.

It is well-known fact that there is no statutory provision specifically forbidding a women to have sexual intercourse with a boy of 14. But what s 15 of the Sexual Offences Act 1956, under which this case was brought, says is as follows:

> '(1) It is an offence for a person to make an indecent assault on man.
> (2) A boy under the age of sixteen cannot in law give any consent which would prevent an act being an assault for the purposes of this section. . .'

The way in which counsel for the appellant, in his attractive argument to this court, has put the matter is as follows. He submits that, since the act of sexual intercourse in these circumstances is not an offence on the part of the woman, therefore that touching of the boy as a prelude to, or as part of, or as postlude to, the act of sexual intercourse cannot in logic itself be an offence.

He submits, secondly, if, for example, in an act of sexual intercourse, in the way described by Wien J in *R v Upward* (7th October 1976, unreported), to which reference will be made later, a woman lies passively and does nothing at all except let the boy have sexual intercourse, that, suggests counsel, would be no offence; whereas if she took any part in the act, by touching the boy for instance on the buttock during the act of sexual intercourse, it would be an offence. That, counsel submits, is contrary to common sense and contrary to logic and therefore, he goes on to argue, it cannot be right that the act of sexual intercourse under any circumstances can amount to indecent assault by the woman on the boy.

We have been referred to a number of authorities and it is right, both for the purpose of clarity and in deference to the arguments addressed to us, that I should refer to them. The first case we were referred to was *R v Hare* [1934] 1 KB 354, [1933] All ER Rep 550. The appellant was a woman who had been convicted under s 62 of the Offences against the Person Act 1861 (which was a precursor of the 1956 Act) of indecent assault on a boy of 12. In so far as it was material, that section of the 1861 Act read: 'Whosoever . . . shall be guilty . . . of any indecent Assault upon any Male Person shall be guilty of a misdemeanour . . .'

The judgment of the court was delivered by Avory J. Having stated the facts, he went on as follows ([1934] 1 KB 354 at 355–356, [1933] All ER Rep 550 at 551–552):

'We are asked in this case to hold that it was not competent to the Recorder to leave the case to the jury or for the jury to convict the appellant. The argument put forward on behalf of the appellant is that the charge being laid under s 62 of the Offences against the Person Act, 1861, no woman can be convicted of the offences charged. The boy, being under the age of sixteen, was by law incompetent to consent to any such conduct as took place between him and the appellant. There is no question that the nature of that which took place between them was indecent. The whole question is, as has been concisely put by counsel for the appellant, whether the offence under s 62 is to be limited to an indecent assault of a sodomitical character . . . there is no reason for saying that the phrase: ''Whosoever . . . shall be guilty . . . of any indecent assault'' does not include a woman.'

That case provides a formidable hurdle for counsel for the appellant to clear.

The next case to which we were referred was *Director of Public Prosecutions v Rogers* [1953] 2 All ER 644, [1953] 1 WLR 1017. That was a case where the facts were somewhat special, as will be observed. The headnote reads (37 Cr App R 137):

'On two occasions, the respondent, when alone in the house with his daughter aged 11, put his arm round her and led her upstairs, and when they were upstairs exposed his person and invited her to masturbate him, which she did. No compulsion or force was used by the defendant, and the child neither objected nor resisted, but submitted to the defendant's request. Justices dismissed informations charging the defendant with indecent assault on the child.'

The Divisional Court held, on those facts, 'that as the defendant had not used compulsion or force, or acted in a hostile manner towards the child, there had been no assault, and consequently no indecent assault on her, and that the decision of the justices was, therefore, right'. The facts were that the father, being alone in the house with the little daughter, put his arms round her and said 'come upstairs'. She made no objection or resistance and no force was used on either of the two occasions. That was the basis for the decision of the court, namely that the justices were right and the appeal was dismissed.

It seems to me that the circumstances there were exceptional. There was no reason why the father should not put his arm round the shoulder of his daughter; there was a lawful excuse for doing that, because he was the father. There was no touching of the child in an indecent way.

The next case was *R v Mason* (1968) 53 Cr App R 12. The headnote reads as follows:

'The defendant, a married woman, was arraigned on a number of counts, each alleging indecent assault against one of six different boys, all between the ages of fourteen and sixteen years. Over a substantial period of time she had been visited by the boys, sometimes singly, sometimes more than one at a time, and had had sexual intercourse with them. There was no suggestion that she had used any force or committed any hostile act against any of the boys. Intercourse had taken place sometimes at her suggestion, sometimes at the suggestion of the boys themselves. *Held*, that as there was no evidence of the use of any force or of any hostile act by the defendant, there had been no assault, and consequently no indecent assault, so that the counts must be quashed.'

I read one passage from the judgment of Veale J, which was really the high spot of counsel's argument (at 18):

'I am further prepared to hold that acts of touching readily submitted to and enjoyed during or preliminary to intercourse in such circumstances should be regarded as part of the intercourse and are equally not an assault by the woman on the boy.'

Those words were echoed in a different form in a case to which we have been referred, *R v Upward* (7th October 1976, unreported) which was heard at Caernarvon before Wien J and a jury. Wien J was there, in the passage to which we have been referred, informing the jury of the reason why he was directing them to acquit the woman in similar circumstances to those which I have described in *Mason*. Wien J, as I say, echoed and expanded the words used by Veale J in *Mason*.

One turns now to consider whether those two passage correctly reflect the law as it stands at the moment and in order to reach that decision it is necessary to look at two more recent decisions. The first is *R v McCormack* [1969] 3 All ER 371, [1969] 2 QB 442. That was a decision of the Court of Appeal, Criminal Division, before Fenton Atkinson LJ, Melford Stevenson and James JJ. The headnote reads as follows (53 Cr App R 514):

'A charge of unlawful sexual intercourse with a girl under sixteen necessarily includes an allegation of indecent assault on the same girl and, where there is clear evidence of indecent assault, the judge should leave this lesser offence also to the jury, even though the prosecution have not relied on it. When a man inserts his finger into the vagina of a girl under sixteen, this is an indecent assault, however willing and co-operative the girl may be.'

I read a passage from the judgment of the court delivered by Fenton Atkinson LJ ([1969] 3 All ER 371 at 373, [1969] 2 QB 442 at 445);

'Then there followed an argument by counsel for the appellant, which he has repeated to this court and put very attractively before us, whether in view of the girl's consent, there could be a conviction of indecent assault, there being here a willing girl and no evidence of any compulsion or hostility; and he referred to a line of authorities such as *Fairclough v Whipp* ([1951] 2 All ER 834) and *Director of Public Prosecutions v Rogers* ([1953] 2 All ER 644, [1953] 1 WLR 1017), cases which have shown that where the accused adult invites a child, for example, to touch his private parts, but exercises no sort of compulsion and there is no hostile act, the charge of indecent assault is not appropriate. But, in our view, that line of authorities has no application here, and, in the view of the members of this court, it is plain beyond argument that if a man inserts a finger into the vagina of a girl under sixteen that is an indecent assault, in view of her age, and is it an indecent assault however willing and co-operative she may in fact be.'

Finally, so far as authorities are concerned, I turn to *R v Sutton* [1977] 3 All ER 476, [1977] 1 WLR 1086. In that case the facts were that the appellant took three boys, all under the age of 14, to his home and photographed them partially clothed and in the nude. He remained fully clothed. He neither touched or fondled the boys, except touch them on the hands and legs and bodies in order to arrange their poses for the purpose of photography. The boys consented to these acts.

The appellant was charged with indecently assaulting the boys contrary to s 15(1) of the 1956 Act. The jury were directed that any touching without consent was an assault and the law did not permit persons under 16 to consent to the touching, if it was accompanied by circumstances of indecency. The jury convicted. On appeal it was held by the Court of Appeal, Criminal Division, that they had been misdirected.

The holding was (66 Cr App R 21):

'that whereas section 15(2) of the Sexual Offences Act 1956 bars consent from preventing an act with a boy under 16 from being an indecent assault—i e if the act alleged to constitute the assault is itself an indecent act—and thus the defence of consent will not avail a defendant; in the present case the touching of the boys by the appellant, which was merely to indicate a pose, was not of itself indecent, was consented to and was not hostile or threatening, the consent of the boys to the acts complained of prevented such acts being an assault, and, therefore, an indecent assault; thus the question of indecency did not arise; accordingly, the jury had been misdirected and the appeal would be allowed and the conviction quashed.'

One turns, in the light of those authorities, to the present case. First of all what is an assault? An assault is any intentional touching of another person without the consent of that person and without lawful excuse. It need not necessarily be hostile or rude or aggressive, as some of the cases seem to indicate. If the touching is an indecent touching, as in this case it plainly was because the appellant took hold of the boy's penis, then the provisions of s 15(2) of the Sexual Offences Act 1956 come into play: 'A boy under the age of sixteen cannot in law give any consent which would prevent an act being an assault for the purposes of this section.' Consequently, the touching undoubtedly being indecent, the boy in this case, being aged 14, could not consent to it. It was intentional touching; it was touching without lawful excuse, and in view of s 15(2) it was a touching to which the boy could not in law consent and therefore did not consent. Accordingly, as I see it, one has all the necessary ingredients of the offence of indecent assault, and the consequence is that the recorder was correct in the conclusion to which he came.

The question which is asked by the case is as follows:

'. . . whether the acts of the appellant to which the complainant consented in pulling him on top of her and touching his penis immediately before sexual intercourse by him with her were an indecent assault by the appellant on the complainant contrary to s 15(1) of the Sexual Offences Act, 1956?'

The answer I would give to that is Yes, it was an indecent assault. In my judgment the decision of Veale J in *Mason* was wrong, and in so far as it is necessary to refer to the matter, where Wien J was making explanation to the jury, he was likewise in error.

For these reasons I would dismiss this appeal.

[**Boreham J** and **Drake J** delivered concurring judgments.]

Appeal dismissed

(1) THE REQUIREMENT OF AN ASSAULT

The term 'assault' here is used both in its strict sense, as where P is made to apprehend a contact, and to include a battery where there is an actual contact. It follows that if P consents then (subject to the limitations on consent considered above, p 357) there can be no assault and it is irrelevant to further consider whether what is consented to is indecent. But this is not quite the position where P is under 16 years of age. The general rule is the same in that there is no assault where P, being under 16, consents to the contact by D (as in sports or medical treatment for example) but a person under 16 cannot consent to an indecent contact by D. Hence an indecent contact by D on P is an *indecent* assault (though not a *common* assault) though P consents. According to *DPP v Rogers* (considered in *Faulkner v Talbot*) an indecent contact by P on D, even at D's invitation is not an indecent assault by D on P at least if D remains inactive during the contact. The one act in *Rogers* which might have constituted an indecent assault was when D put his arm round P and led her upstairs with intent that she should masturbate him. Why was this not an indecent assault? What if D had threatened P with violence if she did not masturbate him? Indecent assault?

(2) CIRCUMSTANCES OF INDECENCY

Obviously there is an indecent assault where D, intending to indecently assault, makes P apprehend an indecent contact or makes an indecent contact. In *Beal v Kelley* [1951] 2 All ER 763 D exposed his person to a 14-year-old boy and asked him to handle it, and when the boy refused D grabbed his arm and pushed the boy towards himself. An argument that the contact itself must be indecent was rejected and the court held that it sufficed that the assault was 'accompanied by circumstances of indecency' on D's part. The circumstances here may include words spoken by D evincing an indecent intention on D's part.

The more difficult case is where D intends to act indecently but nothing in his conduct evinces that intention. In *George* [1956] Crim LR 52 D attempted to remove a girl's shoe from her foot because it gave him perverted sexual gratification. Streatfeild J, rejecting the argument that the indecent motive made this an indecent assault, held that circumstances of indecency must be proved and that there was no evidence of them in this case. Suppose that in *Rogers* D had the following day again put his arm round P to lead her upstairs. Though nothing is said, P realises that D's intentions are indecent. Has D been indecently assaulted?

In *Pratt* [1984] Crim LR 41 two boys were fishing at midnight on a lonely quay when they were approached by D wearing a stocking mask. By pretending he had a gun D obliged the boys to undress so as to reveal their private parts. He then had the boys shine a torch on each other and claimed that his motive in so doing was to search for cannabis which he thought the boys had stolen from him the previous afternoon. On a charge of indecent assault the prosecution argued that it was enough to show an assault in circumstances of indecency but the Assistant Recorder ruled that it was necessary for the prosecution to prove an indecent intention. Suppose, however, that D's story about the cannabis had been bogus and he had forced the boys to strip to satisfy his prurient interest. Would this constitute an indecent assault?

While an indecent motive (at least if P is unaware of it) cannot convert an objectively innocent act into an indecent assault, a decent motive may justify what would otherwise be an indecent act. Touching of the body is not indecent if done in the course of a proper medical examination. Would it make any difference that the doctor derived sexual satisfaction from conducting what was otherwise a proper medical examination? Consider *Bolduc and Bird* (p 359, above). Supposing that the patient had been under 16, would she have been indecently assaulted?

What is 'indecent'? Suppose P's girlfriend sends him a 'kissogram' on his birthday. D, the girl who delivers the greeting, insists on kissing P though he indicates his lack of consent. D is guilty of an assault but is she guilty of an indecent assault? What of the boss who pinches his secretary's bottom?

(3) MENS REA

The mens rea may be regarded as having two aspects: (i) in relation to the assault; and (ii) in relation to the indecency.

As to the former see *Venna* ([1976] QB 421, [1975] 3 All ER 788, CA, p 355, above) and *Kimber* ([1983] 3 All ER 316, [1983] 1 WLR 1118, CA, p 237, above). As to the latter there is no ruling by an appellate court but the Assistant Recorder in *Pratt* (supra) was surely right in ruling that it was not enough to prove an assault in circumstances of indecency and that an intention to indecently assault must be shown. It can hardly be supposed that if Archimedes in his excitement on discovering that a body displaces its own weight in water had rushed naked from his house and had then assaulted a passer-by who sought to dispute his theory that Archimedes would thereby have been guilty of an indecent assault.

(4) INDECENCY WITH CHILDREN

Cases such as *Fairclough v Whipp, DPP v Rogers, Mason,* and *Sutton* are now covered by the Indecency with Children Act 1960 provided the child is under 14 and the indecency is 'gross'. When does 'indecency' become 'gross indecency'? Is it possible to articulate any satisfactory test? Should the matter simply be regarded as one of fact since magistrates or a jury can be expected to tell the difference between indecency and gross indecency when they see it?

(5) PROPOSALS FOR REFORM

The CLRC (Cmnd 9213, para 4.1–4.31) proposes to confine indecent assault to assault properly so called and to rid the law of the problems presently created by the consensual indecent assault of persons under 16. Nor will the CLRC proposals draw any distinction between indecent assaults on males or females. The Committee did not favour the creation of degrees of indecent assault but suggested lines along which an offence of aggravated indecent assault might be defined. Consistently with their view that 16 should be the age of consent for heterosexual conduct, the Committee (para 7.1–7.28) recommended that the age in the offence of indecency with children should be raised to sixteen.

With the exception of the offence of intercourse with a girl under thirteen, the CLRC has recommended that in relation to all sexual offences where the age of the victim is relevant that an honest belief that the victim is above the relevant age should be a defence.

CHAPTER 20

Theft and related offences

The law relating to offences of theft is to be found in the Theft Acts 1968 and 1978. These Acts were largely based on the recommendations of the Criminal Law Revision Committee (*Eighth Report, Theft and Related Offences*, Cmnd 2977 (1966); and *Thirteenth Report, Section 16 of the Theft Act 1968*, Cmnd 6733 (1977)) which had decided (Cmnd 2977, para 7) that the time had come 'for a new law of theft and related offences, based on a fundamental reconsideration of the principles underlying this branch of the law and embodied in a modern statute.'

So far as the law of *theft* is concerned these Acts constitute the authoritative, comprehensive and exclusive source of the law. But, of course, a law of theft assumes laws relating to ownership. In general terms a man cannot steal his own property and can only steal property belonging to another. While s 5 of the Theft Act states when property is to be treated as belonging to another it is immediately apparent that in order to determine whether P has 'a proprietary right or interest' or whether property is 'subject to a trust' or whether a person is 'under an obligation to make restoration' reference must be made to civil cases, whether decided before or after the coming into force of the Theft Acts which are authoritative as explaining these concepts. Hence whether D is guilty of theft may involve a consideration of the law of contract, the Sale of Goods Acts 1979, or principles of equity. But in cases decided under the Acts the courts have on occasion displayed some impatience with arguments based on the civil law. In *Baxter* ([1971] 2 All ER 359, 363, CA; and see also the observations of Lord Roskill in *Morris* [1983] 3 All ER 288, below) Sachs LJ said:

> 'At this juncture it is convenient in connection with the older authorities concerned with obtaining money or chattels by false pretences to mention a point of some importance in relation to the Theft Act 1968. That is an Act designed to simplify the law—it uses words in their natural meaning and is to be construed thus to produce sensible results; when that Act is under examination this court deprecates attempts, to bring into close consideration the finer distinctions in civil law as to the precise moment when contractual communications take effect or when property passes.'

This attitude, though laudable in its aim to achieve simplicity, cannot be defended. All offences relating to the appropriation of property can be defined intelligibly only in relation to a law of property. That law is the civil law and sometimes the question of mine and thine (and this is a fundamental question in this context) must involve fine questions of civil law. (See Smith, 'Civil Law Concepts in the Criminal Law' [1972B] CLJ 197; Williams, 'Theft, Consent and Illegality' [1977] Crim LR 127 and 205).

Otherwise reference to prior cases would rarely be permissible. One case where such reference may be made is where the Acts use expressions taken from earlier legislation which have acquired a settled meaning. For example it would be permissible to refer to earlier decisions to elucidate the meaning of 'menaces' in connection with the offence of blackmail under s 21 of the 1968 Act. Strictly the earlier cases on the meaning of 'menaces' are no longer authoritative but reference to them would be legitimate and most likely they would be followed. The word 'menaces' had acquired a special meaning which was rather wider than that which it had in ordinary parlance and accordingly it may be assumed, since the draftsman could have chosen another word such as 'threats', that by retaining 'menaces' the intention was to retain its earlier meaning. But this process cannot be carried too far and certainly affords no pretext for any wholesale reference to earlier law. Before any reference can be made it must be clear from the context in which the expression is used in the Act that it is being used in its special sense. For example, it would not be relevant to consider earlier decisions on the meaning of 'robbery' since s 8 of the 1968 Act itself defines robbery exhaustively and that definition may or may not accord with the former position.

One other general point may be made. In their interpretation of the Acts the courts have aimed to give words and expressions their ordinary meaning so as to avoid undue technicality and subtlety. This is a sensible approach clearly enough but it has led, and not only in the context of the Theft Acts, to the practice of leaving the interpretation, at least of 'ordinary' words and expressions to be decided by the jury. This may be a less desirable development. The interpretation even of ordinary words would seem to be pre-eminently a matter for the court if consistency of interpretation is to be achieved. To leave interpretation in the hands of the jury is to risk juries taking different views on comparable facts. Even such ordinary words in the Acts as 'dishonesty', 'force', 'building' may involve definitional problems on which a jury requires guidance if like is to be treated as like. But there is House of Lords authority (*Brutus v Cozens* [1973] AC 854, [1972] 2 All ER 1297) for this innovation and it looks as though we shall have to live with it for some time yet.

1. Theft

Theft Act 1968, s 1(1), p 565, below

(1) APPROPRIATION

Theft Act 1968, s 3, p 565, below

R v Morris, Anderton v Burnside [1983] 3 All ER 288, House of Lords (Lords Fraser of Tullybelton, Edmund-Davies, Roskill, Brandon of Oakbrook and Brightman)

Lord Roskill. My Lords, these two consolidated appeals, one from the Court of Appeal, Criminal Division, the other from the Divisional Court, have been brought by leave of your Lordships' House in order that controversial questions of law arising from the dishonest practice of label-switching in connection with shoplifting in supermarkets may be finally decided. These matters have been in controversy for some time and have been the subject of judicial decisions which are not always easy to reconcile as well as disagreement between distinguished academic lawyers.

The facts giving rise to these appeals are simple. Morris, the appellant from the Court of

Appeal, Criminal Division, on 30 October 1981 took goods from the shelves of a supermarket. He replaced the price labels attached to them with labels showing a lesser price than the originals. At the check-out point he was asked for and paid those lesser prices. He was then arrested. Burnside, the appellant from the Divisional Court, was seen to remove a price label from a joint of pork in the supermarket and attach it to a second joint. This action was detected at the check-out point but before he had paid for that second joint which at that moment bore a price label showing a price of £2.73 whereas the label should have shown a price of £6.91½. Burnside was then arrested.

The only relevant difference between the two cases is that Burnside was arrested before he had dishonestly paid the lesser price for the joint of pork. Morris was arrested after he had paid the relevant lesser prices. Morris was tried in the Crown Court at Acton on two charges of theft contrary to s 1(1) of the Theft Act 1968. A third count of obtaining property by deception contrary to s 15 of that Act appeared in the indictment but the assistant recorder did not take a verdict on it and ordered that count to remain on the file. Morris appealed. The Court of Appeal, Criminal Division (Lord Lane CJ, O'Connor LJ and Talbot J) ([1983] 2 All ER 448, [1983] 2 WLR 768) dismissed his appeal in a reserved judgment given on 8 March 1983 by Lord Lane CJ.

Burnside was convicted at Manchester Magistrates' Court on 27 January 1982 on a single charge of theft contrary to s 1(1) of the 1968 Act. He appealed by way of case stated. On 5 November 1982, the Divisional Court (Ackner LJ and Webster J) dismissed the appeal.

Both the Court of Appeal, Criminal Division and the Divisional Court granted certificates. The former certificate read thus:

> 'If a person has substituted on an item of goods displayed in a self-service store a price label showing a lesser price for one showing a greater price, with the intention of paying the lesser price and then pays the lesser price at the till and takes the goods, is there at any stage a "dishonest appropriation" for the purposes of section 1 of the Theft Act 1968, and if so, at what point does such appropriation take place?'

The certificate in the latter case reads:

> 'If a person has substituted on an item of goods displayed in a self-service store a price label showing a lesser price for one showing a greater price, with the intention of paying the lesser price, and then pays the lesser price at the till and takes the goods, is there at any stage a "dishonest appropriation" for the purposes of section 1 of the Theft Act 1968.'

The two certificates though clearly intended to raise the same point of law are somewhat differently worded and, with respect, as both counsel ultimately accepted during the debate before your Lordships, do not precisely raise the real issue for decision, at least in the terms in which it falls to be decided.

My Lords, in his submissions for the appellants, which were conspicuous both for their clarity and their brevity, counsel for the appellants urged that on these simple facts neither appellant was guilty of theft. He accepted that Morris would have had no defence to a charge under s 15(1) of obtaining property by deception for he dishonestly paid the lesser prices and passed through the check-point having done so before he was arrested. But Morris, he said, was not guilty of theft because there was no appropriation by him before payment at the check-point sufficient to support a charge of theft, however dishonest his actions may have been in previously switching the labels.

Counsel for the appellants pointed out that if, as he accepted, an offence was committed against s 15(1) and if the prosecution case were right, Morris would be liable to be convicted of obtaining property by deception which he had already stolen, a situation which counsel suggested was somewhat anomalous.

As regards Burnside, counsel for the appellants submitted that for the same reason there was no appropriation before his arrest sufficient to support a charge of theft. He also submitted that Burnside's actions however dishonest would not support a charge of attempting to obtain property by deception contrary to s 15(1) since his dishonest act was no more than an act preparatory to obtaining property by deception and was not sufficiently proximate to an attempt to obtain property by deception.

My Lords, if these submissions be well founded it is clear that however dishonest their actions, each appellant was wrongly convicted of theft. The question is whether they are well founded. The answer must depend on the true construction of the relevant sections of the 1968 Act and it is to these that I now turn. For ease of reference I set them out [his Lordship read ss 1, 2, 3 and 4(1)].

It is to be observed that the definition of 'appropriation' in s 3(1) is not exhaustive. But ss 1(1) and 3(1) show clearly that there can be no conviction for theft contrary to s 1(1) even if all the other ingredients of the offence are proved unless 'appropriation' is also proved.

The starting point of any consideration of the submissions of counsel for the appellants must, I think, be the decision of this House in *Lawrence v Comr of Police for the Metropolis* [1971] 2 All ER 1253, [1972] AC 626; *affg* [1970] 3 All ER 933, [1971] 1 QB 373. In the leading speech, Viscount Dilhorne expressly accepted the view of the Court of Appeal, Criminal Division in that case that the offence of theft involved four elements: (1) a dishonest (2) appropriation (3) of property belonging to another, (4) with the intention of permanently depriving the owner of it. Viscount Dilhorne also rejected the argument that even if these four elements were all present there could not be theft within the section if the owner of the property in question had consented to the acts which were done by the defendant. That there was in that case a dishonest appropriation was beyond question and the House did not have to consider the precise meaning of that word in s 3(1).

Counsel for the appellants submitted that the phrase in s 3(1) 'Any assumption by a person of *the rights* [my emphasis] of an owner amounts to an appropriation' must mean any assumption of '*all* the rights of an owner'. Since neither appellant had at the time of the removal of the goods from the shelves and of the label-switching assumed *all* the rights of the owner, there was no appropriation and therefore no theft. Counsel for the prosecution, on the other hand, contended that *the* rights in this context only meant *any* of the rights. An owner of goods has many rights: they have been described as 'a bundle or package of rights'. Counsel for the prosecution contended that on a fair reading of the subsection it cannot have been the intention that every one of an owner's rights had to be assumed by the alleged thief before an appropriation was proved and that essential ingredient of the offence of theft established.

My Lords, if one reads the words 'the rights' at the opening of s 3(1) literally and in isolation from the rest of the section, the submission of counsel for the appellants undoubtedly has force. But the later words 'any later assumption of a right' in sub-s (1) and the words in sub-s (2) 'no later assumption by him of rights' seem to me to militate strongly against the correctness of the submission. Moreover, the provisions of s 2(1)(a) also seem to point in the same direction. It follows therefore that it is enough for the prosecution if they have proved in these cases the assumption by the defendants of *any* of the rights of the owner of the goods in question, that is to say, the supermarket concerned, it being common ground in these cases that the other three of the four elements mentioned in Viscount Dilhorne's speech in *Lawrence's* case had been fully established.

My Lords, counsel for the prosecution sought to argue that any removal from the shelves of the supermarket, even if unaccompanied by label-switching, was without more an appropriation. In one passage in his judgment in *Morris's* case, Lord Lane CJ appears to have accepted the submission, for he said:

'. . . It seems to us that in taking the article from the shelf the customer is indeed assuming one of the rights of the owner, the right to move the article from its position on the shelf to carry it to the check-out . . .'

With the utmost respect, I cannot accept this statement as correct. If one postulates an honest customer taking goods from a shelf to put in his or her trolley to take to the check-point there to pay the proper price, I am unable to see that any of these actions involves any assumption by the shopper of the rights of the supermarket. In the context of s 3(1), the concept of appropriation in my view involves not an act expressly or impliedly authorised by the owner but an act by way of adverse interference with or usurpation of those rights. When the honest shopper acts as I have just described, he or she is acting with the implied authority of the owner of the supermarket to take the goods from the shelf, put them in the trolley, take them to the check-point and there to pay the correct price, at which moment the property in the goods will pass to the shopper for the first time. It is with the consent of the owners of the supermarket, be that consent express or implied, that the shopper does these acts and thus obtained at least control if not actual possession of the goods preparatory, at a later stage, to obtaining the property in them on payment of the proper amount at the check-point. I do not think that s 3(1) envisages any such act as an 'appropriation', whatever may be the meaning of that word in other fields such as contract or sale of goods law.

If, as I understand all of your Lordships to agree, the concept of appropriation in s 3(1) involves an element of adverse interference with or usurpation of some right of the owner, it is necessary next to consider whether that requirement is satisfied in either of these cases. As I have already said, in my view mere removal from the shelves without more is not an appropriation. Further, if a shopper with some perverted sense of humour, intending only to create confusion and nothing more, both for the supermarket and for other shoppers, switches labels, I do not think that the act of label-switching alone is without more an appropriation, though it is not difficult to envisage some cases of dishonest label-switching which could be. In cases such as the present, it is in truth a combination of these actions, the removal from the shelf and the switching of the labels which evidences adverse interference with or usurpation of the right of the owner. Those acts, therefore, amount to an appropriation and if they are accompanied by proof of the other three elements to which I have referred, the offence of theft is established. Further, if they are accompanied by other acts such as putting the goods so removed and relabelled into a receptacle, whether a trolley or the shopper's own bag or basket, proof of appropriation within s 3(1) becomes overwhelming. It is the doing of one or more acts which individually or collectively amount to such adverse interference with or usurpation of the owner's rights which constitute appropriation under s 3(1) and I do not think it matters where there is more than one such act in which order the successive acts take place, or whether there is any interval of time between them. To suggest that it matters whether the mislabelling precedes or succeeds removal from the shelves is to reduce this branch of the law to an absurdity.

My Lords, it will have been observed that I have endeavoured so far to resolve the question for determination in these appeals without reference to any decided cases except *Lawrence's case* which alone of the many cases cited in argument is a decision of this House. If your Lordships accept as correct the analysis which I have endeavoured to express by reference to the construction of the relevant sections of the 1968 Act, a trail through a forest of decisions, many briefly and indeed inadequately reported, will tend to confuse rather than to enlighten. There are, however, some to which brief reference should perhaps be made.

First, *R v McPherson* [1973] Crim LR 191. Your Lordships have had the benefit of a transcript of the judgment of Lord Widgery CJ. I quote from the transcript:

> 'Reducing this case to its bare essentials we have this. Mrs McPherson in common design with the others takes two bottles of whisky from the stand, puts them in her shopping bag; at the time she intends to take them out without paying for them, in other words she intends to steal them from the very beginning. She acts dishonestly as the jury found, and the sole question is whether that is an appropriation of the bottles within the meaning of s 1. We have no hesitation whatever in saying that it is such an appropriation and indeed we content ourselves with a judgment of this brevity because we have been unable to accept or to find any argument to the contrary, to suggest that an appropriation is not effective in those simple circumstances.'

That was not, of course, a label-switching case, but it is a plain case of appropriation effected by the combination of the acts of removing the goods from the shelf and of concealing them in the shopping bag. *R v McPherson* is to my mind clearly correctly decided as are all the cases which have followed it. It is wholly consistent with the principles which I have endeavoured to state in this speech.

It has been suggested that *R v Meech* [1973] 3 All ER 939, [1974] QB 549, *R v Skipp* [1975] Crim LR 114, (your Lordships also have a transcript of the judgment in this case), and certain other cases are inconsistent with *R v McPherson*. I do not propose to examine these or other cases in detail. Suffice it to say that I am far from convinced that there is any inconsistency between them and other cases as has been suggested once it is appreciated that facts will vary infinitely. The precise moment when dishonest acts, not of themselves amounting to an appropriation, subsequently, because of some other and later acts combined with those earlier acts, do bring about an appropriation within s 3(1), will necessarily vary according to the particular case in which the question arises.

Of the other cases referred to, I understand all your Lordships to agree that *Anderton v Wish* (1980) 72 Cr App R 23 was rightly decided for the reasons given. I need not therefore refer to it further. *Eddy v Niman* (1981) 73 Cr App R 237 was in my view also correctly decided on its somewhat unusual facts. I think that Webster J, giving the first judgment, asked the right question (at 241), though, with respect, I think that the phrase 'some overt act . . . inconsistent with the true owner's rights' is too narrow. I think that the act need not necessarily be 'overt'.

Dip Kaur v Chief Constable of Hampshire [1981] 2 All ER 430, [1981] 1 WLR 578 is a difficult case. I am disposed to agree with Lord Lane CJ that it was wrongly decided but without going into further detail I respectfully suggest that it is on any view wrong to introduce into this branch of the criminal law questions whether particular contracts are void or voidable on the ground of mistake or fraud or whether any mistake is sufficiently fundamental to vitiate a contract. These difficult questions should so far as possible be confined to those fields of law to which they are immediately relevant and I do not regard them as relevant questions under the 1968 Act.

My Lords, it remains briefly to consider any relationship between s 1 and s 15. If the conclusion I have reached that theft takes place at the moment of appropriation and before any payment is made at the check-point be correct it is wrong to assert, as has been asserted, that the same act of appropriation creates two offences, one against s 1(1) and the other against s 15(1), because the two offences occur at different points of time: the s 15(1) offence is not committed until payment of the wrong amount is made at the check-point while the theft has been committed earlier. It follows that in cases such as *Morris* two offences were committed. I do not doubt that it was perfectly proper to add the third count under s 15(1) in this case. I think the assistant recorder was right to leave all three counts to the jury. While one may sympathise with his preventing them from returning a verdict on the third count once they convicted on the theft counts if only in the interests of simplification, the counts were not alternative as he appears to have treated them. They were cumulative and once they were left to the jury verdicts should have been taken on all of them.

My Lords, these shoplifting cases by switching labels are essentially simple in their facts and their factual simplicity should not be allowed to be obscured by ingenious legal arguments on the 1968 Act which for some time have bedevilled this branch of the criminal law without noticeably contributing to the efficient administration of justice, rather the reverse. The law to be applied to simple cases, whether in magistrates' courts or the Crown Court, should if possible be equally simple. I see no reason in principle why, when there is clear evidence of both offences being committed, both offences should not be charged. But where a shoplifter has passed the check-point and quite clearly has, by deception, obtained goods either without paying or by paying only a lesser price than he should, those concerned with prosecutions may in future think it preferable in the interests of simplicity to charge only an offence against s 15(1). In many cases of that kind it is difficult to see what possible defence there can be and that course may well avoid any opportunity for further ingenious legal arguments on the first few sections of the 1968 Act. Of course when the dishonesty is detected before the defendant has reached the check-point and he or she is arrested before that point so that no property has been obtained by deception, then theft is properly charged and if appropriation, within the meaning I have attributed to that word in this speech, is proved as well as the other three ingredients of the offence of theft, the defendant is plainly guilty of that offence.

My Lords, as already explained I have not gone through all the cases cited though I have mentioned some. Of the rest, those inconsistent with this speech must henceforth be treated as overruled.

I would answer the certified questions in this way: there is a dishonest appropriation for the purposes of the Theft Act 1968 where by the substitution of a price label showing a lesser price on goods for one showing a greater price, a defendant either by that act alone or by that act in conjunction with another act or other acts (whether done before or after the substitution of the labels) adversely interferes with or usurps the right of the owner to ensure that the goods concerned are sold and paid for at that greater price.

I would dismiss these appeals.

[Lords Fraser of Tullybelton, Edmund-Davies, Brandon of Oakbrook and **Brightman** concurred.]

Appeals dismissed

In his speech Lord Roskill refers with approval to *McPherson*, *Eddy v Niman*, *Anderton v Wish*, *Skipp*, and *Meech*.

In *McPherson* it was held that D appropriated the goods when she took them from the stand and placed them in her own shopping bag. In *Eddy v Niman* D, bent on stealing goods from a store, placed the goods in the wire basket provided by the store. D, however, changed his mind and abandoned the basket in the store. It was held that D had not appropriated the goods. *Anderton v Wish* was an earlier case involving the switching of price labels; it was held that D appropriated goods when she covered the price label on them with a price label taken from cheaper goods though she subsequently went through the check-out and paid the lower price.

In *Skipp* D, posing as a genuine haulage contractor, obtained instructions to collect three loads of goods from separate places and, having done so, made off with them. Convicted on a single count which charged him with the appropriation of all three loads, he argued on appeal that since there were three separate appropriations the count was bad for duplicity. It was held that there was only one appropriation which took place when D diverted the goods from their true destination. *Meech* is to the same effect though factually more complicated. D was asked by P to cash a cheque but because the cheque was for £1,450 the bank asked D to wait until it was cleared. Before clearance D discovered that P had dishonestly come by the cheque so D resolved to cheat P by staging a false robbery to be effected by his confederates E and F while D was ostensibly taking the money to P. This was done but the fraud was discovered and D, E and F were convicted of stealing the money. On appeal E and F argued that D had stolen the money when he withdrew it from the bank and that while they were liable as handlers they were not liable as thieves. It was held, however, that the appropriation took place at the time the fake robbery was staged for it was then that 'the performance of the obligation [by D to P] finally became impossible.'

Lord Roskill disapproved of the 'difficult case' of *Dip Kaur v Chief Constable of Hampshire*. There D was looking at shoes, some priced £6.99 and some £4.99. She noticed that one pair of £6.99 shoes carried a £6.99 label on one shoe and a £4.99 label on the other. Without making any attempt to conceal the labels she presented the shoes at the check-out hoping that the cashier would see only the £4.99 label and charge that price. The cashier did. Quashing D's conviction for theft the court said that the transaction between the store and D was merely voidable and not void. Consequently D became the owner of the goods at the check-out and the issue of appropriation did not arise.

NOTES AND QUESTIONS

1. What are the rights of an owner? Is it helpful to speak of 'the rights of an owner' when the expression is nowhere exhaustively defined?

2. Is s 3(1) ambiguous in that it might be read, as counsel for the appellants in *Morris* submitted, as meaning any assumption of *all* the owner's rights, or, as counsel for the prosecution submitted, as meaning any assumption of *any* of the owner's rights? The House of Lords adopted the latter view. Are there any compelling arguments for adopting the former view? However that question is answered, it has to be accepted, of course, that the prevailing view favours the latter.

3. Lord Roskill says that the prankster who switches labels on goods simply to cause confusion has not appropriated the goods. Why not? Obviously the prankster cannot be convicted of theft if other elements of theft (most obviously an intention permanently to deprive) are not present, but why is such conduct not an appropriation? Appropriation must require a mental element. A shopper who, for example, smashes a bottle when he inadvertently knocks it from a shelf could not be said to have appropriated the bottle. What is the mental element in relation to appropriation and does the prankster lack it?

4. In determining whether there has been an appropriation the cases make it clear that a relevant (the only?) consideration is whether P consents to what D does with the property. Clearly the storekeeper does not consent to D placing articles in his pocket or carrier. But does he any more consent when the dishonest shopper places the goods in the basket provided so that he can later transfer them to his own carrier in a less well observed part of the store? Why is there no appropriation by the shopper until something is done with the goods which evidences adverse interference with the rights of the owner? The court in *Eddy v Niman* spoke of the necessity for 'some overt act' but Lord Roskill thought that the act need not necessarily be 'overt'. There are certain difficulties with the concept of a non-overt act. What might Lord Roskill have had in mind? Cf *Fritschy* [1985] Crim LR 745. On P's instructions D bought Krugerrands in London which, again on P's instructions, he removed to Switzerland. P then heard no more so he called in the police and D was charged with stealing the Krugerrands in England. The judge directed the jury that D might be convicted of theft if when he collected the Krugerrands he dishonestly intended to dispose of them regardless of P's rights. Quashing D's conviction the court referred to Lord Roskill's view that the act need not necessarily be overt and said:

> 'We have found this comment difficult to understand and we were tempted to say that some subsequent act on the part of an accused person, for example in the present instance disposing of the goods in Switzerland, could be evidence to justify a finding of an earlier appropriation: in this instance at the time when [D] received the Krugerrands [in London]. But having regard to Lord Roskill's earlier requirement of an act by way of adverse interference with or usurpation of an owner's rights, we found this conclusion impossible. There was here no evidence of any act by [D] within the jurisdiction that was not authorised by [P]. That, in the light of . . . *Morris* is fatal to the charge of theft.'

5. Suppose that in *Skipp* the owner at the second place, P, had realised shortly after D left that he had been defrauded. P telephones to Q at the third place who calls in the police. Acting on police advice Q allows D to load the goods though he is not of course taken in by D's representations. Once D has loaded the goods the police step in. Has D appropriated the third load? The tenor of the foregoing cases (and cf *Grundy v Fulton* [1981] 2 Lloyds Rep 666; affd [1983] 1 Lloyd's Rep 16, CA, which is to the same effect) suggests not, but in *Lawrence* [1972] AC 626, [1971] 2 All ER 1253 p 434, below) the House of Lords held that s 1(1) of the Theft Act 1968 was not to be read as though it contained the words 'without the consent of the owner'. This problem will be reconsidered following *Lawrence*, p 434, below.

6. In the foregoing cases D has acquired possession, or at least custody or control, of P's property. But s 3(1) does not in terms require any assumption of possession by D; it merely requires an assumption of the rights of an owner and this invites a consideration of when, if at all, D may appropriate P's property though at no stage does he have possession, custody or control. In *Pitham and Hehl* (1976) 65 Cr App Rep 45, CA, p 512, below, X, knowing that P was in prison and in no position to interfere, planned a fraud. He took D and E to P's house, showed them the furniture and offered it to them at a considerable undervalue. D and E agreed to buy. It was held that X stole the furniture when he appropriated it by inviting D and E to buy it. The case is severly criticised by Williams (*Textbook of Criminal Law*, 2nd edn, pp 763–765). How he asks, can an offer by X to sell property not in his possession and in which he can pass no title, intelligibly be regarded as an appropriation? Williams supposes the case of a butler who has the key to his employer's safe and who authorises the parlourmaid to take silver from the safe. It would be preposterous, says Williams, to say that because only the employer may lawfully authorise a removal of the silver that accordingly the butler has assumed the rights of an owner. Is it preposterous? Is the butler's case the same as that of X in *Pitham and Hehl*?

7. 'The exclusion of P from possession without D's actually getting his hands on the property could be theft, as where P is looking for his property and D, knowing where it is and intending to steal it, misdirects P so that he will not find it.' (Griew, *The Theft Acts 1968 and 1978*, 4th edn, para 2–51.) Do you agree?

8. May an appropriation be constituted by an omission? In *Monaghan* [1979] Crim LR 673, CA, D, a supermarket cashier, took £3.99 from a customer for a purchase. She placed the money in the till but did not ring up the purchase and subsequently admitted that she had done so dishonestly, intending to remove the money from the till at a later stage. The Court of Appeal, affirming her conviction for theft, held that she had appropriated the money when she failed to ring it up in order that the money should accrue to herself and not to her employers. But what did D do with *the money* that was unauthorised? Suppose that D borrows P's cycle for a week. At the end of the week he fails to return it having decided to steal it though he takes no active steps in relation to the cycle which is left standing in his garage. Has he appropriated the cycle? Can it be said that D is 'keeping . . . it as owner'?

9. As to s 3(2) the CLRC observed (Cmnd 2977, para 37),

> 'A person may buy something in good faith, but may find out afterwards that the seller had no title to it, perhaps because the seller or someone else had no title to it. If the buyer nevertheless keeps the thing or otherwise deals with it as owner, he could, on the principles stated above, be guilty of theft. It is arguable that this would be right; but on the whole it seems to us that, whatever view is taken of the buyer's moral duty, the law would be too strict if it made him guilty of theft.'

(2) PROPERTY

Theft Act 1968, s 4, p 565, below

The broad effect of s 4 is that all property may be stolen subject to certain exceptions in relation to land, wild growth and wild creatures.

While gas is tangible property (which may be stolen by placing a by-pass on the meter) and so is air (strictly it may be theft to let out the air from someone else's car tyres), there has always been a doubt as to whether electricity is tangible property. The CLRC (Cmnd 2977, para 85) thought that 'owing to its nature electricity is excluded from the definition of stealing' and accordingly made separate provision for the dishonest use, wasting or diverting of electricity in s 13. The CLRC view was confirmed in *Low v Blease* [1975] Crim LR 513, DC, where it was held that since electricity was not property capable of appropriation, D could not be convicted of burglary where he entered premises as a trespasser and made an unauthorised telephone call. Oddly enough D may steal a battery but not the electricity it contains though the battery is of no value or use to D without its charge of electricity.

Section 4 provides that some kinds of property cannot be stolen in certain circumstances. Mushrooms growing wild on P's land constitute property belonging to P which P is entitled to protect by recourse to the civil law but the taker, unless he has a commercial purpose, cannot commit theft. While s 4 identifies certain kinds of property which cannot be stolen, it does not otherwise provide a definition of property, whether tangible or intangible, which is capable of being stolen. To determine what is property for this purpose recourse has to be made to the civil law. Merely because something has a value does not mean that it constitutes property:

Oxford v Moss [1979] Crim LR 119, Queen's Bench Division
(Lord Widgery CJ, Wien and Smith JJ)

In 1976, M was an engineering student at Liverpool University. He acquired the proof of an examination paper for a Civil Engineering examination at the University. An information was preferred against him by O, alleging that he stole certain intangible property, i e confidential information, being property of the Senate of the University. It was agreed that he never intended to permanently deprive the owner of the piece of paper on which the questions were printed.

Held, by the stipendiary at Liverpool: on the facts of the case, confidential information is not a form of intangible property as opposed to property in the paper itself, and that confidence consisted in the right to control the publication of the proof paper and was a right over property other than a form of intangible property. The owner had not been permanently deprived of any intangible property. The charge was dismissed.

On appeal by the prosecutor, as to whether confidential information can amount to property within the meaning of section 4 of the Theft Act 1968.

Held: there was no property in the information capable of being the subject of a charge of theft, i e it was not intangible property within the meaning of section 4. Appeal dismissed.

Intangible property includes such things as debts, copyright, or shares in a company. The difficulty lies not in determining what constitutes intangible property but in determining how such property is appropriated and the owner permanently deprived of it. Suppose that D without permission publishes P's poems. This is a breach of copyright but is the copyright stolen? Since D does not intend to deprive P *of the copyright* the case would seem to be analagous to a dishonest use by D of P's car which is not theft in the absence of intention permanently to deprive. So how does D set about stealing P's copyright?

One case where it is easy to see how intangible property is appropriated is where D is a trustee of it. Supposing that D is a trustee of money held in a bank account for the benefit of P. If D dishonestly causes this account to be debited and his own to be credited he has appropriated a chose. But what if D, a bank clerk, by manipulating the bank's computer causes the account of P to be debited and his own to be credited? This is just what was done in *Thompson* [1984] 3 All ER 565, [1984] 1 WLR 962, CA, where it was held that D did not thereby obtain a chose in action. The Court said (at 569):

> 'We think, however, that one may legitimately ask: of what property did the appellant in that way obtain control . . . ? What was the nature of that property? The reply of counsel for the appellant, as we understand it, was that the appellant obtained the control of those credit balances on his savings accounts, which were effectively choses in action, and were such until the bank discovered his fraud. With all respect to counsel's persuasive argument, we think that when it is examined it is untenable. We do not think that one can describe as a chose in action a liability which has been brought about by fraud, one where the action to enforce that liability is capable of immediate defeasance as soon as the fraud is pleaded. It is neither here nor there, we think, that the person defrauded, in this case the bank, may not have been aware that one of its employees had been fraudulent in this way until a later time. The ignorance of the bank in no way, in our view, breathes life into what is otherwise a defunct situation brought about entirely by fraud. One has only to take a simple example. Discard for the moment the modern sophistication of computers and programmes and consider the old days when bank books were kept in manuscript in large ledgers. In effect all that was done by the appellant through the modern computer in the

present case was to take a pen and debit each of the five accounts in the ledger with the relevant sums and then credit each of his own five savings accounts in the ledger with corresponding amounts. On the face of it his savings accounts would then have appeared to have in them substantially more than in truth they did have, as the result of his forgeries; but we do not think that by those forgeries any bank clerk in the days before computers would in law have thus brought into being a chose in action capable either of being stolen or of being obtained by deception contrary to s 15 of the 1968 Act.

In so far as the customers whose accounts had been fraudulently debited and who had to be reimbursed by the bank, as counsel for the appellant submitted, are concerned, we prefer the approach of counsel for the Crown. He submitted that properly considered it was not a question of reimbursement: it was merely a question of correcting forged documents, forged records, to the condition in which they ought to have been but for the fraud.'

Is it possible to fault this reasoning? Is it different if the fraud causes the bank's employee to debit P's and credit D's account? How does D, other than where he is a trustee, set about stealing a debt?

(3) BELONGING TO ANOTHER

Theft Act 1968, s 5, p 566, below

At first sight it is a perfectly obvious proposition that a man may steal only the property of another and, equally, that he cannot steal his own property. Usually the issue of mine-and-thine is clear cut. So D is guilty of theft if, with mens rea, he snatches P's handbag; the handbag being owned and possessed by P and D having no proprietary interest in it whatever. Conversely if D arranges for the 'disappearance' of his own property in order to perpetrate a fraud on insurers (cf *Robinson* [1915] 2 KB 342, p 275, above) it may be that D will commit other offences but it is plain that he cannot be convicted of theft.

But not all cases are so straightforward. P may have some interest in the property less than ownership. The handbag snatched from P might have been lent by N (the owner) to O (who thereby acquired possession) and O has in turn asked P to hold it while O unlocks her car door. Here P has mere custody of the handbag but this suffices under s 5(1) and the handbag is stolen from her. It is also stolen from N and O but it is equally stolen from P.

There is no oddity in extending theft to an appropriation of property from someone who is not the exclusive owner of the property. Nor is there any oddity in holding that a person may be guilty of theft though he himself has a proprietary right or interest in the property. If in the illustration concerning the handbag O (the possessor) dishonestly intending to keep it for herself, tells N (the owner) that it was stolen from her by D then both in law and good sense it can be said that O has stolen from N. Even if D is an owner of property he may yet steal it. So in *Bonner* [1970] 2 All ER 97n, CA, it was held that where property is held by a partnership, one partner, even though he is a joint owner of all partnership property, may steal partnership property if he appropriates it to himself intending to defeat the interests of the other partners. The essential idea is that D may be guilty of theft where in respect of particular property he acts so as to usurp the interests that others have in that property.

**R v Woodman [1974] 2 All ER 955 Court of Appeal, Criminal Division
(Lord Widgery CJ, Ashworth and Mocatta JJ)**

The judgment of the court was delivered by:

Lord Widgery CJ. . . . The facts of the case were these. On 20 March 1973 the appellant and his son, and another man called Davey who was acquitted, took a van to some premises at Wick near Bristol and loaded on to the van one ton six cwt of scrap metal, which they proceeded to drive away.

The premises from which they took this scrap metal were a disused factory belonging to English China Clays, and the indictment alleged that the scrap metal in question was the property of English China Clays. Whether that was entirely true or not depends on the view one takes of the events immediately preceding this taking of scrap metal, because what had happened, according to the prosecution evidence, was that the business run by English China Clays at this point had been run down. In August 1970 the business had ceased. There was at that time a great deal of miscellaneous scrap metal on the site, and English China Clays, wishing to dispose of this, sold the scrap metal to the Bird Group of companies, who thereupon had the right and title to enter on the site and remove the scrap metal which they had bought. They or their sub-contractor went on to the site. They took out the bulk of the scrap metal left there by English China Clays, but a certain quantity of scrap was too inaccessible to be removed to be attractive to the Bird Group of companies so that it was left on the site and so it seems to have remained for perhaps a couple of years until the appellant and his son came to take it away, as I have already recounted.

Also in the history of the matter, and important in it, is the fact that when the site had been cleared by the Bird Group of companies a barbed wire fence was erected around it obviously to exclude trespassers. The site was still in the ownership of the English China Clays and their occupation, and the barbed wire fence was no doubt erected by them. Within the barbed wire fence were these remnants of scrap which the Bird Group had not taken away.

English China Clays took further steps to protect their property because a number of notices giving such information as 'Private Property. Keep Out' and 'Trespassers will be prosecuted' were exhibited around the perimeter of the site. A Mr Brooksbank, who was an employee of English China Clays, gave evidence that he had visited the site about half a dozen times over a period of two or three years, and indeed he had visited it once as recently as between January and March 1973. He did not notice that any scrap metal had been left behind, and it is perfectly clear that there is no reason to suppose that English China Clays or their representatives appreciated that there was any scrap remaining on the site after the Bird Group had done their work.

When this matter came on before the Bristol Crown Court, at the close of the prosecution case where evidence had been led to deal with the facts I have referred to, a submission was made to the recorder that there was no case to answer, because it was said that on that evidence there was no ground in law for saying that the theft had been committed.

By now of course it is the Theft Act 1968 which governs the matter, and so one must turn to see what it says. Section 1(1) provides: 'A person is guilty of theft if he dishonestly appropriates property belonging to another . . . ' I need not go further because the whole of the debate turns on the phrase 'belonging to another'.

Section 5(1) of the 1968 Act expands the meaning of the phrase in these terms:

> 'Property shall be regarded as belonging to any person having possession or control of it, or having in it any proprietary right or interest . . .'

The recorder took the view that the contract of sale between English China Clays and the Bird Group had divested English China Clays of any proprietary right to any scrap on the site. It is unnecessary to express a firm view on that point, but the court are not disposed to disagree with that conclusion that the proprietary interest in the scrap had passed.

The recorder also took the view on the relevant facts that it was not possible to say that English China Clays were in possession of the residue of the scrap. It is not quite clear why he took that view. It may have been because he took the view that difficulties arose by reason of the fact that English China Clays had no knowledge of the existence of this particular scrap at any particular time. But the recorder did take the view that so far as control was concerned there was a case to go to the jury on whether or not this scrap was in the control of English China Clays, because if it was, then it was to be regarded as their property for the purposes of a larceny charge even if they were not entitled to any proprietary interest.

The contention before us today is that the recorder was wrong in law in allowing this issue to go to the jury. Put another way, it is said that as a matter of law English China Clays could not on these facts have been said to be in control of the scrap.

We have formed the view without difficulty that the recorder was perfectly entitled to do what he did, that there was ample evidence that English China Clays were in control of the site and had taken considerable steps to exclude trespassers as demonstrating the fact that they were in control of the site, and we think that in ordinary and straightforward cases if it is once established that a particular person is in control of a site such as this, then prima facie he is in control of articles which are on the site.

The point was well put in an article written by no less a person than Oliver Wendell Holmes Jnr, in his book *The Common Law* [(1881) pp 222–224], dealing with possession. Considering the very point we have to consider here, he said:

> 'There can be no *animus domini* unless the thing is known of; but an intent to exclude others from it may be contained in the larger intent to exclude others from the place where it is, without any knowledge of the object's existence . . . In a criminal case [*Rowe* (1859) 8 Cox CC 139], the property in iron taken from the bottom of a canal by a stranger was held well laid in the canal company, although it does not appear that the company knew of it, or had any lien upon it. The only intent concerning the thing discoverable in such instances is the general intent which the occupant of land has to exclude the public from the land, and thus, as a consequence, to exclude them from what is upon it.'

So far as this case is concerned, arising as it does under the Theft Act 1968, we are content to say that there was evidence of English China Clays being in control of the site and prima facie in control of articles on the site as well. The fact that it could not be shown that they were conscious of the existence of this or any particular scrap iron does not destroy the general principle that control of a site by excluding others from it is prima facie control of articles on the site as well.

There has been some mention in argument of what would happen if, in a case like the present, a third party had come and placed some article within the barbed wire fence and thus on the site. The article might be an article of some serious criminal consequence such as explosives or drugs. It may well be that in that type of case the fact that the article has been introduced at a late stage in circumstances in which the occupier of the site had no means of knowledge would produce a different result from that which arises under the general presumption to which we have referred, but in the present case there was in our view ample evidence to go to the jury on the question of whether English China Clays were in control of the scrap at the relevant time. Accordingly the recorder's decision to allow the case to go to the jury cannot be faulted and the appeal is dismissed.

Appeal dismissed

Generally possession or control is shown by some measure of control in fact accompanied by an intention to exclude others. Obviously a householder retains possession or control (indeed he retains ownership) of 'unwanted' items which he consigns to his attic or cellar even though he cannot itemise them. Even household rubbish consigned to the dustbin remains in his disposition for he would certainly not want any Tom, Dick or Harry looking for items of value in his dustbin. But what of the men sent by the local authority to empty the dustbins? In *Williams v Phillips* (1957) 41 Cr App Rep 5, DC, a decision under the former law, it was held that dustmen stole refuse which they placed in the corporation's cart and which they subsequently appropriated. Once placed in the corporation's cart the refuse came into the possession of the corporation and could then be stolen by others, including the corporation's employees. Suppose, though, that the dustmen had removed the valuable rubbish before placing it in their employer's cart. Would they be guilty of stealing from their employer or from the householder or both?

In *Woodman* the appellants were convicted of stealing the metal from English China Clays. The court appeared to lay stress on the facts that the company had erected a barbed wire fence and had erected notices against trespassing. Would it have made any difference if the company had taken neither of these steps?

All the scrap on the site had been sold to the Bird Group. What would the position have been if the appellants had been charged with stealing the scrap from the Bird Group?

The court in *Woodman* considered, without decisively determining, what the position might have been if some stranger had deposited goods (drugs, explosives) behind the wire fence which the appellants had then appropriated. From the cases (most of them are civil and it can hardly be supposed that different considerations apply in criminal cases) it appears that only exceptionally will a third party acquire a better title to goods than the owner of the land where the goods are found. According to *Parker v British Airways Board* [1982] QB 1004, [1982] 1 All ER 834, CA, the finder of goods on another's property obtains a title better than the owner only where he is lawfully on the owner's premises, the property is not attached to the land and the owner has not manifested an intention to exercise control over the premises and things which may be upon it.

R v Turner (No 2) [1971] 2 All ER 441 Court of Appeal, Criminal Division (Lord Parker CJ, Widgery LJ and Bridge J)

[**Lord Parker CJ** delivered the judgment of the court:]

. . . The facts need not to be stated at great length, although there is considerable disparity in the accounts given on behalf of the Crown and the defence. The appellant was at the material time living in Seymour Road, East Ham, with a Miss Nelson and their children. Three miles away a man called Arthur Edwin Brown ran a garage in Carlyle Road, Manor Park. There is no doubt that at some time prior to 7 March 1969, the appellant took a Sceptre car of which he was the registered owner to Brown's garage for repairs. It was Mr Brown's case that he did those repairs, that as he was short of space he left the car in Carlyle Road some 10 to 20 yards from the garage. The ignition key had been handed to him by the appellant, and this he retained on the keyboard in his office. According to Mr Brown, on 7 March 1969 the appellant called at the garage and asked if the car was ready. On being told that it was except that it might require to be tuned, the appellant said that he would return on the next day, i e Saturday 8 March 1969, and would pay Mr Brown for the repairs and pick up the car. A few hours later, however, Mr Brown found that the Sceptre car had gone; moreover whoever had taken it had had a key, because the key that Mr Brown had was still on the keyboard. He reported the matter to the police.

Apparently night after night thereafter until 16 March 1969 Mr Brown, according to him, went round the neighbouring streets to see if he could find the car, and sure enough on Sunday 16 March 1969 he found it parked in a street near to the appellant's flat. It was, moreover, his evidence that he did not know the appellant's full name or his address and only knew of him as Frank. What Mr Brown then did was to take the car back to his garage, to take out the engine and then tow it back less the engine to the place from which he had taken it. Meanwhile, the police made enquiries of the appellant and there is no doubt in the light of what happened afterwards, that he, the appellant, told lie after lie to the police. He said that Mr Brown had never had his Sceptre car at all, that the car had never been to the garage, and the only work that Mr Brown had done was to a Zephyr car on an earlier occasion. However, a time came when he abandoned those denials and agreed that he had taken the car to the garage, and that he had taken it away and had never paid for it. In saying that, he however emphasised that he had taken it away with the consent of Mr Brown. It was on those short facts the the jury, as I have said by a majority, found the appellant guilty of the theft of his own car.

The trial lasted, we are told, six days, in the course of which every conceivable point seems to have been taken and argued. In the result, however, when it comes to this court two points, and two only are taken. It is said in the first instance that while Mr Brown may have had possession or control in fact, that is not enough, and that it must be shown before it can be said that the property 'belonged to' Mr Brown, those being the words used in s 1(1) of the Theft Act 1968, that that possession is, as it is said, a right superior to that in Mr Brown. It is argued from that, in default of proof of a lien—and the judge in his summing-up directed the jury that they were not concerned with the question of whether there was a lien—that Mr Brown was merely a bailee at will and accordingly that he had no sufficient possession.

The words 'belonging to another' are specifically defined in s 5 of the Act. Section 5 (1) provides:

'Property shall be regarded as belonging to any person having possession or control of it, or having in it any proprietary right or interest . . .'

As I have said, the judge directed the jury that they were not concerned in any way with lien and the sole question was whether Mr Brown had possession or control. This court is quite satisfied that there is no ground whatever for qualifying the words 'possession or control' in any way. It is sufficient if it is found that the person from whom the property is taken, or to use the words of the Act, appropriated, was at the time in fact in possession or control. At the trial there was a long argument whether that possession or control must be lawful, it being said that by reason of the fact that this car was subject to a hire-purchase agreement, Mr Brown could never even as against the appellant obtain lawful possession or control. As I have said, this court is quite satisfied that the judge was quite correct in telling the jury that they need not bother about lien, and that they need not bother about hire-purchase agreements. The only question was: was Mr Brown in fact in possession or control?

The second point that is taken relates to the necessity for proving dishonesty. Section 2 (1) provides:

'A person's appropriation of property belonging to another is not to be regarded as dishonest—(a) if he appropriates the property in the belief that he has in law the right to deprive the other of it, on behalf of himself or of a third person . . .'

The judge, in dealing with this matter, said, and I am only taking passages from his summing-up:

'Fourth and last, they must prove that [the appellant] did what he did dishonestly and this may be the issue which lies very close to the heart of this case.'

He then went on to give them a classic direction in regard to claim of right, emphasising that it is immaterial that there exists no basis in law for such belief. He reminded the jury that the appellant had said categorically in evidence: 'I believe that I was entitled in law to do what I did.' At the same time he directed the jury to look at the surrounding circumstances. He said this:

'The Prosecution say that the whole thing reeks of dishonesty, and if you believe Mr Brown that the [appellant] drove the car away from Carlyle Road, using a duplicate key, and having told Brown that he would come back tomorrow and pay, you may think the Prosecution are right.'

What counsel for the appellant says on this point is this. He says again that if in fact one disregards lien entirely as the jury were told to do, then Mr. Brown was a bailee at will, and the car could have been taken back by the appellant perfectly lawfully at any time whether any money was due in regard to repairs or whether it was not. He says, as the court understands it, first that if there was the right, then there cannot be theft at all, and secondly, that if and insofar as the mental element is relevant, namely belief, the jury should have been told that he had this right and be left to judge, in the light of the existence of that right, whether they thought he may have believed, and he said, that he did have a right.

This court, however, is quite satisfied that there is nothing in this point whatever. The whole test of dishonesty is the mental element of belief. No doubt, although the appellant may for certain purposes be presumed to know the law, he would not at the time have the vaguest idea whether he did have in law a right to take the car back again, and accordingly when one looks at his mental state, one looks at it in the light of what he believed. The jury were properly told that if he believed that he had a right, albeit there was none, he would nevertheless fall to be acquitted. This court, having heard all that counsel for the appellant has said, is quite satisfied that there is no manner in which this summing-up can be criticised, and that accordingly the appeal against conviction should be dismissed . . .

Appeal and application dismissed

R v Meredith [1973] Crim LR 253 Manchester Crown Court
(Judge John Da Cunha)

The defendant, who owned a car, left it in a road while he attended a football match. The car was removed to a police station yard under regulation 4 of the

Removal and Disposal of Vehicles Regulations 1968. After the match the defendant went to the police station adjacent to the yard; it was crowded and he went to the yard not having paid any sum to the police. He found his car with a police Krooklok on the steering wheel and, without consent or authority from the police he drove the car away. Two days later he was seen by the police, to whom he handed the Krooklok, and he was arrested and charged with its theft contrary to ss 1 and 7 of the Theft Act 1968. While he was at the police station an entry relating to his car in the found property book was signed by him and his having received his car, the column relating to a £4 charge [under regulation 17(1)(a)(iii)] being marked 'not paid' by a police officer. Later he was charged also with theft of the car, the property of the police, contrary to ss 1 and 7 of the 1968 Act, and with taking the vehicle without consent of the owner or other lawful authority, contrary to s 12 of the 1968 Act, and he was committed for trial on the three charges. Subsequently he received a demand from the police for £4, the cost of impounding his car. At his trial no evidence was offered on the count under s 12. At the close of the prosecution's evidence he submitted that he had no case to answer.

Held, upholding the submission, that the reality of the situation was that the police were removing the car to another situation for the owner to collect it subsequently. An owner was liable to pay the statutory charge only if the car originally caused an obstruction, and he had three choices on going to the police station: to pay the £4, admitting that his car caused an obstruction; to refuse to pay, whereupon inevitably he would face a prosecution for having caused an obstruction; or to agree to pay, and then, no doubt, receive a bill. In all three eventualities he would be allowed to take the car away, for the police had no right, as against the owner, to retain it. Consequently, a charge of theft against the defendant was improper. As to the count of theft of the Krooklok, not merely was it a (comparatively) minor offence, but so short was the time elapsing between its being taken and the defendant's admission that he had it, that he should no longer be in jeopardy of conviction for dishonesty. Accordingly, the jury would be directed to find the defendant not guilty on all three counts.

Questions

1. Can the decision in *Meredith* be reconciled with the decision in *Turner*?

2. In *Turner* the jury was told to disregard the possibility that the repairer had a lien on the appellant's car. On that hypothesis how could the car be regarded as 'belonging to another', viz the repairer? Suppose Don lends his copy of Cheshire and Fifoot to Peter for a day. Several days later Peter has still not returned it and Don sees it on Peter's desk. Don surreptitiously retakes his book and says nothing to Peter. Is Don a thief? Would it make any difference to your answer if Don subsequently charged Peter with the loss of the book?

R v Hall [1972] 2 All ER 1009 Court of Appeal, Criminal Division
(Edmund Davies, Stephenson LJJ and Boreham J)

[**Edmund Davies LJ** read the judgment of the court:]

During 1968 the appellant and two others started trading in Manchester as travel agents under the title of 'People to People'. The other partners received no remuneration, played purely insignificant parts, and were called as Crown witnesses. Each of the seven counts related to money received by the appellant as deposits and payments for air trips to America. In some instances a lump sum was paid by school-masters in respect of charter flights for their pupils; in other instances individuals made payments in respect of their own projected flights. In none of the seven cases covered by the indictment did the flights materialise, in none of them was there any refund of the moneys paid, and in each case the appellant admitted that he was unable to make any repayment. In some cases he disputed all liability on the grounds that the other parties had unjustifiably cancelled the proposed trips, in others he denied dishonesty. He claimed to have paid into the firm's general trading account all the sums received by him, asserted that those moneys had become his own property and had been applied by him in the conduct of the firm's business, and submitted that he could not be convicted of theft simply because the firm had not prospered and that in consequence not a penny remained in the bank.

Two points were presented and persuasively developed by the appellant's counsel: (1) that, while the appellant has testified that all moneys received had been used for business purposes, even had he been completely profligate in its expenditure he could not in any of the seven cases be convicted of 'theft' as defined by the Theft Act 1968; there being no allegation in any of the cases of his having *obtained* any payments by deception, counsel for the appellant submitted that, having received from a client, say £500 in respect of a projected flight, as far as the criminal law is concerned he would be quite free to go off immediately and expend the entire sum at the races and forget all about his client; (2)[omitted] . . .

Point (1) turns on the application of s 5(3) of the Theft Act 1968, which provides:

> 'Where a person receives property from or on account of another, and is under an obligation to the other to retain and deal with that property or its proceeds in a particular way, the property or proceeds shall be regarded (as against him) as belonging to the other.'

Counsel for the appellant submitted that in the circumstances arising in these seven cases there arose no such 'obligation' on the appellant. He referred us to a passage in the Eighth Report of the Criminal Law Revision Committee [Theft and Related Offences, Cmnd 2977 (1966), p 127] which reads as follows:

> '*Subsection* (3) [of cl 5 "Belonging to Another"] provides for the special case where property is transferred to a person to retain and deal with for a particular purpose and he misapplies it or its proceeds. An example would be the treasurer of a holiday fund. The person in question is in law the owner of the property; but the subsection treats the property, as against him, as belonging to the persons to whom he owes the duty to retain and deal with the property as agreed. He will therefore be guilty of stealing from them if he misapplies the property or its proceeds.'

Counsel for the appellant submitted that the example there given is, for all practical purposes, identical with the actual facts in *Pulham*, where, incidentally, s 5 (3) was not discussed, the convictions there being quashed, as we have already indicated, owing to the lack of a proper direction as to the accused's state of mind at the time he appropriated. But he submits that the position of a treasurer of a solitary fund is quite different from that of a person like the appellant, who was in general (and genuine) business as a travel agent, and to whom people pay money in order to achieve a certain object—in the present cases, to obtain charter flights to America. It is true, he concedes, that thereby the travel agent undertakes a contractual obligation in relation to arranging flights and at the proper time paying the airline and any other expenses. Indeed, the appellant throughout acknowledged that this was so, although contending that in some of the seven cases it was the other party who was in breach. But what counsel for the appellant resists is that in such circumstances the travel agent 'is under an obligation' to the client 'to retain and deal with . . . in a particular way' sums paid to him in such circumstances.

What cannot of itself be decisive of the matter is the fact that the appellant paid the money into the firm's general trading account. As Widgery J said in *Yule* [[1964] 1 QB 5 at 10; [1963] 2 All ER 780 at 784], decided under s 20 (1) (iv) of the Larceny Act 1916:

'The fact that a particular sum is paid into a particular banking account . . . does not affect the right of persons interested in that sum or any duty of the solicitor either towards his client or towards third parties with regard to disposal of that sum.'

Nevertheless, when a client goes to a firm carrying on the business of travel agents and pays them money, he expects that in return he will, in due course, receive the tickets and other documents necessary for him to accomplish the trip for which he is paying, and the firm are 'under an obligation' to perform their part to fulfil his expectation and are liable to pay him damages if they do not. But, in our judgment, what was not here established was that these clients expected them 'to retain and deal with that property or its proceeds in a particular way', and that an 'obligation' to do so was undertaken by the appellant. We must make clear, however, that each case turns on its own facts. Cases could, we suppose, conceivably arise where by some special arrangement (preferably evidenced by documents), the client could impose on the travel agent an 'obligation' falling within s 5 (3). But no such special arrangement was made in any of the seven cases here being considered. It is true that in some of them documents were signed by the parties; thus, in respect of counts 1 and 3 incidents there was a clause to the effect that the People to People organisation did not guarantee to refund deposits if withdrawals were made later than a certain date; and in respect of counts 6, 7 and 8 the appellant wrote promising 'a full refund' after the flights paid for failed to materialise. But neither in those nor in the remaining two cases (in relation to which there was no documentary evidence of any kind) was there, in our judgment, such a special arrangement as would give rise to an obligation within s 5 (3).

It follows from this that, despite what on any view must be condemned as scandalous conduct by the appellant, in our judgment on this ground alone this appeal must be allowed and the convictions quashed. But as, to the best of our knowledge, this is one of the earliest cases involving s 5 (3), we venture to add some observations.

(A) Although in *Pulham* [(1971) 15 June (unreported)], s 5 (3) was not referred to and the case turned on s 2 (1) (b) of the Act, it is equally essential for the purposes of the former provision that dishonesty should be present at the time of appropriation. We are alive to the fact that to establish this could present great (and maybe insuperable) difficulties when sums are on different dates drawn from a general account. Nevertheless, they must be overcome if the Crown is to succeed.

(B) Where the case turns, wholly or in part, on s 5 (3) a careful exposition of the subsection is called for. Although it was canvassed by counsel in the present case, it was nowhere quoted or even paraphrased by the commissioner in his summing-up. Instead he unfortunately ignored it and proceeded on the assumption that, as the appellant acknowledged the purpose for which clients had paid him money, ipso facto there arose an 'obligation . . . to retain and deal with' it for that purpose. He therefore told the jury:

'The sole issue to be determined in each count is this. Has it been proved that the money was stolen in the sense I have described, dishonestly appropriated by him for purposes other than the purpose for which the moneys were handed over? Bear in mind that this is not a civil claim to recover money that has been lost.'

We have to say respectfully that this will not do, as cases under s 20 (1) (iv) of the Larceny Act 1916 illustrate. Thus in *Sheaf* [(1925) 134 LT 127] it was held that whether money had been 'entrusted' to the defendant for and on account of other persons was a question of fact for the jury and must therefore be the subject of an express direction, Avory J saying [(1925) 134 LT at 128]:

'It is not sufficient to say that if the question had been left they might have determined it against the appellant. When we once arrive at the conclusion that a vital question of fact has not been left to the jury the only ground on which we can affirm a conviction is that we can say that there has been no miscarriage of justice . . . '

The same point was made in *Bryce* [(1955) 40 Cr App Rep 62].

(C) Whether in a particular case the Crown has succeeded in establishing an 'obligation' of the kind coming within s 5 (3) of the new Act may be a difficult question. Happily, we are not called on to anticipate or solve for the purposes of the present case the sort of difficulties that can arise. But, to illustrate what we have in mind, mixed questions of law and fact may call for consideration. For example, if the transaction between the parties is wholly in writing, is it for the judge to direct the jury that, as a matter of law, the defendant had thereby undertaken an 'obligation' within s 5 (3)? On the other hand, if it is wholly (or partly) oral, it would appear that it is for the judge to direct them that, if they find certain facts proved, it would be open to them to find that an 'obligation' within s 5 (3) had been undertaken—but presumably not that they must so find, for so to direct them would be to invade their territory. In effect, however, the commissioner unhappily did something closely resembling that in the present case by his above-quoted direction that the only issue for their consideration was whether the appellant was proved to have been actuated by dishonesty.

We have only to add that counsel for the Crown submitted that, even if the commissioner's failure to deal with s 5 (3) amounted to a misdirection, this was a fitting case to apply the proviso. But point (1), successfully taken by defence counsel, is clearly of such a nature as to render that course impossible. We are only too aware that, in the result, there will be many clients of the appellant who, regarding themselves as cheated out of their money by him, will think little of a law which permits him to go unpunished. But such we believe it to be, and it is for this court to apply it.

Appeal allowed. Conviction quashed

NOTES AND QUESTIONS

1. Edmund Davies LJ said that 'what was not here established was that clients expected them "to retain and deal with that property or its proceeds in a particular way", and that an "obligation" to do so was undertaken by the appellants.' What exactly were the expectations of the clients in relation to the deposits paid? What if to a man they had (not unreasonably?) maintained that they expected the agency to use the money to make bookings on their behalf and for no other purpose? What exactly was the obligation, if any, of the appellant?

2. Evidently the 'obligation' under s 5(3) must be a legal obligation (why?) and the courts have frequently affirmed this. Whether there is a legal obligation is a matter of law for the judge. Of course whether there is a legal obligation depends on the facts and the facts may be disputed. Since it is the province of the jury to determine the facts, the judge should direct the jury on which factual findings a legal obligation would be established.

3. In *Cullen* (1974) unreported, No 968/c/74, P gave his mistress, D, two sums of money to buy food for the house and to pay certain domestic debts. D spent the money on herself and did not return. D relied on *Balfour v Balfour* [1919] 2 KB 571 as showing that the transactions in question were not legally enforceable but, upholding D's conviction for theft, Roskill LJ, on behalf of the Court of Appeal, said that 'one could hardly imagine a plainer case of theft.' He added that there was plainly a legal obligation to deal with the money as P directed and it did not cease to be a legal obligation because she was his mistress at the time. But was there a legal obligation? Consider in this connection *Meech* [1973] 3 All ER 939, CA, the facts of which are given above, p 416. To the argument that Meech was not under a legal obligation the court said (at 942):

Starting from this premise—that 'obligation' means 'legal obligation'—it was argued that even at the time when Meech was ignorant of the dishonest origin of the cheque, as he was at the time when he agreed to cash the cheque and hand the proceeds less the £40 to McCord, McCord could never have enforced that obligation because McCord had acquired the cheque illegally. In our view this submission is unsound in principle. The question has to be looked at from Meech's point of view not McCord's. Meech plainly assumed an 'obligation' to McCord which on the facts then known to him he remained obliged to fulfil and on the facts as found he must be taken at that time honestly to have intended to fulfill. The fact that on the true facts if known McCord might not and indeed would not subsequently have been permitted to enforce that obligation in a civil court does not prevent that 'obligation' on Meech having arisen. The argument confuses the creation of the obligation with the subsequent discharge of that obligation either by performance or otherwise. That the obligation might have become impossible of performance by Meech or of enforcement by McCord on grounds of illegality or for reasons of public policy is irrelevant. The opening words of s 5 (3) clearly look to the time of the creation of or the acceptance of the obligation by the bailee and not to the time of performance by him of the obligation so created and accepted by him.

It is further to be observed in this connection that s 5 (3) deems property (including the proceeds of property) which does not belong to the bailor to belong to the bailor so as to render a bailee who has accepted an obligation to deal with the property or to account for it in a particular way but then dishonestly fails to fulfill that obligation, liable to be convicted of theft whereas previously he would have been liable to have been convicted of fraudulent conversion though not of larceny. It was not seriously disputed in argument that before 1968 Meech would have had no defence to a charge of fraudulent conversion.

The first branch of the argument therefore clearly fails. The second argument (as already indicated) was that even if Meech initially became under an obligation to McCord, that obligation ceased to bind Meech once Meech discovered McCord had acquired the cheque by fraud. It was argued that once Meech possessed this knowledge, performance of his pre-existing obligation would have involved him in performing an 'obligation' which he knew to be illegal. Thus, it was said, he was discharged from performance and at the time of his dishonest mis-appropriation had ceased to be bound by his obligation so that he could not properly be convicted of theft by virtue of s 5 (3).

This submission was advanced at considerable length before the trial judge. It is not necessary to relate those arguments more fully. They will be found set out in the transcript which this court has read. The judge rejected the arguments and he directed the jury in the following terms so far as relevant. After saying that there were three considerations which Meech said affected his mind and led him not to carry out his agreement with McCord, the judge dealt correctly with the first two of the three matters. He continued as follows:

'Thirdly, he says that he was worried about being involved in the offence of obtaining money by fraud; that he knew this to be, as he described it, a "dodgy" cheque—knew not at the time that he was handed it, but knew before he drew the cash; that he alleges that from enquiries made on 11 and 12 September he discovered what was seemingly common knowledge among some motor dealers of High Wycombe, that McCord was involved in a dishonest transaction. His knowledge of this was limited and inaccurate, since he thought that there was a name Harris involved. He is not entitled in law to repudiate his agreement merely on the basis of suspicions about McCord. The only basis on which he was entitled to refuse payment was that he refused because if he had honoured the agreement he, Meech, would have committed a criminal offence, or that was his belief. Only if that was the basis—or if you thought on the evidence that may have been the basis—was there no obligation to pay. Otherwise, although you may well think many people had a better right than McCord, so far as Meech was concerned it was his obligation to deal with the proceeds of the cheque in the way that he had agreed with McCord that he would.'

The judge thus emphasised that the obligation to McCord remained but that Meech would be excused performance if performance would have involved commission of a criminal offence or if Meech genuinely believed that such performance would involve commission of a criminal offence. Of course if Meech acted as he did honestly and had an honest reason for not performing his obligation and for claiming relief from performance of that obligation, this would clearly be the end of any criminal charge against him. But the jury, as already pointed out, clearly negatived any such honest intention or belief on Meech's part. The argument before this court was that even though he was found to have acted dishonestly, he still could not be convicted of theft . . .

The answer to the main contention is that Meech being under the initial obligation already mentioned, the proceeds of the cheque continued as between him and McCord to be deemed to be McCord's property so that if Meech dishonestly misappropriated those proceeds he was by reason of s 5 (3) guilty of theft even though McCord could not have enforced performance of that obligation against Meech in a civil action. Some reliance was placed on a passage in Professor Smith's book [*The Law of Theft* (2nd edn, 1972, p 31, para 76)]:

'Thus there is no redress in civil or criminal law against a client who is accidentally over-paid by a bookmaker. The same principle no doubt governs other cases where the transaction is void or illegal by statute or at common law. If this is a defect in the law, the fault lies with the civil law and not with the Theft Act. If the civil law says that the defendant is the exclusive owner of the money and under no obligation to repay even an equivalent sum, it would be incongruous for the criminal law to say he had stolen it.'

It must be observed that the passage was written with reference to s 5 (4) of the Theft Act 1968 and not with reference to s 5 (3) of that Act. It immediately follows a discussion of the Gaming

Act cases. We do not think the learned author had a case such as the present in mind. On no view could it be said in the present case that the common law would regard Meech as the 'exclusive owner' of the original cheque or of its proceeds. The true owner of the proceeds was the hire purchase finance company. They could have sued Meech to judgment for the full value of the original cheque. But Meech having received the original cheque from McCord under the obligation we have mentioned, the criminal law provides that as between him and McCord the cheque and its proceeds are to be deemed to be McCord's property so that a subsequent dishonest misappropriation of the cheque or its proceeds makes Meech liable to be convicted of theft. We are therefore clearly of the view that Meech was properly convicted of theft just as under the old law he would have been liable to have been convicted of fraudulent conversion. We therefore think that the judge was quite right in leaving this case to the jury and that the direction which he gave was correct. If it be open to criticism at all, the criticism might be that the direction was arguably too favourable to the appellants.

Appeals dismissed. The court certified that the decision involved the following points of law of general public importance but refused leave to appeal to the House of Lords: 1. What is the true construction of the phrase 'is under an obligation' in s 5 (3) of the Theft Act 1968? 2. Whether where an 'obligation' is created and accepted in good faith by a defendant in relation to stolen property and the defendant subsequently dishonestly misappropriates that property he is liable by s 5 (3) to be convicted of theft notwithstanding that that 'obligation' could not have been enforced against him at common law?

Questions

1. How would you answer the first question certified by the court? If 'obligation' means legal obligation, was Meech at any stage of the transaction under a legal obligation to pay the proceeds of the cheque to McCord? Is it enough that the recipient of the property believes himself to be under an obligation?

2. How would you answer the second question certified by the court?

3. Was it necessary for the court to have relied on s 5 (3) at all? Did not McCord have a proprietary right or interest in the cheque under s 5 (1) since Meech was merely his agent for the purpose of cashing it? Cf commentary on *Meech* in [1973] Crim LR 771.

4. Is it ever strictly necessary to rely on s 5 (3)? If the defendant, as against another, is 'under an obligation to the other to retain and deal with the property or its proceeds in a particular way' does it not follow that the other must have a proprietary right or interest within s 5 (1)?

5. If Meech had been charged with stealing the proceeds of the cheque from the finance company from whom McCord got the cheque by means of a forged instrument, would he have had any answer to the charge?

Of all the provisions in s 5, subsection (4) certainly appears to be the most complicated and an explanation of its genesis may be helpful. In *Moynes v Coopper* [1956] 1 QB 439, [1956] 1 All ER 450, D, an employee of P, was given an advance of pay by the site agent amounting to £6.19.6½d. Unaware that this advance had been made, P's wages clerk paid D his full weekly wage of £7.3.4d and D on discovering the mistake dishonestly decided to keep all of the money. The difficulty with this case is that in law ownership of the £7.3.4d passed to D on delivery of the pay packet and hence D had not taken money belonging to another. D's acquittal, affirmed by the DC, provoked much criticism and Moynes was probably a significant, if unwitting, cause of the reference of the law of theft to the CLRC.

At all events the CLRC considered it important to bring this kind of conduct within the net of the criminal law, hence s 5(4). But how does s 5(4) trap Moynes? If the facts of *Moynes v Coopper* were to be repeated (and making necessary adjustments for decimalisation) Moynes still becomes the owner of the money so how is he to be regarded as appropriating property 'belonging to another'? The answer which the CLRC provided was that D may steal property got by P's mistake if, and only if, the effect in law (the civil law of course) is that D is under a (legal) obligation to make restoration of the property or its proceeds or the value thereof.

Any reader who has acquaintance with the law of contract will know of the difficulties attendant upon mistake and that mistakes have different effects. Consideration of *Cundy v Lindsay* (1878) 3 App Cas 459, HL, and *King's Norton Metal Co v Edridge Merrett & Co Ltd* (1897) 14 TLR 98, CA, may be helpful in this context. In the former, one Blenkarn ordered goods on credit from Lindsay & Co in the name of Blenkiron & Co, Blenkirons being a firm known to Lindsays as highly respectable and creditworthy. Having obtained the goods Blenkarn sold them to Cundy and made off with the proceeds. In the latter, one Wallis adopted the name of Hallam & Co and in that name ordered goods on credit from King's Norton which he subsequently sold to Edridges and made off with the proceeds.

In terms of dishonesty there is nothing to choose between the frauds of Blenkarn and Wallis. Both might now be convicted of obtaining by deception. But the point under discussion here is whether either or both are also now guilty of theft by virtue of s 5(4). There is, as students of the law of contract will appreciate, an important distinction between the two cases. In *Cundy v Lindsay* it was held that the transaction between Lindsays and Blenkarn was void, no property in the goods passed to Blenkarn which he could pass to Cundys and Lindsays all along retained ownership of the goods. The case is now clearly caught by s 5(4); Blenkarn gets the goods by a mistake and since ownership remains with Lindsays he is under an obligation to make restoration of the property (or of its value or proceeds). It might be asked in passing; is s 5(4) *necessary* to make a thief of Blenkarn? Is Blenkarn not also a thief by virtue of s 5(1)?

In *King's Norton*, on the other hand, the contract was merely voidable. It served to pass a voidable title which was good until such time as the contract was set aside by *King's Norton* and since they had not done so at the time of the sale to Edridges, the latter obtained a good title. Here again it can properly be said that Wallis gets the property under a mistake and the critical question becomes: *is* Wallis under an obligation to make restoration of the property or its value or proceeds? The layman might say that he ought to be because he is a rogue who has no intention of paying for the goods. But in law the goods belong to *Wallis* until such time as the contract is set aside. Edridges on discovering the fraud might, if they so wish, affirm the contract and sue Wallis for the price.

An illustration of the operation of s 5(4) is provided by *A-G's Reference (No 1 of 1983)* [1984] 3 All ER 369, CA. The respondent, a woman police officer, received her pay from her employer by way of direct debit. On one occasion she was overpaid by £74.74 but when she became aware of this she decided to take no action about it though she did not subsequently withdraw any of this money. At the close of the prosecution's case the judge directed an acquittal but on a reference by the A-G, Lord Lane CJ, on behalf of the court, said this (at 372):

"The debt here was a thing in action, therefore the property was capable of being stolen.

It will be apparent that, at first blush, that debt did not belong to anyone except the respondent herself. She was the only person who had the right to go to her bank and demand the handing over of that £74.74. Had there been no statutory provision which altered that particular situation that would have been the end of the case, but if one turns to s 5(4) of the 1968 Act one finds these words: [his Lordship read s 5(4)]

In order to determine the effect of that subsection on this case one has to take it piece by piece to see what the result is read against the circumstances of this particular prosecution. First of all: did the respondent get property? The word 'get' is about as wide a word as could possibly have been adopted by the draftsman of the Act. The answer is Yes; the respondent in this case did get her chose in action, that is her right to sue the bank for the debt which they owed her, money which they held in their hands to which she was entitled by virtue of the contract between bank and customer.

Second: did she get it by another's mistake? The answer to that is plainly Yes, the Receiver of the Metropolitan Police made the mistake of thinking she was entitled to £74.74 when she was not entitled to that at all.

Was she under an obligation to make restoration of either the property or its proceeds or its value? We take each of those in turn. Was she under an obligation to make restoration of the 'property', the chose in action? The answer to that is No, it was something which could not be restored in the ordinary meaning of the word. Was she under an obligation to make restoration of its proceeds? The answer to that is No, there were no proceeds of the chose in action to restore. Was she under an obligation to make restoration of the value thereof, the value of the chose in action? The answer to that seems to us to be Yes.

I should say here, in parenthesis, that a question was raised during the argument this morning whether 'restoration' is the same as 'making restitution'. We think that, on the wording of s 5(4) as a whole, the answer to that question is Yes. One therefore turns to see whether, under the general principles of restitution, the respondent was obliged to restore or pay for the benefit which she received. Generally speaking the respondent in these circumstances, is obliged to pay for a benefit received when the benefit has been given under a mistake as to a material fact on the part of the giver. The mistake must be as to a fundamental or essential fact and the payment must have been due to that fundamental or essential fact. The mistake here was that this police officer had been working on a day when she had been at home and not working at all. The authority for that proposition is to be found in *Norwich Union Fire Insurance Society Ltd v William H Price Ltd* [1934] AC 455, [1934] All ER Rep 352. That sets out the principles we have in précis form endeavoured to describe.

In the present case, applying that principle to the facts of this case, the value of the chose in action (the property) was £74.74 and there was a legal obligation on the respondent to restore that value to the receiver when she found that the mistake had been made. One continues to examine the contents of s 5(4). It follows from what has already been said that the extent of that obligation, the chose in action, has to be regarded as belonging to the person entitled to restoration, that is the Receiver of the Metropolitan Police.

As a result of the provisions of s 5(4) the debt of £74.74 due from the respondent's bank to the respondent notionally belonged to the Receiver of the Metropolitan Police, therefore the prosecution, up to this point, have succeeded in proving (remarkable though it may seem) that the 'property' in this case belonged to another within the meaning of s 1 in the 1968 Act from the moment when the respondent became aware that this mistake had been made and that her account had been credited with the £74.74 and she consequently became obliged to restore the value. Furthermore, by the final words of s 5(4), once the prosecution succeed in proving that the respondent intended not to make restoration, that is notionally to be regarded as an intention to deprive the receiver of that property which notionally belongs to him.

That would leave two further matters on which the prosecution would have to satisfy the jury. First, that there was an appropriation under the wording of s 1, if that is not already established by virtue of the application of the facts of s 3(1), which reads:

> 'Any assumption by a person of the rights of an owner amounts to an appropriation, and this includes, where he has come by the property (innocently or not) without stealing it, any later assumption of a right to it by keeping or dealing with it as owner.'

The second matter on which the prosecution would have to satisfy the jury is that the respondent had acted dishonestly. Whether they would have succeeded in proving either of those two matters we do not pause to inquire. . . ."

Even though the respondent did not in any way deal with the £74.74, it is clear that any possible argument as to whether she intended to permanently deprive is forestalled by the provision in s 5(4) that 'an intention not to make restoration shall be regarded accordingly as an intention to deprive that person of the property or proceeds.' Lord Lane adds that the prosecution must also prove an appropriation but does not pause to inquire whether there was an appropriation on these facts. Was there an appropriation? She intended to act dishonestly but in what way did she assume the rights of an owner?

It is all very well saying, as s 5(4) does, that D may be guilty of theft if he is under an obligation to make restoration of the property etc, but when is D under such an obligation? How is this issue to be determined?

R v Gilks [1972] 3 All ER 280, Court of Appeal, Criminal Division (Cairns, Stephenson LJJ, and Willis J)

Cairns LJ. The judgment I am about to read is the judgment of the court . . . the appellant was convicted of theft . . .

The facts were as follows. On 27 March 1971 the appellant went into Ladbrokes' betting shop at North Cheam and placed some bets on certain horses: one of his bets was on a horse called 'Fighting Scot'. 'Fighting Scot' did not get anywhere in the race which was in fact won by a horse called 'Fighting Taffy'. Because of a mistake on the part of the relief manager in the betting shop, the appellant was paid out as if he had backed the successful horse with the result that he was overpaid to the extent of £106.63. He was paid £117.25 when the amount he had won (on other races) was only £10.62. At the very moment when he was being paid the appellant knew that a mistake had been made and that he was not entitled to the money, but he kept it. He refused to consider repaying it, his attitude being that it was Ladbrokes' hard lines.

The questions of law arise under the following sections of the Theft Act 1968. [His Lordship read s 1 (1), s 2 (1) and s 5 (4).]

The deputy chairman gave rulings in law to the following effect. He ruled that at the moment when the money passed it was money 'belonging to another' and that that ingredient in the definition of theft in s 1 (1) of the Act was therefore present. Accordingly, s 5 (4) had no application to the case. If he was wrong about that then, he said, 'obligation' in s 5 (4) included an obligation which was not a legal obligation. He told the jury that it was open to them to convict the appellant of theft in respect of the mistaken overpayment. And he directed them that the test of dishonesty was whether the appellant believed that 'when dealing with your bookmaker if he makes a mistake you can take the money and keep it and there is nothing dishonest about it'.

In the grounds of appeal it is contended that all these directions were wrong. The main foundation of one branch of the appellant's case at the trial and in this court was the decision of the Court of Appeal in *Morgan v Ashcroft* [[1938] 1 KB 49; [1937] 3 All ER 92]. In that case a bookmaker, by mistake, overpaid a client £24. It was held that the bookmaker was not entitled to recover the money by action because that would involve taking accounts of gaming transactions which were void under the Gaming Act 1845. The argument proceeded as follows. When Ladbrokes paid the appellant they never supposed that they were discharging a legal liability; even if he had won they need not, in law, have paid him. They simply made him a gift of the money. The deputy chairman was wrong in saying that at the moment of payment the money 'belonged to another'. At that very moment its ownership was transferred and therefore the appellant could not be guilty of theft unless the extension given by s 5 (4) to the meaning of the words 'belonging to another' could be brought into play. But s 5 (4) had no application because under the rule in *Morgan v Ashcroft* the appellant had no obligation to repay.

The deputy chairman did not accept this line of argument. He held that it was unnecessary for the prosecution to rely on s 5 (4) because the property in the £106.63 never passed to the appellant. In the view of this court that ruling was right. The sub-s introduced a new principle into the law of theft but long before it was enacted it was held in *Middleton* [(1873) LR 2 CCR 38] that where a person was paid by mistake (in that case by a post office clerk) a sum in excess of that properly payable, the person who accepted the overpayment with knowledge of the excess was guilty of theft. Counsel for the appellant seeks to distinguish the present case from that one on the basis that in *Middleton* the depositor was entitled to withdraw 10s from his Post Office Savings Bank account and the clerk made a mistake in thinking he was entitled to withdraw more than £8, whereas in the present case there was no mistake about the appellant's rights—whether his horse won or lost he had no legal right to payment. In our view this argument is fallacious. A bookmaker who pays out money in the belief that a certain horse has won, and who certainly would not have made the payment but for the belief, is paying by mistake just as much as the Post Office clerk in *Middleton*.

The gap in the law which s 5 (4) was designed to fill was, as the deputy chairman rightly held, that which is illustrated by the case of *Moynes v Coopper*. There a workman received a pay-packet containing £7 more than was due to him but did not become aware of the overpayment until he opened the envelope some time later. He then kept the £7. This was held not to be theft because there was no *animus furandi* at the moment of taking, and *Middleton* was distinguished on that ground. It was observed that the law as laid down in *Middleton* was reproduced and enacted in s 1 (2) (i) of the Larceny Act 1916. It would be strange indeed if s 5 (4) of the 1968 Act, which was designed to bring within the net of theft a type of dishonest behaviour which escaped before, were to be held to have created a loophole for another type of dishonest behaviour which was always within the net.

An alternative ground on which the deputy chairman held that the money should be regarded as belonging to Ladbrokes was that 'obligation' in s 5 (4) meant an obligation whether a legal one or not. In the opinion of this court that was an incorrect ruling. In a criminal statute, where a person's criminal liability is made dependent on his having an obligation, it would be quite wrong to construe that word so as to cover a moral or social obligation as distinct from a legal one. As, however, we consider that the deputy chairman was right in ruling that the prosecution did not need to rely on s 5 (4), his ruling on this alternative point does not affect the result . . .

Appeal dismissed

Questions

1. The court in *Gilks* appears to suggest that the problem arising from *Moynes v Coopper* with which s 5(4) was intended to deal was that, as the law then stood, Moynes could not be convicted of theft because his intent to steal (animus furandi) did not accompany the taking of the money. Would it have been necessary to enact s 5(4) at all in order to deal with that difficulty?

2. While refusing leave to appeal the court certified two points of law. The first was whether the identified recipient of an identified voluntary payment steals the sum so paid if, without any antecedent deception on his part, he accepts the sum knowing that it would not have been paid if the person making the payment had knowledge of all the relevant facts. How is this question to be answered?

3. The court says that Gilks might have been convicted without s 5(4). Do you agree? In this connection consider *Lawrence*, below.

Lawrence v Commissioner of Police for the Metropolis [1971] 2 All ER 1253, House of Lords
(Viscount Dilhorne, Lords Pearson, Donovan, Diplock and Cross of Chelsea)

Viscount Dilhorne. My Lords, the appellant was convicted on 2 December 1969 of theft contrary to s 1 (1) of the Theft Act 1968. On 1 September 1969 a Mr Occhi, an Italian who spoke little English, arrived at Victoria Station on his first visit to this country. He went up to a taxi driver, the appellant, and showed him a piece of paper on which an address in Ladbroke Grove was written. The appellant said that it was very far and very expensive. Mr Occhi got into the taxi, took £1 out of his wallet and gave it to the appellant who then, the wallet being still open, took a further £6 out of it. He then drove Mr Occhi to Ladbroke Grove. The correct lawful fare for the journey was in the region of 10s 6d. The appellant was charged with and convicted of the theft of the £6.

In cross-examination, Mr Occhi when asked whether he had consented to money being taken, said that he had 'permitted'. He gave evidence through an interpreter and it does not appear that he was asked to explain what he meant by the use of the word. He had not objected when the £6 were taken. He had not asked for the return of any of it. It may well be that when he used the word 'permitted', he meant no more than that he had allowed the money to be taken. It certainly was not established at the trial that he had agreed to pay to the appellant a sum far in excess of the legal fare for the journey and so had consented to the acquisition of the appellant of the £6.

The main contention of the appellant in this House and in the Court of Appeal [[1971] 1 QB 373; [1970] 3 All ER at 933] was that Mr Occhi had consented to the taking of the £6 and that, consequently, his conviction could not stand. In my opinion, the facts of this case to which I have referred fall far short of establishing that Mr Occhi had so consented.

Prior to the passage of the Theft Act 1968, which made radical changes in and greatly simplified the law relating to theft and some other offences, it was necessary to prove that the property alleged to have been stolen was taken 'without the consent of the owner' (Larceny Act 1916, s 1 (1)).

These words are not included in s 1 (1) of the Theft Act 1968, but the appellant contended that the subsection should be construed as if they were, as if they appeared after the word 'appropriates'. Section 1 (1) provides:

'A person is guilty of theft if he dishonestly appropriates property belonging to another with the intention of permanently depriving the other of it; and 'thief' and 'steal' shall be construed accordingly.'

I see no ground for concluding that the omission of the words 'without the consent of the owner' was inadvertent and not deliberate, and to read the subsection as if they were included is, in my opinion, wholly unwarranted. Parliament by the omission of these words has relieved the prosecution of the burden of establishing that the taking was without the owner's consent. That is no longer an ingredient of the offence.

Megaw LJ, delivering the judgment of the Court of Appeal [[1971] 1 QB at 376, [1970] 3 All ER at 935], said that the offence created by s 1 (1) involved four elements: '(i) a dishonest (ii) appropriation (iii) of property belonging to another (iv) with the intention of permanently depriving the owner of it.' I agree. That there was appropriation in this case is clear. Section 3 (1) states that any assumption by a person of the rights of an owner amounts to an appropriation. Here there was clearly such an assumption. That an appropriation was dishonest may be proved in a number of ways. In this case it was not contended that the appellant had not acted dishonestly. Section 2 (1) provides, inter alia, that a person's appropriation of property belonging to another is not to be regarded as dishonest if he appropriates the property in the belief that he would have the other's consent if the other knew of the appropriation and the circumstances of it. A fortiori, a person is not to be regarded as acting dishonestly if he appropriates another's property believing that with full knowledge of the circumstances that other person has in fact agreed to the appropriation. The appellant, if he believed that Mr Occhi, knowing that £7 was far in excess of the legal fare, had nevertheless agreed to pay him that sum, could not be said to have acted dishonestly in taking it. When Megaw LJ said that if there was true consent, the essential element of dishonesty was not established, I understand him to have meant this. Belief or the absence of belief that the owner had with such knowledge consented to the appropriation is relevant to the issue of dishonesty, not to the question whether or not there has been an appropriation. That may occur even though the owner has permitted or consented to the property being taken. So proof that Mr Occhi had consented to the appropriation of £6 from his wallet without agreeing to paying a sum in excess of the legal fare does not suffice to show that there was not dishonesty in this case. There was ample evidence that there was.

I now turn to the third element 'property belonging to another'. Counsel for the appellant contended that if Mr Occhi consented to the appellant taking the £6, he consented to the property in the money passing from him to the appellant and that the appellant had not, therefore, appropriated property belonging to another. He argued that the old distinction between the offence of false pretences and larceny had been preserved. I am unable to agree with this. The new offence of obtaining property by deception created by s 15 (1) of the Theft Act 1968 also contains the words 'belonging to another'. 'A person who by any deception dishonestly obtains property belonging to another with the intention of permanently depriving the owner of it. . .' commits that offence. 'Belonging to another' in s 1 (1) and in s 15 (1) in my view signifies no more than that, at the time of the appropriation or the obtaining, the property belonged to another with the words 'belonging to another' having the extended meaning given by s 5. The short answer to this contention on behalf of the appellant is that the money in the wallet which he appropriated belonged to another, to Mr Occhi. There was no dispute about the appellant's intention being permanently to deprive Mr Occhi of the money.

The four elements of the offence of theft as defined in the Theft Act 1968 were thus clearly established and, in my view, the Court of Appeal [[1971] 1 QB 373, [1970] 3 All ER 933] was right to dismiss the appeal. Having done so, they granted a certificate that a point of law of general public importance was involved and granted leave to appeal to this House. Under the

Administration of Justice Act 1960, s 1 (1), they have power to grant such leave if they think that a point of law of general public importance is involved and also that the point is one which ought to be considered by this House. The certificate granted does not state that they thought that the point was one which ought to be considered by this House but I infer that they were of that opinion from the fact that leave to appeal was granted.

The first question posed in the certificate was:

> 'Whether section 1 (1) of the Theft Act 1968, is to be construed as though it contained the words 'without having the consent of the owner' or words to that effect.'

In my opinion, the answer is clearly No.

The second question was:

> 'Whether the provisions of section 15 (1) and of section 1 (1) of the Theft Act 1968, are mutually exclusive in the sense that if the facts proved would justify a conviction under section 15 (1) there cannot lawfully be a conviction under section 1 (1) on those facts.'

Again, in my opinion, the answer is No. There is nothing in the Act to suggest that they should be regarded as mutually exclusive and it is by no means uncommon for conduct on the part of an accused to render him liable to conviction for more than one offence. Not infrequently there is some overlapping of offences. In some cases the facts may justify a charge under s 1 (1) and also a charge under s 15 (1). On the other hand, there are cases which only come within s 1 (1) and some which are only within s 15 (1). If in this case the appellant had been charged under s 15 (1), he would, I expect, have contended that there was no deception, that he had simply appropriated the money and that he ought to have been charged under s 1 (1). In my view, he was rightly charged under that section.

I must confess to some surprise that a certificate for leave to appeal should have been granted in this case. While it may be true to say that few points of law affecting the general criminal law of the country are not points of general public importance, the second limb of s 1 (1) of the Administration of Justice Act 1960 is one to which great regard should be had, namely, that the point is one which ought to be considered by this House. I can say with some confidence that prior to the Administration of Justice Act 1960, it is most unlikely that the Attorney General's fiat would have been granted for an appeal to this House in a case such as this.

For the reasons I have stated, in my opinion this appeal should be dismissed.

[Lords Donovan, Pearson, Diplock and **Cross of Chelsea** agreed.]

Appeal dismissed

NOTES AND QUESTIONS

1. Occhi handed the first £1 note to Lawrence and Lawrence was not charged with stealing that even though, as Lawrence knew, the correct fare was 10s 6d. Could Lawrence have been convicted of stealing the £1 or of 9s 6d? Cf Williams, *Textbook, Criminal Law*, 2nd edn, at p 809 and Smith, *Theft*, 5th edn, para 39.

2. Suppose that P authorises D, his secretary, to take £5 from the petty cash. D goes into the adjoining room and, unseen by P, removes £10 from the cashbox. This would seem a plain case of theft of £5 by D. Was not Lawrence, in effect, doing precisely the same in that, authorised to take the correct fare from the wallet, he took in excess of that? Or does it make a difference that Occhi, unlike P, saw what Lawrence did? Did Occhi 'consent' to the taking of the £6? Would it have made any difference if Occhi had himself taken the £6 from his wallet and tendered these to Lawrence in the belief that they represented the fare?

3. There are further difficulties with *Lawrence* in relation to appropriation. In *Morris* (p 411, above) Lord Roskill said that there was in *Lawrence* an appropriation 'was beyond question'. Was it? It seems to follow from *Morris* that an authorised act is not an appropriation even though D in doing that act

has a dishonest intent. Yet in *Lawrence* Viscount Dilhorne appears to treat consent as not relevant 'to the question whether or not there has been an appropriation' and in *Morris* Lord Roskill appears to approve of Viscount Dilhorne's rejection of the argument that there could be no theft if the owner had consented to the acts which were done by the defendant. But is it possible to reconcile *Lawrence* with *Morris*?

(4) DISHONESTY

The partial definition of dishonesty in s 2 makes it clear that where it applies D's *belief* is of paramount importance. If D believes he has a legal right to property he cannot be convicted of theft however unreasonable his belief may be. If he believes that P has consented to the appropriation he cannot be accounted dishonest though only a fool (which D is) could have believed that P was giving the consent. If D finds and appropriates property in circumstances in which any man who gave thought to it would realise the owner could be traced by taking reasonable steps, D is not dishonest if this thought does not occur to him. But the definition in s 2 is only partial.

R v Ghosh [1982] 2 All ER 689, Court of Appeal, Criminal Division
(Lord Lane CJ, Lloyd and Eastham JJ)

[Lord Lane CJ read the following judgment of the court:]

. . . the appellant was convicted on four counts of an indictment laid under the Theft Act 1968: on count 1, attempting to procure the execution of a cheque by deception; on count 2, attempting to obtain money by deception; on counts 3 and 4, obtaining money by deception. Count 1 was laid under s 20(2) and the remainder under s 15(1). He was fined the sum of £250 on each count with a term of imprisonment to be served in default of payment.

At all material times the appellant was a surgeon acting as a locum tenens consultant at a hospital. The charges alleged that he had falsely represented that he had himself carried out a surgical operation to terminate pregnancy or that money was due to himself or an anaesthetist for such an operation, when in fact the operation had been carried out by someone else, and/or under the national health service provisions.

His defence was that there was no deception; that the sums paid to him were due for consultation fees which were legitimately payable under the regulations, or else were the balance of fees properly payable; in other words that there was nothing dishonest about his behaviour on any of the counts.

The effect of the jury's verdict was as follows: as to count 1, that the appellant had falsely represented that he had carried out a surgical operation and had intended dishonestly to obtain money thereby; that as to count 2 he had falsely pretended that an operation had been carried out under the national health service; that as to count 3 he had falsely pretended that money was due to an anaesthetist; and that as to count 4 that he had obtained money by falsely pretending that an operation had been carried out on a fee-paying basis when in fact it had been conducted under the terms of the national health service.

The grounds of appeal are simply that the judge misdirected the jury as to the meaning of dishonesty.

What the judge had to say on that topic was as follows:

'Now, finally dishonesty. There are, sad to say, infinite categories of dishonesty. It is for you. Jurors in the past and, whilst we have criminal law in the future, jurors in the future have to set the standards of honesty. Now it is your turn today, having heard what you have, to consider contemporary standards of honesty and dishonesty in the context of all that you have heard. I cannnot really expand on this too much, but probably it is something rather like getting something for nothing, sharp practice, manipulating systems and many other matters which come to your mind.'

The law on this branch of the Theft Act 1968 is in a complicated state and we embark on an examination of the authorities with great diffidence.

When *R v McIvor* [1982] 1 All ER 491, [1982] 1 WLR 409 came before the Court of Appeal, there were two conflicting lines of authority. On the one hand there were cases which decided that the test of dishonesty for the purposes of the Theft Act 1968 is, what we venture to call, subjective, that is to say, the jury should be directed to look into the mind of the defendant and determine whether he knew he was acting dishonestly: see *R v Landy* [1981] 1 All ER 1172 at 1181, [1981] 1 WLR 355 at 365 where Lawton LJ, giving the reserved judgment of the Court of Appeal said:

> 'An assertion by a defendant that throughout a transaction he acted honestly does not have to be accepted but has to be weighed like any other piece of evidence. If that was the defendant's state of mind, or may have been, he is entitled to be acquitted. But if the jury, applying their own notions of what is honest and what is not, conclude that he could not have believed he was acting honestly, then the element of dishonesty will have been established. What a jury must not do is to say to themselves: "If we had been in his place we would have known we were acting dishonestly, so he must have known he was." '

On the other hand there were cases which decided that the test of dishonesty is objective. Thus in *R v Greenstein, R v Green* [1976] 1 All ER 1 at 6, [1975] 1 WLR 1353 at 1359 the judge in the court below had directed the jury:

> '. . . there is nothing illegal in stagging. The question you have to decide and what this case is all about is whether these defendants, or either of them, carried out their stagging operations in a dishonest way. To that question you apply your own standards of dishonesty. It is no good, you see, applying the standards of anyone accused of dishonesty otherwise everybody accused of dishonesty, if he were to be tested by his own standards, would be acquitted automatically, you may think. The question is essentially one for a jury to decide and it is essentially one which the jury must decide by applying its own standards.'

The Court of Appeal, in a reserved judgment, approved that direction.

In *R v McIvor* [1982] 1 All ER 491 at 497, [1982] 1 WLR 409 at 417 the Court of Appeal sought to reconcile these conflicting lines of authority. They did so on the basis that the subjective test is appropriate where the charge is conspiracy to defraud, but in the case of theft the test should be objective. We quote the relevant passage in full:

> 'It seems elementary, first, that where the charge is conspiracy to defraud the prosecution must prove actual dishonesty in the minds of the defendants in relation of the agreement concerned, and, second, that where the charge is an offence contrary to s 15 of the Theft Act 1968 the prosecution must prove that the defendant knew or was reckless regarding the representation concerned. The passage in my judgment in *R v Landy* [1981] 1 All ER 1172 at 1181, [1981] 1 WLR 355 at 365 per Lawton LJ to which we have referred should be read in relation to charges of conspiracy to defraud, and not in relation to charges of theft contrary to s 1 of the 1968 Act. Theft is in a different category from conspiracy to defraud, so that dishonesty can be established independently of the knowledge or belief of the defendant, subject to the special cases provided for in s 2 of the Act. Nevertheless, where a defendant has given evidence of his state of mind at the time of the alleged offence, the jury should be told to give that evidence such weight as they consider right, and they may also be directed that they should apply their own standards to the meaning of dishonesty.'

The question we have to decide in the present case is, first, whether the distinction suggested in *R v McIvor* is justifiable in theory and, second, whether it is workable in practice.

In *Scott v Comr of Police for the Metropolis* [1974] 3 All ER 1032, [1975] AC 819 the House of Lords had to consider whether deceit is a necessary element in the common law crime of conspiracy to defraud. They held that it is not. It is sufficient for the Crown to prove dishonesty. In the course of his speech Viscount Dilhorne traced the meaning of the words 'fraud', 'fraudulently' and 'defraud' in relation to simple larceny, as well as the common law offence of conspiracy to defraud. After referring to *Stephen's History of the Criminal Law of England* ((1883) vol 2, pp 121–122) and *East's Pleas of the Crown* ((1803) vol 2, pp 553) he continued as follows ([1974] 3 All ER 1032 at 1036, [1975] AC 819 at 836–837):

> 'The Criminal Law Revision Committee in their eighth report on "Theft and Related Offences" (Cmnd 2977 (1966)) in para 33 expressed the view that the important element of larceny, embezzlement and fraudulent conversion was "undoubtedly the dishonest

appropriation of another person's property''; in para 35 that the words ''dishonestly appropriates'' meant the same as ''fraudulently converts to his own use or benefit, or the use or benefit of any other person'', and in para 39 that ''dishonestly'' seemed to them a better word than ''fraudulently''. Parliament endorsed these views in the Theft Act 1968, which by s 1(1) defined theft as the dishonest appropriation of property belonging to another with the intention of permanently depriving the other of it. Section 17 of that Act replaces ss 82 and 83 of the Larceny Act 1861 and the Falsification of Accounts Act 1875. The offences created by those sections and by that Act made it necessary to prove that there had been an ''intent to defraud''. Section 17 of the Theft Act 1968 substitutes the words ''dishonestly with a view to gain for himself or another or with intent to cause loss to another'' for the words ''intent to defraud''. If ''fraudulently'' in relation to larceny meant ''dishonestly'' and ''intent to defraud'' in relation to falsification of accounts is equivalent to the words now contained in s 17 of the Theft Act 1968 which I have quoted, it would indeed be odd if ''defraud'' in the phrase ''conspiracy to defraud'' has a different meaning and means only a conspiracy which is to be carried out by deceit.'

Later on in the same speech Viscount Dilhorne continued as follows ([1974] 3 All ER 1032 at 1038, [1975] AC 819 at 839):

'As I have said, words take colour from the context in which they are used, but the words ''fraudulently'' and ''defraud'' must ordinarily have a very similar meaning. If, as I think, and as the Criminal Law Revision Committee appears to have thought, ''fraudulently'' means ''dishonestly'', then ''to defraud'' ordinarily means, in my opinion, to deprive a person dishonestly of something which is his or of something to which he is or would or might but for the perpetration of the fraud be entitled.'

In *Scott* the House of Lords were only concerned with the question whether deceit is an essential ingredient in cases of conspiracy to defraud; and they held not. As Lord Diplock said ([1974] 3 All ER 1032 at 1040, [1975] AC 819 at 841), 'dishonesty of any kind is enough'. But there is nothing in *Scott* which supports the view that, so far as the element of dishonesty is concerned, 'theft is in a different category from conspiracy to defraud'. On the contrary the analogy drawn by Viscount Dilhorne between the two offences, and indeed that whole tenor of his speech, suggests the precise opposite.

Nor is there anything in *R v Landy* itself which justifies putting theft and conspiracy to defraud into different categories. Indeed the court went out of its way to stress that the test for dishonesty, whatever it might be, should be the same whether the offence charged be theft or conspiracy to defraud. This is clear from the reference to *R v Feely* [1973] 1 All ER 341, [1973] QB 530, which was a case under s 1 of the Theft Act 1968. Having set out what we have for convenience called the subjective test, the court in *R v Landy* [1981] 1 All ER 1172 to 1181, [1981] 1 WLR 355 at 365 continued:

'In our judgment this is the way *R v Feely* should be applied in cases where the issue of dishonesty arises. It is also the way in which the jury should have been directed in this case . . .'

In support of the distinction it is said that in conspiracy to defraud the question arises in relation to an agreement. But we cannot see that this makes any difference. If A and B agree to deprive a person dishonestly of his goods, they are guilty of conspiracy to defraud: see *Scott's* case. If they dishonestly and with the necessary intent deprive him of his goods, they are presumably guilty of theft. Why, one asks respectfully, should the test be objective in the case of simple theft, but subjective where they have agreed to commit a theft?

The difficulties do not stop there. The court in *McIvor* evidently regarded cases under s 15 of the Theft Act 1968 as being on the subjective side of the line, at any rate so far as proof of deception is concerned. This was the way they sought to explain *R v Greenstein*. In that case, after directing the jury in the passage which we have already quoted, the judge in the court below continued as follows ([1976] 1 All ER 1 at 7, [1975] 1 WLR 1353 at 1360):

'Now in considering whether Mr Green or Mr Greenstein had or may have had an honest belief in the truth of their representations . . . the test is a subjective one. That is to say, it is not what you would have believed in similar circumstances. It is what you think they believed and if you think that they, or either of them, had an honest belief to that effect, well then, of course, there would not be any dishonesty. On the other hand, if there is an absence of reasonable grounds for so believing, you might think that that points to the conclusion that they or either of them, as the case may be, had no genuine belief in the truth of their representations. In which case, applying your own standards, you may think that they acted dishonestly and it would be for you to say whether it has been established by the prosecution that they had no such honest belief . . .'

The Court of Appeal in *R v Greenstein* appear to have approved that passage. At any rate they expressed no disapproval.

In *R v McIvor* [1982] 1 All ER 491 at 496, [1982] 1 WLR 409 at 415 the court reconciled the two passages quoted from the judge's summing up as follows:

> 'It seems that those two passages are concerned with different points. The first, which follows and adopts the standards laid down in *R v Feely*, is concerned with the element of dishonesty in s 15 offences, whilst the second is specifically concerned with the mental element in relation to the false representation the subject matter of the charge. Clearly, if a defendant honestly believes that the representation made was true the prosecution cannot prove that he knew or, or was reckless as to, its falsity.'

The difficulty with s 15 of the Theft Act 1968 is that dishonesty comes in twice. If a person knows that he is not telling the truth he is guilty of dishonesty. Indeed deliberate deception is one of the two most obvious forms of dishonesty. One wonders therefore whether 'dishonestly' in s 15(1) adds anything, except in the case of reckless deception. But assuming it does, there are two consequences of the distinction drawn in *McIvor*. In the first place it would mean that the legislation has gone further than its framers intended. For it is clear from paras 87–88 of the Criminal Law Revision Committee's eighth report that 'deception' was to replace 'false pretence' in the old s 32(1) of the Larceny Act 1916, and 'dishonestly' was to replace 'with intent to defraud'. If the test of dishonesty in conspiracy to defraud cases is subjective, it is difficult to see how it could have been anything other than subjective in considering 'intent to defraud'. It follows that, if the distinction drawn in *McIvor* is correct, the Criminal Law Revision Committee were recommending an important change in the law by substituting 'dishonestly' for 'with intent to defraud'; for they were implicitly substituting an objective for a subjective test.

The second consequence is that in cases of deliberate deception the jury will have to be given two different tests of dishonesty to apply: the subjective test in relation to deception and the objective test in relation to obtaining. This is indeed what seems to have happened in *R v Greenstein*. We cannot regard this as satisfactory from a practical point of view. If it be sought to obviate the difficulty by making the test subjective in relation to both aspects of s 15, but objective in relation to s 1, then that would certainly be contrary to what was intended by the Criminal Law Revision Committee. For in para 88 they say:

> 'The provision in clause 12(1) making a person guilty of criminal deception if he "dishonestly obtains" the property replaces the provision in the 1916 Act, section 32 (1) making a person guilty of obtaining by false pretences if he "with intent to defraud, obtains" the things there mentioned. The change will correspond to the change from "fraudulently" to "dishonestly" in the definition of stealing (contained in section 1).'

We feel, with the greatest respect, that in seeking to reconcile the two lines of authority in the way we have mentioned, the Court of Appeal in *McIvor* was seeking to reconcile the irreconcilable. It therefore falls to us now either to choose between the two lines of authority or to propose some other solution.

In the current supplement to *Archbold's, Pleading, Evidence and Practice in Criminal Cases* (40th edn, 1979) para 1460, the editors suggest that the observations on dishonesty by the Court of Appeal in *R v Landy* can be disregarded 'in view of the wealth of authority to the contrary'. The matter, we feel, is not as simple as that.

In *R v Waterfall* [1969] 3 All ER 1048, [1970] 1 QB 148 the defendant was charged under s 16 of the 1968 Act with dishonestly obtaining a pecuniary advantage from a taxi driver. Lord Parker CJ, giving the judgment of the Court of Appeal, said ([1969] 3 All ER 1048 at 1049–1050, [1970] 1 QB 148 at 150–151):

> 'The sole question as it seems to me in this case revolves round the third ingredient, namely, whether that what was done was done dishonestly. In regard to that the deputy recorder directed the jury in this way: ". . . if on reflection and deliberation you came to the conclusion that [the appellant] never did have any genuine belief that [the appellant's accountant] would pay the taxi fare, then you would be entitled to convict him . . ." In other words, in that passage the deputy recorder is telling the jury they had to consider what was in this particular appellant's mind; had he a genuine belief that the accountant would provide the money? That, as is seems to this court, is a perfectly proper direction subject to this, that it would be right to tell the jury that they can use as a test, although not a conclusive test, whether there were any reasonable grounds for that belief. Unfortunately, however, just before the jury retired, in two passages of the transcript the

deputy recorder, as it seems to this court, was saying that one cannot hold that the appellant had a genuine belief unless he had reasonable grounds for that belief.'

Lord Parker CJ then sets out the passages in question and continues:

'. . . the court is quite satisfied that those directions cannot be justified. The test here is a subjective test, whether the appellant had an honest belief, and of course whereas the absence of reasonable ground may point strongly to the fact that that belief is not genuine, it is at the end of the day for the jury to say whether or not in the case of this particular man he did have that genuine belief.'

That decision was criticised by academic writers. But it was followed shortly afterwards in *R v Royle* [1971] 3 All ER 1359, [1971] 1 WLR 1764, another case under s 16 of the 1968 Act. Edmund Davies LJ, giving the judgment of the court, said ([1971] 3 All ER 1359 at 1365, [1971] 1 WLR 1764 at 1769-1770):

'The charges being that debts had been dishonestly "evaded" by deception, contrary to s 16(2)(a), it was incumbent on the commissioner to direct the jury on the fundamental ingredient of dishonesty. In accordance with *R v Waterfall* they should have been told that the test is whether the accused had an honest belief and that, whereas the absence of reasonable ground might point strongly to the conclusion that he entertained no genuine belief in the truth of his representation, it was for them to say whether or not it had been established that the appellant had no such genuine belief.'

It is to be noted that the court in that case treated the 'fundamental ingredient of dishonesty' as being the same as whether the defendant had a genuine belief in the truth of the representation.

In *R v Gilks* [1972] 3 All ER 280, [1972] 1 WLR 1341, which was decided by the Court of Appeal the following year, the appellant had been convicted of theft contrary to s 1 of the 1968 Act. The facts were that he had been overpaid by a bookmaker. He knew that the bookmaker had made a mistake, and that he was not entitled to the money. But he kept it. The case for the defence was that 'bookmakers are a race apart'. It would be dishonest if your grocer gave you too much change and you kept it, knowing that he had made a mistake. But it was not dishonest in the case of a bookmaker.

The deputy chairman of the court below directed the jury as follows:

'Well, it is a matter for you to consider, members of the jury, but try and place yourselves in [the appellant's] position at that time and answer the question whether in your view he thought he was acting honestly or dishonestly.'

(See [1972] 3 All ER 280 at 283, [1972] 1 WLR 1341 at 1345)

Cairns LJ, giving the judgment of the court of appeal held that that was, in the circumstances of the case, a proper and sufficient direction on the matter of dishonesty. He continued ([1972] 3 All ER 280 at 283, [1972] 1 WLR 1341 at 1345):

'On the face of it the appellant's conduct was dishonest; the only possible basis on which the jury could find that the prosecution had not established dishonesty would be if they thought it possible that the appellant did have the belief which he claimed to have.'

A little later *R v Feely* came before a court of five judges. The case is often treated as having laid down an objective test of dishonesty for the purpose of s 1 of the 1968 Act. But what it actually decided was (i) that it is for the jury to determine whether the defendant acted dishonestly and not for the judge, (ii) that the word 'dishonestly' can only relate to the defendant's own state of mind, and (iii) that it is unnecessary and undesirable for judges to define what is meant by 'dishonestly'.

It is true that the court said ([1973] 3 All ER 341 at 345, [1973] QB 530 at 537-538):

'Jurors, when deciding whether an appropriation was dishonest can be reasonably expected to, and should, apply the current standards of ordinary decent people.'

It is that sentence which is usually taken as laying down the objective test. But the passage goes on:

'In their own lives they have to decide what is and what is not dishonest. We can see no reason why, when in a jury box, they should require the help of a judge to tell them what amounts to dishonesty.'

The sentence requiring the jury to apply current standards leads up to the prohibition of judges from applying *their* standards. That is the context in which the sentence appears. It seems to be reading too much into that sentence to treat it as authority for the view that 'dishonesty can be established independently of the knowledge or belief of the defendant'. If it could, then any reference to the state of mind of the defendant would be beside the point.

This brings us to the heart of the problem. Is 'dishonestly' in s 1 of the 1968 Act intended to characterise a course of conduct? Or is it intended to describe a state of mind? If the former, then we can well understand that it could be established independently of the knowledge or belief of the accused. But if, as we think, it is the latter, then the knowledge and belief of the accused are at the root of the problem.

Take for example a man who comes from a country where public transport is free. On his first day here he travels on a bus. He gets off without paying. He never had any intention of paying. His mind is clearly honest; but his conduct, judged objectively by what he had done, is dishonest. It seems to us that, in using the word 'dishonestly' in the 1968 Act, Parliament cannot have intended to catch dishonest conduct in that sense, that is to say conduct to which no moral obloquy could possibly attach. This is sufficiently established by the partial definition in s 2 of the Theft Act 1968 itself. All the matters covered by s 2(1) relate to the belief of the accused. Section 2(2) relates to his willingness to pay. A man's belief and his willingness to pay are things which can only be established subjectively. It is difficult to see how a partially subjective definition can be made to work in harness with the test which in all other respects is wholly objective.

If we are right that dishonesty is something in the mind of the accused (what Professor Glanville Williams calls 'a special mental state'), then if the mind of the accused is honest, it cannot be deemed dishonest merely because members of the jury would have regarded it as dishonest to embark on that course of conduct.

So we would reject the simple uncomplicated approach that the test is purely objective, however attractive from the practical point of view that solution may be.

There remains the objection that to adopt a subjective test is to abandon all standards but that of the accused himself, and to bring about a state of affairs in which 'Robin Hood would be no robber' (see *R v Greenstein*). This objection misunderstands the nature of the subjective test. It is no defence for a man to say, 'I knew that what I was doing is generally regarded as dishonest; but I do not regard it as dishonest myself. Therefore I am not guilty.' What he is, however, entitled to say is, 'I did not know that anybody would regard what I was doing as dishonest.' He may not be believed; just as he may not be believed if he sets up 'a claim of right' under s 2(1) of the 1968 Act, or asserts that he believed in the truth of a misrepresentation under s 15 of the 1968 Act. But if he *is* believed, or raises a real doubt about the matter, the jury cannot be sure that he was dishonest.

In determining whether the prosecution has proved that the defendant was acting dishonestly, a jury must first of all decide whether according to the ordinary standards of reasonable and honest people what was done was dishonest. If it was not dishonest by those standards, then the jury must consider whether the defendant himself must have realised that what he was doing was by those standards dishonest. In most cases, where the actions are obviously dishonest by ordinary standards, there will be no doubt about it. It will be obvious that the defendant himself knew that he was acting dishonestly. It is dishonest for a defendant to act in a way which he knows ordinary people consider to be dishonest, even if he asserts or genuinely believes that he is morally justified in acting as he did. For example, Robin Hood or those ardent anti-vivisectionists who remove animals from vivisection laboratories are acting dishonestly, even though they may consider themselves to be morally justified in doing what they do, because they know that ordinary people would consider these actions to be dishonest.

Cases which might be described as borderline, such as *Boggeln v Williams* [1978] 2 All ER 1061, [1978] 1 WLR 873, will depend on the view taken by the jury whether the defendant may have believed what he was doing was in accordance with the ordinary man's idea of honesty. A jury might have come to the conclusion that the defendant in that case was disobedient or impudent, but not dishonest in what he did.

So far as the present case is concerned, it seems to us that once the jury had rejected the defendant's account in respect of each count in the indictment (as they plainly did), the finding of dishonesty was inevitable, whichever of the tests of dishonesty was applied. If the judge had asked the jury to determine whether the defendant might have believed that what he did was in accordance with the ordinary man's idea of honesty, there could have only been one answer, and that is No, once the jury had rejected the defendant's explanation of what happened.

In so far as there was a misdirection on the meaning of dishonesty, it is plainly a case for the application of the proviso to s 2(1) of the Criminal Appeal Act 1968.

This appeal is accordingly dismissed.

Appeal dismissed

NOTES AND QUESTIONS

1. While *Ghosh* clarifies the earlier law in some respects it still leaves the jury to determine as a matter of fact whether D's conduct would be regarded as dishonest by the ordinary standards of reasonable and honest people. This view has its critics (see, for example, Griew, *Dishonesty and the Jury*, Leicester University Press 1974 and 'Dishonesty, the Objections to *Feely* and *Ghosh*' [1985] Crim LR 341, and Elliott, 'Dishonesty in Theft: A Dispensable Concept' [1982] Crim LR 395; but it has its defenders (see Samuels, [1974] Crim LR 493). The CLRC said that dishonesty is 'something which laymen can easily recognise when they see it'. Can you easily recognise dishonesty when you see it? Do you think that you would always agree with your fellows on what is and what is not dishonest? If not, is it satisfactory to settle the matter by vote after discussion which is presumably what a jury would do where opinions differ?

2. In *Salvo* [1980] VR 401 the Full Court of Victoria declined to follow the approach of English courts to the interpretation of dishonesty. Concluding that it was for the judge to direct the jury on the meaning of dishonesty, Fullager J said in the context of similar Victorian legislation (at 431):

> 'The alleged proposal of the [CLRC] . . . is in my opinion based upon a clear and fundamental fallacy. First, it is simply untrue to say that every citizen "knows dishonesty when he sees it" or knows the meaning of the word generally, let alone in the context of a . . . statute. Secondly, that is simply not the question that arises under the Acts; it is a different question altogether to ask whether a deprivation by deception has been achieved dishonestly. The word "dishonestly" is in my opinion used in a somewhat special sense in its special context in the Theft Act 1973 and it is simply not true to say that every citizen knows what the word "dishonestly" means in the context of this statute . . . . In my opinion the word "dishonestly" in s 81(1) imports that the accused person must obtain the property (with intent to deprive), without any belief that he has in law the right to deprive the other of the property.'

But is it any more satisfactory to leave dishonesty to be defined by the judges? Is Fullager J's definition a satisfactory one?

3. Would it be possible and desirable to enact an exhaustive definition of dishonesty? Suppose the partial definition in the 1968 Act had been made an exhaustive definition; would this adequately meet the case?

4. In *Feely* [1973] 1 All ER 341 at 346, CA, Lawton LJ instanced the case of a shop manager, under instructions not to take money from the till, who takes 40p from the till to pay a taxi driver because he has nothing less than a £5 note which the driver cannot change. Assuming that the manager intends to repay the 40p as soon as he has change, Lawton LJ thought that to hold that such a taking was dishonest would bring the law into contempt. Would it? Assume the owner has made it clear that in no circumstances whatever is an employee to take money from the till, does not the manager know that he has not a shred of right to take the 40p? Assuming the manager is not accounted dishonest, at what point do such 'borrowings' become dishonest? Is this to be determined by the amount taken, the time it will take D to restore the amount, or what?

(5) INTENTION PERMANENTLY TO DEPRIVE

Theft Act, s 6, p 566, below

R v Lloyd & others [1985] 2 All ER 661, Court of Appeal, Criminal Division (Lord Lane CJ, Farquharson and Tudor Price JJ)

[**Lord Lane CJ** delivered the following judgment of the court:] . . . The first count of conspiracy to steal of course was that on which the conviction was recorded . . .

At all material times the appellant Lloyd was employed as chief projectionist at the Odeon cinema at Barking. The other two appellants with whom we are concerned, namely Ali and Bhuee, were employed by a man called Mustafa, who was also named in the indictment who pleaded guilty to the charge of conspiracy to steal. They were employed at premises at 3 Plumstead Road, Barking. The case against the appellants was that over a period of months Lloyd had been clandestinely removing feature films which were due to be shown at the Odeon cinema at Barking and lending them to his co-defendants, who had sophisticated equipment at their premises at 3 Plumstead Road. That sophisticated equipment enabled them to copy the feature films on to a master videotape, and, as a result of the preparation of that master video-tape, they or others were enabled to produce a very large quantity of pirated versions of the film.

The process of copying was done rapidly. The films were only out of the cinema and out of the hands of Lloyd for a few hours and were always back in time for their projection to take place at the advertised times to those people who attended the cinema to see them.

It was important that the film should be returned rapidly, because if it was not it would soon become apparent that the film had been illegally removed and steps would be taken to prevent a recurrence.

The pirated copies prepared from the master tape would be put on the market to the great financial benefit of the pirates and the great financial detriment of the lawful owners, the film distributors and those who would derive money from the film enterprise. The detriment would occur in a number of different ways, and that indeed was proved before the jury. First of all it would occur through a lowering of cinema attendances to see the particular film and secondly through the legitimate sales of cassettes of the film being undermined by the sale of the pirated copies. The profits apparently, so it was stated in evidence, to the film pirates are enormous and the loss to the legitimate trade is potentially crippling.

In the upshot the appellants were caught red-handed in the process of copying a film called 'The Missionary' on to the master tape.

The trial judge issued his certificate by posing the following question:

> 'Whether the offence of conspiracy to steal is committed when persons dishonestly agree to take a film from a cinema without authority intending it should be returned within a few hours but knowing that many hundreds of copies will be subsequently made and that the value of the film so returned will thereby be substantially reduced?'

The complaint by the appellants is this, that the judge misdirected the jury first of all in leaving the question for them to decide whether the removal of a film in these circumstances could amount to theft, and secondly, in allowing them to consider s 6(1) of the Theft Act 1968 as being relevant at all in the circumstances of this case.

The point is a short one. It is not a simple one. It is not without wider importance, because if the judge was wrong in leaving the matter in the way in which he did for the jury to consider, it might mean, as we understand it, that the only offence of which a person in these circumstances could be convicted would be a conspiracy to commit a breach of the Copyright Act 1956. At the time when this particular case was being tried, the maximum penalties available for the substantive offence under the Copyright Act were minimal. Those penalties have now been increased by the provisions of the Copyright (Amendment) Act 1983, and in the light of that Act it can be said that, although Parliament perhaps has not entirely caught up with this type of prevalent pirating offence, it is at least gaining on it.

We turn now to the provisions of the Theft Act 1968, the conspiracy alleged being a breach of that particular Act. Section 1(1) of the 1968 Act provides: [His Lordship read s 1(1)] . . .

On that wording alone these appellants were not guilty of theft or of conspiracy to steal. The success of their scheme and their ability to act with impunity in a similar fashion in the future, depended, as we have already said, on their ability to return the film to its rightful place in the hands of the Odeon cinema at Barking as rapidly as possibly, so that its absence should not be noticed. Therefore the intention of the appellants could more accurately be described as an intention temporarily to deprive the owner of the film and was indeed the opposite of an intention permanently to deprive.

What then was the basis of the prosecution case and the basis of the judge's direction to the jury? It is said that s 6(1) of the Theft Act 1968 brings such actions as the appellants performed here within the provisions of s 1. The judge left the matter to the jury on the basis that they had to decide whether the words of s 6(1) were satisfied by the prosecution or not. Section 6(1) reads as follows:

> 'A person appropriating property belonging to another without meaning the other permanently to lose the thing itself is nevertheless to be regarded as having the intention of permanently depriving the other of it if his intention is to treat the thing as his own to dispose of regardless of the other's rights; and a borrowing or lending of it may amount to so treating it if, but only if, the borrowing or lending is for a period and in circumstances making it equivalent to an outright taking or disposal.'

That section has been described by J R Spencer in 'The Metamorphosis of Section 6 of the Theft Act' [1977] Crim LR 653 as a section which 'sprouts obscurities at every phrase', and we are inclined to agree with him. It is abstruse. But it must mean, if nothing else, that there are circumstances in which a defendant may be deemed to have the intention permanently to deprive, even though he may intend the owner eventually to get back the object which has been taken.

We have had the benefit of submissions by counsel for the appellants in this case. His first submission is that the definition of 'property' in s 4 of the Theft Act 1968 does not include value, and he submits that it was on the basis of loss of value or loss of virtue of the films that the prosecution of the case proceeded. In order to substantiate that submission, he referred us to the decision of the House of Lords in *Rank Film Distributors Ltd v Video Information Centre* [1981] 2 All ER 76, [1982] AC 380. Relying on that case he sought to demonstrate to us that the provisions of the Theft Act 1968 do not cover the stealing of copyright or kindred matters.

We are indebted to counsel for the appellants for his careful arguments on this point, namely to the effect that copyright probably cannot be the subject of theft, but we are not concerned with that proposition here, so it seems to us, except perhaps incidentally, because the allegation here was one of conspiracy to steal feature films, not the copyright in them, and the allegation that the appellants conspired together to steal feature films depends on proof by the prosecution that that is the thing that they were conspiring to steal.

Counsel for the appellants next cited to us a series of helpful cases, which are these. First of all, *R v Warner* (1970) 55 Cr App R 93. This was a case in which the judgment of the court was delivered by Edmund Davies LJ. Having cited the the words in which the chairman directed the jury, Edmund Davies LJ continued (at 96–97):

> 'But unfortunately his direction later became confused by his references to section 6, the object of which he may himself have misunderstood. There is no statutory definition of the words "intention of permanently depriving," but section 6 seeks to clarify their meaning in certain respects. Its object is in no wise to cut down the definition of "theft" contained in section 1. It is always dangerous to paraphrase a statutory enactment, but its apparent aim is to prevent specious pleas of a kind which have succeeded in the past providing, in effect, that it is no excuse for an accused person to plead absence of the necessary intention if it is clear that he appropriated another's property intending to treat it as his own, regardless of the owner's rights. Section 6 thus gives illustrations, as it were, of what can amount to the dishonest intention demanded by section 1(1). But it is a misconception to interpret it as watering down section 1.'

Those observations we must bear in mind, because that it is a decision which of course is binding on this court.

Then counsel for the appellants referred us to *R v Duru* [1973] 3 All ER 715, [1974] 1 WLR 2. That was a case involving cheques. The allegation was that the defendant had obtained certain cheques from the local authority by deception with the intention of permanently depriving the council of them. That was contrary to s 15(1) of the Theft Act 1968, but s 6(1) was equally applicable in that case as it would have been had the allegation been one simply of theft. Megaw LJ, delivering the judgment of the court, said ([1973] 3 All ER 715 at 720, [1974] 1 WLR 2 at 8):

> 'So far as the cheque itself is concerned, true it is a piece of paper. But it is a piece of paper which changes its character completely once it is paid, because then it receives a rubber stamp on it saying it has been paid and it ceases to be a thing in action, or at any rate it ceases to be, in its substance, the same thing as it was before: that is, an instrument

on which payment falls to be made. It was the intention of the appellants, dishonestly and by deception, not only that the cheques should be made out and handed over, but also that they should be presented and paid, thereby permanently depriving the Greater London Council of [the cheques in their substance as things in action]. The fact that the mortgagors were under an obligation to repay the mortgage loans does not affect the appellants' intention permanently to deprive the council of these cheques. If it were necessary to look to s 6(1) of the Theft Act 1968, this court would have no hesitation in saying that that subsection, brought in by the terms of s 15(3), would also be relevant, since it is plain that the appellants each had the intention of causing the cheque to be treated as the property of the person by whom it was to be obtained, to dispose of, regardless of the rights of the true owner.'

Finally counsel for the appellants referred us to *R v Downes* (1983) 77 Cr App R 260. That was a case similar in essence to *R v Duru* [1973] 3 All ER 715, [1974] 1 WLR 2. The judgment of the court in *R v Downes* was delivered by Nolan J who said this (at 266–267):

'It is of some interest to note in *Duru* the Court was referred to the earlier case of *Warner* ((1970) 55 Cr App R 93, which Mr Lodge cited in support of the narrower reading of section 6(1) for which he contended. *Warner* does not however appear to us, as evidently it did not appear to this Court in *Duru* to have any significant bearing on the point at issue. It follows that, for substantially the same reasons as those given by the learned judge, we consider that the charge of theft is made out, the vouchers having been dishonestly appropriated with the intention of destroying their essential character and thus depriving the owners, the Inland Revenue, of the substance of their property. In our judgment therefore the appeal must be dismissed.'

In general we take the same view as Professor Griew in his book *The Theft Acts 1968 and 1978* (4th edn, 1982) para 2–73, namely that s 6 should be referred to in exceptional cases only. In the vast majority of cases it need not be referred to or considered at all.

Deriving assistance from another distinguished academic writer, namely Professor Glanville Williams, we would like to cite with approval the following passage from his *Textbook of Criminal Law* (2nd edn, 1983) p 719:

'In view of the grave difficulties of interpretation presented by section 6, a trial judge would be well advised not to introduce it to the jury unless he reaches the conclusion that it will assist them, and even then (it may be suggested) the question he leaves to the jury should not be worded in terms of the generalities of the subsection but should reflect those generalities as applied to the alleged facts. For example, the question might be; "Did the defendant take the article, intending that the owner should have it back only on making a payment? If so, you would be justified as a matter of law in finding that he intended to deprive the owner permanently of his article, because the taking of the article with that intention is equivalent to an outright taking." '

Bearing in mind the observations of Edmund Davies LJ in *R v Warner* (1970) 55 Cr App R 93, we would try to interpret s 6 in such a way as to ensure that nothing is construed as an intention permanently to deprive which would not prior to the 1968 Act have been so construed. Thus the first part of s 6(1) seems to us to be aimed at the sort of case where a defendant takes things and then offers them back to the owner for the owner to buy if he wishes. If the taker intends to return them to the owner only on such payment, then, on the wording of s 6(1), that is deemed to amount to the necessary intention permanently to deprive: see for instance *R v Hall* (1849) 1 Den 381, 169 ER 291, where the defendant took fat from a candlemaker and then offered it for sale to the owner. His conviction for larceny was affirmed. There are other cases of similar intent: for instance, 'I have taken your valuable painting. You can have it back on payment to me of £X,000. If you are not prepared to make that payment, then you are not going to get your painting back'.

It seems to us that in this case we are concerned with the second part of s 6(1), namely the words after the semi-colon: 'and a borrowing or lending of it may amount to so treating it if, but only if, the borrowing or lending is for a period and in circumstances making it equivalent to an outright taking or disposal.'

These films, it could be said, were borrowed by Lloyd from his employers in order to enable him and the others to carry out their 'piracy' exercise.

Borrowing is ex hypothesi not something which is done with an intention permanently to deprive. This half of the subsection, we believe, is intended to make it clear that a mere borrowing is never enough to constitute the necessary guilty mind unless the intention is to return the 'thing' in such a changed state that it can truly be said that all its goodness or virtue has gone.

For example *R v Beecham* (1851) 5 Cox CC 181, where the defendant stole railway tickets intending that they should be returned to the railway company in the usual way only after the journeys had been completed. He was convicted of larceny. The judge in the present case gave another example, namely the taking of a torch battery with intention of returning it only when its power is exhausted.

That being the case, we turn to inquire whether the feature films in this case can fall within this category. Our view is that they cannot. The goodness, the virtue, the practical value of the films to the owners has not gone out of the article. The film could still be projected to paying audiences, and, had everything gone according to the conspirators' plans, would have been projected in the ordinary way to audiences at the Odeon cinema, Barking, who would have paid for their seats. Our view is that those particular films which were the subject of this alleged conspiracy had not themselves diminished in value at all. What had happened was that the borrowed film had been used or was going to be used to perpetrate a copyright swindle on the owners whereby their commercial interests were grossly and adversely affected in the way that we have endeavoured to describe at the outset of this judgment. The borrowing, it seems to us, was not for a period, or in such circumstances, as made it equivalent to an outright taking or disposal. There was still virtue in the film.

For those reasons we think that the submissions of counsel for the appellants on this aspect of the case are well founded. Accordingly, the way in which the trial judge directed the jury was mistaken, and accordingly this conviction of conspiracy to steal must be quashed. . . .

Appeals allowed, convictions quashed

NOTES AND QUESTIONS

1. In *Warner* (referred to in *Lloyd*) D removed a toolbox from P's workshop next door and when questioned by the police denied that he had taken it. There had been some ill-feeling between D and P concerning the parking of motor cars and D later said that it was his intention to return the toolbox and that he told lies to the police because he had panicked. It was held that the trial judge had misdirected the jury in saying that D could be convicted of theft if his intention was that P should lose the use of his tools indefinitely.

2. The court in *Lloyd* indicated that when the 'thing' is returned to P there is deemed to be a permanent deprivation only where 'the goodness, the virtue, the practical value' has been exhausted. Since the film could still be screened, for paying viewers (at least in Barking!) its value was not exhausted. Consider *Oxford v Moss*, p 417, above. Was not the borrowing of the paper equivalent to an outright taking in that the examination paper, once its contents were disclosed, was valueless to the university?

3. When introducing s 6 to an expectant and hushed House of Commons, the Under Secretary of State for the Home Department said:

> 'The case which comes most readily to mind in this connection is that of a person borrowing, say, a season ticket. If he borrows it merely to keep it for any reason whatever as a piece of cardboard having an intrinsic value of a fraction of a penny, no offence can be committed under the [section]. But let us assume that he uses the ticket to gain admittance to a certain performance or series of performances—let us say he uses it for 19 or 20 performances. He has, by that act, used the season ticket in a situation which shows that he is not any longer acting as borrower but as . . . owner of the ticket.'

Do you agree that the taker of the season ticket is (a) not guilty of theft on the first hypothesis, but (b) guilty of theft on the second?

4. Suppose that D offers to sell to P, an unusually gullible tourist, the Crown jewels for £500. Realising that this is something of a bargain, P accepts and pays £500. Obviously a case of obtaining by deception, but has D stolen the Crown jewels? Whether in such circumstances D has appropriated the jewels has been considered p 417, above but, assuming there is an appropriation, has D, by virtue of s 6, an intention permanently to deprive the owner?

5. D must *intend* permanent deprivation. Suppose D takes P's car in Nottingham which he later abandons in Leeds. D realises that the car may be restored to P but it is a matter of indifference to him whether it is or no. It would seem that D does not *intend* permanently to deprive P. But can it be said that he has treated the car as his own 'to dispose of regardless of the other's rights' and this is 'in circumstances making it equivalent to an outright taking or disposal'?

6. A problem which has much exercised the courts in recent years is whether D may be convicted of theft where his intention permanently to deprive is conditional, as where D has not specific property in mind but has resolved to steal if there is anything worth his while to take. Commonly, for example, rogues enter cars on the look-out for anything that may be of value to them while realising that there may be nothing in the car that interests them. Obviously the rogue cannot be convicted of theft if in fact he appropriates nothing, but may he be convicted of attempted theft, and, if so, of attempting to steal what? The problem was further complicated by *Haughton v Smith* (p 291, above) which held that attempt could not be committed where the *actus reus* was physically impossible to achieve. The difficulty created by *Haughton v Smith* has now been removed by legislation (p 298, above) and the other difficulties (cf *A-G's References (Nos 1 and 2 of (1979)* [1980] QB 180, [1979] 2 All ER 143, CA) have been shown to be formal rather than substantive. Of course D cannot be convicted of attempting to steal that which he does not intend to steal. If the car contains only articles (tissues, road maps) of no interest to D, D cannot be convicted of attempting to steal these. But if it is D's intention to steal the car radio then he may be convicted of attempting to steal the radio thought the car has no radio. And if D is on a fishing expedition having no specific property in mind it appears that he may be convicted of attempting to steal property of P from the car.

2. Robbery

Theft Act 1968, s 8, p 566, below

'Robbery' by JA Andrews, [1966] Crim LR 524, 525

A considerable advantage of the new definition is that it does not require that the property should be in the 'immediate and personal care and protection' of the person against whom force is used or threatened. Whereas historically it might have been sufficient for the scope of robbery to be confined to protecting the person of the owner or custodian of the stolen property, obviously in the context of modern robbery it is necessary to extend the ambit of the crime to cover situations where it is bystanders or customers of banks or post offices against whom force is used or threatened.

Another advantage of the new definition is that the crime of robbery is not restricted to stealing from the person or in the presence of the person against whom force is used or threatened. This covers the *Smith v Desmond* [see *Smith v Desmond* [1965] AC 960 at 979–981] type of situation. However a problem does arise even under the new definition. Let us take the case of a defendant who assaults and binds someone and then proceeds to his victim's property some distance away where minutes or even hours later he steals. Is he guilty of robbery? The fact that the theft is away from the presence of the victim would no longer be a problem, but the new definition does restrict the scope of robbery to circumstances where the defendant 'immediately before or at the time of [stealing] wilfully uses force on any person or wilfully puts or seeks to put any person in fear of being then and there subjected to force'. Has the force been used 'immediately before' in our example? Does immediate mean seconds, minutes or hours? Presumably it is not intended to cover the situation where the violence precedes the stealing by a matter of days. Nor can one argue that the force or fear is a continuing factor if the victim remains under continuing fear or restraint, because what must be immediate is the wilful use of force not the continuing effect of it, or alternatively the putting of the person in fear or seeking to put him in fear must be immediate, not merely the continuing fear. The matter might be better put if the words 'immediately before or at the time of doing of doing so' were left out of the definition. The crime of robbery would still be limited to where the person uses force or fear 'in order to [steal]'. This would meet the Criminal Law Revision Committee's point that 'force used only to get away after committing a theft does not seem naturally to be regarded as robbery'. [Cmnd 2977, para 65] Such force would not be used in order to steal, but in order to avoid apprehension. To further restrict it in terms of temporal proximity of force and theft is to make a defence of the criminal's divorcing in time the violence and the stealing and there seems no great reason in that. The real issue should surely be whether the force or threat of force was used *in order to steal*.

It could be argued that this would bring within the ambit of the crime the man who uses force against a person when taking a car which he intends to use in order to steal. Force used in taking a car—as opposed to stealing the car—would not be robbery, but if the car is to be used in a subsequent shopbreaking and is so used it might make the crime robbery. But why shouldn't this amount to robbery? If in order to commit a theft the wrongdoer uses or threatens force against a person at any stage up to the completion of the crime then surely he is exhibiting just those traits that the severity of the law on robbery seeks to guard society against.

The force must be used against a person or a man must wilfully seek to put a person in fear of force before he is guilty of robbery. This will exclude the bag-snatcher whose force is directed only toward the bag. If, however, he makes efforts to put fear of the use of force into the carrier of the bag or another this will make his crime robbery. It will also be robbery if he and the bag-carrier struggle for possession of the bag, since this will amount to force against the person of the carrier. This distinction is reasonably sound and worth preserving.

Enactment of the Theft Bill would remove from the criminal law such issues as whether threats to accuse of unnatural offences or threats of damage to the victim's property will ground a conviction for robbery [See Smith & Hogan, *Criminal Law*, 1965, p 395]. They will not do so in the future. Threats to the safety of other people such as the intended victim's children would only result in a conviction for robbery if the defendant actually used force against them or wilfully put or sought to put them in fear of being then and there subjected to force. Threats made to one person that force would be used against another would not in themselves suffice.

It is important to realise that the scope of the crime of robbery would be indirectly extended by acceptance of the new definition of theft. [[1966] Crim LR 415] This new definition is based on appropriation rather than on a taking and this same change would have application to robbery. There is food for thought here. The traditional idea of 'taking' has the advantage that it is a once and for all thing. Once a thing is taken the matter is over and done with and the larceny is complete. The issue of whether force or threats of force were used to assist the taking is relatively clear cut. But an 'appropriation' is not as rigid a thing as a 'taking'. This is its advantage in avoiding the fictions which have had to be attached to the concept of taking, but it might confuse the issue of robbery. If I come by your watch innocently but then discover I am not entitled to keep it this subsequent dishonest retention may amount to larceny under the new Bill. Clause 3(1) reads

> 'Any assumption by a person of the rights of an owner amounts to an appropriation, and this includes, where he has come by the property (innocently or not) without stealing it, any later assumption of a right to it by keeping or dealing with it as owner.'

Subsection (2) specifically protects appropriation by one who has given value for it in good faith. Clause 1(1) defines theft in terms of a dishonest appropriation intended permanently to deprive the person to whom the property belongs and specifically states that 'steals' shall be construed accordingly.

If I have come by your watch innocently but without giving value and you now approach me and claim it as your own and I refuse to hand it over intending to keep it permanently this will amount to stealing. If at the same time I threaten to beat you if you lay a hand on the watch intending to frighten you off this must make it robbery. Does the Criminal Law Revision Committee intend to extend the scope of robbery so far?

NOTES AND QUESTIONS

1. In *Smith v Desmond* [1965] AC 960, [1965] 1 All ER 976, HL, D and E were held to have robbed P and Q, respectively nightwatchman and maintenance engineer in a bakery, where force was used on them in order to steal from an office some distance away on the premises. Their employer's property was in their immediate care and protection. The case is obviously within the terms of s 8 which extends to any case in which force is used on any person in order to steal.

2. Robbery is essentially a form of aggravated stealing so proof of theft is essential to a conviction. In *Robinson* [1977] Crim LR 173, CA, D ran a clothing club to which P's wife owed £7. Meeting P, D and others threatened him and in the fight which followed £5 fell from P's pocket which D took, claiming he was still owed £2. Quashing D's conviction for robbery, it was held that all D had to show was an honest belief in entitlement to the money and not that he honestly believed that he was entitled to take it in the way he did.

3. Force must be used 'in order to' steal. If D knocks P senseless in a fight and then decides to make off with P's watch which has fallen from his pocket it would not be robbery. Conversely if D steals property without using force but subsequently uses or threatens force to retain it or in effecting an escape it would not be robbery. In *Hale* (1978) 68 Cr App Rep 415, CA, D and E entered P's house and while D was upstairs stealing a jewellery box, E was downstairs tying up P. The Court of Appeal declined to quash their convictions for robbery though they might have appropriated the jewellery box before the force was used. The Court said (at 418):

> '[T]he act of appropriation does not suddenly cease. It is a continuous act and it is a matter for the jury to decide whether or not the act of appropriation has finished. Moreover, it is quite clear that the intention to deprive the owner permanently, which accompanied the assumption of the owner's rights was a continuing one at all material times. This Court therefore rejects the contention that the theft had ceased by the time [P] was tied up. As a matter of common sense [E] was in the course of committing theft; he was stealing.'

4. Force must be used on a person. The CLRC said it would not regard a mere snatching of property, a handbag for example, from an unresisting owner as a use of force for this purpose. But it requires very little to turn such a case into one of robbery; a push or nudge causing the victim to lose his balance is enough (*Dawson and James* (1976) 64 Cr App Rep 170, CA).

5. The robbery is complete when the theft is complete, that is when the appropriation takes place. So in *Corcoran v Anderton* (1980) 71 Cr App Rep 104, DC, where D and E sought to take P's handbag by force, it was held the theft was complete when D snatched the handbag from P's grasp though it then fell from D's hands and the defendants made off without it. Their contention that this was only an attempt was rejected since the snatching of the handbag from P constituted an appropriation.

6. D is about to go out one day to steal a new suit from a clothiers. He tells his wife of his plan and she threatens to telephone the police. D pushes her into the broom cupboard and locks the door and does not free her till he returns later wearing his new suit. Robbery?

7. Do you agree with Andrews that it would be robbery where I come across your watch innocently and, having been made aware that the watch is yours, threaten to beat you should you try to take it back?

3. Offences involving deception

Theft Act 1968, ss 15 and 16, p 569, below, and Theft Act 1978, ss 1 and 2, p 581, below

The offences involving deception have certain common features in relation to the obtaining, the deception and dishonesty, and these common features are dealt with here before turning to the differences that exists in relation to what may be obtained.

(1) OBTAINING BY DECEPTION

R v Lambie [1981] 2 All ER 776, House of Lords
(Lord Diplock, Lord Fraser of Tullybelton, Lord Russell of Killowen, Lord Keith of Kinkel, Lord Roskill)

Their Lordships concurred in the speech of Lord Roskill.

Lord Roskill. My Lords, on 20th April 1977 the respondent was issued by Barclays Bank Ltd ('the bank') with a Barclaycard ('the card'). That card was what today is commonly known as a credit card. It was issued subject to the Barclaycard current conditions of use, and it was an express condition of its issue that it should be used only within the respondent's credit limit. That credit limit was £200 as the respondent well knew, since that figure had been notified to her in writing when the card was issued. The then current conditions of use included an undertaking by the respondent, as its holder, to return the card to the bank on request. No complaint was, or indeed could be, made of the respondent's use of the card until 18th November 1977. Between that date and 5th December 1977 she used the card for at least 24 separate transactions, thereby incurring a debt of some £533. The bank became aware of this debt and thereupon sought to recover the card. On 6th December 1977 the respondent agreed to return the card on 7th December 1977. She did not, however, do so. By 15th December 1977 she had used the card for at least 43 further transactions, incurring a total debt to the bank of £1,005.26.

My Lords, on 15th December 1977 the respondent entered into the transaction out of which this appeal arises. She visited a Mothercare shop in Luton. She produced the card to a departmental manager at Mothercare named Miss Rounding. She selected goods worth £10.35. Miss Rounding completed the voucher, checked that the card was current in date, that it was not on the current stop list and that the respondent's signature on the voucher corresponded with her signature on the card. Thereupon, the respondent took away the goods which she had selected. In due course, Mothercare sent the voucher to the bank and were paid £10.35 less that appropriate commission charged by the bank. On 19th December 1977 the respondent returned the card to the bank.

My Lords, at her trial at the Crown Court at Bedford on 1st and 2nd August 1979 before his Honour Judge Counsell and a jury, the respondent faced two charges of obtaining a pecuniary advantage by deception contrary to s 16(1) of the Theft Act 1968. These were specimen charges. The first related to an alleged offence on 5th December 1977 and the second to the events which took place at the Mothercare shop at Luton which I have just related. The particulars of each charge were that she dishonestly obtained for herself a pecuniary advantage 'namely, the evasion of a debt for which she then made herself liable by deception, namely, by false representations that she was authorised to use a Barclaycard . . . to obtain goods to the value of £10.35'.

The jury acquitted the respondent on the first charge. She was, however, convicted on the second. The evidence of dishonesty in relation to the Mothercare transaction which was the subject of the second charge was overwhelming, and before your Lordships' House counsel for the respondent did not seek to suggest otherwise. Presumably the acquittal on the first count was because the jury were not certain that at the earlier date, 5th December 1977, the respondent was acting dishonestly.

My Lords, during the hearing in this House your Lordships inquired of counsel for the appellant prosecutor why no count of obtaining property by deception on 15th December 1977 contrary to s 15 of the Theft Act 1968 had been included in the indictment. Your Lordships were told that such a charge had indeed been preferred at the magistrates' court during the committal proceedings but had been rejected by the magistrates on a submission made on behalf of the respondent during those proceedings. My Lords, if this be so, I find it difficult to see on what basis such a submission could properly have succeeded, or what defence there could have been had such a charge been the subject of a further count in the indictment once the jury were convinced, as they were, of the respondent's dishonesty on 15th December 1977. Had that course been taken, the complications which in due course led to the Court of Appeal, Criminal Division, quashing the conviction on the second count, and consequently, to the prosecutor's appeal to this House, with your Lordships' leave, following the grant of a certificate by the Court of Appeal, Criminal Division, would all have been avoided. But the course of adding a count charging an offence against s 15 of the Theft Act 1968 was not followed, and accordingly your Lordships have now to determine whether the Court of Appeal, Criminal Division, was correct in quashing the conviction on the second count. If it was, then, as that court recognised in the concluding paragraph of its judgment, a gateway to successful fraud has been opened for the benefit of the dishonest who in circumstances such as the present cannot be proceeded against and punished at least for offences against s 16 of the Theft Act 1968.

My Lords, the committal proceedings were what is sometimes called 'old fashioned', that is to say, that advantage was not taken of s 1 of the Criminal Justice Act 1967. Witnesses were called in the magistrates' court and cross-examined. These witnesses included Miss Rounding, the departmental manager. Your Lordships were shown a copy of her deposition. Miss Rounding was not called at the trial at the Crown Court. Her deposition was read to the jury. It emerged from her evidence, and other evidence given or read, that, as one would expect, there was an agreement between Mothercare and the bank. That agreement does not appear to have been properly proved at the trial, but, by consent, your Lorships were given a pro forma copy of what is known as a 'merchant member agreement' between the bank and its customer, setting out the conditions on which the customer will accept and the bank will honour credit cards such as Barclaycards.

My Lords, at the close of the case for the prosecution, counsel for the respondent invited the judge to withdraw both counts from the jury on, it seems from reading the judge's clear ruling on this submission, two grounds: first, that as a matter of law there was no evidence from which a jury might properly draw the inference that the presentation of the card in the circumstances I have described was a representation by the respondent that she was authorised by the bank to use the card to create a contract to which the bank would be a party, and, second, that as a matter of law there was no evidence from which a jury might properly infer that Miss Rounding was induced by any representation which the respondent might have made to allow the transaction to be completed and the respondent to obtain the goods. The foundation for this latter submission was that it was the existence of the agreement between Mothercare and the bank that was the reason for Miss Rounding allowing the transaction to be completed and the goods to be taken by the respondent, since Miss Rounding knew of the arrangement with the bank, so that Mothercare was in any event certain of payment. It was not, it was suggested, any representation by the respondent which induced Miss Rounding to complete the transaction and to allow the respondent to take the goods.

My Lords, the judge rejected these submission. He was clearly right to do so, as indeed was conceded in argument before your Lordships' House, if the decision of this House in *Metropolitan Police Comr v Charles* [1976] 3 All ER 112, [1977] AC 177 is of direct application. In that appeal this House was concerned with the dishonest use, not as in the present appeal of a credit card, but of a cheque card. The appellant defendant was charged and convicted on two counts of obtaining a pecuniary advantage by deception, contrary to s 16 of the Theft Act 1968. The Court of Appeal, Criminal Division, and your Lordships' House both upheld those convictions. Your Lordships unanimously held that where a drawer of a cheque which is accepted in return for goods, services or cash, uses a cheque card he represents to the payee that he has the actual authority of the bank to enter on its behalf into the contract expressed on the card that it would honour the cheque on presentation for payment.

My Lords, I venture to quote in their entirety three paragraphs from the speech of my noble and learned friend Lord Diplock ([1976] 3 All ER 112 at 114, [1977] AC 177 at 182–183) which, as I venture to think, encapsulate the reasoning of all those members of your Lordships' House who delivered speeches:

> 'When a cheque card is brought into the transaction, it still remains the fact that all the payee is concerned with is that the cheque should be honoured by the bank. I do not think that the fact that a cheque card is used necessarily displaces the representation to be implied from the act of drawing the cheque which has just been mentioned. It is, however, likely to displace that representation at any rate as the main inducement to the payee to take the cheque, since the use of the cheque card in connection with the transaction gives to the payee a direct contractual right against the bank itself to payment on presentment,

provided that the use of the card by the drawer to bind to pay the cheque was within the actual or ostensible authority conferred on him by the bank.

'By exhibiting to the payee a cheque card containing the undertaking by the bank to honour cheques drawn in compliance with the conditions endorsed on the back and drawing the cheque accordingly, the drawer represents to the payee that he has actual authority from the bank to make a contract with the payee on the bank's behalf that it will honour the cheque on presentment for payment.

'It was submitted on behalf of the accused that there is no need to imply a representation that the drawer's authority to bind the bank was actual and not merely ostensible, since ostensible authority alone would suffice to create a contract with the payee that was binding on the bank; and the drawer's possession of the cheque card and the cheque book with the bank's consent would be enough to constitute his ostensible authority. So, the submission goes, the only representation needed to give business efficacy to the transaction would be true. This argument stands the doctrine of ostensible authority on its head. What creates ostensible authority in a person who purports to enter into a contract as agent for a principal is a representation made to the other party that he has the actual authority of the principal for whom he claims to be acting to enter into the contract on that person's behalf. If (1) the other party has believed the representation and on the faith of that belief has acted on it and (2) the person represented to be his principal has so conducted himself towards that other party as to be estopped from denying the truth of the representation, then, and only then, is he bound by the contract purportedly made on his behalf. The whole foundation of liability under the doctrine of ostensible authority is a representation, believed by the person to whom it is made, that the person claiming to contract as agent for a principal has the actual authority of the principal to enter into the contract on his behalf.'

If one substitutes in the passage the words 'to honour the voucher' for the words 'to pay the cheque', it is not easy to see why mutatis mutandis the entire passages are not equally applicable to the dishonest misuse of credit cards as to the dishonest misuse of cheque cards.

But the Court of Appeal in a long and careful judgment delivered by Cumming-Bruce LJ felt reluctantly impelled to reach a different conclusion. The crucial passage in the judgment which the learned Lord Justice delivered reads thus ([1981] 1 All ER 332 at 339–340, [1981] 1 WLR 78 at 86–87):

'We would pay tribute to the lucidity with which the learned judge presented to the jury the law which the House of Lords had declared in relation to deception in a cheque card transaction. If that analysis can be applied to this credit card deception, the summing up is faultless. But, in our view, there is a relevant distinction between the situation described in *Metropolitan Police Comr v Charles* and the situation devised by Barclays Bank for transactions involving use of their credit cards. By their contract with the bank, Mothercare had bought from the bank the right to sell goods to Barclaycard holders without regard to the question whether the customer was complying with the terms of the contract between the customer and the bank. By her evidence Miss Rounding made it perfectly plain that she made no assumption about the appellant's credit standing at the bank. As she said: "The company rules exist because of the company's agreement with Barclaycard." The flaw in the logic is, in our view, demonstrated by the way in which the judge put the question of the inducement of Miss Rounding to the jury: "Is that a reliance by her, Miss Rounding of Mothercare, on the presentation of the card as being due authority *within the limits as at that time* as with count 1?" In our view, the evidence of Miss Rounding could not found a verdict that necessarily involved a finding of fact that Miss Rounding was induced by false representation that the appellant's credit standing at the bank gave her authority to use the card.'

I should perhaps mention, for the sake of clarity, that the person referred to as the appellant in that passage is the present respondent.

It was for that reason that the Court of Appeal, Criminal Division, allowed the appeal, albeit with hesitation and reluctance. That court accordingly certified the following point of law as of general public importance, namely:

'In view of the proved differences between a cheque card transaction and a credit card transaction, were we right in distinguishing this case from that of *Metropolitan Police Comr v Charles* [1976] 3 All ER 112, [1977] AC 177 on the issue of inducement?'

My Lords, as the appellant says in his printed case, the Court of Appeal, Criminal Division, laid too much emphasis on the undoubted, but to my mind irrelevant, fact that Miss Rounding said she made no assumption about the respondent's credit standing with the bank. They reasoned from the absence of assumption that there was no evidence from which the jury could conclude that she was 'induced by a false representation that the [respondent's] credit standing at the bank gave her authority to use the card'. But, my Lords, with profound respect to Cumming-Bruce LJ, that is not the relevant question. Following the decision of this house in *Charles*, it is in my view clear that the representation arising from the presentation of a credit card has nothing to do with the respondent's credit standing at the bank but is a representation of actual authority to make the contract with, in this case, Mothercare on the bank's behalf that the bank will honour the voucher on presentation. On that view, the existence and terms of the agreement between the bank and Mothercare are irrelevant, as is the fact that Mothercare, because of that agreement, would look to the bank for payment.

That being the representation to be implied from the respondent's actions and use of the credit card, the only remaining question is whether Miss Rounding was induced by that representation to complete the transaction and allow the respondent to take away the goods. My Lords, if she had been asked whether, had she known the respondent was acting dishonestly and, in truth, had no authority whatever from the bank to use the credit card in this way, she (Miss Rounding) would have completed the transaction, only one answer is possible: 'No'. Had an affirmative answer been given to this question, Miss Rounding would, of course, have become a participant in furtherance of the respondent's fraud and a conspirator with her to defraud both Mothercare and the bank. Leading counsel for the respondent was ultimately constrained, rightly as I think, to admit that had that question been asked of Miss Rounding and answered, as it must have been, in the negative, this appeal must succeed. But both he and his learned junior strenuously argued that as Lord Edmund-Davies pointed out in his speech in *Charles* [1976] 3 All ER 112 at 122, [1977] AC 177 at 192–193, the question whether a person is or is not induced to act in a particular way by a dishonest representation is a question of fact, and, since what they claimed to be the crucial question had not been asked of Miss Rounding, there was no adequate proof of the requisite inducement. In her deposition, Miss Rounding stated, no doubt with complete truth, that she only remembered this particular transaction with the respondent because someone subsequently came and asked her about it after it had taken place. My Lords, credit card frauds are all too frequently perpetrated, and if conviction of offenders for offences against s 15 or s 16 of the Theft Act 1968 can only be obtained if the prosecution are able in each case to call the person on whom the fraud was immediately perpetrated to say that he or she positively remembered the particular transaction and, had the truth been known, would never have entered into that supposedly well-remembered transaction, the guilty would often escape conviction. In some cases, of course, it may be possible to adduce such evidence if the particular transaction is well remembered. But where as in the present case no one could reasonably be expected to remember a particular transaction in detail, and the inference of inducement may well be in all the circumstances quite irresistible, I see no reason in principle why it should not be left to the jury to decide, on the evidence in the case as a whole, whether that inference is in truth irresistible as to my mind it is in the present case. In this connection it is to be noted that the respondent did not go into the witness box to give evidence from which that inference might conceivably have been rebutted.

My Lords, in this respect I find myself in agreement with what was said by Humphreys J giving the judgment of the Court of Criminal Appeal in *R v Sullivan* (1945) 30 Cr App R 132 at 136:

> 'It is, we think, undoubtedly good law that the question of the inducement acting upon the mind of the person who may be described as the prosecutor is not a matter which can only be proved by the direct evidence of the witness. It can be, and very often is, proved by the witness being asked some question which brings the answer: "I believed that statement and that is why I parted with my money"; but it is not necessary that there should be that question and answer if the facts are such that it is patent that there was only one reason which anybody could suggest for the person alleged to have been defrauded parting with his money, and that is the false pretence, if it was a false pretence.'

It is true that in *R v Laverty* [1970] 3 All ER 432 Lord Parker CJ said that the Court of Appeal, Criminal Division, was anxious not to extend the principle in *Sullivan* further than was necessary. Of course, the Crown must always prove its case and one element which will always be required to be proved in these cases is the effect of the dishonest representation on the mind of the person to whom it is made. But I see no reason why in cases such as the present, where what Humphreys J called the direct evidence of the witness is not and cannot reasonably be expected to be available, reliance on a dishonest representation cannot be sufficiently established by proof of facts from which an irresistible inference of such reliance can be drawn.

My Lords, I would answer the certified question in the negative and would allow the appeal and restore the conviction of the respondent on the second count in the indictment which she faced at the Crown Court.

Certified question answered in the negative; order appealed from reversed; conviction on count 2 of the indictment restored.

NOTES AND QUESTIONS

1. Lord Roskill refers to *Metropolitan Police Comr v Charles, Sullivan* and *Laverty*. In *Charles* D was provided by his bank with a chequebook and cheque card and authorised to overdraw his account up to £100. The cheque card was in commmon form and contained an undertaking by the bank that any cheque not exceeding £30 would be honoured by the bank if the specified conditions were met. In the course of one evening at a gambling club D drew 25 cheques for £30 each made out to Mr Cersell, the manager of the club, for which he received gaming chips. In *Sullivan* D represented that he was the 'actual maker' of dartboards which he offered for sale and for which he received a number of orders. No purchaser ever received a dartboard nor was any money returned and D had neither premises nor plant for making dartboards. D's conviction for obtaining by false pretences was upheld though no purchaser said he had parted with his money because of D's claim that he was the 'actual maker' and those that were asked why they had said that it was because they wanted a dartboard. The Court of Appeal, Criminal Division held that there was no conceivable reason for their parting with the money other than the language of the advertisement which began with the words 'actual maker'. In *Laverty* D changed the number plates on a car which he then sold to P. It was held that this constituted a representation that the car was the original car to which these numbers had been assigned. D's conviction for obtaining by deception was quashed because it was not proved that this deception had operated on P's mind.
2. In *Charles* Mr Cersell said that it was 'totally irrelevant' to him whether D had authority to draw the cheque and in *Lambie* Miss Rounding was, if anything, even more adamant on this. 'We will honour the card,' she said, 'if the conditions are satisfied whether the bearer has authority to use it or not.' So how could it be said that the deception in either case was an operative cause of the obtaining? In both cases reliance is placed on the fact that had Mr Cersell or Miss Rounding known that the defendants were acting without authority they would not have entered into the transacton. Is this a relevant consideration? Suppose Miss Rounding had said to D, 'I would not enter into this transaction if I thought you had no authority to use the credit card but you look honest enough to me and I'll assume that you are authorised.' Would she then have been deceived by D's representation of authority? Does it follow from *Charles* and *Lambie* that the deception in *Laverty* equally caused P to buy the car? He had no reason to question the number plates but if he had known that they were not the number plates belonging to that car he would presumably have declined to buy the car.
3. Lord Roskill thought that in *Lambie* it would have simplified the issues had D been charged with obtaining the goods from Mothercare by deception contrary to s 15. Is it clear that D obtained the goods from Mothercare by deception?

R v Doukas [1978] 1 All ER 1061, Court of Appeal, Criminal Division
(Geoffrey Lane LJ, Milmo and Watkins JJ)

The applicant, a waiter employed at an hotel, was found in the hotel with six bottles of wine. The wine was not of a type stocked or sold by the hotel. A search of his car revealed bottles of spirits. On a charge under s 25 (1) the prosecution's case was that the applicant intended, on receipt of orders by customers for the hotel's wine, to substitute his own and pocket the money. The applicant was convicted.

[**Geoffrey Lane LJ** delivered the judgment of the court:]
. . . The only criticism which is levelled against the conviction is that the judge was wrong in law in rejecting the submission, made by the defence at the close of the prosecution case, that the evidence could not prove the offence alleged; the facts of this case, in all material respects, were the same as in *Rashid* [[1977] 2 All ER 237, [1977] 1 WLR 298]. Then it goes on to a second ground which must be dealt with hereafter. This court has to decide whether the judge was wrong in law in rejecting the applicant's submission.

[His Lordship referred to s 25 (1) and s 15]

Combining those two sections of the 1968 Act, ss 25 and 15, which are apposite, one reaches this result: 'A person shall be guilty of an offence if, when not in his place of abode, he has with him any article for use in the course of or in connection with, any deception, whether deliberate or reckless, by words or conduct, as to fact or as to law, for purposes of dishonestly obtaining property belonging to another with the intention of permanently depriving the other of it'.

If one analyses that combined provision, one reaches the situation that the following items have to be proved. First of all that there was an article for use in connection with the deception; here the bottles. Secondly, that there was a proposed deception: here the deception of the guests into believing that the proffered wine was hotel wine and not the waiter's wine. Thirdly, an intention to obtain property by means of the deception, and the property here is the money of the guests which he proposes to obtain and keep. Fourthly, dishonesty. There is twofold dishonesty in the way the Crown put the case. First of all the dishonesty in respect of his employers, namely putting into his pocket the money which really should go to the hotel and, more important, the second dishonesty, vis-à-vis the guests, the lying to or misleading of the guests into believing that the wine which had been proffered was the hotel wine and not the waiter's wine. Fifthly, there must be proof that the obtaining would have been, wholly or partially, by virtue of the deception.

The prosecution must prove that nexus between the deception and obtaining. It is this last and final ingredient which, as we see it in the present case, is the only point which raises any difficulty. Assuming, as we must, and indeed obviously was the case, that the jury accepted the version of the police interviews and accepted that this man had made the confession to which I have referred, then the only question was, would this obtaining have in fact been caused by the deception practised by the waiter?

We have, as in the notice of appeal, been referred to the decision in *Rashid* which was a decision by another division of this court. That case concerned not a waiter in a hotel, but a British Railways waiter who substituted not bottles of wine for the railway wine but his own tomato sandwiches for the railway tomato sandwiches; and it is to be observed in that case the basis of the decision was that the summing-up of the judge to the jury was inadequate. On that basis the appeal was allowed. But the court went on [[1977] 2 All ER 237 at 240, [1977] 1 WLR 298 at 302, per Bridge LJ] to express its views obiter on the question whether in these circumstances it could be said that the obtaining was by virtue of deception and it came to the conclusion, as I say obiter, that the answer was probably No.

Of course each case of this type may produce different results according to the circumstances of the case and according, in particular, to the commodity which is being proffered. But, as we see it, the question has to be asked of the hypothetical customer: why did you buy this wine? or, if you had been told the truth, would you or would you not have bought the commodity? It is, at least in theory, for the jury in the end to decide that question.

Here, as the ground of appeal, is simply the judge's action in allowing the case to go to the jury, we are answering that question, so to speak, on behalf of the of the judge rather than the jury. Was there evidence of the necessary nexus fit to go to the jury? Certainly so far as the wine is concerned, we have no doubt at all that the hypothetical customer, faced with the waiter saying to him: 'This of course is not hotel wine, this is stuff which I imported into the hotel myself and I am going to put the proceeds of the wine, if you pay, into my own pocket', would certainly answer, so far as we can see, 'I do not want your wine, kindly bring me the hotel carafe wine'. Indeed it would be a strange jury that came to any other conclusion, and a stranger guest who gave any other answer, for several reasons. First of all the guest would not know what was in the bottle which the waiter was proffering. True he may not know what was in the carafe which the hotel was proffering, but he would at least be able to have recourse to the hotel if something was wrong with the carafe wine, but he would have no such recourse with the waiter; if he did, it would be worthless.

It seems to us that the matter can be answered on a much simpler basis. The hypothetical customer must be reasonably honest as well as being reasonably intelligent and it seems to us incredible that any customer, to whom the true situation was made clear, would willingly make himself a party to what was obviously a fraud by the waiter on his employers. If that conclusion is contrary to the obiter dicta in *Rashid*, then we must respectfully disagree with those dicta. It is not necessary to examine the question any further whether we are differing from *Rashid* or not. But it seems to us beyond argument that the judge was right in the conclusion he reached and was right to allow the matter to go to the jury on the basis which he did.

There are two other matters which are raised on behalf of the applicant. The first is the question of the gin, whisky, brandy and Cointreau which was found in the applicant's car, which was also included in the indictment as being part of the articles which were being used for cheating. The jury were invited, if they wished, to come to a separate conclusion on the spirits from that which they reached on the wine. They did not make any distinction and counsel for the applicant suggests that they must have been wrong so far as the spirits were concerned on the basis that any customer who was proffered a sealed bottle of a proprietary brand of spirits, either brandy, whisky or gin, would be certain, or might reasonably be expected to say 'Yes' to the waiter's offer, although he may have said 'No' so far as the wine was concerned. We think that the same reasoning can be applied to that. No reasonable customer would lend himself to such a swindle, whether the basis of the swindle was wine or spirits.

Finally, the last part of the notice of appeal reads:

> '. . . the terms of the [applicant's] alleged confession, which was the basis of the prosecution case, did not preclude the possibility that the customers would be willing parties to the defendant's scheme.'

With respect to counsel for the applicant it is not altogether clear what that means but I think the way he explained it to us was this. The way in which the applicant answered the questions of the police in the passage which I have read, did not preclude his giving the customers a choice, namely 'There is carafe wine of the hotel if you wish it. There is also the wine which I have here, which is my wine, if you wish that. Kindly select which you would prefer.' It seems to us that that is an unreal hypothetical situation which would never, in the circumstances of this case, have arisen.

For the reasons which we have endeavoured to explain in this judgment, we are of the view that there is no basis on which this application can properly be founded. Consequently the application is refused.

Application refused

NOTES AND QUESTIONS

1. Suppose the customers had said after the arrest of Doukas, 'We never gave any thought to whose wine it was but had we thought about it we would have assumed it was the proprietor's'. Would they have been deceived?

2. D buys a knife to murder his wife but he does not tell the seller this since he assumes (correctly) that the seller would not sell him the knife if he knew this. Has the knife been obtained by deception? Is there not an implicit representation by D that he requires the knife for a lawful purpose?

3. For a deception to take place it would seem implicit that some human mind must be deceived. 'For a deception to take place', said Lord Morris in *DPP v Ray* [1973] 3 All ER 131 at 137, 'there must be some person or persons who will have been deceived.' It follows that a machine cannot be deceived. If, however, D uses a washer to get goods from a machine he may be convicted of stealing the goods just as much as if he had used a jemmy to force the machine open: *Hands* (1887) 16 Cox CC 188.

4. In many cases D may obtain by making representations which are both true and false and here D may be convicted provided the representations which are false are an effective, though not necessarily the exclusive, cause of the obtaining. But it does not follow that a false representation is an effective cause of the obtaining because P would never had entered the transaction had he known of the falsity. In *Clucas* [1949] 2 KB 226, [1949] 2 All ER 40, CCA, D and E falsely represented to P, a bookmaker, that they were acting as commission agents on behalf of several other persons and by this representation P was induced to allow them to bet on credit; the horse backed won and P paid the bet. It was held under the former law that their false representation was too remote a cause of the obtaining; they obtained the money because they backed the winning horse. Similarly where D gets employment by misrepresenting his qualifications he cannot be convicted of obtaining his salary by deception since the salary is paid for work done. These two cases are now specifically provided for by s 16(2)(c) of the 1968 Act but the principle is otherwise unaffected.

(2) THE DECEPTION

Director of Public Prosecutions v Ray [1973] 3 All ER 131, House of Lords
(Lords Reid, MacDermott, Morris of Borth-y-Gest, Hodson and Pearson)

Four men, including the respondent, entered a restaurant and ordered a meal. The respondent did not have enough money to pay but one of the others had agreed to lend him enough to pay for the meal. After eating the meal, and while the waiter was still in the dining room, they all decided not to pay and to run out of the restaurant. Some ten minutes later, and while the waiter had left the dining room to go into the kitchen, all four ran off without making payment. This was an appeal against the quashing by the Divisional Court of the respondent's conviction for obtaining a pecuniary advantage by deception contrary to s 16 (1) of the Act.

Lord Reid . . . If a person induces a supplier to accept an order for goods or services by a representation of fact, that representation must be held to be a continuing representation lasting until the goods or services are supplied. Normally it would not last any longer. A restaurant supplies both goods and services: it supplies food and drink and the facilities for consuming them. Customers normally remain for a short time after consuming their meal, and I think that it can properly be held that any representation express or implied made with a view of obtaining a meal lasts until the departure of the customers in the normal course.

In my view, where a new customer orders a meal in a restaurant, he must be held to make an implied representation that he can and will pay for it before he leaves. In the present case the respondent must be held to have made such a representation. But when he made it it was not dishonest: he thought he would be able to borrow money from one or his companions.

After the meal had been consumed the respondent changed his mind. He decided to evade payment. So he and his companions remained seated where they were for a short time until the waiter left the room and then ran out of the restaurant.

Did he thereby commit an offence against s 16 of the Theft Act 1968? It is admitted, and rightly admitted, that if the waiter had not been in the room when he changed his mind and he had immediately run out he would not have committed an offence. Why does his sitting still for a short time in the presence of the waiter make all the difference?

The section requires evasion of his obligation to pay. That is clearly established by his running out without paying. Secondly, it requires dishonesty: that is admitted. There would have been both evasion and dishonesty if he had changed his mind and run out while the waiter was absent.

The crucial question in this case is whether there was evasion 'by any deception'. Clearly there could be no deception until the respondent changed his mind. I agree with the following quotation from the judgment of Buckley J in *Re London and Globe Finance Corpn Ltd* [[1903] 1 Ch 728 at 723, [1900–3] All ER Rep 891 at 893]:

'To deceive is, I apprehend, to induce a man to believe that a thing is true which is false, and which the person practising the deceit knows or believes to be false.'

So the respondent, after he changed his mind, must have done something intended to induce the waiter to believe that he still intended to pay before he left. Deception, to my mind, implies something positive. It is quite true that a man intending to deceive can build up a situation in which his silence is as eloquent as an express statement. But what did the accused do here to create a situation? He merely sat still . . . The justices stated that they were of opinion that:

'. . . having changed his mind as regards payment, by remaining in the restaurant for a further ten minutes as an ordinary customer who was likely to order a sweet or coffee, the [respondent] practised a deception.'

I cannot read that as a finding that after he changed his mind he intended to deceive the waiter into believing that he still intended to pay. And there is no finding that the waiter was in fact induced to believe that by anything the respondent did after he changed his mind. I would infer from the case that all that he intended to do was to take advantage of the first opportunity to escape and evade his obligation to pay.

Deception is an essential ingredient of the offence. Dishonest evasion of an obligation to pay is not enough. I cannot see that there was, in fact, any more than that in this case. I agree with the Divisional Court that [[1973] 1 All ER 860 at 865, per Talbot J]:

'His plan was totally lacking in the subtlety of deception and to argue that his remaining in the room until the coast was clear amounted to a representation to the waiter is to introduce an artificiality which should have no place in the Act.'

I would therefore dismiss this appeal.

Lord MacDermott. . . . To prove the charge against the respondent the prosecution had to show that he (i) by a deception (ii) had dishonestly (iii) obtained for himself (iv) a pecuniary advantage . . .

No issue . . . arises on the ingredients I have numbered (iii) and (iv). Nor is there any controversy about ingredient (ii). If the respondent obtained a pecuniary advantage as described he undoubtedly did so dishonestly. The case is thus narrowed to ingredient (i) and that leaves two questions for consideration. First, do the facts justify a finding that the respondent practised a deception? And secondly, if he did, was his evasion of the debt obtained by that deception?

The first of these questions involves nothing in the way of words spoken or written. If there was deception on the part of the respondent it was by his conduct in the course of an extremely common form of transaction which, because of its nature, leaves much to be implied from conduct. Another circumstance affecting the ambit of this question lies in the fact that, looking only to the period *after* the meal had been eaten and the respondent and his companions had decided to evade payment, there is nothing that I can find in the discernible conduct of the respondent which would suffice in itself to show that he was then practising a deception. No doubt he and the others stayed in their seats until the waiter went into the kitchen and while doing so gave all the appearance of ordinary customers. But in my opinion, nothing in this or in anything else which occured *after* the change of intention went far enough to afford proof of deception. The picture, as I see it, presented by this last stage of the entire transaction, is simply that of a group which had decided to evade payment and were awaiting the opportunity to do so.

There is, however, no sound reason that I can see for restricting the enquiry to this final phase. One cannot, so to speak, draw a line through the transaction at the point where the intention changed and search for evidence of deception only in what happened before that or only in what happened after that. In my opinion the transaction must for this purpose be regarded in its entirety, beginning with the respondent entering the restaurant and ordering his meal and ending with his running out without paying. The different stages of the transaction are all linked and it would be quite unrealistic to treat them in isolation.

Starting then at the beginning one finds in the conduct of the respondent in entering and ordering his meal evidence that he impliedly represented that he had the means and the intention of paying for it before he left. That the respondent did make such a representation was not in dispute and in the absence of evidence to the contrary it would be difficult to reach a different conclusion. If this representation had then been false and matters had proceeded thereafter as they did (but without any change of intention) a conviction for the offence charged would, in my view, have had ample material to support it. But as the representation when originally made in this case was not false there was therefore no deception at that point. Then the meal is served and eaten and the intention to evade the debt replaces the intention to pay. Did this change of mind produce a deception?

My Lords, in my opinion it did. I do not base this conclusion merely on the change of mind that had occurred for that in itself was not manifest at the time and did not amount to 'conduct' on the part of the respondent. But it did falsify the representation which had already been made because that initial representation must, in my view, be regarded not as something then spent and past but as a continuing representation which remained alive and operative and had already resulted in the respondent and his defaulting companions being taken on trust and treated as ordinary, honest customers. It covered the whole transaction up to and including payment and must therefore, in my opinion, be considered as continuing and still active at the time of the change of mind. When that happened, with the respondent taking (as might be expected) no step to bring the change to notice, he practised to my way of thinking a deception just as real and just as dishonest as would have been the case if his intention all along had been to go out without paying.

Holding for these reasons that the respondent practised a deception, I turn to what I have referred to as the second question. Was the respondent's evasion of the debt obtained by that deception?

I think the material before the justices was enough to show that it was. The obvious effect of the deception was that the respondent and his associates were treated as they had been previously, that is to say as ordinary, honest customers whose conduct did not excite suspicion or call for precautions. In consequence the waiter was off his guard and vanished into the kitchen. That gave the respondent the opportunity of running out without hindrance and he took it. I would therefore answer this second question in the affirmative.

I would, accordingly, allow the appeal and restore the conviction.

Lord Morris of Borth-y-Gest. . . . In the present case the person deceived was the waiter. Did the respondent deceive the waiter as to what were his intentions? Did the respondent so conduct himself as to induce the waiter to believe that he (the respondent) intended to pay his bill before he left the restaurant whereas at the relevant time he did not so intend?. . .

In the present case it is found as a fact that when the respondent ordered his meal he believed that he would be able to pay. One of his companions had agreed to lend him money. He therefore intended to pay. So far as the waiter was concerned the original implied representation made to him by the respondent must have been a continuing representation so long as he (the respondent) remained in the restaurant. There was nothing to alter the representation. Just as the waiter was led at the start to believe that he was dealing with a customer who by all that he did in the restaurant was indicating his intention to pay in the ordinary way, so the waiter was led to believe that that state of affairs continued. But the moment came when the respondent decided and therefore knew that he was not going to pay: but he also knew that the waiter still thought that he was going to pay. By ordering his meal and by his conduct in assuming the role of an ordinary customer the respondent had previously shown that it was his intention to pay. By continuing in the same role and behaving just as before he was representing that his previous intention continued. That was a deception because his intention, unknown to the waiter, had become quite otherwise. The dishonest change of intention was not likely to produce the result that the waiter would be told of it. The essence of the deception was that the waiter should not know of it or be given any sort of clue that it (the change of intention) had come about. Had the waiter suspected that by a change of intention a secret exodus was being planned, it is obvious that he would have taken action to prevent its being achieved.

A further contention on behalf of the respondent was that the debt was not in whole or in part evaded. It was said that on the facts as found there was an evasion of the payment of a debt but no evasion of the debt and that a debt (which denotes an obligation to pay) is not evaded unless it is released or unless there is a discharge of it which is void or voidable. I cannot accept this contention. Though a 'debt', as referred to it in the section does denote an obligation to pay, the obligation of the respondent was to pay for his meal before he left the restaurant. When he left without paying he had, in my view, evaded his obligation to pay before leaving. He dodged his obligation. Accordingly he obtained a 'pecuniary advantage'.

The final question which arises is whether, if there was deception and if there was pecuniary advantage, it was by the deception that the respondent obtained the pecuniary advantage. In my view, this must be a question of fact and the justices have found that it was by his deception that the respondent dishonestly evaded payment. It would seem to be clear that if the waiter had thought that if he left the restaurant to go to the kitchen the respondent would at once run out, he (the waiter) would not have left the restaurant and would have taken suitable action. The waiter proceeded on the basis that the implied representation made to him (ie of an honest intention to pay) was effective. The waiter was caused to refrain from taking certain courses of action which but for the representation he would have taken. In my view, the respondent during the whole time that he was in the restaurant made and by his continuing conduct continued to make a representation of his intention to pay before leaving. When in place of his original intention he substituted the dishonest intention of running away as soon as the waiter's back was turned, he was continuing to lead the waiter to believe that he intended to pay. He practised a deception on the waiter and by so doing he obtained for himself the pecuniary advantage of evading his obligation to pay before leaving. That he did so dishonestly was found by the justices who, in my opinion, rightly convicted him.

I would allow the appeal.

Lord Hodson. . . . .There is no doubt that the respondent evaded payment of the debt by walking out of the restaurant with his companions, but the prosecution has always accepted that there was no deception in the first instance because the intention was to pay for the meal when ordered. It is argued, however, that a representation having been made at the time the credit was honestly obtained, the respondent later dishonestly decided to evade payment by failing to correct the original representation.

To answer the submitted question it is necessary to follow the definition of deceit which I have cited from s 15(4). The deceit is in essence the same as that long recognised when a person is charged with obtaining property by fraud. There must be some deceit spoken, written or acted to constitute a false pretence: see *Jones* [[1898] 1 QB 119].

There having been no deception in the first instance, since the respondent and his companions intended to pay for the meal, the question is, was a deception practised so as to evade the debt or obligation when having consumed the meal they left without paying for it?

One who enters into a contract is taken to have the intention of carrying it out, but if he changes his mind and decides not to pay he may be guilty of a breach of his contractual obligation but not necessarily of evading the debt by deception. The deception must be proved whereby a pecuniary advantage was obtained.

The vital question is whether by sitting in the restaurant for ten minutes after having consumed the meal the respondent was guilty of deception when he departed without paying.

If he had no intention of paying at the outset *cadit quaestio*. If, on the other hand, his representation made at the outset was honest, I find it difficult to accept that the effect of the original representation continues so as to make subsequent failure to pay his creditor, automatically, so to speak, an evasion of debt obtained by deception.

Whether any evidence was given by a waiter is not disclosed. The case states that the waiter had gone to the kitchen and that during his absence the respondent and his four companions ran out of the restaurant after having been there for nearly an hour and maintaining the demeanour of ordinary customers. Would the reasonable man say that a deception had been practised on him? Evade the debt the respondent did, but no more than any other debtor who, having originally intended to pay for a pecuniary advantage, subsequently changes his mind and evades his contractual obligation by not paying.

In order to succeed the prosecution must rely on the original representation honestly made by the respondent when he entered the restaurant as a continuing representation which operated and lulled the restaurant proprietor into a sense of security so that the respondent was enabled to leave as he did.

I do not recollect that the prosecution put the case in this way but I think it is most formidable if so presented, for if the representation continued it was falsified by the change of mind of the respondent.

It is trite law and common sense that an honest man entering into a contract is deemed to represent that he has the present intention of carrying it out but if, as in this case, having accepted the pecuniary advantage involved in the transaction he does not necessarily evade his debt by deception if he fails to pay his debt.

Nothing he did after his change of mind can be characterised as conduct which would indicate that he was then practising a deception.

To rely on breach of a continuous representation I suggest that in administering a criminal statute this is going too far and seems to involve that the ordinary man who enters into a contract intending to carry it out can be found guilty of a criminal offence if he changes his mind after incurring the obligation to pay unless he has taken a step to bring the change of mind to the notice of his creditor.

The appellant sought to support the argument, that there was a duty on the respondent to correct his original representation, by authority.

With v O'Flanagan [[1936] Ch 575; [1936] 1 All ER 727] is good authority for the proposition that if a person who makes a representation, which is not immediately acted on, finds that the facts are changing he must, before the representation is acted on, disclose the change to the person to whom he had made the representation.

That case concerned the sale of a medical practice. The seller, a doctor, represented that his practice was profitable. This was true when the representation was made but by the time the contract was signed the practice had dwindled to practically nothing. This was not disclosed to the purchaser who, on discovery, sought rescission. It was held that the statement made, though true at the time, had become untrue during the negotiations and that there was an obligation to disclose the fact to the purchaser.

The earlier case of *Traill v Baring* [(1864) 4 De GJ & Sm 318] was cited. It contains the following passage from the judgment of Turner LJ [(1864) 4 De GJ & Sm at 329]:

> 'I take it to be clear, that if a person makes a representation by which he induces another to take a particular course and the circumstances are afterwards altered to the knowledge of the party making the representation, but not to the knowledge of the party to whom the representation is made, and are so altered that the alteration of the circumstances may affect the course of conduct which may be pursued by the party to whom the representation is made it is the imperative duty of the party who has made the representation to communicate to the party to whom the representation has been made the alteration of those circumstances; and that this Court will not hold the party to whom the representation has been made bound unless such a communication has been made.'

This authority does not assist the appellant as to continuity of representation generally. The position there taken was based on a duty to communicate a change of circumstances which had occurred after a representation, true when made, had been falsified by the time the contract was entered into. Here no contract was entered into following a deception of any kind.

The respondent was in breach of his obligation to pay his debt but I agree with the conclusion of the Divisional Court that there was no evidence that he evaded it by deception.

I would dismiss the appeal.

Lord Pearson. . . . In my view, the justices could and did reasonably imply from the course of conduct a representation by the respondent that he had a present intention of paying for his meal before leaving the restaurant. It was a continuing representation in the sense that I have indicated, being made at every moment throughout the course of conduct. Insofar as it was being made before the decision to run out without paying, it was according to the justices' finding a true representation of the respondent's then present intention. Insofar as it was being made after that decision, it was a false representation of the respondent's then present intention, and of course false to his knowledge. That false representation deceived the waiter, inducing him to go the kitchen, whereby the respondent, with his companions, was enabled to make his escape from the restaurant and so dishonestly evade his obligation to pay for his meal. Thus by deception he obtained for himself the pecuniary advantage of evading the debt.

In my opinion, the respondent was rightly convicted by the justices. I would allow the appeal and restore the conviction and sentence.

Appeal allowed

NOTES AND QUESTIONS

1. What was the deception in *Ray*? Did the deception cause the waiter to leave the dining room so that he was in no position to prevent the appellant from decamping without payment?

2. What would the position have been in *Ray* if (a) the respondent had formed the intent not to pay and had decamped while the waiter was in the dining room; or (b) the respondent had formed the intent not to pay while the waiter was in the kitchen and had decamped before the waiter returned to the dining room?

3. The deception must be 'deliberate or reckless'. The *Caldwell* test for recklessness was expressly said to be applicable where recklessness appeared in a modern statute but the requirement for dishonesty would appear to rule out its use here. No amount of negligence can make a dishonest man of an honest man (cf *Derry v Peek* (1889) 14 App Cas 337, HL).

4. A deception may be made by conduct other than the use of words. In *Barnard* (1837) 7 C & P 784, D went into an Oxford shop wearing a fellow-commoner's cap and gown and induced the shopkeeper to give him credit by claiming to be a fellow-commoner. It was said that there would have been a deception even had he said nothing. But there must be some conduct of D's for passive acquiescence by D in the self-deception of P will not ordinarily render a resulting contract between D and P voidable, let alone amount to a deception. On the other hand if D makes a statement which is true, or believed by him to be true when made, which is discovered by him to be false before P acts on it, there would seem to be no reason why this cannot be treated as deliberate deception made by D; cf *Ray*, p 458, above and *Miller*, p 23, above.

5. A common form of obtaining by deception is where D, in return for goods or services provided by P, gives a cheque which D knows will not be met, or has reason to believe may not be met, when presented by P. In giving a cheque D does not represent that he then had funds in his account to meet the cheque for he may have a facility to overdraw his account, or intend himself or pay in sufficient funds before the cheque is presented or expect a third party to do so. In *Hazelton* (1874) LR 2 CCR 134, it was thought to be settled law that a person tendering a cheque impliedly makes three representaions: (i) that he had an account at the bank on which the cheque is drawn; (ii) that he has has authority to draw on the bank for the amount specified; and (iii) that the cheque as drawn is a valid order for that amount but in *Metropolitan Police Comr v Charles* [1977] AC 177, [1976] 3 All ER 112, HL, it was held that in substance there is only one representation, namely, that the cheque will be honoured on presentation; and if D postdates the cheque that it will be met on the due date (*Gilmartin* [1983] QB 953, [1983] 1 All ER 829, CA).

A case which is not at first sight easy to reconcile with these principles is *Greenstein* [1976] 1 All ER 1, [1975] 1 WLR 1353, CA. D and others applied to P for large numbers of shares and with each application they enclosed a cheque to cover the purchase price. They knew that they did not have funds in the bank to meet the cheque *at the time of the application*, but they also knew from experience that they would be allocated only a proportion of the shares applied for and that when the shares were allocated P would return a cheque for the difference between their cheque for the full purchase price and the actual purchase price. P's cheque would then be promptly paid into the defendants' account so that their own cheque, which was presented by P after the allocation of shares, would be met either on first or, at worst, second presentation. To put this simply: suppose D has £5,000 in his bank account. He applies to P for £10,000's worth of shares knowing that the issue will be oversubscribed and that at best he will be allocated 40% of his application. P allocates D 40%, confirms this allocation to D and encloses a cheque for £6,000. D promptly banks this so that he has £11,000 standing to his credit when D's cheque for £10,000 is presented by P for payment.

The defendants had been told by their bankers that this practice (known as 'stagging') was irregular, and the defendants knew that P would not have issued the shares had they realised that by this scheme the defendants were getting for themselves a larger number of shares than bona fide applicants. Indeed to combat the practice of stagging P had in some cases asked applicants to give an assurance that their cheques would be met on first presentation and, when asked, the defendants had given this assurance.

The defendants claimed that they did not dishonestly obtain the shares by deception since their experience in these stagging operations showed that the cheques would be met (it was only in 14 out of 136 transactions that the defendants' cheques were not met on first presentation because P's return cheque had not been cleared in time). But it was held that, in so far as the defendants represented that each cheque was a valid order, it was not because, as they knew, they had no authority whatever to draw cheques for such large amounts—cheques which could only be met if the defendants succeeded in deceiving P into thinking their applications were genuine. But does a cheque cease to be a valid order because D does not have the funds in the bank to meet it at the time it is drawn if he expects that there will be sufficient funds at the time of presentation? Does it follow from *Greenstein* that if D buys goods from P with a cheque for £10,000 he is guilty of obtaining by deception if he has only £5,000 to his account but believes that a rich uncle will pay into his account a further £5,000 before P presents his cheque?

In those cases where the defendants had given an undertaking that their cheques would be met on first presentation the case against them seems clearer. They might have hoped that their cheques would be met on first presentation but they were aware of the risk (since in 14 cases their cheques had not been so met) that they might not hence it could be said that there was a reckless deception.

6. In *Charles* [1976] 3 All ER 112 at 116, Viscount Dilhorne said, 'Until the enactment of the Theft Act 1968 it was necessary in order to obtain a conviction for false pretences to establish that there had been a false pretence of an existing fact.' Has the Theft Act dispensed with this requirement? By s 15(4) 'deception' includes 'a deception as to the present intentions of the person using the deception'. Where this qualification applies, is it unnecessary for the prosecution to prove a deception as to an existing fact? What statement as to existing fact did the defendants make in *Greenstein*?

7. A statement of opinion is not a statement of fact but there is usually implicit in a statement of opinion a statement of fact. If D says that in his opinion X is honest or that certain spoons are made of silver these assertions contain the implicit statement of fact that he knows of nothing that makes his assertion untrue.

(3) DISHONESTY

All offences of deception require dishonesty. Although no definition of dishonesty is provided for the deception offences under ss 15 and 16 of the 1968 Act and for ss 1 and 2 of the 1978 Act, nor is there any adaptation of the partial definition of dishonesty relating to theft in s 2, the CLRC seems to have thought that dishonesty for the purposes of ss 15 and 16 should bear, so far as the case admits, the same meaning for these offences as it has for theft. 'Owing to the words "dishonestly obtains",' said the Committee (Cmnd 2977, para 88):

> 'a person who uses deception in order to obtain property to which he believes himself entitled will not be guilty; for though the deception may be dishonest the obtaining is not. In this respect . . . the offence will be in line with theft, because a belief in legal

right to deprive an owner of property is for the purpose of theft inconsistent with dishonesty and is specifically made a defence by the partial definition of "dishonestly" in [s]2(1)(a). (The partial definition of "dishonestly" in [s]2(1) is not repeated in [s]5(1). It would be only partly applicable to the offence of criminal deception, and it seems unnecessary and undesirable to complicate the [Act] by including a separate definition in [s]15).'

It can hardly be supposed that the CLRC had some different definition of dishonesty in mind for the (remaining) offences under s 16 of the 1968 Act or for the offences under ss 1 and 2 of the 1978 Act.

In cases not involving a claim of right *Ghosh* (p 437, above) where the charge was laid under s 15, governs the issue of dishonesty. *Greenstein* (p 463, above) may illustrate the practical difficulties of the test. How is a jury to determine whether the conduct in question would be regarded as dishonest by the standards of ordinary man? How many ordinary men know the first thing about stagging and by what yardstick is it to be regarded as dishonest? Is it to be settled by reference to what bankers and issuing houses think?

In *Greenstein* the CA said that it would be no bar to the conviction of the defendants that no one lost a penny by the scheme. In *Potger* (1970) 55 Cr App Rep 42, CA, where D induced P to subscribe for magazines by the false representation that he was a student taking part in a points competition, it was no answer that the magazines to be delivered were worth what was asked for them. Cf s 2(2) of the 1968 Act—'A person's appropriation of property may be dishonest notwithstanding that he is willing to pay for the property.'

(4) WHAT MAY BE OBTAINED

Most commonly it is tangible property (money or goods) that is obtained by deception but there would be serious gaps in the law if only tangible property could be the subject of a charge. D may by deception obtain gains to himself or inflict losses on another other than in terms of tangible property. He may, for example, by deception persuade P to forgo a debt which D owes to P, or he may obtain a service by deception. Separate provision is made in the Theft Acts 1968 and 1978 according to the nature of what is obtained. It should not be thought, however, that these provisions are mutually exclusive and on given facts D may fall foul of more than one provision. Take what might be one of the most common frauds of all where D obtains goods on credit having no intention to pay. Here D commits an offence under s 15 of the Theft Act 1968 in obtaining goods by deception but he also commits an offence under s 1 of the 1978 Act because he has caused P to do an act (deliver the goods) which confers a benefit on D and this amounts to a service.

A word of explanation about the Theft Act 1978. Before this Act, cases where D obtained by deception something other than tangible property were provided for mainly, though not exclusively, in s 16(2)(a) of the 1968 Act. This provision which was not the work of the CLRC was drafted in some haste as the Bill was going through Parliament. Its interpretation was attended by so much difficulty (Edmund Davies LJ once referred to it as a 'judicial nightmare') that it was repealed and replaced by ss 1 and 2 of the 1978 Act.

(a) Theft Act 1968, s 15, p 569, below: property belonging to another

By s 34(1) of the 1968 Act (p 572, below) the definition of property for the purpose of theft in s 4(1) is applied for the purposes of s 15. Thus the qualifications to the general definition in s 4(1) do not apply to the s 15 offence. One difference of significance is that while land, in general, cannot be stolen, it may be obtained by deception. Why?

(b) Theft Act 1968, s 16, p 569, below: pecuniary advantage

All that remains of s 16 are the two particular cases instanced by paras (b) and (c) and the offence of obtaining a pecuniary advantage has no application whatsoever outside these two instances (*DPP v Turner* [1974] AC 357, [1973] 3 All ER 124, HL).

(c) Theft Act 1978, s 1, p 581, below: services

'The Theft Act 1978' by J.R. Spencer, [1979] Crim LR 24 at 28

The definition of obtaining services requires the victim of the offence not merely to 'do some act, or cause or permit some act to be done,' but to *confer a benefit* thereby. It seems, therefore, that P must be induced to do something which is of some use to somebody. Possibly, this means that P must be induced to do something which is of *economic value* to D or someone else—meaning that he must, at the end of the day, be finincially better off than he would otherwise have been. To some extent as yet uncertain, therefore, the use of the word 'benefit' cuts down the extreme wideness of the phrases which follow it.

The benefit which P is induced to confer must involve 'doing some act, or causing or permitting some act to be done.' In many or most of the cases at which section 1 is aimed, P will be induced to confer a benefit by doing some act: repairing D's car, painting D's house, carrying D in his taxi, or doing some other sort of work for him. Were the benefit limited to the doing of some act, however, certain recurrent cases would fall outside the section. Where D lies his way into P's hotel, cinema or car-park, for example, P's acts in providing the benefit are done for a large number of people, and would be done whether or not D told P lies in order to share it; P is not induced to show his film or to make up the hotel beds solely because D deceives him. The only thing which D actually induces P to do which he would not have done anyway—and hence the only conduct of P's causally linked to D's deception— is to *allow* D to use the facility, and this D would no doubt have argued was an omission, not an act. Presumably it was with this problem in mind that the section includes conferring a benefit by 'permitting some act to be done.' Presumably the benefit may also be conferred by 'causing some act to be done' in order to make it obtaining services from P where P, an employer or manager, is deceived into commanding one of his servants or underlings to do some act of benefit to D—as where a garage proprietor is deceived into telling his mechanic to service D's car. 'Doing some act' might have been sufficient to produce this result without the addition of 'causing some act to be done,' but the addition of 'causing' relieves the courts of the need to construe 'doing' in an extensive sense.

A person 'is induced to confer a benefit by doing some act' inter alia where he is persuaded to hand over propery to another. Thus there appears to be a considerable overlap between this offence and obtaining property by deception contrary to section 15 of the Theft Act 1968. *Some* overlap is desirable. Two mutually exclusive offences would be excessively inconvenient, because many transactions involve both materials and services: the trickster who obtains bed and breakfast by deception would have to be charged under section 15 of the Theft Act 1968 for the breakfast and under section 1 of the Theft Act 1978 for the bed, and the man who by deception gets a silicone damp-course injected into the walls of his house would be guaranteed an appeal to the House of Lords, whichever offence he were charged with! If *any* transfer of property counts as 'conferring a benefit by doing some act' and hence performing services, so that any contravention of section 15 of the Theft Act 1969 is automatically a breach of section 1 of the Theft Act 1978 as well, no great injustice would result, since section 1 carries only half the punishment available under section 15. However, an offence of obtaining services by deception that also included all cases of obtaining property by deception would be unsightly. This result can be avoided if subsection (2) is interpreted as *limiting*, but not extending, the word 'services' in subsection (1). On this view, conduct would only amount to 'services' if it could fairly be described as 'services' in normal speech. The new offence would then cover obtaining property by deception where work was provided as well, but not obtaining property pure and simple.

'. . . on the understanding that the benefit has been or will be paid for'

This phrase imposes an important limitation on what conduct conferring a benefit amounts to 'services' within the section. If P's intention were to do something for D free of charge, then, notwithstanding the fact that D might in everyday language be said to have dishonestly obtained services by deception, he has not in law committed the criminal offence. Thus if D gets P, his neighbour, to drive him to the station free of charge by telling him a lie about a dying relative that he has to visit, D would not contravene section 1 of the Theft Act 1978. It would be no different even if P were a taxi-driver who normally charges his passengers, but was induced to make an exception in this case—though here there would appear to be an offence under section 2(1)(c) of this Act.

The range of dishonesty which this limitation leaves unpunished depends on when a benefit is 'paid for.' At its narrowest, a benefit would only be 'paid for' when a specific fee was paid in respect of a specific benefit. Thus where a motorist paid an annual fee to the Automobile Association for example, and was then entitled to the 'free' use of their breakdown service if he needed it, the benefit would not on this view be 'paid for.' On a broader view of 'paid for,' however, this sort of indirect payment would be sufficient. It is to be hoped that the broader view will be adopted.

It is sufficient if P believes either that he will be paid, or that he *has been paid*. Thus provision is made for the man who gets into a rugby international by lying that he has lost his ticket.

A benefit counts as services if it is conferred 'on the understanding' that it has been or will be paid for, not 'on the *mis*understanding.' The phrase occurs, be it noted, in the definition of what amounts to 'obtaining services' not in a limitation of what sort of deception is necessary to commit the offence. Thus, unless the courts are willing to read in words in favour of the accused, the offence does not require D's deception to be as to payment. So D commits an offence if, on payment of the appropriate fee, he obtains a service available only to a member of a restricted group to which he falsely pretends to belong: if he gets the use of a bed in a YHA hostel on payment, for example, having pretended to be a YHA member; or if he impersonates a member of a trade association in order to obtain, on payment, confidential information about debtors available only to members.

It appears to be enough that P should understand that the benefit has been or will be paid for. It does not seem to be necessary for P to believe that D can be, or could have been, legally made to pay. Thus an offence appears to be committed even where D tricks P into performing an unlawful act for him, as long as P understands that he has been or will be paid. So the man who induces a prostitute to have intercourse with him on a false promise of payment seems to be guilty of obtaining services by deception.

(d) Theft Act 1978, s 2, p 581, below: evasion of liability

CLRC Thirteenth Report, paras 13–16

13. Clause 1 of the draft Bill at Annex 1 deals with the common frauds to which section 16(2)(a) applies where there is a deception at the outset of a transaction. In our Working Paper we suggested that part of the balance of section 16(2)(a) could be brought within the scope of an offence of obtaining relief from debt by deception and we suggested that this offence should be limited to cases where by deception a debtor obtains remission of the whole or part of any liability to make payment, including a liability that would be incurred but for the remission, and cases where there is an existing liability to make payment and the debtor by deception induces the creditor to wait for payment intending never to pay. When we subsequently worked on the detail of this proposal we found it convenient to divide this offence into three parts and to use 'liability' throughout rather than 'debt'. The resulting provision appears as clause 2 of our draft Bill. Subsection (1)(a) covers the deception which dishonestly secures the remission of the whole or part of an existing liability to make a payment. An example would be where a man borrows £100 from a neighbour and, when repayment is due, tells a false story of some family tragedy which makes it

impossible for him to find the money; this deception persuades the neighbour to tell him that he need never repay the loan.

14. Clause 2(1)(b) is concerned with the stalling debtor. It provides that a creditor who by deception dishonestly induces his creditor to wait for payment or to forego payment is guilty of an offence if, and only if, he intends to make permanent default in whole or in part of his liability to pay. This final limitation makes the offence narrower than the corresponding offence in section 16(2)(a) for the reasons which have been given in paragraph 6 above. We recognise that the practical difficulties of proving an intention never to pay will have the consequence that there will be few prosecutions under this head, but this is consistent with our view that the criminal law should not apply to the debtor who is merely trying to delay making a payment. Sir Rupert Cross and Professor Williams are opposed to the inclusion of clause 2(1)(b) in the draft Bill. Professor Williams' views are set out in the Note at the end of this Report.

15. Clause 2(1)(c) is concerned with a type of fraud which can conveniently be brought within the scope of the offence of obtaining relief from liability by deception although it differs from the other cases covered by the offence in that it can include frauds where the offender has been acting dishonestly from the outset of the transaction. In paragraph 7 of Appendix 2 we note that certain enactments creating offences of fraudulently evading charges or obtaining allowances or relief were repealed by the Theft Act 1968 on the basis that the conduct at which they were aimed would involve offences under section 16. Clause 2(1)(c) will ensure that such conduct remains an offence. For there to be an offence under this provision there must be dishonesty and a deception which obtains any exemption from or abatement of liability to make a payment. To take an example, section 49(8) of the General Rate Act 1967 (one of the enactments repealed in 1968) provided a penalty for false statements made to obtain rate rebates. The ratepayer who makes a false statement in order to obtain a rebate to which he is not entitled is acting dishonestly and is practising a deception in order to obtain an abatement of his liability to pay rates and, accordingly, would be guilty of an offence under clause 2(1)(c). The wording of this provision, 'where a person by any deception . . . dishonestly obtains any exemption from or abatement of liability to make a payment' is intended to cover cases where the deception has induced the victim to believe that there is nothing due to him or that the amount due to him is less than would be the case if he knew the true facts. [it is the 'liability to make a payment' from which exemption (or of which abatement) is obtained and it is not necessary for there to be 'any existing liability' which is reduced or extinguished.] Another example of the application of this part of clause 2 is the case where a person by deception obtains services at a reduced rate (for example, air travel at a special rate for students when the traveller is not a student). . . .

16. Subsection (2) of clause 2 makes it clear that the clause does not apply in relation to a liability that has not been accepted or established to pay compensation for a wrongful act or omission. Without this provision there would be room for argument that subsection (1)(a) of the clause applies where, for example, a person lies about the circumstances of an accident in order to avoid the bringing of civil proceedings for negligence against him. We think that the dividing line is reached where liability is not disputed even though the amount of that liability is. On this basis it would be an offence under clause 2(1)(a) for an antique dealer to lie about the age and value of jewellery sent to him for valuation which had been lost as a result of his admitted negligence, but not for him to lie about the circumstances of the loss in disputing an allegation of negligence. We see no justification for extending the criminal law to cases where the existence of any liability is disputed: the claimant can launch civil proceedings if he thinks he had been deceived when he absolved the other from liability.

NOTES AND QUESTIONS

1. At the end of para 13 the CLRC gives an example of the operation of s 2(1)(a). In such a case D does not secure the 'remission' of an existing liability to make a payment if remission means the extinction in law of the debt. In law D continues to owe his neighbour £100 and the neighbour would no doubt enforce that liability once he becomes aware of the fraud so how can it be said that D has secured the remission of an existing liability? Griew, however, argues (*Theft Acts 1968 and 1978*, paras 8–11) that,

'It must be immaterial that the creditor's agreement is not binding on him, because it was obtained by fraud and that the debtor whose fraud is uncovered may in the result . . . gain temporary relief only.' The same issue arises in connection with s 2(1)(c) in that there would in law be no exemption from the prospective liability.

2. The operation of s 2(1)(b) may be illustrated by reference to the facts of *DPP v Turner* [1974] AC 357, [1973] 3 All ER 124, HL. D, who owed P some £38 for work done and was being pressed for payment, told P that he had no ready cash and persuaded P to accept a cheque knowing that it would be dishonoured. Such conduct falls within s 2(1)(b) if, and only if, D intends to make permanent default. If, as seemed likely in *Turner*, D simply wanted to give himself a breathing space, and was bent on settling the debt at a later stage, he would not commit the offence.

3. Does D commit an offence, and if so under which provision relating to deception, in any of the following circumstances?

(i) He obtains free admission to Wembley on Cup Final day by falsely pretending to be the referee.

(ii) He obtains a haircut at half price by falsely representing to be an old age pensioner.

(iii) He obtains the services of a prostitute at half price by falsely representing that he is an old age pensioner.

(iv) Being an infant he gets flying lessons from P on credit, having no intention of paying for them.

4. Making off without payment

Theft Act 1978, s 3, p 581, below

CLRC Thirteenth Report, paras 19–21

18. Our proposed offences of deception as to prospect of payment and obtaining relief from liability by deception would replace section 16(2)(a). In our Working Paper we discussed *DPP v Ray* [[1973] 3 All ER 131]. The facts were that the defendant ordered a meal in a restaurant and after he had eaten it waited until the waiter went out into the kitchen before running out of the restaurant without paying his bill. The magistrates' court found that when the defendant ordered the meal he intended to pay for it and that his conduct in remaining seated at the table after he had finished eating amounted to a deception which obtained for him the opportunity of evading his liability by running out of the restaurant. If the defendant had entered the restaurant with the intention of not paying for his meal he would have been guilty of an offence under section 15, and in our Working Paper we asked whether that section is, in practice, an adequate weapon to use against restaurant bilking and similar frauds or whether there are sufficient cases where the accused claims an original innocent intention to make it necessary to consider creating a new offence. We explained that any new offence should not be an offence of deception, because the mischief would have been as great in *Director of Public Prosecutions v Ray* if the diner had run out of the restaurant immediately he decided not to pay the bill; and we commented that it must be very rare to be able to allege any deception of the waiter. The comments which we received from those with practical experience of the conduct of prosecutions showed that there were many cases in which the accused claimed an original innocent intention; and there was general support for our suggestion that where the customer knows that he is expected to pay on the spot for goods supplied to him or services done for him it should be an offence for him dishonestly to go away without having paid and intending never to pay. We have developed this proposal into clause 3 of our draft Bill and have given the offence the label 'making off without payment'.

19. The proposed new offence is confined to circumstances where goods are supplied or a service is done on the basis that payment will be made there and then. The obvious example is the restaurant where everyone knows that the meal is supplied on the understanding that the bill will be paid before the diner leaves the restaurant. The clause also covers hotel bills which the traveller is expected to pay before he leaves. The clause will equally apply to bills for board and lodging alone, in boarding houses or elsewhere, where the arrangements are such that payment on the spot is required. It will not apply where there is a lease of premises because the lease will not require the tenant to pay the rent on the premises when it is due and before he goes away from them. In the discussion of this proposal in our Working Paper we commented that it could be represented as producing a risk that the threat of prosecution would be used by the creditors to enforce their claims, in particular where lodgers leave their lodgings without paying the out-standing rent. Comments on our proposal made it clear that there is a need for an offence to deal with the dishonest guest who leaves an hotel without paying his bill but who cannot be proved to have practised any deception on the hotel management. We have found it impossible to devise a satisfactory limitation on the scope of the offence which would apply it to hotels but exclude payment for accommodation in other premises. We have concluded that the advantages of extending the criminal law as we propose in clause 3 outweigh the possible risks to which we referred in our Working Paper. The clause applies also to the collection of goods on which work has been done or in respect of which service has been provided: examples are the collection from a shop of shoes which have been repaired or clothes which have been cleaned, and for the purposes of the clause it does not matter whether the work was done on the premises. As the new offence is essentially a protection for the legitimate business we have not thought it right that it should extend to transactions where the supply of the goods or the doing of the service is contrary to law, or where the service done is such that payment is not legally enforceable, and clause 3(3) imposes this limitation.

20. Further examples of the application of the clause are the passenger who at the end of his journey in a taxi runs off without paying his fare; and the motorist who has had his car's petrol tank filled at a garage and when the attendant is called to the telephone drives off without paying for the petrol.

21. Among the comments on our Working Paper was the suggestion that this proposed offence should be extended to cover obtaining entry to premises without paying the admission charge. We were told that young people frequently enter cinemas through fire exits or cloakroom windows and that they cannot be prosecuted when they are caught. We can see that there is a case for creating a summary offence to deal with that and similar misconduct (e g climbing over the wall into a football ground to avoid paying at the turnstiles). The essence of that offence would be *entering* premises knowing that a charge was made for admission and without paying that charge. This cannot be combined in one provision with the offence in clause 3 of *making off* without paying when payment on the spot for goods or services is required or expected. Clause 3 is a natural extension of our proposals for replacing section 16(2)(a) but we do not think it right to go any further away from the offences of deception which our terms of reference required us to review and so we must leave it to others to decide whether it would be desirable to create a summary offence of entering premises without paying the admission charge.

NOTES AND QUESTIONS

1. According to the OED 'makes off' means to depart suddenly 'often with a disparaging implication'. But while making off is usually thought of as having the disparaging implication of cowardice or secrecy or stealth, it is not confined to such cases. It simply means to decamp and in *Brooks and Brooks* (1982) 76 Cr App Rep 66 at 69, CA, the court said that it 'may be an exercise accompanied by the sound of trumpets or a silent stealing away after a folding of tents.'

Difficulties arise where D leaves the spot where payment is required with the consent of P. It may be supposed that when presented with the bill after a meal D says that his wallet is in his car in the street nearby and is given permission to fetch it; or E says that he has left his wallet at home and is allowed to leave on the understanding that he will return the following day to settle up. Assuming that in both cases D is acting dishonestly and does not return, is the offence committed? Must the offence extend to both or neither, or is it possible to distinguish between them? Does 'on the spot' have a temporal as well as geographical connotation so that it might be said that in D's case P still expects payment on the spot (i e now as well as here) whereas E is expected to make payment here but not now?

J.R. Spencer would regard both cases as falling within s 3. He says ([1983] Crim LR 573):

> Obviously, section 3 is partly concerned to prevent the legitimate expectations of restaurateurs, hoteliers, etc being disappointed by people failing to pay their bills. But equally obviously, the section is aimed at some specific mischief narrower than this. If non-payment had been all that Parliament was concerned with, presumably it would have phrased the offence as 'dishonestly failing to pay.' If mere failure to pay was the true mischief of the offence, there was no need for 'making off' as an ingredient in it at all, whether it means 'leaves' as Professor Smith and others say, or whether it means 'leaves with guilty haste' as Francis Bennion suggests. So we must assume, surely, that 'makes off' points to some additional element of mischief which renders the case significantly worse than simply failing to pay, and to see what 'making off' really is, we ought to consider what conduct is, in practical terms, significantly worse than merely failing to pay. It can hardly be *leaving* without paying, because this, as such, does not worsen the creditor's position. It must surely be *disappearing: leaving in a way that makes it difficult for the debtor to be traced*.
>
> On this view, 'making off' would cover, obviously, the man who runs away. It would also cover the man who tells a lie to get outside, and then runs away. It would also cover a man who leaves a cheque signed in a false name. But it would not cover the person who leaves his correct name and an address at which he may readily be found. Nor would it usually cover the person who leaves behind him a cheque, drawn on his own account, in circumstances where it is likely to be dishonoured. In this case, although D has left, he has not as a rule made it difficult for P to trace him.
>
> I also think this interpretation of 'makes off' is the right one because it solves a problem which otherwise arises in connection with section 3(4): 'Any person may arrest without warrant any one who is, or whom he, with reasonable cause, suspects to be, committing or attempting to commit an offence under this section,' Years ago the common law set its face against giving hoteliers, restaurateurs and suchlike the power to arrest those who merely fail to pay their bills. Yet if we interpret 'makes off' as synonymous with 'leaves' we give them precisely this. On this view, any customer who sought to leave having failed to pay his bill would—subject to what the jury make of 'dishonestly'—commit the offence of making off without payment, and the hotelier or restaurateur would be able lawfully to detain him. To me, at least, it seems highly undesirable that hoteliers, etc should be given this power, at any rate when they know who the non-paying customer is and where he may later be found. On the other hand, if 'makes off' is limited as I suggest, there is no question of the hotelier having the power to arrest a customer who leaves his name backed with some plausible identification.

On this view, presumably, D would not commit the offence where, being well known to P, he dishonestly decides not to pay the bill and decamps via the lavatory window. But does not such a case fall four-square within s 3 however unlikely it is that D will get away with it?

2. The offence requires that goods be *supplied* or a service *done*. If D enters a jeweller's shop and steals a ring it could be said that he makes off without payment when payment on the spot is required. But, and while such a case is obviously one of theft, D does not commit an offence under s 3 since it cannot be said that the ring was supplied to him. It could hardly make any difference (or could it?) that the jeweller, believing D to be a bona fide customer, had placed the ring in D's hands for inspection. Section 3 appears to contemplate a supply in connection with an agreed, or at least proposed sale.

On the other hand goods may be supplied, or services done, though many or all of the physical acts are done by D. All commentators are agreed that petrol is supplied by P at self-service filling stations though the customer serves himself. Similarly a service is done by P at a self-service car wash though P is not on the premises and the machinery is operated by D.

A more difficult case is the self-service store. Suppose that D takes goods from the shelves which he places in his pocket and leaves the store with them. Obviously theft but does he also commit the offence under s 3? A.T.H. Smith ([1981] Crim LR 590) thinks that this case is to be distinguished from the self-service petrol station in that in the latter 'the customer does not just take possession of the petrol, but makes himself owner of it by pouring it into his tank.'

3. Payment ordinarily presents no problems. One problem concerns payment by cheque. If the cheque is supported by a cheque card which the bank must then honour it would seem clear that P has been paid though D has exceeded his authority as between himself and the bank, and the same would follow where a credit card is used. But what if P accepts a cheque from D which D knows will not be honoured. There is a suggestion in *Hammond* [1982] Crim LR 611 that P has been paid because a cheque taken without a banker's card is always taken at risk by the recipient. The judge in *Hammond* added that he did not see how in such a case it could be said that D made off.

R v Allen [1985] 2 All ER 641, House of Lords
(Lords Hailsham LC, Scarman, Diplock, Bridge of Harwich and Brightman)

Lord Hailsham of St Marylebone LC. . . . The facts, which are not disputed, and which I draw from the case for the appellant, were as follows. The respondent, Christopher Allen, booked a room at a hotel for ten nights from 15 January 1983. He stayed on thereafter and finally left on 11 February 1983 without paying his bill in the sum of £1,286.94. He telephoned two days later to explain that he was in financial difficulties because of some business transactions and arranged to return to the hotel on 18 February 1983 to remove his belongings and leave his Australian passport as security for the debt. He was arrested on his return and said that he genuinely hoped to be able to pay the bill and denied he was acting dishonestly. On 3 March 1983 he was still unable to pay the bill and provided an explanation to the police of his financial difficulties.

The respondent's defence was that he had acted honestly and had genuinely expected to pay the bill from the proceeds of various business ventures.

After a fairly lengthy summing up by the trial judge to which, in the light of what happened, I need make no special reference, the jury retired at 1 pm and came back at 2.18 pm with a note containing the following specific question for guidance by the judge:

> 'Regarding count 2 of the indictment, the words "and with intent to avoid payment of the £1,286.94", do you refer to permanent intention or one applying only to the dates mentioned in the charge?'

To this question the judge gave the following explicit answer:

> 'The answer is: one applying only to 8 and 11 February 1983. You see it says in count 2: "knowing that payment on the spot for goods supplied and services done was required or expected from him . . ." "On the spot" means the day you leave. There was no payment on the spot when he should have paid. It contrasts sharply with count 1 where the intent there is permanent; that is not so in count 2 where he was required to pay on the spot; and there has been a failure to do that. Will you please, once more, retire to consider you verdict?'

The original summing up had contained the same direction, but in view of what happened there is no need to refer to it separately, for the effect on the jury of this specific reply was immediate and decisive. Within five minutes they returned the verdict of guilty.

Despite some (though not unanimous) textbook opinions in an opposite sense (see Smith *The Law of Theft* (5th edn, 1984) para 250, p 130, Griew *The Theft Acts 1968 and 1978* (4th edn, 1982) para 11-14, p 155 and, less strongly, Glanville Williams *Textbook of Criminal Law* (2nd edn, 1983) p 878), I consider this answer to be clearly erroneous.

Section 3(1) of the 1978 Act, under which count 2 was laid, reads as follows:

[His Lordship read s 3(1).]

The offence thus created is triable only on indictment and attracts a maximum penalty of two years.

The Crown's contention was that the effect of this section is to catch not only those who intend permanently to avoid payment of the amount due, but also those whose intention is to avoid payment on the spot, which, after all, is the time at which, ex hypothesi, payment has been 'expected or required', and the time, therefore, when the 'amount' became 'due'.

The judgment of the Court of Appeal, with which I agree, was delivered by Boreham J. He said ([1985] 1 All ER 148 at 154, [1985] 1 WLR 50 at 57):

'To secure a conviction under s 3 of the 1978 Act the following must be proved: (1) that the defendant in fact made off without making payment on the spot; (2) the following mental elements: (a) knowledge that payment on the spot was required or expected of him; and (b) dishonesty; and (c) intent to avoid payment [sc 'of the amount due'].'

I agree with this analysis. To this the judge adds the following comment:

'If (c) means, or is taken to include, no more than an intention to delay or defer payment of the amount due, it is difficult to see what it adds to the other elements. Anyone who knows that payment on the spot is expected or required of him and who then dishonestly makes off without paying as required or expected must have at least the intention to delay or defer payment. It follows, therefore, that the conjoined phrase "and with intent to avoid payment of the amount due" adds a further ingredient: an intention to do more than delay or defer, an intention to evade payment altogether.'

My own view, for what it is worth, is that the section thus analysed is capable only of this meaning. But counsel for the Crown very properly conceded that, even if it were equivocal and capable of either meaning, in a penal section of this kind any ambiguity must be resolved in favour of the subject and against the Crown. Accordingly, the appeal falls to be dismissed either if on its true construction it means unambiguously that the intention must be permanently to avoid payment, or if the clause is ambiguous and capable of either meaning. Even on the assumption that, in the context, the word 'avoid' without the addition of the word 'permanently' is capable of either meaning, which Boreham J was inclined to concede, I find myself convinced by his final paragraph, which reads:

'Finally, we can see no reason why, if the intention of Parliament was to provide, in effect, that an intention to delay or defer payment might suffice, Parliament should not have said so in explicit terms. This *might* have been achieved by the insertion of the word "such" before payment in the phrase in question. It *would* have been achieved by a grammatical reconstruction of the material part of s 3(1) thus, "dishonestly makes off without having paid and with intent to avoid payment of the amount due as required or expected". To accede to the Crown's submission would be to read the section as if it were constructed in that way. That we cannot do. Had it been intended to relate the intention to avoid "payment" to "payment as required or expected" it would have been easy to say so. The section does not say so. At the very least it contains an equivocation which should be resolved in favour of [the respondent].'

There is really no escape from this argument. There may well be something to be said for the creation of a criminal offence designed to protect, for instance, cab drivers and restaurant keepers against persons who dishonestly abscond without paying on the spot and without any need for the prosecution to exclude an intention to pay later, so long as the original act of 'making off' could be described as dishonest. Unlike that in the present section, such an offence might very well as with the railway ticket offence, be triable summarily, and counsel for the Crown was able to call in aid the remarks of Cumming-Bruce LJ in *Corbyn v Saunders* [1978] 2 All ER 697 at 699, [1978] 1 WLR 400 at 403 which go a long way to support such a view. But, as the Court of Appeal remarked, that decision was under a different statute and a differently worded section which did not contain both the reference to 'dishonestly' and the specific intention 'to avoid payment' as two separate elements in the mens rea of the offence. In order to give the section now under consideration the effect required the section would have to be remodelled in the way suggested by Boreham J in the passage quoted above, or the word 'and' in the ultimate phrase would have to be read as if it meant 'that is to say' so that the required intent would be equated with 'dishonestly' in the early part of the subsection.

Apart from the minor matter not relevant to the judgment there is nothing really to be added to the judgment delivered by Boreham J.

The minor matter to which I have just referred was the disinclination of the Court of Appeal to consider the Criminal Law Revision Committee's Thirteenth Report (Section 16 of the Theft Act 1968) (Cmnd 6733 (1977)) which led to the passing of the 1978 Act. In accordance with the present practice, this, for the purpose of defining the mischief of the Act but not to construe it, their Lordships in fact have done. The 'mischief' is covered by paras 18 to 21 of the report and it is significant that the report was accompanied by a draft Bill, cl 3 of which is in terms identical with s 3 of the Act, save that the proposed penalty was three years instead of two. Though we did not use it as an aid to construction, for the purpose of defining the mischief to be dealt with by the section, I consider it to be relevant. The discussion had originated from the decision in *DPP v Ray* [1973] 3 All ER 131, [1974] AC 370 and the committee defined the mischief in the following terms (para 18):

> '. . . there was general support for our suggestion that where the customer knows that he is expected to pay on the spot for goods supplied to him or services done for him it should be an offence for him dishonestly to go away without having paid *and intending never to pay.*' (My emphasis.)

From this it is plain beyond doubt that the mischief aimed at by the authors of the report was precisely that which the Court of Appeal, construing the section without reference to the report, attributed to the section by the mere force of grammatical construction.

In the result I agree with the judgment of the Court of Appeal and apart from my reference to the Criminal Law Revision Committee report can add nothing usefully to it. . . .

[**Lords Scarman, Diplock, Bridge of Harwich** and **Brightman** agreed.]

Appeal dismissed

5. Temporary deprivation

A temporary taking of property can be every bit as much of a nuisance, though not ultimately as damaging, as a permanent deprivation. Most students will have experienced the problem when a book or article which they are recommended to read disappears from the library shelves and is not returned until it is too late to make use of it. The CLRC, however, decided against creating a general offence of dishonest use since they did not think such a considerable extension of the criminal law was called for by any existing social evil.

But there are particular cases in which temporary deprivation is a serious evil. The most obvious is the taking of a motor vehicle, first made an offence in 1930, and this was followed by a similar offence in relation to the taking of vessels in 1967. The Theft Act 1968, s 12, continues these offences and extends them to a greater range of conveyances. The CLRC also recommended, and s 11 introduced, an offence of removing articles from public places which was inspired by a number of notorious 'removals' such as the removal from the National Gallery of Goya's portrait of the Duke of Wellington and the removal of the Coronation Stone from Westminster Abbey.

(1) REMOVAL OF ARTICLES FROM PLACES OPEN TO THE PUBLIC

Theft Act 1968, s 11, p 567, below

While the CLRC recommended the creation of this offence, the Committee did not include a provision for it in its Draft Bill. The section was drafted at a subsequent stage and, as a glance at it will show, it is one of some difficulty.

The essential aim of the offence, to protect things which are put at risk by being displayed to the public, is clear enough but 'the section is drafted with a complexity disproportionate to the complexity of the offence' (Griew, *The Theft Acts 1968 and 1978*, 4th edn, at 5–03).

(2) TAKING CONVEYANCES

Theft Act 1968, s 12, p 568, below

**R v Bow (1976) 64 Cr App Rep 54, Court of Appeal, Criminal Division
(Bridge LJ, Wien and Kenneth Jones JJ)**

The appellant, together with his brother and father, drove in the brother's motor car to a country estate; all had air rifles. At the estate they were approached by gamekeepers who asked for their names and addresses. When these were refused, the head gamekeeper sent for the police and parked his Land Rover so as to obstruct the only escape route for the brother's car. Since the head gamekeeper refused to remove the Land Rover, the appellant got into it, released the handbrake and allowed it to coast some 200 yards so that his brother could drive his car away. The appellant was convicted of an offence under s 12 (1).

[**Bridge LJ** delivered the judgment of the court:]
. . . Mr Toulson, for whose interesting and careful argument we are extremely grateful, makes two submissions in summary. First, he submits that the case should have been withdrawn from the jury on the footing that there was indeed no evidence that the taking of Land Rover was for the appellant's own use. Secondly, and alternatively, if he is wrong on the first submission he says that in any event the issue raised a question of fact which should have been left by the judge to be determined by the jury.

It is convenient to say at the outset that no point turns in this appeal on the fact that the Land Rover's engine was not used by the appellant. Mr Toulson does not suggest that the case falls to be decided any differently because the appellant was able to coast downhill for 200 yards than if he had driven 200 yards using the engine.

It is appropriate to recall that the present statutory offence created by section 12 of the Act of 1968 is defined in two respects in significantly different language from the language which was used in earlier statutes, the latest embodiment prior to 1968 having been in section 217 of the Road Traffic Act 1960. Under that Act the offence was defined as committed by 'a person who takes and drives away a motor vehicle without having either the consent of the owner or other lawful authority.'

Some arguments have been addressed to us with respect to the supposed intention of the legislature in effecting those changes in the definition of the offence, but in the event, having regard to the conclusion the Court has reached on a narrow point which we think is decisive of this appeal, it is unnecessary for us to express any opinion on those wider arguments

Mr Toulson's basic submission is in these terms. He contends that if a person moves a vehicle for the sole reason that it is in his way and moves it no further than is necessary to enable him to get past the obstruction, he is not taking that vehicle for his own use. The starting point of the argument is the decision of this court in *Bogacki* (1973) 57 Cr App R 593, [1973] QB 832. In that case the three defendants were charged with attempting to take without authority a motor bus. The evidence showed that they had gone to a bus garage late at night and attempted to start the engine of a bus without success. The trial judge directed the jury as follows, adverting specifically to the change of language between section 12 of the Act of 1968 and section 217 of the Act of 1960. He said:

'The offence is not, I repeat, the offence is not taking and driving away, it is merely taking and "taking," members of the jury, means assuming possession of an object for your own unauthorised use, however temporary that assumption of possession might be. May I give you an example. Suppose that you left your motorcar parked in the car park behind a cinema, and you forgot to lock the door but you shut the door, and suppose that a man and a woman, some time later, when the motorcar was unattended, came along, opened the door, got into the car, and had sexual intercourse in the car. This particular offence would then have been committed by them.'

Later he said with respect to the defendants before him: 'The question is: Did they, without the permission of the owners, acquire possession, for however short a time, for their own unauthorised purpose? That is the question.'

In giving the judgment of this Court in that case Roskill LJ said at pp 598 and 837 of the respective reports:

'The word "take" is an ordinary simple English word and it is undesirable that where Parliament has used an ordinary simple English word elaborate glosses should be put upon it. What is sought to be said is that "take" is the equivalent of "use" and that mere unauthorised user of itself constitutes an offence against section 12. It is to be observed that if one treats "takes" as a synonym for "uses," the subsection has to be read in this way: "if . . . he uses any conveyance for his own or another's use. . . ." That involves the second employment of the word "use" being tautologous, and this court can see no justification where Parliament has used the phrase "if . . . he takes any conveyance for his own or another's use" for construing this language as meaning if he "uses any conveyance for his own or another's use," thus giving no proper effect to the words "for his own or another's use." For those reasons the court accepts Mr Lowry's submission that there is still built in, if I may use the phrase, to the word "takes" in the subsection the concept of movement and that before a man can be convicted of the completed offence under section 12 (1) it must be shown that he took the vehicle, that is to say, that there was an unauthorised taking possession or control of the vehicle by him adverse to the rights of the true owner or person otherwise entitled to such possession or control, coupled with some movement, however small . . . of that vehicle following such unauthorised taking.'

Basing himself on that decision, Mr Toulson submits, cogently as we think, that since the concept of taking in the definition of the offence already involves moving the vehicle taken, the words 'for his own or anothers's use' must involve something over and above mere movement of the vehicle. What then is the concept embodied in this phrase 'for his own or another's use'?

On this point the argument ranged widely, but we hope that at the end of the day it is an adequate summary of the final submission made on it by Mr Toulson to say that he contends that what is involved is that the conveyance should have been used as a conveyance, i e should have been used as a means of transport. That submission seems to us to be well-founded. Mr Toulson points out that the mischief at which this section is aimed has been appropriately defined as 'stealing a ride.' The interpretation of the phrase 'for his own or another's use' as meaning 'for his own or another's use as a conveyance' would fall into line, we think, with the discriminations suggested in Smith and Hogan's *Criminal Law*, 3rd edn (1973) at p 462, where the following passage occurs:

'But subject to the requirement of taking, the offence does seem, in essence, to consist in stealing a ride. This seems implicit in the requirement that the taking be for "his own or another's *use*," Thus if D releases the handbrake of a car so that it runs down an incline, or releases a boat from its moorings so that it is carried off by the tide this would not as such be an offence within the section.'

Pausing at that point in the quotation from the textbook, the reason why neither of those examples would constitute an offence within the section would be that in neither case, although the conveyance had been moved, would it have been used as a conveyance.

The quotation from the textbook goes on: 'The taking must be for D's use or the use of another and if he intends to make no use of the car or boat there would be no offence under section 12. But it would be enough if D were to release the boat from its moorings so that he would be carried downstream in the boat.' In that case, since he would be carried downstream in the boat there would be a use of the boat as a conveyance, as a means of transporting him downstream.

So far the court is in agreement with Mr Toulson's submissions. But then the next step has to be taken. The next step is, as Mr Toulson submits that merely to move a vehicle which constitutes an obstruction so that it shall be an obstruction no more cannot involve use of the vehicle as a conveyance. It is at this point that the submission requires to be carefully analysed.

Clearly one can envisage instances in which an obstructing vehicle was merely pushed out of the way a yard or two which would not involve any use of it as a conveyance. But the facts involved in the removal of the obstructing vehicle must be examined in each case.

Mr Matheson, for the Crown, meets this submission squarely by pointing to the circumstance that here the Land Rover was in the ordinary sense of the English language driven for 200 yards. Attention has already been drawn to the fact that no distinction was relied upon by Mr Toulson between a vehicle driven under its own power and a vehicle driven by being allowed to coast down hill. Mr Matheson says that again, as a matter of ordinary use of English, in the course of driving the vehicle a distance of 200 yards the appellant was inevitably using it as a conveyance and that his motive for so doing is immaterial. This submission for the Crown, it is pointed out to us, is in line with another suggestion by Professor Smith in his textbook on the *Law of Theft*, 2nd edn (1972), paragraph 317, where he says: 'Probably driving, whatever the motive, would be held to be "use." '

In reply, Mr Toulson submits that even if it be right that the appellant had in the ordinary sense of the word to drive the Land Rover for 200 yards, and even if that did involve its use as a conveyance, nevertheless the offence was still not made out because the purpose of the taking was not to use the conveyance as a conveyance but merely to remove it as an obstruction. He emphasises that the words of the section are: 'takes for his own use,' not 'takes and uses.' This is in our judgment a very subtle and refined distinction and if it were admitted it would open a very wide door to persons who take conveyances without authority and use them as such to dispute their guilt on the ground that the motive of the taking was something other than the use of the conveyance as such.

The short answer, we think, is that where as here, a conveyance is taken and moved in a way which necessarily involves its use as a conveyance, the taker cannot be heard to say that the taking was not for that use. If he has in fact taken the conveyance and used it as such, his motive in so doing is, as Mr Matheson submits, quite immaterial. It follows, in our judgment, that the trial judge was right, not only to reject the submission of no case, but also to direct the jury, as he did, that on the undisputed facts the appellant had taken the Land Rover for his own use. Accordingly the appeal will be dismissed.

Appeal Dismissed

McKnight v Davies [1974] RTR 4, Queen's Bench Division
(Lord Widgery CJ, Bridge and May JJ)

Lord Widgery CJ . . . The justices convicted the defendant and found the following facts. The defendant was employed as a lorry driver. His duty was to deliver goods from his employer's depot to shops, and on completion of deliveries to return the lorry to the depot. On the evening of 30 November 1972 the defendant, having completed his deliveries, was driving the lorry back to the depot when the roof of the lorry struck a low bridge. When he saw the damage to the lorry he was scared, and he drove it to a public house and had a drink. After that he drove three men to their homes on the outskirts of Cardiff, drove back to the centre of the city and had a drink at another public house, and then drove to the area where he lived and parked the lorry near his home. He drove the lorry to his employer's depot at 6.20 am on 1 December, the following day.

The question for this court is whether on those relatively simple facts the defendant was guilty of the offence charged.

Section 12 of the Theft Act 1968, so far as relevant, reads:

'(1) Subject to subsections (5) and (6) below, a person shall be guilty of an offence if, without having the consent of the owner or other lawful authority, he takes any conveyance for his own or another's use . . .'

There can, I think, be little doubt that the lorry was being used, following the accident with the bridge, for the defendant's own use, and the argument centres on whether on the facts found he can be said to have 'taken' the conveyance at all.

A similar question arose under s 28 of the Road Traffic Act 1930 in *Mowe v Perraton* [1952] 1 All ER 423. In that case a lorry driver had made an unauthorised deviation from his route in the course of his working day in order to pick up a radiogram and take it to the address of a friend. He had no authority from his employers to use the vehicle for a private purpose of that character, and he was charged with a breach of the corresponding provision in the Road Traffic Act 1930. In this court it was held that he had not committed the offence charged, Lord Goddard CJ pointing out that s 28 of the Act of 1930—and, I quote, 35 Cr App Rep 194 at 196:

'. . . was intended to deal with a case where a person takes a motor car which does not belong to him, drives it away and then abandons it . . . This is a case of a man who took and drove a motor vehicle during his work. What he did was an unauthorised thing, but that does not make the taking or the driving away a criminal offence under section 28.'

That authority on its face suggests that the offence could not be committed by a man who was lawfully entrusted with a vehicle for a limited purpose, but subsequently used it in excess of the purpose for which it had been given to him.

The point was next raised in this court in *Wibberley* [1966] 2 QB 214, [1965] 3 All ER 718, where a driver employed to drive a vehicle had taken it home at the end of the day and parked it outside his house. It was within the authority of his employers to leave the vehicle outside overnight instead of taking it back to the depot. Having so parked it, and after an interval, the defendant took the vehicle out on a private mission of his own, and it was held that he was properly convicted of taking the vehicle for the purpose of the present legislation. The earlier decision in *Mowe v Perraton* [1952] 1 All ER 423 was distinguished on the footing that, since the driver had finished his working day and parked the vehicle in the place where it should be parked for the night, it was possible to say that when he returned to the vehicle and began to drive it he had taken it for present purposes.

The third authority to which I would refer is *Phipps, McGill* [1970] RTR 209, a decision of the Court of Appeal. That case fell to be decided under s 12 of the Theft Act 1968, and I will read the headnote, in (1970) 54 Cr App Rep 301:

> 'Where a defendant has been given permission by the owner of a motor vehicle to take and use it for a limited purpose, but on the completion of that purpose fails to return it and thereafter uses it without any reasonable belief that the owner would consent, the defendant is guilty of taking the vehicle without the consent of the owner, contrary to s 12 of the Theft Act 1968.'

That decision, as I understand it, is inconsistent with the judgment of Lord Goddard CJ, in *Mowe v Perraton* [1952] 1 All ER 423. In *Phipps, McGill* [1970] RTR 209 the Court of Appeal clearly rejected the argument that a lawful acquisition of possession or control of the vehicle meant that an unauthorised use by the driver could never amount to a taking for the purpose of s 12.

In my judgment we must choose between those two decisions, and I have no hesitation in saying that we should follow the decision of the Court of Appeal in *Phipps, McGill* [1970] RTR 209. It is, therefore, not in itself an answer in the present case for the defendant to say that he was lawfully put in control of the vehicle by his employers. The difficulty which I feel is in defining the kind of unauthorised activity on the part of the driver, whose original control of the vehicle is lawful, which will amount to an unlawful taking for the purpose of s 12. Not every brief, unauthorised diversion from his proper route by an employed driver in the course of his working day will necessarily involve a 'taking' of the vehicle for his own use. If, however, as in *Wibberley* [1966] 2 QB 214, [1965] 3 All ER 718, he returns to the vehicle after he has parked it for the night and drives it off on an unauthorised errand, he is clearly guilty of the offence. Similarly, if in the course of his working day, or otherwise while his authority to use the vehicle is unexpired, he appropriates it to his own use in a manner which repudiates the rights of the true owner, and shows that he has assumed control of the vehicle for his own purposes, he can properly be regarded as having taken the vehicle within s 12.

As Professor Smith puts it (in Smith's *Law of Theft*, 2nd edn (1972), p 113) he has

> ' . . . altered the character of his control over the vehicle, so that he no longer held as servant but assumed possession of it in the legal sense.'

In the present case I think that the defendant took the vehicle when he left the first public house. At that point he assumed control for his own purposes in a manner which was inconsistent with his duty to his employer to finish his round and drive the vehicle to the depot. I think that the justices reached the correct conclusion and I would dismiss the appeal.

I am authorised by Bridge J to say that he agrees with the judgment that I have just delivered.

May J. I also agree.

Appeal dismissed

Questions

1. *Bow* Suggests that to fall within the provision the conveyance must be taken for use as a conveyance. In *Pearce* [1973] Crim LR 321, CA, a conviction was upheld where D took an inflatable rubber dinghy from outside a life-boat depot, putting it on a trailer and driving it away. The court rejected D's contention that the conveyance must be moved in its own element, water in this case. Perhaps D had it in mind to use the dinghy as a conveyance at some future stage, but what if he was minded to use it as a paddling pool for his children? Cf *Stokes* [1982] Crim LR 695, CA, where it was held that D did not commit the offence when, as a practical joke, he pushed P's car round the corner so that P would think it had been stolen.

2. In *Bow* Bridge LJ said that clearly there would be cases in which an obstructing vehicle was moved a yard or two which would not involve the use of the vehicle as conveyance. Suppose D lives in a cul-de-sac and finds that P's car obstructs his access to the highway. Is it to make a difference if in order to gain access to the highway D has to move P's car 2 yards, 20 yards or 200 yards?

Whittaker and another v Campbell [1983] 3 All ER 582, Queen's Bench Division (Robert Goff LJ and Glidewell J)

Two brothers, Wilson Coglan Whittaker and Stewart Whittaker, purchased coal at an advantageous price but were required to provide their own means of transport. The former had no driving licence while the latter had only a provisional licence and neither had a vehicle of his own. Somehow they came into the possession of a full driving licence belonging to one Derek Dunn. They then hired a van by W.C. Whittaker representing himself as Derek Dunn and by producing to the hirer the driving licence in that name. The hirer said that he believed W.C. Whittaker to be Derek Dunn and the holder of a full licence; had he known that this was not the case the brothers would not have been allowed to hire any of their vehicles.

The judgment of the court was delivered by:

Robert Goff LJ. . . . The case raises for decision a point of construction of s 12 (1) of the Theft Act 1968, relating to the meaning of the words 'without having the consent of the owner' in the offence which is committed under that subsection if a person, without having the consent of the owner or other lawful authority, takes any conveyance for his own or another's use . . . The justices convicted the two appellants of such an offence. . . .

Before the Crown Court it was contended by the appellants that they had the consent of the owner to take the conveyance, that consent having been given by Mr Robson to the persons with whom he was dealing, namely the appellants, and that consent not having been vitiated by the misrepresentation of Wilson Coglan Whittaker that he was in fact Derek Dunn and the holder of a full driving licence. The misrepresentations as to identity and the holding of a full driving licence were not fundamental so as to vitiate the consent given, but were merely misrepresentations as to the representor's attributes, such as to render a contract voidable and not void ab initio. The mere fact that Mr Robson would not have consented to parting with possession of the vehicle if he had known of the true position was not conclusive against the appellants; nor was the fact that the appellants would not be insured to drive the vehicle.

The respondent, on the other hand, contended that the appellants were guilty of the offence because in law and in fact they did not have the consent of the vehicle owner or other lawful authority to take the vehicle in question. Although the vehicle owner gave his de facto consent to the appellants taking the vehicle, that consent was not a true consent or a consent at all in law or in fact because it was vitiated by the fraudulent misrepresentations as to identity and the holding of a full driving licence made by the appellants which induced the owner to part with possession of his vehicle. These misrepresentations were fundamental to the transaction in that the owner would not have parted with possession had he known of the true position because the hirer would not have been insured to drive the vehicle.

These arguments were repeated and developed in the submissions made by counsel before this court. We, like the Crown Court, were referred to certain authorities, some of which we shall consider later in this judgment. The conclusion of the Crown Court was that the appellants' misrepresentations were fundamental in that the vehicle owner would not have contemplated handing over the vehicle had he known the true position, and that his consent was therefore vitiated by the fraudulent misrepresentation of the appellants. We quote from the case:

> 'The question in the present appeals was whether the vehicle owner gave his consent to the Appellants taking the vehicle. In my opinion he did not. He consented to someone called Derek Dunn with a full driving licence taking the vehicle. I accordingly held that in law the Appellants were guilty of the offence under Section 12(1) of the Theft Act 1968.'

The following questions were stated for the opinion of the court:

> '(1) Whether in law the de facto consent to take a conveyance namely a motor vehicle given by the vehicle owner to a person hiring that vehicle is vitiated by reason of its being induced by the false representations of the person hiring the vehicle as to his identity and the holding of a full driving licence, so that the person taking the vehicle under the contract of hire is guilty of taking a conveyance without the owner's consent or other lawful authority contrary to Section 12(1) of the Theft Act 1968. (2) Whether, on the facts found by me and having regard to the cases cited, the Crown Court was wrong in law in rejecting the appeals of the Appellants.'

We are concerned in the present case with the construction of certain words, viz 'without having the consent of the owner', in their context in a particular subsection of a criminal statute. However, the concept of consent is relevant in many branches of the law, including not only certain crimes but also the law of contract and the law of property. There is, we believe, danger in assuming that the law adopts a uniform definition of the word 'consent' in all its branches. . . .

What is the effect of fraud? Fraud is, in relation to a contract, a fraudulent misrepresentation by one party which induces the other to enter into a contract or apparent contract with the representor. Apart from the innocent party's right to recover damages for the tort of deceit, the effect of the fraud is simply to give the innocent party the right, subject to certain limits, to rescind the contract. These rights are similar to (though not identical with) the rights of a party who has been induced to enter into a contract by an innocent, as opposed to a fraudulent, misrepresentation, though there the right to recover damages derives from statute, and the limits to rescission are somewhat more severe. It is plain, however, that in this context fraud does not 'vitiate consent', any more than an innocent misrepresentation 'vitiates consent'. Looked at realistically, a misrepresentation, whether fraudulent or innocent, induces a party to enter into a contract in circumstances where it may be unjust that the representor should be permitted to retain the benefit (the chose in action) so acquired by him. The remedy of rescission, by which the unjust enrichment of the representor is prevented, though for historical and practical reasons treated in books on the law of contract, is a straightforward remedy in restitution subject to limits which are characteristic of that branch of the law . . .

Similar criteria to those applied in order to ascertain whether property in goods had passed in circumstances such as these were at one time of particular relevance in criminal law. This was because, under the old law of larceny, the crime of larceny as the result of a mistake was only committed if the mistake was sufficient to prevent the property from passing to the accused; and the crime of larceny by a trick was only committed if the accused, having the relevant mens rea, induced the owner to transfer possession of the goods to him, though the owner did not intend to convey the property to the accused. If the owner was induce to convey the property to the accused, the latter could not be guilty of larceny but could be guilty of obtaining by false pretences. The nature of the mistake in cases of larceny as the result of a mistake and the distinction between larceny by a trick and obtaining by false pretences were, not surprisingly, fruitful sources of dispute and of nice distinctions. But one purpose of the Theft Act 1968 was to avoid, as far as possible, problems of this kind. And even under the old law of larceny it could not be said that fraud 'vitiated consent', for the existence of the crime of larceny as the result of a mistake demonstrates that the 'vitiating' of the consent of the owner to part with the property in the goods was not dependent on fraud on the part of the accused.

It is against this background that we turn to the problem in the instant case. There being no general principle that fraud vitiates consent, we see the problem simply as this: can a person be said to have taken a conveyance for his own or another's use 'without having the consent of the owner or other lawful authority' within those words as used in s 12(1) of the Theft Act 1968 if he induces the owner to part with possession of the conveyance by a fraudulent misrepresentation of the kind employed by the appellants in the present case?

Now there is no doubt about the mischief towards which this provision (like its predecessors, ss 28(1) and 217(1) of the Road Traffic Acts 1930 and 1960, respectively) is directed. It is directed against persons simply taking other persons' vehicles for their own purposes, for example, for use in the commission of a crime, or for a joyride, or just to get home, without troubling to obtain the consent of the owner but without having the animus furandi necessary for theft. In the vast majority of circumstances, no approach is made to the owner at all: the vehicle is just taken. But is the crime committed when the owner is approached, and when he is compelled to part with his possession by force, or when he is induced to part with his possession by fraud?

Now it may be that, if the owner is induced by force to part with possession of his vehicle, the offence is committed, because a sensible distinction may be drawn between consent on the one hand and submission to force on the other. This is a point which, however, we do not have to decide, though we comment that, in the generality of such cases the accused is likely to have committed one or more other offences with which he could perhaps be more appropriately charged.

But where the owner is induced by fraud to part with the possession of his vehicle, no such sensible distinction can be drawn. In commonsense terms, he has consented to part with the possession of his vehicle, but his consent has been obtained by the fraud. In such a case no offence under this subsection will have been committed unless, on a true construction, a different meaning is to be placed on the word 'consent' in the subsection. We do not however consider that any such construction is required.

It is to be observed, in the first instance, that the presence or absence of consent would be as much affected by innocent as by fraudulent misrepresentation. We do not however regard this point as persuasive, for the answer may lie in the fact that, where the misrepresentation is innocent, the accused would lack the mens rea which, on the principle in *R v Tolson* (1889) 23 QBD 168, [1886–90] All ER Rep 26, may well be required as a matter of implication (a point which, once again, we do not have to decide). It is also to be observed that the owner's consent may, to the knowledge of the accused, have been self-induced, without any misrepresentation, fraudulent or innocent, on the part of the accused. More compelling, however, is the fact that it does not appear sensible to us that, in cases of fraud, the commission of the offence should depend not on the simple question whether possession of the vehicle had been obtained by fraud but on the intricate question whether the effect of the fraud had been such that it precluded the existence of objective agreement to part with possession of the car, as might for example be the case where the owner was only willing to part with possession to a third party and the accused fraudently induced him to do so by impersonating that third party.

We find it very difficult to accept that the commission of an offence under this subsection should depend on the drawing of such a line, which, having regard to the mischief to which this subsection is directed, appears to us to be irrelevant. The judge in the Crown Court felt it necessary to inquire, on the appeal before him, whether this line had been crossed before he could hold that the appellants had committed the offence. An inquiry of this kind is by no means an easy one, as is demonstrated by, for example, the disagreement on a similar point among the members of the Court of Appeal in *Ingram v Little* [1960] 3 All ER 332, [1961] 1 QB 31, and by the subsequent preference by the Court of Appeal in *Lewis v Averay* [1971] 3 All ER 907, [1972] 1 QB 198, for the dissenting judgment of Devlin LJ in the earlier case. Indeed, we would (had we thought it necessary to do so) have reached a different conclusion on the point from that reached by the judge in the Crown Court in the present case, considering that the effect of the appellants' fraud was not that the owner parted with possession of his vehicle to a different person from the one to whom he intended to give possession but that the owner believed that the person to whom he gave possession had the attribute, albeit a very important attribute, of holding a driving licence. However, on our view of the subsection, the point does not arise.

In circumstances such as those of the present case, the criminality (if any) of the act would appear to rest rather in the fact of the deception, inducing the person to part with the possession of his vehicle, rather than in the fact (if it be the case) that the fraud has the effect of inducing a mistake as to, for example, 'identity' rather than 'attributes' of the deceiver. It would be very strange if fraudulent conduct of this kind has only to be punished if it happened to induce a fundamental mistake; and it would be even more strange if such fraudulent conduct has only to be punished where the chattel in question happened to be a vehicle. If such fraudulent conduct is to be the subject of prosecution, the crime should surely be classified as one of obtaining by deception, rather than an offence under s 12(1) of the 1968 Act, which appears to us to be directed to the prohibition and punishment of a different form of activity. It was suggested to us in argument that, in the present case, the appellants could have been accused of dishonestly obtaining services by deception contrary to s 1(1) of the Theft Act 1978; the submission was that, having regard to the broad definition of 'services' inherent in s 1(2) of the 1978 Act, the hiring of a vehicle could, untypically, be regarded as a form of services. Since we did not hear full argument on the point, we express no opinion on it, commenting only that, in a comprehensive law of theft and related offences, a decision of policy has to be made whether a fraudulent obtaining of temporary possession of a vehicle or other goods should be punishable, irrespective of any of the nice distinctions which the Crown Court felt required to consider in the present case.

We are fortified in our conclusion by the opinion expressed by Sachs LJ in *R v Peart* [1970] 2 All ER 823, [1970] 2 QB 672. In that case, on comparable facts, the Court of Appeal held that no offence had been committed under s 12(1) of the 1968 Act, because the fraudulent misrepresentation did not relate to a fact which was sufficiently fundamental. But Sachs LJ, in delivering the judgment of the court, expressly reserved the question whether, in any case where consent had been induced by fraud, an offence would be committed under the subsection; and it is plain from his comments that he had serious misgivings whether any such offence would be committed in those circumstances ([1970] 2 All ER 823 at 825, [1970] 2 QB 672 at 676). These misgivings we share in full measure, and it is our conclusion that the subsection on its true construction contemplates no such offence.

We wish to add that our judgment is confined to the construction of s 12(1) of the Theft Act 1968. We are not to be understood to be expressing any opinion on the meaning to be attached to the word 'consent' in other parts of the criminal law, where the word must be construed in its own particular context.

It follows that we answer the first question posed for our decision in the negative and the second question in the affirmative, and that the convictions of the appellants under s 12(1) of the Theft Act 1968 will be quashed.

Appeal allowed. Convictions quashed. Leave to appeal to the House of Lords refused.

NOTES AND QUESTIONS

1. In *Peart* [1970] 2 QB 672, [1970] 2 All ER 823, CA, D had persuaded P to lend him a van by saying that he needed it for an urgent appointment in Alnwick and that he would be able to return it by 7.30 pm. In fact D wanted the van for a journey to Burnley where he was found with the van by the police at 9.30 pm. D knew all along that P would not have consented to lending the van for a trip to Burnley but it was held that P's consent was not vitiated by the deception. It should be noted that the court had to consider the situation at 2.30 pm when the van was borrowed in the afternoon since no issue was left to the jury as to whether there might not have been a fresh taking at some time after 2.30 pm. But if D admits, as he did in *Peart*, that it was his intention all along to go to a destination not agreed to by P, why should this not be a taking for his own use from the outset?

2. Assume that in *Whittaker v Campbell* the brothers had told the hirer that they required the van to transport coal and the hirer agreed to this. Supposing the brothers intended all along to transport stolen goods, would they commit the offence?

3. Suppose that in *Cundy v Lindsay* ((1878) 3 App Cas 459, p 431, above) Blenkarn had by his fraud induced Lindsays to deliver a hire car to his premises which Blenkarn then used. Is it to be supposed that Lindsays, who believe they are dealing with their trusted customer Blenkiron, have consented to the use by Blenkarn?

4. 'Conveyance' has been held to connote a mechnical contrivance of some kind; it does not include a horse since this ancient form of transport is not 'constructed or adapted' for the carriage of persons: *Neal v Gribble* (1978) 68 Cr App Rep 9. What of the student who uses a lift reserved for the Vice-Chancellor? What of someone who borrows a parachute? What of someone who borrows another's roller-skates? While pedal cycles are excluded from the definition of conveyance, provision is made in s 12(5) for the taking of them.

5. The offence may be committed not merely by one who takes the conveyance but also by one who, knowing the conveyance has been taken without authority, drives it or allows himself to be carried in or on it. If the taking by D is aided by E then E is a secondary party in the ordinary way, but E is also guilty of the offence where, subsequent to the taking, he becomes aware that it has been taken without consent or other lawful authority and allows himself to be carried in or on it.

6. Blackmail

Theft Act 1968, s 21 and s 34, pp 570, 572, below

Originally the word blackmail was used to describe the tribute paid to Scottish chieftains by landowners in the border countries to secure immunity from raids on their lands. In the early years of its development it seems to have been pretty well coextensive with robbery and attempted robbery (the simplistic money-or-your-life approach) but over the years it has been extended to more subtle forms of extortion. Ordinarily the blackmailer's demand is for money or other property but s 21(2) provides that 'the nature of the act or omission demanded is immaterial'. This is not as far-reaching as may appear because the offence may be committed only where D has a view to gain or an intent to cause loss, and this refers to gain and loss in money or other property. The Theft Act is concerned with the invasion of economic interests so if D by menaces demands, say, sexual favours, other provisions of the criminal law must be looked to.

(1) THE DEMAND

The demand may take any form and may be implicit as well as explicit. The essence of the matter is that D's communication to P, however phrased, conveys to P that a menace will materialise on P's failure to comply.

The offence is committed when D 'makes any . . . demand'. The offence is thus complete when the demand is made irrespective of whether P hears it or understands it as a demand or is not intimidated by it. In *Treacy v DPP* [1971] AC 537, [1971] 1 All ER 110, HL, it was held that a demand is made when it is posted so that D could be convicted of blackmail where his demand, addressed to P in Germany, was posted in England.

(2) MENACES

R v Harry [1974] Crim LR 32, Chelmsford Crown Court
(Judge Francis Petre)

H was indicted on two counts of blackmail. As treasurer of a college rag committee he sent letters to 115 shopkeepers asking them to buy indemnity posters for amounts between £1 and £5, the money to go to charity. The purchase of a poster was to 'protect you from any Rag Activity which could in any way cause you inconvenience'. The letter continued: 'The Committee sincerely hope that you will contribute, as we are sure you will agree that these

charities are worthy causes which demand the support of all the community.'
The poster read 'These premises are immune from all rag '73 activities
whatever they may be.' Fewer than six traders complained about the letter.
None who complained had paid. One witness said in evidence that his
objection was to the veiled threat contained in the words 'protect you from
. . . inconvenience'. The President of the local Chamber of Trade said that he
thought the letter was ill-conceived but that he took no serious view about it;
because it was so loosely worded it was apt to be misconstrued.

The prosecution submitted that the letter contained 'the clearest threat or
menace however nicely it was couched, and that there was no need for direct
evidence that anyone thought it was a threat.'

Defence counsel submitted that there was no or no sufficient evidence to
leave the jury. Not every threat, veiled or otherwise, was within the section
but only if it satisfied the test in *Clear* [1968] 2 WLR 122 at 130 of being 'of
such a nature and extent that the mind of an ordinary person of normal
stability and courage might be influenced or made apprehensive so as to
accede unwillingly to the demand.' There was no evidence from any victim or
possible victim that the letter had that effect at all.

The judge ruled that he was not satisfied there were any menaces within the
definition in *Clear*. That case had stiffened the law as previously laid down in
Thorne v Motor Trade Association [1937] AC 797 at 817. Normally a
demand with menaces was made to one person; in this case it was made to
over 100 people. To some extent one could be guided by their reaction.
Exercising a broad general judgment commonsense indicated that no
menaces had been proved such as fell within the Act. In directing the jury to
return verdicts of not guilty on both counts, Judge Petre said: 'Menaces is a
strong word. You may think that menaces must be of a fairly stern nature to
fall within the definition.'

NOTES AND QUESTIONS

1. In *Thorne v Motor Trade Association* [1937] AC 797, [1937] 3 All ER 157,
HL, Lord Wright said, at 167:

> 'I think the word menace is to be liberally construed, and not as limited to threats
> of violence, but as including threats of any action detrimental to or unpleasant to the
> person addressed. It may also include a warning that, in certain events, such action is
> intended.'

Should menaces in the context of s 21 also receive a 'liberal' construction?

2.   'Words or conduct which would not intimidate or influence anyone to respond to the
demand would not be menaces . . . but threats and conduct of such a nature and extent
that the mind of an ordinary person of normal stability and courage might be influenced
or made apprehensive so as to accede unwillingly to the demand would be sufficient for a
jury's consideration. The demand must be accompanied . . . by menaces . . . There may
be special circumstances unknown to an accused which would make the threats innocuous
and unavailing for the accused's demand, but such circumstances would have no bearing
on the accused's state of mind and his intention. If an accused knew that what he
threatened would have no effect on the victim it might be different.'

— *Clear* [1968] 1 All ER 74 at 80, CA, considering the offence of demanding
with menaces contrary to s 30 of the Larceny Act 1916. See also *Lawrence
and Pomroy* (1971) 57 Cr App R 64, p 491, below.

3. In *Harry* the trial judge pointed out that D's letters had been sent to over 100 people and only a handful had complained. The judge obviously thought that regard must be had to the general reaction. Was the judge directing himself to the right question? The shopkeepers might well have thought themselves capable of dealing with any trouble caused by students but were they not threatened by D with 'action detrimental or unpleasant' to themselves? The majority of shopkeepers did not view the threat seriously but then nor did Wellington when he replied, 'Publish and be damned'. Is it relevant where D makes a demand coupled with a threat of something detrimental or unpleasant to consider whether D knows he is dealing with (a) an unduly timorous soul; (b) a person of ordinary firmness; or (c) the Duke of Wellington who does not know fear?

(3) UNWARRANTED DEMAND

CLRC, Eighth Report, Theft, paras 121–122

The essential feature of the offence will be that the accused demands something with menaces when he knows either that he has no right to make the demand or that the use of the menaces is improper. This, we believe, will limit the offence to what would ordinarily be thought should be included in blackmail. The true blackmailer will know that he has no reasonable grounds for demanding money as the price of keeping his victim's secret: the person with a genuine claim will be guilty unless he believes that it is proper to use the menaces to enforce his claim. It is likely that, as at present, only those kinds of cases which resemble blackmail in the generally accepted sense will be prosecuted. In doubtful cases the test proposed will, we believe, be one which a jury will find easy to apply. Obviously much would depend on the circumstances. The size of the demand may show whether the accused was seeking genuine compensation or merely trying to make money; and a repetition of a demand once met is likely to be strong evidence of the latter. On this test we should expect that Dymond probably (assuming that the facts were as the defence wished to prove), and Bernhard certainly, would easily establish that they believed that they had reasonable grounds for making the demand. Whether they would establish that they believed that the use of the menaces was a proper means of reinforcing the demand would depend on the facts. A deliberate and unjustified refusal to pay a debt might cause a creditor to believe that he could properly threaten to tell the debtor's wife or employer about the debt. A threat to do some harm disproportionate to the amount of a disputed claim would be strong evidence of the absence of any belief in the propriety of the threat.

At first we proposed to include a requirement that a person's belief that he has reasonable grounds for making the demand or that the use of the menaces is proper should be a reasonable belief. There would be a case for this in policy; for it may be thought that a person who puts pressure on another by menaces of a kind which any reasonable person would think ought to be blackmail should not escape liability merely because his moral standard is too low, or his intelligence too limited, to enable him to appreciate the wrongness of his conduct. The requirement might also make the decision easier for a jury; for if they found that the demand was unwarranted or that the menaces were improper, they would not have to consider whether the accused believed otherwise. But we decided finally not to include the requirement. To require that an honest belief, in order to be a defence, should be reasonable would have the result that the offence of blackmail could be committed by mere negligence (for example, in not consulting a lawyer or, as did Bernhard, in consulting the wrong kind of lawyer). The requirement would also be out of keeping with the rest of the Bill, because all the major offences under it depend expressly or by implication on dishonesty. In particular, the provision in clause 2 (1) making it a defence to a charge of theft that the defendant believed that he had the right to deprive the owner does not require that the belief should be reasonable.

NOTES

In the above passage the CLRC refers to the cases of *Dymond* [1920] 2 KB 260, CCA, and *Bernhard* [1938] 2 KB 264, [1938] 2 All ER 140, CCA, both decided under the former law of blackmail. In the former case D wrote to P accusing him of having indecently assaulted her and added, 'I leave this to you to think what you are going to do, paid or gett summons . . . if you don't send to and apologize I shall let everybody knowed in the town it.' In the latter case P, some time after D had ceased to be his mistress, promised her money but later failed to honour his promise. D was informed, incorrectly, that she was legally entitled to the money but having been refused payment she threatened to expose him to his wife and to the Press.

'Blackmail' by Sir Brian MacKenna [1966] Crim LR 467 at 468

4. The two issues, the reasonableness of the grounds and the propriety of using menaces, are each to be decided by a subjective test. In other words the question for the jury will be whether the defendant believed that he had reasonable grounds and that it was proper to use the menaces. Had the test been objective the question would have been whether the jury, as reasonable men, believed that the defendant's grounds were reasonable and that his menaces were properly used.
5. A man's belief that he has reasonable grounds for making a demand depends on two matters:
(a) his belief that the facts of the case are such-and-such; and
(b) his opinion upon these facts that it would be reasonable to make the demand.
In a particular case one man's belief that there are reasonable grounds for making a demand may differ from another's because of a difference in their beliefs about the facts (one believing the facts to be X, the other to be Y), or because of a difference in their opinions upon the same facts (one opining that those facts give a reasonable ground for making the demand, the other that they do not).
6. 'Reasonable grounds' in clause 17 (1) (a) cannot be limited to such as are believed to give a legally enforceable claim. To many it would seem reasonable to demand satisfaction of a claim recognised by the law as valid though unenforceable by legal action for some technical reason, such as the want of a writing or the expiration of the period of limitation. To some it would seem equally reasonable to demand payment of a claim incapable in any circumstances of being enforced by action, such as the claim to be paid a winning bet. There may be many other cases in which a moral, as distinct from a legal right, would seem to some at least a reasonable ground for making a demand. On these questions there could be differences of opinion, particularly as to whether on the facts of the case the person demanding had a moral right to the thing demanded. There could be similar 'moral' differences about the propriety of using threats.
7. The Committee intend that the test shall be subjective in both the respects indicated in 5 above: (i) the facts shall be taken to be those which the defendant believed to exist, and (ii) his opinion as to whether those facts gave him a reasonable ground for making a demand (or made it proper for him to use threats) will be the only relevant one. His own moral standards are to determine the rightness or wrongness of his conduct. This appears from a sentence in paragraph 122 where the Committee discuss (and dismiss) the possible objection to clause 17 (1) that 'it may be thought that a person who puts pressure on another by menaces of a kind which any reasonable person would think ought to be blackmail should not escape liability merely because his moral standard is too low, or his intelligence too limited, to enable him to appreciate the wrongness of his conduct.'
8. That a sane man's guilt or innocence should depend in this way on his own opinion as to whether he is acting rightly or wrongly is, I think, an innovation in our criminal law.
9. The claim of right which excuses a taking that might otherwise be theft under s 1 of the Larceny Act 1916, may of course be a mistaken claim, and the mistake may be one of law or of fact. A man's mistaken belief that the rules of the civil law make him the owner of a certain thing is as good an excuse as his mistaken belief that the thing is X when it is in fact Y. But clause 17 (1) goes further than this, and gives efficacy to the defendant's moral judgments whatever they may be. That is surely something different. It is one thing to hold that the defendant is excused if he believes the civil law to be X when it is Y. It is another to excuse him in any case where he thinks that what he is doing is morally right, though according to ordinary moral notions he may be doing something very wrong.

10. Dr Glanville Williams observes [*Criminal Law, General Part,* 2nd edn, p 100] that negligence has an objective meaning in the law of tort, and that the same rule prevails in criminal law. I am sure that this is so. If it is, then the analogy is much against the proposed new rule for blackmail. If on a charge of manslaughter by negligence it is no defence for the defendant to prove that he thought it reasonable to act as he did in a case where the ordinary man would think his conduct unreasonable, why should a different rule prevail in blackmail?

11. The Committee give their reasons in paragraph 118 which I shall now examine (I have numbered the sentences for convenient reference):

'118. [1] As to the illegality of making the demand we are decidedly of the opinion that the test should be subjective, namely whether the person in question honestly believes that he has the right to make the demand. [2] This means in effect adopting the test whether there is a claim of right, as in 1916 s 30 and not the test whether there is in fact a reasonable cause for making the demand, as in 1916 s 29 (1) (i). [3] Since blackmail is in its nature an offence of dishonesty, it seems wrong that a person should be guilty of the offence by making a demand which he honestly believes to be justified. [4] Moreover to adopt the objective test seems to involve almost insuperable difficulty. [5] It would be necessary either to set out the various kinds of demands which it was considered should be justified or to find an expression which would describe exactly these kinds but not others. [6] The former course might in theory be possible; but the provision would have to be very elaborate, and it would involve the risk which attends any attempt to list different kinds of conduct for the purpose of a criminal offence—that of including too much or too little. [7] Moreover, there is much room for disagreement as to what kinds of demand should or should not be treated as justified. [8] The latter course seems impossible having regard to the results which have followed from making liability depend on the absence of a 'reasonable or probable cause'. [9] Any general provision would probably have to use some such uninformative expression, and it would be almost bound to cause similar difficulty and uncertainty.'[Similar reasons are said to justify clause 17 (1) (b), op cit para 120.]

12. Sentences [1] to [3] must be read with the following passage from paragraph 122 in which the Committee justify their rejection of the requirement that the defendant's belief as to the reasonableness of his grounds should be a reasonable one:

'The requirement would also be out of keeping with the rest of the Bill, because all the major offences under it depend expressly or by implication on dishonesty. In particular, the provision in clause 2 (1) making it a defence to a charge of theft that the defendant believed that he had the right to deprive the owner does not require that the belief should be reasonable.'. . .

13. In paragraph 118 the Committee apparently treat as one and the same thing the defendant's belief that he has a legal right to that which is demanded and his belief that he has reasonable grounds for demanding it. But the two things are different, as I have tried to show in 7 an 9 above. The difference is between mistaking the law and making a wrong moral judgment. Clause 2 (1) would be analogous to clause 17 (1) only if it provided that the appropriation of anything should not be theft if the person making the appropriation thought it reasonable to do so. That is not what clause 2 (1) provides.

14. Sentence [5] states the draftsman's alternatives, either to express his thought in general or in particular terms. Sentences [6] and [7] point out the objection to the use of particular terms: (a) too much or too little may be included, and (b) those listing the cases which are to be included may have difficulty in agreeing about them. Sentences [8] and [9] point out the objection to the use of general terms: there may be difficulty in interpreting them, the kind of difficulty which caused the disagreement between the Court of Criminal Appeal in *Denyer* [1926] 2 KB 258 and the Court of Appeal in *Hardie and Lane Ltd v Chilton* [1928] 2 KB 306]. Sentence [4] suggests that all these difficulties may be eliminated by the use of a subjective test. But is this so? Whether the justification for the demand is to be (a) the existence of a state of things (the objective test), or (b) the defendant's belief that that state of things exists (the subjective test), the draftsman must still describe the state of things, using either general or particular terms to do so. Whether the form of the enactment is 'if X exists' or 'if X is believed to exist', X must still be given a value, and there is no means of doing this except by words, which must be either general or particular.

15. The objections to the use of general terms are not fully stated in sentences [8] and [9]. As in the case of particular terms, there is a danger of too much or too little being included. If when general words are used there are fewer disagreements among the drafting committee about particular cases, it can only be that the members understand the same general words in different senses or that in choosing those words they do not advert to the particular cases which the words may (or may not) include. These are not necessarily good things.

16. The Committee's solution is to choose the most general expressions ('reasonable grounds' in (a) and 'proper means' in (b)) and to make the defendant himself the judge of what are

'reasonable grounds' under (a) and of what is a 'proper means' under (b). This solution perhaps reduces the possibility of disagreement at the drafting stage and certainly eliminates it at any subsequent stage. When Denyer decides for himself what is reasonable or proper, there is no possibility of any conflict on the point between the two Courts of Appeal. Though this may be convenient, there are disadvantages. These are twofold. If a defendant has acted disgracefully by making a certain demand reinforced by threats of a particular kind, I see no injustice in holding him responsible in a criminal court, even though he may have acted according to his own standard in these matters. On the other hand I see some danger to our general standards of right and wrong if each man can claim to act according to his own, however low that standard may be. That is one objection. Another is the difficulty of the jury's ascertaining the defendant's standard, so that it may be decided whether in the case before them he acted in accordance with it. A man whose standard is below the general may fail in a particular case to observe even his own standard in which event he would, I suppose, be punishable under clause 17. (What is the position to be if his standard is above the general and he does not act in accordance with it?) But are questions of this kind triable?

R v Harvey, Uylett and Plummer, (1980) 72 Cr App Rep 139, Court of Appeal (Shaw LJ, Wien and Bingham JJ)

The appellants had entered into a supposed transaction with a rogue named Scott, the basis of which was that Scott would procure a large quantity of cannabis for a sum in excess of £20,000. Scott had no intention of supplying the cannabis but he produced a purported sample, which was in fact cannabis and followed that up by delivering what turned out to be a load of rubbish. The appellants were accountable to others who had made their contribution to the £20,000 and were much enraged. They then kidnapped Scott's wife and small child. They also kidnapped Scott and subjected him to threats of what would happen to him, and his wife and child, if he did not give them their money back. The appellants were convicted of various offences against the person and of blackmail. The judgment of the court was delivered by:

Bingham J. Section 21 (1) of the Theft Act 1968 is in these terms:

'A person is guilty of blackmail if, with a view to gain for himself or another or with intent to cause loss to another, he makes any unwarranted demand with menaces; and for this purpose a demand with menaces is unwarranted unless the person making it does so in the belief—(a) that he has reasonable grounds for making the demand; and (b) that the use of the menaces is a proper means of reinforcing the demand.'

The learned judge in his direction to the jury quoted the terms of the subsection and then continued as follows:

'Now where the defence raise this issue, in other words, where they say that the demand is warranted and where they say they believe they had reasonable cause for making the demand and that the use of the menaces was a proper way of reinforcing the demand, it is for the prosecution to negative that allegation. It is not for the defendants to prove it once they have raised it. It is for the prosecution to prove that they had no such belief. Now is that clear? It is not easy and I do not want to lose you on the way. It has been raised in this case so you have got to ask yourself this. Has the prosecution disproved that these defendants or those who have raised the matter believed that they had *reasonable* grounds for making the demand? Certainly you may say to yourselves that they had been ripped off to the tune of £20,000. They had been swindled . . . As I say, on this question of reasonable ground for making a demand, you may say to yourselves: 'Well, they did have reasonable ground for making the demand in this sense, that they had put money into this deal, they had been swindled by Scott, and it was reasonable to demand the return of their money.' So you may say: 'Well, the prosecution have not negatived that but what about the second leg of the proviso the belief that the use of menaces is a proper method of reinforcing the demand?' Now it is for you to decide what, if any, menaces were made, because that is a question of evidence. If you decide that the threats or menaces made by these accused, or any of them, were to kill or to maim or to rape, or any of the other matters that have been mentioned in evidence—I mention about three that come into my mind—then those menaces or threats are threats to commit a criminal act, a threat to murder, a threat to rape, or a threat to blow your legs or kneecaps off, those are threats to commit a criminal offence and surely everybody in this country, including the defendants, knows those are criminal offences. The point is that this is a matter of law. It cannot be a proper means of reinforcing the demand to make threats to commit serious criminal offences. So I say to you that if you look at these two counts of blackmail and you decide that these defendants, or any of them, used menaces, dependent upon the menaces you decide were used, the threats that were used, but if you decide that these threats were made by these men to commit criminal offences against Scott, they cannot be heard to say on this blackmail charge that they had reasonable belief that the use of those threats was a proper method of reinforcing their demand.'

Later, when prosecuting counsel drew attention to the learned judge's erroneous reference to 'reasonable' belief, he added the following:

'I do not think it affects the point I was seeking to make, that where the demand or the threat is to commit a criminal offence, and a serious criminal offence like murder and maiming and rape, or whatever it may be, it seems hard for anybody to say that the defendants had a belief that was a proper way of reinforcing their demand. That is the point.'

For the appellants it was submitted that the learned judge's direction, and in particular the earlier of the passages quoted, was incorrect in law because it took away from the jury a question properly falling within their province of decision, namely, what the accused in fact believed. He was wrong to rule as a matter of law that a threat to perform a serious criminal act could never be thought by the person making it to be a proper means. While free to comment on the unlikelihood of a defendant believing threats such as were made in this case to be a proper means, the judge should nonetheless (it was submitted) have left the question to the jury. For the Crown it was submitted that a threat to perform a criminal act can never as a matter of law be a proper means within the subsection, and that the learned judge's direction was accordingly correct. Support for both these approaches is to be found in academic works helpfully brought to the attention of the Court.

The answer to this problem must be found in the language of the subsection, from which in our judgment two points emerge with clarity: (1) The subsection is concerned with the belief of the individual defendant in the particular case: '. . . a demand with menaces is unwarranted unless *the person making it* does so in the belief . . .' (added emphasis). It matters not what the reasonable man, or any man other than the defendant, would believe save in so far as that may throw light on what the defendant in fact believed. Thus the factual question of defendant's belief should be left to the jury. To that extent the subsection is subjective in approach, as is generally desirable in a criminal statute. (2) In order to exonerate a defendant from liability his belief must be that the use of the menaces is a 'proper' means of reinforcing the demand. 'Proper' is an unusual expression to find in a criminal statute. It is not defined in the Act, and no definition need be attempted here. It is, however, plainly a word of wide meaning, certainly wider than (for example) 'lawful.' But the greater includes the less and no act which was not believed to be lawful could be believed to be proper within the meaning of the subsection. Thus no assistance is given to any defendant, even a fanatic or a deranged idealist, who knows or suspects that his threat, or the act threatened, is criminal, but believes it to be justified by his end or his peculiar circumstances. The test is not what he regards as justified, but what he believes to be proper. And where, as here, the threats were to do acts which any sane man knows to be against the laws of every civilised country no jury would hesitate long before dismissing the contention that the defendant genuinely believed the threats to be a proper means of reinforcing even a legitimate demand.

It is accordingly our conclusion that the direction of the learned judge was not strictly correct. If it was necessary to give a direction on this aspect of the case at all (and in the absence of any evidence by the defendants as to their belief we cannot think that there was in reality any live issue concerning it) the jury should have been directed that the demand with menaces was not to be regarded as unwarranted unless the Crown satisfied them in respect of each defendant that the defendant did not make the demand with menaces in the genuine belief both: (a) that he had had reasonable grounds for making the demand; and (b) that the use of the menaces was in the circumstances a proper (meaning for present purposes a lawful, and not a criminal) means of reinforcing the demand.

The learned judge could, of course, make appropriate comment on the unlikelihood of the defendants believing murder and rape or threats to commit those acts to be lawful or other than criminal.

On the facts of this case we are quite satisfied that the misdirection to which we have drawn attention could have caused no possible prejudice to any of the appellants. Accordingly, in our judgment, it is appropriate to apply the proviso to section 2 (1) of the Criminal Appeal Act 1968, and the appeals are dismissed.

Appeals against conviction dismissed.

NOTES AND QUESTIONS

1. In *Lambert* [1972] Crim LR 422, D suspected his wife, W, to be having an affair with P, W's sales manager. D contacted P and informed him that for £250 P could buy D's rights to W and that if P did not accept this offer D would inform P's employer and P's wife of his suspicions. D was charged with blackmail and in directing the jury the trial judge (Deputy Circuit Judge John Arnold) said that a demand was unwarranted unless D made it in the belief that he had reasonable grounds. This did not mean that D's belief be reasonable, only that he honestly thought that it was reasonable. 'The defendant's belief.' the judge continued,

> 'need not be reasonable. The question is whether the defendant held this belief is to ask the question—what did the defendant himself believe? His guilt or innocence depends upon his own opinion whether he was acting rightly or wrongly in the circumstances. . . . The main question in the case was this. Was the demand with menaces unwarranted? Did the defendant honestly believe he had the right on reasonable grounds for making the demand, and did he honestly believe it was proper to reinforce that demand? . . . The prosecution must establish that the defendant did not have that belief. The defendant's guilt or innocence depends on his own opinion as to whether he was acting rightly or wrongly at the time.'

The defendant was acquitted.

2. Is the effect of s 21, as Sir Brian MacKenna suggest, that the defendant's 'own moral standards are to determine the rightness or wrongness of his conduct'?

3. No doubt a lawyer (and even the ordinary man in the street?) would have appreciated in *Harvey* that the defendants were not in law entitled to recover the £20,000 paid for the cannabis. But the court said that it was for the jury to determine as a matter of fact whether they believed their demand to be reasonable. How is the jury to set about this task? How can a jury answer the question: in what circumstances may a person involved in illegal drug trafficking believe that it is reasonable to recover a payment for drugs not delivered? Is not the only possible answer: Never?

4. The court in *Harvey* appears to assume that if D knows that his menace constitutes a threat of action that is criminal then the menace is necessarily improper. Why? If the reasonableness of his demand, however divorced from legal niceties, is to be judged as a matter of fact, why not the menace? If the standards of the Mafia are to be accepted in relation to what they consider to be a reasonable demand, why should not their standards be equally applicable to what they consider to be a proper menace?

(4) VIEW TO GAIN OR INTENT TO CAUSE LOSS

Normally the blackmailer intends a gain to himself and a loss to the victim but either will suffice. D may commit blackmail where he secures employment by P through menaces though his intention is to restore the failing fortunes of

P's firm. Conversely D might by menaces cause P to do something, revoke a will for example, which confers no benefit on D but causes loss to others.

A question which arises here is whether D has an intent to gain or cause loss where he has, or believes he has, a claim of right to the property demanded. In *Lawrence and Pomroy* (1971) 57 Cr App Rep 64, D and E were convicted of blackmail where they threatened to use force in order to collect a debt owed for roofing repairs effected by D. That D may have had a claim of right to the money demanded was not discussed but in *Parkes* [1973] Crim LR 358, the trial judge (Judge Dean QC) rejected a submission that D could not be guilty of blackmail where by menaces he demanded what was lawfully owing to him.

A person cannot be convicted of theft nor of robbery where he appropriated property under a claim of legal right (p 437, above). The CLRC characterised blackmail as an offence of dishonesty but, if so, does s 21 carry out their intentions? Is there an invasion of P's economic interests where D demands that P pay a debt that is due or believed to be due? In *Robinson* [1977] Crim LR 173, CA, p 450, above, D could not be convicted of robbery. But can he be convicted of blackmail?

(5) UNLAWFUL HARASSMENT OF DEBTORS

Administration of Justice Act 1970, s 40, p 572, below

Payne Committee Report, 1969, Cmnd 3909, paras 1231–1234 (footnotes omitted)

Under the present law, so long as no unlawful means are employed, no restrictions are placed upon the creditor or his representative resorting to any device to obtain payment of his debt; and even if the device is unfair, callous or wicked there is no protection for the debtor nor sanction against the creditor. The result is that comparatively little is known about the various reprehensible forms of pressure which are employed or about their harmful effect on debtors and their families.

1232. We have received factual information from the John Hilton Bureau of the *News of the World* which cites several kinds of pressure by debt collectors against readers of that newspaper:
(i)   'the blue frightener', ie a printed notice of intention to institute proceedings in a county court but printed in black letters on blue paper so as to simulate a county court summons;
(ii) 'the red frightener', ie a printed notice with large red letters on white paper under the rubric 'You have four days in which to reduce your debt';
(iii) frequent calls at the home of the debtor leaving threatening cards;
(iv) informing neighbours of the debtor about the indebtedness of the debtor under the guise of seeking information;
(v) informing local shopkeepers of the indebtedness of the debtor under the guise of seeking information;
(vi) threatening to paint over a motor car with the statement that it is the property of the creditor;
(vii) writing to the employer of the debtor about his indebtedness under the guise of avoiding the need for the debtor to absent himself from work to attend court;
(viii) threats to send a 'Bad Debt Collection Van', ie a van with the words 'Bad Debt Collection' painted in large letters on the side, to make a personal call on the debtor at his home or place of employment.
1233. Through the kindness of the Independent Television Authority we saw a documentary film entitled 'Easy Credit Bad Debts' which had been shown as part of the normal Independent Television programme. This film showed two forms of extra-judicial pressure:
(i)   visiting the home of the debtor in the early hours of the morning, even on Sunday morning under the guise of collecting chattels let under a hire purchase agreement; and
(ii) implied threat to use force under the guise that any force used against the collector would be met by force.
1234. We have also material from other sources showing that other forms of pressure are

used. They include visiting the debtor at his place of work, calling on a shopkeeper/debtor and demanding payment in the presence of his customers, calling with an alsatian dog to collect from the debtor, sending obvious demand notes for debts but wrongly addressed to the debtor's neighbours, threatening to paint the debtor's premises, and other similar measures of intimidation.

Questions

1. Is it now true to say that 'so long as no unlawful means are employed, no restrictions are placed upon the creditor .'. . resorting to any device to obtain payment'? And is it correct to say that there is no sanction against the creditor even if his device is 'unfair, callous or wicked'?

2. Which, if any, of the illustrations given by the Payne Committee of debt collecting practices would amount to blackmail?

7. Burglary

Theft Act 1968, s 9, p 567, below

R v Collins [1972] 2 All ER 1105, Court of Appeal, Criminal Division
(Edmund Davies, Stephenson LJJ and Boreham J)

[**Edmund Davies LJ** delivered the judgment of the court:]

This is about as extraordinary a case as my brethren and I have ever heard either on the Bench or while at the Bar, Stephen William George Collins was convicted on 29 October 1971 at Essex Assizes of burglary with intent to commit rape and he was sentenced to 21 months' imprisonment. He is a 19 year old youth, and he appeals against that conviction by the certificate of the trial judge. The terms in which that certificate is expressed reveals that the judge was clearly troubled about the case and the conviction.

Let me relate the facts. Were they put into a novel or portrayed on the stage, they would be regarded as being so improbable as to be unworthy of serious consideration and as verging at times on farce. At about two o'clock in the early morning of Saturday, 24 July 1971, a young lady of 18 went to bed at her mother's home in Colchester. She had spent the evening with her boyfriend. She had taken a certain amount of drink, and it may be that this fact affords some explanation of her inability to answer satisfactorily certain crucial questions put to her. She has the habit of sleeping without wearing night apparel in a bed which is very near the lattice-type window of her room. At one stage in her evidence she seemed to be saying that the bed was close up against the window which, in accordance with her practice, was wide open. In the photographs which we have before us, however, there appears to be a gap of some sort between the two, but the bed was clearly quite near the window. At about 3.30 to 4.00 am she awoke and she then saw in the moonlight a vague form crouched in the open window. She was unable to remember, and this is important, whether the form was on the outside of the window sill or on that part of the sill which was inside the room, and for reasons which will later become clear, that seemingly narrow point is of crucial importance. The young lady then realised several things: first of all that the form in the window was that of a male; secondly that he was a naked male; and thirdly that he was a naked male with an erect penis. She also saw in the moonlight that his hair was blond. She thereupon leapt to the conclusion that her boyfriend, with whom for some time she had been on terms of regular and frequent sexual intimacy, was paying her an ardent nocturnal visit. She promptly sat up in bed, and the man descended from the sill and joined her in bed and they had full sexual intercourse. But there was something about him which made her think that things were not as they usually were between her and her boyfriend. The length of his hair, his voice as they had exchanged what was described as 'love talk', and other features led her to the conclusion that somehow there was something different. So she turned on the bed-side light, saw that her companion was not her boyfriend and slapped the face of the intruder, who was none other than the appellant. He said to her, 'Give me a good time tonight', and got hold of her arm, but she bit him and told him to go. She then went into the bathroom and he promptly vanished.

The complainant said that she would not have agreed to intercourse if she had known that the person entering her room was not her boyfriend. But there was no suggestion of any force having been used on her, and the intercourse which took place was undoubtedly effected with no resistance on her part.

The appellant was seen by the police at about 10.30 am later that same morning. According to the police, the conversation which took place then elicited these points: He was very lustful the previous night. He had taken a lot of drink, and we may here note that drink (which to him is a very real problem) had brought this young man into trouble several times before, but never for an offence of this kind. He went on to say that he knew the complainant because he had worked around her house. On this occasion, desiring sexual intercourse—and according to the police evidence he had added that he was determined to have a girl, by force if necessary, although that part of the police evidence he challenged—he went on to say that he walked around the house, saw a light in an upstairs bedroom, and he knew that this was the girl's bedroom. He found a step ladder, leaned it against the wall and climbed up and looked into the bedroom. What he could see inside through the wide open window was a girl who was naked and asleep. So he descended the ladder and stripped off all his clothes, with the exception of his socks, because apparently he took the view that if the girl's mother entered the bedroom it would be easier to effect a rapid escape if he had his socks on than if he was in his bare feet. That is a matter about which we are not called on to express any view, and would in any event find ourselves unable to express one. Having undressed, he then climbed the ladder and pulled himself up on to the window sill. His version of the matter is that he was pulling himself in when she awoke. She then got up and knelt on the bed, she put her arms around his neck and body, and she seemed to pull him into the bed. He went on:

> '. . . I was rather dazed, because I didn't think she would want to know me. We kissed and cuddled for about ten or fifteen minutes and then I had it away with her but found it hard because I had so much to drink.'

The police officer said to the appellant:

> 'It appears that it was your intention to have intercourse with this girl by force if necessary and it was only pure coincidence that this girl was under the impression that you were her boyfriend and apparently that is why she consented to allowing you to have sexual intercourse with her.'

It was alleged that he then said:

> 'Yes, I feel awful about this. It is the worst day of my life, but I know it could have been worse.'

Thereupon the officer said to him—and the appellant challenged this—'What do you mean, you know it could have been worse?' to which he is alleged to have replied:

> 'Well, my trouble is drink and I got very frustrated. As I've told you I only wanted to have it away with a girl and I'm only glad I haven't really hurt her.'

Then he made a statement under caution, in the course of which he said:

> 'When I stripped off and got up the ladder I made my mind up that I was going to try and have it away with this girl. I feel terrible about this now, but I had too much to drink. I am sorry for what I have done.'

In the course of his testimony, the appellant said that he would not have gone into the room if the girl had not knelt on the bed and beckoned him into the room. He said that if she had objected immediately to his being there or to his having intercourse he would not have persisted. While he was keen on having sexual intercourse that night, it was only if he could find someone who was willing. He strongly denied having told the police that he would, if necessary, have pushed over some girl for the purpose of having intercourse.

There was a submission of no case to answer on the ground that the evidence did not support the charge, particularly that ingredient of it which had reference to entry into the house 'as a trespasser'. But the submission was overruled, and, as we have already related, he gave evidence.

Now, one feature of the case which remained at the conclusion of the evidence in great obscurity is where exactly the appellant was at the moment when, according to him, the girl manifested that she was welcoming him. Was he kneeling on the sill outside the window or the inner sill? It was a crucial matter, for there were certainly three ingredients that it was incumbent on the Crown to establish. Under s 9 of the Theft Act 1968, which renders a person guilty of burglary if he enters any building or part of a building as a trespasser and with the intention of committing rape, the entry of the appellant into the building must first be proved. Well, there is no doubt about that, for it is common ground that he did enter this girl's bedroom. Secondly, it must be proved that he entered as a trespasser. We will develop that point a little later. Thirdly it must be proved that he entered as a trespasser with intent at the time of entry to commit rape therein.

The second ingredient of the offence—the entry must be as a trespasser—is one which has not, to the best of the our knowledge, been previously canvassed in the courts. Views as to its ambit have naturally been canvassed by the textbook writers, and it is perhaps not wholly irrelevant to recall that those who were advising the Home Secretary before the Theft Bill was presented to Parliament had it in mind to get rid of some of the frequently absurd technical rules which had been built up in relation to the old requirement in burglary of a 'breaking and entering'. The cases are legion as to what this did or did not amount to, and happily it is not now necessary for us to consider them. But it was in order to get rid of those technical rules that a new test was introduced, namely that the entry must be 'as a trespasser'.

What does that involve? According to the learned editors of Archbold [*Criminal Pleading, Evidence and Practice* (37th edn, 1969), p 572, para 1505]:

> 'Any intentional, reckless or negligent entry into a building will, it would appear, constitute a trespass if the building is in the possession of another person who does not consent to the entry. Nor will it make any difference that the entry was the result of a reasonable mistake on the part of the defendant, so far as trespass is concerned.'

If that be right, then it would be no defence for this man to say (and even were he believed in saying), 'Well, I honestly thought that this girl was welcoming me into the room and I therefore entered, fully believing that I had her consent to go in'. If Archbold is right, he would nevertheless be a trespasser, since the apparent consent of the girl was unreal, she being mistaken as to who was at her window. We disagree. We hold that, for the purpose of s 9 of the Theft Act 1968, a person entering a building is not guilty of trespass if he enters without knowledge that he is trespassing or at least without acting recklessly as to whether or not he is unlawfully entering.

A view contrary to that of the learned editors of Archbold was expressed in Professor J.C. Smith's book on *The Law of Theft* [(1968), pp 123, 124, para 462], where, having given an illustration of an entry into premises, the learned author comments:

> 'It is submitted that . . . D should be acquitted on the ground of lack of mens rea. Though, under the civil law, he entered as a trespasser, it is submitted that he cannot be convicted of the criminal offence unless he knew of the facts which caused him to be a trespasser or, at least, was reckless.'

The matter has also been dealt with by Professor Griew [*The Theft Act 1968*, pp 52, 53, para 4–05] who in his work on the Theft Act 1968 had this passage:

> 'What if D wrongly believes that he is not trespassing? His belief may rest on facts which, if true, would mean that he was not trespassing: for instance, he may enter a building by mistake, thinking that it is the one he has been invited to enter. Or his belief may be based on a false view of the legal effect of the known facts: for instance, he may misunderstand the effect of a contract granting him a right of passage through a building. Neither kind of mistake will protect him from tort liability for trespass. In either case, then, D satisfies the literal terms of section 9(1): he "enters . . . as a trespasser." But for the purposes of criminal liability a man should be judged on the basis of the facts as he believed them to be, and this should include making allowances for a mistake as to rights under the civil law. This is another way of saying that a serious offence like burglary should be held to require mens rea in the fullest sense of the phrase: D should be liable for burglary only if he knowingly trespasses or is reckless as to whether he trespasses or not. Unhappily it is common for Parliament to omit to make clear whether mens rea is intended to be an element in a statutory offence. It is also, though not equally, common for the courts to supply the mental element by construction of the statute.'

We prefer the view expressed by Professor Smith and Professor Griew to that of the learned editors of Archbold. In the judgment of this court, there cannot be a conviction for entering premises 'as a trespasser' within the meaning of s 9 of the Theft Act 1968 unless the person entering does so knowing that he is a trespasser and nevertheless deliberately enters, or, at the very least, is reckless whether or not he is entering the premises of another without the other party's consent.

Having so held, the pivotal point of this appeal is whether the Crown established that the appellant at the moment that he entered the bedroom knew perfectly well that he was not welcome there or, being reckless whether he was welcome or not, was nevertheless determined to enter. That in turn involves consideration as to where he was at the time that the complainant indicated that she was welcoming him into her bedroom. If, to take an example that was put in the course of argument, her bed had not been near the window but was on the other side of the bedroom, and he (being determined to have her sexually even against her will) climbed through the window and crossed the bedroom to reach her bed, then the offence charged would have been established. But in this case, as we have related, the layout of the room was different, and it became a point of nicety which had to be conclusively established by the Crown as to where he was when the girl made welcoming signs, as she unquestionably at some stage did.

How did the learned judge deal with this matter? We have to say regretfully that there was a flaw in his treatment of it. Referring to s 9, he said:

'. . . there are three ingredients. First is the question of entry. Did he enter into that house? Did he enter as a trespasser? That is to say, did he—was the entry, if you are satisfied there was an entry, intentional or reckless? And, finally, and you may think this is the crux of the case as opened to you by [counsel for the Crown], if you are satisfied that he entered as a trespasser, did he have the intention to rape this girl?'

The judge then went on to deal in turn with each of these three ingredients. He first explained what was involved in 'entry' into a building. He then dealt with the second ingredient. But he here unfortunately repeated his earlier observation that the question of entry as a trespasser depended on 'was the entry intentional or reckless?' We have to say that this was putting the matter inaccurately. This mistake may have been derived from a passage in the speech of counsel for the Crown when replying to the submission of 'No case'. Counsel for the Crown at one stage said:

'Therefore, the first thing that the Crown have got to prove, my Lord, is that there has been a trespass which may be an intentional treapass, or it may be a reckless trespass.'

Unfortunately the trial judge regarded the matter as though the second ingredient in the burglary charged was whether there had been an intentional or reckless entry, and when he came to develop this topic in his summing-up that error was unfortunately perpetuated. The trial judge told the jury:

'He had no right to be in that house, as you know, certainly from the point of view of [the girl's mother], but if you are satisfied about entry, did he enter intentionally or recklessly? What the Prosecution say about this is, you do not really have to consider recklessness because when you consider his own evidence he intended to enter that house, and if you accept the evidence I have just pointed out to you, he, in fact, did so. So, at least, you may think, it was intentional. At the least, you may think it was reckless because as he told you he did not know whether the girl would accept him.'

We are compelled to say that we do not think the trial judge by these observations made it sufficiently clear to the jury the nature of the second test about which they had to be satisfied before the appellant could be convicted of the offence charged. There was no doubt that his entry into the bedroom was 'intentional'. But what the appellant had said was, 'She knelt on the bed, she put her arms around me and then I went in'. If the jury thought he might be truthful in that assertion, they would need to consider whether or not, although entirely surprised by such a reception being accorded to him, this young man might not have been entitled reasonably to regard her action as amounting to an invitation to him to enter. If she in fact appeared to be welcoming him, the Crown do not suggest that he should have realised or even suspected that she was so behaving because, despite the moonlight, she thought he was someone else. Unless the jury were entirely satisfied that the appellant made an effective and substantial entry into the bedroom without the complainant doing or saying anything to cause him to believe that she was consenting to his entering it, he ought not to be convicted of the offence charged. The point is a narrow one, as narrow maybe as the window sill which is crucial to this case. But this is a criminal charge of gravity and, even though one may suspect that his *intention* was to commit the offence charged, unless the facts show with clarity that he in fact committed it he ought not to remain convicted.

Some question arose whether or not the appellant can be regarded as a trespasser ab initio. But we are entirely in agreement with the view expressed in Archbold [*Criminal Pleading, Evidence and Practice* (37th edn, 1969) p 572, para 1505] that the common law doctrine of trespass ab initio has no application to burglary under the Theft Act 1968. One further matter that was canvassed ought perhaps to be mentioned. The point was raised that, the complainant not being the tenant or occupier of the dwelling-house and her mother being apparently in occupation, this girl herself could not in any event have extended an effective invitation to enter, so that even if she had expressly and with full knowledge of all material facts invited the appellant in, he would nevertheless be a trespasser. Whatever be the position in the law of tort, to regard such a proposition as acceptable in the criminal law would be unthinkable.

We have to say that this appeal must be allowed on the basis that the jury were never invited to consider the vital question whether this young man did enter the premises as a trespasser, that is to say knowing perfectly well that he had no invitation to enter or reckless of whether or not his entry was with permission. The certificate of the trial judge, as we have already said, demonstrated that he felt there were points involved calling for further consideration. That consideration we have given to the best of our ability. For the reasons we have stated, the outcome of the appeal is that this young man must be acquitted of the charge preferred against him. The appeal is accordingly allowed and his conviction quashed.

Appeal allowed. Conviction quashed

R v Jones, R v Smith [1976] 3 All ER 54, Court of Appeal, Criminal Division (James, Geoffrey Lane LJJ and Cobb J)

Two television sets were removed in the early hours of the morning from the home in Farnborough of Mr Alfred Smith without his knowledge or consent. The sets were subsequently found in the possession of the appellants, Christopher Smith (who lived in Arborfield and was the son of Alfred Smith) and his friend John Jones. At their trial for burglary Alfred Smith said that Christopher would not be a trespasser in his house at any time. The appellants were convicted of burglary.

[James LJ delivered the judgment of the court:]

. . . The next ground of appeal relied on by counsel for the appellants in his argument is that which is put forward as the first ground in each of the appellant's grounds. It is the point on which counsel had laid the greatest stress in the course of his argument. The argument is based on the wording of the Theft Act 1968, s 9(1) [his Lordship read s 9(1)]. . . .

The important words from the point of view of the argument in this appeal are 'having entered any building . . . as a trespasser'.

It is a section of an Act of Parliament which introduces a novel concept. Entry as a trespasser was new in 1968 in relation to criminal offences of burglary. It was introduced in substitution for, as an improvement on, the old law, which required considerations of breaking and entering and involved distinctions of nicety which had bedevilled the law for some time.

Counsel for the appellants argues that a person who had a general permission to enter premises of another person cannot be a trespasser. His submission is as short and as simple as that. Related to this case he says that a son to whom a father has given permission generally to enter the father's house cannot be a trespasser if he enters it even though he had decided in his mind before making the entry to commit a criminal offence of theft against the father once he had got into the house and had entered that house solely for the purpose of committing that theft. It is a bold submission. Counsel frankly accepts that there has been no decision of the court since this Act was passed which governs particularly this point. He had reminded us of the decision in *Byrne v Kinematograph Renters Society Ltd*[1], which he prays in aid of his argument. In that case persons had entered a cinema by producing tickets not for the purpose of seeing the show, but for an ulterior purpose. It was held in the action, which sought to show that they entered as trespassers pursuant to a conspiracy to trespass, that in fact they were not trespassers. The important words in the judgment are[2]: 'They did nothing that they were not invited to do . . .' That provides a distinction between that case and what we consider the position to be in this case.

Counsel has also referred us to one of the trickery cases, *Boyle*[3], and in particular to a passage in the judgment of that case[4]. He accepts that the trickery cases can be distinguished from such a case as the present because in the trickery cases it can be said that that which would otherwise have been consent to enter was negatived by the fact that consent was obtained by a trick. We do not gain any help in the particular case from that decision.

We were also referred to *Collins*[5] and in particular to the long passage of Edmund Davies LJ[6] where he commenced the consideration of what is involved by the words 'the entry must be "as a trespasser" '. Again it is unnecessary to cite that long passage in full; suffice it to say that this court on that occasion expressly approved the view expressed in Professor Smith's book on the

Law of Theft[7], and also the view of Professor Griew[8] in his publication on the Theft Act 1968 on this aspect of what is involved in being a trespasser.

In our view the passage there referred to is consonant with the passage in the well-known case of *Hillen and Pettigrew v ICI (Alkali) Ltd*[9] where, in the speech of Lord Atkin, these words appear:

'My Lords, in my opinion this duty to an invitee only extends so long as and so far as the invitee is making what can reasonably be contemplated as an ordinary and reasonable use of the premises by the invitee for the purposes for which he has been invited. He is not invited to use any part of the premises for purposes which he knows are wrongfully dangerous and constitute an improper use. As Scrutton LJ has pointedly said[10]: "When you invite a person into your house to use the staircase you do not invite him to slide down the banisters." '

That case of course was a civil case in which it was sought to make the defendant liable for a tort.

The decision in *Collins* in this court, a decision on the criminal law, added to the concept of trespass as a civil wrong only the mental element of mens rea, which is essential to the criminal offence. Taking the law as expressed in *Hillen and Pettigrew v ICI (Alkali) Ltd* and in *Collins*, it is our view that a person is a trespasser for the purpose of s 9(1)(b) of the Theft Act 1968 if he enters premises of another knowing that he is entering in excess of the permission that has been given to him, or being reckless whether he is entering in excess of the permission that has been given to him to enter, providing the facts are known to the accused which enable him to realise that he is acting in excess of the permission given or that he is acting recklessly as to whether he exceeds that permission, then that is sufficient for the jury to decide that he is in fact a trespasser.

In this particular case it was a matter for the jury to consider whether, on all the facts, it was shown by the prosecution that the appellants entered with the knowledge that entry was being effected against the consent or in excess of the consent that had been given by Mr Alfred Smith to his son Christopher. The jury were, by their verdict, satisfied of that. It was a novel argument that we heard, interesting but one without, in our view, any foundation. . . .

Finally, before parting with the matter, we would refer to a passage of the summing-up to the jury which I think one must read in full. In the course of that the recorder said:

'I have read out the conversations they had with Detective Sergeant Tarrant and in essence Smith said, "My father gave me leave to take these sets and Jones was invited along to help." If that account may be true, that is an end of the case, but if you are convinced that that night they went to the house and entered as trespassers and had no leave or licence to go there for that purpose and they intended to steal these sets and keep them permanently themselves, acting dishonestly, then you will convict them. Learned counsel for the prosecution did mention the possibility that you might come to the conclusion that they had gone into the house with leave or licence of the father and it would be possible for you to bring in a verdict simply of theft but, members of the jury, of course it is open to you to do that if you felt that the entry to the house was as a consequence of the father's leave or licence, but what counts of course for the crime of burglary to be made out is the frame of mind of each person when they go into the property. If you go in intending to steal, then your entry is burglarious, it is to trespass because no one gave you permission to go in and steal in the house.'

Then the recorder gave an illustration of the example of a person who is invited to go into a house to make a cup of tea and that person goes in and steals the silver and he went on:

'I hope that illustrates the matter sensibly. Therefore you may find it difficult not to say, if they went in there they must have gone in order to steal because they took elaborate precautions, going there at dead of night, you really cannot say that under any circumstances their entry to the house could have been other than trespass.'

In that passage that I have just read the recorder put the matter properly to the jury in relation to the aspect of trespass and on this ground of appeal as on the others we find that the case is not made out, that there was not misdirection, as I have already indicated early in the judgment, and in those circumstances the appeal will be dismissed in the case of each of the appellants.

Appeals dismissed

1. [1958] 2 All ER 579, [1958] 1 WLR 762.
2. [1958] 2 All ER at 593, [1958] 1 WLR at 776, per Harman J.
3. [1954] 2 QB 292, [1954] 2 All ER 721.
4. [1954] 2 QB at 295, [1954] 2 All ER at 721, 722.

5. [1973] QB 100, [1972] 2 All ER 1105.
6. [1973] QB at 104, [1972] 2 All ER at 1109, 1110.
7. (1968) pp 123, 124, para 462.
8. (1968) pp 52, 53, para 4-05.
9. [1936] AC 65 at 69, [1935] All ER Rep 555 at 558.
10. *The Carlgarth, The Otarama* [1972] P 93 at 110.

(1) ENTRY

In *Collins* Edmund Davies LJ said that the entry must be 'substantial and effective' but did not expand on this. At common law any insertion of D's body (a finger through an opening) constituted an entry whether that part of the body was inserted as part of the process of entry or to effect a theft. The use of 'substantial' might seem to exclude such a case. In *Brown* [1985] Crim LR 212, CA, it was said that while an entry must be 'effective' it did not help to add 'substantial'. It was held there was an entry where D was found bending through a broken shop window and rummaging inside it. Though his feet may have been on the highway outside it seemed an 'astonishing proposition' to the court that a person could break a shop window, put his hand inside and not be held as having entered as a trespasser. But effective for what purpose? To steal (or commit one of the other ulterior offences) or merely to effect entry? What if D put his arm through a broken window to release a window latch? And what if the only 'entry' is by an implement, a jemmy for instance? Would it make any difference that the jemmy was inserted to break a lock or was used by D to pull goods out of the building? What if Taffy trains his dog to steal the leg of beef?

(2) AS A TRESPASSER

1. What must D know to render him a trespasser for the purpose of burglary?
2. For the purposes of staging a sit-in, students enter the main administrative offices of the university. They believe (wrongly) that, as students of the university, they are entitled to go anywhere on university premises. One of them steals a file from the registry office. Is he a burglar?
3. Dan, who is courting Stella, knows that Peter, Stella's father, has formed a strong dislike for him and has forbidden him ever to enter Peter's house. But, at Stella's invitation, he enters the house one evening without Peter's knowledge. Just before he leaves, Dan steals Peter's riding boots. Is Dan a burglar? Would it make any difference to your answer if Dan had accepted Stella's invitation only because he wished to steal Peter's riding boots?
4. Suppose that in *Jones and Smith* Smith had lived at the Farnborough house with his parents. Would he have been guilty of burglary? Would Jones?
5. 'The decision [in *Jones and Smith*] runs counter to *Collins*, where it must have been held . . . that the defendant was not a trespasser although, since he intended to commit rape if necessary, he knew that his intention was "in excess of the permission." The court in *Jones and Smith* evidently did not realise this aspect of *Collins*. If Jones and Smith is right, Collins should have been convicted of burglary.'—Glanville Williams, *Textbook of Criminal Law*, (2nd edn) at p 849. Do you agree? Cf *Barker* (1983) 57 ALJR 426, High

Court of Australia, where D, asked to look after P's house during P's absence, entered and stole certain goods. His conviction for burglary was upheld. Murphy J, dissenting, said that to regard such a case as one of burglary would depart very far from the traditional concept of burglary; it would mean that one who accepted an invitation to dinner would be guilty of burglary if he intended to steal a teaspoon.

(3) BUILDING OR PART OF A BUILDING

1. In *Stevens v Gourley* (1859) 7 CBNS 99, a question arose whether a wooden structure measuring 16 by 13 feet and intended to be used as a shop was a building for the purposes of the Metropolitan Building Act 1855 though it was not let into the ground and merely rested on timbers laid on the surface. In his judgment Byles J said, at p 112:

> 'The only question is, whether the subject-matter of this contract was a "building" within the fair meaning and contemplation of the act. And that brings us to the very difficult inquiry, What is a "building"? Now, the verb "to build" is often used in a wider sense than the substantive "building". Thus, a ship or a barge-builder is said to build a ship or a barge, a coach-builder to build a carriage; so, birds are said to build nests: but neither of these when constructed can be a "building". It is a well-established rule, that the words of an act of parliament, like those of any other instrument, must if possible be construed according to their ordinary grammatical sense. The imperfection of human language renders it not only difficult, but absolutely impossible, to define the word "building" with any approach to accuracy. One may say of this or that structure, this or that is not a building; but no general definition can be given; and our lexicographers do not attempt it. Without, therefore, presuming to do what others have failed to do, I may venture to suggest, that, by "a building" is usually understood a structure of considerable size, and intended to be permanent, or at least to endure for a considerable time. A church, whether constructed of iron or wood, undoubtedly is a building. So, a "cowhouse" or "stable" has been held to be a building the occupation of which as tenant entitles the party to be registered as a voter under the . . . Reform Act . . . On the other hand, it is equally clear that a bird-cage is not a building, neither is a wig-box, or a dog-kennel, or a hen-coop—the very value of these things being their portability. It seems to me that the structure in question, which was erected for a shop, and is of considerable dimensions, and intended for the use of human creatures, is clearly a "building", in the common and ordinary understanding of the word. If we look at the object and intention of the act, we find that this construction is the only one which will bear it out. The intention—the main intention—was, to prevent the metropolis from being covered with combustible structures. Looking, therefore, at the ordinary meaning of the word, and at the intention of the legislature, I think we are well warranted in coming to the conclusion that this was a "building" within the prohibition of the statute. . .'

It was held in *B and S v Leathley* [1979] Crim LR 314 (Carlisle CC) that a freezer container about 25 feet long and 7 feet square cross section which was resting on railway sleepers in a farmyard was a building. Cf [1986] Crim LR 167

In *Walkington* [1979] 2 All ER 716, CA, D entered the 'counter area' (a rectangle made up from moveable counters which housed a till and which was reserved to staff) of a department store and was there observed to open and shut the till drawer. It was held, upholding D's conviction for burglary, that whether the counter area was sufficient to amount to an area from which the public were excluded was a matter for the jury; there was ample evidence from which the jury could conclude that it was such an area and that D knew it.

2. Does Dan, a law student, commit burglary in any of the following cases?

(i) He enters a telephone kiosk with intent to break open the meter and steal its contents.

(ii) He enters the law library and, seeing that no one is around, he goes behind the library counter and steals a bottle of champagne that the library assistant had brought for her lunch.

(iii) He enters the departmental secretary's room intending to pass through into the office of the Head of Department in order to steal the criminal law examination paper, but is stopped by the secretary before he reaches the office.

(iv) He enters a hall of residence intending to enter any study that might have been left unlocked and in order to steal therein.

(v) He falls asleep in a cinema and wakes to find the building closed. On his way out through the foyer he helps himself to some cigarettes from the kiosk which stands near the entrance.

(vi) Owing to acute pressure on space in the law department, the university has hired a caravan which is placed outside the department and used by Smart, a law lecturer, as his office. Dan enters this caravan and steals a copy of *Russell on Crime*.

(4) MENS REA

1. The mens rea involves two elements: (a) as to the trespassory entry and (b) as to the ulterior offence.

As to (a) *Collins* shows that D must be proved to know (or be reckless as to) the facts which constitute him a trespasser.

As to (b) it must be shown that D either (i) entered with intent to steal, or to inflict grievous bodily harm, or to commit rape, or to do unlawful damage to the building or anything therein; or (ii) entered and committed, or attempted to commit, the offence of stealing or of inflicting grievous bodily harm. It is not immediately apparent why D if he enters a building as a trespasser without intent to commit any offence is not a burglar if he thereafter decides to set it alight but is a burglar if he steals some trinket.

Stealing clearly means theft contrary to s 1 of the 1968 Act. So was D in *Morris* (p 411, above) a burglar? Was D a burglar in *McPherson* (p 415, above)?

Grievous bodily harm must extend to those offences where the infliction of grievous bodily harm is an offence (viz ss 20 and 23 of the Offences against the Person Act 1861). Whether it extends to the s 18 offence which uses 'causes' rather than inflicts, or whether it extends to murder, is undecided but it would certainly be surprising if it did not do so.

There are differences depending on whether reliance is placed on s 9(1)(a) or s 9(1)(b). Under the former *intent* must be proved in relation to the ulterior offence at the time of entry but under the latter recklessness would suffice if it suffices for the ulterior offence. Another distinction seems to be suggested by *Jenkins* [1983] 1 All ER 1000, CA. It will be noticed that while s 9(1)(a) refers to 'offences of . . . inflicting on any person therein any grievous bodily harm' s 9(1)(b) merely refers to the infliction (or attempt to inflict) any grievous bodily harm without specifying that it must be an offence. This led the Court of Appeal in *Jenkins*, at 1004, to give the following example:

'An intruder gains access to the house without breaking in (where there is an open window for instance). He is on the premises as a trespasser and his intrusion is observed by someone in the house of whom he may not even be aware, and as a result that person suffers a severe shock with a resulting stroke . . . Should such an event fall outside the provisions of s 9 when causing some damage to property falls fairly within it?'

What arguments are there for saying that this event should fall within or without s 9? The House of Lords allowed the appeal in *Jenkins* [1984] AC 242, [1983] 3 All ER 448, without expressing any opinion on this matter.

2. Must there be some nexus between the invasion of the building and the commission of the ulterior crime? Would D commit burglary when having attacked P in order to rape her he drags her into Q's barn so that he cannot be seen from the highway? If D and E, two tramps, squat for the night in P's empty building, does D become a burglar because he attacks E and inflicts on him grievous bodily harm?

8. Aggravated burglary

Theft Act 1968, s 10, p 567, below

NOTES AND QUESTIONS

1. It must be proved that D had the article of aggravation with him *at the time* of the commission of the burglary. Where the charge is one of entry with intent this is the time of the entry; where it is one of committing a specified offence, having entered etc, it is the time of commission of the specified offence. In *Francis* [1982] Crim LR 363, CA, the Ds who were armed with sticks were allowed by P to enter after they noisily demanded entry. They then discarded their sticks and subsequently stole articles in the house. Their convictions for aggravated burglary were quashed.

2. 'Has with him' would presumably be interpreted to require knowledge by D that he has the article with him since what aggravates the burglary, and attracts the higher penalty, must be D's decision to have the article of aggravation with him.

3. Where D knowingly has with him a firearm or a weapon of offence or an explosive he commits aggravated burglary though he has no intention of using the article for offensive purposes or causing an explosion. Under paras (b) and (c) D's intent may become relevant. If, for example, D has with him an article not made or adapted for causing injury (a clothes-line, a jemmy) he is guilty of aggravated burglary only if he has the clothes-line with him in order to tie up the occupier or has the jemmy with a view to causing him injury.

4. In *Ohlson v Hylton* [1975] 2 All ER 490, [1975] 1 WLR 724, it was held for the purposes of s 1 of the Prevention of Crime Act 1953 that D, a carpenter on his way home from work did not have with him an offensive weapon when during an altercation with P he took a hammer from his tool bag and struck P with it. Does it follow that if D, surprised by the occupier, then decides to use his jemmy as a weapon of offence and attacks the occupier with it that D has not committed aggravated burglary? What if D realises he has disturbed the occupier's sleep and hears him descending the stairs, takes up a nearby poker and attacks the occupier when moments later he enters the kitchen?

9. Possession of housebreaking implements etc

Theft Act 1968, s 25, p 571, below

In *Bundy* [1977] 2 All ER 382, CA, the appellant had been convicted under s 25(1) where the articles had been found in his car. He argued that his car was his 'place of abode' because he lived in it travelling from place to place. Affirming his conviction, the court said (at p 384):

'In that context [*sc* s 25(1)] it is manifest that no offence is committed if a burglar keeps the implements of his criminal trade in his "place of abode". The phrase "place of abode" . . . connotes, first of all, a site. That is the ordinary meaning of the word "place". It is a site at which the occupier intends to abide. So, there are two elements in the phrase "place of abode", the element of site and the element of intention. When the appellant took the motor car to a site with the intention of abiding there, then his motor car on that site could be said to be his "place of abode", but when he took it from that site to another site where he intended to abide, the motor car could not be said to be his "place of abode" during transit. When he was arrested by the police he was not intending to abide on the site where he was arrested. It follows that he was not then at his "place of abode".'

The requirement 'for use in the course of or in connection with' refers to a future use. In *Ellames* [1974] 3 All ER 130, CA, where it had been proved that the appellant was in possession of certain articles after but not before a robbery, his conviction was quashed:

'An intention to use must necessarily relate to use in the future. . . . the words "for use" govern the whole of the words which follow. The object and effect of the words "in connection with" is to add something to "in the course of". It is easy to think of cases where an article could be intended for use "in connection with" though not "in the course of" a burglary, etc, e g articles intended to be used while doing preparatory acts or while escaping after the crime. . . . In our view, to establish an offence under s 25(1) the prosecution must prove that the defendant was in possession of the article, and intended the article to be used in the course of or in connection with some future burglary, theft or cheat; it is enough to prove a general intention to use it for *some* burglary, theft or cheat; we think that this view is supported by the use of the word "any" in s 25(1). Nor, in our view, is it necessary to prove that the defendant intended to use it himself; it will be enough to prove that he had it with him with the intention that it should be used by someone else. For example, if in the present case it had been proved that the defendant was hiding away these articles, which had already been used for one robbery, with the intention that they should later be used by someone for some other robbery, he would be guilty of an offence under s 25(1).'

While s 25 does not in terms require an *intent* to use in the course of any burglary etc, it seems clear that only an intended use is contemplated. No doubt it would suffice that D intended to use the article should the occasion for its use present itself, but it is not enough to prove that D had the article and that he might have used it: *Hargreaves* [1985] Crim LR 243, CA.

CLRC, Theft, para 148

[T]he offence under the [section] applies to possessing articles of any kind. There is no reason for listing particular kinds of articles . . . anything intended for use in committing any of the offences referred to should be included. The offence will apply, for example, to firearms and other offensive weapons, imitation firearms, housebreaking implements, any articles for the purpose of concealing identity (for example masks, rubber gloves and false car number-plates) and . . . [a variety of] car keys and confidence tricksters' outfits. The reference to the offender having the article for use 'in the course of or in connection with' any of the offences mentioned will secure that the offence under the clause will apply to having an article (for example a motor car) for getting to the place of the crime or getting away afterwards.

R v Doukas [1978] 1 All ER 1061, Court of Appeal, Criminal Division (Geoffrey Lane LJ, Milmo and Watkins JJ)

The case is set out at p 458, above.

NOTES AND QUESTIONS

1. In *Cooke and Sutcliffe* [1985] Crim LR 215, CA, which also involved the provision by a British Rail steward of his own sandwiches, the court said that the ownership of the sandwiches would matter vitally to the customers if they were poisonous since the Board could pay damages when the steward could not.
2. The CLRC considered that a motor car may fall within the offence if it is used 'for getting to the place of the crime or getting away afterwards.' What if D drives to a shop with a view to ordering goods for which he does not intend to pay? When the respondent in *Comer v Bloomfield*, p 276, above, crashed his van and hid it in the woods, did he then have the van with him in connection with a cheat?

10. Handling stolen goods

Theft Act 1968, s 22, p 570, below

(1) STOLEN GOODS

'Goods' are defined in s 34(2)(b) of the 1968 Act, p 572, below. The effect seems to be that with minor exceptions the property which can be the subject of handling is co-extensive with that which can be the subject of theft. While things in action are not expressly mentioned in s 34(2) they must be included in the words 'every other description of property except land'. Perhaps a thing in action cannot be 'received' (a word more apt to describe taking control of tangible property) but there would seem to be no reason why a thing in action cannot be 'realised' or 'disposed of'. In *A-G's Reference (No 4 of 1979)* [1981] 1 All ER 1193 at 1198, CA, the court said:

> '[I]t is clear that a balance in a bank account, being a debt, is itself a thing in action which falls within the definition of goods and may therefore be goods which directly or indirectly represent stolen goods for the purposes of s 24(2)(a).'

This makes sense. If D steals £500 and gives £250 in cash to E while opening a bank account in F's favour for the remainder it would be absurd that E might be a handler while F might not.

When goods are 'stolen' is defined by s 24(4) of the 1968 Act, p 571, below.

(2) WHEN GOODS CEASE TO BE STOLEN

When goods cease to be stolen is governed by s 24(3) of the 1968 Act. The subsection was considered in:

Re Attorney-General's Reference (No 1 of 1974) [1974] 2 All ER 899, Court of Appeal, Criminal Division
(Lord Widgery CJ, Ashworth and Mocatta JJ)

Lord Widgery CJ. This is a reference to the court by the Attorney-General of a point of law seeking the opinion of the court pursuant to s 36 of the Criminal Justice Act 1972. It is in fact the first occasion on which the Attorney-General has exercised his power under this section to refer a question for our opinion : . .

The facts of the present case, which I take from the terms of the reference itself, are these:

> 'A Police Constable found an unlocked unattended car containing packages of new clothing which he suspected, and which in fact subsequently proved to be, stolen. The Officer removed the rotor arm from the vehicle to immobilise it, and kept observation. After about ten minutes, the accused appeared, got into the van and attempted to start the engine. When questioned by the Officer, he gave an implausible explanation, and was arrested.'

On those facts two charges were brought against the respondent: one of stealing the woollen goods, the new clothing, which was in the back of the car in question, and secondly and alternatively of receiving those goods knowing them to be stolen. The trial judge quite properly ruled that there was no evidence to support the first charge, and that he would not leave that to the jury, but an argument developed whether the second count should be left to the jury or not. Counsel for the respondent in the court below had submitted at the close of the prosecution case that there was no case to answer, relying on s 24(3) of the Theft Act 1968. Section 24(3) provides:

> '. . . no goods shall be regarded as having continued to be stolen goods after they have been restored to the person from whom they were stolen or to other lawful possession or custody . . .'

The rest of the subsection is not relevant and I do not read it. It was therefore contended in the court below on the facts to which I have already referred that by virtue of s 24(3) the goods had been restored to other lawful possession or custody, namely the custody or possession of the police officer, before the respondent appeared on the scene and sought to drive the car away. If that argument was sound, of course it would follow that there was no case for the respondent to answer, because if in fact the police constable had restored the stolen goods to his own lawful possession or custody before the act relied on as an act of receiving occurred, it would follow that they would not be stolen goods at the material time.

After hearing argument, the judge accepted the submission of the respondent and directed the jury that they should acquit on the receiving count. That has resulted in the Attorney-General referring the following point of law to us for an opinion under s 36 of the 1972 Act. He expresses the point in this way:

> 'Whether stolen goods are restored to lawful custody within the meaning of Section 24(3) of the Theft Act 1968 when a Police Officer, suspecting them to be stolen, examines and keeps observation on them with a view to tracing the thief or a handler.'

One could put the question perhaps in a somewhat different way by asking whether on the facts set out in the reference the conclusion as a matter of law was clear to the effect that the goods had ceased to be stolen goods. In other words, the question which is really in issue in this reference is whether the trial judge acted correctly in law in saying that those facts disclosed a defence within s 24(3) of the 1968 Act.

Section 24(3) is not perhaps entirely happily worded. It has been pointed out in the course of argument that in the sentence which I have read there is only one relevant verb, and that is 'restore'. The section contemplates that the stolen goods should be restored to the person from whom they were stolen or to other lawful possession or custody. It is pointed out that the word 'restore', although it is entirely appropriate when applied to restoration of the goods to the true owner, is not really an appropriate verb to employ if one is talking about a police officer stumbling on stolen goods and taking them into his own lawful custody or possession.

We are satisfied that despite the absence of another and perhaps more appropriate verb, the effect of s 24(3) is to enable a defendant to plead that the goods had ceased to be stolen goods if the facts are that they were taken by a police officer in the course of his duty and reduced into possession by him.

Whether or not s 24(3) is intended to be a codification of the common law or not, it certainly deals with a topic on which the common law provides a large number of authorities. I shall refer to some of them in a moment, although perhaps not all, and it will be observed that from the earliest times it has been recognised that if the owner of stolen goods resumed possession of them, reduced them into his possession again, that they thereupon ceased to be stolen goods for present purposes and could certainly not be the subject of a later charge of receiving based on events after they had been reduced into possession. It is to be observed that in common law nothing short of a reduction into possession, either by the true owner or by a police officer acting in the execution of his duty, was regarded as sufficient to change the character of the goods from stolen goods into goods which were no longer to be so regarded.

I make that assertion true by a brief reference from the cases to which we have been referred. The first is *Dolan* [(1855) 6 Cox CC 449]. The facts there were that stolen goods were found in the pocket of a thief by the owner. The owner sent for a policeman, and the evidence given at the subsequent trial showed that after the policeman had taken the goods from the thief, the thief, the policeman and the employer went towards the shop owned and occupied by the prisoner at which the thief had asserted that he was hoping to sell the stolen goods. When they got near the shop the policeman gave the goods to the thief, who then went on ahead into the shop with a view to selling the goods, closely followed by the owner and the policeman, who proceeded to arrest the shopkeeper. It was held there:

> 'that the prisoner was not guilty of feloniously receiving stolen goods, inasmuch as they were delivered to him under the authority of the owner by a person to whom the owner had bailed them for that purpose.'

Put another way, one can explain that decision on the broad principle to which I have already referred: the goods had already been returned to the possession of the owner before they were released by him into the hands of the thief in order that the thief might approach the receiver with a view to the receiver being arrested. The principle thus enunciated is one which, as I have already said, is to be found in the other authorities to which we have been referred.

The next case which is similar is *Schmidt* [(1866) LR 1 CCR 15]. The reference in the headnote suffices:

> 'Four thieves stole goods from the custody of a railway company and afterwards sent them in a parcel by the same company's line addressed to the prisoner. During the transit the theft was discovered; and, on the arrival of the parcel at the station for its delivery, a policeman in the employ of the company opened it, and then returned it to the porter whose duty it was to deliver it, with instructions to keep it until further orders. On the following day the policeman directed the porter to take the parcel to its address, when it was received by the prisoner, who was afterwards convicted of receiving goods knowing them to be stolen . . .'

And it was held by the Court of Crown Cases Reserved:

> 'that the goods had got back into the possession of the owner, so as to be no longer stolen goods, and that the conviction was wrong.'

Again unquestionably they had been reduced into the possession of the owner by the hand of the police officer acting on his behalf. They had not been allowed to continue their course unaffected. They had been taken out of circulation by the police officer, reduced into the possession of the owner or of the officer, and it matters not which, and thus had ceased to be stolen goods for present purposes. Mellor J, in giving a brief judgment, said [LR 1 CCR at 19]:

> 'The property is rightly laid in the company [that is the railway company] because at the time of the larceny there was a bailment to them by the true owners. I concur in the propriety of the decision in *Dolan*; but there the goods got back into the possession of the true owner. In this case the policeman merely looked at the goods, and did not take possession of them.'

It is to be observed that he was taking a different view of the effect of the acts of the police officer, but the principle as far as we can see is unaffected by that decision.

Then there is a helpful case, *Villensky* [[1892] 2 QB 597]. Again it is a case of a parcel in the hands of carriers. This parcel was handed to the carriers in question for conveyance to the consignees, and whilst in the carriers' depot it was stolen by a servant of the carriers who removed the parcel to a different part of the premises and placed on it a label addressed to the prisoners by a name by which they were known and at a house where they resided. The superintendent of the carriers, on receipt of information as to this and after inspection of the parcel, directed it to be replaced in the place from which the thief had removed it and to be sent with a special delivery receipt in a van accompanied by two detectives to the address shown on the label. At that address it was received by the prisoners under circumstances which clearly showed knowledge on their part that it had been stolen. The property in the parcel was laid in the indictment in the carriers and an offer to amend the indictment by substituting the names of the consignees was declined. The carriers' servant pleaded guilty to a count for larceny in the same indictment. It was there held by the Court of Crown Cases Reserved:

> 'that as the person in which the property was laid [ie the carriers] had resumed possession of the stolen property before its receipt by the prisoners, it had then ceased to be stolen property, and the prisoners could not be convicted of receiving it knowing it to have been stolen.'

In the same report there is a brief and valuable judgment by Pollock B, in these terms [[1892] 2 QB at 599]:

> 'The decisions in *Dolan* and *Schmidt* are, in my judgment, founded on law and on solid good sense, and they should not be frittered away. It is, of course, frequently the case that when it is found that a person has stolen property he is watched; but the owner of the property, if he wishes to catch the receiver, does not resume possession of the stolen goods; here the owners have done so, and the result is that the conviction must be quashed.'

We refer to that brief judgment because it illustrates in a few clear words what is really the issue in the present case. When the police officer discovered these goods and acted as he did, was the situation that he had taken possession of the goods, in which event, of course, they ceased to be stolen goods, or was it merely that he was watching the goods with a view to the possibility of catching the receiver at a later stage? I will turn later to a consideration of those two alernatives.

Two other cases should, I think, be mentioned at this stage. The next one is *King* [[1938] 2 All ER 662]. We are now getting to far more recent times because the report is published in 1938. The appellant here was convicted with another man of receiving stolen goods knowing them to have been stolen. A fur coat had been stolen and shortly afterwards the police went to a flat where they found the man Burns and told him they were enquiring about some stolen property. He at first denied that there was anything there, but finally admitted the theft and produced a parcel from a wardrobe. While the policeman was in the act of examining the contents of the parcel, the telephone bell rang. Burns answered it and the police heard him say: 'Come along as arranged'. The police then suspended operations and about 20 minutes later the appellant arrived and being admitted by Burns, said: 'I have come for the coat. Harry sent me.' This was heard by the police, who were in hiding at the time. The coat was handed to the appellant by Burns, so that he was actually in possession of it. It was contended that the possession by the police amounted to possession by the owner of the coat, and that, therefore, the coat was not stolen property at the time the appellant received it. It was held by the Court of Criminal Appeal that 'the coat had not been in the possession of the police, and it was therefore still stolen property when the appellant received it.'

Counsel for the Attorney-General, appearing in support of this reference, showed some hesitation in relying on this case, because he clearly took the view that it was perhaps a rather unlikely decision, the policemen having started to examine the coat and then stopped for 20 minutes until the prisoner arrived and then claiming that the coat was not in his possession. It might be thought to be a rather bold decision to say that the police action in that case had not reduced the coat into their possession. But nevertheless that was the view of this court in the judgment of Humphreys J. All the authorities, as I say, point in the same direction.

The most recent case on the present topic, but of little value in the present problems is *Haughton v Smith* [[1975] AC 476 [1973] 3 All ER 1109; p 291 above]. The case being of little value to us in our present problems, I will deal with it quite briefly. It is a case where a lorry-load of stolen meat was intercepted by police, somewhere in the north of England, who discovered that the lorry was in fact full of stolen goods. After a brief conference they decided to take the lorry on to its destination with a view to catching the receivers at the London end of the affair. So the lorry set off for London with detectives both in the passenger seat and in the back of the vehicle, and in due course was met by the defendant at its destination in London. In that case before this court it was conceded, as it had been conceded below, that the goods had been reduced into the possession of the police when they took possession of the lorry in the north of England, so no dispute in this court or later in the House of Lords was raised on that issue. It is, however, to be noted that three of their Lordships, when the matter got to the House of Lords, expressed some hesitation as to the propriety of the prosecution conceding in that case that the goods had been reduced to the possession of the police when the lorry was first intercepted. Since we cannot discover on what ground those doubts were expressed either from the report of the speeches or from the report of the argument, we cannot take advantage of that case in the present problem.

Now to return to the present problem again with those authorities in the back-ground did the conduct of the police officer, as already briefly recounted, amount to a taking of possession of the woollen goods in the back seat of the motor car? What he did, to repeat the essential facts, was: seeing these goods in the car and being suspicious of them because they were brand new goods and in an unlikely position, he removed the rotor arm and stood by in cover to interrogate any driver of the car who might subsequently appear. Did that amount to a taking possession of the goods in the back of the car? In our judgment it depended primarily on the intentions of the police officer. If the police officer seeing these goods in the back of the car had made up his mind that he would take them into custody, that he would reduce them into his possession or control, take charge of them so that they could not be removed and so that he would have the disposal of them, then it would be a perfectly proper conclusion to say that he had taken possession of the goods. On the other hand, if the truth of the matter is that he was of an entirely open mind at that stage as to whether the goods were to be seized or not and was of an entirely open mind as to whether he should take possession of them or not, but merely stood by so that when the driver of the car appeared he could ask certain questions of that driver as to the nature of the goods and why they were there, then there is no reason whatever to suggest that he had taken the goods into his possession or control. It may be, of course, that he had both objects in mind. It is possible in a case like this that the police officer may have intended by removing the rotor arm both to prevent the car from being driven away and to enable him to assert control over the woollen goods as such. But if the jury came to the conclusion that the proper explanation of what had happened was that the police officer had not intended at that stage to reduce the goods into his possession or to assume the control of them, and at that stage was merely concerned to ensure that the driver, if he appeared, could not get away without answering questions, then in that case the proper conclusion of the jury would have been to the effect that the goods had not been reduced into the possession of the police and therefore a defence under s 24 (3) of the 1968 Act would not be of use to this particular defendant.

In the light of those considerations it has become quite obvious that the trial judge was wrong in withdrawing the issue from the jury. As a matter of law he was not entitled to conclude from the facts which I have set out more than once that these goods were reduced into the possession of the police officer. What he should have done in our opinion would have been to have left that issue to the jury for decision, directing the jury that they should find that the prosecution case was without substance if they thought that the police officer had assumed control of the goods as such and reduced them into his possession. Whereas, on the other hand, they should have found the case proved, assuming that they were satisfied about its other elements, if they were of the opinion that the police officer in removing the rotor arm and standing by and watching was doing no more than ensure that the driver should not get away without interrogation and was not at that stage seeking to assume possession of the goods as such at all. That is our opinion.

Determination accordingly

NOTES AND QUESTIONS

1. In determining whether goods have ceased to be stolen which issues are for the judge and which for the jury? Considering *Haughton v Smith,* do you think that, had the prosecution not conceded the point, it would have been successfully argued that the goods on the lorry remained stolen goods, i e they had not been restored to the possession or control of the police?

2. In *A-G's Reference (No 1 of 1974)* was not the only possible interpretation of the police officer's conduct, and especially his immobilisation of the car, that he had taken 'custody' of the car and its contents? If so, was not the trial judge right to withdraw the case from the jury? The police officer's intention may have been conditional (I will let D drive away with the goods in the back of the car only if he satisfies me that they are not stolen) but even if it was so conditioned, should this make any difference?

3. Goods representing those originally stolen may be stolen goods: s 24(2). If D steals an Austin car from P which he sells to E for £5,000, that £5,000 is 'stolen' because it represents the proceeds and if F receives the £5,000 knowing its provenance he may be convicted of handling. It will be appreciated that there might soon be a multiplicity of stolen goods in circulation since the car might be resold several times and the money might also change hands and be converted into other goods. A limitation is accordingly imposed by s 24(2) which in effect provides that once the proceeds of the stolen goods come into the hands of an innocent party (for example F uses the £5,000 to buy a Bentley from the innocent Q) whatever the innocent party acquires with those proceeds will cease to be stolen goods. The originally stolen goods (in our example the Austin car) continues to be stolen until they are restored to the owner or other lawful custody, or the owner ceases to have a right of restitution (as where the Austin is sold in market overt and the buyer acquires a good title).

(3) FORMS OF HANDLING

Under the former law it was an offence to 'receive' stolen property which was interpreted as requiring that D should have exclusive control over the property or should be acting in concert with the thief so as to have joint control of the property. This meant that if, say, D helped E to load stolen goods onto a lorry, or allowed E to leave them in D's garage overnight, or put E into contact with a prospective buyer, D did not thereby become guilty of receiving. The CLRC was in favour of enlarging the offence and s 22 extends not only to receiving but to what the CLRC referred to (Cmnd 2977, para 127) as 'other kinds of meddling with stolen property'. The offence may be committed in the following ways: (i) by *receiving* the goods; (ii) by *undertaking* the retention, removal, disposal or realisation of the goods by another person; (iii) by *assisting* in the retention, removal, disposal or realisation of the goods by another person, and (iv) by *arranging* to do (i), (ii) or (iii). The words of the section, it was said in *Deakin* [1972] 3 All ER 803 at 808, 'are obviously intended to throw the net very wide'.

R v Kanwar [1982] 2 All ER 528, Court of Appeal, Criminal Division
(Dunn LJ, Cantley and Sheldon JJ)

[**Cantley J** read the following judgment of the court:]

In counts 7 and 9 of an indictment on which she was tried with others, the appellant was charged with dishonestly assisting in the retention of stolen goods for the benefit of Maninder Singh Kanwar, who was her husband. She was convicted and by way of sentence was given a conditional discharge. She now appeals against her conviction.

Her husband had brought the stolen goods to their house where the goods were used in the home. It was conceded that the appellant was not present when the goods were brought to the house. She was in hospital at the time.

On 2 November 1978 police officers, armed with a search warrant, came to the house to look for and take away any goods which they found there which corresponded with a list of stolen goods in their possession. The appellant arrived during the search and was told of the object of the search. She replied: 'There's no stolen property here.'

She was subsequently asked a number of questions with regard to specific articles which were in the house and in reply to those questions, she gave answers which were lies. It is sufficient for present purposes to take two examples. She was asked about a painting which was in the living room and she replied: 'I bought it from a shop. I have a receipt.' The officer said: 'That's not true.' She said: 'Yes, I have.' He said: 'If you can find a receipt, please have a look.' She made some pretence of looking for the receipt but none was produced and ultimately she at least tacitly admitted there was none. The painting is one of the articles in the particulars to count 9.

She was also asked about a mirror which was in the kitchen. This is one of the articles in the particulars to count 7. The officer said: 'What about the mirror?' She said: 'I bought it from the market.' The officer asked: 'When?' She said: 'Sometime last year.' There is no dispute that that answer was a lie as was the answer about the painting. Later on, she was warned that she was telling lies and that the property was stolen. She said: 'No, it isn't. We're trying to build up a nice home.' Ultimately, although the officer had had no intention of arresting her when he came to the house, he did arrest her and she was subsequently charged.

The appellant did not give evidence and the evidence of the police officer stood uncontradicted.

In *R v Thornhill*, decided in this court on 15 May 1981, and in *R v Sanders*, decided in this court on 25 February 1982, both unreported, it was held that merely using stolen goods in the possession of another does not constitute the offence of assisting in their retention. To consitute the offence, something must be done by the offender, and done intentionally and dishonestly, for the purpose of enabling the goods to be retained. Examples of such conduct are concealing or helping to conceal the goods, or doing something to make them more difficult to find or to identify. Such conduct must be done knowing or believing the goods to be stolen and done dishonestly and for the benefit of another.

We see no reason why the requisite assistance should be restricted to physical acts. Verbal representations, whether oral or in writing, for the purpose of concealing the identity of stolen goods may, if made dishonestly and for the benefit of another, amount to handling stolen goods by assisting in their retention within the meaning of s 22 of the Theft Act 1968.

The requisite assistance need not be successful in its object. It would be absurd if a person dishonestly concealing stolen goods for the benefit of a receiver could establish a defence by showing that he was caught in the act. In the present case, if, while the police were in one part of the house, the appellant, in order to conceal the painting had put it under a mattress in the bedroom, it would not alter the nature of her conduct that the police subsequently looked under the mattress and found the picture because they expected to find it there or that they caught her in the act of putting it there.

The appellant told these lies to the police to persuade them that the picture and the mirror were not the stolen property which they had come to take away but were her lawful property which she had bought. If that was true, the articles should be left in the house. She was, of course, telling these lies to protect her husband, who had dishonestly brought the articles there but, in our view, she was nonetheless, at the time, dishonestly assisting in the retention of the stolen articles.

In his summing up, the judge directed the jury as follows:

> 'It would be quite wrong for you to convict this lady if all she did was to watch her husband bring goods into the house, even if she knew or believed that they were stolen goods because, no doubt, you would say to yourselves, "What would she be expected to do about it?" Well, what the Crown say is that she knew or believed them to be stolen and that she was a knowing and willing party to their being kept in that house in those circumstances. The reason the Crown say that, and we shall be coming to the evidence, is that when questioned about a certain number of items, [the appellant] gave answers which the Crown say were not true and that she could not possibly have believed to be true and that she knew perfectly well were untruthful. So, say the prosecution, she was not just an acquiescent wife who could not do much about it, she was, by her conduct in trying to put the police officers as best she could off the scent, demonstrating that she was a willing and knowing part of those things being there and that she was trying to account for them. Well, it will be for you to say, but you must be satisfied before you can convict her on either of these counts, not only that she knew or believed the goods to be stolen, but that she actively assisted her husband in keeping them there; not by just passive acquiescence in the sense of saying, "What can I do about it?" but in the sense of saying, "How nice to have these things in our home, although they are stolen goods".'

In so far as this direction suggests that the appellant would be guilty of the offence if she was merely willing for the goods to be kept and used in the house and was thinking that it was nice to have them there, although they were stolen goods, it is a misdirection. We have considered whether on that account the conviction ought to be quashed. However, the offence was established by the uncontradicted evidence of the police officer which, looked at in full, clearly shows that in order to mislead the officer who had come to take away stolen goods, she misrepresented the identity of the goods which she knew or believed to be stolen. We are satisfied that no miscarriage of justice has occurred and the appeal is accordingly dismissed.

Appeal dismissed.

R v Pitchley (1972) 57 Cr App Rep 30, Court of Appeal, Criminal Division (Cairns LJ, Nield and Croom-Johnson JJ)

On 5 November the appellant was handed £150 by his son, Brian, and was asked to look after it. On 6 November the appellant paid the money into his post office savings account. The money was in fact stolen but the appellant claimed that his son told him that he had won the money on the horses and, while he thought this explanation strange, he did not become aware that it was stolen until 7 November. Having become aware of this he had no wish to take his son to the police so he allowed the money to remain in his account and it was still there when he was seen by the police on 11 November. The appellant was convicted of handling the money.

Cairns LJ. . . . The main point that has been taken by Mr Kalisher, who is appearing for the appellant in this Court, is that, assuming that the jury were not satisfied that the appellant received the money knowing it to have been stolen, and that is an assumption which clearly it is right to make, then there was no evidence after that, that from the time when the money was put into the savings bank, that the appellant had done any act in relation to it. His evidence was, and there is no reason to suppose that the jury did not believe it, that at the time when he put the money into the savings bank he still did not know or believe that the money had been stolen—it was only at a later stage that he did. That was on the Saturday according to his evidence, and the position was that the money had simply remained in the savings bank from the Saturday, to the Wednesday when the police approached the appellant. It is fair to say that from the moment when he was approached he displayed the utmost frankness to the extent of correcting them when they said it was £100 to £150 and telling them where the post office savings book was so that the money could be got out again and restored to its rightful owner.

But the question is: Did the conduct of the appellant between the Saturday and the Wednesday amount to an assisting in the retention of this money for the benefit of his son Brian? The Court has been referred to the case of *Brown* (1969) 53 Cr App Rep 527 which was a case where stolen property had been put into a wardrobe at the appellant's house and when police came to inquire about it the appellant said to them: 'Get lost'. The direction to the jury had been on the basis that it was for them to consider whether in saying: 'Get lost', instead of helping the police constable, he was dishonestly assisting in the retention of stolen goods. This Court held that that was a misdirection but there are passages in the judgment in the case of *Brown* (supra) which, in the view of this Court, are of great assistance in determining what is meant by 'retention' in this section. I read first of all from p 528 setting out the main facts a little more fully: 'A witness named Holden was called by the prosecution. He gave evidence that he and others had broken into the café and had stolen the goods, and that he had brought them to the appellant's flat, where, incidentally, other people were sleeping, and had hidden them there; and he described how he had taken the cigarettes out of the packets, put them in the plastic bag and hidden them in the wardrobe. Holden went on to say that later and before the police arrived he told the appellant where the the cigarettes were; in other words, he said that the appellant well knew that the cigarettes were there and that they had been stolen'. There was no evidence that the appellant had done anything active in relation to the cigarettes up to the time when the police arrived. The Lord Chief Justice, Lord Parker, in the course of his judgment at p 530 said this: 'It is urged here that the mere failure to reveal the presence of the cigarettes, with or without the addition of the spoken words "Get lost", was incapable itself of amounting to an assisting in the retention of the goods within the meaning of the subsection. The Court has come to the conclusion that that is right. It does not seem to this Court that the mere failure to tell the police, coupled if you like with the words: "Get lost", amounts in itself to an assisting in their retention. On the other hand, those matters did afford strong evidence of what was the real basis of the charge here, namely, that knowing that they have been stolen, he permitted them to remain there or, as it has been put, provided accommodation for these stolen goods in order to assist Holden to retain them.' Having said that the direction was incomplete, the Lord Chief Justice went on to say: 'The Chairman should have gone on to say: "But the fact that he did not tell the constable that they were there and said 'Get lost' is evidence from which you can infer, if you think right, that this man was permitting the goods to remain in his flat, and to that extent assisting in their retention by Holden." '

In this present case there was no question on the evidence of the appellant himself, that he was permitting the money to remain under his control in his savings bank book, and it is clear that this Court in the case of *Brown* (supra) regarded such permitting as sufficient to constitute retention within the meaning of retention. That is clear from the passage I have already read, emphasised in the next paragraph, the final paragraph of the judgment, where the Lord Chief Justice said (at p 531): 'It is a plain case in which the proviso should be applied. It seems to this Court that the only possible inference in these circumstances, once Holden was believed is that this man was assisting in their retention by housing the goods and providing accommodation for them, by permitting them to remain there.' It is important to realise that that language was in relation to a situation where there was no evidence that anything active had been done by the appellant in relation to the goods.

In the course of the argument, Nield J cited the dictionary meaning of the word 'retain'—keep possession of, not lose, continue to have. In the view of this Court, that is the meaning of the word 'retain' in this section. It was submitted by Mr Kalisher that, at any rate, it was ultimately for the jury to decide whether there was retention or not and that even assuming that what the appellant did was of such a character that it could constitute retention, the jury ought to have been directed that it was for them to determine as a matter of fact, whether that was so or not. The Court cannot agree with that submission. The meaning of the word 'retention' in the section is a matter of law in so far as the construction of the word is necessary. It is hardly a difficult question of construction because it is an ordinary English word and in the view of this Court, it was no more necessary for the Deputy Chairman to leave to the jury the question of whether or not what was done amounted to retention, than it would be necessary for a judge in a case where goods had been handed to a person who knew that they had been stolen for him to direct the jury it was for them to to decide whether or not that constituted receiving . . .

Appeal dismissed

Questions

1. Are *Pitchley* and *Brown* authority for the proposition that handling may be constituted by omission?

2. Dan's wife, Ena, makes her living by stealing fur coats which she keeps in the garage to Dan's house. Dan is well aware of this but considers it no business of his to interfere so long as he can get his car in and out of the garage. Is Dan a handler?

3. Don tells Eric that he plans to steal a load of whisky the next day if he can get the right price for it. He adds that the driver of the lorry on which the whisky is carried is a former associate of his, has already provided Don with duplicate keys and has arranged to take his lunch at a particular rendezvous so that Don can drive off with the lorry. The plan strikes Eric as foolproof and he immediately agrees to pay Don £1,000 c.o.d. Is Eric guilty at this stage of handling the whisky?

(4) THE RELATIONSHIP BETWEEN HANDLING AND THEFT

CLRC, Eighth Report, Theft paras 131, 132

The extension of the offence to giving assistance in the ways mentioned involves two problems about the relation between the thief and the handler. First, if two persons join in stealing and each helps the other to carry off the property, the extension might in the absence of a special provision have the effect of making each of them guilty of handling on account of undertaking or assisting in the disposal of the property. It would be wrong to make the thief in such a case guilty of handling stolen goods when the latter offence will be punishable with the higher penalty of fourteen year's imprisonment. This is prevented by the provision in [s 22(1)] that the offence shall apply to things done 'otherwise than in the course of the stealing'. This provision is in accordance with the present law of receiving. Secondly, under the definition a thief may be liable for handling if, after the theft is complete, he does some of the things mentioned in the definition for someone else, for example if he helps a receiver to dispose of the goods. Since it might be thought too severe to make a thief guilty of handling in such a case, we thought of providing that a thief should not be guilty of handling by reasons of doing any of the things mentioned in the definition in respect of goods which he has himself stolen. But we decided not to include the provision. If after the theft is complete the thief takes part in a separate transaction for the disposal of the goods, it seems right that he should be guilty of handling like anybody else involved in the transaction .'. . but since the offence will apply only to undertaking or assisting in the disposal or other dealing 'by or for the benefit of another person', a thief will not be guilty of handling by keeping or disposing of the goods for his own benefit.

In para 131 we mentioned that a thief may be guilty of handling goods which he has stolen. It should be noted also that a person guilty of handling stolen goods will often be guilty at the same time of stealing them. This is because what he does in relation to them will be likely to amount to an appropriation within the meaning of [section] 3 as it would if they had not been stolen (cf para 35 and the reference there to *Walters v Lunt* [1951] 2 All ER 645). We see no reason of principle or convenience why a receiver of stolen goods in the present sense of receiving should not be guilty of stealing them. He dishonestly appropriates something with the intention of permanently depriving the owner. Moreover a person who receives goods otherwise than for value, but is not guilty of handling because he does not know that they are stolen, will be guilty of theft if he dishonestly keeps the goods when he finds out that they were stolen (para 36). It seems right therefore that, if he knows at the time of receiving that the goods were stolen, the receiving should amount also to theft. It would be more natural in ordinary cases to charge the offender with handling, and there would be two practical reasons for doing so. First, the penalty will be higher. Secondly, certain evidence will be admissible under [section 27 (3)] on a charge of handling which would not be admissible on a charge of stealing (paras 156–8).

In *Pitham and Hehl* (1976) 65 Cr App Rep 45, CA, one Millman, knowing that his friend McGregor was in prison and in no position to interfere, planned to steal the furniture from McGregor's house. He told the appellants that he had some furniture to sell, took them with him to McGregor's house, and there sold them such furniture as they wished to buy at a considerable undervalue. Millman was convicted of stealing the furniture and the appellants of handling it. They argued that as their handling was 'in the course of the stealing' they could not be convicted of handling. Affirming the conviction, the court said, at p 48:

> 'Section 22(1) of the Theft Act provides: "A person handles stolen goods if (otherwise than in the course of the stealing)"—I emphasise the words "otherwise than in the course of the stealing"—"knowing or believing them to be stolen goods he dishonestly receives the goods, or dishonestly undertakes or assists in their retention, removal, disposal or realisation by or for the benefit of another person, or if he arranges to do so." Now, the two conflicting academic views can be summarised in this way. Professor Smith's view in his book [*The Law of Theft* (3rd edn, 1977)], para 400, seems to be that "in the course of the stealing" can be a very short time or it can be a very long period of time. Professor Griew in his book [*The Theft Act 1968* (2nd edn, 1974)] paras 8-18, 8-19, seems to be of the opinion that, "in the course of the stealing," embraces not only the act of stealing as defined by section 1 of the Theft Act 1968, but in addition making away with the goods. In the course of expounding their differing views in their books on the Theft Act the two professors have both referred to ancient authorities. Both are of the opinion that the object of the words, "otherwise than in the course of the stealing" was to deal with the situation where two men are engaged in different capacities in a joint enterprise. In those circumstances, unless some such limiting words as those to which I have referred were included in the definition of handling, a thief could be guilty of both stealing and receiving. An illustration of the sort of problem which arises is provided by Professor Smith's reference to the old case of *Coggins* (1873) 12 Cox CC 517. In his book on the Theft Act at paragraph 400, he summarises the facts of *Coggins* (supra) in these terms: "If a servant stole money from his master's till and handed it to an accomplice in his

master's shop, the accomplice was guilty of larceny and not guilty of receiving." He added another example. It was the case of *Perkins* (1852) 5 Cox CC 554. He summarises that case as follows: "Similarly, if a man committed larceny in the room in which he lodged and threw a bundle of stolen goods to an accomplice in the street, the accomplice was guilty of larceny and not guilty of receiving."

In our judgment the words to which I have referred in section 22(1), were designed to make it clear that in those sorts of situations a man could not be guilty under the Theft Act of both theft and handling. As was pointed out to Mr Murray by my brother, Bristow J, in the course of argument, the Theft Act in section 1 defines theft. It has been said in this Court more than once that the object of that definition was to make a fresh start so as to get rid of all the subtle distinctions which had arisen in the past under the old law of larceny. Subsection (1) of section 1 has a side heading, "Basic definition of theft." That definition is in these terms: "A person is guilty of theft if he dishonestly appropriates property belonging to another with the intention of permanently depriving the other of it; and 'thief' and 'steal' shall be construed accordingly." What Parliament meant by "appropriate" was defined in section 3(1): "Any assumption by a person of the rights of an owner amounts to an appropriation, and this includes, where he has come by the property (innocently or not) without stealing it, any later assumption of a right to it by keeping or dealing with it as owner."

Mr Murray's submission—a very bold one—was that the general words with which section 3(1) opens, namely, "Any assumption by a person of the rights of an owner amounts to an appropriation, " are limited by the words beginning "and this includes." He submitted that those additional words bring back into the law of theft something akin to the concept of appropriation, which was one of the aspects of the law of larceny which the Theft Act 1968 was intended to get rid of. According to Mr Murray, unless there is something which amounts to "coming by" the property there cannot be an appropriation. We disagree. The final words of section 3(1) are words of inclusion. The general words at the beginning of section 3(1) are wide enough to cover *any* assumption by a person of the right of an owner.

What was the appropriation in this case? The jury found that the two appellants had handled the property *after* Millman had stolen it. That is clear from their acquittal of these two appellants on count 3 of the indictment which had charged them jointly with Millman. What had Millman done? He had assumed the right of the owner. He had done that when he took the two appellants to 20 Parry Road, showed them the property and invited them to buy what they wanted. He was then acting as the owner. He was then, in the words of the statute, "assuming the rights of the owner." The moment he did that he appropriated McGregor's goods to himself. The appropriation was complete. After this appropriation had been completed there was no question of these two appellants taking part, in the words of section 22, in dealing with the goods "in the course of the stealing."

It follows that no problem arises in this case. It may well be that some of the situations which the two learned professors envisage and discuss in their books may have to be dealt with at some future date, but not in this case. The facts are too clear.

Mr Murray suggested the learned judge should have directed the jury in some detail about the possibility that the appropriation had not been an instantaneous appropriation, but had been one which had gone on for some time. He submitted that it might have gone on until such time as the furniture was loaded into the appellant's van. For reasons we have already given that was not a real possibility in this case. It is no part of a judge's duty to give the jury the kind of lecture on the law which may be appropriate for a professor to give to a class of undergraduates. We commend the judge for not having involved himself in a detailed academic analysis of the law relating to this case when on the facts it was as clear as anything could be that either these appellants had helped Millman to steal the goods, or Millman had stolen them and got rid of them by sale to these two appellants. We can see nothing wrong in the learned judge's approach to this case and on that particular ground we affirm what he did and said.'

Questions

1. Consider *Haughton v Smith* [1973] 3 All ER 1109, HL, p 291, above. Could the respondent have been convicted of stealing the consignment of corned beef?

2. In the light of *Pitham and Hehl* do you think the accomplices in *Coggins* and *Perkins* could be convicted of handling?

R v Bloxham [1982] 1 All ER 582, House of Lords
(Lords Diplock, Scarman, Bridge of Harwich and Brandon of Oakbrook)

Lord Bridge of Harwich. My Lords, in January 1977 the appellant purchased a motor car for £1,300. He paid the seller £500 in cash and was to pay the balance when the seller produced the car's registration document, but in the event this never happened. The car had in fact been stolen. It is accepted by the Crown that the appellant did not know or believe this when he acquired the car. In December 1977 he sold the car for £200 to an unidentified third party who was prepared to take the car without any registration document.

The appellant was charged under s 22(1) of the Theft Act 1968 with handling stolen goods, the particulars of the relevant count in the indictment alleging that he:

> 'dishonestly undertook or assisted in the disposal or realization of certain stolen goods, namely a Ford Cortina motor car registered number SJH 606M, by or for the benefit of another, namely the unknown purchaser knowing or believing the same to be stolen goods.'

At the trial it was submitted that the count disclosed no offence in that the disposal or realisation of the car had been for the appellant's own benefit, not for the benefit of the unknown purchaser, and that in any event the purchaser was not within the ambit of the categories of 'other person' contemplated by s 22(1). The judge ruled that the purchaser derived a benefit from the transaction, in that, although he got no title, he had the use of the car, there was no reason to give any restricted construction to the words 'another person' in the subsection, and that, accordingly, on the undisputed facts, the appellant had undertaken the disposal or realisation of the car for the benefit of another person within the meaning of s 22(1). In face of this ruling the appellant entered a plea of guilty, thereby, it may be noted, confessing both his guilty knowledge and his dishonesty in relation to the December transaction.

On appeal against conviction to the Court of Appeal, the court affirmed the trial judge's ruling and dismissed the appeal (see [1981] 2 All ER 647, [1981] 1 WLR 859). The court certified the following point of law of general public importance as involved in their decision:

> 'Does a bona fide purchaser for value commit an offence of dishonestly undertaking the disposal or realisation of stolen property for the benefit of another if when he sells the goods on he knows or believes them to be stolen?'

The present appeal is brought by leave of your Lordships' House.

The full text of s 22(1) of the Theft Act 1968 reads: [his Lordship read s 22(1).]

It is, I think, now well settled that this subsection creates two distinct offences, but no more than two. The first is equivalent to the old offence of receiving under s 33 of the Larceny Act 1916. The second is a new offence designed to remedy defects in the old law and can be committed in any of the various ways indicated by the words from 'undertakes' to the end of the subsection. It follows that the new offence may and should be charged in a single count embodying in the particulars as much of the relevant language of the subsection, including alternatives, as may be appropriate to the circumstances of the particular case, and that such a count will not be bad for duplicity. It was so held by Geoffrey Lane J delivering the judgment of the Court of Appeal in *R v Willis, R v Syme* [1972] 3 All ER 797, [1972] 1 WLR 1605 and approved by that court in *R v Deakin* [1972] 3 All ER 803, [1972] 1 WLR 1618. So far as I am aware, this practice has been generally followed ever since.

The critical words to be construed are 'undertakes . . . their . . . disposal or realisation . . . for the benefit of another person'. Considering these words first in isolation, it seems to me that, if A sells his own goods to B, it is a somewhat strained use of language to describe this as a disposal or realisation of the goods for the benefit of B. True it is that B obtains a benefit from the transaction, but it is surely more natural to say that the disposal or realisation is for A's benefit than for B's. It is the purchase, not the sale, that is for the benefit of B. It is only when A is selling as agent for a third party C that it would be entirely natural to describe the sale as a disposal or realisation for the benefit of another person.

But the words cannot, of course, be construed in isolation. They must be construed in their context, bearing in mind, as I have pointed out, that the second half of the section creates a single offence which can be committed in various ways. I can ignore for present purposes the concluding words 'or if he arranges to do so', which throw no light on the point at issue. The preceding words contemplate four activities (retention, removal, disposal, realisation). The offence can be committed in relation to any one of these activities in one or other of two ways. First, the offender may himself undertake the activity *for the benefit* of another person. Second, the activity may be undertaken *by* another person and the offender may assist him. Of course, if the thief or an original receiver and his friend act together in, say, removing the stolen goods, the friend may be committing the offence in both ways. But this does not invalidate the analysis, and if the analysis holds good it must follow, I think, that the category of other persons contemplated by the subsection is subject to the same limitations in whichever way the offence is committed. Accordingly, a purchaser, as such, of stolen goods cannot, in my opinion, be 'another person' within the subsection, since his act of purchase could not sensibly be described as a disposal or realisation of the stolen goods *by* him. Equally, therefore, even if the sale to him could be described as a disposal or realisation for his benefit, the transaction is not, in my view, within the ambit of the subsection. In forming this opinion I have not overlooked that in *R v Deakin* [1972] 3 All ER 803 at 808, [1972] 1 WLR 1618 at 1624 Phillimore LJ said of the appellant, a purchaser of stolen goods who was clearly guilty of an offence under the first half of s 22(1) but had only been charged under the second half, that he was 'involved in the realisation'. If he meant to say that a purchase of goods is a realisation of those goods by the purchaser, I must express my respectful disagreement.

If the foregoing considerations do not resolve the issue of construction in favour of the appellant, at least they are, I believe, sufficient to demonstrate that there is an ambiguity. Conversely, it is no doubt right to recognise that the words to be construed are capable of the meaning which commended itself to the learned trial judge and to the Court of Appeal. In these circumstances, it is proper to test the question whether the opinion I have expressed in favour of a limited construction of the phrase 'for the benefit of another person' is to be preferred to the broader meaning adopted by the courts below, by any available aids to construction apt for the resolution of statutory ambiguities.

As a general rule, ambiguities in a criminal statute are to be resolved in favour of the subject, sc in favour of the narrower rather than the wider operation of an ambiguous penal provision. But here there are, in my opinion, more specific and weightier indications which point in the same direction as the general rule.

First, it is significant that the Theft Act 1968, notwithstanding the wide ambit of the definition of theft provided by ss 1 and 3(1), specifically protects the innocent purchaser of goods who subsequently discovers that they were stolen, by s 3(2) which provides: [his Lordship read s 3(2).]

It follows that, though some might think that in this situation honesty would require the purchaser, once he knew the goods were stolen, to seek out the true owner and return them, the criminal law allows him to retain them with impunity for his own benefit. It hardly seems consistent with this that, if he deals with them for the benefit of a third party in some way that falls within the ambit of the activities referred to in the second half of s 22(1), he risks prosecution for handling which carries a heavier maximum penalty (14 years) than theft (10 years). The force of this consideration is not, in my view, significantly weakened by the possibility that the innocent purchaser of stolen goods who sells them after learning they were stolen may commit the quite distinct offences of obtaining by deception (if he represents that he has a good title) or, conceivably, of aiding and abetting the commission by the purchaser of the offence of handling by receiving (if both know the goods were stolen).

Second, it is clear that the words in parenthesis in s 22(1) ('otherwise than in the course of the stealing') were designed to avoid subjecting thieves, in the ordinary course, to the heavier penalty provided for handlers. But most thieves realise the goods they have stolen by disposing of them to third parties. If the judge and the Court of Appeal were right, all such thieves are liable to prosecution as principals both for theft and for handling under the second half of s 22(1).

Finally, we have the benefit of the Eighth Report of the Criminal Law Revision Committee (Cmnd 2977), which led to the passing of the Theft Act 1968 including the provisions presently under consideration in the same form as they appeared in the draft Bill annexed to the report, to assist us in ascertaining what was the mischief which the Act, and in particular the new offence created by s 22(1), was intended to cure. We are entitled to consider the report for this purpose to assist us in resolving any ambiguity, though we are not, of course, entitled to take account of what the committee thought their draft Bill meant: see *Black-Clawson International Ltd v Papierwerke Waldhof-Aschaffenburg AG* [1975] 1 All ER 810, [1975] AC 591.

There is a long section in the report headed 'Handling Stolen Goods etc' from paras 126 to 144. The committee, after drawing attention to the limitations of the existing offence of receiving, say in para 127:

'. . . we are in favour of extending the scope of the offence to certain other kinds of meddling with stolen property. This is because the object should be to combat theft by making it more difficult and less profitable to dispose of stolen property. Since thieves may be helped not only by buying the property but also in other ways such as facilitating its disposal, it seems right that the offence should extend to these kinds of assistance.'

This gives a general indication of the mischief aimed at. The ensuing paragraphs, after setting out the proposed new provision in the terms which now appear in s 22(1) of the Act, give numerous illustrations of the activities contemplated as proper to attract the same criminal sanction as that previously attaching to the old offence of receiving. Throughout these paragraphs there is no hint that a situation in any way approximating to the circumstances of the instant case lay within the target area of the mischief which the committee intended their new provision to hit.

For these reasons I have reached the conclusion that any ambiguity in the relevant language of s 22(1) should be resolved in favour of the narrower meaning suggested earlier in this opinion. I would accordingly answer the certified question in the negative and allow the appeal. The costs of both parties should be paid out of central funds.

[**Lords Diplock**, **Scarman** and **Brandon of Oakwood** concurred.]
Certified question answered in the negative; order appealed from reversed; conviction quashed.

(5) MENS REA

The mens rea contains two elements: (i) dishonesty; and (ii) knowledge or belief that the goods are stolen. No doubt dishonesty bears the same meaning as it does for the purpose of other Theft Acts offences (see p 437, above). As to knowledge or belief the CLRC appeared to think (Cmnd 2977, para 134) that the formula would cover the case of the man who buys goods at a ridiculously low price from an unknown seller whom he meets in a public house. Such a man may not *know* that the goods are stolen but if he has considered that they might be and decided to take the risk he ought to be guilty of handling. But the formula chosen—'knowing or believing'—has been repeatedly held not to extend to one who suspects that the goods may be stolen, or closed his eyes to the obvious: *Hall* [1985] Crim LR 377, CA. So in *Reader* (1977) 66 Cr App Rep 33, CA, it was held a misdirection to tell the jury that the formula was satisfied if D thought it more likely than not that the goods were stolen. The court said (at 36):

> 'We are clearly of opinion that to have in mind that it is more likely that they are stolen than they are not, which is the test which the judge told the jury to apply, is not sufficient to comply with the terms of the section. To believe that the goods are probably stolen is not to believe that the goods are stolen, and in our view this was a misdirection by the learned judge and one which was not a misdirection which was in favour of the appellant but which was against him. The jury were being told to accept a lower state of guilty mind than the section actually requires.
> Our attention was drawn to two cases, *Grainge* (1973) 59 Cr App R 3; [1974] 1 WLR 619, and *Griffiths* (1974) 60 Cr App R 14, where two other directions about suspicion were considered by this Court. In the case of Grainge (supra) in giving the judgment of the Court, Eveleigh J pointed out that where there are simple words it is undesirable for the judge to try to explain what those words mean, and we entirely agree with that. If the learned judge had left the word "belief" entirely alone and left the jury to decide what is belief, that is something which everybody is concerned with almost every day of their lives and they would have been able to come to a proper conclusion without any explanation being given. In his mistaken attempt to give an explanation he erred. He erred in a sense in two ways, not only by putting the degree of belief wrong, but also in confusing the jury in our view by adding balance of probabilities into the concept which they had to be satisfied about. Accordingly there was in our view a material misdirection in this case.'

If D knows or believes that the goods are stolen it does not have to be proved that he knew the nature of the goods: *McCullum* [1973] Crim LR 582, CA.

Is the word 'knowing' in s 22(1) superfluous?

As to dishonesty, see *Roberts* [1986] Crim LR 122, CA.

CHAPTER 21

Forgery

Forgery is now regulated by the Forgery and Counterfeiting Act 1981. This Act is largely based on the recommendations of the Law Commission (Law Com No 55, *Report on Forgery and Counterfeit Currency* (1973)).

Forgery is usually done as a preparatory step to the commission of some other crime, most often a crime involving deception, which will result in some material advantage (most obviously money or other property) to the forger.

1. The subject matter of forgery

Forgery and Counterfeiting Act 1981, ss 1 and 8, pp 583 and 584, below

The *Oxford English Dictionary* defines forgery as 'the making of a thing in fraudulent imitation of something' and in common parlance the production of any fake article (whether a painting, a violin or a camera) is called a forgery. Forgery in the legal sense, however, has only extended to documents or writings, and the Act now prefers the word 'instrument'. The Act offers some guidance on this. An instrument is 'any document whether of a formal or informal character' (s 8(1)(a)) and 'any disc, tape, sound track or other device on or in which information is recorded or stored by mechanical, electronic or other means' (s 8(1)(d)).

It will be readily appreciated that an instrument may be expressed in any language in any form (code, hieroglyphic) on any substance (a tally stick for example). There is thus no reason why it should not extend to information electronically recorded on tape even though this cannot be read by the human eye but para (d) puts the matter beyond doubt. Even so a line has to be drawn somewhere. Under earlier legislation it has been held that a letter purporting to come from an employee requesting money of the employer (*Cade* [1914] 2 KB 209), a telegram antedated to defraud a bookmaker (*Riley* [1896] 1 QB 309), a certificate of competency to drive (*Potter* [1958] 2 All ER 51) and a football coupon (*Butler* (1954) 38 Cr App Rep 57) were all 'documents' and there is no reason to suppose that they would not now be 'instruments'. A vehicle excise licence is clearly an instrument but what of the car's number plates which may be altered to give a false impression of the car's age?

The essence of forgery, in our view, is the making of a false document intending that it be used to induce a person to accept and act upon the message contained in it, as if it were contained in a genuine document. In the straightforward case a document usually contains messages of two distinct kinds—first a message about the document itself (such as the message that the document is a cheque or a will) and secondly a message to be found in the words of the document that is to be accepted and acted upon (such as the message that a banker is to pay a specified sum or that property is to be distributed in a particular way). In our view it is only documents which convey not only the first type of message but also the second type that need to be protected by the law of forgery. Forgery should not be concerned, for example, with the false making of the autograph of a celebrity on a plain piece of paper, but it should be concerned with the false making of a signature as an endorsement on the back of a promissory note. The autograph conveys only the message that the signature was written by the person who bears that name; the endorsement conveys not only that the signatory made the endorsement, but also that he has authorised delivery of the note and has made himself liable to the holder in due course.

(Law Com No 55, para 22.) Is there anything in the Act which suggests that something may be a document only if it conveys messages of two kinds? The *Oxford English Dictionary* defines document as 'Something written, inscribed etc which furnishes evidence or information on any subject.' Would this definition include the car number plate or the celebrity's autograph? Is there a tenable distinction between something which conveys two messages and something that conveys only one? Cannot it be said that the celebrity's autograph conveys two messages: (i) that it is a genuine autograph; and (ii) that the recipient is intended to act upon it as such, eg by buying it from the defendant?

The Law Commission had intended specifically to exclude documents of historical interest only from the definition of document but there is no provision to this effect in the Act. Suppose that D makes a false copy of Shakespeare's will with a view to selling it as genuine. Does this fall within the Act's definition of instrument? Assuming that the Shakespeare will and the celebrity's autograph are excluded from the ambit of forgery, is there any convincing reason why they should be so excluded?

The Law Commission planned to define instrument as 'any instrument *in writing*' so as to make it clear that such things as 'a painting purporting to bear the signature of the artist, the false autograph and any writing on manufactured articles indicating the name of the manufacturer or the country of origin' stood excluded but the Act does not so qualify 'instrument'. In *Closs* (1858) Dears & B 460, CCR, it was held that a painting purporting to be the work of X and to bear X's signature was not 'a document or writing' and the argument that the signature was in the nature of an authentication certificate was rejected; the signature was said to be no more than a means for identifying the painting. Obviously an authentication certificate in the form of a statement by an acknowledged expert ascribing a particular painting to a particular artist is a document (it was so held in *Pryse-Hughes* (1958) Times, 14 May) and it is no less a document because it is pasted to the painting. In *Douce* [1972] Crim LR 105, QS, where the facts were essentially similar to *Closs*, the court concluded that 'document' for the purposes of the Forgery Act 1913 bore a wider meaning than it did at common law and held that the signatures on the paintings were documents 'as they purported to tell you something about the paintings'. Does the signature on the painting convey two messages or only one? Does it matter?

It seems to have mattered in *Smith* (1858) Dears & B 566, though again this was a decision under the common law. D had sold wrappers substantially representing the wrappers of one George Borwick, a well-known manufacturer of baking powder. It was held that the wrappers were not within the ambit of forgery since they were not documents. The same result would appear to follow on the Law Commission view. The wrappers conveyed only one message, that they were George Borwick wrappers, and conveyed no further message concerning the genuineness of the goods. They may have conveyed a second message about the lineage of the baking powder but there was no second message (or was there?) conveying the notion that the *wrapper* was to be acted on as such. How is this case to be decided under the Act? Is not a wrapper or label containing information at least a document of an 'informal' character?

2. The forgery

Forgery and Counterfeiting Act 1981, s 9, p 585, below

(1) FALSITY IN GENERAL

41. The present Act [viz Forgery Act 1913] contains no exhaustive definition of a false document, and it is to the common law that one must look to ascertain the meaning of the word in the context of forgery. By the middle of the nineteenth century it was established that for the purposes of the law of forgery the fact that determined whether a document was false was not that it contained lies, but that it told a lie about itself. It was in *R v Windsor* [(1865) 10 Cox CC 118 at 123] that Blackburn J said:

'Forgery is the false making of an instrument purporting to be that which it is not, it is not the making of an instrument which purports to be what it really is, but which contains false statements. Telling a lie does not become a forgery because it is reduced into writing'.

This test was recently applied in the Court of Appeal in *R v Dodge and Harris* [[1972] 1 QB 416], which makes it clear that any *dicta* to the contrary in *R v Hopkins and Collins* [(1957) 41 Cr App Rep 231] do not correctly state the law. Section 1 (2) of the Forgery Act 1913 puts into statutory form a series of decisions as to what at common law could amount to a false document, but is not intended to be an exhaustive definition. It provides that a document is false if the whole or any material part of it purports to be made by any person who did not make it or authorise its making; or if the time or place of making, where either is material, or in the case of a document identified by number or mark, the number or any distinguishing mark identifying the document, is falsely stated in it.

42. As we have said in Part III, the primary reason for retaining a law of forgery is to penalise the making of documents which, because of the spurious air of authenticity given to them, are likely to lead to their acceptance as true statements of the facts related in them. We do not think that there is any need for the extension of forgery to cover falsehoods that are reduced to writing, and we do not propose any change in the law in this regard.

43. The essential feature of a false instrument in relation to forgery is that it is an instrument which 'tells a lie about itself' in the sense that it purports to be made by a person who did not make it (or altered by a person who did not alter it) or otherwise purports to be made or altered in circumstances in which it was not made or altered. Falsity needs to be defined in these terms to cover not only, for example, the obvious case of forging a testator's signature to a will, but also the case where the date of a genuine will is altered to make it appear that the will was executed later than it in fact was, and therefore after what in truth was the testator's last will.

(Law Com No 55.)

In its ordinary application the distinction between a document that tells a lie and one that tells a lie about itself is easy enough to grasp. If an applicant for a job falsely states his qualifications in his letter of application, the letter is not a forgery; but if he writes a reference which purports to come from his employer, the reference is a forgery.

The application of s 9(1) (a) is straightforward and no serious difficulties are likely to be encountered with it or with the application of the next three cases instanced in the subsection. Paragraph (b) deals with the case where D makes a document which purports to be made on P's authority (even though it does not purport to be made by P himself) when P's authority has not been given. It can make no difference, incidentally, if D has the same name as P provided that D intends his signature, or his authorisation, to be taken for the signature or authorisation of P.

Paragraphs (e) and (f) contain further parallel provisions in relation to alterations. Usually the maker of an instrument is at liberty to alter it (he may, for instance, alter the name of the payee or the amount to be paid on a cheque); but where another alters, the alteration purporting to be made or authorised by the maker, the other makes a false instrument. In this connection the facts of *Hopkins and Collins* (1957) 41 Cr App Rep 231, CCA, provide a convenient illustration. D and E, the secretary and treasurer of a football supporters club, received monies raised by members and made disbursements on behalf of the club. Over a period of time they (i) entered in the books amounts less than were paid in; (ii) entered amounts in excess of what was paid out; and (iii) altered certain of the entries. It is clear that their accounts were inaccurate but to keep inaccurate accounts is not a forgery. So far as (i) and (ii) are concerned the accounts merely told a lie; they purported to be the accurate accounts of D and E when they were the inaccurate accounts of D and E. But what of (iii), the alterations? Paragraphs (e) and (f) do not render a document false merely because it has been altered; the alteration makes the document false only if it purports to be made or authorised by one who did not make or authorise it. Thus so long as the alterations were made or authorised by D and E they are not forgeries.

Of course if only E, the treasurer, had been authorised to keep the accounts and if D, the secretary, had without E's authority altered entries to make it appear that the alterations were made or authorised by E then the accounts would have been false. To constitute an instrument false the hand or authorisation of Jacob must appear as the hand or authorisation of Esau.

Paragraph (g) of s 9(1) deals with the case where the document appears to be made or altered on a date or at a place 'or otherwise in circumstances in which it was not in fact made or altered'. This would deal, for example, with the case where D alters the date on a will or deed to make it appear to antedate another will or deed. Nor is the will or deed any less false because it is D's own will or deed; a will or deed which purports to be executed on the 1st of the month tells a lie about itself if it was in fact executed on the 10th and D, provided he acts with mens rea, is guilty of forgery.

R v Donnelly (1984) 79 Cr App Rep 76, Court of Appeal, Criminal Division (Lawton LJ, Kilner Brown and Beldam, JJ)

[T] the appellant was convicted of making a false instrument contrary to section 1 of the Forgery and Counterfeiting Act 1981. . . .

The appellant was the manager of a jeweller's shop at Tooting. It was owned by a well-known company, Peter Alexander Ltd. On August 23, 1982, in collaboration with a man named Mohammed Aslam, he made out and signed what purported to be a written valuation of six items of jewellery. The total value attributed to them was £13,634. A printed form issued by the National Association of Goldsmiths of Great Britain and Northern Ireland was used. The heading on the valuation was in these terms: 'This valuation for insurance is based on values current at the undermentioned date (which was given as August 23, 1982). It is valid only for the purpose specified above.' There then followed a schedule describing in detail items of jewellery, with their weights, which did not exist. At the end of this schedule the appellant signed a statement in these terms: 'I have examined the articles scheduled above and in my opinion the figures given represent the value of such articles for the purpose stated.'

Underneath the appellant's signature was stamped the name of the owners of the shop and its address. This valuation was intended to be used for the purpose of defrauding an insurance company.

He appealed on a point of law, viz, did what the appellant was proved to have done, namely, making in writting what purported to be a jewellery valuation certificate, when there was no jewellery to be valued, with intent to induce somebody to accept it as genuine, amount in law to forgery contrary to section 1 of the Forgery and Counterfeiting Act 1981?

Lawton LJ read the judgment of the Court. . . .

Mr Peddie, on behalf of the appellant, accepted that this valuation was an instrument within the meaning of sections 1 and 8 of the 1981 Act but submitted that it was not a false one, just a lying one, and that an instrument was not a forgery if it did no more than on its face tell a lie, not being a lie as to what it was.

Mr Bevan for the prosecution conceded that both at common law and under the Forgery Act 1913 this valuation would not have been a forgery. He submitted, however, that the 1981 Act made new law and specifically enacted in section 9 what made an instrument a false one. There can be no doubt that in 1981 Parliament intended to make new law. The long title of the Act starts with these words: 'An Act to make fresh provision . . . with respect to forgery and kindred offences.' The trial judge was of the opinion that this valuation was a false instrument within the meaning of section 9(1)(g) which is in these terms: 'An instrument is false for the purposes of this part of this Act— . . . (g) if it purports to have been made or altered on a date on which, or at a place at which, or otherwise in circumstances in which, it was not in fact made or altered.'

Following the wording of paragraph (g) the judge directed the jury as follows: 'An instrument can be false if it purports to be made in circumstances in which it was not in fact made.'

In our judgment the words coming at the end of paragraph (g) 'otherwise in circumstances . . .' expand its ambit beyond dates and places to *any* case in which an instrument purports to be made when it was not in fact made. This valuation purported to be made *after* the appellant had examined the items of jewellery set out in the schedule. He did not make it after examining these items because they did not exist. That which purported to be a valuation after examination of items was nothing of the kind: it was a worthless piece of paper. In our judgment the trial judge's direction was correct. This purported valuation was a forgery. The appeal is dismissed.

Appeal dismissed.

Questions

1. Did the valuation certificates tell a lie about themselves or merely tell a lie? Did the court form any view on this issue?

2. The Law Commission intended to preserve the principle that for forgery the document must tell a lie about itself (p 519, above) but statutes do not always have their intended effect. In a literal sense it could be said that the certificates purported to be made 'in circumstances in which [they were] not made' because, as the court said, they purported to be made after an examination of jewellery which could not have taken place since the jewellery did not exist. Can it be argued that so far as para (g) is concerned there is no requirement that the document should tell a lie about itself? How might this argument be countered?

3. D makes an application for a job in which he claims prior experience which he does not have. Is the letter false within para (g) in that it purports to be made in circumstances in which it was not made? If so it would seem that very little is left of the principle that the document must tell a lie about itself but can such a case be distinguished from *Donnelly*?

(2) FALSITY AND FICTITIOUS PERSONS

Suppose that D and E apply for a job and in order to bolster their prospects D falsely makes a reference purporting to come from Sir George X (who does not exist) while E falsely makes a reference purporting to come from Sir Peter Y (who does exist). E's reference is clearly a forgery and, on the face of it, there is no reason for treating D's case differently and D's case seems clearly to fall within s 9(1)(h).

The invention of a fictitious person may be distinguished from the use of an alias. A man called X may write books under the pseudonym Y and open a bank account in the name of Y into which his royalties are paid. When X draws on this account in the name of Y it can hardly be supposed that his cheque is a false document by virtue of para (h). Y is not a fictitious person; he is a real person, X, styling himself Y. Nor would it make any difference that the bank knows him only as Y and is unaware that his true name is X. The bank may be unaware of, or even have been misled as to, the true name of their customer but so far as Y is concerned there is nothing fictitious about him. If the bank manager is told that Y is really called X he might say, 'Well, I thought he was called Y,' but he could hardly say, 'Well, I never knew that Y did not exist.'

Consider the facts of *Hassard and Devereux* [1970] 2 All ER 647, [1970] 1 WLR 1109, D, a company bookkeeper made out cheques in favour of a creditor of the company called B.S.A. and, after these cheques had been signed by the directors, he altered the cheques to B.S. Andrews and handed them to his confederate E. Obviously these cheques were forgeries (s 9(1)(b)) and no problem arises in connection with them. But D and E now needed to cash these cheques so they gave them to F who opened an account in the name B.S. Andrews and paid in the cheques. F represented herself as being B.S. Andrews, which was not of course her real name, but she did give her correct address. F then drew on this account. The question is whether the cheques drawn by F are forgeries by virtue of para (h). Literally the case seems to fall within para (h) because the cheque purported to be made by an existing person (B.S. Andrews) when B.S. Andrews was the invention of D, E and F and did not really exist. But is the case any different from the case in which an alias is used? Does the fact that D, E and F are acting fraudulently distinguish this case from that supposed above of the writer X assuming the pseudonym Y? If so, would X become guilty of forgery if his purpose in having his royalties paid into his Y account was to defraud the Revenue?

Suppose D writes begging letters purporting to emanate from distressed servicemen A, B and C, these being names that D has invented. The case seems clearly to fall within para (h). But what if D is in fact a distressed serviceman who while using the names A, B and C otherwise makes no misrepresentations and gives his correct address?

3. Mens rea: intent to prejudice

Forgery and Counterfeiting Act 1981, s 10, p 585, below

Sections 1–5 of the Act create various offences involving forgery. For purposes of convenience the mens rea of the various offences may be regarded as having two aspects. There is first of all the mental element required in relation to the making, using or possession of the false instrument and this aspect is considered in relation to the specific offences, p 526, below. The second aspect, which governs the offences under ss 1–4 and certain of the offences under s 5, is the requirement that D should intend that P should be induced, by reason of accepting the false instrument as genuine, to act or omit to act to his own or another's prejudice. It is this aspect which is discussed here.

Traditionally forgery required an intent to defraud or, in some cases, an intent to deceive. The meaning of these concepts was subject to controversy and the Law Commission sought a more precise and exhaustive definition of the mens rea of forgery.

32. It is obviously not satisfactory in a codification of the law of forgery merely to retain the phrase 'with intent to defraud' leaving its meaning to be ascertained from the many cases on the earlier statutes. This is particularly so when the cases, while not putting any precise limitation upon the nature of the disadvantage which must be intended, have not limited the disadvantage to economic loss, a limitation which the ordinary person might think follows from such a word as defraud. The essential feature of the mental element in forgery is an intention to induce another to accept the forged instrument as genuine and, by reason of that, to do or refrain from doing some act. Indeed in the Australian and Canadian Codes the required intention is defined in this way. Such a definition, however, creates a very wide offence which would penalise such practical jokes as the making of a forged invitation to a social function made with no more wicked intent than of raising a laugh at another's expense by inducing him to act upon the invitation. We do not think that such conduct should be within a serious offence such as forgery. Accordingly we have sought for a formula to limit the width of the offence.

33. We explored many possibilities in a search for a way of defining the intent required and at one stage we thought that the right result could be obtained simply by providing that there should be an intent to induce another to act upon the forged instrument to his or another's prejudice. 'Prejudice', however, is not a word which in the field of criminal law has acquired a precise meaning, and we feared that the use of this word undefined might lead to a series of decisions on the meaning to be given to it, thus defeating one of our objects in re-stating and clarifying the law. We turned, therefore, to a consideration of the main fields in which forgery most commonly occurs, with a view to determining what needed to be covered by the offence. Forgery most commonly occurs in connection with obtaining money or other property at the expense of another, and we decided to put in the forefront of our definition the intention to induce another to suffer a loss of money or other property, whether permanently or only temporarily—loss being defined, as it is in the Theft Act 1968, to include not getting what one might get, as well as parting with what one has. Such a definition would not cover an intention to induce another to give an opportunity to earn remuneration, for the remuneration is paid in return for the work done. Nevertheless the forging of any instrument, such as a testimonial or certificate evidencing a qualification, in order to obtain employment should be covered. Indeed, this is the present law and our consultations do not suggest that it should be changed. But even a definition of an intention to cause a loss cast in these terms would be insufficient to cover the variety of circumstances in which the making of a false instrument is at present an offence and, in our view, should continue to be penalised. The making of a forged security pass to obtain access to a building, the forging of a certificate of competency to drive a vehicle in order to obtain a driving licence, or the forging of documents in the circumstances of a case such as *Welham v DPP* [[1960] 1 All ER 805] would not be within the intention to cause a loss to another. In each of these cases the forgery is intended to be used to induce another to perform a duty which he has in a way in which he would not have performed it had he not accepted the instrument as genuine, and should also be covered. Again, this is, in effect, the present law and our consultations do not suggest that it should be changed.

34. There is some authority that it is forgery under the present law to make a false document to obtain payment of what is due, unless the maker of the document also believed that he was entitled to make the false document. It may be that such a fact situation as arose in *R v Parker* [(1910) 74 JP 208] would not fall within the part of our definition of prejudice which relates to a person suffering a loss; the debtor in paying what is due by him does not suffer a loss. However, it could be said that he has performed his duty to repay in a way in which he would not have performed it had he not accepted the instrument as genuine; but in our view it should not be forgery to make a false instrument to induce another to do what he is obliged to do or refrain from doing what he is not entitled to do. Cases where the forged instrument contained menaces would be caught in appropriate cases by section 21 of the Theft Act 1968 as blackmail if the instrument were used. That we think is the stage at which such an offence should be prosecuted, the determining factor being whether the person believed that the use of the menaces was a proper means of reinforcing the demand.

35. We have considered whether this definition of the mental element should be further refined by the addition of the word 'dishonestly'. This word is used in sections 15–16 of the Theft Act

1968 in penalising a person who by any deception obtains property belonging to another or a pecuniary advantage. Although the Act does not define the word, the effect of section 2 is to exclude from the operation of those sections a person who uses deception to obtain property, or a pecuniary advantage, to which he believes he is entitled. In forgery, however, as we propose that it should be defined, we are dealing with the more specific concept of intention to prejudice by the use of a false instrument as if it were genuine, and we do not think that the addition of a further qualification of 'dishonestly' is either necessary or helpful. If a person makes a false instrument intending that it be used as genuine to prejudice another by inducing him to act contrary to his duty it is irrelevant that that person may genuinely believe that he is entitled to what he is trying to obtain. However firmly he may believe, for example, that he is entitled to a driving licence, he intends to induce another to act contrary to his duty if he intends to induce him to issue such a licence against a false certificate of competence to drive a vehicle, as it is the issuing officer's duty to issue a licence only against the presentation of a valid certificate of competence.

36. It will be appreciated that an essential feature of the mental element, as we propose that it should be defined, is an intent that the false instrument be used to induce another to accept it as genuine, and by reason of that to do or refrain from doing some act. This postulates the use of an instrument to deceive a person, and does not appropriately meet the case where the intention is to use a false instrument to cause a machine to operate. The increasing use of more sophisticated machines has led us to include within 'instruments' capable of being forged the discs, tapes and other devices mentioned in paragraph 25, which may cause machines into which they are fed to respond to the information or instructions upon them, and, of course, these are machines which are designed to respond to an instrument in writing. It is necessary, therefore, to make provision to cover in such cases the intention to cause a machine to respond to a false instrument as if it were a genuine instrument. There also has to be provision for treating the act or omission intended to flow from the machine responding to the instrument as an act or omission to a person's prejudice.

Conclusion

37. *We recommend* that the mental element of the offence of forgery should be an intention that the false instrument shall be used with the intention of inducing someone to accept it as genuine and, by reason of that, to do or refrain from doing some act to the prejudice of himself or of any other person. An act intended to be induced should be to a person's prejudice only if it is one which, if it occurs:

(a) will result in loss by that person in money or other property,

(b) will take the form of giving an opportunity to earn remuneration or greater remuneration, or

(c) will be attributable to his having accepted the false instrument as genuine in connection with the performance by him of a duty.

It should not, however, be to a person's prejudice for him to be induced to do some act which he has an enforceable duty to do, or to refrain from doing some act which he is not entitled to do. It will be necessary to make special provisions for such a case, and also to provide that the requisite intention is present when there is an intention to cause a machine to respond to an instrument as if it were genuine.

(Law Com No 55.)

R v Campbell (1985) 80 Cr App Rep 47, Court of Appeal, Criminal Division (Ackner LJ, Bristow and Popplewell JJ)

The following facts are taken from the judgment.

The facts are very simple and they were not essentially in dispute. About March 30, 1982, the appellant came into possession of a cheque for £5,363.67 made out on the account of Boleyn Car Sales Ltd and payable to G.N. Croydon. This cheque was provided to her by a plausible lady called Mrs Vincent, who was employed by Boleyn Car Sales Ltd, and who told her friend, the appellant, that she had purchased a car from the company, had decided that it was not what she wanted and the only way in which she could get her money back from the company was if the cheque was made out to a fictitious name and was then negotiated through a banking account. The appellant then obligingly endorsed the cheque with the fictitious name 'G.N. Croydon,' following that name with her own name and bank account number. She paid the cheque into her bank account. Within a day she withdrew the selfsame sum in cash and paid it over to the no doubt delighted Mrs. Vincent. She explained to the police, when she was asked, what her part was in the case and the prosecution accepted those facts.

She appealed on the grounds that the trial judge erred in ruling (i) that dishonesty was no longer a necessary element in the offence of forgery, and (ii) that there was an intention by the appellant to do some act to another's prejudice. For although prejudice was created by her act of forgery there was no intention to cause temporary or permanent loss.

Ackner LJ. On August 10, 1983, in the Crown Court at Knightsbridge the appellant pleaded guilty on re-arraignment to forgery (count 3). As a result she was sentenced to a fine of £20 or one day's imprisonment in default. She had originally pleaded not guilty to this count, but as a result of the learned judge indicating to counsel that he considered it she had no defence in law, the plea was altered. The appeal comes before us because it is submitted that the judge was wrong in taking the view that in law there was no defence.

The learned Lord Justice stated the facts and continued:

The offence of forgery under section 1 of the Forgery and Counterfeiting Act 1981 arises '. . . if [a person] makes a false instrument, with the intention that he or another shall use it to induce somebody to accept it as genuine, and by reason of so accepting it to do or not to do some act to his own or any other person's prejudice.' It is common ground that the intention which the statute requires contains two ingredients. One is the intention that the false instrument shall be used to induce somebody to accept it as genuine and the other is the intention to induce somebody by reason of so accepting it to do or not to do some act to his own or any other person's prejudice. It is common ground, as it has to be on these facts, that the appellant did make a false instrument because she endorsed the fictitious name on the back of the cheque thereby giving the impression that the cheque had been properly made out to G. N. Croydon, and that G. N. Croydon had endorsed the cheque over to her. It is conceded that she did that with the intention to induce somebody—that is the bank—to accept it as genuine. So the first of the ingredients of the intention was properly made out by the prosecution. In fact it was not in issue.

That which is in issue is whether the prosecution on the facts which we have recounted have established the second ingredient, namely that the intention was to induce somebody by reason of so accepting that false document to do some act to his own or any other person's prejudice. Again so far as the law is concerned it is common ground that section 10 of the Act exhaustively defines 'induce' and 'prejudice' for the purpose of this second ingredient. It is a lengthy section. We need only read that part of the section which relates to the facts of this case. Subsection (1):

'Subject to subsections (2) and (4) below, for the purposes of this Part of this Act an act or omission intended to be induced is to a person's prejudice if, and only if, it is one which, if it occurs— . . . (c) will be the result of his having accepted a false instrument as genuine . . . in connection with his performance of any duty.'

It is common ground that in the context of this case 'his' means 'the bank,' so it will read: 'will be the result of the bank having accepted a false instrument as genuine in connection with the bank's performance of any duty.'

Mr. Tabor seeks to rely before us, though he did not before the learned judge, on subsection (2). Again we read only those words that can relate to this case: 'An act which a person has an enforceable duty to do . . . shall be disregarded for the purposes of this Part of this Act.' In our judgment, that subsection provides no assistance to the appellant for this simple reason, that it was the bank's duty to pay out only on a valid instrument and it is common ground in this case that that which was presented to the bank, and which was accepted by the bank, was a false instrument which it was not part of the bank's duty to honour. On the contrary, had the bank known of the true status of that document, they would have wholly rejected it. In these circumstances it seems plain to us that the offence was properly established. It would be remarkable if such a situation was not covered one way or another by this far-embracing, recent piece of legislation.

Accordingly the appeal against conviction is dismissed.

Appeal dismissed.

Question

In what sense did Campbell intend to prejudice the bank when, as it seems to have been assumed, she thought there was nothing improper in what she did? Is an *intent* to prejudice required?

NOTE

The Law Commission thought that in an age where machines are increasingly used to respond to instructions it was necessary to make provision for cases where a machine is made to respond to a false instrument as though it were a genuine one and ss 10(3) and (4) implement the Commission's view.

Take the card issued by banks to enable customers to obtain money from automatic tills. Electronically encoded on the card is certain information, usually the customer's account number, the branch where the account is held and the customer's pass number. Such a card is an instrument within s 8 and to make a facsimile of the card would render the instrument false within s 9. But if the matter rested there the offence of forgery would not be committed because the maker does not intend to induce any act or omission to a *person's* prejudice. The maker intends to use the card to operate the machine but he does not intend any person by reason of accepting the card as genuine to act or fail to act to his prejudice. The Act, however, provides for this case; the false card was made with a view to 'inducing the machine to respond' as if the card were genuine (s 9(3)) and by s 10(4) the resulting prejudice '*shall* be treated' as an act to a person's prejudice.

The above is a case where economic loss is caused. But prejudice is not confined to economic loss and extends to causing a person to act in contravention of a duty. We are to assume, it seems, that a machine may act in contravention of its duty! Many hotels now have sophisticated locks which are operated by a magnetially encoded card and similar devices are commonly used to gain access to car parks. Would it really be forgery to make facsimiles to gain access? Are such things instruments within s 8?

4. The offences

(1) FORGERY

Forgery and Counterfeiting Act 1981, s 1, p 583, below.

To constitute forgery the instrument must be made false in order to induce another to accept it as genuine. Making a copy intending to pass it off as a copy is not forgery. In *Woodward* (1796) 2 Leach 782n, D signed a promissory note in his own name and subsequently passed off the note as coming from his sergeant-major who had the same name. Would D now be guilty of forgery? The point is perhaps of little practical importance because D will usually commit an offence under ss 2, 3 or 4 which merely require knowledge or belief (as to which see p 516, above) that the instrument *is* false, not that it was *made* false with the requisite intention.

(2) COPYING A FALSE INSTRUMENT

Forgery and Counterfeiting Act 1981, s 2, p 583, below.

39. It is also necessary to provide for the making of a copy of a false instrument. In *R v Harris* [[1965] 3 All ER 206n] the court, in the context of section 6 of the present Act which deals with

the using of a false document, left open the question whether the mere making of a photostat copy of a forged document is itself using a forged document, though it held that making the copy and sending it out as a copy of a genuine document with the requisite intention was within the prohibition of the section. With the increasing use of photocopying machines there is increasing reliance being placed on copies of original documents, which assume more the character of duplicate originals than of copies of the original. For this reason we propose that the making of a copy of an instrument which the maker knows or believes to be a false instrument should, if it is made with the intention of inducing another to accept the copy as a copy of a genuine instrument and by reason of that to do or refrain from doing some act to his or another's prejudice, be an offence of the same nature as making a forgery.

(Law Com No 55)

Strictly it might be argued that a photocopy of a false instrument is not itself a false instrument (why?) but s 2 now covers the case.

(3) USING A FALSE INSTRUMENT AND COPIES

Forgery and Counterfeiting Act 1981, ss 3 and 4, p 583, below.

Any communication of a false instrument would amount to a use; even to photocopy a false instrument would appear to be a use of it though this is expressly governed by s 2.

Sometimes D may use a false instrument to begin a chain of events which will result in a gain to himself or a loss to another. D may furnish false instruments to P with a view to inducing P to affirm D's creditworthiness to Q who then delivers property to D. Here Q has been induced by D's fraud to extend credit to D but he has not been so induced by the false instruments. In such a case it is only P who, by virtue of accepting the false instruments as genuine, has been induced to act to his own or another's prejudice.

(4) POSSESSION OFFENCES

Forgery and Counterfeiting Act 1981, s 5, p 583, below.

The possession offences extend only to the instruments listed in s 5(5). The Act, on the recommendation of the Law Commission, eschews the word 'possession' because of the technicalities associated with that concept and prefers 'custody or control'. The former is apt to cover D's personal custody of the instrument while the latter is apt where the instrument is at a place or with a person subject to access or control by D.

While s 5 creates four offences, there are in essence two pairs of offences. All four have the common element of custody or control but the offences under s 5(1) and (3) are more serious than the offences under s 5(2) and (4):

68. Having regard to the nature of the instruments referred to . . . it is easy to envisage circumstances where possession of such instruments might be of great social danger, particularly where there is an intention that the instruments should be used to induce another to act to his prejudice in the belief that they are genuine. On the other hand the possession of a false postage stamp or even of a false share certificate if unaccompanied by such an intention will normally have less serious implications. For this reason we feel that there should be two offences in relation to possession of the listed instruments, the one requiring an intention that the instruments be used as genuine to induce another to act to his prejudice, and the other requiring only possession without lawful authority or excuse. The first offence should carry the same penalty as the forgery and the using offence, whereas the second offence should carry a maximum penalty of two years'

imprisonment. We think that the provision of two offences with differing mental elements will provide adequate protection against possession by persons who have such false instruments for the purpose of a fraudulent scheme, and yet not penalise too heavily those who come into possession of such false instruments and yet with knowledge of their falsity continue to hold them instead of delivering them up to the authorities.

Neither the Act nor the Law Commission's report offers guidance as to what constitutes 'lawful authority or excuse'. The expression is one which is found in other contexts in the criminal law and its judicial interpretation in those contexts affords no grounds for thinking that it will be generously interpreted. Lawful authority must extend to the police officer who acquires the false instrument as part of his duties and to the citizen who intends to act in accordance with the law. Excuse would certainly be apt where D has some general defence (infancy, duress) to crime available to him. It is thought unlikely that an innocent intention (as where a false instrument is kept as a curio or where a dye is kept simply for the purpose of producing illustrations in a magazine or newspaper) will suffice since the potential for mischief remains irrespective of the present intention of the possessor.

CHAPTER 22

Offences of damage to property

The principal offences of damage to property are governed by the Criminal Damage Act 1971 which is in the main the work of the Law Commission: see The Law Commission (Law Com No 29) *Criminal Law: Report on Offences of Damage to Property* (1970), hereinafter referred to as Law Com No 29.

1. Destroying or damaging property of another

Criminal Damage Act 1971, s 1 (1), p 575, below

(1) DESTROY OR DAMAGE

The *Oxford English Dictionary* defines 'damage' as 'To do or cause damage to; to hurt, harm, injure; now commonly to injure (a thing) so as to lessen its value'. And 'destroy' is defined as 'To undo, break up, reduce into a useless form, consume, or dissolve'. In *Barnet London Borough Council v Eastern Electricity Board* [1973] 2 All ER 319 DC, which was concerned with whether there had been a 'destruction' of certain trees for the purposes of s 29 (1) of the Town and Country Planning Act 1962, May J, said:

> 'The respondents in their turn point to the dictionary meanings of "destroy" . . . To destroy, they say, is to render useless or to kill and they ask, pertinently enough, how it can be said that the respondents have destroyed at least the two trees still standing and which are still alive? Even if any act of the respondents can be said to have initiated any "destruction" of any of the trees, that process is not complete, and a person cannot be convicted of this contravention of the order at least until the tree is dead.
> We have not found this at all an easy point of construction. In the first place we think it right as a matter of language not necessarily to treat "destruction" as a synonym for "obliteration"; a glass vase is destroyed when it falls to the ground and shatters, even though the fragments which once comprised it still remain. On the other hand "destruction" must have at least elements of finality and totality about it and must in our judgment go further than merely a material change in the life-span or stability of the tree. The difficulty in this case is to say precisely how much further one must go and how clearly to define in words the point at which one should stop.
> We think it right to start consideration of the problem with one of the dictionary definitions of destroy to which we have already referred, namely "to render useless". Before a tree can be said to be destroyed we feel that it must have been rendered useless—but rendered useless as what? This last enquiry raises immediately the question of the purpose for which the use of the tree may or may not continue to exist. Consequently in our judgment one must bear in mind in this case that the underlying purpose of the relevant legislation is the preservation of trees and woodlands as amenities, as living creatures providing pleasure, protection and shade; it is their use as such that is sought to be preserved and a tree the subject of a tree preservation order is destroyed in the present context when as a result of that which is done to it, it ceases to have any use as an amenity,

as something worth preserving. For example, if a person intentionally inflicts on a tree so radical an injury that in all the circumstances any reasonably competent forester would in consequence decide that it ought to be felled, then in our opinion that person wilfully destroys the tree within the meaning of that word in the relevant legislation and order.'

In *A (a Juvenile) v R* [1978] Crim LR 689 (Kent CC) D's conviction for damaging a police officer's raincoat by spitting on it was quashed. 'Spitting at a garment,' Judge Streeter said,

'could be an act capable of causing damage. However, one must consider the specific garment which has been allegedly damaged. If someone spat upon a satin wedding dress, for example, any attempt to remove the spittle might in itself leave a mark or stain. The court would find no difficulty in saying that an article had been rendered "imperfect" if, after a reasonable attempt at cleaning it, a stain remained. An article might also have been rendered "inoperative" if, as a result of what happened, it had been taken to dry cleaners. However, in the present case, no attempt had been made, even with soap and water, to clean the raincoat, which was a service raincoat designed to resist the elements. Consequently, there was no likelihood that if wiped with a damp cloth, the first obvious remedy, there would be any trace or mark remaining on the raincoat requiring further cleaning.'

But why was the raincoat not damaged if it could be wiped clean with a dry cloth but was damaged if it required 'further cleaning' at a dry cleaners? In *Samuels v Stubbs* [1972] 4 SASR 200 (SC of S Aust) it was held that a 'temporary functional derangement' of a police officer's cap as a result of its being stamped upon by D constituted damage though it could be pushed back to its former shape. Is there (should there be?) a principle of *de minimis* in relation to damage?

May something be damaged merely by removing or disconnecting a part? Under the former law it was held to constitute damage to dismantle a machine (*Getty v Antrim County Council* [1950] NI 114), and even to remove an iron bar from a machine though it was a simple matter to re-screw the bar to make the machine operational again (*Tacey* (1821) Russ & Ry 452). But can it be said that a car is damaged by disconnecting the battery terminals, or by removing the ignition key?

(2) PROPERTY

Criminal Damage Act 1971, s 10 (1), p 576, below

Offences of criminal damage to property in the context of the present law connote physical damage in their commission, and for that reason we have not included intangible things the class of property, damage to which should constitute an offence. On the other hand, the context of damage to property there is no reason to distinguish, as does the Theft Act between land and other property . . . We recommend, therefore, that the property which can be the subject of an offence of criminal damage should be all property of a tangible nature, whether real or personal.

(Law Com No 29, paras 34, 35.)

(3) BELONGING TO ANOTHER

Criminal Damage Act 1971, s 10 (2), p 576, below

The offence under s 1 (1) may be committed only where D destroys or damages property 'belonging to another'. Since there are similar policy considerations s 10(2) of the Criminal Damage Act is similar to, though not identical with, s 5 of the Theft Act 1968. It is accordingly enough that P has some proprietary interest in the property which D damages and it does not have to be shown that P is the owner of the property; D may, for example, damage property of which P is the lessee or bailee. Further, D may commit an offence where he is the owner of the property provided that P also has a proprietary interest in the property and that D acts with *mens rea*.

But if no third party has any interest in the property D cannot by destroying that property, nor by authorising its destruction, commit an offence under s 1(1) even if this is done in order to perpetrate a fraud by making a claim against insurers:

R v Appleyard Lexis, No 6771/B/84; [1985] Crim LR 723 Court of Appeal, Criminal Division
(Lord Lane CJ, Skinner and Macpherson JJ)

The Lord Chief Justice. . . . . There is no need to detail the facts relating to the offences other than that alleged in count 4. Count 4 was based upon an allegation made by the Crown that on 15th June 1982, allegedly with a man called Lawford, who was in fact acquitted, this man set fire to a store belonging to a limited company called Pontefract Tape Ltd.

The appellant and Lawford were seen at the premises shortly after 5.30 in the evening in a Volvo motor car. The fire brigade was called some 20 minutes later by a neighbour who had seen smoke issuing from the premises. The engine arrived at 5.57 and there was no doubt upon the scientific examination of the premises that the fire had been deliberately started, because traces of paraffin were found upon the floor. According further to the scientific evidence, the fire had not been burning for very much longer than 20 minutes before the fire engine arrived. Consequently it was at least possible, if not strongly probable, that the appellant had something to do with the starting of the fire . . .

At the close of the prosecution case Mr Steer, appearing for the defendant then as he does for him as the appellant now, submitted that there was no case to answer, amongst other counts, on count 4. It was argued by him that since the appellant was in effect the owner of the premises, he must be entitled to set fire to them if he wanted to. It could not therefore be said that he was acting without lawful excuse as the statute requires. After a very lengthy submission indeed, the learned Judge rejected that submission, the trial continued and, as already indicated, the jury convicted.

The first and main issue at the trial was the question whether it was proved to the satisfaction of the jury so that they felt sure that this man had started the fire. The jury came to the conclusion, not surprisingly, that they were so satisfied.

The next problem was that raised by the words of the statute itself. Let me therefore read the terms of section 1 of the Criminal Damage Act 1971: [His Lordship read s (1) and 1 (3) of the Act.]

The submission made by Mr Steer and rejected by the learned Judge, has been repeated here today. The only point of this appeal is whether the Judge was right in rejecting that submission or not. Mr Steer confines his argument today to section 1 and does not rely on the provisions of section 5(2), to which it is therefore not necessary for us to refer.

The basis of Mr Steer's submission, as he was eventually driven to concede, was a statement by this Court in *R v Denton* (1982) 74 Cr App R 81. Let me just read the headnote relating the facts of that case in order to show the way it is distinguished from the present circumstances. It reads as follows:

'The appellant, who was employed by one T, set fire to T's business premises and was charged with arson contrary to section 1(1) and (3) of the Criminal Damage Act 1971. At his trial he gave evidence that T had asked him to start the fire because T's company was in difficulties and a fire might improve the financial circumstances of the company. The appellant relied on section 5(2) of the Act of 1971 providing him with a defence to the charge in that T had consented to the damage caused by the fire and intended to make a fraudulent insurance claim in respect of it. The trial judge ruled that "entitled" in section 5(2)(a) carried a connotation of general lawfulness and that T could not be said to have been entitled to consent to damage for a fraudulent purpose, so that the defence under section 5(2) was not open to the appellant, whereupon the latter changed his plea to one of guilty. On appeal against the judge's ruling,

Held, that no offence was committed under section 1(1) and (3) of the Criminal Damage Act 1971 by a person who burnt down his own premises; nor could that act become unlawful because of an inchoate intent to defraud the insurers; accordingly, the judge's ruling was wrong; and as the appellant's plea of guilty had been based upon that ruling, the appeal would be allowed and the conviction quashed.

It will therefore be seen that the point at issue in that case was nothing to do with the point in issue in the present case. Moreover in that case it was the servant of the company who had set light to the machinery and not T. In the present case it is the managing director or, as Mr Steer chooses inaccurately to call him, the proprietor of the business who had, according to the jury's finding, set fire to the property.

Therefore in order to support his argument and, as he concedes, as the basis of his argument, Mr Steer relies upon a passage at the top of page 84 of the judgment, which runs as follows:

'It was agreed on all hands for the purpose of this case that T was the person who, any evil motives apart, was entitled to consent to the damage. It was likewise conceded that the appellant Denton honestly believed that T occupied that position and was entitled to consent.'

Basing himself upon that and basing himself upon the similarity of the position of T to the position of the appellant in the present case, Mr Steer argues that therefore this appellant must be taken to have been entitled to consent to the damage.

The fundamental fallacy of that argument scarcely needs pointing out. It was a concession in Denton that was assumed for the purposes of argument, for the simple reason that it was the servant and not the so called proprietor who was being charged. To seek to base a proposition of law upon a concession which was made simply for the purpose of argument in another case, is a fruitless exercise.

There is nothing in this appeal and it is dismissed.

Appeal dismissed

Questions

Is *Denton* overruled by *Appleyard*? In *Denton* D evidently thought that T was in a position to authorise the destruction of the company's premises; he was, as *Appleyard* shows, mistaken in this belief but would his mistaken belief save him from liability for criminal damage? What if in *Appleyard* D had genuinely, though mistakenly, believed that, as managing director, he was entitled to destroy the company's premises?

(4) INTENTION AND RECKLESSNESS

R v Caldwell [1981] 1 All ER 961, HL

The case is set out at p 68, above.

Elliott v C(a minor) [1983] 2 All ER 1005, DC

The case is set out at p 73, above.

R v Stephen Malcolm R (1984) 79 Cr App Rep 334, CA

The case is set out at p 76, above.

Caldwell has been considered in its general application in the criminal law, p 68, above. Whatever uncertainty exists about that, it has to be accepted that it authoritatively defines recklessness in relation to criminal damage which is the concern of this section.

Some commentators thought at first that *Caldwell* did not entirely rule subjective factors out of account. In it Lord Diplock talked of a risk 'obvious if any thought were given to the matter *by the doer of the act*' [1981] 1 All ER 961 at 965, (italics supplied) and in the related case of *Lawrence* [1981] 1 All ER 974, at 982, p 72, above,) he said that regard must also be given 'to any explanation [D] gives as to his state of mind which may displace the inference.' But *Elliott v C (a minor)* and *Stephen Malcolm*, pp 73, 76, above, despite the misgivings expressed, seem to rule out consideration of subjective factors, certainly such factors as age, or lack of experience and intellect. The Court of Appeal held that *Caldwell* established that the risk needed to be obvious to an 'ordinary prudent individual'. But how far is this process to be taken? Suppose that D, unable to locate the light switch in a darkened store strikes a match. There is in fact an overpowering smell of petrol fumes to which, owing to a heavy cold, D is completely oblivious and the store is consumed by fire. Or suppose that E, a blind man, knocks over and destroys a statue placed in a corridor which E has previously found free from obstruction. Are D and E reckless on the *Caldwell* view? Can their cases be sensibly distinguished from those of the defendants in *Caldwell*, *Elliott v C* and *Stephen Malcolm* ? Would it be a relevant consideration that D entered the store with intent to steal, or that E failed to use his white stick?

What of the situation where D in fact foresees the risk but decides to take it? Consider *Pembliton* (1874) LR 2 CCR 119, p 81 above. When he threw the stone at the people with whom he was fighting Pembliton might have (i) failed to consider the risk of breaking the window; or (ii) realised there was a risk of breaking the window but thought that it was so remote as to be worth taking; or (iii) considered the risk of breaking the window but was so sure of his aim that he thought there was no risk involved for him. On hypothesis (i) Pembliton may now be convicted of criminal damage if what he did created an obvious risk. But how does he stand on hypotheses (ii) and (iii)?

Intention, unlike recklessness, appears to have no objective connotations. It is not enough to prove that D intentionally did the act (threw the stone, fired the gun) that in the result caused damage to property unless that result was also intended. But in such cases the prosecution may rely on recklessness since D is liable to conviction if his intentional throwing of the stone or firing the gun creates an obvious risk even though it is not foreseen by him.

It is apprehended that the doctrine of transferred intent continues to apply under the Act:

> 'For the simple offence we think that the necessary mental element should be expressed as an intention to destroy or damage the property of another or as recklessness in that regard. The intention or the recklessness need not be related to the particular property damaged, provided that it is related to another's property. If, for example, a person throws a stone at a passing motor car intending to damage it, but misses and breaks a shop window, he will have the necessary intention in respect of the damage to the window as he intended to damage the property of another. But if in a fit of anger he throws a stone at his own car and breaks a shop window behind the car he will not have the requisite intention. In the latter case the question of whether he has committed an offence will depend upon whether he was reckless as to whether any property belonging to another would be destroyed or damaged.'

(Law Com No 29, para 45.) But in the Law Commission's illustration does the person who breaks the shop window any more intend to break that window where he throws the stone at another's car as where he throws the stone at his own car? Is it sensible to say that if D intends to damage *some* property he therefore intends to damage *any* property? The Law Commission assumes that if D intends to damage his own car but misses and breaks a shop window then he is not guilty of criminal damage to the window. Is this assumption well founded?

Suppose that D, bent on stealing from a gas meter, knowingly fractures the gas pipe and this leads to a fire in which the premises are destroyed. D is clearly guilty of criminal damage to the pipe but is he guilty of arson? Professor Glanville Williams thinks not ([1983] CLJ 85 at 86) because, and though damage caused by fire is simply one way of causing damage, arson carries a higher maximum punishment than criminal damage. 'The reasonable view,' he says, 'is that arson is a separate offence, so that the intention cannot be transferred.' But what if the gas leak caused an explosion, without any attendant fire, which destroyed the premises?

Obviously *mens rea* cannot be supplied by an afterthought. If D inadvertently breaks P's window he cannot be liable when, having learned that P is a tax inspector, he rejoices in the harm caused. On the other hand, as *Miller* [1983] 2 AC 161, [1983] 1 All ER 978, HL, p 23, above shows, if D inadvertently sets fire to P's property and subsequently becomes aware that he has done so, he may be criminally liable if, intending or being reckless that *further* damage may ensue to P's property, he lets the fire take its course when it lies within his power to prevent or minimise that further damage.

(5) LAWFUL EXCUSE

Criminal Damage Act 1971, s 5, p 575, below

In most cases there is a clear distinction between the mental element and the element of unlawfulness, and in the absence of one or the other element no offence will be committed, notwithstanding that damage may have been done to another's property. For example, a police officer who, in order to execute a warrant of arrest, has to force open the door of a house is acting with a lawful excuse although he intends to damage the door or the lock. On the other hand a person playing tennis on a properly fenced court who inadvertently hits a ball on to a greenhouse roof, breaking a pane of glass, acts without lawful excuse, but will escape liability because he has not the requisite intention.

(Law Com No 29, para 49.)

R v Smith (David Raymond) [1974] 1 All ER 632, Court of Appeal,
Criminal Division
(Roskill, James, LJJ and Talbot J)

[James LJ read the following judgment of the court:]

. . . The question of law in this appeal arises in this way. In 1970 the appellant became the tenant of a ground floor flat at 209 Freemasons Road, London, E16. The letting included a conservatory. In the conservatory the appellant and his brother, who lived with him, installed some electric wiring for use with stereo equipment. Also, with the landlord's permission, they put up roofing material and asbestos wall panels and laid floor boards. There is no dispute that the roofing, wall panels and floor boards became part of the house and, in law, the property of the landlord. Then in 1972 the appellant gave notice to quit and asked the landlord to allow the appellant's brother to remain as tenant of the flat. On 18 September 1972 the landlord informed the appellant that his brother could not remain. On the next day the appellant damaged the roofing, wall panels and floorboards he had installed in order—according to the appellant and his brother—to gain access to and remove the wiring. The extent of the damage was £130. When interviewed by the police, the appellant said, 'Look, how can I be done for smashing my own property. I put the flooring and that in, so if I want to pull it down it's a matter for me.' The offence for which he was indicted is in these terms:

> 'Damaging property contrary to Section 1 (1) of the Criminal Damage Act 1971. *Particulars of Offence*: [The appellant] and Steven John Smith on the 19th day of September 1972 in Greater London, without lawful excuse, damaged a conservatory at 209, Freemasons Road, E16, the property of Peter Frank Frand, intending to damage such property or being reckless as to whether such property would be damaged.'

The Steven John Smith jointly charged is the appellant's brother. He was acquitted.

The appellant's defence was that he honestly believed that the damage he did was to his own property, that he believed that he was entitled to damage his own property, and therefore he had a lawful excuse for his action causing the damage.

In the course of his summing-up the deputy judge directed the jury in these terms:

> 'Now, in order to make the offence complete, the person who is charged with it must destroy or damage that property belonging to another, "without lawful excuse", and that is something that one has got to look at a little more, members of the jury, because you have heard here that, so far as each defendant was concerned, it never occurred to them, and, you may think, quite naturally never occurred to either of them, that these various additions to the house were anything but their own property . . . But, members of the jury, the Act is quite specific, and so far as the [appellant] is concerned . . . lawful excuse is the only defence which has been raised. It is said he had a lawful excuse by reason of his belief, his honest and genuinely held belief that he was destroying property which he had a right to destroy if he wanted to. But, members of the jury, I must direct you as a matter of law, and you must, therefore, accept it from me, that belief by the [appellant] that he had the right to do what he did is not lawful excuse within the meaning of the Act. Members of the jury, it is an excuse, it may even be a reasonable excuse, but it is not, members of the jury, a lawful excuse, because, in law, he had no right to do what he did. Members of the jury, as a matter of law, the evidence, in fact, discloses, so far as [the appellant] is concerned, no lawful excuse at all, because, as I say, the only defence which he has raised is the defence that he thought he had the right to do what he did. I have directed you that that is not a lawful excuse, and members of the jury, it follows from that that so far as [the appellant] is concerned, I am bound to direct you as a matter of law that you must find him guilty of this offence with which he is charged.'

It is contended for the appellant that that is a misdirection in law, and that, as a result of the misdirection, the entire defence of the appellant was wrongly withdrawn from the jury . . .

The offence created [by s 1 (1) of the Criminal Damage Act] includes the elements of intention or recklessness and the absence of lawful excuse. There is in s 5 of the Act a partial 'definition' of lawful excuse. . . .[His Lordship referred to s 5 (2), s 5 (3) and s 5 (5), pp 575–576, below].

It is argued for the appellant that an honest, albeit erroneous, belief that the act causing damage or destruction was done to his own property provides a defence to a charge brought under s 1 (1). The argument is put in three ways. First, that the offence charged includes the act causing the damage or destruction and the element of mens rea. The element of mens rea relates to all the circumstances of the criminal act. The criminal act in the offence is causing damage to or destruction of 'property belonging to another' and the element of mens rea, therefore, must relate to 'property belonging to another'. Honest belief, whether justifiable or not, that the property is the defendant's own negatives the element of mens rea. Secondly, it is argued that by the terms of s 5, in particular the words of sub-s (2), 'whether or not he would be treated for the purposes of this Act as having a lawful excuse apart from this subsection', and the words in sub-s (5), the appellant had a lawful excuse in that he honestly believed he was entitled to do as he did to property he believed to be his own. This it seems is the way the argument was put at the trial. Thirdly, it is argued, with understandable diffidence, that if a defendant honestly believes he is damaging his own property he has a lawful excuse for so doing because impliedly he believes that he is the person entitled to give consent to the damage being done and that he has consented: thus the case falls within s 5 (2) (a) of the Act.

We can dispose of the third way in which it is put immediately and briefly. Counsel for the Crown argues that to apply s 5 (2) (a) to a case in which a defendant believes that he is causing damage to his own property involves a tortuous and unjustifiable construction of the wording. We agree. In our judgment, to hold that those words of s 5 (2) (a) are apt to cover a case of a person damaging the property of another in the belief that it is his own would be to strain the language of the section to an unwarranted degree. Moreover, in our judgment, it is quite unnecessary to have recourse to such a construction.

Counsel for the Crown invited our attention to *Cambridgeshire and Isle of Ely County Council v Rust* [[1972] 2 QB 426, [1972] 3 All ER 232], a case under the Highways Act 1959, s 127, concerning the pitching of a stall on a highway without lawful excuse. The case is cited as authority for the proposition that in order to establish a lawful excuse as a defence it must be shown that the defendant honestly but mistakenly believed on reasonable grounds that the facts were of a certain order, and that if those facts were of that order his conduct would have been lawful. Applying that proposition to the facts of the present case, counsel argues that the appellant cannot be said to have had a lawful excuse because in law the damaged property was part of the house and owned by the landlord. We have no doubt as to the correctness of the decision in the case cited. The proposition is argued here in relation to the appellant's contention that he had a lawful excuse and does not touch the argument based on absence of mens rea.

It is conceded by counsel for the Crown that there is force in the argument that the element of mens rea extends to 'property belonging to another'. But, it is argued, the section creates a new statutory offence and that it is open to the construction that the mental element in the offence relates only to causing damage to or destroying property. That if in fact the property damaged or destroyed is shown to be another's property the offence is committed although the defendant did not intend or foresee damage to another person's property.

We are informed that so far as research has revealed this is the first occasion on which this court has had to consider the question which arises in this appeal.

It is not without interest to observe that under the law in force before the passing of the Criminal Damage Act 1971, it was clear that no offence was committed by a person who destroyed or damaged property belonging to another in the honest but mistaken belief that the property was his own or that he had a legal right to do the damage. In *Twose* [(1879) 14 Cox CC 327] the prisoner was indicted for setting fire to furze on a common. Persons living near the common had occasionally burned the furze in order to improve the growth of grass but without the right to do so. The prisoner denied setting fire to the furze and it was submitted that even if it were proved that she did she could not be found guilty if she bona fide believed she had a right to do so whether the right were a good one or not. Lopes J ruled that if she set fire to the furze thinking she had a right to do so that would not be a criminal offence.

On the facts of the present appeal the charge, if brought before the 1971 Act came into force, would have been laid under s 13 of the Malicious Damage Act 1861, alleging damage by a tenant to a building. It was a defence to a charge under that section that the tenant acted under a claim of right to do the damage.

If the direction given by the deputy judge in the present case is correct, then the offence created by s 1 (1) of the 1971 Act involves a considerable extension of the law in a surprising direction. Whether or not this is so depends on the construction of the section. Construing the language of s 1(1) we have no doubt that the actus reus is 'destroying or damaging any property belonging to another'. It is not possible to exclude the words 'belonging to another' which describe the 'property'. Applying the ordinary principles of mens rea, the intention and recklessness and the absence of lawful excuse required to constitute the offence have reference to property belonging to another. It follows that in our judgment no offence is committed under this section if a person destroys or causes damage to property belonging to another if he does so in the honest though mistaken belief that the property is his own, and provided that the belief is honestly held it is irrelevant to consider whether or not it is a justifiable belief.

In our judgment, the direction given to the jury was a fundamental misdirection in law. The consequence was that the jury were precluded from considering facts capable of being a defence to the charge and were directed to convict . . .

Appeal allowed. Conviction quashed

The Law Commission says that in most cases there is a clear distinction between 'the mental element' and 'the element of unlawfulness' and the Act deals separately with these elements. Is there any such clear distinction? Was the conviction in *Smith (DR)* quashed because D lacked the mental element or because he had a lawful excuse? Does it matter to determine which? Cf *Jaggard v Dickinson*, p 99, above.

In *Denton* [1982] 1 All ER 65, CA, p 531, above, D obviously contemplated a fraudulent claim against insurers and the trial judge ruled that he could not rely on s 5(2) because the section carried a general connotation of lawfulness and it could not be said that the owner was 'entitled' to consent to damage for a fraudulent purpose. Quashing D's conviction the Court of Appeal pointed out that had T been charged he would (on the admission made in that case) have to be acquitted since it is no crime for a man to set fire to his own property. But if the Crown's contention was right someone whom the owner directed to set fire to the property could be convicted. The court concluded (at 68):

> 'Quite apart from any other consideration, that is such an anomalous result that it cannot possibly be right. The answer is this: that one has to decide whether or not an offence is committed at the moment that the acts are alleged to be committed. The fact that somebody may have had a dishonest intent which in the end he was going to carry out, namely to claim from the insurance company, cannot turn what was not originally a crime into a crime. There is no unlawfulness under the 1971 Act in burning a house. It does not become unlawful because there may be an inchoate attempt to commit fraud contained in it; that is to say it does not become a crime under the 1971 Act, whatever may be the situation outside of the Act.
>
> Consequently it is apparent to us that the judge, in his ruling in this respect, was wrong. Indeed it seems to us, if it is necessary to go as far as this, that it was probably unnecessary for the defendant to invoke s 5 of the 1971 Act at all, because he probably had a lawful excuse without it, in that T was lawfully entitled to burn the premises down. The defendant believed it. He believed that he was acting under the directions of T and that on its own, it seems to us, may well have provided him with a lawful excuse without having resort to s 5.'

On the face of it the conduct of Denton falls four-square with s 5(2)(a) but the court thought he probably had a lawful excuse without it. On this view is s 5(2)(a) superfluous?

Smith (DR) is overtly based on the premise (and *Denton* implicitly so) that the mens rea of criminal damage lies not merely in intentionally or recklessly damaging property but in intentionally or recklessly damaging property *of another*. 'It is not possible', the court said in *Smith (DR)*, 'to exclude the words 'belonging to another' which describe the 'property'. Applying the ordinary principles of mens rea, the intention and recklessness and the absence of lawful excuse required to constitute the offence have reference to property belonging to another.' No doubt D would commit an offence where, not sure whether property which was really P's belonged to himself or P, he nevertheless went ahead and destroyed the property. But *Caldwell* goes further and says that a person may be convicted though it never occurred to him that *any* property would be damaged though such a person, ex hypothesi, can give no thought to damaging property *of another*. The passage just cited from *Smith (DR)* therefore requires some modification. The *Caldwell* rule clearly applies to 'the mental element' but does it also apply to 'the element of unlawfulness'? *Satnam, Kewal* (1983) 78 Cr App Rep 149, p 400, above suggest that *Caldwell* recklessness is confined to results and does not extend to circumstances. Are the issues whether property belongs to another or whether there is a lawful excuse matters of result or circumstance? Suppose that Professor D, who is notoriously absent-minded, destroys a cardboard box and its contents. D, who has no recollection of even checking the contents of the box, had simply assumed that the box contained papers of his but it is now shown that it contained papers belonging to his employer, the University. Assuming it would be obvious to the ordinary prudent individual that the box contained property belonging to another, how does D stand? Is it to be said that there was an obvious risk of destroying property belonging to another to which he gave no thought, or had he, by believing that the box contained his own property, formed the view that his conduct involved no risk of destroying the property of another? If yes, didn't *Caldwell* believe that there was no risk to the occupants of the hotel when he started the fire? Had not *Caldwell* formed the view that there was no risk to the occupants?

Section 5(2) is couched in highly subjective terms and might be said to provide a warrant for the most extravagant action. Would, for instance, D have a lawful excuse for burning down P's factory because effluent from the factory was ruining his tomatoes so long as D believed this to be reasonable? In *Day* (1844) 8 JP 186, a case decided under the former law, it was held that D was not guilty of an offence in maiming P's sheep which D had distrained where D did so in the honest belief that he was so entitled on P's refusal to pay compensation for damage done by the sheep. At this point there does appear to be a distinction between measures taken to protect person and property in that the former must meet an objective standard. Under the Draft Criminal Code Bill (cll 47, 89; see Law Com No 143, para 13.33 and p 233, above) a common standard would be applied.

The definition of lawful excuse in s 5(2) is partial only. Other cases where D may have a lawful excuse include cases where D acts under a belief in ownership or under a-claim of right, defence of the person, or where D has available to him some general defence such as duress or necessity.

2. Destroying etc property with intent to endanger life

Criminal Damage Act 1971, s 1 (2), p 575, below

This proposed offence gives effect to our view that the policy of the criminal law is, and should continue to be, to select certain offences as attracting exceptionally high maximum penalties, because these offences are accompanied by aggravating factors. There are examples of this approach in ss 8-10 of the Theft Act 1968 dealing with robbery, burglary and aggravated burglary, which may be regarded as theft accompanied by aggravating circumstances . . . None of our commentators suggested that the test should be objective in the sense that one should look only to the consequences or potential consequences of the offender's conduct. All were agreed that the criterion for the aggravated offence was to be found in the offender's state of mind, namely, his intention to endanger the personal safety of another or his recklessness in that regard . . . [I]f no such offence is created, a considerable gap in the law is left, especially where the offender is reckless as to endangering personal safety and yet no injury is caused. In such a case the offender cannot be convicted of an attempt to commit an offence under the Offences against the Person Act 1861, in an attempt to commit an offence, intention and not merely recklessness is necessary . . . We think that the proper criterion should be related to the endangering of life, a concept which appears in s 2 of the Explosive Substances Act 1883 and in s 16 of the Firearms Act 1968. It is not, therefore, a novel one likely to give rise to difficulties of interpretation, and we think that it correctly expresses the necessary seriousness. It is true that in adopting the criterion of endangering life there may still be some overlapping with offences against the person . . .

(Law Com No 29, paras 21-27.)

By s 5(1) (p 575, below) of the Act the provisions of that section relating to lawful excuse do not apply to the offence under s 1(2). Even if D has a lawful excuse independently of s 5(2) he may still commit this offence, as where for example D sets fire to his own house intending to endanger the life of his wife. On the other hand s 5(5) makes it clear that nothing in s 5 shall be construed as casting any doubt on any defence recognised by law as a defence to criminal charges; obviously defences such as infancy, insanity or duress would provide an answer to a charge under s 1(2) just as they provide an answer to any other charge.

Questions

1. Do you agree with the Law Commission that but for the creation of this offence 'a considerable gap is left in the law'? How does this offence differ from attempted murder?
2. Consider *Cunningham* [1957] QB 396, [1957] 2 All ER 412, p 63, above. Could Cunningham be convicted of an offence under this section?
3. Suppose that D while effecting repairs on his car disconnects the brake cable. He breaks off work for a cup of tea and his wife then says she needs the car to do some shopping. D says nothing but lets his wife drive off in the car hoping he will never see her again. Has D committed any offence?

3. Arson

The Law Commission recommended that there should be no separate offence of damaging property by fire (see Law Com No 29, paras 28–33) but this recommendation proved unacceptable to Parliament and s 1(3) of the Act, p 575, below, provides for arson.

A person may therefore be charged with an offence under s 1(1) and (3), to which the definition of lawful excuse in s 5 applies; or with an offence under s 1(2) and (3), to which the definition in s 5 does not apply. In order to constitute arson there must be some damage, however slight, done by fire.

4. Other offences

By s 2 of the Criminal Damage Act, p 575, below, it is an offence to threaten to destroy etc property, and by s 3 it is an offence to possess anything intending to destroy etc property.

Appendix I: Statutes

The following selection of statutes has been amended up to 31 October 1985.

Accessories and Abettors Act 1861
(24 & 25 Vict c 94)

1-7. (*Repealed*)

8. Abettors in misdemeanours
Whosoever shall aid, abet, counsel, or procure the commission of any indictable offence, whether the same be an offence at common law or by virtue of any Act passed or to be passed, shall be liable to be tried, indicted, and punished as a principal offender.

9-11. (*Repealed*)

10. (*Not printed in this work*)

Offences against the Person Act 1861
(24 & 25 Vict c 100)

1. [The operation of s 1 was temporarily suspended by the Murder (Abolition of Death Penalty) Act 1965, and made permanent by affirmative resolutions of both Houses of Parliament in 1969.]

2-3. (*Repealed*)

4. Conspiring or soliciting to commit murder
. . . whosoever shall solicit, encourage, persuade, or endeavour to persuade, or shall propose to any person, to murder any other person, whether he be a subject of Her Majesty or not, and whether he be within the Queen's dominions or not, shall be guilty of [an offence], and being convicted thereof shall be liable . . . to [imprisonment for life].

5. Manslaughter
Whosoever shall be convicted of manslaughter shall be liable, at the discretion of the court, to [imprisonment for life].

6-8. (*Repealed*)

9. Murder or manslaughter abroad
Where any murder or manslaughter shall be committed on land out of the United

Kingdom, whether within the Queen's dominions, or without, and whether the person killed were a subject of Her Majesty or not, every offence committed by any subject of Her Majesty in respect of any such case, whether the same shall amount to the offence of murder or of manslaughter, . . . may be dealt with, inquired of, tried, determined, and punished . . . in England or Ireland . . . Provided, that nothing herein contained shall prevent any person from being tried in any place out of England or Ireland for any murder or manslaughter committed out of England or Ireland, in the same manner as such person might have been tried before the passing of this Act.

10. Provision for the trial of murder and manslaughter where the death or cause of death only happens in England or Ireland

Where any person being criminally stricken, poisoned, or otherwise hurt upon the sea, or at any place out of England or Ireland, shall die of such stroke, poisoning, or hurt in England or Ireland, or, being criminally stricken, poisoned, or otherwise hurt in any place in England or Ireland, shall die of such stroke, poisoning, or hurt upon the sea, or at any place out of England or Ireland, every offence committed in respect of any such case, whether the same shall amount to the offence of murder or of manslaughter, . . . may be dealt with, inquired of, tried, determined, and punished . . . in England or Ireland . . .

11–15. (*Repealed*)

16. Threats to kill

A person who without lawful excuse makes to another a threat, intending that that other would fear it would be carried out, to kill that other or a third person shall be guilty of an offence and liable on conviction on indictment to imprisonment for a term not exceeding ten years.

Acts causing or tending to cause Danger of Life or Bodily Harm

17. Impeding a person endeavouring to save himself or another from shipwreck

Whosoever shall unlawfully and maliciously prevent or impede any person, being on board of or having quitted any ship or vessel which shall be in distress, or wrecked, stranded, or cast on shore, in his endeavour to save his life, or shall unlawfully and maliciously prevent or impede any person in his endeavour to save the life of any such person as in this section first aforesaid, shall be guilty of [an offence], and being convicted thereof shall be liable . . . to [imprisonment] for life . . .

18. Shooting or attempting to shoot or wounding with intent to do grievous bodily harm, or to resist apprehension

Whosoever shall unlawfully and maliciously by any means whatsoever wound or cause any grievous bodily harm to any person . . . with intent . . . to do some . . . grievous bodily harm to any person, or with intent to resist or prevent the lawful apprehension or detainer of any person, shall be guilty of [an offence], and being convicted thereof shall be liable, . . . to [imprisonment] for life . . .

19. (*Repealed*)

20. Inflicting bodily injury, with or without weapon

Whosoever shall unlawfully and maliciously wound or inflict any grievous bodily harm upon any other person, either with or without any weapon or instrument, shall be guilty of [an offence], and being convicted thereof shall be liable . . . to [a term of imprisonment not exceeding five years].

21. Attempting to choke, etc, in order to commit or assist in the committing of any indictable offence

Whosoever shall, by any means whatsoever, attempt to choke, suffocate, or strangle any other person, or shall by any means calculated to choke, suffocate, or strangle, attempt to render any other person insensible, unconscious, or incapable of resistance, with intent in any of such cases thereby to enable himself or any other person to commit, or with intent in any such cases thereby to assist any other person in committing any indictable offence, shall be guilty of [an offence], and being convicted thereof shall be liable . . . to [imprisonment] for life . . .

22. Using chloroform, etc, to commit or assist in the committing of any indictable offence

Whosoever shall unlawfully apply or administer to or cause to be taken by, or attempt to apply or administer to or attempt to cause to be administered to or taken by, any person, any chloroform, laudanum, or other stupefying or overpowering drug, matter, or thing, with intent in any of such cases thereby to enable himself or any other person to commit, or with intent in any of such cases thereby to assist any other person in committing, any indictable offence, shall be guilty of [an offence], and being convicted thereof shall be liable . . . to [imprisonment] for life . . .

23. Maliciously administering poison, etc, so as to endanger life or inflict grievous bodily harm

Whosoever shall unlawfully and maliciously administer to or cause to be administered to or taken by any other person any poison or other destructive or noxious thing, so as thereby to endanger the life of such person, or so as thereby to inflict upon such person any grievous bodily harm shall be guilty of [an offence], and being convicted thereof shall be liable . . . to [imprisonment] for any term not exceeding ten years . . .

24. Maliciously administering poison, etc, with intent to injure, aggrieve, or annoy any other person

Whosoever shall unlawfully and maliciously administer to or cause to be administered to or taken by any other person any poison or other destructive or noxious thing, with intent to injure, aggrieve, or annoy such person, shall be guilty of [an offence], and being . . . convicted thereof shall be liable to [imprisonment for a term not exceeding five years].

25. Person charged with [an offence] under s 23 may be found guilty of [an offence] under s 24

If, upon the trial of any person for [an offence under s 23], the jury shall not be satisfied that such person is guilty thereof, but shall be satisfied that he is guilty of [an offence under s 24], then and in every such case the jury may acquit the accused of [an offence under s 23], and find him guilty of [an offence under s 24], and thereupon he shall be liable to be punished in the same manner as if convicted upon an indictment for [an offence under s 24].

26. Not providing apprentices or servants with food, etc, or doing bodily harm, whereby life is endangered, or health permanently injured

Whosoever, being legally liable, either as a master or mistress, to provide for any apprentice or servant necessary food, clothing, or lodging, shall wilfully and without lawful excuse refuse or neglect to provide the same, or shall unlawfully and maliciously do or cause to be done any bodily harm to any such apprentice or servant, so that the life of such apprentice or servant shall be endangered, or the health of such apprentice or servant shall have been or shall be likely to be permanently injured, shall be guilty of [an offence], and being convicted thereof shall be liable . . . to [imprisonment for a term not exceeding five years] . . .

27. Exposing child, whereby life is endangered, or health permanently injured

Whosoever shall unlawfully abandon or expose any child, being under the age of two years, whereby the life of such child shall be endangered, or the health of such child shall have been or shall be likely to be permanently injured, shall be guilty of [an offence], and being convicted thereof shall be liable . . . to [imprisonment for a term not exceeding five years].

28. Causing bodily injury by gunpowder
Whosoever shall unlawfully and maliciously, by the explosion of gunpowder or other explosive substance, burn, maim, disfigure, disable, or do any grievous bodily harm to any person, shall be guilty of [an offence], and being convicted thereof shall be liable, at the discretion of the court, to [imprisonment] for life . . .

29. Causing gunpowder to explode, or sending to any person an explosive substance, or throwing corrosive fluid on a person, with intent to do grievous bodily harm
Whosoever shall unlawfully and maliciously cause any gunpowder or other explosive substance to explode, or send or deliver to or cause to be taken or received by any person any explosive substance or any other dangerous or noxious thing, or put or lay at any place, or cast or throw at or upon or otherwise apply to any person any corrosive fluid or any destructive or explosive substance with intent in any of the cases aforesaid to burn, maim, disfigure, or disable any person, or to do some grievous bodily harm to any person, shall, whether any bodily injury be effected or not, be guilty of [an offence] and being convicted thereof shall be liable, at the discretion of the court, to [imprisonment] for life . . .

30. Placing gunpowder near a building, etc, with intent to do bodily injury to any person
Whosoever shall unlawfully and maliciously place or throw in, into, upon, against, or near any building, ship, or vessel any gunpowder or other explosive substance, with intent to do any bodily injury to any person, shall, whether or not any explosion take place, and whether or not any bodily injury be effected, be guilty of [an offence], and being convicted thereof shall be liable, at the discretion of the court, to [imprisonment] for any term not exceeding fourteen years . . .

31. Setting or allowing to remain spring guns, etc, with intent to inflict grievous bodily harm
Whosoever shall set or place, or cause to be set or placed, any spring gun, man trap, or other engine calculated to destroy human life or inflict grievous bodily harm, with the intent that the same or whereby the same may destroy or inflict grievous bodily harm upon a trespasser or other person coming in contact therewith, shall be guilty of [an offence], and being convicted thereof shall be liable . . . to [imprisonment for a term not exceeding five years] . . .; and whosoever shall knowingly and wilfully permit any such spring gun, man trap, or other engine which may have been set or placed in any place then being in or afterwards coming into his possession or occupation by some other person to continue so set or placed, shall be deemed to have set and placed such gun, trap, or engine with such intent as aforesaid: Provided, that nothing in this section contained shall extend to make it illegal to set or place any gin or trap such as may have been or may be usually set or placed with the intent of destroying vermin: Provided also, that nothing in this section shall be deemed to make it unlawful to set or place, or cause to be set or placed, or to be continued set or placed, from sunset to sunrise, any spring gun, man trap, or other engine which shall be set or placed, or caused or continued to be set or placed, in a dwelling-house, for the protection thereof.

32. Placing wood, etc, on railway, taking up rails, turning points, showing or hiding signals, etc, with intent to endanger passengers
Whosoever shall unlawfully and maliciously put or throw upon or across any railway any wood, stone, or other matter or thing, or shall unlawfully and maliciously take up, remove, or displace any rail, sleeper, or other matter or thing belonging to any railway, or shall unlawfully and maliciously turn, move, or divert any points or other machinery belonging to any railway, or shall unlawfully and maliciously make or

show, hide or remove, any signal or light upon or near to any railway, or shall unlawfully and maliciously do or cause to be done any other matter or thing, with intent, in any of the cases aforesaid, to endanger the safety of any person travelling or being upon such railway, shall be guilty of [an offence], and being convicted thereof shall be liable, at the discretion of the court, to [imprisonment] for life . . .

33. Casting stone, etc, upon a railway carriage, with intent to endanger the safety of any person therein, or in any part of the same train
Whosoever shall unlawfully and maliciously throw, or cause to fall or strike, at, against, into, or upon any engine, tender, carriage, or truck used upon any railway, any wood, stone, or other matter or thing, with intent to injure or endanger the safety of any person being in or upon such engine, tender, carriage, or truck, or in or upon any other engine, tender, carriage, or truck of any train of which such first-mentioned engine, tender, carriage, or truck shall form part, shall be guilty of [an offence], and being convicted thereof shall be liable . . . to [imprisonment] for life . . .

34. Doing or omitting anything so as to endanger passengers by railway
Whosoever, by any unlawful act, or by any wilful omission or neglect, shall endanger or cause to be endangered the safety of any person conveyed or being in or upon a railway, or shall aid or assist therein, shall be guilty of [an offence], and being convicted thereof shall be liable, at the discretion of the court, to be imprisoned for any term not exceeding two years . . .

35. Drivers of carriages injuring persons by furious driving
Whosoever, having the charge of any carriage or vehicle, shall by wanton or furious driving or racing, or other wilful misconduct, or by wilful neglect, do or cause to be done any bodily harm to any person whatsoever, shall be guilty of [an offence], and being convicted thereof shall be liable, at the discretion of the court, to be imprisoned for any term not exceeding two years,. . .

Assaults

36. Obstructing or assaulting a clergyman or other minister in the discharge of his duties in place of worship or burial place, or on his way thither
Whosoever shall, by threats or force, obstruct or prevent or endeavour to obstruct or prevent, any clergyman or other minister in or from celebrating divine service or otherwise officiating in any church, chapel, meeting house, or other place of divine worship, or in or from the performance of his duty in the lawful burial of the dead in any churchyard or other burial place, or shall strike or offer any violence to, or shall, upon any civil process, or under the pretence of executing any civil process, arrest any clergyman or other minister who is engaged in, or to the knowledge of the offender is about to engage in, any of the rites or duties in this section aforesaid, or who to the knowledge of the offender shall be going to perform the same or returning from the performance thereof, shall be guilty of [an offence] and being convicted thereof shall be liable, at the discretion of the court, to be imprisoned for any term not exceeding two years,. . .

37. Assaulting a magistrate, etc, on account of his preserving wreck
Whosoever shall assault and strike or wound any magistrate, officer, or other person whatsoever lawfully authorized, in or on account of the exercise of his duty in or concerning the preservation of any vessel in distress, or of any vessel, goods, or effects wrecked, stranded, or cast on shore, or lying under water, shall be guilty of [an offence], and being convicted thereof shall be liable . . . to [imprisonment] for any term not exceeding seven years . . .

38. Assault with intent to [resist arrest]
Whosoever . . . shall assault any person with intent to resist or prevent the lawful

apprehension or detainer of himself or of any other person for any offence, shall be guilty of [an offence], and being convicted thereof shall be liable, at the discretion of the court, to be imprisoned for any term not exceeding two years . . .

39. Assaults with intent to obstruct the sale of grain, or its free passage

Whosoever shall beat, or use any violence or threat of violence to any person, with intent to deter or hinder him from buying, selling, or otherwise disposing of, or to compel him to buy, sell, or otherwise dispose of, any wheat or other grain, flour, meal, malt, or potatoes, in any market or other place, or shall beat or use any such violence or threat to any person having the care or charge of any wheat or other grain, flour, meal, malt, or potatoes, whilst on the way to or from any city, market town, or other place, with intent to stop the conveyance of the same, shall on conviction thereof before two justices of the peace be liable to be imprisoned for any term not exceeding three months: Provided, that no person who shall be punished for any such offence by virtue of this section shall be punished for the same offence by virtue of any other law whatsoever.

40. Assaults on seamen, etc

Whosoever shall unlawfully and with force hinder or prevent any seaman, keelman, or caster from working at or exercising his lawful trade, business, or occupation, or shall beat or use any violence to any such person with intent to hinder or prevent him from working at or exercising the same, shall on conviction thereof before two justices of the peace be liable to be imprisoned for any term not exceeding three months: Provided, that no person who shall be punished for any such offence by reason of this section shall be punished for the same offence by virtue of any other law whatsoever.

41. (*Repealed*)

42. Persons comitting any common assault or battery may be imprisoned or compelled by two magistrates to pay fine and costs not exceeding £200

Where any person shall unlawfully assault or beat any other person, two justices of the peace, upon complaint by or on behalf of the party aggrieved, may hear and determine such offence, and the offender shall, upon conviction thereof before them, at the discretion of the justices, either be committed to the common gaol or house of correction, there to be imprisoned . . ., for any term not exceeding two months, or else shall forefeit and pay such fine as shall appear to them to be meet, not exceeding, together with costs (if ordered), the sum of [£200]; and if such fine as shall be so awarded, together with the costs (if ordered), shall not be paid, either immediately after the conviction or within such period as the said justices shall at the time of the conviction appoint, they may commit the offender to the common gaol or house of correction, there to be imprisoned . . ., for any term not exceeding two months, unless such fine and costs be sooner paid.

43. Persons convicted of aggravated assaults on females and boys under fourteen years of age may be imprisoned or fined, and bound over to keep the peace

When any person shall be charged before two justices of the peace with an assault or battery upon any male child whose age shall not in the opinion of such justices exceed fourteen years, or upon any female, either upon the complaint of the party aggrieved or otherwise, the said justices, if the assault or battery is of such an aggravated nature that it cannot in their opinion be sufficiently punished under the provisions hereinbefore contained as to common assaults and batteries, may proceed to hear and determine the same in a summary way, and, if the same be proved, may convict the person accused; and every such offender shall be liable to be imprisoned in the common gaol or house of correction . . . for any period not exceeding six months, or to pay a fine not exceeding (together with costs) the sum of [£500] and in default of payment to be imprisoned in the common gaol or house of correction for any period not exceeding six months, unless such fine and costs be sooner paid . . .

44–46. (*Not printed in this work*)

47. Assault occasioning bodily harm—Common assault

Whosoever shall be convicted upon an indictment of any assault occasioning actual bodily harm shall be liable . . . to [imprisonment for five years] . . .; and whosoever shall be convicted upon an indictment for a common assault shall be liable at the discretion of the court, to be imprisoned for any term not exceeding one year . . .

48–55. (*Repealed*)

Child-stealing

56. (*Repealed*)

Bigamy

57. Bigamy

Whosoever, being married, shall marry any other person during the life of the former husband or wife, whether the second marriage shall have taken place in England or Ireland or elsewhere, shall be guilty of [an offence], and being convicted thereof shall be liable to [imprisonment] for any term not exceeding seven years . . .: Provided, that nothing in this section contained shall extend to any second marriage contracted elsewhere than in England and Ireland by any other than a subject of Her Majesty, or to any person marrying a second time whose husband or wife shall have been continually absent from such person for the space of seven years then last past, and shall not have been known by such person to be living within that time, or shall extend to any person who, at the time of such second marriage, shall have been divorced from the bond of the first marriage, or to any person whose former marriage shall have been declared void by the sentence of any court of competent jurisdiction.

Attempts to procure Abortion

58. Administering drugs or using instruments to procure abortion

Every woman, being with child, who, with intent to procure her own miscarriage, shall unlawfully administer to herself any poison or other noxious thing, or shall unlawfully use any instrument or other means whatsoever with the like intent, and whosoever, with intent to procure the miscarriage of any woman, whether she be or be not with child, shall unlawfully administer to her or cause to be taken by her any poison or other noxious thing, or shall unlawfully use any instrument or other means whatsoever with the like intent, shall be guilty of [an offence], and being convicted thereof shall be liable . . . to [imprisonment] for life . . .

59. Procuring drugs, etc, to cause abortion

Whosoever shall unlawfully supply or procure any poison or other noxious thing, or any instrument or thing whatsoever, knowing that the same is intended to be unlawfully used or employed with intent to procure the miscarriage of any woman, whether she be or be not with child, shall be guilty of [an offence], and being convicted thereof shall be liable . . . [to imprisonment for a term not exceeding five years]. . .

Concealing the Birth of a Child

60. Concealing the birth of a child

If any woman shall be delivered of a child, every person who shall, by any secret disposition of the dead body of the said child, whether such child died before, at, or after its birth, endeavour to conceal the birth thereof, shall be guilty of [an offence], and being convicted thereof shall be liable, at the discretion of the court, to be imprisoned for any term not exceeding two years,. . .

61–63. (*Repealed*)

64. Making or having gunpowder, etc, with intent to commit or enable any person to commit any felony mentioned in this Act
Whosoever shall knowingly have in his possession, or make or manufacture, any gunpowder, explosive substance, or any dangerous or noxious thing, or any machine, engine, instrument, or thing, with intent by means thereof to commit, or for the purpose of enabling any other person to commit, any of the [offences] in this Act mentioned shall be guilty of [an offence], and being convicted thereof shall be liable, at the discretion of the court, to be imprisoned for any term not exceeding two years . . .

65, 68, 76 and **78.** (*Not printed in this work*)

66, 67, 69–75, 77 and **79.** (*Repealed*)

Trial of Lunatics Act 1883
(46 & 47 Vict c 38)

1. (*Not printed in this work*)

2. Special verdict where accused found guilty, but insane at date of act or omission charged, and orders thereupon
(1) Where in any indictment or information any act or omission is charged against any person as an offence, and it is given in evidence on the trial of such person for that offence that he was insane, so as not to be responsible, according to law, for his actions at the time when the act was done or omission made, then, if it appears to the jury before whom such person is tried that he did the act or made the omission charged, but was insane as aforesaid at the time when he did or made the same, the jury shall return [a special verdict that the accused is not guilty by reason of insanity].

Infant Life (Preservation) Act 1929
(19 & 20 Geo 5 c 34)

1. Punishment for child destruction
(1) Subject as hereinafter in this subsection provided, any person who, with intent to destroy the life of a child capable of being born alive, by any wilful act causes a child to die before it has an existence independent of its mother, shall be guilty of [an offence], to wit, of child destruction, and shall be liable on conviction thereof on indictment to [imprisonment] for life:
    Provided that no person shall be found guilty of an offence under this section unless it is proved that the act which caused the death of the child was not done in good faith for the purpose only of preserving the life of the mother.
    (2) For the purposes of this Act, evidence that a woman had at any material time been pregnant for a period of twenty-eight weeks or more shall be primâ facie proof that she was at that time pregnant of a child capable of being born alive.

2. Prosecution of offences
(1) (*Repealed*)
    (2) Where upon the trial of any person for the murder or manslaughter of any child, or for infanticide, or for an offence under section fifty-eight of the Offences against the Person Act 1861 (which relates to administering drugs or using instruments to procure abortion), the jury are of opinion that the person charged is not guilty of murder, manslaughter or infanticide, or of an offence under the said section

fifty-eight, as the case may be, but that he is shown by the evidence to be guilty of the [offence] of child destruction, the jury may find him guilty of that [offence], and thereupon the person convicted shall be liable to be punished as if he had been convicted upon an indictment for child destruction.

(3) Where upon the trial of any person for the [offence] of child destruction the jury are of opinion that the person charged is not guilty of that [offence], but that he is shown by the evidence to be guilty of an offence under the said section fifty-eight of the Offences against the Person Act, 1861, the jury may find him guilty of that offence, and thereupon the person convicted shall be liable to be punished as if he had been convicted upon an indictment under that section.

(4) (*Repealed*)

(5) (*not printed in this work*)

Infanticide Act 1938
(1 & 2 Geo 6 c 36)

1. Offence of infanticide

(1) Where a woman by any wilful act or omission causes the death of her child being a child under the age of twelve months, but at the time of the act or omission the balance of her mind was disturbed by reason of her not having fully recovered from the effect of giving birth to the child or by reason of the effect of lactation consequent upon the birth of the child, then, notwithstanding that the circumstances were such that but for this Act the offence would have amounted to murder, she shall be guilty of [an offence], to wit of infanticide, and may for such offence be dealt with and punished as if she had been guilty of the offence of manslaughter of the child.

(2) Where upon the trial of a woman for the murder of her child, being a child under the age of twelve months, the jury are of opinion that she by any wilful act or omission caused its death, but that at the time of the act or omission the balance of her mind was disturbed by reason of her not having fully recovered from the effect of giving birth to the child or by reason of the effect of lactation consequent upon the birth of the child, then the jury may, notwithstanding that the circumstances were such that but for the provisions of this Act they might have returned a verdict of murder, return in lieu thereof a verdict of infanticide.

(3) (*Not printed in this work*)

Sexual Offences Act 1956
(4 & 5 Eliz 2 c 69)

PART I. OFFENCES, AND THE PROSECUTION AND PUNISHMENT OF OFFENCES

Intercourse by force, intimidation, etc

1. Rape

(1) It is [an offence] for a man to rape a woman.

(2) A man who induces a married woman to have sexual intercourse with him by impersonating her husband commits rape.

2. Procurement of woman by threats

(1) It is an offence for a person to procure a woman, by threats or intimidation, to have unlawful sexual intercourse in any part of the world.

(2) A person shall not be convicted of an offence under this section on the evidence of one witness only, unless the witness is corroborated in some material particular by evidence implicating the accused.

3. Procurement of woman by false pretences

(1) It is an offence for a person to procure a woman, by false pretences or false representations, to have unlawful sexual intercourse in any part of the world.

(2) A person shall not be convicted of an offence under this section on the evidence of one witness only, unless the witness is corroborated in some material particular by evidence implicating the accused.

4. Administering drugs to obtain or facilitate intercourse

(1) It is an offence for a person to apply or administer to, or cause to be taken by, a woman any drug, matter or thing with intent to stupefy or overpower her so as thereby to enable any man to have unlawful sexual intercourse with her.

(2) A person shall not be convicted of an offence under this section on the evidence of one witness only, unless the witness is corroborated in some material particular by evidence implicating the accused.

Intercourse with girls under sixteen

5. Intercourse with girl under thirteen

It is [an offence] for a man to have unlawful sexual intercourse with a girl under the age of thirteen.´

6. Intercourse with girl under sixteen

(1) It is an offence, subject to the exceptions mentioned in this section, for a man to have unlawful sexual intercourse with a girl . . . under the age of sixteen.

(2) Where a marriage is invalid under section two of the Marriage Act 1949, or section one of the Age of Marriage Act 1929 (the wife being a girl under the age of sixteen), the invalidity does not make the husband guilty of an offence under this section because he has sexual intercourse with her, if he believes her to be his wife and has reasonable cause for the belief.

(3) A man is not guilty of an offence under this section because he has unlawful sexual intercourse with a girl under the age of sixteen, if he is under the age of twenty-four and has not previously been charged with a like offence, and he believes her to be of the age of sixteen or over and has reasonable cause for the belief.

In this subsection, 'a like offence' means an offence under this section or an attempt to commit one, or an offence under paragraph (1) of section five of the Criminal Law Amendment Act, 1885 (the provision replaced for England and Wales by this section).

Intercourse with defectives

7. Intercourse with defective

(1) It is an offence, subject to the exception mentioned in this section, for a man to have unlawful sexual intercourse with a woman who is a defective.

(2) A man is not guilty of an offence under this section because he has unlawful sexual intercourse with a woman if he does not know and has no reason to suspect her to be a defective.

8. (*Repealed*)

9. Procurement of defective

(1) It is an offence, subject to the exception mentioned in this section, for a person to procure a woman who is a defective to have unlawful sexual intercourse in any part of the world.

(2) A person is not guilty of an offence under this section because he procures a defective to have unlawful sexual intercourse, if he does not know and has no reason to suspect her to be a defective.

Incest

10. Incest by a man
(1) It is an offence for a man to have sexual intercourse with a woman whom he knows to be his grand-daughter, daughter, sister or mother.

(2) In the foregoing subsection 'sister' includes half-sister, and for the purposes of that subsection any expression importing a relationship between two people shall be taken to apply notwithstanding that the relationship is not traced through lawful wedlock.

11. Incest by a woman
(1) It is an offence for a woman of the age of sixteen or over to permit a man whom she knows to be her grandfather, father, brother or son to have sexual intercourse with her by her consent. ·

(2) In the foregoing subsection 'brother' includes half-brother, and for the purposes of the subsection any expression importing a relationship between two people shall be taken to apply notwithstanding that the relationship is not traced through lawful wedlock.

Unnatural offences

12. Buggery
(1) It is [an offence] for a person to commit buggery with another person or with an animal.
(2) (*Repealed*)
(3) (*Repealed*)

13. Indecency between men
It is an offence for a man to commit an act of gross indecency with another man, whether in public or private, or to be a party to the commission by a man of an act of gross indecency with another man, or to procure the commission by a man of an act of gross indecency with another man.

Assaults

14. Indecent assault on a woman
(1) It is an offence, subject to the exception mentioned in subsection (3) of this section, for a person to make an indecent assault on a woman.

(2) A girl under the age of sixteen cannot in law give any consent which would prevent an act being an assault for the purposes of this section.

(3) Where a marriage is invalid under section two of the Marriage Act, 1949, or section one of the Age of Marriage Act, 1929 (the wife being a girl under the age of sixteen), the invalidity does not make the husband guilty of any offence under this section by reason of her incapacity to consent while under that age, if he believes her to be his wife and has reasonable cause for the belief.

(4) A woman who is a defective cannot in law give any consent which would prevent an act being an assault for the purposes of this section, but a person is only to be treated as guilty of an indecent assault on a defective by reason of that incapacity to consent, if that person knew or had reason to suspect her to be a defective.

15. Indecent assault on a man
(1) It is an offence for a person to make an indecent assault on a man.

(2) A boy under the age of sixteen cannot in law give any consent which would prevent an act being an assault for the purposes of this section.

(3) A man who is a defective cannot in law give any consent which would prevent an act being an assault for the purposes of this section, but a person is only to be treated

as guilty of an indecent assault on a defective by reason of that incapacity to consent, if that person knew or had reason to suspect him to be a defective.

(4) (*Repealed*)

(5) (*Repealed*)

16. Assault with intent to commit buggery

(1) It is an offence for a person to assault another person with intent to commit buggery.

(2) (*Repealed*)

(3) (*Repealed*)

Abduction

17. Abduction of woman by force or for the sake of her property

(1) It is [an offence] for a person to take away or detain a woman against her will with the intention that she shall marry or have unlawful sexual intercourse with that or any other person, if she is so taken away or detained either by force or for the sake of her property or expectations of property.

(2) In the foregoing subsection, the reference to a woman's expectations of property relates only to property of a person to whom she is next of kin or one of the next of kin, and 'property' includes any interest in property.

18. (*Repealed*)

19. Abduction of unmarried girl under eighteen from parent or guardian

(1) It is an offence, subject to the exception mentioned in this section, for a person to take an unmarried girl under the age of eighteen out of the possession of her parent or guardian against his will, if she is so taken with the intention that she shall have unlawful sexual intercourse with men or with a particular man.

(2) A person is not guilty of an offence under this section because he takes such a girl out of the possession of her parent or guardian as mentioned above, if he believes her to be of the age of eighteen or over and has reasonable cause for the belief.

(3) In this section 'guardian' means any person having the lawful care or charge of the girl.

20. Abduction of unmarried girl under sixteen from parent or guardian

(1) It is an offence for a person acting without lawful authority or excuse to take an unmarried girl under the age of sixteen out of the possession of her parent or guardian against his will.

(2) In the foregoing subsection 'guardian' means any person having the lawful care or charge of the girl.

21. Abduction of defective from parent or guardian

(1) It is an offence, subject to the exception mentioned in this section, for a person to take a woman who is a defective out of the possession of her parent or guardian against his will, if she is so taken with the intention that she shall have unlawful sexual intercourse with men or with a particular man.

(2) A person is not guilty of an offence under this section because he takes such a woman out of the possession of her parent or guardian as mentioned above, if he does not know and has no reason to suspect her to be a defective.

(3) In this section 'guardian' means any person having the lawful care or charge of the woman.

Prostitution, procuration, etc

22. Causing prostitution of women

(1) It is an offence for a person:

(a) to procure a woman to become, in any part of the world, a common prostitute; or

(b) to procure a woman to leave the United Kingdom, intending her to become an inmate of or frequent a brothel elsewhere; or

(c) to procure a woman to leave her usual place of abode in the United Kingdom, intending her to become an inmate of or frequent a brothel in any part of the world for the purposes of prostitution.

(2) A person shall not be convicted of an offence under this section on the evidence of one witness only, unless the witness is corroborated in some material particular by evidence implicating the accused.

23. Procuration of girl under twenty-one

(1) It is an offence for a person to procure a girl under the age of twenty-one to have unlawful sexual intercourse in any part of the world with a third person.

(2) A person shall not be convicted of an offence under this section on the evidence of one witness only, unless the witness is corroborated in some material particular by evidence implicating the accused.

24. Detention of woman in brothel or other premises

(1) It is an offence for a person to detain a woman against her will on any premises with the intention that she shall have unlawful sexual intercourse with men or with a particular man, or to detain a woman against her will in a brothel.

(2) Where a woman is on any premises for the purpose of having unlawful sexual intercourse or is in a brothel, a person shall be deemed for the purpose of the foregoing subsection to detain her there if, with the intention of compelling or inducing her to remain there, he either withholds from her her clothes or any other property belonging to her or threatens her with legal proceedings in the event of her taking away clothes provided for her by him or on his directions.

(3) A woman shall not be liable to any legal proceedings, whether civil or criminal, for taking away or being found in possession of any clothes she needed to enable her to leave premises on which she was for the purpose of having unlawful sexual intercourse or to leave a brothel.

25. Permitting girl under thirteen to use premises for intercourse

It is [an offence] for a person who is the owner or occupier of any premises, or who has, or acts or assists in, the management or control of any premises, to induce or knowingly suffer a girl under the age of thirteen to resort to or be on those premises for the purpose of having unlawful sexual intercourse with men or with a particular man.

26. Permitting girl under the age of sixteen to use premises for intercourse

It is an offence for a person who is the owner or occupier of any premises, or who has, or acts or assists in, the management or control of any premises, to induce or knowingly suffer a girl . . . under the age of sixteen, to resort to or be on those premises for the purpose of having unlawful sexual intercourse with men or with a particular man.

27. Permitting defective to use premises for intercourse

(1) It is an offence, subject to the exception mentioned in this section, for a person who is the owner or occupier of any premises, or who has, or acts or assists in, the management or control of any premises, to induce or knowingly suffer a woman who is a defective to resort to or be on those premises for the purpose of having unlawful sexual intercourse with men or with a particular man.

(2) A person is not guilty of an offence under this section because he induces or knowingly suffers a defective to resort to or be on any premises for the purposes mentioned, if he does not know and has no reason to suspect her to be a defective.

28. Causing or encouraging prostitution of, intercourse with, or indecent assault on, girl under sixteen

(1) It is an offence for a person to cause or encourage the prostitution of, or the commission of unlawful sexual intercourse with, or of an indecent assault on, a girl under the age of sixteen for whom he is responsible.

(2) Where a girl has become a prostitute, or has had unlawful sexual intercourse or has been indecently assaulted, a person shall be deemed for the purposes of this section to have caused or encouraged it, if he knowingly allowed her to consort with, or to enter or continue in the employment of, any prostitute or person of known immoral character.

(3) The persons who are to be treated for the purposes of this section as responsible for a girl are (subject to the next following subsection):

(a) any person who is her parent or legal guardian; and

(b) any person who has actual possession or control of her, or to whose charge she has been committed by her parent or legal guardian or by a person having the custody of her; and

(c) any other person who has the custody, charge or care of her.

(4) In the last foregoing subsection:

(a) 'parent' does not include, in relation to any girl, a person deprived of the custody of her by order of a court of competent jurisdiction but (subject to that), in the case of a girl who . . . is illegitimate . . ., means her mother and any person who has been adjudged to be her putative father;

(b) 'legal guardian' means, in relation to any girl, any person who is for the time being her guardian, having been appointed according to law by deed or will or order of a court of competent jurisdiction.

(5) If, on a charge of an offence against a girl under this section, the girl appears to the court to have been under the age of sixteen at the time of the offence charged, she shall be presumed for the purposes of this section to have been so, unless the contrary is proved.

29. Causing or encouraging prostitution of defective

(1) It is an offence, subject to the exception mentioned in this section, for a person to cause or encourage the prostitution in any part of the world of a woman who is a defective.

(2) A person is not guilty of an offence under this section because he causes or encourages the prostitution of such a woman, if he does not know and has no reason to suspect her to be a defective.

30. Man living on earnings of prostitution

(1) It is an offence for a man knowingly to live wholly or in part on the earnings of prostitution.

(2) For the purposes of this section a man who lives with or is habitually in the company of a prostitute, or who exercises control, direction or influence over a prostitute's movements in a way which shows he is aiding, abetting or compelling her prostitution with others, shall be presumed to be knowingly living on the earnings of prostitution, unless he proves the contrary.

31. Woman exercising control over prostitute

It is an offence for a woman for purposes of gain to exercise control, direction or influence over a prostitute's movements in a way which shows she is aiding, abetting or compelling her prostitution.

Solicitation

32. Solicitation by men

It is an offence for a man persistently to solicit or importune in a public place for immoral purposes.

Suppression of brothels

33. Keeping a brothel
It is an offence for a person to keep a brothel, or to manage, or act or assist in the management of, a brothel.

34. Landlord letting premises for use as brothel
It is an offence for the lessor or landlord of any premises or his agent to let the whole or part of the premises with the knowledge that it is to be used, in whole or in part, as a brothel, or, where the whole or part of the premises is used as a brothel, to be wilfully a party to that use continuing.

35. Tenant permitting premises to be used as a brothel
(1) It is an offence for the tenant or occupier, or person in charge, of any premises knowingly to permit the whole or part of the premises to be used as a brothel.

(2) Where the tenant or occupier of any premises is convicted (whether under this section or, for an offence committed before the commencement of this Act, under section thirteen of the Criminal Law Amendment Act 1885) of knowingly permitting the whole or part of the premises to be used as a brothel, the First Schedule to this Act shall apply to enlarge the rights of the lessor or landlord with respect to the assignment or determination of the lease or other contract under which the premises are held by the person convicted.

(3) Where the tenant or occupier of any premises is so convicted, or was so convicted under the said section thirteen before the commencement of this Act and either:
  (a)   the lessor or landlord, after having the conviction brought to his notice, fails or failed to exercise his statutory rights in relation to the lease or contract under which the premises are or were held by the person convicted; or
  (b)   the lessor or landlord, after exercising his statutory rights so as to determine that lease or contract, grants or granted a new lease or enters or entered into a new contract of tenancy of the premises to, with or for the benefit of the same person, without having all reasonable provisions to prevent the recurrence of the offence inserted in the new lease or contract;
then, if subsequently an offence under this section is committed in respect of the premises during the subsistence of the lease or contract referred to in paragraph (a) of this subsection or (where paragraph (b) applies) during the subsistence of the new lease or contact, the lessor or landlord shall be deemed to be a party to that offence unless he shows that he took all reasonable steps to prevent the recurrence of the offence.

References in this subsection to the statutory rights of a lessor or landlord refer to his rights under the First Schedule to this Act or under subsection (1) of section five of the Criminal Law Amendment Act 1912 (the provision replaced for England and Wales by that Schedule).

36. Tenant permitting premises to be used for prostitution
It is an offence for the tenant or occupier of any premises knowingly to permit the whole or part of the premises to be used for the purposes of habitual prostitution.

37–38. (*Not printed in this work*)

39–40. (*Repealed*)

41–43. (*Not printed in this work*)

Interpretation

44. Meaning of 'sexual intercourse'
Where, on the trial of any offence under this Act, it is necessary to prove sexual inter-

course (whether natural or unnatural), it shall not be necessary to prove the completion of the intercourse by the emission of seed, but the intercourse shall be deemed complete upon proof of penetration only.

45. Meaning of 'defective'
In this Act 'defective' means a person suffering from [a state of arrested or incomplete development of mind which includes severe impairment of intelligence and social functioning.]

46. Use of words 'man', 'boy', 'woman' and 'girl'
The use in any provision of this Act of the word 'man' without the addition of the word 'boy', or vice versa, shall not prevent the provision applying to any person to whom it would have applied if both words had been used, and similarly with the words 'woman' and 'girl'.

47. Proof of exceptions
Where in any of the foregoing sections the description of an offence is expressed to be subject to exceptions mentioned in the section, proof of the exception is to lie on the person relying on it.

Part II. (*Not printed in this work*)

Homicide Act 1957
(5 & 6 Eliz 2 c 11)

PART I. AMENDMENTS OF LAW OF ENGLAND AND WALES AS TO FACT OF MURDER

1. Abolition of 'constructive malice'
(1) Where a person kills another in the course or furtherance of some other offence, the killing shall not amount to murder unless done with the same malice aforethought (express or implied) as is required for a killing to amount to murder when not done in the course or furtherance of another offence.

(2) For the purposes of the foregoing subsection, a killing done in the course or for the purpose of resisting an officer of justice, or of resisting or avoiding or preventing a lawful arrest, or of effecting or assisting an escape or rescue from legal custody, shall be treated as a killing in the course or furtherance of an offence.

2. Persons suffering from diminished responsibility
(1) Where a person kills or is a party to the killing of another, he shall not be convicted of murder if he was suffering from such abnormality of mind (whether arising from a condition of arrested or retarded development of mind or any inherent causes or induced by disease or injury) as substantially impaired his mental responsibility for his acts and omissions in doing or being a party to the killing.

(2) On a charge of murder, it shall be for the defence to prove that the person charged is by virtue of this section not liable to be convicted of murder.

(3) A person who but for this section would be liable, whether as principal or as accessory, to be convicted of murder shall be liable instead to be convicted of manslaughter.

(4) The fact that one party to a killing is by virtue of this section not liable to be convicted of murder shall not affect the question whether the killing amounted to murder in the case of any other party to it.

3. Provocation
Where on a charge of murder there is evidence on which the jury can find that the

person charged was provoked (whether by things done or by things said or by both together) to lose his self-control, the question whether the provocation was enough to make a reasonable man do as he did shall be left to be determined by the jury; and in determining that question the jury shall take into account everything both done and said according to the effect which, in their opinion, it would have on a reasonable man.

4. Suicide pacts
(1) It shall be manslaughter, and shall not be murder, for a person acting in pursuance of a suicide pact between him and another to kill the other or be a party to the other . . . being killed by a third person.

(2) Where it is shown that a person charged with the murder of another killed the other or was a party to his . . . being killed, it shall be for the defence to prove that the person charged was acting in pursuance of a suicide pact between him and the other.

(3) For the purposes of this section 'suicide pact' means a common agreement between two or more persons having for its object the death of all of them, whether or not each is to take this own life, but nothing done by a person who enters into a suicide pact shall be treated as done by him in pursuance of the pact unless it is done while he has the settled intention of dying in pursuance of the pact.

Part II. (*Not printed in this work*)

Indecency With Children Act 1960
(8 & 9 Eliz 2 c 33)

1. Indecent conduct towards young child
(1) Any person who commits an act of gross indecency with or towards a child under the age of fourteen, or who incites a child under that age to such an act with him or another, shall be liable on conviction on indictment to imprisonment for a term not exceeding two years, or on summary conviction to imprisonment for a term not exceeding six months, to a fine not exceeding [the prescribed sum], or to both.

(2), (3), (4) (*Not printed in this work*)

2–3. (*Not printed in this work*)

Suicide Act 1961
(9 & 10 Eliz 2 c 60)

1. Suicide to cease to be a crime
The rule of law whereby it is a crime for a person to commit suicide is hereby abrogated.

2. Criminal liability for complicity in another's suicide
(1) A person who aids, abets, counsels or procures the suicide of another, or an attempt by another to commit suicide, shall be liable on conviction on indictment to imprisonment for a term not exceeding fourteen years.

(2) If on the trial of an indictment for murder or manslaughter it is proved that the accused aided, abetted, counselled or procured the suicide of the person in question, the jury may find him guilty of that offence.

(3) (*Not printed in this work*)

(4) . . . no proceedings shall be instituted for an offence under this section except by or with the consent of the Director of Public Prosecutions.

Criminal Procedure (Insanity) Act 1964
(1964 c 84)

1. Acquittal on grounds of insanity

The special verdict required by section 2 of the Trial of Lunatics Act 1883 (hereinafter referred to as a 'special verdict') shall be that the accused is not guilty by reason of insanity; and accordingly in subsection (1) of that section for the words from 'a special verdict' to the end there shall be substituted the words 'a special verdict that the accused is not guilty by reason of insanity'.

2–3. (*Repealed*)

4. Unfitness to plead

(1) Where on the trial of a person the question arises (at the instance of the defence or otherwise) whether the accused is under disability, that is to say under any disability such that apart from this Act it would constitute a bar to his being tried, the following provisions shall have effect.

(2) The court, if having regard to the nature of the supposed disability the court are of opinion that it is expedient so to do and in the interests of the accused, may postpone consideration of the said question (hereinafter referred to as 'the question of fitness to be tried') until any time up to the opening of the case for the defence, and if before the question of fitness to be tried falls to be determined the jury return a verdict of acquittal on the count or each of the counts on which the accused is being tried that question shall not be determined.

(3) Subject to the foregoing subsection, the question of fitness to be tried shall be determined as soon as it arises.

(4) The question of fitness to be tried shall be determined by a jury; and:

(a) where it falls to be determined on the arraignment of the accused, then if the trial proceeds the accused shall be tried by a jury other than that which determined that question;

(b) where it falls to be determined at any later time it shall be determined by a separate jury or by the jury by whom the accused is being tried, as the court may direct.

(5) Where in accordance with subsection (2) or (3) of this section it is determined that the accused is under disability, the trial shall not proceed or further proceed.

5. Orders for admission to hospital

(1) Where:

(a) a special verdict is returned, or

(b) . . .

(c) a finding is recorded that the accused is under disability, or

(d) . . .

the court shall make an order that the accused be admitted to such hospital as may be specified by the Secretary of State.

(2) (*repealed*)

(3) The provisions in that behalf of Schedule I to this Act shall have effect in relation to orders for admission to hospital made under this section.

(4) Subject to the provisions of the said Schedule, if while a person is detained in pursuance of an order under paragraph (c) of subsection (1) of this section the Secretary of State, after consultation with the responsible medical officer, is satisfied that the said person can properly be tried, the Secretary of State may remit that person to prison, or to a remand centre provided under section 43 of the Prison Act 1952, for trial . . . and on his arrival at the prison or remand centre the order under subsection (1) (c) shall cease to have effect.

In relation to persons ordered under section 2 of the Criminal Lunatics Act 1800 to be kept in custody this subsection and paragraph 2(2) of Schedule I to this Act shall apply as if the order were an order under subsection (1) (c) of this section.

(5) (*Repealed*)

6. Evidence by prosecution of insanity or diminished responsibility

Where on a trial for murder the accused contends:

(a) that at the time of the alleged offence he was insane so as not to be responsible according to law for his actions; or

(b) that at that time he was suffering from such abnormality of mind as is specified in subsection (1) of section 2 of the Homicide Act 1957 (diminished responsibility),

the court shall allow the prosecution to adduce or elicit evidence tending to prove the other of those contentions, and may give directions as to the stage of the proceedings at which the prosecution may adduce such evidence.

7–8. (*Not printed in this work*)

Police Act 1964
(1964 c 48)

51. Assaults on constables

(1) Any person who assaults a constable in the execution of his duty, or a person assisting a constable in the execution of his duty, shall be guilty of an offence and liable on summary conviction to a fine not exceeding £1000 or to imprisonment for a term not exceeding six months or to both.

(2) Subsection (2) of section 23 of the Firearms Act 1937 (additional penalty for possession of firearms when committing certain offences) shall apply to offences under subsection (1) of this section.

(3) Any person who resists or wilfully obstructs a constable in the execution of his duty, or a person assisting a constable in the execution of his duty, shall be guilty of an offence and liable on summary conviction to imprisonment for a term not exceeding one month or to a fine not exceeding [level 5 on the standard scale], or to both.

(*None of the other sections is printed in this work*)

Criminal Law Act 1967
(1967 c 58)

PART I. FELONY AND MISDEMEANOUR

1. Abolition of distinction between felony and misdemeanour

(1) All distinctions between felony and misdemeanour are hereby abolished.

(2) Subject to the provisions of this Act, on all matters on which a distinction has previously been made between felony and misdemeanour, including mode of trial, the law and practice in relation to all offences cognisable under the law of England and Wales (including piracy) shall be the law and practice applicable at the commencement of this Act in relation to misdemeanour.

2. (*Repealed*)

3. Use of force in making arrest, etc

(1) A person may use such force as is reasonable in the circumstances in the prevention of crime, or in effecting or assisting in the lawful arrest of offenders or suspected offenders or of persons unlawfully at large.

(2) Subsection (1) above shall replace the rules of the common law on the question when force used for a purpose mentioned in the subsection is justified by that purpose.

4. Penalties for assisting offenders

(1) Where a person has committed an arrestable offence, any other person who, knowing or believing him to be guilty of the offence or of some other arrestable offence, does without lawful authority or reasonable excuse any act with intent to impede his apprehension or prosecution shall be guilty of an offence.

(2) If on the trial of an indictment for an arrestable offence the jury are satisfied that the offence charged (or some other offence of which the accused might on that charge be found guilty) was committed, but find the accused not guilty of it, they may find him guilty of any offence under subsection (1) above of which they are satisfied that he is guilty in relation to the offence charged (or that other offence).

(3) A person committing an offence under subsection (1) above with intent to impede another person's apprehension or prosecution shall on conviction on indictment be liable to imprisonment according to the gravity of the other person's offence, as follows:

(a) if that offence is one for which the sentence is fixed by law, he shall be liable to imprisonment for not more than ten years;

(b) if it is one for which a person (not previously convicted) may be sentenced to imprisonment for a term of fourteen years, he shall be liable to imprisonment for not more than seven years;

(c) if it is not one included above but is one for which a person (not previously convicted) may be sentenced to imprisonment for a term of ten years, he shall be liable to imprisonment for not more than five years;

(d) in any other case, he shall be liable to imprisonment for not more than three years.

(4) No proceedings shall be instituted for an offence under subsection (1) above except by or with the consent of the Director of Public Prosecutions:

(5) (*Repealed*)

(6) For purposes of the Extradition Acts 1870 to 1935 offences in relation to an extradition crime which in England would be offences under subsection (1) above shall be extradition crimes and be deemed to be included in Schedule 1 to the Extradition Act 1870.

(7) (*Repealed*)

5. Penalties for concealing offences or giving false information

(1) Where a person has committed an arrestable offence, any other person who, knowing or believing that the offence or some other arrestable offence has been committed, and that he has information which might be of material assistance in securing the prosecution or conviction of an offender for it, accepts or agrees to accept for not disclosing that information any consideration other than the making good of loss or injury caused by the offence, or the making of reasonable compensation for that loss or injury, shall be liable on conviction on indictment to imprisonment for not more than two years.

(2) Where a person causes any wasteful employment of the police by knowingly making to any person a false report tending to show that an offence has been committed, or to give rise to apprehension for the safety of any persons or property, or tending to show that he has information material to any police inquiry, he shall be liable on summary conviction to imprisonment for not more than six months or to a fine of not more than level 4 on the standard scale.

(3) No proceedings shall be instituted for an offence under this section except by or with the consent of the Director of Public Prosecutions.

(4) (*Repealed*)

(5) The compounding of an offence other than treason shall not be an offence otherwise than under this section.

6. Trial of offences

(1) Where a person is arraigned on an indictment:

    (a) he shall in all cases be entitled to make a plea of not guilty in addition to any demurrer or special plea;

    (b) he may plead not guilty of the offence specifically charged in the indictment but guilty of another offence of which he might be found guilty on that indictment;

    (c) if he stands mute of malice or will not answer directly to the indictment, the court may order a plea of not guilty to be entered on his behalf, and he shall then be treated as having pleaded not guilty.

(2) On an indictment for murder a person found not guilty of murder may be found guilty:

    (a) of manslaughter, or of causing grievous bodily harm with intent to do so; or

    (b) of any offence of which he may be found guilty under an enactment specifically so providing, or under section 4(2) of this Act; or

    (c) of an attempt to commit murder, or of an attempt to commit any other offence of which he might be found guilty;

but may not be found guilty of any offence not included above.

(3) Where, on a person's trial on indictment for any offence except treason or murder, the jury find him not guilty of the offence specifically charged in the indictment, but the allegations in the indictment amount to or include (expressly or by implication) an allegation of another offence falling within the jurisdiction of the court of trial, the jury may find him guilty of that other offence or of an offence of which he could be found guilty on an indictment specifically charging that other offence.

(4) For purposes of subsection (3) above any allegation of an offence shall be taken as including an allegation of attempting to commit that offence; and where a person is charged on indictment with attempting to commit an offence or with any assault or other act preliminary to an offence, but not with the completed offence, then (subject to the discretion of the court to discharge the jury with a view to the preferment of an indictment for the completed offence) he may be convicted of the offence charged notwithstanding that he is shown to be guilty of the completed offence.

(5) Where a person arraigned on an indictment pleads not guilty of an offence charged in the indictment but guilty of some other offence of which he might be found guilty on that charge, and he is convicted on that plea of guilty without trial for the offence of which he has pleaded not guilty, then (whether or not the two offences are separately charged in distinct counts) his conviction of the one offence shall be an acquittal of the other.

(6) Any power to bring proceedings for an offence by criminal information in the High Court is hereby abolished.

(7) Subsections (1) to (3) above shall apply to an indictment containing more than one count as if each count were a separate indictment.

7. (*Repealed*)

8–15. (*Not printed in this work*)

Sexual Offences Act 1967
(1967 c 60)

1. Amendment of law relating to homosexual acts in private

(1) Notwithstanding any statutory or common law provision, but subject to the provisions of the next following section, a homosexual act in private shall not be an offence provided that the parties consent thereto and have attained the age of twenty-one years.

(2) An act which would otherwise be treated for the purposes of this Act as being done in private shall not be so treated if done:

(a) when more than two persons take part or are present; or

(b) in a lavatory to which the public have or are permitted to have access, whether on payment or otherwise.

(3) A man who is suffering from severe mental handicap cannot in law give any consent which, by virtue of subsection (1) of this section, would prevent a homosexual act from being an offence, but a person shall not be convicted, on account of the incapacity of such a man to consent, of an offence consisting of such an act if he proves that he did not know and had no reason to suspect that man to be suffering from severe mental handicap.

(4) Section 128 of the Mental Health Act 1959 (prohibition on men on the staff of a hospital, or otherwise having responsibility for mental patients, having sexual intercourse with women patients) shall have effect as if any reference therein to having unlawful sexual intercourse with a woman included a reference to committing buggery or an act of gross indecency with another man.

(5) Subsection (1) of this section shall not prevent an act from being an offence (other than a civil offence) under any provision of the Army Act 1955, the Air Force Act 1955 or the Naval Discipline Act 1957.

(6) It is hereby declared that where in any proceedings it is charged that a homosexual act is an offence the prosecutor shall have the burden of proving that the act was done otherwise than in private or otherwise than with the consent of the parties or that any of the parties had not attained the age of twenty-one years.

(7) For the purposes of this section a man shall be treated as doing a homosexual act if, and only if, he commits buggery with another man or commits an act of gross indecency with another man or is a party to the commission by a man of such an act.

2. Homosexual acts on merchant ships

(1) It shall continue to be:

(a) an offence under section 12 of the Act of 1956 and at common law for a man to commit buggery with another man in circumstances in which by reason of the provisions of section 1 of this Act it would not be an offence (apart from this section); and

(b) an offence under section 13 of that Act for a man to commit an act of gross indecency with another man, or to be party to the commission by a man of such an act in such circumstances as aforesaid,

provided that the act charged is done on a United Kingdom merchant ship, wherever it may be, by a man who is a member of the crew of that ship with another man who is a member of the crew of that or any other United Kingdom merchant ship.

(2) Section 11 of the Criminal Justice Act 1925 (venue in indictable offences) shall apply to an act which is an offence by virtue of this section as if it were an offence when done on land.

(3) In this section:

'member of the crew' in relation to a ship, includes the master of the ship and any. apprentice to the sea service serving in that ship;

'United Kingdom merchant ship' means a ship registered in the United Kingdom habitually used or used at the time of the act charged for the purposes of carrying passengers or goods for reward.

3. (*Not printed in this work*)

4. Procuring others to commit homosexual acts

(1) A man who procures another man to commit with a third man an act of buggery which by reason of section 1 of this Act is not an offence shall be liable on conviction on indictment to imprisonment for a term not exceeding two years.

(2) (*Repealed*)

(3) It shall not be an offence under section 13 of the Act of 1956 for a man to

procure the commission by another man of an act of gross indecency with the first-mentioned man which by reason of section 1 of this Act is not an offence under the said section 13.

5. Living on earnings of male prostitution
(1) A man or woman who knowingly lives wholly or in part on the earnings of prostitution of another man shall be liable:
  (a) on summary conviction to imprisonment for a term not exceeding six months; or
  (b) on conviction on indictment to imprisonment for a term not exceeding seven years.
(2) (*Repealed*)
(3) Anyone may arrest .without a warrant a person found committing an offence under this section.

6. Premises resorted to for homosexual practices
Premises shall be treated for purposes of sections 33 to 35 of the Act of 1956 as a brothel if people resort to it for the purpose of lewd homosexual practices in circumstances in which resort thereto for lewd heterosexual practices would have led to its being treated as a brothel for the purposes of those sections.

7. Time limit on prosecutions
(1) No proceedings for an offence to which this section applies shall be commenced after the expiration of twelve months from the date on which that offence was committed.
(2) This section applies to:
  (a) any offence under section 13 of the Act of 1956 (gross indecency between men);
  (b) (*Repealed*)
  (c) any offence of buggery by man with another man not amounting to an assault on that other man and not being an offence by a man with a boy under the age of sixteen.

8. Restriction on prosecutions
No proceedings shall be instituted except by or with the consent of the Director of Public Prosecutions against any man for the offence of buggery with, or gross indecency with, another man . . . or for aiding, abetting, counselling, procuring or commanding its commission where either of those men was at the time of its commission under the age of twenty-one: . . .

9. (*Repealed*)

10–11. (*Not printed in this work*)

Criminal Justice Act 1967
(1967 c 80)

8. Proof of criminal intent
A court of jury, in determining whether a person has committed an offence,:
  (a) shall not be bound in law to infer that he intended or foresaw a result of his actions by reason only of its being a natural and probable consequence of those actions; but
  (b) shall decide whether he did intend or foresee that result by reference to all the evidence, drawing such inferences from the evidence as appear proper in the circumstances.

(*None of the other sections is printed in this work*)

Abortion Act 1967
(1967 c 87)

1. Medical termination of pregnancy
(1) Subject to the provisions of this section, a person shall not be guilty of an offence under the law relating to abortion when a pregnancy is terminated by a registered medical practitioner if two registered medical practitioners are of the opinion, formed in good faith:

    (a) that the continuance of the pregnancy would involve risk to the life of the pregnant woman, or of injury to the physical or mental health of the pregnant woman or any existing children of her family, greater than if the pregnancy were terminated; or

    (b) that there is a substantial risk that if the child were born it would suffer from such physical or mental abnormalities as to be seriously handicapped.

(2) In determining whether the continuance of a pregnancy would involve such risk of injury to health as is mentioned in paragraph (a) of subsection (1) of this section, account may be taken of the pregnant woman's actual or reasonably foreseeable environment.

(3) Except as provided by subsection (4) of this section, any treatment for the termination of pregnancy must be carried out in a hospital vested in the Secretary of State for the purposes of his functions under the National Health Service Act 1977 or the National Health Service (Scotland) Act 1978 or in a place approved for the purposes of this section by the Secretary of State.

(4) Subsection (3) of this section, and so much of subsection (1) as relates to the opinion of two registered medical practitioners, shall not apply to the termination of a pregnancy by a registered medical practitioner in a case where he is of the opinion, formed in good faith, that the termination is immediately necessary to save the life or to prevent grave permanent injury to the physical or mental health of the pregnant woman.

2. Notification
(1) The Minister of Health in respect of England and Wales, and the Secretary of State in respect of Scotland, shall by statutory instrument make regulations to provide:

    (a) for requiring any such opinion as is referred to in section 1 of this Act to be certified by the practitioners or practitioner concerned in such form and at such time as may be prescribed by the regulations, and for requiring the preservation and disposal of certificates made for the purposes of the regulations;

    (b) for requiring any registered medical practitioner who terminates a pregnancy to give notice of the termination and such other information relating to the termination as may be so prescribed;

    (c) for prohibiting the disclosure, except to such persons or for such purposes as may be so prescribed, of notices given or information furnished pursuant to the regulations.

(2) The information furnished in pursuance of regulations made by virtue of paragraph (b) of subsection (1) of this section shall be notified solely to the Chief Medical Officers of the Ministry of Health and the Scottish Home and Health Department respectively.

(3) Any person who wilfully contravenes or wilfully fails to comply with the requirements of regulations under subsection (1) of this section shall be liable on summary conviction to a fine not exceeding level 5 on the standard scale.

(4) Any statutory instrument made by virtue of this section shall be subject to annulment in pursuance of a resolution of either House of Parliament.

3. (*Not printed in this work*)

4. Conscientious objection to participation in treatment

(1) Subject to subsection (2) of this section, no person shall be under any duty, whether by contract or by any statutory or other legal requirement, to participate in any treatment authorised by this Act to which he has a conscientious objection:

Provided that in any legal proceedings the burden of proof of conscientious objection shall rest on the person claiming to rely on it.

(2) Nothing in subsection (1) of this section shall affect any duty to participate in treatment which is necessary to save the life or to prevent grave permanent injury to the physical or mental health of a pregnant woman.

(3) (*Not printed in this work*)

5. Supplementary provisions

(1) Nothing in this Act shall affect the provisions of the Infant Life (Preservation) Act 1929 (protecting the life of the viable foetus).

(2) For the purposes of the law relating to abortion, anything done with intent to procure the miscarriage of a woman is unlawfully done unless authorised by section 1 of this Act.

6. Interpretation

In this Act, the following expressions have meanings hereby assigned to them:

> 'the law relating to abortion' means sections 58 and 59 of the Offences against the Person Act 1861, and any rule of law relating to the procurement of abortion;

> 'the National Health Service Acts' means the National Health Service Acts 1946 to 1966 or the National Health Service (Scotland) Acts 1947 to 1966.

Criminal Appeal Act 1968
(1968 c 19)

1–11. (*Not printed in this work*)

12. Appeal against verdict of not guilty by reason of insanity

A person in whose case there is returned a verdict of not guilty by reason of insanity may appeal to the Court of Appeal against the verdict:

(a) on any ground of appeal which involves a question of law alone; and

(b) with the leave of the Court of Appeal, on any ground which involves a question of fact alone, or a question of mixed law and fact, or on any other ground which appears to the Court of Appeal to be a sufficient ground of appeal;

but if the judge of the court of trial grants a certificate that the case is fit for appeal on a ground which involves a question of fact, or a question of mixed law and fact, an appeal lies under this section without the leave of the Court of Appeal.

13–14. (*Not printed in this work*)

15. Right of appeal against finding of disability

(1) Where there has been a determination under s 4 of the Criminal Procedure (Insanity) Act 1964 of the question of a person's fitness to be tried, and the jury has returned a finding that he is under disability, the person may appeal to the Court of Appeal against the finding.

(2) An appeal under this section may be:

(a) on any ground of appeal which involves a question of law alone; and

(b) with the leave of the Court of Appeal, on any ground which involves a question of fact alone, or a question of mixed law and fact, or on any other ground which appears to the Court of Appeal to be a sufficient ground of appeal;

but if the judge of the court of trial grants a certificate that the case is fit for appeal on a ground which involves a question of fact, or a question of mixed law and fact, an appeal lies under this section without the leave of the Court of Appeal.

16-55. (*Not printed in this work*)

Theft Act 1968
(1968 c 60)

Definition of 'theft'

1. Basic definition of theft
(1) A person is guilty of theft if he dishonestly appropriates property belonging to another with the intention of permanently depriving the other of it; and 'thief' and 'steal' shall be construed accordingly.

(2) It is immaterial whether the appropriation is made with a view to gain, or is made for the thief's own benefit.

(3) The five following sections of this Act shall have effect as regards the interpretation and operation of this section (and, except as otherwise provided by this Act, shall apply only for purposes of this section).

2. 'Dishonestly'
(1) A person's appropriation of property belonging to another is not to be regarded as dishonest:
  (a) if he appropriates the property in the belief that he has in law the right to deprive the other of it, on behalf of himself or of a third person; or
  (b) if he appropriates the property in the belief that he would have the other's consent if the other knew of the appropriation and the circumstances of it; or
  (c) (except where the property came to him as trustee or personal representative) if he appropriates the property in the belief that the person to whom the property belongs cannot be discovered by taking reasonable steps.

(2) A person's appropriation of property belonging to another may be dishonest notwithstanding that he is willing to pay for the property.

3. 'Appropriates'
(1) Any assumption by a person of the rights of an owner amounts to an appropriation, and this includes, where he has come by the property (innocently or not) without stealing it, any later assumption of a right to it by keeping or dealing with it as owner.

(2) Where property or a right or interest in property is or purports to be transferred for value to a person acting in good faith, no later assumption by him of rights which he believed himself to be acquiring shall, by reason of any defect in the transferor's title, amount to theft of the property.

4. 'Property'
(1) 'Property' includes money and all other property, real or personal, including things in action and other intangible property.

(2) A person cannot steal land, or things forming part of land and severed from it by him or by his direction, except in the following cases, that is to say:
  (a) when he is a trustee or personal representative, or is authorised by power of attorney, or as liquidator of a company, or otherwise, to sell or dispose of land belonging to another, and he appropriates the land or anything forming part of it by dealing with it in breach of the confidence reposed in him; or
  (b) when he is not in possession of the land and appropriates anything forming part of the land by severing it or causing it to be severed, or after it has been severed; or
  (c) when, being in possession of the land under the tenancy, he appropriates the whole or part of any fixture or structure let to be used with the land.

For purposes of this subsection 'land' does not include incorporeal hereditaments; 'tenancy' means a tenancy for years or any less period and includes an agreement for such a tenancy, but a person who after the end of a tenancy remains in possession as statutory tenant or otherwise is to be treated as having possession under the tenancy, and 'let' shall be construed accordingly.

(3) A person who picks mushrooms growing wild on any land, or who picks flowers, fruit or foliage from a plant growing wild on any land, does not (although not in possession of the land) steal what he picks, unless he does it for reward or for sale or other commercial purpose.

For purposes of this subsection 'mushroom' includes any fungus, and 'plant' includes any shrub or tree.

(4) Wild creatures, tamed or untamed, shall be regarded as property; but a person cannot steal a wild creature not tamed nor ordinarily kept in captivity, or the carcase of any such creature, unless either it has been reduced into possession by or on behalf of another person and possession of it has not since been lost or abandoned, or another person is in course of reducing it into posession.

5. 'Belonging to another'

(1) Property shall be regarded as belonging to any person having possession or control of it, or having in it any proprietary right or interest (not being an equitable interest arising only from an agreement to transfer or grant an interest).

(2) Where property is subject to a trust, the persons to whom it belongs shall be regarded as including any person having a right to enforce the trust, and an intention to defeat the trust shall be regarded accordingly as an intention to deprive of the property any person having that right.

(3) Where a person receives property from or on account of another, and is under an obligation to the other to retain and deal with that property or its proceeds in a particular way, the property or proceeds shall be regarded (as against him) as belonging to the other.

(4) Where a person gets property by another's mistake, and is under an obligation to make restoration (in whole or in part) of the property or its proceeds or of the value thereof, then to the extent of that obligation the property or proceeds shall be regarded (as against him) as belonging to the person entitled to restoration, and an intention not to make restoration shall be regarded accordingly as an intention to deprive that person of the property or proceeds.

(5) Property of a corporation sole shall be regarded as belonging to the corporation notwithstanding a vacancy in the corporation.

6. 'With the intention of permanently depriving the other of it'

(1) A person appropriating property belonging to another without meaning the other permanently to lose the thing itself is nevertheless to be regarded as having the intention of permanently depriving the other of it if his intention is to treat the thing as his own to dispose of regardless of the other's rights; and a borrowing or lending of it may amount to so treating it if, but only if, the borrowing or lending is for a period and in circumstances making it equivalent to an outright taking or disposal.

(2) Without prejudice to the generality of subsection (1) above, where a person, having possession or control (lawfully or not) of property belonging to another, parts with the property under a condition as to its return which he may not be able to perform, this (if done for purposes of his own and without the other's authority) amounts to treating the property as his own to dispose of regardless of the other's rights.

Theft, robbery, burglary, etc

7. Theft

A person guilty of theft shall on conviction on indictment be liable to imprisonment for a term not exceeding ten years.

8. Robbery

(1) A person is guilty of robbery if he steals, and immediately before or at the time of

doing so, and in order to do so, he uses force on any person or puts or seeks to put any person in fear of being then and there subjected to force.

(2) A person guilty of robbery, or of an assault with intent to rob, shall on conviction on indictment be liable to imprisonment for life.

9. Burglary

(1) A person is guilty of burglary if:

   (a) he enters any building or part of building as a trespasser and with intent to commit any such offence as is mentioned in subsection (2) below; or

   (b) having entered any building or part of a building as a trespasser he steals or attempts to steal anything in the building or that part of it or inflicts or attempts to inflict on any person therein any grievous bodily harm.

(2) The offences referred to in subsection (1)(a) above are offences of stealing anything in the building or part of a building in question, of inflicting on any person therein any grievous bodily harm or raping any woman therein, and of doing unlawful damage to the building or anything therein.

(3) References in subsections (1) and (2) above to a building shall apply also to an inhabited vehicle or vessel, and shall apply to any such vehicle or vessel at times when the person having a habitation in it is not there as well as at times when he is.

(4) A person guilty of burglary shall on conviction on indictment be liable to imprisonment for a term not exceeding fourteen years.

10. Aggravated burglary

(1) A person is guilty of aggravated burglary if he commits any burglary and at the time has with him any firearm or imitation firearm, any weapon of offence, or any explosive; and for this purpose:

   (a) 'firearm' includes an airgun or air pistol, and 'imitation firearm' means anything which has the appearance of being a firearm, whether capable of being discharged or not; and

   (b) 'weapon of offence' means any article made or adapted for use for causing injury to or incapacitating a person, or intended by the person having it with him for such use; and

   (c) 'explosive' means any article manufactured for the purpose of producing a practical effect by explosion, or intended by the person having it with him for that purpose.

(2) A person guilty of aggravated burglary shall on conviction on indictment be liable to imprisonment for life.

11. Removal of articles from places open to the public

(1) Subject to subsections (2) and (3) below, where the public have access to a building in order to view the building or part of it, or a collection or part of a collection housed in it, any person who without lawful authority removes from the building or its grounds the whole or part of any article displayed or kept for display to the public in the building or that part of it or in its grounds shall be guilty of an offence.

For this purpose 'collection' includes a collection got together for a temporary purpose, but references in this section to a collection do not apply to a collection made or exhibited for the purpose of effecting sales or other commercial dealings.

(2) It is immaterial for purposes of subsection (1) above, that the public's access to a building is limited to a particular period or particular occasion; but where anything removed from a building or its grounds is there otherwise than as forming part of, or being on loan for exhibition with, a collection intended for permanent exhibition to the public, the person removing it does not thereby commit an offence under this section unless he removes it on a day when the public have access to the building as mentioned in subsection (1) above.

(3) A person does not commit an offence under this section if he believes that he has lawful authority for the removal of the thing in question or that he would have it if the person entitled to give it knew of the removal and the circumstances of it.

(4) A person guilty of an offence under this section shall, on conviction on indictment, be liable to imprisonment for a term not exceeding five years.

12. Taking motor vehicle or other conveyance without authority

(1) Subject to subsections (5) and (6) below, a person shall be guilty of an offence if, without having the consent of the owner or other lawful authority, he takes any conveyance for his own or another's use or, knowing that any conveyance has been taken without such authority, drives it or allows himself to be carried in or on it.

(2) A person guilty of an offence under subsection (1) above shall on conviction on indictment be liable to imprisonment for a term not exceeding three years.

(3) (*Repealed*)

(4) If on the trial of an indictment for theft the jury are not satisfied that the accused committed theft, but it is proved that the accused committed an offence under subsection (1) above, the jury may find him guilty of the offence under subsection (1).

(5) Subsection (1) above shall not apply in relation to pedal cycles; but, subject to subsection (6) below, a person who, without having the consent of the owner or other lawful authority, takes a pedal cycle for his own or another's use, or rides a pedal cycle knowing it to have been taken without such authority, shall on summary conviction be liable to a fine not exceeding level 3 on the standard scale.

(6) A person does not commit an offence under this section by anything done in the belief that he has lawful authority to do it or that he would have the owner's consent if the owner knew of his doing it and the circumstances of it.

(7) For purposes of this section:
- (a) 'conveyance' means any conveyance constructed or adapted for the carriage of a person or persons whether by land, water or air, except that it does not include a conveyance constructed or adapted for use only under the control of a person not carried in or on it, and 'drive' shall be construed accordingly; and
- (b) 'owner', in relation to a conveyance which is the subject of a hiring agreement or hire-purchase agreement, means the person in possession of the conveyance under the agreement.

13. Abstracting of electricity

A person who dishonestly uses without due authority, or dishonestly causes to be wasted or diverted, any electricity shall on conviction on indictment be liable to imprisonment for a term not exceeding five years.

14. Extension to thefts from mails outside England and Wales, and robbery etc. on such a theft

(1) Where a person:
- (a) steals or attempts to steal any mail bag or postal packet in the course of transmission as such between places in different jurisdictions in the British postal area, or any of the contents of such a mail bag or postal packet; or
- (b) in stealing or with intent to steal any such mail bag or postal packet or any of its contents, commits any robbery, attempted robbery or assault with intent to rob;

then, notwithstanding that he does so outside England and Wales, he shall be guilty of committing or attempting to commit the offence against this Act as if he had done so in England or Wales, and he shall accordingly be liable to be prosecuted, tried and punished in England and Wales without proof that the offence was committed there.

(2) In subsection (1) above the reference to different jurisdictions in the British postal area is to be construed as referring to the several jurisdictions of England and Wales, of Scotland, of Northern Ireland, of the Isle of Man and of the Channel Islands.

(3) For purposes of this section 'mail bag' includes any article serving the purpose of a mail bag.

Fraud and blackmail

15. Obtaining property by deception

(1) A person who by any deception dishonestly obtains property belonging to another, with the intention of permanently depriving the other of it, shall on conviction on indictment be liable to imprisonment for a term not exceeding ten years.

(2) For purposes of this section a person is to be treated as obtaining property if he obtains ownership, possession or control of it, and 'obtain' includes obtaining for another or enabling another to obtain or to retain.

(3) Section 6 above shall apply for purposes of this section, with the necessary adaptation of the reference to appropriating, as it applies for purposes of section 1.

(4) For purposes of this section 'deception' means any deception (whether deliberate or reckless) by words or conduct as to fact or as to law, including a deception as to the present intentions of the person using the deception or any other person.

16. Obtaining pecuniary advantage by deception

(1) A person who by any deception dishonestly obtains for himself or another any pecuniary advantage shall on conviction on indictment be liable to imprisonment for a term not exceeding five years.

(2) The cases in which a pecuniary advantage within the meaning of this section is to be regarded as obtained for a person are cases where:

(a) (*Repealed*)

(b) he is allowed to borrow by way of overdraft, or to take out any policy of insurance or annuity contract, or obtains an improvement of the terms on which he is allowed to do so; or

(c) he is given the opportunity to earn remuneration or greater remuneration in an office or employment, or to win money by betting.

(3) For purposes of this section 'deception' has the same meaning as in section 15 of this Act.

17. False accounting

(1) Where a person dishonestly, with a view to gain for himself or another or with intent to cause loss to another,:

(a) destroys, defaces, conceals or falsifies any account or any record or document made or required for any accounting purpose; or

(b) in furnishing information for any purpose produces or makes use of any account, or any such record or document as aforesaid, which to his knowledge is or may be misleading, false or deceptive in a material particular;

he shall, on conviction on indictment, be liable to imprisonment for a term not exceeding seven years.

(2) For purposes of this section a person who makes or concurs in making in an account or other document an entry which is or may be misleading, false or deceptive in a material particular, or who omits or concurs in omitting a material particular from an account or other document, is to be treated as falsifying the account or document.

18. Liability of company officers for certain offences by company

(1) Where an offence committed by a body corporate under section 15, 16 or 17 of this Act is proved to have been committed with the consent or connivance of any director, manager, secretary or other similar officer of the body corporate, or any person who was purporting to act in any such capacity, he as well as the body corporate shall be guilty of that offence, and shall be liable to be proceeded against and punished accordingly.

(2) Where the affairs of a body corporate are managed by its members, this section shall apply in relation to the acts and defaults of a member in connection with his functions of management as if he were a director of the body corporate.

19. False statements by company directors, etc

(1) Where an officer of a body corporate or unincorporated association (or person purporting to act as such), with intent to deceive members or creditors of the body corporate or association about its affairs, publishes or concurs in publishing a written statement or account which to his knowledge is or may be misleading, false or deceptive in a material particular, he shall on conviction on indictment be liable to imprisonment for a term not exceeding seven years.

(2) For purposes of this section a person who has entered into a security for the benefit of a body corporate or association is to be treated as a creditor of it.

(3) Where the affairs of a body corporate or association are managed by its members, this section shall apply to any statement which a member publishes or concurs in publishing in connection with his functions of management as if he were an officer of the body corporate or association.

20. Suppression, etc of documents

(1) A person who dishonestly, with a view to gain for himself or another or with intent to cause loss to another, destroys, defaces or conceals any valuable security, any will or other testamentary document or any original document of or belonging to, or filed or deposited in, any court of justice or any government department shall on conviction on indictment be liable to imprisonment for a term not exceeding seven years.

(2) A person who dishonestly, with a view to gain for himself or another or with intent to cause loss to another, by any deception procures the execution of a valuable security shall on conviction on indictment be liable to imprisonment for a term not exceeding seven years; and this subsection shall apply in relation to the making, acceptance, indorsement, alteration, cancellation or destruction in whole or in part of a valuable security, and in relation to the signing or sealing of any paper or other material in order that it may be made or converted into, or used or dealt with as, a valuable security, as if that were the execution of a valuable security.

(3) For purposes of this section 'deception' has the same meaning as in section 15 of this Act, and 'valuable security' means any document creating, transferring, surrendering or releasing any right to, in or over property, or authorising the payment of money or delivery of any property, or evidencing the creation, transfer, surrender or release of any such right, or the payment of money or delivery of any property, or the satisfaction of any obligation.

21. Blackmail

(1) A person is guilty of blackmail if, with a view to gain for himself or another or with intent to cause loss to another, he makes any unwarranted demand with menaces; and for this purpose a demand with menaces is unwarranted unless the person making it does so in the belief:

(a)   that he has reasonable grounds for making the demand; and

(b)   that the use of the menaces is a proper means of reinforcing the demand.

(2) The nature of the act or omission demanded is immaterial, and it is also immaterial whether the menaces relate to action to be taken by the person making the demand.

(3) A person guilty of blackmail shall on conviction on indictment be liable to imprisonment for a term not exceeding fourteen years.

Offences relating to goods stolen, etc

22. Handling stolen goods

(1) A person handles stolen goods if (otherwise than in the course of the stealing) knowing or believing them to be stolen goods he dishonestly receives the goods, or dishonestly undertakes or assists in their retention, removal, disposal or realisation by or for the benefit of another person, or if he arranges to do so.

(2) A person guilty of handling stolen goods shall on conviction on indictment be liable to imprisonment for a term not exceeding fourteen years.

23. Advertising rewards for return of goods stolen or lost

Where any public advertisement of a reward for the return of any goods which have been stolen or lost uses any words to the effect that no questions will be asked, or that the person producing the goods will be safe from apprehension or inquiry, or that any money paid for the purchase of the goods or advanced by way of loan on them will be repaid, the person advertising the reward and any person who prints or publishes the advertisement shall on summary conviction be liable to a fine not exceeding level 3 on the standard scale.

24. Scope of offences relating to stolen goods

(1) The provisions of this Act relating to goods which have been stolen shall apply whether the stealing occurred in England or Wales or elsewhere, and whether it occurred before or after the commencement of this Act, provided that the stealing (if not an offence under this Act) amounted to an offence where and at the time when the goods were stolen; and references to stolen goods shall be construed accordingly.

(2) For purposes of those provisions reference to stolen goods shall include, in addition to the goods originally stolen and parts of them (whether in their original state or not),:

(a) any other goods which directly or indirectly represent or have at any time represented the stolen goods in the hands of the thief as being the proceeds of any disposal or realisation of the whole or part of the goods stolen or of goods so representing the stolen goods; and

(b) any other goods which directly or indirectly represent or have at any time represented the stolen goods in the hands of a handler of the stolen goods or any part of them as being the proceeds of any disposal or realisation of the whole or part of the stolen goods handled by him or of goods so representing them.

(3) But no goods shall be regarded as having continued to be stolen goods after they have been restored to the person from whom they were stolen or to other lawful possession or custody, or after that person and any other person claiming through him have otherwise ceased as regards those goods to have any right to restitution in respect of the theft.

(4) For purposes of the provisions of this Act relating to goods which have been stolen (including subsections (1) to (3) above) goods obtained in England or Wales or elsewhere either by blackmail or in the circumstances described in section 15(1) of this Act shall be regarded as stolen; and 'steal', 'theft' and 'thief' shall be construed accordingly.

Possession of housebreaking implements, etc

25. Going equipped for stealing, etc

(1) A person shall be guilty of an offence if, when not at his place of abode, he has with him any article for use in the course of or in connection with any burglary, theft or cheat.

(2) A person guilty of an offence under this section shall on conviction on indictment be liable to imprisonment for a term not exceeding three years.

(3) Where a person is charged with an offence under this section, proof that he had with him any article made or adapted for use in committing a burglary, theft or cheat shall be evidence that he had it with him for such use.

(4) Any person may arrest without warrant anyone who is, or whom he, with reasonable cause, suspects to be, committing an offence under this section.

(5) For purposes of this section an offence under section 12 (1) of this Act of taking a conveyance shall be treated as theft, and 'cheat' means an offence under section 15 of this Act.

26-33. (*Not printed in this work*)

Supplementary

34. Interpretation

(1) Sections 4 (1) and 5 (1) of this Act shall apply generally for purposes of this Act as they apply for purposes of section 1.

(2) For purposes of this Act:

(a) 'gain' and 'loss' are to be construed as extending only to gain or loss in money or other property, but as extending to any such gain or loss whether temporary or permanent; and:

(i) 'gain' includes a gain by keeping what one has, as well as a gain by getting what one has not; and

(ii) 'loss' includes a loss by not getting what one might get as well as a loss by parting with what one has;

(b) 'goods', except in so far as the context otherwise requires, includes money and every other description of property except land, and includes things severed from the land by stealing.

35–36. (*Not printed in this work*)

Administration of Justice Act 1970
(1970 c 31)

40. Punishment for unlawful harassment of debtors

(1) A person commits an offence if, with the object of coercing another person to pay money claimed from the other as a debt due under a contract, he:

(a) harasses the other with demands for payment which, in respect of their frequency or the manner or occasion of making any such demand, or of any threat or publicity by which any demand is accompanied, are calculated to subject him or members of his family or household to alarm, distress or humiliation;

(b) falsely represents, in relation to the money claimed, that criminal proceedings lie for failure to pay it;

(c) falsely represents himself to be authorised in some official capacity to claim or enforce payment; or

(d) utters a document falsely represented by him to have some official character or purporting to have some official character which he knows it has not.

(2) A person may be guilty of an offence by virtue of subsection (1)(a) above if he concerts with others in the taking of such action as is described in that paragraph, notwithstanding that his own course of conduct does not by itself amount to harassment.

(3) Subsection (1)(a) above does not apply to anything done by a person which is reasonable (and otherwise permissible in law) for the purpose:

(a) of securing the discharge of an obligation due, or believed by him to be due, to himself or to persons for whom he acts, or protecting himself or them from future loss; or

(b) of the enforcement of any liability by legal process.

(4) A person guilty of an offence under this section shall be liable on summary conviction to a fine of not more than £100, and on a second or subsequent conviction to a fine of not more than level 5 on the standard scale.

(*None of the other sections is printed in this work*)

Misuse of Drugs Act 1971
(1971 c 38)

1–3. (*Not printed in this work*)

4. Restriction of production and supply of controlled drugs

(1) Subject to any regulations under section 7 of this Act for the time being in force, it shall not be lawful for a person:

    (a)   to produce a controlled drug; or

    (b)   to supply or offer to supply a controlled drug to another.

(2) Subject to section 28 of this Act, it is an offence for a person:

    (a)   to produce a controlled drug in contravention of subsection (1) above; or

    (b)   to be concerned in the production of such a drug in contravention of that subsection by another.

(3) Subject to section 28 of this Act, it is an offence for a person:

    (a)   to supply or offer to supply a controlled drug to another in contravention of subsection (1) above; or

    (b)   to be concerned in the supplying of such a drug to another in contravention of that subsection; or

    (c)   to be concerned in the making to another in contravention of that subsection of an offer to supply such a drug.

5. Restriction of possession of controlled drugs

(1) Subject to any regulations under section 7 of this Act for the time being in force, it shall not be lawful for a person to have a controlled drug in his possession.

(2) Subject to section 28 of this Act and to subsection (4) below, it is an offence for a person to have a controlled drug in his possession in contravention of subsection (1) above.

(3) Subject to section 28 of this Act, it is an offence for a person to have a controlled drug in his possession, whether lawfully or not, with intent to supply it to another in contravention of section 4(1) of this Act.

(4) In any proceedings for an offence under subsection (2) above in which it is proved that the accused had a controlled drug in his possession, it shall be a defence for him to prove:

    (a)   that, knowing or suspecting it to be a controlled drug, he took possession of it for the purpose of preventing another from committing or continuing to commit an offence in connection with that drug and that as soon as possible after taking possession of it he took all such steps as were reasonably open to him to destroy the drug or to deliver it into the custody of a person lawfully entitled to take custody of it; or

    (b)   that, knowing or suspecting it to be a controlled drug, he took possession of it for the purpose of delivering it into the custody of a person lawfully entitled to take custody of it and that as soon as possible after taking possession of it he took all such steps as were reasonably open to him to deliver it into the custody of such a person.

(5) (*Repealed*)

(6) Nothing in subsection (4) above shall prejudice any defence which it is open to a person charged with an offence under this section to raise apart from that subsection.

6. Restriction of cultivation of cannabis plant

(1) Subject to any regulations under section 7 of this Act for the time being in force, it shall not be lawful for a person to cultivate any plant of the genus *Cannabis*.

(2) Subject to section 28 of this Act, it is an offence to cultivate any such plant in contravention of subsection (1) above.

7. (*Not printed in this work*)

Miscellaneous offences involving controlled drugs etc

8. Occupiers etc of premises to be punishable for permitting certain activities to take place there

A person commits an offence if, being the occupier or concerned in the management

of any premises, he knowingly permits or suffers any of the following activities to take place on those premises, that is to say:
- (a) producing or attempting to produce a controlled drug in contravention of section 4(1) of this Act;
- (b) supplying or attempting to supply a controlled drug to another in contravention of section 4(1) of this Act, or offering to supply a controlled drug to another in contravention of section 4(1);
- (c) preparing opium for smoking;
- (d) smoking cannabis, cannabis resin or prepared opium.

9. Prohibition of certain activities etc relating to opium

Subject to section 28 of this Act, it is an offence for a person:
- (a) to smoke or otherwise use prepared opium; or
- (b) to frequent a place used for the purpose of opium smoking; or
- (c) to have in his possession:
    (i) any pipes or other utensils made or adapted for use in connection with the smoking of opium, being pipes or utensils which have been used by him or with his knowledge and permission in that connection or which he intends to use or permit others to use in that connection; or
    (ii) any utensils which have been used by him or with his knowledge and permission in connection with the preparation of opium for smoking.

10–27. (*Not printed in this work*)

Miscellaneous and supplementary provisions

28. Proof of lack of knowledge etc to be a defence in proceedings for certain offences

(1) This section applies to offences under any of the following provisions of this Act, that is to say section 4 (2) and (3), section 5 (2) and (3), section 6 (2) and section 9.

(2) Subject to subsection (3) below, in any proceedings for an offence to which this section applies it shall be a defence for the accused to prove that he neither knew of nor suspected nor had reason to suspect the existence of some fact alleged by the prosecution which it is necessary for the prosecution to prove if he is to be convicted of the offence charged.

(3) Where in any proceedings for an offence to which this section applies it is necessary, if the accused is to be convicted of the offence charged, for the prosecution to prove that some substance or product involved in the alleged offence was the controlled drug which the prosecution alleges it to have been and it is proved that the substance or product in question was that controlled drug, the accused:
- (a) shall not be acquitted of the offence charged by reason only of proving that he neither knew nor suspected nor had reason to suspect that the substance or product in question was the particular controlled drug alleged but
- (b) shall be acquitted thereof:
    (i) if he proves that he neither believed nor suspected nor had reason to suspect that the substance or product in question was a controlled drug; or
    (ii) if he proves that he believed the substance or product in question to be a controlled drug, or controlled drug of a description, such that, if it had in fact been that controlled drug or a controlled drug of that description, he would not at the material time have been committing any offence to which this section applies.

(4) Nothing in this section shall prejudice any defence which it is open to a person charged with an offence to which this section applies to raise apart from this section.

(*The remaining provisions are not printed in this work*)

Criminal Damage Act 1971
(1971 c 48)

1. Destroying or damaging property
(1) A person who without lawful excuse destroys or damages any property belonging to another intending to destroy or damage any such property or being reckless as to whether any such property would be destroyed or damaged shall be guilty of an offence.

(2) A person who without lawful excuse destroys or damages any property, whether belonging to himself or another:
   (a) intending to destroy or damage any property or being reckless as to whether any property would be destroyed or damaged; and
   (b) intending by the destruction or damage to endanger the life of another or being reckless as to whether the life of another would be thereby endangered;
shall be guilty of an offence.

(3) An offence committed under this section by destroying or damaging property by fire shall be charged as arson.

2. Threats to destroy or damage property
A person who without lawful excuse makes to another a threat, intending that that other would fear it would be carried out,:
   (a) to destroy or damage any property belonging to that other or a third person; or
   (b) to destroy or damage his own property in a way which he knows is likely to endanger the life of that other or a third person;
shall be guilty of an offence.

3. Possessing anything with intent to destroy or damage property
A person who has anything in his custody or under his control intending without lawful excuse to use it or cause or permit another to use it:
   (a) to destroy or damage any property belonging to some other person; or
   (b) to destroy or damage his own or the user's property in a way which he knows is likely to endanger the life of some other person;
shall be guilty of an offence.

4. Punishment of offences
(1) A person guilty of arson under section 1 above or of an offence under section 1 (2) above (whether arson or not) shall on conviction on indictment be liable to imprisonment for life.

(2) A person guilty of any other offence under this Act shall on conviction on indictment be liable to imprisonment for a term not exceeding ten years.

5. 'Without lawful excuse'
(1) This section applies to any offence under section 1 (1) above and any offence under section 2 or 3 above other than one involving a threat by the person charged to destroy or damage property in a way which he knows is likely to endanger the life of another or involving an intent by the person charged to use or cause or permit the use of something in his custody or under his control so to destroy or damage property.

(2) A person charged with an offence to which this section applies shall, whether or not he would be treated for the purposes of this Act as having a lawful excuse apart from this subsection, be treated for those purposes as having a lawful excuse:
   (a) if at the time of the act or acts alleged to constitute the offence he believed that the person or persons whom he believed to be entitled to consent to the destruction of or damage to the property in question had so consented, or would have so consented to it if he or they had known of the destruction or damage and its circumstances; or

(b) if he destroyed or damaged or threatened to destroy or damage the property in question or, in the case of a charge of an offence under section 3 above, intended to use or cause or permit the use of something to destroy or damage it, in order to protect property belonging to himself or another or a right or interest in property which was or which he believed to be vested in himself or another, and at the time of the act or acts alleged to constitute the offence he believed:

   (i) that the property, right or interest was in immediate need of protection; and

   (ii) that the means of protection adopted or proposed to be adopted were or would be reasonable having regard to all the circumstances.

(3) For the purposes of this section it is immaterial whether a belief is justified or not if it is honestly held.

(4) For the purposes of subsection (2) above a right or interest in property includes any right or privilege in or over land, whether created by grant, licence or otherwise.

(5) This section shall not be construed as casting doubt on any defence recognised by law as a defence to criminal charges.

6. (*Not printed in this work*)

7. Jurisdiction of magistrates' courts

(1) (*Repealed*)

(2) No rule of law ousting the jurisdiction of magistrates' courts to try offences where a dispute of title to property is involved shall preclude magistrates' courts from trying offences under this Act, or any other offences of destroying or damaging property.

8. (*Repealed*)

9. (*Not printed in this work*)

10. Interpretation

(1) In this Act 'property' means property of a tangible nature, whether real or personal, including money and:

   (a) including wild creatures which have been tamed or are ordinarily kept in captivity, and any other wild creatures or their carcasses if, but only if, they have been reduced into possession which has not been lost or abandoned or are in the course of being reduced into possession; but

   (b) not including mushrooms growing wild on any land or flowers, fruit or foliage of a plant growing wild on any land.

For the purposes of this subsection 'mushroom' includes any fungus and 'plant' includes any shrub or tree.

(2) Property shall be treated for the purposes of this Act as belonging to any person:

   (a) having the custody or control of it;

   (b) having in it any proprietary right or interest (not being an equitable interest arising only from an agreement to transfer or grant an interest); or

   (c) having a charge on it.

(3) Where property is subject to a trust, the persons to whom it belongs shall be so treated as including any person having a right to enforce the trust.

(4) Property of a corporation sole shall be so treated as belonging to the corporation notwithstanding a vacancy in the corporation.

11–12. (*Not printed in this work*)

Road Traffic Act 1972
(1972 c 20)

Offences connected with driving of motor vehicles

1. Causing death by reckless driving
(1) A person who causes the death of another person by the driving of a motor vehicle on a road recklessly shall be guilty of an offence.

2. Reckless driving
A person who drives a motor vehicle on a road recklessly shall be guilty of an offence.

3. Careless, and inconsiderate, driving
If a person drives a motor vehicle on a road without due care and attention, or without reasonable consideration for other persons using the road, he shall be guilty of an offence.

[*Sections 1 and 2 were substituted by s 50 of the Criminal Law Act 1977 (1977 c 45)*]

(*The remaining sections are not printed in this work*)

Sexual Offences (Amendment) Act 1976
(1976 c 82)

1. Meaning of 'rape' etc
(1) For the purposes of section 1 of the Sexual Offences Act 1956 (which relates to rape) a man commits rape if:
  (a) he has unlawful sexual intercourse with a woman who at the time of the intercourse does not consent to it; and
  (b) at the time he knows that she does not consent to the intercourse or he is reckless as to whether she consents to it;
and references to rape in other enactments (including the following provisions of this Act) shall be construed accordingly.

(2) It is hereby declared that if at a trial for a rape offence the jury has to consider whether a man believed that a woman was consenting to sexual intercourse, the presence or absence of reasonable grounds for such a belief is a matter to which the jury is to have regard, in conjunction with any other relevant matters, in considering whether he so believed.

2. Restrictions on evidence at trials for rape etc
(1) If at a trial any person is for the time being charged with a rape offence to which he pleads not guilty, then, except with the leave of the judge, no evidence and no question in cross-examination shall be adduced or asked at the trial, by or on behalf of any defendant at the trial, about any sexual experience of a complainant with a person other than that defendant.

(2) The judge shall not give leave in pursuance of the preceding subsection for any evidence or question except on an application made to him in the absence of the jury by or on behalf of a defendant; and on such an application the judge shall give leave if and only if he is satisfied that it would be unfair to that defendant to refuse to allow the evidence to be adduced or the question to be asked.

(3) In subsection (1) of this section 'complainant' means a woman upon whom, in a charge for a rape offence to which the trial in question relates, it is alleged that rape was committed, attempted or proposed.

(4) Nothing in this section authorises evidence to be adduced or a question to be asked which cannot be adduced or asked apart from this section.

3–6. (*Not printed in this work*)

7. Citation, interpretation, commencement and extent

(1) This Act may be cited as the Sexual Offences (Amendment) Act 1976, and this Act and the Sexual Offences Acts 1956 and 1967 may be cited together as the Sexual Offences Acts 1956 to 1976.

(2) In this Act:

'a rape offence' means any of the following, namely rape, attempted rape, aiding, abetting, counselling and procuring rape or attempted rape, and incitement to rape; and

references to sexual intercourse shall be construed in accordance with section 44 of the Sexual Offences Act 1956 so far as it relates to natural intercourse (under which such intercourse is deemed complete on proof of penetration only);

and section 46 of that Act (which relates to the meaning of 'man' and 'woman' in that Act) shall have effect as if the reference to that Act included a reference to this Act.

(3)–(6) (*Not printed in this work*)

Criminal Law Act 1977
(1977 c 45)

PART I. CONSPIRACY

1. The offence of conspiracy

(1) Subject to the following provisions of this Part of this Act, if a person agrees with any other person or persons that a course of conduct shall be pursued which, if the agreement is carried out in accordance with their intentions, either:

(a) will necessarily amount to or involve the commission of any offence or offences by one or more of the parties to the agreement, or

(b) would do so but for the existence of facts which render the commission of the offence or any of the offences impossible.

he is guilty of conspiracy to commit the offence or offences in question.

(2) Where liability for any offence may be incurred without knowledge on the part of the person committing it of any particular fact or circumstance necessary for the commission of the offence, a person shall nevertheless not be guilty of conspiracy to commit that offence by virtue of subsection (1) above unless he and at least one other party to the agreement intend or know that that fact or circumstance shall or will exist at the time when the conduct constituting the offence is to take place.

(3) Where in pursuance of any agreement the acts in question in relation to any offence are to be done in contemplation or furtherance of a trade dispute (within the meaning of the Trade Union and Labour Relations Act 1974) that offence shall be disregarded for the purposes of subsection (1) above provided that it is a summary offence which is not punishable with imprisonment.

(4) In this Part of this Act 'offence' means an offence triable in England and Wales, except that it includes murder notwithstanding that the murder in question would not be so triable if committed in accordance with the intentions of the parties to the agreement.

2. Exemptions from liability for conspiracy

(1) A person shall not by virtue of section 1 above be guilty of conspiracy to commit any offence if he is an intended victim of that offence.

(2) A person shall not by virtue of section 1 above be guilty of conspiracy to commit any offence or offences if the only other person or persons with whom he agrees are (both initially and at all times during the currency of the agreement) persons of any one or more of the following descriptions, that is to say:

(a) his spouse;

(b) a person under the age of criminal responsibility; and

(c) an intended victim of that offence or of each of those offences.

(3) A person is under the age of criminal responsibility for the purposes of subsection (2) (b) above so long as it is conclusively presumed, by virtue of section 50 of the Children and Young Persons Act 1933, that he cannot be guilty of any offence.

3. Penalties for conspiracy

(1) A person guilty by virtue of section 1 above of conspiracy to commit any offence or offences shall be liable on conviction on indictment:

(a) in a case falling within subsection (2) or (3) below, to imprisonment for a term related in accordance with that subsection to the gravity of the offence or offences in question (referred to below in this section as the relevant offence or offences); and

(b) in any other case, to a fine.

Paragraph (b) above shall not be taken as prejudicing the application of section 30 (1) of the Powers of Criminal Courts Act 1973 (general power of court to fine offender convicted on indictment) in a case falling within subsection (2) or (3) below.

(2) Where the relevant offence or any of the relevant offences is an offence of any of the following descriptions, that is to say:

(a) murder, or any other offence the sentence for which is fixed by law;

(b) an offence for which a sentence extending to imprisonment for life is provided; or

(c) an indictable offence punishable with imprisonment for which no maximum term of imprisonment is provided,

the person convicted shall be liable to imprisonment for life.

(3) Where in a case other than one to which subsection (2) above applies the relevant offence or any of the relevant offences is punishable with imprisonment, the person convicted shall be liable to imprisonment for a term not exceeding the maximum term provided for that offence or (where more than one such offence is in question) for any one of those offences (taking the longer or the longest term as the limit for the purposes of this section where the terms provided differ).

In the case of an offence triable either way the references above in this subsection to the maximum term provided for that offence are references to the maximum term so provided on conviction on indictment.

4. Restrictions on the institution of proceedings for conspiracy

(1) Subject to subsection (2) below proceedings under section 1 above for conspiracy to commit any offence or offences shall not be instituted against any person except by or with the consent of the Director of Public Prosecutions if the offence or (as the case may be) each of the offences in question is a summary offence.

(2) In relation to the institution of proceedings under section 1 above for conspiracy to commit:

(a) an offence which is subject to a prohibition by or under any enactment on the institution of proceedings otherwise than by, or on behalf or with the consent of, the Attorney General, or

(b) two or more offences of which at least one is subject to such a prohibition,

subsection (1) above shall have effect with the substitution of a reference to the Attorney General for the reference to the Director of Public Prosecutions.

(3) Any prohibition by or under any enactment on the institution of proceedings for any offence which is not a summary offence otherwise than by, or on behalf or with the consent of, the Director of Public Prosecutions or any other person shall apply also in relation to proceedings under section 1 above for conspiracy to commit that offence.

(4) Where:

(a) an offence has been committed in pursuance of any agreement; and

(b) proceedings may not be instituted for that offence because any time limit applicable to the institution of any such proceedings has expired,

proceedings under section 1 above for conspiracy to commit that offence shall not be instituted against any person on the basis of that agreement.

5. Abolitions, savings, transitional provisions, consequential amendment and repeals

(1) Subject to the following provisions of this section, the offence of conspiracy at common law is hereby abolished.

(2) Subsection (1) above shall not affect the offence of conspiracy at common law so far as relates to conspiracy to defraud, and section 1 above shall not apply in any case where the agreement in question amounts to a conspiracy to defraud at common law.

(3) Subsection (1) above shall not affect the offence of conspiracy at common law if and in so far as it may be committed by entering into an agreement to engage in conduct which:

(a)   tends to corrupt public morals or outrages public decency; but

(b)   would not amount to or involve the commission of an offence if carried out by a single person otherwise than in pursuance of an agreement.

(4) Subsection (1) above shall not affect:

(a)   any proceedings commenced before the time when this Part of this Act comes into force;

(b)   any proceedings commenced after that time against a person charged with the same conspiracy as that charged in any proceedings commenced before that time; or

(c)   any proceedings commenced after that time in respect of a trespass committed before that time;

but a person convicted of conspiracy to trespass in any proceedings brought by virtue of paragraph (c) above shall not in respect of that conviction be liable to imprisonment for a term exceeding six months.

(5) Section 1 and 2 above shall apply to things done before as well as to things done after the time when this Part of this Act comes into force, but in the application of section 3 above to a case where the agreement in question was entered into before that time:

(a)   subsection (2) shall be read without the reference to murder in paragraph (a); and

(b)   any murder intended under the agreement shall be treated as an offence for which a maximum term of imprisonment of ten years is provided.

(6) The rules laid down by sections 1 and 2 above shall apply for determining whether a person is guilty of an offence of conspiracy under any enactment other than section 1 above, but conduct which is an offence under any such other enactment shall not also be an offence under section 1 above.

(7) Incitement . . . to commit the offence of conspiracy (whether the conspiracy incited . . . would be an offence at common law or under section 1 above or any other enactment) shall cease to be offences.

(8) The fact that the person or persons who, so far as appears from the indictment on which any person has been convicted of conspiracy, were the only other parties to the agreement on which his conviction was based have been acquitted of conspiracy by reference to that agreement (whether after being tried with the person convicted or separately) shall not be a ground for quashing his conviction unless under all the circumstances of the case his conviction is inconsistent with the acquittal of the other person or persons in question.

(9) Any rule of law or practice inconsistent with the provisions of subsection (8) above is hereby abolished.

(10) In section 4 of the Offences against the Person Act 1861:

(a)   the words preceding 'whosoever' shall cease to have effect; and

(b)   for the words from 'be kept' to 'years' there shall be substituted the words 'imprisonment for life'.

(11) Section 3 of the Conspiracy and Protection of Property Act 1875 shall cease to have effect.

Parts II–III. (*Not printed in this work*)

Theft Act 1978
(1978 c 31)

1. Obtaining services by deception
(1) A person who by any deception dishonestly obtains services from another shall be guilty of an offence.

(2) It is an obtaining of services where the other is induced to confer a benefit by doing some act, or causing or permitting some act to be done, on the understanding that the benefit has been or will be paid for.

2. Evasion of liability by deception
(1) Subject to subsection (2) below, where a person by any deception:
- (a) dishonestly secures the remission of the whole or part of any existing liability to make a payment, whether his own liability or another's; or
- (b) with intent to make permanent default in whole or in part on any existing liability to make a payment, or with intent to let another do so, dishonestly induces the creditor or any person claiming payment on behalf of the creditor to wait for payment (whether or not the due date for payment is deferred) or to forgo payment; or
- (c) dishonestly obtains any exemption from or abatement of liability to make a payment;

he shall be guilty of an offence.

(2) For purposes of this section 'liability' means legally enforceable liability; and subsection (1) shall not apply in relation to a liability that has not been accepted or established to pay compensation for a wrongful act or omission.

(3) For purposes of subsection (1) (b) a person induced to take in payment a cheque or other security for money by way of conditional satisfaction of a pre-existing liability is to be treated not as being paid but as being induced to wait for payment.

(4) For purposes of subsection (1) (c) 'obtains' includes obtaining for another or enabling another to obtain.

3. Making off without payment
(1) Subject to subsection (3) below, a person who, knowing that payment on the spot for any goods supplied or service done is required or expected from him, dishonestly makes off without having paid as required or expected and with intent to avoid payment of the amount due shall be guilty of an offence.

(2) For purposes of this section 'payment on the spot' includes payment at the time of collecting goods on which work has been done or in respect of which service has been provided.

(3) Subsection (1) above shall not apply where the supply of the goods or the doing of the service is contrary to law, or where the service done is such that payment is not legally enforceable.

(4) Any person may arrest without warrant anyone who is, or whom he, with reasonable cause, suspects to be, committing or attempting to commit an offence under this section.

4. Punishments
(1) Offences under this Act shall be punishable either on conviction on indictment or on summary conviction.

(2) A person convicted on indictment shall be liable:
- (a) for an offence under section 1 or section 2 of this Act, to imprisonment for a term not exceeding five years; and
- (b) for an offence under section 3 of this Act, to imprisonment for a term not exceeding two years.

(3) A person convicted summarily of any offence under this Act shall be liable:
- (a) to imprisonment for a term not exceeding six months; or

(b) to a fine not exceeding the prescribed sum for the purposes of [section 32 of the Magistrates' Courts Act 1980] (punishment on summary conviction of offences triable either way; £2,000 or other sum substituted by order under that Act),

or to both.

5. Supplementary
(1) For purposes of sections 1 and 2 above 'deception' has the same meaning as in section 15 of the Theft Act 1968, that is to say, it means any deception (whether deliberate or reckless) by words or conduct as to fact or as to law, including a deception as to the present intentions of the person using the deception or any other person; and section 18 of that Act (liability of company officers for offences by the company) shall apply in relation to sections 1 and 2 above as it applies in relation to section 15 of that Act.

(2) Sections 30 (1) (husband and wife), 31 (1) (effect on civil proceedings) and 34 (interpretation) of the Theft Act 1968, so far as they are applicable in relation to this Act, shall apply as they apply in relation to that Act.

(3) In the Schedule to the Extradition Act 1873 (additional list of extradition crimes), after 'Theft Act 1968' there shall be inserted 'or the Theft Act 1978'; and there shall be deemed to be included among the descriptions of offences set out in Schedule 1 to the Fugitive Offenders Act 1967 any offence under this Act.

(4) In the Visiting Forces Act 1952, in paragraph 3 of the Schedule (which defines for England and Wales 'offence against property' for purposes of the exclusion in certain cases of the jurisdiction of United Kingdom courts) there shall be added at the end:

'(j) the Theft Act 1978'.

(5) In the Theft Act 1968 section 16 (2) (a) is hereby repealed.

6. and 7. (*Not printed in this work*)

Magistrates' Courts Act 1980
(1980 c 43)

44. Aiders and abettors
(1) A person who aids, abets, counsels or procures the commission by another person of a summary offence shall be guilty of the like offence and may be tried (whether or not he is charged as a principal) either by a court having jurisdiction to try that other person or by a court having by virtue of his own offence jurisdiction to try him.

(2) Any offence consisting in aiding, abetting, counselling or procuring the commission of an offence triable either way (other than an offence listed in Schedule 1 to this Act) shall by virtue of this subsection be triable either way.

45. Incitement
(1) Any offence consisting in the incitement to commit a summary offence shall be triable only summarily.

(2) Subsection (1) above is without prejudice to any other enactment by virtue of which any offence is triable only summarily.

(3) On conviction of an offence consisting in the incitement to commit a summary offence a person shall be liable to the same penalties as he would be liable to on conviction of the last-mentioned offence.

101. Onus of proving exceptions, etc
Where the defendant to an information or complaint relies for his defence on any exception, exemption, proviso, excuse or qualification, whether or not it accompanies the description of the offence or matter of complaint in the enactment creating the offence or on which the complaint is founded, the burden of proving the exception,

exemption, proviso, excuse or qualification shall be on him; and this notwithstanding that the information or complaint contains an allegation negativing the exception, exemption, proviso, excuse or qualification.

(*None of the other sections is printed in this work*)

Forgery and Counterfeiting Act 1981
(1981 c 45)

1. The offence of forgery
A person is guilty of forgery if he makes a false instrument, with the intention that he or another shall use it to induce somebody to accept it as genuine, and by reason of so accepting it to do or not to do some act to his own or any other person's prejudice.

2. The offence of copying a false instrument
It is an offence for a person to make a copy of an instrument which is, and which he knows or believes to be, a false instrument, with the intention that he or another shall use it to induce somebody to accept it as a copy of a genuine instrument, and by reason of so accepting it to do or not to do some act to his own or any other person's prejudice.

3. The offence of using a false instrument
It is an offence for a person to use an instrument which is, and which he knows or believes to be, false, with the intention of inducing somebody to accept it as genuine, and by reason of so accepting it to do or not to do some act to his own or any other person's prejudice.

4. The offence of using a copy of a false instrument
It is an offence for a person to use a copy of an instrument which is, and which he knows or believes to be, a false instrument, with the intention of inducing somebody to accept it as a copy of a genuine instrument, and by reason of so accepting it to do or not to do some act to his own or any other person's prejudice.

5. Offences relating to money orders share certificates passports, etc
(1) It is an offence for a person to have in his custody or under his control an instrument to which this section applies which is, and which he knows or believes to be, false, with the intention that he or another shall use it to induce somebody to accept it as genuine, and by reason of so accepting it to do or not to do some act to his own or any other person's prejudice.

(2) It is an offence for a person to have in his custody or under his control, without lawful authority or excuse, an instrument to which this section applies which is, and which he knows or believes to be, false.

(3) It is an offence for a person to make or to have in his custody or under his control a machine or implement, or paper or any other material, which to his knowledge is or has been specially designed or adapted for the making of an instrument to which this section applies, with the intention that he or another shall make an instrument to which this section applies which is false and that he or another shall use the instrument to induce somebody to accept it as genuine, and by reason of so accepting it to do or not to do some act to his own or any other person's prejudice.

(4) It is an offence for a person to make or to have in his custody or under his control any such machine, implement, paper or material, without lawful authority or excuse.

(5) The instruments to which this section applies are:
(a) money orders;
(b) postal orders;
(c) United Kingdom postage stamps;

    (d)   Inland Revenue stamps;
    (e)   share certificates;
    (f)   passports and documents which can be used instead of passports;
    (g)   cheques;
    (h)   travellers' cheques;
    (i)   cheque cards;
    (j)   credit cards;
    (k)   certified copies relating to an entry in a register of births, adoptions, marriages or deaths and issued by the Registrar General, the Registrar General for Northern Ireland, a registration officer or a person lawfully authorised to register marriages; and
    (l)   certificates relating to entries in such registers.

(6) In subsection (5) (e) above 'share certificate' means an instrument entitling or evidencing the title of a person to a share or interest:

    (a)   in any public stock, annuity, fund or debt of any government or state, including a state which forms part of another state; or
    (b)   in any stock, fund or debt of a body (whether corporate or unincorporated) established in the United Kingdom or elsewhere.

Penalties etc

6. Penalties for offences under Part I

(1) A person guilty of an offence under this Part of this Act shall be liable on summary conviction:

    (a)   to a fine not exceeding the statutory maximum; or
    (b)   to imprisonment for a term not exceeding six months; or
    (c)   to both.

(2) A person guilty of an offence to which this subsection applies shall be liable on conviction on indictment to imprisonment for a term not exceeding ten years.

(3) The offences to which subsection (2) above applies are offences under the following provisions of this Part of this Act:

    (a)   section 1;
    (b)   section 2;
    (c)   section 3;
    (d)   section 4;
    (e)   section 5(1); and
    (f)   section 5(3).

(4) A person guilty of an offence under section 5(2) or (4) above shall be liable on conviction on indictment to imprisonment for a term not exceeding two years.

(5) In this section 'statutory maximum', in relation to a fine on summary conviction, means the prescribed sum, within the meaning of section 32 of the Magistrates' Courts Act 1980 (£2,000 or another sum fixed by order under section 143 of that Act to take account of changes in the value of money); and those sections shall extend to Northern Ireland for the purposes of the application of this definition.

7. (*Not printed in this work*)

Interpretation of Part I

8. Meaning of 'instrument'

(1) Subject to subsection (2) below, in this Part of this Act 'instrument' means:

    (a)   any document, whether of a formal or informal character;
    (b)   any stamp issued or sold by the Post Office;
    (c)   any Inland Revenue stamp; and
    (d)   any disc, tape, sound track or other device on or in which information is recorded or stored by mechanical, electronic or other means.

(2) A currency note within the meaning of Part II of this Act is not an instrument for the purposes of this Part of this Act.

(3) A mark denoting payment of postage which the Post Office authorise to be used instead of an adhesive stamp is to be treated for the purposes of this Part of this Act as if it were a stamp issued by the Post Office.

(4) In this Part of this Act 'Inland Revenue stamp' means a stamp as defined in section 27 of the Stamp Duties Management Act 1891.

9. Meaning of 'false' and 'making'

(1) An instrument is false for the purposes of this Part of this Act:

- (a) if it purports to have been made in the form in which it is made by a person who did not in fact make it in that form; or
- (b) if it purports to have been made in the form in which it is made on the authority of a person who did not in fact authorise its making in that form; or
- (c) if it purports to have been made in the terms in which it is made by a person who did not in fact make it in those terms; or
- (d) if it purports to have been made in the terms in which it is made on the authority of a person who did not in fact authorise its making in those terms; or
- (e) if it purports to have been altered in any respect by a person who did not in fact alter it in that respect; or
- (f) if it purports to have been altered in any respect on the authority of a person who did not in fact authorise the alteration in that respect; or
- (g) if it purports to have been made or altered on a date on which, or at a place at which, or otherwise in circumstances in which, it was not in fact made or altered; or
- (h) if it purports to have been made or altered by an existing person but he did not in fact exist.

(2) A person is to be treated for the purposes of this Part of this Act as making a false instrument if he alters an instrument so as to make it false in any respect (whether or not it is false in some other respect apart from that alteration).

10. Meaning of 'prejudice' and 'induce'

(1) Subject to subsections (2) and (4) below, for the purposes of this Part of this Act an act or omission intended to be induced is to a person's prejudice if, and only if, it is one which, if it occurs:

- (a) will result:
  - (i) in his temporary or permanent loss of property; or
  - (ii) in his being deprived of an opportunity to earn remuneration or greater remuneration; or
  - (iii) in his being deprived of an opportunity to gain a financial advantage otherwise than by way of remuneration; or
- (b) will result in somebody being given an opportunity:
  - (i) to earn remuneration or greater remuneration from him; or
  - (ii) to gain a financial advantage from him otherwise than by way of remuneration; or
- (c) will be the result of his having accepted a false instrument as genuine, or a copy of a false instrument as a copy of a genuine one, in connection with his performance of any duty.

(2) An act which a person has an enforceable duty to do and an omission to do an act which a person is not entitled to do shall be disregarded for the purposes of this Part of this Act.

(3) In this Part of this Act references to inducing somebody to accept a false instrument as genuine, or a copy of a false instrument as a copy of a genuine one, include references to inducing a machine to respond to the instrument or copy as if it were a genuine instrument or, as the case may be, a copy of a genuine one.

(4) Where subsection (3) above applies, the act or omission intended to be induced

by the machine responding to the instrument or copy shall be treated as an act or omission to a person's prejudice.

(5) In this section 'loss' includes not getting what one might get as well as parting with what one has.

11–12. (*Not printed in this work*)

13. Abolition of offence of forgery at common law
The offence of forgery at common law is hereby abolished for all purposes not relating to offences committed before the commencement of this Act.

(*The remaining sections not printed in this work*)

Criminal Attempts Act 1981
(1981 c 47)

1. Attempting to commit an offence
(1) If, with intent to commit an offence to which this section applies, a person does an act which is more than merely preparatory to the commission of the offence, he is guilty of attempting to commit the offence.

(2) A person may be guilty of attempting to commit an offence to which this section applies even though the facts are such that the commission of the offence is impossible.

(3) In any case where:
- (a) apart from this subsection a person's intention would not be regarded as having amounted to an intent to commit an offence; but
- (b) if the facts of the case had been as he believed them to be, his intention would be so regarded,

then, for the purposes of subsection (1) above, he shall be regarded as having had an intent to commit that offence.

(4) This section applies to any offence which, if it were completed, would be triable in England and Wales as an indictable offence, other than:
- (a) conspiracy (at common law or under section 1 of the Criminal Law Act 1977 or any other enactment);
- (b) aiding, abetting, counselling, procuring or suborning the commission of an offence;
- (c) offences under section 4(1) (assisting offenders) or 5(1) (accepting or agreeing to accept consideration for not disclosing information about an arrestable offence) of the Criminal Law Act 1967.

2. Application of procedural and other provisions to offences under s 1
(1) Any provision to which this section applies shall have effect with respect to an offence under section 1 above of attempting to commit an offence as it has effect with respect to the offence attempted.

(2) This section applies to provisions of any of the following descriptions made by or under any enactment (whenever passed):
- (a) provisions whereby proceedings may not be instituted or carried on otherwise than by, or on behalf or with the consent of, any person (including any provisions which also make other exceptions to the prohibition);
- (b) provisions conferring power to institute proceedings;
- (c) provisions as to the venue of proceedings;
- (d) provisions whereby proceedings may not be instituted after the expiration of a time limit;
- (e) provisions conferring a power of arrest or search;
- (f) provisions conferring a power of seizure and detention of property;
- (g) provisions whereby a person may not be convicted or committed for trial on

the uncorroborated evidence of one witness (including any provision requiring the evidence of not less than two credible witnesses);

(h) provisions conferring a power of forfeiture, including any power to deal with anything liable to be forfeited;

(i) provisions whereby, if an offence committed by a body corporate is proved to have been committed with the consent or connivance of another person, that person also is guilty of the offence.

3. Offences of attempt under other enactments

(1) Subsections (2) to (5) below shall have effect, subject to subsection (6) below and to any inconsistent provision in any other enactment, for the purpose of determining whether a person is guilty of an attempt under a special statutory provision.

(2) For the purposes of this Act an attempt under a special statutory provision is an offence which:

(a) is created by an enactment other than section 1 above, including an enactment passed after this Act; and

(b) is expressed as an offence of attempting to commit another offence (in this section referred to as 'the relevant full offence').

(3) A person is guilty of an attempt under a special statutory provision if, with intent to commit the relevant full offence, he does an act which is more than merely preparatory to the commission of that offence.

(4) A person may be guilty of an attempt under a special statutory provision even though the facts are such that the commission of the relevant full offence is impossible.

(5) In any case where:

(a) apart from this subsection a person's intention would not be regarded as having amounted to an intent to commit the relevant full offence; but

(b) if the facts of the case had been as he believed them to be, his intention would be so regarded,

then, for the purposes of subsection (3) above, he shall be regarded as having had an intent to commit that offence.

(6) Subsections (2) to (5) above shall not have effect in relation to an act done before the commencement of this Act.

Trial etc of offences of attempt

4. Trial and penalties

(1) A person guilty by virtue of section 1 above of attempting to commit an offence shall:

(a) if the offence attempted is murder or any other offence the sentence for which is fixed by law, be liable on conviction on indictment to imprisonment for life; and

(b) if the offence attempted is indictable but does not fall within paragraph (a) above, be liable on conviction on indictment to any penalty to which he would have been liable on conviction on indictment of that offence; and

(c) if the offence attempted is triable either way, be liable on summary conviction to any penalty to which he would have been liable on summary conviction of that offence.

(2) In any case in which a court may proceed to summary trial of an information charging a person with an offence and an information charging him with an offence under section 1 above of attempting to commit it or an attempt under a special statutory provision, the court may, without his consent, try the informations together.

(3) Where, in proceedings against a person for an offence under section 1 above, there is evidence sufficient in law to support a finding that he did an act falling within subsection (1) of that section, the question whether or not his act fell within that subsection is a question of fact.

(4) Where, in proceedings against a person for an attempt under a special statutory provision, there is evidence sufficient in law to support a finding that he did an act falling within subsection (3) of section 3 above, the question whether or not his act fell within that subsection is a question of fact.

(5) Subsection (1) above shall have effect:

(a)   subject to section 37 of and Schedule 2 to the Sexual Offences Act 1956 (mode of trial of and penalties for attempts to commit certain offences under that Act); and

(b)   notwithstanding anything:

(i)   in section 32(1) (no limit to fine on conviction on indictment) of the Criminal Law Act 1977; or

(ii)   in section 31(1) and (2) (maximum of six months' imprisonment on summary conviction unless express provision made to the contrary) of the Magistrates' Courts Act 1980.

5. (*Not printed in this work*)

6. Effect of Part I on common law

(1) The offence of attempt at common law and any offence at common law of procuring materials for crime are hereby abolished for all purposes not relating to acts done before the commencement of this Act.

(2) Except as regards offences committed before the commencement of this Act, references in any enactment passed before this Act which fall to be construed as references to the offence of attempt at common law shall be construed as references to the offence under section 1 above.

Child Abduction Act 1984
(1984 c 37)

PART I.   OFFENCES UNDER LAW OF ENGLAND AND WALES

1. Offence of abduction of child by parent, etc

(1)   Subject to subsections (5) and (8) below, a person connected with a child under the age of sixteen commits an offence if he takes or sends the child out of the United Kingdom without the appropriate consent.

(2)   A person is connected with a child for the purposes of this section if:

(a)   he is a parent or guardian of the child; or

(b)   there is in force an order of a court in England or Wales awarding custody of the child to him, whether solely or jointly with any other person; or

(c)   in the case of an illegitimate child, there are reasonable grounds for believing that he is the father of the child.

(3)   In this section 'the appropriate consent', in relation to a child, means:

(a)   the consent of each person:

(i)   who is a parent or guardian of the child; or

(ii)   to whom custody of the child has been awarded (whether solely or jointly with any other person) by an order of a court in England or Wales; or

(b)   if the child is the subject of such a custody order, the leave of the court which made the order; or

(c)   the leave of the court granted on an application for a direction under section 7 of the Guardianship of Minors Act 1971 or section 1(3) of the Guardianship Act 1973.

(4)   In the case of a custody order made by a magistrates' court, subsection (3)(b) above shall be construed as if the reference to the court which made the order included

a reference to any magistrates' court acting for the same petty sessions area as that court.

(5) A person does not commit an offence under this section by doing anything without the consent of another person whose consent is required under the foregoing provisions if:

   (a) he does it in the belief that the other person:

        (i) has consented; or

        (ii) would consent if he was aware of all the relevant circumstances; or

   (b) he has taken all reasonable steps to communicate with the other person but has been unable to communicate with him; or

   (c) the other person has unreasonably refused to consent.

but paragraph (c) of this subsection does not apply where what is done relates to a child who is the subject of a custody order made by a court in England or Wales, or where the person who does it acts in breach of any direction under section 7 of the Guardianship of Minors Act 1971 or section 1(3) of the Guardianship Act 1973.

(6) Where, in proceedings for an offence under this section, there is sufficient evidence to raise an issue as to the application of subsection (5) above, it shall be for the prosecution to prove that that subsection does not apply.

(7) In this section:

   (a) 'guardian' means a person appointed by deed or will or by order of a court of competent jurisdiction to be the guardian of a child; and

   (b) a reference to a custody order or an order awarding custody includes a reference to an order awarding legal custody and a reference to an order awarding care and control.

(8) This section shall have effect subject to the provisions of the Schedule to this Act in relation to a child who is in the care of a local authority or voluntary organisation or who is committed to a place of safety or who is the subject of custodianship proceedings or proceedings or an order relating to adoption.

2. Offence of abduction of child by other persons

(1) Subject to subsection (2) below, a person not falling within section 1(2)(a) or (b) above commits an offence if, without lawful authority or reasonable excuse, he takes or detains a child under the age of sixteen:

   (a) so as to remove him from the lawful control of any person having lawful control of the child; or

   (b) so as to keep him out of the lawful control of any person entitled to lawful control of the child.

(2) In proceedings against any person for an offence under this section, it shall be a defence for that person to show that at the time of the alleged offence:

   (a) he believed that the child had attained the age of sixteen; or

   (b) in the case of an illegitimate child, he had reasonable grounds for believing himself to be the child's father.

3. Construction of references to taking, sending and detaining

For the purposes of this Part of this Act:

   (a) a person shall be regarded as taking a child if he causes or induces the child to accompany him or any other person or causes the child to be taken;

   (b) a person shall be regarded as sending a child if he causes the child to be sent; and

   (c) a person shall be regarded as detaining a child if he causes the child to be detained or induces the child to remain with him or any other person.

(None of the other sections is printed in this work)

Police and Criminal Evidence Act 1984
(1984 c 60)

ARREST

24. Arrest without warrant for arrestable offences

(1) The powers of summary arrest conferred by the following subsections shall apply:
  (a) to offences for which the sentence is fixed by law;
  (b) to offences for which a person of 21 years of age or over (not previously con-
       victed) may be sentenced to imprisonment for a term of five years (or might be
       so sentenced but for the restrictions imposed by section 33 of the Magistrates'
       Courts Act 1980); and
  (c) to the offences to which subsection (2) below applies,
and in this Act 'arrestable offence' means any such offence.

(2) The offences to which this subsection applies are:
  (a) offences for which a person may be arrested under the customs and excise
       Acts, as defined in section 1(1) of the Customs and Excise Management Act
       1979;
  (b) offences under the Official Secrets Act 1911 and 1920 that are not arrestable
       offences by virtue of the term of imprisonment for which a person may be
       sentenced in respect of them;
  (c) offences under section 14 (indecent assault on a woman), 22 (causing prostitu-
       tion of women) or 23 (procuration of girl under 21) of the Sexual Offences Act
       1956;
  (d) offences under section 12(1) (taking motor vehicle or other conveyance
       without authority etc) or 25(1) (going equipped for stealing, etc) of the Theft
       Act 1968; and
  (e) offences under section 1 of the Public Bodies Corrupt Practices Act 1889
       (corruption in office) or section 1 of the Prevention of Corruption Act 1906
       (corrupt transactions with agents).

(3) Without prejudice to section 2 of the Criminal Attempts Act 1981, the powers
of summary arrest conferred by the following subsections shall also apply to the
offences of:
  (a) conspiring to commit any of the offences mentioned in subsection (2) above;
  (b) attempting to commit any such offence;
  (c) inciting, aiding, abetting, counselling or procuring the commission of any such
       offence;
and such offences are also arrestable offences for the purposes of this Act.

(4) Any person may arrest without a warrant:
  (a) anyone who is in the act of committing an arrestable offence;
  (b) anyone whom he has reasonable grounds for suspecting to be committing such
       an offence.

(5) Where an arrestable offence has been committed, any person may arrest
without a warrant:
  (a) anyone who is guilty of the offence;
  (b) anyone whom he has reasonable grounds for suspecting to be guilty of it.

(6) Where a constable has reasonable grounds for suspecting that an arrestable
offence has been committed, he may arrest without a warrant anyone whom he has
reasonable grounds for suspecting to be guilty of the offence.

(7) A constable may arrest without a warrant:
  (a) anyone who is about to commit an arrestable offence;
  (b) anyone whom he has reasonable grounds for suspecting to be about to commit
       an arrestable offence.

25. General arrest conditions

(1) Where a constable has reasonable grounds for suspecting that any offence which
is not an arrestable offence has been committed or attempted, or is being committed
or attempted, he may arrest the relevant person if it appears to him that service of a

summons is impracticable or inappropriate because any of the general arrest conditions is satisfied.

(2) In this section 'the relevant person' means any person whom the constable has reasonable grounds to suspect of having committed or having attempted to commit the offence or of being in the course of committing or attempting to commit it.

(3) The general arrest conditions are:

(a) that the name of the relevant person is unknown to, and cannot be readily ascertained by, the constable;

(b) that the constable has reasonable grounds for doubting whether a name furnished by the relevant person as his name is his real name;

(c) that:

(i) the relevant person has failed to furnish a satisfactory address for service; or

(ii) the constable has reasonable grounds for doubting whether an address furnished by the relevant person is a satisfactory address for service;

(d) that the constable has reasonable grounds for believing that arrest is necessary to prevent the relevant person:

(i) causing physical injury to himself or any other person;

(ii) suffering physical injury;

(iii) causing loss of or damage to property;

(iv) committing an offence against public decency; or

(v) causing an unlawful obstruction of the highway;

(e) that the constable has reasonable grounds for believing that arrest is necessary to protect a child or other vulnerable person from the relevant person.

(4) For the purposes of subsection (3) above an address is a satisfactory address for service if it appears to the constable:

(a) that the relevant person will be at it for a sufficiently long period for it to be possible to serve him with a summons; or

(b) that some other person specified by the relevant person will accept service of a summons for the relevant person at it.

(5) Nothing in subsection (3)(d) above authorises the arrest of a person under subparagraph (iv) of that paragraph except where members of the public going about their normal business cannot reasonably be expected to avoid the person to be arrested.

(6) This section shall not prejudice any power of arrest conferred apart from this section.

117. Power of constable to use reasonable force

Where any provision of this Act:

(a) confers a power on a constable; and

(b) does not provide that the power may only be exercised with the consent of some person, other than a police officer,

the officer may use reasonable force, if necessary, in the exercise of the power.

(None of the other sections is printed in this work)

Appendix II: Some recent cases

1. Intention and murder (pp 54 and 313, above)

R v Hancock and Shankland [1986] 1 All ER 641, House of Lords
(Lords Scarman, Keith of Kinkel, Roskill, Brightman and Griffiths)

Hancock (H) and Shankland (S) were miners on strike. They objected to a miner (X) going to work. X was going to work in a taxi driven by the deceased, Wilkie (W). H and S pushed a concrete block weighing 46 lbs and a concrete post weighing 65 lbs from a bridge over the road along which X was being driven by W with a police escort. The block struck the taxi's windscreen and killed W. H and S were prepared to plead guilty to manslaughter but the Crown decided to pursue the charge of murder. The defence was that H and S intended to block the road but not to kill or do serious bodily harm to anyone. Mann J directed the jury in accordance with the *Moloney* 'guidelines', p 58, above:

'You may think that critical to the resolution of this case is the question of intent. In determining whether a person intended to kill or to cause really serious injury, you must have regard to all of the evidence which has been put before you, and draw from it such inferences as to you seem proper and appropriate. You may or may not, for the purpose of considering what inferences to draw, find it helpful to ask: Was death or serious injury a natural consequence of what was done? Did a defendant foresee that consequence as a natural consequence? That is a possible question which you may care to ask yourselves. If you find yourselves not satisfied so as to be sure that there was an intent to kill or to cause really serious injury, then it is open to you to return a verdict of not guilty of murder, but guilty of manslaughter.'

H and S were convicted of murder. The Court of Appeal quashed their conviction.

[**Lord Lane CJ**, having cited Lord Bridge's statement in *Moloney*, p 55 at p 56, above that 'the probability of the consequence taken to have been foreseen must be little short of overwhelming before it will suffice to establish the necessary intent,' continued:]

Unfortunately in the passage . . . in which the guidelines are set out [p 58, above], there is no corresponding definition of what is meant by 'natural consequence'. The submission of the appellants here is that without such definition a jury might understand the words as including something which followed in an unbroken causal chain from the initial event, whether it was highly likely or not. They would not confine the words to the limited meaning which Lord Bridge intended they should bear.

We think there is substance in that submission. Indeed Mr Thomas, on behalf of the Crown, as we understood him, was driven to concede that the expression 'natural consequence' without more is potentially misleading. We hope that we are not guilty of any discourtesy to their Lordships in saying what we do. It is a matter which can be put right with ease by any Judge who feels that he is obliged to direct a jury according to the guidelines in *Moloney* by explaining to the jury that 'natural consequence' in the guidelines means that it must have been highly likely that the defendant's act would cause death or serious injury before the inference can be drawn that he had the necessary intent.

Thus the Judge in the present case was unwittingly led into misdirecting the jury by reason of the way in which the guidelines in *Moloney* were expressed.

The real problem is to decide to what extent the high degree of likelihood (viewed objectively) of death or serious injury resulting can be taken into account by the jury in determining the defendant's intention. It seems to us that the law is now back to the situation in which it was when the Court of Criminal Appeal delivered judgment in *R v Smith* [1960] 2 All ER 450. That view is reinforced by the fact that Lord Bridge himself at page 667 cites with approval the very same passage from *R v Steane* [1947] KB at p 1004 as was relied on by the Court of Criminal Appeal in *R v Smith* [1960] 2 All ER at p 453.

If one adapts the judgment in *Smith* to cater for what seems to us to be an ambiguity in the words 'natural consequence', one arrives at a formulation which can perhaps best be explained to a jury by relating it to the evidence and the burden of proof.

In cases in which the defendant's motive or purpose was not primarily to kill or injure, the Judge should ask the jury to consider some such questions as these:

(a) Are you sure that the defendant did the act which caused death, knowing what he was doing and intending to do it? If no, you must find him not guilty of both murder and manslaughter. If yes, go on to consider the next question.

(b) Are you sure that the defendant's act was of a kind which was highly likely to cause death or really serious bodily injury? If no, you must find him not guilty of murder, but he may be guilty of manslaughter. If yes, go on to consider the next question.

(c) On the evidence considered as a whole, which will of course include the defendant's evidence and that of his witnesses, are you sure that the defendant appreciated that what he did was highly likely to cause death or really serious bodily injury? If your answer is 'no', you must not find him guilty of murder, but he may be guilty of manslaughter. If your answer is 'yes', there is evidence before you from which you can infer that the defendant intended to cause death or really serious bodily injury, but you must not find him guilty of murder unless you feel sure that he so intended. If however you are sure, the fact that he may not have desired that result is irrelevant. Desire and intent are two different things.

The Crown appealed to the House of Lords.

Lord Scarman. The question for the House is . . . whether the *Moloney* guidelines are sound. In *Moloney*'s case the ratio decidendi was that the judge never properly put to the jury the defence, namely that the accused was unaware that the gun was pointing at his stepfather. The House, however, held it necessary in view of the history of confusion in this branch of the law to attempt to clarify the law relating to the establishment of the mental element necessary to constitute the crime of murder and to lay down guidelines for assisting juries to determine in what circumstances it is proper to infer intent from foresight. The House certainly clarified the law. First, the House cleared away the confusions which had obscured the law during the last 25 years laying down authoritatively that the mental element in murder is a specific intent, the intent to kill or to inflict serious bodily harm. Nothing less suffices: and the jury must be sure that the intent existed when the act was done which resulted in death before they can return a verdict of murder.

Secondly, the House made it absolutely clear that foresight of consequences is no more than evidence of the existence of the intent; it must be considered, and its weight assessed, together with all the evidence in the case. Foresight does not necessarily imply the existence of intention, though it may be a fact from which when considered with all the other evidence a jury may think it right to infer the necessary intent. Lord Hailsham of St Marylebone LC put the point succinctly and powerfully in his speech in *Moloney* [1985] AC 905, 913 E-F:

> 'I conclude with the pious hope that your Lordships will not again have to decide that foresight and foreseeability are not the same thing as intention although either may give rise to an irresistible inference of such, and that matters which are essentially to be treated as matters of inference for a jury as to a subjective state of mind will not once again be erected into a legal presumption. They should remain, what they always should have been, part of the law of evidence and inference to be left to the jury after a proper direction as to their weight, and not part of the substantive law.'

Thirdly, the House emphasised that the probability of the result of an act is an important matter for the jury to consider and can be critical in their determining whether the result was intended.

These three propositions were made abundantly clear by Lord Bridge of Harwich. His was the leading speech and received the assent of their other Lordships, Lord Hailsham of

St Marylebone LC, Lord Fraser of Tullybelton, Lord Edmund-Davies, and Lord Keith of Kinkel. His speech has laid to rest ghosts which had haunted the case law ever since the unhappy decision of your Lordships' House in *Reg v Smith* [1961] AC 290 and which were given fresh vigour by the interpretation put by some upon the speeches of members of this House in [*Hyam v DPP*] [1975] AC 55.

It is only when Lord Bridge of Harwich turned to the task of formulating guidelines that difficulty arises. It is said by the Court of Appeal that the guidelines by omitting any express reference to probability are ambiguous and may well lead a jury to a wrong conclusion. The omission was deliberate. Lord Bridge omitted the adjective 'probable' from the time-honoured formula 'foresight of the natural and probable consequences of his acts' because he thought that 'if a consequence is natural, it is really otiose to speak of it as also being probable,' [1985] AC 905, 929 B. But is it?

Lord Bridge of Harwich did not deny the importance of probability. He put it thus, p 925H:

> 'But looking on their facts at the decided cases where a crime of specific intent was under consideration, including [*Hyam v DPP*] [1975] AC 55 itself, they suggest to me that the probability of the consequence taken to have been foreseen must be little short of overwhelming before it will suffice to establish the necessary intent.'

In his discussion of the relationship between foresight and intention, Lord Bridge of Harwich reviewed the case law since the passing of the Homicide Act 1957 and concluded at p 928 F that

> 'foresight of consequences, as an element bearing on the issue of intention in murder, or indeed any other crime of specific intent, belongs, not to the substantive law, but to the law of evidence.'

He referred to the rule of evidence that a man is presumed to intend the natural and probable consequences of his acts, and went on to observe that the House of Lords in *Smith*'s case [1961] AC 290 had treated the presumption as irrebuttable, but that Parliament intervened by section 8 of the Criminal Justice Act 1967 to return the law to the path from which it had been diverted, leaving the presumption as no more than an inference open to the jury to draw if in all the circumstances it appears to them proper to draw it.

Yet he omitted any reference in his guidelines to probability. He did so because he included probability in the meaning which he attributed to 'natural'. My Lords, I very much doubt whether a jury without further explanation would think that 'probable' added nothing to 'natural'. I agree with the Court of Appeal that the probability of a consequence is a factor of sufficient importance to be drawn specifically to the attention of the jury and to be explained. In a murder case where it is necessary to direct a jury on the issue of intent by reference to foresight of consequences the probability of death or serious injury resulting from the act done may be critically important. Its importance will depend on the degree of probability: if the likelihood that death or serious injury will result is high, the probability of that result may, as Lord Bridge of Harwich noted and the Lord Chief Justice emphasised, be seen as overwhelming evidence of the existence of the intent to kill or injure. Failure to explain the relevance of probability may, therefore, mislead a jury into thinking that it is of little or no importance and into concentrating exclusively on the causal link between the act and its consequence. In framing his guidelines Lord Bridge of Harwich emphasised [1985] AC 905, 929G, that he did not believe it necessary to do more than to invite the jury to consider his two questions. Neither question makes any reference (beyond the use of the word 'natural') to probability. I am not surprised that when in this case the judge faithfully followed this guidance the jury found themselves perplexed and unsure. In my judgment, therefore, the *Moloney* guidelines as they stand are unsafe and misleading. They require a reference to probability. They also require an explanation that the greater the probability of a consequence the more likely it is that the consequence was foreseen and that if that consequence was foreseen the greater the probability is that that consequence was also intended. But juries also require to be reminded that the decision is theirs to be reached upon a consideration of all the evidence.

Accordingly, I accept the view of the Court of Appeal that the *Moloney* guidelines are defective. I am, however, not persuaded that guidelines of general application, albeit within a limited class of case, are wise or desirable. The Lord Chief Justice formulated in this case guidelines for the assistance of juries but for the reason which follows, I would not advise their use by trial judges when summing up to a jury.

I fear that their elaborate structure may well create difficulty. Juries are not chosen for their understanding of a logical and phased process leading by question and answer to a conclusion but are expected to exercise practical common sense. They want help on the practical problems encountered in evaluating the evidence of a particular case and reaching a conclusion. It is better,

I suggest, notwithstanding my respect for the comprehensive formulation of the Court of Appeal's guidelines, that the trial judge should follow the traditional course of a summing up. He must explain the nature of the offence charged, give directions as to the law applicable to the particular facts of the case, explain the incidence and burden of proof, put both sides' cases making especially sure that the defence is put; he should offer help in understanding and weighing up all the evidence and should make certain that the jury understand that whereas the law is for him the facts are for them to decide. Guidelines, if given, are not to be treated as rules of law but as a guide indicating the sort of approach the jury may properly adopt to the evidence when coming to their decision on the facts.

In a case where foresight of a consequence is part of the evidence supporting a prosecution submission that the accused intended the consequence, the judge, if he thinks some general observations would help the jury, could well, having in mind section 8 of the Criminal Justice Act 1967, emphasise that the probability, however high, of a consequence is only a factor, though it may in some cases be a very significant factor, to be considered with all the other evidence in determining whether the accused intended to bring it about. The distinction between the offence and the evidence relied on to prove it is vital. Lord Bridge's speech in *Moloney* made the distinction crystal clear: it would be a disservice to the law to allow his guidelines to mislead a jury into overlooking it.

For these reasons I would hold that the *Moloney* guidelines are defective and should not be used as they stand without further explanation. The laying down of guidelines for use in directing juries in cases of complexity is a function which can be usefully exercised by the Court of Appeal. But it should be done sparingly, and limited to cases of real difficulty. If it is done, the guidelines should avoid generalisation so far as is possible and encourage the jury to exercise their common sense in reaching what is their decision on the facts. Guidelines are not rules of law: judges should not think that they must use them. A judge's duty is to direct the jury in law and to help them upon the particular facts of the case.

[Lords Keith, Roskill, Brightman and **Griffiths** agreed.]

Appeal dismissed

Questions

1. Intention is a state of mind. When the jury has found that the defendant was aware that it was highly probable that his act would cause serious injury, what further mental element must they find existed before they are sure that the defendant 'intended' the injury?

2. Is it possible to infer a further state of mind from a defendant's knowledge that a result is hightly probable (other than, eg, that he did not care whether he caused that result or not—which is not in issue)?

3. Does the case leave it open to the jury to decide that the defendant's knqwledge that the result is highly probable amounts to intention if they wish to convict him; and that it does not amount to intention if they do not? If this is the position, is it satisfactory?

2. Attempt and impossibility (pp 270 and 287, above)

In *Shivpuri* [1985] QB 1029, [1985] 1 All ER 143, CA, the appellant was arrested by customs officials while in possession of a suitcase. He admitted that he knew that it contained prohibited drugs. Analysis showed that the material in the suitcase was not a prohibited drug but a vegetable material akin to snuff. He was convicted of attempting to be knowingly concerned in dealing with and harbouring a prohibited drug, contrary to s 1 (1) of the Criminal Attempts Act 1981, p 586, above, and s 170 (1)(b) of the Customs and Excise Management Act 1979. His appeal was dismissed following the decision of the Divisional Court in *Anderton v Ryan*, p 296, above. Shivpuri's appeal to the House of Lords was pending when the House decided *Anderton v Ryan*. The certificate granted by the Divisional Court took an unusual form in that it asked two hypothetical questions, one of which was whether a person would be guilty of an attempt if he imported a substance which he believed to be heroin but which was in fact a harmless white powder. Lord Roskill noted that the question had been posed before the decision of the Court of Appeal in *Shivpuri* and that it would be wrong to engage in any discussion of that question in view of the pending appeal. Lord Edmund-Davies, dissenting, after referring to *Shivpuri*, said that he had refrained from considering situations basically indistinguishable, adding:

> 'It is no fault of mine if, despite such restraint, what I have perforce said has made obvious the short answer I would unavoidably have given had it been necessary to deal in its entirety with the question here certified by the Divisional Court.'

NOTE

At the time of writing the House has heard argument in the case of *Shivpuri* but has asked for further argument on the Practice Statement (Judicial Precedent) [1966] 1 WLR 1234 under which the House may depart from its previous decisions. Clearly, the House has in mind the possibility of not following *Anderton v Ryan*, p 296, above. See Hogan, 'The Principle of Legality' (1986) 136 NLJ 267.

Question

Is it possible to attempt to be 'knowingly concerned'? Is there any difference between the state of mind of a person who knows and that of a person who thinks (wrongly) that he knows? If not, does not the latter person have the mens rea of the offence?

R v Tulloch [1986] Crim LR 50, Court of Appeal
(Stephen Brown LJ, Bristow and Otton JJ)

The appellant was charged with attempting to supply a controlled drug contrary to section 1(1) of the Criminal Attempts Act 1981. At a pop music festival the appellant was with a group who were heard to shout 'acid for sale.' A police officer in plain clothes asked the price of the 'tabs' and bought three papers from the appellant for £6. He believed they were LSD 'smiley faces' containing lysergide but on analysis no controlled drugs were detected. They were merely three pieces of plain paper. After his arrest the appellant told the police he had bought four 'acid trips' at the festival for £1.50 each. He had sold three to the officer and given the other one away. The prosecution [sic] accepted that the appellant had made the purchase in the belief that the papers were impregnated with LSD. At the trial the appellant pleaded guilty in the light of the Court of Appeal's decision in *Anderton v Ryan*. A few days after the appellant had been sentenced the House of Lords delivered their judgment in *Anderton v Ryan* [p 296, above] reversing the Court of Appeal. The appellant appealed against his conviction (the trial judge having granted a certificate) on the ground that had the House of Lords decided *Anderton v Ryan* before the Crown Court hearing the appellant would have had a complete defence to the charge. The respondent submitted that since the House of Lord's decision it was still possible for a person to be guilty of an attempt in cases where a full offence was not committed because of the person's mistake of fact as to the physical nature of the object at which his attention was directed. Thus a mistake of fact as to the physical nature to the substance which was sold as a dangerous drug was still an offence under the 1981 Act even though it would not have been a crime at common law. He relied on *Shivpuri* [1985] 1 All ER 143.

Held, dismissing the appeal, that leave to appeal to the House of Lords had been granted in *Shivpuri*. The question certified in *Shivpuri* was the very question to be decided in the instant case. Lord Roskill in *Anderton v Ryan* had said that it would be wrong to discuss the situation raised in that case as the appeal had yet to be heard and he was not to be taken as accepting that no offence against section 1(1) had been committed on the facts of *Shivpuri*. Until the appeal in *Shivpuri* was heard the Court of Appeal was therefore bound by the Court of Appeal's decision in *Shivpuri* and the appellant's submissions had to be rejected.

(The Court certified a point of law of general public importance and granted leave to appeal to the House of Lords).

Questions

1. Is there a material distinction between a mistake as to the physical nature of a thing and a mistake as to what has happened to a thing—eg, that it has been stolen?

2. One suggested test is that a person may be guilty of an attempt where, but only where, he would have committed a crime if he had achieved his objective. According to that test, would Tulloch have been guilty of attempt (i) to possess a controlled drug when he bought the papers believing them to be LSD 'smiley faces' or (ii) to supply a controlled drug when he sold the papers in the same belief?

NOTE

In *Smith and Smith* [1986] Crim LR 166, CA, it was held that the appellants were rightly convicted of attempting to steal 'some or all of the contents of a handbag' belonging to a named victim although there was no evidence that there was anything capable of being stolen in the handbag. Hodgson J said 'The Criminal Attempts Act 1981, however it may otherwise have missed some of its intended targets, has been entirely efficacious in removing the "pickpocket's defence".' Following *A-G's References (Nos 1 and 2 of 1979)* [1980] QB 180 the Court rejected as fallacious a submission that by alleging 'some or all of the contents of a handbag' the prosecution averred that there was property in the handbag which they could not prove.

What if there had been evidence of the nature of the contents and the defendants had sworn that they would not have taken any of those? Cf *Easom* [1971] 2 QB 315.

3. Duress and accessories (pp 135 and 205, above)

R v Burke, Clarkson, Howe and Bannister [1986] Crim LR 331, Court of Appeal (Lord Lane CJ, Russell and Taylor JJ)

Bannister and Howe were charged in two counts with murder. Their defence was that they feared that they would be killed by Murray if they did not carry out his instructions. On the first count they were in the position of principals in the second degree and on the second count, principals in the first degree. Jupp J left duress to the jury on the first but not the second count. They were convicted on both counts.

In a separate trial, Burke and Clarkson were charged with murder, Burke as the 'principal in the first degree'. His defences were (i) that, though he had agreed to shoot Botton, when it came to the event, the gun went off accidentally and that the killing was only manslaughter; and (ii) that he was acting under a threat to his life by Clarkson. Clarkson's defence was that he had nothing to do with the shooting at all. Burke and Clarkson were convicted of murder.

The appeals in both cases were heard together.

Bannister, Howe and Burke appealed on the ground that the judges ought to have left their defence of duress to the jury. Burke also appealed on the ground that the judge had wrongly directed the jury that the culpability of a secondary party can be no higher than that of the principal so that, if they found Burke guilty of manslaughter, Clarkson could be guilty at the most of manslaughter and, if they acquitted Burke on the ground of duress, Clarkson must be acquitted altogether. It was submitted that this may have induced the jury to return a perverse verdict against Burke to ensure that they could convict Clarkson whom they believed to be the real villain.

[Having reviewed the authorities, **Lane LCJ** said:]

In our judgment the two Judges in the present cases were correct in their view as to what the law is at present and their directions to the jury accurately reflected the true position.

It is true that to allow the defence to the aider and abettor but not to the killer may lead to illogicality, as was pointed out by this Court in *Graham* [p 208, above] where the question in issue in the instant case was not argued, but that is not to say that any illogicality should be cured by making duress available to the actual killer rather by removing it from the aider and abettor.

Assuming that a change in the law is desirable or necessary, we may perhaps be permitted to express a view. The whole matter was dealt with in extenso by Lord Salmon in his speech in *Abbott* [p 214, above] to which reference has already been made. He dealt there with the authorities. It is unnecessary for us in the circumstances to repeat the citations which he there makes. It would moreover be impertinent for us to try to restate in different terms the contents of that speech with which we respectfully agree. Either the law should be left as it is or the defence of duress should be denied to anyone charged with murder, whether as a principal in the first degree or otherwise. It seems to us that it would be a highly dangerous relaxation in the law to allow a person who has deliberately killed, maybe a number of innocent people, to escape conviction and punishment altogether because of a fear that his own life or those of his family might be in danger if he did not; particularly so when the defence of duress is so easy to raise and may be so difficult for the prosecution to disprove beyond reasonable doubt, the facts of necessity being as a rule known only to the defendant himself. That is not to say that duress may not be taken into account in other ways, for example by the Parole Board.

Even if, contrary to our views, it were otherwise desirable to extend the defence of duress to the actual killer, this is surely not the moment to make any such change, when acts of terrorism are commonplace and opportunities for mass murder have never been more readily to hand.

In any event, if it is to be permitted as a defence to murder at all, duress should in our view, by analogy with provocation, only reduce the offence to manslaughter and not result in an outright acquittal. That would mean that the effect and gravity of the duress in a particular case could fairly be reflected in the sentence imposed.

We turn now to consider the second ground of appeal advanced on behalf of Burke, namely that the Judge was wrong in directing the jury that if Burke was guilty of manslaughter and not of murder, then Clarkson could be found guilty at the worst only of manslaughter.

The learned Judge based himself on a decision of this Court in *Richards* [p 135, above]. [Lord Lane stated the facts and quoted from the judgment in *Richards* and continued:] The decision in *Richards* has been the subject of some criticism (see for example Smith and Hogan, *Criminal Law*, 5th Edition, page 140).

Counsel before us posed the situation where A hands a gun to D informing him that it is loaded with blank ammunition only and telling him to go and scare X by discharging it. The ammunition is in fact live (as A knows) and X is killed. D is convicted only of manslaughter, as he might be on those facts. It would seem absurd that A should thereby escape conviction for murder.

We take the view that *Richards* was incorrectly decided, but it seems to us that it cannot properly be distinguished from the instant case. In those circumstances we are obliged to follow the decision until such time as it is overruled. Our liberty to depart from a precedent which we think to be erroneous is restricted, generally speaking, to cases where the departure is in favour of the appellant: see *DPP v Merriman* (1972) 56 Cr App R 766, per Lord Diplock, page 794.

In cases such as the present where an accessory before the fact has prevailed upon another to commit a criminal act, a more satisfactory rule would be to allow each to be convicted of the offence appropriate to his intention, whether or not that would involve the accessory in being convicted of a more serious offence than the principal. In our view the learned Judge was in the circumstances right to direct the jury as he did.

The Court dismissed the appeals and certified the following points of law of general public importance:

(1) Is duress available as a defence to a person charged with murder as a principal in the first degree (actual killer)?

(2) Can one who incites or procures by duress another to kill or to be a party to a killing be convicted of murder if that other is acquitted by reason of duress?

(3) Does the defence of duress fail if the prosecution prove that a person of reasonable firmness sharing the characteristics of the defendant would not have given way to the threats as did the defendant?

The Court granted leave to appeal to the House of Lords.

Questions

1. If duress is not to be a defence to murder should it be a defence to (i) attempted murder or (ii) causing grievous bodily harm with intent, contrary to s 18 of the Offences against the Person Act 1861? Can it be the law that an act done with intent to kill or to cause grievous bodily harm is excusable so long as it does not result in death—but becomes inexcusable if death results within a year and a day?

2. The *Richards* principle is applicable if the actual killer is guilty only of manslaughter and the abettor has the mens rea of murder; but does it apply where the actual killer is acquitted on the ground of duress?

4. Involuntary manslaughter (p 332, above)

R v Goodfellow (1986) Times, 1 March
(Lord Lane CJ, Boreham and Taylor JJ)

The appellant (G) was having difficulties with two men one of whom had been fined for damaging the front door of G's council house. G wanted to move but had no chance of exchanging his council house for another. He decided to set the house on fire, making it appear that this had been done by a petrol bomb. He poured petrol over the furniture and set fire to it. His wife, another woman and his son, aged two, died in the fire. He was convicted of manslaughter and appealed on the ground that the judge failed to direct the jury properly and, particularly, did so on the basis of the passage in *Archbold* (41st edn), criticised in *Kong Cheuk Kwan*, p 348, above.

Lord Lane CJ said that the passage in *Archbold* had been criticised for confusing manslaughter by an illegal act of violence with what had been said in *Caldwell*, p 68, above, *Lawrence*, p 72, above, and *Bateman*, p 342, above. The instant case was capable of falling within either or both types of manslaughter. On the *Lawrence* aspect, the jury might well have been satisfied that G was acting in such a manner as to create an obvious and serious risk of causing physical injury to some person and, second, that he, having recognised that some risk was involved, nevertheless had gone on to take it. His lordship rejected a submission that the present was not a case of 'unlawful act' manslaughter because the act was not 'directed at' the victim as, it was submitted, *Dalby*, p 338, above, required. What Waller LJ was there intending to say was that there must be no fresh intervening cause between the act and the death. Their Lordships doubted the assertions in Smith & Hogan, *Criminal Law* (5th edn) that because the House of Lords refused the prosecutor leave to appeal in *Dalby*, that case must be taken to represent the law.

The questions for the jury were: (i) Was the act intentional? (ii) Was it unlawful? (iii) Was it an act which any reasonable person would realise was bound to subject some other human being to the risk of physical harm, albeit not necessarily serious harm? (iv) Was the act the cause of death?

The direction was, if anything, too favourable to G.

Appeal dismissed

Question

Does not *Dalby*, as interpreted in *Goodfellow*, represent the law? Must not a judge be taken to mean what judges in subsequent cases say he meant?

Index